TRADE MARKS IN EUROPE

A PRACTICAL JURISPRUDENCE

TRADE MARKS IN EUROPE

A PRACTICAL JURISPRUDENCE

Spyros Maniatis
*Centre for Commercial Law Studies,
Queen Mary, University of London*

Dimitris Botis
*Office for Harmonisation in the
Internal Market*

SWEET & MAXWELL  THOMSON REUTERS

First Edition 2006 by Syros Maniatis
Published in 2009 by Thomson Reuters (Professional) UK Limited
trading as Sweet & Maxwell, Friars House, 160 Blackfriars Road,
London SE1 8EZ
(Registered in England & Wales, Company No 1679046.
Registered Office and address for service:
2nd Floor, 1 Mark Square, Leonard Street, London EC2A 4EG)

Typeset by LBJ Typesetting of Kingsclere
Printed and bound by CPI Group (UK) Ltd, Croydon, CR0 4YY

No natural forests were destroyed to make this product;
only farmed timber was used and replanted

A C.I.P. catalogue record for this book is available from the British Library

ISBN: 9781847039040

All rights reserved. Crown copyright legislation is reproduced with the permission of the Controller of HMSO and the Queen's Printer for Scotland.

No part of this publication may be reproduced or transmitted in any form or by any means, or stored in any retrieval system of any nature without prior written permission, except for permitted fair dealing under the Copyright, Designs and Patents Act 1988, or in accordance with the terms of a licence issued by the Copyright Licensing Agency in respect of photocopying and/or reprographic reproduction. Application for permission for other use of copyright material including permission to reproduce extracts in other published works shall be made to the publishers. Full acknowledgement of author, publisher and source must be given.
No natural forests were destroyed to make this product, only farmed timber was used and replanted.

Thomson Reuters and the Thomson Reuters Logo are trademarks of Thomson Reuters. Sweet & Maxwell is a registered trademark of Thomson Reuters (Legal) Limited.

© 2010 Thomson Reuters (Professional) UK Limited

FOREWORD

European trade mark law consists of the (first) Directive for the approximation of trade mark law of the Member States of the European Union, adopted in 1988 and since "codified" (in 2008), and of the Community Trade Mark Regulation, adopted in 1993 and also since codified in 2009. Its interpretation and application is a matter for national authorities, in the case of the "harmonised" national law and in all infringement matters, and for the (aptly titled) Office for Harmonisation in the Internal Market (OHIM), the European Union's trade marks and designs office in Alicante. However, the true "source" of European trade mark law today, aside from the often bland language of the statutes, is the European Court of Justice (ECJ) and the Court of First Instance (CFI) in Luxembourg. The CFI has competence to review decisions of OHIM's Boards of Appeal. The ECJ hears appeals from the CFI, limited to points of law, and issues preliminary rulings when called upon to do so by national courts referring questions of interpretation of the Directive or of the Regulation.

Since the first judgment of the ECJ interpreting the Directive, the famous Sabèl/Puma case, close to 100 preliminary rulings have enlightened and confused trade mark lawyers everywhere, and since the equally famous Baby-Dry judgment close to 100 appeals have been decided by the ECJ, with many hundreds of judgments having been pronounced by the CFI.

The Luxembourg pronouncements need to be ordered, classified, analysed, and compared with each other, so as to create some degree of order out of the universe of decisions often "oracle"-like, difficult to understand and reconcile with each other.

The book provides analysis and commentary, placing European trade mark law into the legal order of the European Community, and covers as well the interfaces with competition law and unfair practices law. As a bonus, European law is compared with the often equally difficult to understand US American law as interpreted by the US Supreme Court.

Professor Spyiros Maniatis and Dimitris Botis have prepared the menu admirably. It is for us to enjoy.

Dr Alexander von Mühlendahl, J.D., LL.M. (Northwestern University)
Attorney-at-Law, Munich, Germany
Former Vice-President of the Office for Harmonisation in the Internal Market (Trade Marks and Designs) (1994–2005)

ACKNOWLEDGMENTS

Numerous people have contributed to the second edition of *Trade Marks in Europe: A Practical Jurisprudence*. Sweet and Maxwell have been a constant source of assistance and encouragement; the publishing, editorial, and marketing teams led by Jo Slinn, Paul Crick, Lisa Mitchell, Joanna Suckling, and Bronwen Edwards have been exceptionally effective and I am grateful to all of them.

Colleagues at CCLS and elsewhere have challenged my ideas and commented on the first edition. Equally inspiring have been my research, LLM, ITMA, and Certificate students. Marilee Owens has helped me with the proofs.

Above all, I was extremely fortunate to find in Dimitris Botis the perfect co-author: his enthusiasm about the subject, his insightful knowledge, his motivation and energy, became a catalyst that has genuinely transformed the first edition into a new book.

Finally, I am delighted and honoured that Alexander von Mühlendahl is contributing a foreword. He has been the inspiration and driving force behind the Community Trade Mark system. We owe a lot to him; his vision for European trade mark law is behind the subject matter of this work.

On a personal note, Kiki Maniatis, Maria Michalis, and Natalia Marina Maniatis have always been generous with their love, patience, and support.

Spyros Maniatis

When Spyros asked me to contribute to the second edition of *Trade Marks in Europe*, it sounded like an invitation to enter a labyrinth with no real end, which just gets deeper the longer you venture inside. On second thoughts, however, I decided to give in and take up the challenge, as I realised that the book does not need to reveal where the exit is, or is supposed to be; it suffices to follow the course of the case-law, step by step, hoping that after this turn, or perhaps the next, the shadows will recede and the glimpse of the sun will get stronger.

So I thank Spyros for the opportunity he gave me to follow this path, all my colleagues at the OHIM for the endless talks on this or that Judgment and, above all, my wife Alex for her understanding and my daughters Artemis and Elli, for setting the appropriate time-frame:

Dad, how many pages until you finish that book at last?

Finally, I thank Alexander von Mühlendahl not only for his kind guidance and support all these years in Alicante, but also for showing us all how trade mark law can become a real passion.

Dimitris Botis

CONTENTS

	Page
Foreword	v
Acknowledgments	vii
Table of Cases	xix
Table of Legislation	lxi

CHAPTER 1

	Para
Introduction	1–001

CHAPTER 2

Community Trade Mark Law: The Directive and the Regulation

	Para
1. Introduction	2–001
2. The "Harmonisation" Directive	2–005
3. The Community Trade Mark Regulation	2–009
(1) The architecture of coexistence	2–010
(2) The Community Trade Mark	2–011
(3) The expansion of the Community Trade Mark	2–021
4. The Peculiarities of the Community Trade Mark	2–023
(1) Conversion	2–023
(2) Seniority	2–024
(3) Other aspects of coexistence	2–025
5. Conclusion	2–027

CHAPTER 3

The Court of Justice of The European Communities: The Role and Interpretive Principles and Techniques of the Court

1. Introduction	3–001
2. Forms of Action	3–004
(1) Actions against Member States in breach of Community Law	3–004
(2) Actions against a Community institution for failure to act	3–005
(3) Annulment actions	3–006

(4) Appeals	3–008
(5) References for a preliminary ruling	3–009
3. The Composition and Mechanics of the Court of Justice	3–013
(1) The composition of the Court	3–013
(2) Direct actions	3–014
(3) Preliminary rulings—procedural differences	3–018
(4) Interlocutory proceedings	3–020
(5) Expedited procedure	3–021
4. The Court of First Instance—Specialist Tribunals	3–022
(1) The basics	3–022
(2) The composition and mechanics of the Court of First Instance	3–024
5. The Interpretive Principles and Techniques of the Court	3–026
(1) Direct effect	3–028
(2) Supremacy of Community law	3–041
(3) The development of the "indirect effect" of Community law	3–046
(4) The competence of the Court of Justice—the acte clair doctrine	3–047
(5) Looking for the essence of the question	3–049
(6) Fundamental rights	3–050
6. Judicial Review and the Community Trade Mark	3–053
(1) Arcol—the "institutional architecture" in trade mark cases	3–053
(2) Scope and limits of administrative and judicial review	3–058
(3) The value of precedents	3–064
7. Conclusion	3–069

CHAPTER 4

Absolute Grounds

1. Introduction	4–001
2. The Provisions of the Directive and the Regulation	4–003
(1) Article 2—signs of which a trade mark may consist	4–003
(2) Article 3—grounds for refusal or invalidity	4–004
(3) Article 7 of the Regulation	4–005
3. What is a Sign	4–006
(1) Dyson—the fundamental question	4–006
(2) Pre-Dyson jurisprudence—setting the ground	4–007
(3) Dyson—the fundamental requirement	4–013
4. Capable of being Represented Graphically	4–031
(1) Sieckmann—the purpose of graphical representation—non-visual signs—scents—the general conditions	4–032
(2) Shield mark—graphical representation of sounds—general policy considerations	4–052

    (3) Libertel—colour samples—public policy
considerations 4–069
    (4) Heidelberger Bauchemie—abstract combinations of
colours 4–079
5. Capable of Distinguishing 4–086
    (1) Philips—setting the principles 4–086
    (2) Capable of distinguishing—the limited effect of
article 3(1)(a) 4–095
    (3) Some guidelines for interpreting article 3 4–097
6. Article 3(1)(b)—Devoid of any Distinctive Character 4–103
    (1) Companyline—article 7(1)(b)—balancing between
Baby-Dry and Postkantoor 4–103
    (2) "SAT.2"—back to Baby-dry? 4–117
    (3) BioID—the limited effect of "SAT.2" 4–133
    (4) Nichols—no special conditions for surnames 4–152
    (5) Erpo—registrability of slogans 4–161
    (6) Libertel—the distinctiveness of colours 4–175
    (7) Heidelberger Bauchemie—combinations of
colours—replaying Libertel 4–190
    (8) KWS—colours—broader functionality considerations ... 4–193
    (9) Mag—distinctive character of shapes of products 4–200
    (10) Linde, Winward, and Rado—products shapes—a
broader perspective 4–216
    (11) Henkel—the assimilation of packaging and product
shapes 4–228
    (12) Glaverbel—aesthetic functionality? 4–241
    (13) The washing tablets cases 4–243
    (14) SiSi-Werke—article 7(1)(b) and packaging 4–279
    (15) Eurocermex–article 7(1)(b), three-dimensional shapes,
and the concept of a product 4–301
    (16) Storck I—the shape of a sweet 4–311
    (17) Storck II—the distinctive character of packaging 4–320
7. Article 3(1)(c)—Descriptive Signs or Indications 4–346
    (1) Windsurfing Chiemsee—geographical names—
setting the general principles 4–346
    (2) Baby-Dry—composite words—a permissive
approach 4–355
    (3) Doublemint—a more nuanced approach 4–375
    (4) Postkantoor—a parallel approach 4–394
    (5) Streamserve—consolidating Doublemint 4–421
    (6) Telefon & Buch—following Doublemint 4–432
    (7) BVBA—challenging the procedural points of
Postkantoor 4–439
    (8) Matratzen—article 3(1)(c) and free movement of goods
considerations 4–459

  (9) Celltech—burden of proof: technical and scientific terms 4–464
  (10) Develey—burden of proof: consumer goods 4–468
8. Article 3(1)(d)—Signs or Indications that have become Customary 4–471
  (1) Bravo—the link with the specification 4–471
  (2) Alcon—article 7(1)(d) and acronyms 4–483
  (3) Procordia—expanding the class of persons determining distinctiveness 4–492
9. Article 3(1)(e)—Functional Shapes 4–503
  (1) Philips—the overriding scope of article 3(1)(e) 4–503
  (2) Benetton—attractiveness v distinctiveness 4–514
10. Article 3(1)(g)—Trade Marks of a Deceptive Nature 4–521
  (1) Elizabeth Emanuel—trade mark assignments 4–521
  (2) Free movement of goods and deceptive use 4–538
11. Article 3(1)(h)—State Emblems 4–561
  (1) Maple Leaf—applicability of article 6ter to services 4–561
12. Article 3(2)(d)—Bad Faith 4–578
  (1) Lindt & Sprüngli—what is bad faith? 4–578
13. Article 3(3)—Distinctive Character Acquired Through Use ... 4–589
  (1) Windsurfing Chiemsee—the test for assessing acquired to distinctive character 4–589
  (2) Philips—reinforcing Windsurfing Chiemsee 4–598
  (3) Kit-Kat—combined use 4–602
  (4) Storck I—article 7(3)—sales figures—amount spent on advertising 4–608
  (5) Storck II—sales figures in abstract 4–620
  (6) Europolis—acquired distinctive character in the Benelux—linguistic and geographical considerations 4–627
  (7) Pure Digital—the relevant point in time 4–638
14. Conclusion 4–645

CHAPTER 5

Relative Grounds

1. Introduction 5–001
2. The Provisions of the Directive and the Regulation 5–002
  (1) The Trade Marks Directive 5–002
  (2) The Community Trade Mark Regulation 5–003
3. LTJ Diffusion—Establishing Identity Between Marks 5–004
4. Confusion, Similarity, and Distinctiveness 5–010
  (1) Sabel—confusion and association: alternative concepts? 5–011
  (2) Canon—distinctiveness, confusion, and association 5–017

(3)	Lloyd Schuhfabrik—properly substantiated and genuine confusion	5–020
(4)	Marca Mode—revisiting Sabel—a positive finding on confusion	5–023
(5)	Lloyd—the distinctiveness factors	5–028
(6)	The average consumer	5–030

5. Establishing Confusion—Global Appreciation 5–031
   (1) The three tests 5–031
   (2) The test for confusion 5–032
   (3) Canon—global appreciation in a wider context 5–035
   (4) Vedial—cumulative similarity/identity conditions 5–038
   (5) Sabel—comparing the marks 5–043
   (6) Lloyd—aural similarity 5–045
   (7) Mühlens—a challenge to Lloyd 5–048
   (8) Matratzen I—similarity between a figurative and a word mark 5–056
   (9) Flexi Air—distinctiveness as part of a multifactor assessment 5–066
   (10) Comparing the goods or services 5–074
6. Levi Strauss—The Timing of the Assessment 5–078
7. Revisiting Global Appreciation 5–094
   (1) Picasso/Picaro—the limitations of Arsenal 5–095
   (2) Rossi—protection of surnames—global appreciation—the Community Trade mark registration process 5–106
   (3) Medion—the importance of dominant elements 5–137
   (4) Praktiker—a special case for retail services? 5–141
   (5) Travatan—the mediation of professionals: pharmaceuticals 5–146
   (6) Limoncello—Quicky—La Española: composite marks ... 5–152
   (7) Armafoam—confusion in part of the Community 5–164
8. Marks with a Reputation 5–169
   (1) General Motors—the factors for assessing reputation ... 5–169
   (2) Fincas Tarragona—marks well known "in a Member State" 5–173
   (3) Pago—reputation "in the Community" 5–180
   (4) Davidoff v Gofkid—the scope of article 5(2) 5–191
   (5) Fitnessworld—the interpretive limits of Davidoff v Gofkid 5–197
   (6) Adidas v Fitnessworld—global appreciation in the context of article 5(2) 5–201
   (7) Adidas v Fitnessworld—use as a trade mark 5–204
   (8) Intel—proof of dilution: chasing the chimera? 5–207
   (9) Bellure—unfair advantage 5–230
   (10) Nasdaq—putting the Intel into perspective? 5–240
9. Conclusion 5–247

CHAPTER 6

Scope of Protection, Limitations, and Enforcement

1. Introduction 6–001
2. The Provisions of the Directive and the Regulation 6–002
   (1) The Trade Marks Directive 6–002
   (2) The Community Trade Mark Regulation 6–004
3. Identical Signs and Goods or Services—The Scope
   of Protection 6–008
   (1) Hölterhoff—limiting the scope of protection 6–009
   (2) Arsenal—a counterbalancing exercise 6–014
   (3) Adam Opel—challenging the limits of protection 6–024
   (4) Marca II—availability and scope of protection 6–040
   (5) Smirnoff—use by intermediaries 6–051
   (6) Bellure—broadening the scope of protection 6–056
   (7) Google—taking a step back—the relevance
       of context 6–066
4. The Conflict between Trade Marks and Trade Names 6–080
   (1) Robelco—trade marks and trade names 6–080
   (2) Céline—trade names performing a distinguishing
       function 6–084
5. Limitations to Trade Mark Rights 6–094
   (1) BMW—setting the principles 6–094
   (2) Gerolsteiner Brunnen—the scope of article 6(1)(b) 6–116
   (3) Gillette—indicating compatibility 6–125
   (4) Adam Opel 6–139
6. Enforcing the Community Trade Mark 6–141
   (1) Nokia—adequate enforcement 6–141
   (2) Davidoff III—seizure of infringing goods 6–151
7. Conclusion 6–157

CHAPTER 7

Challenging or Maintaining the Registration

1. Introduction 7–001
2. The Legislative Context 7–002
   (1) The provisions of the Directive 7–002
3. The Case law of the Court 7–007
   (1) Ansul—the concept of "genuine use" 7–007
   (2) Laboratoire de la Mer—subjective and objective
       perspectives 7–024
   (3) Radetzky—use in respect of non-profitable activities 7–030
   (4) Silberquelle—use on promotional items 7–038

(5) Nasdaq—complementary services offered free of charge	7–049
(6) Lidl—start of the use requirement and proper reasons for non-use	7–054
(7) Bainbridge—defensive registrations	7–066
4. Challenging a Community Trade Mark	7–074
(1) Sunrider—evidence of use; the burden of proof	7–074
5. Conclusion	7–089

CHAPTER 8

Parallel Imports

1. Introduction	8–001
2. The General Principles	8–002
(1) The legislative framework	8–002
(2) Duties and taxes	8–006
(3) Quantitative restrictions	8–011
(4) The equality proviso	8–028
(5) Public policy considerations	8–030
(6) Protection of health and life of humans	8–036
(7) Codacons—labelling requirements—the residual power of the free movement of goods rationale	8–040
(8) Commission v Ireland—hallmarks and public interest	8–045
3. Free Movement of Goods and Intellectual Property	8–047
(1) The existence–exercise dichotomy	8–051
(2) The specific subject-matter of the right	8–053
(3) "Independent" rights	8–054
4. Free Movement of Goods and Trade Mark Law	8–056
(1) The early days—the essential function and the specific subject-matter of trade marks	8–056
(2) Developing the concept of consent	8–058
(3) Hag I—a restrictive approach	8–059
(4) Terrapin—consent and independent rights	8–061
(5) Merck v Stephar—lack of protection	8–062
(6) Pharmon v Hoechst—compulsory licence	8–063
(7) Centrafarm v American Home Products—changing direction	8–065
(8) HAG II—the concept of consent, the role and function of trade marks	8–067
(9) Ideal Standard—voluntary assignment	8–071
(10) Repackaging and parallel imports—Hoffmann-La Roche—setting the principles	8–075
5. Free Movement of Goods and the New Trade Mark Regime	8–089

(1) Bristol Myers Squibb and the related cases–article 7 of the Directive and the free movement of goods rules–the fifth repackaging condition 8–089
6. Pharmacia & Upjohn—Replacing The Trade Mark—The Requirement of Necessity 8–142
7. Boehringer—Revisiting Repackaging 8–155
8. Ballantine—Trade Mark Infringement and Policing Channels Of Trade 8–170
9. Dior—Beyond the Origin Function 8–190
10. Silhouette—the Territorial Scope of Exhaustion 8–209
11. Sebago—"Specific" Consent 8–223
12. Davidoff—"Clear" Consent 8–228
13. Peak Holding—The Concept of "Putting Goods on The Market" 8–243
14. Class International—Goods in Transit 8–247
15. Boehringer II—Revisiting Repackaging, Overstickering and Reboxing 8–253
16. Wellcome v Paranova—Is There a Requirement of Minimum Intervention?—The Extent Of Disclosure 8–282
17. Conclusion 8–290

CHAPTER 9

Competition and Trade Marks

1. Introduction 9–001
2. Competition Rules 9–004
3. The Scope of the Competition Provisions 9–005
   (1) The multiple tasks of European competition law 9–005
   (2) Direct applicability 9–008
4. The Application of Article 81 9–014
   (1) The concept of undertakings 9–014
   (2) The scope and the form of an agreement 9–016
   (3) Concerted practices 9–022
   (4) Hugin—the boundaries between Community and national competition law 9–023
   (5) Consten and Grundig—the interaction with trade mark law—the starting point 9–024
   (6) Société Technique Minière—a rule of reason analysis? 9–035
   (7) Volk v Vervaecke—significant effect 9–036
   (8) Beguelin—the relevance of context 9–037
   (9) Delimitis—a web of agreements—closer to a rule of reason analysis 9–038
   (10) EMI and Nungesser—existence and the way the right is exercised 9–052

CONTENTS

 (11) Pronuptia de Paris—the benefits of franchising agreements 9–057
 (12) BAT—competition and trade mark law—delimitation agreements 9–062
 (13) The position of the Commission on delimitation agreements 9–064
 (14) The Commission on repackaging bans 9–066
 (15) Campari—an example of the application of article 81(3) by the Commission 9–067
 (16) Javico—the Contrast with Silhouette 9–072
5. The Application of Article 82 9–079
 (1) Dominance 9–079
 (2) Dominance and intellectual property 9–088
 (3) Der Grüne Punkt—dominance and trade marks—the function of the sign 9–121
6. Conclusion 9–134

CHAPTER 10

The Spillover Effect

1. Introduction 10–001
2. Comparative Advertising 10–002
 (1) Toshiba—the interplay between trade marks and comparative advertising 10–005
 (2) Pippig—the contradictions of article 7(2) of Directive 84/450 10–025
 (3) Siemens—reconfirming the Court's permissive approach 10–040
 (4) DeLandtsheer Emmanuel—designations of origin—the competitive relationship 10–049
 (5) O2—use of a similar sign—the indispensability challenge 10–059
 (6) L'Oréal v Bellure—taking a step back? 10–065
3. Geographical Indications 10–072
 (1) Feta—consumer confusion and a misappropriation rationale 10–072
 (2) Bavaria—the coexistence between trade mark and geographical indication protection 10–091
 (3) Grana Padano—trade marks v geographical indication—the concept of genericity 10–103
4. The Budweiser Tetralogy 10–106
 (1) Geographical indications, bilateral agreements, and free movement of goods 10–107
 (2) Bud II—replaying Bud I 10–119

    (3) European trade mark law and the TRIPs
        Agreement—protecting trade names 10–133
    (4) The European Court of Human Rights—geographical
        indications, trade marks and property rights 10–155
5. Conclusion 10–166

CHAPTER 11

The Contemporary Jurisprudence of the US Supreme Court

1. Introduction 11–001
    (1) Unfair competition foundations 11–001
    (2) The distinction between registered trade mark
        infringement and unfair competition 11–002
    (3) Introduction to unfair competition 11–003
    (4) Registered trade marks 11–006
    (5) The jurisprudence of the Supreme Court 11–015
2. The Trade Dress Cases 11–016
    (1) Two Pesos—a permissive approach 11–016
    (2) Qualitex—a state of ambivalence 11–026
    (3) Wal Mart—taking a step back 11–032
3. Traffix—Functionality 11–037
    (1) Functionality as a public policy 11–037
    (2) The judgment in Traffix 11–041
4. Other Limitations to Trade Mark Protection 11–047
    (1) Dastar—the scope of section 43(a) and copyright 11–047
    (2) KP Permanent—a balancing exercise 11–053
5. Victoria's Secret—The Uncertainties of Dilution 11–058
    (1) The basics of dilution 11–058
    (2) The Gay Olympic Games—protecting the
        Olympic symbols 11–060
    (3) The 1995 Act—section 43(c) 11–068
    (4) Establishing dilution 11–070
    (5) Victoria's Secret—the sceptic's stance 11–071
6. Parallel Imports 11–077
    (1) The exhaustion principle—universality v territoriality 11–077
    (2) Legislative context 11–081
    (3) The competition question 11–082
    (4) Material differences 11–083
    (5) K MART—parallel imports 11–084
7. Conclusion 11–101

CHAPTER 12

    Conclusion 12–001

TABLE OF CASES

National Cases by Jurisdiction

Benelux

P Ferrero & Co S.p.A v Alfred Ritter Schokoladefabrik Gmbh (Kinder), 19 January 1981, NJ 1981, 294 4–403

France

Baccarat, C.A. de Nancy, P.I.B.D. 1980 III 227 4–357
Cass. Commerc., P.I.B.D. 1982, No.312, III 238 4–357
L'Oreal SA v Bellure NV [2006] E.C.D.R. 16 C d'A (Paris) 4–038

Germany

Muhlens GMBH & Co KG v Zirh International Corp [2005] E.T.M.R. 55,
 LG (Hamburg) 5–052
Shell [1996] E.I.P.R. D45 5–191

Portugal

Beyeler v Italy [GC] no.33202/96, E.C.H.R., 2000–1 10–162
Broniowski v Poland [GC] no.31443/96 at E.C.H.R. 2004–v 10–162
Gratzinger and Gratzingerova v The Czech Republic [GC] no.39794/98,
 E.C.H.R. 2002-VII 10–163
Iatridis v Greece [GC] no.31107/96, E.C.H.R. 199-11 10–164
Smith Kline and French Laboratories Ltd v The Netherlands (12633/87)
 October 4, 1990 (DR) 66 10–162

Netherlands

Jullien v Verschuere [1983] Jur. Vol. 4, p.36 5–022
Turmac v Reynolds (A80/1) [1981] E.C.C. 346 7–008

Sweden

Koninklijke Philips Electronics NV v Rotary Shaver Sweden AB [2005]
 E.T.M.R. 103, HR (Stockholm) 4–086

United Kingdom

Arsenal Football Club Plc v Reed (No.1) [2001] 2 C.M.L.R. 23; [2001]
 E.T.M.R. 77; [2001] R.P.C. 46; (2001) 24(6) I.P.D. 24037, Ch D 6–014

TABLE OF CASES

Arsenal Football Club Plc v Reed (No.2) [2003] EWCA Civ 696; [2003] 3 All E.R. 865; [2003] 2 C.M.L.R. 25; [2003] Eu. L.R. 641; [2003] E.T.M.R. 73; [2003] R.P.C. 39; (2003) 26(7) I.P.D. 26045; (2003) 147 S.J.L.B. 663, CA (Civ Div) 6–022, 6–023

BP Amoco Plc v John Kelly Ltd [2001] N.I. 25; [2002] F.S.R. 5; [2001] E.T.M.R. CN14, CA (NI) 4–177

Boehringer Ingelheim KG v Swingward Ltd (Form of Reference to ECJ); Boehringer Ingelheim KG v Dowelhurst Ltd (Form of Reference to ECJ); Glaxo Group Ltd v Swingward Ltd (Form of Reference to ECJ); Glaxo Group Ltd v Dowelhurst Ltd (Form of Reference to ECJ); Smithkline Beecham Plc v Dowelhurst Ltd (Form of Reference to ECJ); Eli Lilly & Co v Dowelhurst Ltd (Form of Reference to ECJ) [2004] EWCA Civ 757; [2004] 3 C.M.L.R. 4; [2004] Eu. L.R. 959; (2004) 27(7) I.P.D. 27075; (2004) 148 S.J.L.B. 789, CA (Civ Div) 8–250

Boehringer Ingelheim KG v Swingward Ltd (Harm to Trade Mark Rights: Repackaging); Glaxo Group Ltd v Dowelhurst Ltd (Harm to Trade Mark Rights: Repackaging); Eli Lilly & Co v Dowelhurst Ltd (Harm to Trade Mark Rights: Repackaging); SmithKline Beecham Plc v Dowelhurst Ltd (Harm to Trade Mark Rights: Repackaging); Glaxo Group Ltd v Swingward Ltd (Harm to Trade Mark Rights: Repackaging); Boehringer Ingelheim KG v Dowelhurst Ltd (Harm to Trade Mark Rights: Repackaging) [2004] EWCA Civ 129; [2004] 3 C.M.L.R. 3; [2004] Eu. L.R. 757; [2004] E.T.M.R. 65; (2004) 27(6) I.P.D. 27057, CA (Civ Div) 8–250

British Sugar Plc v James Robertson & Sons Ltd [1997] E.T.M.R. 118; [1996] R.P.C. 281; (1996) 19(3) I.P.D. 19023, Ch D 5–076

Dyson Ltd v Registrar of Trade Marks; sub nom. Dyson Ltd's Trade Mark Application; Dyson Ltd v Registrar of Trade Marks [2003] EWHC 1062 (Ch); [2003] 1 W.L.R. 2406; [2003] E.T.M.R. 77; [2003] R.P.C. 47; (2003) 26(7) I.P.D. 26047; (2003) 100(28) L.S.G. 31, Ch D 4–014

European Economic Community v Syntex Corp; European Economic Community v Synthelabo [1990] 4 C.M.L.R. 343; [1990] F.S.R. 529, CEC 9–064

HP Bulmer Ltd v J Bollinger SA (No.2) [1974] Ch. 401; [1974] 3 W.L.R. 202; [1974] 2 All E.R. 1226; [1974] 2 C.M.L.R. 91; [1974] F.S.R. 334; [1975] R.P.C. 321; (1974) 118 S.J. 404, CA (Civ Div) 3–026, 3–029

John Lewis of Hungerford Ltd's Trade Mark Application [2001] E.T.M.R. 104; [2001] R.P.C. 28, App Person 4–038

Joseph Crosfield & Sons Ltd, Re; California Fig Syrup Co, Re; HN Brock & Co Ltd, Re;sub nom. California Fig Syrup Co's Trade Mark Application [1910] 1 Ch. 130; (1909) 26 R.P.C. 846, CA 4–536

Macarthys Ltd v Smith (Reference to ECJ) 1979] 1 W.L.R. 1189; [1979] 3 All E.R. 325; [1979] 3 C.M.L.R. 381; [1979] 3 C.M.L.R. 44; [1979] I.C.R. 785; [1979] I.R.L.R. 316; (1979) 123 S.J. 603, CA (Civ Div) 3–029

Mag Instrument Inc v California Trading Co Norway, Ulsteen (E2/97) [1998] 1 C.M.L.R. 331; [1998] E.T.M.R. 85, EFTA 8–211

Marca Mode CV v Adidas AG [1999] E.T.M.R. 791, HR (NL) 5–023

PERSIL Trade Mark, Re [1978] 1 C.M.L.R. 395; [1978] F.S.R. 348, CEC 9–064

Paranova A/S v Merck & Co Inc (E3/02) [2003] 3 C.M.L.R. 7; [2004] E.T.M.R. 1, EFTA 8–260, 8–273, 8–281

Philips Electronics NV v Remington Consumer Products Ltd (No.1) [1999] E.T.M.R. 816; [1999] R.P.C. 809; (1999) 22(9) I.P.D. 22084, CA (Civ Div) 4–007, 4–086

xx

TABLE OF CASES

Wagamama Ltd v City Centre Restaurants Plc [1997] Eu. L.R. 313; [1996] E.T.M.R. 23; [1995] F.S.R. 713, Ch D 5–014
Zino Davidoff SA v A&G Imports Ltd (No.1) [2000] Ch. 127; [1999] 3 W.L.R. 849; [1999] 3 All E.R. 711; [1999] 2 C.M.L.R. 1056; [1999] E.T.M.R. 700; [1999] I.T.C.L.R. 392; [1999] R.P.C. 631; (1999) 22(8) I.P.D. 22078, Ch D 8–228

United States of America

A Bourjois & Co v Katzel 260 U.S. 689, 43 S. Ct. 244 (1923) 11–078, 11–087, 11–094, 11–095, 11–100
A Leschen & Sons Rope Co v Broderick & Bascom Rope Co, 201 U.S. 166, 26 S.Ct. 425 (1906) 11–031
AHP Subsidiary Holding Co v Stuart Hale Co, 1 F. 3d 611, 27 U.S.P.Q. 2d 1758 (7th Cir. 1993) 11–058
AJ Canfield Co v Honickman, 808 F.2d 291 (3rd Cir. 1986) 11–018
ALPO Petfoods, Inc v Ralston Purina Co, 913 F.2d 958 (C.A.D.C. 1990) 11–049
AbBrit, Inc v Kraft, Inc, 812 F.2d 1531 (11th Cir. 1986)), cert. denied, 481 U.S. 1041, 107 S.Ct. 1983, 95 L.Ed.2d 822 (1987) 11–025
Abercrombie & Fitch Co v Hunting World, Inc, 537 F.2d 4 (2nd Cir. 1976) 11–018, 11–027, 11–034
Alfred Dunhill, Ltd v Interstate Cigar Co, 499 F.2d 232 (2nd Cir. 1974) 11–049
AmBrit, Inc v Kraft, Inc, 812 F.2d 1531 .... 11–018, 11–023
American Greetings Corp v Dan-Dee Imports, Inc, 807 F.2d 1136 (3rd Cir. 1986) 11–018
American Philatelic Soc v Claibourne, 3 Cal. 2d 689, 46 P.2d 135 (1935) 11–004
American Steel Foundries v Robertson, 269 U.S. 372 (1926) 11–011
American Washboard Co v Saginaw Mfg Co, 103 F.281 (6th Cir. 1900) 11–024
Amsted Industries, Inc v West Coast Wire Rope & Rigging Inc, 2 U.S.P.Q.2d 1755 (TTAB 1987) 11–030
Artic Electronics Co, Re 220 U.S.P.Q. 836 (T.T.A.B. 1983) 11–012
Ashley Furniture Industries, Inc v Sangiacomo N.A., Ltd, 187 F.3d 363 (4th Cir. 1999) 11–034
Autozone, Inc, et al v Tandy Corp, 71 U.S.P.Q.2d 1385 (6th Cir. 2004) 11–101
Baglin v Cusenier Co, 221 U.S. 580, 31 S.Ct. 669 (1911) 11–055
Beer Nuts Inc v Clover Club Foods Co, 805 F.2dn 920 (10th Cir. 1986) 11–056
Bell Bio-Medical v Cin-Bad, Inc, 864 F.2d 1253 (5th Cir. 1989) 11–017
Blue Chip Stamps v Manor Drug Stores, 421 U.S. 723, 95.S.Ct. 1917 (1975) 11–063
Blum v Yaretsky, 457 U.S. 991, 102 S.Ct. 2777 (1982) 11–066
Bonito Boats, Inc v Thunder Craft Boats, Inc, 489 U.S. 141, 109 S.Ct. 971 (1989) 11–043, 11–051, 11–052
Brunswick Corp v British Seagull Ltd, 35 F.3d 1527 (CA Fed. 1994) 11–031
Brunswick Corp v Spirit Reel Co, 832 F.2d 513 (10th Cir. 1987) 11–018
COPIAT v United States, 252 U.S.App.D.C. 342, 790 F.2d 903 (1986) 11–084, 11–092, 11–096
Campbell Soup Co v Armour & Co, 175 F.2d 795 (3rd Cir. 1949) 11–030
Canal Co v Clark, 13 Wall. 311, 20 L.Ed. 581 (1872) 11–055, 11–056
Car-Freshner Corp v SC Johnson & Son, Inc, 70 F.3d 267 (2nd Cir. 1995) 11–057
Car-Freshner Corp v Turtle Wax, Inc, 268 F.Supp 162 (SDNY 1967) 11–027
Central Hudson Gas & Electric Corp v Public Service Comm'n of New York, 447 U.S. 557, 100 S.Ct. 2343 (1980) 11–064

xxi

TABLE OF CASES

Chevron Chemical Co v Voluntary Purchasing Groups, Inc, 659 F.2d 695
  (5th Cir. 1981) 11–019, 11–023, 11–024
City Council of Los Angeles v Taxpayers for Vincent, 466 U.S. 789, 104
  S.Ct. 2118 (1984) 11–064
Clarke, Re, 17 U.S.P.Q. 2d 1238 (TTAB 1990) 4–038, 11–027
Clock & Radio Co v Vacheron & Constantin–Le Coultre Watches, 105
  U.S.P.Q. 160 (2nd Cir. 1955) 11–012
Co v National Biscuit Co, 305 U.S. 111 (1938) 11–018
Coca Cola v Gemini Rising, 346 F. Supp. 1183, 175 U.S.P.Q. 56
  (E.D.N.Y. 1972) 11–059
Coca-Cola Co v Koke Co of America, 254 U.S. 143, 41 S.Ct.113 (1920) 11–031
Cohen v California, 403 U.S. 15, 91 S.Ct. 1780 (1971) 11–063
Cosmetically Sealed Industries, Inc v Chesebrough-Pond's USA Co, 125
  F.3d 28 (2nd Cir. 1997) 11–054, 11–057
Crescent Tool Co v Kilborn and Bishop Co, 247 F. 299 (1917) 11–023, 11–024
Dastar Corp v Twentieth Century Fox Film Corp, 539 U.S. 23, 123 S.Ct.
  2041 (2003) 11–047, 11–049
Deere & Co v Farmland, Inc, 560 F. Supp. 85 (721 F.2d 253 (8th Cir. 1983) 11–031
Dial-A-Matress Franchise Corp v Page, 880 F.2d 675 (2nd Cir. 1989) 11–030
Eastern Wine Corp v Winslow Warren Ltd, 137 F.2d 955, 57 USPQ 565 (2dn
  Cir. 1943) 11–003
Eldred v Ashcroft, 537 U.S. 186, 123 S.Ct. 769 11–052
EI Du Pont de Nemours & Co, Re 476 F.2d 1357, 177 U.S.P.Q. 563
  (C.C.P.A. 1973) 11–013
Everett O Fisk & Co v Fisk Teachers' Agency, Inc, 3 F.2d 7, (8th Cir. 1924) ... 11–096
Fashion Two Twenty Inc v Steinberg, 339 F. Supp. 836, 172 USPQ 102
  (E.D.N.Y. 1971) 11–003
Federal-Mogul-Bower Bearings, Inc v Azzof, 313 F.2d 405 (6th Cir. 1963) 11–049
Ferrero, Re 178 U.S.P.Q. 167 (C.C.P.A. 1973) 11–011
First Brands Corp v Fred Meyers, Inc, 809 F.2d 1378 (9th Cir. 1987) 11–018
Flagg Mfg Co v Holway, 178 Mass. 83 (1901) 11–024
Friedman v Rogers, 440 U.S. 1, 99. S.Ct. 887 (1979) 11–064
Gibson Guitar Corp v Paul Reed Smith Guitars, LP, 126 S.Ct. 2355 (2006) ... 11–103
Gibson Guitar Corp v Paul Reed Smith Guitars, LP, 423 F.3d 539
  (6th Cir. 2005) 11–103
Hanover Star Milling Co v Metcalf, 240 U.S. 403, 415, 36 S.Ct. 357, 361
  (1916) 11–100
Hard Rock Café Licensing corp v Concessions Services Inc, 955 F.3d 1143
  (7th Cir. 1992) 6–069
Harper & Row Publishers, Inc v Nation Enterprises, 471 U.S. 539, 105 S.Ct.
  2218 (1985) 11–065
Hermes Intern v Lederer de Paris Fifth Ave Inc, 55 U.S.P.Q.2d 1360 (2nd
  Cir. 2000) 11–012
Herring-Hall-Marvin Safe Co v Hall's Safe Co, 208 U.S. 554, 28 S.Ct. 350
  (1908) 11–055
Hibbs v Winn, 542 U.S. 88, 124 S.Ct 2276 (2004) 11–056
Hodes-Lange Corp, Re 167 U.S.P.Q. 256 (TTAB 1970) 11–030
INS Cardoza-Fonseca, 480 U.S. 421 (1987) 11–096
Independent Baking Powder Co v Boorman, 175 F. 448, (CC NJ 1910) 11–096
International News Service v Associated Press, 248 U.S. 215, 39
  S.Ct. 68 (1918) 11–063, 11–065
Inwood Laboratories, Inc v Ives Laboratories, Inc, 456 U.S. 844 (1982) 6–069,
                                                            11–016, 11–018,
                                                            11–024, 11–027,

TABLE OF CASES

11–028, 11–031, 11–037,
11–046, 11–052
J Wiss & Sons Co v WE Bassett Co, 59 C.C.P.A. 1269 (Pat.), 462 F.2d 569 (1972) 11–027
John H Harland Co v Clarke Checks, Inc, 711 F.2d 966 (11th Cir. 1983) 11–017
KP Permanent Make-Up, Inc v Lasting Impression Inc, 543 U.S. 111, 125 S.Ct. 542 11–053
K Mart Corp v Cartier Inc, et al. 47th Street Photo Inc, 486 U.S. 281, 108 S.Ct. 1811 (1988) 11–023,
11–081, 11–084
Kellogg Co v Exxon Corp, 209 F.3d 562 (6th Cir. 2000) 11–073
Kellogg Co v National Biscuit Co, 305 U.S. 111, 59 S.Ct. 109 (1938) 11–028,
11–039
Knitwaves, Inc v Lollytogs, Ltd, 71 F.3d 996 (2nd Cir. 1995) 11–034
L'Aiglon Apparel, Inc v Lana Lobell Inc, 214 F.2d 649 (3rd Cir. 1954) 11–023
LeSportsac, Inc v K Mart Corp, 754 F.2d 71 (2nd Cir. 1985) 11–021,
11–023
Lever Bros Co v United States 981 F.2d 1330, 25 USPQ2d 1579 (D.C. Cir. 1993) 11–083
Lever Brothers Co v United States, 652 F.Supp. 403 (DC 1987) 11–092
Life Savers Corp v Curtiss Candy Co, 182 F.2d 4 (7th Cir. 1950) 11–031
Lone Star Steakhouse and Saloon, Inc v Alpha of Virginia, Inc, 43 F.3d 922 (4th Cir. 1995) 11–055
Mackey v Lanier Collection Agency & Service, Inc, 486 U.S. 825, 108 S.Ct. 2182 (1988) 11–051
McLean v Fleming, 96 U.S. 245 (1878) 11–031
Macmahan Pharmacal Co v Denver Chemical Mfg Co, 113 F. 468, 475 (8th Cir. 1901) 11–096
McNeil–PPC v Guardian Drug Co, 45 U.S.P.Q.2d 1437 (E.D. Mich. 1997) 11–012
Master Distributors, Inc v Pako Corp, 986 F.2d 219 (8th Cir. 1993) 11–027
Maternally Yours, Inc v Your Maternity Shop, Inc, 234 F.2d 538 (2nd Cir. 1956) 11–023
Mead Data Central Inc v Toyota, 875 F.2d 1026, 10 U.S.P.Q.2d 1961 (2nd Cir.) 11–058
Mishawaka Rubber & Woolen Mfg Co v SS Kresge Co, 316 U.S. 203, 62 S.Ct. 1022 (1942) 11–065
Mobil Oil Corp v Pegasus Petroleum Corp, 2 U.S.P.Q.2d 1677 (2nd Cir. 1987) 11–012
Morton Norwich Products Inc, Re 671 F2d 1332, 213 U.S.P.Q. 9 (C.C.P.A. 1982) 11–038, 11–039
Moseley v Victoria Secret Catalogue 537 U.S. 418, 123 S.Ct. 1115 ..... 11–071, 11–074
Moskal v United States, 498 U.S. 103, 111 S.Ct. 461 (1990) 11–023
Nabisco, Inc v PF Brands, Inc, 51 U.S.P.Q.2d 1882 (2nd Cir. 1999) 11–068,
11–070, 11–073
New West Corp v NYM Co of California, Inc, 595 F.2d 1194 (9th Cir. 1979) ... 11–023
Nikon, Inc v Ikon Corp, 987 F. 2d 91, 25 U.S.P.Q. 2d 2021 (2d Cir. 1993) 11–058
Nor-Am Chemical v O.M. Scott & Sons Co, 4 U.S.P.Q.2d 1316 (ED Pa. 1987) 11–031
NutraSweet Co v Stadt Corp, 917 F.2d 1024 (7th Cir. 1990) 11–027
Olympus Corp v United States, 792 F.2d 315 (2nd Cir. 1986), aff'g 627 F.Supp. 911 (EDNY 1985) 11–092
Optimum Technologies Inc v Henkel Consumer Adhesives Inc, 496 F.3d 1231 (11th Cir. 2007) 6–069

TABLE OF CASES

Osawa & Co v B & H Photo, 589 F. Supp. 1163, 223 U.S.P.Q. 124 (S.D.N.Y. 1984) 11–078
Owens-Corning Fiberglas Corp, Re 774 F.2d 1116 (CA Fed. 1985) 11–027, 11–031
PACCAR Inc v Telescan Technologies, LLC, 319 F.3d 243 (6th Cir. 2003) 11–054
Pagliero v Wallace China Co, 198 F.2d 339, 95 U.S.P.Q. 45 (9th Cir. 1952) 11–040
Park 'N Fly, Inc v Dollar Park and Fly, Inc, 469 U.S. 189, 224 U.S.P.Q.2d 327 (1985) 11–018, 11–021, 11–057
Philadelphia Novelty Mfg Co v Rouss, 40 F. 585 (CC SDNY 1889) 11–024
Polaroid Corp v Polarad Electronics Corp, 287 F.2d 492, 128 U.S.P.Q. 411 (2dn Cir. 1961) 11–013
Posadas de Puerto Rico Assoc v Tourism Company of Puerto Rico, 478 U.S. 328, 106 S.Ct. 2968 (1986) 11–064
Punta Operations, Inc v Universal Marine Co, 543 F.2d 1107 (5th Cir. 1976) 11–049
Qualitex Co v Jacobson Products Co, 514 U.S. 159, 34 U.S.P.Q.2d 1161 (1995) 4–178, 11–026, 11–029, 11–034, 11–035, 11–040, 11–046, 11–051, 11–074
Rendell-Baker v Kohn, 457 U.S. 830, 102 S.Ct. 2764 (1982) 11–066
Ringling Bros–Barnum & Bailey Combined Shows, Inc v Utah Division of Travel Dev, 170 F.3d 449 (4th Cir. 1999) 11–073
Rolex Watch USA v Meece, 158 F.3d 816 (5th Cir. 1998) 6–069
Russello v United States, 464 U.S. 16, 104 S.Ct. 296 11–055
San Francisco Arts & Athletics, Inc v United States Olympic Committee 483 U.S. 522, 3 U.S.P.Q.2d 1145 (1987) 11–060
Sarkisian v Winn-Proof Corp, 697 F.2d 1313 (9th Cir. 1983) 11–044
Scandinavia Belting Co v Asbestos & Rubber Works of America, Inc, 257 F. 937, (2nd Cir. 1919) 11–096, 11–100
Seabrook Foods, Inc v Bar-Well Foods, Ltd, 568 F.2d 1342 (1977) 11–035
Sear, Roebuck & Co v Stiffel Co, 376 U.S. 225, 84 S.Ct. 784 (1964) 11–051
Shakespeare Co v Silstar Corp of Am, 110 F.3d 234 (4th Cir. 1997) 11–054, 11–056, 11–057
Sheet & Tube Co v Tallman Conduit Co, 149 U.S.P.Q. 656 (TTAB 1966) ... 11–030
Smith v Montoro, 648 F.2d 602 (9th Cir. 1981) 11–049
Sony Corp of America v Universal City Studios Inc, 464 US 417 (1984) 6–076
Stop the Olympic Prison v United States Olympic Committee, 489 F.Supp. 1112 (S.D.N.Y. 1980) 11–064
Stormy Clime Ltd v ProGroup, Inc, 809 F.2d 971 (2nd Cir. 1987) ... 11–018, 11–023
Stuart Hall Co, Inc v Ampad Corp, 51 F.3d 780 (8th Cir. 1995) 11–034
Sunbeam Products, Inc v West Bend Co, F.3d 246 (5th Cir. 1997) 11–042
Sunmark, Inc v Ocean Spray Cranberries, Inc, 64 F.3d 1055 (7th Cir. 1995) 11–054, 11–057
Swift & Co v United States, 276 U.S. 311, 48 S.Ct. 311 11–076
Thompson Medical Co v Pfizer Inc, 753 F.2d 208 (2nd Cir. 1985) 11–018, 11–021
Tiger v Western Investment Co, 221 U.S. 286, 31 S.Ct. 578 11–024
Trade Mark Cases, 100 U.S. 82, 25 L. Ed. 550 (1879) 11–005
TrafFix Devices, Inc v Marketing Displays, Inc, 532 U.S. 23, 58 U.S.P.Q.2d 1001 (2001) 11–039, 11–041, 11–051, 11–052
Two Pesos, Inc v Taco Cabana, Inc, 505 U.S. 763, 23 U.S.P.Q.2d 1081 (1992) 11–016, 11–025, 11–027, 11–029, 11–034, 11–036, 11–046, 11–055

TABLE OF CASES

United States Jaycees v Philadelphia Jaycees, 639 F.2d 134 (3rd Cir. 1981) 11–056
United States v Guerlain, Inc 78 S. Ct. 285, 19 USPQ 501 (1958) 11–082
United States v O'Brien, 391 U.S. 367, 88 S.Ct. 1673 (1968) 11–064
United States v Turkette, 452 U.S. 576, 101 S.Ct. 2524 11–023
United States v Wong Kim Bo, 472 F.2d 720 (5th Cir. 1972) 11–055
University of Georgia Athletic Assn v Laite, 756 F.2d 1535 (11th Cir. 1985) 11–018
Valu Enginnering, Inc v Rexnord Corp, 278 F.3d 1268, 61 U.S.P.Q.2d 1422 (Fed. Cir. 2002) 11–038
Vibrant Sales, Inc v New Body Boutique, Inc, 652 F.2d 299 (2nd Cir. 1981) 11–016, 11–021, 11–023
Villeroy & Boch Keramiche Werke KG v THC Sys, Inc, 999 F.2d 619, 27 U.S.P.Q.2d 1866 (2nd Cir. 1993) 11–040
Virginia Pharmacy Bd v Virginia Citizens Consumer Council, Inc, 425 U.S. 748, 96 S.Ct. 1817 (1976) 11–064
Vivitar–Corp v United States, 761 F.2d 1552 (CA Fed. 1985), aff'g 593 F.Supp. 420 (Ct.Int'l Trade 1984) 11–092
Vornado Air Circulation Systems, Inc, v Duracraft Corp, 58 F.3d 1498 (10th Cir. 1995) 11–042, 11–046
WT Rogers Co v Keene, 778 F.2d 334 (7th Cir. 1985) 11–031
Wal-Mart Stores, Inc v Samara Bros, Inc, 529 U.S. 205, 54 U.S.P.Q.2d 1065 (2000) 11–032, 11–043, 11–052
Weil Ceramics & Glass, Inc v Dash, 878 F.2d 659, 11 USPQ2d 1001 (3d Cir. 1989) 11–080
William R Warner & Co v Elli Lilly & Co, 265 U.S. 526, 44 S.Ct. 615 (1924) 11–055
Yale Electric Corp v Robertson, 26 F.2d 972 (2nd Cir. 1928) 11–024
Zatarains, Inc v Oak Grove Smokehouse, 698 F.2d 786 (5th Cir. 1983) 11–054

TABLE OF EUROPEAN CASES

Cases before the European Court of Justice, Court of First Instance and European Court of Human Rights

ACF Chemiefarma NV v Commission of the European Communities
(41/69) [1970] E.C.R. 661, ECJ 9-016
AKZO Chemie BV v Commission of the European Communities (C-62/86)
[1991] E.C.R. I-3359; [1993] 5 C.M.L.R. 215; [1994] F.S.R. 25, ECJ
(5th Chamber) 9-085, 9-086
AMS Advanced Medical Services GmbH v OHIM (T-425/03) unreported ... 7-051
ASM Brescia SpA v Comune di Rodengo Saiano (C-347/06) [2008] 3
C.M.L.R. 35, ECJ (2nd Chamber) 5-236
Adam Opel AG v Autec AG (C-48/05) [2007] C.E.C. 204; [2007] E.T.M.R.
33, ECJ (1st Chamber) 3-015, 6-024, 6-034, 6-035,
6-036, 6-037, 6-039,
6-059, 6-063, 6-069
Adam P.H Blomefield v Commission of the European Communities
(190/82) [1983] E.C.R. 3981, ECJ 3-065
Adeneler v Ellinikos Organismos Galaktos (ELOG) (C-212/04) [2007] All
E.R. (EC) 82; [2006] E.C.R. I-6057; [2006] 3 C.M.L.R. 30; [2006]
I.R.L.R. 716, ECJ 8-277
Adidas AG v Marca Mode CV (Marca II) (C-102/07) [2008] E.T.M.R. 44;
[2008] F.S.R. 38, ECJ (1st Chamber) 6-040, 6-046,
6-047, 6-048,
6-049, 6-050
Adidas-Salomon AG v Fitnessworld Trading Ltd (C-408/01) [2004] Ch. 120;
[2004] 2 W.L.R. 1095; [2003] E.C.R. I-12537; [2004] 1 C.M.L.R. 14;
[2004] C.E.C. 3; [2004] E.T.M.R. 10; [2004] F.S.R. 21, ECJ (6th
Chamber) 3-027, 5-197, 5-200, 5-201,
5-203, 5-204, 5-206, 5-207,
5-209, 5-211, 5-218,
5-221, 5-236, 5-239
Administration des Douanes et Droits Indirects v Rioglass SA (C-115/02)
[2003] E.C.R. I-12705; [2006] 1 C.M.L.R. 12; [2004] E.T.M.R. 38; [2004]
F.S.R. 35, ECJ (6th Chamber) 8-245
Alcon Inc v Office for Harmonisation in the Internal Market (Trade Marks
and Designs) (OHIM) (C192/03 P) [2004] E.C.R. I-8993; [2005]
E.T.M.R. 69, ECJ (6th Chamber) 4-102, 4-490, 4-491,
4-492, 4-493, 4-614, 5-149
Alcon Inc v Office for Harmonisation in the Internal Market (Trade Marks
and Designs) (OHIM) (C-412/05 P) [2007] E.T.M.R. 68; [2007] Bus.
L.R. D85, ECJ 5-147, 5-149,
5-150, 5-151
Alcon Inc v Office for Harmonisation in the Internal Market (Trade Marks
and Designs) (OHIM) (T-130/03) [2005] E.C.R. II-3859, CFI 5-148

TABLE OF EUROPEAN CASES

American Clothing Associates v OHIM (Representation of a maple leaf)
  (T-215/06) [2008] E.C.R. II-303 .... 4-570, 4-571, 4-580,
                                                                4-581, 4-582,
                                                                4-583, 4-584
Amministrazione delle Finanze dello Stato v Meridionale Industria Salumi
  Srl (212/80) [1981] E.C.R. 2735, ECJ 6-096
Amministrazione delle Finanze dello Stato v Schiavon Silvano (A Firm)
  (C230/98) [2000] E.C.R. I-3547, ECJ 4-469
Amministrazione delle Finanze dello Stato v Simmenthal SpA (106/77);
  sub nom. Italian Tax and Revenue Administration v SA Simmenthal,
  Monza (Italy) (106/77) [1978] E.C.R. 629; [1978] 3 C.M.L.R. 263, ECJ 3-043
Ampafrance SA v Office for Harmonisation in the Internal Market (Trade
  Marks and Designs) (OHIM) (T-164/03) [2005] E.C.R. II-1401; [2005]
  E.T.M.R. 107, CFI (3rd Chamber) 3-061
Amsterdam Bulb BV v Produktschap voor Siergewassen (C-50/76) [1977]
  E.C.R. 137; [1977] 2 C.M.L.R. 218, ECJ 3-032
Angonese v Cassa di Risparmio di Bolzano SpA (C-281/98) [2000] All E.R.
  (EC) 577; [2000] E.C.R. I-4139; [2000] 2 C.M.L.R. 1120; [2000] C.E.C.
  374, ECJ 3-037
Anheuser-Busch Inc v Budejovicky Budvar Narodni Podnik (C-245/02)
  [2004] E.C.R. I-10989; [2005] E.T.M.R. 27, ECJ 6-030, 6-033,
                                                                6-069, 6-080,
                                                                6-086, 6-088,
                                                                6-093, 6-140,
                                                              10-064, 10-133
Anheuser-Busch Inc v Portugal (73049/01) [2006] E.T.M.R. 43; (2007) 44
  E.H.R.R. 42, ECHR 3-069,
                                                                       10-156,
                                                              10-162, 10-163
Ansul BV v Ajax Brandbeveiliging BV (C-40/01) [2005] Ch. 97; [2004] 3
  W.L.R. 1048; [2003] E.C.R. I-2439; [2005] 2 C.M.L.R. 36; [2003]
  E.T.M.R. 85; [2003] R.P.C. 40; (2005) 28(4) I.P.D. 28022, ECJ 4-283, 6-026,
                                                                6-126, 7-007, 7-018,
                                                                7-021, 7-022, 7-023,
                                                                7-025, 7-026, 7-034,
                                                                7-035, 7-044, 7-046,
                                                                7-047, 7-048, 7-053,
                                                                7-063, 7-086
Antartica Srl v Office for Harmonisation in the Internal Market (Trade
  Marks and Designs) (OHIM) (C-320/07 P), ECJ 7-073
Antartica Srl v Office for Harmonisation in the Internal Market (Trade
  Marks and Designs) (OHIM) (T-47/06) [2007] E.T.M.R. 77, CFI (3rd
  Chamber) 5-240, 5-244,
                                                                7-049, 7-052
Apple and Pear Development Council v KJ Lewis Ltd (C222/82) [1983]
  E.C.R. 4083; [1984] 3 C.M.L.R. 733, ECJ 8-017
Aragonesa de Publicidad Exterior SA v Departmento de Sanidad y
  Seguridad Social de la Generalitat de Cataluna (C-1/90); Publivia SAE
  v Departmento de Sanidad y Seguridad Social de la Generalitat de
  Cataluna (C-176/90) [1991] E.C.R. I-4151; [1994] 1 C.M.L.R. 887, ECJ ... 8-038
Arbeitsgemeinschaft Deutscher Rundfunkanstalten (ARD) v Pro Sieben
  Media AG (C6/98) [2000] All E.R. (EC) 3; [1999] E.C.R. I-7599; [1999]
  3 C.M.L.R. 769; [2000] C.E.C. 59; [2000] E.M.L.R. 349, ECJ (6th
  Chamber) 4-500

TABLE OF EUROPEAN CASES

Bayerische Motorenwerke AG v Deenik (C-63/97) BMW AG v Deenik
(C-63/97)[1999] All E.R. (EC) 235; [1999] E.C.R. I-905; [1999] 1
C.M.L.R. 1099; [1999] C.E.C. 159; [1999] E.T.M.R. 339, ECJ 4-026, 4-183,
4-240, 4-480, 4-507,
6-011, 6-012, 6-026,
6-027, 6-035, 6-086, 6-088,
6-094, 6-108, 6-110, 6-113,
6-114, 6-115, 6-121, 6-122, 6-123,
6-124, 6-129, 6-132, 6-134,
6-135, 6-137, 8-189, 8-223,
8-261, 8-262, 8-286, 10-018,
10-022, 10-027, 10-060
Becker v European Parliament (C-41/88) [1989] E.C.R. 3807, ECJ 3-065
Becker v Finanzamt Munster-Innenstadt (8/81) [1982] E.C.R. 53; [1982] 1
C.M.L.R. 499, ECJ 3-036
Beguelin Import Co v Import Export SA GL (C22/71) [1971] E.C.R. 949;
[1972] C.M.L.R. 81, ECJ 9-014, 9-037
Belgische Radio en Televisie v SABAM SV (127/73) (No.1) [1974] E.C.R.
51, ECJ 9-008,
9-011, 9-048
Belgium v Commission of the European Communities (C142/87); sub
nom. Aid to Tubemeuse, Re (C142/87) [1990] E.C.R. I-959; [1991] 3
C.M.L.R. 213, ECJ 10-082
Benetton Group SpA v G-Star International BV (C-371/06) [2008]
E.T.M.R. 5, ECJ (6th Chamber) 4-521,
4-525, 4-526
Best Buy Concepts Inc v Office for Harmonisation in the Internal Market
(Trade Marks and Designs) (OHIM) (T122/01) [2003] E.C.R. II-2235;
[2004] E.T.M.R. 19, CFI (2nd Chamber) 4-164
Bic SA v Office for Harmonisation in the Internal Market (Trade Marks
and Designs) (OHIM) (T262/04) (Unreported, December 15, 2005),
CFI 4-648
BioID AG v Office for Harmonisation in the Internal Market (Trade Marks
and Designs) (OHIM) (T-91/01) [2002] E.C.R. II-5159; [2003]
E.T.M.R. 60, CFI (2nd Chamber) 4-132
Bioid AG (In Liquidation) v Office for Harmonisation in the Internal
Market (Trade Marks and Designs) (OHIM) (C-37/03) [2005] E.C.R.
I-7975, ECJ 3-066, 4-132,
4-145, 4-147, 4-150,
4-296, 4-298, 4-299,
5-055, 5-082, 5-132, 7-084
Biret International SA v Council of the European Union (C-93/02 P) [2003]
E.C.R. I-10497; [2006] 1 C.M.L.R. 17, ECJ 4-197
Bjornekulla Fruktindustrier AB v Procordia Food AB (C371/02) [2004]
E.C.R. I-5791; [2005] 3 C.M.L.R. 16; [2004] E.T.M.R. 69; [2004] R.P.C.
45, ECJ (6th Chamber) 4-499
Boehringer Ingelheim Pharma KG v Swingward Ltd (C-143/00) [2002]
E.C.R. I-3759 .... 8-154, 8-163,
8-164, 8-165, 8-168,
8-250, 8-252, 8-254,
8-259, 8-263, 8-265,
8-271, 8-272, 8-273,
8-274, 8-275, 8-280,
8-282, 8-285, 9-109

TABLE OF EUROPEAN CASES

Armacell Enterprise GmbH v Office for Harmonisation in the Internal
  Market (Trade Marks and Designs) (OHIM) (T-172/05) [2006] E.C.R.
  II-4061, CFI 5-164
Arsenal Football Club Plc v Reed (C-206/01) [2003] Ch. 454; [2003] 3
  W.L.R. 450; [2003] All E.R. (EC) 1; [2002] E.C.R. I-10273; [2003] 1
  C.M.L.R. 12; [2003] C.E.C. 3; [2003] E.T.M.R. 19; [2003] R.P.C. 9;
  (2002) 152 N.L.J. 1808, ECJ 4-062, 4-532,
                                                              4-541, 5-009, 5-010,
                                                              5-088, 5-100, 5-105,
                                                              5-195, 6-008, 6-011,
                                                              6-014, 6-017, 6-018,
                                                              6-019, 6-020, 6-021,
                                                              6-026, 6-028, 6-033,
                                                              6-059, 6-063, 6-069,
                                                              6-070, 6-086, 6-119,
                                                              6-126, 6-134, 7-012,
                                                              10-064, 10-140, 10-147
Aslanidou v Ypourgos Ygeias & Pronoias (C142/04) [2005] E.C.R. I-7181,
  ECJ 3-035
Association des Centres Distributeurs Edouard Leclerc v Au Ble Vert Sarl
  (C-229/83) [1985] E.C.R. 1; [1985] 2 C.M.L.R. 286, ECJ 8-033,
                                                                          8-034
Atlanta Fruchthandelsgesellschaft mbH v Bundesamt fur Ernahrung und
  Forstwirtschaft (C-465/93) [1996] All E.R. (E.C.) 31; [1995] E.C.R.
  I-3761; [1996] 1 C.M.L.R. 575, ECJ 3-049
August Storck KG v Office for Harmonisation in the Internal Market
  (Trade Marks and Designs) (OHIM) (C-24/05) [2006] E.C.R. I-5677,
  ECJ 4-311, 4-320,
                                                              4-325, 4-340,
                                                              4-628, 4-633,
                                                              4-634, 4-645, 5-087
Australian Mining & Smelting Europe Ltd v Commission of the European
  Communities (155/79); sub nom. AM&S Europe Ltd v Commisson of
  the European Communities (155/79) [1983] Q.B. 878; [1983] 3 W.L.R.
  17; [1983] 1 All E.R. 705; [1982] E.C.R. 1575; [1982] 2 C.M.L.R. 264;
  [1982] F.S.R. 474; (1983) 127 S.J. 410, ECJ 3-052
Azienda Agricola Monte Arcosu Srl v Regione Autonoma della Sardegna
  (C403/98) [2001] E.C.R. I-103; [2002] 2 C.M.L.R. 14, ECJ (6th
  Chamber) 3-032
BAT Cigaretten-Fabriken GmbH v Commission of the European
  Communities (C35/83) [1985] E.C.R. 363; [1985] 2 C.M.L.R. 470;
  [1985] F.S.R. 533, ECJ 9-062, 9-063
BVBA Management Training & Consultancy v Benelux-Merkenbureau
  (C-239/05) [2007] E.T.M.R. 35, ECJ (2nd Chamber) 4-447,
                                                                   4-462, 4-463,
                                                                   4-464, 4-477
Bank fur Arbeit und Wirtschaft AG v Office for Harmonisation in the
  Internal Market (Trade Marks and Designs) (OHIM) (T87/00) [2001]
  E.C.R. II-1259; [2001] C.E.C. 73; [2001] E.T.M.R. 68, CFI 4-163
Bauhuis v Netherlands (46/76) [1977] E.C.R. 5, ECJ 8-019
Bayer AG v Commission of the European Communities (C-195/91) [1994]
  E.C.R. I-5619, AGO 9-066
Bayerische Motorenwerke AG v ALD Auto-Leasing D GmbH (C-70/93)
  [1995] E.C.R. I-3439; [1996] 4 C.M.L.R. 478, ECJ 9-076, 9-078

TABLE OF EUROPEAN CASES

Boehringer Mannheim GmbH v Commission of the European
  Communities (45/69) [1970] E.C.R. 769, ECJ 9-016
Booker Aquaculture Ltd (t/a Marine Harvest McConnell) v Scottish
  Ministers (C20/00); Hydro Seafood GSP Ltd v Scottish Ministers
  (C64/00) [2003] E.C.R. I-7411; [2003] 3 C.M.L.R. 6; [2003] N.P.C. 89,
  ECJ 6-074
Bovemij Verzekeringen NV v Benelux-Merkenbureau (C-108/05) [2006]
  E.C.R. I-7605; [2007] E.T.M.R. 29, ECJ (1st Chamber) 4-635
Brasserie de Haecht SA v Wilkin (23/67) [1967] E.C.R. 407; [1968]
  C.M.L.R. 26, ECJ 9-040, 9-074
Brasserie du Pecheur SA v Germany (C-46/93); R. v Secretary of State for
  Transport Ex p. Factortame Ltd (C-48/93) [1996] Q.B. 404; [1996] 2
  W.L.R. 506; [1996] All E.R. (EC) 301; [1996] E.C.R. I-1029; [1996] 1
  C.M.L.R. 889; [1996] C.E.C. 295; [1996] I.R.L.R. 267, ECJ 3-039
Brauerei A Bilger Sohne GmbH v Jehle (43/69) [1970] E.C.R. 127; [1974]
  1 C.M.L.R. 382, ECJ 9-042
Bristol Myers Squibb Co v Paranova A/S (C-427/93); Bayer AG v Paranova
  A/S (C-436/93); CH Boehringer Sohn v Paranova A/S (C-
  429/93) [2003] Ch. 75; [2002] 3 W.L.R. 1746; [1996] E.C.R. I-3457;
  [1997] 1 C.M.L.R. 1151; [1996] C.E.C. 716; [1996] E.T.M.R. 1; [1997]
  F.S.R. 102; (1997) 34 B.M.L.R. 59, ECJ 4-504, 5-065,
                                                   8-088, 8-089, 8-090, 8-091,
                                                   8-111, 8-122, 8-123, 8-126,
                                                   8-129, 8-130, 8-131, 8-132,
                                                   8-133, 8-134, 8-139, 8-143,
                                                   8-145, 8-150, 8-163, 8-164,
                                                   8-174, 8-175, 8-176, 8-178,
                                                   8-180, 8-182, 8-184, 8-185,
                                                   8-188, 8-193, 8-195, 8-205,
                                                   8-255, 8-257, 8-263, 8-272,
                                                   8-280, 8-282, 8-283
British Airways Plc v Commission of the European Communities
  (C-95/04 P) [2007] 4 C.M.L.R. 22; [2007] C.E.C. 607, ECJ (3rd Chamber) ... 9-115
British Leyland Plc v Commission of the European Communities
  (C226/84) [1986] E.C.R. 3263; [1987] R.T.R. 136; [1987] 1 C.M.L.R.
  185, ECJ (5th Chamber) 9-131
Buchler & Co v Commission of the European Communities (44/69) [1970]
  E.C.R. 733, ECJ 9-016
Budejovicky Budvar Narodni Podnik v Rudolf Ammersin GmbH
  (C216/01) [2003] E.C.R. I-13617; [2005] 1 C.M.L.R. 56; [2004]
  E.T.M.R. 21, ECJ 10-106, 10-119
Buet v Ministere Public (C-382/87) [1989] E.C.R. 1235; [1993] 3 C.M.L.R.
  659, ECJ (5th Chamber) 4-554
Bundeskartellamt v Volkswagen AG (C-266/93) [1995] E.C.R. I-3477,
  ECJ 9-015,
                                                                     9-075
Bundesverband der Arzneimittel Importeure eV v Bayer AG (C-2/01 P); sub
  nom. Bayer AG v Commission of the European Communities (C-2/01
  P) [2004] All E.R. (EC) 500; [2004] E.C.R. I-23; [2004] 4 C.M.L.R. 13;
  [2004] E.T.M.R. 100; [2005] I.C.R. 834; (2004) 78 B.M.L.R. 91, ECJ 9-018,
                                                              9-019, 9-020, 9-021
Buy Irish Campaign, Re (C249/81); sub nom. Commission of the European
  Communities v Ireland (C249/81) [1982] E.C.R. 4005; [1983] E.C.R.
  4005; [1983] 2 C.M.L.R. 104, ECJ 8-016

TABLE OF EUROPEAN CASES

CIA Security International SA v Signalson SA (C194/94) [1996] All E.R.
(EC) 557; [1996] E.C.R. I-2201; [1996] 2 C.M.L.R. 781, ECJ 3-039
CILFIT Srl v Ministero della Sanita (283/81): sub nom. CILFIT Srl v
Ministro della Sanita (283/81)[1982] E.C.R. 3415; [1983] 1 C.M.L.R.
472, ECJ 3-012,
3-047, 4-502
CT Control v Commission of the European Communities (C-121/91)
[1993] E.C.R. I-3873, ECJ (5th Chamber) 6-096
Campina Melkunie BV v Benelux-Merkenbureau (C-265/00) [2004] E.C.R.
I-1699; [2005] 2 C.M.L.R. 9; [2005] C.E.C. 676; [2004] E.T.M.R. 58, ECJ
(6th Chamber) 4-123, 4-127,
4-145, 4-638
Campus Oil Ltd v Minister for Industry and Energy (72/83) [1984] E.C.R.
2727; [1984] 3 C.M.L.R. 544, ECJ 8-015,
8-034, 8-035
Canadane Cheese Trading AMBA v Greece (C317/95) [1997] E.C.R.
I-4681, ECJ 10-078,
10-079, 10-080
Canon Kabushiki Kaisha v Metro Goldwyn Mayer Inc (C-39/97) [1998] All
E.R. (EC) 934; [1998] E.C.R. I-5507; [1999] 1 C.M.L.R. 77; [1998] C.E.C.
920; [1999] E.T.M.R. 1; [1999] F.S.R. 332; [1999] R.P.C. 117, ECJ 4-043,
4-075, 4-091,
4-185, 4-186, 4-488,
5-017, 5-018, 5-019,
5-024, 5-035, 5-036,
5-037, 5-042, 5-067,
5-071, 5-074, 5-077,
5-113, 5-114, 5-115, 5-121,
5-193, 5-195, 5-203, 6-101
Carbonari v Universita degli Studi di Bologna (C131/97) [1999] E.C.R.
I-1103, ECJ (5th Chamber) 3-033
Carl Kuhne GmbH & Co KG v Jutro Konservenfabrik GmbH & Co KG
(C269/99) [2001] E.C.R. I-9517; [2003] E.T.M.R. 3, ECJ (6th
Chamber) 10-105
Celine Sarl v Celine SA (C-17/06) [2007] E.T.M.R. 80, ECJ (Grand
Chamber) 6-069, 6-070, 6-084, 6-091, 6-093
Centrafarm BV v American Home Products Corp (C-3/78) [1978]
E.C.R. 1823; [1979] 1 C.M.L.R. 326; [1979] F.S.R. 189, ECJ 8-065,
8-066, 8-097, 8-104,
8-126, 8-144, 8-151, 8-174
Centrafarm BV v Sterling Drug Inc (C-15/74); Centrafarm BV v Winthrop
BV (C-16/74) [1974] E.C.R. 1147; [1974] E.C.R. 1183; [1974] 2
C.M.L.R. 480; [1975] F.S.R. 161, ECJ 8-053, 8-076,
8-099, 8-101
Centrafarm BV v Winthrop BV (16/74) [1974] E.C.R. 1183, ECJ 8-056, 8-057,
8-062, 8-076,
8-077, 8-101,
8-125, 8-129,
8-173, 8-207, 8-230
Centrosteel Srl v Adipol GmbH (C456/98) [2000] E.C.R. I-6007; [2000] 3
C.M.L.R. 711; [2000] C.E.C. 527, ECJ (1st Chamber) 3-046
Chocoladefabriken Lindt & Sprungli AG v Franz Hauswirth GmbH
(C-529/07), unreported 4-585, 4-592,
4-594, 4-595

TABLE OF EUROPEAN CASES

Chronopost SA v Union Francaise de l'Express (UFEX) (C-341/06 P); La
  Poste v Union Francaise de l'Express (UFEX) (C-342/06 P) [2008] 3
  C.M.L.R. 19, ECJ (Grand Chamber) 9-132
Ciola v Land Vorarlberg (C-224/97) [1999] E.C.R. I-2517; [1999] 2
  C.M.L.R. 1220, ECJ 3-042
Citigroup Inc v Office for Harmonisation in the Internal Market (Trade
  Marks and Designs) (OHIM) (T-181/05) [2008] E.T.M.R. 47, CFI (1st
  Chamber) 5-228, 5-229
Class International BV v Colgate-Palmolive Co (C-405/03) [2006] Ch. 154;
  [2006] 2 W.L.R. 507; [2005] E.C.R. I-8735; [2006] 1 C.M.L.R. 14; [2006]
  C.E.C. 193; [2006] E.T.M.R. 12, ECJ 5-093, 8-244,
                                                                8-247, 8-248, 8-249
Claudia de Angelis v Commission of the European Communities (246/83)
  [1985] E.C.R. 1253, ECJ 3-065
Clean Car Autoservice GmbH v Stadt Wien (C472/99) [2001] E.C.R.
  I-9687; [2003] 2 C.M.L.R. 40; [2003] C.E.C. 529, ECJ (6th Chamber) 4-457,
                                                                        4-463, 6-150
Cnl-Sucal NV SA v Hag GF AG (C10/89) [1990] E.C.R. I-3711; [1990] 3
  C.M.L.R. 571; [1991] F.S.R. 99, ECJ 3-015, 4-026,
                                                                4-035, 4-183, 4-480,
                                                                4-484, 4-533, 5-019,
                                                                5-033, 6-112, 6-115,
                                                                6-134, 8-067, 8-073,
                                                                8-097, 8-125, 8-129,
                                                                8-173, 8-197
Comitato di Coordinamento per la Difesa della Cava v Regions Lombardia
  (C-236/92) [1994] E.C.R. I-483; [1994] Env. L.R. 281, ECJ 3-030
Comite du Personnel de la Banque Centrale Europeenne v European
  Central Bank (C-467/00 P) [2001] E.C.R. I-6041, ECJ 4-114
Commission of the European Communities v Anic Partecipazioni SpA (C-
  49/92 P) [1999] E.C.R. I-4125; [2001] 4 C.M.L.R. 17, ECJ (6th
  Chamber) 9-022
Commission of the European Communities v Atlantic Container Line AB
  (C149/95 P (R)) [1995] All E.R. (EC) 853; [1995] E.C.R. I-2165; [1997]
  5 C.M.L.R. 167, ECJ 9-013
Commission of the European Communities v BASF (C-137/92 P) [1994]
  E.C.R. I-2555, ECJ (5th Chamber) 9-013
Commission of the European Communities v Belgium (C-2/90) [1992]
  E.C.R. I-4431, AGO 8-014
Commission of the European Communities v Camar Srl (C312/00); Camar
  Srl v Council of the European Union (T260/97); Tico Srl v
  Commission of the European Communities (T117/98); sub nom.
  Camar Srl v Commission of the European Communities
  (T79/96) [2000] E.C.R. II-2193, CFI 3-005, 5-051
Commission of the European Communities v Ceva Sante Animale SA
  (C198/03 P) [2005] E.C.R. I-6357; [2005] 3 C.M.L.R. 30, ECJ 5-131
Commission of the European Communities v Chambre Syndicale
  Nationale des Entreprises de Transport de Fonds et Valeurs (Sytraval)
  (C-367/95 P) [1998] E.C.R. I-1719, ECJ 4-197, 10-090
Commission of the European Communities v Council of Ministers of the
  European Communities (C-11/88) [1989] E.C.R. 3799, ECJ 10-095
Commission of the European Communities v Denmark (106/84); sub
  nom. Taxation of Wine, Re (106/84) [1986] E.C.R. 833; [1987] 2
  C.M.L.R. 278, ECJ 8-008

TABLE OF EUROPEAN CASES

Commission of the European Communities v France (168/78); sub nom.
French Taxation of Spirits, Re (168/78) [1980] E.C.R. 347; [1981] 2
C.M.L.R. 631, ECJ 8-008
Commission of the European Communities v France (C-152/78); sub nom.
Advertising of Alcoholic Beverages, Re (C-152/78) [1980] E.C.R. 2299;
[1981] 2 C.M.L.R. 743, ECJ 8-036
Commission of the European Communities v Germany (12/74); sub nom.
German Sparkling Wines and Brandies, Re [1975] E.C.R. 181; [1975]
1 C.M.L.R. 340, ECJ 10-084
Commission of the European Communities v Germany (C-18/87); sub
nom. Animals Inspection Fees, Re (C-18/87) [1988] E.C.R. 5427;
[1990] 1 C.M.L.R. 561, ECJ 8-006
Commission of the European Communities v Greece (C-240/86); sub nom
Foreign Currency Permits, Re[1988] E.C.R. 1835; [1989] 3 C.M.L.R.
578, ECJ 3-004
Commission of the European Communities v Greece (C-391/92); sub nom.
Infant Milk Imports, Re [1995] All E.R. (E.C.) 802; [1995] E.C.R.
I-1621; [1996] 1 C.M.L.R. 359; (1996) 30 B.M.L.R. 131, ECJ 8-028
Commission of the European Communities v Greencore Group Plc
(C-123/03 P) [2004] E.C.R. I-11647; [2005] 4 C.M.L.R. 1, ECJ (2nd
Chamber) 8-040, 8-043
Commission of the European Communities v Ireland (C13/00); sub nom.
Berne Convention, Re (C13/00) [2002] E.C.R. I-2943; [2002] 2
C.M.L.R. 10; [2002] E.C.D.R. 30, ECJ 3-004
Commission of the European Communities v Ireland (C30/99) [2001]
E.C.R. I-4619; [2001] 3 C.M.L.R. 28, ECJ (5th Chamber) 4-233,
8-045
Commission of the European Communities v Italy (24/68); sub nom.
Statistical Levy, Re (24/68) [1969] E.C.R. 193; [1971] C.M.L.R. 611,
ECJ 8-006
Commission of the European Communities v Italy (39/72); sub nom.
Premiums for Reducing Dairy Production, Re (39/72)[1973] E.C.R.
101; [1973] C.M.L.R. 439, ECJ 3-032
Commission of the European Communities v Italy (7/68); sub nom. Export
Tax on Art Treasures, Re (7/68) [1968] E.C.R. 423; [1969] C.M.L.R. 1,
ECJ 8-006
Commission of the European Communities v Italy (78/82) [1983] E.C.R.
1955, ECJ 8-025
Commission of the European Communities v Italy (C184/85) [1987] E.C.R.
2013, ECJ 8-010
Commission of the European Communities v Italy (C365/97) [1999] E.C.R.
I-7773; [2003] Env. L.R. 1; [2001] Env. L.R. D8, ECJ 3-030
Commission of the European Communities v Jego-Quere et Cie SA
(C-263/02 P) [2005] Q.B. 237; [2005] 2 W.L.R. 179; [2004] All E.R.
(EC) 983; [2004] E.C.R. I-3425; [2004] 2 C.M.L.R. 12; [2004] C.E.C.
284, ECJ (6th Chamber) 3-010
Commission of the European Communities v Luxembourg (2/62) [1962]
E.C.R. 425; [1963] C.M.L.R. 199, ECJ 8-007
Commission of the European Communities v Luxembourg (C473/93); sub
nom. Public Service Employment, Re (C473/93)[1996] E.C.R. I-3207;
[1996] 3 C.M.L.R. 981, ECJ 3-043
Commission of the European Communities v Netherlands (C-89/76); sub
nom. Inspection Fees on Exported Plants, Re (C-89/76) [1977] E.C.R.
1355; [1978] 3 C.M.L.R. 630, ECJ 8-006

TABLE OF EUROPEAN CASES

Commission of the European Communities v Portugal (C84/98) [2000]
  E.C.R. I-5215, ECJ 10-118
Commission of the European Communities v United Great Britain and
  Northern Ireland (170/78) [1983] E.C.R. 2265, AGO 8-009
Commission of the European Communities v United Kingdom (C207/83);
  sub nom. Origin Marking of Retail Goods, Re (C207/83) [1985]
  E.C.R. 1201; [1985] 2 C.M.L.R. 259; [1985] I.C.R. 714; (1985)
  4 Tr. L. 194, ECJ 8-017, 8-018,
                                                                  8-019
Commission of the European Communities v United Kingdom (C-300/95);
  sub nom. Product Liability Directive, Re (C-300/95)[1997] All E.R.
  (EC) 481; [1997] E.C.R. I-2649; [1997] 3 C.M.L.R. 923, ECJ (5th
  Chamber) 3-046
Community Concepts AG v Office for Harmonisation in the Internal
  Market (Trade Marks and Designs) (OHIM) (T360/99) [2000] E.C.R.
  II-3545; [2001] E.T.M.R. 17, CFI (4th Chamber) 4-437
Compagnie Royale Asturienne des Mines SA v Commission of the
  European Communities (29/83) [1984] E.C.R. 1679; [1985] 1 C.M.L.R.
  688, ECJ (4th Chamber) 9-074
Conceria Daniele Bresciani v Amministrazione delle Finanze (87/75)
  [1976] E.C.R. 129; [1976] 2 C.M.L.R. 62, ECJ 8-006
Conegate v Customs and Excise Commissioners (C-121/85) [1987] Q.B.
  254; [1987] 2 W.L.R. 39; [1986] 2 All E.R. 688; [1986] E.C.R. 1007;
  [1986] 1 C.M.L.R. 739; (1987) 84 L.S.G. 743; (1987) 131 S.J. 75, ECJ
  (4th Chamber) 8-032
Conserchimica Srl v Amministrazione delle Finanze dello Stato (C261/96)
  [1997] E.C.R. I-6177, ECJ (1st Chamber) 6-096
Consorzio Italiano della Componentistica di Ricambio per Autoveicoli v
  Regie Nationale des Usines Renault (C53/87); Maxicar v Regie
  Nationale des Usines Renault (C53/87) [1988] E.C.R. 6039; [1990] 4
  C.M.L.R. 265; [1990] F.S.R. 544, ECJ 9-092
Consorzio per la Tutela del Formaggio Gorgonzola v Kaserei Champignon
  Hofmeister GmbH & Co KG (C-87/97) [1999] E.C.R. I-1301; [1999] 1
  C.M.L.R. 1203; [1999] E.T.M.R. 454, ECJ 4-539, 10-094,
                                                              10-109, 10-123
Consorzio per la Tutela del Formaggio Grana Padano v Office for
  Harmonisation in the Internal Market (Trade Marks and Designs)
  (OHIM) (T-291/03); sub nom. Biraghi's Community Trade Mark
  Application [2008] E.T.M.R. 3, CFI (4th Chamber) 10-103,
                                                              10-104, 10-105
Cooperatieve Vereniging de Verenigde Bloemenveilingen Aalsmeer BA
  (VBA) v Florimex BV (C-265/97 P) [2000] E.C.R. I-2061; [2001] 5
  C.M.L.R. 37, ECJ (5th Chamber) 4-173, 4-197
Cooperatieve Vereniging Suiker Unie UA v Commission of the European
  Communities (40/73); sub nom. European Sugar Cartel, Re (40/73);
  Suiker Unie v Commission of the European Communities (40/73)
  [1975] E.C.R. 1663; [1976] 1 C.M.L.R. 295; [1976] F.S.R. 443, ECJ 9-015
Coote v Granada Hospitality Ltd (C-185/97) [1998] All E.R. (EC) 865;
  [1998] E.C.R. I-5199; [1998] 3 C.M.L.R. 958; [1999] C.E.C. 515; [1999]
  I.C.R. 100; [1998] I.R.L.R. 656, ECJ 3-052, 5-200
Costa v Ente Nazionale per l'Energia Elettrica (ENEL) (6/64) [1964]
  E.C.R. 585; [1964] C.M.L.R. 425, ECJ 3-011, 3-030,
                                                                3-042, 3-043,
                                                                3-049

xxxv

TABLE OF EUROPEAN CASES

Criminal Proceedings against Arcaro (C168/95) [1997] All E.R. (EC) 82;
[1996] E.C.R. I-4705; [1997] 1 C.M.L.R. 179; [1998] Env. L.R. 39, ECJ
(4th Chamber) 3-046
Criminal Proceedings against Bigi (C66/00); sub nom. Bigi, Re (C66/00)
[2002] E.C.R. I-5917; [2002] 3 C.M.L.R. 3; [2003] E.T.M.R. 55,
ECJ 10-103, 10-108
Criminal Proceedings against Bluhme (C67/97) [1998] E.C.R. I-8033;
[1999] 1 C.M.L.R. 612; [2000] Env. L.R. D1, ECJ (5th Chamber) 8-014
Criminal Proceedings against Guimont (C448/98); sub nom. Guimont, Re
(C448/98) [2000] E.C.R. I-10663; [2003] 1 C.M.L.R. 3; [2001] E.T.M.R.
14, ECJ 10-105, 10-108, 10-116
Criminal Proceedings against Keck (C-267/91); Criminal Proceedings
against Mithouard (C-268/91)[1993] E.C.R. I-6097; [1995]
1 C.M.L.R. 101, ECJ 4-554, 4-561, 8-024,
8-026, 8-027,
8-028, 8-029
Criminal Proceedings against Lemmens (C226/97) [1998] All E.R. (EC)
604; [1998] E.C.R. I-3711; [1998] 3 C.M.L.R. 261, ECJ 3-039
Criminal Proceedings against Vanacker (C-37/92) [1993] E.C.R. I-4947,
ECJ 10-109
DKV Deutsche Krankenversicherung AG v Office for Harmonisation in
the Internal Market (Trade Marks and Designs) (OHIM) (C-104/00
P) [2002] E.C.R. I-7561; [2003] E.T.M.R. 20, ECJ (5th Chamber) 3-008,
3-062, 4-098,
4-103, 4-208,
4-210, 4-258, 4-269,
4-277, 4-295, 4-296,
4-316, 4-395, 4-439,
4-446, 4-497, 5-063,
5-073, 5-098, 5-132
Da Costa en Schaake NV v Nederlandse Belastingadministratie (28/62)
[1963] E.C.R. 31; [1963] C.M.L.R. 224, ECJ 3-011, 3-012
DaimlerChrysler AG v Office for Harmonisation in the Internal Market
(Trade Marks and Designs) (OHIM) (T356/00); sub nom. CARCARD
Trade Mark (T356/00)[2002] E.C.R. II-1963; [2003] E.T.M.R. 61;
(2002) 25(5) I.P.D. 25036, CFI (2nd Chamber) 4-473
DaimlerChrysler Corp v Office for Harmonisation in the Internal Market
(Trade Marks and Designs) (OHIM) (T128/01) [2003] E.C.R. II-701;
[2003] E.T.M.R. 87; (2003) 26(5) I.P.D. 26035, CFI (4th Chamber) 5-128
Davidoff & Cie SA v Gofkid Ltd (C292/00) [2003] 1 W.L.R. 1714; [2003] All
E.R. (EC) 1029; [2003] E.C.R. I-389; [2003] 1 C.M.L.R. 35; [2003] C.E.C.
208; [2003] E.T.M.R. 42; [2003] F.S.R. 28, ECJ (6th Chamber) 4-299,
5-191, 5-196,
5-197, 5-198,
5-236, 5-239, 10-148
De Landtsheer Emmanuel SA v Comite Interprofessionnel du Vin de
Champagne (C-381/05) [2007] Bus. L.R. 1484; [2008] All E.R. (EC) 1068;
[2007] 2 C.M.L.R. 43; [2007] E.T.M.R. 69, ECJ (1st Chamber) 10-049,
10-055, 10-056,
10-058, 10-062,
10-066, 10-071
Defrenne v SA Belge de Navigation Aerienne (SABENA) (43/75); sub
nom. Defrenne v SABENA (43/75)[1981] 1 All E.R. 122; [1976] E.C.R.
455; [1976] 2 C.M.L.R. 98; [1976] I.C.R. 547, ECJ 3-030, 3-037

TABLE OF EUROPEAN CASES

Delimitis v Henninger Brau AG (C234/89) [1991] E.C.R. I-935; [1992] 5
   C.M.L.R. 210, ECJ 9-003, 9-011, 9-013,
                                                      9-038, 9-041, 9-042,
                                                      9-043, 9-044, 9-048,
                                               9-049, 9-073, 9-074, 9-075
Denmark v Commission of the European Communities (C-289/96); France
   v Commission of the European Communities (C-299/96); Germany v
   Commission of the European Communities (C-293/96) [1999] E.C.R.
   I-1541; [2001] 1 C.M.L.R. 14; [1999] E.T.M.R. 478; (1999) 22(12)
   I.P.D. 22121, ECJ 10-075
Der Grune Punkt – Duales System Deutschland v Commission of the
   European Communities (T-151/01) [2001] E.C.R. II-3295, CFI 9-121, 9-129
Deutsche Grammophon Gesellschaft GmbH v Metro SB Grossmarkte
   GmbH & Co KG (78/70) [1971] E.C.R. 487; [1971] C.M.L.R. 631, ECJ ... 8-051,
                                                                8-052, 8-054,
                                                                8-076, 8-096,
                                                                8-173, 8-231
Deutsche Krankenversicherung AG (DKV) v Office for Harmonisation in
   the Internal Market (Trade Marks and Designs) (OHIM) (T359/99)
   [2001] E.C.R. II-1645; [2001] E.T.M.R. 81, CFI (2nd Chamber) 4-104, 4-473
Deutsche Milchkontor GmbH v Germany (205/82) [1983] E.C.R. 2633;
   [1984] 3 C.M.L.R. 586, ECJ 8-109
Deutsche Post AG v Sievers (C270/97); Deutsche Post v Schrage
   (C271/97) [2000] E.C.R. I-929, ECJ 4-090
Deutsche Renault AG v Audi AG (C317/91) [1993] E.C.R. I-6227; [1995] 1
   C.M.L.R. 461; [1995] F.S.R. 738, ECJ 5-033, 8-070
Deutsche SiSi-Werke GmbH & Co Betriebs KG v Office for Harmonisation in
   the Internal Market (Trade Marks and Designs) (OHIM) (C173/04 P)
   [2006] E.C.R. I-551; [2006] E.T.M.R. 41, ECJ (2nd Chamber) 3-066,
                                                                4-279, 4-293,
                                                               4-294, 4-298,
                                                               4-299, 4-300,
                                                               4-301, 4-319
Develey Holding GmbH & Co Beteiligungs KG v Office for Harmonisation
   in the Internal Market (Trade Marks and Designs) (OHIM)
   (T-129/04) [2006] E.T.M.R. 85, CFI (2nd Chamber) 3-059
Develey Holding GmbH & Co Beteiligungs KG v Office for Harmonisation in
   the Internal Market (Trade Marks and Designs) (OHIM) (C-238/06 P)
   [2008] E.T.M.R. 20, ECJ (8th Chamber) 3-062, 3-068,
                                                                4-476, 4-477
Dorsch Consult Ingenieurgesellschaft mbH v Bundesbaugesellschaft
   Berlin mbH (C-54/96) [1998] All E.R. (EC) 262; [1997] E.C.R. I-4961;
   [1998] 2 C.M.L.R. 237, ECJ................................... 4-540, 7-060
Dorsch Consult Ingenieurgesellschaft mbH v Council of the European
   Union (C-237/98 P) [2000] E.C.R. I-4549; [2002] 1 C.M.L.R. 41, ECJ
   (5th Chamber) 4-497
Douwe Egberts NV v Westrom Pharma NV (C239/02) [2004] E.C.R. I-
   7007; [2005] 2 C.M.L.R. 55, ECJ (2nd Chamber) 8-039
Dsg Dradenauer Stahlgesellschaft mbH v Commission of the European
   Communities (C-323/00 P) [2002] E.C.R. I-3919, ECJ 4-114
Dyson Ltd v Registrar of Trade Marks (C-321/03) [2007] Bus. L.R. 787;
   [2007] 2 C.M.L.R. 14; [2007] C.E.C. 223; [2007] E.T.M.R. 34; [2007]
   R.P.C. 27, ECJ (3rd Chamber) 3-069, 4-006,
                                                                4-028, 4-030

TABLE OF EUROPEAN CASES

EMI Records Ltd v CBS United Kingdom Ltd (C51/75); EMI v CBS
  Grammofon A/S (C86/75); EMI v CBS Schallplatten GmbH (C96/75)
  [1976] E.C.R. 811; [1976] 2 C.M.L.R. 235; [1976] F.S.R. 457, ECJ 8-213,
                                                                              8-214, 9-023,
                                                                              9-053, 9-089
Eau de Cologne und Parfumerie-Fabrik Glockengasse No.4711 KG v
  Provide Srl (C150/88); sub nom. Kommanditgesellschaft Eau de
  Cologne & Parfumerie-Fabrik Gockengass No.4711 v Provide Srl
  [1989] E.C.R. 3891; [1991] 1 C.M.L.R. 715, ECJ (6th Chamber) 4-553
ECopy Inc v Office for Harmonisation in the Internal Market (Trade Marks
  and Designs) (OHIM) (T247/01) [2002] E.C.R. II-5301; [2003]
  E.T.M.R. 99, CFI (4th Chamber) 4-648,
                                                                       5-128, 5-129
Eden SARL v Office for Harmonisation in the Internal Market (Trade
  Marks and Designs) (OHIM) (T305/04) [2005] E.C.R. II-4705; [2006]
  E.T.M.R. 14, CFI 4-051
EI Du Pont de Nemours Italiana SpA v Unita Sanitaria Locale No.2 di
  Carrara (C21/88) [1990] E.C.R. I-889; [1991] 3 C.M.L.R. 25, ECJ 8-015
El Corte Ingles SA v Office for Harmonisation in the Internal Market
  (Trade Marks and Designs) (OHIM) (T-8/03) [2004] E.C.R. II-4297,
  CFI 4-648
Elliniki Radiophonia Tileorassi AE (ERT) v Dimotiki Etairia Pliroforissis
  (DEP) (C260/89); Elliniki Radiophonia Tileorassi AE (ERT) v Sotirios
  Kouvelas[1991] E.C.R. I-2925; [1994] 4 C.M.L.R. 540, ECJ 3-052
El-Yassini v Secretary of State for the Home Department (C-416/96) [1999]
  All E.R. (EC) 193; [1999] E.C.R. I-1209; [1999] 2 C.M.L.R. 32; [1999]
  I.N.L.R. 131; (1999) 96(31) L.S.G. 43, ECJ 4-540
Emanuel v Continental Shelf 128 Ltd (C-259/04) [2006] E.C.R. I-3089;
  [2006] E.T.M.R. 56, ECJ (3rd Chamber) 4-528, 4-541,
                                                                      4-543, 4-544
Emesa Sugar (Free Zone) NV v Aruba (C17/98 R) [2000] E.C.R. I-665,
  ECJ 4-540
Enderby v Frenchay HA (C127/92) [1994] 1 All E.R. 495; [1993] E.C.R.
  I-5535; [1994] 1 C.M.L.R. 8; [1994] I.C.R. 112; [1993] I.R.L.R. 591, ECJ
  (1st Chamber) 4-453
Erpo Mobelwerk GmbH v Office for Harmonisation in the Internal Market
  (Trade Marks and Designs) (OHIM) (T138/00); sub nom. DAS
  PRINZIP DER BEQUEMLICHKEIT Trade Mark[2001] E.C.R. II-3739;
  [2002] C.E.C. 49; [2002] E.T.M.R. 39, CFI (4th Chamber) 4-160, 4-611
Estee Lauder Cosmetics GmbH & Co OHG v Lancaster Group GmbH
  (C220/98) [2000] All E.R. (EC) 122; [2000] E.C.R. I-117; [2000] 1
  C.M.L.R. 515; [2000] C.E.C. 317, ECJ (5th Chamber) 4-205, 4-233,
                                                                      10-036, 10-121
Etablissements Biret & Cie SA v Council of the European Union (C-94/02)
  [2003] E.C.R. I-10565, ECJ 4-197
Etablissements Consten Sarl v Commission of the European Economic
  Community (56/64); Grundig-Verkaufs GmbH v Commission of the
  European Economic Community (58/64) [1966] E.C.R. 299; [1966]
  C.M.L.R. 418, ECJ 9-024, 9-056,
                                                                      9-061, 9-074, 9-076
Etablissements Delhaize Freres & Compagnie Le Lion SA v Promalvin SA
  & AGE Bodegas Unidas SA (C47/90) [1992] E.C.R. I-3669, ECJ 4-554, 8-124
Eurim-Pharm Arzneimittel GmbH v Beiersdorf AG (C71/94); Eurim-
  Pharm Arzneimittel GmbH v Boehringer Ingelheim KG (C72/94);

TABLE OF EUROPEAN CASES

Eurim-Pharm Arzneimittel GmbH v Farmitalia Carlo Erba GmbH
(C73/94) [1996] E.C.R. I-3603; [1997] 1 C.M.L.R. 1222, ECJ 4-240, 8-092,
8-093, 8-126,
8-130, 8-139
Eurocermex SA v Office for Harmonisation in the Internal Market (Trade
Marks and Designs) (OHIM) (C-286/04 P) [2005] E.C.R. I-5797;
[2005] E.T.M.R. 95, ECJ (1st Chamber) 4-301
Eurocermex SA v Office for Harmonisation in the Internal Market (Trade
Marks and Designs) (OHIM) (T399/02) [2004] E.C.R. II-1391; [2004]
E.T.M.R. 95, CFI 4-301, 4-303,
4-304, 4-305, 4-307
Eurocool Logistik GmbH v Office for Harmonisation in the Internal
Market (Trade Marks and Designs) (OHIM) (T34/00) [2002] E.C.R.
II-683; [2003] E.T.M.R. 4; (2002) 25(4) I.P.D. 25027, CFI (4th
Chamber) 3-061
European Ombudsman v Lamberts (C234/02 P) [2004] E.C.R.
I-2803, ECJ 4-309
European Parliament v Council of Ministers of the European Communities
(C302/87) [1988] E.C.R. 5615, ECJ 3-005
Europemballage Corp and Continental Can Co Inc v Commission of the
European Communities (6/72 R) (No.1) [1972] E.C.R. 157; [1972]
C.M.L.R. 690, ECJ 9-081
Exportur SA v Lor SA and Confiserie du Tech (C3/91) [1992] E.C.R.
I-5529, ECJ 10-109, 10-110,
10-115, 10-117
Extramet Industrie SA v Council of the European Communities (C-358/89)
[1991] E.C.R. I-2501; [1993] 2 C.M.L.R. 619, ECJ (6th Chamber) 3-010
F Hoffmann La Roche & Co AG v Centrafarm Vertriebsgesellschaft
Pharmazeutischer Erzeugnisse mbH (102/77) [1978] E.C.R. 1139;
[1978] 3 C.M.L.R. 217; [1978] F.S.R. 598, ECJ 3-016,
4-126, 4-298, 5-033,
5-082, 6-019, 6-026,
6-119, 6-126, 6-134,
8-074, 8-075, 8-082,
8-085, 8-096, 8-100,
8-104, 8-107, 8-126,
8-129, 8-132, 8-134, 8-144,
8-174, 8-175, 8-178, 8-187,
8-257, 8-259, 8-263
Faccini Dori v Recreb Srl (C91/92) [1995] All E.R. (E.C.) 1; [1994] E.C.R.
I-3325; [1995] 1 C.M.L.R. 665Times, August 4, 1994; Financial Times,
August 2, 1994, ECJ 3-033, 3-037, 6-096,
6-107, 8-139
Falck SpA v Commission of the European Communities (C-74/00 P); sub
nom. Acciaierie di Bolzano SpA v Commission of the European
Communities (C-75/00 P) [2002] E.C.R. I-7869, ECJ 4-197
Ferriere Nord SpA v Commission of the European Communities (C-219/95 P)
[1997] E.C.R. I-4411; [1997] 5 C.M.L.R. 575, ECJ (6th Chamber) 4-508, 9-073
Finanzamt Kassel-Goethestrasse v Viessmann KG (C280/91); sub nom.
Finanzamt Kassel-Goethestrasse v KommanditgesellschaftViessmann
[1993] E.C.R. I-971; [1993] 3 C.M.L.R. 153, ECJ (1st Chamber) 4-008,
4-070
Firma Foto Frost v Hauptzollamt Lubeck-Ost (314/85) [1987] E.C.R. 4199;
[1988] 3 C.M.L.R. 57, ECJ 3-048

TABLE OF EUROPEAN CASES

Ford Motor Co v Office for Harmonisation in the Internal Market (Trade
   Marks and Designs) (OHIM) (T91/99) [2000] E.C.R. II-1925; [2000] 2
   C.M.L.R. 276; [2000] C.E.C. 251; [2000] E.T.M.R. 554; (2000) 23(7)
   I.P.D. 23049, CFI (4th Chamber) 4-640, 4-644
Foster v British Gas Plc (C-188/89) [1991] 1 Q.B. 405; [1991] 2 W.L.R. 258;
   [1990] 3 All E.R. 897; [1990] E.C.R. I-3313; [1990] 2 C.M.L.R. 833;
   [1991] I.C.R. 84; [1990] I.R.L.R. 353, ECJ 3-039
Francovich v Italy (C-6/90); Bonifacti v Italy (C-9/90) [1991] E.C.R. I-5357;
   [1993] 2 C.M.L.R. 66; [1995] I.C.R. 722; [1992] I.R.L.R. 84, ECJ 3-036, 3-039
Fratelli Costanzo SpA v Comune di Milano (103/88) [1989] E.C.R. 1839;
   [1990] 3 C.M.L.R. 239, ECJ 3-039
Fratelli Graffione SNC v Fransa (C313/94); sub nom. Fratelli Graffione
   SNC v Ditta Fransa (C313/94) [1996] E.C.R. I-6039; [1997] 1 C.M.L.R.
   925; [1997] E.T.M.R. 71; [1997] F.S.R. 538, ECJ 4-470, 4-563
Fratelli Variola SpA v Amministrazione Italiana delle Finanze (34/73)
   [1973] E.C.R., ECJ 3-032
Gantner Electronic GmbH v Basch Exploitatie Maatschappij BV (C111/01)
   [2003] E.C.R. I-4207; [2003] I.L.Pr. 37, ECJ (5th Chamber) 4-064
Gaston Schul Douane-Expediteur BV v Minister van Landbouw, Natuur en
   Voedselkwaliteit (C461/03) [2005] E.C.R. I-10513, ECJ 3-049
Gateway Inc v Office for Harmonisation in the Internal Market (Trade
   Marks and Designs) (OHIM) (T-434/05) [2008] C.E.C. 318, CFI (5th
   Chamber) 5-164
Geddo v Ente Nazionale Risi (2/73) [1973] E.C.R. 865; [1974] 1 C.M.L.R.
   13, ECJ 8-012
Gemeente Almelo v Energiebedrijf Ijsselmij NV (C393/92); sub nom.
   Commune d'Almelo ea v NV Energiebedrijf Ijsselmij (C393/92);
   Municipality of Almelo v NV Energiebedrijf Ijsselmij (C393/92) [1994]
   E.C.R. I-1477; [1994] 2 C.E.C. 281, ECJ (5th Chamber) 9-077
General Motors Corp v Yplon SA (C-375/97) [1999] All E.R. (EC) 865;
   [1999] E.C.R. I-5421; [1999] 3 C.M.L.R. 427; [1999] C.E.C. 528; [1999]
   E.T.M.R. 950; [2000] R.P.C. 572; (1999) 22(11) I.P.D. 22112, ECJ 4-641,
                                                                    4-642, 4-645,
                                                                    5-169, 5-171,
                                                                    5-172, 5-173,
                                                                    5-174, 5-178,
                                                                    5-180, 5-183,
                                                                    5-193, 5-202,
                                                                    5-207, 5-218,
                                                                    5-219, 5-222
Germany v Commission of the European Communities (C465/02) [2005]
   E.C.R. I-9115; [2006] E.T.M.R. 16, ECJ 10-072
Germany v Council of the European Communities (C280/93) [1994] E.C.R.
   I-4973, ECJ (5th Chamber) 10-096
Gerolsteiner Brunnen GmbH & Co v Putsch GmbH (C100/02) [2004]
   E.C.R. I-691; [2004] E.T.M.R. 40; [2004] R.P.C. 39, ECJ (5th
   Chamber) 6-116, 6-123,
                                                           6-124, 6-126,
                                                           6-132, 6-134,
                                                           6-137, 10-151
Gillette Co v LA-Laboratories Ltd Oy (C228/03) [2005] All E.R. (EC) 940;
   [2005] E.C.R. I-2337; [2005] 2 C.M.L.R. 62; [2005] C.E.C. 734; [2005]
   E.T.M.R. 67; [2005] F.S.R. 37, ECJ (3rd Chamber) 6-125, 6-134,
                                                                 6-135, 6-137

xl

TABLE OF EUROPEAN CASES

Gimenez Zaera v Instituto Nacional de la Seguridad Social (C126/86)
  [1987] E.C.R. 3697; [1989] 1 C.M.L.R. 827, ECJ (6th Chamber) 3-030
Glaverbel SA v Office for Harmonisation in the Internal Market (Trade
  Marks and Designs) (OHIM) (C445/02 P) [2004] E.C.R. I-6267;
  [2005] E.T.M.R. 70, ECJ (5th Chamber) 4-157,
                                                                  4-158, 4-241
Glawischnig v Bundesminister fur Soziale Sicherheit (C316/01) [2003]
  E.C.R. I-5995, ECJ 8-044
Glencore Grain Ltd v Commission (C-24/01 P) [2002] E.C.R. I-10119, ECJ 4-213
Google France Inc v CNRRH Others (C-238/09), 22 September 2009 6-066
Google France Inc v Louis Vuitoon Malletier (C-236/08), 22 September 2009 ... 6-066
Google France Inc v Viaticum Luteciel (C-237/08), 22 September 2009 6-066
Gottrup-Klim Grovvareforeninger v Dansk Landsbrugs Grovvareselskab
  AmbA (C250/92) [1994] E.C.R. I-5641; [1996] 4 C.M.L.R. 191, ECJ
  (5th Chamber) 9-073, 9-116
Grad v Finanzamt Traunstein (9/70) [1970] E.C.R. 825; [1971] C.M.L.R.
  1, ECJ 3-040
Groupement d'Achat Edouard Leclerc v Commission of the European
  Communities (T19/92) [1996] E.C.R. II-1851; [1997] 4 C.M.L.R. 995,
  CFI (2nd Chamber) 8-198, 9-072
Gut Springenheide GmbH v Oberkreisdirektor des Kreises Steinfurt – Amt
  fur Lebensmitteluberwachung (C210/96) [1998] E.C.R. I-4657; [1999]
  1 C.M.L.R. 1383, ECJ (5th Chamber) 4-154, 4-205,
                                                                  4-225, 4-233,
                                                                  4-534, 5-030,
                                                                  10-121, 10-128
Harbinger Corp v Office for Harmonisation in the Internal Market (Trade
  Marks and Designs) (OHIM) (T345/99) [2000] E.C.R. II-3525; [2001]
  E.T.M.R. 2, CFI (4th Chamber) 4-437
Hasselblad (GB) Ltd v Commission of the European Communities (86/82)
  [1984] E.C.R. 883; [1984] 1 C.M.L.R. 559; [1984] F.S.R. 321, ECJ 9-076
Hauer v Land Rheinland-Pfalz (44/79) [1979] E.C.R. 3727; [1980] 3
  C.M.L.R. 42; (1981) 3 E.H.R.R. 140, ECJ 3-052
Haupl v Lidl Stiftung & Co KG (C-246/05) [2007] E.T.M.R. 61; [2007] Bus.
  L.R. D89, ECJ (3rd Chamber) 7-054, 7-064, 7-065
Health Inspection Charges, Re (C314/82); sub nom. Commission of the
  European Communities v Belgium (C314/82) [1984] E.C.R. 1543;
  [1985] 3 C.M.L.R. 134, ECJ 8-006
Heidelberger Bauchemie GmbH's Trade Mark Application (C49/02)
  [2004] E.C.R. I-6129; [2004] E.T.M.R. 99, ECJ (2nd Chamber) 4-016,
                                                                  4-018, 4-024,
                                                                  4-075, 4-079,
                                                                  4-085, 4-096,
                                                                  4-189, 4-190,
                                                                  4-196, 10-144,
                                                                  10-150
Henkel KGaA v Deutsches Patent- und Markenamt (C218/01) [2004]
  E.C.R. I-1725; [2005] E.T.M.R. 45, ECJ (6th Chamber) 4-156, 4-158,
                                                                  4-164, 4-208,
                                                                  4-209, 4-228,
                                                                  4-288, 4-292,
                                                                  4-296, 4-470,
                                                                  4-508, 6-043,
                                                                  10-145

TABLE OF EUROPEAN CASES

Henkel KGaA v Office for Harmonisation in the Internal Market (Trade
  Marks and Designs) (OHIM) (C-456/01 P) [2004] E.C.R. I-5089;
  [2005] E.T.M.R. 44, ECJ (6th Chamber) 4-093,
    4-097, 4-121, 4-127,
    4-135, 4-169, 4-171,
    4-201, 4-208, 4-236,
    4-253, 4-266, 4-268, 4-269,
    4-272, 4-273, 4-292, 4-319
Henkel KGaA v Office for Harmonisation in the Internal Market (Trade
  Marks and Designs) (OHIM) (T337/99) [2001] E.C.R. II-2597; [2001]
  C.E.C. 266, CFI (2nd Chamber) 4-243,
    4-245, 4-247,
    4-249, 4-266
Henkel KGaA v Office for Harmonisation in the Internal Market (Trade
  Marks and Designs) (OHIM) (T308/01) [2003] E.C.R. II-3253; [2004]
  E.T.M.R. 74, CFI (2nd Chamber) 7-080,
    7-081
Henri Cullet and Chambre Syndicale des Reparateurs Automobiles et
  Detaillants de Produits Petroliers v Centre Leclerc A Toulouse and
  Centre Leclerc A Saint-orens-de-gameville (231/83) [1985] E.C.R. 305,
  AGO 8-034, 8-035
Herbert Karner Industrie Auktionen GmbH v Troostwijk GmbH (C71/02)
  [2004] E.C.R. I-3025; [2004] 2 C.M.L.R. 5; [2004] C.E.C. 327; [2005]
  E.T.M.R. 59, ECJ (5th Chamber) 6-074
Hermes International v FHT Marketing Choice BV (C53/96) [1998] E.C.R.
  I-3603; [1998] E.T.M.R. 425; [1998] I.L.Pr. 630; [1999] R.P.C. 107, ECJ 4-024,
    8-212
Hilti AG v Commission of the European Communities (C-53/92 P) [1994]
  E.C.R. I-667; [1994] 4 C.M.L.R. 614; [1994] F.S.R. 760, ECJ 4-315,
    5-051,
    9-093
Hilti AG v Commission of the European Communities (T-30/89) [1991]
  E.C.R. II-1439; [1992] 4 C.M.L.R. 16; [1992] F.S.R. 210, CFI (2nd
  Chamber) 9-093
Hoefner v Macrotron GmbH (C41/90) [1991] E.C.R. I-1979; [1993] 4
  C.M.L.R. 306; (1991) 135 S.J.L.B. 54, ECJ (6th Chamber) 9-014
Holterhoff v Freiesleben (C2/00) [2002] All E.R. (EC) 665; [2002] E.C.R. I-
  4187; [2002] E.T.M.R. 79; [2002] F.S.R. 52, ECJ 6-008,
    6-011, 6-013,
    6-016, 6-028,
    6-064, 6-074,
    6-119, 10-060
Hugin Kassaregister AB v Commission of the European Communities
  (C22/78); Hugin Cash Registers v Commission of the European
  Communities (C22/78) [1979] E.C.R. 1869; [1979] 3 C.M.L.R. 345,
  ECJ 9-023,
    9-084, 9-090
Huls AG v Commission of the European Communities (C-199/92 P) [1999]
  E.C.R. I-4287; [1999] 5 C.M.L.R. 1016, ECJ (6th Chamber) 4-497
Humblot v Directeur des Services Fiscaux (112/84) [1985] E.C.R. 1367;
  [1987] E.C.R. 1367; [1986] 2 C.M.L.R. 338, ECJ 8-007
Hydrotherm Geratebau GmbH v Compact de Dott Ing Mario Andredi &
  CSAS (C170/83) [1984] E.C.R. 2999; [1985] 3 C.M.L.R. 224, ECJ (4th
  Chamber) 9-073

TABLE OF EUROPEAN CASES

IHT Internationale Heiztechnik GmbH v Ideal Standard GmbH (C-9/93)
   [1994] E.C.R. I-2789; [1994] 3 C.M.L.R. 857; [1995] F.S.R. 59, ECJ 5-033,
                                                                                                                     5-165, 8-070,
                                                                                                                     8-096, 8-125,
                                                                                                                     8-129, 8-231

IMS Health GmbH & Co OHG v NDC Health GmbH & Co KG (C418/01)
   [2004] All E.R. (EC) 813; [2004] E.C.R. I-5039; [2004] 4 C.M.L.R. 28;
   [2004] E.C.D.R. 23, ECJ (5th Chamber) 9-100, 9-101, 9-102,
                                                                                                                         9-106, 9-107, 9-110

Il Ponte Finanziaria SpA v Office for Harmonisation in the Internal Market
   (Trade Marks and Designs) (OHIM) (C-234/06) [2008] E.T.M.R. 13;
   [2007] Bus. L.R. D121, ECJ 3-060, 7-066, 7-067,
                                                                                                                                      7-068, 7-069, 7-071

Imagination Technologies Ltd v Office for Harmonisation in the Internal
   Market (Trade Marks and Designs) (OHIM) (T-461/04) [2008]
   E.T.M.R. 10, CFI (3rd Chamber) 4-647

Imperial Chemical Industries (ICI) Ltd v Commission of the European
   Communities (48/69) [1972] E.C.R. 619; [1972] C.M.L.R. 557, ECJ 9-022

Indorata-Servicos e Gestao Lda v Office for Harmonisation in the Internal
   Market (Trade Marks and Designs) (OHIM) (T204/04) (Unreported,
   February 15, 2007), CFI 3-066

Ingmar GB Ltd v Eaton Leonard Technologies Inc (C-381/98) [2001] All
   E.R. (EC) 57; [2001] 1 All E.R. (Comm) 329; [2000] E.C.R. I-9305;
   [2001] 1 C.M.L.R. 9, ECJ (5th Chamber) 8-229

Institut fur Lernsysteme GmbH v Office for Harmonisation in the Internal
   Market (Trade Marks and Designs) (OHIM) (T388/00) [2002] E.C.R.
   II-4301; [2004] E.T.M.R. 17, CFI (4th Chamber) 3-061

Intel Corp Inc v CPM United Kingdom Ltd (INTEL) (C-252/07),
   unreported 5-207, 5-218, 5-219,
                                                                                                          5-220, 5-221, 5-222,
                                                                                                                   5-225, 5-228, 5-234,
                                                                                                                     5-243, 5-244

Intermodal Transports BV v Staatssecretaris van Financien (C495/03)
   [2005] E.C.R. I-8151; [2006] 1 C.M.L.R. 32, ECJ 3-049, 7-026

International Chemical Corp SpA v Amministrazione delle Finanze dello
   Stato (C66/80) [1981] E.C.R. 1191; [1983] 2 C.M.L.R. 593, ECC 3-012

Internationale Handelsgesellschaft mbH v Einfuhr- und Vorratsstelle fur
   Getreide und Futtermittel (11/70); Einfuhr und Vorratsstelle fur
   Getreide und Futtermittel v Firma Koster, Berodt & Co (25/70);
   Einfuhr und Vorratsstelle fur Getreide und Futtermittel v Firma
   Gunther Henck (26/70); Firma Ottoscheer v Einfuhr und
   Vorratsstelle fur Getreide und Futtermittel (30/70) [1970] E.C.R. 1125;
   [1972] C.M.L.R. 255, ECJ 3-051

Ireland v Commission of the European Communities (C199/03) [2005]
   E.C.R. I-8027, ECJ 5-133

Ismeri Europa Srl v Court of Auditors of the European Communities
   (C-315/99 P) [2001] E.C.R. I-5281, ECJ 4-213

Istituto Chemioterapico Italiano SpA v Commission of the European
   Communities (6/73); sub nom. Commercial Solvents Corp v
   Commission of the European Communities (7/73) [1974] E.C.R. 223;
   [1974] 1 C.M.L.R. 309, ECJ 9-087,
                                                                                                                                           9-115, 9-118

Italy v Commission of the European Communities (C178/00) [2003] E.C.R.
   I-303, ECJ 5-133

TABLE OF EUROPEAN CASES

Italy v Council of the European Economic Community (32/65) [1966]
E.C.R. 389; [1969] C.M.L.R. 39, ECJ 3-006
J Nold Kohlen- und Baustoffgrosshandlung v Commission of the European
Communities (4/73) [1974] E.C.R. 491; [1975] E.C.R. 985; [1974] 2
C.M.L.R. 338, ECJ 3-052
Jersey Produce Marketing Organisation Ltd v Jersey (C293/02) [2006] All
E.R. (EC) 1126; [2005] E.C.R. I-9543; [2006] 1 C.M.L.R. 29, ECJ 8-014
John Walker & Sons Ltd v Ministeriet for Skatter og Afgifter (243/84)
[1986] E.C.R. 875, ECJ 8-010
Jose Alejandro SL v Office for Harmonisation in the Internal Market
(Trade Marks and Designs) (OHIM) (T129/01) [2003] E.C.R. II-2251;
[2004] E.T.M.R. 15; (2003) 26(11) I.P.D. 26072, CFI (2nd Chamber) 3-061
KBA – Berlin GmbH v Commission of the European Communities
(T126/99); sub nom. Graphischer Maschinenbau GmbH v
Commission of the European Communities (T126/99); Koenig &
Bauer-Albert AG (Berlin) v Commission of the European
Communities (T126/99) [2002] E.C.R. II-2427, CFI 5-129
KWS Saat AG v Office for Harmonisation in the Internal Market (Trade
Marks and Designs) (OHIM) (T-173/00) [2002] E.C.R. II-3843; [2003]
E.T.M.R. 23, CFI (2nd Chamber) 4-192
KWS Saat AG v Office for Harmonisation in the Internal Market (Trade
Marks and Designs) (OHIM) (C-447/02 P) [2004] E.C.R. I-10107;
[2005] E.T.M.R. 86, ECJ (2nd Chamber) 4-451
Kapniki Michailidis AE v Idrima Kinonikon Asphaliseon (IKA) (C441/98);
sub nom. Kapniki Mikhailidis AE v Idrima Kinonikon Asphaliseon
(IKA) (C441/98) [2000] E.C.R. I-7145; [2001] 1 C.M.L.R. 13, ECJ (5th
Chamber) 8-006
Keurkoop BV v Nancy Kean Gifts BV (C144/81) [1982] E.C.R. 2853; [1982]
Com. L.R. 212; [1983] 2 C.M.L.R. 47; [1983] F.S.R. 381, ECJ 8-231,
9-091
Kik v Office for Harmonisation in the Internal Market (Trade Marks
and Designs) (OHIM) (C-361/01 P) [2003] E.C.R. I-8283; [2004]
E.T.M.R. 30, ECJ 2-016,
2-017
Kik v Office for Harmonisation in the Internal Market (Trade Marks
and Designs) (OHIM) (T-120/99) [2001] E.C.R. II-2235; [2001]
E.T.M.R. 93; (2001) 24(9) I.P.D. 24060, CFI (4th Chamber) 2-016
Koelman v Commission of the European Communites (T56/92) [1993]
E.C.R. II-1267, CFI 3-060
Koninklijke KPN Nederland NV v Benelux-Merkenbureau (C-363/99)
[2006] Ch. 1; [2005] 3 W.L.R. 649; [2005] All E.R. (EC) 19; [2004]
E.C.R. I-1619; [2005] 2 C.M.L.R. 10; [2005] C.E.C. 216; [2004]
E.T.M.R. 57, ECJ (6th Chamber) 3-027, 3-049,
4-009, 4-010, 4-095,
4-098, 4-099, 4-100,
4-102, 4-103, 4-105,
4-127, 4-135, 4-136,
4-145, 4-203, 4-211,
4-240, 4-269, 4-396,
4-403, 4-447, 4-456,
4-457, 4-459, 4-470,
4-471, 4-637, 4-639, 7-010
Koninklijke Philips Electronics NV v Remington Consumer Products Ltd
(C-299/99); sub nom. Philips Electronics NV v Remington Consumer

TABLE OF EUROPEAN CASES

Products Ltd (C-299/99) [2003] Ch. 159; [2003] 2 W.L.R. 294; [2002]
All E.R. (EC) 634; [2002] E.C.R. I-5475; [2002] 2 C.M.L.R. 52; [2002]
C.E.C. 525; [2002] E.T.M.R. 81; [2003] R.P.C. 2; (2002) 25(9) I.P.D.
25060, ECJ 4-022, 4-043,
4-086, 4-093, 4-120,
4-126, 4-156, 4-164, 4-165,
4-176, 4-183, 4-205, 4-219,
4-221, 4-225, 4-226, 4-233,
4-239, 4-273, 4-298, 4-316,
4-411, 4-425, 4-510, 4-517,
4-518, 4-519, 4-520, 4-525,
4-606, 4-613, 4-615,
4-624, 4-630, 4-632,
4-639, 5-082, 6-026,
6-043, 6-134
Konsumentombudsmannen (KO) v Gourmet International Products AB
(C-405/98) [2001] All E.R. (EC) 308; [2001] E.C.R. I-1795; [2001] 2
C.M.L.R. 31; [2001] C.E.C. 98, ECJ (6th Chamber) 8-029, 8-037
Koubi v Office for Harmonisation in the Internal Market (Trade Marks and
Designs) (OHIM) (T10/03) [2004] E.C.R. II-719; [2004] E.T.M.R. 61,
CFI (4th Chamber) 5-069
Kvaerner Plc v Staatssecretaris van Financien (C191/99) [2002] Q.B. 385;
[2001] 3 W.L.R. 1663; [2001] S.T.C. 1007; [2001] E.C.R. I-4447; [2001]
3 C.M.L.R. 2; [2001] C.E.C. 157; [2002] Lloyd's Rep. I.R. 68; [2001]
B.T.C. 8018, ECJ 4-071
L&D SA v Office for Harmonisation in the Internal Market (Trade Marks
and Designs) (OHIM) (C-488/06 P) [2008] E.T.M.R. 62, ECJ (2nd
Chamber) 7-072, 7-073
LC Nungesser KG v Commission of the European Communities
(C-258/78) [1981] E.C.R. 45; [1982] E.C.R. 2015; [1983] Com. L.R. 64;
[1983] 1 C.M.L.R. 278; [1983] F.S.R. 309, ECJ 9-052, 9-053, 9-056
L'Oreal (C-487/07) [2009] E.C.R. I-0000 6-074
L'Oreal NV v De Nieuwe AMCK PVBA (C31/80) [1980] E.C.R. 3775;
[1981] 2 C.M.L.R. 235; [1981] F.S.R. 507, ECJ........................ 9-085
L'Oreal SA, Lancome Parfums et Beaute & Cie, Laboratoire Garnier & Cie
v Bellure NV, Malaika Investments Ltd, Starion International Ltd
(C-487/07) not yet reported 10-065,
10-070, 10-071
L'Oreal SA v Office for Harmonisation in the Internal Market (Trade
Marks and Designs) (OHIM) (T112/03) [2005] E.C.R. II-949, CFI 5-066,
5-067, 5-068,
5-069, 5-072
L'Oreal SA v Office for Harmonisation in the Internal Market (Trade
Marks and Designs) (OHIM) (C235/05) [2006] E.C.R. I-57, ECJ 5-066
LTJ Diffusion SA v Sadas Vertbaudet SA (C-291/00) [2003] E.C.R. I-2799;
[2003] C.E.C. 283; [2003] E.T.M.R. 83; [2003] F.S.R. 34, ECJ 4-186,
4-395, 5-004,
5-009, 10-148
La Mer Technology Inc v Laboratoires Goemar SA (C259/02); sub nom.
Laboratories Goemar SA's Trade Marks (Nos.1338514 and 1402537)
(C259/02) [2004] E.C.R. I-1159; [2004] E.T.M.R. 47; [2004] F.S.R. 38,
ECJ (3rd Chamber) 4-498, 7-025,
7-028, 7-030,
7-034, 7-086

xlv

TABLE OF EUROPEAN CASES

Laboratoires Pharmaceutiques Bergaderm SA v Commission of the
European Communities (C-352/98 P) [2000] E.C.R. I-5291, ECJ 4-309
Laboratorios RTB SL v Office for Harmonisation in the Internal Market
(Trade Marks and Designs) (OHIM) (T162/01) [2003] E.C.R. II-2821;
[2004] E.T.M.R. 51, CFI (4th Chamber) 5-121
Lancome SA v Etos BV (99/79); Cosparfrance Nederland BV v Albert
Heijn Supermart BV [1980] E.C.R. 2511; [1981] E.C.R. 2511; [1981] 2
C.M.L.R. 164; [1981] F.S.R. 490, ECJ 9-076
Land Baden-Wurttemberg v Schilling (C63/00) [2002] E.C.R. I-4483, ECJ
(6th Chamber) 4-500
Lange v Georg Schunemann GmbH (C350/99) [2001] All E.R. (EC) 481;
[2001] E.C.R. I-1061; [2001] I.R.L.R. 244; [2001] Emp. L.R. 247, ECJ
(5th Chamber) 4-008, 4-070
Lenzing AG v Commission of the European Communities (T-36/99) [2004]
E.C.R. II-3597; [2006] 1 C.M.L.R. 46, CFI (5th Chamber) 4-163
Levi Strauss & Co v Casucci SpA (C-145/05) [2006] E.C.R. I-3703; [2006]
E.T.M.R. 71; [2007] F.S.R. 8, ECJ (3rd Chamber) 5-044, 5-078,
5-088, 5-089, 5-090,
5-091, 5-092, 5-093
Libertel Groep BV v Benelux-Merkenbureau (C-104/01) [2004] Ch. 83;
[2004] 2 W.L.R. 1081; [2003] E.C.R. I-3793; [2005] 2 C.M.L.R. 45;
[2003] E.T.M.R. 63; [2004] F.S.R. 4, ECJ 3-015, 4-008,
4-017, 4-021, 4-055, 4-069,
4-076, 4-078, 4-081, 4-084,
4-096, 4-097, 4-101, 4-121,
4-136, 4-155, 4-166, 4-172,
4-174, 4-181, 4-184, 4-185,
4-186, 4-187, 4-188, 4-190,
4-191, 4-196, 4-198, 4-211,
4-258, 4-259, 4-265, 4-273,
4-316, 4-417, 4-421, 4-425,
4-451, 4-503, 4-626, 4-638,
4-642, 5-091, 5-205, 6-043
Limburgse Vinyl Maatschappij NV (LVM) v Commission of the European
Communities (C-238/99 P); DSM Kunststoffen BV v Commission of
the European Communities (C-244/99 P) [2002] E.C.R. I-8375; [2003]
4 C.M.L.R. 10, ECJ 9-133
Linde AG's Trade Mark Application (C53/01); Rado Uhren AG's Trade
Mark Application (C55/01); Winward Industrie Inc's Trade Mark
Application (C54/01); sub nom. Linde AG v Deutsches Patent- und
Markenamt (C53/01)[2003] E.C.R. I-3161; [2005] 2 C.M.L.R. 44;
[2003] E.T.M.R. 78; [2003] R.P.C. 45, ECJ 4-021, 4-062,
4-090, 4-098, 4-136,
4-157, 4-164, 4-171,
4-183, 4-215, 4-216, 4-227,
4-237, 4-239, 4-268, 4-269,
4-316, 4-397, 4-400, 4-417,
4-422, 4-425, 4-438, 4-503, 4-638
Lithgow v United Kingdom (A/102); sub nom. Lithgow v United Kingdom
(9006/80); Vosper Plc v United Kingdom (9262/81); English Electric
Co Ltd v United Kingdom (9263/81); Banstonian Co v United
Kingdom (9265/81); Yarrow Plc v United Kingdom (9266/81);
Vickers Plc v United Kingdom (9313/81); Dowsett Securities Ltd v
United Kingdom (9405/81) (1986) 8 E.H.R.R. 329, ECHR 10-165

TABLE OF EUROPEAN CASES

Lloyd Schuhfabrik Meyer & Co GmbH v Klijsen Handel BV (C-342/97)
[1999] All E.R. (EC) 587; [1999] E.C.R. I-3819; [1999] 2 C.M.L.R. 1343;
[1999] C.E.C. 285; [1999] E.T.M.R. 690; [2000] F.S.R. 77; (1999) 22(11)
I.P.D. 22111, ECJ 4-126, 4-154,
4-164, 4-182, 4-205,
4-233, 4-277, 4-501, 5-007,
5-020, 5-022, 5-028, 5-029,
5-030, 5-045, 5-047, 5-049,
5-050, 5-052, 5-071, 5-098,
5-099, 5-121, 5-146, 5-202, 10-021
Loendersloot (t/a F Loendersloot Internationale Expeditie) v George
Ballantine & Son Ltd (C349/95) [1997] E.C.R. I-6227; [1998] 1
C.M.L.R. 1015; [1998] E.T.M.R. 10; [1998] F.S.R. 544, ECJ 4-043,
4-091, 4-480, 4-488,
5-088, 6-107, 8-068,
8-086, 8-145, 8-169, 8-172,
8-177, 8-187, 8-188, 8-253,
8-254, 8-257, 8-259, 8-280, 8-285
Luxembourg v Linster (C287/98) [2000] E.C.R. I-6917; [2001] Env. L.R. D3,
ECJ 7-018, 7-063
MPA Pharma Gmbh v Rhone-Poulenc Pharma GmbH (C232/94) [1996]
E.C.R. I-3671, ECJ 8-094, 8-105,
8-126, 8-130,
8-140, 8-174, 8-217
Mag Instrument Inc v Office for Harmonisation in the Internal Market
(Trade Marks and Designs) (OHIM) (C-136/02 P); sub nom. Mag
Instrument Inc v Office for Harmonisation in the Internal Market
(Trade Marks and Designs) (OHIM) (T-88/00) [2004] E.C.R. I-9165;
[2005] E.T.M.R. 46, ECJ (2nd Chamber) 4-199, 4-200,
4-203, 4-204, 4-209,
4-211, 4-212, 4-286,
4-292, 4-295, 4-296,
4-309, 4-626, 8-211
Mangold v Helm (C-144/04) [2006] All E.R. (EC) 383; [2005] E.C.R. I-9981;
[2006] 1 C.M.L.R. 43; [2006] C.E.C. 372; [2006] I.R.L.R., ECJ 3-037
Marca Mode CV v Adidas AG (C-425/98) [2000] All E.R. (EC) 694; [2000]
E.C.R. I-4861; [2000] 2 C.M.L.R. 1061; [2000] C.E.C. 395; [2000]
E.T.M.R. 723, ECJ (6th Chamber) 3-003, 5-023,
5-026, 5-027, 5-195,
5-202, 5-218, 6-040, 6-072
Marks & Spencer Plc v Customs and Excise Commissioners (C62/00)
[2003] Q.B. 866; [2003] 2 W.L.R. 665; [2002] S.T.C. 1036; [2002] E.C.R.
I-6325; [2002] 3 C.M.L.R. 9; [2002] C.E.C. 572; [2002] B.T.C. 5477;
[2002] B.V.C. 622; [2002] S.T.I. 1009, ECJ (5th Chamber) 3-036
Marleasing SA v La Comercial Internacional de Alimentacion SA
(C-106/89) [1990] E.C.R. I-4135; [1993] B.C.C. 421; [1992] 1 C.M.L.R.
305, ECJ (6th Chamber) 3-033, 3-046,
4-508, 6-096, 6-107,
8-139, 8-216, 8-219
Marshall v Southampton and South West Hampshire AHA (152/84) [1986]
Q.B. 401; [1986] 2 W.L.R. 780; [1986] 2 All E.R. 584; [1986] E.C.R. 723;
[1986] 1 C.M.L.R. 688; [1986] I.C.R. 335; [1986] I.R.L.R. 140; (1986) 83
L.S.G. 1720; (1986) 130 S.J. 340, ECJ 3-036, 6-096,
8-095, 8-139

xlvii

TABLE OF EUROPEAN CASES

Marshall v Southampton and South West Hampshire AHA (C271/91)
[1994] Q.B. 126; [1993] 3 W.L.R. 1054; [1993] 4 All E.R. 586; [1993]
E.C.R. I-4367; [1993] 3 C.M.L.R. 293; [1993] I.C.R. 893; [1993] I.R.L.R.
445, ECJ 3-046
Masterfoods Ltd (t/a Mars Ireland) v HB Ice Cream Ltd (C344/98) [2001]
All E.R. (EC) 130; [2000] E.C.R. I-11369; [2001] 4 C.M.L.R. 14, ECJ 9-003,
9-009, 9-011,
9-012, 9-013
Matratzen Concord AG v Hukla Germany SA (C421/04) [2006] E.C.R.
I-2303; [2006] C.E.C. 621; [2006] E.T.M.R. 48, ECJ (1st Chamber) 4-467,
4-469, 4-470,
4-471, 4-639
Matratzen Concord GmbH v Office for Harmonisation in the Internal
Market (Trade Marks and Designs) (OHIM) (C-3/03 P) [2004] E.C.R.
I-3657, ECJ 5-056, 5-059,
5-060, 5-073,
5-139, 5-141
Matratzen Concord GmbH v Office for Harmonisation in the Internal
Market (Trade Marks and Designs) (OHIM) (T6/01) [2002] E.C.R.
II-4335; [2003] E.T.M.R. 31, CFI (4th Chamber) 5-056, 5-057,
5-059, 5-062,
5-063, 5-070
Medion AG v Thomson Multimedia Sales Germany & Austria GmbH
(C120/04) [2005] E.C.R. I-8551; [2005] C.E.C. 720; [2006] E.T.M.R. 13,
ECJ (2nd Chamber) 5-009, 5-137,
5-139, 5-141,
6-069
Merck & Co Inc v Primecrown Ltd (C267/95); Beecham Group Plc v
Europharm of Worthing Ltd (C268/95) [1996] E.C.R. I-6285; [1997] 1
C.M.L.R. 83; [1997] F.S.R. 237, ECJ 8-062, 8-232
Merck & Co Inc v Stephar BV (C187/80); Merck & Co Inc v Exler
(C187/80) [1981] E.C.R. 2063; [1981] 3 C.M.L.R. 463; [1982] F.S.R. 57,
ECJ 8-067, 8-099
Merck Sharp & Dohme GmbH v Paranova Pharmazeutika Handels GmbH
(C443/99) [2003] Ch. 27; [2002] 3 W.L.R. 1697; [2002] All E.R. (EC)
581; [2002] E.C.R. I-3703; [2002] E.T.M.R. 80; (2002) 25(8)
I.P.D. 25053, ECJ 8-154, 8-168
Merz & Krell GmbH & Co v Deutsches Patent- und Markenamt (C517/99);
sub nom. Merz & Krell GmbH & Co's Trade Mark Application
(C517/99) [2002] All E.R. (EC) 441; [2001] E.C.R. I-6959; [2002]
E.T.M.R. 21, ECJ 4-035, 4-164,
4-165, 4-168, 4-171,
4-283, 4-425, 4-479,
4-491, 4-495, 4-504,
4-507, 6-134, 7-010
Messe Munchen GmbH v Office for Harmonisation in the Internal Market
(Trade Marks and Designs) (OHIM) (T-32/00) [2000] E.C.R. II-3829;
[2001] C.E.C. 3; [2001] E.T.M.R. 13; (2001) 24(1) I.P.D. 24002, CFI
(4th Chamber) 4-436
Metro SB-Grossmarkte GmbH & Co KG v Cartier SA (C376/92) [1994]
E.C.R. I-15; [1994] 5 C.M.L.R. 331, ECJ (5th Chamber) 9-075
Metronome Musik GmbH v Music Point Hokamp GmbH (C200/96) [1998]
E.C.R. I-1953; [1998] 3 C.M.L.R. 919; [2000] E.C.D.R. 11; [1999]
E.M.L.R. 93; [1999] F.S.R. 576, ECJ 8-229

TABLE OF EUROPEAN CASES

Metso Paper Automation Oy v Office for Harmonisation in the Internal
Market (Trade Marks and Designs) (OHIM) (T-19/04) [2005]
E.C.R. II-2383; [2007] E.T.M.R. 2, CFI (4th Chamber) 4-147
Michael v Commission of the European Communities (343/82) [1983]
E.C.R. 4023, ECJ 3-065
Microsoft Corp v Commission of the European Communities (T201/04 R 1)
[2004] E.C.R. II-2977; [2004] 5 C.M.L.R. 21, CFI 9-103, 9-105,
9-106
Milchwerke Heinz Wohrmann & Sohn KG v Commission of the European
Economic Community (31/62); Alfons Lutticke GmbH v Commission
of the European Economic Community (33/62) [1962] E.C.R. 501;
[1963] C.M.L.R. 152, ECJ 3-007
Milk Marketing Board v Cricket St Thomas Estate (C372/88) [1990]
E.C.R. I-1345; [1990] 2 C.M.L.R. 800, ECJ (6th Chamber) 4-500
Miller International Schallplatten GmbH v Commission of the European
Communities (C19/17) [1978] E.C.R. 131; [1978] 2 C.M.L.R. 334;
[1978] F.S.R. 524, ECJ 9-076
Ministere Public v Cognet (C355/85) [1986] E.C.R. 3231; [1987] 3
C.M.L.R. 942, ECJ (3rd Chamber) 8-013
Ministere Public v Deserbais (C286/86) [1988] E.C.R. 4907; [1989] 1
C.M.L.R. 516, ECJ 9-097
Ministere Public v Mutsch (C137/84) [1985] E.C.R. 2681; [1986] 1
C.M.L.R. 648, ECJ 3-052
Ministero delle Finanze v IN.CO.GE.'90 Srl (C10/97) [1998] E.C.R. I-6307;
[2001] 1 C.M.L.R. 31, ECJ 3-044
Moccia Irme SpA v Commission of the European Communities (C-280/99)
[2001] E.C.R. I-4717, ECJ 4-114
Monsanto Agricoltura Italia SpA v Presidenza del Consiglio dei Ministri
(C236/01) [2003] E.C.R. I-8105, ECJ 8-044
Muhlens GmbH & Co KG v Office for Harmonisation in the Internal
Market (Trade Marks and Designs) (OHIM) (C-206/04 P) [2006]
E.C.R. I-2717; [2006] E.T.M.R. 57, ECJ 5-048,
5-049, 5-054
Muhlens GmbH & Co KG v Office for Harmonisation in the Internal
Market (Trade Marks and Designs) (OHIM) (T-355/02) [2004] E.C.R.
II-791; [2004] E.T.M.R. 101, CFI (4th Chamber) 5-048
Mulhens GmbH & Co KG v Office for Harmonisation in the Internal
Market (Trade Marks and Designs) (OHIM) (T-93/06) [2008]
E.T.M.R. 69, CFI 5-234
Musik-Vertrieb Membran GmbH v GEMA (C55/80); sub nom. Musik-
Vertrieb Membran GmbH v Gesellschaft fur Musikalische
Auffuhrungs- und Mechanische Vervielfaltigungsrechte (GEMA)
(C55/80) [1981] E.C.R. 147; [1981] 2 C.M.L.R. 44; [1981] F.S.R. 433,
ECJ 8-201,
8-205
Musique Diffusion Francaise SA v Commission of the European
Communities (100/80); Pioneer High Fidelity (GB) Ltd v Commission
of the European Communities (103/80); Pioneer Electronic (Europe)
NV v Commission of the European Communities (102/80); C
Melchers & Co v Commission of the European Communities (101/80)
[1983] E.C.R. 1825; [1983] 3 C.M.L.R. 221, ECJ 9-076
Mystery Drinks GmbH v Office for Harmonisation in the Internal Market
(Trade Marks and Designs) (OHIM) (T99/01) [2003] E.C.R. II-43;
[2004] E.T.M.R. 18, CFI (2nd Chamber) 5-049

TABLE OF EUROPEAN CASES

NV Algemene Transport- en Expeditie Onderneming van Gend en Loos v
  Nederlandse Administratie der Belastingen (26/62) [1963] E.C.R. 1;
  [1963] C.M.L.R. 105, ECJ 3-029,
                                                        3-041, 3-042
Neri v European School of Economics (C153/02) [2003] E.C.R. I-13555;
  [2004] 1 C.M.L.R. 16, ECJ (5th Chamber) 5-236
Nichols Plc v Registrar of Trade Marks (C404/02) [2005] 1 W.L.R. 1418;
  [2005] All E.R. (EC) 1; [2004] E.C.R. I-8499; [2005] C.E.C. 160; [2005]
  E.T.M.R. 21; [2005] R.P.C. 12, ECJ (2nd Chamber) 4-011, 4-151,
                                                        4-156, 4-157,
                                                        4-159, 4-533, 4-542
Nijman, Re (125/88); sub nom. Criminal Proceedings against Nijman
  (125/88) [1989] E.C.R. 3533; [1991] 1 C.M.L.R. 92, ECJ (3rd
  Chamber) 10-116
Nokia Corp v Wardell (C-316/05) [2007] 1 C.M.L.R. 37; [2007] C.E.C. 393;
  [2007] E.T.M.R. 20; [2007] Bus. L.R. D16, ECJ (1st Chamber) 6-141
Northern Ireland Fish Producers Organisation Ltd (NIFPO) v Department
  of Agriculture for Northern Ireland (C4/96); Northern Ireland
  Fishermen's Federation v Department of Agriculture for Northern
  Ireland (C4/96) [1998] E.C.R. I-681; [1998] 1 C.M.L.R. 1288, ECJ 10-097
Nuno v Franquet (C-328/06) [2008] E.T.M.R. 12, ECJ (2nd Chamber) ... 5-173, 5-180
O2 Holdings Ltd v Hutchison 3G UK Ltd (C-533/06) [2008] 3 C.M.L.R. 14;
  [2008] C.E.C. 899; [2008] E.T.M.R. 55, ECJ (1st Chamber) 6-069
O2 Holdings Ltd v Hutchison 3G UK Ltd (C-533/06) [2008] 3 C.M.L.R. 14;
  [2008] C.E.C. 899; [2008] E.T.M.R. 55, ECJ (1st Chamber) 10-059,
                                                        10-062, 10-063,
                                                        10-067, 10-070
Oakley Inc v OHIM (The O Store) (T-116/06) unreported 6-092
Oceano Grupo Editorial v Rocio Murciano Quintero (C-240-244/98) [2000]
  E.C.R. I-4491 3-046
Office for Harmonisation in the Internal Market (Trade Marks and
  Designs) (OHIM) v Zapf Creation AG (C-498/01 P) [2004] E.C.R.
  I-11349; [2005] E.T.M.R. 68, ECJ (2nd Chamber) 6-025, 6-039
Office for Harmonisation in the Internal Market (Trade Marks and
  Designs) (OHIM) v Erpo Mobelwerk (C-64/02 P) [2004] E.C.R.
  I-10031; [2005] E.T.M.R. 58, ECJ 4-135, 4-146,
                                                        4-160, 4-170, 4-171
Office for Harmonisation in the Internal Market (Trade Marks and
  Designs) (OHIM) v Kaul GmbH (C-29/05) [2007] E.T.M.R. 37, ECJ 3-054
Office for Harmonisation in the Internal Market (Trade Marks and
  Designs) (OHIM) v Wm Wrigley Jr Co (C-191/01 P) [2004] 1 W.L.R.
  1728; [2004] All E.R. (EC) 1040; [2003] E.C.R. I-12447; [2005] 3
  C.M.L.R. 21; [2004] E.T.M.R. 9; [2004] R.P.C. 18, ECJ 4-136, 4-141,
                                                        4-168, 4-376, 4-385,
                                                        4-399, 4-424, 4-427,
                                                        4-429, 4-438, 4-440,
                                                        4-445, 4-654
Office for Harmonisation in the Internal Market (Trade Marks
  and Designs) (OHIM) v Celltech R&D Ltd (C-273/05 P) [2007]
  E.T.M.R. 52, ECJ 4-472, 4-473,
                                                        4-474, 4-475
Office National de l'Emploi v Ioannidis (C258/04) [2006] All E.R. (EC) 926;
  [2005] E.C.R. I-8275; [2005] 3 C.M.L.R. 47; [2006] C.E.C. 960, ECJ
  (1st Chamber) 6-036

Officier van Justitie v Sandoz BV (174/82) [1983] E.C.R. 2445; [1984]
3 C.M.L.R. 43, ECJ (5th Chamber) 8-110
Oosthoek's Uitgeversmaatschappij BV (C286/81) [1982] E.C.R. 4575;
[1983] 3 C.M.L.R. 428, ECJ 8-024
Openbaar Ministerie v van der Veldt (C17/93) [1994] E.C.R. I-3537; [1995]
1 C.M.L.R. 621, ECJ (5th Chamber) 8-030
Oscar Bronner GmbH & Co KG v Mediaprint Zeitungs- und
Zeitschriftenverlag GmbH & Co KG (C7/97) [1998] E.C.R. I-7791;
[1999] 4 C.M.L.R. 112; [1999] C.E.C. 53, ECJ (6th Chamber) 9-098,
9-099, 9-100, 9-101
Osterreichische Unilever GmbH v Smithkline Beecham Markenartikel
GmbH (C77/97) [1999] E.C.R. I-431; [2001] 2 C.M.L.R. 50, ECJ (5th
Chamber) 3-039
Pafitis v Trapeza Kentrikis Ellados AE (C441/93) [1996] E.C.R. I-1347;
[1996] 2 C.M.L.R. 551; [1997] C.E.C. 646, ECJ 3-039
Pall Corp v PJ Dahlhausen & Co (C238/89) [1990] E.C.R. I-4827, ECJ 3-069,
4-446, 4-553,
4-556, 4-561, 4-565
Parfums Christian Dior SA v Evora BV (C337/95) [1997] E.C.R. I-6013;
[1998] 1 C.M.L.R. 737; [1998] C.E.C. 91; [1998] E.T.M.R. 26; [1998]
R.P.C. 166, ECJ 4-533, 5-009,
6-060, 6-099, 6-112,
8-189, 8-202, 8-203,
8-204, 8-223, 8-234,
8-261, 8-262, 8-286
Parfums Christian Dior SA v Tuk Consultancy BV (C-300/98); Assco
Geruste GmbH v Wilhelm Layher GmbH & Co KG (C-392/98) [2000]
E.C.R. I-11307; [2001] E.T.M.R. 26; [2001] E.C.D.R. 12, ECJ ... 10-134, 10-140,
10-144, 10-145
Parke Davis & Co v Probel (24/67) [1968] E.C.R. 55; [1968] C.M.L.R. 47;
[1968] F.S.R. 393, ECJ 9-088, 9-089
Parti Ecologiste Les Verts v European Parliament (294/83); sub nom. Les
Verts, Parti Ecologiste v European Parliament (294/83) [1986]
E.C.R. 1339; [1987] 2 C.M.L.R. 343, ECJ 3-026, 3-065
Peak Holding AB v Axolin-Elinor AB (C16/03) [2005] Ch. 261; [2005] 2
W.L.R. 650; [2005] All E.R. (EC) 723; [2004] E.C.R. I-11313; [2005] 1
C.M.L.R. 45; [2005] C.E.C. 481; [2005] E.T.M.R. 28, ECJ 8-240,
8-242, 8-243
Pedro Diaz SA v Office for Harmonisation in the Internal Market (Trade
Marks and Designs) (OHIM) (T85/02) [2003] E.C.R. II-4835; [2004]
E.T.M.R. 42, CFI 5-113
Pfeiffer v Deutsches Rotes Kreuz Kreisverband Waldshut eV (C-397/01)
[2004] E.C.R. I-8835; [2005] 1 C.M.L.R. 44; [2005] I.C.R. 1307; [2005]
I.R.L.R. 137, ECJ 3-044, 3-045
Pfizer Inc v Eurim-Pharm GmbH (C1/81) [1981] E.C.R. 2913; [1982] 1
C.M.L.R. 406; [1982] F.S.R. 269, ECJ (1st Chamber) 8-096, 8-099,
8-107, 8-136
Pharmacia & Upjohn SA (formerly Upjohn SA) v Paranova A/S (C379/97);
sub nom. Upjohn SA Danmark v Paranova A/S (C379/97) [2000]
Ch. 571; [2000] 3 W.L.R. 303; [1999] All E.R. (EC) 880; [1999] E.C.R.
I-6927; [2000] 1 C.M.L.R. 51; [1999] C.E.C. 630; [1999] E.T.M.R.
937; [2000] F.S.R. 621; (2001) 62 B.M.L.R. 150; (2000) 18 Tr. L.R. 457,
ECJ 8-151, 8-153,
8-163, 8-273

TABLE OF EUROPEAN CASES

Pharmon BV v Hoechst AG (C19/84) [1985] E.C.R. 2281; [1985]
3 C.M.L.R. 775; [1986] F.S.R. 108, ECJ 8-063, 8-064,
8-099, 8-173
Phillips Van Heusen Corp v Office for Harmonisation in the Internal
Market (Trade Marks and Designs) (OHIM) (T292/01) [2003] E.C.R.
II-4335; [2004] E.T.M.R. 60; (2003) 26(11) I.P.D. 26074, CFI (2nd
Chamber) 5-049, 5-118
Phytheron International SA v Jean Bourdon SA (C352/95) [1997] E.C.R.
I-1729; [1997] 3 C.M.L.R. 199; [1997] E.T.M.R. 211; [1997] F.S.R. 936,
ECJ (5th Chamber) 8-257
Pippig Augenoptik GmbH & Co KG v Hartlauer Handelsgesellschaft mbH
(C-44/01) [2004] All E.R. (EC) 1156; [2003] E.C.R. I-3095; [2004] 1
C.M.L.R. 39; [2004] E.T.M.R. 5, ECJ 10-025, 10-035,
10-036, 10-046,
10-061, 10-062
Polydor Ltd v Harlequin Record Shops Ltd (270/80) [1982] E.C.R. 329;
[1982] Com. L.R. 112; [1982] 1 C.M.L.R. 677; [1982] F.S.R. 358, ECJ 8-215
Praktiker Bau- und Heimwerkermarkte AG v Deutsches Patent- und
Markenamt (C418/02) [2006] Ch. 144; [2006] 2 W.L.R. 195; [2005]
E.C.R. I-5873; [2006] 3 C.M.L.R. 29; [2005] E.T.M.R. 88, ECJ (2nd
Chamber) 3-010, 5-141,
5-144, 5-145, 6-092
Prasident Ruhrkolen Verkaufsgesellschaft mbh v High Authority of the
European Coal and Steel Community (36/59) [1960] E.C.R. 423, ECJ ... 3-050
PreussenElektra AG v Schleswag AG (C379/98) [2001] All E.R. (EC) 330;
[2001] E.C.R. I-2099; [2001] 2 C.M.L.R. 36; [2001] C.E.C. 217; [2002]
Env. L.R. 3, ECJ 10-114
Procter & Gamble Co v Office for Harmonisation in the Internal
Market (Trade Marks and Designs) (OHIM) (T-163/98) [2000] 1
W.L.R. 91; [1999] All E.R. (EC) 648; [1999] E.C.R. II-2383; [1999] 2
C.M.L.R. 1442; [1999] C.E.C. 329; [1999] E.T.M.R. 767, CFI (2nd
Chamber) 3-054, 4-176
Procter & Gamble Co v Office for Harmonisation in the Internal Market
(Trade Marks and Designs) (OHIM) (T63/01) [2002] E.C.R. II-5255;
[2003] E.T.M.R. 43, CFI (4th Chamber) 3-054
Procter & Gamble Co v Office for Harmonisation in the Internal Market
(Trade Marks and Designs) (OHIM) (C-468/01 P) [2004] E.C.R. I-
5141; [2004] E.T.M.R. 88, ECJ (6th Chamber) 4-121, 4-158, 4-172,
4-208, 4-243, 4-276
Procter & Gamble Co v Office for Harmonisation in the Internal Market
(Trade Marks and Designs) (OHIM) (C-473/01 P) [2004] E.C.R.
I-5173; [2004] E.T.M.R. 89, ECJ (6th Chamber) 4-121, 4-278
Procter & Gamble Co v Office for Harmonisation in the Internal Market
(Trade Marks and Designs) (OHIM) (C383/99 P) [2001] E.C.R.
I-6251; [2001] E.T.M.R. 75; [2002] R.P.C. 16, AGO 4-002, 4-103,
4-107, 4-108, 4-152,
4-155, 4-203, 4-221,
4-378, 4-388, 4-407,
4-411, 4-427, 4-438,
4-443, 4-445, 4-469, 4-654
Procter & Gamble Co v Office for Harmonisation in the Internal Market
(Trade Marks and Designs) (OHIM) (T117/00) [2001] E.C.R. II-2723;
[2002] E.T.M.R. 14, CFI (2nd Chamber) 4-248, 4-249,
4-250, 4-276

Procter & Gamble Co v Office for Harmonisation in the Internal Market
(Trade Marks and Designs) (OHIM) (T118/00) [2001] E.C.R. II-2731,
CFI (2nd Chamber) 4-248, 4-276
Procter & Gamble Co v Office for Harmonisation in the Internal Market
(Trade Marks and Designs) (OHIM) (T119/00) [2001] E.C.R. II-2761,
CFI 4-248, 4-276
Procter & Gamble Co v Office for Harmonisation in the Internal Market
(Trade Marks and Designs) (OHIM) (T120/00) [2001] E.C.R. II-2769,
CFI 4-248, 4-276
Procter & Gamble Co v Office for Harmonisation in the Internal
Market (Trade Marks and Designs) (OHIM) (T121/00); sub nom.
Procter & Gamble France's Community Trade Mark Application
(R 529/1999-1) [2001] E.C.R. II-2777, CFI 4-248, 4-276
Procter & Gamble Co v Office for Harmonisation in the Internal Market
(Trade Marks and Designs) (OHIM) (T128/00) [2001] E.C.R. II-2785,
CFI 4-251, 4-278
Procter & Gamble Co v Office for Harmonisation in the Internal Market
(Trade Marks and Designs) (OHIM) (T129/00) [2001] E.C.R. II-2793;
[2001] C.E.C. 313, CFI (2nd Chamber) 4-251, 4-278
Procureur de la Republique, Besancon v Bouhelier (C53/76) [1977] E.C.R.
197; [1977] 1 C.M.L.R. 436, ECJ 8-015
Procureur du Roi v Dassonville (8/74); sub nom. Dassonville v
Commission of the European Communities (8/74) [1974] E.C.R. 837;
[1974] 2 C.M.L.R. 436; [1975] F.S.R. 191, ECJ 4-547,
4-561, 4-565,
8-012, 8-027
Pronuptia de Paris GmbH v Prounptia de Paris Irmgard Schillgalis
(C161/84) [1986] E.C.R. 353; [1986] 1 C.M.L.R. 414, ECJ 9-057,
9-059, 9-061
Pubblico Ministero v Ratti (148/78) [1979] E.C.R. 1629; [1980] 1 C.M.L.R.
96, ECJ 3-035, 3-036
Punto Casa SpA v Sindaco Del Commune di Capena (C69/93) [1994]
E.C.R. I-2355, ECJ (6th Chamber) 8-028
R. v Henn (Maurice Donald) (34/79); R.v Darby (John Frederick) (34/79)
[1980] 2 W.L.R. 597; [1980] 2 All E.R. 166; [1979] E.C.R. 3795; [1980]
1 C.M.L.R. 246, ECJ 8-031,
8-032, 8-038
R. v Immigration Appeal Tribunal Ex p. Antonissen (C292/89) [1991]
E.C.R. I-745; [1991] 2 C.M.L.R. 373; (1991) 135 S.J. 6, ECJ 4-071
R. v Ministry of Agriculture, Fisheries and Food Ex p. Federation
Europeene de la Sante Animale (FEDESA) (C331/88) [1990] E.C.R.
I-4023; [1991] 1 C.M.L.R. 507, ECJ (5th Chamber) 3-052
R. v Ministry of Agriculture, Fisheries and Food Ex p. JH Cooke & Sons
(C372/98) [2000] E.C.R. I-8683, ECJ (6th Chamber) 4-500
R. v Secretary of State for Transport Ex p. Factortame Ltd (C-213/89)
[1990] 2 Lloyd's Rep. 351; [1990] E.C.R. I-2433; [1990] 3 C.M.L.R. 1;
(1990) 140 N.L.J. 927, ECJ 3-043
R. v Secretary of State for Transport Ex p. Factortame Ltd (C-213/89)
[1990] 2 Lloyd's Rep. 351; [1990] E.C.R. I-2433; [1990] 3 C.M.L.R. 1;
(1990) 140 N.L.J. 927, ECJ 8-217
R. (on the application of Swedish Match AB) v Secretary of State for
Health (C210/03); sub nom. Swedish Match AB v Secretary of State
for Health (C210/03) [2004] E.C.R. I-11893; [2005] 1 C.M.L.R. 26,
ECJ 4-469, 4-540

TABLE OF EUROPEAN CASES

R. (on the application of Wells) v Secretary of State for Transport, Local
Government and the Regions (C-201/02); sub nom. Wells v Secretary
of State for Transport, Local Government and the Regions (C-201/02)
[2005] All E.R. (EC) 323; [2004] E.C.R. I-723; [2004] 1 C.M.L.R. 31;
[2004] Env. L.R. 27; [2004] N.P.C. 1, ECJ (5th Chamber) 3-037
Radio Telefis Eireann v Commission of the European Communities
(C-241/91 P); Independent Television Publications Ltd v Commission
of the European Communities (C-242/91 P); sub nom. Magill Case,
Re (C-241/91 P) 1995] All E.R. (E.C.) 416; [1995] E.C.R. I-743; [1995]
4 C.M.L.R. 718; [1995] E.M.L.R. 337; [1995] F.S.R. 530; [1998] Masons
C.L.R. Rep. 58, ECJ 9-094, 9-095,
9-096, 9-097, 9-098,
9-099, 9-101, 9-107, 9-108
Raimund Vidrbnyi v Commission of the European Communities
(C-283/90) [1991] E.C.R. I-4339, ECJ 4-497
Ramondin SA v Commission of the European Communities (C186/02 P)
[2004] E.C.R. I-10653; [2005] 1 C.M.L.R. 32, ECJ (2nd Chamber) 4-344
Ravil Sarl v Bellon Import Sarl (C469/00) [2003] E.C.R. I-5053; [2004]
E.T.M.R. 22; (2003) 26(6) I.P.D. 26038, ECJ 4-469
Ravil Sarl v Bellon Import Sarl (C469/00) [2003] E.C.R. I-5053; [2004]
E.T.M.R. 22; (2003) 26(6) I.P.D. 26038, ECJ 10-130
Reemark Gesellschaft fur Markenkooperation mbH v Office for
Harmonisation in the Internal Market (Trade Marks and Designs)
(OHIM) (T22/04) [2005] E.C.R. II-1559, CFI 5-140
Regie Networks (C-333/07) [2008] E.C.R. I-0000 10-125
Rene Lancry SA v Direction Generale des Douanes (C363/93) [1994]
E.C.R. I-3957, ECJ 8-014
Restrictions on Importation of Souvenirs, Re (C113/80); sub nom.
Commission of the European Communities v Ireland (C113/80)
[1981] E.C.R. 1625; [1982] 1 C.M.L.R. 706, ECJ 8-018, 8-020,
8-021, 8-030, 8-033
Rewe Zentral AG v Office for Harmonisation in the Internal Market (Trade
Marks and Designs) (OHIM) (T79/00); sub nom. LITE Community
Trade Mark (T79/00) [2002] E.C.R. II-705; [2002] E.T.M.R. 91, CFI
(4th Chamber) 4-133, 4-547,
4-561, 4-565
Rewe-Zentral AG v Bundesmonopolverwaltung fur Branntwein (120/78);
sub nom. Cassis de Dijon, Re (120/78) [1979] E.C.R. 649; [1979] 3
C.M.L.R. 494, ECJ 8-020, 8-022,
8-023, 8-027, 8-046
Reyners v Belgium (2/74) [1974] E.C.R. 631; [1974] 2 C.M.L.R. 305, ECJ 3-031
Riksskatteverket v Gharehveran (C-441/99) [2001] E.C.R. I-7687, ECJ (5th
Chamber) 3-035
Ritter-Coulais v Finanzamt Germersheim (C-152/03) [2006] All E.R. (EC)
613; [2006] S.T.C. 1111; [2006] E.C.R. I-1711; [2006] 2 C.M.L.R. 31;
[2006] C.E.C. 531; [2006] S.T.I. 529, ECJ 4-028
Robelco NV v Robeco Groep NV (C-23/01) [2002] E.C.R. I-10913; [2003]
E.T.M.R. 52, ECJ (6th Chamber) 4-532, 5-199,
6-080, 6-083, 10-149
Ruiz-Picasso v Office for Harmonisation in the Internal Market (Trade
Marks and Designs) (OHIM) (T-185/02) [2004] E.C.R. II-1739; [2005]
E.T.M.R. 22, CFI (2nd Chamber) 3-059, 4-102,
4-621, 4-626,
5-051, 5-095, 5-096

liv

TABLE OF EUROPEAN CASES

Ruiz-Picasso v Office for Harmonisation in the Internal Market (Trade
  Marks and Designs) (OHIM) (C-361/04 P) [2006] E.C.R. I-643; [2006]
  E.T.M.R. 29, ECJ (1st Chamber) 5-055, 5-095,
  5-096, 5-097, 5-101,
  5-102, 5-103, 5-104,
  5-105, 5-146, 10-148
Rutili v Ministre de l'Iinterieur (36/75) [1975] E.C.R. 1219; [1976] 1
  C.M.L.R. 140, ECJ 3-052
SAT.1 Satellitenfernsehen GmbH v Office for Harmonisation in the
  Internal Market (Trade Marks and Designs) (OHIM) (T323/00)
  [2002] E.C.R. II-2839; [2003] E.T.M.R. 49, CFI 4-116, 4-123,
  4-126, 4-128, 4-131,
  4-145, 4-148, 4-164,
  4-297, 4-298, 4-299,
  4-304, 4-307, 4-308,
  5-082, 6-043
SIGLA SA v Office for Harmonisation in the Internal Market (Trade Marks
  and Designs) (OHIM) (T-215/03) [2007] E.T.M.R. 79; [2007] Bus.
  L.R. D53, CFI (5th Chamber) 5-234
SMW Wintersekt GmbH v Land Rheinland-Pfalz (C306/93) [1994] E.C.R.
  I-5555; [1995] 2 C.M.L.R. 718, ECJ 10-096
Sabel BV v Puma AG (C-251/95) [1997] E.C.R. I-6191; [1998] 1 C.M.L.R.
  445; [1998] C.E.C. 315; [1998] E.T.M.R. 1; [1998] R.P.C. 199, ECJ 4-277,
  4-352, 4-484,
  4-502, 5-007, 5-011,
  5-016, 5-021, 5-022,
  5-024, 5-027, 5-032, 5-034,
  5-036, 5-043, 5-044, 5-071,
  5-083, 5-099, 5-118, 5-139,
  5-191, 5-193, 5-195, 5-197,
  5-202, 5-203, 6-101, 6-132, 8-197
Sadas SA v Office for Harmonisation in the Internal Market (Trade Marks
  and Designs) (OHIM) (T346/04) [2006] E.T.M.R. 27, CFI (3rd
  Chamber) 5-004
Salomon SA v Commission of the European Communities (T123/97)
  146034[1999] E.C.R. II-2925, CFI 5-129
Samar SpA v Office for Harmonisation in the Internal Market (Trade
  Marks and Designs) (OHIM) (T115/03) [2004] E.C.R. II-2939, CFI 5-128
Schieving-Nijstad VOF v Groeneveld (C89/99); sub nom. VOF Schieving-
  Nijstad v Groeneveld (C89/99) [2001] E.C.R. I-5851; [2001] 3 C.M.L.R.
  44; [2002] E.T.M.R. 4; [2002] F.S.R. 22, ECJ 10-134, 10-137,
  10-144, 10-149
Schutzverband gegen Unwesen in der Wirtschaft EV v Warsteiner
  Brauerei Haus Cramer GmbH & Co KG (C312/98) [2000] E.C.R.
  I-9187; [2001] 2 C.M.L.R. 11; [2003] E.T.M.R. 6, ECJ 10-109,
  10-115, 10-123
Sebago Inc v GB Unic SA (C173/98) [2000] Ch. 558; [2000] 2 W.L.R. 1341;
  [1999] All E.R. (EC) 575; [1999] E.C.R. I-4103; [1999] 2 C.M.L.R. 1317;
  [1999] C.E.C. 273; [1999] E.T.M.R. 681; [2000] R.P.C. 63, ECJ (5th
  Chamber) 8-220, 8-227,
  8-236, 8-237, 8-239
Sergio Rossi SpA v Office for Harmonisation in the Internal Market (Trade
  Marks and Designs) (OHIM) (C214/05) [2006] E.C.R. I-7057, ECJ 3-057,
  5-106

lv

TABLE OF EUROPEAN CASES

Sergio Rossi SpA v Office for Harmonisation in the Internal Market
(Trade Marks and Designs) (OHIM) (T-169/03), [2005] E.C.R. II-685,
CFI 5-106, 5-112, 5-113,
5-116, 5-117, 5-118,
5-121, 5-122, 5-123,
5-133, 5-136
Shaker di L Laudato & C SAS v Office for Harmonisation in the Internal
Market (Trade Marks and Designs) (OHIM) (T7/04) [2005] E.C.R.
II-2305; [2006] E.T.M.R. 51, CFI (3rd Chamber) 5-153
Shield Mark BV v Kist (t/a Memex) (C-283/01) [2004] Ch. 97; [2004] 2
W.L.R. 1117; [2004] All E.R. (EC) 277; [2003] E.C.R. I-14313; [2005] 1
C.M.L.R. 41; [2004] C.E.C. 228; [2004] E.T.M.R. 33; [2004] R.P.C. 17,
ECJ (6th Chamber) 4-052, 4-066,
4-068, 4-081
Sieckmann v Deutsches Patent- und Markenamt (C-273/00) [2003] Ch.
487; [2003] 3 W.L.R. 424; [2004] All E.R. (EC) 253; [2002] E.C.R.
I-11737; [2005] 1 C.M.L.R. 40; [2004] C.E.C. 404; [2003] E.T.M.R. 37;
[2003] R.P.C. 38, ECJ 4-006, 4-007,
4-012, 4-018, 4-032,
4-052, 4-055, 4-058,
4-059, 4-066, 4-068, 4-073,
4-077, 4-081, 5-205, 7-015
Siemens AG v VIPA Gesellschaft fur Visualisierung und
Prozessautomatisierung mbH (C59/05) [2006] E.C.R. I-2147; [2006] 2
C.M.L.R. 32; [2006] C.E.C. 752; [2006] E.T.M.R. 47, ECJ (1st
Chamber) 10-040, 10-046,
10-047, 10-048
Silberquell GmbH v Maselli Strickmode GmbH (C-495/07) unreported 7-039,
7-047
Silhouette International Schmied GmbH & Co KG v Hartlauer
Handelsgesellschaft mbH (C-355/96) [1999] Ch. 77; [1998] 3 W.L.R.
1218; [1998] All E.R. (EC) 769; [1998] E.C.R. I-4799; [1998] 2 C.M.L.R.
953; [1998] C.E.C. 676; [1998] E.T.M.R. 539; [1998] F.S.R. 729; (1998)
21(10) I.P.D. 21110, ECJ 7-018, 8-206,
8-227, 8-236,
8-255, 9-072
Simitzi v Kos (C485/93) [1995] E.C.R. I-2655, ECJ 8-014
Simmenthal Spa v Commission of the European Communities (92/78)
[1978] E.C.R. 1129, ECJ 3-007
Sirena Srl v Eda Srl (40/70) [1971] E.C.R. 69; [1971] C.M.L.R. 260; [1971]
F.S.R. 666, ECJ 8-053
Sociale Verzekeringsbank v Van der Vecht (19/67) [1967] E.C.R. 345;
[1968] C.M.L.R. 151, ECJ 4-508
Societa Eridania Zuccherifici Nazionali v Commission of the European
Communities (10/68) [1969] E.C.R. 459, ECJ 3-005
Societa Italiana Petroli SpA (IP) v Borsana Srl (C2/97) [1998] E.C.R.
I-8597; [2001] 1 C.M.L.R. 27, ECJ 9-012
Societe des Produits Nestle SA v Mars UK Ltd (C353/03) [2006] All E.R.
(EC) 348; [2005] E.C.R. I-6135; [2005] 3 C.M.L.R. 12; [2006] C.E.C. 3;
[2005] E.T.M.R. 96; [2006] F.S.R. 2; (2005) 28(10) I.P.D. 28071, ECJ
(2nd Chamber) 4-610, 4-615,
4-620, 4-624,
4-632, 7-072,
7-073

TABLE OF EUROPEAN CASES

Societe des Produits Nestle SA v Office for Harmonisation in the Internal
   Market (Trade Marks and Designs) (OHIM) (T74/04) (Unreported,
   February 22, 2006), CFI 5-155, 5-156,
                                                                   5-157, 5-158
Societe Provencale d'Achat et de Gestion (SPAG) SA v Office for
   Harmonisation in the Internal Market (Trade Marks and Designs)
   (OHIM) (T57/03) [2005] E.C.R. II-287; [2005] E.T.M.R. 116, CFI (2nd
   Chamber) 3-059
Societe Technique Miniere v Maschinenbau Ulm GmbH (56/65) [1966]
   E.C.R. 235; [1966] C.M.L.R. 357, ECJ 9-035, 9-047,
                                                                   9-074, 9-076
Spain v Commission of the European Communities (C-276/02) [2004] 3
   C.M.L.R. 47, ECJ (2nd Chamber) 5-129
Staatssecretaris van Financien v Shipping & Forwarding Enterprise Safe
   BV (C-320/88) [1991] S.T.C. 627; [1990] E.C.R. I-285; [1993] 3
   C.M.L.R. 547, ECJ (6th Chamber) 5-022, 7-024
Stauder v City of Ulm (29/69) [1969] E.C.R. 419; [1970] C.M.L.R. 112, ECJ 3-051
Stora Kopparbergs Bergslags AB v Commission of the European
   Communities (C-286/98 P) [2000] E.C.R. I-9925; [2001] 4 C.M.L.R. 12,
   ECJ (5th Chamber) 9-015
Storck KG v Office for Harmonisation in the Internal Market (Trade Marks
   and Designs) (OHIM) (T396/02) [2004] E.C.R. II-3821, CFI 4-311,
                                                                    4-320, 4-321,
                                                                  4-322, 4-340, 4-344,
                                                                4-616, 4-624, 4-626, 4-627
Streamserve Inc v Office for Harmonisation in the Internal Market (Trade
   Marks and Designs) (OHIM) (C150/02 P) [2004] E.C.R. I-1461;
   [2005] E.T.M.R. 57, ECJ 4-299, 4-429, 4-431,
                                                                  4-435, 4-436, 4-439, 5-063
Sunrider Corp v Office for Harmonisation in the Internal Market (Trade
   Marks and Designs) (OHIM) (C416/04) [2006] E.C.R. I-4237, ECJ 3-057,
                                                                      4-454, 7-001,
                                                                    7-016, 7-019, 7-075
Sunrider Corp v Office for Harmonisation in the Internal Market (Trade
   Marks and Designs) (OHIM) (T24/00) [2001] E.C.R. II-449; [2001]
   E.T.M.R. 56, CFI (2nd Chamber) 4-437
Sunrider Corp v Office for Harmonisation in the Internal Market (Trade
   Marks and Designs) (OHIM) (T-203/02) [2004] E.C.R. II-2811; [2004]
   C.E.C. 424, CFI (2nd Chamber) 7-075
Swaddling v Adjudication Officer (C90/97) [1999] All E.R. (EC) 217; [1999]
   E.C.R. I-1075; [1999] 2 C.M.L.R. 679; [1999] C.E.C. 184; [1999] 2 F.L.R.
   184; [1999] Fam. Law 382, ECJ (5th Chamber) 4-008, 4-070
Sykes Enterprises Inc v Office for Harmonisation in the Internal Market
   (Trade Marks and Designs) (OHIM) (T130/01) [2002] E.C.R. II-5179;
   [2003] C.E.C. 29; [2003] E.T.M.R. 57, CFI (2nd Chamber) 4-164
Synetairismos Farmakopoion Aitolias & Akarnanias (SYFAIT) v
   Glaxosmithkline Plc (C53/03) [2005] E.C.R. I-4609; [2005] 5
   C.M.L.R. 1, ECJ 7-060, 7-061, 9-109, 9-113
TEPEA BV v Commission of the European Communities (C28/77) [1978]
   E.C.R. 1391; [1978] 3 C.M.L.R. 392; [1979] F.S.R. 11, ECJ 9-053
TWD Textilwerke Deggendorf GmbH v Germany (C188/92) [1994]
   E.C.R. I-833; [1995] 2 C.M.L.R. 145, ECJ 3-010, 10-092
Taurus Film GmbH & Co v Office for Harmonisation in the Internal
   Market (Trade Marks and Designs) (OHIM) (T135/99); sub nom.

TABLE OF EUROPEAN CASES

CINE ACTION Trade Mark (T135/99)[2001] E.C.R. II-379; [2001]
E.T.M.R. 55; (2001) 24(6) I.P.D. 24041, CFI (2nd Chamber) 4-163
Team Srl v Commission of the European Communities (C-13/99 P) [2000]
E.C.R. I-4671, ECJ 9-132
Telefon & Buch Verlags Gmbh v Office for Harmonisation in the Internal
Market (Trade Marks and Designs) (OHIM) (C-326/01 P) [2004]
E.C.R. I-1371; [2005] E.T.M.R. 50, ECJ (4th Chamber) 4-136, 4-299,
4-440, 4-497,
5-063, 5-073
Telefon & Buch Verlags GmbH v Office for Harmonisation in the Internal
Market (Trade Marks and Designs) (OHIM) (T357/99) [2001] E.C.R.
II-1705; [2001] 3 C.M.L.R. 3; [2001] C.E.C. 151; [2001] E.T.M.R. 91,
CFI (4th Chamber) 4-440, 4-445
Terrapin (Overseas) Ltd v Terranova Industrie CA Kapferer & Co (119/75)
[1975] E.C.R. 1039; [1976] E.C.R. 1039; [1976] 2 C.M.L.R. 482; [1976]
F.S.R. 557, ECJ 4-470, 5-033,
5-065, 8-054, 8-055,
8-061, 8-067, 8-076
Theodor Kohl KG v Ringelhan & Rennett SA (C177/83) [1984] E.C.R.
3651; [1985] 3 C.M.L.R. 340; [1986] F.S.R. 8, ECJ 8-021, 8-033
Thyssen Stahl AG v Commission of the European Communities (C-194/99 P)
(Unreported, October 2, 2003), ECJ 4-210
Toshiba Europe GmbH v Katun Germany GmbH (C-112/99) [2002] All
E.R. (EC) 325; [2001] E.C.R. I-7945; [2002] 3 C.M.L.R. 7; [2002] C.E.C.
438; [2002] E.T.M.R. 26; [2002] F.S.R. 39, ECJ (5th Chamber) 6-132
Toshiba Europe GmbH v Katun Germany GmbH (C-112/99) [2002] All
E.R. (EC) 325; [2001] E.C.R. I-7945; [2002] 3 C.M.L.R. 7; [2002] C.E.C.
438; [2002] E.T.M.R. 26; [2002] F.S.R. 39, ECJ (5th Chamber) 10-005,
10-017, 10-018, 10-019,
10-022, 10-023, 10-024,
10-027, 10-034, 10-035,
10-036, 10-041, 10-042, 10-051
Traunfellner GmbH v Osterreichische Autobahnen- und
Schnellstrassenfinanzierungs AG (C421/01) [2003] E.C.R. I-11941,
ECJ 5-145
Trojani v Centre Public d'Aide Sociale de Bruxelles (CPAS) (C-456/02)
[2004] All E.R. (EC) 1065; [2004] E.C.R. I-7573; [2004] 3 C.M.L.R. 38;
[2005] C.E.C. 139, ECJ 6-036, 10-150
Tzoanos v Commission of the European Communities (C-191/98 P) [1999]
E.C.R. I-8223, ECJ 4-497
UDV North America Inc v Brandtraders NV (Smirnoff Ice) (C-62/08) unre
ported 6-051,
6-054, 6-055
Unilever Italia SpA v Central Food SpA (C443/98) [2000] E.C.R. I-7535;
[2001] 1 C.M.L.R. 21, ECJ 3-039
Union de Pequenos Agricultores v Council of the European Union
(C-50/00 P) [2003] Q.B. 893; [2003] 2 W.L.R. 795; [2002] All E.R. (EC)
893; [2002] E.C.R. I-6677; [2002] 3 C.M.L.R. 1, ECJ 3-010
Union Deutsche Lebensmittelwerke Gmbh v Schutzverband gegen
Unwesen in der Wirtschaft eV (C101/98) [1999] E.C.R. I-8841, ECJ
(6th Chamber) 8-043
Union Nationale des Entraineurs et Cadres Techniques Professionnels du
Football (UNECTEF) v Heylens (222/86) [1987] E.C.R. 4097; [1989] 1
C.M.L.R. 901, ECJ 4-451, 4-462

lviii

TABLE OF EUROPEAN CASES

Union Royale Belge des Societes de Football Association (ASBL) v
  Bosman (C415/93); sub nom. Royal Club Liegois SA v Bosman
  (C415/93); Union des Associations Europeennes de Football (UEFA)
  v Bosman (C415/93) [1996] All E.R. (EC) 97; [1995] E.C.R. I-4921;
  [1996] 1 C.M.L.R. 645; [1996] C.E.C. 38, ECJ 4-064
United Brands Co v Commission of the European Communities (27/76)
  [1978] E.C.R. 207; [1978] 1 C.M.L.R. 429, ECJ 9-005, 9-079,
    9-083, 9-115,
    9-118, 9-120
United Kingdom v Commission of the European Communities (C180/96)
  [1998] E.C.R. I-2265; [1998] 2 C.M.L.R. 1125; (1998) 17 Tr. L.R. 243,
  ECJ 10-095
Vaassen (nee Gobbels) v Beambtenfonds voor het Mijnbedrijf (61/65)
  [1966] E.C.R. 261; [1966] C.M.L.R. 508, ECJ 4-540
Vag Sverige AB, Re (C329/95) [1997] E.C.R. I-2675, ECJ 4-071
Van den Bergh Foods Ltd v Commission of the European Communities
  (T65/98) [2005] All E.R. (EC) 418; [2003] E.C.R. II-4653; [2004] 4
  C.M.L.R. 1, CFI (5th Chamber) 9-009, 9-010
Van Duyn v Home Office (41/74) [1975] Ch. 358; [1975] 2 W.L.R. 760;
  [1975] 3 All E.R. 190; [1974] E.C.R. 1337; [1975] 1 C.M.L.R. 1; (1974)
  119 S.J. 302, ECJ 3-033, 3-034,
    3-035, 8-055
Van Zuylen Freres v Hag AG (192/73); sub nom. Van Zuylen Bros v Hag
  AG (192/73) [1974] E.C.R. 731; [1974] 2 C.M.L.R. 127; [1974]
  F.S.R. 511, ECJ 8-059, 8-060,
    8-066, 8-067, 8-076
Vedial SA v Office for Harmonisation in the Internal Market (Trade Marks
  and Designs) (OHIM) (C-106/03 P) [2004] E.C.R. I-9573; [2005]
  E.T.M.R. 23, ECJ (2nd Chamber) 5-038, 5-042
Vedial SA v Office for Harmonisation in the Internal Market (Trade Marks
  and Designs) (OHIM) (T-110/01) [2002] E.C.R. II-5275; [2004]
  E.T.M.R. 102, CFI 5-038
Vennootschap Onder Firma Senta Aromatic Marketing's Application
  [1999] E.T.M.R. 429, OHIM (2nd Bd App) 4-038
Verband Sozialer Wettbewerb eV v Clinique Laboratories SNC (C315/92)
  [1994] E.C.R. I-317, ECJ (5th Chamber) 4-552, 4-555,
    4-564, 4-566, 8-124
Verbraucherschutzverein EV v Sektkellerei GC Kessler GmbH & Co
  (C303/97) [1999] E.C.R. I-513; [1999] 1 C.M.L.R. 756; [1999] E.T.M.R.
  269, ECJ (5th Chamber) 4-233
Verein Gegen Unwesen in Handel und Gewerbe Koln eV v Mars GmbH
  (C470/93) [1995] E.C.R. I-1923; [1995] 3, ECJ (5th Chamber) 4-559,
    4-565, 4-566
Verein Radetzky-Orden v Bundesvereinigung Kameradschaft
  "Feldmarschall Radetzky" (C-442/07) unreported 7-031, 7-035,
    7-036, 7-047
Volk v Etablissements J Vervaecke SPRL (5/69) [1969] E.C.R. 295; [1969]
  C.M.L.R. 273, ECJ 9-036, 9-074, 9-076
Volvo AB v Erik Veng (UK) Ltd (238/87) [1988] E.C.R. 6211; [1989] 4
  C.M.L.R. 122, ECJ 9-090, 9-091,
    9-092, 9-101, 9-106
Von Colson v Land Nordrhein-Westfahlen (C14/83); Harz v Deutsche
  Tradax GmbH (C79/83) [1984] E.C.R. 1891; [1986] 2 C.M.L.R. 430,
  ECJ 3-033, 3-046, 5-200, 8-095

TABLE OF EUROPEAN CASES

Warner Brothers Inc v Christiansen (158/86) [1988] E.C.R. 2605; [1990] 3
  C.M.L.R. 684; [1991] F.S.R. 161, ECJ 8-205
Weber v Freistaat Bayern (C328/00) [2002] E.C.R. I-1461, ECJ 10-090
Weigel v Finanzlandesdirektion fur Vorarlberg (C-387/01) [2004] E.C.R.
  I-4981; [2004] 3 C.M.L.R. 42, ECJ (6th Chamber) 4-028
Wellcome Foundation Ltd v Paranova Pharmazeutika Handels GmbH
  (C-276/05) unreported 8-278, 8-184, 8-285
Williams v Court of Auditors of the European Communities (134/84)
  [1985] E.C.R. 2225, ECJ 4-117
Willy Kempter KG v Hauptzollamt Hamburg-Jonas (C-2/06) [2008] 2
  C.M.L.R. 21, ECJ (Grand Chamber) 10-128
Windsurfing Chiemsee Produktions- und Vertriebs GmbH v Boots- und
  Segelzubehor Walter Huber (C108/97) 115569; Windsurfing
  Chiemsee Produktions und Vertriebs GmbH v Attenberger
  (C109/97) [2000] Ch. 523; [2000] 2 W.L.R. 205; [1999] E.C.R. I-2779;
  [1999] E.T.M.R. 585, ECJ 4-002, 4-020, 4-035,
                                                     4-088, 4-092, 4-094, 4-097,
                                                     4-120, 4-121, 4-126, 4-136,
                                                     4-154, 4-164, 4-183, 4-187,
                                                     4-217, 4-221, 4-226, 4-227,
                                                     4-270, 4-271, 4-346, 4-360,
                                                     4-361, 4-362, 4-363, 4-373,
                                                     4-386, 4-400, 4-409, 4-411,
                                                     4-421, 4-431, 4-438, 4-446,
                                                     4-470, 4-488, 4-503, 4-505,
                                                     4-506, 4-507, 4-597, 4-602,
                                                     4-603, 4-605, 4-607, 4-608,
                                                     4-609, 4-614, 4-630, 4-632,
                                                     4-638, 4-639, 4-645, 4-653,
                                              5-029, 6-037, 6-043, 6-120, 10-121
Witte v European Parliament (188/83) [1984] E.C.R. 3465, ECJ 4-117
Wm Wrigley Jr Co v Office for Harmonisation in the Internal Market
  (Trade Marks and Designs) (OHIM) (T-193/99) [2001] E.C.R. II-417;
  [2001] E.T.M.R. 58; (2001) 24(5) I.P.D. 24033, CFI (2nd Chamber) 4-376,
                                                                    4-385, 4-386
Yves Rocher GmbH, Re (C126/91); sub nom. Schutzverband gegen
  Unwesen in der Wirtschaft v Yves Rocher GmbH, Re (C126/91) [1993]
  E.C.R. I-2361, ECJ (1st Chamber) 4-561, 4-565
Yves Saint Laurent Parfums SA v Javico International (C306/96); sub nom.
  Javico International v Yves Saint Laurent Parfums SA (C306/96)
  [1999] Q.B. 477; [1998] 3 W.L.R. 1200; [1998] E.C.R. I-1983; [1998] 5
  C.M.L.R. 172; [1998] C.E.C. 813, ECJ 8-214, 9-072,
                                                             9-076, 9-077
Zino Davidoff SA v A&G Imports Ltd (C-414/99); Levi Strauss & Co v
  Tesco Stores Ltd (C-415/99); Levi Strauss & Co v Costco Wholesale
  UK Ltd (C-416/99) [2002] Ch. 109; [2002] 2 W.L.R. 321; [2002] All E.R.
  (EC) 55; [2001] E.C.R. I-8691; [2002] 1 C.M.L.R. 1; [2002] C.E.C. 154;
  [2002] E.T.M.R. 9; [2002] R.P.C. 20, ECJ 5-199, 7-009, 7-019,
                                                          8-225, 8-245, 8-249
Zino Davidoff SA v Bundesfinanzdirektion Sudost (Davidoff III)
  (C-302/08) 6-151, 6-152
Zwartveld, Re (C2/88 Imm) [1990] E.C.R. I-3365; [1990] 3 C.M.L.R. 457,
  ECJ 9-051

TABLE OF EUROPEAN LEGISLATION

Treaties & Conventions

1883 Paris Convention for the
 Protection of Industrial
 Property 5–015, 5–177,
 7–035
 art.5C 7–009
 art.6(3) 8–070
 art.6bis 2–013, 5–170, 5–173
 B(2) 4–070, 4–403,
 4–480, 4–481
 C(1) 4–188, 4–406, 4–416
 art.6quarter 8–070
 art.6ter 4–572, 4–577, 4–582
 (1) 4–569, 4–571,
 4–575, 4–580
 art.8 ... 10–142, 10–153, 10–154
 art.219 10–133
1886 Berne Convention for the
 Protection of Literary
 and Artistic Works 9–097
 art.9(1) 9–097
 (2) 9–097
1891 Madrid Agreement
 Concerning the
 International Registration
 of Marks 2–003
 art.3(4) 7–055
 art.9ter 8–070
1947 General Agreement on
 Tariffs and Trade 2–003
1950 European Convention on
 Human Rights 10–155
 art.6 .... 4–306, 9–132
1951 Treaty of Paris 3–026
1957 Treaty establishing the
 European
 Community 3–009, 3–026,
 3–039, 8–001,
 8–123
 art.2 3–030
 art.3 4–024
 (g) 9–004
 art.6 3–065

(1) 3–050
art.7 .... 3–001, 3–050
art.10 ..... 3–033, 3–041, 3–043,
 3–046, 5–053, 5–084,
 8–051, 9–012, 9–051
art.12 3–043
art.14 5–195
arts.23–25 8–003
art.23 8–002
 (1) 8–002
 (2) 8–003
art.24 8–247
art.25 ..... 3–029, 3–030, 8–006
arts.28–31 .... 8–003, 8–004
art.28 ..... 4–469, 4–470, 4–564,
 4–565, 8–005, 8–011,
 8–013, 8–015, 8–017,
 8–018, 8–024, 8–025, 8–026,
 8–027, 8–029, 8–030, 8–033,
 8–039, 8–046, 8–071, 8–095,
 8–101, 8–125, 8–177, 10–108,
 10–114, 10–116, 10–117,
 10–119, 10–127
art.29 .... 8–005, 8–011,
 8–015, 8–030
art.30 ..... 4–469, 4–470, 4–565,
 5–059, 5–064, 5–065,
 8–005, 8–018, 8–030, 8–033,
 8–034, 8–038, 8–039, 8–052,
 8–053, 8–067, 8–071, 8–076,
 8–081, 8–087, 8–095, 8–099,
 8–101, 8–102, 8–110, 8–124,
 8–125, 8–128, 8–171, 8–176,
 8–177, 8–201, 8–205, 8–255,
 9–032, 10–108, 10–109,
 10–110, 10–114, 10–116,
 10–117, 10–123, 10–126,
 10–127, 10–129
art.31(1) 8–005
 (2) 8–005
 (3) 8–005
art.33 10–095
art.34 10–096
art.37 .... 10–095, 10–096

art.39 3–037	art.232(3) 3–005
art.43 3–031	art.234 . . . . 3–009, 3–010, 3–048,
art.44(2) 3–031	4–430, 4–540, 7–024,
art.47(1) 3–031	7–060, 8–177, 8–192,
art.49 4–114	8–202, 9–112, 10–092
arts.61–69 3–009	(1)(a) 3–009
art.68 3–009	(b) 3–009
art.81 . . . . . 8–033, 8–073, 9–001,	(c) 3–009
9–004, 9–008, 9–011,	art.235 9–0133
9–014, 9–026, 9–027,	art.241 3–006
9–032, 9–035, 9–037,	art.249 . . . . 3–032, 3–033,
9–049, 9–059, 9–062,	3–040, 3–046,
9–064, 9–067	4–240, 9–013
(1) 9–009, 9–011, 9–016,	art.253 4–197
9–018, 9–020, 9–021,	art.254 3–037
9–022, 9–024, 9–026,	art.288 9–133
9–030, 9–031, 9–036,	art.295 9–032
9–037, 9–039, 9–040,	arts.296–298 8–035
9–044, 9–045, 9–047,	art.307 . . . . 10–112, 10–113,
9–048, 9–050, 9–051,	10–114, 10–118
9–052, 9–056, 9–064,	1973 Trade Mark Registration
9–065, 9–066, 9–068,	Treaty 2–003
9–069, 9–070, 9–074,	1976 Agreement on the
9–075, 9–076, 9–077,	protection of indications
9–078, 9–088	of source, designations
(3) 9–003, 9–009, 9–011,	of origin and other
9–024, 9–025, 9–033,	designations referring to
9–034, 9–038, 9–048,	the source of agricultural
9–056, 9–061, 9–066,	and industrial
9–070, 9–071, 9–072	products 10–107
art.82 . . . . . 8–033, 8–081, 8–087,	1978 Vienna Convention on
9–001, 9–004, 9–008,	the Law of Treaties . . . 10–112
9–011, 9–023, 9–026,	art.31 10–113
9–048, 9–051, 9–062,	art.34(1) 10–112
9–089, 9–097, 9–098,	1989 Protocol relating to the
9–099, 9–100, 9–103,	Madrid Agreement
9–109, 9–115,	concerning the
9–116, 9–131	international registration
art.85(1) 8–051	of marks 6–151
art.90(1) 8–007	art.4(1) 6–154
(2) 8–007, 8–009	1992 Treaty on European
art.95 8–212	Union 3–050
art.141 3–037	art.6 4–206
art.189 . . . . 6–107, 8–217	art.35 3–009
art.217 2–016	1994 Agreement on Trade-
art.220 3–001	Related Aspects of
art.225 . . . . 3–022, 3–060, 3–062,	Intellectual Property
4–197, 4–210, 5–051	Rights 5–015, 10–106,
(3) 3–024	10–134, 10–145
art.226 3–004	art.2 . . . . 10–142, 10–156
art.228 3–004	(1) . . . 7–009, 10–133, 10–153
art.229(a) 3–023	art.6 8–213
art.230 . . . . 3–002, 3–006,	art.7 4–024
3–010, 10–092	art.15 . . . . . 4–072, 4–082, 10–149

TABLE OF EUROPEAN LEGISLATION

    (1) 4–072
art.16 .... 10–140, 10–143
    (1) 5–005, 10–133,
              10–138, 10–139,
              10–144, 10–146,
              10–147, 10–153,
                    10–154
    (2) 5–177
    (3) 5–170, 5–174
art.17 10–150
art.19 7–059
    (1) 7–064
art.21 4–531
art.24(5) 10–156
art.44(1) 6–147
art.61 6–147
art.70 10–133
    (1) 10–144
    (2) 10–144
Trade Mark Law Treaty
art.16 .... 4–569, 4–571
art.19 7–009
2001 Treaty of Nice 3–023
2004 Treaty Establishing a
     Constitution for Europe
     [2004] O.J. C310/1 3–003

Regulations

1962 Reg.17/62 covering
     agreements in existence
     prior to March 13, 1962
     [1962] O.J. L13/204 ... 9–049
1967 Reg.67/67 [1967] O.J.
     L57/849 9–061
     art.2 9–061
1968 Reg.1612/68 3–033
1983 Reg.1983/83 on block
     exemptions [1983] O.J.
     L173/1 9–073
     art.1 .... 9–073, 9–078
     Reg.1984/83 relating to
     exlcusive purchasing
     agreements [1983] O.J.
     L173/5 .. 9–038, 9–046, 9–048
     art.6 9–038
1984 Reg.2349/84 on patent
     licences [1984] O.J.
     L219/15 9–001
1989 Reg.556/89 on know–how
     licences [1989] O.J.
     L61/1 9–001
1992 Reg.2081/92 on agricultural
     products and foodstuffs

     [1992] O.J. L208/1 4–354,
                 10–054, 10–073,
                 10–092, 10–096,
                 10–103, 10–109,
                 10–110, 10–123
art.2 4–354
    (2)(a) 10–073, 10–084,
                       10–086
    (b) 10–093, 10–115,
                      10–126
    (3) 10–073, 10–084
art.3 10–104
    (1) .. 10–074, 10–087, 10–093
art.6(2) 10–086
art.13 .. 10–054, 10–094, 10–104
    (1) 10–104
art.14(2) 10–102
    (3) .. 10–100, 10–101, 10–102
art.17(1) 10–097
    (2) 10–093
Reg.2913/92 [1992] O.J.
     L302/1 8–244
art.91(1) 8–244
art.92 8–244
1995 Reg.2868/95 implementing
     Reg.40/94 [1995] O.J.
     L303/1 .... 2–009, 3–054
     art.22(2)–(3) 7–016
1996 Reg.216/96 laying down
     Rules of Procedure of
     the Boards of Appeal of
     OHIM 3–061
Reg.240/96 known as the
     Technology Transfer
     Regulation [1996]
     O.J. L31/2 9–001
Reg.1107/96 on the registration of
     geographical indications
     and designations of
     origin [1996] O.J.
     L148/1 ...... 10–075, 10–103
1997 Reg.258/97 [1997]
     O.J. L43/1 8–044
1998 Reg.1139/98 relating to
     foodstuffs [2000] O.J.
     L6/13 .... 8–040, 8–043,
                       8–044
     art.1(1) 8–042
     art.2(2)(b) 8–040, 8–043
1999 Reg.2790/99 on the
     application of Art.81(3)
     to categories of vertical
     agreements [1999] O.J.
     L336 9–002

TABLE OF EUROPEAN LEGISLATION

2000 Reg.2658/2000 on
specialisation agreements
[2000] O.J. L304/3 9–002
Reg.2659/2000 on research and
development agreements
[2000] O.J. L304/7 9–002
2001 Reg.1347/2001 on the
registration of geographical
indications and
designations of origin
[2001] O.J.
L182/3 ...... 10–092, 10–095
art.14 .... 10–093, 10–094
2002 Reg.178/2002 on
requirements of food
law [2002] O.J.
L31/1 .... 10–093, 10–095
art.2 .... 10–093, 10–095
Reg.1400/2002 on vertical
agreements in the motor
vehicle sector [2002]
O.J. L203/30 9–002
Reg.1829/2002 regarding the
name "feta" [2002]
O.J. L227/10 10–075
2003 Reg.1/2003 on the
implementation of the
rules on competition
[2003] O.J. L1/1 9–003
Reg.692/2003 on the protection
of geographical indications
and designations of origin
for agricultural products
[2003] O.J. L99/1 10–074
Reg.1383/2003 concerning customs
and infringement of
intellectual property
rights [2003] O.J.
L296/7 .... 6–151, 6–153
art.2 6–151
art.5(1) 6–151
(4) 6–151, 6–152
Reg.1992/2003 amending
Reg.40/94 to give effect
to the accession of the
Madrid Agreement ... 2–009,
6–151, 6–153,
6–154
2004 Reg.772/2004 on the
application of Art.81(3)
to technology agreements
[2004] O.J. L123/11 ... 9–002
Reg.918/2004 introducing
transitional arrangements for
agricultural products and
foodstuffs [2004] O.J.
L163/88 10–132
2006 Reg.510/2006 [2006]
O.J. L93 10–122,
10–123, 10–130
2009 Reg.207/2009 on the
Community Trade
Mark 2–002, 2–009,
2–014, 2–027, 3–064,
3–070, 5–134, 5–184
art.1 2–011
arts.4–6 7–068
art.4 ...... 2–012, 4–370, 4–371,
4–372, 4–379
art.6 2–012
art.7 ...... 2–012, 4–005, 4–255,
4–370, 4–371, 4–474,
4–578, 4–652
(1) 4–105, 4–127, 4–148,
4–171, 4–255, 4–273,
4–297, 4–382,
4–437, 4–642
(a) 4–118, 4–119,
4–164, 4–371
(b)–(e) 4–117, 4–121,
4–122, 4–135
(b) ... 4–103, 4–106, 4–108,
4–112, 4–114, 4–115,
4–116, 4–118, 4–119,
4–120, 4–123, 4–124,
4–126, 4–129, 4–130,
4–131, 4–132, 4–133,
4–134, 4–136, 4–145,
4–146, 4–148, 4–160,
4–161, 4–163, 4–164,
4–167, 4–168, 4–171,
4–192, 4–196, 4–199,
4–200, 4–201, 4–211,
4–212, 4–239, 4–241,
4–243, 4–245, 4–248,
4–251, 4–253, 4–257,
4–258, 4–263, 4–264,
4–265, 4–269, 4–270,
4–273, 4–276, 4–278,
4–279, 4–281, 4–290,
4–298, 4–300, 4–311,
4–314, 4–316, 4–319,
4–323, 4–325, 4–342,
4–365, 4–369, 4–378,
4–388, 4–429, 4–437,
4–440, 4–442, 4–472,
4–631, 4–634, 4–646,
4–647, 7–072

TABLE OF EUROPEAN LEGISLATION

(c) ... 4–104, 4–106, 4–112,
4–114, 4–116, 4–117,
4–120, 4–123, 4–132,
4–133, 4–134, 4–136,
4–148, 4–160, 4–163,
4–168, 4–199, 4–201,
4–246, 4–263, 4–264,
4–290, 4–299, 4–365,
4–366, 4–367, 4–368,
4–369, 4–372, 4–373,
4–376, 4–378, 4–379,
4–380, 4–382, 4–383,
4–384, 4–385, 4–386,
4–388, 4–395, 4–298,
4–399, 4–400, 4–401,
4–402, 4–429, 4–431,
4–437, 4–438, 4–439,
4–440, 4–442, 4–443,
4–444, 4–445,
4–646, 4–647
(d) ... 4–120, 4–146, 4–168,
4–171, 4–264, 4–386,
4–480, 4–481, 4–490,
4–491, 4–494,
4–504, 4–646
(e) 4–120, 4–264,
4–583
(f) 4–256
(h) 4–568, 4–569,
4–570, 4–571,
4–579, 4–583
(i) 4–583
(j) 4–583
(k) 4–583
(2) 2–012, 4–104,
4–112, 4–382, 4–631,
4–634, 4–642, 5–164
(3) ... 4–119, 4–166, 4–211,
4–241, 4–247, 4–259,
4–278, 4–305, 4–310,
4–311, 4–314, 4–323,
4–365, 4–371, 4–378,
4–386, 4–490, 4–494,
4–619, 4–629, 4–631,
4–634, 4–646, 4–647,
4–648, 4–650
(4) 4–194
art.8 2–013
(1)(b) 4–284, 5–059,
5–062, 5–067, 5–069,
5–070, 5–113, 5–125,
5–131, 5–151, 5–155,
5–160, 5–162, 5–165,
7–067

(2) 2–025, 5–165
(c) 5–173, 5–174
(4) 2–013, 2–025
(5) 5–160, 5–173, 5–174,
5–195, 5–227, 5–228,
5–229, 5–234, 5–240,
5–241, 7–049, 7–050,
7–051, 7–0
art.9 6–004
(1) 6–052, 6–054,
6–144, 6–145,
8–244, 8–247
(a) 6–051, 6–053
(c) 5–173, 5–180,
5–182, 5–185,
5–186, 5–187,
5–188
(2) 6–052
(b) 8–244, 8–248
(c) 8–244, 8–247
(d) 6–051, 6–053
art.10 6–005
art.11 6–006
art.12 6–007
(b) 4–104, 4–112,
4–114, 4–162,
4–168, 4–172,
4–257, 4–372,
4–376, 4–379,
4–397, 4–444,
5–059, 5–063
art.13 8–215
art.14 .... 5–052, 6–149
art.15 .... 2–014, 7–019
(2)(a) 7–067, 7–071
art.16 2–020
art.21 2–020
art.28 4–467
art.30 4–467
arts.34–35 2–024
art.37 4–112
(2) 4–112
(3) 4–112
art.39 3–033
art.40 2–013
art.41 2–013
art.42 .... 7–067, 7–068,
7–069
(2) 7–074
(3) 7–074
(5) 4–466
art.43 4–465
art.45 4–466
art.46 4–466

TABLE OF EUROPEAN LEGISLATION

art.51 7–019
   (1)(a) 5–185
art.52 4–255
   (1) 4–255, 4–490
     (a) 4–652
     (b) 4–256, 4–585,
                    4–588, 4–651
     (c) 4–256
   (2) 4–255, 4–646,
                 4–650, 4–651
art.53 2–014
art.54(2) 2–025
art.55 4–466
art.57(2) 7–069
arts.58–64 2–019
art.64 4–366
   (1) 3–053, 3–055, 3–056
art.65 5–134
   (2) 3–057
   (3) 4–430
   (6) 3–061, 4–430
arts.66–74 2–011
art.66(2) 4–373
art.75 . . . . 4–314, 4–315,
                     4–322, 4–323,
                     4–344, 5–128,
                     5–136
arts.76–78 2–019
art.76 4–315
   (1) 3–059, 4–314, 4–322,
             4–323, 4–326, 4–343,
             4–344, 4–474, 4–476,
             5–128, 5–135
   (2) 3–054
art.95 2–020
art.100(7) 5–053
art.101(3) 5–025
art.102(1) 6–142, 6–143,
                      6–147, 6–148,
                      6–149, 6–150
   (2) 5–025
art.104 5–053
art.109 5–053
art.110 2–025
   (2) 2–026
art.111 2–026
arts.112–114 2–023
art.112(2)(b) 5–167
art.119(4) 2–016
art.136(4) 3–053
art.147 . . . . 4–631, 10–104
art.151 6–151
   (2) 6–154
art.165 2–021

Directives

1964   Dir.64/221 3–033
1970   Dir.70/50 [1970] O.J.
         L13/29
         art.2(3) 8–012
1976   Dir.76/768 relating to
         cosmetic products [1976]
         O.J. L262/169 4–553
         art.6(2) 4–555
1979   Dir.79/112 relating to
         certain foodstuffs [1979]
         O.J. L33/1 . . . . . 8–042, 8–044
         art.3 8–042
         art.4(2) 8–042
1980   Dir.80/777 relating to the
         exploitation and
         marketing of natural
         mineral waters
         [1980] O.J. L229/1 6–122,
                                     6–123
1983   Dir.83/189 laying down a
         procedure for the
         provision of information
         in the field of technical
         standards and
         regulations [1983]
         O.J. L109/8 3–039
1984   Dir.84/450 concerning
         misleading advertising
         [1984] O.J.
         L250/17 4–551,
                4–553, 5–232, 6–012,
                6–066, 10–002,
                10–019, 10–050
         art.1 10–060
         art.2 10–003
            (1) 6–062, 10–017,
                           10–070
            (2) 10–003, 10–004,
                           10–035
              (a) 6–012, 6–062,
                      10–003, 10–007,
                      10–034
            (2a) 10–017, 10–056,
                        10–062, 10–066
         art.3 . . . . 10–004, 10–035
         art.3a 10–018, 10–029,
                     10–031, 10–060,
                     10–061
            (1) 6–062, 10–004,
                       10–008, 10–029,
                   10–037, 10–038, 10–057,
                   10–063, 10–067, 10–068

TABLE OF EUROPEAN LEGISLATION

  (a) 10–030, 10–032
  (c) 10–008, 10–039,
        10–041
  (d) 10–036, 10–063
  (e) 10–036, 10–061
  (f) 10–054, 10–058
  (g) 10–036, 10–058,
      10–061, 10–069,
        10–071
  (h) 10–071
 (2) 10–030
art.7 10–004,
        10–028
 (1) 10–035
 (2) 10–029, 10–031,
        10–035

1989 Dir.89/398 concerning labelling, presentation and advertising of certain products
art.4 8–042
art.7(1) 8–043
 (4) 8–043

1990 Dir.90/220 [1996] O.J. L107/10 8–044

1991 Dir.91/321 concerning labelling of infant formulae 8–042

1993 Dir.93/104 concerning certain aspects of the organisation of working time [1993] O.J. L307/18 3–044
art.6(2) 3–045

1996 Dir.96/5 determining rules on labelling of infant formulae 8–042

1997 Dir.97/55/EC concerning misleading advertising and comparative advertising [1997] O.J. L290/18 . . . 6–012,
      6–132, 10–002,
      10–005, 10–006,
      10–019, 10–022,
      10–036, 10–039,
      10–046, 10–062
art.3a(1)(a) 10–028
 (b) 10–056
 (c) 10–027
 (g) 10–011, 10–027

2000 Dir.2000/31/EC on electronic commerce [2000] O.J. L178/1 6–066
art.12 6–077

art.13 6–077
art.14 6–077
art.15 6–007

2008 Dir.2008/95 relating to Trade Marks . . 2–002, 2–005,
       2–008, 2–027,
       3–064, 3–069,
       3–070, 4–057,
       4–403, 5–019,
       6–002, 6–066,
      8–277, 10–019
art.1 7–061
art.2 . . . . . . 4–001, 4–003, 4–006,
     4–008, 4–010, 4–011,
     4–015, 4–016, 4–017,
     4–018, 4–020, 4–022,
     4–028, 4–029, 4–030,
     4–034, 4–, 4–071,
     4–076, 4–080, 3–082,
     4–092, 4–096, 4–151,
     4–153, 4–176, 4–191,
     4–196, 4–216, 4–218,
     4–222, 4–225, 4–231,
     4–370, 7–044, 10–149
art.3 . . . . 4–004, 4–008, 4–070,
     4–151, 4–183, 4–226,
     4–416, 4–417, 4–421,
     4–425, 4–455, 4–456,
     4–469, 4–508, 4–543,
     4–651, 6–042, 6–046,
      6–047, 7–044
 (1) 4–007, 4–010, 4–087,
     4–097, 4–098, 4–221,
      4–237, 4–512
  (a) 4–007, 4–010,
     4–086, 4–087, 4–091,
      4–092, 4–093,
      4–095, 4–097
  (b)–(d) 4–645
  (b) . . . 4–001, 4–007, 4–009,
     4–010, 4–069, 4–086,
     4–087, 4–092, 4–093,
     4–095, 4–097, 4–112,
     4–127, 4–152, 4–154,
     4–155, 4–156, 4–158,
     4–186, 4–215, 4–217,
     4–218, 4–222, 4–228,
     4–229, 4–265, 4–273,
     4–350, 4–426, 4–471,
     4–483, 4–598, 4–601,
     4–610, 4–611, 4–637,
     4–638, 4–639, 4–640,
     4–643, 4–644, 5–086,
     6–043, 6–044, 6–045

(c) ... 3–067, 4–010, 4–086,
        4–087, 4–092, 4–093,
        4–097, 4–112, 4–153,
        4–183, 4–215, 4–220,
        4–221, 4–222, 4–226,
        4–227, 4–228, 4–229,
        4–232, 4–237, 4–346,
        4–347, 4–348, 4–350,
        4–351, 4–353, 4–354,
        4–357, 4–358, 4–361,
        4–362, 4–363, 4–370,
        4–403, 4–409, 4–410,
        4–414, 4–422, 4–423,
        4–424, 4–426, 4–468,
        4–471, 4–483, 4–485,
        4–489, 4–490, 4–503,
        4–505, 4–506, 4–601,
        4–606, 4–637, 4–638,
        4–639, 4–640, 4–643,
        4–644, 5–205, 6–043,
        6–044, 6–045,
        6–120, 10–094
(d) ... 4–010, 4–086, 4–087,
        4–092, 4–093, 4–215,
        4–222, 4–350, 4–426,
        4–479, 4–480, 4–481,
        4–482, 4–483, 4–485,
        4–486, 4–487, 4–488,
        4–489, 4–490, 4–503,
        4–504, 4–601, 4–606
(e) ... 4–013, 4–022, 4–024,
        4–026, 4–087, 4–089,
        4–183, 4–215, 4–216,
        4–217, 4–220, 4–221,
        4–222, 4–223, 4–225,
        4–226, 4–228, 4–229,
        4–232, 4–237, 4–414,
        4–423, 4–510, 4–511,
        4–512, 4–513, 4–517,
        4–519, 4–521, 4–524,
        4–526, 4–427, 4–606,
        5–205, 6–043
(f) 4–512
(g) 4–512, 4–528,
        4–529, 4–542,
        4–543, 4–544,
        10–094
(h) 4–568
(2)(d) 4–585
(3) 4–006, 4–022, 4–026,
        4–028, 4–093, 4–186,
        4–218, 4–225, 4–227,
        4–410, 4–483, 4–503,
        4–505, 4–506, 4–512,

        4–517, 4–525, 4–526,
        4–527, 4–597, 4–598,
        4–601, 4–602, 4–606,
        4–610, 4–611, 4–612,
        4–613, 4–615, 4–635,
        4–636, 4–640, 4–641,
        4–655, 4–646, 4–650, 7–072
(4) 6–096
art.4 .... 5–002, 7–044
(1) 2–006, 5–145, 5–195,
        7–044
(a) 5–008
(b) .. 4–501, 5–011, 5–018,
        5–019, 5–034, 5–035,
        5–036, 5–037, 5–044,
        5–193
(2) 2–006
(b) 5–173, 5–177,
        10–143
(d) 5–179, 10–143
(3) 2–006
(4) 2–006, 5–191, 5–196
(a) ... 5–025, 5–170, 5–173,
        5–191, 5–192, 5–193,
        5–195, 5–209, 5–215,
        5–218, 5–219, 5–220,
        5–224, 5–227
(b) 5–177, 5–179
(5) 2–006
(6) 2–006, 6–096
arts.5–7 8–242
art.5 ...... 2–012, 4–612, 5–092,
        5–199, 6–010, 6–015,
        6–044, 6–047, 6–090,
        6–096, 6–108, 6–119,
        7–041, 7–044, 8–203,
        8–218, 8–227, 8–255,
        9–130, 10–140
(1)–(4) 6–083
(1) 4–468, 5–009, 5–089,
        5–105, 5–145, 5–195,
        5–201, 5–204, 6–010,
        6–011, 6–013, 6–015,
        6–016, 6–020, 6–047,
        6–054, 6–057, 6–062,
        6–082, 6–086, 6–087,
        6–091, 6–109, 7–044,
        8–067, 8–210, 8–236,
        8–244, 8–247, 8–248,
        8–254, 10–059, 10–062,
        10–063, 10–064,
        10–065, 10–067
(a) ... 5–004, 5–008, 5–009,
        5–205, 5–232, 6–013,

6-026, 6-027, 6-031,
6-032, 6-033, 6-034,
6-035, 6-038, 6-039,
6-051, 6-056, 6-057,
6-058, 6-059, 6-060,
6-061, 6-062, 6-063,
6-064, 6-065, 6-074,
6-084, 6-086, 6-092,
6-098, 6-109, 6-111,
8-216, 8-217, 10-060,
10-068
(b) 4-501, 5-009,
5-024, 5-025,
5-026, 5-141,
5-196, 5-203,
6-013, 6-048,
6-056, 6-057,
6-063, 6-074,
6-096, 6-101,
10-060, 10-064
(2) 4-641, 5-025, 5-169,
5-170, 5-171, 5-173,
5-178, 5-188, 5-191,
5-192, 5-193, 5-195,
5-196, 5-197, 5-198,
5-201, 5-202, 5-203,
5-204, 5-205, 5-206,
5-209, 5-215, 5-218,
5-227, 5-230, 5-232,
5-233, 6-016, 6-036,
6-038, 6-049, 6-059,
6-060, 6-062, 6-064,
6-065, 6-074, 6-082,
6-087, 6-091, 6-096,
6-102, 6-109, 6-110,
10-062, 10-063,
10-065, 10-067
(3) 5-084, 5-090, 6-057,
6-070, 6-087, 6-110
(a) 6-033
(b) 6-033, 8-242,
8-244, 8-248
(c) 8-242, 8-244,
8-247
(d) 6-051, 6-072,
8-191, 8-194
(4) 6-096, 6-107
(5) 5-205, 6-080, 6-081,
6-082, 6-083, 6-084,
6-091, 6-103, 6-109,
6-110, 10-149
art.6 ...... 2-007, 4-155, 5-199,
6-003, 6-010, 6-012,
6-104, 6-108, 6-111,

6-119, 6-121, 6-126,
6-134, 8-191, 8-218,
8-227, 8-255
(1) 4-153, 6-011, 6-012,
6-014, 6-044, 6-105,
6-124, 6-130,
6-134, 6-139
(a) 4-155, 4-156,
4-159, 6-088,
6-091, 6-093,
10-150, 10-151
(b) 4-355, 4-357,
4-361, 4-468,
5-232, 6-010,
6-027, 6-037,
6-038, 6-039,
6-044, 6-045,
6-047, 6-050,
6-118, 6-120,
6-123, 6-124,
6-139, 6-140
(c) 6-037, 6-104,
6-114, 6-125,
6-127, 6-134,
6-136, 10-014,
10-018
(2) 5-179
art.7 ...... 2-007, 5-199, 6-108,
6-111, 6-112, 8-095,
8-098, 8-107, 8-108,
8-109, 8-116, 8-123,
8-124, 8-128, 8-191,
8-193, 8-203, 8-210,
8-215, 8-218, 8-227,
8-236, 8-255
(1) 6-099, 8-107, 8-108,
8-125, 8-126, 8-193,
8-194, 8-195, 8-203,
8-206, 8-207, 8-209,
8-210, 8-215, 8-216,
8-217, 8-219, 8-222,
8-223, 8-230, 8-233,
8-235, 8-240, 8-241,
8-243, 8-254
(2) 6-099, 6-112, 6-113,
8-107, 8-108, 8-126,
8-127, 8-128, 8-189,
8-195, 8-203, 8-208,
8-222, 8-224, 8-234,
8-254, 8-255, 8-257,
8-260, 8-262, 8-284
(3) 4-615
art.8 .... 2-007, 5-003
(2) 9-130

art.9 .... 5–085, 7–044
  (1) 5–091
  (c) 5–227
arts.10–15 .... 7–019, 7–044,
                7–063, 7–073
art.10 ...... 7–002, 7–007, 7–041
  (1) 4–612, 7–048, 7–054,
            7–058, 7–059, 7–061
  (2)(a) 7–071
  (3) 7–021
art.11 7–003
art.12 ..... 4–508, 5–085, 5–086,
        6–047, 7–004, 7–007,
                      7–033
  (1) 5–091, 7–008, 7–030,
           7–031, 7–034, 7–035,
           7–036, 7–048, 7–054,
           7–059, 7–062, 7–064,
                      7–065
  (2) 5–091, 5–092
    (a) 4–499, 4–503,
                4–505, 4–506,
                4–509, 5–089,
                      6–046
  (b) 4–539, 4–544,
                4–564, 4–567,
                    10–094
art.13 ..... 4–456, 4–459, 4–460,
                4–462, 7–005
art.14 7–006
art.15(2) 4–361, 4–373
art.19 4–531

Decisions

1994 Council Decision 94/800
      [1994] O.J. L336/1 4–072
2003 Council Decision
      2003/793 [2003] O.J.
      L296/20 6–151
2004 Council Decision of
      November 2, 2004
      establishing the
      European Union Civil
      Service Tribunal [2004]
      O.J. L333/7 3–023

CHAPTER 1

1. INTRODUCTION

1–001 Trade mark law has been growing rapidly in Europe during the last 15 years as a result of the harmonisation process and the introduction of the Community Trade Mark system. Until the introduction of the new European regime, national schemes of protection had been developed following contradictory models, ranging from pure deposit systems to registries that wished to protect consumers and competitors first and trade mark owners second. At the same time national courts had been applying their own distinct and often disparate trade mark law doctrines, whereas for the Court of Justice trade mark rights were primarily potential anti-competitive tools and barriers to intra-Community trade. From the early 1990s onwards, the new European regime has changed all that. National laws have had to adapt following the same substantive principles and national systems to coexist with a new, and truly federal, competing system of protection.

As a result, the Court of Justice has been deluged by references from national courts and appeals against the judgments of the Court of First Instance. Within this relatively short period of time, the Court of Justice had to face down persistent legal traditions and build up concepts that took the United States Supreme Court decades to delineate in a much less disparate environment. The Court also found that it had to deal with trade marks in a dual capacity, as an interpretive court but also as a supreme court dealing with appeals.

The aim of this book is to focus on trade marks from that new angle, the jurisprudence of the Court of Justice, and combine a comprehensive review of case law with an analysis of the conceptual core of European trade mark law. It aspires to provide a comprehensive—though not exhaustive—review of the case law of the Court of Justice on trade marks.

1–002 The judgments of the Court of First Instance are examined only to the extent that they have been appealed before the Court of Justice. Some matters of administrative and court procedure are covered to the extent that they have influenced the outcome of a judgment of the Court. Note that it has been attempted to follow developments before the Court of Justice up to September 2009.

The book starts with three brief introductory chapters. Chapter 2 provides an outline of the European trade mark regime. Chapter 3 looks at the role of the Court of Justice in the legal order of the European Union.

The next part of the book moves on to the heart of the European trade mark regime, considering what can be protected as a trade mark and the scope of protection. Chapter 4 covers the requirements for obtaining a trade mark right and the absolute grounds on the basis of which that protection can be denied. Chapter 5 examines relative grounds and Chapter 6 the scope of protection. Chapter 7 considers use as a requirement for maintaining a registration.

1–003 The third part of the book examines the interaction between trade marks and other areas of law. First, it traces the development of trade marks from their early EEC days to their current status within the framework of free movement of goods, in Chapter 8, and competition rules, in Chapter 9. Note that the exhaustion cases are discussed in Chapter 8. Chapter 10 posits trade marks amidst the broader context of unfair competition, with illustrations from the fields of comparative advertising, the protection of geographical indications and trade names, and the human rights/property aspects of a trade mark.

Chapter 11 provides a brief overview of the contemporary trade mark jurisprudence of the United States Supreme Court in order to allow the reader to draw some comparative conclusions.

Finally, Chapter 12 brings together some key points that have been resurfacing throughout the book.

CHAPTER 2

COMMUNITY TRADE MARK LAW: THE DIRECTIVE AND THE REGULATION

1. Introduction	2–001
2. The "Harmonisation" Directive	2–005
3. The Community Trade Mark Regulation	2–009
(1) The architecture of coexistence	2–010
(2) The Community Trade Mark	2–011
(3) The expansion of the Community Trade Mark	2–021
4. The Peculiarities of the Community Trade Mark	2–023
(1) Conversion	2–023
(2) Seniority	2–024
(3) Other aspects of coexistence	2–025
5. Conclusion	2–027

1. INTRODUCTION

"European" trade mark law at a supra-national level has developed following two parallel paths. One led to the harmonisation of disparate national systems of trade mark protection; the other, to the creation of a "federal" trade mark right, effective throughout the territory of the European Union. **2–001**

The Court of Justice built a third path that often crossed the other two and influenced their direction; here, national trade mark rights were considered as obstacles to intra-Community trade or mechanisms that could affect competition.

The aim of this chapter is to describe briefly the destinations reached by the "harmonisation" and the "federal" paths. These destinations form the background of Chs 4, 5, 6 and 9. The third path is charted in Chs 7 and 8.

The history of "European" trade mark law starts in 1964 with the circulation of a Preliminary Draft of a Convention of a European Trade Mark that remained unpublished. A period of inactivity, caused by French opposition to integration, ended in 1973 with the recirculation and publication of the draft.[1] In July 1976 the "Memorandum on an EEC Trade Mark" was adopted **2–002**

---

[1] Department of Trade and Industry: Proposed European Trade Mark–Unofficial Translation of a Preliminary Draft of a Convention for a European Trade Mark (HMSO, 1973).

by the Commission.² The Memorandum described a European market where national markets in branded goods predominated. "There is as yet, to the disadvantage of consumers, distributors and manufacturers, no common market for branded goods and thus no internal market for a substantial proportion of goods for sale."³ Trade marks deserved to be protected because they enabled consumers to choose. "To make the right choice, the consumer needs to be able to identify and distinguish these goods according and to recognize a connection between a particular product, its quality and its reputation."⁴

The stance taken in the Memorandum was radical. A new Community Trade Mark would be introduced. The new right could ultimately replace the existing divergent national laws and create a new Community-wide system of protection. However, the Memorandum acknowledged that conversion of national rights to Community rights would be a long and difficult process and accepted that a regime of coexistence between the Community and national systems would be the only realistic solution. The proposal proved controversial and a new dual parallel approach was developed. The aim should be to harmonise to a certain extent national laws and at the same time create a new Community-wide right. New national systems would coexist with the Community right.⁵

The First Council Directive to Approximate the Laws of the Member States Relating to Trade Marks was adopted in 1988 and the Community Trade Mark Regulation in 1993.

Alexander von Mühlendahl, one of the most influential Community Trade Mark visionaries, described the setting and the basic principles behind the "new" Community Trade Mark in the following way.⁶

2–003
Compared with the situation in the 1950s the picture of trade mark law in Europe has been transformed. New national laws have been adopted (e.g. France, Benelux) and the European Community has expanded to include Member States with strong, but different, trade mark traditions (e.g. the United Kingdom). Expanding the scope of trade mark law to cover new areas (e.g. service marks) whilst imposing new conditions on their owners (e.g. use requirements) has become an international trend.

At the international stage, the Trade Mark Registration Treaty has been a disappointment. The Madrid Agreement Concerning the International Registration of Marks has been considering ways for becoming more appealing to new Member States and users of the system. And finally, at the

---

² Memorandum on the Creation of an EEC Trade Mark, Bulletin of the European Communities, Supplement 8/76.
³ Memorandum on the Creation of an EEC Trade Mark, Bulletin of the European Communities, Supplement 8/76, para.10.
⁴ Memorandum on the Creation of an EEC Trade Mark, Bulletin of the European Communities, Supplement 8/76, para.11.
⁵ New Trade Mark System for the Community–Proposed Directive and Regulation, Bulletin of the European Communities, Supplement 5/80.
⁶ Alexander von Mühlendahl, "The Future Community Trade Mark System" (1989) 20 I.I.C. 583.

2. THE "HARMONISATION" DIRECTIVE

global level trade mark law has become one of the issues considered under the aegis of the General Agreement on Tariffs and Trade.

Negotiations regarding the Community Trade Mark were focusing on the location of the Office and its working languages. The substance of the new right—and of the harmonisation process—in terms of scope and procedure has been less controversial.

The intention was to provide for:

2–004

(a) a broad definition of registrable trade marks;

(b) an examination system that ex officio would focus exclusively on absolute grounds;

(c) opposition proceedings for the owners of prior rights;

(d) the widening of the definition of the exclusive rights of the trade mark owner to cover the right to prevent importation and exportation;

(e) the establishment of identity or similarity of the signs and of the goods or services as the decisive criteria for protection;

(f) broader protection for marks with a "reputation" in appropriate situations;

(g) exceptions from the scope of protection including exhaustion of trade mark rights, acquiescence, and a fair use provision;

(h) the introduction of a requirement to use the trade mark;

(i) the ability to assign a trade mark without the respective business or goodwill; and

(j) trade mark licensing and infringement in some cases where the terms of a licence agreement have been breached.

2. THE "HARMONISATION" DIRECTIVE

The aim of the Directive[7] is to achieve partial harmonisation of the Member States' national trade mark laws. The harmonisation focused on the substantive provisions of national trade mark laws that could impede the completion and effective operation of an internal, single European market, in particular if they diverged from one Member State to another.

2–005

The Recitals also stress the significance of ensuring that a registered trade mark enjoys the same protection under the legal systems of all the

---

[7] First Council Directive 89/104/EEC to Approximate the Laws of the Member States Relating to Trade Marks [1989] OJ L40/1. The Directive has recently been codified by Directive 2008/95/EC of the European Parliament and of the Council to Approximate the Laws of the Member States Relating to Trade Marks [2008] OJ L299/25.

Member States. It is the function of a trade mark as an indication of origin that primarily justifies protection and delineates its scope.

To achieve harmonisation the Directive sets detailed principles through provisions, the introduction of which into national trade mark laws is mandatory.

2–006 On the other hand the Directive allows Member States to provide wider protection. It sets the ground through provisions the adoption of which is not compulsory. For example art.4 of the Directive provides in ss.(1) (2) and (3) the relative grounds on the basis of which an application for registration must be refused. The introduction of these grounds into national law is mandatory. They cover first, identical marks used on identical goods or services where protection of the earlier mark appears to be absolute, because the information carried by the later trade mark cannot be trusted. They also cover similar marks and similar goods or services, but in this case a further condition must be fulfilled: there must be a likelihood of confusion, including association. Only when there is confusion is there a risk that the function of the trade mark is undermined.

Sections (4), (5), and (6) of art.4 provide further relative grounds, including protection against later similar marks in respect of dissimilar goods where the earlier mark has a reputation or rights based on applications rather than registrations. The adoption of these grounds remains at the discretion of each Member State.

2–007 In summary, the Directive deals mainly with the definition of a trade mark; grounds for refusal, revocation, invalidity, and infringement.

It also refers briefly to licensing in art.8.

Articles 6 and 7 refer to the limitations and exhaustion of trade mark rights.

2–008 The Directive leaves at the discretion of Member States the type of the system of registration, the establishment of registry and court procedures, and provisions on ownership as well as the regulation of rights acquired through use, unfair competition, civil liability, and consumer protection.

3. THE COMMUNITY TRADE MARK REGULATION

2–009 The scope of the Regulation[8] is the establishment of a unitary right—a single trade mark right that is effective throughout the territory of the European Union. The Recitals set the harmonious development of economic activities

---

[8] Council Regulation (EC) 207/2009 on the Community Trade Mark [2009] OJ L78/1 that codified Council Reg. (EC) No.40/94 on the Community trade mark [1994] OJ L11/1 (the Regulation) and Commission Reg. (EC) No.2868/95 implementing Council Reg. (EC) No.40/94 on the Community trade mark [1995] OJ L303/1 are available at: *http://oami.europa.eu* following the links. Note that the Community Trade Mark system has become a member of the Protocol to the Madrid Agreement: Council Reg. (EC) No.1992/2003 amending Regulation (EC) No.40/94 on the Community trade mark to give effect to the accession of the European Community to the Protocol relating to the Madrid Agreement concerning the international registration of marks [2003] OJ L296/1.

3. THE COMMUNITY TRADE MARK REGULATION

and a continuous and balanced expansion of the common market as the targets of the Regulation. They will be achieved by completing an internal market which functions properly and offers conditions which are similar to those obtained in a national market.

It is, therefore, essential to enable marketers to use one trade mark to identify their products throughout the territory of the European Union. Such a trade mark must be protected by a uniform community right, directly applicable in all Member States. It is stressed that the protection afforded by the Community Trade Mark right should aim in particular to guarantee the trade mark as an indication of origin.

(1) The Architecture of Coexistence

The approach of the Community Trade Mark system to prior rights was "probably the single most contentious issue to be resolved".[9] There were two issues the new system had to settle. First, it would have to decide the future of existing national trade mark rights, balancing between an equitable solution and the need to offer an attractive new right. Secondly, it would have to choose between incompatible, at that time, national trade mark systems. The Benelux system combined a "deposit system" approach with an official search for prior rights. France and Italy had not adopted either a search process or opposition proceedings. Germany provided for opposition proceedings based on earlier registered trade mark rights but had no search procedure. Denmark, Greece, Ireland, Spain and the United Kingdom were all examining ex officio for prior rights and providing an opposition procedure. In order to accommodate existing national rights and deal with the impossible task of resolving conflicts as to which national right should lead to the grant of a Community Trade Mark at the exclusion of other national rights, the Community Trade Mark system is erected according to the architecture of "coexistence". It lives together with the harmonised national trade mark systems of the Member States. Each system confers individual and independent, but interacting, rights.

2–010

According to this principle Community Trade Mark rights are granted on a first come/first served basis. An earlier national right does not confer to its owner a preferential "right to apply" for a Community Trade Mark; it can be used however, in order to block or challenge a subsequent unconnected and unauthorised Community Trade Mark application or registration.

At the same time a Community Trade Mark right does not destroy an earlier national trade mark right that has not been raised against it. It simply bypasses it and the two coexist in some sort of harmony.[10] It can be used, though, in order to block or challenge a subsequent application or registration at the national level.

---

[9] Von Mühlendahl (1989), p.589.
[10] See para.2–023, below.

(2) The Community Trade Mark

2–011   The essence of the Community Trade Mark system is the establishment of a unitary right that is effective throughout the territory of the European Union. This right is conferred by registration with the "Office for Harmonisation in the Internal Market (Trade Marks and Designs)", in Spain, in the city of Alicante.[11]

The Community Trade Mark is one indivisible entity. It has equal effect throughout the Union. It can be registered, transferred, surrendered or revoked only for the entirety of the European Union. It can, however, be licensed for parts of the Union.

It is defined in art.1 as a trade mark for goods or services which is registered in accordance with the conditions contained in the Regulation. Articles 64–72 provide for Community collective marks. There is no provision for Community certification marks.

2–012   The two primary registration requirements are set out in art.4. Community Trade Marks may consist of a sign that is capable of being represented graphically and capable of distinguishing the goods or services of one undertaking from those of other undertakings.

Article 6 provides that a Community Trade Mark Right shall be obtained by registration. Any person can file an application for registration according to art.5.

The Regulation covers the almost identical, with the Directive, absolute grounds for refusing registration in art.7; art.7(2) provides that they will block registration even if they apply only in part of the Community. The only difference with the Directive is that "bad faith" is an absolute ground that can be used only for the invalidation, rather than the refusal, of registration.

2–013   Article 8 provides that earlier trade mark registrations or applications which can block an application for a Community Trade Mark comprise:

(a) existing Community Trade Marks;

(b) national or Benelux trade marks;

(c) international registrations effective in one of the Member States or the Benelux; and

(d) well-known marks according to art.6bis of the Paris Convention.

The proprietor of rights acquired through use can oppose a subsequent Community Trade Mark application provided that its use is "of more than mere local significance" (art.8(4)).

---

[11] The location of the Office has been another controversial issue. A number of cities, including London, Munich, The Hague, and Luxembourg, appeared as contenders at different stages of the negotiating process. Spain played the card of Madrid. The Office was finally allocated to Alicante.

3. THE COMMUNITY TRADE MARK REGULATION

Article 42 provides that opposition proceedings can be instituted only by entitled persons. The entitlement rules vary depending on the ground invoked. According to art.41 any person may make observations objecting to registration on the basis of absolute grounds.

Article 15 provides that genuine use in the Community by the proprietor or with his consent will constitute sufficient use to maintain the mark on the register. Genuine use includes use of the sign in a form that does not alter the distinctiveness of the mark as registered, as well as use solely for export purposes.

2–014

Article 52 provides that invalidation proceedings can also be based on a right of personal portrayal, rights to a name, copyright, or other industrial property right. These are only mentioned in the Regulation as grounds for invalidation, not opposition. The assumption is that the complexity of those grounds requires a more detailed examination which is incompatible with the expedient character of opposition proceedings.

And, as a consequence of the principle of the free movement of goods, the Regulation also provides that the proprietor of a Community Trade Mark is not entitled to prohibit its use by a third party in relation to products which have been put into circulation within the territory of the Union under that trade mark, with the consent of the proprietor, unless there are legitimate reasons for the proprietor to oppose further commercialisation of these products.

(a) Procedural matters

Applications for registration must be filed either directly with OHIM or with a national Registry which will then forward the application to OHIM.

2–015

The application can be filed in any official language of the Union but must indicate a second language from the five Office languages, namely, English, French, German, Italian or Spanish.

The language rule was challenged before the Court in *Kik*.[12]

The Court of First Instance had noted that art.217 EC empowered the Council to establish and alter language rules for the institutions of the European Union. It accepted that the language rule "was adopted for the legitimate purpose of reaching a solution on languages in cases where opposition, revocation or invalidity proceedings ensue between parties who do not have the same language preference and cannot agree between themselves on the language of proceedings"[13] and that the Council had made "an appropriate

2–016

---

[12] *Kik v Office for the Harmonisation in the Internal Market (Trade Marks and Designs)* (C-361/01 P) [2003] E.C.R. I-8283. The case was an appeal against the decision of the Court of First Instance in *Kik v Office for the Harmonisation in the Internal Market (Trade Marks and Designs)* (T-120/99) [2001] E.C.R. II-2235, dismissing an action against the decision of the Board of Appeal in Case R 65/98-3, March 19, 1999.
[13] *Kik v Office for the Harmonisation in the Internal Market (Trade Marks and Designs)* (T-120/99) [2001] E.C.R. II-2235, para.62.

and proportionate choice, even if the official languages of the Community were treated differently".[14]

The Court of Justice first delineated the scope of art.115(4) of the Regulation: "the language of proceedings before the Office is to be the language used for filing the application for a Community trade mark, although the second language chosen by the applicant may be used by the Office to send him written communications. It follows from that provision that the option of using a second language for written communications is an exception to the principle that the language of proceedings be used, and that the term 'written communications' must therefore be interpreted strictly".[15]

This meant that "any document that is required or prescribed by the Community legislation for the purposes of processing an application for a Community trade mark or necessary for such processing, be they notifications, requests for correction, clarification or other documents ... must ... be drawn up by [the Office] in the language used for filing the application".[16]

2–017 Following this interpretation, that resulted in a change of practice on behalf of OHIM, the Court accepted the reasoning of the Court of First Instance. In addition, it made a distinction between all citizens and economic operators: "the Community trade mark was created for the benefit not of all citizens, but of economic operators, and that economic operators are not under any obligation to make use of it".[17] "Whilst the monopoly right to use a trade mark is recognised by a public authority, the trade mark right is essentially a tool used by economic operators in the context of their professional activities to produce profits. The legislature is therefore free to require that they should bear, in whole or at least in part, the operating costs of a body created to register Community trade marks."[18]

It accepted that the Council was pursuing the legitimate aim of seeking an appropriate linguistic solution to the difficulties arising from the failure of the parties to agree on a common language. And, taking into account the public interest of keeping registration costs at a reasonable level, it added that "even if the Council did treat official languages of the Community differently, its choice to limit the languages to those which are most widely known in the European Community is appropriate and proportionate".[19]

(b) Examination procedure (arts 40–43)

2–018 The Office will examine the application as to formalities, entitlement, and absolute grounds.

---

[14] *Kik* (T-120/99) [2001] E.C.R. II-2235, para.63.
[15] *Kik* (C-361/01 P) [2003] E.C.R. I-8283, para.45.
[16] *Kik* (C-361/01 P) [2003] E.C.R. I-8283, para.46.
[17] *Kik* (C-361/01 P) [2003] E.C.R. I-8283, para.88. It can be argued that such statements potentially undermine the wider justificatory basis of trade mark rights.
[18] *Kik* (C-361/01 P) [2003] E.C.R. I-8283, para.89.
[19] *Kik* (C-361/01 P) [2003] E.C.R. I-8283, para.94.

3. THE COMMUNITY TRADE MARK REGULATION

Compromising between the diverse national examination systems the Regulation provides that a search of the Community register will be conducted. The application will be communicated to national Offices that have declared their intention to conduct a search for prior rights. This, though, does not constitute an examination of the application on the basis of relative grounds; simply the results of the searches will be communicated to the applicant who can then decide whether to proceed with the application.

The application will then be published for opposition or observation purposes.

Oppositions must be filed within three months following the publication of the application. Note that opponents based on an earlier Community Trade Mark or national Member State registration may have to prove genuine use within the preceding five-year period in order to oppose the subsequent Community Trade Mark application.

2–019

There are provisions (arts 74–76) for the submission of evidence, the conduct of hearings, and the notification and publication of decisions of the Office.

The decisions of the Office are subject to an appeal before the Board of Appeal (arts 57–62) and from there to the Court of First Instance.

(c) Enforcement—court proceedings

There is provision in art.91 and onwards that each Member State must nominate particular courts as Community Trade Mark Courts of first and second instance. According to art.16, jurisdiction is based on the Member State of the defendant's domicile. If there is no such State then we look for the Member State of the defendant's establishment. If there is no such State then we look for the Member State, and then for the Member State of the plaintiff's domicile or establishment. The Spanish Community Trade Mark Courts are the last resort.

2–020

The Community Trade Mark courts have exclusive jurisdiction on the following subject matter:

(a) infringement proceedings;

(b) actions for declaration of non-infringement;

(c) actions for compensation for infringing acts during the application period; and

(d) counter-claims for revocation of Community Trade Mark registrations or for declarations of their invalidity.

Finally, for the purposes of property and transactions a Community Trade Mark is dealt with as a national trade mark registered in the State where the proprietor has its seat or domicile on the relevant date. If there is no such

State, the State where the proprietor has an establishment will have jurisdiction, or if there is no such State then jurisdiction over the case moves to Spain (art.16).

Article 21 provides that where bankruptcy proceedings are filed then the Community Trade Mark registration may only be involved in the proceedings which started first.

(3) The expansion of the Community Trade Mark

2–021 On May 1, 2004, 10 new Member States—Cyprus, Czech Republic, Estonia, Hungary, Latvia, Lithuania, Malta, Poland, Slovakia and Slovenia—joined the European Union. These were followed in 2006 by Bulgaria and Romania.

Community Trade Mark registrations and applications filed prior to the accession date have been automatically extended to the new Member States (art.159a).

Community Trade Mark applications filed up to six months prior to the enlargement date could be opposed by the owner of a national trade mark in a new Member State on the basis of an "interim opposition procedure" provided the earlier right was not obtained in bad faith.

2–022 Community Trade Mark applications filed more than six months before the enlargement cannot be opposed or declared invalid on the basis of national trade marks registered in a new Member State.

Note that earlier national rights may prevent use of a Community Trade Mark in the relevant new Member State.

4. THE PECULIARITIES OF THE COMMUNITY TRADE MARK

(1) Conversion

2–023 Articles 108–110 provide that a Community Trade Mark registration or application may be converted into one or more national trade mark applications. The filing date of the Community Trade Mark application will be deemed to be the filing date of the national applications. This is a safe fall-back position in case the Community Trade Mark is considered to fail absolute or relative grounds that exist only in part of the European Union and as a result the application is rejected or the registration is invalidated or revoked.

Inevitably conversion will not be possible in respect of the Member State that triggered the fall of the Community Trade Mark. Conversion will also cover any seniority claims. Partial conversion is possible.

4. THE PECULIARITIES OF THE COMMUNITY TRADE MARK

(2) Seniority

Articles 34–35 provide that the proprietor of a national registration may also file for registration of its mark as a Community Trade Mark claiming seniority. This means that if the Community Trade Mark application proceeds to registration and the national registration subsequently lapses or is abandoned then the Community Trade Mark registration is deemed to provide (at the national level and in addition to the Community Trade Mark protection), the same protection as the protection that would be afforded by the earlier national registration.

2–024

It is possible to claim seniority in respect of more than one jurisdiction, according to the existing national registrations.

The purpose of seniority is to make the Community Trade Mark an attractive option to those who have already registered a trade mark at the national level and wish to retain rights they enjoyed as a result of a national registration. It allows the proprietor of a Community Trade Mark to retain the advantages of a national registration without the costs and inconvenience of renewal. Note that seniority does not backdate the effect of the Community Trade Mark right in the relevant jurisdictions. It simply allows the national registrations to live next to the Community Trade Mark right retaining their earlier filing dates.

(3) Other Aspects of Coexistence

The owner of an earlier national right can oppose the application of a conflicting Community Trade Mark. If it fails to do so, it can attack the Community Trade Mark registration by seeking its invalidation. If it fails to act within a five-year period from the date it became aware of the use of the Community Trade Mark then the registration becomes incontestable according to art.53(2).

2–025

Nevertheless, according to art.106, this incontestability shall not affect the right existing under the laws of the Member State to invoke claims for infringement of earlier rights within the meaning of art.8 or art.52(2) in relation to the use of a later Community Trade Mark.

Claims for infringement of earlier rights within the meaning of art.8(2) and (4) may, however, no longer be invoked if the proprietor of the earlier right may no longer apply for a declaration that the Community Trade Mark is invalid in accordance with art.53(2).

Article 106(2) provides that the Community Trade Mark Regulation, unless otherwise provided, "shall not affect the right to bring proceedings under the civil, administrative or criminal law of a Member State or under provisions of Community law for the purpose of prohibiting the use of a Community Trade Mark to the extent that the use of a national trade mark may be prohibited under the law of that Member State or under Community law".

2–026

Article 107 deals with prior rights applicable to particular localities. It provides that the proprietor of an earlier right which only applies to a particular locality may oppose the use of the Community Trade Mark in the territory where its right is protected insofar as the law of the Member State concerned so permits.

This right shall cease to apply if the proprietor of the earlier right has acquiesced in the use of the Community Trade Mark in the territory where its right is protected for a period of five successive years, being aware of such use, unless the Community Trade Mark was applied for in bad faith. In this case the proprietor of the Community Trade Mark shall not be entitled to oppose use of the right mentioned above even though that right may no longer be invoked against the Community Trade Mark.

5. CONCLUSION

2–027 There are two points that must be highlighted at the end of this chapter.

First, that the Directive and the Regulation cannot be seen as two distinct pieces of legislation covering parallel areas. They share a common historical background and their common aim is to establish a European trade mark regime. In essence there is no hierarchical distinction between them.

Secondly, that the new regime has been constructed on the basis of a principle of coexistence. The aim is for the Community Trade Mark system to become an attractive alternative to national systems of protection rather than take over them. The bigger aim is for national and Community rights to contribute to the creation and functioning of a growing European market.

CHAPTER 3

THE COURT OF JUSTICE OF THE EUROPEAN COMMUNITIES: THE ROLE AND INTERPRETIVE PRINCIPLES AND TECHNIQUES OF THE COURT

1. Introduction — 3–001
2. Forms of Action — 3–004
   (1) Actions against Member States in breach of Community Law — 3–004
   (2) Actions against a Community institution for failure to act — 3–005
   (3) Annulment actions — 3–006
   (4) Appeals — 3–008
   (5) References for a preliminary ruling — 3–009
3. The Composition and Mechanics of the Court of Justice — 3–013
   (1) The composition of the Court — 3–013
   (2) Direct actions — 3–014
   (3) Preliminary rulings—procedural differences — 3–018
   (4) Interlocutory proceedings — 3–020
   (5) Expedited procedure — 3–021
4. The Court of First Instance—Specialist Tribunals — 3–022
   (1) The basics — 3–022
   (2) The composition and mechanics of the Court of First Instance — 3–024
5. The Interpretive Principles and Techniques of the Court — 3–026
   (1) Direct effect — 3–028
   (2) Supremacy of Community law — 3–041
   (3) The development of the "indirect effect" of Community law — 3–046
   (4) The competence of the Court of Justice—the acte clair doctrine — 3–047
   (5) Looking for the essence of the question — 3–049
   (6) Fundamental rights — 3–050
6. Judicial Review and the Community Trade Mark — 3–053
   (1) Arcol—the "institutional architecture" in trade mark cases — 3–053
   (2) Scope and limits of administrative and judicial review — 3–058
   (3) The value of precedents — 3–064
7. Conclusion — 3–069

1. INTRODUCTION

The purpose of this chapter is to provide a basic introductory background on the role and the workings of the Court of Justice.[1] According to its own mission-statement the responsibility of the Court is to:

3–001

---

[1] The reader should note that the selection of cases is purely illustrative.

"ensure that the law is observed in the interpretation and application of the Treaties establishing the European Communities and of the provisions laid down by the competent Community institutions".[2]

The Court of Justice is one of the five principal equal institutions of the European Union that according to art.7 of the EC Treaty must, acting within the limits imposed by the Treaty, carry out the tasks entrusted to the Community.

The Council, composed of government ministers from the Member States, has legislative and decision-making powers and is the body that expresses the political will of the Member States. The European Commission, the independent "administration" of the European Union, is another player in the legislative and decision-making process, often the instigator of legislation. The European Parliament is an influential, albeit not ultimately determinative link in the legislative process. The European Parliament can reject the Council's legislative proposal if it does not agree with it, but cannot replace it with its own. The Court of Auditors is the internal controller and auditor of the financial management of the European Union.

3–002 The Court of Justice has no direct role in the formal legislative process, except in the drafting and, with the approval of the Council, the adoption of its own Rules of Procedure and of those of the Court of the First Instance. This distancing of the Court from the formal legislative process has been characterised as "essential to avoid prejudicing the Court's approach to any future judicial proceedings which might arise".[3]

The role of the Court however becomes critical when we turn to the law, the product of the legislative process, and the relationships of institutions of the Community between themselves on the one hand and with the Member States on the other. The Court applies the law directly, interprets the law, and adjudicates on the institutional power struggles.

The Court is the judiciary side in the European legislature–government –judiciary triangle. A commanding side, since its decisions cannot be reversed by an act of the legislature. On the contrary, any measure having legal effect can be annulled by the Court if it considers it contrary to the Treaties or other provisions of Community law. The Court can and must enforce the law against the Community institutions but also against the contracting parties to the Treaties.[4]

---

[2] Available following the links at *http://curia.europa.eu*. Article 220 of the EC Treaty appears open ended, it provides that the role of the Court of Justice and the Court of first Instance is to "ensure that in the interpretation and application of the Treaty the law is observed".
[3] Brown and Kennedy (eds), *The Court of Justice of the European Communities*, 5th edn (London: Sweet and Maxwell, 2000), p.11.
[4] Article 230: The Court of Justice shall review the legality of acts adopted jointly by the European Parliament and the Council, of acts of the Council, of the Commission and of the ECB, other than recommendations and opinions, and of acts of the European Parliament intended to produce legal effects vis-à-vis third parties. It shall for this purpose have jurisdiction in actions brought by a Member State, the European Parliament, the Council or the Commission on

1. INTRODUCTION

A ruling of the Court can be reversed only by the Court itself in a subsequent case, or by amendment of the Treaties.[5] Amending the Treaties requires unanimous agreement between the Member States and subsequent ratification by all the Member States. The misfortune of the European "Constitution"[6] shows the complications of this process:

3–003

> "Conversely, the political obstacles to amending the Treaties lend added significance to the Court's rulings on their interpretation, especially as the Court... has been ready to interpret boldly in the face of political deadlock between the Council and the Commission."[7]

The boldness of the Court can also be evidenced in the exercise of its jurisdiction. In theory, the jurisdiction of the Court is conferred upon it and delineated by the Treaties or by a convention. However, its guardianship of the Treaties function, that it shares with the Commission, enables the Court to assume a jurisdiction that, in practice at least, appears to be innate to the Court itself.[8]

For example, the Member States did not intend the Treaty of Rome to confer judicially enforceable rights on private legal entities. Still, the Court inferred rights from provisions such as those requiring Member States to remove national obstacles to intra-Community trade:

> "Legal integration is therefore largely a record of how the ECJ has made creative use of its discretionary powers to remake the Treaty, and how private actors, national judges, and political elites have responded to these moves."[9]

Sometimes, this interpretive and jurisdictional boldness, particularly when combined with national obstinacy about legal principles and apprehension regarding sovereignty, can make national courts behave in unreceptive ways.[10]

---

grounds of lack of competence, infringement of an essential procedural requirement, infringement of this Treaty or of any rule of law relating to its application, or misuse of powers. The Court of Justice shall have jurisdiction under the same conditions in actions brought by the Court of Auditors and by the ECB for the purpose of protecting their prerogatives. Any natural or legal person may, under the same conditions, institute proceedings against a decision addressed to that person or against a decision which, although in the form of a regulation or a decision addressed to another person, is of direct and individual concern to the former. The proceedings provided for in this article shall be instituted within two months of the publication of the measure, or of its notification to the plaintiff, or, in the absence thereof, of the day on which it came to the knowledge of the latter, as the case may be.

[5] Indeed, the Court appears impervious regarding the doctrinal debate over the status of its jurisprudence; see Barceló, "Precedent in European Community Law", in MacCormick and Summers (eds), *Interpreting Precedents: A Comparative Study* (Ashgate/Dartmouth, 1997), pp.420–424.

[6] Treaty Establishing a Constitution for European [2004] OJ C310/1.

[7] Brown and Kennedy (2000), p.6.

[8] For a view supporting that the Court has inherent jurisdiction see Arnull, "Does the Court of Justice Have Inherent Jurisdiction?" (1992) 27 C.M.L.Rev. 683.

[9] Stone Sweet, *The Judicial Construction of Europe* (Oxford University Press, 2004), p.24.

[10] See, for example, the judicial debate on conclusion and association in *Marca Mode CV v Adidas AG & Adida Berelux BV* (C-425/98) [2000] E.C.R. I-4861, discussed in Ch.5.

2. FORMS OF ACTION

(1) Actions against Member States in breach of Community Law

3-004 This is the second part of a two-tiered procedure that is available against Member States that are considered to act in breach of Community law[11]; the scope of the action is very wide, it may cover Member States' positive actions, omissions, breaches of the Treaty and secondary legislation, failures in implementing directives, or breaking of any rule that has become part of the Community legal order.[12] The procedure is initiated in most cases by the Commission, but it can also be activated by a complaint submitted by another Member State. The Commission may also act in response to a complaint submitted by an individual.[13]

The Member State is given the opportunity to respond during a preliminary procedure performed by the Commission. It can explain its position and may opt to change its practice in order to reach a compromise with the Commission. If this informal process is unsuccessful, a formal letter is issued by the Commission and the Member State has another opportunity to respond, and resolve the issue. In the absence of a resolution a reasoned opinion is issued by the Commission and if the Member State does not conform an action may be brought by the Commission before the Court.[14]

According to its findings, the Court may find, in a declaratory judgment, that the Member State has infringed the Treaty. Further proceedings can be instituted by the Commission against a Member State that has not complied

---

[11] Article 226 EC provides:

"[I]f the Commission considers that a Member State has failed to fulfil an obligation under this Treaty, it shall deliver a reasoned opinion on the matter after giving the State concerned the opportunity to submit its observations.

If the State concerned does not comply with the opinion within the period laid down by the Commission, the latter may bring the matter before the Court."

[12] For example *Commission v Ireland* (C-13/00) [2002] E.C.R. I-2943 concerned a breach in the area of the Community's external competence. See the reviews of Snyder, "The Effectiveness of European Community Law: Institutions, Processes, Tools and Techniques" (1993) 56 M.L.R. 19; and Rawlings, "Engaged Elites: Citizen Action and Institutional Attitudes in Commission Enforcement" (2000) 6 E.L.J. 4. For a US-based comparative perspective see Pfander, "Member State Liability and Constitutional Change in the United States and Europe" (2003) 51 Am.J.Comp.L. 237.

[13] The European Community Ombudsman has a role to play here, acting as a conduit, investigating how the Commission responds to individual complaints, and reviewing the Commission's enforcement procedures. For the role of the Ombudsman see its own website http://www.euro-ombudsman.eu.int/; and Leino, "The Wind Is in the North: the First European Ombudsman" (2004) 10 European Public Law 333–367; Cadeddu, "The Proceedings of the European Ombudsman" (2004) 68 Law & Contemp. Probs. 161; and Peters, "The European Ombudsman and the European Constitution" (2005) 42 C.M.L.Rev. 697.

[14] An action may be admitted even if the Member State has complied with the reasoned opinion of the Commission, for example where it is required to establish liability in order for the Member State to fulfil its obligations against those to whom rights have accrued as a result of its failure, *Commission v Greece* (C-240/86) [1988] E.C.R. 1835.

2. FORMS OF ACTION

with such a judgment; the Court may then impose financial penalties against the Member State according to art.228 EC.

(2) Actions against a Community institution for failure to act

The other side of the coin is the action against a Community institution that can be brought by a Member State, another Community institution, or an individual for its failure to act despite having been prompted to do so.[15] If the Court decides that the failure to act has been unlawful, the institution must take the appropriate measures to end its failure.[16]

3–005

Individuals, according to art.232(3) EC, can bring actions regarding acts that have a legal effect, not recommendations or opinions. The jurisprudence of the Court of Justice in the *Comitology* case implies that Member States and Community institutions can challenge failure to act even if it is in respect of recommendations or opinions.[17]

(3) Annulment actions

Measures taken by Community institutions can be attacked directly or through an action for annulment of the underlying regulation.[18] The action can be brought primarily by directly affected individuals, but also by Community institutions and Member States.[19]

3–006

Article 241 does not create an independent cause of action; rather, it provides an attacking tool to parties to proceedings involving a Community measure[20]:

> "It is clear from the wording and the general scheme of this Article that a declaration of the inapplicability of a Regulation is only contemplated in proceedings brought before the Court of Justice itself under some other provision of the Treaty, and then only incidentally and with limited effect.

---

[15] EC Treaty art.232 EC.
[16] Applications for compensation for non contractual liability can be filed with the Court of First Instance.
[17] *European Parliament v Council* (302/87) [1988] E.C.R. 5615. See Hartley, *The Foundations of European Community Law* (Oxford University Press, 1998), pp.333–341. In principle an individual has standing to bring an action if it is directly and individually concerned, without being necessary to be individually addressed by the relevant decision; see *Società "Eridania" Zuccherifici Nazionali v Commission* (C-10 and 18/68) [1969] E.C.R. 459; and *Camar Srl and Tico Srl v Commission* (C-117/98) [2000] E.C.R. II-2193.
[18] See art.230 EC.
[19] See the Opinion of A.G. Roemer in *Italy v Commission* (32/65) [1996] E.C.R. 389, p.414.
[20] Article 241 EC provides:

> "[N]otwithstanding the expiry of the period laid down in the fifth paragraph of Article 230, any party may, in proceedings in which a regulation adopted jointly by the European Parliament and the Council, or a regulation of the Council, of the Commission or of the ECB is at issue, plead the grounds specified in the second paragraph of Article 230, in order to invoke before the Court of Justice the inapplicability of that regulation."

More particularly, it is clear from the reference to the time limit laid down in Article [230] that Article [241] is applicable only in the context of proceedings brought before the Court of Justice and that it does not permit the said time limit to be avoided.

The sole object of Article [241] is thus to protect an interested party against the application of an illegal Regulation, without thereby in any way calling in issue the Regulation itself, which can no longer be challenged because of the expiry of the time limit laid down in Article [230]."[21]

3-007 According to the text of the Treaty only the effect of regulations can be challenged in this way, however the Court of Justice in *Simmenthal* has ensured that it covers any act which in substance functions as a regulation:

"As the Court... has already held in connexion with Article 36 of the ECSC Treaty, Article [241 EC] gives expression to a general principle conferring upon any party to proceedings the right to challenge, for the purpose of obtaining the annulment of a decision of direct and individual concern to the party, the validity of previous acts of the institutions which form the legal basis of the decision which is being attacked, if that party was not entitled under Article [230 EC] to bring a direct action challenging those acts by which it was thus affected without having been in a position to ask that they be declared void.

The field of application of the said article must therefore include acts of the institutions which although they are not in the form of a Regulation, nevertheless produce similar effects and on those grounds may not be challenged under Article [230] by natural or legal persons other than Community institutions and Member States.

This wide interpretation of Article [241] derives from the need to provide those persons who are precluded by the second paragraph of Article [230] from instituting proceedings directly in respect of general acts with the benefit of judicial review of them at the time when they are affected by implementing decisions which are of direct and individual concern to them."[22]

(4) Appeals

3-008 The judgments of the Court of First Instance can be challenged on points of law following an appeal to the Court of Justice. The Court will consider the admissibility and the basis of the appeal. If the appeal is valid it will set aside

---

[21] *Milchewerke Heinz Wohrmann & Sohn KG and Alfons Lütticke GmbH v Commission* (31 and 33/62) [1962] E.C.R. 501, p.507.
[22] *Simmenthal SpA v Commission* (92/78) [1979] E.C.R. 777, paras 39–41.

2. FORMS OF ACTION

the judgment of the Court of First Instance and according to the nature of the proceedings will either decide the case itself or refer the case back to the Court of First Instance to be reconsidered according to the decision given on appeal.[23]

Note that following the introduction of specialist tribunals attached to the Court, the Court of Justice retained for itself the role of reviewing in exceptional circumstances the appeal decisions of the Court of First Instance.

(5) References for a preliminary ruling

Here the Court acts as a mentor of national courts and custodian of the Community legal order. This "preliminary" function of the Court has transformed it from an ordinary supreme—or even federal supreme—court to the powerhouse of Community law. It is through art.234 that the Court of Justice has developed doctrines such as direct effect and supremacy.[24]

3–009

A dispute between individuals or between an individual and a national authority falls within the jurisdiction of the appropriate national court or tribunal rather than the jurisdiction of the Court of Justice. However, a national court during the administration of justice involving Community law is often confronted with interpretive dilemmas. Does its own national legislation conform with the Community legislation that led to its adoption? Is the relevant Community legislation clear enough to allow a finding on conformity? Is a change of direction required when the national court identifies that on a comparable situation it follows a divergent route from other national courts? Is an act of a Community institution valid?[25]

---

[23] See for example *DKV Deutsche Krankenversicherung AG v Office for Harmonisation in the Internal Market (Trade Marks and Designs)* (C-104/00 P) [2002] E.C.R. I-7561.

[24] Article 234 provides:

"The Court of Justice shall have jurisdiction to give preliminary rulings concerning:

(a) the interpretation of this Treaty;
(b) the validity and interpretation of acts of the institutions of the Community and of the ECB;
(c) the interpretation of the statutes of bodies established by an act of the Council, where those statutes so provide".

[25] Where such a question is raised before any court or tribunal of a Member State, that court or tribunal may, if it considers that a decision on the question is necessary to enable it to give judgment, request the Court of Justice to give a ruling thereon.

Where any such question is raised in a case pending before a court or tribunal of a Member State against whose decisions there is no judicial remedy under national law, that court or tribunal shall bring the matter before the Court of Justice.

For the purposes of this book the general procedure under art.234 EC is the most relevant. Preliminary rulings can also be obtained according to art.68 EC in the context of Title IV of the EC Treaty arts 61–69, on "Visas, Asylum, Immigration and Other Policies Concerning the Free Movement of Persons". Article 35 of the TEU provides for a narrower version of preliminary rulings in the field of "Police and Judicial Co-operation in Criminal Matters". These provisions are specific to the general EC Rules.

To solve the riddles the national court has to turn to the Court of Justice to clarify a particular point of Community law set in the EC Treaty, including all the Treaties amending or supplementing the EC Treaty (art.234(1)(a)),[26] or consider the validity and interpretation of an act of a Community institution (art.234(1)(b).[27]

3–010   Individuals even have the right to demand that the national court considers seeking clarifications from the Court of Justice.[28] If the national court considers it appropriate and necessary it will formulate a question— often a long list of questions—in the form of a reference to the Court of Justice for a preliminary ruling.

The Court of Justice has no other option but to consider the question; only in exceptional cases will the Court of Justice refuse to consider a reference. It cannot ignore it; at most it can rephrase it in order to retrieve—or in some cases bypass—its essence.[29]

The parties to the national proceedings, Member States, and the Commission can participate in the proceedings before the Court.[30]

3–011   The Court's response to the national court is neither a decision on the facts of a case nor a simple authoritative opinion on the interpretation of a legal provision. In *Costa v ENEL*, the Court of Justice delineated between the functions of the Court of Justice and the national court, the role of the Court of Justice is not to investigate the facts of the case and the grounds and purpose of the request for a preliminary ruling.[31]

The Court of Justice does not function as an appeal court or a trendsetter. The response to the national court is a judgment, or reasoned order, that sets a principle and binds the referring court. The national court has to

---

[26] Note that the Court of Justice is not deciding whether a national law is valid or not; this remains in the jurisdiction of the national court that has to decide the particular case that gave rise to the request. See ECJ–Guidance on References by National Court for Preliminary Rulings [1997] 1 C.M.L.R. 78.

[27] Article 234(1)(c) is viewed as a limitation on the effect of art.234(1)(b) in respect of instruments governing the operation of Community institutions, see Craig and De Búrca (2003), p.435; and Hartley, *The Foundations of European Community Law* (Clarendon Press, 1998), p.262–265.
The Court of Justice has expanded the scope of art.234 EC by holding that a request may also be submitted in respect of provisions of national laws based or referring to Community law.

[28] Indeed parties that do not have standing under art.230 EC can use the art.234 EC procedure. For an authoritative comment on this see the Opinion of A.G. Jacobs in *Extramet Industrie SA v Council* (C-358/89) [1991] E.C.R. I-2501. And more recently, in *Unión de Pequeÿnos Agricultores v Council* (C-50/00) [2002] E.C.R. I-6677. See further *Commission v Jégo Quévé* (C-263/02 P) [2004] E.C.R. I-3425; and *TWD v Germany* (C-188/92) [1994] E.C.R. I-833.

[29] See for example *Praktiker Bau- und Heimwerkermärkte AG v Deutsches Patent- und Markenamt* (C-418/02) [2005] E.C.R. I-5873, as discussed in Ch.5.

[30] For the role of governments in the judicial process at this level, see Everling, "The Member States of the European Community before their Court of Justice" (1984) 9 E.L.Rev. 215; and Granger, "When Governments Go to Luxembourg... The Influence of Governments on the Court of Justice" (2004) 29 E.L.Rev. 3, examining their litigation strategies. Three motives are identified: defence of national interests; promotion of national visions of Europe; furthering of EU interests.

[31] *Costa v Ente Nazionale per l'Energia Elettrica (ENEL)* (6/64)[1964] E.C.R. 585, p.593.

2. FORMS OF ACTION

decide its case on the basis of its own facts following the interpretive direction chosen by the Court of Justice.

In addition, the judgment of the Court of Justice has a wider ambit. Subsequent courts facing analogous factual scenarios have to conform, unless they prefer to ask the Court one more time, maybe longing for a different answer. The position of the Court of Justice has been stated clearly in *Da Costa*. Having answered the question in an earlier case does not render a new request inadmissible; if there is no new issue, factor, or argument to be examined, it will simply refer the national court to its earlier judgment.[32]

This, in turn, means that national courts can rely on the precedents set by the jurisprudence of the Court of Justice. In *CILFIT* and *ICC* the Court elaborated further on its ruling in *Da Costa*:

3–012

> "It must be remembered... that in... Da Costa the Court ruled that: 'Although paragraph 3 of Article [234] unreservedly requires courts or tribunals of a Member State against whose decision there is no judicial remedy... to refer to the Court every question of interpretation raised before them, the authority of an interpretation under Article [234] already given by the Court may deprive the obligation of its purpose and thus empty it of its substance. Such is the case especially when the question raised is materially identical with a question which has already been the subject of a preliminary ruling in a similar case'. The same effect, as regards the limits set to the obligation laid down by paragraph (3) of Article [234], may be produced where previous decisions of the Court have already dealt with the point of law in question, irrespective of the nature of the proceedings which led to those decisions, even though the questions at issue are not strictly identical.
>
> However, it must not be forgotten that in all such circumstances national courts and tribunals, including those referred to in paragraph (3) of Article [234], remain entirely at liberty to bring a matter before the Court of Justice if they consider it appropriate to do so."[33]

In *ICC* the Court strengthened the principle that its judgments constitute precedents that national courts have to follow:

> "When the Court is moved under Article [234 EC] to declare an act of one of the institutions to be void there are particularly imperative requirements concerning legal certainty in addition to those concerning the uniform application of Community law. It follows from the very nature of

---

[32] *Da Costa en Schaake NV, Jacob Meijer NV and Hoechst-Holland NV v Nederlandse Belastingadministratie* (C-28/62, C-29/62 & C-30/62) [1963] E.C.R. 31.
[33] *Srl CILFIT and Lanificio di Gavardo SpA v Ministry of Health* (283/81) [1982] E.C.R. 3415, at paras 13–15.

such a declaration that a national court may not apply the act declared void without once more creating serious uncertainty as to the Community law applicable."[34]

The development of precedent in the preliminary rulings process led to the creation of a European judicial system where national courts and the Court of Justice co-operate as "Community" courts.

3. THE COMPOSITION AND MECHANICS OF THE COURT OF JUSTICE

(1) The composition of the Court

3–013 The Court of Justice is currently composed of 27 Judges and 8 Advocates General. Judges and Advocates General are hierarchically equal. The Judges represent all the nationalities of the European Union and sit together in various formations to deliberate and decide a case.[35] The representative nature of its composition renders to the Court a moral authority that rises above national borders and equips it with the specialisation required to deal with individual national legal systems and languages. The Judges select one amongst them as President of the Court for a renewable term of three years.

Advocates General assist the Court in its task and function individually. They deliver an Opinion that must be impartial and independent in each case, unless the Court decides that there is no such need because a particular case does not raise a new point of law.

Judges and Advocates General are appointed by common accord of the governments of the Member States and remain in office for a renewable term of six years. They are chosen from the wider legal community. In their previous careers, they may have been national judges, practicing lawyers, academics, or otherwise legal experts.[36] They must possess independence

---

[34] *International Chemical Corp v Amministrazione delle Finanze dello Stato* (66/80) [1981] E.C.R. 1191.
[35] The Statute of the Court of Justice and the latest consolidated edition of The Regulations of the Court of Justice can be found following the links at: *http://curia.europa.eu/*. The Court of Justice sits as a full Court in exceptional circumstances provided by the Treaty, for example where it considers retiring a member of the European Commission. It can also sit in a Grand Chamber, composed of 13 judges, if this is requested by a Community institution or for a case the Court considers to be exceptionally complicated or important. Normally cases are heard by Chambers of five or three judges that select their own presidents for three- or one-year periods respectively.
[36] Formal legal training is not a requirement; in as early as 1964 it has been remarked that the broad knowledge some of the Judges had in fields like economics or administration and their influence during judicial interaction may be one factor behind "decisions which transcend narrow judicial considerations and which reflect an application of the Treaties with a keen eye on the purpose of the Communities and with an appreciation for the future"; Feld, *The Court of the European Communities: New Dimension in International Adjudication* (Martinus Nijhoff, 1964), p.32.

3. THE COMPOSITION AND MECHANICS OF THE COURT OF JUSTICE

that is beyond doubt and the qualifications required for appointment to the highest judicial offices in their respective countries or recognised competence.

The Court has its own administration headed by the Registrar of the Court.

(2) Direct actions

Direct actions are brought before the Court by written application addressed to the Registry that is recorded on the Court register. The language of the case may be any of the official languages of the Union.[37]

3–014

A notice of the action and the applicant's claims is published in the Official Journal of the European Union. This is followed by the appointment of a Judge-Rapporteur and an Advocate General. The action is served on the defendant who has a one-month period to respond. The applicant may submit a reply and the defendant a rejoinder within respective one-month periods; extensions may be granted by the President. Following the written procedure the parties must state, within a further one-month period, whether they wish a hearing to be arranged.

The Court then considers the report of the Judge-Rapporteur and the views of the Advocate General in order to decide the appropriate bench for the case. The Judge-Rapporteur prepares a Hearing Report summing up the facts and the arguments of the parties and the interveners. The report is made public at the hearing in the language of the case. The parties argue their case before the Judges and the Advocate General who may prompt them with questions.

At a later stage, the Advocate General delivers his Opinion in open court in his own language. The Opinion is an analytical review of the legal aspects of the case building up to a proposal regarding its outcome.

3–015

In terms of style, Opinions are nothing like the formal Decisions. They are longer, lucid, even passionate sometimes, documents reflecting the individual style of the Advocate General.

In terms of substance, the Advocate General posits the case within a wider legal and factual context. Opinions consider the actual text of the law, the case law of the Court of Justice, the views of legal writers ("la doctrine"), but also the writings of philosophers, historians, economists or literary figures. They can also discuss in detail the circumstances and the facts of the case and examine them from a wider legal, social, economic, and political perspective. For example, from a legal viewpoint Opinions can point to special features of the case[38] or suggest a change in the approach of the

---

[37] When the defendant is a Member State or a legal or natural person that is a national of a Member State, the language of the case will be the official language of that Member State. If the State has more than one official language, the applicant may choose which he prefers.

[38] See for example *Libertel Groep BV v Benelux-Merkenbureau* (C-104/01) [2003] E.C.R. I-3793, on the objections raised in relation to the registrability of colours, discussed in Ch.4.

Court.[39] From a policy angle they may debate the potential impact of a judgment to competition[40] or European integration.[41]

3-016 The next stage of the judicial process is closed to the parties, the public, and the Advocate General. Here, French becomes the working language of the Court. The Judges discuss the case using a draft judgment drawn up by the Judge-Rapporteur as their chart.

Historically, French influence has not been confined to the selection of a convenient working language. The style of the judgment followed French legal tradition. The whole judgment was delivered in the form of a single sentence: the facts of the case, the procedural steps, and the legal reasons were all recited as subordinate clauses leading to the "the Court hereby rules" main sentence as an apogee. Gradually, this "single sentence" has been abandoned. The essence and the structure remain the same—almost always divided into facts, procedure, and legal reasoning, all leading to the Court's ruling—but the sentences have been separated. Traditionally the judgments of the Court were short decisions[42]; in many areas of law, including trade marks, this is gradually changing in parallel with the increasing complexity of factual scenarios, the growth of Community law, and the technicality of legal instruments. It is becoming more and more difficult to rule by relying on basic principles.

The stylistic approach combined with persistent case themes introduced to the case law of the Court certain "leitmotifs that recur through whole sequences of its decisions. Phrases or passages will be repeated in case after case, sometimes in identical terms, sometimes with subtle variations. By constant rehearsal the Court, like a Welsh choir, finds the exact note it wants to sound. Examples abound of this technique whereby phrase-building becomes law making . . .".[43]

3-017 The Decisions of the Court of Justice are reached by majority and they must be signed by all the participating Judges. They contain rulings regarding substance and costs.[44] The judgments of the Court and the

---

[39] *SA CNL-SUCAL NV v Hag GF AG* (C-10/89) [1990] E.C.R. I-3711, is discussed in Ch.8 as one of the few examples where the Court changed its position.
[40] *Adam Opel AG v Autec AG* (C-48/05), Opinion of the Advocate General, March 7, 2006, on the effect the judgment might have on the market of toys, is discussed in Ch.5.
[41] *Hoffmann-la Roche & Co AG and Hoffmann-la Roche AG v Centrafarm Vertriebsgesellschaft Pharmazeutischer Erzeugnisse mbH* (102/77) [1978] E.C.R. 1139, on the balancing between free movement of goods and the creation of a common market on the one hand and protection of intellectual property rights on the other, is discussed in Ch.8.
[42] "ECJ decisions are rather short, terse, and magisterial decisions that offer condensed factual descriptions, impersonally clipped and collegial legal reasoning, and ritualized stylistic forms": Lasser, *Judicial Deliberations—A Comparative Analysis of Judicial Transparency and Legitimacy* (Oxford University Press, 2004), p.104.
[43] Brown and Kennedy (2000), p.57; the link of all the major developments in trade mark law with the function of a trade mark is a good example.
[44] A party unable to meet all or part of the costs of the case may apply for legal aid. The application must include all supporting evidence. The Chamber to which the Judge-Rapporteur belongs decides whether or not to grant legal aid. Intervening governments carry the costs for their observations.

3. THE COMPOSITION AND MECHANICS OF THE COURT OF JUSTICE

Opinions of the Advocates General are available on the website of the Court of Justice on the day they are read.[45] They are subsequently published in the Court's Reports of Cases (E.C.R.).

The collegiate nature of the Decision means that dissenting judgments or consenting judgments that are based on a different reasoning are not made public. The Court speaks in "institutional third person singular".[46] A code of secrecy permeates the deliberations of the Court. Only the judges themselves know whether their decision was reached unanimously or by a majority. Compromises and diverging opinions are sometimes accommodated into the final agreed text adding to the judgment a flavour of Delphic ambivalence. Still, secrecy and collegiality allow the Judges to act independently, free from national constraints; and where a Member State's interests or sensitivities are at stake the Judge "representing" the Member State can discuss openly, even in practical and political terms, what the case involves.

(3) Preliminary rulings—procedural differences

In terms of procedure[47] there are some differences between direct actions and preliminary rulings. The term "preliminary ruling" in itself is somewhat misleading. "The ruling is requested and given, not before the case comes to the national court, but in the course of the proceedings before it. It is therefore an interlocutory ruling, a step in the proceeding before the national court. But it is a step which may be taken, and is frequently best taken, before the case comes to trial. Thus references are commonly made in the course of interlocutory proceedings. The French "renvoi prejudiciel" is clearer: that is, the submission of an issue for prior judgment before determining the principal issue".[48]

3–018

The reference for a preliminary ruling is communicated to the Court of Justice by a national court. The language used by the national court becomes the official language of the case.

The reference is translated into all the Community languages, served on the parties to the main national proceedings, and notified to Member States and Community institutions. A notice in the Official Journal indicates the referring court, the names of the parties, and the theme of the question.

The parties, the Member States, and the institutions can submit written observations within a two-month period and may also present their arguments at the hearing.

3–019

Further, where the Court considers that the answer to a reference for a preliminary ruling has already been given in an identical earlier reference,

---

[45] *http://curia.europa.eu.*
[46] Lasser (2004), p.107.
[47] See the procedural "flowchart" of the Court at: *http://curia.europa.eu/en/instit/presentationfr/index-cje.htm.*
[48] Brown and Kennedy (2000), p.206.

or where the answer to the question admits of no reasonable doubt, or where the answer may be deduced from existing case law, the Court of Justice may inform the national court accordingly, hear the views of the parties concerned, consider the position of the Advocate General and give its decision by Reasoned Order, citing the previous relevant case law.

(4) Interlocutory proceedings

3–020 It is also possible to file an application for interim suspension of the operation of a measure adopted by an institution or an interim measure that is necessary to prevent serious and irreparable damage. Interlocutory proceedings are ancillary to the main proceedings.

(5) Expedited procedure

3–021 Finally, where there is a particular urgency to decide a case any of the parties in a direct action or the national court in a reference for a preliminary ruling can request from the President of the Court to follow an expedited procedure. The President of the Court will hear the other parties and decide on the request.

4. THE COURT OF FIRST INSTANCE—SPECIALIST TRIBUNALS

(1) The basics

3–022 The Court of First Instance is an independent court attached to the Court of Justice. It has the task of "ensuring that the law is observed in the interpretation and application of the Treaties constituting the European Communities and the provisions adopted by the competent Community institutions".[49]

The Court of First Instance was created in 1989 in order to lift some of the judicial burden the Court of Justice had to carry. Concerns, that were shared by the Court itself, about the efficiency—dealing with an increased number of cases inevitably led to delays—and efficacy—cases gradually became longer, more complex and specialised—of the Court of Justice culminated in the adoption of art.225 EC with the ratification of the Single European Act. That opened the way to the Council at the request of the Court of Justice and following consultation with the Commission and the European Parliament, to "attach" to the Court of Justice a Court with jurisdiction to hear and decide at first instance certain classes of actions or proceedings brought by natural or legal persons. Today the jurisdiction of the Court of First Instance extends to all direct actions brought by

---

[49] *http://curia.europa.eu/en/instit/presentationfr/index-cje.htm.*

4. THE COURT OF FIRST INSTANCE—SPECIALIST TRIBUNALS

individuals and the Member States against Community institutions,[50] with the exception of those to be assigned to a "judicial panel" and those reserved for the Court of Justice.

All cases heard at first instance by the Court of First Instance may be subject to a right of appeal to the Court of Justice, but only on points of law.

In order to lift some of the burden that is now being carried by the Court of First Instance the Treaty of Nice provides for the creation of "judicial panels" covering specific types of disputes.[51] The first such tribunal—the European Union Civil Service Tribunal that considers at first instance disputes involving the European civil service—was introduced on November 2, 2004. Its decisions are subject to a right of appeal before the Court of First Instance on points of law only. In exceptional cases the appeal decisions of the Court of First Instance may be subject to review by the Court of Justice.[52]

3–023

Article 229(a), also introduced by the Treaty of Nice, provides specifically for the field of industrial property: "Without prejudice to the other provisions of this Treaty, the Council, acting unanimously on a proposal from the Commission and after consulting the European Parliament, may adopt provisions to confer jurisdiction, to the extent that it shall determine, on the Court of Justice in disputes relating to the application of acts adopted on the basis of this Treaty which create Community industrial property rights. The Council shall recommend those provisions to the Member States for adoption in accordance with their respective constitutional requirements".

Indeed the process for the creation of a patent tribunal had already been initiated by the Commission in 2003.[53] Subsequently there has been a suggestion to establish an industrial property tribunal attached to the Court of First Instance with broader jurisdiction over industrial property matters.[54]

---

[50] Its jurisdiction covers all matters, including agriculture, State aid, competition, commercial policy, regional policy, social policy, institutional law, trade mark law, transport, and Staff Regulations.

[51] Article 225(a) EC inserted by the Treaty of Nice goes further and provides for the creation of judicial panels. "The Council, acting unanimously on a proposal from the Commission and after consulting the European Parliament and the Court of Justice or at the request of the Court of Justice and after consulting the European Parliament and the Commission, may create judicial panels to hear and determine at first instance certain classes of action or proceeding brought in specific areas . . .".

[52] Council Decision of November 2, 2004 establishing the European Union Civil Service Tribunal [2004] OJ L333/7; Decision of the President of the Court of Justice recording that the European Union Civil Service Tribunal has been constituted in accordance with law [2005] OJ L325/1.

[53] COM (2003) 827 final, December 23, 2003, Proposal for a Council Decision conferring jurisdiction on the Court of Justice in disputes relating to the Community patent, Celex No. 503PC0827; COM (2003) 828 final, December 23, 2003, Proposal for a Council Decision establishing the Community Patent Court and concerning appeals before the Court of First Instance, Celex No. 503PC0828.

[54] Opinion of the European Economic and Social Committee on the proposal for a Council Decision conferring jurisdiction on the Court of Justice in disputes relating to the Community patent (COM (2003) 827 final–2003/0326 (CNS)) [2004] OJ C112/81.

If either one of the proposals materialises the Court of First Instance will probably be transformed to a court of appeal and the Court of Justice would become the court where the decisions of the court of appeal could be reviewed. Appeals against the decisions of the "Community Patent Courts" both on points of fact and law will be directed to the Court of First Instance that will give a final judgment unless the First Advocate General of the Court of Justice requests a review of the judgment because the unity or consistency of Community law is jeopardised.[55]

(2) The composition and mechanics of the Court of First Instance

3–024 The Court of First Instance is currently composed of 27 Judges, at least one from each Member State, appointed for a renewable term of six years by common accord of the governments of the Member States.[56] Its members shall be chosen from "persons whose independence is beyond doubt and who possess the ability required for appointment to judicial office" (art.225(3)). It has been suggested that the slight difference in the wording of the required qualifications compared with those required for the Judges of the Court of Justice implied that the members of the Court of First Instance should possess the necessary practical skills and experience for a fact-finding role.[57] In practice, there is evidence of a revolving door between the two Courts regarding a significant minority of appointments. This "may bring advantages, such as continuity of judicial approach and practice, but also possible disadvantages, such as a reluctance to depart from established ways and even some deference [from the Court of First Instance to the Court of Justice]".[58]

The Members of the Court of First Instance elect amongst themselves a President of the Court of First Instance and the Presidents of the Chambers of five Judges for a renewable three-year term. There is no provision for a Court of First Instance Advocate General post. The task of an Advocate General may be performed in a limited number of cases by a Judge.

The Court of First Instance appoints its own Registrar, but its administration is part of the administration of the Court of Justice.

3–025 The Court of First Instance has its own Rules of Procedure.[59] In general, they are similar to those followed by the Court of Justice. Actions are

---

[55] See Lavranos, "The New Speacialised Courts within the European Judicial System" (2005) 30 E.L.Rev. 261.
[56] The Court of First Instance may sit in Grand Chamber or as a full court in particularly important cases. Normally, it sits in chambers composed of three or five Judges. In certain cases it may even be constituted by a single Judge.
[57] Brown and Kennedy (2000), pp.81–82.
[58] Brown and Kennedy (2000), p.84.
[59] The Rules of Procedure of the Court of First Instance of the European Communities of May 2, 1991 [1991] OJ L136/1. For the up to date consolidated version follow the links at http://curia.europa.eu/.

5. THE INTERPRETIVE PRINCIPLES AND TECHNIQUES OF THE COURT

brought before the Court by written application. This triggers the written phase of the proceedings. The language chosen by the applicant becomes the language of the case.

A Judge-Rapporteur, who is appointed by the President of the Court, follows closely the course of the proceedings.

At the close of the written procedure and, as the case may be, on adoption of measures of inquiry, the case is argued orally in open court.[60] The Judges then deliberate on the basis of a draft judgment prepared by the Judge-Rapporteur. The judgment is delivered in open court.

5. THE INTERPRETIVE PRINCIPLES AND TECHNIQUES OF THE COURT

Dehousse describes succinctly the constitutionalisation of the community legal order by the Court of Justice. The creation of the Coal and Steel Community, the precursor of the European Union, with the Treaty of Paris on April 18, 1951, a revolutionary political development in itself, for the jurist took the "rather banal form of an international treaty".[61] This was followed by subsequent, ever expanding Treaties. The content was innovative, often eroding considerably national sovereignty. The format and the structure resembled the classic international treaty model. But, it was the absence of interpretation clauses that allowed the Court to take up a new role. According to Lord Denning the EC Treaty lays down general principles, it expresses its aims and purposes, all "in sentences of moderate length and commendable style. But it lacks precision. It uses words and phrases without defining what they mean. An English lawyer would look for an interpretation clause, but . . . there is none".[62]

3–026

Thirty years later, in *Les Verts*[63] the Court did not hesitate to describe the Treaty of Rome as the "Constitutional Charter" of the Community. In 1991, it went on to suggest that some parts of the Treaty were so important that Member States could not modify them at will.[64] "A detached observer of Community life could well have seen this as either a rhetorical device, or the expression of a pious wish. A meticulous lawyer could have pointed out the inappropriateness of such views in relation to what remained an

---

[60] Note, however, that after the enactment of art.135(a), which was added to the Rules of Procedure of the Court of First Instance in 2008, the Court may rule on the action without an oral procedure, unless one of the parties submits an application setting out the reasons for which he wishes to be heard. That provision is expected to reduce the number of hearings in trade mark cases, as well as to speed up proceedings in general. In 2008, the average length of the proceedings in intellectual property cases was over 20 months.
[61] Dehousse, *The European Court of Justice* (Macmillan, 1998).
[62] *HP Bulmer Ltd v Bollinger SA* [1974] 2 C.M.L.R. 91, para.40.
[63] *Parti Ecologiste "Les Verts" v Parliament* (294/83) [1986] E.C.R. 1339.
[64] Opinion of the Court 1/91 [1991] E.C.R. I-6079.

international agreement. In reality, however, none of this happened and there was little criticism."[65]

The advance of the Court's jurisprudence over the years has reshaped the Treaties into a constitutional type of structure. In parallel, the need for legal integration within the European Union and effectiveness in the application of the new legal order led the Court to adapt the legal tools it possessed. Four themes—the doctrine of direct effect, the supremacy of Community law, the case law on its own competence, and the case law on fundamental rights—have pushed the "classic treaty" elements to the periphery and pictured the new structure as the logical conclusion of a long process of integration.

3-027 Subsequently, the Court partly recognising the limitations of the institutions of the Community, partly as a policy manoeuvre, took a step back and acknowledged two new themes: subsidiarity and proportionality. This did not alter the nature of the legal order; it simply fine-tuned its inherent checks and balances. And, it did not diminish the Court's own role; to the contrary, the Court has become once again the arbiter in determining the borders between Community institutions and Member States on the one hand and between Community institutions themselves on the other.

Tridimas identifies three trends in the field of EU judicial protection: formalisation, equivalence, and selective deference:

> "Formalisation refers to the tendency to provide for the express declaration and entrenchment of rights in constitutional texts. This trend began with the Treaty on European Union, which, for the first time, enshrined respect for fundamental rights at Treaty level and provided expressly for fundamental constitutional doctrines, such as the principles of attribution of powers, subsidiarity and proportionality."[66]

The trend towards equivalence means that the Court "increasingly subjects the Community institutions and the Member States to the same standards of scrutiny and accountability".[67]

Selective deference means that in some areas the Court "is content to defer to choices made at national level, uphold the powers of the Member States or leave matters to the national courts to decide. But in other areas, the ECJ is willing to provide leadership and dictate the results".[68]

---

[65] Dehousse (1998), pp.36–37.
[66] Tridimas, "Judicial Federalism and the European Court of Justice" in Fedthe and Markesinis (eds), *Patterns of Federalism and Regionalism: Lessons for the UK* (Hart, 2006), p.152.
[67] Tridimas, "Judicial Federalism and the European Court of Justice", p.154. In the field of trade marks this is evident in the often repeated statement that the registrability provisions should be applied following the same standards throughout the European Union both by national registration authorities and OHIM, see for example *Koninklijke KPN Nederland NV v Benelux-Merkenbureau* (C-363/99) [2004] E.C.R. I-1619.
[68] Tridimas, "Judicial Federalism and the European Court of Justice", p.154–155. *Adidas-Salomon AG and Adidas Benelux BV v Fitnessworld Trading Ltd* (C-408/01) [2003] E.C.R. I-12537 is a good example of the Court opting for the second more activist choice.

5. THE INTERPRETIVE PRINCIPLES AND TECHNIQUES OF THE COURT

(1) Direct effect

States that become contracting parties of international agreements have their own national constitutional rules determining the effect of the agreement in their internal legal order. Some accept that the provisions of the agreements have direct effect and may be invoked before their own national courts; others require a national law that gives to the international agreement effect in the national legal order. Would Community law, the result of an international agreement, require national legislation to become effective in the Member States belonging to the second category?

3–028

(a) The direct effect of the Treaties

The Court dealt with this problem back in 1963, in *Van Gend en Loos*,[69] a reference for a preliminary ruling from The Netherlands. The question was whether art.12[70] of the Treaty of Rome that prohibited the increase of customs' duties in respect of imported goods could be raised by Van Gend en Loos, a Dutch company, before the courts in order to challenge a decision which set a higher duty on imported goods. To interpret the provision A.G. Roemer followed a purposive approach. He supported that the intention of those drafting the provision was to impose an obligation on Member States, not to create a legal norm of a general nature. The reference to the intention of the parties was after all a common interpretive tool regarding international agreements.

3–029

The Court however did not follow the suggestion of the Advocate General. The tools for determining the effect of the provision were "the spirit, the general scheme and the wording" of the provision.[71] Literal interpretation came after the spirit—the objectives of the Treaty described in the Preamble—and the general scheme—the positioning of the provision within the Treaty but also within the wider institutional framework of the Community.

---

[69] *NV Algemente Transporten Expeditie Onderneming van Gend en Loos v Nederlandse Administratie der Belastingen* (C-26/62) [1963] E.C.R. 1.

[70] Article 12 provided: "Member States shall refrain from introducing between themselves any new customs duties on imports or exports or any charges having equivalent effect, and from increasing those which they already apply in their trade with each other".

[71] *NV Algemente Transporten Expeditie Onderneming van Gend en Loos v Nederlandse Administratie der Belastingen* (C-26/62) [1963] E.C.R. 1. at 12. Lord Denning in *HP Bulmer Ltd v Bollinger SA* [1974] 2 C.M.L.R. 91 continues in para.40, "[A]ll the way through there are gaps and lacunae. These have to be filled in by the judges, or by regulations or directives ... [para.42] [English courts] must follow the European pattern. No longer must they argue about the precise grammatical sense. They must look to the purpose and intent ... They must divine the spirit of the Treaty and gain inspiration from it. If they find a gap, they must fill it as best they can ... These are the principles on which the European Court acts". However, Lord Denning has also stated that if "the time should come when Parliament deliberately passes an Act with the intention of repudiating the Treaty or any provision of it or intentionally of acting inconsistently with it and says so in express terms, then I should have thought it would be the duty of our courts to follow the statute of our Parliament", *Macarthys Ltd v Smith* [1979] All E.R. 325 at 329.

Citizens of the Member States were asked to co-operate in the functioning of the Community through institutional intermediaries.[72] At the same time the existence in itself of the "preliminary reference" system signified that they were directly concerned by Community law. The nature of the Treaty was beyond an agreement creating obligations between the Member States. The Community "constitutes a new legal order of international law for the benefit of which the states have limited their sovereign rights, albeit within limited fields and the subjects of which comprise not only Member States but also their nationals".[73] The Community legal order confers obligations as well as rights upon individuals, Member States, and Community institutions.

3–030 Having painted its own liberal and idealistic version of the Community legal order as the background for the provision,[74] the Court focused on the detail of art.12 (art.25 EC): it contained a clear and unconditional prohibition, a negative obligation, not qualified by any reservation that would render its implementation conditional upon a positive legislative measure. And then, it contextualised the detail within the Community legal order. By its nature, the provision was ideally suitable to produce direct legal effects between Member States and their citizens.

The Court drew the line at "particularly aspirational"[75] Treaty provisions such as art.2 or provisions that required further implementation in order to be capable of comparable judicial, rather than political, application throughout the Union.[76]

---

[72] Dehousse (1998) points out that in 1963 the European Parliament was not directly elected and the members of the Economic and Social Committee were, and still are, appointed by the governments of the Member States. This could be an indication of the indirectness—rather than the directness—of the involvement of the citizen in the Community legal order.

[73] *NV Algemene Transporten Expeditie Onderneming van Gend en Loos* (C-26/62) [1963] E.C.R. 1, p.12.

[74] Pescatore (a former Judge of the Court of Justice), in "The Doctrine of 'Direct Effect': An Infant Disease of Community Law" (1983) 8 E.L.Rev. 155 at 158 describes the concept that individuals must be visualised as subjects of Community law as the "consequence of a democratic ideal, meaning that in the Community, as well as in a modern constitutional State, Governments may not say any more what they are used to doing in international law: L' Etat, c'est moi. Far from it; the Community calls for participation of everybody, with the result that private individuals are not only liable to burdens and obligations, but that they have also prerogatives and rights which must be legally protected. It was thus a highly political idea, drawn from a perception of the constitutional system of the Community, which is at the basis of Van Gend en Loos and which continues to inspire the whole doctrine flowing from it".

[75] Craig and De Búrca, *EU Law* (Oxford University Press, 2003), p.188.

[76] For example, *Fernando Roberto Giménez Zaera v Instituto Nacional de la Seguridad Social* (C-126/86) [1987] E.C.R. 3697. According to the questions referred and the individual factual scenarios the results have sometimes been contradictory. For example, Craig and De Búrca, (2003) cite *Comitato di Coordinamento per la Difesa della Cava v Regione Lombardia* (C-236/92) [1994] E.C.R. I-483; and *Commission v Italy* (C-365/97) [1999] E.C.R. I-7773 where a provision of a directive on waste disposal was found in the first case to be insufficiently precise or unconditional to have direct effect and in the second to be sufficiently clear to have direct effect.

5. THE INTERPRETIVE PRINCIPLES AND TECHNIQUES OF THE COURT

The Court continued gaining inspiration by the doctrine of "direct effect" in subsequent case law. In *Costa v ENEL*[77] *and Defrenne II*[78] the doctrine has been applied against Member States that had failed to implement their obligations under Community.

The turn of Community institutions came in *Reyners*[79] where the Court looked at art.43 EC in relation to a case of discrimination based on nationality: a Dutch national who studied law in Belgium was refused admission to the Belgian Bar. Article 43 provides that restrictions on freedom of establishment of Community nationals in Member States other than that of their own nationality are to be abolished within a wider framework according to the procedure under arts 44(2) and 47(1).

3–031

The Court had no difficulty holding that art.43, by laying down that freedom of establishment shall be attained at the end of the transitional period, imposes "an obligation to attain a precise result, the fulfilment of which had to be made easier by, but not made dependent on, the implementation of a programme of progressive measures".[80] After the expiry of the transitional period the directives included in the progressive measures have become superfluous, and failure on behalf of the Council to issue the directives should not be invoked against the direct effect of freedom of establishment. The doctrine expanded to cover failure of a Community institution.

The next step in the development of the doctrine was its application in respect of "secondary" European legislation: regulations, directives, and decisions.

(b) The direct effect of regulations

The language of art.249 EC, stating that a regulation "shall be binding in its entirety and directly applicable in all Member States", provides a strong foundation for the argument that regulations have direct effect unless their provisions are not "sufficiently clear, precise and relevant to the situation of an individual litigant".[81]

3–032

Indeed, the Court of Justice has declared that regulations are, as such, directly applicable in all Member States and come into force solely by virtue of their publication in the Official Journal of the Communities, as from the date specified in them, or in the absence thereof, as from the date provided in the Treaty".[82] And, the consequence is that implementing methods that would create an obstacle to direct application or jeopardise simultaneous and uniform application throughout the European Union would be against

---

[77] *Costa v Ente Nazionale per l'Energia Elettrica (ENEL)* (6/64) [1964] E.C.R. 585.
[78] *Defrenne v Société Anonyme Belge de Navigation Aérienne* (43/75) [1976] E.C.R. 455.
[79] *Reyners v Belgium* (2/74) [1974] E.C.R. 631.
[80] *Reyners* (2/74) [1974] E.C.R. 631, para.26.
[81] Craig and De Búrca (2003), p.190.
[82] *Commission v Italy* (39/72) [1973] E.C.R. 101, para.17.

the EC Treaty. Member States can not choose which elements of a regulation will have effect within their jurisdiction. Its application is independent of any measure of reception into national law.[83]

Implementing measures at the national level are acceptable only if, and to the extent that, they are necessary in order to implement specific provisions of a regulation.[84] One of the reasons that the Court is apprehensive of implementing national laws is that they can disguise the "Community law" nature of a regulation. This is linked with the actual understanding and acceptance of the European character and direct application of a regulation by European citizens, the perceived supremacy that European law often enjoys. But, also with the real in legal terms "supremacy" of "Community law" over "national law", a theme that is discussed later.[85]

(c) The direct effect of directives

3–033 The application of the doctrine of direct effect becomes more complicated in the case of directives. Article 249 EC provides that a directive "shall be binding as to the result to be achieved, upon each Member State to which it is addressed, but shall leave to the national authorities the choice of form and methods". The text of the provision indicates clearly the distinction between a directive and a regulation. As our more detailed discussion of trade mark law in Europe will also show, directives primarily aim to harmonise national legal orders rather than create a new European Union-wide legal order. They often accommodate national differences. They may allow the discretionary application of some of their provisions. However, according to art.249 EC and the jurisprudence of the Court of Justice, the effect of a directive is binding. Member States are under an obligation to achieve the result envisaged by the directive and under art.10 EC to take all appropriate measures, general or particular, to ensure the fulfilment of that obligation.[86]

The length of each legal leap forward taken by a directive is co-determined by the description of its aim and the precision and detail of its measures. But, once again, the Court of Justice is the official that reads the distance.

The "direct effect" of a directive was first considered in *Van Duyn*,[87] a case involving the rights of a Dutch national who was refused leave to enter the

---

[83] *Fratelli Variola SpA v Amministrazione Italiana delle Finanze* (34/73) [1973] E.C.R. 981.
[84] See for example *Azienda Agricola Monte Arcosu v Regione Autonoma della Sardegna* (403/98) [2001] E.C.R. I-103.
[85] See for example *Amsterdam Bulb BV v Produktschap voor Siergewassen* (50/76) [1977] E.C.R. 137.
[86] The obligation covers all the authorities of the Member States, including courts. *Von Colson and Kamann v Land Nordhein-Westfalen* (14/83) [1984] E.C.R. 1891; see also *Marleasing v La Comercial Internacional de Alimentacion* (C-106/89) [1990] E.C.R. I-4135, *Faccini Dori v Recreb Srl* (C-91/92) [1994] E.C.R. I-3325; and *Carbonari v Universita degli Studi di Bologna* (C-131/97) [1999] E.C.R. I-1103. See Tridimas, "Black White and Shades of Grey: Horizontality of Directives Revisited" [2002] 21 Y.E.L. 327.
[87] *Van Duyn v Home Office* (41/74) [1974] E.C.R. 1337.

5. THE INTERPRETIVE PRINCIPLES AND TECHNIQUES OF THE COURT

United Kingdom because she aimed to work there for the Church of Scientology. Scientology was considered by the UK government to be socially harmful; nevertheless there were no legal restrictions against it. The Court of Justice was asked by the High Court whether the provisions of Directive 64/221[88] had direct effect.

The Court built its decision around the binding effect of directives and noted again that each provision of a directive must be viewed in its context in order to determine whether it has direct effect:

3-034

"It would be incompatible with the binding effect attributed to a directive by Article [249] to exclude in principle, the possibility that the obligation which it imposes may be invoked by those concerned. In particular, where the Community authorities have, by directive, imposed on Member States the obligation to pursue a particular course of conduct, the useful effect of such an act would be weakened if individuals were prevented from relying on it before their national courts and if the latter were prevented from taking into consideration as an element of Community law. Article [234], which empowers national courts to refer to the Court questions concerning the validity and interpretation of all acts of the Community institutions, without distinction implies furthermore that these acts may be invoked by individuals in the national courts. It is necessary to examine, in every case, whether the nature, general scheme and wording of the provision in question are capable of having direct effects on the relations between Member States and individuals."[89]

So, in principle a directive can have "vertical direct effect", it can create rights that individuals may invoke against a national government.

The context of the provisions on allowable, discretionary restrictions based on public policy included in the directive was provided by another provision that measures taken on public policy grounds had to relate to the individual's conduct, an obligation that was clear, precise, and legally complete. This meant that the degree of a Member State's discretion could be challenged before a national court.

Along the same line of argument the Court decided in subsequent cases that Member States could not re-invent their discretion once they had exercised it or chosen not to exercise it on implementation.[90]

3-035

---

[88] Free movement of workers was then regulated by art.48 [now art.39] EC, Reg.1612/68, and Dir.64/221.
[89] *Van Duyn* (41/74) [1974] E.C.R. 1337, para.12.
[90] See for example, *Riksskateverket v Charehveran Sindicato de Médicos de Asistencia Pública (SIMAP) v Conselleria de Sanidad y Consumo de la Generalidad Valenciana* (C-441/99) [2000] E.C.R. I-7963. In *Aslanidou v Ypourgos Ygeias & Pronoias* (C-142/04) [2005] E.C.R. I-7181 the Court repeated that a Member State which has failed to fulfil its obligation to transpose the provisions of a directive into national law can no more rely, as against Community citizens, upon the limitations laid down by those provisions than it can require that they perform the obligations laid down by that directive.

Ratti[91] elaborates on the doctrine of "direct effect" in two seemingly opposing ways.

First, "perhaps in response to ... criticisms" by some Member States that with *Van Duyn* the Court "had gone too far in advancing its conception of Community law at the expense of the clear language of the Treaty, and the obvious limitations on directives as a form of legislation"[92] the Court added to its general argument a more specific line of reasoning based on the concept of "estoppel", requiring Member States not to use their own implementation failures as a cyclical defensive tool when challenged before a court because of their failures. Secondly, however, by linking the doctrine of direct effect with a potent reasoning based on fundamental justice the Court responded to criticism by strengthening its argument rather than retreating from its position.

3-036 Ratti marketed solvents in Italy following the packaging and labelling requirements imposed by the relevant directives. Italy, however, had not implemented the directives and applied more demanding standards. Ratti relied on the direct effect of the directives during criminal proceedings against him.[93]

The Court held that "a national court requested by a person who has complied with the provisions of a directive not to apply a national provision incompatible with the directive not incorporated into the internal legal order of a defaulting Member State, must uphold that request if the obligation in question is unconditional and sufficiently precise".[94] It concluded however that "it is only at the end of the prescribed period and in the event of the Member State's default that the directive ... will be able to have the effects described [above]. Until that date the Member States remain free in that field".[95]

The repositioning of the Court continued with *Marshall*[96] where it held that the direct effect of a directive could be relied upon against a Member State, but not against an individual.

3-037 Advocate General Slynn in his Opinion made a distinction between directives addressed to Member States and directives addressed to individuals. Accepting that all directives automatically have a "horizontal effect" would make the legal division between regulations and directives meaningless. In principle directives in most cases would have a "vertical effect", and as we have seen above this "vertical effect" could be direct. The Court approached the question from a literal interpretation perspective and relied on

---

[91] *Pubblico Ministero v Tullio Ratti* (148/78) [1979] E.C.R. 1629.
[92] Craig and De Búrca (2003), p.204.
[93] The Court has also sanctioned proactive rather than defensive reliance on the direct effect of directives, see for example *Becker v Finanzamt Münster-Innenstadt* (8/81) [1982] E.C.R. 53.
[94] *Pubblico Ministero* (148/78) [1979] E.C.R. 1629, para.23.
[95] *Pubblico Ministero* (148/78) [1979] E.C.R. 1629, paras 43–44. See also *Francovich and Bonifici v Italy* (C-6/90 & C-9/90) [1991] E.C.R. I-5357; and *Marks & Spencer v Commissioners of Customs & Excise* (C-62/00) [2002] E.C.R. I-6325.
[96] *Marshall v Southampton and South-West Hampshire Area Health Authority (Teaching)* (C-152/84) [1986] E.C.R. 723.

5. THE INTERPRETIVE PRINCIPLES AND TECHNIQUES OF THE COURT

the text of art.254 providing that the binding effect of a directive covers the Member States that it addresses. Craig and De Búrca note that, some years earlier, the Court had followed a different approach regarding the effect of art.141 EC that is also addressed only to Member States.[97]

Nevertheless, the Court applied the precedent of Marshall consistently.[98] Negating horizontal direct effect to directives—directives do not create rights and obligations between private entities—has been often criticised as an anomaly. Here, it is supported that the Court through this approach achieved three objectives.

First, it reinforced the hierarchy between the Treaties and legislation that is the result of the Treaties. The Treaties have direct horizontal effect, as well as regulations because the Treaties provide so. The Treaties play the role of a constitution from which all other powers derive.

Secondly, it responded to criticisms by Member States targeting the Court's drive and enthusiasm by showing some restraint in its integrationist jurisprudence.

3–038

Thirdly, it did not give away much regarding the efficiency and effectiveness of European law.

In its constant search for a new equilibrium, the Court of Justice, having established that directives do not have a horizontal direct effect, then went on to dilute its reasoning by strengthening the concept of "vertical direct effect". It expanded the notion of what constitutes a public body that would be bound by a directive. In *Marshall* itself, the Court decided that Ms Marshall could rely on the provisions of the Directive since the Health Authority should be regarded as an organ of the Member State that was bound by it.

In addition it broadened the definition of authorities that could recognise the direct effect of a directive and, as a result, should apply its provisions even without implementation at the national level; the direct effect of a directive could be sought before virtually any public authority.[99]

3–039

---

[97] It took a similar path in *Angonese v Cassa di Risparmio di Bolzano* (C-281/98) [2000] E.C.R. I-4139 regarding the horizontal effect of art.39 EC (free movement of workers); and *Defrenne v Sabena* (43/75) [1976] E.C.R. 455 on the horizontal effect of art.141 EC (principal of equal pay). All these cases considered gender discrimination. Craig and De Búrca (2003), p.207.

[98] *Faccini Dori v Recreb Srl* (C-91/92) [1994] E.C.R. I-3325; and *Wells v Secretary of State for Transport, Local Government and the Regions* (C-201/02) [2004] E.C.R. I-723. Note too that a directive may produce vertical direct effect if it gives effect to a pre-existing general principle of Community law; see *Werner Mongold v Rüdiger Helm* (C-144/04) [2005] E.C.R. I-9981.

[99] In *Fratelli Costanzo SpA v Comune di Milano* (103/88) [1989] E.C.R. 1839 the Court decided that when the conditions under which individuals may rely on the provisions of a directive before the national courts are met then all organs of the administration are obliged to apply those provisions. In *Foster v British Gas Plc* (C-188/89) [1990] E.C.R. I-3313 the Court reviewed its case law, stating that it had found that directives could be relied upon against tax authorities, local or regional authorities, constitutionally independent authorities responsible for the maintenance of public order and safety, and public authorities providing public health services. It added that, irrespective of its legal form, a body which has been made responsible by a measure of the State for providing a public service under the Control of the State and has, for that purpose, special powers beyond those covered by normal rules applicable in relations between individuals, is included among such organs.

A further diluting step was the attribution to some directives of "incidental horizontal effects", directives can cause effects between individuals without imposing directly legal obligations. In *CIA Security*[100] the Court targeted primarily the implementation of Directive 83/189[101] by Belgian state authorities. Failure to notify draft technical regulations for alarm systems to the Commission before their adoption meant that the disputed technical regulations were inapplicable; the collateral effect of their inapplicability was that the defendant, a private entity, could be found liable for unfair trading because it could not rely on the technical regulations as part of its defence.[102]

The Court of Justice delineated the effect of *CIA Security* with its judgment in *Lemmens*,[103] where a drunken driver challenged the prosecution by claiming that the regulations for the particular breathalyzer used had not been properly notified. The Court held that the directive could be invoked when the marketing of a product is restricted, affecting the free movement of goods principle, but not when there was no link with this principle.[104]

Finally, the Court ensured that Member States would think twice before undermining the effect of directives by establishing State liability in damages for non-implementation:

> "[F]ull effectiveness of Community rules would be impaired and the protection of the rights which they grant would be weakened if individuals were unable to obtain compensation when their rights are infringed by a breach of Community law for which a Member State can be held responsible. The possibility of compensation by the Member State is particularly indispensable where... the full effectiveness of Community rules is subject to prior action on the part of the State and consequently individuals cannot, in the absence of such action, enforce

---

[100] *CIA Security International SA v Signalson SA and Securitel SPRL* (C-194/94) [1996] E.C.R. I-2201.
[101] Council Directive 83/189 laying down a procedure for the provision of information in the field of technical standards and regulations [1983] OJ L109/8.
[102] For a similar result see *Panagis Pafitis v Trapeza Kentrikis Ellados AE* (C-441/93) [1996] E.C.R. I-1347; and *österreichische Unilever GmbH v Smithkline Beecham* (C-77/97) [1999] E.C.R. I-431. In *Unilever Italia SpA v Central Food SpA* (C-443/98) [2000] E.C.R. I-7535 the Court held that non compliance with other provisions of the directive—in this case a standstill clause—could have the same effect with non-notification. For an analysis of the effect of such cases see Dougan, "The 'Disguised' Vertical Direct Effect of Directives" (2000) 59 C.L.J. 586; and Sara Drake, "Twenty Years After Von Colson: The Impact of 'Indirect Effect' on the Protection of the Individual's Community Rights" (2005) 30 E.L.Rev. 329.
[103] *Lemmens* (C-226/97) [2000] E.C.R. I-3711.
[104] Note that the initial scheme established by the Rome Treaty focused on three pylons supporting the creation of a single market: free movement of goods, services, labour, and capital; common external customs policy; common system of market regulation.

5. THE INTERPRETIVE PRINCIPLES AND TECHNIQUES OF THE COURT

the rights granted to them by Community law before the national courts."[105]

(d) The direct effect of decisions

According to art.249 EC a decision is a Community act that is "binding in its entirety upon those to whom it is addressed". It does not have the effect of a regulation because it is not a general measure; it addresses a specific audience. The Court of Justice considered whether a decision can be directly applicable in *Franz Grad*,[106] a case that is also a precursor of the Court's jurisprudence in relation to directives. It accepted that art.249 EC was silent regarding the direct effect of decisions and directives whereas it explicitly referred to the direct applicability of regulations. Nevertheless, this would not preclude the possibility of a decision having a direct effect, in particular where the obligation imposed by the decision is sufficiently unconditional, clear and precise:

3–040

"It would be incompatible with the binding effect attributed to decisions by Article [249] to exclude in principle the possibility that persons affected may invoke the obligation imposed by a decision. Particularly in cases where, for example, the Community authorities by means of a decision have imposed an obligation on a Member State or all the Member States to act in a certain way, the effectiveness (l'effet utile) of such a measure would be weakened if the nationals of that State could not invoke it in the courts and the national courts could not take it into consideration as part of Community law".[107]

(2) Supremacy of Community law

The doctrine of supremacy of Community over national law has been described as the second "constitutionalising" tool.[108] It is applied whenever directly applicable Community law is concerned. "The combination of the

3–041

---

[105] *Francovich and Bonifaci v Italy* (C-6 & 9/90) [1991] E.C.R. I-5357, paras 33–34. The Court imposed three conditions: the result imposed by the directive should entail the grant of rights to individuals; the content of these rights should be identified by the directive; a causal link between the breach of the State's obligations and the harm suffered by the injured parties. In *Brasserie du Pêcheur SA v Germany* and *R. v Secretary of State for Transport Ex p. Factortame Ltd* (C-46/93 & C-48/93) [1996] E.C.R. I-1029 it developed an analogy between Member State and Community institution non contractual liability and referred to the factors that must be taken into account, like the degree of discretion available to the author of the act, the complexity of the situations covered by the legislation, and the difficulties in the application or interpretation of the relevant texts. So when a Member State does not have a wide discretion in implementing Community policies there are three conditions that must be met in order to establish liability: the rule of law must be intended to confer rights to individuals; the breach must be sufficiently serious; a direct causal link must exist between the breach of the State's obligation and the damage sustained by the injured parties.
[106] *Franz Grad v Finanzamt Traunstein* (9/70) [1970] E.C.R. 825.
[107] *Franz Grad* (9/70) [1970] E.C.R. 825, para.5.
[108] Weiler, *The Constitution of Europe* (Cambridge University Press, 1999), p.20.

two doctrines means that Community norms that produce direct effects are not merely the law of the land but the 'higher law' of the land. Parallels to this kind of constitutional architecture may, with very few exceptions, be found only in the internal constitutional order of federal states".[109] This has occurred despite the fact that unlike some federal constitutions the EC Treaty does not include a "supremacy clause".

The EC Treaty is silent on the supremacy point; art.10 EC provides that Member States shall take "all appropriate measures, whether general or particular, to ensure fulfilment of the obligations arising out of this Treaty".[110]

The starting point in the development of the doctrine is *Van Gend en Loos*[111] where the Court chose to bypass A.G. Roemer's point that the constitutional laws of some Member States did not accord primacy to international treaties over national law. The Court stated that the legal order created by the Treaty was an entirely new system, something more than an agreement which merely creates mutual obligations between contracting states. It stressed the establishment by the Treaty of Institutions endowed with sovereign rights and noted that for the benefit of this new legal order the Member States have limited their sovereign rights.

3–042   *Van Gend en Loos* was a great example of teleological reasoning. The Court combined self-apodictic statements with references to the aims and the spirit of the Treaty to draw the wider picture; it then used the detail of the direct applicability of regulations to give to the picture the tone that dominates; and finally, applied the practical difficulties, as the finishing touches that reinforce the tone. This may not be a picture that is sufficiently close to the textual image of the Treaty, but it has proven to be catching, evocative, and, above all, lingering.[112]

The Court of Justice became more explicit in *Costa*.[113] The facts of the case show how individuals have influenced legal developments in Europe by challenging national establishments. Costa, an Italian citizen, refused to pay the equivalent of €3 for an electricity bill protesting against the nationalisation of the industry in Italy; he was a shareholder in one of the expropriated companies and claimed that the nationalisation process violated EC rules against discriminatory favouritism for national monopolies.

---

[109] Weiler, pp.21–22.
[110] Dehousse (1998), p.41, describes the question from an international law perspective as follows: "It was thus clear that Community law, like international law, required that incompatible national legislation be set aside, as treaty commitments have to be honoured. But the real issue was whether this claim to supremacy would convince national courts, which play a crucial role in ensuring the effectiveness of EC law".
[111] *NV Algemene Transporten Expeditie Onderneming van Gend en Loos* (C-26/62) [1963] E.C.R. 1.
[112] The Court reinforced the principle by rejecting a Member State's claim that the principle of primacy should not apply, at least automatically, to specific individual administrative acts. To the contrary, it held that it must be applied whenever directly effective law is concerned; *Ciola v Land Voralberg* (C-224/97) [1999] E.C.R. I-2517.
[113] *Costa v Ente Nazionale per l'Energia Elettrica (ENEL)* (6/64) [1964] E.C.R. 585 at 593.

5. THE INTERPRETIVE PRINCIPLES AND TECHNIQUES OF THE COURT

The Court of Justice started by asserting, without referring to concrete instances from the constitutional law or jurisprudence of the Member States, that the Treaty has become an integral part of the legal systems of the Member States which their courts are bound to apply. It employed the explicit direct applicability of regulations to strengthen its own argument: the unlimited duration of the Treaty, the institutions of the Community, its autonomous personality, legal capacity, and capacity of representation at the international level, all led to the conclusion that the Member States have created a body of law which binds both their nationals and themselves. The integration of such provisions into their own national laws and "more generally the terms and the spirit of the Treaty, make it impossible for the states, as a corollary, to accord precedence to a unilateral and subsequent measure over a legal system accepted by them on the basis of reciprocity".[114]

It elaborated on the basic decisive argument by supporting that the executive force of Community law can not vary from one State to another according to subsequent national laws. Otherwise the objectives of the Treaty set out in art.10 would be jeopardised together with the principle of non-discrimination established by art.12. And the direct applicability of regulations would become meaningless:

3–043

> "It follows ... that the law stemming from the Treaty, an independent source of law, could not, because of its special and original nature, be overridden by domestic legal provisions, however framed, without being deprived of its character as Community law and without the legal basis of the Community itself being called into question."[115]

The effect of the rights and obligations imposed by the Treaty is a permanent limitation against which an incompatible with the concept of the Community and unilateral act cannot prevail.[116]

Case law developed further in two ways. First, the Court held that the status of a conflicting national legal measure in the domestic legal order is irrelevant; Community law will always takes precedence.[117] And secondly, that the validity of Community measures may be judged only under the light

---

[114] *Costa* (6/64) [1964] E.C.R. 585 at 593.
[115] *Costa* (6/64) [1964] E.C.R. 585.
[116] Interestingly Costa's specific claims have been found by the Court to be unfounded.
[117] *Commission v Luxembourg* (C-473/93) [1996] E.C.R. I-3207. The general position has been expressed with strong words in *Amministrazione delle Finanze dello Stato v Simmenthal SpA* (C-106/77) [1978] E.C.R. 629, para.17: "In accordance with the principle of the precedence of Community law, the relationship between provisions of the Treaty and directly applicable measures of the institutions on the one hand and the national law of Member States on the other is such that those provisions and measures not only by their entry into force render automatically inapplicable any conflicting provision of current national law but—in so far as they are an integral part of, and take precedence in, the legal order applicable in the territory of each of the Member States—also preclude the valid adoption of new legislative measures to the extent to which they would be incompatible with Community provisions".

of Community law, not according to national legal rules or concepts of law.[118] The next logical step in this direction was to declare that every national court, within its jurisdiction, must apply Community law in its entirety and set aside prior or subsequent provisions of national law which may conflict with Community law.[119] In practice, this gave to national courts a power that they did not previously enjoy within their national context. To an extent they too became Community courts.

3–044   For example, clarifying the effect of supremacy, the Court of Justice noted that it cannot "be inferred from the judgment in *Simmenthal* that the incompatibility with Community law of a subsequently adopted rule of national law has the effect of rendering that rule of national law non-existent. Faced with such a situation, the national court is, however, obliged to disapply that rule, provided always that this obligation does not restrict the power of the competent national courts to apply, from among the various procedures available under national law, those which are appropriate for protecting the individual rights conferred by Community law".[120] The national court will not determine the validity of the contested provision, it will refrain from applying it.

Advocate General Ruiz Zarabo succinctly depicted the weight of "primacy" in the legal order of the Community in *Bernhard Pfeiffer*.[121] Having reviewed the relevant case law of the Court of Justice he noted that to "disregard those developments would entail a serious set-back for respect for the principle of the primacy of Community law, would compromise the authority of the Court of Justice to impose a uniform interpretation of that law throughout the territory of the European Union and would demoralise national courts in the exercise of their function as Community courts, in particular those which have followed the recommendations of preliminary rulings relevant for the "interpretation in conformity of their legal provisions".[122]

He supported that every time a Community provision is believed to preclude a national provision, the 40-year-old principle of primacy must be

---

[118] *Internationale Handelsgesellschaft mbH v Einfuhr-und Vorratsstelle für Getreide und Futtermittel* (11/70) [1970] E.C.R. 1125.

[119] The question was raised in *Amministrazione delle Finanze dello Stato* (106/77) [1978] E.C.R. 629; the Court held that it was not necessary for the national court to request from the Italian Constitutional Court to set aside the provision. Further impetus was provided by *R. v Secretary of State for Transport Ex p. Factortame Ltd* (C-213/89) [1990] E.C.R. I-2433 where it was decided that even interim relief should be granted if such relief would be granted if it were not for a rule of national law that should be set aside.

[120] *Ministero delle Finanze v IN.CO.GE.'90 Srl* (C-10–22/97) [1998] E.C.R. I-6307, para.21.

[121] *Bernhard Pfeiffer* (C-397/01), *Wilhelm Roith* (C-398/01), *Albert Su\s* (C-399/01), *Michael Winter* (C-400/01), *Klaus Nestvogel* (C-401/01), *Roswitha Zeller* (C-402/01), *Matthias Dobele* (C-403/01) *v Deutsches Rotes Kreuz, Kreisverband Waldshut eV* [2004] E.C.R. I-8835; the cases involved the interpretation of Council Dir. 93/104/EC concerning certain aspects of the organization of working time [1993] OJ L307/18.

[122] *Bernhard Pfeiffer* (C-397/01), *Wilhelm Roith* (C-398/01), *Albert Su\s* (C-399/01), *Michael Winter* (C-400/01), *Klaus Nestvogel* (C-401/01), *Roswitha Zeller* (C-402/01), *Matthias Dobele* (C-403/01) *v Deutsches Rotes Kreuz, Kreisverband Waldshut eV* [2004] E.C.R. I-8835, point 36.

5. THE INTERPRETIVE PRINCIPLES AND TECHNIQUES OF THE COURT

reiterated, irrespective of the Community source: the Treaty, a regulation or a directive.

In its judgment the Court distinguished between the correct implementation by the Member State of the relevant provision of a directive—in this case art.6(2) of Directive 93/104—and the direct effect the same provision might have; "the first concerns the interpretation of Article 6(2) of Directive 93/104 for the purpose of enabling the national court to decide whether the relevant rules of national law are compatible with the requirements of Community law, whilst the second concerns whether, if the Member State concerned has transposed Article 6(2) into national law incorrectly, that provision satisfies the conditions which would enable an individual to rely on it before the national courts in circumstances such as those in the main proceedings".[123]

3–045

According to the circumstances of the case, the Court found that the implementing domestic provision was not compatible with the requirements of art.6(2) of the Directive. As to the direct effect of art.6(2) it noted that: "it is clear from the settled case-law of the Court that, whenever the provisions of a directive appear, so far as their subject-matter is concerned, to be unconditional and sufficiently precise, they may be relied upon before the national courts by individuals against the State where the latter has failed to implement the directive in domestic law by the end of the period prescribed or where it has failed to implement the directive correctly".[124]

Indeed, art.6(2) fulfilled all the conditions necessary to produce direct effect. However, the Court also acknowledged its case law that a directive cannot of itself impose obligations on an individual and cannot therefore be relied upon as such against an individual. Still, the objective of the directive is binding national authorities; it is the "the responsibility of the national courts in particular to provide the legal protection which individuals derive from the rules of Community law and to ensure that those rules are fully effective".[125]

"Thus, when it applies domestic law, and in particular legislative provisions specifically adopted for the purpose of implementing the requirements of a directive, the national court is bound to interpret national law, so far as possible, in the light of the wording and the purpose of the directive concerned in order to achieve the result sought by the directive and consequently comply with the third paragraph of Article 249 EC."[126]

---

[123] *Bernhard Pfeiffer* (C-397/01), *Wilhelm Roith* (C-398/01), *Albert Su\s* (C-399/01), *Michael Winter* (C-400/01), *Klaus Nestvogel* (C-401/01), *Roswitha Zeller* (C-402/01), *Matthias Dobele* (C-403/01) *v Deutsches Rotes Kreuz, Kreisverband Waldshut eV* [2004] E.C.R. I-8835, para.88.
[124] *Bernhard Pfeiffer* (C-397/01), *Wilhelm Roith* (C-398/01), *Albert Su\s* (C-399/01), *Michael Winter* (C-400/01), *Klaus Nestvogel* (C-401/01), *Roswitha Zeller* (C-402/01), *Matthias Dobele* (C-403/01) *v Deutsches Rotes Kreuz, Kreisverband Waldshut eV* [2004] E.C.R. I-8835, para.103.
[125] *Bernhard Pfeiffer* (C-397/01), *Wilhelm Roith* (C-398/01), *Albert Su\s* (C-399/01), *Michael Winter* (C-400/01), *Klaus Nestvogel* (C-401/01), *Roswitha Zeller* (C-402/01), *Matthias Dobele* (C-403/01) *v Deutsches Rotes Kreuz, Kreisverband Waldshut eV* [2004] E.C.R. I-8835, para.110.
[126] *Bernhard Pfeiffer* (C-397/01), *Wilhelm Roith* (C-398/01), *Albert Su\s* (C-399/01), *Michael Winter* (C-400/01), *Klaus Nestvogel* (C-401/01), *Roswitha Zeller* (C-402/01), *Matthias Dobele* (C-403/01) *v Deutsches Rotes Kreuz, Kreisverband Waldshut eV* [2004] E.C.R. I-8835, para.113.

National courts must look at the relevant specific provisions but also consider national law as a whole in order to assess to what extent it may be applied so as "not to produce a result contrary to that sought by the directive".[127]

The indirect effect of Community law has been equally influential in shaping the principle of "supremacy".

(3) The development of the "indirect effect" of Community law

3–046   The essence of the indirect effect of Community law is that national courts must interpret a national provision in a way that is compatible with the relevant Community legal context. From a negative perspective, the provision must not be in conflict with the Community legal order; viewed positively, it must seek to achieve the result sought by the corresponding Community legislation.

The "indirect effect" principle of interpretation of national law has become a popular route in the field of directives. It allows the Court to emancipate and empower a directive even if it has not been properly implemented at the national level. In *Von Colson*[128] the Court of Justice noted the obligations of Member States under art.10 EC regarding the attainment of the result envisaged by a directive according to art.249 EC and, building up the notion of an ongoing dialogue between "Community" courts, it attributed to national courts the responsibility of interpreting their own national law in the light and of the wording and purpose of a directive in order to achieve its binding effect. "It is for the national courts to interpret and apply the legislation adopted for the implementation of the directive in conformity with the requirements of community law, in so far as it is given discretion to do so under national law".[129]

As we have seen above *Von Colson*[130] involved a state authority; *Marleasing*[131] however expanded the "indirect effect" principle to cases involving individuals even where the disputed national provision predates the directive. Craig and De Búrca highlight a paragraph from the Opinion of A.G. Van Gerven as setting the parameters of the principle:

"The obligation to interpret a provision of national law in conformity with a directive arises whenever the provision in question is to any extent open to interpretation. In those circumstances the national court must, having

---

[127] *Bernhard Pfeiffer* (C-397/01), *Wilhelm Roith* (C-398/01), *Albert Sü\s* (C-399/01), *Michael Winter* (C-400/01), *Klaus Nestvogel* (C-401/01), *Roswitha Zeller* (C-402/01), *Matthias Dobele* (C-403/01) *v Deutsches Rotes Kreuz, Kreisverband Waldshut eV* [2004] E.C.R. I-8835, para.115; note the "negative" language chosen by the Court; the national court must ensure that the result is not contrary to the directive.
[128] *Von Colson and Kamann v Land Nordrhein-Westfalen* (14/83) [1984] E.C.R. 1891.
[129] *Von Colson and Kamann* (14/83) [1984] E.C.R. 1891, para.28.
[130] See 3–033 fn 86 above.
[131] *Marleasing SA* (C-106/89) [1990] E.C.R. I-4135.

5. THE INTERPRETIVE PRINCIPLES AND TECHNIQUES OF THE COURT

regard to the usual methods of interpretation in its legal system, give preference to the method which enables it to construe the national provision concerned in a manner consistent with the directive."[132]

Note that the Court of Justice ruled that the national Spanish court was precluded from interpreting national law in any way not complying with the directive.[133] According to the facts of the particular case the interpretation of the national law did not impose a legal obligation on either party; nevertheless, it shifted the balance because according to the directive the statute establishing the defendant legal entity could not be declared void as it would have been according to national law. The *Marleasing* line has been followed consistently by the Court of Justice; as we have seen above it has almost led to accepting that directives have incidental horizontal effects.[134]

(4) The competence of the Court of Justice—the acte clair doctrine

It is telling that regarding the legitimacy of requests for a preliminary ruling from national courts when a Court of Justice precedent does not exist, the Court of Justice has approached the issue from a negative perspective. The

3–047

---

[132] *Marleasing SA* (C-106/89) [1990] E.C.R. I-4135, para.8; Craig and De Búrca (2003), p.214, note "[e]ven if, as the Advocate general suggested it is essentially a matter for resolution in accordance with national principles of interpretation, the Treaty-derived obligation on national courts to take all measures possible to comply with Community law clearly constrains the interpretative discretion they would otherwise have under national law".

[133] As to whether the Court of Justice would require a national court to decide a case against its own national law in order to satisfy a directive the position is not yet settled. Some cases imply that a *contra legem* decision can be justified, *Marshall v Southampton and South-West Hampshire Area Health Authority* (C-271/91) [1993] E.C.R. I-4367 where the Court does not contradict the statement to that effect of A.G. Van Gerven. Other cases appear to imply the opposite, *Commission v UK* (C-300/95) [1997] E.C.R. I-2649, where the Court indirectly, at least, dismisses such an argumentation. In general the Court leaves it to national courts to decide whether national law can be interpreted according to a directive. Another limitation to "indirect effect" is that it cannot lead to retroactively imposed criminal liability; this has been expressed in a rather vague language in Luciano Arcaro (C-168/95) [1996] E.C.R. I-4705 that could appear to undermine the "indirect effect" principle in its entirety; see Craig, "Directives: Direct Effect, Indirect Effect and the Construction of National Legislation" (1997) 22 E.L.Rev. 519. A.G. Jacobs has subsequently commented on this point in *Centrosteel Srl v Adipol GmbH* (C-456/98) [2000] E.C.R. I-6007, point 35: "the national court must ... interpret national law, as far as possible, in the light of the wording and purpose of relevant directives. While that process of interpretation cannot, of itself and independently of a national law implementing the directive, have the effect of determining or aggravating criminal liability, it may well lead to the imposition upon an individual of civil liability or a civil obligation which would not otherwise have existed". The Court of Justice in its judgment applauded those national courts that had already interpreted national law according to the relevant directive and corresponding case law of the Court of Justice. In *Océano Grupo Editorial v Rocio Murciano Quintero* (C-240–244/98) [2000] E.C.R. I-4491 the Court even declared, para.32 that the "requirement for an interpretation in conformity with the Directive requires the national court, in particular, to favour the interpretation that would allow it to decline of its own motion the jurisdiction conferred on it by virtue of an unfair term".

[134] See 3–039 above.

Court of Justice has considered when a national court can refuse to make a reference in a *CILFIT* holding, that when the correct application of Community law is so obvious that it leaves "no scope for any reasonable doubt as to the manner in which the question raised is to be resolved"[135] that the national court does not have to make a court reference, provided that it is convinced that the matter is equally obvious to the courts of other Member States and to the Court of Justice. This approach has become know as the "acte clair" doctrine.

Determining whether a specific question constitutes an "acte clair" however is not a finding based on the intuition of the national court, the following must be considered in order to ensure that specific characteristics of Community law, the particular difficulties caused by its interpretation, and the risk of national divergences are taken into account: the different language versions of the provision, terminological peculiarities, the meaning of relevant legal concepts in Community law and national laws. Finally, the Community provision "must be placed in its context and interpreted in the light of the provisions of Community law as a whole, regard being had to the objectives thereof and to its state of evolution at the date on which the provision in question is to be applied".[136]

In jurisprudential terms *CILFIT* has been a particularly interesting decision; the Court covered two fundamental issues[137] by attempting a difficult balancing exercise between broadening its jurisdiction and strengthening its legitimacy.[138]

3–048 A national court can not itself decide that an act of a Community institution is invalid; the Court of Justice interpreted the lacuna of art.234 EC in a way that delivered to itself this jurisdictional advantage:

---

[135] *Srl CILFIT and Lanificio di Gavardo SpA v Ministry of Health* (238/81) [1982] E.C.R. 3415, para.16.
[136] *Srl CILFIT and Lanificio di Gavardo SpA* (238/81) [1982] E.C.R. 3415, para.20.
[137] See Brown & Kennedy (2000), p.393.
[138] Tellingly commentators have read *CILFIT* in different ways. Craig and De Búrca (2003) compare three influential articles. Mancini and Keeling, "From CILFIT to ERT: The Constitutional Challenge Facing the European Court" (1991) Y.B.E.L. 1 at 4, discuss the "the subtlety displayed by the Court ... together with an acute understanding of judicial psychology ... The Court, recognizing that it could not in any case coerce the national courts into accepting its jurisdiction concedes something—a great deal in fact, nothing less than the right not to refer if the Community measure is clear—to the professional or national pride of the municipal judge, but then ... restricts the circumstances in which the clarity of the provision may legitimately be sustained to cases so rare that the nucleus of its own authority is preserved intact". Arnull, "The Use and Abuse of Article 177" [now 234 EC] (1989) 52 M.L.R. 622, concludes, at 637, that English judicial practice illustrates how *CILFIT* can be used to justify refusing to make a reference in cases where the national court has chosen a particular interpretative path, it is "a serious matter when a decision of the European Court of Justice is used by the English Courts as a reason for failing to take a step which it might otherwise have been more difficult to avoid". Rasmussen, "Remedying the Crumbling EC Judicial System" (2000) 37 C.M.L.Rev. 1071, would like to see a CILFIT II that would allow national courts to view more Community acts as "actes clairs" by giving back to national judges the initiative to solve on their own less straightforward questions of interpretation of Community law.

5. THE INTERPRETIVE PRINCIPLES AND TECHNIQUES OF THE COURT

"In enabling national courts against whose decisions there is a judicial remedy under national law to refer to the Court for a preliminary ruling question on interpretation or validity, Article [234 EC] did not settle the question whether those courts themselves may declare that acts of Community institutions are invalid.

Those courts may consider the validity of a Community act and, if they consider that the grounds put forward before them by the parties in support of invalidity are unfounded, they may reject them, concluding that the measure is completely valid. By taking that action they are not calling the existence of the Community measure into question.

...

Since Article [234 EC] gives the Court exclusive jurisdiction to declare void an act of a Community institution, the coherence of the system requires that where the validity of a Community act is challenged before a national court the power to declare the act invalid must also be reserved to the Court of Justice.

...

It should be added that the rule that national courts may not themselves declare Community acts to be invalid may have to be qualified in certain circumstances in the case of proceedings relating to an application for interim measures..."[139]

(5) Looking for the essence of the question

Another technique commonly used by the Court is to search for the essence of the question referred to it; in some cases deservedly given the tendency of some national courts to pose detailed and unwieldy questions. In other cases, however, this could appear to function as a screen, allowing the Court to consider only some elements of the reference:

3–049

"the Court has power to extract from a question imperfectly formulated by the national court those questions which alone pertain to the interpretation of the Treaty. Consequently a decision should be given by the Court not upon the validity of [a national] law in relation to the Treaty, but

---

[139] *Firma Foto-Frost v Hauptzollamt Lübeck-Ost* (314/85) [1987] E.C.R. 4199, paras 13, 14, 17, and 19. In *Atlanta Fruchthandelsgesellschaft mbH v Bundesamt für Ernährung und Forstwirtschaft* (C-465/93) [1995] E.C.R. I-3761 the Court set the considerations that national courts must take into account before granting interim relief: there must be serious doubt about the validity of the Community measure, a reference must have been made to the Court of Justice (the decision of which must ultimately be respected by the national court), the relief must be necessary to prevent serious and irreparable damage to the claimant, Community interests must be taken into account. For recent reiterations of the acte clair doctrine see *Gaston Schul Douane-Expediteur BV v Minister van Landbouw* (C-461/03) [2005] E.C.R. I-105123; and *Intermodal Transports BV Financiën* (C-495/03) [2005] E.C.R. I-8151.

only upon the interpretation of the [relevant provisions for the Treaty] in the context of the points of law stated by the [national judge]."[140]

(6) Fundamental rights

3–050 The original Treaties focused on economic rather than political European integration. Wider integration had been considered in the 1950s but French reluctance to join a European Defence Treaty made economic development a much more fertile ground for the European adventure.[141] Economic integration though brought significant socio-political repercussions the effects of which became more visible and apprehensible though the doctrine of "direct effect". Economic measures affected and were affected by fundamental rights. This cross fertilisation has become acknowledged by the Treaty of the European Union. Article 6 adopted in Maastricht and amended in Amsterdam, declares that respect for fundamental rights and freedoms constitutes one of the pylons supporting the European Union; art.6(1) states "The Union is founded on the principles of liberty, democracy, respect for human rights and fundamental freedoms, and the rule of law, principles which are common to the Member States". Article 7 provides a mechanism for sanctioning Member States that violate these principles.

The role of the Court of Justice has once again been fundamental and multifaceted. Through the "direct effect" doctrine it made Member States realise that Community measures could undermine their national principles on fundamental rights. It responded by incorporating these principles into its interpretative tools that it then used in order to expand further the European Union's and its own jurisdiction into areas that Member States considered impenetrable.

At the beginning the Court of Justice was cautious, not because it doubted the value of the fundamental values invoked but rather because it worried about the "danger of subordinating EC law to national constitutional law".[142] In *Geitling* it declared that "Community law ... does not contain any general principle, express or otherwise, guaranteeing the maintenance of vested rights".[143]

---

[140] *Costa v Ente Nazionale per l'Energia Elettrica (ENEL)* (6/64) [1964] E.C.R. 585; see the comments of A.G. Ruiz Zarabo in *Koninklijke KPN Nederland NV* (C-363/99) [2004] E.C.R. I-1619.
[141] See Dauses, "The Protection of Fundamental Rights in the Community Legal Order" (1985) 10 E.L.Rev. 398; Trachtman, "L'Etat, C'est Nous: Sovereignty, Economic Integration and Subsidiarity", 33 Harvard Int. L.J. 459 (1992); and De Búrca, "The Constitutional Challenge of New Governance in the European Union" (2003) 28 E.L.Rev. 814.
[142] Craig and De Búrca (2003), p.320; there was concern regarding the source of the values, rather than the values themselves.
[143] The cases involved the ECSC Treaty; *Präsident Ruhrkolen-Verkaufsgesellschaft mbH, Geitling Ruhrkohlen-Verkaufsgesellschaft mbH, Mausegatt Ruhrkohlen-Verkaufsgesellschaft mbH and I. Nold KG v High Authority of the European Coal and Steel Community* (36, 37, 38 & 40/59) [1960] E.C.R. 423.

5. THE INTERPRETIVE PRINCIPLES AND TECHNIQUES OF THE COURT

Accordingly, fundamental, albeit national, principles could not override provisions of the Treaties.[144]

Gradually, though, the Court shifted its position. In *Stauder*[145] it looked at a specific claim from a comparative perspective. It considered the relevant measure, a decision of the Commission, in its different language versions concluding that the contested requirement was not necessary; in this way the conflict with the fundamental right involved could be avoided. At the same time, the comparative approach allowed the Court to refer to fundamental human rights in general without taking a stance as to their source. "Interpreted in this way the provision at issue contains nothing capable of prejudicing the fundamental human rights enshrined in the general principles of Community law and protected by the Court".[146]

3–051

The facts of subsequent cases did not give the Court similar space for manoeuvre. On the one hand the Court stressed that the validity or effect of a Community measure "can only be judged in the light of Community law ... [it] cannot be affected by allegations that it runs counter to either fundamental rights as formulated by the constitution of that State or the principles of a national constitutional structure".[147]

On the other, it also noted that "respect for fundamental rights forms an integral part of the general principles of Community law protected by the Court of Justice. The protection of such rights, whilst inspired by the constitutional traditions common to the Member States, must be ensured within the framework of the structure and objectives of the Community. It must therefore be ascertained ... whether [the relevant measure] has infringed rights of a fundamental nature, respect for which must be ensured in the Community legal system".[148]

Along similar lines the Court talked about inspiration from common constitutional traditions and guidelines from international treaties signed by the Member States.[149] In its case law the Court of Justice kept on applying

3–052

---

[144] *Sgarlata v Commission* (40/64) [1965] E.C.R. 215.
[145] *Stauder v City of Ulm* (29/69) [1969] E.C.R. 419. A German national successfully claimed that a Community scheme to give away butter to social security recipients in order to reduce surpluses violated the right to dignity because the beneficiaries had to declare their names and addresses.
[146] *Stauder* (29/69) [1969] E.C.R. 419, para.7.
[147] *Internationale Handelsgesellschaft v Einfuhr und Vorratstelle für Getreide und Futtermittel* (11/70) [1970] E.C.R. 1125, para.3.
[148] *Internationale Handelsgesellschaft* (11/70) [1970] E.C.R. 1125, para.3.
[149] See for example *Nold v Commission* (4/73) [1974] E.C.R. 491 for the general combined approach; *Rutili v Minister for the Interior* (36/75) [1975] E.C.R. 1219; and *Coote v Granada Hospitality* (C-185/97) [1998] E.C.R. I-5199 for principles and guidelines derived from the European Convention on Human Rights; *Ministère Public v Mutsch* (137/84) [1985] E.C.R. 2681 provides a more critical examination of the actual standards set by the ECHR, probably lower from the standards achieved in most Member States; *Hauer v Land Rheinland-Pfalz* (44/79) [1979] E.C.R. 3727; and *AM & S Europe Ltd v Commission* (155/79) [1982] E.C.R. 1575 for principles derived from common national legal traditions. For the "special significance" of the ECHR see *ERT v DEP* (C-260/89) [1991] E.C.R. I-2925 and Opinion 2/94 on Accession by the Community to the ECHR [1996] E.C.R. I-1759.

general principles of law by incorporating them into the Community legal order rather than individualising and developing specific rights on the basis of national constitutional norms or international obligations.

Here too, the approach of the Court is characterised by balancing exercises. For example in *Fedesa*[150] the Court held that the lawfulness of a prohibition of an economic activity should be subject to the condition that the prohibitory measures are appropriate and necessary in order to achieve the legitimate objectives pursued by the legislation and the disadvantages must not be disproportionate to the aims. Accordingly where there is a choice between alternative measures the least onerous should be the most appropriate. However, the Court added that:

> "with regard to judicial review of compliance with those conditions it must be stated that in matters concerning the common agricultural policy the Community legislature has a discretionary power which corresponds to the political responsibilities given to it by Articles 40 and 43 of the Treaty. Consequently, the legality of a measure adopted in that sphere can be affected only if the measure is manifestly inappropriate having regard to the objective which the competent institution is seeking to pursue".[151]

Tridimas identifies the following general principles of Community law on the basis of which a measure can be annulled by the Court:

(a) the right to judicial protection;

(b) the principle of equal treatment or non-discrimination;

(c) the principle of proportionality;

(d) the principle of legal certainty;

(e) the principle of the protection of legitimate expectations;

(f) the protection of fundamental rights;

(g) the rights of defence.

"These principles have constitutional status. They are binding on the Community institutions and a measure, whether legislative or administrative, which infringes one of them is illegal and may be annulled by the Court. They are also binding on Member States".[152]

---

[150] *R. v Ministry of Agriculture, Fisheries and Food Ex p. Federation Europeene de la Sante Animale (FEDESA)* (C-331/88) [1990] E.C.R. I-4023.
[151] *R. v Ministry of Agriculture, Fisheries and Food Ex p. Federation Europeene de la Sante Animale (FEDESA)* (C-331/88) [1990] E.C.R. I-4023, para.14.
[152] Tridimas, *The General Principles of EC Law* (Oxford University Press, 2006), p.6.

He notes that a common characteristic of the above principles is that "they have been derived by the Court from the laws of the Member States, sometimes with little assistance from the text of the Treaty".[153]

6. JUDICIAL REVIEW AND THE COMMUNITY TRADE MARK

(1) Arcol—the "institutional architecture" in trade mark cases

3–053

Conflicts concerning the registration of Community trade marks involve up to four levels of scrutiny: on the one hand, there is a two-tier administrative examination system within the OHIM, whereby parties are entitled to appeal unfavourable decisions of the departments dealing with the case at first instance to the Office's Boards of Appeal, which enjoy independence in the performance of their duties[154]; on the other hand, the Regulation also provides for the subsequent judicial review of the decisions of the Boards by the Community Judicature.

The scope of the decision-making powers of the Boards is laid down in art.62(1) CTMR (new art.64) according to which, in deciding on the appeal, the Boards may "either exercise any power within the competence of the department responsible for the decision appealed, or remit the case to that department for further prosecution".

That formulation, however, does not fully reveal the extent of the Boards' powers of review. In particular, it does not clarify whether the Boards have the right to re-examine the case ab initio, for example by taking into account facts and evidence produced for the first time before them, or whether their jurisdiction is actually confined to a mere re-assessment of the factual and legal matrix on which the first instance decision was based.

3–054

That issue reached the Court of Justice in *Arcol*,[155] by way of an appeal concerning the interpretation of art.74(2) CTMR (new art.76) which provides that the Office "may disregard facts or evidence not submitted in due time by the parties".

In that case, the appellant had produced new evidence before the Board of Appeal with a view to remedying the deficiencies in the substantiation of its opposition that had led to its rejection at first instance. The Board dismissed that evidence as belated, on the grounds that it had been filed after the expiry of the peremptory time limits provided for in the Implementing Regulation[156] in relation to opposition proceedings.

---

[153] Tridimas, *The General Principles of EC Law* (Oxford University Press, 2006), p.6.
[154] According to art.131(4) CTMR the President, Chairmen and Members of the Boards of Appeal are independent in the sense that "in their decisions they shall not be bound by any instructions".
[155] *OHIM/Kaul GmbH (ARCOL)* (C-029/05 P).
[156] Commission Regulation (EC) No 2868/95 of 13 December 1995, implementing Council Regulation No 40/94 on the Community trade mark, as revised and amended

THE COURT OF JUSTICE OF THE EUROPEAN COMMUNITIES

The appellant filed an action before the Community Courts seeking the annulment of the Board's decision. The Court of First Instance[157] granted the request. Referring to its settled case law,[158] it recalled that the "continuity in terms of functions" between the decision-making instances of OHIM actually "requires the Boards of Appeal to base their decisions on all the matters of fact and of law invoked by the parties either at first instance or, subject only to Article 74(2) CTMR [new art.76], in the appeal".

3–055   OHIM appealed to the Court of Justice arguing that art.62(1) CTMR (new art.64) does not require the Boards to take into account facts and evidence presented out of time and that such an interpretation of "functional continuity" would ultimately render the provisions relating to the fixing of time limits devoid of purpose.

The Court set the framework for its analysis by referring to the role of the various decision-making instances intervening at each stage of the proceedings and by comparing the scope of the examination performed by OHIM to the judicial review of its decisions carried out by the Community Courts.

3–056   **(i) The nature of the proceedings before the Boards of Appeal.** Dealing, first, with the nature of the proceedings before the Boards of Appeal, it stated that art.62(1) CTMR (new art.64) had to be interpreted in the light of the "institutional architecture" introduced by the Regulation,[159] while stressing that "in spite of the independence enjoyed by their members, the Boards remain nonetheless departments of OHIM".[160]

Thus, the Court considered that, when seized of an appeal, the Board is required to "give judgment on the case itself by either rejecting the relevant claim or declaring it to be founded, thereby either upholding or reversing the contested decision" and that "through the effect of the appeal brought before it, the Board of Appeal is called upon to carry out a new, full examination of the merits of the case, in terms of both law and fact".[161]

Accordingly, it found that "there was no reason of principle related to the nature of the proceedings before the Board that precludes it from taking into account facts produced for the first time at the appeal stage" and that unless otherwise specified, the various decision-making departments of the Office have "wide discretionary powers" to accept evidence filed late,[162] in particular where "the material produced late is, on the face of it, likely to be relevant to the outcome", provided however that "the stage of the

---

[157] *Kaul v OHIM – Bayer (ARCOL)* (T-164/02) [2004] E.C.R. II-3807, paras 25–34.
[158] *Procter & Gamble v OHIM (BABY-DRY)* (T-163/98) [1999] E.C.R. II-2383, paras 38–44; *Procter & Gamble v OHIM (Soap bar shape)* (T-63/01) [2002] E.C.R. II-5255, para.21; and *Henkel v OHIM LHS (UK) (KLEENCARE)* (T-63/01) [2003] E.C.R. II-3253, paras 24–32.
[159] para.55.
[160] para.51.
[161] paras 56–57.
[162] paras 41–43.

proceedings and the surrounding circumstances do not speak against such an acceptance".[163]

(ii) The nature of Court proceedings. Next, the Court contrasted the full re-examination performed by the Boards with the judicial review of their decisions, observing that pursuant to art.63(2) CTMR (new art.65) the Court of First Instance may annul or alter a decision of a Board of Appeal of OHIM only on grounds of lack of competence, infringement of an essential procedural requirement, infringement of the Treaty, of the Regulation or of any rule of law relating to their application, or misuse of power. 3–057

Hence, the Court inferred that the Court of First Instance has the power to "either annul or alter a decision against which an action has been brought only if, at the time that decision was adopted, it was vitiated by one of those grounds for annulment or alteration", which means that the Court of First Instance "may not annul or alter that decision on grounds which come into existence subsequent to its adoption".[164]

Accordingly, the Court concluded that the function of the Court of First Instance is "to assess the legality of the decision of the Board by reviewing the application of Community law made by it, particularly in the light of facts which were submitted to the latter; by contrast, that Court cannot carry out such a review by taking into account matters of fact newly produced before it".[165]

(2) Scope and limits of administrative and judicial review

It follows from *Arcol* that the jurisdictional differences between the Office and the Courts in trade mark registration cases are a direct consequence of their distinct institutional roles. While the subject-matter of proceedings before the Office is the complete examination of a ground of refusal pursuant to the Regulations, the object of the dispute before the Court is the Office's decision and the control of its legality, as delimited by the application for annulment. 3–058

(i) The scope of the administrative proceedings. In that regard, the Court of First Instance has referred to the scope of the "full" examination conducted by OHIM by stressing that "the criteria for applying a relative ground for refusal or any other provision relied on in support of arguments put forward by the parties are naturally part of the matters of law submitted for examination by OHIM. It should be borne in mind in this regard that a matter of law may have to be ruled on by OHIM even when it has not been raised by the parties if it is necessary to resolve that matter in order to 3–059

---

[163] para.44.
[164] para.53; citing *Sunrider v OHIM* (C-416/04 P) [2006] E.C.R. I-4237, paras 54–55.
[165] para.54; citing *Rossi v OHIM* (C-214/05 P) [2006] E.C.R. I-7057, para.50.

ensure a correct application of the Regulation having regard to the facts, evidence and arguments provided by the parties".[166]

Thus, although art.74(1) (new art.76) *in fine* of the Regulation requires the Office, at least when dealing with relative grounds of refusal, to "restrict its examination to the facts, evidence and arguments provided by the parties and the relief sought", this does not relieve it from the obligation to examine all the points of law and fact necessary for adjudicating on the matter pending before it.

In addition, the Court has held that art.74(1) CTMR (new art.76) does not preclude OHIM (or, mutatis mutandis, the Court), from also basing its conclusions, where appropriate, on "generally known facts arising from common experience, or on facts which may be obtained from generally accessible sources",[167] a statement equally valid for both absolute and relative grounds examination.

3–060 **(ii) The scope of judicial review.** On the other hand, the control of legality exercised by the judicature is more closely linked to the claims and pleas put forward in the action or in the appeal, while its main features are defined by the Courts' Rules of Procedure. In that sense, the Courts are not called upon to conduct a new, full examination of the case, by addressing points that were not raised in the application, but rather only to review the legality of the contested decision within the confines of, and for the reasons contained in, the application for annulment. As stressed by the Court, "if the applicant does not precisely indicate the contested elements which he seeks to have set aside, or give clear reasons and arguments to that effect, the relevant points cannot be examined".[168]

That obligation to clearly delimit the subject-matter of the dispute to the points raised in the action for annulment is imposed by art.225 EC and art.58 of the Statute of the Court, in conjunction with art.112(1) of its Rules of Procedure. Moreover, according to art.21 of the Statute and art.38(1)(c) of the same Rules (which is identical to art.44(1)(c) of the Rules of the Court of First Instance) the statement of the grounds of appeal must be sufficiently clear and precise to enable the defendant to exercise its right of defence and the Court to perform its control, without having recourse to extraneous information or supporting documents. Rather, all the essential matters of law and fact must be apparent from the text of the action itself.

Note that the Court tends to apply those requirements quite literally, considering that its role is not to "take the place of the applicant, or his

---

[166] *Société provençale d'achat et de gestion (SPAG) SA/OHIM* (HOOLIGAN/OLLY GAN)) T-57/03) [2005] E.C.R. II-287, para.21.
[167] *Develey Holding GmbH & Co Beteiligungs KG/OHIM* (PLASTIKFLASCHENFORM) (T-129/04) [2007] E.C.R. II-811, paras 19–22; and *Succession Picasso/OHIM* (PICASSO) (T-185/02) [2005] E.C.R. II-1739, para.29.
[168] *Il Ponte Finanziaria Spa /OHIM* (BAINBRIDGE) (C-234/06P) [2007] E.C.R. I-7333, para.44.

6. JUDICIAL REVIEW AND THE COMMUNITY TRADE MARK

counsel, by trying to locate and identify itself among the documents on the file the information which it might regard as supporting the claims formulated in the application".[169]

Exceptionally, however, the Court may annul a decision for reasons not raised by the claimant, notably when the contested decision is vitiated by a defect that infringes against procedure rules or principles relating to public order. In those cases, the Court not only can, but actually *must* raise the relevant ground of its own motion. Such types of inherent vice typically include formal deficiencies, the breach of the duty to state reasons, as well as all sorts of substantial procedural violations and omissions.[170]

3–061

The judicial review carried out by the Courts is also limited as to its effects by virtue of art.63(6) CTMR (new art.65), according to which the Office is required to take "all the necessary measures in order to comply with the judgments of the Community Courts". This means that although the Court has the competence to control the legality of the Office's decisions and to either annul, or amend them, as the case may be, it cannot take directly administrative measures or issue orders to the Office to perform a specific act, other than those clearly inherent in the annulment of its decision.[171]

Rather, it is for the Office to take the appropriate measures for complying with the Court's judgment, by deciding whether a separate decision of the Boards or another department is necessary to that effect. In practice, that means that where a decision of the Boards is annulled, but the Court has not fully and finally adjudicated on the substance of the dispute, the Office is bound to reopen the file and continue the prosecution of the case.[172]

(iii) The Appeal to the Court of Justice. The scope of the appeal to the Court of Justice is defined by art.225 EC and the first paragraph of art.58 of its Statute, according to which an appeal is limited to points of law only. As repeatedly stressed by the Court, it is the exclusive jurisdiction of the Court of First Instance to make findings of fact and to appraise the evidence when exercising its powers of review. Moreover, the Court has made clear that "that assessment does not, save where the clear sense of the evidence

3–062

---

[169] Order in *Koelman v Commission* (T-56/92) [1993] E.C.R. II-1267, para.23.
[170] *Institut für Lernsysteme GmbH / OHIM* (ELS) (T-388/00) paras 58–59.
[171] *Mitsubishi HiTec Paper Bielefeld GmbH/OHIM* (GIROFORM) (T-331/99) [2001] E.C.R. II-433, para.33; *Eurocool Logistik GmbH/OHIM* (EUROCOOL) (T-34/00) [2002] E.C.R. II-683, para.12; *José Alejandro, SL/OHIM* (BUDMEN/BUD) (T-129/01) [2007] E.C.R. II-2251, para.22; *Ampafrance SA/OHIM* (MONBEBE/BEBE) (T-164/03) [2005] E.C.R. II-1401, para.24.
[172] See in that connection art.1(d) of Commission Regulation (EC) No. 216/96, of 5 February 1996, laying down the Rules of Procedure of the Boards of Appeal of OHIM, according to which "if pursuant to Article 63 (6) of the Regulation, the measures necessary to comply with a Judgment of the Court of Justice annulling all or part of a decision of a Board of Appeal or of the Grand Board include re-examination by the Boards of Appeal of the case which was the subject of that decision, the Presidium shall decide if the case shall be referred to the Board which adopted that decision, or to another Board, or to the Grand Board".

has been distorted, constitute a point of law which is subject, as such, to review by the Court of Justice on appeal".[173]

Such a distortion occurs where the corresponding findings are demonstrably inaccurate and lead to errors of assessment capable of materially affecting the outcome. In that regard, the Court has pointed out that the resulting inaccuracy, omission or contradiction "must be obvious from the documents on file, without it being necessary to undertake a fresh assessment of the facts".[174] In other words, the alleged distortion can only become actionable if it is objectively manifest from the contents of the file, or where it is in apparent contradiction with facts or circumstances which are well-known to everyone.

The Court of Justice considers as questions of fact not only matters that are strictly connected to the factual sub-stratum of the case, but also assessments of mixed character, like those concerning the similarity between the signs or the goods, the existence of a reputation, the fulfilment of the requirement of genuine use, as well as the existence of a likelihood of confusion, detriment or unfair advantage.[175]

3–063 The strict application by the Court of art.58 of the Statute and its widespread tendency to summarily dismiss as inadmissible claims that relate to virtually every kind of assessment made in the context of trade mark examination, has led to the rejection of a high number of appeals filed against judgments of the Court of First Instance in intellectual property cases without addressing their merits.

It follows that while the review carried out by the Court of First Instance effectively involves a genuine reassessment of the findings of the Board, the role of the Court of Justice is strictly limited to examining whether the Court of First Instance has reached its decision by applying the correct legal norms, without however entering into the question whether the relevant rules are consistently applied to the facts. Rather, that assessment can only be invalidated if the judgment under appeal has failed to give sufficient reasons in support of its conclusions, or if its findings are manifestly inconsistent.

(3) The value of precedents

3–064 Another issue arising from the interaction between Community and national trade mark law is the extent to which prior decisions of administrative or judicial authorities in trade mark cases are binding on other such bodies dealing with identical or similar cases in the same or another Member State, or at Community level.

---

[173] *DKV v OHIM* (C-104/00 P) [2002] E.C.R. I-7561, para.22; and *Develey Holding GmbH & Co Beteiligungs KG/OHIM (shape of a plastic bottle)* (C-238/06P) [2007] E.C.R. I-9375, para.97.
[174] ECJ, Judgment of 8 May 2008, *Eurohypo* AG/OHIM (EUROHYPO) (Case C-304/06P).
[175] See, for instance, *alecansan SL/OHIM (CompUSA)* (C-196/06 P) [2007]; *Zipcar Inc., v OHIM (ZIPCAR/CICAR* (C-394/08 P) [2009]; and *Antarctica Srl v OHIM* (NASDAQ) (C-320/07 P) [2009].

6. JUDICIAL REVIEW AND THE COMMUNITY TRADE MARK

That question is particularly important in view of the harmonising objective of the Directive and its close similarity to the Community Trade Mark Regulation, especially since the parallel existence of Community and national trade mark rights covering the same sign often gives rise to a plurality of disputes within the European Union which have, essentially, the same subject-matter.

It has even been argued[176] that insofar as trade mark examination is inevitably encumbered by a considerable degree of subjectivity, the coherent application of trade mark law can only be guaranteed by extensively relying on the general principles of equality and legitimate expectations when deciding subsequent cases. That view thus advocates in favour of a strict adherence to precedents, as the only possible means of achieving a maximum degree of legal certainty and harmonisation under the Directive.

The Court, however, tends to take a more orthodox view: In a series of judgments, it has made abundantly clear that the principles of legitimate expectations and equal treatment cannot be given precedence over the correct application of the relevant legal provisions: first and foremost, the European Union is a community based on the rule of law, as clearly recognised by art.6 of the EC Treaty and as repeatedly confirmed by the Court of Justice.[177]

3–065

Hence, the application of the principle of equal treatment in trade mark conflicts and, by extension, the idea that the authority is always bound by its own acts, finds its limits in the rule of law, in the sense that there can be no equality in injustice.

Applying this maxim in administrative practice, the Court has also held that the publication of guidelines based on precedents cannot override legally binding provisions and that erroneous decisions can therefore not oblige the authority to apply the same standard in the future.[178]

As regards specifically the registration of Community trade marks, the Court has consistently held that "the decisions that OHIM is called on to take under the Regulation are adopted in the exercise of circumscribed powers and are not a matter of discretion" and that, accordingly, the legality of those decisions "must be assessed solely on the basis of the Regulation, as interpreted by the Community judicature and not on the basis of the previous decision-making practice of either OHIM or its Boards of Appeal".[179]

3–066

As a result, the Court systematically rejects claims based on the alleged violation of the principle of equal treatment by the Office or by the Court of

---

[176] See David T. Keeling, *Continuity and Change in EU Law: Essays in Honour of Sir Francis Jacobs* (2008), pp.283, 294.
[177] Judgment of 23 April 1986, *Les Verts/European Parliament* (C-294/83) [1986] E.C.R. 1339.
[178] *Adam PH Blomefield/Commission* (C-190/82) [1983] E.C.R. 3981; *Christos Michael/Commission* (C-343/82) [1983] E.C.R. 4023; *Claudia de Angelis/Commission* (C-246/83) [1986] E.C.R. 1253; *Mathilde Becker and Josyane Starquit/Parliament* (C-41/88) [1989] E.C.R. 3807.
[179] *BioID AG/OHIM (BioID)* (C-37/03 P) [2005] E.C.R. I-7975, para.47; *Deutsche SiSi-Werke GmbH & Co Betriebs KG/OHIM (STANDBEUTEL)* (C-173/04 P) [2006] E.C.R. I-551, para.48.

First Instance, as manifestly unfounded, without even addressing their merits.[180]

Similarly, the Court of First Instance has held that precisely because precedents are not binding, but mere factors that may be taken into consideration in assessing whether a sign is suitable for registration, the Boards of Appeal are not required to give specific reasons for the fact that they departed from a previous decision by another Board, in an identical or similar case.[181]

3–067 Essentially the same issue, but his time concerning national practice under the Directive, was brought before the Court of Justice in *Volkshandy*,[182] a request for a preliminary ruling asking whether national trade mark authorities are compelled, when applying an absolute ground of refusal, to give decisive value to prior registrations of signs composed of similar or identical elements.

The Court was not impressed. Answering by way of reasoned order, it merely made reference to its settled case law on the matter, before stressing once more that the competent authority "is not entitled to disregard the grounds of refusal laid down by Article 3(1)(b) and (c) of the Directive, or to accept the mark merely on the grounds that the sign applied for is structured in an identical or comparable manner to another mark that has already been registered by the same authority".

As concerns, finally, the interaction between Community and national law, the Court has additionally pointed out that national decisions cannot constitute valid precedents for Community authorities also because the regime introduced by the CTMR is "an autonomous system with its own set of objectives and rules peculiar to it, that applies independently of any national system".

3–068 Consequently, "the mark must be examined only on the basis of the relevant Community rules and the national decision can under no circumstances call in question the legality of either the contested decision or the judgment under appeal".[183]

The Court therefore takes the view that a prior decision can constitute a valid precedent only if it was correct in its own right; while the legality of the second decision eventually depends on its correct application of the law and not on its alignment with prior decisions. In the end, if the first decision is correct, it should be followed for that reason only and not because it is prior or binding; whereas if it is wrong, it simply must not be followed.

Thus, by practically reserving the final word in all legal matters for itself, the Court has effectively assumed the role of the absolute guardian of

---

[180] *Indorata-Serviços e Gestão, Lda/OHIM (HAIRTRANSFER)* (C-212/07P), para.44.
[181] *Paul Reber GmbH & Co KG/OHIM (MOZART/MOZART)* (T-304/06), para.53.
[182] *Bild digital GmbH & Co KG, ZVS Zeitungsvertrieb Stuttgart GmbH/Präsident des Deutschen Patent- und Markenamts* (C-039/08 & C-043/08), not yet published.
[183] *Develey Holding GmbH & Co Beteiligungs KG/OHIM (shape of a plastic bottle)* (C-238/06P) [2007] E.C.R. I-9375, paras 66–67.

7. CONCLUSION

Community trade mark law, to whom the privilege to shape up future developments and the responsibility to provide Europe with a harmonised system of trade mark law ultimately belongs.

7. CONCLUSION

To illustrate the interaction of the principles described above with the application of trade mark law the reader should consider, for example, the importance of the principle of legal certainty for the graphical representation requirement,[184] the trade mark proprietors reliance on the right of property in cases like *Anheuser-Busch*,[185] or the catalytic application of proportionality in cases involving consumer protection from deceptive use of distinctive signs.[186]

In setting the background for the analysis of the trade mark jurisprudence of the Court, three particular points discussed in this chapter must be underlined.

First, the provisions of the Directive and the Regulation can only be examined and interpreted in their specific and wider legislative context. The aim of a provision, its interrelationship with fundamental principles, its place within the Directive or the Regulation, and the broader rationale of trade mark law within the European project could be equally important with its literal wording.

Secondly, that in an integrated European Union the Directive and the Regulation should be seen as two parts that interact and complete the European trade mark regime according to the architecture of coexistence mentioned in Ch.2. Accordingly, the essentially identical substantive provisions of the Directive and the Regulation should be interpreted and applied by the Court in the same way. In addition, the Court would be expected to interpret the provisions of the Directive in a way that would bring the national trade mark regimes closer with each other and the Community Trade Mark Regulation.

Thirdly, the Court often relies in repeating statements and using them as paving stones to build up a judgment. As we will see in the case of trade marks their function has been the most commonly used one.

3–069

3–070

---

[184] See for instance the Opinion of the Advocate General in *Dyson Ltd v Registrar of Trade Marks* (C-321/03) [2003] E.C.R. I-687; the Opinion was posted on the website of the Court of Justice on September 14, 2006. This issue is discussed in Ch.4.
[185] *Anheuser-Busch Inc v Portugal* [2006] E.T.M.R. 43, discussed in Ch.10.
[186] See for instance *Pall Corp v P J Dahlhausen & Co* (C-238/89) [1990] E.C.R. I-4827, discussed in Ch.4.

CHAPTER 4

ABSOLUTE GROUNDS

1. Introduction	4–001
2. The Provisions of the Directive and the Regulation	4–003
(1) Article 2—signs of which a trade mark may consist	4–003
(2) Article 3—grounds for refusal or invalidity	4–004
(3) Article 7 of the Regulation	4–005
3. What is a Sign	4–006
(1) Dyson—the fundamental question	4–006
(2) Pre-Dyson jurisprudence—setting the ground	4–007
(3) Dyson—the fundamental requirement	4–013
4. Capable of being represented Graphically	4–031
(1) Sieckmann—the purpose of graphical representation—non-visual signs—scents—the general conditions	4–032
(2) Shield mark—graphical representation of sounds—general policy considerations	4–052
(3) Libertel—colour samples—public policy considerations	4–069
(4) Heidelberger Bauchemie—abstract combinations of colours	4–079
5. Capable of Distinguishing	4–086
(1) Philips—setting the principles	4–086
(2) Capable of distinguishing—the limited effect of article 3(1)(a)	4–095
(3) Some guidelines for interpreting article 3	4–097
6. Article 3(1)(b)—Devoid of any Distinctive Character	4–103
(1) Companyline—article 7(1)(b)—balancing between Baby-Dry and Postkantoor	4–103
(2) "SAT.2"—back to Baby-dry?	4–117
(3) BioID—the limited effect of "SAT.2"	4–133
(4) Nichols—no special conditions for surnames	4–152
(5) Erpo—registrability of slogans	4–161
(6) Libertel?the distinctiveness of colours	4–175
(7) Heidelberger Bauchemie—combinations of colours—replaying Libertel	4–190
(8) KWS—colours—broader functionality considerations	4–193
(9) Mag—distinctive character of shapes of products	4–200
(10) Linde, Winward, and Rado—products shapes—a broader perspective	4–215
(11) Henkel—the assimilation of packaging and product shapes	4–228

	(12) Glaverbel—aesthetic functionality?	4–241
	(13) The washing tablets cases	4–243
	(14) SiSi-Werke—article 7(1)(b) and packaging	4–279
	(15) Eurocermex–article 7(1)(b), three-dimensional shapes, and the concept of a product	4–301
	(16) Storck I—the shape of a sweet	4–311
	(17) Storck II—the distinctive character of packaging	4–320
7.	Article 3(1)(c)—Descriptive Signs or Indications	4–346
	(1) Windsurfing Chiemsee—geographical names—setting the general principles	4–346
	(2) Baby-Dry—composite words—a permissive approach	4–355
	(3) Doublemint—a more nuanced approach	4–375
	(4) Postkantoor—a parallel approach	4–394
	(5) Streamserve—consolidating Doublemint	4–421
	(6) Telefon & Buch—following Doublemint	4–432
	(7) BVBA—challenging the procedural points of Postkantoor	4–439
	(8) Matratzen—article 3(1)(c) and free movement of goods considerations	4–459
	(9) Celltech—burden of proof: technical and scientific terms	4–464
	(10) Develey—burden of proof: consumer goods	4–468
8.	Article 3(1)(d)—Signs or Indications that have become Customary	4–471
	(1) Bravo—the link with the specification	4–471
	(2) Alcon—article 7(1)(d) and acronyms	4–483
	(3) Procordia—expanding the class of persons determining Distinctiveness	4–492
9.	Article 3(1)(e)—Functional Shapes	4–503
	(1) Philips—the overriding scope of article 3(1)(e)	4–503
	(2) Benetton—attractiveness v distinctiveness	4–514
10.	Article 3(1)(g)—Trade Marks of a Deceptive Nature	4–521
	(1) Elizabeth Emanuel—trade mark assignments	4–521
	(2) Free movement of goods and deceptive use	4–538
11.	Article 3(1)(h)—State Emblems	4–561
	(1) Maple Leaf—applicability of article 6ter to services	4–561
12.	Article 3(2)(d)—Bad Faith	4–578
	(1) Lindt & Sprüngli—what is bad faith?	4–578
13.	Article 3(3)—Distinctive Character Acquired Through Use	4–589
	(1) Windsurfing Chiemsee—the test for assessing acquired to distinctive character	4–589
	(2) Philips—reinforcing Windsurfing Chiemsee	4–698
	(3) Kit-Kat—combined use	4–602
	(4) Storck I—article 7(3)—sales figures—amount spent on advertising	4–608

(5)	Storck II—sales figures in abstract	4–620
(6)	Europolis—acquired distinctive character in the Benelux—linguistic and geographical considerations	4–627
(7)	Pure Digital—the relevant point in time	4–638
14. Conclusion		4–645

1. INTRODUCTION

This chapter will examine the jurisprudence of the Court of Justice on what can function and be protected as a trade mark. **4–001**

The provisions of the Directive and the Regulation appear quite permissive: there is no definition of the concept of a sign and the list in art.2 is open ended. The key for obtaining trade mark protection is distinctiveness; nevertheless the concept possesses a split personality. Article 2 requires the sign to be capable of distinguishing, whereas art.3(1)(b) demands the trade mark made up by the sign that is capable of distinguishing not to be devoid of any distinctive character. At the same time distinctiveness acquired through use can overcome an objection based on art.3(1)(b) but not one based on art.2.

There is also a special provision dealing with shapes rather than the external appearance of a product, aiming to maintain "functional" shapes outside the scope of exclusive trade mark rights.

The possibility of obtaining trade mark protection for new types of signs meant the Community and national Trade Mark Offices were inundated with applications, with some of them intending to test the limits of the new regime and a small number bordering on irreverence.

The Court of Justice had to deal within a limited, at least from a broader historical perspective, period of time with references from national courts that felt the need to apply their trusted principles rather than adopt a more liberal approach. Some were particularly concerned about the combination of a broader scope of protection with an expansive list of signs. They sensed, indeed German courts had already experienced it in the past, that this could lead to more conflicts and uncertainty in the market place. **4–002**

As if this were not enough the Court had also to function as the ultimate arbiter for Community Trade Mark applications; its role was to consider legal issues rather than examine actual facts, nevertheless we all know how difficult it is to separate legal principles from factual scenarios in the application of trade mark law.

The intent for this chapter is to build around a logical rather than historical structure, attempting to answer some basic questions regarding registrability through the case law of the Court following the text of the Directive.

Initially, the Court appeared to vacillate between contradictory routes: the first was described in *Windsurfing Chiemsee*[1]; the second, which appeared to be a fast track towards registration, in *Baby-Dry*.[2]

2. THE PROVISIONS OF THE DIRECTIVE AND THE REGULATION

(1) Article 2—signs of which a trade mark may consist

4–003 A trade mark may consist of any sign capable of being represented graphically, particularly words, including personal names, designs, letters, numerals, the shape of goods or of their packaging, provided that such signs are capable of distinguishing the goods or services of one undertaking from those of other undertakings.

(2) Article 3—grounds for refusal or invalidity

4–004 1. The following shall not be registered or if registered shall be liable to be declared invalid:
   a. signs which cannot constitute a trade mark;
   b. trade marks which are devoid of any distinctive character;
   c. trade marks which consist exclusively of signs or indications which may serve, in trade, to designate the kind, quality, quantity, intended purpose, value, geographical origin, or the time of production of the goods or of rendering of the service, or other characteristics of the goods;
   d. trade marks which consist exclusively of signs or indications which have become customary in the current language or in the bona fide and established practices of the trade;
   e. signs which consist exclusively of:
      — the shape which results from the nature of the goods themselves, or
      — the shape of goods which is necessary to obtain a technical result, or
      — the shape which gives substantial value to the goods;
   f. trade marks which are contrary to public policy or to accepted principles of morality;

---

[1] *Windsurfing Chiemsee Produktions- und Vertriebs GmbH v Boots- und Segelzubehör Walter Huber and Franz Attenberger* (C-108/97 & C-109/97) [1999] E.C.R. I-2779; see paras 4–336 and following.

[2] *Procter & Gamble Co v Office for Harmonisation in the Internal Market (Trade Marks and Designs)* (C-383/99 P) [2001] E.C.R. I-6251; see paras 4–355 and following.

2. THE PROVISIONS OF THE DIRECTIVE AND THE REGULATION

g. trade marks which are of such a nature as to deceive the public, for instance as to the nature, quality or geographical origin of the goods or service; and

h. trade marks which have not been authorised by the competent authorities and are to be refused or invalidated pursuant to art.6ter of the Paris Convention for the Protection of Industrial Property, hereinafter referred to as the "Paris Convention".

2. Any Member State may provide that a trade mark shall not be registered or, if registered, shall be liable to be declared invalid where and to the extent that:

   a. the use of that trade mark may be prohibited pursuant to provisions of law other than trade mark law of the Member State concerned or of the Community;

   b. the trade mark covers a sign of high symbolic value, in particular a religious symbol;

   c. the trade mark includes badges, emblems and escutcheons other than those covered by art.6ter of the Paris Convention and which are of Public interest, unless the consent of the appropriate authorities to its registration has been given in conformity with the legislation of the Member State; and

   d. the application for registration of the trade mark was made in bad faith by the applicant.

3. A trade mark shall not be refused registration or be declared invalid in accordance with para.1(b), (c) or (d) if, before the date of application for registration and following the use which has been made of it, it has acquired a distinctive character. Any Member State may in addition provide that this provision shall also apply where the distinctive character was acquired after the date of application for registration or after the date of registration.

4. Any Member State may provide that, by derogation from the preceding paragraphs, the grounds of refusal of registration or invalidity in force in that State prior to the date on which the provisions necessary to comply with this Directive enter into force, shall apply to trade marks for which application has been made prior to that date.

(3) Article 7 of the Regulation

1. The following shall not be registered: 4–005

   (a) signs which do not conform to the requirements of Article 4;

   (b) trade marks which are devoid of any distinctive character;

(c) trade marks which consist exclusively of signs or indications which may serve, in trade, to designate the kind, quality, quantity, intended purpose, value, geographical origin or the time of production of the goods or of rendering of the service, or other characteristics of the goods or service;

(d) trade marks which consist exclusively of signs or indications which have become customary in the current language or in the bona fide and established practices of the trade;

(e) signs which consist exclusively of:
- (i) the shape which results from the nature of the goods themselves; or
- (ii) the shape of goods which is necessary to obtain a technical result; or
- (iii) the shape which gives substantial value to the goods;

(f) trade marks which are contrary to public policy or to accepted principles of morality;

(g) trade marks which are of such a nature as to deceive the public, for instance as to the nature, quality or geographical origin of the goods or service;

(h) trade marks which have not been authorized by the competent authorities and are to be refused pursuant to Article 6ter of the Paris Convention;

(i) trade marks which include badges, emblems or escutcheons other than those covered by Article 6ter of the Paris Convention and which are of particular public interest, unless the consent of the appropriate authorities to their registration has been given;

(j) trade marks for wines which contain or consist of a geographical indication identifying wines or for spirits which contain or consist of a geographical indication identifying spirits with respect to such wines or spirits not having that origin;

(k) trade marks which contain or consist of a designation of origin or a geographical indication registered in accordance with Regulation (EEC) No 2081/92 when they correspond to one of the situations covered by Article 13 of the said Regulation and regarding the same type of product, on condition that the application for registration of the trade mark has been submitted after the date of filing with the Commission of the application for registration of the designation of origin or geographical indication.

2. Paragraph 1 shall apply notwithstanding that the grounds of non-registrability obtain in only part of the Community.

3. Paragraph 1(b), (c) and (d) shall not apply if the trade mark has become distinctive in relation to the goods or services for which registration is requested in consequence of the use which has been made of it.

3. WHAT IS A SIGN

(1) Dyson—the fundamental question

4–006 Until *Dyson*[3] the Court of Justice had not dealt directly with the issue of what constitutes a sign. *Dyson*, a reference from the High Court of the United Kingdom, provided the Court with an opportunity to consider the question.

The contested sign was described in the broadest possible terms as a "transparent bin or collection chamber forming part of the external surface of a vacuum cleaner as shown in the representation" that was a representation of Dyson's vacuum cleaners. Vacuum cleaners were included in the specification of the application. The High Court sought from the Court to interpret art.3(3) of the Directive.

However the Commission in its intervention submitted a new argument: the application should be rejected for failing the fundamental requirement of being a sign under art.2; it covered a concept rather than a sign; a clear collection chamber for a vacuum cleaner that was not capable of perception by one of the five senses. In addition it claimed that the representations of the concept did not satisfy the *Sieckmann*[4] requirements for graphical representation since, in principle, they did not correspond to any particular shape.

The Court decided to stay proceedings in the interests of the proper administration of justice because the Court of First Instance was dealing with the same issue regarding two parallel applications for Community Trade Marks, because "it is common ground that Article 2 of Directive 89/104 and Article 4 of Regulation No 40/94, which are drafted in almost identical terms, must be given and are in fact given the same interpretation".[5] The applications were withdrawn and the Court of First Instance decided not to adjudicate.[6] As a result the Court revived the original case.

(2) Pre-Dyson jurisprudence—setting the ground

4–007 Elements of this fundamental, at least in terms of theory,[7] question had also been covered by the Court in two ways. First, in its general discussions on

---

[3] *Dyson Ltd v Registrar of Trade Marks (CLEAR BIN)* (C-321/03) [2007] E.C.R. I-687.
[4] *Sieckmann v Deutsches Patent-und Markenamt* (C-273/00) [2002] E.C.R. I-11737.
[5] C-321/03 R [2004] E.C.R. 000, para.14.
[6] *Dyson Ltd v Office for Harmonisation in the Internal Market (Trade Marks and Designs)* (T-278/02) [2002] OJ C-289/28.
[7] In *Philips Electronics NV v Remington Consumer Products Ltd* [1998] R.P.C. 283, Jacob J. asked the question: "What is a 'sign'? Can the thing itself also be a 'sign'? If one is not careful one is likely here to end up discussing metaphysical points—hardly the sort of thing appropriate for a law designed for men of commerce. I think a 'sign' is anything which can convey information.

the structure of art.3(1)[8] and, second, through its attempts to clarify the specific relationship between signs that are "not capable of distinguishing" according to art.3(1)(a)[9] and signs that are devoid of any distinctive character according to art.3(1)(b).[10]

Finally in *Sieckmann*[11] there were two particular points that could be linked with the question of what constitutes a sign.

The first was made by A.G. Ruiz-Jarabo Colomer who appeared to indicate that in principle any message capable of perception by the senses could function as a trade mark.[12]

The second formed part of the judgment of the Court. It found that a chemical formula was not a sufficient representation of a scent, partly because it represented the substance itself rather than its odour,[13] although this distinction had not been clearly identified as a condition for satisfying the graphical representation requirement.

(a) Libertel—the relevance of "context"

4–008 In *Libertel*,[14] a case that concerned the registrability of a colour per se, A.G. Léger remarked that although the questions submitted to the Court centred on the interpretation of art.3, the starting point should be whether a colour per se fell within the meaning of art.2. The Court should expand the scope of the enquiry[15] and "consider whether [art.2] ... should be interpreted as meaning that a colour per se, without any shape or contour, constitutes a sign capable of being represented graphically and of distinguishing the goods and services of one undertaking from those of other undertakings".[16]

I appreciate that this is extremely wide, but I can see no reason to limit the meaning of the word.... What I conclude is confirmed by recital 7(b), which emphasises the necessity to list the examples of 'sign'—note the contrast with recital 7(c) which sets out the need to list the grounds of invalidity 'in an exhaustive manner'. You need the examples of a sign to see just how wide the meaning is. What the examples have in common is the ability to convey information. At this point it does not matter what sort of information is conveyed. It is the proviso to Recital 7(b), 'capable of distinguishing', which serves to limit the sort of sign which can be registered. Here, on my findings of fact, the picture does convey a message ... So it is a 'sign'."

[8] See paras 4–086 and following.
[9] Through its reference to signs which cannot constitute a trade mark.
[10] See paras 4–103 and following below.
[11] *Sieckmann* (C-273/00) [2002] E.C.R. I-11737.
[12] *Sieckmann* (C-273/00) [2002] E.C.R. I-11737, point 21.
[13] *Sieckmann* (C-273/00) [2002] E.C.R. I-11737, para.69.
[14] *Libertel Groep BV v Benelux-Merkenbureau* (C-104/01) [2003] E.C.R. I-3793.
[15] This was feasible because according to the Court's case law it is its duty to interpret all provisions of Community law which referring courts need in order to decide the actions pending before them, even if those provisions are not expressly indicated in the questions referred to it; *Finanzamt Kassel-Goethestrasze v Kommanditgesellschaft Viessmann* (C-280/91) [1993] E.C.R. I-971; *Wolfgang Lange v Georg Schunemann GmbH* (C-350/99) [2001] E.C.R. I-1061; and *Robin Swaddling v Adjudication Officer* (C-90/97) [1999] E.C.R. I-1075.
[16] *Libertel Groep BV* (C-104/01) [2003] E.C.R. I-3793, point 35.

3. WHAT IS A SIGN

Colour was a sensation rather than a pre-existing objective reality; its perception would vary according to the circumstances of its experience. On the other hand colour functioned as a language, provoking feelings, and conveying information. In all cases however colours did not exist independently, they were the attributes of something else.

The Court accepted that it was necessary to start its analysis from art.2 which set three conditions for a colour to be registered as a trade mark. First, it had to be a sign. Secondly, that sign should be capable of graphic representation. Thirdly, it should be capable of distinguishing the goods or services of one undertaking from those of other undertakings.[17]

It ruled that a colour carried within it the potential to satisfy the "sign" requirement:

> "Normally a colour is a simple property of things. Yet it may constitute a sign. That depends on the context in which the colour is used. None the less, a colour per se is capable, in relation to a product or service, of constituting a sign."[18]

(b) *Postkantoor—article 2 and signs in abstract*

In *Postkantoor*,[19] however, the Court appeared to adopt a different stance regarding the purpose of art.2; the difference is immaterial once the provision is positioned within the bigger structure of the Directive where the sign rediscovers its context in art.3(1)(b). Still, the wording chosen appears contradictory:

4–009

> "The purpose of Article 2 . . . is to define the types of signs of which a trade mark may consist, irrespective of the goods or services for which protection might be sought. It provides that a trade mark may consist inter alia of words and letters, provided that they are capable of distinguishing the goods or services of one undertaking from those of other undertakings".[20]

(c) *Philips—linking the concept of the sign with graphical representation and distinctiveness*

Postkantoor should probably be read in the light of the earlier judgment of the Court in *Philips*[21] where the Court of Justice provided a framework, the most comprehensible so far, for interpreting art.3(1).

4–010

---

[17] The Court agreed with the A.G. that the Joint Declaration OHIM OJ 5/96, p.607, did not affect the interpretation of the provision. See paras 25 and 26 of the judgment.
[18] *Libertel Groep BV* (C-104/01) [2003] E.C.R. I-3793, para.27.
[19] *Koninklijke KPN Nederland NV v Benelux-Merkenbureau* (C-363/99) [2004] E.C.R. I-1619.
[20] *Koninklijke KPN Nederland NV* (C-363/99) [2004] E.C.R. I-1619, para.80.
[21] *Koninklijke Philips Electronics NV v Remington Consumer Products Ltd* (C-299/99) [2002] E.C.R. I-5475.

Part of it was the recognition that art.2 provided that all signs satisfying its two requirements, capable of distinguishing and of being represented graphically, could become registered trade marks.

Article 3(1)(a) excluded "signs which are not generally capable of being a trade mark and thus cannot be represented graphically and/or are not capable of distinguishing the goods or services of one undertaking from those of other undertakings".[22]

To provide a meaning for the term "generally" it linked art.3(1)(a) with art.3(1)(b), art.3(1)(c), and art.3(1)(d): ". . . Article 3(1)(a) . . . like the rule laid down by Article 3(1)(b), (c) and (d), precludes the registration of signs or indications which do not meet one of the two conditions imposed by Article 2 of the Directive, that is to say, the condition requiring such signs to be capable of distinguishing the goods or services of one undertaking from those of other undertakings".[23]

(d) Nichols—the "list of examples"

4–011 The list of art.2 should not be seen as limiting the types of signs that can function, and as a result be protected, as trade marks.

In *Nichols*,[24] where the Court considered the conditions for the registration of surnames, it stated: "Article 2 . . . contains a list, described as a 'list of examples' in the seventh recital in the preamble to that Directive, of signs which may constitute a trade mark, provided that such signs are capable of distinguishing the goods or services of one undertaking from those of other undertakings, that is to say to fulfil the trade mark's function as an indicator of origin."[25]

(e) Sieckmann—the non-exhaustive character of the list

4–012 In *Sieckmann*,[26] the first case that tested the registrability of a non-visual sign, the Court added that the art.2 list was a list of examples, thus not exhaustive ". . . as is clear from the language of both Article 2 of the Directive and the seventh recital in the preamble thereto, which refers to 'a list [of] examples' of signs which may constitute a trade mark, that list is not exhaustive. Consequently, that provision, although it does not mention signs which are not in themselves capable of being perceived visually, such as odours, does not, however, expressly exclude them".[27]

---

[22] *Koninklijke Philips Electronics NV* (C-299/99) [2002] E.C.R. I-5475, para.37.
[23] *Koninklijke Philips Electronics NV* (C-299/99) [2002] E.C.R. I-5475, para.38.
[24] *Nichols Plc v Registrar of Trade Marks* (C-404/02) [2004] E.C.R. I-8499.
[25] *Nichols Plc* (C-404/02) [2004] E.C.R. I-8499, para.22.
[26] *Sieckmann* (C-273/00) [2002] E.C.R. I-11737.
[27] *Sieckmann* (C-273/00) [2002] E.C.R. I-11737, para.44.

3. WHAT IS A SIGN

(3) Dyson—the fundamental requirement

(a) The legal background

As mentioned above the Court of Justice came back to the reference of the High Court once the Community Trade Mark applications were withdrawn. 4–013

By the time *Dyson* came back before the Court, the Court had ample opportunity to consider distinctiveness and functionality in relation to almost every type of sign; functionality considerations had influenced its case law both on the graphical representation and the distinctiveness requirements. Overall, but not without contradictions, the Court appeared to adopt a more restrictive approach.

Dyson posed a dilemma to the Court; would it enhance and formalise this approach transforming art.3(1)(e) into a public policy doctrine, would it confront the question of what constitutes a sign, or would it choose to decide the case on the basis of the graphical representation requirement?

The questions regarding the registrability of the shape of the Dyson vacuum cleaner came before the Court as a reference from the English High Court.[28] Dyson had applied in the United Kingdom for the registration of a sign consisting of a transparent plastic container that was the central element of its bagless vacuum cleaners functioning as a dirt collector. There were two applications that shared a common description: "The mark consists of a transparent bin or collection chamber forming part of the external surface of a vacuum cleaner as shown in the representation". The applications depicted a representation of a Dyson model with a transparent bin; a different model was used for each application. The specification covered "apparatus for cleaning, polishing and shampooing floors and carpets; vacuum cleaners; carpet shampooers; floor polishers; parts and fittings for all the aforesaid goods" in Class 9 of the Nice Agreement. 4–014

The applications were rejected at the Trade Mark Registry, the sign being considered devoid of any distinctive character and serving to designate the kind and the intended purpose of the specified products. Dyson appealed before the High Court, which agreed with the Registry and raised an additional point regarding the monopoly that Dyson would obtain in the event of a successful application. Looking at the evidence of distinctiveness acquired through use it noted that consumers associated the container with the product in a market where Dyson enjoyed a de facto monopoly; inevitably this created a link with Dyson. However the sign as such had never been promoted as a trade mark.

Accordingly the national court stayed proceedings and referred the following questions to the Court:

---

[28] *Dyson Ltd's TM Application* [2003] R.P.C. 47.

"1. In a situation where an applicant has used a sign (which is not a shape) which consists of a feature which has a function and which forms part of the appearance of a new kind of article, and the applicant has, until the date of application, had a de facto monopoly in such articles, is it sufficient, in order for the sign to have acquired a distinctive character within the meaning of Article 3(3) of Directive 89/104/EEC, that a significant proportion of the relevant public has by the date of application for registration come to associate the relevant goods bearing the sign with the applicant and no other manufacturer?

2. If that is not sufficient, what else is needed in order for the sign to have acquired a distinctive character and, in particular, is it necessary for the person who has used the sign to have promoted it as a trade mark?"[29]

(b) The opinion of the Advocate General

4–015 Advocate General Léger started his analysis by taking up an issue raised by the Commission: was the particular mark applied for capable of constituting a trade mark in the first place under art.2 of the Directive?

4–016 **(i) The first requirement: what constitutes a sign.** The first requirement imposed by art.2 was that the mark applied for should constitute a sign. The Advocate General reminded the Court that "the purpose of that requirement is in particular to prevent the abuse of trade mark law in order to obtain an unfair competitive advantage".[30]

He found the bin to be "first and foremost functional and utilitarian",[31] it replaced vacuum cleaner bags and filters and in addition functioned as an indicator of fullness. He added that it also possessed an aesthetic function to the extent that it formed an integral part of the appearance of a product.

Advocate General Léger agreed with the Commission that what Dyson sought to protect was in essence a concept for collecting, storing and emptying waste. Looking for the meaning of "concept"—a general and abstract mental representation of an object[32]—he noted that "when a concept is developed, it can lead to the creation of a wide range of objects".[33] Accordingly, the application sought to obtain exclusive rights over all possible appearances of a functional feature; indeed the two representations of the mark applied for registration on the application form showed two distinct containers:

"The protection claimed is not limited to a shape, a composition, or a particular arrangement since this feature must only form part of the

---

[29] Reproduced under point 24 of the Opinion of A.G. Léger, *Dyson Ltd (CLEAR BIN)* (C-321/03) [2009] ECR I-697 (Dyson Ltd (CLEAR BIN)).
[30] Point 44 of the Opinion of A.G. Léger, citing in particular para.24 of *Heidelberger Bauchemie (Colours blue and yellow)* C-49/02 [2002] E.C.R. I-6129.
[31] Point 46 of the Opinion of A.G. Léger.
[32] *Le Petit Robert, Dictionnaire de la Langue Française* (Paris, Éditions Dictionnaires Le Robert, 2004).
[33] Point 48 of the Opinion of A.G. Léger.

external surface of the vacuum cleaner and allow the user to see through the container. There are many possibilities as regards the shape, the dimensions, the presentation and even the composition of that collection chamber in relation to the product in question, depending not only on the vacuum cleaner models developed by the applicant, but also on technological innovations. As far as transparency is concerned, it allows many colours to be used."[34]

The Advocate General accepted the argument that a concept appealed to our imagination rather than our senses. And because our imagination could not be limited, the multitudiness of potential forms a concept could take was in conflict with the essential function of a trade mark that required some sort of stability that a concept could not satisfy. A trade mark had to enable the consumer, without any possibility of confusion, to distinguish the marked product or service from others which have another origin; this objective could not be "achieved by a sign which is capable of being perceived by human beings in such diverse ways. As a result, a concept cannot, in my opinion, constitute an indication for the consumer and, consequently, cannot be a sign capable of fulfilling a trade mark's distinguishing function".[35] 4–017

Note that the Advocate General appeared to admit that the particular concept could be a sign in the first place; however, for the purposes of trade mark law he linked the sign requirement with the distinguishing function in order to deny trade mark protection based on the lack of the most fundamental requirement of art.2, "a functional feature like that at issue in the present case is not capable of constituting a sign within the meaning of Article 2".[36]

(ii) The second requirement—graphical representation. Advocate General Léger supported that the applications also failed the second requirement, that a trade mark might consist only of signs capable of being represented graphically. 4–018

According to *Sieckmann*,[37] art.2 required the sign to be represented visually, particularly by means of images, lines or characters, so that it could be precisely identified and defined. This would enable the determination of the precise subject of protection and contribute to legal certainty. Accordingly the representation had to be clear, precise, self-contained, easily accessible, intelligible, durable and objective.[38]

---

[34] Point 51 of the Opinion of A.G. Léger.
[35] Point 54 of the Opinion of A.G. Léger. Note that in *Libertel Groep BV* (C-104/01) [2003] E.C.R. I-3793 the Advocate General had remarked that for colours we employ our feelings to conceive them.
[36] Point 55 of the Opinion of A.G. Léger.
[37] *Sieckmann* (C-273/00) [2002] E.C.R. I-11737. See para.4–031, below.
[38] The Advocate had already made the point in *Heidelberger Bauchemie GmbH* (C-49/02) [2004] E.C.R. I-6129 that the graphical representation requirement had a dual objective: first to allow the competent authorities to know with clarity and precision the nature of the signs in order to

Instead of identifying which of the above conditions were not satisfied the Advocate General then chose to refer to *Heidelberger Bauchemie*[39] where the Court had distilled some of them into a requirement that a sign should be represented unambiguously and uniformly. This, together with the durability requirement, was what such a functional feature failed to fulfil: "... the functionality for whose registration Dyson is applying can clearly take on a multitude of different shapes and appearances which will depend not only on the vacuum cleaner models developed by the applicant, but also on technological developments. In so far as the protection conferred by the trade mark right can be for an unlimited duration ... it is highly likely, in my view, that the appearance of the transparent collecting bin and the way in which it is integrated into the vacuum cleaner will change over the years".[40]

4-019 Note, the use of the term "functionality" to describe the feature for which protection was sought.

The imprecision of the graphic representation on how the bin would actually be integrated into the product went against the principle of legal certainty on which the graphical representation requirement was founded.

4-020 **(iii) The third requirement—capable of distinguishing.** Advocate General Léger suggested that the application should also fail the distinctiveness requirement.

Here, his analysis was based on the distinction between distinctive character in general—the requirement that the sign could serve to identify the product as originating from a particular undertaking, and thus to distinguish that product from goods of other undertakings[41]—and intrinsic distinctive character—the assessment of which should be independent of the use of the sign, depending solely on whether the sign was capable in itself of having a distinctive character. Article 2 required intrinsic distinctive character.

Functionality was again the determinative factor. What had to be assessed was whether the functional feature served to convey precise information as to the origin of the product. The answer should be negative for two reasons.

4-021 First, it was not possible to determine with any certainty how "that functionality will be integrated into the products for which registration is sought ... an assessment of whether or not a sign is capable of having a distinctive character requires that one should be able to know exactly what the sign is".[42]

---

carry out the examination of an application for registration and maintain an appropriate and precise register; and, secondly, to enable third parties to identify with clarity and precision what is already protected.

[39] *Heidelberger Bauchemie GmbH* (C-49/02) [2004] E.C.R. I-6129, para.31 in particular.
[40] Point 62 of the Opinion of A.G. Léger.
[41] Citing *Windsurfing Chiemsee Produktions- und Vertriebs GmbH v Boots- und Segelzubehör Walter Huber and Franz Attenberger* (C-108/97 & C-109/97) [1999] E.C.R. I-2779; and *Linde AG, Winward Industries Inc and Rado Uhren AG* (C-53/01 to C-55/01) [2003] E.C.R. I-3161.
[42] Point 70 of the Opinion of A.G. Léger, citing his Opinion in *Libertel Groep BV* (C-104/01) [2003] E.C.R. I-3793.

Secondly, the "functionality" in question would not be able to indicate to consumers the origin of the marked product. Here, the application sought to protect a concept or, at least, all possible appearances it could take; "it is not possible to take the view that a functional feature like that at issue in the main proceedings can have a sufficiently precise meaning to indicate the origin of the product without any possible confusion".[43]

(iv) Functionality—the application of article 3(1)(e). The Advocate General added that even if the Court were to adopt the opposite position regarding art.2, the functionality provision of the Directive, art.3(1)(e), should preclude registration. The application concerned a shape—or a graphic representation of that shape according to *Philips*[44]—that was necessary to obtain a technical result. 4–022

He reminded the Court that in *Philips* the Court found that art.3(1)(e) was intended to prevent the extension of trade mark protection beyond signs which served to distinguish a product from those offered by competitors, "so as to form an obstacle preventing competitors from freely offering for sale products incorporating such technical solutions or functional characteristics in competition with the proprietor of the trade mark".[45] The second indent of the provision in particular, that should also be applied in the current case, required that "a shape whose essential characteristics perform a technical function is not reserved to one undertaking alone and may be freely used by all".[46] He noted that the availability of other shapes that could achieve the same result would not affect the application of that ground. The Court had also precluded the application of art.3(3) for signs originally covered by art.3(1)(e).

(v) Article 3(1)(e)—beyond shapes? Potentially expanding the scope of the provision beyond three-dimensional signs the Advocate General stated: "... it is clear that this reasoning applies legitimately to a functional feature which forms part of the appearance of a product. Although that article refers only to signs which consist exclusively of the shape of a product, I think that the general interest which underlies that provision requires that registration of a functionality like that at issue in the main proceedings be refused".[47] 4–023

Advocate General Léger developed four lines of supporting arguments.

First, registration of the particular "functionality" would mean that according to art.5(1) the trade mark proprietor could reserve for itself the exclusive use of a technical solution, potentially without any time limitation.

---

[43] Point 73 of the Opinion of A.G. Léger.
[44] Citing para.76 of *Koninklijke Philips Electronics NV* (C-299/99) [2002] E.C.R. I-5475.
[45] Point 83 of the Opinion of A.G. Léger.
[46] Point 84 of the Opinion of A.G. Léger.
[47] Point 88 of the Opinion of A.G. Léger.

4–024 The effect in this case would be "a monopoly on a technical and functional feature which a consumer is likely to seek in bagless vacuum cleaners manufactured by competing undertakings".[48]

Secondly, since the exclusive right would cover a multitude of shapes the functional feature might take, competing undertakings would be unable to determine precisely whether and how they might still use that feature. "Granting such a monopoly would therefore be likely to restrict their freedom excessively in a sector where technical progress is based on a process of ongoing improvement of earlier innovations."[49] Ultimately, such a monopoly might prevent new players from entering the particular product market, wipe out competition in innovative ideas, and harm free competition. All these would be against the aims of the Directive and the EC Treaty.[50]

The third line of argument was based on TRIPs; following the case law of the Court in *Hermès*[51] and *Heidelberger Bauchemie*[52] he underlined that the second indent of art.3(1)(e) should be interpreted so far as possible in the light of the wording and purpose of TRIPs.

Article 7 of TRIPs provided that: "The protection and enforcement of intellectual property rights should contribute to the promotion of technological innovation and to the transfer and dissemination of technology, to the mutual advantage of producers and users of technological knowledge and in a manner conducive to social and economic welfare, and to a balance of rights and obligations". The Advocate General supported that the wider context drawn for intellectual property rights by that provision precluded the protection of such a feature under trade mark law.

4–025 **(vi) Trade marks and other IP rights: policy considerations.** Accordingly, the Advocate General discussed the relationship between trade mark and other intellectual property rights.

Trade mark registration "could result in a situation where exclusive rights are acquired or perpetuated through trade mark law over inventions which are in reality patentable, contrary to the legitimate objective pursued by Article 3(1)(e), second indent, of the directive".[53]

The application of trade mark law should not result to an "unfair competitive advantage".[54] He agreed with the referring court that the function of a trade mark was not to create a monopoly in new developments in technology.

---

[48] Point 90 of the Opinion of A.G. Léger.
[49] Point 92 of the Opinion of A.G. Léger.
[50] Citing in particular art.3(g) and (m) EC referring, respectively, to "... a system ensuring that competition in the internal market is not distorted" and the "the strengthening of the competitiveness of Community industry".
[51] *Hermès v FHT Marketing Choice BV* (C-53/96) [1998] E.C.R. I-3603.
[52] *Heidelberger Bauchemie GmbH* (C-49/02) [2004] E.C.R. I-6129.
[53] Point 95 of the Opinion of A.G. Léger.
[54] Point 96 of the Opinion of A.G. Léger.

3. WHAT IS A SIGN

4–026 Citing *HAG II*[55] and *BMW*[56] he noted that the jurisprudence of the Court of Justice viewed trade marks as an essential element in the system of undistorted competition envisaged by the Treaty; Community legislature pursued the same aim through the adoption of the Directive. However, he reminded the Court that trade mark protection was potentially unlimited in terms of duration, and some undertakings might attempt to circumvent the time limitations of other intellectual property rights through the attainment of trade mark rights. Technological innovations he supported should be achieved only through the grant of a patent and not through a trade mark. He concluded that "Article 3(1)(e), second indent, of the directive precludes the registration as a trade mark of a functional feature which forms part of the appearance of a product".[57]

Closing his analysis he reminded the Court that art.3(3) could not affect the application of art.3(1)(e).

4–027 **(vii) The conclusions of the Advocate General.** Given the potential importance of the Opinion of the Advocate General it is worth reproducing in full the suggested conclusions of the Advocate General:

"(1) A visible functional feature of a product which is capable of taking on a multitude of appearances does not fulfil the necessary conditions to constitute a trade mark within the meaning of Article 2 of [the Directive] since it does not constitute a sign capable of being represented graphically and capable of distinguishing goods and services of one undertaking from those of other undertakings.

(2) In any event, Article 3(1)(e), second indent, of [the Directive] precludes the registration as a trade mark of a visible functional feature of a product."[58]

Note the reference to "visible functional features" rather than three-dimensional signs.

(c) The judgment of the Court

4–028 **(i) Resetting the Ground.** The High Court had sought from the Court of Justice to interpret art.3(3) of the Directive, the provision on distinctiveness acquired through use.

However, the Court turned its attention to the definition of a trade mark. In its recitation of the factual background of the case it highlighted the finding that consumers recognised the transparent bin as an indication of a

---

[55] *SA CNL-SUCAL NV v Hag GF AG* (C-10/89) [1990] E.C.R. I-3711.
[56] *Bayerische Motorenwerke AG and BMW Nederland BV v Deenik* (C-63/97) [1999] E.C.R. I-905.
[57] Point 102 of the Opinion of A.G. Léger.
[58] Point 106 of the Opinion of A.G. Léger.

bagless vacuum cleaner; it was advertising and the lack of any rival products that indicated that bagless vacuum cleaners were manufactured by Dyson. In itself, the bin had not been actively promoted as a trade mark.

It acknowledged that the two questions concerned the interpretation of art.3(3) of the Directive. However as it had become clear during the hearing that the trade mark application covered all conceivable shapes of a transparent collecting bin forming part of the external surface of a vacuum cleaner, the Court decided to focus on art.2 of the Directive. The Court noted:

> "As Dyson has stated on a number of occasions both in its written observations and at the hearing, and as the national court itself noted in its order for reference, the application does not seek to obtain registration of a trade mark in one or more particular shapes of transparent collecting bin—the shapes represented graphically on the application form being only examples of such a bin—but rather to obtain registration of a trade mark in the bin itself. It is, moreover, common ground that those marks consist not of a particular colour, but rather in the absence of any particular colour, namely transparency, which enables the consumer to see how much dust has been collected in the collecting bin and to know when the bin is full."[59]

The Court should not be precluded from providing the national court with all the elements for the interpretation of Community law that might contribute to the adjudication of the case pending before it.[60]

4–029   **(ii) The "sign" requirement.** The Court repeated that the list of signs mentioned in art.2 was purely indicative. However, it added, "if that condition is not to be deprived of all substance, it cannot be accepted that the subject-matter of any trade mark application necessarily constitutes a sign ...".[61] It agreed with the Advocate General that the purpose of the requirement was in particular to prevent the abuse of trade mark law in order to obtain an unfair competitive advantage.

In this case, the subject-matter of the application consisted of all the conceivable shapes of a collecting bin. Accordingly, it was not capable of being perceived visually; the two representations were, as accepted by Dyson, examples of the subject-matter rather than specific signs. It appears that the Court considered relevant for the interpretation of art.2 the multitude of different appearances the subject-matter could take rather than its inability to be visually perceived.

---

[59] *Dyson Ltd (CLEAR BIN)* (C-321/03) [2007] E.C.R. I-687, para.19.
[60] Citing *Weigel* (C-387/01) [2004] E.C.R. I-4981; and *Ritter-Coulais* (C-152/03) [2006] E.C.R. I-1711.
[61] *Dyson Ltd (CLEAR BIN)* (C-321/03) [2007] E.C.R. I-687, para.33.

4. CAPABLE OF BEING REPRESENTED GRAPHICALLY

The Court noted that the purpose of art.2 was in particular to prevent the abuse of trade mark law in order to obtain an unfair competitive advantage.

Turning to the facts of the case it stressed that the subject-matter of the application in the main proceedings was not a particular type of transparent collecting bin but, in a general and abstract manner, all its conceivable shapes.

4–030

The two graphic representations could not be assimilated to the subject-matter of the application because, "as pointed out by Dyson on a number of occasions, they are merely examples of it".[62] The subject-matter of the application "is capable of taking on a multitude of different appearances and is thus not specific".[63]

The Court further agreed with the Advocate General that what could make the subject-matter specific—i.e. its shape, dimensions, presentation and composition—depended on the models developed by Dyson and technological innovations. Transparency on the other hand meant that a variety of colours could be used. So, an exclusive right over such non-specific subject-matter would give an unfair competitive advantage to its owner who would be entitled to prevent its competitors from marketing vacuum cleaners incorporating any kind of transparent bin on their external surface.

As a result the Court concluded that art.2 "is to be interpreted as meaning that the subject-matter of an application for trade mark registration, such as that lodged in the main proceedings, which relates to all the conceivable shapes of a transparent bin or collection chamber forming part of the external surface of a vacuum cleaner, is not a 'sign' within the meaning of that provision and therefore is not capable of constituting a trade mark within the meaning thereof".[64]

4. CAPABLE OF BEING REPRESENTED GRAPHICALLY

The first fundamental requirement that a sign has to satisfy in order to gain registered trade mark protection is to be capable of being represented graphically.

4–031

So far, the Court has considered the conditions for satisfying this requirement in a number of cases involving both visual and non visual signs.

(1) Sieckmann—the purpose of graphical representation—non-visual signs—scents—the general conditions

Here the Court took four considerable interpretive steps forward. First, it described the underlying reasoning and the function of the graphical

4–032

---

[62] *Dyson Ltd (CLEAR BIN)* (C-321/03) [2007] E.C.R. I-687, para.36.
[63] *Dyson Ltd (CLEAR BIN)* (C-321/03) [2007] E.C.R. I-687, para.37.
[64] *Dyson Ltd (CLEAR BIN)* (C-321/03) [2007] E.C.R. I-687, para.40.

representation requirement; secondly, it unequivocally accepted that non-visual signs could be represented graphically; thirdly, it looked at ways for representing scents; and, fourthly, in doing so, it came up with the general conditions that had to be satisfied in order to fulfil the requirement.

Sieckmann[65] was a reference by the German Federal Patents Court (Bundespatentgericht). It was a trade mark practitioner who triggered the case. Sieckmann had applied to register a scent as a trade mark for services in classes 35, 41, and 42, including "legal services", "advertising", "education", "entertainment and sporting and cultural activities", "providing of food and drink", "medical, hygienic and beauty care", and "veterinary and agricultural services".

The sign was described in a number of ways:

"... the pure chemical substance methyl cinnamate (= cinnamic acid methyl ester), whose structural formula is set out below. Samples of this olfactory mark can also be obtained via local laboratories listed in the Gelbe Seiten (Yellow Pages) of Deutsche Telekom AG or, for example, via the firm E. Merck in Darmstadt.

$C6H5 - CH = CHCOOCH3$."[66]

A verbal description of the scent as "balsamically fruity with a slight hint of cinnamon" had been added to the application and a container with a sample of the scent had also been attached.

4-033 A declaration of consent to an inspection of the files relating to the deposited mark had also been filed together with the application.

The application was originally rejected because the sign (i) was not capable of constituting a trade mark and of being represented graphically; and (ii) lacked distinctive character.

On appeal the Bundespatentgericht took a more enlightened approach and held that in principle scents might be capable of distinguishing but referred to the Court of Justice two questions regarding graphical representation.

4-034 First, it enquired whether the graphical representation requirement of art.2 of the Directive allowed the registration only of signs that could be reproduced directly in their visible form rather than signs, like odours, that could not be perceived visually per se but could be reproduced indirectly.

Secondly, in case the more liberal approach were to be followed by the Court, whether the same requirement would be satisfied (a) by a chemical formula; (b) by a description; (c) by means of a deposit; or (d) by a combination of the above mentioned reproductions.

---

[65] *Sieckmann* (C-273/00) [2002] E.C.R. I-11737.
[66] Reproduced in para.11.

4. CAPABLE OF BEING REPRESENTED GRAPHICALLY

(a) The Opinion of the Advocate General

Advocate General Ruiz-Jarabo Colomer viewed the two questions as a plea from the national court to clarify the concept of a "sign capable of being represented graphically", in particular the possibility and the conditions for registering an odour as a trade mark.

4–035

To answer the question he had to start from a review of the functions of a trade mark from a wider, than the purely legal, perspective, linking capability to distinguish with consumer's freedom to choose and effective competition.[67] From a consumer's perspective this meant identifying goods and services by their origin and quality.[68]

(i) Trade marks: fiats of communication.

4–036

"The matter is thus one of establishment of a dialogue between manufacturer and consumer... A trade mark is in reality communication. Communication means one person imparting something that he knows to another. Consequently, every act of communication requires a sender, a message, a medium or channel for its transmission, and a recipient who can decipher or decode it. The code in which it can be expressed depends on the type of decoder the recipient uses to receive, comprehend and assimilate it... perception of signs by consumers can be as varied as the senses at their disposal."[69]

(ii) The viewpoint of the individual sensing the sign.

In principle, any message capable of perception by the senses could function as a trade mark.[70]

4–037

However, because taste and touch were inextricably linked with the article they referred to and could not be perceived independently from it, A.G. Ruiz-Jarabo Colomer limited the signs that prima facie could function

---

[67] Citing *SA CNL-SUCAL NV v Hag GF AG* (C-10/89) [1990] E.C.R. I-3711; and *Merz and Krell GmbH & Co v Deutches Patent-und Markenamt* (C-517/99) [2001] E.C.R. I-6959 as precedents on the function of a trade mark.

[68] He cited the Opinion of A.G. Cosmas in *Windsurfing Chiemsee Produktions- und Vertriebs GmbH v Boots- und Segelzubehör Walter Huber and Franz Attenberger* (C-108/97 & C109/97) [1999] E.C.R. I-2779 and, in more general terms Fernández Novoa, "Fundamentos de Derecho de Marcas" Editorial Montecorvo, (1984), pp.46–49; and Baylos Corroza, "Tratado de derecho industrial", Editorial Civitas, (2nd edn, 1993), p.817, who linked the distinguishing function with the origin function by supporting that the aim is not to identify a product with one undertaking in particular, but to indicate that all products bearing the same trade mark originate from the same manufacturer, regardless of that manufacturer's identity.

[69] Points 19, 20, and 21. The A.G. referred amongst others to Maniatis, "Scents as Trademarks: Propertisation of Scents and Olfactory Poverty" in Bently and Flynn (eds), *Law and The Senses–Sensational Jurisprudence* (Pluto Press, 1996), pp.217–235; and Polasso, La Comunicación Inteligente in Humaniora, website of the Faculty of Arts at the University of Göteborg (*http://www.hum.gu.se*), p.61 and following on how humans communicate and the communicative value of trade marks.

[70] Through a reference to Goethe's *Preface for his Theory of Colours* (republished by MIT Press, 1970) the A.G. describes the interplay between our senses and the variety of ways that we can perceive nature.

as trade marks to those that can be perceived independently and spatially: visual, auditory, and olfactory signs.[71]

On the other hand he suggested that tactile, visual, and auditory signs were easier to comprehend because they related to the concept of shape and form whereas taste and olfactory signs lacked precise rules for determining their content.[72]

He warned, however, against sweeping generalisations because, at the end, the description of all signs depended on the perception of the individual sensing them. He hinted, for example, that, because of their numerous variations, colours and scents would pose similar problems.

4-038   (iii) **Visual and olfactory signs.** The major relevant difference between visual and olfactory signs was that whereas "the eye sees not just colours, but also shapes, the sense of smell only permits perception of the colour of an odour and never its outline. The sense of sight operates over a wider range and therefore has a wider range of perception".[73]

Still, there was no doubt, according to the Advocate General, that the sense of smell could fulfil an identification function.[74]

For the Advocate General the obstacle that a scent could not overcome was the graphical representation requirement of art.2.

4-039   (iv) **The reasoning underlying the graphical representation requirement.** The reason behind the graphical representation requirement was legal certainty. The public register had to depict the "nature and scope of the signs ... the symbols so claimed must be known very precisely so

---

[71] Perot-Morel, "Les Difficultés Relatives aux Marques de Forme et à quelques Types Particuliers de Marques dans le Cadre Communautaire", Rivista di Diritto Industriale, Year XLV (1996), Pt 1, 247, had made that distinction.

[72] Referring to Laligant, "Des Oeuvres aux Marches du Droit d'Auteur: les Oeuvres de l'Esprit Perceptibles par l'Odorat, le Goût et le Toucher", Revue de Recherche Juridique, Droit Prospectif, 1992, No.1.

[73] Point 28, referring to "Diderot's Notes on Painting" in *Diderot on Art–1* (Yale University Press, 1995), p.196.

[74] Searching for examples in the world of literature the A.G. mentioned Baudelaire's poem Le Parfum (from *Les Fleurs du Mal*, Ed. Gallimard (La Pléiade), 1971, p.39) to the sensory triggers behind Proust's à la Recherche du Temps Perdu (Bloom (ed.), *Remembrance of Things Past* (Chelsea House Publishers, 1987)) and in particular the scent of madeleines (Doubrousky, La Place de la Madeleine, "écriture et fantasme chez Proust", Ed. Mercure de France, Paris, 1974) or the scent of public toilets in the Champs élysées (Beckett, Proust, Ed. Nostromo, 1975). From a more practical legal perspective the Advocate General mentioned the "plumeria blossom" and registration for sewing thread and embroidery yarn granted in the United States, (see *In Re Clarke*, 17 U.S.P.Q. 2d 1238 (TTAB 1990)) the one-off registration of the smell of freshly-cut grass as a Community Trade Mark (see Case R156/199862 *Venootschap onder Firma Senta Aromatic Marketing's Application* [1999] E.T.M.R. 429), the change in the position of the United Kingdom's Patent and Trade Mark Office that had registered scents for car tyres and dart flights but rejected the scent of cinnamon for furniture (*John Lewis of Hungerford Ltd's Trade Mark Application*) [2001] R.P.C. 28), the more permissive approach of the Benelux Trade Mark Registry that allowed the registration of scents for cosmetic products, and the possibility of protecting a fragrance under copyright in France (see *L'Oréal SA v Bellure NV* [2006] E.C.D.R. 16 C d'A (Paris)).

4. CAPABLE OF BEING REPRESENTED GRAPHICALLY

that other people may be properly guided. For reasons of legal certainty, the requirement of graphical representation is thus linked with the identification function, the primary and essential function of trade marks",[75] that also justified the exclusive nature of the right.

(v) The conditions for fulfilling the graphical representation requirement. The concept of "graphical representation" required drawing the sign on paper "in a comprehensible manner, since comprehension is a precondition of discernment".[76] It must be: 4–040

> "complete, clear and precise . . . and intelligible to those persons having an interest in inspecting the register, in other words other manufacturers and consumers".[77]

Alas, a scent could not be drawn on paper.

(vi) Representing a scent. Examining the alternatives indicated in the reference he noted that the chemical formula represented the substance itself rather than the odour of the substance. In addition it lacked clarity and precision and it would be intelligible by very few individuals. Finally, according to concentration, the ambient temperature, or the substance bearing the odour the same substance could emit different scents according to the circumstances. 4–041

Describing the sign in written language was a graphical representation but it would fail the requirements of clarity and precision. Juxtaposing designs with music, colours, and scents he suggested that designs could be described with objectivity. The description of scents, in this case, was more subjective and therefore relative.[78] The terms "balsamically" and "fruity" exemplified this. Similarly, the "slight hint of cinnamon" lacked information regarding intensity. A longer, more detailed, description would face similar problems. Language on its own was unable to objectively describe a scent.

Depositing a sample of the scent could be permissible but did not constitute a graphical representation; and in any case the scent of the sample would change with time.

The combination of all these ways would only create more uncertainty. Increasing the messages intended to identify the sign would increase the risk of different interpretations. 4–042

However, he refrained from excluding scents as such from registrability. In the future it might become possible to describe a scent adequately. "It is

---

[75] Point 36 of the Opinion of A.G. Ruiz-Jarabo Colomer.
[76] Point 37. For the A.G. distinctive character and graphical representability shared a common purpose: enabling the products on the market to be selected by potential buyers on the basis of their origin. The graphical representation of distinctive signs had to be such as to allow users of the register to distinguish between the protected signs.
[77] Point 38 of the Opinion of A.G. Ruiz-Jarabo Colomer.
[78] For example the same wine was described in different ways, fn.56 of the Opinion.

ABSOLUTE GROUNDS

not necessary expressly to exclude certain signs from legal provisions regarding trade marks. They exclude themselves, because they are unable to comply with the requirements of trade mark law."[79]

(b) The judgment of the Court

4–043   **(i) The context of article 2.** The Court started its analysis from the context of art.2, reminding us that according to the Tenth Recital "the function of the protection afforded by a trade mark is in particular to guarantee the mark as an indication of origin".[80] It added that the essential function of a trade mark was to guarantee the identity of the origin of the marked product by enabling the consumer or end-user, without any possibility of confusion, to distinguish that product from those with a different origin, and that in order to achieve this the trade mark should offer a guarantee that all the goods or services bearing it had been manufactured or supplied under the control of a single undertaking which was responsible for their quality.[81]

Registration was the key element of trade mark protection. "The registration system constitutes an essential element of their protection, which contributes, in respect of both Community law and the different national laws, to legal certainty and sound administration."[82]

Trade mark rights could also be obtained through use at the national level however the Directive applied only to registered trade marks and the Community Trade Mark system was based on registration.

4–044   **(ii) Article 2—non-visual signs.** Within this context the Court had to consider whether art.2 covered signs not capable of being perceived visually. It admitted that the list of examples in art.2 referred only to visual signs but it was clear from the language of the provision and the Seventh Recital that the list was not exhaustive and that art.2 did not expressly exclude non visual signs. A trade mark "may consist of a sign which is not in itself capable of being perceived visually, provided that it can be represented graphically".[83]

4–045   **(iii) The underlying reasons and the conditions for the graphical representation requirement.** The main requirement the Court set for graphical representation was that it had to enable the sign to be represented visually, particularly by means of images, lines or characters, so that it can be precisely identified. The Court gave a number of reasons for this

---

[79] Point 45 of the Opinion of A.G. Ruiz-Jarabo Colomer.
[80] *Sieckmann*, para.34.
[81] Citing *Frits Loendersloot v George Ballantine & Son* (C-349/95) [1997] E.C.R. I-6227; *Canon Kabushiki Kaisha v Metro-Goldwyn-Mayer Inc* (C-39/97) [1998] E.C.R. I-5507; and *Koninklijke Philips Electronics NV* (C-299/99) [2002] E.C.R. I-5475.
[82] *Sieckmann* (C-273/00) [2002] E.C.R. I-11737, para.37.
[83] *Sieckmann* (C-273/00) [2002] E.C.R. I-11737, para.45.

4. CAPABLE OF BEING REPRESENTED GRAPHICALLY

requirement, which, in turn, constitute the eight conditions a graphical representation has to satisfy.

Graphical representation: clear and precise. The first two conditions were clarity and precision. They were necessary because graphic representation defined the mark in order to determine the precise subject of protection and its inclusion in a public register informed the competent authorities—that had to fulfil obligations regarding examination of applications, publication of registrations, and maintenance of a register—and the public, particularly economic operators—that should be able to locate information about the rights of their existing or potential competitors. 4–046

Graphical representation: self contained, accessible, and intelligible. The second set of conditions, namely that the graphical representation had to be self-contained, easily accessible and intelligible, aimed to enable users of the register determine the precise nature of a mark on the basis of its registration. 4–047

Graphical representation: durable. Durability, the sixth condition, was linked with the indication of origin function of a trade mark. Trade marks rights were potentially perpetual and the signs that constitute them must always be perceived unambiguously and in the same way. 4–048

Graphical representation: unequivocal and objective. The last two conditions were that the graphical representation had to be unequivocal and objective and they intended to avoid any element of subjectivity in the process of identification and perception of the sign. 4–049

Representing olfactory scents. The Court then considered whether an olfactory sign would have been represented adequately in the ways mentioned by the referring court against the general framework it had constructed. 4–050

The chemical formula was rejected by the Court, first, because it would not be sufficiently intelligible, secondly, because it represented the substance itself rather than its odour, and, third, because it was not sufficiently clear and precise.

Note that the second ground appears to be essentially new or at least not developed in detail as part of the general framework. Perhaps it functions as an indication of how the Court would deal with the question of what constitutes a sign.

The description of the odour was graphic, but lacked in clarity, precision, and objectivity. 4–051

The deposit of the sample did not constitute a graphic representation and it was not sufficiently stable—again something not directly mentioned in the general framework—or durable.

Finally, the combination of the above would fail to satisfy the requirements set by the Court, in particular the conditions of clarity and precision.[84]

(2) Shield mark—graphical representation of sounds—general policy considerations

4-052 The next type of signs that the Court had to consider in relation to the graphical representation requirements was sounds. It followed the conditions it had adopted in *Sieckmann*[85]; however, it is becoming apparent that wider policy considerations, like the scope of protection, the expansion of protectable types of signs, or the relation between trade mark and copyright law, are gaining relevance when applying the graphical representation requirement.

Shield Mark[86] was a reference from the Netherlands by the Hoge Raad (Supreme Court of the Netherlands). Shield Mark was the owner of a number of trade marks registered in the Benelux consisting of sounds; the specifications varied from, amongst others, computer software to business management, education, training, and, once again, legal services.

A number of marks consisted of the first nine notes of Beethoven's Für Elise[87] represented in a variety of ways: a musical stave with the notes; the words "the first nine notes of Für Elise"; the sequence of musical notes E, D#, E, D#, E, B, D, C, A; some registrations were accompanied by explanatory notes indicating a sound mark and the medium—a piano—on which the melody would be played.

4-053 Two trade marks consisted of the denomination Kukelekuuuuu, with one of them indicating that the sign constituted an onomatopoeia suggesting, in Dutch, a cockcrow.

Another registration consisted of a cockcrow with the explanatory statement: Sound mark, the trade mark consists of the cockcrow as described.

The Für Elise signs were used in Shield Mark's advertising; the cockcrow was incorporated as a sound in software marketed by Shield Mark.

---

[84] In *Eden SARL v Office for Harmonisation in the Internal Market (Trade Marks and Designs)* (T-305/04) [2006] E.T.M.R. 14, Celex No. 604A0305 the Court of First Instance found the "smell of ripe strawberries" to be not capable of being represented graphically. A combination of the description with a photograph of a strawberry was not sufficient. "The image represented only the fruit which emitted the smell of strawberries, not the smell itself. Furthermore, contrary to what the applicant claims, the image adds no additional information in relation to the description in words. The information purportedly added, that is, the state of ripeness in which a strawberry emits the smell in question, is already contained in the description given, since that description states that it is the smell of 'ripe' strawberries. Thus, since the two elements in the representation convey the same information, their combination cannot amount to more than the sum of the two parts and cannot overcome the criticisms raised against each of them individually" (para.46).
[85] *Sieckmann* (C-273/00) [2002] E.C.R. I-11737.
[86] *Shield Mark BV v Kist* (C-283/01) [2003] E.C.R. I-14313.
[87] Originally composed to be played by a child, as the A.G. indicated in his Opinion citing Kinderman, *Beethoven* (Oxford University Press, 1995), p.146.

4. CAPABLE OF BEING REPRESENTED GRAPHICALLY

Shield Mark started trade mark infringement and unfair competition proceedings against Kist, a communications consultant involved with the organisation of intellectual property seminars and publishing, who used in his advertising a melody consisting of the first nine notes of Für Elise and sold a computer program which emitted a cockcrow when starting up.

4–054

The case reached on appeal the Hoge Raad, which referred the following questions to the court for a preliminary ruling:

"1. (a) Must Article 2 of the Directive be interpreted as precluding sounds or noises from being regarded as trade marks?

(b) If the answer to question 1(a) is in the negative, does the system established by the Directive require that sounds or noises must be capable of being regarded as trade marks?

2. (a) If the answer to question 1(a) is in the negative, what requirements does the Directive lay down for sound marks as regards the reference in Article 2 to the need for the sign to be capable of being represented graphically and, in conjunction therewith, as regards the way in which the registration of such a trade mark must take place?

(b) In particular, are the requirements referred to in (a) satisfied if the sound or the noise is registered in one of the following forms: musical notes; a written description in the form of an onomatopoeia; a written description in some other form; a graphical representation such as a sonogram; a sound recording annexed to the registration form; a digital recording accessible via the internet; a combination of those methods; some other form and, if so, which?"[88]

(a) The Opinion of the Advocate General

Advocate General Ruiz-Jarabo Colomer saw the case as belonging to the same line as *Sieckmann*[89]—that had already been decided by the Court—and *Libertel*[90]—that was then still pending—and started by answering the question whether sounds functioned and deserved to be protected as trade marks.

4–055

(i) Limiting the scope of the reference. Expressing his own, and increasingly common, dislike of speculative doctrinal references he stated:

4–056

"The Hoge Raad's request that, irrespective of the facts of the case and in the abstract, the Court of Justice should rule on different forms of representation of a sound ignores the nature of the judicial process, the purpose of which is to provide an answer which will be useful to the determination

---

[88] Reproduced in para.25.
[89] *Sieckmann* (C-273/00) [2002] E.C.R. I-11737.
[90] *Libertel Groep BV* (C-104/01) [2003] E.C.R. I-3793.

of the dispute. Furthermore, the very nature of that procedure and the absence of expert evidence would make it difficult to rule on questions of a highly technical content."[91]

Accordingly the Court should not deal with sonograms, spectrograms, and sound and digital recordings that were outside the factual scenario of the case before the Hoge Raad.

4-057 **(ii) Sounds as trade marks.** Sounds were perceived by our senses, could communicate messages, and possessed the capacity to distinguish.[92] So, in principle, auditory messages could constitute trade marks, although not specifically mentioned in the Directive.[93]

Indeed, a number of Member States specifically listed sounds as signs that might serve as trade marks.[94] "In so far as the Directive has not precluded sounds, no Member State can prevent a message of that type from being registered as a trade mark, on the clear understanding that it satisfies the mandatory requirements: capacity to distinguish and capability of being represented graphically."[95]

4-058 **(iii) The importance of precision.** Precision was the key issue in the graphical representation requirement, linking the subject of protection with the scope of protection: "If an undertaking reserves certain signs and references for itself in order to distinguish its goods and services from those of other undertakings, the symbols so claimed must be known very precisely".[96]

4-059 **(iv) Graphical representation of sounds.** Following the path he had signposted in *Sieckmann*, not without some apparent hesitation,[97] he found that sounds could be represented graphically. Given the link between written and oral communications he believed that in the abstract, the capacity of sounds to be reproduced in writing was undeniable.

---

[91] Point 34 of the Opinion of A.G. Ruiz-Jarabo Colomer.
[92] Citing Proust and Schopenhauer, he discussed music's ability to identify as a result of its evocative intensity, converting sounds into a specific language or interpreting the intimate essence of things: Proust, "A la Recherche du Temps Perdu", *La Prisonniere* (Ed. Gallimard, La Pleiade, 1988), Vol. III, at 762–763; and Schopenhauer, "Le Monde Comme Volonte et Comme Representation" translated by Burdeau (1888), revised and corrected by Roos (Ed. P.U.F. 1966), at 340.
[93] He noted, though, that words in essence are sounds capable of being represented graphically. Indicatively, he referred to the Spanish, French, English, and German definitions of "word" as a combination of sounds that is expressive of an idea.
[94] Germany, Austria, Spain, France, Greece, Italy, and Portugal.
[95] Point 21 of the Opinion of A.G. Ruiz-Jarabo Colomer.
[96] Point 26; reiterating the point expressed in *Sieckmann* (C-273/00) [2002] E.C.R. I-11737.
[97] In point 32 he characterised his answer as more nuanced than the negative one he delivered in *Sieckmann*, definitely not a categorically positive response.

4. CAPABLE OF BEING REPRESENTED GRAPHICALLY

He stressed that he adequacy of the representation in each actual case was an issue that the national courts had to determine. The Court could only provide general guidance.

Musical notation. Musical notation formed part of the case and the Advocate General found it an acceptable way for representing a sound provided that the notes were set on a musical stave. This would ensure that the sound that the notes "are perfectly recognisable and leave no room for doubt... With that universal language, the diffused drawing consisting of the sequence of notes, called by name, seems to be clear, with its precise contours to identify it, differentiating it from others. The notes written on the stave, together with the key, which determines the tonality, the time signature, which determines the rhythm, and the relative value of each note, and also an indication of the instruments which are to interpret them, are a faithful photograph of the sequence of sounds which are represented; if I may say so, they are their fingerprint".[98]

4–060

Note that he accepted that the majority of those viewing musical notation would be unable to decipher it, still he stressed that once the score is read by an expert the uninformed would be enabled to understand the sign without confusing its identity.

Other ways for describing sounds. Other ways of describing sounds, including onomatopoeia and reference to the title of the composition, appeared vague and lacking in clarity and precision, in particular in a trade mark system based on registration rather than use.[99]

4–061

Normally they would be insufficient, however this was a matter to be determined by the national courts in each case[100] applying the criteria adopted by the Court of Justice in *Sieckmann*.

(v) Wider policy considerations. The closing remarks of A.G. Ruiz-Jarabo Colomer reveal two things. First, that wider public policy considerations influence the Court in determining issues like graphical representation that appear to be narrow technical trade mark questions. Secondly, that the perceived "monopolisation" of the sign is a significant factor in the interpretation of trade mark law.

4–062

Looking beyond the abstract question, he noted that the contested signs were a cockcrow and the first notes of, probably, the best-known piece for piano in the history of music.

In such cases, balancing between the monopoly conferred to the owner of the trade mark and the rights of others was critical. He repeated his statement

---

[98] Point 39 of the Opinion of A.G. Ruiz-Jarabo Colomer.
[99] Citing Tarzan's cry as an example of a sign that had acquired distinctiveness through use in the United States.
[100] Point 44, citing as example OHIM's decision to reject the registration of a sound mark consisting of the sound of a click, Déclic (R-1/1996–2), of October 7, 1998.

in *Arsenal* that any extension of the catalogue of signs capable of constituting this form of industrial property must be accompanied by a precise delimitation of the rights which registration conferred on the owner[101] and added that "particular care must also be exercised when a person is granted the exclusive use on the market of a sign, whatever sense it is perceived by".[102]

He believed that the public interest that certain signs should be left free to be used by other traders covered natural indications and signs that were a direct manifestation of nature[103] but also creations of the mind that had become part of the universal cultural heritage. He did not accept that such signs "should be appropriated indefinitely by a person to be used on the market in order to distinguish the goods he produces or the services he provides with an exclusivity which not even its author's estate enjoys".[104]

4–063   **(vi) Trade mark rights and copyright.** The last point—the juxtaposition between copyright and trade mark rights—led the Advocate General to remark that when a sign constituted a trade mark and at the same time is an original work protected by copyright then it was necessary to regulate their reciprocal interrelations.[105]

(b)   The judgment of the Court

4–064   **(i) Limiting the scope of the reference.** Before responding to the second question the Court took a step back and reconsidered its own jurisdiction. Citing *Bosman*,[106] it accepted that where the questions submitted by the national court concerned the interpretation of Community law, the Court of Justice was, in principle, bound to give a ruling. However, the Court could examine the conditions in which the case was referred to it, because the "spirit of co-operation which must prevail in the preliminary-ruling procedure requires the national court, for its part, to have regard to the function entrusted to the Court of Justice, which is to assist in the administration of justice in the Member States and not to deliver advisory opinions on general or hypothetical questions",[107] and refuse to consider hypothetical problems.[108] So, the Court agreed with the Advocate General and found that representations in the form of a sonogram, a sound

---

[101] Point 61 of *Arsenal Football Club Plc v Matthew Reed* (C-206/01) [2002] E.C.R. I-10273.
[102] Point 50 of the Opinion of A.G. Ruiz-Jarabo Colomer.
[103] Citing point 19 and following of his Opinion in *Linde AG* (C-53/01), *Winward Industries Inc* (C-54/01) and *Rado Uhren AG* (C-55/01) [2003] E.C.R. I-3161.
[104] Point 52 of the Opinion of A.G. Ruiz-Jarabo Colomer.
[105] Citing Bercovitz, "Marcas y Derecho de Autor", Revista de Derecho Mercantil" (2001), No.240, 405–419.
[106] *Union Royale Belge des Societes de Football Association ASBL v Jean-Marc Bosman* (C-415/93) [1995] E.C.R. I-4921; [1996] 1 C.M.L.R. 645.
[107] *Union Royale Belge des Societes de Football Association ASBL* (C-415/93) [1995] E.C.R. I-4921; [1996] 1 C.M.L.R. 645, para.52.
[108] Citing *Gantner Electronic GmbH v Basch Exploitatie Maatschappy BV* (C-111/01) [2003] E.C.R. I-4207.

4. CAPABLE OF BEING REPRESENTED GRAPHICALLY

recording, a digital recording or a combination of those methods, were not relevant in this case and would not be examined by the Court.

(ii) Sounds as trade marks. The first issue confronted by the Court was whether sounds could be signs of which a trade mark might exist. It repeated that the list of art.2 was not exhaustive and did not exclude signs which were not in themselves capable of being perceived visually. Further, sound signs were not "by nature incapable of distinguishing"[109] the goods or services of one undertaking from those of other undertakings. Accordingly, sounds could constitute a trade mark and Member States could not preclude their registration as a matter of principle.

4–065

(iii) Sounds—the general framework. The Court then repeated its interpretation of art.2 in *Sieckmann* and ruled that the same conditions were "also binding on sound signs, which, like olfactory signs, are not in themselves capable of visual perception".[110] National courts would have to apply the conditions and determine registrability on a case by case basis.

4–066

The Court of Justice felt that in this case it could provide guidance regarding the types of representation that were relevant, albeit in a quite prescriptive manner.

(iv) Graphical representation—the application must indicate the type of sign. First, the Court required emphatically that the application had to indicate that the sign is a sound sign. Otherwise, the sign would have to be examined as a word or figurative mark.

4–067

(v) Graphical representation—ways for representing sounds. Secondly, although the Court would not preclude the possibility that the representation of a sound sign by a description in written language might satisfy the *Sieckmann* conditions, it held that a graphical representation such as the first nine notes of Für Elise or a cockcrow lacked precision and clarity.

4–068

Thirdly, regarding onomatopoeia, it found a lack of consistency between the onomatopoeia itself, as pronounced, and the actual signified sound. So, it would remain questionable whether the registration covered the pronunciation of the onomatopoeia itself or the signified sound. Further, it could be perceived differently by different individuals or in different Member States. The national variations in the onomatopoeia of a cockrow were indeed a good example.

Fourthly, a sequence of notes without more detail would be neither clear, nor precise, nor self-contained.

However, a stave divided into bars and showing, in particular, a clef, musical notes, and rests whose form indicates the relative value and, where

---

[109] *Shield Mark BV* (C-283/01) [2003] E.C.R. I-14313, para.36.
[110] *Shield Mark BV* (C-283/01) [2003] E.C.R. I-14313, para.56.

appropriate, accidentals might constitute a faithful representation of the sequence of sounds forming the relevant melody. The Court accepted that such a representation would not be immediately intelligible; still, it found that it could become "easily intelligible"[111] allowing traders, in particular, to identify the sound sign with precision.

(3) Libertel—colour samples—public policy considerations

4–069 "Colours" was the next type of signs the registrability of which was considered by the Court. Because *Libertel*[112] involved questions on distinctiveness as well as graphical representation public policy considerations found their way into the discussion of the graphical representation requirements almost by osmosis.

The case was a reference by the Hoge Raad (Supreme Court of the Netherlands). Libertel, a Dutch telecommunications company, had applied to register as a trade mark for telecommunication goods and services in the Benelux a shade of orange. On the application form the mark was described as "orange", without a reference to the usual colour coding systems, and reproduced by an orange rectangle.

The application was rejected as devoid of any distinctive character. The case reached on appeal the Hoge Raad that referred the following questions to the Court for a preliminary ruling:

"(1) Is it possible for a single specific colour which is represented as such or is designated by an internationally applied code to acquire a distinctive character for certain goods or services within the meaning of Article 3(1)(b) of the Directive?

(2) If the answer to the first question is in the affirmative:

> (a) in what circumstances may it be accepted that a single specific colour possesses a distinctive character in the sense used above?
> (b) does it make any difference if registration is sought for a large number of goods and/or services, rather than for a specific product or service, or category of goods or services respectively?

(3) In the assessment of the distinctive character of a specific colour as a trade mark, must account be taken of whether, with regard to that colour, there is a general interest in availability, such as can exist in respect of signs which denote a geographical origin?

(4) When considering the question whether a sign, for which registration as a trade mark is sought, possesses the distinctive character referred to in Article 3(1)(b) of the Directive, must the Benelux Trade Mark Office

---

[111] *Shield Mark BV* [2003] E.C.R. I-14313, para.63.
[112] *Libertel Groep BV* (C-104/01) [2003] E.C.R. I-3793.

4. CAPABLE OF BEING REPRESENTED GRAPHICALLY

confine itself to an assessment in abstracto of distinctive character or must it take account of all the actual facts of the case, including the use made of the sign and the manner in which the sign is used?"[113]

(a) The Opinion of the Advocate General

Before considering the provisions of the Directive A.G. Léger took a step further back and started his review of relevant law from the Paris Convention, "the text on which all international rules governing industrial property rights are based",[114] and noted that it did not contain any definition of signs capable of constituting a trade mark.[115]

4–070

The Advocate General remarked that although the questions concerned the interpretation of art.3, the starting point should be the issue of whether a colour per se fell within the meaning of art.2. He suggested that the Court should thus expand the scope of the enquiry[116] and "consider whether [Article 2] ... should be interpreted as meaning that a colour per se, without any shape or contour, constitutes a sign capable of being represented graphically and of distinguishing the goods and services of one undertaking from those of other undertakings".[117]

Libertel, the Commission, the Benelux Trade Mark Office, and the Governments of the Netherlands and the United Kingdom supported that a colour per se could be registered as a trade mark, it constituted a visual statement and possessed communicative characteristics.[118]

Albeit, the Advocate General held the opposite view; he maintained that a colour per se failed both the requirements of art.2.

(i) The function of graphical representation. Graphical representation was the first legal requirement he considered, looking at the text of the provision but taking also into account the context and the objectives of art.2.[119]

4–071

---

[113] Reproduced in para.20.
[114] Point 3 of the Opinion of A.G. Léger.
[115] Article 6quinquies B(2) covered signs that should be denied registration.
[116] This was feasible because according to the Court's case law it is its duty to interpret all provisions of Community law which referring courts need in order to decide the actions pending before them, even if those provisions are not expressly indicated in the questions referred to it; *Finanzant Kassel-Goethestrasze v Kommanditgesell Schaft Viessmann* (C-280/91) [1993] E.C.R. I-971; *Wolfgang Lange v Georg Schunemann GmbH* (C-350/99) [2001] E.C.R. I-1061; and *Robin Swaddling v Adjudication Officer* (C-90/97) [1999] E.C.R. I-1075.
[117] Point 35 of the Opinion of A.G. Léger.
[118] Support for this position was also sought from the joint declaration of the Council of the European Union and the Commission at the meeting of the Council adopting the Directive. It stated that art.2 does not exclude the possibility of registering as a trade mark a combination of colours or one colour alone (OJ OHIM No.5/96, p.607) and the position adopted by OHIM's Third Board of Appeal in R-122/1998–3, LIGHT GREEN, December 19, 1998.
[119] Citing *Kvaerner Plc v Staatssecretaris van Financien* (C-191/99) [2001] E.C.R. I-447.

The open-ended wording of the provision–resulting from the combination of the expression "any sign" with an indicative rather than exhaustive list of signs—had resulted in diverse approaches at the national level.[120]

The ambiguity could not be resolved by reference to the joint declaration of the Council and the Commission because there was no reference to it in the provision.[121]

4–072 And, turning again to the wider legislative picture he remarked that art.15 of the Agreement on Trade-related Aspects of Intellectual Property Rights—to which both the European Union[122] and its Member States have acceded—referred only to "combinations of colours".[123]

Graphical representation was a critical requirement, because it enabled examining the application without evidence of use.

Following registration it allowed immediate protection without use but also acted as the point of reference for determining whether the trade mark proprietor had put the mark into actual use:

> "It therefore follows from the scheme of the Directive that it is the graphic representation of the sign set out in the application for registration that allows an assessment to be carried out as to whether all the conditions relating to the acquisition of rights to the trade mark are complied with and which determines the rights and obligations conferred by its registration."[124]

4–073 Since, at the time, the Court had not adopted the *Sieckmann*[125] criteria A.G. Léger cited with approval the Opinion of A.G. Ruiz-Jarabo Colomer and set two broader conditions.

---

[120] At the time German law allowed the registration of colours; Portuguese law allowed only combinations of colours; French law referred to shades of colours; Italian law to chromatic tonalities. The laws of the Benelux, Denmark, Greece, Ireland, Austria, Finland, Sweden, Spain, and the United Kingdom were silent.

[121] Citing *Antonissen v Council and Commission* (C-292/89) [1991] E.C.R. I-745; and *VAG Sverige AB* (C-329/95) [1997] E.C.R. I-2675. In any case he noted the Declaration clearly stated in its Preamble: The declarations of the Council and the Commission set out below not forming part of the legislative text, they do not seek to pre-empt the interpretation of the latter by the Court of Justice of the European Communities.

[122] Council Decision 94/800, [1994] OJ L336/1.

[123] Article 15(1): Any sign, or any combination of signs, capable of distinguishing the goods or services of one undertaking from those of other undertakings, shall be capable of constituting a trademark. Such signs, in particular words including personal names, letters, numerals, figurative elements and combinations of colours as well as any combination of such signs, shall be eligible for registration as trademarks. Where signs are not inherently capable of distinguishing the relevant goods or services, Members may make such registrability depend on distinctiveness acquired through use. Members may require, as a condition of registration, that signs be visually perceptible.

The A.G. also mentioned the legislative history of art.15; its original version referred to colours, however its scope as adopted appeared to be narrower.

[124] Point 60 of the Opinion of A.G. Léger.

[125] *Sieckmann* (C-273/00) [2002] E.C.R. I-11737.

4. CAPABLE OF BEING REPRESENTED GRAPHICALLY

First, the representation had to be clear and precise; secondly it had to be intelligible.

(ii) Graphical representation of colours. Colours failed both these requirements irrespective of whether the representation was by reproduction of the colour as such or by reference to codes. 4–074

The second route was rejected outright because it demanded unreasonable effort from a consumer or a competitor that would like to determine what is the sign that is protected.

Reproduction failed because a colour did not possess, according to the Advocate General, an independent existence and it would not be possible to determine how it would appear on the specified goods.

Services faced the same obstacle, because there the colour had to be applied on documents or objects related with their supply. 4–075

The trade mark monopoly would be too broad in its coverage[126] and in addition it would be difficult to determine, first, whether in practice the colour formed part of a composite sign, secondly, whether it was purely ornamental, and thirdly, whether there was a likelihood of confusion between shades of the same colour.

The difficulty of competitors in determining what remained outside the scope of trade mark protection by inspecting the Register was seen as an additional point, linked with the likelihood of confusion issue above.

Citing *Canon*,[127] as recognising the importance of the principle of legal certainty in the field of trade marks, he found that graphical representation of colours as such, without shape or contour, would fail this requirement irrespective of the form or method of representation.

(b) The judgment of the Court

The Court accepted that it was necessary to start its analysis from art.2 which set three conditions for a colour to be registered as a trade mark: First, it had to be a sign. Secondly, that sign should be capable of graphic representation. Thirdly, it should also be capable of distinguishing the goods or services of one undertaking from those of other undertakings[128]: 4–076

> "Normally a colour is a simple property of things. Yet it may constitute a sign. That depends on the context in which the colour is used. None the less, a colour per se is capable, in relation to a product or service, of constituting a sign."[129]

---

[126] Citing *Heidelberger Bauchemie GmbH* (C-49/02) [2004] E.C.R. I-6129.
[127] Case *Canon Kabushiki Kaisha v Metro-Goldwyn-Mayer Inc* (C-39/97) [1998] E.C.R. I-5507.
[128] The Court agreed with the Advocate General that the Joint Declaration, OHIM O.J.N. 5/96, p.607 did not affect the interpretation of the provision.
[129] *Libertel, Groep BV* (C-104/01) [2003] E.C.R. I-3793, para.27.

4–077	**(i) Graphical representation of colours.** Graphical representation had to satisfy the *Sieckmann*[130] requirements: it had to enable the sign to be represented visually, particularly by means of images, lines or characters; and it had to be clear, precise, self-contained, easily accessible, intelligible, durable and objective.

Depositing a mere sample of a colour would fail in particular the durability requirement, because the shade could change with the passage of time.

A verbal description of a colour had to be examined according to the circumstances of each individual case, however in principle it could satisfy the *Sieckmann* standards.

4–078	Accordingly the combination of a sample with a verbal description could also satisfy the same standards.

In cases where the above combination failed, lacking for example precision, this "could be remedied by adding a colour designation from an internationally recognised identification code".[131]

As part of its conclusion regarding the first question the Court ruled that a colour could be capable of functioning and being protected as a trade mark "provided that, inter alia, it may be represented graphically in a way that is clear, precise, self-contained, easily accessible, intelligible, durable and objective. The latter condition cannot be satisfied merely by reproducing on paper the colour in question, but may be satisfied by designating that colour using an internationally recognised identification code".[132]

(4) Heidelberger Bauchemie—abstract combinations of colours

4–079	The Court then considered abstract combinations of colours in *Heidelberger Bauchemie*.[133] The German Patent and Trade Mark Office had refused to register as a trade mark for goods used in the building trade a colour combination.

On the form the sign had been reproduced by a rectangular piece of paper, the upper part of which was blue and the lower half yellow and described in the following terms:

> "The trade mark applied for consists of the applicant's corporate colours which are used in every conceivable form, in particular on packaging and labels.
> The specification of the colours is:
> RAL 5015/HKS 47 – blue
> RAL 1016/HKS 3 – yellow."[134]

---

[130] *Sieckmann* (C-273/00) [2002] E.C.R. I-11737.
[131] *Libertel Groep BV* (C-104/01) [2003] E.C.R. I-3793, para.38.
[132] *Libertel Groep BV* (C-104/01) [2003] E.C.R. I-3793, para.68.
[133] *Heidelberger Bauchemie GmbH* (C-49/02) [2004] E.C.R. I-6129.
[134] Reproduced in para.10.

4. CAPABLE OF BEING REPRESENTED GRAPHICALLY

The product specification included adhesives, solvents, paints, and insulating materials.

Originally, the German Office had rejected the application, holding that the sign was not capable of constituting a trade mark, was not capable of being represented graphically, and was devoid of any distinctive character. However, at a later stage[135] it reviewed its position as to the first two grounds but considered that the sign still lacked distinctive character. The case reached the Federal Patents Court (Bundespatentgericht) that queried whether graphical representation of abstract signs satisfied the precision and legal certainty principles that it deemed art.2 to encapsulate. Accordingly it referred the following questions to the Court of Justice:

4–080

"Do colours or combinations of colours which are the subject of an application for registration as a trade mark, claimed in the abstract, without contours and in shades which are named in words by reference to a colour sample (colour specimen) and specified according to a recognised colour classification system, satisfy the conditions for capability of constituting a trade mark for the purposes of article 2 of [the Directive]?

In particular, for the purposes of article 2 of the Directive, is such an (abstract) colour mark:

(a) a sign,
(b) sufficiently distinctive to be capable of indicating origin,
(c) capable of being represented graphically?"[136]

(a) The Opinion of the Advocate General

Advocate General Léger delivered another sceptical Opinion as to whether colours in abstract could be registered. He started by reminding the requirements set by the Court in *Libertel*,[137] *Sieckmann*,[138] and *Shield Mark*.[139]

4–081

(i) Colour combinations as trade marks. He supported that the current case was not covered by the recent jurisprudence of the Court because it covered colour combinations rather than single colours as such. Article 2 of the Directive was silent, whereas art.15 of TRIPs referred to "combinations of colours" however this should not infer that abstract combinations of colours as such could become protectable signs.

4–082

He also noted that linguistically the term could refer to distinct concepts. In English and Spanish for example the terms "combination" and "combinaciones" did not imply a special arrangement or organisation; in French,

---

[135] And following the decision in "black/yellow colour mark" [1999] I.I.C. 809 of the German Federal Court of Justice of December 10, 1998.
[136] Reproduced in para.14.
[137] *Libertel Groep BV* (C-104/01) [2003] E.C.R. I-3793.
[138] *Sieckmann* (C-273/00) [2002] E.C.R. I-11737.
[139] *Shield Mark BV* (C-283/01) [2003] E.C.R. I-14313.

though, the term "combinaison" was narrower requiring a specific arrangement of the combined elements.

The interpretation given to art.2 in relation to a single colour should also cover combinations of two or more colours; thus, it would appear that colour combinations could be protected.

Even so A.G. Léger disagreed with the existing case law and sought from the Court to re-examine the issue, noting that the Court had given the Bundespatentgericht the opportunity to re-assess whether it was worth pursuing further the reference before the Court of Justice, given its judgment in Libertel, but the German court insisted in receiving an answer from the Court.

He asked from the Court to look again at the reasoning developed in his Opinion in Libertel and chose to concentrate here on why two colours should not be protected as such.

4–083   (ii) **Representing abstract colour combinations.** Developing the theme of legal certainty further he doubted whether the designation of two colours through international identification codes could enable national authorities and economic operators to determine whether a trade mark consisting of two colours per se was identical or similar with another such sign:

> "... the graphic representation of the trade mark must enable the competent authorities and the other economic operators to compare the overall impressions created by the sign and the trade mark in question, bearing in mind their distinctive and dominant elements. Clearly, the competent authorities would have the greatest difficulty in making such a comparison where the trade mark consists of two colours per se. In reality, such a trade mark may assume very different forms. It is undeniable that, depending on the arrangement in which the colours appear and, in particular, the proportion of each colour in relation to the other, the overall impression created by the trade mark, as well as its distinctive and dominant elements, may be very different."[140]

The same applied to economic operators. The resulting uncertainty showed that the legal certainty condition would not be observed.

(b)   The judgment of the Court

4–084   The Court adapted its ruling in *Libertel*[141] taking, to some extent, account of the reflections of the Advocate General.

4–085   (i) **Systematic arrangement.** It required that a graphic representation of two or more colours, designated in the abstract and without contours,

---
[140] Point 60 of the Opinion of A.G. Léger.
[141] *Libertel Groep BV* (C-104/01) [2003] E.C.R. I-3793.

should be "systematically arranged by associating the colours concerned in a predetermined and uniform way".[142]

Looking at it from a negative perspective it found that the:

> "mere juxtaposition of two or more colours, without shape or contours, or a reference to two or more colours 'in every conceivable form', as is the case with the trade mark which is the subject of the main proceedings, does not exhibit the qualities of precision and uniformity required by Article 2 of the Directive...".[143]

5. CAPABLE OF DISTINGUISHING

(1) Philips–setting the Principles

4–086
The concept of the capability of distinguishing was first considered by the Court in a case that involved a three-dimensional sign. In *Philips*[144] the Court of Appeal of England and Wales had to resolve an infringement case. The trade mark registered by Philips in the United Kingdom consisted of a two-dimensional representation of the three-dimensional shape of an electric razor, the shape of a Philishave.[145] Remington marketed a similar shaver. The Court of Appeal referred to the Court of Justice a list of seven questions, in an attempt to clarify the "functionality" provisions of the Directive but also to obtain a framework for determining distinctiveness and the scope of protection.

The first question had to do with the difference between "capable of distinguishing" and "devoid of any distinctive character". The Court of Appeal wanted to know whether there was a category of signs that did not fail the requirements set by art.3(1)(b), art.3(1)(c), or art.3(1)(d) but nevertheless would be excluded from registration by art.3(1)(a) of the Directive.

The second question focused on shapes from a distinctiveness perspective; when the sign for which registration was sought was the shape of the specified product did it need to incorporate some capricious addition, an embellishment that had no functional purpose, in order to be capable of distinguishing?

(a) *The Opinion of the Advocate General*

4–087
The analysis of A.G. Ruiz-Jarabo Colomer concentrated on art.3(1)(e)(ii) that he considered to be primarily relevant to the outcome of the case. And

---

[142] *Heidelberger Bauchemie* (C-49/02) [2004] E.C.R. I-6129, para.33.
[143] *Heidelberger Bauchemie* (C-49/02) [2004] E.C.R. I-6129, para.34.
[144] *Koninklijke Philips Electronics NV* (C-299/99) [2002] E.C.R. I-5475. See also paras 4–503 and following and paras 4–598 and following, below.
[145] For a comparison see *Koninklijke Philips Electronics NV v Rotary Shaver Sweden AB* [2005] E.T.M.R. 103 HR (Stockholm); and *Philips Electronics NC v Remington Consumer Products Ltd* [1999] R.P.C. 809; [1999] E.T.M.R. 816.

his overview of the reasoning behind art.3(1) of the Directive looked more at the specific provisions of art.3(1) rather than art.3(1)(a).

Article 3(1)(b), covered signs "which do not fulfil the primary purpose of distinguishing the goods and which, therefore, do not make it possible to identify their origin, that is to say their manufacturer".[146] Article 3(1)(c) and art.3(1)(d) excluded signs because of their generic nature or their customary character.

He believed that all these specific provisions considered aspects of distinctiveness; they contained "a partial legal definition of the concept of distinctive character".[147] The similarity between these three grounds had been recognised by the legislator who provided through art.3(3)— acquiring distinctiveness through use—a common route for overcoming them, but not art.3(1)(a).

Having dealt in detail with the "functionality" question he turned very briefly his attention to the remaining questions that he really considered irrelevant for resolving the matter that concerned the Court of Appeal.

4–088 **(i) Potentiality and actuality.** The answer to the first question, he suggested, should be negative. The terminology expressed a distinction between potentiality, expressed by "capable of distinguishing", and actuality, expressed by "distinctive character". He found the Court's approach in *Windsurfing Chiemsee*[148] as supporting his analysis.

4–089 **(ii) Arbitrary addition and technical result.** On the second question he repeated, what he had already discussed under the functionality part of his Opinion, that art.3(1)(e) was not connected with distinctiveness. Still, he stated that "if 'arbitrary addition' means any element the essential features of which do not seek to achieve a technical result, the answer must be in the affirmative. Only if a shape contains an addition of this type will it be appropriate to consider whether it has a distinctive character, assuming that it is not a shape dictated by its nature or which gives substantial value to the goods".[149]

(b) The judgment of the Court

4–090 The Court started by ruling on a procedural issue. Philips had requested the reopening of the oral procedure or the joinder of *Linde*[150] in order to take into account the views of the German referring court. The Court

---

[146] Point 13 of the Opinion of A.G. Ruiz-Jarabo Colomer.
[147] Point 14 of the Opinion of A.G. Ruiz-Jarabo Colomer.
[148] *Windsurfing Chiemsee Produktions- und Vertriebs GmbH v Boots- und Segelzubehör Walter Huber and Franz Attenberger* (C-108/97 & C-109/97) [1999] E.C.R. I-2779.
[149] Point 47 of the Opinion of A.G. Ruiz-Jarabo Colomer.
[150] *Linde AG* (C-53/01), *Winward Industries Inc* (C-54/01) and *Rado Uhren AG* (C-55/01) [2003] E.C.R. I-3161.

5. CAPABLE OF DISTINGUISHING

dismissed the application because it considered it had all the information necessary in order to answer the questions referred by the English court.[151]

The Court adhered partially to the advice of the Advocate General regarding the questions that deserved to be answered; the first two questions were discussed by the Court in considerable detail.

(i) Article 3(1)(a)—the essential function of a trade mark. On the first question Remington supported that signs which are not capable to distinguish, failing art.3(1)(a), should not be registered even with evidence of extensive use. Philips supported the opposite. 4–091

The analysis of the Court started from the essential function of a trade mark as a guarantee for the consumer of the identity of the origin of the marked product.[152] It stressed that the registrability provisions should be interpreted in view of that essential function.

(ii) No distinction between different categories of trade marks. From the wording of art.2 it was clear that it made no distinction between different categories of trade marks. "The criteria for assessing the distinctive character of three-dimensional trade marks are thus no different from those to be applied to other categories...".[153] 4–092

According to the analysis of the Court art.3(1)(a) was the mirror image of art.2 expressed in a negative way. Article 3(1)(b), art.3(1)(c), and art.3(1)(d) provided specific reasons for which a mark should not be registered.[154]

Article 3(3) provided that through use a sign that failed art.3(1)(b), art.3(1)(c), or art.3(1)(d) could overcome this barrier through evidence of acquired distinctive character. In *Windsurfing Chiemsee*[155] the Court had already observed that this meant that the mark ought to identify the specified product as originating from a particular undertaking, and thus to distinguish that product from goods of other undertakings.

Perhaps it would suffice for the Court to underline the above statement; however it felt that it had to offer some justification for the obvious textual discrepancy and reconcile the shades of distinctiveness within the legislative context of the Directive.

(iii) The continuum of distinctiveness. Accordingly, on the basis of the language of the provision and the structure of the Directive it viewed art.3(1)(a) as excluding "signs which are not generally capable of being a 4–093

---

[151] Rules of Procedure art.61; *Deutsche Post AG v Elisabeth Sievers, Brunhilde Schrage* (C-270/97 & C-271/97) [2000] E.C.R. I-929.
[152] Citing the Tenth Recital of the Preamble to the Directive and *Frits Loendersloot v George Ballantine & Son* (C-349/95) [1997] E.C.R. I-6227; and *Canon Kabushiki Kaisha v Metro-Goldwyn-Mayer Inc* (C-39/97) [1998] E.C.R. I-5507.
[153] *Philips*, para.48.
[154] Citing *Windsurfing Chiemsee Produktions- und Vertriebs GmbH v Boots- und Segelzubehör Walter Huber and Franz Attenberger* (C-108/97 & C-109/97) [1999] E.C.R. I-2779.
[155] *Windsurfing Chiemsee*, para.46.

trade mark and thus cannot be represented graphically and/or are not capable of distinguishing the goods or services of one undertaking from those of other undertakings".[156]

However, all the distinctiveness provisions were linked; in a way it viewed them as part of the same continuum:

"... Article 3(1)(a) ... like the rule laid down by Article 3(1)(b), (c) and (d), precludes the registration of signs or indications which do not meet one of the two conditions imposed by Article 2 of the Directive, that is to say, the condition requiring such signs to be capable of distinguishing the goods or services of one undertaking from those of other undertakings".[157]

The Court, as the result of this admittedly unclear statement, concluded that there was no category of marks which was not excluded from registration according to art.3(1)(b), (c) and (d) and art.3(3) but could still be excluded under art.3(1)(a).

Note however, that this is a one way only conclusion. In *Henkel*,[158] the Court stressed that point in relation to the Regulation:

"The fact that a sign, is in general capable of constituting a trade mark within the meaning of Article 4 [of the Regulation] does not mean that the sign necessarily has distinctive character for the purposes of Article 7(1)(b) in relation to a specific product or service."[159]

4–094 **(iv) Three-dimensional Signs—No Requirement for a Capricious Addition.** The answer to the second question followed the same logic, based on the premise that all a mark has to do is to distinguish a product from other products on the basis of commercial origin. This constituted the basic requirements and the Directive made no other distinction between categories of mark including shapes. Accordingly, there was no requirement of a capricious addition; the only requirement the shape had to satisfy was to function as a trade mark.

Note that, from contrasting positions, the submissions of both *Philips* and *Remington* had been based on descriptiveness, perhaps influenced by the stance of the Court in *Windsurfing Chiemsee*.[160]

---

[156] *Philips*, para.37.
[157] *Philips*, para.38.
[158] *Henkel KGaA v Office for Harmonisation in the Internal Market (Trade Marks and Designs)* (C-456/01 P and C-457/01 P) [2004] E.C.R. I-5089.
[159] *Philips*, para.32.
[160] *Windsurfing Chiemsee Produktions- und Vertriebs GmbH v Boots- und Segelzubehör Walter Huber and Franz Attenberger* (C-108/97 & C-109/97) [1999] E.C.R. I-2779.

(2) Capable of distinguishing—the limited effect of article 3(1)(a)

In its subsequent case law the Court considered distinctiveness overwhelmingly under art.3(1)(b) and the requirement of distinctive character. 4–095

The effect of art.3(1)(a) appears to be quite limited.

For example, in *Postkantoor*[161] the Court found that there was "no reason to find that a word like Postkantoor is not, in respect of certain goods or services, capable of fulfilling the essential function of a trade mark...".[162]

In respect of colours the Court having admitted that colours possessed little inherent capacity for communicating specific information went on to assert that: 4–096

> "that factual finding would not justify the conclusion that colours per se cannot, as a matter of principle, be considered to be capable of distinguishing the goods or services of one undertaking from those of other undertakings. The possibility that a colour per se may in some circumstances serve as a badge of origin ... cannot be ruled out".[163]

Similarly in *Heidelberger Bauchemie*,[164] it limited further the possibility of a colour functioning as a trade mark. The wording it employed in this case is further evidence of the fact that the Court views distinctiveness as one issue with many different aspects. Referring to art.2 it appeared to describe the distinctiveness requirement mentioned therein as initial distinctive character:

> "Save in exceptional cases, colours do not initially have a distinctive character, but may be capable of acquiring such character as the result of the use made of them in relation to the goods or services claimed."[165]

Nevertheless, this should not raise an obstacle to registration according to art.2:

> "Subject to the above, it must be accepted that for the purposes of article 2 ... colours and combinations of colours, designated in the abstract and without contours, may be capable of distinguishing the goods or services of one undertaking from those of other undertakings."[166]

---

[161] *Koninklijke KPN Nederland NV* (C-363/99) [2004] E.C.R. I-1619.
[162] *Postkantoor*, para.81.
[163] *Libertel Groep BV* (C-104/01) [2003] E.C.R. I-3793, para.41.
[164] *Heidelberger Bauchemie GmbH* (C-49/02) [2004] E.C.R. I-6129.
[165] *Heidelberger Bauchemie GmbH* (C-49/02) [2004] E.C.R. I-6129, para.39.
[166] *Heidelberger Bauchemie GmbH* (C-49/02) [2004] E.C.R. I-6129, para.40.

(3) Some guidelines for interpreting article 3

(a) Public interest, independence, and interdependence

4–097 Despite the limited role art.3(1)(a) played in the development of trade mark law in terms of distinctiveness the concept of distinctiveness has become a considerable barrier to registrability as a result of art.3(1)(b) and the notion that behind each one of the specific provisions of art.3(1) there is an underlying public interest.

The Court having explicitly rejected in *Windsurfing Chiemsee*[167] the need to interpret the provisions of the Directive and the registrability of a geographical name according to general policy doctrines; however, it stressed that, in that occasion, art.3(1)(c) had to be interpreted according to the public interest behind it.

The same applied to other categories of types of marks and the remaining provisions of art.3(1).

In *Libertel*[168] it ruled that the "possibility of registering a trade mark may be limited for reasons relating to public interest".[169]

In *Henkel*[170] it added that the public interest underlying each of that grounds of art.3(1) "may, or even must, reflect different considerations, depending upon which ground for refusal is at issue".[171]

(b) The independence of each ground

4–098 In *Linde*[172] it underlined that "[e]ach of the grounds for refusal to register listed in article 3(1) . . . is independent of the others and calls for separate examination".[173]

Successfully overcoming one of the grounds would not guarantee the same result for the others. For example in *Postkantoor*[174] the Court ruled that:

> "it is not . . . open to the competent authority to conclude that a mark is not devoid of any distinctive character in relation to certain goods or services purely on the ground that it is not descriptive of them".[175]

---

[167] *Windsurfing Chiemsee Produktions- und Vertriebs GmbH v Boots- und Segelzubehör Walter Huber and Franz Attenberger* (C-108/97 & C-109/97) [1999] E.C.R. I-2779.
[168] *Libertel Groep BV* (C-104/01) [2003] E.C.R. I-3793.
[169] *Libertel Groep BV* (C-104/01) [2003] E.C.R. I-3793, para.50.
[170] *Henkel KGaA v Office for Harmonisation in the Internal Market (Trade Marks and Designs)* (C-456/01 P and C-457/01 P) [2004] E.C.R. I-5089.
[171] *Henkel* (C-456/01 P and C-457/01 P) [2004] E.C.R. I-5089, para.46.
[172] *Linde AG* (C-53/01), *Winward Industries Inc* (C-54/01) and *Rado Uhren AG* (C-55/01) [2003] E.C.R. I-3161.
[173] *Linde, AG* (C-53/01), para.67.
[174] *Koninklijke KPN Nederland NV* (C-363/99) [2004] E.C.R. I-1619.
[175] *Koninklijke KPN Nederland NV* (C-363/99) [2004] E.C.R. I-1619, para.70.

5. CAPABLE OF DISTINGUISHING

And failing one of the grounds would be enough to negate registration. In *Companyline*[176] the Court looking at the equivalent provision of the Regulation, art.7(1) it stressed that "it is quite evident from the wording of article 7(1) ... that it is sufficient that one of the absolute grounds for refusal listed in that provision applies for the sign at issue not to be registrable as a Community trade mark".[177]

However, probably as a result of the continuum of distinctiveness, failing one of the grounds could cause a domino effect.   **4–099**

In *Postkantoor*[178] the Court found that a:

"word mark which is descriptive of characteristics of goods or services for the purposes of article 3(1)(c) ... is, on that account, necessarily devoid of any distinctive character with regard to the same goods or services within the meaning of article 3(1)(b)".[179]

(c) The link with the specification, the relevant consumer, and timing

Another critical interpretive issue that has arisen from the case law of the Court is that the assessment of absolute grounds is not an exercise that can be concluded in abstract. To the contrary, context is everything.   **4–100**

We will see below how the Court has incorporated the context it has found relevant for each ground into the respective test or assessment criteria it has adopted. But there are three elements that appear to be common.

First, registrability is linked with the specification. In *Postkantoor*[180] the Court has indicated this link in broad terms:

"Where registration of a mark is sough in respect of various goods or services, the competent authority must check, in relation to each of the goods or services claimed, that none of the grounds for refusal listed in Article 3(1) of the Directive applies to the mark and may reach different conclusions depending upon the goods or services in question."[181]

Secondly, registrability is considered from the perspective of the public; not the public in general, but the public that is relevant for the specified goods or services.   **4–101**

---

[176] *DKV Deutsche Krankenversicherung AG v Office for Harmonisation in the Internal Market (Trade Marks and Designs)* (C-104/00 P) [2002] E.C.R. I-7561.
[177] *DKV Deutsche Krankenversicherung AG* (C-104/00 P) [2002] E.C.R. I-7561, para.29.
[178] *Koninklijke KPN Nederland NV v Benelux-Merkenbureau* (C-363/99) [2004] E.C.R. I-1619.
[179] *Koninklijke KPN Nederland NV* (363/99) [2004] E.C.R. I-1619, para.86.
[180] *Koninklijke KPN Nederland NV* (C-363/99) [2004] E.C.R. I-1619.
[181] *Koninklijke KPN Nederland NV* (363/99) [2004] E.C.R. I-1619, para.73.

In *Libertel*,[182] the Court has made this clear, again in broad registrability terms:

> "For the purposes of determining whether a sign is registrable as a trade mark it is necessary to take as a standpoint that of the relevant public."[183]

Finally, there are two "timing" points to be made.

4–102 First, from the consumer's perspective the Court has indicated that the critical time for determining distinctive character, at least, is that of making a choice:

> "it is when making his choice between different products in the category concerned that the average consumer exhibits the highest level of attention[184] ... so that the question whether or not the average consumer sees the mark at the time of purchase is of particular importance for determining whether the mark has acquired distinctive character through use".[185]

Secondly, from the perspective of the authority administering the system of registration the relevant date for establishing the registrability criteria is the date of filing the application. The Court has indicated this clearly in relation to the Community Trade Mark regime:

> "The date of filing the application for registration of the Community trade mark is the material date for the examination."[186]

Indeed the Court of First Instance when reviewing a decision of the Office should consider the situation on that date:

> "... the Court of First Instance could without inconsistency in its reasoning or error of law take account of material which, although subsequent to the date of filing the application, enabled the drawing of conclusions on the situation as it was on that date."[187]

---

[182] *Libertel Groep BV* (C-104/01) [2003] E.C.R. I-3793.
[183] *Libertel Groep BV* (C-104/01) [2003] E.C.R. I-3793, para.45. See also para.4-409.
[184] Citing *Ruiz-Picasso v Office for Harmonisation in the Internal Market (Trade Marks and Designs)* (C-361/04 P) [2006] E.C.R. I-643.
[185] *Koninklijke KPN Nederland NV* (C-363/99) [2004] E.C.R. I-1619, para.72.
[186] *ALCON v Office for Harmonisation in the Internal Market (Trade Marks and Designs)* (C-192/03 P) [2004] E.C.R. I-8993, para.40.
[187] *ALCON* (C-192/03 P) [2004] E.C.R. I-8993, para.41.

6. ARTICLE 3(1)(b)—DEVOID OF ANY DISTINCTIVE CHARACTER

(1) Companyline—article 7(1)(b)—balancing between Baby-Dry and Postkantoor

Companyline[188] was a post *Baby-Dry*[189] case where the Court reconsidered distinctive character and descriptiveness in the context of composite marks, this time from the perspective of art.7(1)(b) of the Regulation.[190]

4–103

(a) The judgment of the Court of First Instance

The case came as an appeal against a judgment of the Court of First Instance[191] dismissing the action against the refusal by the Board of Appeal to allow DKV's application for registration of COMPANYLINE as a Community Trade Mark for insurance and financial affairs services. The Court of First Instance, in a judgment issued before the publication of the judgment of the Court in *Baby-Dry*, found the mark to be devoid of distinctive character, since the sign consisted of two generic words simply coupled together. "Company" indicated that the services were intended for companies and "line", a branch, a line, or a group of services.

4–104

It declined to consider the application of art.7(1)(c) by the Board since failure under one ground would suffice and also rejected a third plea regarding misuse of powers.

DKV, before the Court of Justice, claimed that the Court of First Instance had: misinterpreted—by not determining the assessment criteria—and misapplied—by not considering the overall impression—art.7(1)(b); failed to consider art.7(1)(c); did not take into account art.12(b)[192]; applied art.7(2) from the wrong perspective, without focusing on ordinary consumers of the specified services and without having regard to the approach taken by the trade mark offices of the Member States; and failed to assess the objective evidence of misuse of powers.

(b) The Opinion of the Advocate General

Advocate General Ruiz-Jarabo Colomer distinguished *Baby-dry* from the current case based on the structure of the two signs: the former comprised

4–105

---

[188] *DKV Deutsche Krankenversicherung AG* (C-104/00 P) [2002] E.C.R. I-7561.
[189] *Procter & Gamble Co* (C-383/99 P) [2001] E.C.R. I-6251.
[190] Contrast with *Koninklijke KPN Nederland NV* (C-363/99) [2004] E.C.R. I-1619.
[191] *Deutsche Krankenversicherung AG (DKV)* (T-353/99) [2001] E.C.R. II-1645.
[192] Article 12(b) of the Reg. provides: A Community Trade Mark shall not entitle the proprietor to prohibit a third party from using in the course of trade: (b) indications concerning the kind, quality, quantity, intended purpose, value, geographical origin, the time of production of the goods or of rendering of the service, or other characteristics of the goods or service.

two familiar words separated by a hyphen whereas the current involved a "neologism", a combination of two words.

In a way he viewed his Opinion as closely linked with that delivered in *Postkantoor*.[193] Here, for example, he would pay less attention to the "availability" public interest considerations that did not form part of the case; instead he would attempt to build some guiding principles, "clear pointers"[194] that the legislature had failed to provide, regarding the interpretation of art.7(1) of the Regulation.

His starting point was that all the criteria had to be evaluated separately from each other; and because of the overlap courts had to be cautious in their application.

4-106 The nature of composite marks complicated things further. Here for example, the Board based on the descriptive nature of the two components had found that the application failed both art.7(1)(b) and art.7(1)(c). The Court of First Instance relied on the lack of distinctive character of a combination of two customary English words.

Advocate General Colomer, would have preferred the opposite approach, "the sign could in principle be refused registration on the basis of Article 7(1)(c), and only once it is clear that it is purely descriptive can Article 7(1)(b) be pleaded. In other words, lack of distinctive character is assumed from the sign's descriptiveness and not the other way around. That is how word marks should as a rule be assessed".[195]

4-107 **(i) The way forward—a different view.** Before examining the substance of his Opinion in detail it is worth mentioning his view about the role of the Court of Justice as an appellate court.

Advocate General Ruiz-Jarabo Colomer was against the idea of the Court deciding on the registrability of specific signs, contrary to what the Court appeared to do in *Baby-Dry*.[196]

He accepted that this would be advantageous in terms of procedural efficiency. However, and because the Court was the highest interpreter of law in the field of Community trade mark law,[197] its function should be to lay down principles of general application, leaving their implementation to the Court of First Instance and the Office.

Even procedural efficiency would suffer at the end if large number of applications would be left for the Court to decide; this was outside the scope

---

[193] *Koninklijke KPN Nederland NV* (C-363/99) [2004] E.C.R. I-1619.
[194] Point 34 of the Opinion of A.G. Ruiz-Jarabo Colomer.
[195] Point 43 of the Opinion of A.G. Ruiz-Jarabo Colomer.
[196] *Procter & Gamble Co* (C-383/99 P) [2001] E.C.R. I-6251.
[197] The A.G. used the term in the "field of Community trade marks" in point 59, however the fact that in reality the Court is the interpreter not only of the law applied as a result of the Regulation but also of the laws adopted as a result of the Directive strengthens further his argument.

6. ARTICLE 3(1)(b)—DEVOID OF ANY DISTINCTIVE CHARACTER

but also the ability of the Court that lacked the necessary resources to function in that way.

(ii) Distinctive character and perceptible differences. Turning to the substance of the appeal, he considered, first, the application of art.7(1)(b). Re-adjusting the *Baby-Dry* judgment, in the same way he did in *Postkantoor* for descriptiveness, he suggested that "a difference should be considered to be perceptible if it affects significant elements either of the appearance of the mark claimed or of its semantic content".[198]

4–108

(iii) The perspective for determining registrability. The Advocate General adopted a pragmatic approach in order to strengthen the point he had already made in *Postkantoor*:

4–109

"the standpoint from which the assessment is to be made must move away from formal criteria to reflect the actual characteristics of the class of persons targeted. The fact that there are many applications for trade marks composed of English words in itself shows that applicants assume a certain level of understanding of English, even where consumers have a different mother tongue".[199]

The whole gamut of possible ways in which such consumers might be expected to respond should be explored before reaching a decision.

(iv) Registrability of *Companyline*. Advocate General Ruiz-Jarabo Colomer believed that the finding of the Court of First Instance on the nature of the two words was one of fact.

4–110

He accepted that it had not assessed the descriptiveness of the compound sign as such, but there was nothing to suggest that "taking the expression company line as a whole invalidates the Court of First Instance's view—rather the reverse is true".[200]

He found that the position of the Court of First Instance, that the mere coupling of these words failed to generate an additional characteristic that would make the sign "capable of distinguishing the appellant's services from those of other undertakings",[201] was also correct.

Accordingly its finding that the sign lacked distinctiveness should stand.

(v) Descriptiveness should be assessed first. He did have some criticism though on the way the Court of First Instance reached its decision. "It would have been appropriate to begin by finding that the significant

4–111

---

[198] Point 51 of the Opinion of A.G. Ruiz-Jarabo Colomer.
[199] Point 56 of the Opinion of A.G. Ruiz-Jarabo Colomer.
[200] Point 64 of the Opinion of A.G. Ruiz-Jarabo Colomer.
[201] Point 65 of the Opinion of A.G. Ruiz-Jarabo Colomer.

components of the mark claimed were wholly descriptive, and on that basis to declare the mark devoid of any distinctive character. That flaw in logic cannot lead to annulment of the contested decision, since the final assessment is in conformity with law."[202]

4–112 **(vi) The remaining grounds of appeal.** The Advocate General supported that all the remaining grounds should also be dismissed; from his analysis it is worth mentioning here four particular points.

First, he repeated that failing one provision sufficed to reject the application, therefore relying on only one ground "whilst it may be open to criticism as to expediency, does not give rise to questions of legality".[203]

Secondly, art.12(b) delimited the scope of the right following registration. It did not determine the conditions for registration.

4–113 Further, disclaimers under art.38—that the applicant at some stage of the procedure offered to undertake—did not affect the application of art.3(1)(b) and art.3(1)(c).:

> "It is certainly true ... that in BABY-DRY the Court alluded to article 12 ... when stating the legal basis for its subsequent reasoning. But it did not go on to draw any practical consequence from that provision whatsoever."[204]

Thirdly, he underlined that art.7(2) of the Regulation provided that a sign is to be refused registration even where the grounds for refusal obtain in only part of the Community. Once the Court of First Instance had determined that the sign was descriptive in part of the Community there was no reason to consider the impression conveyed by that sign to speakers of other Community languages. It would however be the opposite "if they had decided that the sign raised no problems under Art.7(1)(b) or (c) of the Regulation for speakers of the language in which the sign was expressed. Where that is the case, there is ... no reason why a sign's eligibility for registration as a trade mark should not be assessed taking account of the perception of that sign among consumers in other countries".[205]

4–114 **(vii) The practice of the office as "precedent".** Fourthly, DKV had argued that the Office had misused its powers because in the past other

---

[202] Point 69 of the Opinion of A.G. Ruiz-Jarabo Colomer.
[203] Point 76 of the Opinion of A.G. Ruiz-Jarabo Colomer.
[204] Point 82. Article 38(2) of the Reg. provides that 2. Where the trade mark contains an element which is not distinctive, and where the inclusion of said element in the trade mark could give rise to doubts as to the scope of protection of the trade mark, the Office may request, as a condition for registration of said trade mark, that the applicant state that he disclaims any exclusive right to such element. Any disclaimer shall be published together with the application or the registration of the Community trade mark, as the case may be. Article 38(3) provides that the "application shall not be refused before the applicant has been allowed the opportunity of withdrawing or amending the application or of submitting his observations".
[205] Point 92 of the Opinion of A.G. Ruiz-Jarabo Colomer.

6. ARTICLE 3(1)(b)—DEVOID OF ANY DISTINCTIVE CHARACTER

compound trade marks ending in LINE and that the reason for rejecting was to prevent the applicant from becoming the owner of a group of LINE marks.

He rejected the claim, liberating the Office from having to follow to its past decisions, even if they were wrong. "The mere fact that the Office treated other signs ending in the suffix line differently, if indeed it did, is no reason to assume that it was exercising a power arbitrarily or to support an allegation of misuse of powers."[206]

(c) The judgment of the Court

(i) Inadmissibility—appraisal of facts—new pleas. The Court dismissed the appeal, primarily based on the delineation of its jurisdiction that excluded the assessment and appraisal of facts. The actual application of the provisions, as interpreted by the Court, to the facts of the case involved findings of factual nature and the appraisal of those findings; both were exclusively within the jurisdiction of the Court of First Instance. There were two exceptions: where a substantive inaccuracy in its findings was attributable to the documents submitted to it; and where the clear sense of the evidence before it had been distorted. Only then there is a question of law that allows the Court of Justice to review the appraisal of the facts.[207]

4–115

The claim based on art.12(b) was rejected without being considered in its substance because it had been raised exclusively before the Court of First Instance in relation to art.7(1)(c). Raising the same point in relation to art.7(1)(b) at the appeal stage constituted a new plea that was inadmissible.[208]

Partly responding to the reservations of the Advocate General regarding the role of the Court in trade mark appeals, it found the misuse of power plea to be an unsubstantiated "request for re-examination of the application before the Court of First Instance, which the Court of Justice, by virtue of article 49 of its EC Statute, has no jurisdiction to entertain".[209]

(ii) The interpretation of article 7(1)(b). In terms of substance, first, it accepted that the Court of First Instance was "entitled to confine itself to considering that [art.7(1)(b)] question, and was under no obligation to rule on the possible dividing line between the concept of lack of distinctiveness and that of minimum distinctiveness".[210]

4–116

Then, it found that its interpretation of art.7(1)(b) was not wrong, "in examining whether two generic terms coupled together possess any additional

---

[206] Point 96 of the Opinion of A.G. Ruiz-Jarabo Colomer.
[207] Citing *Moccia Irme v Commission* (C-280/99 to C-282/99) [2001] E.C.R. I-4717; and *DSG v Commission* (C-323/00 P) [2002] E.C.R. I-3919.
[208] The Court referred to its Order of September 13, 2001 in *Staff Committee of the ECB v ECB* (C-467/00 P) [2001] E.C.R. I-6041.
[209] *DKV Deutsche Krankenversicherung AG* (C-104/00 P) [2002] E.C.R. I-7561, para.44.
[210] *DKV Deutsche Krankenversicherung AG* (C-104/00 P) [2002] E.C.R. I-7561, para.20.

characteristic such as to confer on the sign, taken as a whole, a distinctive character, the Court of First Instance did not err in law in its interpretation of Article 7(1)(b)".[211]

It also found that the Court of First Instance had considered not only the distinctive character of each individual component but of the compound mark as well.

(2) "SAT.2"—back to Baby-dry?

4–117 And when we all thought that the Court has become more conservative in its approach on distinctiveness in *SAT.2*[212] the Court appeared to take yet another turn. The case was an appeal against the judgment of the Court of First Instance.[213] The appellant had applied to register as a Community Trade Mark the sign "SAT.2" for goods in several classes and services in Classes 35, 38, 41 and 42. The specification enumerated the services in detail. The examiner rejected the application in respect of all the services in so far as they referred to satellites or to satellite television in the widest sense. The Second Board of Appeal[214] upheld the examiner's decision in respect of Classes 38, 41 and 42, holding that the sign lacked distinctive character and was descriptive, failing both art.7(1)(b) and art.7(1)(c) of the Regulation.

(a) The judgment of the Court of First Instance

4–118 The Court of First Instance annulled the Board of Appeal's decision to the extent that it had failed to rule on the part of the appeal regarding services in Class 35 and insofar as it concerned services not connected with satellite broadcasting. Further, whilst the Court of First Instance accepted that the sign was not exclusively descriptive, according to art.7(1)(c), in respect of all the relevant services, it held that it lacked distinctive character in respect of services that had to do with broadcasting via satellite. According to the Court of First Instance, the absolute grounds for refusal in art.7(1) sub-paras (b) to (e) were public interest provisions, ensuring that the signs they covered remained free for all to use. "SAT.2" lacked distinctiveness because SAT was an established and common abbreviation of a characteristic—a link to satellite broadcasting—of most of the services concerned, and thus devoid of distinctive character. "2" was a number, and numbers were commonly used in trade for the presentation of the same services. And the element "." was commonly used in trade for the presentation of all goods and services. The

---

[211] *DKV Deutsche Krankenversicherung AG* (C-104/00 P) [2002] E.C.R. I-7561, para.21.
[212] *SAT.1 SatellitenFernsehen GmbH v Office for Harmonisation in the Internal Market (Trade Marks and Designs)* (C-329/02 P) [2004] E.C.R. I-8317.
[213] *SAT.1 SatellitenFernsehen v Office for Harmonisation in the Internal Market (Trade Marks and Design)* (T-323/00) [2002] E.C.R. II-2839.
[214] Case R-312/1999-2, August 2, 2000.

6. ARTICLE 3(1)(b)—DEVOID OF ANY DISTINCTIVE CHARACTER

sign as a whole was devoid of any distinctive character because of the weaknesses of its constituent elements. In this case, according to the Court of First Instance, there was no evidence that the composite mark was greater than the sum of its parts, a characteristic that could render the mark distinctive. It also rejected the plea that the Office had breached the principle of equal treatment by changing its position regarding alpha numeric signs; a decision wrongly accepting a sign for registration should not be the basis for annulling a later decision to the contrary.[215] The principle of equal treatment should be balanced with the principle of legality.

Before the Court of Justice SAT.1 submitted that the Court of First Instance was wrong to consider that art.7(1)(b) pursued the public-interest aim of keeping certain signs available to be freely used by all. It had applied a criterion—likelihood of use in trade for the presentation of the relevant products, not included in the provision—therefore, it had failed to assess the distinctiveness of the mark as a whole but merely examined each part separately. Finally, it claimed that it had misinterpreted its plea on non-discrimination by considering the issue of previous individual decisions rather than the Office's past consistent practice.

(b) The Opinion of the Advocate General

4–119 Advocate General Jacobs started his deliberation of the plea on the misinterpretation of art.7(1)(b) with a general comment on the concept of distinctiveness and the difference between art.7(1)(a) and art.7(1)(b).

4–120 **(i) The difference between article 7(1)(a) and article 7(1)(b).** He claimed that the answer could be found in art.7(3) setting that distinctiveness through use is relevant only in the case of art.7(1)(b). Accordingly, art.7(1)(a) referred to the abstract capacity to distinguish between products of different origins, whereas art.7(1)(b) referred to distinctiveness in relation to the class of product in question. For example, the element "." on its own would lack the distinctiveness of both art.7(1)(a) and art.7(1)(b), but the distinctiveness of SAT would have to be established in the context of the specification, according to art.7(1)(b).

4–121 **(ii) Interpreting article 7(1)(b)—a permissive perspective.** Turning to art.7(1)(b) in particular, SAT.1 claimed that whereas *Windsurfing Chiemsee*[216] had established that art.7(1)(c) sought to ensure that descriptive signs remain free for others to use, the Court of Justice had avoided to give the same scope to art.7(1)(b), and instead it had been

---

[215] Citing *Witte v Parliament* (188/83) [1984] E.C.R. 3465; *Williams v Court of Auditors* (134/84) [1985] E.C.R. 2225.
[216] *Windsurfing Chiemsee Produktions- und Vertriebs GmbH v Boots- und Segelzubehör Walter Huber and Franz Attenberger* (C-108/97 & C-109/97) [1999] E.C.R. I-2779.

stressing that the essential function of a trade mark was to distinguish between products of different origins and to guarantee, in a system of undistorted competition, that all the products bearing it originated under the control of a single undertaking, responsible for their quality, which should be in a position to keep its customers by virtue of that quality.

The Office counter-argued that it was clearly in the public interest to exclude from registration signs that lacked distinctive character. The principles of legal certainty and sound administration necessitated that trade marks that could successfully be challenged before the courts should not be registered. Therefore, the distinctiveness of signs comprising simply one of a limited series of elements in common use (e.g. letters, numerals, or basic colours) was limited; numerals in particular had to remain available to designate quantities.

Advocate General Jacobs accepted that each ground for refusing registration should be interpreted in the light of the underlying public interest. Interestingly he adopted a similar position with that of A.G. Ruiz-Jarabo Colomer accepting that art.7(1)(c), art.7(1)(d), and art.7(1)(e) could be interpreted following analogous arguments.[217]

4–122 Still, according to the Advocate General, some analogous reasoning could not be imposed on art.7(1)(b), because there was no obvious reason why signs which lacked distinctive character, in relation to the specified goods or services, should be kept free for general use. Lack of distinctive character did not imply the relationship specified in sub-paras (c) to (e).

He bypassed the ambiguities of *Libertel*[218] where the Court had referred to the general interest in not unduly restricting the availability of colours for other traders by distinguishing the language used by the Court. *Libertel* was not about signs to be "freely used by all" but about "not unduly restricting" the availability of some types of signs, where there is a limited range of them".[219] In this case, he supported, there was a much wider range of numbers that a consumer could recognise as distinctive. He elaborated on this by stressing that a visual trade mark consisted of at least one colour from the limited range available whereas it is a matter of choice "whether to use any element at all from other types of limited range, such as numbers or punctuation marks".[220] He also stated that the registration of a colour per se, as opposed to a specific shape or form bearing that colour, might be

---

[217] Citing *Koninklijke Philips Electronics NV* (C-299/99) [2002] E.C.R. I-5475.
[218] *Libertel Groep BV* (C-104/01) [2003] E.C.R. I-3793.
[219] Citing para.47 of the judgment and point 81 of A.G. Ruiz-Jarabo Colomer's Opinion in *Henkel KGaA* (C-456/01 P & C-457/01 P) [2004] E.C.R. I-5089; *Procter & Gamble* (C-468/01 P to C-472/01 P) [2004] E.C.R. I-5141; and *Procter & Gamble* (C-473/01 P & C-474/01 P) [2004] E.C.R. I-5173.
[220] Point 27. He had attempted to do the same with *Windsurfing Chiemsee Produktions- und Vertriebs GmbH v Boots- und Segelzubehör Walter Huber and Franz Attenberger* (C-108/97 &C-109/97) [1999] E.C.R. I-2779 on descriptiveness in *Procter & Gamble Co* (C-383/99 P) [2001] E.C.R. I-6251.

6. ARTICLE 3(1)(b)—DEVOID OF ANY DISTINCTIVE CHARACTER

likened to the registration of any expression of duality, as opposed to the specific digit "2".

Accordingly, he found that the statement at para.36 of the judgment under appeal "to the effect that the aim of Article 7(1)(b) is to keep the signs to which it refers available to be freely used by all", went appreciably further than what he considered to be a correct interpretation of the law:

> "Although perhaps not decisive in itself, that statement is likely to have influenced the final assessment of the registrability of 'SAT.2'; the application of a test whose aim is to keep signs available to be freely used by all will inevitably be more severe than that of a test aimed simply at not unduly restricting the availability of other types of sign whose range is limited".[221]

(iii) Assessing distinctive character. SAT.1 had submitted that the commonality argument against each one of the elements of the sign should be considered as a ground under art.7(1)(c) or (e) rather than art.7(1)(b) which should only cover signs which were exclusively descriptive. Citing *Baby-dry*, it claimed that innovative, non-descriptive terms were capable of distinctiveness.

4–123

The Office argued that the sign was not descriptive as a whole and could not be refused under art.7(1)(c). Instead, art.7(1)(b) should be applied, because the sign was a combination of a descriptive—non-distinctive—element with an element that was neither descriptive nor distinctive. The sign as a whole was not distinctive because the combination failed to create a whole that was greater than its parts. SAT.1's reasoning, that any non descriptive sign ought to have the capacity to distinguish, would deprive art.7(1)(b) of any independent scope. Further, Baby-dry should be distinguished from the current case because it concerned the descriptiveness of an inventive and syntactically unusual juxtaposition of two descriptive elements rather than the distinctiveness of the addition of a non-distinctive element to a descriptive one. In any case the criterion of "any perceptible difference" could not be satisfied by the addition of a banal element such as a numeral.

Advocate General Jacobs started by pointing out what he found to be correct in the judgment of the Court of First Instance: the assessment under art.7(1)(b) had to be of the mark as a whole, although, at an intermediate stage, it might be helpful to examine each one of the components of the mark.

Regarding the element SAT he agreed that the term was both descriptive and lacking distinctiveness and added that in some cases there was a degree of overlap between the different situations covered by art.7(1)(b) and art.7(1)(c), whilst the respective aims of the provisions were distinct.[222]

4–124

---

[221] Point 28 of the Opinion of A.G. Jacobs.
[222] Citing *Campina Melkunie BV v Benelux-Merkenbureau* (C-265/00) [2004] E.C.R. I-1699.

He disagreed though, first, with its assessment regarding the element "2", that "numbers in general and the number '2' in particular are commonly used, in trade, for the presentation of the services concerned"[223] and therefore lacked distinctive character in that regard. He believed that a descriptive element commonly used in trade was very likely to lack distinctiveness, however this reasoning could not be automatically extended to non-descriptive elements. Numbers, in particular, were widely used to distinguish between categories of items, goods, or services, mentioning administrative forms, golf clubs and bus routes as examples. In some cases use of numbers would be descriptive, for example when they indicated size, but there was "no inherent reason why numerals—which are expressly included in the list in article 4 of the Regulation—should not also distinguish between the products of different suppliers. The approach taken by the Court of First Instance appears however to conflate the criterion of distinctiveness in article 7(1)(b) with that of descriptiveness in article 7(1)(c)".[224]

There should be no automatic presumption that a mark, which consisted exclusively of elements that individually lacked distinctive character, lacked itself distinctiveness, in the absence of an additional factor.

The Court of First Instance, according to the Advocate General, had failed to examine the sign as a whole and, only then, determine whether it is greater than the sum of its parts.

4–125 **(iv) Registrability of "SAT.2".** Regarding the substance of the action he supported that under art.61 of the Court's Statute, it was possible, and in the interests of procedural economy, to decide whether the sign "SAT.2" as a whole lacked distinctive character, within the meaning of art.7(1)(b).

He characterised the mark as a compound sign of a format that is very common in the field of broadcasting. The presence of a numerical identifier according to the Advocate General was clearly designed to ensure distinctiveness; the "very commercial use of these signs to designate television channels and associated products seems ample proof of the success of that approach. If the average consumer of television programmes and spin-offs had difficulty in identifying such signs as differentiating between products and their origins, they would not be used, particularly since the commercial pressures of advertising revenue and audience ratings create a powerful need for product loyalty".[225]

As to the aim of "not unduly restricting" the availability of certain signs, which was admittedly one of the aims of art.7(1)(b), he remarked that the number of possible distinctive and distinguishable combinations of a numerical with a non numerical element was very high. "If consumers can identify,

---

[223] *Campina Melkunie BV* (C-265/00) [2004] E.C.R. I-1699, para.46. *SAT.1 SatellitenFernsehen* (T-323/00) [2002] E.C.R. II-2839.
[224] Point 42 of the Opinion of A.G. Jacobs.
[225] Point 57 of the Opinion of A.G. Jacobs.

6. ARTICLE 3(1)(b)—DEVOID OF ANY DISTINCTIVE CHARACTER

for example, a satellite television channel by means of a sign such as 'SAT.2', they can clearly distinguish it from other combinations involving different letters and/or numbers which other broadcasters might wish to register as trade marks."[226]

(v) The principle of non-discrimination. Having reached a conclusion on the first ground of appeal, he looked briefly at the alternative ground of appeal, the applicability of the principle of equal treatment. He found the approach followed by the Court of First Instance to be the right one. If a previous decision of the Office were wrong, it should not be relied on to support the annulment of a subsequent correct decision, no person should be allowed to rely, in support of his claim, on unlawful acts committed in favour of another. 4–126

He also stated that the Boards of Appeal exercised circumscribed, not discretionary, powers when they decide on registrability, but accepted that a degree of subjectivity is inevitable when assessing the distinctiveness of a mark, even if the law had been applied correctly. In this context he emphasised the importance of maintaining consistency.

(c) The judgment of the Court

(i) The five parameters. From the judgment of the Court we can identify five parameters regarding the application of art.7(1)(b). 4–127

First, it linked the scope of the provision with the essential function of a trade mark,[227] in particular in view of the extent of protection afforded to a trade mark. "Article 7(1)(b) ... is thus intended to preclude registration of trade marks which are devoid of distinctive character which alone renders them capable of fulfilling that essential function".[228]

Secondly, it held that the viewpoint of the relevant public should determine registrability. In the case of products "intended for all consumers, the relevant public must be deemed to be composed of the average consumer, reasonably well-informed and reasonably observant and circumspect".[229]

Thirdly, distinctive character, like all the other grounds for refusal under art.7(1), was independent of the others and had to be examined separately from them. 4–128

---

[226] Point 58 of the Opinion of A.G. Jacobs.
[227] The essential function as described in *Hoffmann-la Roche & Co AG and Hoffmann-la Roche AG v Centrafarm Vertriebsgesellschaft Pharmazeutischer Erzeugnisse mbH* (102/77) [1978] E.C.R. 1139 and, after the Directive, in *Koninklijke Philips Electronics NV v Remington Consumer Products Ltd* (C-299/99) [2002] E.C.R. I-5475.
[228] *SAT.2*, para.23.
[229] *SAT.2*, para.24. *Lloyd Schuhfabrik Meyer & Co GmbH v Klijsen Handel BV* (C-342/97) [1999] E.C.R. I-3819; and *Libertel Groep BV v Benelux-Merkenbureau* (C-104/01) [2003] E.C.R. I-3793. Contrast with *Windsurfing Chiemsee Produktions- und Vertriebs GmbH v Boots- und Segelzubehör Walter Huber and Franz Attenberger* (C-108/97 & C-109/97) [1999] E.C.R. I-2779.

Fourthly, distinctive character, again like all the other grounds, should be seen in the light of the "general interest"[230] specifically underlying the provision. The Court reminded that in the context of *Libertel*[231]—registration of colours as such, not spatially delimited—art.3(1)(b) of the Directive was interpreted as aiming at the need not to restrict unduly the availability of colours for other undertakings offering for sale goods or services of the same type. Setting the barrier, in relation to "SAT.2", the Court noted: "Registration of a sign as a trade mark is not subject to a finding of a specific level of linguistic or artistic creativity or imaginativeness on the part of the proprietor of the trade mark. It suffices that the trade mark should enable the relevant public to identify the origin of the goods or services protected thereby and to distinguish them from those of other undertakings".[232]

Fifthly, for marks comprising words or a word and a digit, distinctiveness had to be assessed on the basis of the whole comprised by its parts. The fact that each part on its own is devoid of distinctive character did not mean that their combination also lacked distinctive character.[233]

4–129 **(ii) The application of article 7(1)(b).** The Court found that the Court of First Instance had correctly stated that assessing the distinctive character of a compound trade mark required considering it as a whole; however, it failed to base its decision on such an examination.

The Court accepted that the findings of the Court of First Instance on the lack of distinctive character of each individual element could not be challenged before the Court.[234]

But, the Court of First Instance had erred by relying on a separate analysis of each of the elements of the mark and concluding that "the fact that a compound trade mark consists only of elements devoid of distinctive character generally justifies the conclusion that that trade mark, considered as a whole, is also capable of being commonly used, in trade, for the presentation of the goods or services concerned".[235] The Court of First Instance had also added that such a conclusion would be invalidated only if there were concrete evidence showing that the mark was greater than the sum of its parts.

4–130 The second error of the Court of the First Instance was its position that trade marks which are capable of being commonly used, in trade, for the

---

[230] *SAT.2*, para.25; citing *Henkel KGaA v Office for Harmonisation in the Internal Market (Trade Marks and Designs)* (C-456/01 P and C-457/01 P) [2004] E.C.R. I-5089.
[231] *Libertel Groep BV* (C-104/01) [2003] E.C.R. I-3793.
[232] *SAT.2*, para.41.
[233] Citing *Campina Melkunie BV* (C-265/00) [2004] E.C.R. I-1699; and *Koninklijke KPN Nederland NV* (C-363/99) [2004] E.C.R. I-1619.
[234] The Court of First Instance had accepted the decision of the Board of Appeal that "SAT" lacked distinctive character in respect of services related with broadcasting via satellite and that the elements "2" and the element "." were or could be commonly used in trade, for the presentation of the goods or services concerned and were thus devoid of any distinctive character.
[235] *SAT.2*, para.49. *SAT.1 SatellitenFernsehen* (T-323/00) [2002] E.C.R. II-2839.

6. ARTICLE 3(1)(b)—DEVOID OF ANY DISTINCTIVE CHARACTER

presentation of the relevant goods or services in should not be registered. That, according to the Court, was a criterion relevant for the application of art.7(1)(c), but it was not the "yardstick against which art.7(1)(b) ... should be judged".[236] The Court of First Instance had deviated from the fourth parameter mentioned above. It must be stressed here that the Court itself avoided to describe clearly the public interest behind art.7(1)(b). Instead it preferred to refer to *Libertel* whilst highlighting the facts that characterised that case.

So, without having to examine the remaining grounds of the Appeal, the Court ruled that the contested judgment had to be set aside.

(iii) Registrability of "SAT.2". The Court chose to give itself a final judgment regarding the challenge against the decision of the Board of Appeal rather than refer the case back to the Court of First Instance.

It found that the Board had failed to explain why a combination of elements that was not considered to be descriptive was nevertheless found to fail art.7(1)(b) without any further explanation. In a way the Office had failed to discharge its burden of proof.

Further, such a combination could not be considered to be in principle devoid of any distinctive character because of the frequent use of trade marks consisting of such combinations in the field of telecommunications.

The Office had supported that in this case the additional elements were so weak that there could be no comparison with other signs incorporating "SAT". The Court disagreed. "The fact that the element associated with 'SAT' is in this case the digit '2' and a point, rather than another verbal element has ... no bearing on that analysis. Furthermore, the Office did not, at any stage in the proceedings, give as a reason for the difference in the treatment afforded to the appellant's application the likelihood of confusion between the sign which the latter sought to register and any previously registered trade mark."[237]

"In those circumstances, the contested decision must be annulled insofar as the Second Board of Appeal of the OHIM rejected, on the basis of Article 7(1)(b) of the regulation the application to register the term 'SAT.2' as a Community trade mark. Since the Court of First Instance has already held, in the contested judgment, that the contested decision could not be based on Article 7(1)(c) of that provision and, secondly, that the Second Board of Appeal of the OHIM had, in the aforementioned decision, failed to rule in the appeal brought before it so far as concerns the services falling within Class 35, the contested decision must be annulled as a whole."[238]

---

[236] *SAT.2*, para.36.
[237] *SAT.2*, para.46.
[238] *SAT.2*, para.48.

(3) BioID—the limited effect of "SAT.2"

4–133 The effect of "SAT.1" was tested in *BioID*, another appeal against a judgment of the Court of First Instance.[239]

BioID AG applied to register the sign BioID® as a Community Trade Mark for goods and services in Classes 9, 38, and 42 of the Nice Agreement, all in relation with "the computer-aided identification and/or verification of live organisms based on one or more specific biometric characteristics". The Bio component of the mark and the full stop after the ID component were depicted in bold; different fonts were used in respect of the Bio and the ID components. The application was refused on the basis of art.7(1)(b) and art.7(1)(c). The Board of Appeal confirmed the refusal[240]; the sign constituted a shortened form of the words "biometric identification" that described the characteristics of the specified goods and services and the additional graphic elements failed to bestow the sign with any distinctive character.

(a) The judgment of the Court of First Instance

4–134 According to the Court of First Instance's delineation of the scope of art.7(1)(b), it aimed to exclude, in particular, signs commonly used in trade in connection with the presentation of the specified goods or services; this also covered goods or services which could be used in that way. The reason behind this interpretation was that such signs could not enable the relevant public to repeat or avoid the experience of a purchase of the specified goods or services.[241]

The Court of First Instance also considered the method for assessing the applicability of art.7(1)(b). The sign had to be assessed as a whole; however, this was not inconsistent with a successive examination of the different composite elements of the mark. It also found that a sign should not be rejected under art.7(1)(b) when even one of its components possessed a distinctive character.

Applying its interpretive statements the Court of First Instance found that the relevant public would understand BioID as meaning "biometrical identification" and that it would be likely to be commonly used in trade for the presentation of the specified goods or services. The typeface and presentation of the sign—Arial in different degrees of boldness—were commonly used in trade for the presentation of all types of goods and services and

---

[239] *BioID AG v Office for Harmonisation in the Internal Market (Trade Marks and Designs)* (C-37/03 P) [2005] E.C.R. I-7975; *BioID AG v Office for Harmonisation in the Internal Market (Trade Marks and Designs)* (T-91/01) [2002] E.C.R. II-5159.
[240] Case R 538/1999-2, February 20, 2001.
[241] Citing *Rewe-Zentral v Office for Harmonisation in the Internal Market (Trade Marks and Designs)* (T-79/00) [2002] E.C.R. II-705.

6. ARTICLE 3(1)(b)—DEVOID OF ANY DISTINCTIVE CHARACTER

were equally devoid of any distinctive character. The same applied for the full stop at the end of the sign, a common indication that the word was an abbreviation, as well as the ® symbol. It concluded that the mark was composed of a combination of elements that each one of them was likely to be used, in trade, to present goods and services in the categories claimed by that trade mark and was therefore devoid of distinctive character in respect of the specified goods or services. However, its consideration of the mark went further than that; it also stated that there was no concrete evidence to indicate that the compound trade mark, taken as a whole, was greater than the sum of its parts. Only then the Court of First Instance confirmed that the trade mark was devoid of any distinctive character.

BioID AG claimed before the Court of Justice first that the Court of First Instance had misinterpreted and misapplied art.7(1)(b)—based on four lines of argument—and secondly that it had failed to examine whether the sign should be refused under art.7(1)(c) and find that it should not be refused registration according to that provision either, in essence asking the Court to decide that the mark was not descriptive.

(b) The Opinion of the Advocate General

(i) Limiting the scope of the appeal. Advocate General Léger viewed the second ground as a request for the Court to decide that the sign did not fail art.7(1)(c) in the case that it also found that it could overcome the art.7(1)(b) objection. Without considering this claim further he concluded that in fact there was only one plea, namely infringement of art.7(1)(b). 4–135

(ii) Interpreting the case law. The Advocate General started with his own analysis of the existing case law. This time the starting point was the overlap between the provisions rather than their individual nature. 4–136

First, he highlighted the overlap in scope between art.7(1)(b), art.7(1)(c), and art.7(1)(d); indeed he was inclined "to think that the signs referred to in Article 7(1)(c) and (d) constitute subsets of the broader category of signs devoid of any distinctive character within the meaning of Article 7(1)(b)".[242] *Postkantoor*[243] was an example of this approach, showing that a descriptive word mark was "on that account, necessarily devoid of any distinctive character within the meaning of Article 7(1)(b)".[244]

Secondly, he viewed the earlier statements of the Court on the individual character of each ground for refusal that had to be interpreted and applied independently from the others as simply meaning that the "circumstances required for a sign to fall within that subset are specific and must be

---

[242] Point 29 of the Opinion of A.G. Léger.
[243] *Koninklijke KPN Nederland NV* (C-363/99) [2004] E.C.R. I-1619.
[244] Point 29 of the Opinion of A.G. Léger.

interpreted in accordance with the general interest inherent in that ground for refusal".[245]

4-137   Third, he described the aim of art.7(1)(c)[246] as intending to leave freely available to all economic operators signs which may be used to designate the specified goods or services or characteristics of those products or services.

Fourthly, attempting to reconcile *Libertel*[247] with *SAT.1*,[248] he noted that the aim of availability should not be extended as the underlying general interest of art.7(1)(b) to all the kinds of signs which fell within its scope. Instead the Court found that the general interest behind art.7(1)(b) was "indissociable"[249] from the essential function of the trade mark, precluding from registration signs that were incapable of fulfilling the function of a trade mark for the specified goods and services concerned.

Finally, the assessment of distinctive character should consider the overall impression conveyed by the sign,[250] because consumers usually perceive a trade mark as a whole without examining its details. This did not prevent a separate examination of each element, it simply meant that the application of art.7(1)(b) should not rely exclusively on such an examination.

4-138   **(iii) Overall impression—the relevant public.** BioID's claim was twofold. First, it challenged the perspective of the examination. The Court of First Instance considered the relevant consumers to be well-informed whereas, according to BioID the specified goods or services were intended for the general public.

The Advocate General found this to be a question of fact, within the exclusive jurisdiction of the Court of First Instance.

4-139   **(iv) Overall impression—assessing the sign as a whole.** The second part of the claim supported that the Court of First Instance had failed to assess the sign as a whole, something it had itself accepted to be required.

---

[245] Point 30. The general interest behind each ground reflected different considerations, citing *Office for Harmonisation in the Internal Market (Trade Marks and Designs) v Erpo Möbelwerk* (C-64/02 P) [2004] E.C.R. I-0031; and *Henkel KGaA v Office for Harmonisation in the Internal Market (Trade Marks and Designs)* (C-456/01 P & C-457/01 P) [2004] E.C.R. I-5089.

[246] Referring to *Office for Harmonisation in the Internal Market (Trade Marks and Designs) v WM Wrigley Jr Co* (C-191/01 P) [2003] E.C.R. I-12447; the order in *Telefon & Buch v Office for Harmonisation in the Internal Market (Trade Marks and Designs)* (C-326/01 P) [2004] E.C.R. I-1371; *Windsurfing Chiemsee Produktions- und Vertriebs GmbH v Boots- und Segelzubehör Walter Huber and Franz Attenberger* (C-108/97 and C-109/97) [1999] E.C.R. I-2779; *Linde AG* (C-53/01), *Winward Industries Inc* (C-54/01) and *Rado Uhren AG* (C-55/01) [2003] E.C.R. I-3161; *Libertel Groep BV* (C-104/01) [2003] E.C.R. I-3793; and *Koninklijke KPN Nederland* (C-363/99) [2004] E.C.R. I-1619.

[247] *Libertel Groep BV* (C-104/01) [2003] E.C.R. I-3793.

[248] *SAT.1 SatellitenFernsehen GmbH* (C-329/02 P) [2004] E.C.R. I-8317.

[249] Point 37 of the Opinion of A.G. Léger.

[250] Citing *Koninklijke KPN Nederland NV* (C-363/99) [2004] E.C.R. I-1619.

6. ARTICLE 3(1)(b)—DEVOID OF ANY DISTINCTIVE CHARACTER

The Advocate General agreed with BioID on this. He supported that the Court of First Instance had carried out a separate appraisal of the various elements composing the sign and then relied on the presumption that devoid of distinctive character elements could not, once combined, have a distinctive character, examining the overall impression only as a secondary consideration.

On the other hand the Advocate General also disapproved the interpretive stance that if one of the elements of the sign possessed distinctive character it would attribute that character to the sign as a whole.

He believed that the Court of First Instance had wrongly applied in relation to distinctive character a criterion that was relevant in respect of descriptiveness. The criterion was whether the elements composing the sign might be used, in trade, for the presentation of the specified goods and services:

4–140

> "although that criterion is relevant in respect of an element descriptive of the goods or services covered by the application for registration or of their characteristics, as is the word element 'BioID' in this case, it is not relevant with regard to figurative elements like letters written in the Arial typeface; a simple full-stop or the element ®. The fact that those elements, which are not in themselves descriptive of the goods and services concerned, may be used for their presentation in trade does not, in itself, mean that they are devoid of any distinctive character in relation to those goods and services".[251]

(v) Word v figurative elements. Instead, he suggested a balancing exercise in order to ensure that no proprietary rights would be granted over wholly descriptive words:

4–141

> "a figurative sign composed of a wholly descriptive word element cannot be regarded as having a distinctive character unless it contains figurative elements which are individually distinctive and have a sufficient impact on the minds of the relevant public to keep their attention instead of that word element, or figurative elements capable of 'overriding' the meaning of that word element, and bestowing a distinctive effect on the overall sign".[252]

In practice, he admitted, this would be difficult to establish because usually it is easier to remember word rather than figurative elements.

(vi) The burden of proof. The second claim of BioID was that the Court of First Instance had failed to take into account that it could not be proved that the contested sign was actually used by the public or its competitors.

4–142

---

[251] Point 79 the Opinion of A.G. Léger.
[252] Point 75 of the Opinion of A.G. Léger.

The Advocate General reminded that in *Doublemint*[253] the Court held that it was sufficient that the sign could be used in a descriptive way; it was not necessary to show that the sign was actually used in that way.

4–143 **(vii) Registration of comparable marks.** BioID further claimed that the Court of First Instance had failed to take into account its argument that the Office had registered similar marks in the past. Advocate General Léger found that here the Court of First Instance had adopted the correct approach by holding that factual or legal grounds contained in a previous decision of the Office might constitute arguments supporting a plea alleging infringement of a provision of the Regulation.

Whether the appellant had produced any evidence to support its specific claim remained a question of fact within the exclusive jurisdiction of the Court of First Instance. Similarly, a claim based on the principle of equal treatment[254] should be rejected because even if the principle as such were applicable the appellant had failed to establish that the finding of the Court of First Instance was based on a distortion of the facts.

4–144 **(viii) Registrability of BioID.** Having proposed to set aside the contested judgment the Advocate General turned to the registrability of the sign.

According to the facts of the case it had been established that BioID was wholly descriptive of a characteristic of the specified goods and services. Similarly, he accepted that none of the figurative elements had "in itself a specific distinctive character"[255] in relation to the same goods and services.

Looking at the mark as a whole he found that the interaction between its elements did not give it a distinctive character. The figurative elements accentuated rather than diluted the descriptiveness of the abbreviation.

As a result the appeal against of the Board of Appeal should be dismissed.

(c) The judgment of the Court

4–145 The Court of Justice divided the appeal regarding the interpretation of art.7(1)(b) into four separate claims.

---

[253] *Office for Harmonisation in the Internal Market (Trade Marks and Designs) v WM Wrigley Jr Co* (C-191/01 P) [2003] E.C.R. I-12447.
[254] The A.G. doubted whether the principle was indeed applicable in such a case because of the following paradox: "either the conflicting decision taken by the Office authorising registration of a mark comparable to the sign in question is in accordance with the regulation and, if so, the Court of First Instance must logically find that the decision refusing registration of that sign has infringed the relevant provisions of the regulation, or the conflicting decision taken by the Office is not lawful and no person may rely, in support of his claim, on an error committed in favour of another" (fn.34).
[255] Point 104 of the Opinion of A.G. Léger.

6. ARTICLE 3(1)(b)—DEVOID OF ANY DISTINCTIVE CHARACTER

(i) The overall impression. The first claim concerned the overall impression produced by the trade mark. The Court repeated first that art.7(1)(b) intended to preclude registration of trade marks which were devoid of distinctive character "which alone renders them capable of fulfilling" their function.[256] Secondly, that distinctive character had to be determined from the viewpoint of the relevant public. Thirdly, that for compound marks the distinctive character had to be assessed according to the overall perception of the mark; the distinctive character of each one of the elements might be assessed separately but this should not lead to presumptions about the distinctive character of the compound mark.[257]

4–146

So the Court of First Instance had "rightly held that . . . is not inconsistent with a successive examination of the different composite elements of the mark to consider that mark as a whole".[258] And although it had found that a compound mark consisting of elements devoid of distinctive character should be itself presumed to be devoid of distinctive character, it had also directed part of its reasoning to considering the sign's distinctiveness as a whole.[259]

(ii) The burden of proof. The Court noted that proving that the trade mark applied for was commonly used by the public or by competitors was relevant under art.7(1)(d) but not under art.7(1)(b).[260] In any case the impact of a trade mark on consumers constituted of fact and remained outside the jurisdiction of the Court.

4–147

(iii) Registration of Comparable Marks. The decisions of the Board of Appeal under the Regulation were "adopted in the exercise of circumscribed powers and [were] not a matter of discretion".[261]

4–148

The legality of the decisions of Boards of Appeal should be assessed solely on the basis of the Regulation, as interpreted by the Community judicature, and not on the basis of a previous decision-making practice of the Boards.[262] Further, each application should be examined in the light of the specified goods or services. "It follows that the identity or similarity of the trade mark applied for in relation to another Community trade mark is irrelevant where, as in this case, elements of fact or of law which have been

---

[256] *BioID*, para.27, citing *SAT.1 SatellitenFernsehen GmbH* (C-329/02 P) [2004] E.C.R. I-8317.
[257] Citing *SAT.1 SatellitenFernsehen GmbH* (C-329/02 P) [2004] E.C.R. I-8317; *Koninklijke KPN Nederland NV* (C-363/99) [2004] E.C.R. I-1619; and *Campina Melkunie BV* (C-265/00) [2004] E.C.R. I-1699.
[258] *BioID*, para.31.
[259] Referring to paras 42, 43, and 44 of the judgment of the Court of First Instance.
[260] Citing *Office for Harmonisation in the Internal Market (Trade Marks and Designs) v Erpo Möbelwerk* (C-64/02 P) [2004] E.C.R. I-10031.
[261] *BioID*, para.47.
[262] Citing *Metso Paper Automation v Office for Harmonisation in the Internal Market (Trade Marks and Designs) (PAPERLAB)* (T-19/04) [2005] E.C.R. I-0000.

put forward in support of the application for that other mark are not put forward by the appellant for the purpose of showing the distinctive character of the trade mark applied for."[263]

In any case the Court of First Instance had accepted that previous decisions could constitute arguments supporting a plea alleging infringement of a provision of the Regulation. Whether the appellant had relied on grounds contained in earlier decisions of the Boards constituted a finding of fact.

4–149 **(iv) The criterion for the application of article 7(1)(b).** The Court held that the Court of First instance had wrongly applied a criterion that was relevant in respect of art.7(1)(c). Each of the grounds listed in art.7(1) had to be examined and applied on its own according to its own underlying interest. In the case of art.7(1)(b) the underlying interest was indissociable from the essential function of a trade mark.[264] Restating its stance in SAT.1 it held that whether the sign was likely to be commonly used in trade was not the yardstick for interpreting that provision.

4–150 **(v) Registrability of BioID.®** The Court taking up the option provided by art.61 of the Statute of the Court of Justice decided to give final judgment regarding the distinctive character of the contested sign. Its examination followed the logic of A.G. Léger.

It started by breaking down the sign into its elements. The abbreviation was indistinguishable from the goods and services covered by the trade mark application and did not possess the character that could guarantee the identity of the origin of the marked product or service to the consumer or end-user from the viewpoint of the relevant public.

Note, here, that there appear to be two audiences that count. First the consumer or end-user that is the recipient of the guarantee of origin. And secondly, the potentially broader, relevant public that determines whether the sign possesses the character to function as a guarantee of origin.

4–151 Then the Court considered the figurative and graphic features of the sign finding that there was no distinctive element therein that could "enable the trade mark applied for to guarantee, to the relevant public, the identity of the origin of the goods and services covered by the trade mark application".[265] This time there was only one relevant audience.

Considering the overall impression conveyed by the sign it found that the abbreviation BioID was the dominant element of that mark. The additional elements did not possess any feature, "in particular in terms of fancifulness or as regards the way in which they are combined, allowing that mark to

---

[263] *BioID*, para.49.
[264] Citing *SAT.1 SatellitenFernsehen GmbH* (C-329/02 P) [2004] E.C.R. I-8317.
[265] *BioID*, para.71.

6. ARTICLE 3(1)(b)—DEVOID OF ANY DISTINCTIVE CHARACTER

fulfil its essential function in relation to the goods and services covered by the trade mark application".[266]

As a result the sign was devoid of any distinctive character and the action against the decision of the Board of Appeal had to be dismissed.

(4) Nichols—no special conditions for surnames

The question of whether registration authorities could impose special conditions for the registration of surnames was considered by the Court in Nichols.[267] This was a reference from the High Court of Justice (England and Wales) that had to deal with a challenge of the practice of the UK's Patent and Trade Mark Office to refuse registration of common surnames without evidence of acquired distinctiveness. A combination of two factors determined commonness, the number of times the name appeared in the London Telephone Directory—names appearing more than two hundred times were considered to be common—and the type and breadth of the specified goods or services.

4–152

The contested application was for the mark Nichols for food and drink products dispensed from vending machines; the sign was considered to be devoid of any distinctive character because Nichols was a common surname and the specification would cover a large number of products originating from an equally large of undertakings. Without evidence of use, consumers would view the sign as a surname rather than a trade mark. The sign had been accepted for vending machines because that market was more specialised.

The High Court referred a list of detailed questions to the Court of Justice, seeking clarifications in relation to arts 2 and 3, but also the scope of art.6 and its interrelation with art.3:

> "1. In what circumstances, if any, must a trade mark (i.e. a 'sign' which complies with the requirements of art.2 of the Trade Marks Directive 89/104/EC) consisting of a single surname be refused registration as being in itself 'devoid of any distinctive character' within the meaning of article 3(1)(b) of the Directive?
>
> 2. In particular (a) must or (b) may such a sign, before it has acquired distinctive character by use, be refused registration if it is a common surname in the Member State in which the trade mark is sought to be registered or if it is a common surname in one or more of the other Member States?
>
> 3. If the answer to either Question 2(a) or (b) is in the affirmative, is it appropriate for national authorities to determine the matter by reference to the presumed expectations of an average customer in relation to the

---

[266] *BioID*, para.74.
[267] *Nichols Plc v Registrar of Trade Marks* (C-404/02) [2004] E.C.R. I-8499.

goods/services in question in the Member State, taking into account the commonness of the surname, the nature of the goods/services at issue, and the prevalence (or otherwise) of the use of surnames in the relevant trade?

4. Is it of significance for the purpose of determining whether a surname is 'devoid of any distinctive character' within article 3(1)(b) of the Directive that the effects of registration of the trade mark are restricted under article 6(1)(a)?

5. If so, (a) is the word 'person' in article 6(1) of the Directive to be understood as including a corporation or a business and (b) what amounts to 'honest practices in industrial or commercial matters'; in particular, does that expression apply where (i) the Defendant is not, in practice, deceiving the public by the use of his own name or (ii) the Defendant is merely causing unintentional confusion thereby?"[268]

(a) The Opinion of the Advocate General

4-153 Advocate General Ruiz-Jarabo Colomer expressed some sympathy for the position of the English court:

> "The national court, rather than taking a purely theoretical approach, prefers to take a realistic view of the functioning of the registered trade mark system. Accordingly, he [Mr Justice Jacob] suggests that attention be paid to the risk of monopolisation deriving from the registration of a common surname to cover a wide range of goods or services. In view of that danger, the possibility, which is costly in terms of time and money, of challenging some of those indications on the ground of non-use, after the expiry of five years following registration, does not seem to be an effective remedy. For the same reasons, it is inappropriate to take account, when analysing the distinctiveness of a trade mark, of considerations concerning the limitation of its effects, even though that seems to be the approach adopted in paragraph 37 of the Baby-Dry[269] judgment. In practice, favourable treatment is accorded to whoever has secured registration".[270]

He examined the first three questions posed by the English court together, simplifying their essence: are common surnames subject to specific distinctiveness conditions, in particular under art.3(1)(b)?

4-154 **(i) Registrability of Surnames.** Article 2 specifically included personal names in its indicative list and in practice surnames were frequently used as

---

[268] *Nichols*, para.6.
[269] *Procter & Gamble Co v Office for Harmonisation in the Internal Market (Trade Marks and Designs)* (C-383/99 P) [2001] E.C.R. I-6251.
[270] Point 18 of the Opinion of A.G. Ruiz-Jarabo Colomer.

6. ARTICLE 3(1)(b)—DEVOID OF ANY DISTINCTIVE CHARACTER

trade marks. The wording of art.6(1) and the absence of surnames from the list of art.3(1)(c) meant that they were not considered in principle to be generic or descriptive. So, he rejected the application of "keep free for other traders to use" considerations.

From a more practical perspective the Commission had underlined in its intervention that the policy of the UK Trade Mark Office was arbitrary and at odds with the Directive.

(ii) Surnames—distinctive character. The Advocate General accepted that determining distinctiveness inevitably involved a degree of subjectivity. However, he was not satisfied with the reasoning, submitted by the United Kingdom in support of its interpretive derogation, that in respect of common surnames recognition of a trade mark in the marketplace was not enough. It supported that its formula ensured that only surnames that identified the products of an undertaking could be protected as trade marks.

4–155

The Advocate General was willing to accept only that the distinguishing capability of surnames could vary from one sector of the economy to another. However, these variations were covered by the criteria imposed by the Court whilst there was no room for a new policy regarding surnames under art.3(1)(b):

> "The distinctive character must be analysed from the viewpoint of the average consumer of such types of products or services, the consumer being deemed to be reasonably well informed and reasonably observant and circumspect."[271]

This covered:

> "the particularity that, in certain sectors, common names or surnames are assiduously used to designate a commercial origin, sometimes by way of trade mark. If that is the case, there is nothing to prevent the registration authorities from finding that the mark has no capacity to distinguish. Such a finding must be specific and must not be made in an all-embracing or abstract manner".[272]

The commonness of the surname would be one of the factors that had to be taken into account, but on its own should not be seen as decisive.

4–156

Article 3(1)(b) on the other hand prohibited "the registration of signs which are devoid of any real distinctive character, that is to say, those signs

---

[271] Point 40, citing *Windsurfing Chiemsee Produktions- und Vertriebs GmbH v Boots- und Segelzubehör Walter Huber and Franz Attenberger* (C-108/97 & C-109/97) [1999] E.C.R. I-2779; *Gut Springenheide and Tusky v Oberkreisdirektor des Kreises Steinfurt—AMT für Lebensmittelüberwachung* (Case C-210/96) [1998] E.C.R. I-4657; and *Lloyd Schuhfabrik Meyer & Co GmbH v Klijsen Handel BV* (C-342/97) [1999] E.C.R. I-3819.
[272] Point 41 of the Opinion of A.G. Ruiz-Jarabo Colomer.

which the average consumer, who is reasonably well informed and reasonably observant and circumspect, does not identify as reliably indicating the commercial origin of the product".[273]

Considering the interaction between art.3(1)(b) and art.6(1)(a) he suggested that the limitations of the latter should not affect the application of the former. "Nothing in the directive requires a less rigorous examination for the purposes of classification, having regard to the existence of provisions restricting the effects of the trade mark."[274] The reference to art.12 of the Regulation—the equivalent of art.6 of the Directive—in Baby-Dry[275] was not relevant because "that judgment does not draw any practical inference whatsoever from that reference".[276] This was confirmed in *Libertel*[277] where the Court opted for a stringent and thorough examination at the time of the application ensuring that only signs that deserved trade mark protection would benefit from the broad infringement provisions.

(b) The judgment of the Court

4–157 The Court considered the first four conditions together: "the national court seeks essentially to ascertain what conditions apply to the assessment, in the context of Article 3(1)(b) of Directive 89/104, of the distinctiveness or otherwise of a trade mark constituted by a surname, particularly where that surname is common, and whether the fact that the effects of registration of the trade mark are limited pursuant to Article 6(1)(a) of the same directive has an impact on that assessment".[278] Article 6(1)(a) provides that the trade mark shall not entitle the proprietor to prohibit a third party from using, in the course of trade his own name or address.

The inclusion of personal names in the art.2 list combined with the interpretation and assessment of distinctive character under art.3(1)(b) were the determinative factors. Distinctive character should not be assessed in abstract, but following a specific assessment, in relation to the specified goods or services and from the perspective of the relevant consumer.[279]

4–158 **(i) Same criteria for all types of marks.** There was "no distinction between different categories of trade mark",[280] the same criteria applied to

---

[273] Point 43 of the Opinion of A.G. Ruiz-Jarabo Colomer.
[274] Point 49 of the Opinion of A.G. Ruiz-Jarabo Colomer.
[275] *Procter & Gamble Co* (C-383/99 P) [2001] E.C.R. I-6251.
[276] Point 50 of the Opinion of A.G. Ruiz-Jarabo Colomer.
[277] *Libertel Groep BV* (C-104/01) [2003] E.C.R. I-3793.
[278] *Nichols*, para.17.
[279] Citing *Koninklijke Philips Electronics NV* (C-299/99) [2002] E.C.R. I-5475; and *Henkel KGaA v Deutches Patent- und Markenamt* (C-218/01) [2004] E.C.R. I-1725.
[280] *Nichols*, para.24, citing *Linde AG* (C-53/01), *Winward Industries Inc* (C-54/01) and *Rado Uhren AG* (C-55/01) [2003] E.C.R. I-3161; and *Glaverbel SA v Office for Harmonisation in the Internal Market (Trade Marks and Designs)* (C-445/02 P) [2004] E.C.R. I-6267.

6. ARTICLE 3(1)(b)—DEVOID OF ANY DISTINCTIVE CHARACTER

personal names. In an absolute manner the Court stated that stricter criteria could not be applied.

(ii) Consumer perception. In the context of the specific assessment it might prove more difficult to find distinctive character for some categories of marks as a result of consumer perception.[281] However this should not lead to a priori assumptions regarding distinctive character or the acquirement of distinctive character through use. 4–159

Note that the Court talks about the distinctive character of marks rather than the capability of some signs to distinguish. In general it appears that distinctiveness questions are more likely to be resolved under art.3(1)(b).

(iii) Competition considerations. The Court also rejected the argument that registration would give an advantage to the first of those bearing the same surname to apply. First, because the Directive contained "no provision to that effect, regardless, moreover, of the category to which the trade mark whose registration is sought belongs".[282] 4–160

In any case, the Court added, art.6(1)(a) limited the right following registration "that is to say after the existence of the mark's distinctive character has been established. It cannot therefore be taken into account for the purposes of the specific assessment of the distinctive character of the trade mark before the trade mark is registered".[283] Article 6(1)(a) should have no impact on the assessment of distinctive character.

(5) Erpo—registrability of slogans

Registrability of slogans came before the Court[284] as an appeal against a decision of the Court of First Instance[285] annulling a decision of the Board of Appeal that had rejected the application for registering as a Community Trade Mark the slogan "DAS PRINZIP DER BEQUEMLICHKEIT" (the principle of comfort) for land vehicles and parts therefore, and household furniture on the basis of art.7(1)(b) and 7(1)(c).[286] 4–161

---

[281] Citing *Henkel KGaA v Deutches Patent- und Markenamt* (C-281/01) [2004] E.C.R. I-1725; *Procter & Gamble v Office for Harmonisation in the Internal Market (Trade Marks and Designs)* (C-468/01 P to C-472/01 P) [2004] E.C.R. I-5141; and *Glaverbel SA v Office for Harmonisation in the Internal Market (Trade Marks and Designs)* (C-445/02 P) [2004] E.C.R. I-6267.
[282] *Nichols*, para.31.
[283] *Nichols*, para.33.
[284] *Office for Harmonisation in the Internal Market v Erpo Möbelwerk* (C-64/02) [2004] E.C.R. I-10031.
[285] *ErpoMöbelwerk v Office for Harmonisation in the Internal Market* (T-138/00) [2001] E.C.R. II-3739.
[286] Case R-392/1999-3, March 23, 2000. Note that the Board had accepted the registrability of the slogan for hand-operated tools and cutlery.

(a) The judgment of the Court of First Instance

4-162 The Office's appeal targeted the interpretation of art.7(1)(b) by the Court of First Instance which had stated that the "dismissal, on the basis of Art.7(1)(b) of Reg.No.40/94, of the appeal brought before the Board of Appeal would have been justified only if it had been demonstrated that the combination of the words 'das Prinzip der ...' ('the principle of ...') alone with a term designating a characteristic of the goods or services concerned is commonly used in business communications and, in particular, in advertising. The contested decision does not contain any finding to that effect and neither in its written pleadings nor at the hearing has the Office asserted that such a usage exists".[287]

Note that the Board of Appeal had appeared to require specifically for slogans an additional element of imagination.

The Office supported that by holding that refusing registration should be limited to cases where it is demonstrated that the sign in question is commonly used in the relevant commercial circles, the Court of First Instance had introduced a new criterion in the application of art.7(1)(b).

4-163 It held the view that slogans, like colours and three-dimensional marks, had to incorporate something additional in order to gain the necessary distinctive character because in most cases they fulfilled an advertising function.

Erpo on the other hand viewed the contested decision as simply stating that the Board's decision did not contain an objective statement of the reasons for refusing registration rather than imposing a new criterion. Further, it stressed that art.12(b) of the Regulation would ensure that competition would not suffer as a result of a liberal policy regarding the registration of slogans.

(b) The Opinion of the Advocate General

4-164 Advocate General Maduro noted that the paragraph challenged by the Office should not be seen in isolation; the preceding paragraphs provided a fuller picture.[288]

He started by exploring the correct criteria for the interpretation and application of the provision. The next steps would be to determine the

---

[287] Judgment of the Court of First Instance, para.46.

[288] "43. Furthermore, the Board of Appeal again noted, in para.30 of the contested decision, that DAS PRINZIP DER BEQUEMLICHKEIT was characterised by the lack of any additional element of imagination. In addition, the Office submitted in its response that, in order to be able to serve as marks, slogans must possess an additional element ... of originality and that the term at issue had such originality.

44. In that regard, it is clear from the case-law of the Court of First Instance that lack of distinctiveness cannot be found because of lack of imagination or of an additional element of originality (Case T-135/99 *Taurus-Film v Office for Harmonisation in the Internal Market (Trade Marks and Designs)* [2001] E.C.R. II-379, paragraph 31; Case T-136/99 *Taurus-Film v Office for Harmonisation in the Internal Market (Trade Marks and Designs)* [2001] E.C.R. II-397, paragraph 31; and Case T-87/00 Bank für Arbeit und Wirtschaft v Office for

6. ARTICLE 3(1)(b)—DEVOID OF ANY DISTINCTIVE CHARACTER

compatibility, first, of the contested statement of the Court of First Instance and, secondly, of the position of the Board of Appeal with the criteria adopted by the Court.

Before concentrating on art.7(1)(b), however, he commented on the relationship between art.7(1)(b) and art.7(1)(c) and noted that the two provisions may, but need not necessarily, overlap.

A purely descriptive trade mark would in principle be devoid of distinctive character. But failing or passing the obstacle of art.7(1)(c) should not be seen as an indication of lack or existence of distinctive character.

4–165

Concurring with A.G. Jacobs[289] he supported that art.7(1)(b) did not simply repeat the "capable of distinguishing" requirement of art.4 and art.7(1)(a). The "distinctive character" requirement covered distinctiveness in relation to the specified products; it did not refer to the general, absolute, and abstract capacity to distinguish.[290]

He described the "criterion" for assessing distinctive character as a two-tiered process, referring first "to the goods or services in respect of which registration is sought and which it is intended to distinguish and, secondly, to the perception of the relevant persons, namely the consumers of the goods or services in question. That means that it must be examined in the light of the presumed perception of an average consumer of the category of goods or services in question, who is reasonably well informed and reasonably observant and circumspect".[291]

(i) Registrability of slogans. Regarding slogans in particular the Court of Justice had already ruled in *Merz and Krell*[292] that registration of

4–166

Harmonisation in the Internal Market (Trade Marks and Designs) [2001] E.C.R. II-1259, paragraphs 39 and 40). Furthermore, it is not appropriate to apply to slogans criteria which are stricter than those applicable to other types of sign.

45. To the extent that the Board of Appeal, in paragraph 31 of the contested decision, again points out the lack of any conceptual tension which would create surprise and so make a striking impression, it must be stated that that point is really only a paraphrase of the Board of Appeal's finding of additional element of imagination."

[289] *SAT.1 SatellitenFernsehen GmbH* (C-329/02 P) [2004] E.C.R. I-8317.

[290] *Windsurfing Chiemsee Produktions- und Vertriebs GmbH v Boots- und Segelzubehör Walter Huber and Franz Attenberger* (C-108/97 & C-109/97) [1999] E.C.R. I-2779; *Koninklijke Philips Electronics NV* (C-299/99) [2002] E.C.R. I-5475; *Linde AG* (C-53/01), *Winward Industries Inc* (C-54/01) and *Rado Uhren AG* (C-55/01) [2003] E.C.R. I-3161; and *Henkel KGaA v Deutches Patent- und Markenamt* (C-218/01) [2004] E.C.R. I-1725, confirmed this link with the specified in the application goods or services. The Court of First Instance followed the same route in cases like *Sykes Enterprises Inc v Office for Harmonisation in the Internal Market (Trade Marks and Designs)* (T-130/01) [2002] E.C.R. II-5179 ;and *Best Buy Concepts Inc v Office for Harmonisation in the Internal Market (Trade Marks and Designs)* (T-122/01) [2003] E.C.R. II-2235.

[291] Point 29, codifying the principles of, amongst others, *Lloyd SchuhfabrikMeyer & Co GmbH v Klijsen Handel BV* (C-342/97) [1999] E.C.R. I-3819; and *Merz&Krell GmbH & Co v Deutches Patent- und Markenamt* (C-517/99) [2001] E.C.R. I-6959.

[292] *Merz&Krell GmbH & Co v Deutches Patent- und Markenamt* (C-517/99) [2001] E.C.R. I-6959.

ABSOLUTE GROUNDS

a sign or indication also used as an advertising slogan was not excluded as such.

Here, though, the question was whether there should be different requirements for the registration of slogans.

Advocate General Maduro rejected the adoption of stricter criteria for slogans. The Court of Justice had ruled that there should be no distinction made between different categories of trade marks.[293] In practice, he added, registrability of any trade mark had to be specifically assessed for each particular case and this did entail considering the nature and the particular characteristics of each individual mark.

4–167 The Court had accepted that some types of signs, for example colours,[294] were perceived in different ways by consumers; the same should be applied to slogans conveying a promotional message:

> "In those circumstances, an average consumer will not perceive the combination of words praising the quality of a product as an indication of the commercial origin of that product as distinct from another product in the same category produced by a different undertaking. This does not apply to word combinations of a different sort, such as invented terms (for example, XTPO33) which have no inherent meaning such as to commend qualities generally associated with all the products in a certain category. Nor does it apply to cases where the slogan includes an element which enables the average consumer to distinguish the commercial origin of the product for which registration is sought from other products in the same category but of a different commercial origin."[295]

Slogans originally lacking the necessary distinctive character could still obtain it through use and the application of art.7(3) of the Regulation.

So, did the contested judgment assess the distinctive character of this slogan properly? He believed that the Court of First Instance had failed to follow the criteria ascertained in the case law of the Court of Justice.

4–168 The Court of First Instance had rightly decided that a slogan should not be rejected merely because it did not display any additional element of imagination, however it was wrong to suggest that, in assessing in practice the distinctive character of a slogan, the competent authority might not find that it lacked any additional element of imagination that would render it capable of distinguishing products according to origin:

> "An assessment, in a particular case, of the capacity of a slogan, from the point of view of the average consumer, to establish in the minds of the public to which it is addressed a link between the owner of the trade mark

---

[293] He cited *Koninklijke Philips Electronics NV* (C-299/99) [2002] E.C.R. I-5475.
[294] Citing *Libertel Groep BV* (C-104/01) [2003] E.C.R. I-3793.
[295] Point 37 of the Opinion of A.G. Maduro.

6. ARTICLE 3(1)(b)—DEVOID OF ANY DISTINCTIVE CHARACTER

and the goods or services whose commercial origin it is supposed to identify, must take into account the nature and the particular characteristics of the combination of words in respect of which registration is sought".[296]

He found that the burden of proof it imposed on the Office violated art.7(1)(b). The Office had to prove that "that combination of words is commonly used in trade",[297] a new requirement incompatible with the "criterion" identified by the Advocate General.

The Advocate General also mentioned approvingly the argument that such slogans should be left free for competing undertakings to use.

Article 12(b) of the Regulation would not always provide a compensating mechanism once the mark has been registered following the adoption of a broad registrability criterion. New competitors "ought to be free to invoke the same qualities in presenting their products, without any legal constraints".[298]

4–169

Referring to *Doublemint*[299] he transposed the interpretation of art.7(1)(c) regarding potentially descriptive terms to art.7(1)(b). The Office was right to underline that requiring proof of use in business communications and advertising in order to refuse registration was in conflict with art.7(1)(c). The Court of First Instance had added to art.7(1)(b) what in reality should be examined under art.7(1)(d).[300]

(c) The judgment of the Court

The Court of Justice agreed with A.G. Maduro and the Court of First Instance that it was inappropriate to apply to slogans stricter criteria than those applied to other types of sign.

4–170

However, citing *Henkel* and *Procter and Gamble*,[301] it added that in applying those criteria, it might become apparent that the relevant public's perception is not necessarily the same for each of those categories. In practice it could prove more difficult to establish distinctiveness for some categories of marks.

(i) The function of slogans. For slogans the difficulty arose from their promotional function that the Office had brought to the fore. It would be more difficult to find distinctiveness for a slogan:

4–171

---

[296] Point 46 of the Opinion of A.G. Maduro.
[297] Point 51 of the Opinion of A.G. Maduro.
[298] Point 54 of the Opinion of A.G. Maduro.
[299] *WM Wrigley Jr Co* (C-191/01 P) [2003] E.C.R. I-12447.
[300] Citing *Merz&Krell GmbH & Co* (C-517/99) [2001] E.C.R. I-6959.
[301] *Henkel KGaA* (C-456/01 P and C-457/01 P) [2004] E.C.R. I-5089.

"in particular if it were established ... that it served a promotional function consisting, for example, of commending the quality of the product in question and that the importance of that function was not manifestly secondary to its purported function as a trade mark, namely that of guaranteeing the origin of the product.

Indeed, in such a case, the authorities may take account of the fact that average consumers are not in the habit of making assumptions about the origin of products on the basis of such slogans".[302]

This though should not lead to the adoption of "specific criteria supplementing or derogating from the criterion of distinctiveness".[303]

The Court of First Instance was right to annul the decision of the Board of Appeal because it had imposed a different and stricter criterion for advertising slogans.

4–172 Albeit, it was wrong to adopt a new criterion for the application of art.7(1)(b), a criterion that was adapted to assist in the application of another provision, art.7(1)(d). The Court repeated that each of the grounds for refusal listed in art.7(1) was independent of the others and called for separate examination.[304]

Turning to the registrability of slogans the Court noted that the fact that they might also function as advertising slogans should not automatically lead to rejection.[305]

The real issue was whether it made it possible to identify the specified product "as originating from a given undertaking and therefore to distinguish the product from those of other undertakings and, therefore, is able to fulfil the essential function of the trade mark".[306]

4–173 The assessment of distinctiveness was a two-tiered exercise. According to Procter and Gamble[307] distinctiveness had to be assessed, first, in relation to the specified goods or services and, secondly, in relation to the perception of them by the relevant public.

This should be the only applicable test; Erpo's argument that the effect of art.12(b) should also be taken into account was rejected.[308]

---

[302] *Erpo*, para.35.
[303] *Erpo*, para.36.
[304] *Henkel KGaA* (C-456/01 P and C-457/01 P) [2004] E.C.R. I-5089.
[305] *Merz&Krell GmbH* (C-517/99) [2001] E.C.R. I-6959.
[306] *Erpo*, para.42; *Procter & Gamble* (C-468/01 P to C-472/01 P) [2004] E.C.R. I-5141; *Merz&Krell GmbH & Co* (C-517/99) [2001] E.C.R. I-6959; and *Linde AG* (C-53/01), *Winward Industries Inc* (C-54/01) and *Rado Uhren AG* (C-55/01) [2003] E.C.R. I-3161.
[307] *Procter & Gamble* (C-468/01 P to C-472/01 P) [2004] E.C.R. I-5141.
[308] Repeating what the Court had already ruled in *Libertel Groep BV* (C-104/01) [2003] E.C.R. I-3793.

6. ARTICLE 3(1)(b)—DEVOID OF ANY DISTINCTIVE CHARACTER

(ii) Wrong reasoning. Right outcome. Concluding, in this domino of errors, the Court accepted that the judgment of the Court of First Instance was vitiated by an error of law. Albeit, this did not alter the outcome of the dispute, since the Court of First Instance had also held, correctly this time, that the decision of the Board should be annulled. The operative part of the contested judgment remained justified.[309]

4–174

(6) Libertel—the distinctiveness of colours

In *Libertel*,[310] the referring court had focused on whether colours could have sufficient distinctive character to function and be protected as trade marks. It referred the following questions to the Court:

4–175

"(1) Is it possible for a single specific colour which is represented as such or is designated by an internationally applied code to acquire a distinctive character for certain goods or services within the meaning of Article 3(1)(b) of the Directive?

(2) If the answer to the first question is in the affirmative: (a) in what circumstances may it be accepted that a single specific colour possesses a distinctive character in the sense used above? (b) does it make any difference if registration is sought for a large number of goods and/or services, rather than for a specific product or service, or category of goods or services respectively?

(3) In the assessment of the distinctive character of a specific colour as a trade mark, must account be taken of whether, with regard to that colour, there is a general interest in availability, such as can exist in respect of signs which denote a geographical origin?

(4) When considering the question whether a sign, for which registration as a trade mark is sought, possesses the distinctive character referred to in Article 3(1)(b) of the Directive, must the Benelux Trade Mark Office confine itself to an assessment in abstracto of distinctive character or must it take account of all the actual facts of the case, including the use made of the sign and the manner in which the sign is used?"[311]

(a) The Opinion of the Advocate General

Advocate General Léger looked at distinctiveness from a broader perspective, taking into account art.2 considerations.

4–176

---

[309] The Court cited *VBA v Florimex* (C-265/97 P) [2000] E.C.R. I-2061 as an example of its case law setting that if the grounds of a judgment of the Court of First Instance revealed an infringement of Community law but the operative part appeared well founded on other legal grounds, the appeal should be dismissed.

[310] *Libertel Groep BV* (C-104/01) [2003] E.C.R. I-3793.

[311] Reproduced in para.20.

In an introductory consideration of the concept of a colour he characterised as a sensation rather than a pre-existing objective reality; its perception would vary according to the nature and intensity of light and the eye of the observer.[312]

The Advocate General focused on the limited number of available colours starting from Newton's seven principal colours and the three primary colours of painters and finishing with the limited number of words that originally refer to colours.[313] And he maintained that despite the millions of industrially produced shades or tonalities defined according to chromatic dictionaries, like the Pantone or the Acoat Colour Codification systems, the human eye could distinguish only a limited number of shades with certainty.[314]

4–177 A second observation he made was that colour was a language, provoking feelings and conveying information. However, these were "purely cultural phenomena...based on conventions"[315]; colours did not exist independently, instead they were the attributes of something else.

Colours per se failed the distinctiveness requirement, that, in the context of art.2, he perceived it to require the signs to be intrinsically capable of having a distinctive character.[316]

A colour per se did not have a distinctive character having regard only to its intrinsic characteristics because, first, the application for its registration "would not allow determination of the sign actually appearing on the goods or in association with the services in question",[317] and, secondly, because it would be unable to fulfil the task of indicating the origin of goods or services as a result without any possibility of confusion. Following his earlier analysis of the concept of colours he repeated that any significance a colour might have was because of social conventions and depended on the conditions in which the colour was seen. "It follows that a colour can only be clearly defined if it is seen in the context of a particular shape or design."[318]

---

[312] Citing La Couleur, Dossier pour la Science No.27, and Manuel de la Couleur (Solar, 2001).
[313] White, red, black, green, yellow, blue, grey, brown, pink, violet, and orange. Other words are borrowed from different contexts, for example lemon or rust.
[314] Up to 200, but commonly under 100 of shades, citing M. Pastoureau, *Dictionnaire des Couleurs de Notre Temps* (Bonneton, 1999).
[315] Point 45 of the Opinion of A.G. Léger.
[316] Citing the interpretation of the Court of First Instance in *Procter and Gamble (Baby Dry)* (T-163/98) [1999] E.C.R. II-2383; and of the Court of Justice in *Koninklijke Philips Electronics NV* (C-299/99) [2002] E.C.R. I-5475 that linked distinctiveness with the specification of the application, and, in the case of Philips that art.3(1)(a) precluded the registration of signs which were not generally capable of being a trade mark.
[317] Point 85 of the Opinion of A.G. Léger.
[318] Point 87, referring to an example given by Klinkenberg, in Qu'est-ce que le Signe? in Dorties (Ed), *Le Langage* (Editions Sciences Humaine, 2001) at 105: in the context of the highway code, red in a round shape signified a prohibition, red in a triangular shape signified a danger.

6. ARTICLE 3(1)(b)—DEVOID OF ANY DISTINCTIVE CHARACTER

Reviewing a number of decisions of the Office to accept the registration of a colour as such[319] he noted that they have been granted in very exceptional cases. He questioned however whether they truly functioned as trade marks. **4–178**

He would have required evidence that the colours on their own would lead consumers to a purchasing decision. "If this other thing is lacking, consumers will no longer be able to identify the origin of the goods or services concerned with certainty. In other words, if the logo or the series of letters that they were used to seeing on goods or their wrapping were no longer to be there, or if the shape of goods were to have changed, consumers might be in doubt as to their origin, even though the colour remained the same."[320]

So, he accepted the logic of national registrations in the United Kingdom and Ireland of colours applied on premises or uniforms.[321]

He also noted that in *Qualitex* the Supreme Court of the United States of America accepted that a particular shade of a colour applied on the external surface of a specific product could be protected as a trade mark following evidence of distinctiveness acquired through use, a practice followed by the United States Patent and Trade Mark Office.[322] **4–179**

From an interpretive perspective the reference to the US jurisprudence and practice is particularly interesting, evidencing openness to foreign practice.

The Advocate General supported that all these cases showed that a colour that functioned as a trade mark could be protected without having to be registered as such; unfair competition, civil liability, and consumer protection laws could also contribute to protection.

(i) Competition considerations. In addition, protection of a colour per se raised competition questions; for example because of its indeterminate representation protection of a particular shade of blue, would at the end result in an exclusive right of the colour blue. The limited number of colours that were actually used in practice for particular goods or services combined with the growing use of colours to attract the attention of consumers rendered the competition issue even more pertinent. "It would thus be enough for several colours per se to be registered as trade marks to confer a real monopoly of use of the colour on a few traders. Such a monopoly could distort competition."[323] It "could even stop new traders entering a particular market".[324] **4–180**

---

[319] Lilac for chocolate, Registration of October 27, 1999, No.31336; magenta for telecommunication goods and services, Registration of August 3, 2000, No.212787; and yellow for anticorrosion products; Registration of January 9, 2001, No.396176.
[320] Point 91 of the Opinion of A.G. Léger.
[321] Respectively: *BP Amoco Plc v John Kelly Ltd and Glenshane Tourist Services Ltd* [2001] F.S.R. 21; and a United Parcels Service in the USA registration no. 221818, October 27, 1998.
[322] *Qualitex*, 514 U.S. 159 (1995); Registration no. 1633711; see paras 11–026 and following.
[323] Point 101 of the Opinion of A.G. Léger.
[324] Point 103 of the Opinion of A.G. Léger.

So, having found that colour per se did not satisfy the conditions of art.2 A.G. Léger decided he did not have to look at the art.3 questions referred by the Court.

(b) The judgment of the Court

4–181   The Court accepted that it was necessary to start its analysis from art.2 which set three conditions for a colour to be registered as a trade mark.

4–182   **(i) Distinctiveness of colours.** Regarding distinctiveness of colours the Court remarked that although colours were capable of conveying certain associations of ideas and arousing feelings, they possessed "little inherent capacity for communicating specific information".[325] However, this would not justify a blanket conclusion.

In some circumstances a colour per se might function as a trade mark.

4–183   **(ii) Registrability of colours—the general interest—article 3(1)(c) and article 3(1)(e) considerations.** Having reached the opposite conclusion from the Advocate General the Court turned to consider whether in order to determine registrability recourse had to be given to the general interest that a particular colour had to remain available for other competitors to use.

The right angle for resolving this was the perspective of the average consumer, reasonably well-informed and reasonably observant and circumspect[326] rather than the availability or not of a large number of colours.

From that perspective the:

> "number of colours which that public is capable of distinguishing is limited, because it is rarely in a position directly to compare products in various shades of colour. It follows that the number of different colours that are in fact available as potential trade marks to distinguish goods or services must be regarded as limited".[327]

4–184   The Court repeated that trade marks constitute an essential element in the system of undistorted competition which the EC Treaty seeks to establish and maintain[328]; this, together with the fact that trade mark rights are potentially perpetual had to be taken into account when considering the rights and powers they confer.

---

[325] *Libertel*, para.40.
[326] According to *Lloyd Schuhfabrik Meyer & Co GmbH v Klijsen Handel BV* (C-342/97) [1999] E.C.R. I-3819.
[327] *Libertel*, para.47.
[328] Citing *SA CNL-SUCAL NV v Hag GF AG* (C-10/89) [1990] E.C.R. I-3711; and *Bayerische Motorenwerke AG and BMW Nederland BV v Deenik* (C-63/97) [1999] E.C.R. I-905.

6. ARTICLE 3(1)(b)—DEVOID OF ANY DISTINCTIVE CHARACTER

Citing *Philips*[329] the Court reiterated that the public interest might limit trade mark rights and art.3 should be interpreted according to the public interest underlying each one of the grounds of the provision. The public interest under art.3(1)(c) was that "the signs and indications descriptive of the categories of goods or services for which registration is sought may be freely used by all"[330] whereas under art.3(1)(e) shapes whose "essential characteristics perform a technical function and were chosen to fulfil that function may be freely used by all".[331]

For colours the Court raised a general objection based on their nature and linked with the aims of art.3(1)(c) and art.3(1)(e).

It opted to adopt the colour depletion theory holding that the registration of colours per se, not spatially delimited, coupled with the limited number of actually available colours meant that:

4–185

> "a small number of trade mark registrations for certain services or goods could exhaust the entire range of the colours available.
>
> Such an extensive monopoly would be incompatible with a system of undistorted competition, in particular because it could have the effect of creating an unjustified competitive advantage for a single trader. Nor would it be conducive to economic development or the fostering of the spirit of enterprise for established traders to be able to register the entire range of colours that is in fact available for their own benefit, to the detriment of new traders".[332]

The public interest was "in not unduly restricting the availability of colours for the other operators who offer for sale goods or services of the same type as those in respect of which registration is sought".[333]

Broad specifications would exacerbate the conflict with the public interest.

The contention of the Commission that art.6 covered that public interest was rejected. The Court aware of the historical development of the German doctrine resisted the shift in terms of time and competence from the time of examining the application to the time of enforcing the right; the Directive necessitated a review prior to registration, not posteriori. "It must be a stringent and full examination, in order to prevent trade marks from being

4–186

---

[329] *Koninklijke Philips Electronics NV* (C-299/99) [2002] E.C.R. I-5475.
[330] *Windsurfing Chiemsee Produktions- und Vertriebs GmbH v Boots- und Segelzubehör Walter Huber and Franz Attenberger* (C-108/97 & C-109/97) [1999] E.C.R. I-2779; and *Linde AG* (C-53/01), *Winward Industries Inc* (C-54/01) and *Rado Uhren AG* (C-55/01) [2003] E.C.R. I-3161.
[331] *Koninklijke Philips Electronics NV* (C-299/99) [2002] E.C.R. I-5475; and *Linde AG* (C-53/01), *Winward Industries Inc* (C-54/01) and *Rado Uhren AG* (C-55/01) [2003] E.C.R. I-3161.
[332] *Libertel*, para.54.
[333] *Libertel*, para.55.

improperly registered. As the Court has already held, for reasons of legal certainty and good administration, it is necessary to ensure that trade marks whose use could successfully be challenged before the courts are not registered."[334]

It concluded that:

> "in assessing the potential distinctiveness of a given colour as a trade mark, regard must be had to the general interest in not unduly restricting the availability of colours for the other traders who offer for sale goods or services of the same type as those in respect of which registration is sought".[335]

4–187   (iii) **Distinctive character of a colour per se.** The Court then considered the issue of distinctiveness of a colour per se under art.3(1)(b) and art.3(3) based on the essential function of guaranteeing the identity of the origin of the marked products, adding that "regard must be had both to the ordinary use of trade marks as a badge of origin in the sectors concerned and to the perception of the relevant public",[336] in this case an average consumer, reasonably well-informed and reasonably observant and circumspect who only rarely has the chance to make a direct comparison between the different marks but must place his trust in the imperfect picture of them that s/he has kept in his/her mind.[337]

4–188   (iv) **The importance of public perception.** The Court contrasted between word and figurative signs on the one hand and colours per se on the other:

> "While the public is accustomed to perceiving word or figurative marks instantly as signs identifying the commercial origin of the goods, the same is not necessarily true where the sign forms part of the look of the goods in respect of which registration of the sign as a trade mark is sought. Consumers are not in the habit of making assumptions about the origin of goods based on their colour or the colour of their packaging, in the absence of any graphic or word element, because as a rule a colour per se is not, in current commercial practice, used as a means of identification. A colour per se is not normally inherently capable of distinguishing the goods of a particular undertaking."[338]

---

[334] *Libertel*, para.59, citing *Canon Kabushiki Kaisha v Metro-Goldwyn-Mayer Inc* (C-39/97) [1998] E.C.R. I-5507.
[335] *Libertel*, para.60.
[336] *Libertel*, para.62.
[337] Citing *Lloyd Schuhfabrik Meyer & Co GmbH* (C-342/97) [1999] E.C.R. I-3819; and *LTJ Diffusion SA v Sadas Vertbaudet SA* (C-291/00) [2003] E.C.R. I-2799.
[338] *Libertel*, para.65.

6. ARTICLE 3(1)(b)—DEVOID OF ANY DISTINCTIVE CHARACTER

So, in principle a colour per se would require distinctiveness acquired through use according to art.3(3) as interpreted in *Windsurfing Chiemsee*.[339] The Court left open a very narrow gap for "exceptional circumstances, and particularly where the number of goods or services for which the mark is claimed is very restricted and the relevant market very specific".[340]

Concluding on the first question the Court ruled that:

"a colour per se, not spatially delimited, may, in respect of certain goods and services, have a distinctive character within the meaning of Article 3(1)(b) and Article 3(3) of the Directive, provided that, inter alia, it may be represented graphically in a way that is clear, precise, self-contained, easily accessible, intelligible, durable and objective. The latter condition cannot be satisfied merely by reproducing on paper the colour in question, but may be satisfied by designating that colour using an internationally recognised identification code".[341]

On question 2(a) the Court ruled that:

4–189

"a colour per se may be found to possess distinctive character within the meaning of Article 3(1)(b) and Article 3(3) of the Directive, provided that, as regards the perception of the relevant public, the mark is capable of identifying the product or service for which registration is sought as originating from a particular undertaking and distinguishing that product or service from those of other undertakings".[342]

The answer on question 2(b) stressed that, in the case of colours, the breadth of the specification was relevant in assessing:

"both the distinctive character of the colour in respect of which registration is sought, and whether its registration would run counter to the general interest in not unduly limiting the availability of colours for the other operators who offer for sale goods or services of the same type as those in respect of which registration is sought".[343]

The fourth question confirmed that trade mark law is linked with what is happening in the marketplace. An application for registration should not be examined in abstract for distinctiveness. Distinctiveness is determined according to the specification of the application and "in assessing whether a trade mark has distinctive character within the meaning of Article 3(1)(b)

---

[339] *Windsurfing Chiemsee Produktions- und Vertriebs GmbH* (C-108/97 & C-109/97) [1999] E.C.R. I-2779.
[340] *Libertel*, para.66.
[341] *Libertel*, para.68.
[342] *Libertel*, para.69.
[343] *Libertel*, para.71.

and Article 3(3) of the Directive, the competent authority for registering trade marks must carry out an examination by reference to the actual situation, taking account of all the circumstances of the case and in particular any use which has been made of the mark".[344]

(7) Heidelberger Bauchemie—combinations of colours—replaying Libertel

4–190 In *Heidelberger Bauchemie*[345] A.G. Léger adapted the arguments he had developed in *Libertel* to the fact that this application was for a combination of colours.

The intention of Heidelberger Bauchemie was to protect the two colours in relation to the specified products irrespective of any arrangement between them. Such a combination would not be capable of distinguishing in the sense of art.2 because the number of combinations between them would be unlimited.

The trade mark proprietor would be given the exclusive right to use them as blue and yellow ribbons appearing on the surface of the product or coloured geometrical shapes, for instance a blue circle on a yellow background.

4–191 However their ability to distinguish would differ according to the way they would appear on the relevant product. So, and given that the Court had accepted in *Libertel* that colours can communicate specific information only to a limited degree, two colours would be capable of distinguishing only in the context of a specific arrangement.

Granting trade mark protection to the colours as such would equate granting protection to a number of letters because in a particular combination the same number of letters forms a word that can be protected as a trade mark.[346]

He also rejected the possibility that a colour combination in a particular, specified, arrangement would satisfy the distinctiveness requirement:

> "... to accept that two colours per se are capable of having distinctive character on the ground that they may satisfy that condition, but only in the context of certain specified arrangements, would amount, in my view, to misinterpreting the very purpose of the application for registration, which seeks exclusive rights in all the possible forms in which those colours may appear. In the case of a word mark, that would amount to

---

[344] *Libertel*, para.77. The Court referred to 12th Recital in the Preamble to the Directive linking the Directive with the Paris Convention and, accordingly, to art.6quinquies C(1) of the Paris Convention that stated: "[I]n determining whether a mark is eligible for protection, all the factual circumstances must be taken into consideration, particularly the length of time the mark has been in use".
[345] *Heidelberger Bauchemie GmbH* (C-49/02) [2004] E.C.R. I-6129.
[346] Point 47 of the Opinion of A.G. Léger.

6. ARTICLE 3(1)(b)—DEVOID OF ANY DISTINCTIVE CHARACTER

accepting that a number of letters may have distinctive character and that each of them may be the subject of exclusive rights on the ground that, where those letters form a certain word, they are capable of having distinctive character."[347]

(a) The judgment of the Court

The Court approached the issue of distinctiveness by asking "whether or not those colours or combinations of colours are capable of conveying precise information, particularly as regards the origin of a product or service".[348]

4–192

It reminded its approach in *Libertel*[349] and added that subject to the conditions raised therein "it must be accepted that for the purposes of Article 2 of the Directive colours and combinations of colours, designated in the abstract and without contours, may be capable of distinguishing the goods or services of one undertaking from those of other undertakings".[350]

It then stressed that the registration authority would also have to examine whether the mark applied for satisfied art.3 taking into account the public interest described in *Libertel*.[351]

(8) KWS–Colours–Broader Functionality Considerations

The case came before the Court as an appeal against a judgment of the Court of First Instance.[352] KWS Saat AG (KWS) had applied for the registration of a shade of orange, using the standard reference "Orange HKS7", as a Community Trade Mark for treatment installations for seeds, agricultural, horticultural and forestry products, and technical and business consultancy in the seed sector. The Second Board of Appeal found the mark devoid of any distinctive character under art.7(1)(b) of the Regulation since it was common practice to use colorants to identify treated seed.[353]

4–193

(a) The judgment of the Court of First Instance

The Court of First Instance upheld in part the application brought by KWS, finding that with regard to consultancy services the shade of orange per se was capable of enabling the relevant public to distinguish the services concerned from those of a different commercial origin when they come to make a choice for a subsequent purchase.

4–194

---

[347] Point 49 of the Opinion of A.G. Léger.
[348] *Heidelberger Bauchemie*, para.37.
[349] *Libertel Groep BV v Benelux-Merkenbureau* (C-104/01) [2003] E.C.R. I-3793.
[350] Point 40 of the Opinion of A.G. Léger.
[351] *Libertel Groep BV v Benelux-Merkenbureau* (C-104/01) [2003] E.C.R. I-3793.
[352] *KWS Saat AG v Office for Harmonisation in the Internal Market (Trade Marks and Designs)* (T-173/00) [2002] E.C.R. II 3843.
[353] Case R-282/1999-2, April 19, 2000.

For treated seed it found that use of colours, including the contested shade of orange or very similar shades, was common. The sign applied for would not enable the relevant public immediately and with certitude to distinguish the applicant's goods from those of other undertakings in other shades of orange. Similarly, for treatment installations, it concurred with the Board of Appeal that it was not rare to come across machines in that or a similar colour. Orange had become a commonplace colour that the relevant public would perceive as an element of the finish of the installations.

KWS appealed further to the Court of Justice in relation to the goods covered in the specification. The Office expressed doubts, but did not bring a cross-appeal regarding the consultancy services.

4–195 The first three grounds were about the judicial process before the Board of Appeal and the Court of First Instance.

First, KWS claimed that the Office had failed to conduct a sufficiently detailed examination of the facts, according to art.74(1) of the Regulation, and in particular that it had based its findings on usage of colours in this field on a single website of a manufacturer in the United States.

With the second ground KWS supported that its right to a fair hearing was infringed in the proceedings before the Board of Appeal and the Court of First Instance because the decision of the Office was based on a single document, the internet address mentioned above.

4–196 With the third ground KWS contended that both the Board of Appeal and the Court of First Instance had not stated sufficiently the reasons for their decisions.

The fourth ground introduced the argument that the distinctive character of a colour should be assessed in the same way with word and figurative signs. The availability of other colours to indicate product characteristics should be irrelevant. Public perception would be a more appropriate consideration. If competing undertakings use distinct colours to indicate particular characteristics, consumers would see each colour as indicating two things. Accordingly, the Court of First Instance had erred, applying a more stringent criterion for colours.

(b) The Opinion of the Advocate General

4–197 Regarding the fourth ground in particular A.G. Léger reminded the Court that in *Libertel*[354] and *Heidelberg Bauchemie*[355] he had supported that a colour per se did not satisfy art.2 of the Directive.

The Court of First Instance had followed the judgment of the Court in *Libertel*, it did not err in holding that although art.7(1)(b) of the Regulation did not differentiate between types of signs, the relevant public did not

---

[354] *Libertel Groep BV* (C-104/01) [2003] E.C.R. I-3793.
[355] *Heidelberger Bauchemie GmbH* (C-49/02) [2004] E.C.R. I-6129.

6. ARTICLE 3(1)(b)—DEVOID OF ANY DISTINCTIVE CHARACTER

necessarily perceive in the same way a sign consisting of a colour per se and a sign that is independent from the external appearance of the product in relation to which it is used.[356]

To the contrary, he criticised the finding of the Court of First Instance regarding the consultancy services supporting that it had not applied the *Libertel* criteria in their entirety or that it had erred in their application. However this remained outside the scope of this judgment.[357]

(c) The judgment of the Court

The Court found the first ground to be inadmissible; according to art.225 EC and art.58 of the Statute of the Court of Justice an appeal could be based only on grounds relating to breaches of rules of law, and on the appraisal of facts.

4–198

In respect of the second ground the Court accepted that the Office had infringed KWS's right to a fair hearing because it mentioned that document for the first time in the contested decision. The Board of Appeal had failed under art.73 of the Regulation that required from the Board of Appeal to base its decision only on matters of fact or of law on which the parties have been able to set out their views. However it found that the overall decision of the Board should stand because it was only partially based on that document. The remaining underpinnings of the decision that colours per se do not have a distinctive character without evidence of use and that competitors might have an interest in using that colour remained valid. The contested document was "merely confirmatory in character".[358]

On the third ground the Court reminded that the statement of reasons under art.253 EC had to "disclose in a clear and unequivocal manner the reasoning ... in such a way as to enable the persons concerned to ascertain the reasons for the measure and to enable the competent Community Court to exercise its power of review. It is not necessary for the reasoning to go into all the relevant facts and points of law, since the question whether the statement of reasons meets the requirements of Article 253 EC must be assessed with regard not only to its wording but also to its context and to all the legal rules governing the matter in question".[359] It found that in both instances there had been full and precise statements of reasons.

---

[356] Point 77 of the Opinion of A.G. Léger.
[357] Point 86 of the Opinion of A.G. Léger.
[358] *KWS*, para.50, citing *Falck and Acciaierie di Bolzano v Commission* (C-74/00 P and C-75/00 P) [2002] E.C.R. I7869; *Biret International SA v Council of the European Union* (C-93/02 P) [2003] E.C.R. I-10497; and *Etablissements Biret et Cie SA v Council of the European Union* (C-94/02 P) [2003] E.C.R. I-10565.
[359] *KWS*, para.65, citing *Commission v Chambre Syndicale Nationale des Entreprises de Transport de Fonds et Valeurs (Sytraval) and Brink's France SARL* (C-367/95 P) [1998] E.C.R. I-1719; and *Coöperatieve Vereniging de Verenigde Bloemenveilingen Aalsmeer BA (VBA) v Florimex* (C-265/97 P) [2000] E.C.R. I-2061.

4–199   Regarding the fourth ground the Court repeated its position in Libertel.[360] "[W]hile the public is accustomed to perceiving word or figurative marks immediately as signs identifying the commercial origin of the goods, the same does not necessarily hold true where the sign forms part of the external appearance of the goods".[361]

It is suggested that the reference to the external appearance of the goods carries the seeds of a European theory of functionality that is much broader than the provisions on shapes.

(9)   Mag—distinctive character of shapes of products

4–200   Registrability of shapes was reconsidered by the Court in *Mag*.[362] The applicant had unsuccessfully applied to register as Community Trade Mark five cylindrical shapes of torches for "Accessories for apparatus for lighting, in particular for flashlights (torches)"; and "Apparatus for lighting, in particular flashlights (torches), including parts and accessories for the above-named goods" in Classes 9 and 11 of the Nice Agreement. The shapes were the actual shapes of torches marketed by Mag. The applications were rejected for failing art.7(1)(b).

The Board of Appeal rejected the appeal. The decision stated that in order for the shape of a product alone to function as an indication of its origin it had to display some features that were different from the usual shape of the specified goods so that a prospective consumer would perceive the shape as an indication of origin rather than a representation of the goods themselves. In the latter case the shape would be descriptive and fall within the scope of art.7(1)(c) of the Regulation.

It added that attractiveness did not render a sign inherently distinctive and, in the same trend, that a mere trace of distinctive character would not confer to the sign the distinctiveness that is necessary to overcome the objections based on art.7(1)(b).

(a)   The judgment of the Court of First Instance

4–201   The applicant claimed before the Court of First Instance that the Board had infringed art.7(1)(b). The Court of First Instance dismissed the application.[363]

It held that the provision did not make any distinctions between categories of signs; accordingly the distinctiveness criteria should be the same. It found that the distinctive characteristic of the torches was their cylindrical shape, a common shape for torches, indicating their nature rather than their

---

[360] *Libertel Groep BV* (C-104/01) [2003] E.C.R. I-3793.
[361] *Libertel*, para.78.
[362] *Mag Instrument Inc v Office for Harmonisation in the Internal Market (Trade Marks and Designs)* (C-136/02 P) [2004] E.C.R. I-9165.
[363] *Mag Instrument Inc v Office for the Harmonisation in the Internal Market (Trade Marks and Designs)* (T-88/00) [2002] E.C.R. II-467.

6. ARTICLE 3(1)(b)—DEVOID OF ANY DISTINCTIVE CHARACTER

origin. The aesthetic qualities and original design of the product simply rendered the shape a variant of a common torch shape rather than a shape capable of differentiating them from other torches. It left open the possibility of applying art.7(3) noting that the applicant had chosen not to invoke the provision, despite the fact that its arguments pointed towards this, rather than the inherent, form of distinctiveness.

Some of Mag's arguments relied on experts' reports and references in books regarding the distinctiveness, originality, and creativity of its torch shapes. It had also claimed that often counterfeiters exploited the original design of the torches without having to use the Mag Lite name.

Before the Court of Justice Mag claimed that the Court of First Instance had misinterpreted misapplied art.7(1)(b). In particular it supported that it (i) had wrongly appraised the distinctiveness of the sign as a whole; (ii) failed to take relevant evidence into account; (iii) infringed its right to a hearing; (iv) based its findings on distinctiveness on arbitrary assumptions; (v) employed unsubstantiated assumptions in its appraisal of distinctiveness; (vi) applied excessively stringent criteria; and, (vii) it wrongly took the view that the contested shapes were usual shapes.

(b) *The Opinion of the Advocate General*

Advocate General Ruiz-Jarabo Colomer started his analysis by stating that, although the Court of Justice had to consider only the applicability of art.7(1)(b), on which the decision of the Court of First Instance was based, he still felt art.7(1)(c) constituted a better starting point for determining the registrability of shapes.[364] He classified the grounds under three parts: misappraisal of specific distinctiveness, misappraisal of the facts relating to distinctiveness, infringement of a right to hearing. 　4–202

(i) **Misappraisal of specific distinctiveness.**

Misappraisal of the distinctiveness of the sign as a whole The appellant argued that the Court of First Instance had failed to take into account the detailed description of the visual and aesthetic aspects, specific to each one of the torches. Seeing them from an overall perspective the Court should hold that the signs were not devoid of any distinctive character. The Office counterclaimed that the appellant's detailed descriptions failed to perceive each sign as a whole, instead they separated them to their component parts. 　4–203

---

[364] Referring to his views expressed in *Henkel KGaA* (C-456/01 P and C-457/01 P) [2004] E.C.R. I-5089 he stated that this would allow the examiner to consider whether the sign "essentially conveys the idea of the goods formed by the average consumer and if not he would have to refuse it registration on the basis of Article 7(1)(c) because it constitutes a new graphic description of the goods" (para.20).

The Advocate General supported that this claim should be rejected, since the Court of First Instance had not undertaken an examination of all the parts of the signs in question without addressing the impression they conveyed as a whole. It had simply stated that the, usual for torches, cylindrical shapes did not enable the consumer to differentiate the product or to associate it with any particular commercial origin.

4–204 *Misappraisal of distinctiveness as a result of applying excessively stringent criteria.* According to the appellant, and in respect of shape marks, any perceptible difference compared to usual goods should confer the sign the necessary distinctiveness. Following *Baby-Dry*[365] a "variant" of the ordinary shape should be accepted for registration.

The Advocate General rejected this ground as a misinterpretation both of the judgment under appeal and *Baby-Dry*. The term "variants" in the judgment of the Court of First Instance meant, according to the Advocate General, "manifestations" of that common shape. It had also found that the signs "correspond to shapes commonly used by other torch manufacturers on the market".[366] He also attacked the test of "any perceptible difference"as minimal, because it would comprise "any difference however small" and thus would fail to "guarantee that the trade marks fulfil their identificatory function".[367]

Repeating the position expressed in *Postkantoor*[368] on the form of a sign he stated that a difference should be regarded truly perceptible only if it affected important components of either the form of the sign or its meaning; a sign could be refused trade mark protection even if it comprised certain differences compared with the usual presentation of the specified products.

He concluded that the Court of First Instance had not applied more stringent criteria than those applied in the case of other categories of trade mark.

4–205 *Misappraisal of distinctiveness as a result of taking the view that the shapes were usual shapes.* According to the appellant the finding of the Court of First Instance that "the average consumer is accustomed to seeing shapes similar to those at issue here in a wide variety of designs"[369] should lead to the conclusion that the average consumer perceived the variants as an indication of origin.

Again, the Advocate General supported that the appellant had misconstrued the meaning of a statement that really meant that the signs were not sufficiently different from other torches.

---

[365] *Procter & Gamble Co* (C-383/99 P) [2001] E.C.R. I-6251.
[366] *Mag Instrument Inc* (T-88/00) [2002] E.C.R. II-467, para.36.
[367] Point 30 of the Opinion of A.G. Ruiz-Jarabo Colomer.
[368] *Koninklijke KPN Nederland NV* (C-363/99) [2004] E.C.R. I-1619.
[369] *Mag Instrument Inc* (T-88/00) [2002] E.C.R. II-467, para.37.

6. ARTICLE 3(1)(b)—DEVOID OF ANY DISTINCTIVE CHARACTER

(ii) Misappraisal of the facts relating to distinctiveness. Advocate General Ruiz-Jarabo Colomer discussed together the second, fourth, and fifth grounds because all three of them were based on an incorrect interpretation of the way in which the Court assessed a sign's distinctiveness. This had been settled in *Güt Springenheide and Tusky*[370] where it had adopted a uniform criterion of general application. The applicability of this criterion in trade mark cases has been endorsed in *Lloyd Schuhfabrik*[371] and for shapes in particular in *Philips*.[372]

4–206

So, if:

"a sign's capacity to distinguish can be assessed on the basis of a presumption as to what the average consumer who is reasonably well informed, reasonably circumspect and observant is capable of perceiving, it would seem to be unnecessary to undertake further investigations, analytical or comparative studies, expert's opinions or statistical research. Nor, further, do any of those forms of evidence by their existence relieve the Examiner or the Court of the need to exercise their own discretion based on the yardstick of the average consumer as defined by Community law".[373]

This was the correct criterion, he argued, in particular in respect of signs intended for the general public, because it "does not entail actual comparison of the signs sought to be registered with those in current use but with an ideal model composed of elements which naturally convey to the mind an image of the shape of the product".[374] Only when the relevant authorities were in doubt or the case involved specialist goods or services they should seek outside evidence such as studies or opinions.

Finally, in respect of the second ground of appeal in particular he noted that it referred to evidence which in fact should not be considered material.

(iii) Infringement of the right to a hearing. With the third ground the appellant supported that the Court of First Instance, because of its failure to examine the facts and the relevant evidence, had infringed its right to be heard contrary to the second paragraph of art.6 EU in conjunction with art.6 of the European Convention on the Protection of Human Rights and Fundamental Freedoms and the first indent of para.2 of art.41 of the Charter of Fundamental Rights of the European Union.

4–207

---

[370] *Gut Springenheide and Tusky v Oberkreisdirektor des Kreises Steinfurt—AMT für Lebensmittelüberwachung* (C-210/96) [1998] E.C.R. I-4657.
[371] *Lloyd Schuhfabrik Meyer & Co GmbH v Klijsen Handel BV* (C-342/97) [1999] E.C.R. I-3819.
[372] *Koninklijke Philips Electronics NV* (C-299/00) [2002] E.C.R. I-5475.
[373] Point 48, citing A.G. Fennelly in *Esteé Lauder Cosmetics GmbH & Co OHG v Lancaster Group GmbH* (C-220/98) [2000] E.C.R. I-117.
[374] Point 49 of the Opinion of A.G. Ruiz-Jarabo Colomer.

The Advocate General suggested that his findings under Pt B meant that this ground was inadmissible.

(c) The judgment of the Court

4–208　The Judgment of the Court considered all the grounds of appeal following the route indicated by the Advocate General.

4–209　**(i) The first ground—overall impression.** The Court repeated that distinctive character should be assessed by reference, first, to the specified goods or services and, secondly, to the perception of the relevant public,[375] adding that the average consumer normally perceived a mark as a whole without analysing its various details. This is why distinctive character should be assessed according to the overall impression conveyed by the sign.[376]

It found that the Court of First Instance had not sought to separate each of the marks into their component parts; rather, it had correctly considered the overall impression given by each one of them.

4–210　**(ii) The sixth ground—the criteria for assessing distinctive character for "product shape" marks.** The Court restated that the criteria for assessing the distinctive character of three-dimensional marks consisting of the shape of the product itself were the same with those applicable to other signs, however:

> "for the purpose of applying those criteria, the relevant public's perception is not necessarily the same... Average consumers are not in the habit of making assumptions about the origin of products on the basis of their shape or the shape of their packaging in the absence of any graphic or word element and it could therefore prove more difficult to establish distinctiveness in relation to such a three-dimensional mark than in relation to a word or figurative mark".[377]

Accordingly, the Court required the shape to depart significantly from the norm or customs of the relevant sector. Being a "variant" of a common shape for that type of product would not be sufficient to establish that the

---

[375] Citing *Henkel KGaA* (C-218/01) [2004] E.C.R. I-1725, para.50 and the case law cited there; see also *Henkel KGaA* (C-456/01 P and C-457/01 P) [2004] E.C.R. I-5089, para.35 and the case law cited there.

[376] Citing *DKV Deutsche Krankenversicherung AG* (C-104/00 P) [2002] E.C.R. I-7561; and, in relation to shapes, *Procter & Gamble* (C-468/01 P to C-472/01 P) [2004] E.C.R. I-5141.

[377] *Mag*, para.30; citing *Henkel KGaA* (C-218/01) [2004] E.C.R. I-1725.

6. ARTICLE 3(1)(b)—DEVOID OF ANY DISTINCTIVE CHARACTER

mark is not devoid of any distinctive character. "It must always be determined whether such a mark permits the average consumer of that product, who is reasonably well informed and reasonably observant and circumspect, to distinguish the product concerned from those of other undertakings without conducting an analytical examination and without paying particular attention."[378]

(iii) The seventh ground—appraising facts. Regarding the seventh ground it found that the Court of First Instance had not taken the view that consumers would, as a matter of principle, fail to recognise the shape of goods as an indication of their origin.

4–211

In addition examining the appellant's argument would constitute an appraisal of the facts of the case and remained outside the jurisdiction of the Court according to art.225.[379]

(iv) The fourth ground—evidence of distinctive character. The Court clarified that art.7(1)(b) was concerned with the ab initio distinctive character of a trade mark whereas art.7(3) with the distinctive character that might be acquired as a result of use.[380] However, for assessing distinctive character the Court of First Instance, "must have regard to all the relevant facts and circumstances".[381]

4–212

Accordingly, "evidence based on the actual perception of the mark by consumers may, in certain cases, provide guidance".[382]

The Court went further and identified what that evidence had to show. The trade mark had to immediately enable consumers to distinguish the marked goods or services from those of competing undertakings. Showing that consumers had become accustomed to the mark would be relevant for art.7(3) but not for art.7(1)(b); otherwise art.7(3) would become redundant.

Since the evidence in the case considered the perception of consumers at a time when the torches had been on the market for a long period of time the Court of First Instance was entitled to find that it could be relevant for establishing acquired—but not ab initio—distinctive character.

(v) The second ground—the meaning of the evidence. The Court divided the evidence into consumer and expert evidence. It repeated that the Court of First Instance had taken the consumer evidence and had decided,

4–213

---

[378] *Mag*, para.32.
[379] Citing *DKV Deutsche Krankenversicherung AG* (C-104/00 P) [2002] E.C.R. I-7561; and *Thyssen Stahl v Commission* (C-194/99 P) [2003] E.C.R. I-10821.
[380] Citing *Libertel Groep BV v Benelux-Merkenbureau* (C-104/01) [2003] E.C.R. I-3793, it noted that "the normal process of familiarising the relevant public" (para.47) could be one of the ways for acquiring distinctive character.
[381] *Mag*, para.48, citing *Koninklijke KPN Nederland NV* (C-363/99) [2004] E.C.R. I-1619.
[382] *Mag*, para.49.

as it was entitled to, that it was not relevant for the purposes of art.7(1)(b). The expert's evidence had also been taken into account and the Court of First Instance had found that the excellence of the design and the aesthetic and functional qualities of the torches did not show that the marks possessed distinctive character ab initio; it was capable only of demonstrating that they might become distinctive through use.

Regarding the international recognition enjoyed by the designs the Court noted that "the fact that goods benefit from a high quality of design does not necessarily mean that a mark consisting of the three-dimensional shape of those goods enables ab initio those goods to be distinguished from those of other undertakings for the purposes of article 7(1)(b)".[383]

4–214   **(vi) The third ground—the right to be heard.** The first part of this ground revisited what the appellant had supported in the second ground and was accordingly rejected. On the second part regarding the expert evidence, the Court stressed that "the Court of First Instance is the sole judge of any need for the information available to it concerning the cases before it to be supplemented".[384] The third part of the same ground referred to the variety of shapes used by other manufacturers; the Court found that this requested a reappraisal of the facts, that was outside the jurisdiction of the Court.

4–215   **(vii) The fifth ground—general propositions.** The Court stated that average consumers were not in the habit of making assumptions about origin on the basis of the shape of a product or the shape of its packaging in the absence of any graphic or word element. The Court of First Instance had simply accepted that the nature of the mark might influence the perception of the relevant public.

The remaining arguments again required the appraisal of facts, that belonged in the jurisdiction of the Court of First Instance.

(10) Linde, Winward, and Rado—Products Shapes—a broader perspective

4–216   Joined Cases *Linde, Winward Industries, and Rado Uhren*,[385] gave the Court the opportunity to consider once again three-dimensional marks, first, from the perspective of distinctiveness and, secondly, in relation to the balance between art.3(1)(e) on the one hand and art.3(1)(b), art.3(1)(c), and art.3(1)(d) on the other. They came before the Court as a reference from

---

[383] *Mag*, para.68.
[384] *Mag*, para.76, citing *Ismeri Europa v Court of Auditors* (C-315/99 P) [2001] E.C.R. I-5281; and *Glencore and Compagnie Continentale v Commission* (C-24/01 P and C-25/01 P) [2002] E.C.R. I-10119.
[385] *Linde AG* (C-53/01), *Winward Industries Inc* (C-54/01) *and Rado Uhren AG* (C-55/01) [2003] E.C.R. I-3161.

6. ARTICLE 3(1)(b)—DEVOID OF ANY DISTINCTIVE CHARACTER

the Bundesgerichtshof dealing with the decisions of the Federal Patent Court that, in turn, considered the Deutsches Patent-und Markenamt's (the German Patent and Trade Mark Office) refusal to register the following marks:

(1) In *Linde*, the shape of a vehicle, as a three-dimensional trade mark, for "motorised trucks and other mobile works vehicles, particularly fork-lift trucks", for lack of distinctive character. The Bundespatentgericht concurred with the Office holding that what the trade saw in the representation of the product was the product itself. The particular shape did not go beyond the parameters of modern industrial design in its non-technical aspects; accordingly it was not so different from standard shapes in order to become a distinctive sign rather than a variation of a familiar shape.

(2) In *Winward*, the shape of a torch, as a three-dimensional trade mark, for torches, again for lack of distinctive character. The shape, according to the Bundespatentgericht, possessed some elegance but was, still, a typical torch shape with minimal differences compared to competing products on the basis of which even an observant consumer would be unable to identify a particular manufacturer from memory.

(3) In *Rado*, the shape of a wrist watch, as a three-dimensional trade mark, for watches, again for lack and distinctiveness but also because there was a need to preserve availability of shapes in a product market characterised by the variety of shapes and designs. The Bundespatentgericht added that protection could be conferred only where an original design could overcome the need to preserve the availability of the elementary shape of the product and its lack of distinctive character.

> "A fairly strict test must be applied for the purposes of establishing the originality of the product or its parts because they themselves are the most important means of description, and if they are monopolised there is a risk that competitors will be impeded in the design of their products and it is at least conceivable that there is a need to preserve availability".[386]

On appeal, the Bundesgerichtshof took the view that three-dimensional trade marks could possess distinctive character in the abstract within the meaning of art.2 of the Directive. It also considered that the, specific for shapes, grounds for refusal set by art.3(1)(e) did not apply, because of additional characteristics that were present in all three signs. So, the issue was whether the signs were devoid of distinctive character or not. According to the Bundespatentgericht's case law the distinctiveness criteria for three-dimensional signs should be more stringent than those for other marks

4–217

---

[386] *Linde, Winward and Rado*, para.16.

because of the need to preserve the availability of shapes that were easily conceived of and because of the difference between trade mark rights on the one hand and design and utility model rights on the other. The Bundesgerichtshof, however disagreed with this approach, supporting that the criteria should be the same for all marks. The:

> "interest in keeping graphic shapes generally available for use should not affect specific distinctiveness within Article 3(1)(b) of the Directive in any way, although that requirement may nevertheless be relevant in the context of Article 3(1)(c)".[387]

Accordingly, it submitted the following questions to the Court:

> "(1) In determining whether a three-dimensional trade mark which depicts the shape of a product has a distinctive character within the meaning of Article 3(1)(b) of the Directive is there a stricter test for distinctive character than in the case of other forms of trade marks?
>
> (2) In the case of three-dimensional trade marks which depict the shape of the product, does Article 3(1)(c) of the Directive have any significance independently of Article 3(1)(e)? If so, when considering Article 3(1)(c)—or alternatively Article 3(1)(e)—must regard be had to the interest of the trade in having the shape of the product available for use, so that registration is, at least in principle, ruled out, and is possible as a rule only in the case of trade marks which meet the requirements of the first sentence of Article 3(3) of the Directive?"[388]

(a) The Opinion of the Advocate General

4–218   **(i) The first question.** Winward supported that the Court had refused to impose additional conditions regarding distinctiveness based on the German doctrine in *Windsurfing Chiemsee*.[389] Winward and Rado also argued that art.3(1)(e) was the only provision in the Directive referring expressly, and thus derogating, to three-dimensional marks.

The Austrian Government submitted that the variety of shapes that may be given to products and their packaging was, in certain trade sectors, likely to make it harder for the relevant persons to recognise the shape of a product or its packaging as a trade mark.

The Austrian and the UK Governments argued that in practice it was harder to establish the distinctive character required by art.3(1)(b) in respect of a three-dimensional shape of product, first, because the main features of such shapes were influenced by their function, introducing a

---

[387] *Linde, Winward and Rado*, para.24.
[388] Reproduced in para.26.
[389] *Windsurfing Chiemsee Produktions- und Vertriebs GmbH v Boots- und Segelzubehör Walter Huber and Franz Attenberger* (C-108/97 and C-109/97) [1999] E.C.R. I-2779.

6. ARTICLE 3(1)(b)—DEVOID OF ANY DISTINCTIVE CHARACTER

"functionality doctrine" element in the interpretation of the provision. And, secondly, because there were many similarities between products of the same type.

4–219 In addition, the UK Government in particular argued that a shape's distinctive character should also be assessed in the context of the normal range of variations for the product in question. If the shape fell within the normal range of variation of the product, it would be unlikely to be accorded trade mark significance by the average consumer.

The Commission submitted that when assessing distinctiveness within the meaning of art.3(1)(b) of the Directive, the same test should be applied to all types of marks.

Advocate General Ruiz-Jarabo Colomer agreed that the Directive did not contain any provision suggesting that three-dimensional product shapes had to be treated differently in respect of the assessment "as to whether they possess actual distinctive character",[390] making a distinction with "capable of distinguishing or potential distinctive character (Article 2 of the Directive) or acquired distinctive character (Article 3(3))".[391]

4–220 He accepted that there were public interest reasons that favoured the application of different rules according to the relevant type of sign. This was reflected in other provisions of the Directive, but the Court had made it clear in *Philips*[392] that the criteria for assessing the distinctive character of three-dimensional trade marks were no different from those to be applied to other categories of trade mark.

Whether in practice it would be harder to demonstrate distinctive character for three-dimensional shapes constituted a practical difficulty linked with the nature of such signs and consumer idiosyncrasies, but this did not mean that the Court followed a stricter approach in the assessment of distinctive character.[393]

4–221 **(ii) The second question.** Linde argued that any need to preserve the availability of a sign, taking account of competitors' actual proven requirements, should be considered under art.3(1)(c) and once it had been established that art.3(1)(e) did not apply.

Winward supported that art.3(1)(e) applied where there was an absolute need to preserve the availability of the shape claimed; the provision ought not to apply where the technical result required could be achieved by using

---

[390] Point 10 of the Opinion of A.G. Ruiz-Jarabo Colomer.
[391] fn.5.
[392] *Koninklijke Philips Electronics NV* (C-299/99) [2002] E.C.R. I-5475.
[393] He noted (point 12) that art.3(1)(e) would preclude the registration of functional shapes but added "inasmuch as shape is dictated by function and similar products are therefore usually similar in appearance, it can be difficult for the original shape to be distinctive, although it may none the less acquire distinctiveness through use, in accordance with article 3(3) of the Directive. In any event, it is unlikely that the average consumer will perceive minor differences as an indication of the product's origin".

alternative shapes. In any case the need to preserve availability fell under art.3(1)(e) rather art.3(1)(c).

Rado claimed that art.3(1)(c) set the same criteria for all types of marks and should not be interpreted in a way that would preclude the registration of three-dimensional marks.

4–222 In its intervention the UK Government submitted that the two provons were independent from each other; art.3(1)(e) should be considered first, and if a purposive construction were to be given to it then art.3(1)(c) would be of limited applicability. The Commission, too, supported the independent and autonomous applicability of each provision. It reminded the existence of earlier case law setting that art.3(1)(c) did not require a current or serious need to leave a sign free, citing *Windsurfing Chiemsee*.[394] The provisions of the Directive were precise in their scope and there was no need to take into account further broad principles; for example, the interest of the relevant trade in keeping certain shapes available had been built into art.3(1)(e).

Advocate General Ruiz-Jarabo Colomer based his analysis on the judgment of the Court in *Philips*.[395] He started by distilling its principles. The Court first, accepted "that when the various grounds for refusal are applied, other underlying general-interest considerations may be taken into account"[396]; this meant that the rationale behind each ground had to be analysed. Secondly, it ruled that the rationale for art.3(1)(e) was to prevent trade mark protection from conferring or a monopoly on technical solutions or functional characteristics of a product that a user would be likely to seek in the products of competitors; the aim of art.3(1)(ii) in particular was to exclude shapes "to the extent to which they perform a technical function".[397] Elaborating further on this the Court, based on that rationale, also set out the conditions for applying art.3(1)(e)(ii). The Advocate General suggested that the same reasoning could be extended to the other cases referred to in art.3(1)(e); registration should be refused when the essential characteristics of a three-dimensional sign consisting of the shape of the product resulted from the nature of the product or gave the product substantial value. Third, it ruled that for "the remainder, the principles relating to the need to preserve availability in the domain of Article 3(1)(c), as formulated in *Windsurfing Chiemsee*, continue to apply".[398]

---

[394] *Windsurfing Chiemsee Produktions- und Vertriebs GmbH* (C-108/97 and C-109/97) [1999] E.C.R. I-2779.

[395] *Koninklijke Philips Electronics NV* (C-299/99) [2002] E.C.R. I-5475.

[396] Point 20; the Court resolved the uncertainty that followed *Windsurfing Chiemsee Produktions- und Vertriebs GmbH v Boots- und Segelzubehör Walter Huber and Franz Attenberger* (C-108/97 and C-109/97) [1999] E.C.R. I-2779; and *Procter & Gamble Co* (C-383/99 P) [2001] E.C.R. I-6251.

[397] Point 21 of the Opinion of A.G. Ruiz-Jarabo Colomer.

[398] Point 23; in turn the general interest in preserving the availability of certain signs was underlying art.3(1)(c).

6. ARTICLE 3(1)(b)—DEVOID OF ANY DISTINCTIVE CHARACTER

A roadmap for product shapes. There were three steps that product shapes **4–223**
had to take before reaching registration.
First, they ought to satisfy the abstract requirements of art.2.
Secondly, avoid falling within the scope of art.3(1)(e). And thirdly, satisfy the requirements of art.3(1)(b), art.3(1)(c), and art.3(1)(d). And although he described the ambit of art.3(1)(e) in very broad and forceful terms he also stressed that avoiding its application should not automatically mean satisfying the remaining grounds of art.3(1).
Finally, art.3(3) provided a potential fourth step, bypassing the obstacles raised by art.3(1)(b), art.3(1)(c), and art.3(1)(d) but not art.3(1)(e). At the end, he acknowledged, many three-dimensional shape-of-product signs would probably fall before reaching registration.

The ambit of article 3(1)(e). The Advocate General stressed that under **4–224**
art.3(1)(e):

> "the purpose of excluding from trade mark protection three dimensional signs which are exclusively dictated by the nature of the product, by the need for a technical result or by the need to give substantial value, reflects the paramount concern not to permit individuals to use trade marks to perpetuate exclusive rights over natural forms, technical developments or aesthetic designs. In keeping with that logic, the legislature did not include subparagraph (e) among the grounds for refusal which may be cured by virtue of the first sentence of Article 3(3). Natural, functional and ornamental shapes are incapable, by express intention of the legislature, of acquiring distinctive character... It cannot be denied that that interpretation means that many unadorned signs... will never be eligible for registration but... that consequence is not disproportionate: the public interest should not have to tolerate even a slight risk that trade mark rights unduly encroach on the field of other exclusive rights which are limited in time, whilst there are in fact other effective ways in which manufacturers may indicate the origin of a product (addition of arbitrary features to a three-dimensional shape, innovative arrangement of the whole, word and figurative marks)".[399]

(b) The judgment of the Court of Justice

(i) The first question. The Court of Justice noted that for the purposes **4–225**
of art.2 a three-dimensional shape of product sign could in principle constitute a trade mark provided that its two conditions are met.[400]

---

[399] Point 29 of the Opinion of A.G. Ruiz-Jarabo Colomer.
[400] Citing *Koninklijke Philips Electronics NV* (C-299/99) [2002] E.C.R. I-5475.

Moving to art.3(1)(b) it added that distinctiveness meant that the trade mark served to identify to the relevant persons the specified product as originating from a particular undertaking, distinguishing it from products of other undertakings. The criteria should be the same for all types of marks.[401]

Article 3(1)(e) was characterised by the Court as a preliminary obstacle that cannot be overcome even with evidence of acquired distinctiveness through use.[402]

However, the Court also accepted that in practice it might be more difficult to establish distinctiveness in relation to a product shape than a word or figurative mark. In these cases art.3(3) would become relevant.

4-226 **(ii) The second question—the Court's roadmap.** The Court repeated that art.3(1)(e) constituted a preliminary obstacle. After this, the remaining provisions had to be applied; each one was independent of the others and called for separate examination.

Further, it held that the art.3 grounds for refusing registration had to be interpreted in the light of the public interest underlying each one of them.[403]

Elaborating on the second situation envisaged by the referring court it added that for certain three-dimensional shape of product signs, it had already held that the rationale of the grounds for refusing registration laid down in art.3(1)(e) is to prevent the grant of a monopoly on technical solutions or functional characteristics of a product which a user is likely to seek in the products of competitors.[404]

4-227 Whereas the public interest behind art.3(1)(c) was to ensure that descriptive signs or indications relating to the characteristics of the specified goods or services could be freely used by all, e.g. as collective marks or as part of complex or graphic marks.[405]

Regarding the application of art.3(1)(c) the Court called again for a balanced approach: robust examination without predetermined outcomes:

"The competent authority called upon to apply Art.3(1)(c) of the Directive to such trade marks must determine, by reference to the goods or services for which registration is sought, in the light of a concrete consideration of all the relevant aspects of the application, and in particular the

---

[401] *Koninklijke Philips Electronics NV* (C-299/99) [2002] E.C.R. I-5475 (para.48); and *Gut Springenheide and Tusky v Oberkreisdirektor des Kreises Steinfurt—AMT für Lebensmittelüberwachung* (C-210/96) [1998] E.C.R. I-4657 (para.31).
[402] Again citing *Koninklijke Philips Electronics NV* (C-299/99) [2002] E.C.R. I-5475.
[403] Citing *Koninklijke Philips Electronics NV* (C-299/99) [2002] E.C.R. I-5475; and *Windsurfing Chiemsee Produktions- und Vertriebs GmbH v Boots- und Segelzubehör Walter Huber and Franz Attenberger* (C-108/97 & C-109/97) [1999] E.C.R. I-2779.
[404] Citing *Koninklijke Philips Electronics NV* (C-299/99) [2002] E.C.R. I-5475.
[405] *Windsurfing Chiemsee Produktions- und Vertriebs GmbH v Boots- und Segelzubehör Walter Huber and Franz Attenberger* (C-108/97 & C-109/97) [1999] E.C.R. I-2779.

6. ARTICLE 3(1)(b)—DEVOID OF ANY DISTINCTIVE CHARACTER

public interest referred to above, whether the ground for refusing registration in that provision applies to the case at hand. The same concrete examination is required in the case of an application for registration of a three dimensional shape of product mark. The authority may not, however, refuse such an application as a matter of principle."[406]

There was no differentiation from the above in respect of three-dimensional shape of product marks, so the answer "to the second limb of the second question must be that, when examining the ground for refusing registration in Article 3(1)(c) of the Directive in a concrete case, regard must be had to the public interest underlying that provision, which is that all three-dimensional shape of product trade marks which consist exclusively of signs or indications which may serve to designate the characteristics of the goods or service within the meaning of that provision should be freely available to all and, subject always to Article 3(3) of the Directive, cannot be registered".[407]

(11) Henkel—the assimilation of packaging and product shapes

In *Henkel KGaA v Deutsches Patent- und Markenamt*[408] it considered the registrability of packaging of goods which are normally traded in packaged form mainly under art.3(1)(b) and art.3(1)(c) of the Directive, but also the relationship of those provisions with art.3(1)(e). 4–228

The case was a reference from the Bundespatentgericht. Henkel had applied for the registration of a coloured three-dimensional trade mark consisting of a tall bottle, narrowing towards the top, with an integral handle, a small pouring opening, and a two-level stopper which could also be used as a measuring cup, for liquid wool detergent. The application was rejected by the Deutsches Patent- und Markenamt for lack of distinctive character. Henkel attacked the decision before the Bundespatentgericht claiming that the combination of the shape with the colours of the container created a distinctive overall impression, in particular in a product market that was accustomed to perceive containers as indicators of origin as evidenced in a survey it had commissioned.

The German court found that there was no ground for the application of art.3(1)(e). However, it queried whether the public interest behind art.3(1)(c) precluded the registration of such a container. It also sought to clarify the criteria for establishing distinctive character under art.3(1)(b).

Accordingly it referred the following questions to the Court: 4–229

"1. In the case of three-dimensional trade marks which consist of the packaging of goods which are normally traded in packaged form (such as

---

[406] *Linde, Windward and Rado*, para.75.
[407] *Linde, Windward and Rado*, para.77.
[408] *Henkel KGaA* (C-218/01) [2004] E.C.R. I-1725.

liquids, for example), is the packaging of the goods to be equated with the shape of the goods for the purpose of trade mark law in such a way that

(a) the packaging of the goods is to be regarded as the shape of the goods for the purpose of Article 3(1)(e) of the Directive; and
(b) the packaging of the goods may serve to designate the (external) quality of the packaged goods for the purpose of Article 3(1)(c) of the Directive?

2. In the case of three-dimensional trade marks which consist of the packaging of goods which are normally traded in packaged form does the establishment of distinctive character within the meaning of Article 3(1)(b) of the Directive turn on whether or not the average consumer, who is reasonably well informed and reasonably observant and circumspect, is able to recognise the characteristic features of the three-dimensional trade mark applied for, which differ from the norm or custom in the sector and are therefore decisive as regards its capability of serving as an indication of origin, without even conducting an analytical or comparative examination and without paying particular attention?

3. Can the necessary assessment of distinctive character be made solely on the basis of the relevant national trade perceptions without further official investigations being necessary to establish whether and to what extent identical or comparable trade marks have been registered or refused registration in other Member States of the European Union?"[409]

(a) The Opinion of the Advocate General

4–230 Advocate General Ruiz-Jarabo Colomer identified two main issues, first whether packaging should be equated with content and, secondly, the test to be applied for the assessment of distinctive character in that case. The effect of registration of comparable marks in other Member States to that assessment was the third point he had to answer.

4–231 (i) **Packaging and content.** Henkel argued that goods that did not have a shape—like liquids—could not acquire a shape by means of their packaging. The two were distinct and this was how consumers perceived them.

The Advocate General, however, viewed packaging as a component of the product: the only visible, distinguishable element of the product. Accordingly, it constituted the only component that was relevant for the purposes of trade mark law. He accepted that according to art.2 packaging appeared to be a separate item from the product. However, he suggested approaching the issue from a teleological perspective taking into account the aim of the Directive.

---

[409] Reproduced in para.19.

6. ARTICLE 3(1)(b)—DEVOID OF ANY DISTINCTIVE CHARACTER

He suggested that packaging was the only shape that consumers could identify as the shape of the product in relation to materials that were devoid of a clearly defined size and form, like liquids, gases, and granulated or highly brittle materials: "For the purpose of trade mark law, the three-dimensional shape of such substances is the shape of the packaging in which they are displayed; therefore, in this context, goods should be taken to mean the container in which they are traded."[410] From a marketing perspective, he added, packaging was often a decisive factor. "The size of the packaging determines the quantity of goods available; its shape, their function; and its material, their weight. In the eyes of a consumer, those characteristics may even be more important than the real or presumed attributes of the liquid itself."[411]

So, when applying the provisions of the Directive, including art.3(1)(c) and art.3(1)(e), this link between the product and its packaging should not be ignored. The public interest underlying art.3(1)(e) in particular would be easily circumvented if the product and its packaging were considered to be distinct from each other.

Concluding, he suggested the following reply to the German court: "for the purpose of Community trade mark law, where goods are normally traded in packaged form, the term three-dimensional goods should be taken to mean the shape of the packaging".[412]

(ii) The test for assessing distinctive character. The Advocate General did not come up with a multi factor test for determining whether the mark possesses distinctive character. Instead he reconfirmed the perspectives from which distinctive character should be judged.

First, citing *Güt Springenheide and Tusky*,[413] he stated that the national court should make the assessment by reference to the presumed expectations of an average consumer who is reasonably well-informed and reasonably observant and circumspect. In principle there should be no need to resort to experts' reports or consumer research polls unless the court is unable to make the assessment on its own.

Secondly, he stressed the link of the trade mark with the marked product. Protection was limited to the goods or services specified in the application. Accordingly, the assessment of distinctive character should be made from the point of view of an average consumer of the same type of goods or services.

---

[410] Point 12 of the Opinion of A.G. Ruiz-Jarabo Colomer.
[411] Point 13 of the Opinion of A.G. Ruiz-Jarabo Colomer.
[412] Point 17 of the Opinion of A.G. Ruiz-Jarabo Colomer.
[413] *Gut Springenheide and Tusky v Oberkreisdirektor des Kreises Steinfurt—AMT für Lebensmittelüberwachung* (C-210/96) [1998] E.C.R. I-4657. The same approach has been consistently adopted by the Court, for example, in *Verbraucherschutzverein eV v Sektkellerei GC Kessler GmbH und Co* (C-303/97) [1999] E.C.R. I-513, *Estée Lauder Cosmetics GmbH & Co OHG v Lancaster Group GmbH* (C-220/98) [2000] E.C.R. I-117; and *Commission v Ireland* (C30–99) [2001] E.C.R. I-4619; and, in the field of trade mark law, *Lloyd Schuhfabrik Meyer & Co GmbH* (C-342/97) [1999] E.C.R. I-3819; and *Koninklijke Philips Electronics NV* (C-299/99) [2002] E.C.R. I-5475.

4–234	Thirdly, he introduced to the assessment the element of territoriality. Trade mark rights were territorial; the assessment should be made from the point of view of an average consumer in the territory in which the application was filed.

Regarding the type of the particular sign in question he noted that there was no reason to depart from that line of reasoning; the assessment should be made from the same perspectives.

4–235	**(iii) The effect of registration in other Member States.** The Advocate General found that national courts and authorities were not required to take account of practices in other Member States; after all, the expectations of consumers might vary according to territory. The only obligation was to interpret national legislation in the light of the wording and purpose of the Directive.

He suggested, however, that in the interests of prudence and mutual good faith, that the reasoning behind the practices followed in other Member States should be viewed as a helpful indication.

(b)   The judgment of the Court

4–236	**(i) Packaging and content.** The Court made a distinction between goods with and without an intrinsic shape.

In the first category belonged goods the shape of which derived from the features of the goods themselves; in such cases, there was, in principle, no sufficiently close relationship between the packaging and the goods.

The second category comprised goods that did not possess an intrinsic shape and had to be packaged in order to be marketed. "The packaging chosen imposes its shape on the goods. In such circumstances, that packaging, for the purposes of examining an application for registration as a mark, must be assimilated to the shape of the product. That applies, for example, to goods manufactured, in particular, in the form of granules, powder or liquid which, because of their very nature, lack a shape of their own."[414]

4–237	Focusing on art.3(1)(e) in particular the Court concluded that "in the case of three-dimensional marks consisting of the packaging of goods which are packaged in trade for reasons linked to the very nature of the goods, the packaging thereof must be assimilated to the shape of the goods, so that that packaging constitutes the shape of the goods within the meaning of Article 3(1)(e) of the Directive".[415]

The Court continued its analysis by repeating that the art.3(1) grounds were independent from each other.[416] Overcoming art.3(1)(e) would not warrant registrability.

---

[414] *Henkel*, para.33.
[415] *Henkel*, para.37.
[416] Citing *Linde AG* (C-53/01), *Winward Industries Inc* (C-54/01) and *Rado Uhren AG* (C-55/01) [2003] E.C.R. I-3161.

6. ARTICLE 3(1)(b)—DEVOID OF ANY DISTINCTIVE CHARACTER

As a result, the response to the second part of the first question was that art.3(1)(c) could still be applied; the public interest underlying that provision was that:

"subject to article 3(3), any trade mark which consists exclusively of a sign or indication which may serve to designate the characteristics of goods or a service within the meaning of that provision must be freely available to all and not be registrable".[417]

It is noted here that the Court described the public interest in broad terms without citing its earlier case law.

4–238

The Court doubted whether that type of packaging could designate characteristics of the packaged product but insisted that the provision should not be overlooked. "Whilst it might be difficult to identify such characteristics, the possibility that the packaging might describe the characteristics of the product, including its quality, cannot be ruled out."[418]

(ii) The assessment of distinctive character. The Court started with a general remark, indicating that art.7(1)(b) should be applied rigorously:

4–239

"a simple departure from the norm or customs of the sector is not sufficient to render inapplicable the ground for refusal given in Article 3(1)(b) of the Directive. In contrast, a trade mark which significantly departs from the norm or customs of the sector and thereby fulfils its essential original function is not devoid of distinctive character".[419]

It repeated its findings on the distinctive character of three-dimensional signs in *Philips*[420] and *Linde*[421] before concluding that:

"for three-dimensional trade marks consisting of the packaging of goods which are packaged in trade for reasons linked to the very nature of the product, their distinctive character ... must be assessed by reference to the perception of the average consumer of such goods, who is reasonably well informed and reasonably observant and circumspect. Such a trade mark must enable such a consumer to distinguish the product concerned from those of other undertakings without conducting an analytical or comparative examination and without paying particular attention".[422]

---

[417] *Henkel*, para.41.
[418] *Henkel*, para.42.
[419] *Henkel*, para.49.
[420] *Koninklijke Philips Electronics NV* (C-299/99) [2002] E.C.R. I-5475.
[421] *Linde AG* (C-53/01), *Winward Industries Inc* (C-54/01) and *Rado Uhren AG* (C-55/01) [2003] E.C.R. I-3161.
[422] *Henkel*, para.53.

4-240   (iii) **The effect of registrations in other Member States.** It is worth referring here to the stance of the Commission that had argued that registrations in other Member States should be useful but not binding in assessing distinctive character because it is "in trade mark law that the effective approximation of trade usage and that of consumers in the internal market can be effectively taken into account".[423]

The Court reminded its holding that the competent authorities must apply and interpret the relevant national law, as far as possible, in the light of the wording and the purpose of the Directive so as to achieve the result it has in view and comply with art.249 EC.[424]

The competent authority of a Member State could take account of the decision on registration in another Member State of an identical trade mark for identical products or services but would not be bound by that decision. However, the fact that a trade mark had been registered in one Member State for certain goods or services could have no bearing on the examination by the competent authority of another Member State of the distinctive character of a similar mark for similar goods or services.[425]

The bottom line was that distinctive character should be assessed solely on the basis of national trade usage.

(12) Glaverbel—aesthetic functionality?

4-241   The interpretation of art.7(1)(b) by the Court of First Instance was challenged again in *Glaverbel*.[426] Glaverbel had applied for registration as a Community Trade Mark of "a design applied to the surface of the goods" for glass products for building and for the manufacture of sanitary installations. The actual sign was an abstract design.

The application was rejected for lack of distinctive character under art.7(1)(b) of the Regulation. The Board of Appeal dismissed the appeal[427] and the case reached the Court of First Instance, that rejected the plea alleging infringement of art.7(1)(b) but upheld another plea on the basis of art.7(3) and annulled the contested decision. Glaverbel insisted and brought the art.7(1)(b) part of the case before the Court.

The Court rejected the appeal by reasoned order under art.119 of the Rules of Procedure; where the appeal is clearly inadmissible or clearly

---

[423] *Henkel*, para.58.
[424] Citing *Eurim-Pharm Arzneimittel GmbH v Beiersdorf AG* (C-71/94 to C-73/94) [1996] E.C.R. I-3603; and *Bayerische Motorenwerke AG and BMW Nederland BV v Deenik* (C-37/97) [1999] E.C.R. I-905.
[425] Citing *Koninklijke KPN Nederland NV* (C-363/99) [2004] E.C.R. I-1619.
[426] *Glaverbel SA v Office for Harmonisation in the Internal Market (Trade Marks and Designs)* (C-445/02 P) [2004] E.C.R. I-6267; the appeal was against the judgment of the Court of First Instance in *Glaverbel SA v Office for Harmonisation in the Internal Market (Trade Marks and Designs)* (T-36/01) [2002] E.C.R. II-3887.
[427] Case R 0986/2004-4, March 1, 2004.

6. ARTICLE 3(1)(b)—DEVOID OF ANY DISTINCTIVE CHARACTER

unfounded, the Court may at any time, acting on a report from the Judge-Rapporteur and after hearing the Advocate General, dismiss the appeal by reasoned order.

The most interesting and challenging part of the appeal was Glaverbel's claim regarding the function of the design applied on the surface of the glass. The Court of First Instance had found that the design, which consisted of countless tiny strokes applied throughout the surface of the sheet of glass, constituted part of the appearance of the product and embodied obvious characteristics of the product. It functioned, and accordingly was perceived in the same way, as a technical means of rendering the glass opaque. It added that the complexity and fancifulness of the design was the result of its ornamental and decorative nature and made its perception as a distinguishing sign difficult and improbable.

4–242

Glaverbel argued that there were thousands of patterns that could make a sheet of glass opaque. It accepted the aesthetic nature of the design by claiming that consumers chose a glass sheet on the basis of its design. However, it viewed this as a counterargument regarding the technical function described by the Court of First Instance, and supported that the complexity and fancifulness of the design would make consumers recognise it and perceive it as a distinguishing sign when seeing it elsewhere.

The Court did not get drawn into this discussion of aesthetic functionality for the purposes of distinctive character. Instead it agreed with the Office and rejected the plea as inadmissible because it saw it as a request to reassess findings of fact.

(13) The washing tablets cases

In the washing tablets cases the Court took a strict approach regarding the application of art.7(1)(b). The cases involved a number of appeals against judgments of the Court of First Instance on the distinctive character of the shape of a number of washing tablets as Community Trade Marks for "washing or dishwashing preparations in tablet form". Another issue in these cases was the timing for the determination of distinctive character.

4–243

The Court of First Instance had bypassed this question in *Henkel*[428] where it had decided that the shapes' lack of distinctive character and their inability to indicate the origin of the product was not affected by the number of similar tablets already on the market.

Consequently, it was not necessary to decide whether their distinctive character should be assessed by reference to the date on which the application for registration was filed or the date of actual registration.

---

[428] *Henkel (rectangular tablet, white and red)* (T-337/99) [2001] E.C.R II-2597.

ABSOLUTE GROUNDS

Advocate General Ruiz-Jarabo Colomer examined all the appeals jointly in one Opinion; the Court considered the appeals in three separate judgments.[429]

(a) The judgments of the Court of First Instance

4–244   **(i) Henkel—the two-layered tablets.** The trade marks in the *Henkel* judgments[430] consisted of two-layered, rectangular tablets. The colours of the layers were white and red in the first mark and white and green in the second.

The applications were rejected for lack of distinctive character. The Board of Appeal confirmed the rejection, holding that in the case of a three-dimensional mark that was simply a reproduction of the product the shape mark had to be sufficiently unique to imprint itself easily on the mind of the relevant consumer and to stand out from what was considered to be normal in the trade.

From a broader justificatory perspective the Board also contrasted between trade mark law and the law of utility models and designs noting that the standard for assessing distinctive character should be higher under trade mark law because of the broad and potentially perpetual scope of trade mark rights.[431]

4–245   The Court of First Instance linked distinctive character with the function of the trade mark as an indicator of origin: the mark should enable:

> "members of the public concerned to distinguish the product or service that it designates from those which have a different trade origin and to conclude that all the products or services that it designates have been manufactured, marketed or supplied under the control of the owner of the mark and that the owner is responsible for their quality".[432]

It accepted that a minimum degree of distinctive character should satisfy the art.7(1)(b) requirement and that the same criteria should be applied in respect of all types of signs. However, it also noted that the perception of the relevant section of the public would not necessarily be the same in relation to a three-dimensional mark consisting of the shape and the colours of the product itself compared with a word mark, a figurative mark or a

---

[429] *Henkel KGaA* (C-456/01 P and C-457/01 P) [2004] E.C.R. I-5089; *Procter & Gamble* (C-468/01 P to C-472/01 P) [2004] E.C.R. I-5141; and *Procter & Gamble* (C-473/01 P and C-474/01 P) [2004] E.C.R. I-5173. For the Opinion of the A.G. see the *Henkel* case.
[430] Case *Henkel KGaA* (T-335/99) [2001] E.C.R. II-2581; and *Henkel KGaA* (T-336/99) [2001] E.C.R. II-2589. For the English version of those cases see the almost identical *Henkel (rectangular tablet, white and red)* (T-337/99) [2001] E.C.R II-2597.
[431] Case R 70/1999–3, Case R 71/1999–3 and Case R 73/1999–3, September 21, 1999.
[432] *Henkel KGaA* (T-337/99) [2001] E.C.R. II-2581, para.43.

three-dimensional mark not consisting of the shape of the product. "Whilst the public is used to recognising the latter marks instantly as signs identifying the product, this is not necessarily so where the sign is indistinguishable from the appearance of the product itself."[433] It also agreed with the Board on the level of consumer attention for everyday goods; setting it in a negative way it found that the level was not high.

Analysing the overall impression conveyed by the sign it examined first each one of its elements, which also constituted features of the product.

The shape was one of the basic geometrical shapes, obvious for such a product.

4–246

Regarding colours it added that consumers were used to seeing different colour features in detergent preparations; indeed, the use of basic colours like blue and green was typical in that sector, whereas the use of other basic colours was found to be one of the most obvious variations on the typical design of these products.

Note that the Court of First Instance perceived colours as elements of the overall product design, indirectly introducing into the debate broader functionality arguments.

It conceded that consumers might get into the habit of recognising the product from its colours, but this should only be relevant for the application of art.7(3).

4–247

Then, it looked at the mark as a whole: "a combination of obvious features typical of the product concerned"[434] that failed to enable consumers to distinguish the specified products according to origin.

(ii) Procter & Gamble—the speckled tablets. The first set of the Procter & Gamble cases concerned five square tablets with slightly rounded edges and corners. Two consisted of two layers (white and pale green,[435] white with green speckles and pale green)[436]; the remaining three of a single layer incorporating speckles (white with yellow and blue speckles,[437] white with blue speckles,[438] and white with green and blue speckles[439]). The specified products were "washing and bleaching preparations and other substances for laundry

4–248

---

[433] *Henkel KGaA* (T-337/99) [2001] E.C.R. II-2581, para.47.
[434] *Henkel KGaA* (T-337/99) [2001] E.C.R. II-2581, para.54.
[435] *Procter & Gamble* (T-117/00) [2001] E.C.R. II-2723; the application was against the decision of the Board of Appeal in Case R-509/1999–1, March 8, 2000.
[436] *Procter & Gamble* (T-118/00) [2001] E.C.R. II-2731; the application was against Case R-516/1999–1, March 3, 2000.
[437] *Procter & Gamble* (T-119/00) [2001] E.C.R. II-2761; the application was against Case R-519/1999–1, February 29, 1999.
[438] *Procter & Gamble* (T-120/00) [2001] E.C.R. II-2769; the application was against Case R-520/1999–1, February 29, 2000.
[439] *Procter & Gamble* (T-121/00) [2001] E.C.R. II-2777; the application was against Case R-529/1999–1, February 29, 1999.

use; cleaning, polishing, scouring and abrasive preparations; preparations for the washing, cleaning and care of dishes; soaps".

The applications were rejected on the basis of art.7(1)(b) of the Regulation.

The Board of Appeal upheld the decision of the examiner finding that the basic geometric shapes were the most obvious shapes for such tablets, there was nothing arbitrary or fanciful in a square tablet as a shape for solid detergents, and that colours failed to confer distinctive character.

4–249 Looking at them from a "functionality" angle, it noted that white was associated with cleanliness and was a traditional colour for soap powders; green, apart from being a basic colour, was attractive and associated with environmental protection. The Board had also referred to the need of competitors to use similar shapes and colours for their own tablets.

Before the Court of First Instance Procter & Gamble stated that it brought the action because the registrability of these signs was an issue that had to be clarified rather than because it believed they deserved trade mark protection.

The Court of First Instance[440] agreed with the Board, following the line of arguments it had established in *Henkel*.[441] Regarding colour combinations and speckles in particular it noted that consumers were used to different colour features in detergent preparations. The coloured particles suggested—but not directly described—certain product qualities; they did not function as indicators of origin.

4–250 The position of the Court of First Instance on colours was again uncompromising:

> "... the use of basic colours, such as blue or green, is commonplace and is even typical of detergents. The use of other basic colours, such as red or yellow, is one of the most obvious variations on the typical design of these products. The same is true of the various shades of those colours. For that reason, the applicant's argument that the mark applied for is distinctive because one of the layers of the tablet is 'pale green' must be dismissed".[442]

In an attempt to discourage further applications based on different combinations it added that although it was possible to vary the basic geometric shapes and add other basic colours as a layer or as speckles such differences would not suffice to transform the tablets to indications of the product's origin, "inasmuch as those differences are, as in the present case, obvious variations on the product's basic shapes".[443]

---

[440] *Procter & Gamble* (T-117/00) [2001] E.C.R. II-2723.
[441] *Henkel KGaA* (T-337/99) [2001] E.C.R. II-2581.
[442] *Procter & Gamble* (T-117/00) [2001] E.C.R. II-2723, para.64.
[443] *Procter & Gamble* (T-117/00) [2001] E.C.R. II-2723, para.73.

6. ARTICLE 3(1)(b)—DEVOID OF ANY DISTINCTIVE CHARACTER

From a doctrinal perspective, it acknowledged that the Board had partially based its decision on the general interest in preventing trade mark law from conferring a monopoly over a product, a criterion that the Court of First Instance did not consider to be directly applicable in relation to art.7(1)(b), however the Board had not automatically precluded the registration of such signs, but required them to display sufficiently unusual and arbitrary features to render them distinctive.

(iii) Procter & Gamble—the inlaid tablets. The second set of the Procter & Gamble cases concerned two tablets—one square[444] and the other rectangular[445]—with chamfered edges, bevelled or slightly rounded corners, speckles, and inlays on the upper surface.   4–251

The Board of Appeal confirmed the decision of the Office to refuse registration according to art.7(1)(b), adding this time that the use of "shouldered" corners, bevelled edges, concave centres and colours did not confer distinctive character on the trade marks.[446]

The Court of First Instance underlined that here the applicant had not claimed a colour. So, the applicant had to establish that "the average consumer, when he sees a rectangular tablet with chamfered edges, speckles and a triangular inlay, will recognise it irrespective of its colour and associate all products presented in that way with the same origin".[447]

It found that the additional elements did not assist the shape in gaining distinctive character, irrespective of the fact that there were no other tablets at the market with the same combination—rectangular tablet/triangular inlay—of shapes.   4–252

Interestingly, the Court of First Instance continued employing "functionality" arguments. It found the slightly rounded corners to be dictated by practical considerations and viewed the chamfered edges as a barely perceptible variant on the basic shape.

Considering the speckles it added that consumers were used to light and dark features in detergent preparations because powder was usually very light grey or beige and appeared to be almost white. Often it contained particles of one or more colours, darker or lighter than its basic colour, which suggested the presence of various active ingredients. Similarly the inlays were seen as one of the most obvious solutions for combining various ingredients in a tabular washing product. The form of the inlays, a slight depression in the tablet's centre in a geometrical shape, and the combined effect of their shape with the shape of the tablet were equally obvious. Whereas the Court of First Instance required something additional that would have an impact on consumers' perception.

---

[444] *Procter & Gamble (Square tablet with inlay)* (T-128/00) [2001] E.C.R. II-2785.
[445] *Procter & Gamble (Rectangular tablet with inlay)* (T-129/00) [2001] E.C.R. II-2793.
[446] Case R-506/1999–1 and Case R-508/1999 March 8, 2000.
[447] *Procter & Gamble* (T-128/00) [2001] E.C.R. II-278, para.55.

(b) The Opinion of the Advocate General

4-253 The Opinion of A.G. Ruiz-Jarabo Colomer covered all the appeals under one roof[448] since they all involved the interpretation and application of art.7(1)(b). He started his analysis by considering the "procedural" question of the timing of the assessment of distinctive character.

4-254 **(i) The critical time for assessing distinctive character.** Henkel claimed that at the time of the application their tablets were readily distinguishable because the product as such, washing tablets, existed only to a limited extent. At the time the actual assessment took place their competitors have incorporated elements of the design of the appellants' products into their own.

It also argued that, from an evidentiary perspective, applicants decided whether or not to file an application on the basis of the facts available to them at the date of the application. Accordingly, the authorities undertaking the examination should take into account only the products known at the time of the application.

The Office claimed that there was no reason for the Court of First Instance to consider this issue because the tablets lacked distinctive character even at the application filing date, although as a matter of principle it supported that the conditions for registration should also be satisfied at the date of registration.

4-255 The Advocate General agreed with the Office's position that the sign applied for had to meet the requisite conditions, both at the time of filing the application and on registration. This would preclude the registration of signs that lost their distinctive character during the process of the examination.

This was, first, based on a joint reading of art.7(1) with art.51[449] providing that a trade mark registered in breach of the provisions of art.7 should be invalidated. If we were to follow the line of the appellants a trade mark could be registered and annulled immediately after registration. This appeared illogical. He felt that his position was strengthened by the wording of art.51(2) that specifically referred to "registration" rather than the filing of the application.[450]

Secondly, he accepted the Office's "undertaking" that in order to avoid denying registration to a sign that had been systematically copied in the course of the examination procedure, it would exclude from its analysis of distinctive character cases where the sign was used solely for that purpose.

---

[448] [2004] E.C.R I-5089.
[449] Article 51(1) provides: "A Community trade mark shall be declared invalid on application to the Office or on the basis of a counterclaim in infringement proceedings, (a) where the Community trade mark has been registered contrary to the provisions of Article 7; (b) where the applicant was acting in bad faith when he filed the application for the trade mark."
[450] Article 51(2) provides; "Where the Community trade mark has been registered in breach of the provisions of Article 7(1)(b), (c) or (d), it may nevertheless not be declared invalid if, in consequence of the use which has been made of it, it has after registration acquired a distinctive character in relation to the goods or services for which it is registered".

6. ARTICLE 3(1)(b)—DEVOID OF ANY DISTINCTIVE CHARACTER

He found that behind this "undertaking" lay either art.7(1)(f) of the Regulation[451] or the "general principle of law proscribing acts committed in bad faith, which is recognised in article 51(1)(b) of the Regulation".[452] In essence the Office should, according to the Regulation, refuse to take account, for the purposes of registration, of any conduct whose sole purpose was to obstruct registration of competitors' marks.

4–256

Thirdly, from a doctrinal perspective he suggested that frequent use of the same elements would be relevant only if the contested judgments had been based on the criterion of relative originality or currency of the signs, that could be more relevant when considering the general interest in preserving the availability of a mark in the context of art.7(1)(c). "In fact, the signs were rejected on other grounds, namely the association of those components with what the Court of First Instance described as obvious features."[453]

(ii) The interpretation and application of article 7(1)(b). The Advocate General divided the remaining grounds of appeal into four categories.

4–257

First, the significance of the existence of similar products in the marketplace and the relationship between art.7(1)(b) and art.12(b); secondly, the angle for viewing and examining distinctive character; thirdly, the relevance of actual distinctive character; and finally the relevance of the need to preserve availability.

The significance of similar products—article 12(b). A number of grounds were covered under this theme.

4–258

First, Henkel argued that searching for similarities with other comparable products should not be an issue under art.7(1)(b), because it would introduce into the examination of registrability a concern that was relevant for determining the scope of protection.

The Advocate General noted from the outset that the Court of First Instance had not undertaken comparisons with existing products. "The Court of First Instance ... preferred to contrast the signs with an image of the ideal representation of the product."[454] But he viewed Henkel's claim as an attempt to "allude to the question of the relationship between the absolute grounds for refusal and the limited extent of the protection afforded by a trade mark, as recognised by article 12(b)".[455]

---

[451] Article 7(1)(f) covers trade marks which are contrary to public policy or to accepted principles of morality.
[452] Point 46 of the Opinion of A.G. Ruiz-Jarabo Colomer.
[453] Point 47 of the Opinion of A.G. Ruiz-Jarabo Colomer.
[454] Point 50 of the Opinion of A.G. Ruiz-Jarabo Colomer.
[455] Point 51. From the A.G.'s perspective this was an opportunity to refer to his earlier Opinion in *DKV Deutsche Krankenversicherung AG* (C-104/00 P) [2002] E.C.R. I-7561 where he expressed his strong opposition to creating a link between the two provisions. *Libertel Groep BV* (C-104/01) [2003] E.C.R. I-3793 he suggested had endorsed his position.

4-259 Following *Libertel*[456] it appeared that the Court had made clear that registrability and enforcement were distinct processes. Accordingly, and without examining further whether the Court of First Instance was entitled to contrast the signs applied for registration with the ideal representation of the product, he concluded that it had not made an error in law in its interpretation of art.7(1)(b). The comparison made by the Court of First Instance was reconsidered by the Advocate General in his discussion of the ground of appeal based on the existence of actual distinctive character.

Secondly, Procter & Gamble suggested that the Court of First Instance should have considered under art.7(1)(b) the possibility that consumers might get used into identifying a product from its colours; this should not be seen as an exclusively art.7(3) issue. One of the counter-arguments employed by the Office was that applicants should not be allowed to enjoy the priority of a Community Trade Mark for such basic and commonplace product. They should be protected as trade marks only where extremely widespread use had given them the necessary distinctive character.

The Advocate General found that this claim targeted an aspect of the Court of First Instance's reasoning that had no impact on the outcome and, in any case, on its own this possibility would not suffice to make the sign distinctive.

Thirdly, Procter & Gamble also supported that if there were no similar tablets on the market at the time of assessment of the sign's distinctive character then it would be appreciably different and possess distinctive character. Again, A.G. Ruiz-Jarabo Colomer rejected the argument:

> "first, what is decisive is not the number of products on the market but the way in which the average consumer perceives them; second, nor is the number of products on the market capable of counteracting, for example, the descriptive nature of their appearance for the purposes of article 7(1)(c) of the Regulation".[457]

4-260 *The average consumer's level of attention.* Henkel challenged the view that the average consumer's level of attention would not be high for everyday consumer goods. It argued that to the contrary consumers paid particular attention to the qualities of detergents.

Procter & Gamble added two further arguments. First, that the everyday use of consumer products heightened the consumer's attention in respect of their appearance and characteristics; the same applied to advertising. Both should be particularly relevant for a product that was sold in packaging that differed from its shape. Secondly, it approached the same issue from a different angle, claiming that at the time of the application dishwasher

---

[456] Referring to *Libertel Groep BV* (C-104/01) [2003] E.C.R. I-3793.
[457] Point 57 of the Opinion of A.G. Ruiz-Jarabo Colomer.

6. ARTICLE 3(1)(b)—DEVOID OF ANY DISTINCTIVE CHARACTER

tablets and washing tablets were not everyday consumer goods; they were placed at the top quality end of the market and enjoyed a high degree of consumer attention.

The Office deduced a different conclusion from the way the tablets were used. It underlined that at the point of sale consumers paid little attention to the exact shape and colour of the tablets because they were not sold loose but in packaging. And during the actual use of the product consumers would hold the tablets for a few seconds without raising any questions concerning the shape of the tablets and its meaning.

The Advocate General found that assessing the precise way consumers perceived a product was a matter of fact, outside the jurisdiction of the Court. In any case he found the Court of First Instance's assertion to be the correct inference to be drawn from the proposition that as regards the relevant public's perception of the trade mark, the attention of the average consumer varied according to the category of products or services in question.

4–261

As to Procter & Gamble's argument based on use and advertising it had not been addressed before the Court of First Instance and could not be raised before the Court of Justice.

Actual distinctive character. Again, a number of claims were dealt by the Advocate General under this heading.

4–262

First, Henkel argued that the correct test for assessing distinctive character should be for the Court of First Instance to examine whether the specific characteristics of the three-dimensional signs were different from those that were typical in the same product market and whether they were necessary for technical reasons, rather than consider their obviousness. Procter & Gamble followed a similar but more direct line focusing on whether the signs differed perceptibly from the usual get-up of such detergents. The right test should be whether the shape of the tablets was at the material time already part of the usual get-up of tablets on the market and, if not, whether the difference was perceptible, rendering it apt to confer distinctive character on the marks.

The Office suggested that "three-dimensional shape-of-product" marks had to be original, unusual or arbitrary in order to possess distinctive character; it viewed this as the result of recurring factual situations rather than the application of a more stringent criterion. Based on the functional nature of the product it supported that basic shapes were obvious and usual shapes for it. Another argument brought forward by the Office was that the above test was in essence the test applied for the registration of designs. It accepted that the same get up could be protected under both trade mark and design rights however it noted that the conditions for the grant of each right should be applied separately and vigorously.

Advocate General Ruiz-Jarabo Colomer categorically supported the approach taken by the Court of First Instance:

4–263

"the test used by the Court of First Instance is not only correct, but is also more appropriate, than the test proposed by the appellants. When the signs for which registration is sought are compared, not with those already current, but with a paradigm composed of features which spring to mind if the shape of the product is imagined, the test performed, although based on objective criteria, does not lean so heavily on the vagaries of the market".[458]

The Court of First Instance had simply adapted the method for assessing distinctive character to take into account the particular features of this type of signs.

This would also ensure that no one undertaking could protect under trade mark law features that its competitors would like to use. Nevertheless, he found that since it remained uncertain whether the need to preserve availability could be raised under art.7(1)(b) of the Regulation the best way for dealing with such concerns would be under art.7(1)(c) that excluded signs that were nothing more than the representation of a graphic description of the product. Article 7(1)(c) also allowed the consideration of factors pertaining to the future.

The second set of claims focused on the significance of specific peculiarities, for example the arrangement of colours or the rounded edges in relation to some of the tablets.

The Advocate General considered these issues to be matters of fact.

4–264 *The need to preserve availability.* The final set of grounds attacked the apparent inclusion in the analysis of the Court of First Instance of the need to preserve the availability of some signs for other undertakings, something that fell within the scope of art.7(1)(c) that was not applicable in this case.

For the Advocate General the purpose of art.7(1)(b) was to:

"to prohibit the registration of signs which are devoid of any real distinctive character, that is to say, those signs which the average consumer, who is reasonably well informed and reasonably observant and circumspect, cannot identify as reliably indicating the commercial origin of the product".[459]

Preventing the appropriation of three-dimensional shapes that were useful from an aesthetic or technical point of view, or the monopolisation of descriptive signs was covered by subparagraphs art.7(1)(e) and art.7(1)(c). Article 7(1)(d) protected the general interest in keeping available for all signs that were customary in the current language or in the bona fide and established practices of the trade.

---

[458] Point 68 of the Opinion of A.G. Ruiz-Jarabo Colomer.
[459] Point 78 of the Opinion of A.G. Ruiz-Jarabo Colomer.

6. ARTICLE 3(1)(b)—DEVOID OF ANY DISTINCTIVE CHARACTER

In *Libertel*[460] the Court of Justice had taken into account the monopolisation of colours in the application of art.3(1)(b) of the Directive, however this should be seen in the particular context of that case:

4–265

> "Those considerations—based, as is recognised in the judgment itself, on the fact that there are a limited number of colours which an average consumer can in practice identify—do not appear to be transferable to the rules relating to trade marks consisting of the shape of the product."[461]

The Advocate General accepted that the reference to such concerns by the Court of First Instance under art.7(1)(b) was problematic. However, it had not employed this criterion improperly in its judgments:

> "Rather, in using the notion of an obvious shape, it assessed distinctive character by reference to an ideal paradigmatic concept of the product or, in other words, to how it instinctively comes to mind, instead of by reference to products already available on the market."[462]

He found the test applied by the Court of First Instance to be an objective one, when properly executed. "In the present case, it is significant that the appellants, who claim that the shapes of the washing tablets were not customary at the time when the application was filed, accept that they are now. That is perhaps the best proof that the test carried out was the right one."[463]

(c) The judgment of the Court in Henkel KgaA[464]

In the first of the three washing tablets cases the Court considered jointly the appeals against two judgments of the Court of First Instance[465] covering four separate issues: the distinctive character of the trade marks; the relevance of the need to preserve the availability of a sign; the assessment of the average consumer's level of attention; and the date for assessing distinctive character.

4–266

Henkel also claimed that the Office had already accepted that comparable signs possessed distinctive character; the Court rejected the claim because it had not been raised before the Court of First Instance. "To allow a party to put forward for the first time before the Court of Justice a plea in law

---

[460] *Libertel Groep BV* (C-104/01) [2003] E.C.R. I-3793.
[461] Point 81 of the Opinion of A.G. Ruiz-Jarabo Colomer.
[462] Point 82 of the Opinion of A.G. Ruiz-Jarabo Colomer.
[463] Point 84 of the Opinion of A.G. Ruiz-Jarabo Colomer.
[464] *Henkel KGaA* (C-456/01 P and C-457/01 P) [2004] E.C.R. I-5089.
[465] *Henkel (rectangular tablet, red and white)* (T-335/99) [2001] E.C.R. II-2581; and *Henkel (rectangular tablet, green and white)* (T-336/99) [2001] E.C.R. II-2589; for the English version see the almost identical *Henkel (rectangular tablet, white and red)* (T-337/99) [2001] E.C.R II-2597.

which it has not raised before the Court of First Instance would be to allow it to bring before the Court, whose jurisdiction in an appeal is limited, a case of wider ambit than that which came before the Court of First Instance. In an appeal the Court's jurisdiction is thus confined to review of the findings of law on the pleas argued before the Court of First Instance".[466]

4–267   **(i) Assessing the distinctive character of a trade mark.** Here the Court dealt with Henkel's claims on distinctive character: what mattered for assessing distinctive character was whether the features of the tablets were different from those in that product market or whether they had to be used because of technical requirements; colours were perceived as individual features of the get-up of a particular product; and, the Court of First Instance had failed to take into account that Henkel was the only player in that market using red on its tablets, this allowed the public to make the link as to origin between the product and Henkel.

The Office's response was based on the functional nature of the product and the requirement for such marks to be original, unusual or arbitrary. Trade mark protection should be granted only if there was evidence of distinctive character acquired through use. Regarding colour combinations in particular it supported that they were perceived by consumers as indications of ingredients with different properties rather than conveyors of detailed information regarding the composition and effect of each product in that form.

The Court held that the Court of First Instance had rightly followed the path mapped by the Court in its earlier jurisprudence. There were no surprises in the Court's statements.

4–268   First, in principle and according to art.4 the shape and colours of product could constitute a trade mark provided they were capable of being represented graphically and capable of distinguishing. However:

> "the fact that a sign is, in general, capable of constituting a trade mark within the meaning of Article 4 ... does not mean that the sign necessarily has distinctive character for the purposes of Article 7(1)(b) ... in relation to a specific product or service".[467]

Secondly, in order to possess distinctive character a mark had to identify the specified product as originating from a particular undertaking, and thus to distinguish that product from those of other undertakings[468]; and distinctive character should be assessed, first, by reference to the specified products

---

[466] *Henkel KGaA*, para.50, citing *Commission v Brazzelli Lualdi* (C-136/92 P) [1994] E.C.R. I-1981; and the Order in *Eridania v Council of the European Union* (Case C-352/99 P) [2001] E.C.R. I-5037.
[467] *Henkel KGaA*, para.32.
[468] Citing *Linde AG* (C-53/01), *Winward Industries Inc* (C-54/01) and *Rado Uhren AG* (C-55/01) [2003] E.C.R. I-3161.

6. ARTICLE 3(1)(b)—DEVOID OF ANY DISTINCTIVE CHARACTER

or services and, secondly, by reference to the perception of the relevant public.[469]

Thirdly, the criteria for assessing distinctive character were the same for all types of trade marks.

Fourthly, for the purposes of those criteria, the relevant public's perception was not necessarily the same in relation to a three-dimensional mark consisting of the shape and colours of the product itself as it would be in relation to a word or figurative mark consisting of a sign independent from the appearance of the products it denoted.

4–269

Average consumers were not in the habit of making assumptions about the origin of products on the basis of their shape or the shape of their packaging in the absence of any graphic or word element and it could therefore prove more difficult to establish distinctiveness in relation to such a three-dimensional mark.[470]

This meant that the more closely the shape for which registration is sought resembled the shape most likely to be taken by the specified product in question, the greater the likelihood of the shape being devoid of any distinctive character for the purposes of art.7(1)(b) of Reg. No.40/94:

> "Only a trade mark which departs significantly from the norm or customs of the sector and thereby fulfils its essential function of indicating origin, is not devoid of any distinctive character for the purposes of that provision".[471]

How those criteria were applied in a particular case remained in the exclusive jurisdiction of the Court of First Instance because it involved findings of a factual nature. The Court could intervene on appeal only in cases of distortion of the evidence produced before the Court of First Instance.[472]

(ii) Article 7(1)(b) and the need to preserve the availability of a sign. Here the Court appeared to alter its position regarding the public interest underlying art.7(1)(b).

4–270

Henkel's arguments and the Office's riposte had both taken up the "functionality" point insinuated in the judgment of the Court of First Instance. The appellant argued that the Court of First Instance had overly relied on its finding that the shapes and colours of the tablets were both "basic". This

---

[469] Citing *Linde AG* (C-53/01), *Winward Industries Inc* (C-54/01) and *Rado Uhren AG* (C-55/01) [2003] E.C.R. I-3161; and *Koninklijke KPN Nederland NV v Benelux-Merkenbureau* (C-363/99) [2004] E.C.R. I-1619.
[470] Citing *Linde AG* (C-53/01), *Winward Industries Inc* (C-54/01) and *Rado Uhren AG* (C-55/01) [2003] E.C.R. I-3161; and *Henkel KGaA v Deutches Patent- und Markenamt* (C-218/01) [2004] E.C.R. I-1725.
[471] *Henkel KGaA*, para.39, citing *Henkel KGaA v Deutches Patent- und Markenamt* (C-218/01) [2004] E.C.R. I-1725.
[472] Citing *DKV Deutsche Krankenversicherung AG* (C-104/00 P) [2002] E.C.R. I-7561.

led to the claim that it had taken into account "need to preserve the availability of a sign" considerations that were relevant only for the application of art.7(1)(b).[473]

Henkel went further and queried whether the "need to preserve the availability of a sign" considerations would preclude the registration of the contested signs. The shape of the tablet was determined freely by the manufacturer; it only had to observe some universal technical requirements that did not dictate the details of the actual shape. From a technical point of view there was no compelling ground for a competitor to use that particular shape.

4–271 The same applied to the colour combinations that, it stressed, followed a specific arrangement. Consumers would not perceive them as indications of technical product characteristics but as a manifestation of the individuality of the product.

It concluded that if there was no need to maintain the availability of each one of the elements of the sign, the same should apply to the combination of those elements.

The Office supported that Henkel's overall approach was wrong because it had misinterpreted the judgment of the Court in *Windsurfing Chiemsee*.[474]

4–272 In addition, it suggested that Henkel's own account of the product development of washing tablets showed that from their early stages competing undertakings had been using rectangular and circular two-layered and two-coloured shapes for their tablets. This should be seen as evidence of the need to ensure that these elements would also remain available to other competitors.

Note that the Office had also submitted, first, that the test for distinctive character suggested by Henkel was appropriate for determining the distinctive character of a design but not of a trade mark and, secondly, that a Community Trade Mark registration should not be used to give a priority right over an obvious product configuration; the story would be different if there was evidence of distinctiveness acquired through use.

The response of the Court was twofold. First, it rejected the basis of Henkel's claim, finding that the Court of First Instance had founded its judgment on lack of distinctive character. Secondly, and more important from a doctrinal perspective, it held that "even on the assumption that the Court of First Instance did include considerations pertaining to the public interest in its assessment of distinctive character, it did not make an error of law in that regard".[475]

---

[473] Citing *Windsurfing Chiemsee Produktions- und Vertriebs GmbH v Boots- und Segelzubehör Walter Huber and Franz Attenberger* (C-108/97 & C-109/97) [1999] E.C.R. I-2779.
[474] *Windsurfing Chiemsee Produktions- und Vertriebs GmbH v Boots- und Segelzubehör Walter Huber and Franz Attenberger* (C-108/97 & C-109/97) [1999] E.C.R. I-2779.
[475] *Henkel KGaA*, para.44.

6. ARTICLE 3(1)(b)—DEVOID OF ANY DISTINCTIVE CHARACTER

But to which public interest did the Court refer? This remained a mute point.   4-273

The Court noted:

"Each of the grounds for refusal to register listed in Article 7(1)(b) of Regulation No 40/94 is independent of the others and calls for separate examination. Furthermore, the various grounds for refusal must be interpreted in the light of the public interest underlying each of them".[476]

The public interest underlying each of those grounds "may, or even must, reflect different considerations, depending upon which ground for refusal is at issue".[477]

De-contextualising *Libertel*[478] from its factual background reminded the Court that there it had ruled that art.3(1)(b) of the Directive was directed at the need not to restrict unduly the availability of colours for other traders. And, looking at the registrability of the contested signs from a negative perspective, it added: "there is no public interest in conferring the benefit of the full protection . . . on a trade mark which does not fulfil its essential function . . .".[479]

Accordingly it rejected Henkel's claim as inadmissible.

(iii) The average consumer's level of attention. The Court ruled that this issue involved findings of fact that were not subject to review by the Court of Justice on appeal.   4-274

(iv) The date for assessing distinctive character. The Court chose to ignore the substance of this question. Functioning as a true court of appeal rather as an interpretive court it accepted that the Court of First Instance was correct in finding that it was not necessary to decide this point since its judgment on distinctive character was not affected by the number of similar tablets on the market.   4-275

(d) The judgment of the Court in the speckled tablets Procter & Gamble cases

In the first *Procter & Gamble*[480] case the Court considered the appeals against the judgments of the Court of First Instance in the square speckled   4-276

---

[476] *Henkel KGaA*, para.45, probably meaning art.7(1) rather than art.7(1)(b). Even if this is a mistake it is perhaps revealing of the fact that the Court views art.7(1) as a distinctiveness continuum rather than a compilation of distinct grounds. Citing *Koninklijke Philips Electronics NV* (C-299/99) [2002] E.C.R. I-5475.
[477] *Henkel KGaA*, para.46.
[478] *Libertel Groep BV* (C-104/01) [2003] E.C.R. I-3793.
[479] *Henkel KGaA*, para.50.
[480] *Procter & Gamble v Office for Harmonisation in the Internal Market (Trade Marks and Designs)* (C-468/01 P to C-472/01 P) [2004] E.C.R. I-5141.

tablets cases.[481] Procter & Gamble claimed that the Court of First Instance had misinterpreted art.7(1)(b) focusing on five issues: the distinctive character of the trade marks; the assessment of the consumer's level of attention; the date for assessing distinctive character; the need to consider the trade mark as a whole; the criterion concerning use of a trade mark.

The Court followed its judgment in *Henkel* regarding the first three issues. So here we will concentrate on the need to consider the mark as a whole and the criterion concerning use of the mark.

4-277   **(i) Considering the mark as a whole.** Procter & Gamble argued that the Court of First Instance had examined each one of the individual components but failed to analyse the overall impression produced by the specific combinations. The Office responded that the Court of First Instance and examination authorities were entitled to start the examination of a trade mark with a separate analysis of the individual components of the marks.

The Court repeated its findings in cases that dealt with conflicts between signs. The average consumer normally perceived a mark as a whole and did not proceed to analyse its various details.[482] Accordingly, the overall impression given by the mark should be considered in order to assess distinctive character.[483] However, this did not mean that the competent authorities "may not first examine each of the individual features of the get-up of that mark in turn. It may be useful, in the course of the competent authority's overall assessment, to examine each of the components of which the trade mark concerned is composed".[484]

This is what the Court of First Instance had done in this case. It examined the shapes of the tablets and their colour arrangements separately and then assessed the overall impression deriving from them.

4-278   **(ii) The criterion concerning use of a trade mark.** The Court summarily rejected Procter & Gamble's argument that use of or advertising for other signs could influence the public to view colours as indicators of origin and that this use should be considered under art.7(1)(b) rather than

---

[481] *Procter & Gamble v Office for Harmonisation in the Internal Market (Trade Marks and Designs) (Square tablet, white and pale green)* (T-117/00) [2001] E.C.R. II-2723; *Procter & Gamble v Office for Harmonisation in the Internal Market (Trade Marks and Designs) (Square tablet, white with green speckles and pale green)* (T-118/00) [2001] E.C.R. II-2731; *Procter & Gamble v Office for Harmonisation in the Internal Market (Trade Marks and Designs) (Square tablet, white with yellow and blue speckles)* (T-119/00) [2001] E.C.R. II-2761; *Procter & Gamble v Office for Harmonisation in the Internal Market (Trade Marks and Designs) (Square tablet, white with blue speckles)* (T-120/00) [2001] E.C.R. II-2769; and *Procter & Gamble v Office for Harmonisation in the Internal Market (Trade Marks and Designs) (Square tablet, white with green and blue speckles)* (T-121/00) [2001] E.C.R. II-2777.
[482] *Sabel BV v Puma AG, Rudolf Dassler Sport* (C-251/95) [1997] E.C.R. I-6191; and *Lloyd Schuhfabrik Meyer & Co GmbH v Klijsen Handel BV* (C-342/97) [1999] E.C.R. I-3819.
[483] *Sabel BV* (C-251/95) [1997] E.C.R. I-6191; and *DKV Deutsche Krankenversicherung AG* (C-104/00 P) [2002] E.C.R. I-7561.
[484] *Procter & Gamble*, para.45.

6. ARTICLE 3(1)(b)—DEVOID OF ANY DISTINCTIVE CHARACTER

art.7(3) by simply stating that the Court of First Instance had correctly applied art.7(1)(b).

(e) The judgment of the Court in the inlaid Procter & Gamble tablets

In the second *Procter & Gamble* case[485] the Court considered the appeals against the judgments of the Court of First Instance concerning the inlaid tablets.[486] The claims were the same with those developed in the first *Procter & Gamble* case. The Court rejected the appeal following the same line it had drawn in the first case.

(14) SiSi-Werke—article 7(1)(b) and packaging

In *SiSi-Werke*[487] the Court looked at the application of art.7(1)(b) of the Regulation in relation to packaging. The case was an appeal against a judgment of the Court of First Instance[488] dismissing the actions against the decisions of the Second Board of Appeal[489] refusing registration of eight three-dimensional trade marks consisting of various pouches for "fruit drinks and fruit juices". The applications were rejected under art.7(1)(b). The Board of Appeal confirmed the decisions of the examiner, holding that consumers would see the pouches purely as packaging rather than indications of origin. The Board also noted that granting such a registration would be against the interests of packaging manufacturers and beverage producers from a competition perspective.

4–279

(a) The judgment of the Court of First Instance

The Court of First Instance agreed with the Board. It rejected the applicant's argument that marketing fruit juices in such a type of packaging was, in itself, unusual:

4–280

> "Since this form of packaging is in general use for liquids for human consumption, including beverages, it is not sufficiently unusual for the average consumer to perceive it, per se, as an indication of the specific commercial origin of a product within that category. This kind of packaging

---

[485] *Procter & Gamble v Office for Harmonisation in the Internal Market (Trade Marks and Designs)* (C-473/01 P and C-474/01 P) [2004] E.C.R. I-5173.
[486] *Procter & Gamble v Office for Harmonisation in the Internal Market (Trade Marks and Designs) (Square tablet with inlay)* (T-128/00) [2001] E.C.R. II-2785; and *Procter & Gamble v Office for Harmonisation in the Internal Market (Trade Marks and Designs) (Rectangular tablet with inlay)* (T-129/00) [2001] E.C.R. II-2793.
[487] *Deutsche SiSi-Werke GmbH & Co Betriebs KG v Office for Harmonisation in the Internal Market (Trade Marks and Designs)* (C-173/04) [2006] E.C.R. I-551; [2004] E.T.M.R. 72.
[488] *Deutsche SiSi-Werke v Office for Harmonisation in the Internal Market (Trade Marks and Designs) (Flat-bottomed pouches)* (T-146/02 to T-153/02) [2004] E.C.R. II-447.
[489] Cases R-719/1999–2 to R-724/1999–2, R-747/1999–2 and R-748/1999–2; February 28, 2002.

for liquids for human consumption is devoid of distinctive character as regards each of the products within that category and, in particular, the beverages concerned in this instance. The expected development of this type of packaging confirms, if confirmation were needed, that its use is unexceptional."[490]

Then it considered all the individual elements of the pouches and the overall impression produced by their combined appearance and found that the pouches were devoid of any distinctive character.

(b) The Opinion of the Advocate General

4–281 Advocate General Ruiz-Jarabo Colomer noted from the outset that the jurisprudence of the Court had already dealt with most of the issues regarding the distinctive character of three-dimensional signs. The exception was the delimitation of the relevant context for verifying whether a three-dimensional sign was capable of fulfilling the essential function of a trade mark.

In addition he criticised the way the appellant approached the appeal process. It had invoked three pleas regarding the interpretation of art.7(1)(b) but went on to present its arguments without specifying the ground that each one of them referred to.

The Advocate General divided the appeal into five parts.

4–282 **(i) The context for determining distinctive character.** With the first part of the first plea, the appellant supported that the Court of First Instance had failed to take account of the sector of the specified product and, accordingly, the shapes of packaging that should form the background for assessing whether the pouches possessed the necessary distinctive character.

It claimed that in the relevant sector, the market for beverages, consumers were accustomed to perceiving the packaging of a product as an indication of origin. And, according to the evidence, in Europe fruit drinks and fruit juices were packaged in glass bottles or in cartons. The Court of First Instance had erred in law by looking at a much wider market than the market for the specific products in Europe.

The Office had responded that the limits of the context for the comparison should be set following a wider set of comparisons, beyond the normal shapes of the specified goods. In addition consumers having recognised and perceived even once pouches as a type of packaging for one product they would respond in the same way and perceive them as the same type of packaging when confronted with pouches in relation to other products.

---

[490] *SiSi-Werke*, para.42.

6. ARTICLE 3(1)(b)—DEVOID OF ANY DISTINCTIVE CHARACTER

In any case, what the Court of First Instance did was to appraise facts; a review of this function remained, in principle, outside the jurisdiction of the Court of Justice.

4–283

The Advocate General supported that taking account of the packaging of a broader category of products rather than those specified in the application was a more pertinent option. He found the appellant's analysis of the relevant case law of the Court to be rather simplistic. If the relevant goods or services affect the perspective from which the distinctive character is assessed, and this was indeed the case according to the jurisprudence of the Court, then the goods and services that would have to be examined should not be exclusively those actually mentioned in the form but equally all those that belonged to the same class, or the same type, or the same species. In other words, all those goods or services that could compete in terms of product choice either because they travelled through similar channels of distribution or because they targeted the same consumers.

Citing his views already expressed in *Merz & Krell*[491] and *Ansul*[492] he stressed that in the assessment of distinctive character it was necessary to take into account the structure of the relevant sector and the channels of commercialisation; in essence A.G. Ruiz-Jarabo Colomer suggested that we should introduce factors that would also be relevant in competition considerations.

It was essential, he added, to examine the whole range of products confronting the consumer. In this particular context we should include all alimentary products in a liquid form.

4–284

He agreed too with the submission of the Office regarding the perception of a consumer who would see for the first time in relation to a particular product a type of packaging that had been used until then only for some other product. It would still function as packaging rather than as an indication of origin.

In terms of "spatial delimitation" the Advocate General suggested that consumer perception in the entirety of the Community should be relevant following the same logic with that underlying art.8(1)b of the Regulation regarding likelihood of confusion.

(ii) The assessment of the marks as "basic geometric shapes". On the same basis the appellant had challenged the finding of the Court of First Instance that the pouches were "basic geometric shapes", in the second part of the first plea. In the absence of other pouches there should not be any basic shape for them.

4–285

The Advocate General found that to a certain extent the plea involved the assessment of evidence.

He looked only at the argument that according to the appellant the Court of First Instance had wrongly incorporated into the assessment the fact that

---

[491] *Merz & Krell GmbH & Co* (C-517/99) [2001] E.C.R. I-6959.
[492] *Ansul BV v Ajax Brandbeveiliging BV* (C-40/01) [2003] E.C.R. I-2439.

the pouches could be used frequently as packaging for fruit juices as part of the general interest behind the provision.

However he found that the Court of First Instance had simply stated that because the particular type of packaging had been commonly used in relation to liquid alimentary products the sign did not present the necessary exceptionality.[493]

4-286 **(iii) The level of the distinctiveness requirement for three-dimensional trade marks.** SiSi Werke had argued—with the first part of the second plea—that the Court of First Instance had set too high a requirement for three-dimensional trade marks. Instead it should have applied the same criterion it applied to other types of marks, according to which even if it were accepted that stand-up pouches constituted normal forms of packaging for fruit drinks and fruit juices in Europe, the designs of those described in the applications possessed sufficient special features to be able to fulfil their indicator of origin function.

The Office supported that the Court of First Instance had only applied the case law of the Court according to which the perception of the public was not necessarily the same in relation to a three-dimensional mark consisting of the appearance of the product as that in relation to a word mark or a figurative mark. In any case, it added, the differences were too insignificant.

The Advocate General's response was that even if the same criteria were to be applied this would not change the finding that because of the nature of the sign ordinary consumers would not normally understand the form of the product as an indication of origin and that in order to be able to function as a trade mark the three-dimensional design would need to be sufficiently distant from the form of the product. Since the packaging of a liquid product would reflect the image of the product a simple variation of the ordinary form of packaging would not possess the necessary distinctive character.[494]

4-287 The Advocate General thought it would be helpful to revert to empirical principles in order to compare the forms and the containers existing on the market, in particular in relation to products that consumers encountered in their everyday lives. He believed that the attention of consumers would veer towards the label rather than the form of the packaging. Accordingly, the examination of commonly used containers and of basic structures was relevant and did not imply the application of a stricter criterion.

He indicated that the Court of First Instance had respected all those rules in its assessment. It had examined all the essential characteristics individually, considered the overall impression, and found that the sign lacked distinctive character.

---

[493] Referring to *Deutsche SiSi-Werke v Office for Harmonisation in the Internal Market (Trade Marks and Designs) (flat-bottomed pouches)* (T-146/02 to T-153/02) [2004] E.C.R. II-447, para.42.
[494] Citing *Mag Instrument Inc* (C-136/02 P) [2004] E.C.R. I-9165.

6. ARTICLE 3(1)(b)—DEVOID OF ANY DISTINCTIVE CHARACTER

(iv) The absence of justification. With the second part of the second plea the appellant supported that since the Office had already allowed registration of other trade marks of the same type in the same sector and the marks applied for had been registered in a number of Member States the Office and the Court of First Instance would need to justify why the marks applied would not be perceived by the average consumer as indications of origin.

4–288

The Office responded that the only requirement the Court of First Instance had to fulfil would be to give reasons for its application of the law; it did not have to justify any divergence between its judgment and the practice of the Office or other national authorities.

The Advocate General noted that following *Henkel*[495] it was clear that registration of a trade mark for a particular product in one Member State did not implicate that the same mark should be accepted or rejected in another Member State.

The same reasoning should apply to applications for Community Trade Mark registrations. He noted that registration was subject to specific rules applied on certain concrete circumstances and this is exactly what the Court of First Instance had decided.

4–289

The Court of First Instance had also shown why past practice of the Office should not be viewed as binding; registrability of a mark could be assessed only on the basis of the relevant Community legislation.

In any case, he added, the applications SiSi Werke referred had been filed and decided at a later date than the date of the contested decisions of the Board, accordingly SiSi Werke would have been unable to rely on them.

(v) The interest of the competitors. With the third plea SiSi Werke complained that the Court of First Instance had overtly relied on the interest of its competitors without considering the interest of consumers and overlooking that for years it had been using these pouches without causing any problem to its competitors.

4–290

It reminded the Court that the interests of the competitors should be considered under art.7(1)(c). The general interest underlying art.7(1)(b), on the other hand, included the interest of the consumer to be able to recognise the goods covered by a trade mark and associate them with a particular manufacturer.

The Office contended that once the trade mark was found to be devoid of distinctive character the general interest of consumers could not block the application of art.7(1)(b); because, by definition, consumers would not perceive a sign that was devoid of distinctive character as an indication of origin.

The Advocate General found that the Court of First Instance had referred to the risk of monopolisation in order to confirm that the marks could not fulfil the essential function of a trade mark.

---

[495] *Henkel KGaA* (C-218/01) [2004] E.C.R. I-1725.

ABSOLUTE GROUNDS

(c) The judgment of the Court

4–291 The Court followed a slightly different pattern in the building up of its judgment, in particular in relation to the first ground. It divided its judgment into three parts. First, it looked at the context of the assessment, the first part of the first plea. Then, it reviewed the distinctive character requirements for three-dimensional marks, the second plea. And thirdly, it combined the second part of the first plea and the third plea that focused on the interests of third parties.

4–292 **(i) The context of the assessment.** The Court repeated that the parameters of the assessment should be set according to the specification and the perception of the marks by the relevant public[496] and that the criteria for assessing distinctive character should be the same for all categories of trade marks. However, the relevant public's perception would not necessarily be the same in the case of a three-dimensional mark consisting of the appearance of the product itself as it would be in the case of a word or figurative mark.[497]

For products in a liquid form, it added, packaging had to enable average consumers of the products, who were reasonably well informed and reasonably observant and circumspect, to distinguish the product concerned from those of other undertakings without conducting an analytical or comparative examination and without paying particular attention.[498]

Accordingly the Court of first Instance was right in holding that the average consumer would see the form of drinks packaging as an indication of origin only if it might be perceived immediately as such; it did not hold that the packaging of liquid goods could never have a distinctive character.

4–293 The Court then referred to its case law stating that:

> "only a mark which departs significantly from the norm or customs of the sector and thereby fulfils its essential function of indicating origin is not devoid of any distinctive character".[499]

In relation to this the Court reinforced and clarified two particular points.

First, that it was not necessary "systematically to restrict the sector for the purposes of comparison to the actual goods in respect of which registration is sought".[500] It could not be excluded that consumers might be influenced, "in their perception of the trade mark which the product bears, by

---

[496] Citing *Henkel KGaA* (C-456/01 P and C-457/01 P) [2004] E.C.R. I-5089.
[497] Citing *Mag Instrument Inc* (C-136/02 P) [2004] E.C.R. I-9165.
[498] Citing *Henkel KGaA* (C-218/01) [2004] E.C.R. I-1725.
[499] *SiSi-Werke*, para.31, citing *Henkel KGaA v Deutches Patent- und Markenamt* (C-218/01) [2004] E.C.R. I-1725; and *Mag Instrument Inc v Office for Harmonisation in the Internal Market (Trade Marks and Designs)* (C-136/02 P) [2004] E.C.R. I-9165.
[500] *SiSi-Werke*, para.32.

6. ARTICLE 3(1)(b)—DEVOID OF ANY DISTINCTIVE CHARACTER

the marketing methods used for other goods which they also use".[501] Depending on the nature of the goods and the trade mark applied for, it might be necessary to take into account a wider sector.

The current case was characterised by two facts that according to the Court made this widening necessary. One was that the product had to be packaged in order to be marketed; and, after *Henkel*,[502] the packaging imposed its shape on the product and had to be assimilated to the shape of the product. Accordingly, the relevant norm or customs applying "in the sector of the packaging of goods which are of the same type and intended for the same consumers as those goods in respect of which registration is sought"[503] may be relevant. The second was a negative assumption more than a fact:

4–294

> "It cannot be excluded that the average consumer, who is accustomed to seeing various products from different undertakings packaged in the same type of packaging, does not at first identify the use of that type of packaging by an undertaking for the marketing of a given product as being, of itself, an indication of origin, when the same product is marketed by competitors of that undertaking in other types of packaging ... the average consumer, who does not make a study of the market, will not know in advance that only one undertaking markets a given product in a certain type of packaging whilst its competitors use other types of packaging for that product."[504]

In essence the Court held that we should not assume that consumers would be aware of what constituted trade knowledge. At the same time it did not preclude the possibility that the packaging could function as a trade mark even in such a factual scenario. Everything, it appears, is a question of fact.

Indeed, this was the second clarificatory point made by the Court: "... restriction of the sector in which the comparison is to be made falls within the appraisal of the facts".[505] And this, in turn, fell within the jurisdiction of the Court of First Instance.[506]

Rejecting the first part of the first plea, the Court concluded that the Court of First Instance could take into consideration the types of packaging used on the European market for liquids for human consumption in general in order to determine whether the use of any one of the contested pouches enabled the average consumer of fruit drinks and fruit juices to distinguish, without conducting an analytical or comparative examination and without paying particular attention, the appellant's goods from those of other undertakings.

4–295

---

[501] *SiSi-Werke*, para.32.
[502] *SiSi-Werke*, para.32.
[503] *SiSi-Werke*, para.33.
[504] *SiSi-Werke*, para.34.
[505] *SiSi-Werke*, para.35.
[506] Citing *DKV Deutsche Krankenversicherung AG* (C-104/00 P) [2002] E.C.R. I-7561; and *Mag Instrument Inc* (C-136/02 P) [2004] E.C.R. I-9165.

Further it could also refer to the "standard shape", the "basic shape", the "standard form" or the "standard appearance" of the pouches on the basis of stand-up pouches used for the marketing of liquids for human consumption on the European market.

4–296 **(ii) The level of the distinctive character requirement for three-dimensional "shape of the product" marks—the powers of the board of appeal.** Regarding the first part of the second plea the Court repeated that in order to possess distinctive character a mark had to identify the specified goods or services as originating from a particular undertaking, and thus to distinguish them from those of other undertakings.[507] Following its analysis above the Court found the claim to be unfounded, to the extent that it challenged the findings regarding the perception of three-dimensional marks consisting of the appearance of the product. To the extent that it challenged the assessment of the Court of First Instance regarding the specific characteristics of the marks the plea was inadmissible.

In relation to the second part of the second plea the Court noted that the decisions of the Board were taken under the Regulation in the exer-cise of circumscribed powers rather than as a matter of discretion. It concurred with the Court of First Instance that the legality of those decisions should be assessed solely on the basis of the Regulation rather than previous practice.[508]

It added that registrations made in Member States were factors that might merely be taken into consideration, without being given decisive weight.[509] Indeed there was no provision in the Regulation requiring the Office or the Court of First Instance to come to the same conclusions on registrability with those reached by national authorities in similar circumstances.[510]

4–297 **(iii) The monopolisation argument.** The Court looked together at the second part of the first plea and the third plea, since both regarded the interest of possible competitors.

It noted that each one of the art.7(1) grounds was independent of the others and required separate examination and, further, should be interpreted in the light of the general interest specifically underlying each one of them.[511]

In order to readdress the interest behind the provision it linked it with the essential function of a trade mark.

4–298 The combination of the citations of the Court regarding the general interest behind art.7(1)(b) is revealing of its continuous efforts to balance between the rights of trade mark proprietors and their competitors. It chose

---

[507] Citing *Mag Instrument Inc* (C-136/02 P) [2004] E.C.R. I-9165.
[508] Citing *BioID AG* (C-37/03 P) [2005] E.C.R. I-7975.
[509] Citing *Henkel KGaA* (C-218/01) [2004] E.C.R. I-1725 in relation to the Directive.
[510] Citing *DKV Deutsche Krankenversicherung AG* (C-104/00 P) [2002] E.C.R. I-7561.
[511] Citing *SAT.1 SatellitenFernsehen GmbH* (C-329/02 P) [2004] E.C.R. I-8317; and *BioID AG* (C-37/03 P) [2005] E.C.R. I-7975.

6. ARTICLE 3(1)(b)—DEVOID OF ANY DISTINCTIVE CHARACTER

Hoffmann-La Roche,[512] from its earlier, pre-harmonisation, free movement of goods jurisprudence, *Philips*,[513] the first case where the Court considered the registrability of shapes from a number of diverse perspectives and followed a restrictive approach, and *SAT.1*,[514] where it appeared to be more permissive.

According to the above, art.7(1)(b) intended to preclude registration of trade marks:

> "which are devoid of distinctive character which alone renders them capable of fulfilling the essential function of a trade mark, which is to guarantee the identity of the origin of the marked product or service to the consumer or end-user by enabling him, without any possibility of confusion, to distinguish the product or service from others which have another origin".[515]

It added, that in view of the extent of protection, the general interest underlying art.7(1)(b) was "manifestly, indissociable from the essential function of a trade mark".[516]

Article 7(1)(c) on the other hand pursued:

4–299

> "an aim which is in the public interest, namely that such signs or indications may be freely used by all. That provision accordingly prevents such signs and indications from being reserved to one undertaking alone because they have been registered as trade marks".[517]

The reference to the "public interest" rather than a "general interest" could be seen as evidence of a stronger basis for article 7(1)(c), however in the German original text the same term is being used.[518]

In any case the Court reminded that:

> "the criterion according to which trade marks which are capable of being commonly used, in trade, for the presentation of the goods or services in

---

[512] *Hoffmann-la Roche & Co AG and Hoffmann-la Roche AG* (102/77) [1978] E.C.R. 1139
[513] *Koninklijke Philips Electronics NV* (C-299/99) [2002] E.C.R. I-5475.
[514] *SAT.1 SatellitenFernsehen GmbH* (C-329/02 P) [2004] E.C.R. I-8317.
[515] *SiSi-Werke*, para.60.
[516] *SiSi-Werke*, para.61, citing *SAT.1 SatellitenFernsehen GmbH* (C-329/02 P) [2004] E.C.R. I-8317; and *BioID AG* (C-37/03 P) [2005] E.C.R. I-7975.
[517] *SiSi-Werke*, para.62, citing *WM Wrigley Jr Co* (C-191/01 P) [2003] E.C.R. I-12447; and the orders in *Telefon & Buch v Office for Harmonisation in the Internal Market (Trade Marks and Designs)* (C-326/01 P) [2004] E.C.R. I-371; and *Streamserve Inc v Office for Harmonisation in the Internal Market (Trade Marks and Designs)* (C-150/02 P) [2004] E.C.R. I-1461.
[518] Imprecise translations are often a problem; see also *Davidoff & Cie SA and Zino Davidoff SA v Gofkid Ltd* (C-292/00) [2003] E.C.R. I-389 discussed in Ch.5 where the term "well known" marks is used instead of marks with a reputation.

question may not be registered is relevant in the context of Article 7(1)(c) of Regulation No 40/94 but it is not the yardstick by which Article 7(1)(b) must be interpreted".[519]

4–300 The Court referred in detail to the relevant part of the judgment of the Court of First Instance stating that trade marks devoid of any distinctive character were in particular those that were commonly used for the presentation of the specified goods or services "or with regard to which there exists, at the very least, concrete evidence justifying the conclusion that they are capable of being used in that manner".[520] The Court of First Instance had found that there was indeed concrete evidence that the pouches were capable of being used in that way and concluded that the expected development of this type of packaging confirmed that its use was unexceptional.

The Court found that the judgment of the Court of First Instance had reached its decision on the basis of the trade marks being devoid of distinctive character[521]:

> "The Court of First Instance thus reached that conclusion on the basis not of the possibility that stand-up pouches may be commonly used in future in the sector of liquids for human consumption—which it used as the framework for its analysis—but of the finding that they are already commonly used. In so doing, the Court of First Instance based its conclusion on a proper criterion."[522]

The statement that the pouches were capable of being used in future by competitors of the appellant was, according to the Court, made for reasons of completeness. The Court of First Instance had accepted that the interest of competitors in itself would not suffice to refuse registration under art.7(1)(b)[523]; in its analysis of distinctive character it had, properly:

> "limited itself to determining whether those trade marks enable the average consumer of fruit drinks and fruit juices to distinguish, without any possibility of confusion, the goods of the appellant from those of a different commercial origin".[524]

---

[519] *SiSi-Werke*, para.63. Citing *SAT.1 SatellitenFernsehen GmbH* (C-329/02 P) [2004] E.C.R. I-8317; and *BioID AG* (C-37/03 P) [2005] E.C.R. I-7975.
[520] *SiSi-Werke*, para.64, referring to para.31 of the judgment of the Court of First Instance, *Deutsche SiSi-Werke* (T-146/02 to T-053/02) [2004] E.C.R. II-447.
[521] Referring to para.42, of the judgment of the Court of First Instance, cited above.
[522] *SiSi-Werke*, para.67.
[523] Judgment of the Court of First Instance, para.32.
[524] *SiSi-Werke*, para.70.

6. ARTICLE 3(1)(b)—DEVOID OF ANY DISTINCTIVE CHARACTER

(15) Eurocermex—article 7(1)(b), three-dimensional shapes, and the concept of a product

Eurocermex[525] was another appeal against a judgment of the Court of First Instance[526]; it involved a sign that could be seen from two perspectives, as a three-dimensional trade mark but, and perhaps even more than that, as a product concept.

4–301

Eurocermex was the distributor of the Mexican beer CORONA in Europe, popularly drunk with an added slice of lime. It applied to register as a Community Trade Mark a three-dimensional mark consisting of a three-dimensional shape of a transparent bottle, filled with a yellow liquid, having a long neck in which a slice of lemon with green skin has been plugged. The pictures of a beer bottle with a piece of lime from three different aspects accompanied the description.

The specification was for "paper, cardboard and goods made from these materials; printed matter, bookbinding materials, photographs; stationery; adhesives for stationery or household purposes; office requisites, except furniture; plastic materials for packaging (not included in other classes); printers' type; printing blocks" in Class 16; "clothing of all kinds, undershirts, shorts and all kinds of trousers; footwear of all kinds; headgear of all kinds" in Class 25; "beers, mineral and aerated waters, fruit juices" in Class 32; and "restaurants, bars, snack bars" in Class 42.

The examiner refused the application for the goods in Class 32 and the services in Class 42 for being devoid of any distinctive character, also finding that Eurocermex had failed to produce evidence that the mark had become distinctive through use.

4–302

The First Board of Appeal[527] set aside the part of the examiner's decision relating to "mineral waters" and upheld the remainder.

Eurocermex brought an action before the Court of First Instance in respect of "beers, aerated waters, fruit juices" and "restaurants, bars, snack bars".

(a) The judgment of the Court of First Instance

The Court of First Instance found that the mark was devoid of any distinctive character.

4–303

Before looking at the details of the application it made two general points. First, it repeated its statement that devoid of any distinctive character were in particular the trade marks which were commonly used, in trade, for the presentation of the goods or services concerned or with regard to which there existed, at the very least, concrete evidence justifying the conclusion

---

[525] *Eurocermex SA v Office for Harmonisation in the Internal Market (Trade Marks and Designs)* (C-286/04 P) [2005] E.C.R. I-5797.
[526] *Eurocermex SA v Office for Harmonisation in the Internal Market (Trade Marks and Designs)* (T-399/02) [2004] E.C.R. II-1391.
[527] Case R 188/2002–1, October 21, 2002.

that they were capable of being used in that manner. Secondly, that in order to assess the distinctive character of the mark, it had to be considered as a whole. However, this was not incompatible with an examination of its individual features.

In respect of "beers, aerated waters, fruit juices" it examined the bottle, the slice of lemon, and the colours, and found that the "the trade mark applied for consists of a combination of features, each of which is capable of being commonly used, in trade, for the presentation of the products referred to in the application for registration and therefore lacks any distinctive character in relation to those products".[528]

4–304 Before concluding on distinctive character in relation to the contested goods the Court of First Instance appeared to make another general point, stating that:

> "if a composite mark comprises only features devoid of any distinctive character in respect of the products and services concerned, it may be concluded that the overall mark is likewise likely to be commonly used, in trade, to present those goods and services... That would only not be the case if concrete evidence, such as, for example, the way in which the various features are combined, were to indicate that the composite trade mark, taken as a whole, is greater than the sum of its parts".[529]

This was a point that the Court of First Instance had already made in its *SAT.1* judgment.[530]

In the absence of such evidence the Court of First Instance found that the mark was devoid of distinctive character in relation to the specified goods. It is worth noting here the reference to the absence of alternatives:

> "The trade mark applied for, which is essentially distinguished by the combination of the three-dimensional shape of a bottle with the colours yellow and green, together with a slice of green lemon, is capable of being commonly used, in trade, for the presentation of the products referred to in the application for registration. With more particular reference to the structure of the mark applied for, which is distinguished by the fact that the slice of lemon is plugged in the neck of the bottle, it is difficult to imagine other ways of combining those elements in a single three-dimensional form. Furthermore, it represents the only way in which a drink can be decorated with a slice or a piece of lemon when the drink is consumed directly from the bottle. It follows that the manner in which the elements of the composite mark in question are combined is not capable of giving it a distinctive character."[531]

---

[528] *Eurocermex*, para.30.
[529] *Eurocermex*, para.31.
[530] *SAT.1 SatellitenFernsehen GmbH* (C-329/02 P) [2004] E.C.R. I-8317.
[531] *Eurocermex*, para.32.

6. ARTICLE 3(1)(b)—DEVOID OF ANY DISTINCTIVE CHARACTER

In relation to the part of the specification covering "restaurants, bars, snack bars", the Court of First Instance found that they were very closely linked with "beers, aerated waters, fruit juices":

4–305

> "it should be noted that the particular aim of those services is the commercialisation of the products concerned. As was stated above, the mark applied for is capable of being commonly used, in trade, for the presentation of those products. That is concrete evidence that that mark is also capable of being commonly used, in trade, for the presentation of those services. It thus lacks a distinctive character in relation to them".[532]

The Court of First Instance then found that the mark had not acquired distinctive character through use according to art.7(3). One of the weaknesses of the evidence identified in the judgment was that it related to use of branded bottles of beer rather than the bottle appearing on the application form: "all bear a label on which appear words such as 'corona', 'corona extra', 'coronita' or even 'estrella' ".[533]

(b) The judgment of the Court

The Court gave its judgment without finding it necessary for the Advocate General to issue an Opinion.[534]

4–306

(i) The overall impression. In the first part of the first plea Eurocermex argued that the Court of First Instance had not taken account of the overall impression conveyed by the mark.

4–307

The Court noted that according to *Procter & Gamble*[535] examination authorities could examine each of the individual features of the mark in the course of their overall assessment. The Court of First Instance had assessed each individual characteristic; in respect of their combined effect it had made the point that it was likely that a mark comprising only features devoid of any distinctive character would be commonly used, in trade, to present those goods and services.[536]

The Court then referred to *SAT.1*[537] as requiring that in assessing whether a composite mark had distinctive character, the overall perception of the mark by the average consumer should be relied upon; it rejected presumptions that combinations of features individually devoid of

---

[532] *Eurocermex*, para.36.
[533] *Eurocermex*, para.50.
[534] The Court heard Advocate General Ruiz-Jarabo Colomer and decided to proceed without an Opinion.
[535] *Procter & Gamble* (C-468/01 to C-472/01 P) [2004] E.C.R. I-5141.
[536] In para.31 of *Eurocermex SA* (T-399/02) [2004] E.C.R. II-1391.
[537] *SAT.1 SatellitenFernsehen GmbH* (C-329/02 P) [2004] E.C.R. I-8317.

distinctive character could not display such character. There the Court had found that the Court of First Instance had examined the overall impression only secondarily.

4–308 Here, however, the Court of First Instance had continued its analysis "by investigating in detail whether or not the mark, taken as a whole, displayed such character".[538] The Court found the statements included in para.32 and para.33 of the judgment of the Court of First Instance to constitute sufficient bases for the Court of First Instance to reach the conclusion that the mark as applied for did not have the necessary distinctive character.

It is suggested that the Court appears once again to take a more cautious approach, compared with *SAT.1*.[539]

Accordingly, this part was rejected as unfounded.

4–309 **(ii) Setting the parameters for an appeal.** With the second part of the first plea the appellant claimed that it was apparent from the documentation referred to by the Board of Appeal that the trade mark was capable of enabling consumers to identify the origin of the products bearing it.

The Court found this claim to be inadmissible. Setting some useful parameters that prospective appellants have to conform to, the Court made two particular points. First, it reminded us that an appeal should indicate precisely the contested elements of the judgment that the appellant sought to have set aside and the legal arguments specifically advanced in support of the appeal had to indicate.[540] And, secondly, it stressed that an appeal was possible only on a point of law, whereas the Court of First Instance had exclusive jurisdiction to find and appraise the relevant facts and to assess the evidence.[541]

In this case, the appellant had asserted that the Court of First Instance had wrongly reached its conclusion without specifying the error it had made in its interpretation and application of the Regulation. In the absence of a distortion of the facts and evidence by the Court of First Instance the claim of the appellant was inadmissible.

4–310 The Court applied the same reasoning to the third part of the first plea, according to which the reasons for rejecting the trade mark for "restaurants, bars and snack bars" had not been substantiated; the appellant had merely reproduced the line of argument followed at first instance.

Similarly the second plea of the appeal, claiming infringement of art.7(3), was rejected because it would involve a re-assessment of the evidence.

---

[538] *Eurocermex*, para.28.
[539] *SAT.1 SatellitenFernsehen GmbH* (C-329/02 P) [2004] E.C.R. I-8317.
[540] Citing *Laboratoires Pharmaceutiques Bergaderm and Goupil v Commission* (C-352/98 P) [2000] E.C.R. I-5291; and *Ombudsman v Lamberts* (C-234/02 P) [2004] E.C.R. I-2803 on the interpretation of art.225 EC, art.58 of the Statute of the Court of Justice, and art.112(1)(c) of the Rules of Procedure of the Court of Justice.
[541] Citing *Mag Instrument Inc* (C-136/02 P) [2004] E.C.R. I-9165 on the application of art.225 EC and art.58 of the Statute of the Court of Justice in an analogous context.

6. ARTICLE 3(1)(b)—DEVOID OF ANY DISTINCTIVE CHARACTER

(16) Storck I—the shape of a sweet

The two *Storck* cases offered the Court the opportunity to elaborate further not only on the distinctive character of three-dimensional signs but also on the differences between the shape of a product—the three-dimensional shape of a sweet, the Werther's Original—on the one hand and the packaging of a sweet—a gold wrapper—on the other. Both cases reached the Court as appeals against judgments of the Court of First Instance.

4–311

The Court dealt first with appeal against the judgment regarding the shape of the product.[542]

Augustus Storck KG (Storck) had applied to register as a Community Trade Mark for "confectionery" a three-dimensional sign in the form of a light-brown sweet. The pictures of a sweet from three different aspects appeared on the application. The application was rejected under art.7(1)(b); the examiner also found that the mark had not acquired distinctive character as a result of use according to art.7(3). The Board of Appeal confirmed the decision.

Storck brought an action before the Court of First Instance claiming that the Board had infringed both art.7(1)(b) and art.7(3).

(a) The judgment of the Court of First Instance

The Court of First Instance concurred with the Board on the lack of distinctive character and accepted the following general points made by the Board.

4–312

In the case of mass consumer goods, consumers did not pay much attention to their shape and colour. As a result it was unlikely that the choice of the average consumer would be determined by the shape of such a product.

Regarding the particular shape it accepted that consumers were accustomed to confectionery products, including sweets, being round, circular, oval, elliptical or cylindrical and that they commonly had rounded sides regardless of their configuration for functional reasons. The two potentially distinguishing criteria, the circular depression in the middle of the sweet and its flat lower surface, were weak as indicators of origin because they did not substantially alter the overall impression given by the shape.

Equally common was the colour.

4–313

The Court of First Instance rejected the argument that the particular shape and colour differed from those of other confectionery products and

---

[542] *August Storck KG v Office for Harmonisation in the Internal Market (Trade Marks and Designs)* (C-24/05 P) [2006] E.C.R. 000; [2006] WL 721555; [2006] WL 1699022 was an appeal against the judgment of the Court of First Instance in *Storck v Office for Harmonisation in the Internal Market (Trade Marks and Designs)* (T-396/02) [2004] E.C.R. II-3849 dismissing an action for annulment of the decision of the Fourth Board of Appeal of the Office for Harmonisation in the Internal Market (Trade Marks and Designs) of October 14, 2002, Case R-187/2001-4.

also found that the mark as a whole did not enable the average consumer to distinguish the products concerned according to origin.

Before the Court of Justice, Storck followed four lines of appeal.

4–314   First, the Court of First Instance had infringed art.7(1)(b) for two reasons: it required the trade mark applied for to be markedly different from other commonly used forms of presentation for such products and failed to ascertain whether the mark possessed in itself a minimum level of distinctiveness irrespective of other similar forms of presentation.

Secondly, it had infringed art.74(1)[543] of the Regulation according to which the Office should examine the facts of its own motion.

Thirdly, it had infringed art.73[544] of the Regulation according to which decisions of the Office had to be based only on reasons or evidence on which the parties had the opportunity to comment.

Fourthly, the Court of First Instance had infringed art.7(3) of the Regulation.[545]

(b)   The Opinion of the Advocate General

4–315   **(i) Admissibility considerations.** Advocate General Ruiz-Jarabo Colomer, agreeing with the submissions of the Office, suggested that a number of grounds were inadmissible.

The second part of the first ground because it was seeking from the Court to substitute its own findings for those of the Court of First Instance.[546]

The second and the third grounds because they introduced new claims before the Court, that had not been presented before the Court of First Instance. He noted that the claims regarding art.73 and art.74 targeted primarily the Board of Appeal and only in a subsidiary fashion the Court of First Instance for adopting the reasoning of the Board; however Storck had failed to raise them before the Court of First Instance.

4–316   **(ii) The criterion for the application of article 7(1)(b).** Regarding the first part of the first ground, the Advocate General accepted that the wording of art.7(1)(b) seemed to suggest clearly that any sign with a minimum degree of distinctiveness should be eligible for registration.

---

[543] Article 74(1) provides: "In proceedings before it [the Office] shall examine the facts of its own motion; however, in proceedings relating to relative grounds for refusal of registration, [the Office] shall be restricted in this examination to the facts, evidence and arguments provided by the parties and the relief sought".

[544] Article 73 provides: "Decisions of [the Office] shall state the reasons on which they are based. They shall be based only on reasons or evidence on which the parties concerned have had an opportunity to present their comments". Article 74(1) of Regulation No 40/94, entitled "Examination of the facts by the Office of its own motion", provides: "In proceedings before it [OHIM] shall examine the facts of its own motion; however, in proceedings relating to relative grounds for refusal of registration, [OHIM] shall be restricted in this examination to the facts, evidence and arguments provided by the parties and the relief sought."

[545] The provision referring to distinctiveness acquired through use.

[546] Citing *Hilti v Commission* (C-53/92 P) [1994] E.C.R. I-667.

6. ARTICLE 3(1)(b)—DEVOID OF ANY DISTINCTIVE CHARACTER

However, the Court's case law on three-dimensional marks had been consistently repeating that although the criteria for assessing the distinctive character of signs consisting of the shape of the product were the same with those applicable for any other type of sign, in practice, it was more difficult to prove distinctive character than in relation to a name or figurative mark.[547]

The Court had also recognised that the perception of the average consumer was not necessarily the same in relation to a three-dimensional sign as with other types of signs that were distinguishable from the appearance of the goods that they covered, since consumers were not accustomed to making assumptions about the origin of goods according to their shape, independently of graphic or word elements.[548]

The Court of First Instance had clearly followed the case law of the Court **4–317** and the first part of the first ground of appeal should be rejected as unfounded.

Note that the Advocate General remarked that the dividing line between minimum distinctive character and absolute lack of distinctiveness remained an issue in relation to graphic and name marks.[549]

(c) The judgment of the Court

The Court agreed with the Advocate General's suggestions regarding **4–318** admissibility and found that the second part of the first ground and second and the third grounds were inadmissible.

(i) Article 7(1)(b)—three-dimensional signs. The first ground of **4–319** appeal was considered in some detail. The Court focused on Storck's two main arguments that had to with the reference to the need for the mark to be markedly different from other forms of product presentation in the relevant product market. This meant that the Court of First Instance had imposed stricter requirements for three-dimensional marks than for word or figurative marks and that it had introduced likelihood of confusion issues into the assessment of distinctive character.

It repeated its general mantra on the assessment of distinctive character,[550] with the "in practice" proviso regarding three-dimensional signs,[551]

---

[547] Citing *Koninklijke Philips Electronics NV* (C-299/99) [2002] E.C.R. I-5475; and *Linde AG* (C-53/01), *Winward Industries Inc* (C-54/01) and *Rado Uhren AG* (C-55/01) [2003] E.C.R. I-3161.

[548] Citing *Henkel KGaA* (C-456/01 P and C-457/01 P) [2004] E.C.R. I-5089, in relation to packaging; and *Libertel Groep BV* (C-104/01) [2003] E.C.R. I-3793 in relation to colours.

[549] Noting in fn.25 of his Opinion that "in DKV the Court of Justice dispensed with the discussion, relieving the Court of First Instance of any obligation to broach such a fine distinction, despite the views expressed in paragraphs 44 to 57 of my Opinion in that case", referring to *DKV Deutsche Krankenversicherung AG* (C-104/00 P) [2002] E.C.R. I-7561.

[550] Citing, however, cases where it had appeared to take a stricter approach: *Henkel KGaA* (C-456/01 P and C-457/01 P) [2004] E.C.R. I-5089; and *Deutsche SiSi-Werke & Co Betriebs KG* (C-173/04 P) [2006] E.C.R.I-551.

[551] Citing *Henkel; Mag Instrument* (C-136/02 P) [2004] E.C.R. I-9165; and *Deutsche SiSi-Werke & Co Betriebs KG v Office for Harmonisation in the Internal Market (Trade Marks and Designs)*.

ABSOLUTE GROUNDS

and the assumptions regarding consumer perception regarding the shape of a product or the shape of its packaging.[552] The outcome was that only a mark which departed significantly from the norm or customs of the sector and thereby fulfilled its essential function of indicating origin should be considered as not devoid of any distinctive character for the purposes of art.7(1)(b).[553]

Accordingly the Court of First Instance had not erred in its interpretation. The "markedly different" condition did not go further than the "significant departure" case law of the Court:

> "It is apparent ... that the Court of First Instance relied on the finding that the mark applied for consists of a combination of presentational features which come naturally to mind and which are typical of the goods in question, that it is a variation of certain basic shapes commonly used in the confectionery sector, that, since the alleged differences are not readily perceptible, it follows that the shape in question cannot be sufficiently distinguished from other shapes commonly used for sweets and that it does not enable the relevant public to distinguish immediately and with certainty the appellant's sweets from those of another commercial origin."[554]

The Court also rejected the claim that the Court of First Instance had required that the mark applied for to be markedly different from similar marks which might exist in the confectionery sector, finding that it was based on an incorrect interpretation of its judgment.

(17) Storck II—the distinctive character of packaging

4–320 The second *Storck* case[555] dealt with packaging. It came before the Court as an appeal against the judgment of the Court of First Instance dismissing an action for annulment of the decision of the Board of Appeal[556] refusing registration of a figurative mark as a Community Trade Mark for sweets for being devoid of any distinctive character.

The mark consisted of a two-dimensional representation in perspective of a sweet in a gold-coloured wrapper with twisted ends.

---

[552] Citing the same cases as above [2004] E.C.R. I-9165; *Deutsche SiSi-Werke & Co Betriebs KG* (C-173/04 P) [2006] E.C.R. I-551.
[553] Citing the same cases as above; note that in the judgment it referred to a mark in general rather than a three-dimensional mark.
[554] *Storck I*, para.29.
[555] *August Storck KG* (C-25/05 P) [2006] E.C.R. 000; [2006] WL 721556; [2006] WL 1699026.
[556] *Storck* (T-402/02) [2004] E.C.R. II-3849 dismissing the action for annulment of the decision of the Second Board of Appeal of the Office for Harmonisation in the Internal Market (Trade Marks and Designs) of October 18, 2002 Case R-256/2001-2, [2006] E.C.R. 000.

6. ARTICLE 3(1)(b)—DEVOID OF ANY DISTINCTIVE CHARACTER

(a)   The judgment of the Court of First Instance

4–321 The Court of First Instance followed a parallel route with that followed in the shape of the product *Storck* case.

It accepted the Board of Appeal's finding that the configuration of the mark "twisted wrapper, light brown or gold coloured" was a normal and traditional shape for a sweet wrapper that did not fundamentally stand out against the other usual presentations in that trade and that the average consumer would perceive the sign as a sweet wrapper rather than an indication of origin.

It also accepted that the Board of Appeal:

"was entitled to refer ... to the risk of monopolisation of the wrapper in question for sweets, since its findings confirmed the lack of distinctive character of that wrapper for those goods, reflecting the general interest underlying the absolute ground for refusal founded on Article 7(1)(b)".[557]

4–322 Storck had also raised, unsuccessfully, two procedural points before the Court of First Instance, based on art.74(1) and art.73.

On the first point it stressed that:

"under the maxim ultra posse nemo obligatur (no one is obliged to do the impossible), and notwithstanding the rule in the first sentence of Article 74(1) of Regulation No 40/94 whereby OHIM 'shall examine the facts of its own motion', OHIM is not bound to examine facts showing that the mark claimed has become distinctive through use within the meaning of Article 7(3) of Regulation No 40/94 unless the applicant has pleaded them".[558]

Regarding the art.73 point, the Court of First Instance viewed the proceedings before the Office as a unified process. The examiner had highlighted the weaknesses of the evidence regarding sale volumes, but Storck failed to produce any additional evidence before the Board regarding the overall size of the market for sweets. Offering to provide the information to the Court of First Instance was futile since it could not consider new evidence.

4–323 And viewing the proceedings before the Office as a unified process it added that the applicant did have the opportunity to present its views.

Before the Court of Justice the applicant raised four grounds of appeal claiming that the Court of First Instance had infringed art.7(1)(b), art.74(1), art.73, and art.7(3) of the Regulation.

---

[557] *Storck II*, para.60.
[558] *Storck II* para.96.

(b) The Opinion of the Advocate General

4-324 **(i) Article 7(1)(b)—re-assessment of facts.** Advocate General Ruiz-Jarabo Colomer suggested that the third part of the first ground, a claim that the Court of First Instance had not fully considered the effect of the colour on the wrapping and wrongly assessed the behaviour of the average consumer, was inadmissible because its examination would involve the re-assessment of the facts of the case.

4-325 **(ii) The application of article 7(1)(b).** With the first part of the first ground Storck argued that the Court of First Instance had imposed a stricter criterion regarding the distinctive character of three-dimensional marks.

The Advocate General, in essence, repeated the line of arguments he developed in the shape of the product *Storck* case,[559] without distinguishing between the shape of the product and its packaging, and supported that the Court should reject that part as unfounded.

The second part of the first ground targeted the reference by the Board of Appeal to the risk of monopolisation. Storck claimed that this was in no way connected with the general interest underlying art.7(1)(b).

The Advocate General accepted the Office's submission that the Court of First Instance had accepted this statement as an additional and confirmatory statement. Before making it the Board had already established that the sign lacked the necessary distinctive character. Accordingly, the second part should be rejected as ineffective.

4-326 **(iii) Article 74(1) and article 73.** The second and the third ground were examined together.

In the second ground the appellant supported that the Board had undertaken its own assessment of the market situation without giving to Storck the opportunity to examine concrete examples of wrappers that were identical to its own according to the Board. By sanctioning this tactic the Court of First Instance had failed to take into account art.74(1).

The Office responded that art.74(1) required the Office to examine the facts—indeed the Office had the exclusive responsibility for examining the facts—without requiring it to support its findings with concrete examples.

4-327 The third ground followed from the second: Storck had been deprived from the opportunity to prove that its wrappers differed substantially from those on which the Board had built its conclusions.

The Office retorted that the third ground was manifestly unfounded. The Board had properly analysed Storck's arguments before rejecting them. And Storck had the opportunity to present its views on this since it had

[559] *August Storck KG* (C-24/05 P) [2006] E.C.R. 000.

6. ARTICLE 3(1)(b)—DEVOID OF ANY DISTINCTIVE CHARACTER

admitted before the Court of First Instance that it had dealt with shapes commonly used for wrappers for sweets.

The Advocate General suggested that Storck had misinterpreted the principles behind the two provisions.

4–328 The procedure before the Office required the examiners and the Board of Appeal to examine the facts of their own motion and establish their accuracy irrespective of the claims of the parties.

However, some limitations were to be imposed on this general principle.

For example the parties were under an obligation to co-operate with the Office; or, from another perspective, the Office was entitled to determine the extent that a simple objective assessment of the facts would suffice for deciding the case.

4–329 In addition the Office had to take into account facts arising from practical experience generally acquired from the marketing of general consumer goods, as the Court of First Instance had remarked. Otherwise, the Office would risk overlooking facts that could influence the outcome of a case.

He stressed that the Court should recognise that the Boards had the option to use facts that were well known to all as part of the examination of absolute grounds without having to assess their accuracy; the burden of proof should pass to the party wishing to challenge them (*ipsa loquitur*).

Accordingly, even if the Court were to accept that Storck had missed the opportunity to express its views before the Board for facts that were well known to all it should hold that it had been given that opportunity by the Court of First Instance that had subsequently decided that its observations were not sufficient to overturn the decision of the Board.

Accordingly the second and the third grounds should be rejected as unfounded.

(c) The judgment of the Court

4–330 **(i) Article 7(1)(b)—requirements.** Looking at the first part of the first ground of appeal, the Court followed closely its findings in the shape of the product *Storck* case,[560] failing to make a distinction between product shapes and packaging, and rejected it as unfounded.

Indeed, the only new point made by the Court reflected the assimilation of a two-dimensional representation of a three-dimensional sign with the three-dimensional sign as such but also the potential assimilation between product shapes and packaging.

The case law "which was developed in relation to three-dimensional trade marks consisting of the appearance of the product itself, also applies where, as in the present case, the trade mark applied for is a figurative mark consisting of the two-dimensional representation of that product. In such a

---

[560] *August Storck KG* (C-24/05 P).

case, the mark likewise does not consist of a sign unrelated to the appearance of the products it covers".[561]

4-331 **(ii) Article 7(1)(b)—general interest.** The Court followed the Advocate General's suggestion that the Court of First Instance had not based its conclusion on the risk of monopolisation of the wrapper applied for registration. It referred to it in a purely confirmatory way.

The second part of the first ground was rejected as unfounded.

4-332 **(iii) Article 7(1)(b)—re-assessment of facts.** The Court noted that since it had found that the Court of First Instance had not erred in law in its application of art.7(1)(b) assessing the distinctive character of the mark or the perception of the relevant consumers would involve a re-assessment of facts.

Accordingly the third part of the first ground was rejected as inadmissible.

4-333 **(iv) Article 74(1).** Under art.74(1) examiners and the Board of Appeal were required to examine the facts of their own motion whilst considering an application for registration under art.7 and they might reach decisions based on facts that had not been alleged by the applicant. In principle they would have to establish the accuracy of such facts in their decisions.

However, when they relied on facts that were well known it was the applicant who would have to challenge their accuracy.

Whether the facts were well known or not was a factual assessment that remained in the jurisdiction of the Court of First Instance.

So, the second ground of appeal was dismissed as unfounded.

4-334 **(v) Article 73.** The third ground of appeal was divided by the Court into two parts.

First, it dealt with an admissibility point. The art.73 ground had not been raised before the Court of First Instance in relation to the proceedings before the Board; the appellant had raised the ground that the Board of Appeal had not shown the accuracy of its findings only in the context of art.74(1). To that extent the claim was rejected as inadmissible because a plea could not be introduced for the first time before the Court of Justice.[562]

Then, the Court dealt with that ground in relation to the proceedings before the Court of First Instance. It ruled that art.73:

"is to be complied with by bodies of OHIM in the context of assessment of applications for registration, but not in the context of proceedings before the Court of First Instance, which are governed by the Statute of

---

[561] *Storck II*, para.29.
[562] Citing *Ramondin SA v Commission* (C-186/02 P and C-188/02 P) [2004] E.C.R. I-10653.

7. ARTICLE 3(1)(c)—DESCRIPTIVE SIGNS OR INDICATIONS

the Court of Justice and by the Rules of Procedure of the Court of First Instance".[563]

In any case, it added, the appellant was in a position to challenge before the Court of First Instance the Board's assertions and its broader rights of defence, including its right to be heard, were observed.

4–335

Accordingly, the third ground was rejected as being partly inadmissible and partly unfounded.

7. ARTICLE 3(1)(c)—DESCRIPTIVE SIGNS OR INDICATIONS

(1) Windsurfing Chiemsee—geographical names—setting the general principles

In *Windsurfing Chiemsee*[564] the Court clarified that geographical names could be registered. It also established two tests: one for determining whether a mark is descriptive and another for establishing distinctive character acquired through use. And dealing with descriptiveness it considered the German theory that there are some signs that must be left free for other traders to use rejecting its applicability as a general public policy doctrine. However, elements of this theory resurfaced as specific considerations underlying the scope of art.3(1)(c).

4–336

The case came before the Court as a reference from the Landgericht München that had to decide whether the word Chiemsee, the name of the largest lake in Bavaria, could be protected as a trade mark. The word Chiemsee as such would have been refused trade mark registration according to German doctrine since it was considered to be a geographical indication that other traders would also want to use.

Windsurfing Chiemsee, a company running a shop near the lake selling sports fashion clothing and sports goods, designed locally but manufactured abroad, had registered the word Chiemsee as part of a number of composite "picture" trade marks combined with graphic design elements; in some cases the word was also accompanied by other words, for example "Chiemsee Jeans" or "Windsurfing—chiemsee—Active Wear". Windsurfing Chiemsee started trade mark infringement proceedings to enjoin two other traders, Attenberger and Huber, from selling t-shirts and other similar types of clothing bearing the term Chiemsee combined with other graphic elements.

Attenberger and Huber attacked the basis of the claim and contended that the term Chiemsee was an indication of geographical origin that should

4–337

---

[563] *Storck II*, para.64.
[564] *Windsurfing Chiemsee Produktions- und Vertriebs GmbH v Boots- und Segelzubehör Walter Huber and Franz Attenberger* (C-108/97 and C-109/97) [1999] E.C.R. I-2779.

be left available for other traders to use. Accordingly, their own use of the term in a different graphic form could not create any likelihood of confusion.

Indeed the referring court explained that according to German practice likelihood of confusion could result only from the similarity between the graphic components of the mark if Chiemsee was considered to be descriptive according to art.3(1)(c).

The Landgericht wanted to know whether the interpretation of this provision was affected by the "need to leave free" (Freihaltebedürfnis) doctrine that had been developed by German courts and provided that some signs, including geographical indications, should be left free for other traders to use.

4–338 German courts had elaborated further on this doctrine applying a more stringent variant when there was a real, current, or serious need, the "serious need to leave free" doctrine. Were the original doctrine found to be valid then Chiemsee would be automatically covered by art.3(1)(c). If the variant were to be applied then the national court would have to take into account the fact that there was no textile industry on the shores of the Chiemsee.

Accordingly the Landgericht München I referred the following questions on art.3(1)(c) to the Court.

> "Is Article 3(1)(c) to be understood as meaning that it suffices if there is a possibility of the designation being used to indicate the geographical origin, or must that possibility be likely in a particular case (in the sense that other such undertakings already use that word to designate the geographical origin of their goods of similar type, or at least that there are specific reasons to believe that that may be expected in the foreseeable future), or must there even be a need to use that designation to indicate the geographical origin of the goods in question, or must there in addition also be a qualified need for the use of that indication of origin, for instance because goods of that kind, produced in that region, enjoy a special reputation?"
>
> "Is it of significance for a broader or narrower interpretation of Article 3(1)(c) with respect to geographical indications of origin that the effects of the mark are restricted under article 6(1)(b)?"
>
> "Do geographical indications of origin under Article 3(1)(c) cover only those which relate to the manufacture of the goods at that place, or does trade in those goods at that place or from that place suffice, or in the case of the production of textiles does it suffice if they are designed in the region designated but then manufactured under contract elsewhere?"[565]

---

[565] Reproduced in para.17.

7. ARTICLE 3(1)(c)—DESCRIPTIVE SIGNS OR INDICATIONS

(a) The Opinion of the Advocate General

4-339 Advocate General Cosmas interpreted the first and the third question as in essence enquiring whether in principle a geographical indication can be protected as a trade mark and the conditions and scope of any such protection.

4-340 **(i) The context of article 3(1).** Within the context of the Directive and keeping in mind the primary function of a trade mark as a source indicator he viewed art.3(1)(b) as an obstacle based on the lack of any distinctive character. And whilst art.3(1)(c) and art.3(1)(d) covered separate grounds, in essence they were partial or more specific or, simply, the most characteristic instances of lack of distinctive character that explained and elucidated the general concept rather than introduced a new genus of, or fundamentally distinct, concepts. Article 3(1)(b) covered cases that were not specifically covered under art.3(1)(c) and art.3(1)(d).[566]

4-341 **(ii) The conditions for the application of article 3(1)(c).** The application of art.3(1)(c) in particular required three conditions.
The trade mark had to consist exclusively of a geographical term.
The term had to be capable of serving in trade as an indication of geographical origin.
And the geographical origin had to be linked with the characteristics of the product.

4-342 **(iii) The first condition.** The exclusivity requirement would bring outside the scope of the provision composite marks with one of their elements functioning in a descriptive way but also incorporating other elements that attributed distinctive character to the mark.
The Court had already indicated in a different context that it was the overall impression conveyed by the mark that authorities had to consider.[567] Advocate General Cosmas criticised the German practice of accepting registration of a geographical term only when combined with other graphic elements. In some cases the phonetic impression of Chiemsee would be the dominating element of the mark, confining the visual impression into a secondary role. In such cases, objectively, there could be a likelihood of confusion irrespective of the differences between the graphic elements. Following the opposite approach and claiming that there would be no likelihood of confusion when the graphic elements differed would allow the registration of a multitude of variations of the same term resulting to total confusion in the marketplace.

---

[566] Point 29 of the Opinion of A.G. Cosmas.
[567] Citing *Sabel BV v Puma AG, Rudolf Dassler Sport* (C-251/95) [1997] E.C.R. I-6191.

4-343 **(iv) The second condition.** According to the second condition the Advocate General excluded from the scope of art.3(1)(c) imaginary, mythical, or non-existent geographical terms, for example Utopia or Atlantis. The same applied to historical terms that no longer existed or were known by a different name, like Byzantium or Babylon. Taking one step further he also suggested that existing geographical terms that no one would associate with the origin of the relevant product were also meant to remain outside the scope of art.3(1)(c), referring to examples such as Mont Blanc for pens and North Pole for bananas. Under the same logic geographical terms that remained obscure for the wider public should also be excluded from its application.

In all the above cases the geographical term because of its nature or due to the circumstances did not indicate geographical origin and accordingly its arbitrary use as a trade mark should be allowed.

The Advocate General's further analysis of the scope of the provision followed the traditional free movement of goods route. He suggested that it intended to exclude from trade mark protection specific geographical indications. And through the inclusion of the phrase "which may serve, in trade" he linked what should be excluded from protection with two concepts, geographical indications and denominations of origin, that were known and established in the Community legal order.

4-344 Article 3(1)(c) should cover terms that have not yet reached that status but carried the potential of functioning in that way. The term should be interpreted by reference to the jurisprudence of the Court in free movement of goods cases that culminated into the definitions provided by art.2 of Reg.2081/92.[568]

So, in order to exclude a sign from trade mark protection he demanded a causal link between the geographical term and the product based on the kind, characteristics, or quality of the product that resulted from its geographical origin. His interpretation was closer to Windsurfing Chiemsee's claims that art.3(1)(c) precluded registration of terms that designated a specified place where several undertakings manufactured the relevant goods and the name of the place had been used to indicate the geographical origin of those goods.

---

[568] Council Reg. (EEC) No. 2081/92 of 14 July 1992 on the protection of geographical indications and designations of origin for agricultural products and foodstuffs [1992] OJ L208/1; art.2 defined a designation of origin as the "the name of a region, a specific place or, in exceptional cases, a country, used to describe an agricultural product or a foodstuff:—originating in that region, specific place or country, and—the quality or characteristics of which are essentially or exclusively due to a particular geographical environment with its inherent natural and human factors, and the production, processing and preparation of which take place in the defined geographical area"; a geographical indication was defined as the "means the name of a region, a specific place or, in exceptional cases, a country, used to describe an agricultural product or a foodstuff:—originating in that region, specific place or country, and—which possesses a specific quality, reputation or other characteristics attributable to that geographical origin and the production and/or processing and/or preparation of which take place in the defined geographical area".

7. ARTICLE 3(1)(c)—DESCRIPTIVE SIGNS OR INDICATIONS

The German doctrine. Acknowledging the existence of the "need to leave free" doctrine developed by German courts he stressed that national provisions and practices could not go against the Directive and noted that in Europe there were two schools regarding the registrability of geographical names.

4–345

The more lenient position—adopted by France, Italy, and the Benelux—followed the requirements set by the Advocate General; the United Kingdom, Germany, and Scandinavian jurisdictions were much stricter, but their historical position appeared to be against the principles of the Directive.

There was only one "availability" requirement set by the Directive and it had to do with signs that were the subject of earlier rights; otherwise geographical terms should follow the same rules with other signs.

He added that the German doctrine was ambiguous as to whether the sign should be kept free to be used by others as a trade mark or as an indication of origin. The first option would be unreasonable, because the first user of the term as a trade mark would have to surrender it to be used as a trade mark by its competitors. The second option, he noted, was specifically regulated through art.6(1)(b) of the Directive.[569]

The third condition. The last of the three requirements suggested by the Advocate General was the link between the geographical indication and the characteristics of the product. Here, he required something more than a common property or quality, the geographical indication had to characterise and distinguish the product. The identity of the producer or of the place, method, and time of production would be relevant only when they, on their own, were considered to be relevant in trade.

4–346

He found the term Chiemsee to be evocative or suggestive but nothing more than that; it lacked the strong relevance he would have required.

The interaction between article 3(1)(c) and article 6(1)(b). Advocate General Cosmas suggested that art.6(1)(b) should not influence the interpretation of art.3(1)(c). The former could only be applied following the application of the latter: once the trade mark had been registered. In any case, he remarked, the provision did not give the right to third parties to use the term as a trade mark. It would only allow use of the term in its original geographical meaning.[570]

4–347

He concluded that a trade mark consisting exclusively of a geographical term would not fall under art.3(1)(c) if the term was imaginary or unknown to the wider public or if there was no direct and indispensable geographical

---

[569] Article 6(1)(b) provided: "The trade mark shall not entitle the proprietor to prohibit a third party from using, in the course of trade, . . . (b) indications concerning the kind, quality, intended purpose, value, geographical origin, the time of production of goods or of rendering of the service, or other characteristics of goods or services."

[570] Citing as example the French case of Baccarat, C. A. de Nancy, P.I.B.D. 1980, III, 227 and Cass. Commerc., P.I.B.D. 1982, No.312, III, 238 that allowed use of the term as part of the address for a company manufacturing crystal products.

indication link between the marked product and the region identified by the term, in particular because the region is, or is likely to become known, for the production of similar products that are valued by consumers because of their characteristics or quality.

(b) The judgment of the Court

4–348 Behind the first set of questions the Court identified two issues: first, whether the application of art.3(1)(c) depended on whether there was a real, current or serious need to leave the sign or indication free; and, secondly what connection there should be between the geographical location and the marked goods.

4–349 **(i) The German doctrine.** First of all, it, too, accepted that the provision covered marks composed exclusively of descriptive signs, narrowing the scope of the provision.

The Court rejected the applicability of the German doctrine; instead it relied for the interpretation of the provision on the specific public interest behind it.

4–350 **(ii) Article 3(1)(c)—the public interest.** The Court described the public interest in the following terms: "descriptive signs or indications relating to the categories of goods or services in respect of which registration is applied for may be freely used by all, including as collective marks or as part of complex or graphic marks".[571]

Descriptive geographical terms in particular had to remain available "not least because they may be an indication of the quality and other characteristics of the categories of goods concerned, and may also, in various ways, influence consumer tastes by, for instance, associating the goods with a place that may give rise to a favourable response".[572]

4–351 **(iii) The interaction between article 3(1)(c) and article 6(1)(b).** Article 15(2) of the Directive indicated further the nature of the public interest the Court had described.[573] The Court also found art.6(1)(b) to work towards the same general objective.

Still, interpretation of art.3(1)(c) did not rely on art.6(1)(b). In terms of scope the latter "does not confer on third parties the right to use the name as a trade mark but merely guarantees their right to use it descriptively, that is to say, as an indication of geographical origin, provided that it is used in accordance with honest practices in industrial and commercial matters".[574]

---

[571] *Windsurfing Chiemsee*, para.25.
[572] *Windsurfing Chiemsee*, para.26.
[573] It provided that signs or indications which may serve to designate the geographical origin of the goods may constitute collective marks.
[574] *Windsurfing Chiemsee*, para.28.

7. ARTICLE 3(1)(c)—DESCRIPTIVE SIGNS OR INDICATIONS

(iv) The factors for the application of article 3(1)(c). It is suggested that the broad description of the public interest expands the scope of the provision. The subsequent uncertain balancing exercises, sometimes contracting sometimes expanding the scope of the provision, or the frequent reference to the limitations of the right is evidence of how the Court attempts to find its way between exclusivity and competition in its interpretation of trade mark law.

4–352

In principle, the Court ruled, art.3(1)(c) "does not ... preclude the registration of geographical names which are unknown to the relevant class of persons—or at least unknown as the designation of a geographical location—or of names in respect of which, because of the type of place they designate (say, a mountain or lake), such persons are unlikely to believe that the category of goods concerned originates there".[575]

The Court then expanded the scope of art.3(1)(c)—supported by the inclusion in the provision of the verb "may"—to cover geographical names designating places currently associated with the category of goods concerned but also names in respect of which "it is reasonable to assume that such an association may be established in the future".[576]

In the latter case "regard must be had more particularly to the degree of familiarity amongst such persons with that name, with the characteristics of the place designated by the name, and with the category of goods concerned".[577]

4–353

As to types of location that could fall under art.3(1)(c) the court ruled that even the name of a lake might function as an indicator of geographical origin for products like sports goods if the name is understood to include the shores of the lake or the surrounding area.

(v) The link between the product and the geographical indication. Regarding the link between the product and the geographical indication in terms of origin the Court found that usually it would be based on manufacture. However, it could also depend on other ties. For example, the geographical location where the goods were conceived and designed could also function as their geographical origin.

4–354

(2) Baby-Dry—composite words—a permissive approach

Baby-Dry[578] was the first case where the distinctiveness of a word combination was considered by the Court. The case reached the Court as an appeal

4–355

---

[575] *Windsurfing Chiemsee*, para.33.
[576] *Windsurfing Chiemsee*, para.31.
[577] *Windsurfing Chiemsee*, para.32.
[578] *Procter & Gamble Co* (C-383/99 P) [2001] E.C.R. I-6251.

against a judgment of the Court of First Instance[579] and carried additional significance as the first such appeal in the field of trade marks.

Procter & Gamble had applied for registration of the sign BABY-DRY as a Community Trade Mark for diapers (disposable diapers and textile diapers). The application was refused under art.7(1)(c) of the Regulation.

The Board of Appeal confirmed the decision of the examiner finding that both art.7(1)(b) and art.7(1)(c) were applicable.[580] It found that existing registrations in some Member States were unpersuasive. Linguistic differences could allow registration in some jurisdictions but for a Community Trade Mark registration all the languages of the Union had to be taken into account.

An additional, and very important, procedural point was that art.7(3) evidence on distinctiveness acquired through use was not taken into account by the Board because the issue of acquired distinctive character had not been raised before the examiner.

(a) The judgment of the Court of First Instance

4–356   In terms of substantive law, the Court of First Instance focused exclusively on art.7(1)(c). It found the sign to be composed exclusively of words which may serve in trade to designate the intended purpose of goods; such signs were inherently incapable of distinguishing the specified products according to origin.

However, in terms of procedure the Court of First Instance favoured Procter & Gamble holding that the Board of Appeal had infringed art.62 of the Regulation.[581]

4–357   **(i) Continuity of the registration process.** The registration process within the Office should be characterised by continuity; the distinction between the examiner and the Board of Appeal should be rejected. Accordingly it annulled the decision of the Board.[582]

---

[579] *Procter & Gamble Co* (T-163/98) [1999] 2 C.M.L.R. 1442.
[580] Case R 35/1998-1, July 31, 1998.
[581] Article 62 provides: "1. Following the examination as to the allowability of the appeal, the Board of Appeal shall decide on the appeal. The Board of Appeal may either exercise any power within the competence of the department which was responsible for the decision appealed or remit the case to that department for further prosecution. 2. If the Board of Appeal remits the case for further prosecution to the department whose decision was appealed, that department shall be bound by the ratio decidendi of the Board of Appeal, in so far as the facts are the same. 3. The decisions of the Boards of Appeal shall take effect only as from the date of expiration of the period referred to in Art.63 (5) or, if an action has been brought before the Court of Justice within that period, as from the date of rejection of such action".
[582] A.G. Jacobs did not express a firm view on the methodology of the Court of First Instance since this was not part of the appeal before the Court of Justice. However, he remarked that it should have done more than simply annul the decision of the Board and leave it to the Office to take the necessary measures to comply with its judgment. It should either rule on the substance of the dispute or remand the case to the examiner.

7. ARTICLE 3(1)(c)—DESCRIPTIVE SIGNS OR INDICATIONS

Procter & Gamble contended that the Court of First Instance had misinterpreted art.7(1)(c). It argued that each trade mark had to be assessed individually taking into account all the facts of the case; even if the words "baby" and "dry" were found to designate the purpose of the diapers, the sign applied for, that the Court of First Instance had failed to consider, was Baby-Dry. By referring to signs that were inherently incapable of distinguishing it had erred in its interpretation of art.7(1)(c).

(b) The Opinion of the Advocate General

(i) The procedural paradox. The procedural paradox, highlighted by A.G. Jacobs, was that the appellant, Procter & Gamble had appealed against a judgment that at the end annulled the decision that Procter & Gamble wanted the Court of Justice to annul.

4–358

Procter & Gamble supported that it had the right to bring an appeal since it had only been partly unsuccessful and it would remain bound by the ruling on art.7(1)(c).[583] The Office accepted that in practice Procter & Gamble did have an interest in challenging the judgment. It preferred to leave the Court decide whether it should itself raise an inadmissibility ground under art.92(2) of the Rules of Procedure.[584]

The Advocate General accepted that the limits on the appeal process were set by the permissive provision of art.49 of the Statute of the Court.

Interpreting "submissions" liberally, he viewed the provision as referring "in general terms to a failure to obtain what was asked for rather than strictly to a failure to have a particular argument accepted or a particular form of order granted".[585]

(ii) The scope of the appeal—article 7(1)(c). Advocate General Jacobs clarified that he intended to examine art.7(1)(c). Article 7(1)(b) was mentioned in the decision of the Board of Appeal, but did not form a further ground of refusal and was not examined by the Court of First Instance.

4–359

The contested judgment raised two issues according to the Advocate General. First, whether there were signs that, should because of their nature, be considered incapable of distinguishing.

The second point was the registrability of Baby-Dry as such.

The distinction between the general doctrine on the one hand and its subsequent application on the other could be particularly useful when the

---

[583] Article 49 of the Statute of the Court of Justice stated that an appeal may be brought by any party which has been unsuccessful, in whole or in part, in its submissions.
[584] Article 92(2) provides that "The Court may at any time of its own motion consider whether there exists any absolute bar to proceeding with a case or declare, after hearing the parties, that the action has become devoid of purpose and that there is no need to adjudicate on it; it shall give its decision in accordance with Art.91(3) and (4) of these Rules".
[585] Point 39 of the Opinion of A.G. Jacobs.

Court functions as a court of appeal. The Opinion and the Judgment of the Court would set the interpretive parameters of art.7(1)(c) by answering the first question. The application of these parameters on the factual scenario of the case should be a secondary issue.

4–360 **(iii) The scope of article 7(1)(c).** In order to unravel the scope of the provision—"not an obviously easy matter"[586]—the Advocate General started by examining its place within art.7 and its relationship with art.4.[587]

Without worrying too much about doctrinal coherence, given that the Regulation and the Directive brought together provisions with different origins and legal traditions, the main principle he adopted was that "at least in the context of the present case, the various provisions should be interpreted each within its own sphere".[588]

Article 4 defined the signs of which a trade mark might consist.

4–361 Article 7 covered the absolute grounds for refusal of registration. Article 7(1)(a) was the negative mirror image of art.4.

The grounds in sub-paras (b) to (d) of art.7 formed "a package"[589] imported from the Paris Convention; they overlapped with each other and with art.7(1)(a) and its mirror image art.4. Those degrees of overlap had to be accepted, "[S]ubparagraphs (b) to (d) . . . include the alignment with the Paris Convention but do not need to be either distinguished from or read in the light of Article 4 or 7(1)(a)".[590]

The existence of one of the grounds would suffice to block registration of a sign; whether more than one ground could be applied was immaterial in practice. The non applicability of art.7(3) in the case of art.7(1)(a) did not alter this conclusion because in practice "if acquired distinctiveness can be established then there must be an underlying capacity to distinguish; if not, the question is immaterial".[591]

4–362 So, although art.7(1)(c) was part of a package it had to be interpreted independently of art.4.

This led the Advocate General first to reject Procter & Gamble's argument that art.7(1)(c) was just an aspect of the "capacity to distinguish" criterion. And, secondly, to support that the Court of First Instance had gone too far by holding that the legislature intended to exclude signs that were by their very nature incapable of distinguishing.

He continued his attempt to delineate art.7(1)(c) through a process of elimination by referring to the Board's holding that the provision intended

---

[586] Point 61 of the Opinion of A.G. Jacobs.
[587] Or for the purposes of the Directive the relationship between art.3(1)(c) and art.2.
[588] Point 67 of the Opinion of A.G. Jacobs.
[589] Point 68; the word "package" was a hint that these grounds, in essence, covered similar territory.
[590] Point 70 of the Opinion of A.G. Jacobs.
[591] Point 71 of the Opinion of A.G. Jacobs.

7. ARTICLE 3(1)(c)—DESCRIPTIVE SIGNS OR INDICATIONS

to prevent traders from taking out of the public domain terms that belonged there. He conceded that this anti-monopolistic concern was amongst the reasons for adopting the equivalent provision of the Paris Convention. However, in the context of the Regulation this was achieved through art.12(b), by limiting the effects of such trade marks:

> "In that light, it may be better to think of Article 7(1)(c) ... as intended not to prevent any monopolising of ordinary descriptive terms but rather to avoid the registration of descriptive brand names for which no protection could be available. If this means that the same words have to be interpreted as having a different import from that which they have in, say, the Paris Convention, that is because they appear in a different context."[592]

(iv) The public interest of Windsurfing Chiemsee. From an interpretive perspective the Advocate General faced the challenge of distinguishing his approach from that adopted in *Windsurfing Chiemsee*[593] without alienating the Court. **4–363**

He suggested that the reference to the public interest expressed in that judgment had to be viewed in the specific context of that case which concerned the use of a geographical name rather than use of descriptive language. Such terms possessed a special status in the Community trade mark protection scheme—being capable of registration as collective marks[594]—but also in the wider Community legal order—through specific to geographical indications legislation.

The facts of that case allowed the Advocate General to extract one of its fundamental legal points and refocus on it from a different wider perspective. And, further, he added, the Court had not embraced the German concept of "real, current or serious need to keep an indication free".

Article 7(1)(c) had to be taken at its face value, it precluded:

> "registration of any proposed trade mark which consists exclusively of signs or indications designating characteristics of the goods or services. It is clear from Art.12(b) that a trade mark may include such signs or indications (or else that provision would serve no purpose) and from Art.7(1)(c) that it may not consist exclusively of them".[595]

(v) Registrability of Baby-Dry. The Advocate General admitted that the words baby and dry were likely to be used in trade to designate the intended purpose of diapers. However, he introduced two qualifications **4–364**

---

[592] Point 78 of the Opinion of A.G. Jacobs.
[593] *Windsurfing Chiemsee Produktions- und Vertriebs GmbH* (C-108/97 & C-109/97) [1999] E.C.R. I-2779.
[594] Article 64(2) of the Regulation and art.15(2) of the Directive.
[595] Point 81 of the Opinion of A.G. Jacobs.

on the perspective from which the sign should be seen for registrability purposes: first impression and hesitation:

> "... it may be doubted whether any reasonably aware person who had not yet encountered the brand name Baby-Dry would think unhesitatingly of diapers when first confronted with it or, when hearing it used in connection with such goods, would regard it as a designation of their intended purpose."[596]

And, although one of the functions of diapers was to keep babies dry, the term baby-dry was not used in ordinary language to refer to them or to their intended purpose.

Confronted with the term Baby-Dry for the first time a consumer might think of a number of diverse products, like talcum powder, or rain hoods for prams, or, even, compact tumble-dryers, or drinks presented in small bottles. Using cautious language he suggested that this "might seem to dilute its power to designate with any precision the intended purpose of diapers".[597]

4-365 Advocate General Jacobs found the interpretation of the scope of the words "exclusively" and "may serve, in trade, to designate" by the Board of Appeal and the Court of First Instance rather narrow. They had concluded that the combination of two terms that could be used to indicate the intended purpose of the product meant that the new sign consisted exclusively of indications which may serve in trade to designate its purpose.

4-366 *Ellipsis, unusual and opaque grammatical structure, incompleteness, inventiveness.* That approach, he supported, did not consider "the extremely elliptical nature of the indication, its unusual structure or its resistance to any intuitive grammatical analysis which would make the meaning immediately clear".[598]

He also suggested that they had failed to look at the case from the opposite perspective and explore what terms would indicate the intended purpose of diapers. Something more that the mere juxtaposition of the words would be required, noting that Baby-Dry did not as such form part of the English language.[599]

---

[596] Point 84 of the Opinion of A.G. Jacobs.
[597] Point 86 of the Opinion of A.G. Jacobs.
[598] Point 90 of the Opinion of A.G. Jacobs.
[599] The A.G. appeared to cite with approval the position adopted by the Court of First Instance in *WM Wrigley Jr Co* (T-193/99) [2001] E.C.R. II-417; albeit, when that case came before the Court he clarified that he agreed with the broader approach to art.7(1)(c) exemplified in several decisions of the Boards of Appeal and the Court of First Instance set out in paras 93 to 95 of the judgment of the Court of first Instance rather than "endorsing the specific reasoning or result in any of those cases"; point 37 of his Opinion in *WM Wrigley Jr Co* (C-191/01 P) [2003] E.C.R. I-12447.

7. ARTICLE 3(1)(c)—DESCRIPTIVE SIGNS OR INDICATIONS

Concluding that the Court of First Instance had erred in its interpretation of art.7(1)(c), he listed the following factors that had not be taken into account: "extreme ellipsis, unusual and opaque grammatical structure, incompleteness as a description and inventiveness".[600] He repeated however that in any case protection would be limited because of art.12(b).

(vi) The suggested way forward. Article 54 of the Statute of the Court provided that in the case of a successful appeal the Court had to quash the decision of the Court of First Instance and then either itself give final judgment or refer the case back to the Court of First Instance.   4–367

Given the length of the appeal process the Advocate General suggested that the best way forward should be to follow the shortest course. The Court should set aside the judgment under appeal, give itself final judgment, and alter the decision of the Board of Appeal.

However, he considered it inappropriate, "a wholly unjustifiable interference"[601] for the Court to order registration of the mark. Instead, the Court should remit the case to the examiner, who, in turn, had to take into account the factors suggested by the Advocate General.

(c) The judgment of the Court

(i) Admissibility considerations. The Court found that the appeal was admissible.[602] The Court of First Instance had dismissed Procter & Gamble's principal claim. The Office could consider the application under art.7(3) without changing its position on art.7(1)(b) and (c).   4–368

(ii) The scope of article 7(1)(c). To interpret art.7(1)(c) the Court also took into account art.12(b) and art.4:   4–369

"It is clear from those two provisions taken together that the purpose of the prohibition of registration of purely descriptive signs or indications as trade marks is, as both Procter & Gamble and the [Office] acknowledge, to prevent registration as trade marks of signs or indications which, because they are no different from the usual way of designating the relevant goods or services or their characteristics, could not fulfil the function of identifying the undertaking that markets them and are thus devoid of the distinctive character needed for that function."[603]

That, it found, was the only interpretation that could be also compatible with art.4.

---

[600] Point 96 of the Opinion of A.G. Jacobs.
[601] Point 108 of the Opinion of A.G. Jacobs.
[602] *Procter & Gamble Co* (C-383/99 P) [2001] E.C.R. I-6251.
[603] *Baby-Dry*, para.37.

4–370 *Defining descriptiveness.* The Court defined the signs that fall under art.7(1)(c) as "those which may serve in normal usage from a consumer's point of view to designate, either directly or by reference to one of their essential characteristics, goods or services such as those in respect of which registration is sought".[604]

4–371 **(iii) The condition for composite marks—the new whole—any perceptible difference.** Following the hint of the Advocate General the Court considered how its general stance on descriptiveness could be applied on composite marks.

A composite mark should not be refused registration unless, "it comprises no other signs or indications and, in addition, the purely descriptive signs or indications of which it is composed are not presented or configured in a manner that distinguishes the resultant whole from the usual way of designating the goods or services concerned or their essential characteristics".[605]

For marks like Baby-Dry descriptiveness had to be determined in relation to each word on its own but also in relation to the new whole they form, because any perceptible difference between the mark as a new whole and the terms as used in common parlance could confer distinctive character to the mark.

4–372 **(iv) The perspective for assessing descriptiveness.** Since art.7(2) provided that art.7(1) would be applied even if the relevant grounds exist in a part of the Community the Court found that descriptiveness in one of the "languages used in trade within the Community"[606] would suffice to trigger art.7(1)(c):

> "In order to assess whether a word combination such as BABY-DRY is capable of distinctiveness, it is therefore necessary to put oneself in the shoes of an English-speaking consumer. From that point of view, and given that the goods concerned in this case are babies' nappies, the determination to be made depends on whether the word combination in question may be viewed as a normal way of referring to the goods or of representing their essential characteristics in common parlance".[607]

4–373 **(v) Registrability of Baby-Dry—unusual juxtaposition—lexical inventions.** The Court found that refusing registration based on art.7(1)(c) was not justified:

---

[604] *Baby-Dry*, para.39.
[605] *Baby-Dry*, para.39.
[606] *Baby-Dry*, para.41; note that the Court referred to languages used in trade within the Community rather than the languages of the Member States.
[607] *Baby-Dry*, para.42.

7. ARTICLE 3(1)(c)—DESCRIPTIVE SIGNS OR INDICATIONS

"Whilst each of the two words in the combination may form part of expressions used in everyday speech to designate the function of babies' nappies, their syntactically unusual juxtaposition is not a familiar expression in the English language, either for designating babies' nappies or for describing their essential characteristics."[608]

"Word combinations like BABY-DRY cannot therefore be regarded as exhibiting, as a whole, descriptive character; they are lexical inventions bestowing distinctive power on the mark so formed and may not be refused registration under article 7(1)(c) of Regulation No 40/94."[609]

(d) The next step

The Court did follow the proposition of the Advocate General. It annulled the relevant part of judgment of the Court of First Instance and the decision of the Board of Appeal "in so far as it dismissed the application for registration of BABY-DRY as a trade mark on the basis of Article 7(1)(c) of Regulation No 40/94"[610] without elaborating further on the way forward for the registration of Baby-Dry.

4–374

(3) Doublemint—a more nuanced approach

Following this apparently permissive interpretation of art.7(1)(c) the Court appeared to take a step back in *Doublemint*, another appeal against a judgment of the Court of First Instance.[611]

4–375

Wrigley had applied to register DOUBLEMINT as a Community Trade Mark for a number of products including chewing gum.[612] The application was rejected under art.7(1)(c) by the examiner and the Board of Appeal that found the sign to be a combination of two English words with no additional fanciful or imaginative element, descriptive of the mint-based composition and the mint flavour of the goods in question.

---

[608] *Baby-Dry*, para.43.
[609] *Baby-Dry*, para.44.
[610] *Baby-Dry*, para.46.
[611] *WM Wrigley Jr Co* (C-191/01 P) [2003] E.C.R. I-12447; *WM Wrigley Jr Co* (T-193/99) [2001] E.C.R. II-417.
[612] The list of products is indicative of the trend towards wide specifications; the application covered: "Class 3 Cosmetics, dentifrices, including chewing gum for cosmetic purposes; Class 5 Pharmaceutical, veterinary and sanitary preparations, including chewing gum for medical purposes, chewing gum with medicinal additives; Class 25 Clothing, footwear, headgear; Class 28 Games and playthings, gymnastic and sporting articles (included in Class 28); decorations for Christmas trees. Class 30 Coffee, tea, cocoa, sugar, rice, tapioca, sago, artificial coffee, coffee substitutes, flour and preparations made from cereals, bread, biscuits, cakes, pastry and confectionery, caramels, ices; honey; treacle, yeast, baking powder, salt, mustard; pepper, vinegar, sauces (condiments), spices; ice; confectionery and chewing gum without medicinal additives, confectionery including chewing gum; sugar-coated chewing gum, chewing gum plain, non-medicated confectionery, chocolate, sugars, candy". Contested in this case where the goods in Classes 3, 5 and 30.

4–376   *(a)   The judgment of the Court of First Instance*

The case came before the Court of First Instance that found that the mark was not exclusively descriptive.[613] Use of the word "double" as a term of praise was unusual, compared with words like "strong" or "extra". "Mint" could refer to spearmint, peppermint, or other types of herbs. The combination of the two words was found to be ambiguous and suggestive rather than exclusively descriptive. It could convey two messages regarding the product; either that it contained twice the usual amount of mint or that it was flavoured with two varieties of mint.

The Office appealed before the Court contending that the Court of First Instance had erred in its application of art.7(1)(c) requiring the sign to be exclusively descriptive to be excluded from registration. It supported that a less rigorous interpretive approach would lead to registering signs that might have more than one meaning but were still descriptive and should not be protected under trade mark law. Instead, it called for interpreting the provision by also taking into account art.7(1)(b), looking at the sign's distinctive character, and art.7(1)(d), considering the sign's customary usage. Descriptive signs were by nature deemed to be incapable of distinguishing.

Wrigley responded that the structure of DOUBLEMINT was unusual and elliptical whereas its meaning was suggestive and ambiguous. It added that nobody would refer to chewing gum or its characteristics by using the word. Anticipating the argument whether the sign was one that should be left free for other traders to use, Wrigley supported that this condition should apply only where there was a reasonably clear and foreseeable need for competitors to use the contested term to describe features of their products. DOUBLEMINT had already been registered for decades in the United States of America and a number of Member States of the European Union and during that time there had been no evidence of competitors seeking to use the sign in descriptive way. This should also be seen as evidence that there was no need to keep the sign in the in the public domain. Finally, it supported that the sign satisfied the requirements set by the Court in *Baby-Dry*,[614] a judgment that came after the judgment of the Court of First Instance in the current case.

The approach the Court would now take, following its initial interpretation of art.7(1)(c) in *Windsurfing Chiemsee*[615] and Baby-Dry, was considered to be critical and as a result there were interventions by the United Kingdom and Germany, supporting the position of the Office and stressing

---

[613] *Wrigley Jr Co* (T-193/99) [2001] E.C.R. II-417.
[614] *Procter & Gamble Co* (C-383/99 P) [2001] E.C.R. I-6251.
[615] *Windsurfing Chiemsee Produktions- und Vertriebs GmbH v Boots- und Segelzubehör Walter Huber and Franz Attenberger* (C-108/97 & C-109/97) [1999] E.C.R. I-2779.

7. ARTICLE 3(1)(c)—DESCRIPTIVE SIGNS OR INDICATIONS

the public interest that the Court had identified in *Windsurfing Chiemsee*[616] as the background of art.7(1)(c). They accepted that for at least part of the specification registration could be obtained at the end as a result of the application of article 7(3).

(b) The Opinion of the Advocate General

4–377

Advocate General Jacobs was given another chance to discuss descriptiveness. Aware of *Baby-Dry's* repercussions, he welcomed the opportunity for the Court to "clarify, refine and develop the indications it gave on the interpretation of that provision in Baby-Dry ... since ... the effect of that judgment has been widely misunderstood".[617]

The current judgment should be annulled on the basis of two apparent flaws.

(i) The meaning of "exclusively". First, he suggested that in the provision the term "exclusively" qualified the verb "consist". It did not refer to the capacity of the elements of the mark to designate characteristics. What the provision required was for all the elements to have a descriptive meaning rather than have no other than a descriptive meaning.

4–378

(ii) The multiplicity of meanings. Secondly, he added, the existence of a multiplicity of meanings should not necessarily lead to the conclusion that the sign did not designate the characteristics of a product. The assumption of the Court of First Instance that the multiplicity of meanings automatically meant that the compound term could not designate a characteristic of the specified products interpreted wrongly art.7(1)(c).

4–379

However it was worth looking at the case from a broader perspective.

The Advocate General supported that art.7(1)(c) should be viewed independently of art.7(1)(b)[618]:

> "It is true that a term which may serve in trade to designate product characteristics will almost certainly be devoid of distinctive character. I nonetheless still consider it preferable, in the legislative context of the Community Trade Mark Regulation, neither to conflate the two criteria nor to view them as inherently interdependent."[619]

(iii) A multi-factor test for assessing descriptiveness. Going through the Opinion of the Advocate General it becomes apparent that he

4–380

---

[616] *Windsurfing Chiemsee Produktions- und Vertriebs GmbH* (C-108/97 & C-109/97) [1999] E.C.R. I-2779.
[617] Point 2 of the Opinion of A.G. Jacobs.
[618] Noting that the Court had appeared to assimilate the concepts of descriptiveness and distinctive character in *Procter & Gamble Co* (C-383/99 P) [2001] E.C.R. I-6251.
[619] Point 53 of the Opinion of A.G. Jacobs.

identified 10 factors that should be considered when determining descriptiveness. It is perhaps unfortunate that these factors have not been combined and branded as a multi-factor test for determining descriptiveness.

4–381 *The first part of the test—four factors.* He suggested, initially, four issues that had to be taken into account before determining whether a sign was descriptive or merely suggestive; a difficult overall exercise since suggestive and descriptive terms were usually linked with a sliding scale rather than delineated by clear dividing lines.

First, descriptiveness had to be assessed in relation to the specification of the trade mark application.

Secondly, the way in which a term related to the product or its characteristics was important:

> "The more factual and objective that relationship, the more likely it is that the term may be used as a designation in trade, so that registration will be precluded by Article 7(1)(c); conversely, the more imaginative and subjective the relationship the more acceptable the term will be for registration".[620]

4–382 Thirdly, the immediacy of the message was also relevant. Ordinary, definite and down-to-earth terms would be readily understood as descriptive designations. "Where at the other extreme the skills of a cryptic-crossword enthusiast are needed in order to detect any connection with the designated characteristic, the grounds for refusing registration are very weak indeed."[621]

Fourthly, the significance of the characteristic for the consumer in relation to the product was equally important:

> "Where the characteristic designated is essential or central to the product, or is of particular importance in a consumer's choice, then the case for refusing registration is compelling; where the designation is of a characteristic that is purely incidental or arbitrary, the case is considerably weaker."[622]

Reminding us that a descriptive term might actually be used in a deceptive manner, he stressed that the question of precision, accuracy or factual correctness should not be relevant to the examination from the above perspectives.

---

[620] Point 62 of the Opinion of A.G. Jacobs.
[621] Point 63 of the Opinion of A.G. Jacobs.
[622] Point 64 of the Opinion of A.G. Jacobs.

7. ARTICLE 3(1)(c)—DESCRIPTIVE SIGNS OR INDICATIONS

And as a final catalyst he added that these questions should be approached with common sense.

Applying the first part of the test. **Doublemint** failed from all the three perspectives suggested by the Advocate General in relation to the goods in question: 4–383

"First, the compound term is a factual, objective reference to mint flavour in some way doubled; secondly, it is readily perceivable as such; and thirdly, such a flavour is a salient feature of the product. The fact that neither the particular variety or varieties of mint involved nor the precise mode of doubling can be discerned in no way detracts from the fact that the term designates a characteristic of doubled mintiness."[623]

The second part of the test—three Baby-Dry factors. Dealing with Wrigley's arguments that *Doublemint* satisfied the requirements set by the Court, the Advocate General accepted that the degree of ellipsis, of unusualness, and of resistance to intuitive analysis should also be taken into account. 4–384

Applying the second part of the test. Compared with *Baby-Dry Doublemint* should also fail the second wave of considerations. In English, *Baby-Dry* constituted an inversion of usual word order, an anastrophe.[624] The contested sign did not display such inversion. 4–385

Further, the combination was neither elliptical not did it resist intuitive grammatical analysis.

Finally, the absence of the term from dictionaries did not compensate the limited degree of lexical invention in creating the word: removing the space between two words that could be otherwise used together descriptively.[625]

More than minimal—the wider context of trade mark law—the eighth factor. To support further his application of the second part of the test the Advocate General also referred to the judgment of the Court in *LTJ Diffusion*[626] that a sign might be considered identical to a trade mark where, viewed as a whole, it contained differences so insignificant that they may go unnoticed by an average consumer. 4–386

---

[623] Point 67 of the Opinion of A.G. Jacobs.
[624] He rejected the view that the A.G. was also anastrophic; he found the term to be a usual sequence of a noun followed by its qualifier, at least when compared with the celebrated critical review of a play titled after an anastrophe by Dorothy Parkers in *The New Yorker*, back in 1933; the review was itself titled "The House Beautiful is The Play Lousy".
[625] The A.G. referred to similar criteria suggested by A.G. Ruiz-Jarabo Colomer in *DKV Deutsche Krankenversicherung AG* (C-104/00 P) [2002] E.C.R. I-7561 then pending before the Court.
[626] *LTJ Diffusion SA v Sadas Vertbaudet SA* (C-291/00) [2003] E.C.R. I-2799; see Ch.5.

Following the same principle, from a different starting point, he stressed that the differences between descriptive terms and registrable trade marks should be more than minimal.

He maintained that in the case of art.7(1)(c):

> "the difference—the addition of at least one element, or the subtraction of some significant element—must be such that it is apparent to both traders and consumers that the mark as a whole is not suitable, in the ordinary language of trade, as a designation of characteristics of the product in question".[627]

4-387 *Adjusting the perspective for viewing descriptiveness—the ninth factor.* Following the critical analysis of his position in *Baby-Dry*,[628] suggesting that an anastrophe that appeared unusual in English would not, necessarily, be seen under the same light in other languages A.G. Jacobs accepted that a sign should be assessed in the light of the perception of consumers in all Member States.

So, the first step should be to look at the sign within the context of its own language. If the sign were found to be descriptive then it would be unnecessary to consider the position of speakers of other languages:

> "However, it may be necessary in some circumstances for a sign consisting of terms drawn from one language to be assessed through the eyes (or ears) of a Community consumer whose language is different."[629]

Still, he rejected the criticism regarding *Baby-Dry* because it appeared to impose the rules of one language, French, to the language of the contested term, "[I]t seems inappropriate to take as a normal yardstick a consumer struggling with an imperfect knowledge of a foreign tongue".[630]

4-388 *Keep free for others to use—article 7(1)(c) and article 12(b).* Repeating his position expressed in *Baby-Dry* A.G. Jacobs stated that a trade mark could include signs or indications designating product characteristics but could not consist exclusively of them:

> "By virtue of article 12(b), the trade mark cannot prevent other traders from using such signs for descriptive purposes. The aim of article 7(1)(c) is to avoid the registration of descriptive brand names for which no

---

[627] Note that the A.G. deliberately chose to refer both to consumers and traders.
[628] He cited the Opinion of A.G. Ruiz-Jarabo Colomer *Koninklijke KPN Nederland NV* (C-363/99) [2004] E.C.R. I-1619; and Kur, "Examining Wordmarks after Baby-Dry Still [a] Worthwhile Exercise?" IPR-Info 2001, 12.
[629] Point 85. The English word "handy" for example signified a mobile phone in Germany; similarly "smoking" signified a tuxedo in other languages.
[630] Point 87 of the Opinion of A.G. Jacobs.

7. ARTICLE 3(1)(c)—DESCRIPTIVE SIGNS OR INDICATIONS

protection could be available rather than to prevent any monopolising of ordinary descriptive terms."[631]

In the same case the Court had appeared to endorse this position.

Albeit, there has been some criticism regarding that view[632] based on the Court's earlier reference to the public interest in *Windsurfing Chiemsee* that should not be influenced by art.12(b).[633]

He accepted that a defence under art.12(b) could be less effective because a trade mark registration would place the owner at a comparatively stronger position. However, the danger would be "obviated"[634] following the more comprehensive interpretation of the criterion of "perceptible difference" as something more than a minimal difference.

Registrations in other jurisdictions—the tenth factor. The Advocate General dismissed Wrigley's argument and noted, with approval, that the Office considered registrations in Member States or non-member countries as evidence of registrability, however it did not necessarily view those registrations as proof that the conditions imposed by art.7(1)(c) were met. 4–389

(c) The judgment of the Court 4–390

The Court followed the Opinion of the Advocate General.[635] However, it took a shortcut; it broadened the scope of art.7(1)(c) but did not explicitly endorse the multi factor test put forward by A.G. Jacobs.

(i) Restating the principles. The Court first reconsidered the scope of art.7(1)(c): 4–391

"signs and indications which may serve in trade to designate the characteristics of the goods or service in respect of which registration is sought are, by virtue of Regulation 40/94, deemed incapable, by their very nature, of fulfilling the indication-of-origin function of the trade mark, without prejudice to the possibility of their acquiring distinctive character through use under article 7(3) of Regulation 40/94".[636]

---

[631] Point 92 of the Opinion of A.G. Jacobs.
[632] Indicatively he referred to the submissions of the Office and the United Kingdom Government in the current case and Tim Pfeiffer, "Descriptive trade marks: The impact of the Baby-Dry Case Considered" [2002] E.I.P.R. 373.
[633] Reaffirmed in *Linde AG* (C-53/01), *Winward Industries Inc* (C-54/01) and *Rado Uhren AG* (C-55/01) [2003] E.C.R. I-3161.
[634] Point 96 of the Opinion of A.G. Jacobs.
[635] *WM Wrigley Jr Co* (C-191/01 P) [2003] E.C.R. I-12447.
[636] *Doublemint*, para.30. In terms of language there is a balancing exercise between strong words regarding the signs, "incapable, by their very nature", and their purpose, "fulfilling the indication-of-origin function" rather than incapable of distinguishing. The effect is the same.

And, secondly, it repeated the public interest behind that provision, noting that:

> "[T]hat provision accordingly prevents such signs and indications from being reserved to one undertaking alone because they have been registered as trade marks".[637]

4–392 **(ii) Future and potential use matters.** The Court then broadened the scope of art.7(1)(c) by holding that it was not necessary for the mark to be actually used in a descriptive way at the time of the application:

> "It is sufficient, as the wording of that provisions itself indicates, that such signs and indications could be used for such purposes. A sign must therefore be refused registration under that provision if at least one of its possible meanings designates a characteristic of the goods or services concerned".[638]

4–393 **(iii) Registrability of DOUBLEMINT.** The Court held that the Court of First Instance had erred as to the scope of art.7(1)(c) because it applied a test based on whether the mark was exclusively descriptive of the specified goods or services or of their characteristics:

> "It thereby failed to ascertain whether the word at issue was capable of being used by other economic operators to designate a characteristic of their goods and services."[639]

The Court chose to annul the decision and refer the case back to the Court of First Instance for judgment.[640]

4–394 **(4) Postkantoor—a parallel approach**

In parallel with *Doublemint*, a reference from The Netherlands sought further clarifications on the interpretation of distinctive character and descriptiveness under the Directive.[641]

Koninklijke KPN Nederland NV (KPN) had applied to register the sign POSTKANTOOR as a Benelux trade mark for a large number of goods and services including paper, card and products manufactured therefrom,

---

[637] *Doublemint*, para.31, citing *Windsurfing Chiemsee Produktions- und Vertriebs GmbH v Boots- und Segelzubehör Walter Huber and Franz Attenberger* (C-108/97 & C-109/97) [1999] E.C.R. I-2779; and *Linde AG* (C-53/01), *Winward Industries Inc* (C-54/01) and *Rado Uhren AG* (C-55/01) [2003] E.C.R. I-3161.
[638] *Doublemint*, para.32.
[639] *Doublemint*, para.35.
[640] Under art.61(2) of the Statute of the Court of Justice.
[641] *Koninklijke KPN Nederland NV* (C-363/99) [2004] E.C.R. I-1619.

7. ARTICLE 3(1)(c)—DESCRIPTIVE SIGNS OR INDICATIONS

postage stamps, and advertising, insurance, construction, telecommunications, transport, education, and technical information and advice services. Postkantoor meant post office in Dutch.

The Benelux Trade Mark Office rejected the application for lack of distinctive character. KPN brought an action before the Dutch Gerechtshof te's-Gravenhage. The Gerechtshof stayed proceedings and referred nine questions to the Court of Justice and the Benelux Court and 15 more questions to the Benelux Court alone. It is worth repeating the questions, almost in their entirety, as an example of how the details, links with the facts of the case, and references to national legislation rather than the relevant Community legislation, sometimes burden the main issues that the national court wishes to clarify:

"1. Must the Benelux Trademarks Office ... have regard not only to the sign as it appears in the application for registration but also to all the relevant facts and circumstances known to it, including those of which it was informed by the applicant (for example, the fact that, prior to the application, the applicant already used the sign widely as a trademark for the relevant products, or the fact that investigation shows that use of the sign for the goods and/or services mentioned in the application will not be of such a nature as to deceive the public)?

2. Does the reply to the [first] question ... also apply to consideration by the Benelux Trademarks Office of the question whether its objections to registration of the application have been removed by the applicant, as well as to its decision to refuse registration in whole or in part, as provided for in Article 6a(4) of the [Uniform Benelux Law] UBL?[642]

3. Does the reply to the [first] question ... also apply to the judicial review to which Article 6b of the UBL refers?[643]

4. In the light of the provisions of Article 6 quinquies (B)(2)of the Paris Convention, do the marks which under Article 3(1)(c) of the Directive are not to be registered ... also include marks composed of signs or indications

---

[642] Article 6a provided: 1. The Benelux-Merkenbureau shall refuse registration where, in its view: (a) the sign applied for does not satisfy the description in Art.1 of a mark, in particular where it is devoid of any distinctive character within the meaning of Art.6 quinquies (B)(2) of the Paris Convention... 2. Refusal of registration must relate to the whole of a sign constituting a mark. It may be limited to one or more of the goods for which the mark is intended. 3. The Benelux Trade Mark Office shall inform the applicant forthwith in writing of its intention to refuse registration wholly or in part, stating the reasons therefor, and shall afford the applicant the possibility of replying within such period as may be laid down in the implementing regulations. 4. If the objections of the Benelux Trade Mark Office to registration are not lifted within the period laid down, registration shall be refused in whole or in part. The office shall forthwith inform the applicant in writing of such refusal, stating the reasons therefor and informing him of his right of action against the decision under Art.6b.

[643] Article 6b provided: Within two months of the notification mentioned in Art.6a(4), the applicant may apply to the *Hof van Beroep* [Court of Appeal] te Brussel, the Gerechtshof te's-Gravenhage, or the *Cour d'appel* [Court of Appeal] de Luxembourg for an order for registration.

which may serve, in trade, to indicate the kind, quality, quantity, intended purpose, value, geographical origin or the time of production of the goods or of rendering of service or other characteristics of the goods or services, even if that configuration is not the (only or most) usual indication used?

Does it make any difference in that connection whether there are many or only a few competitors who may have an interest in using such indications (see the judgment of the Benelux Court of Justice of 19 January 1981, NJ 1981, 294, in P Ferrero & Co S.p.A. v Alfred Ritter Schokoladefabrik GmbH (Kinder))?

Is it also relevant that under Article 13C of the UBL the right to a trademark expressed in one of the national or regional languages of the Benelux area extends automatically to its translation in another of those languages?

5.

(a) In the assessment of the question whether a sign consisting of a (new) word made up of components which in themselves have no distinctive character with regard to the goods or services in respect of which the application is made answers the description given in Article 2 of the Directive (and Article 1 of the UBL)[644] of a mark, must a (new) word of that kind be taken to have in principle a distinctive character?

(b) If not, must a word of that kind (leaving aside the fact that it may have acquired distinctive character through use) be taken to have in principle no distinctive character, it being otherwise only where, because of other circumstances, the combination is more than the sum of its parts?

Is it relevant in that connection whether the sign is the only or an obvious term for indicating the relevant quality or (combination of) qualities, or whether there are synonyms which may reasonably also be used, or that the word indicates a commercially essential or rather an incidental quality of the product or service?

Is it also relevant that, under article 13C of the UBL, the right to a trademark expressed in one of the national or regional languages of the Benelux area extends automatically to its translation in another of those languages?

6. Does the mere fact that a descriptive sign is also lodged for registration as a mark for goods and/or services of which the sign is not descriptive warrant the conclusion that the sign thereby has distinctive character

---

[644] Article 1 provided: The following may be registered as individual marks: names, designs, imprints, stamps, letters, numerals, the shape of goods or their packaging, and any other signs which serve to distinguish the goods of an undertaking. However, shapes which result from the nature of the goods themselves, or which affect the substantial value of the goods, or which give rise to a technical result may not be registered as trade marks.

7. ARTICLE 3(1)(c)—DESCRIPTIVE SIGNS OR INDICATIONS

in relation to those goods and/or services (for example, the sign Postkantoor for furniture)?

If not, in order to determine whether such a descriptive sign has distinctive character for such goods and/or services, must regard be had to the possibility that, in the light of its descriptive meaning or meanings, (a part of) the public will not perceive that sign as a distinctive sign for (all or some of) those goods or services?

7. In the assessment of the abovementioned questions, is significance to be attached to the fact that, since the Benelux countries have chosen to have applications for registration of trademarks examined by the Benelux Trademarks Office as a requirement prior to registration, the appraisal policy of the Office under Article 6a of the UBL, according to the common commentary of the Governments, must be a cautious and restrained one whereby all concerns of commercial life must be taken into account and efforts must be focused on establishing solely which applications are manifestly inadmissible and rectifying or refusing them? If so, under what rules does it fall to be determined whether an application is manifestly inadmissible?

It is assumed that in invalidity proceedings (which may be initiated after registration of a sign) it is not necessary, in addition to reliance on the nullity of the sign lodged as a mark, for the sign to be manifestly inadmissible.

8. Is it consistent with the scheme of the Directive and the Paris Convention for a sign to be registered for specific goods or services subject to the limitation that the registration applies only to those goods and services in so far as they do not possess a specific quality or specific qualities (for example, registration of the sign Postkantoor for the services of direct-mail campaigns and the issue of postage stamps provided they are not connected with a post office)?

9. Is it also material to the answer to be given to the questions whether a corresponding sign for similar goods or services is registered as a GmbH & Co v Deutches Patent- und Markenamt trademark in another Member State?"[645]

(a) The Opinion of the Advocate General 4–395

(i) Limiting the scope of the reference. Advocate General Ruiz-Jarabo Colomer lambasted the approach taken by the national court:

"It is worrying that a court of recognised competence should harbour so many doubts concerning the application of Community trade mark provisions. There appears to be a significant distortion within the system, since it is difficult to believe that the work of the European Union

---

[645] Reproduced in para.18.

legislature could be so lacking in this area, or that those who are responsible for its implementation should fail to understand their role. Regardless of the reason, the Court of Justice is required to supplement and facilitate the work of others within the interpretative role conferred on it under Article 234 EC".[646]

Setting the ground for his Opinion he underlined that he would not deal with parts of the questions that dealt with trade mark application and registration procedures in the Benelux. Member States were free to organise those as they wished. Indeed, the Court could only consider the registrability criteria and their assessment.

Equally the consideration of the compatibility of the existing pre-Directive national case law with the Directive, admittedly an obsession of Dutch courts in particular, was outside the mandate of the Court.

4–396   **(ii) Balancing functions with scope of protection.** The Advocate General started his analysis with a balancing exercise between functions and scope of protection; part of this exercise was the introduction of the requirement of availability:

"The rights of advantage which ownership of a trade mark confers on its owner exist so that consumers will be able to distinguish the marked product or service from products or services of different origins. As such, they may also be subject to restrictions, including restrictions deriving from the fact that it is in the public interest to ensure that certain names remain as widely available as possible (the requirement of availability)."[647]

4–397   **(iii) A roadmap for assessing registrability.** Advocate General Ruiz-Jarabo Colomer untangled the questions submitted by the Dutch court according to their theme. Following the structure of the Directive he started by discussing how should distinctive character be assessed.

According to art.6quinquies (C)(1) of the Paris Convention the assessment of the registrability conditions had to "be specific in nature, in the sense that a variety of factual circumstances must be taken into consideration",[648] including the possibility that the sign had acquired distinctive character through use and the likelihood of confusion.

He drew a roadmap that followed closely the format of the Directive. Each condition was, and should be, examined on its own, independently of the others. The assessment of each condition should be made according to the specification of the application. Some signs would fail more than one condition.

---

[646] Point 28 of the Opinion of A.G. Ruiz-Jarabo Colomer.
[647] Point 32 of the Opinion of A.G. Ruiz-Jarabo Colomer.
[648] Point 38 of the Opinion of A.G. Ruiz-Jarabo Colomer.

7. ARTICLE 3(1)(c)—DESCRIPTIVE SIGNS OR INDICATIONS

To stress the requirement for independent assessment he added that the fact that a sign was not descriptive did not necessarily mean that it possessed distinctive character.

4–398

Diversifying his position slightly from that taken in *Baby-Dry*,[649] he added that the linguistic factor had to be assessed by reference to the average consumer of the specified products.[650]

(iv) Registrability—the practices of national offices. Regarding the administration of national trade mark systems he made two points. First, he noted that there was nothing in the Directive that would preclude the use of disclaimers.

4–399

And, secondly, he stressed that the practices of one Member State could not bind the authorities of another; the only requirement was that they all applied the same principles of interpretation. Registration in one Member State could only constitute a useful indication for the authorities of another Member State.

(v) The scope of article 3(1)(c). Having rejected the admissibility of parts of the questions referring to pre-Directive national Benelux law and its interpretation by national courts A.G. Ruiz-Jarabo Colomer looked at the scope of art.3(1)(c) of the Directive.

4–400

Article 3(1)(c) precluded the registration of descriptive signs because such signs failed "to individualise the goods or services to which they relate".[651] The assessment of whether a sign was descriptive should primarily be made according to the distinguishing function of a trade mark.

However he also admitted that certain public-interest considerations should also be taken into account. The Court had already covered this area in *Windsurfing Chiemsee*.[652]

Same reasoning for all types of signs. Although that case covered geographical indications the same reasoning should apply to all categories of descriptive signs:

4–401

> "The Court of Justice thus held that underlying article 3(1)(c) there is a requirement that any assessment is guided by the fact that it is in the public interest to keep certain signs available but that it is not necessary

---

[649] *Procter & Gamble Co* (C-383/99 P) [2001] E.C.R. I-6251.
[650] "In other words, it is necessary to have regard not so much to whether that consumer speaks the language in which the sign is formulated as to whether, irrespective of the language or languages of the territory concerned, the consumer taken as a reference can reasonably be expected to perceive in the sign a meaning such as to enable it to qualify under article 3(1)(b), (c) and (d)"; point 41.
[651] Point 51 of the Opinion of A.G. Ruiz-Jarabo Colomer.
[652] *Windsurfing Chiemsee Produktions- and Vertriebs GmbH* (C-108/97 & C-109/97) [1999] E.C.R. I-2779.

for that requirement of availability to be real, current or serious as had been held under German case-law".

And making an important distinction between descriptiveness and distinctiveness he added: "[S]uch an assessment is not, however, possible in relation to article 3(3) of the Trade Mark Directive, since this article does not permit any differentiation as regards distinctiveness by reference to the perceived importance of keeping the geographical name available for use by other undertakings."[653]

4–402 *Challenging Baby-Dry.* *Baby-Dry* did not change that interpretation, since "the issue was not specifically debated"[654] therein. According to a different reading of *Baby-Dry*, the Court had opted for a judgment expressed in general terms in order to avoid the debate. Although the Advocate General believed that the principles of *Windsurfing Chiemsee* should be applied he suggested that the Court should dispel the uncertainty "by either approving or overruling expressis verbis its earlier case-law".[655]

Expressing his support for the ruling in *Windsurfing Chiemsee* the Advocate General made another point, indirectly distinguishing first between trade mark law and other types of intellectual property protection and, secondly between trade mark law and competition objectives:

"a trade mark creates a privilege which enables an operator to register a sign in order to designate its goods or services. That privilege becomes all the more excessive when it concerns expressions in everyday use. It is fair and natural that a public authority should be able to reward, with a higher level of protection, signs which demonstrate ingenuity or imagination, and that it should require other signs, which merely reflect aspects or attributes of the products in question, to satisfy more rigorous conditions in order to be eligible for registration. Nor do I think it appropriate for economic development and the promotion of commercial initiatives that established operators should be able to register for their own benefit all the descriptive combinations imaginable, or the most effective such combinations, to the detriment of new operators, who are obliged to use invented names which are more difficult to remember and to establish".[656]

The relationship between trade mark and patent law with competition acting as a catalyst is a theme that the Advocate General had also developed in Philips.[657]

---

[653] Point 57 of the Opinion of A.G. Ruiz-Jarabo Colomer.
[654] Point 59 of the Opinion of A.G. Ruiz-Jarabo Colomer.
[655] Point 59 of the Opinion of A.G. Ruiz-Jarabo Colomer.
[656] Point 61 of the Opinion of A.G. Ruiz-Jarabo Colomer.
[657] *Koninklijke Philips Electronics NV* (C-299/99) [2002] E.C.R. I-5475.

7. ARTICLE 3(1)(c)—DESCRIPTIVE SIGNS OR INDICATIONS

Later, in his Opinion, he explained further why he was quite critical of *Baby-Dry*. First, it was uncertain how well it fitted with *Windsurfing Chiemsee*; secondly, he repeated his point about the linguistic perspective used in that case; thirdly, because it appeared to contain an assessment of factual matters that should remain outside the jurisdiction of an appeal court; fourthly, the test was a "purely minimum"[658] one.   4-403

He accepted, though, that the position of the Court at this stage could not be reversed, because "at issue is a very recent decision, which was, moreover, adopted by the Court in plenary session, for which reason it will probably be of no avail to seek a reversal of precedent".[659]

(vi) The peculiarity of the Benelux. Finally, on the language considerations in the case of the Benelux the Advocate General stated that: 4-404

"[I]f a particular territory has implemented a system of trade mark registration which covers several linguistic regions, it would be in keeping with the aims of the Directive for an assessment of the distinctive character of a sign to be carried out in relation to each of the languages spoken".[660]

(vii) Neologism—more than the mere sum of its parts—form and meaning. Advocate General Ruiz-Jarabo Colomer noted that "a combination of components, each of which is devoid of distinctive character, can have distinctive character, provided that it amounts to more than just a mere sum of its parts".[661]   4-405

In order to find a way for determining whether this was the case he turned first to *Baby-Dry* where the Court accepted that any perceptible difference between the composite mark and its component parts could contribute distinctive character.

Following his criticism, but admitting that the Court would have to live with that judgment for the foreseeable future, he proposed the elaboration of the concept of perceptible difference in two ways. First, a difference should be regarded as perceptible if it affected important components of either the form of the sign or its meaning.

Interestingly he linked this proposal with what he had already suggested in *Philips* regarding functionality. Article 3(1)(c) and art.3(1)(e) had different purposes, however the similarities in their wording necessitated a uniform interpretive approach. There was a common principle in both cases; economic operators should not have to tolerate even the slight risk of trade mark law encroaching either on what should be protected under patent law or on use of descriptive terms.   4-406

---

[658] Point 69 of the Opinion of A.G. Ruiz-Jarabo Colomer.
[659] Point 70 of the Opinion of A.G. Ruiz-Jarabo Colomer.
[660] Point 63. See also the opinion of A.G. Sharpston in Europolis, at para.4-629, below.
[661] Point 65 of the Opinion of A.G. Ruiz-Jarabo Colomer.

Regarding form, he required the "neologism" itself to be more important than the sum of the terms of which it was composed, as a result of the unusual or imaginative nature of the word combination.

On meaning, he required whatever was evoked by the composite sign not to be identical to the sum of that suggested by its descriptive components.

From this stricter interpretive perspective "considerations relating to the existence of synonyms or the essential, or incidental, nature of the descriptive element of a sign are immaterial to the assessment of distinctive character".[662]

4-407   *(b)   The judgment of the Court*

The Court structured its judgment in a different format. Here, the judgment of the Court is divided into five parts. The first part covers the issues that are linked with the registration process; the second descriptiveness; the third and the fourth the relationship between descriptiveness and distinctive character; and the fifth looks at composite marks.

4-408   **(i) The registration process—the parameters for assessing registrability.** The Court based its response on art.6quinquies C(1) of the Paris Convention, that provided that all the factual circumstances had to be taken into account whilst considering whether a mark was eligible for protection. The reference to the Paris Convention was made according to the 12th Recital in the Preamble to the Directive that necessitated that the provisions of the Directive were consistent with the Paris Convention. The Court then described the parameters for assessing registrability.

The first two were linked with the finding that registrability could not be determined in abstract.

First, the competent authority should consider the characteristics peculiar to the mark "including the type of mark (word mark, figurative mark, etc.) and, in the case of a word mark, its meaning, in order to ascertain whether or not any of the grounds for refusal set out in Article 3 . . . apply".[663]

4-409   Secondly, the art.3 grounds had to be assessed specifically by reference to the relevant goods or services.

Distinctive character in particular had to be assessed by reference to the goods or services specified in the application but also by reference to "the perception of them by the relevant public".[664]

In this assessment the competent authority before adopting a final decision on registrability should have regard to all the relevant facts and circumstances, including, where appropriate, the results of surveys submitted by

---

[662] Point 75 of the Opinion of A.G. Ruiz-Jarabo Colomer.
[663] *Postkantoor*, para.32.
[664] *Postkantoor*, para.34, citing *Linde AG* (C-53/01), *Winward Industries Inc* (C-54/01) and *Rado Uhren AG* (C-55/01) [2003] E.C.R. I-3161; and *Libertel Groep BV* (C-104/01) [2003] E.C.R. I-3793.

7. ARTICLE 3(1)(c)—DESCRIPTIVE SIGNS OR INDICATIONS

the applicant. The same applied to a court having to review a decision on registrability, subject to the limits on the exercise of its powers imposed in each jurisdiction.

The case of the Benelux. Regarding the Benelux linguistic peculiarity—the extension of protection to the translations of the trade mark in all the official languages of the Benelux countries—the Court ruled that the competent authority had to ascertain descriptiveness for each one of those translations. **4–410**

Registrability in other Member States. On the effect of registration in one Member State, and given the individualistic character of each application, the Court ruled that registration in one Member State could not have any bearing on registrability of a similar mark in respect of similar goods or services in another Member State. **4–411**

Specification and disclaimers. The Court also considered the question of disclaimers in relation to the specification of a trade mark application. **4–412**

The role of the Nice Agreement is to facilitate the administration of a registration system. Applicants can apply for only some of the goods or services covered in each class of the Agreement and, equally, national authorities can reject parts of a class when the application covers it in its entirety.

However the Court ruled that:

> "where registration is applied for in respect of particular goods or services, it cannot be permitted that the competent authority registers the mark only in so far as the goods or services concerned do not possess a particular characteristic".[665]

The burden imposed on competitors was the justification behind this ruling. Third parties would not normally be aware of such a limitation and they might refrain from using the contested sign despite the existence of the limitation.

The independence of article 3 grounds—thorough examination procedures. Finally, the Court ruled that the competent authority of each Member State must refuse to register any mark caught by one of the grounds for refusal laid down by the Directive, in particular in art.3. **4–413**

The Seventh Recital stated that the conditions for obtaining and maintaining a registration had to be in general, identical in all the Member States; this is why the absolute grounds for refusal of registration were listed exhaustively in the Directive and had to be adopted by all the Member States. "In addition, the scheme of the Directive is founded on review prior

---

[665] *Postkantoor*, para.114.

to registration, even though it also makes provision for ex post facto review."[666] Citing *Libertel*[667] the Court repeated that examination had to be thorough and full. Article 3 did not distinguish between marks which cannot be registered and those which manifestly cannot be registered. Accordingly, it is not open for a national authority to reject only signs that are manifestly inadmissible.

4–414   **(ii) Interpreting and applying article 3(1)(c).** The Court started by clearly reconfirming its position in *Windsurfing Chiemsee*.[668]
The public interest described therein required:

"that all signs or indications which may serve to designate characteristics of the goods or services in respect of which registration is sought remain freely available to all undertakings in order that they may use them when describing the same characteristics of their own goods. Therefore, marks consisting exclusively of such signs or indications are not eligible for registration unless Article 3(3) of the Directive applies".[669]

The Court avoided a detailed test; instead it described in general terms what the competent authority had to do:

"determine whether a trademark for which registration is sought currently represents, in the mind of the relevant class of persons, a description of the characteristics of the goods or services concerned or whether it is reasonable to assume that that might be the case in the future... If, at the end of that assessment, the competent authority reaches the conclusion that that is the case, it must refuse, on the basis of that provision, to register the mark".[670]

4–415   And without making the Advocate General's explicit link with art.3(1)(e) it agreed that it was irrelevant whether there were other, more usual, signs or indications for designating the same characteristics art.3(1)(c) did not require the contested signs or indications to be the only way for designating those characteristics.
On the other hand it did require that the trade mark consisted exclusively of those signs or indications.

---

[666] *Postkantoor*, para.123.
[667] *Libertel Groep BV* (C-104/01) [2003] E.C.R. I-3793.
[668] *Windsurfing Chiemsee Produktions- and Vertriebs GmbH* (C-108/97 & C-109/97) [1999] E.C.R. I-2779. By then it had already been reconfirmed in *Linde AG* (C-53/01), *Winward Industries Inc* (C-54/01) and *Rado Uhren AG* (C-55/01) [2003] E.C.R. I-3161; and *Libertel Groep BV* (C-104/01) [2003] E.C.R. I-3793.
[669] *Postkantoor*, para.55.
[670] *Postkantoor*, para.56; see para.4–408, above.

7. ARTICLE 3(1)(c)—DESCRIPTIVE SIGNS OR INDICATIONS

Similarly, the number of competitors that might have had an interest in using those signs or indications was not decisive; this appeared to be an issue of principle:

"Any operator at present offering, as well as any operator who might in the future offer, goods or services which compete with those in respect of which registration is sought must be able freely to use the signs or indications which may serve to describe characteristics of its goods or services."[671]

Answering the fifth question[672] the Court repeated that a word had to be refused registration if at least one of its possible meanings designates a characteristic of the goods or services concerned.[673] The existence of synonyms for designating those characteristics was irrelevant.

4–416

It also considered it irrelevant whether the characteristics of the relevant goods or services were commercially essential or merely ancillary. Following a literary interpretive path the Court stressed that the wording of art.3(1)(c) drew no distinction by reference to the characteristics which might be designated. The public interest behind art.3(1)(c) required that all undertakings had to able freely to use such signs and indications to describe any characteristic whatsoever of their own goods, irrespective of the commercial significance of that characteristic.

(iii) The independent existence of article 3(1)(b) and article 3(1)(c). Citing its rulings in *Linde*[674] and *Merz & Krell*,[675] the Court confirmed that, despite the overlap in terms of scope, each one of the art.3 grounds was independent of the others and had to be examined separately from the others. In addition each ground had to be interpreted in the light of the respective underlying public interest.[676]

4–417

So, not failing one of the grounds was not a guarantee of not failing the others:

"In particular, it is thus not open to the competent authority to conclude that a mark is not devoid of any distinctive character in relation to

---

[671] *Postkantoor*, para.58.
[672] It re-interpreted the fifth question as essentially asking whether for assessing the applicability of art.3(1)(c) it was relevant (i) whether there were synonyms for the word or (ii) that the characteristics described by the word are commercially essential or merely ancillary.
[673] Citing *WM Wrigley Jr Co* (C-191/01 P) [2003] E.C.R. I-12447.
[674] *Linde AG* (C-53/01), *Winward Industries Inc* (C-54/01) and *Rado Uhren AG* (C-55/01) [2003] E.C.R. I-3161.
[675] *Merz & Krell GmbH & Co* (C-517/99) [2001] E.C.R. I-6959.
[676] Citing *Koninklijke Philips Electronics NV* (C-299/99) [2002] E.C.R. I-5475; and *Libertel Groep BV* (C-104/01) [2003] E.C.R. I-3793.

certain goods or services purely on the ground that it is not descriptive of them."[677]

The Court, patiently, dealt with all the possible combinations raised by the Dutch court. So, it ruled that it was not open to the competent authority to conclude that a mark was not devoid of any distinctive character in relation to certain goods or services purely on the ground that it was descriptive of the characteristics of other goods or services, even where registration is sought in respect of those goods or services as a whole. And, that the fact that a mark was descriptive of certain goods or services should not be seen as a ground for refusing to register that mark for other goods or services.

4–418 **(iv) The overlap between article 3(1)(b) and article 3(1)(c).** The Court, however, in its re-interpretation of the fifth question, also stated that because there was clear overlap between the scope of subparas (b), (c), and (d) of art.3(1):

"[I]n particular, a word mark which is descriptive of characteristics of goods or services for the purposes of Article 3(1)(c) of the Directive is, on that account, necessarily devoid of any distinctive character with regard to the same goods or services within the meaning of Article 3(1)(b) of the Directive. A mark may none the less be devoid of any distinctive character in relation to goods or services for reasons other than the fact that it may be descriptive".[678]

4–419 **(v) Composite marks.** In order to clarify its rulings in *Baby-Dry*[679] and Doublemint[680] the Court provided us with some further guidelines.

The starting point was that descriptiveness of the elements of a composite mark did not automatically mean that the composite mark was also descriptive.

"As a general rule, a mere combination of elements, each of which is descriptive of characteristics of the goods or services in respect of which registration is sought, itself remains descriptive of those characteristics for the purposes of Article 3(1)(c) of the Directive. Merely bringing those elements together without introducing any unusual variations, in particular as to syntax or meaning, cannot result in anything other than a mark consisting exclusively of signs or indications which may serve, in trade, to designate characteristics of the goods or services concerned."[681]

---

[677] *Postkantoor*, para.70.
[678] *Postkantoor*, para.86.
[679] *Procter & Gamble Co* (C-383/99 P) [2001] E.C.R. I-6251.
[680] *WM Wrigley Jr Co* (C-191/01 P) [2003] E.C.R. I-12447.
[681] *Postkantoor*, para.98.

7. ARTICLE 3(1)(c)—DESCRIPTIVE SIGNS OR INDICATIONS

However, and following the Advocate General's rationale regarding conceptual differences and differences as to form between the neologism and its components the Court held that even POSTKANTOOR might not be descriptive if it created an impression:

> "sufficiently far removed from that produced by the simple combination of those elements. In the case of a word mark, which is intended to be heard as much as to be read, that condition must be satisfied as regards both the aural and the visual impression produced by the mark".[682]

Note that the Court appeared to insist that the conceptual differences were the ones that mattered. The differences relating to form had to create an impression that was detached from the specified goods or services:

4–420

> "Thus, a mark consisting of a word composed of elements, each of which is descriptive of characteristics of the goods or services in respect of which registration is sought, is itself descriptive of those characteristics for the purposes of article 3(1)(c) of the Directive, unless there is a perceptible difference between the word and the mere sum of its parts: that assumes either that, because of the unusual nature of the combination in relation to the goods or services, the word creates an impression which is sufficiently far removed from that produced by the mere combination of meanings lent by the elements of which it is composed, with the result that the word is more than the sum of its parts, or that the word has become part of everyday language and has acquired its own meaning, with the result that it is now independent of its components. In the second case, it is necessary to ascertain whether a word which has acquired its own meaning is not itself descriptive for the purpose of the same provision."[683]

(5) Streamserve—consolidating Doublemint

4–421

Streamserve[684] appeared to consolidate the position of the Court of Justice regarding the interpretation of art.7(1)(c) following the line adopted in *Doublemint*.[685]

Intelligent Document Systems Scandinavia AB had filed an application—that it later transferred to Stremaserve Inc—for the registration of

---

[682] *Postkantoor*, para.99.
[683] *Postkantoor*, para.100; this also led to the ruling that the existence of synonyms was irrelevant; the same applied to whether the characterstic was important or ancillary.
[684] *Streamserve Inc, Office for Harmonisation in the Internal Market (Trade Marks and Designs)* (C-150/02 P) [2004] E.C.R. I-1461 an appeal against the judgment of the Court of First Instance in *Streamserve Inc v Office For Harmonisation in the Internal Market (Trade Marks and Designs)* (T-106/00) [2002] E.C.R. II-723, which in turn had dismissed the action against a decision of the Second Board of Appeal Case R-423/1999-2 February 28, 2000.
[685] *WM Wrigley Jr Co* (C-191/01 P) [2003] E.C.R. I-12447.

STREAMSERVE as a Community Trade Mark for "Apparatus for recording, transmitting and reproducing of sounds and images; data processing equipment including computers, computer memories, viewing screens, keyboards, processors, printers and scanners; computer programs stored on tapes, disks, diskettes and other machine-readable media" in Class 9 and "Listed computer programs; manuals; newspapers and publications; education and teaching material" in Class 16. The examiner rejected the application based on art.7(1)(b) and art.7(1)(c) in respect of all the goods except newspapers and publications and education and teaching material.

The Board of Appeal concurred with the examiner on both grounds. Examining the mark it found it to consist of two English words without any additional element that would render it distinctive; to the contrary it was descriptive of the intended use of the goods concerned: a method for transferring digital data from a server enabling the data to be processed as a steady and continuous stream (known as streaming).

4–422   (a)   *The judgment of the Court of First Instance*

(i) The division of powers between the Office and the Court of First Instance. The Court of First Instance dealt first with an admissibility point.

The applicant had sought from it to annul the contested decision and remit the case to the examiner.

The Office supported that, under art.63(3) of the Regulation, the jurisdiction of the Court of First Instance was either to annul or to alter decisions of the Board of Appeal. It remained in the jurisdiction of the Office to take the necessary measures to comply with the judgment of the Court of First Instance.

The Court of First Instance admitted the principle supported by the Office. However, it added that under art.63(6) of the Regulation the Court of First Instance was not entitled to issue directions to the Office. By remitting the case to the examiner, the Court would not be imposing on the Office any obligation to take, or refrain from taking, action. In addition, one of the measures available to the Board of Appeal was to remit the case to the examiner; accordingly it fell within the measures that the Court of First Instance could take in the exercise of its power to amend decisions under art.63(3).

4–423   **(ii) The application of article 7(1)(c).** The Court of First Instance held that for:

"the purpose of applying article 7(1)(c) ... it is necessary only to consider, on the basis of the relevant meaning of the word sign at issue, whether, from the viewpoint of the public addressed, there is a sufficiently direct

7. ARTICLE 3(1)(c)—DESCRIPTIVE SIGNS OR INDICATIONS

and specific relationship between the sign and the goods for which registration is sought".[686]

Citing *Windsurfing Chiemsee*[687] it rejected the claim that the applicant's competitors did not need to use the term to designate the specified goods. The application of art.7(1)(c), did not depend on there being a real, current or serious need to leave a sign or indication free.

It identified the general interest behind the provision in the following terms:

> "Article 7(1)(c) ... prevents the signs or indications referred to in that provision from being reserved to one undertaking alone because they have been registered as a mark. That provision thus pursues an aim which is in the public interest, namely that such signs or indications may be freely used by all."[688]

The Court of First Instance agreed with the Office that the relevant public comprised average English speaking consumers who used the Internet and were interested in its audiovisual aspects, that were deemed to be reasonably well informed and reasonably observant and circumspect. 4–424

The combination of a basic verb with a noun did not appear unusual. In terms of meaning it referred to a technique for transferring digital data from a server, enabling them to be processed as a steady and continuous stream. The fact that the combination could have other meanings was irrelevant. It was sufficient if at least one of the potential meanings designated a characteristic of the specified goods or services.

The Court of First Instance then looked at the relationship between the term and the goods included in the specification. It divided the specification into three parts.

The first covered the categories of goods that STREAMSERVE was directly descriptive of their intended purpose: apparatus for recording, transmitting and reproducing of sounds and images; data processing equipment including computers, computer memories, viewing screens, keyboards, processors, printers and scanners; computer programs stored on tapes, disks, diskettes and other machine-readable media; and listed computer programs. 4–425

For those goods it accepted the submission of the Office that the technique described by the term involved, or indeed required, their use.

---

[686] *Streamserve*, para.40.
[687] *Windsurfing Chiemsee Produktions- und Vertriebs GmbH* (C-108/97 & C-109/97) [1999] E.C.R. I-2779.
[688] *Streamserve*, para.36.

4-426 **(iii) Deciphering the specification—broad specifications.** The second was a subcategory of specific goods covered by the category:

> " 'data processing equipment'—screens, keyboards, processors, printers and scanners—for which it noted that they did not appear as such in the application for registration but were mentioned only as examples of goods falling under the category 'data processing equipment' ".

It held that they should not be taken into account in the appraisal of the descriptive character of the term. Here, this would work against the applicant; even if it were assumed that a sufficiently direct and specific link between the term and those goods were lacking, the appraisal described above would not be undermined.

Further it noted that the applicant had applied for all goods in that category without drawing any distinction between them.

4-427 It appears that unless a more precise specification is drawn, failing in respect of some of the goods covered under class headings or subheadings would result in the rejection of the entire class or subclass.

The third covered the categories of manuals and publications in respect of which the Court of First Instance found that the Office had failed to prove that the term designated one of their characteristics:

> "The technique [described by the term] ... does not require or even involve the use of those goods. Nor can it be alleged, as the Office does in its rejoinder, that the term in question is descriptive of those goods because the technique to which that term refers can also be used for the transfer of texts by electronic means. The transfer of texts by electronic means is, at most, a field of application of that technique but not a technical function of the goods in question. Moreover, the term STREAMSERVE likewise does not appear to designate another characteristic of the abovementioned goods. Accordingly, for the public addressed, there is not a sufficiently direct and specific relationship between the term STREAMSERVE and those goods."[689]

Accordingly it upheld the plea only in relation to "manuals and publications".

4-428 **(iv) The autonomy of the Community Trade Mark regime.** Finally, it held that the "the Community trade mark regime is an autonomous system with its own set of objectives and rules peculiar to it; it is self-sufficient and applies independently of any national system".[690] Registrability of a sign as a

---

[689] *Streamserve*, para.50.
[690] *Streamserve*, para.47, citing its own case law in *Messe München v Office For Harmonisation the Internal Market (Trade Marks and Designs)* (T-32/00) [2000] E.C.R. II-3289.

7. ARTICLE 3(1)(c)—DESCRIPTIVE SIGNS OR INDICATIONS

Community Trade Mark should only be assessed according to the relevant Community rules; registrations of the same sign for the same specification in a Member State or a third country could not bind Office or the Community courts.

(v) The application of article 7(1)(b). The Court of First Instance dealt here with the applicant's contention that the term enjoyed a degree of inventiveness and the argument developed by the Office that signs that were descriptive according to art.7(1)(c) were also devoid of distinctive character under art.7(1)(b).

4–429

It noted that once one of the art.7(1) grounds was found to be applicable the application should be rejected[691]; accordingly in this case it was necessary to consider the substance of the plea only in relation to manuals and publications, since the Board had found the term to fail under art.7(1)(b) because it had also failed under art.7(1)(c).

The Court of First Instance underlined that the decision of the Board and the records of the Office had not shown in any way that the term was not distinctive for goods in the categories manuals and publications.

Accordingly, the plea was upheld in relation to goods in those two categories.

(b) The order of the Court

4–430

The Court found the appeal to be clearly unfounded and dismissed it by reasoned order.

The first ground of the appeal, based on *Baby-Dry*,[692] challenged the stance of the Court of the First Instance regarding the public interest behind art.7(1)(c). Streamserve argued that the provision was intended to preclude the registration of descriptive terms rather than prevent the monopolisation of descriptive terms.

Albeit, the Court disagreed:

"By prohibiting the registration as a Community trade mark of signs or indications which may serve, in trade, to designate the characteristics of the goods or services for which registration is sought, article 7(1)(c) ... pursues an aim which is in the general interest, namely that such signs or indications may be freely used by all. That provision accordingly

---

[691] Citing *Harbinger v Office For Harmonsation a the Internal Market (Trade Marks and Designs)* (T-345/99) [2000] E.C.R. II-3525; *Community Concepts v Office For Harmonsation in the Internal Market (Trade Marks and Designs)* (T-360/99) [2000] E.C.R. II-3545; and *Sunrider v Office For Harmonsation in the Internal Market (Trade Marks and Designs)* (T-24/00) [2001] E.C.R. II-449.
[692] *Procter & Gamble Co* (C-383/99 P) [2001] E.C.R. I-6251.

precludes such signs or indications being reserved to a single undertaking as a result of the registration of the trade mark."[693]

4-431   It held that the Court of First Instance had not erred in its description of the public interest behind art.7(1)(c)[694] and that it had taken into account the objectives of the provision.

With the second ground the appellant argued that the Court of First Instance had misinterpreted the facts in holding that the word Streamserve did not appear unusual for the relevant consumers.

The Court rejected the second ground because it focused on findings of fact rather than points of law.[695]

Furthermore, it held that, based on its findings, the Court of First Instance had correctly applied art.7(1)(c) by concluding that STREAMSERVE could serve, in trade, to designate a characteristic of most of the specified goods.

4-432   **(6) Telefon & Buch—following Doublemint**

Telefon & Buch[696] was one of the first cases that reconsidered the interpretation and application of art.7(1)(c) following *Doublemint*.[697] It came before the Court as an appeal against a judgment of the Court of First Instance.[698]

Telefon & Buch had applied for the registration as Community Trade Marks of the words UNIVERSALTELEFONBUCH (universal telephone directory) and UNIVEVERSALKOMMUNIKATIONSVERZEICHNIS (universal communications directory) for:

"scientific, nautical, surveying, electric, photographic, cinematographic, optical, weighing, measuring, signalling, checking (supervision), lifesaving and teaching apparatus and instruments; apparatus for recording, transmission or reproduction of sound or images; magnetic data carriers and recorded memory media for data processing installations and

---

[693] *Streamserve*, para.25, citing *Windsurfing Chiemsee Produktions- und Vertriebs GmbH* (C-108/97 & C-109/97) [1999] E.C.R. I-2779; *Linde AG* (C-53/01), *Winward Industries Inc* (C-54/01) and *Rado Uhren AG* (C-55/01) [2003] E.C.R. I-3161; and *WM Wrigley Jr Co* (C-191/01 P) [2003] E.C.R. I-12447.

[694] See para.36 of the judgment of the Court of First Instance *Streamserve Inc.* (T-106/00) [2002] E.C.R. II-723.

[695] Citing *DKV Deutsche Krankenversicherung AG* (C-104/00 P) [2002] E.C.R. I-7561.

[696] *Telefon & Buch v Office for Harmonisation in the Internal Market (Trade Marks and Designs)* (C-326/01 P) [2004] E.C.R. I-1371.

[697] *WM Wrigley Jr Co* (C-191/01 P) [2003] E.C.R. I-12447.

[698] *Telefon & Buch v Office for Harmonisation is the Internal Market (Trade Marks and Designs)* (T-357/99 and T-358/99) [2001] E.C.R. II-1705 where the Court of First Instance dismissed the actions against two decisions of the Third Board of Appeal (Cases R-351/1999-3 and R-352/1999-3), October 21, 1999.

7. ARTICLE 3(1)(c)—DESCRIPTIVE SIGNS OR INDICATIONS

apparatus, in particular tapes, discs, CD-ROMs; sound recording discs; automatic vending machines and mechanisms for coin-operated apparatus; cash registers, calculating machines, data processing equipment and computers; fire-extinguishing apparatus" in Class 9;

"paper, cardboard and goods made from these materials, not included in other classes; printed matter, reference works, classified directories; bookbinding material; photographs; stationery; adhesives for stationery or household purposes; artists' materials; paint brushes; typewriters and office requisites (except furniture); instructional and teaching material (except apparatus); plastic materials for packaging (not included in other classes); playing cards; printers' type; printing blocks" in Class 16;

"publishing services, in particular the publication of texts, books, magazines, newspapers" in Class 41;

"editing of written texts" in class 42.

The examiner rejected the terms on the basis of art.7(1)(c) and art.7(1)(b) in respect of "recorded memory media for data processing installations and apparatus, in particular tapes, discs, CD-ROMs" in Class 9; "printed matter, reference works" in Class 16; "publishing services, in particular the publication of texts, books, magazines, newspapers" in Class 41; "editing of written texts" in Class 42.

The Board of Appeal confirmed that in German the two words were descriptive of the specified goods and services indicated by the examiner. It also found them to be devoid of distinctive character.

(a) The judgment of the Court of First Instance 4-433

The Court of First Instance stated that whether the terms were descriptive had to be determined by reference to the goods or services in respect of which registration was sought. It found them to be formed in accordance with the grammatical rules of the German language and composed of common German words. They designated the kind of goods and the intended use of the services concerned; the addition of the adjective universal did not alter its descriptiveness findings, in contrast it functioned as an additional descriptive element.

It then looked at the target public—average German-speaking consumers, reasonably well informed and reasonably circumspect—and found that they would establish, immediately and without further reflection, a specific and direct association between the terms and the specified goods and services. The fact that the terms constituted neologisms did not affect that conclusion.

Note that the Court of First Instance also considered future use of the sign, partly responding to the argument that, until that stage, third parties had not been using the signs:

"Even if universal telephone or communications directories, containing worldwide data, are not currently available on the market, it is very likely that they will exist in the near future, either on paper or on electronic media. In any event, the words UNIVERSALTELEFONBUCH and UNIVERSALKOMMUNIKATIONSVERZEICHNIS may, even now, designate directories which cover or which claim to cover universally, that is to say exhaustively, either the whole of a territory (regional, national or supranational) or a whole sector (professional or social)."[699]

4–434　It did not consider the arguments based on art.7(1)(b) given that the application should be rejected on the basis of art.7(1)(c).

Before the Court of Justice Telefon & Buch claimed that the Court of First Instance had not taken account of the fact that the terms were not exclusively descriptive.

4–435　*(b)　The order of the Court of Justice*

The Court of Justice found the appeal to be clearly unfounded and dismissed it by issuing a reasoned order under art.119 of the Rules of Procedure.

The appellant had employed the language of the Court in *Baby-Dry*[700] in order to strengthen its claims. It argued that the two signs constituted neologisms that consisted of an unusual juxtapositioning of terms. They had no definite meaning and did not convey to the average consumer a clear picture of the goods and services designated by them. Accordingly, it stressed, they were not exclusively descriptive. They were neologisms that remained outside the scope of art.7(1)(c).

It noted that the Office was unable to form a precise idea of the goods in question on the basis of the contested terms and viewed this as evidence that they were not purely descriptive.

4–436　Proactively, it argued that since the terms had not been used before, they were not subject to the requirement of availability that was behind art.12 of the Regulation; in any case the same provision would ensure that third parties would be allowed to use the signs as descriptive indications.

The Office supported a stricter approach. Article 7(1)(c) covered signs that consumers in the Community would understand immediately as designating the goods and services referred to in the application or their characteristics.

It conceded that, post Baby-Dry, where that understanding was not immediate the terms might be registered as trade marks, in particular where the combination of terms was constructed according to an unusual structure.

[699] *Telefon & Buch*, para.30.
[700] *Procter & Gamble Co* (C-383/99 P) [2001] E.C.R. I-6251.

7. ARTICLE 3(1)(c)—DESCRIPTIVE SIGNS OR INDICATIONS

However, it stressed, the fact that the signs were neologisms should not lead to an automatic finding about their descriptiveness. The signs might have had several possible meanings or been constructed according to a slightly different grammatical structure but what mattered was the effect on the decisive factor: "the way in which the sign is immediately understood and perceived by the public".[701]

4–437

The Court repeated the basic points of its case law on art.7(1)(c) until *Doublemint*,[702] failing to cite *Baby-Dry*.[703] Following *Doublemint* it repeated that it:

> "is sufficient, as the wording of that provision itself indicates, that such signs and indications could be used for such purposes. Thus, under article 7(1)(c), registration of a word mark must be refused if at least one of its possible meanings designates a characteristic of the goods or services concerned".[704]

Applying this principle to the current case it held that the Court of First Instance was right to find that:

> "for registration of a descriptive sign to be refused on the basis of article 7(1)(c), it is sufficient that the sign is, in the eyes of the target public, associated with the goods concerned or that it may be reasonably envisaged that such an association will be made in the future and in holding, in paragraph 30 of the judgment under appeal, that the fact that there is currently no market for universal telephone or communication directories does not alter the descriptive character of the words in question ...".[705]

This, the Court held was also in line with the public interest identified in *Windsurfing Chiemsee*.[706]

4–438

The same applied to the possibility that the terms possessed several meanings. The Court stressed again that it was sufficient that at least one of the possible meanings of that sign were descriptive.

The Court concluded that the Court of First Instance had correctly relied on the fact that the terms, in the minds of the public, designated or were capable of designating characteristics of the specified goods or services, rather than the fact that they were exclusively descriptive.

---

[701] para.22.
[702] *WM Wrigley Jr Co* (C-191/01 P) [2003] E.C.R. I-12447.
[703] *Procter & Gamble Co* (C-383/99 P) [2001] E.C.R. I-6251.
[704] *Telefon & Buch*, para.28.
[705] *Telefon & Buch*, para.31, referring to para.30 of the Judgment of the Court of First Instance *Telefon & Buch* (T-357/99 & T-385/99) [2001] E.C.R. II-1705.
[706] *Windsurfing Chiemsee Produktions- und Vertriebs GmbH* (C-108/97 & C-109/97) [1999] E.C.R. I-2779.

The part of the claim supporting that the Court of First Instance was mistaken as to the meaning of the terms was rejected because it merely its assessment of the facts.[707]

4–439 (7) BVBA—challenging the procedural points of Postkantoor

In *BVBA*,[708] another detailed reference, this time from the Belgian Hof van Beroep (Court of Appeal, Brussels), the Court reconsidered some of the procedural repercussions of *Postkantoor*.[709]

BVBA Management Training en Consultancy (BVBA) had applied for the registration in the Benelux of the word mark THE KITCHEN COMPANY for:

> "ovens with control panels, hot plates, refrigerators, microwave ovens, freeze boxes, deep freezers, boilers, electrical chip friers, ovens, built-in grills, extractor hoods, kitchen sinks, taps" in Class 11;
>
> "wooden and plastic kitchen furniture, kitchen chairs, kitchen work surfaces made of wood, plastic, granite, natural stone or tiled" in Class 20;
>
> "kitchen utensils and household and kitchen equipment made of glass, porcelain, non-precious metals, plastic and earthenware" in Class 21;
>
> "the placing and assembly of kitchen furniture and apparatus, maintenance and repair activities" in Class 37; and
>
> "advising in relation to use, nature and application of kitchen apparatus, planning and advising in regard to the installation of kitchens and built-in apparatus, including at the time of purchase" in Class 42.

The Benelux Trade Mark Office rejected the application for lack of distinctive character; its decision did not refer in its conclusion specifically to each one of the goods or services listed in the specification; it was based on the finding that the mark was solely descriptive of the kind, quality, origin or intended purpose of the specified goods and services provided by, for, or in connection with a kitchen company.

4–440 BVBA attacked the decision before the Hof van Beroep that found the mark to be distinctive for "household and kitchen equipment made of glass, porcelain, non-precious metals, plastic and earthenware" in Class 21, since it did not refer to the intended use of the goods. The Benelux Trade Mark Office, however, objected to this separation, because BVBA had not specifically requested the Office to consider registration only for part of the specification.

---

[707] Citing *DKV Deutsche Krankenversicherung AG* (C-104/00 P) [2002] E.C.R. I-7561.
[708] *BVBA Management, Training & Consultancy v Benelux-Merkenbureau* (C-239/05) [2007] E.C.R. I-1445 (the opinion of the A.G. was delivered on July 6, 2006).
[709] *Koninklijke KPN Nederland NV* (C-363/99) [2004] E.C.R. I-1619.

7. ARTICLE 3(1)(c)—DESCRIPTIVE SIGNS OR INDICATIONS

The referring court noted that there appeared to be an inconsistency between the jurisprudence of the Court of Justice as expressed in *Postkantoor*[710] and that of the Benelux Court of Justice in *Vlaamse Toeristenbond*.[711] Indeed, this is a good example of how a national court can challenge the position of a higher court before the Court of Justice. The fact that the higher court whose jurisprudence was challenged was the Benelux Court of Justice, a supra national court functioning in its interpretive capacity, adds more weight and intrigue to the approach of the Court.

There were three particular points in *Postkantoor* that the referring court found to be relevant: the competent authority had to take into account all the relevant facts and circumstances before taking a final decision on registration; the same applied to the national courts reviewing such decisions, subject to the limits on the exercise of their powers as defined by the relevant national legislation; the competent authorities must consider registrability in relation to each one of those goods or services; with potentially different outcomes.

The Benelux court on the other hand had held that according to art.6bis[712] and art.6ter[713] of the Uniform Benelux Law on trade marks the competent courts of appeal were authorised to order registration of a mark for specific goods or services within a class only if the Benelux Trade Mark Office had specifically ruled on those goods or services as such rather than the class as a whole.

4–441

As a result the Hof van Beroep referred the following questions to the Court:

"(1) Is the trade mark authority required, after its examination of all relevant facts and circumstances concerning an absolute ground of refusal, to state in its provisional and in its definitive decision on the application its conclusion in regard to each of the goods and services separately in respect of which trade mark protection is sought?

(2) May the relevant facts and circumstances to be taken into account by the adjudicating authority in the event of an appeal against the decision of the trade mark authority be different as a result of a lapse of time between the two dates on which the decisions are made or must the adjudicating authority only take account of such facts and circumstances as were available at the moment when the trade mark authority made its decision?

---

[710] *Koninklijke KPN Nederland NV* (C-363/99) [2004] E.C.R. I-1619.
[711] Case A 2002/2, judgment of the Benelux court of December 15, 2003.
[712] Article 6bis provides that a refusal to register a mark must concern the sign constituting the mark as a whole, but may be limited to one or several of the products which the mark is intended to cover.
[713] Article 6ter (1) provides that an applicant whose mark has been refused registration may, on appeal to the relevant Court of Appeal seek an order that the mark be registered.

(3) Does the interpretation by the Court of Justice in the Postkantoor judgment preclude national legislation in regard to the competence of the adjudicating authority from being construed as meaning that that authority is prevented from taking account of any alteration in the relevant facts and circumstances or from ruling on the distinctive character of the mark for each of the goods and services in themselves?"[714]

4-442 *(a) The Opinion of the Advocate General*

Advocate General Sharpston divided her Opinion in three parts. First, she covered the general question as to whether art.3 required national authorities to state their conclusions separately for each one of the specified goods or services. Then, she dealt with the time limitations of the facts and circumstances that a court reviewing a decision on registrability could take into account. And, thirdly, whether national rules could preclude a court from ruling on the distinctive character of the mark for each one of the goods and services separately.

4-443 **(i) Article 3—a product by product approach?** The Advocate General suggested that a trade mark registration authority had to examine an application for registration with regard to each of those goods or services. *Libertel*,[715] she reminded the Court, required a stringent and full examination. "How else is the trade mark office to determine the goods or services with regard to which the mark may validly be registered, and thereby ensure compliance with article 13 of the Trade Marks Directive?"[716]

Nevertheless, this should not mean that that the authority had to state its conclusion regarding an absolute ground for refusal separately for each of those individual goods and services. What she required was an adequate justification:

> "Where registration is refused on that basis for an entire group or category of goods or services, it is sufficient that the decision, whether provisional or definitive, so states and explains adequately why the group or category as such is ineligible for registration."[717]

To enable judicial review of the legality of the reasons for the contested decision the decision also had to disclose in:

> "a clear and unequivocal manner the reasoning followed by the institution ... which adopted the measure in question in such a way as to enable the

---

[714] Reproduced in point 3.
[715] *Libertel Groep BV* (C-104/01) [2003] E.C.R. I-3793.
[716] Point 38 of the Opinion of A.G. Sharpston.
[717] Point 39 of the Opinion of A.G. Sharpston.

7. ARTICLE 3(1)(c)—DESCRIPTIVE SIGNS OR INDICATIONS

persons concerned to ascertain the reasons for the measure and to enable the competent court to exercise its power of review".[718]

The reasoning did not have to cover all the relevant facts and points of law, since its assessment would take into account not only its wording but also its context and all the legal rules governing the contested issue.

4–444

The Advocate General supported that using general reasoning could also be useful for practical purposes. Registration authorities received a large number of applications each year and the Nice Classification comprised around 11,000 goods and services. She appeared to accept the Benelux Trade Mark Office's assertion that the only workable method of examination was for the office first to regroup the specified goods and services around the apparent core goods and services, in a way that should be readily apparent to the relevant public.

Once the office indicated why it considered that an absolute ground applied to that category then the burden was on the applicant:

> "to indicate why and demonstrate how the ground for refusal does not hold good for certain specific goods and services.... That will then enable effective judicial review of the decision to be exercised with regard to the office's decision in respect of those goods and services".[719]

The detailed procedure regarding the above would unfold according to national rules, but it seemed to be manifestly disproportionate to require national trade mark offices to set out the reason for refusal to register in respect of each and every product and service in a situation like the one described by the referring court, provided that the decision of the national authority satisfied the criteria set by the Advocate General.

(ii) Article 3—timing considerations. The Advocate General examined the second question together with the first part of the third question, as two sides of the same coin:

4–445

> "The former asks whether, in the light of Article 3, a court of review may take account of intervening facts and circumstances. The latter asks whether, in that light, a court of review may be precluded by national law from taking account of intervening facts and circumstances."[720]

---

[718] Point 40; citing *Heylens* (222/86) [1987] E.C.R. 4097 on the capacity of the courts to request from authorities to present their reasoning and para.65 of *KWS Saat v Harmonisation in the Internal Market (Trade Marks and Designs)* (C-447/02 P) [2004] E.C.R. I-10107 for the field of trade marks in particular.

[719] Point 42 of the Opinion of A.G. Sharpston.

[720] Point 46 of the Opinion of A.G. Sharpston.

She viewed the difference in views on distinctive character between the Benelux Trade Mark Office and the Hof van Beroep as a difference on a question of law rather than one based on an alteration of facts or circumstances but remarked that the reference was expressed in general terms and she would attempt answering it in general terms. It was for the national court to determine the need for a preliminary ruling.[721]

In *Postkantoor* the Court had ruled that a court asked to review a decision of a national authority:

> "must also have regard to all the relevant facts and circumstances, subject to the limits on the exercise of its powers as defined by the relevant national legislation".[722]

4-446 It was:

> "perfectly acceptable for a legal system to prohibit a court from annulling a decision on the basis of subsequent facts. Indeed, this accords with the practice of many judicial bodies when undertaking judicial review of decisions. Community law also recognises that principle".[723]

And in the context of the Community Trade Mark it had been clearly adopted by the Court in *Sunrider*.[724]

Concluding, she suggested that it was for national law to determine whether a court reviewing a decision of a trade mark authority might take account of facts and circumstances which were not available at the time of the original decision and that it was consistent with art.3 for national rules to preclude a court reviewing such a decision from taking account of such facts and circumstances.

4-447 **(iii) Article 3—specification considerations.** In the third part the Advocate General reviewed whether art.3 was compatible with national rules precluding a court reviewing the decision of a trade mark office from ruling on the distinctive character of the mark for each of the goods and services separately.

The question carried an additional charge because the Court's interpretation could affect the judicial freedom not only of the referring court but of all other courts facing a similar scenario.

The juxtaposition of the Benelux Trade Mark Office's stance with that adopted by the intervening German Government reflected the problem well.

---

[721] Citing *Enderby v Frenchay Health Authority and the Secretary of State For Health* (C-127/92) [1993] E.C.R. I-5535.
[722] *Postkantoor*, para.36.
[723] Point 53, citing *France v Commission* (C-214/94) [1996] E.C.R. I-4551 as an example.
[724] *Sunrider v Office For Harmonisation in the Internal Market (Trade Marks and Designs)* (C-416/04 P) [2006] E.C.R. I-0000.

7. ARTICLE 3(1)(c)—DESCRIPTIVE SIGNS OR INDICATIONS

The Benelux Trade Mark Office supported that, after *Postkantoor*,[725] it was clear that the competence of a court of review was subject to the limitations imposed by the relevant national legislation; this, surely, meant that national law could set limits regarding the competence of national courts.

On the other hand the German Government argued that national rules might not limit the power of courts of review to assess distinctive character with regard to separate goods and services. The Directive provided mandatory guidelines for the decisions of trade mark authorities. Courts could review only the lawfulness of those decisions and in their review they had to verify that the guidelines had been applied. In principle they should retain the freedom to rule separately for individual classes.

The Commission supported that the Directive explicitly gave the Member States extensive freedom in respect of trade mark procedure; accordingly such national rules should be considered compatible with art.3. It added that the Benelux Trade Mark Office Trade Mark allowed applicants to indicate specific goods or services in respect of which they wished to pursue further an application for registration that had originally been rejected for the entire specification. This appeared to satisfy art.13 of the Directive.[726]

The Advocate General agreed with the approach taken by the Commission.

She reminded the general principle that in the absence of Community legislation governing a particular matter it was for Member States' domestic legal systems to come up with detailed procedural rules governing court actions for safeguarding rights that individuals enjoyed as a result of Community law, provided that the principles of equivalence and effectiveness were respected.[727]

This had been repeated in *Postkantoor*[728] in the context of trade mark law.

She stressed that the Directive did not undertake full approximation and registration procedures remained in the competence of Member States according to the Fifth Recital, that enjoyed considerable freedom in that respect.

The starting point for answering the question was that it appeared to be consistent with that freedom to authorise partial registration only when the applicant requested it as an alternative to full registration in its application to the trade mark authority.

Equally consistent should be for national rules to preclude a court reviewing the decision of a trade mark office from ruling on the distinctive character of the mark for each of the goods and services separately:

4–448

4–449

4–450

---

[725] *Koninklijke KPN Nederland NV* (C-363/99) [2004] E.C.R. I-1619.
[726] Article 13 of the Directive provides: "Where grounds for refusal of registration or for revocation or invalidity of a trade mark exist in respect of only some of the goods or services for which that trade mark has been applied for or registered, refusal of registration or revocation or invalidity shall cover those goods or services only."
[727] Citing *Clean Car Autoservice GmbH v Stadt Wien and Republic Osterreich* (C-472/99) [2001] E.C.R. I-9687.
[728] *Koninklijke KPN Nederland NV* (C-363/99) [2004] E.C.R. I-1619.

> "It does not seem unreasonable or unduly onerous to expect a trade mark applicant which wishes to preserve its right to apply for partial registration to make that clear in its application for registration. It is, after all, at that stage that the applicant can best assess its commercial interests... and decide whether... it would be content with partial registration of that mark for fewer goods or services, or whether it would prefer to make a fresh application for a different mark for more goods or services."[729]

4–451 The Advocate General, showing again a practical inclination, emphasised that the procedural efficiency would also be better served:

> "if the question of full versus partial registration is considered at the time of application for registration. A national trade mark office is surely a more appropriate forum than an appellate court for the first evaluation of that issue".[730]

As to the spirit of art.13 it would still be "accurately reflected provided that national law ensures that trade mark applicants may in the alternative seek partial registration in their application".[731]

Finally, she interpreted the dictum of the Court in *Postkantoor*[732] that:

> "when registration of a mark is sought in respect of an entire class... the competent authority may, pursuant to article 13 of the Directive, register the mark only in respect of some of the goods and services belonging to that class..."[733]

4–452 As simply invoking art.13 as the basis for giving national trade mark authorities a permissive power.

This interpretation allowed her then to suggest that art.13 did not impose a substantive obligation on a trade mark authority to contemplate partial registration ex officio in all cases and find that there was no conflict between art.13 and national procedural rules requiring an applicant who wanted the trade mark authority to consider partial registration to make that clear in the application:

> "On the contrary, such rules enhance procedural efficiency, are less rather than more cumbersome in the context of the procedure viewed as a whole, and do not make the exercise of Community law rights impossible or unduly difficult."[734]

---

[729] Point 64 of the Opinion of A.G. Sharpston.
[730] Point 65 of the Opinion of A.G. Sharpston.
[731] Point 67 of the Opinion of A.G. Sharpston.
[732] *Koninklijke KPN Nederland NV* (C-363/99) [2004] E.C.R. I-1619.
[733] *Postkantoor*, para.113.
[734] Point 68 of the Opinion of A.G. Sharpston.

7. ARTICLE 3(1)(c)—DESCRIPTIVE SIGNS OR INDICATIONS

In the current case BVBA had failed to make a request for a partial registration at two distinct points of time: when filing its initial application—the provisional stage—and when contesting the provisional decision before the Benelux Trade Mark Office—the final stage. Instead, it made the "subsidiary" application when the case reached the reviewing court. The Advocate General had no sympathy for such an applicant.

(b) The judgment of the Court 4–453

The Court largely concurred with the views expressed by the Advocate General.

(i) The need for a reasonably specific reasoning. The Court started 4–454
its analysis by referring to the requirements in *Postkantoor* that the examination of the absolute grounds for refusal must be thorough and full in order to ensure that trademarks are not improperly registered[735] and that insofar as registration is always sought in respect of particular goods and services, the question whether or not any of the grounds for refusal apply must be assessed specifically by reference to each of those goods or services.[736]

Moreover, it recalled that, according to art.13 of the Directive, where grounds for refusal of registration of a trade mark exist in respect of only some of the goods or services covered by the application, the refusal is to cover those goods or services only. Accordingly, the Court concluded, first, that the examination of absolute grounds must be carried out in relation to each of the goods and services for which registration is sought and, secondly, that the decision refusing registration must, in principle, state reasons in respect of each of those goods or services.[737]

This need further arises from the requirement for any decision of a national authority refusing the benefit of a right conferred by Community law to be subject to judicial review, which is designed to secure the effective protection of that right[738] and applies regardless of whether the application for registration contains subsidiary claims relating to specific goods and services.[739]

However, the Court emphasised that where that same ground of refusal is given for a category or group of goods or services, the competent authority may use only general reasoning for all of the goods and services falling under that category.[740]

---

[735] *Postkantoor*, para.123.
[736] *Postkantoor*, paras 33 and 73.
[737] *BVBA*, para.34.
[738] Citing *Heylens* (222/86) [1987] E.C.R. 4097, paras 14–15.
[739] *BVBA*, paras 35–36.
[740] *BVBA*, para.37.

4–455　**(ii) The overriding effect of national rules.** Then the Court turned to the second part of the third question, dealing with the extent to which the Directive precludes national laws from providing that courts have no competence to consider the various goods and services concerned by the refusal separately.

As a starting point, it noted that according to the third and fifth recitals in its preamble, the Directive is not intended to bring about full-scale approximation of the trade mark laws of the Member States, giving them extensive freedom to fix the procedural rules governing the registration of trade marks.[741]

Moreover, it recalled that according to settled case law, in the absence of specific Community legislation governing a particular matter, it is for the domestic legal system of each Member State to lay down the detailed procedural rules governing court actions for safeguarding rights derived from Community law; however, such rules must not be less favourable than those governing domestic actions (principle of equivalence) and must not render excessively difficult or impossible the exercise of the relevant rights (principle of effectiveness).[742]

Applying those principles to the case, the Court held that national legislation such as the one at issue in the main proceedings, which prevents a court from ruling on the distinctive character of the mark separately for each of the designated goods, cannot be regarded as being contrary to the principle of effectiveness, especially since the interested party could always make a fresh application for registration in case of a partial or total refusal of its mark. It clarified, however, that it is for the referring court to determine whether the principles of equivalence and effectiveness had been observed in the present case.[743]

4–456　**(iii) Time considerations.** Finally, with regard to the question whether the Directive precluded national legislation from providing that the reviewing court could not take into account facts and circumstances subsequent to the refusal, it observed that the national court's duty to have regard to all the relevant factors was subject to the limits imposed on its jurisdiction by the national legislation[744] and that, at all events, the lawfulness of the decision under review depended on the facts and circumstances available at the time of its adoption.[745]

Accordingly, the Court concluded that a national legal order may prevent the court reviewing a decision from taking account of facts and circumstances subsequent to its adoption when exercising the control of its legality.[746]

---

[741] *BVBA*, paras 43–44.
[742] Citing *Clean Car Autoservice* (C-472/99) [2001] E.C.R. I-9687, para.28.
[743] *BVBA*, para.46.
[744] Citing *Postkantoor*, para.36.
[745] *BVBA*, para.60.
[746] *BVBA*, para.61.

7. ARTICLE 3(1)(c)—DESCRIPTIVE SIGNS OR INDICATIONS

(iv) The situation as regards Community Trade Marks. A similar situation arises when Community Trade Mark applications are restricted while the case is pending before the Courts, that is, after the administrative phase of the proceedings has been concluded. OHIM generally considers restrictions filed at that stage to be admissible, given that art.44 CTMR (new art.43) enables the owner to withdraw or restrict the application "at any time", provided of course that the limitation complies with the requirements laid down by the Court in *Postkantoor*.[747]

4–457

On the other hand, the Court does not pronounce itself as to the acceptability of the request, considering it to be an administrative act over which it has no real competence. Rather, it asks OHIM to confirm its prior acceptance before considering the potential impact of such limitations on the proceedings that are under way.

Once the Office confirms its acceptance, two situations may be envisaged: if the restriction is effected by merely deleting specific goods or services from the specification, the Court is inclined to take it into account, considering it to be a partial withdrawal of the application that ultimately has a restrictive effect on the subject-matter of its own proceedings. Conversely, if the limitation is done by adding one or more qualifying clauses to the specification that change the attributes of the goods as well as reducing their number, the Court tends to disregard the restriction, on the assumption that it unduly changes the subject matter of the dispute, forcing it thus to address facts not examined by the contested decision.[748]

However, the practical implications of the Court's refusal to consider the second type of restriction for the purposes of its proceedings ultimately depend on its final decision: if the outcome of the Court case is that the application proceeds, it will be registered as restricted; if, on the other hand, the Court upholds a decision of the Boards rejecting the application, the effects of that rejection go back to the date of filing, as follows from arts 43 (5), 45, 46 and 54 (2) CTMR (new arts 42, 45, 46 and 55).

4–458

Hence, in the latter case the effects of the limitation are in fact overtaken by the retroactivity of the rejection, which means that if the restriction was made by the applicant with a view to reaching an amicable settlement with a third party challenging the application in inter partes proceedings, that party will have to withdraw its opposition or cancellation action before the Court's judgment is handed down, so that the settlement of the parties can take effect and the application is registered as restricted.

---

[747] See *Koninklijke KPN Nederlands (POSTKANTOOR)* (C-363/99) [2004] E.C.R. I-1619, para.117, where the ECJ held that it is not acceptable to add to the specification a condition that the goods or services concerned "do not possess a certain characteristic".

[748] *Ampafrance SA/OHIM, (MONBEBE/BEBE)* (T-164/03) [2005] E.C.R. II-1401, paras 20–22' *Anheuser-Busch, Inc/OHIM, (BUDWEISER/BUDWEISER BUDVAR)* (T-363/05) [2006] E.C.R. II 4255, paras 40–48; *Tegometall International AG/OHIM (TEK)* (T-458/05).

4–459 **(8) Matratzen—article 3(1)(c) and free movement of goods considerations**

In *Matratzen*[749] the Court dealt with the potential anti-competitive effect of the exercise of trade mark rights in Europe. A Spanish court—the Audiencia Provincial de Barcelona—enquired under what conditions a trade mark can be registered in a Member State if it is not distinctive in the language of another Member State but merely denotes or describes the specified product. The case involved registration in Spain of a trade mark incorporating the German word MATRATZEN (translated as mattress in English). Enforcement of the trade mark registration could become a barrier to importation of mattresses from Member States using the German word to describe the product and a disguised restriction on trade between Member States contrary to arts 28 and 30.

4–460 *(a) The Opinion of the Advocate General*

Advocate General Jacobs noted that national authorities were applying national trade mark laws and considering registrability according to the meaning of the word in their own jurisdiction. That, however:

> "does not necessarily mean... that... [they] must never take into account the meaning of a proposed word mark derived from a language which is not the language of the Member State where registration is sought. Since that authority is required to carry out its assessment on the basis of the perception of average consumers of and traders in the product concerned in that Member State, it must also consider whether the word in question is in fact understood by those persons".[750]

He reminded the Court that examination must be stringent and full and ensure that the public interest behind art.3(1)(c)—namely that signs within the scope of the scope of the provision remain freely available for all—is served. He stressed that it is enough that a sign "may serve, in trade" to denote or describe the goods in question for art.3(1)(c) to be applied suggesting that if the sign is understood by a significant number of traders in and consumers of the relevant product in a Member State—rather than the average consumer of that Member State—to be descriptive then registration should be precluded even if the sign was in a language other than that of the Member State concerned.

The Advocate General appeared on the one hand to focus more on the relevant trader and consumer, thus narrowing the circle of the relevant public, but on the other to expand the perimeter so as to cover traders

---
[749] *Matratzen Concord AG v Hukla Germany SA* (C-421/04) [2006] E.C.R. I-2303.
[750] *Matratzen*, para.47.

7. ARTICLE 3(1)(c)—DESCRIPTIVE SIGNS OR INDICATIONS

and consumers irrespective of their language. This, he considered to be a better yardstick that has already been adopted by some national authorities.

Revisiting a familiar theme[751] he concluded that national courts must ensure both that art.5(1) is not abused and that art.6(1)(b) is properly invoked. Registration does not result in an unlimited right. The owner of MATRATZEN in Spain would not be entitled to prevent its use either outside art.5(1) or within art.6(1)(b).

(b) The judgment of the Court 4–461

In order to respond to the question in a useful way the Court noted that it would have to consider provisions of Community law that the referring court had not mentioned in its reference.[752]

It then added that "in a field which has been exhaustively harmonised at Community level, a national measure must be assessed in the light of the provisions of that harmonising measure and not of those of primary law".[753] The Court would focus on art.3 of the Directive rather than arts 28 EC and 30 EC.

Article 3 did not include:

"any ground ... specifically aimed at trade marks constituted by a term borrowed from the language of a Member State other than the State of registration in which it is devoid of distinctive character or descriptive of the goods or services in respect of which registration is sought".[754]

The Court codified its earlier judgments on distinctiveness in the following way: 4–462

"In fact, to assess whether a national trade mark is devoid of distinctive character or is descriptive of the goods or services in respect of which its registration is sought, it is necessary to take into account the perception of the relevant parties, that is to say in trade and or amongst average consumers of the said goods or services, reasonably well-informed and reasonably observant and circumspect, in the territory in respect of which registration is applied for."[755]

---

[751] See also *Procter & Gamble Co* (C-383/99 P) [2001] E.C.R. I-6251.
[752] Citing *Amministrazione delle Finanze dello Stato v Schiavon* (C-230/98) [2000] E.C.R. I-3547; and *Ravil Sarl v Bellon Import Srl and Biraghi SpA* (C-469/00) [2003] E.C.R. I-5053.
[753] *Matratzen*, para.20, citing, amongst others, *Swedish Match AB v Secretary of State For Health* (C-210/03) [2004] E.C.R. I-11893.
[754] *Matratzen*, para.22.
[755] *Matratzen*, para.24, citing *Windsurfing Chiemsee Produktions- und Vertriebs GmbH* (C-108/97 & C-109/97) [1999] E.C.R. I-2779; *Koninklijke KPN Nederland NV* (C-363/99) [2004] E.C.R. I-1619; and *Henkel KGaA* (C-218/01) [2004] E.C.R. I-1725.

And added that because of linguistic, cultural, social and economic differences a trade mark which is devoid of distinctive character or descriptive in one Member State may not be so in another Member State.[756]

The critical issue was whether the relevant parties in the Member State where registration is sought are capable of identifying the meaning of the term, irrespective of its language. Indeed this was in accordance with arts 28 EC and 30 EC.[757]

4–463 The Court had already decided in *Matratzen I*[758] that the principle of the free movement of goods did not prohibit a registration as a national trade mark in one Member State of a sign that is descriptive of the specified goods or devoid of distinctive character in the language of another Member State.

The Court also endorsed the remark of the Advocate General that registration of a sign as a trade mark did not prohibit all other uses of the same sign.[759]

The Court concluded that art.3(1)(b) and (c) "does not preclude the registration in a Member State, as a national trade mark, of a term borrowed from the language of another Member State in which it is devoid of distinctive character or descriptive of the goods or services in respect of which registration is sought, unless the relevant parties in the Member State in which registration is sought are capable of identifying the meaning of the term".[760]

4–464 **(9) Celltech—burden of proof: technical and scientific terms**

In *Celltech*[761] the Court dealt with the evidential standard to be observed by trade mark authorities when determining the descriptiveness of a trade mark. As in the case of lack of distinctiveness, the question whether the sign applied for is descriptive should be assessed by reference to the relevant consumer profile, as defined by the goods concerned and their specific characteristics.

---

[756] Citing by way of analogy an earlier, surprisingly pre-harmonisation, case on misleading trade marks, *Fratelli Graffione SNC v Ditta Fransa* (C-313/94) [1996] E.C.R. I-6039.

[757] Note that the Court in its short review of arts 28 and 30 EC in para.28, made once again clear that the existence/exercise dichotomy has not been abandoned. Citing *Terrapin (Overseas) Ltd v Terranova Industrie CA Kapferer and Co* (119/75) [1976] E.C.R. 1039; and *Dansk Supermarked A/S v A/S Imerco* (58/80) [1981] E.C.R. 181; and the order in *Matratzen Concord GmbH v Office for Harmonisation in the Internal Market (Trade Marks and Designs)* (C-3/03 P) [2004] E.C.R. I-3657 it repeated that the principle of the principle of the free movement of goods, the Treaty does not affect the existence of rights recognised by the legislation of a Member State in matters of intellectual property, but only restricts, depending on the circumstances, their exercise.

[758] *Matratzen Concord GmbH* (C-3/03 P) [2004] E.C.R. I-3657, see para.5-056, below.

[759] Contrast with *Koninklijke KPN Nederland NV v Benelux-Merkenbureau* (C-363/99) [2004] E.C.R. I-1619.

[760] *Matratzen*, para.32.

[761] Cite *OHIM/Celltech R&D Ltd (CELLTECH)* (C-273/05 P).

7. ARTICLE 3(1)(c)—DESCRIPTIVE SIGNS OR INDICATIONS

The case concerned an appeal brought by the Office against the Judgment of the Court of First Instance annulling the decision of its Board of Appeal, which had refused registration of the word mark "CELLTECH" in respect of, essentially, pharmaceutical preparations, medical instruments and biological research, in Classes 5, 10 and 42 of the Nice Classification.

The Board of Appeal held that the term at issue would be immediately and unambiguously understood by the public as designating activities in the field of "cell technology", as well as products, apparatus and equipment used in connection with, or resulting from, those activities.

Hence, it concluded that the connection between the goods and services for which protection is sought and the trade mark applied for, is not sufficiently indirect to endow the mark with the minimum level of inherent distinctiveness required under art.7(1)(b) CTMR.

(a) The judgment of the Court of First Instance 4–465

Although the Court of First Instance[762] recognised that at least one of the possible meanings of the term "CELLTECH" is indeed "cell technology", it observed that neither the examiner nor the Board "had given an explanation of the meaning, in scientific terms, of cell technology", other than producing a dictionary extract showing the definitions of the terms "cell" and "tech", failing thus to explain "in what way those terms give information about the intended purpose and nature of the goods and services and in particular about the way in which they may be applied to cell technology, or result from it".

Referring to its judgments in *Eurohealth*[763] and *Carcard*,[764] the Court further held that the fact that, in view of their medical nature, the goods and services at issue related to bodies composed of cells, did not relieve the Board from the obligation to show that the relevant public would make a "definite and direct association between the goods and services claimed and the meaning of the expression".

Furthermore, even supposing that the goods and services may be used for functional purposes involving cell technology, that fact is not sufficient for a finding that the word "CELLTECH" may serve to designate their intended purpose, since such use constitutes at most one of many possible areas of application, without however revealing their exact technical function.

(b) Findings of the Court 4–466

In the first place, the Court observed, that the Court of First Instance did not annul the contested decision for failure to state reasons, but rather on

---

[762] *Celltech/OHIM (CELLTECH)* (T-260/03) [2005] E.C.R. II-1215.
[763] *DKV/OHIM (EuroHealth)* (T-359/99) [2001] E.C.R. II-1645, para.35.
[764] *DaimlerChrysler/OHIM (CARCARD)* (T-356/00) [2002] E.C.R. II-1963, para.40.

the ground that the Board "had not established that the mark CELLTECH, understood as meaning 'cell technology', was descriptive of the goods and services referred to in the application for registration".[765]

Then, it laid down the framework for its analysis by recalling that, under art.74(1) CTMR (new art.76), the Office is required, when determining whether the sign applied for falls under one of the grounds for refusal provided for in art.7 of the Regulation, to examine the facts of its own motion. That means not only that OHIM may be led to base its decisions on facts which have not been alleged by the applicant, but also that it must establish in its decisions the accuracy of the facts relied on, unless where those facts are well known.[766]

Applying those principles to the case, the Court observed that, by stating that the expression "CELLTECH" will be perceived as designating activities in the field of cell technology, as well as products used in connection with such activities, the Board of Appeal implicitly held, first, that cell technology is a well-known scientific fact and, secondly, that the activities forming part of that method or include the production or manufacture of the designated goods and services.

4–467 It noted, however, that in deciding that the nature of cell technology is not a well-known fact and that it was therefore for the Board of Appeal to establish the correctness of its findings in that regard, the Court of First Instance made a finding of fact which is not subject to review by the Court of Justice on appeal.

Accordingly, the Court concluded that, by not furnishing any evidence that cell technology has the scientific meaning attributed to it, the Board of Appeal did not establish the correctness of the findings on the basis of which it held that the mark "CELLTECH" is descriptive, noting also that the Board "made no attempt to establish the soundness of those findings, for example by referring to scientific literature".[767]

The judgment in *Celltech* thus refined the scope of the evidential rules laid down in *Storck II*, by clarifying that if the case relates to specialised terms, as is for example the case with scientific and technical terminology, the relevant facts cannot qualify as being well-known, within the meaning of the Court's interpretation of art.74(1) CTMR (new art.76).

It follows, that in such cases OHIM bears the procedural burden to provide concrete explanations not only as to the meaning of the relevant expressions, but also as to their specific relationship to the goods and services at issue, if need be by reference to scientific or other specialised literature.

---

[765] *Celltech*, para.37.
[766] Citing *Storck II* (C-25/05 P) [2006] E.C.R. I-5719 paras 50–51.
[767] *Celltech*, para.43.

7. ARTICLE 3(1)(c)—DESCRIPTIVE SIGNS OR INDICATIONS

(10)   Develey—burden of proof: consumer goods   4–468

The judgment in *Develey*[768] came to complement the evidential principles developed in *Celltech*, by clarifying which facts may be regarded as well-known in the context of establishing if a given term is either descriptive or devoid of distinctiveness.

The case concerned the registration of a three-dimensional sign in the form of a plastic bottle in respect of various foodstuffs and drinks in Classes 29, 30 and 32 of the Nice Classification, including in particular seasonings, sauces and creams. OHIM rejected the application on the grounds that the sign merely consisted of the representation of a commonplace ketchup dispenser and thus did not significantly depart from the usual shapes in the sector.

Develey appealed, pleading infringement of art.74(1) CTMR (new art.76) in that OHIM ought to have provided proof of the lack of distinctive character, when noting that the shape in question would be perceived as a common bottle and not as a badge of origin.

The Court of First Instance rejected the action, holding that where the   4–469
Board of Appeal finds that a trade mark applied for is devoid of distinctive character, it may base its analysis "on facts arising from practical experience generally acquired from the marketing of general consumer goods which are likely to be known by anyone and are in particular known by the consumers of those goods", stressing also that since the applicant claimed that the mark was distinctive despite the analysis of the Board, it was for him to provide specific and substantiated information showing that the mark was either intrinsically distinctive, or had acquired the requisite distinctiveness by use.[769]

On appeal, the Court of Justice upheld those findings, stating that the Court of First Instance had not erred in its application of the rules relating to the burden of proof by requiring the applicant to prove its claim that the mark was distinctive, when challenging conclusions of OHIM based on well-known facts.[770]

As regards the complaint that the reasoning of the Court of First Instance made no distinction between the different goods in the application, the Court considered sufficient to that end the observation that the goods at issue are products for everyday consumption and that consumers primarily perceive the bottles in which such goods are contained as a means of packaging. In addition, it held that, since those goods fell within only three classes of the Nice Agreement, there was no need for a more extensive reasoning.[771]

---

[768] *Develey Holding GmbH & Co Beteiligungs KG/OHIM (PLASTIC BOTTLE)* (C-238/06 P).
[769] *Develey Holding GmbH Beteiligungs KG/OHIM (Plastic Bottle)* (T-129/04), para.26.
[770] *Develey*, paras 48–50.
[771] *Develey*, para.91, citing the judgment in *BVBA Management, Training en Consultancy/ Benelux-Merkenbureau (THE KITCHEN COMPANY)* (C-239/05) [2007] E.C.R. I-1455.

4–470 *Develey* and *Celltech* thus suggest that the question whether the facts relating to the distinctive character of a sign are well-known or not mostly depends on the sector concerned: if the goods for which protection is sought are consumer goods targeting the general public, the relevant marketing practices should generally be considered to be known to everyone and, as such, are exempt from proof; if, however, the relevant setting is a more sophisticated one, it is the Office's task to provide specific indications as to the precise meaning of a scientific or technical term and as to its concrete link to the goods.

In any event, it is clear from that case-law that the task of elaborating of more detailed rules in that regard belongs to the Court of First Instance, which is alone competent for deciding whether or not a specific set of facts is to be considered as being well-known for the purposes of trade mark examination.

8. ARTICLE 3(1)(d)—SIGNS OR INDICATIONS THAT HAVE BECOME CUSTOMARY

4–471 **(1) Bravo—the link with the specification**

In *BRAVO*[772] the Court considered the registrability of a laudatory word from the perspective of art.3(1)(d) of the Directive. The case came before the Court as a reference from the German Bundespatentgericht and it concerned an application to register as a trade mark in Germany the word BRAVO for typewriters. The German Patent and Trade Mark Office rejected the application on the ground that BRAVO was a term of praise or an advertising slogan for the specified goods.

4–472 The case reached the Bundespatentgericht that referred to the Court of Justice the following question:

> "Is article 3(1)(d) ... to be interpreted restrictively, contrary to the wording thereof, as meaning that only signs or indications which directly describe goods and services for which registration has specifically been applied, or the essential characteristics or features thereof, are affected by the bar to registration? Or is the provision to be construed as meaning that, in addition to free signs and generic names, signs or indications which have become customary in the current language or in the bona fide and established practices of the trade in the relevant or a similar sector as advertising slogans, indications of quality or incitements to purchase etc., without directly describing the specific characteristics of the goods or

---

[772] *Merz & Krell GmbH & Co* (C-517/99) [2001] E.C.R. I-6959.

8. ARTICLE 3(1)(d)—SIGNS OR INDICATIONS

services for which registration has been applied, may likewise not be registered?"[773]

All the interveners in the case, the German and UK Governments and the Commission, supported that the application of the provision should be linked with the specification of the trade mark application. The Commission had also argued that the provision covered signs that were either generic or had a particular additional connotation.

(a) The Opinion of the Advocate General

(i) The legislative framework. Since this was one of the earliest cases referred to the Court following the adoption of the Directive and the Regulation A.G. Ruiz-Jarabo Colomer started with a thorough analysis of the legislative context starting by international context, the Paris Convention that formed the frame to which the laws of its signatories, but also the agreements and treaties entered into by them, had to adhere.[774]

4–473

From a European perspective he referred to the free movement of goods rules, the Directive, and the Regulation,[775] noting that trade marks were one of the exceptions to the free movement of goods principle, and the relevant provisions of the Directive and the Regulation.[776] The German Law on the Protection of Trade Marks and Other Identification Marks[777] had transposed the Directive in the German legal order.

---

[773] Reproduced in Point 4.
[774] He noted that the Paris Convention should probably be borne in mind when interpreting Community trade mark law. The Twelfth Recital of the Preamble to the Directive and other references to the Paris Convention in the Directive and the Regulation hinted that the Community legislature intended to conform to the Paris Convention framework. In this context, art.6quinquies (B)2 in particular provided that trade marks which "are devoid of any distinctive character, or consist exclusively of signs or indications which may serve, in trade, to designate the kind, quality, quantity, intended purpose, value, place of origin, of the goods, or the time of production, or have become customary in the current language or in the bona fide and established practices of the trade of the country where protection is claimed" could be refused registration or be invalidated.
[775] The Directive and the Regulation had a shared aim and should be seen as complementary. The Directive achieved the partial harmonisation of the areas of trade mark law that most directly affect the internal market. The Regulation created a Community regime for trade marks allowing undertakings to overcome the obstacles caused by the territoriality of national rights.
[776] Article 3(1)(d) of the Directive provided that "trade marks which consist exclusively of signs or indications which have become customary in the current language or in the bona fide and established practices of the trade" could be refused registration or be invalidated. The equivalent provision of the Regulation, art.7(1)(d), covered the same trade marks in identical language; however there was a variation in the German version of the provision that referred to "trade marks which consist exclusively of signs or indications to designate the goods or services which have become customary in the current language or in the bona fide and established practices of the trade".
[777] BGBl. 1994 I, p.3082; art.8(2) covered trade marks "which consist exclusively of signs or indications which have become customary in the current language or in the bona fide and established practices of the trade to designate the goods or services".

Regarding the function of trade marks and trade mark rights he cited *Hag II*.[778] Trade marks rights were an essential element in the system of undistorted competition envisaged in the Treaty; the justification of the exclusive right should be found in the function of trade marks as guarantees of origin. All trade mark provisions—including art.3(1)(d)—should be interpreted according to these objectives and principles:

> "Regard must therefore be had to two interpretation criteria when responding to the question referred in the present proceedings: the teleological criterion, which centres on the function of the trade mark, and the integration criterion which seeks to provide an integrated interpretation of the relevant rule".[779]

4–474   **(ii) The interpretation of article 3(1)(d).** Advocate General Ruiz-Jarabo Colomer started his analysis of the specific provision by highlighting the similarities of the Community provisions with art.6quinquies (B)(2) of the Paris Convention: "an almost literal transcription",[780] with the exception of the German version of art.7(1)(d). He reconciled this discrepancy by focusing on two things: first, on the overwhelmingly identical reading of the same provision in all the other languages[781]; and, secondly, on that the German wording of art.7(1)(d) of the Regulation was not relevant to the interpretation of art.3(1)(d) of the First Directive.

He saw the provision as part of a broader attempt to bar from registration trade marks that lack distinctiveness. "In more general terms, this body of legislation bars the way for the registration of signs which lack the potential to differentiate."[782] Article 3(1)(b) precluded signs which were devoid of any distinctive character, "followed by two specific examples of indications which are not capable of distinguishing goods or services, that is, those which are descriptive (sub-paragraph (c)) and those which are customary (sub-paragraph (d))".[783] The remaining grounds for refusal are based on reasons other than the lack of capacity to distinguish.

4–475   **(iii) A test for the application of article 3(1)(d).** The Advocate General identified two main factors that authorities and courts had to consider before applying art.3(1)(d). The first was the association between the sign and the specified good or services; the distinctive character of

---

[778] *SA CNL-SUCAL NV v Hag GF AG* (C-10/89) [1990] E.C.R. I-3711. Confirmed by the Court at that stage in *Bayerische Motorenwerke AG and BMW Nederland BV v Deenik* (C-63/97) [1999] E.C.R. I-905; and *Frits Loendersloot* (C-349/95) [1997] E.C.R. I-6227.
[779] Point 34 of the Opinion of A.G. Ruiz-Jarabo Colomer.
[780] Point 35 of the Opinion of A.G. Ruiz-Jarabo Colomer.
[781] Citing *Bestuur des Sociale Verzekeringsbank v Vander Vecht* (19/97) [1967] E.C.R. 445; and Case *Stauder v City of Ulm* (29/69) [1969] E.C.R. 419.
[782] Point 37 of the Opinion of A.G. Ruiz-Jarabo Colomer.
[783] Point 39 of the Opinion of A.G. Ruiz-Jarabo Colomer.

8. ARTICLE 3(1)(d)—SIGNS OR INDICATIONS

the sign was the catalyst that brought together the sign and the goods or services. The type and strength of that link constituted the second factor.

The first factor—association and distinctive character. The first factor was **4–476** linked with the primary function of a trade mark, to distinguish, that according to the Advocate General was behind most of the main provisions of Community trade mark law:

> "the raison d'etre of the ground for refusal set out in Article 3(1)(d) ... is that the indications to which it refers do not meet the conditions for qualification as a trade mark laid down in Article 2, namely that they must be capable of distinguishing the goods or services of one undertaking from those of other undertakings".[784]

Article 3(3) that allowed applicants to overcome the barrier of sub-paras (b), (c), and (d) with evidence of acquired distinctive character supported further his interpretation.

Distinctive character was an imprecise legal concept for the Advocate General that could only be clarified in its particular context, in the light of the circumstances and of the particular nature of each individual case.

Returning to the essential function of a trade mark and the judgment of **4–477** the Court in *Hag II*[785] he observed that the exclusive right to use the mark was not the final aim of trade mark law but a step towards allowing consumers to choose according to origin and undertakings to retain their customers by virtue of the quality of their offerings. This remark, that appears to be a step back to his earlier broader discussion on trade marks, allowed the Advocate General to introduce to his test the link with the actual goods or services. Trade mark rights facilitated "the establishment of a bona fide, undistorted system of competition, from which those who seek to gain advantage or to profit from the reputation of others are excluded".[786]

The next point referred to the viewpoint from which capacity to distinguish should be assessed. Citing *Sabel*[787] he chose that of the average consumer of the type of goods or services in question, stressing once again that the specified goods or services should not be overlooked.

In respect of the Directive he concluded that:

> "Article 3(1)(d) ... requires that, for registration of a trade mark to be refused, or, where appropriate, for an existing registration to be declared

---

[784] Point 40 of the Opinion of A.G. Ruiz-Jarabo Colomer.
[785] *SA CNL-SUCAL NV v Hag GF AG* (C-10/89) [1990] E.C.R. I-3711.
[786] Point 42. This was reinforced by the scope and limitations of trade mark rights; they extended as far as necessary for the essential function to be fulfilled. For example the exclusive right to use could only be applied against use that would lead to confusion.
[787] *Sabel BV v Puma AG, Rudolf Dassler Sport* (C-251/95) [1997] E.C.R. I-6191.

invalid, the signs or indications of which it consists must have become customary in the current language or in the bona fide and established practices of the trade relevant to the goods or services which the mark is intended to identify."[788]

4–478 *The second factor—the type and strength of the association.* The second factor considered the heart of the provision. Advocate General Ruiz-Jarabo Colomer started by identifying the meaning of the word "describe". Taking into account its meaning in a number of Community languages he stated that "by describing something, one seeks to define it not by its essential predicates but by providing a general idea of its parts or properties".[789]

On the basis of this definition purely descriptive signs were excluded by art.3(1)(c). Accordingly, art.3(1)(d) did not require the sign or indication to be directly descriptive of the specified goods or services:

> "It merely requires them to be customary in the current language or in the practices of the trade relevant to the goods or services which they are intended to identify, without specifying the degree of association that must exist between them."[790]

The examples provided by the Advocate General linked the provision with the essential function of trade marks and the scope and limitations of trade mark rights. It covered:

> "free signs, generic names and, in general, all graphic representations (whether or not they contain phonemes) which, one way or another, have come to represent in the perception of the public the goods or services to which they refer and which, consequently, may not be appropriated for anyone's exclusive use".[791]

Based on the meaning of a term the Commission had referred to in its submissions—"connotation"—he concluded that the sign had to be "automatically—subconsciously even"[792]—associated with the goods or services it identified.

4–479 **(iv) Registrability of Bravo.** In principle, the contested sign, that in most Community languages functioned as an exclamation, should not be

---

[788] Point 46 of the Opinion of A.G. Ruiz-Jarabo Colomer.
[789] Point 48 of the Opinion of A.G. Ruiz-Jarabo Colomer.
[790] Point 50 of the Opinion of A.G. Ruiz-Jarabo Colomer.
[791] Point 51 of the Opinion of A.G. Ruiz-Jarabo Colomer.
[792] Point 52 of the Opinion of A.G. Ruiz-Jarabo Colomer.

8. ARTICLE 3(1)(d)—SIGNS OR INDICATIONS

excluded from trade mark protection for typewriters on the basis of art.3(1)(d).[793] Registration would be problematic for goods or services in the field of sports where the exclamation was used habitually used.

(b) The judgment of the Court

(i) The legislative framework. The Court chose a narrower legal contextualisation referring exclusively to the Directive and the national trade mark law. Regarding the language of art.3(1)(d) the Court noted that only the Danish and Swedish versions of the provision contained a reference to signs and indications which have become customary in the current language or in the bona fide and established practices of the trade for the goods or services. 4–480

It divided the referred question into two parts. The first part explored the link between the sign and its specification; the second considered the types of signs that should be excluded.

(ii) The link with the specification. The Court repeated the analysis of the Advocate General regarding the essential function of trade marks and the aim of trade mark rights.[794] 4–481

It accepted that art.3(1)(d) did not contain the qualification found in para.8(2)(3) of the Markengesetz. However this did not mean that the connection between the sign and the goods or services should be disregarded.

To the contrary the:

"question whether particular signs or indications possess distinctive character cannot, however, be considered in the abstract and separately from the goods or services those signs or indications are intended to distinguish".[795]

Article 3(1)(d) should be interpreted as:

"only precluding registration of a trade mark where the signs or indications of which the mark is exclusively composed have become customary in the current language or in the bona fide and established practices of

---

[793] He noted that the Office had already accepted BRAVO as a registered trade mark for diesel engines (Application number 000463919, date of registration: September 7, 1999).

[794] Citing *Frits Loendersloot* (C-349/95) [1997] E.C.R. I-6227; and *Canon Kabushiki Kaisha* (C-39/97) [1998] E.C.R. I-5507 from its more recent jurisprudence and the Tenth Recital in the Preamble to the Directive.

[795] *Bravo*, para.29. In *Windsurfing Chiemsee Produktions- und Vertriebs GmbH* (C-108/97 & C-109/97) [1999] E.C.R. I-2779 the Court had already decided that a sign's capacity to distinguish could only be assessed by reference to the goods or services it was meant to distinguish.

the trade to designate the goods or services in respect of which registration of that mark is sought".[796]

4-482 **(iii) The types of signs covered by article 3(1)(d).** The second part of the question targeted the types of signs excluded by the provision, in particular whether it covered only signs or indications describing the properties or characteristics of the specified goods or services or it extended to signs or indications that function as advertising slogans, indications of quality or incentives to purchase that did not necessarily function in the same descriptive way as above.

The Court acknowledged that there was clear overlap between the scope of arts 3(1)(c) and 3(1)(d) of the Directive. So, accepting the stricter interpretation would essentially render art.3(1)(d) ineffective. Marks:

> "covered by article 3(1)(d) are excluded from registration not on the basis that they are descriptive, but on the basis of current usage in trade sectors covering trade in the goods or services for which the marks are sought to be registered".[797]

The sole condition was that indicated by the language of the provision: the sign or indication had to become customary in the current language or in the bona fide and established practices of the trade to designate the goods or services in respect of which registration of that mark is sought. It was immaterial whether they described the properties or characteristics of those goods or services.

The Court added that the exact nature of the contested signs or indications—for example were they advertising slogans or indications of quality—would be inconsequential once it was established that they fell within the scope of the provision. But this should not be seen as a blanket prohibition from registration of signs or indications that were also used as advertising slogans, indications of quality or incitements to purchase the goods or services covered by that mark. National courts had to determine whether the contested signs or indications have become customary in the current language or in the bona fide and established practices of the trade to designate the specified goods or services.

4-483 **(2) Alcon—article 7(1)(d) and acronyms**

In *Alcon*[798] the Court considered the application of art.7(1)(d) of the Regulation in relation to an acronym. Another contested issue in this case was the application of art.7(3).

---

[796] *Bravo*, para.31.
[797] *Bravo*, para.35.
[798] *Alcon* (C-192/03 P) [2007] E.C.R. I-8993.

8. ARTICLE 3(1)(d)—SIGNS OR INDICATIONS

The case was an appeal against a judgment of the Court of First Instance dismissing an action against a decision of the Board of Appeal[799] on the invalidation of a Community Trade Mark registration. Indeed, this was the first invalidity case that reached the Court of Justice.

Alcon had registered the term BSS as a Community Trade Mark for "ophthalmic pharmaceutical preparations; sterile solutions for ophthalmic surgery" in Class 5. Dr Robert Winzer Pharma GmbH (Winzer) challenged the registration under art.51(1)[800] of the Regulation. It claimed that the term was an abbreviation for "balanced salt solution" or "buffered saline solution" and that the registration should be invalidated as descriptive. The Cancellation Division of the Office invalidated the registration on the basis of art.7(1)(d); it also found that the mark had not acquired distinctive character according to art.7(3) and art.51(2) of the Regulation. Alcon appealed, but the Board of Appeal confirmed the decision of the Cancellation Division, finding that both in English and German the acronym was used to describe an ophthalmic solution.

(a) The judgment of the Court of First Instance

(i) The application of article 7(1)(d). The Court of First Instance, 4–484 following the principles set by the Court of Justice in *Merz & Krell*,[801] reviewed the examination of the evidence by the Board and held that it was right to decide that the term had become customary.

First, it identified the target public by reference to the specified goods:

"In view of the intended use of the goods covered by the mark in question, the targeted public comprises medical specialists, particularly ophthalmologists and ophthalmic surgeons. Moreover, given that doctors and pharmacists in the European Union are familiar with scientific terms in English, which is the technical language in this area, the relevant public must be considered to be made up of ophthalmologists and ophthalmic surgeons throughout the whole of the European Union."[802]

---

[799] *Alcon Inc v Office For Harmonisation in the Internal Market (Trade Marks and Designs)— Dr Robert Winzer Pharma (BSS)* (T-237/01) [2003] E.C.R. II-411 dismissing an action against the decision of the First Board of Appeal of the Office for Harmonisation in the Internal Market (Trade Marks and Designs) (Case R-273/2000-1).
[800] Providing that a Community trade mark shall be declared invalid on application to the Office or on the basis of a counterclaim in infringement proceedings (a) where the Community trade mark has been registered contrary to the provisions of art.7 and (b) where the applicant was acting in bad faith when he filed the application for the trade mark.
[801] *Merz & Krell GmbH & Co* (C-517/99) [2001] E.C.R. I-6959.
[802] *Alcon*, para.42.

For that group the term clearly fell within the scope of art.7(1)(d).

> "The evidence submitted by the intervener [Winzer] before the Office as to the customary character of the acronym BSS among ophthalmologic specialists indicates that BSS has become the current generic term for a balanced salt solution. The Court [of First Instance] finds that the chemical, medical and pharmaceutical dictionaries and the scientific articles produced by the intervener demonstrate that the term BSS is regarded by the relevant scientific community as a generic term."[803]

It concluded that by the date of filing of the application for registration of the mark, BSS had become a current generic term.

4–485 **(ii) The application of article 7(3).** The Court of First Instance also concurred with the Board that BSS had not acquired distinctive character as a result of use.

Alcon had relied on a number of documents to establish acquired distinctive character before the Office, including a plan for protecting BSS, titled the Policing BSS schedule, agreements with third parties concerning use of the sign, national trade mark registration certificates of marks containing the letters BSS, and brochures of ALCON BSS and BSS PLUS products, as well as information on turnover and advertising expenditure.

The Court of First Instance had found that this information failed to establish distinctiveness, noting in particular that "the applicant has not advanced any argument in the application on the probative value of those documents".[804]

4–486 In relation to the brochures the Court of First Instance noted that they "might at most indicate that it itself considers that the BSS mark has not acquired a sufficient degree of distinctiveness to be used without any additional element to identify the product".[805]

The appeal claims targeted the relevance of the evidence submitted by Winzer, based on its timing. It claimed that they were produced subsequent to the application filing date and they were not linked with persons that were trading in the relevant goods. The inclusion of the term in dictionaries and publications on its own was not sufficient it argued.

Regarding its own evidence Alcon supported that the Court of First Instance had not taken account of the arguments related to its policy for protecting the BSS mark.

In addition it submitted that the Court of First Instance had failed to fully take into account its own evidence, in contrast with the evidence submitted by Winzer.

---

[803] *Alcon*, para.43.
[804] *Alcon*, para.58.
[805] *Alcon*, para.59.

8. ARTICLE 3(1)(d)—SIGNS OR INDICATIONS

(b) The Order of the Court   4-487

The Court found the appeal to be unfounded and issued a reasoned Order.

The Order can be divided into two parts; the first deals with the legal context of art.7(1)(d). The second covers the broader issue of evidence, in relation both to art.7(1)(d) and art.7(3).

(i) The interpretation and application of article 7(1)(d). The 4-488 Court was satisfied that the Court of First Instance had followed *Merz & Krell*.[806]

First, it had focused on whether the term had become customary rather than descriptive.

Secondly, it had also examined the possibility that the mark might have had acquired distinctive character through use.

The Court stressed that the decisive criterion was not the descriptive 4-489 nature of the mark but its current usage in the relevant sectors.

And, thirdly, the Court of First Instance had correctly adopted the viewpoint of the target public to determine whether the term was customary.

According to the Court those three points constituted the legal context of the case that the Court of First Instance had correctly determined.

It had then found and assessed the evidence within this legal context.

(ii) The findings of fact and the assessment of evidence. The 4-490 findings that Alcon had not produced the necessary evidence to support its claims were findings of fact within the jurisdiction of the Court of First Instance that could not be challenged on appeal.[807]

Similarly, challenging the assessment of the facts without alleging any distortion of the evidence remained outside the scope of an appeal process that covered only points of law.[808]

The Court also rejected a claim that the Court of First Instance had wrongly taken into consideration documents published in the Unites States of America that did not affect the target public. The Court accepted that evidence outside Europe could be relevant:

> "By stating ... that English was the technical language of specialists in the relevant field, and by referring ... to the perception of the term BSS as a generic term by the 'scientific community', the Court of First Instance

---

[806] *Merz & Krell GmbH & Co* (C-517/99) [2001] E.C.R. I-6959.
[807] Citing *Vidrányi v Commission* (C-283/90 P) [1991] E.C.R. I-4339; and *Tzoanos v Commission* (C-191/98 P) [1999] E.C.R. I-8223. Unless the Court of First Instance had distorted the clear sense of the the evidence, *Dorsch Consult v Council and Commission* (C-237/98 P) [2000] E.C.R. I-4549.
[808] Citing *DKV Deutsche Krankenversicherung AG* (C-104/00 P) [2002] E.C.R. I-7561 and the order in *Telefon & Buch* (C-326/01 P) [2004] E.C.R. I-1371.

necessarily considered that those documents, although published outside the European Union, supported the conclusion that the target public regarded that term as having become customary. In so doing it made an assessment of pure fact, which the appellant cannot challenge on appeal."[809]

Finally, Alcon despite its complaints regarding the assessment of its own evidence compared with that of Winzer's evidence had not supported that the Court of First Instance had misapplied the rules on the burden of proof.[810]

4–491   **(iii) The relevant dates for determining invalidity.** The Court noted that in terms of timing the Court of First Instance and the Board of Appeal had correctly and explicitly stated that the term had become customary at the time of Alco's application for registration. It agreed with the Office that the date of filing of the application was the material date for the examination of invalidity.

However, the Court of First Instance was entitled to take account of material subsequent to that date that enabled the drawing of conclusions on the situation as it was on that date.[811]

4–492   **(3)   Procordia—expanding the class of persons determining distinctiveness**

In *Procordia*[812] the Court delineated further the classes of persons whose perception would determine distinctiveness. The case came as a reference from the Swedish Svea Hovratt (Svea Court of Appeal) that had to consider whether the word mark "Bostongurka" had become a generic name for chopped pickled gherkins.

There were contradictory messages from surveys that focused on consumers and a survey targeting leading operators in the grocery, mass catering and food stall sectors. The consumer surveys indicated that the majority considered that the term could be used by any producer of chopped pickled gherkins. Half of the questioned market operators, however, understood the sign as a trade mark for the same product.

The Svea Hovratt referred the following question to the Court: "In cases where a product is handled at several stages before it reaches the consumer what is or are, under Article 12(2)(a) of the Trade Mark Directive, the relevant class or classes of persons for determining whether a trade mark has

---

[809] *Alcon*, para.42.
[810] Citing *Hüls v Commission* (C-199/92 P) [1999] E.C.R. I-4287.
[811] Citing the Order in *La Mer Technology Inc v Laboratoires Goemar SA* (C-259/02) [2004] E.C.R. I-1159.
[812] *Björnekulla Fruktindustrier AB v Procordia Food AB* (C-371/02) [2004] E.C.R. I-5791.

8. ARTICLE 3(1)(d)—SIGNS OR INDICATIONS

become the common name in the trade for a product in respect of which it is registered?"[813]

(a) The Opinion of the Advocate General   4–493

The language of the question reflected the position expressed in the preparatory works behind the Swedish law, A.G. Léger looked at the same question from a broader perspective and described the main issue raised by the Swedish court as to whether art.12(2)(a) of the Directive:

"should be interpreted as meaning that in order to assess whether a trade mark has become a common name in the trade for a product in respect of which the mark is registered, with the result that the trade mark may be revoked, account should be taken of the perception only of those in the trade who deal with the type of goods commercially, or whether the perception of consumers of that type of goods is also relevant."[814]

The fact that the product passed several stages before reaching the consumer only made the issue more relevant.

To answer the question the Advocate General according to the interpretive techniques of the Court suggested considering the wording of the Directive—in all its language versions—its general scheme and its objectives.[815]

The wording of the provision did not identify directly the relevant classes   4–494
of persons: "a trade mark shall . . . be liable to revocation if, after the date on which it was registered, in consequence of acts or inactivity of the proprietor, it has become the common name in the trade for a product or service in respect of which it is registered".

Procordia and the Swedish Government had highlighted the inclusion of the words "in the trade"[816] and contrasted art.12(2)(a) with arts 4(1)(b) and 5(1)(b) of the Directive where the effect "on the part of the public" was considered to be decisive. The Advocate General, however, believed that both expressions did not exclude the viewpoint of persons in the trade:

"Although, according to settled case law, the perception of marks in the mind of the average consumer of the type of goods or services in

---

[813] Reproduced in para.11.
[814] Point 26 of the Opinion of A.G. Léger.
[815] Citing *Milk Marketing Board of England and Wales v Cricket St Thomas Estate* (C-372/88) [1990] E.C.R. I-1345; and *Arbeitsgemeinschaft Deutscher Rundfunkanstalten (ARD) v PRO Sieben Media AG* (C-6/98) [1999] E.C.R. I-7599; as well as his Opinions in *The Queen v Ministry of Agriculture, Fisheries and Food, Ex p. Cooke* (C-372/88) [2000] E.C.R. I-8683; and *Land Baden-Wurttemberg v Schilling and Nehring* (C-63/00) [2002] E.C.R. I-4483 as earlier examples of a similar application of these established interpretive methods.
[816] Added in the amended proposal for the Directive of December 17, 1985, [1985] OJ C351/4. A.G. Léger found the travaux preparatoires unhelpful in explaining why the Commission chose this expression.

question plays a decisive role in the global appreciation of the likelihood of confusion within the meaning of Articles 4(1)(b) and 5(1)(b) of the Directive, it would be wrong to conclude from that that the role is exclusive, that is to say that the perspective of persons in the trade should be entirely excluded from consideration."[817]

4–495 **(i) The meanings of the "in the trade" concept.** He went on to compare the "in the trade" concept in different languages.[818]

Using lexicographic definitions he accepted that in English it appeared to refer to a specific class of persons, "namely persons in the trade who carry on business in a particular commercial or industrial activity, in a specific area or sector" and to exclude consumers.[819] The same applied to the Finnish version. This was not the case though in the other languages. In Italian and Greek the language of the equivalent provision covered all persons who would use the term in their commercial relations, traders and consumers alike. The remaining versions adopted a similar, but less explicit, perspective referring to the marketplace in general, a term that was considered to be inclusive covering both traders and consumers.

4–496 **(ii) The general scheme of the Directive.** This, however, was not enough for the Advocate General. In the absence of a unanimous linguistic position combined with the explanatory inadequacy of the travaux preparatoires he had to turn to the general scheme and the objectives of the Directive.[820]

The analysis of the general scheme was dominated by the essential function of a trade mark as an indication of origin. This is why distinctiveness— including distinctive character under art.3(1)(c) and (d)—was a condition for protection. Distinctiveness could be gained and lost through use. art.12(2)(a) had the converse effect of art.3(3). It applied:

> "where the use of a trade mark has become so widespread that the sign which constitutes the trade mark in question has come to designate the kind, the type or the nature of the goods or services covered by the registration rather than the specific goods or services originating from a particular undertaking".[821]

---

[817] Point 33, citing *Lloyd Schuhfabrik Meyer & Co GmbH* (C-342/97) [1999] E.C.R. I-3819; and *Sabel BV v Puma AG, Rudolf Dassler Sport* (C-251/95) [1997] E.C.R. I-6191.
[818] The Court had already ruled that the different language versions are all equally authentic and that a comparison between them was a valid interpretive tool in *Srl CILFIT and Lanificio di Gavardo SpA v Ministry of Health* (C-283/81) [1982] E.C.R. 3415; and *Bestuur der Sociale Verzekeringsbank v Van der Vecht* (19/67) [1967] E.C.R. 445.
[819] Point 36 of the Opinion of A.G. Léger.
[820] Citing *Bouchereau* (30/77) [1977] E.C.R. 1999; and *Netherlands v Commission* [1979] E.C.R. 245 in support of this interpretive route.
[821] Point 50 of the Opinion of A.G. Léger.

8. ARTICLE 3(1)(d)—SIGNS OR INDICATIONS

Surprisingly, "walkman" was one of the examples A.G. Léger employed; Sony would not be very happy. In such cases the trade mark was stripped from its indication of origin function and became liable to revocation in order to be freely used by all.[822]

All these provisions aimed to safeguard the distinctive character of a trade mark as an indication of origin and had to be interpreted in the same way[823] in particular since the ambiguous concepts were substantially similar. Here the wording and interpretation of art.3(1)(d) proved to be a catalyst. The provision referred to signs or indications that have become customary in the current language or in the bona fide and established practices of the trade.

4–497

In *Merz & Krell*[824] the Court held that registration of a trade mark was precluded where the signs or indications had become customary in the current language or in the bona fide and established practices of the trade to designate the specified goods or services. They had to form part of the language or the bona fide and established practices of the trade but also to become the common name for the goods or services to which they relate. For the Advocate General this expression clearly referred "globally both to the perception of the average consumer of the type of goods or services in question (that is to say to the perception of the reasonably well-informed and reasonably observant and circumspect consumer) and to that of persons in the trade who deal with those goods or services commercially".[825]

Discussing a point also developed by A.G. Ruiz-Jarabo Colomer in *Merz & Krell*[826] he suggested that art.3(1)(d) took into account persons in the trade in two capacities: setting the relevant context but also using the current language, in the manner of the average consumer.[827]

---

[822] Citing *Windsurfing Chiemsee Produktions–und Vertriebs GmbH* (C-108/97 & C-109/97) [1999] E.C.R. I-2779; *Linde AG* (C-53/01), *Winward Industries Inc* (C-54/01) and *Rado Uhren AG* (C-55/01) [2003] E.C.R. I-3161; and *Libertel Groep BV v Benelux-Merkenbureau* (C-104/01) [2003] E.C.R. I-3793.

[823] *Bristol-Myers Squibb v Paranova A/S* (C-427/93) and *CH Boehringer Sohn, Boehringer Ingelheim KG and Boehringer Ingelheim A/S v Paranova A/S* (C-429/93) and *Bayer Aktiengesellschaft and Bayer Danmark A/S v Paranova A/S* (C-436/93) [1996] E.C.R. I-3457 are an example of trade mark cases where the common aim of the relevant provisions played the same unifying role.

[824] *Merz & Krell GmbH & Co* (C-517/99) [2001] E.C.R. I-6959.

[825] Point 58 of the Opinion of A.G. Léger.

[826] Points 51 and 52; *Merz & Krell GmbH & Co* (C-517/99) [2001] E.C.R. I-6959.

[827] A.G. Léger, approvingly, mentioned OHIM's practice in the application of art.7(1)(d) of the Regulation. The Office conducted a global assessment from the perspective of the relevant classes of persons, but introduced variations according to the type of the relevant goods or services. For those with a widespread pattern of consumption particular attention is paid to the meaning of the word in the current language; for those targeting a specialist audience, the attention shifts to the meaning in the bona fide and established practices of the trade. "Bruschetta" (133C 000372920/1) was an example of the first approach; the word was found to be a common description of an Italian dish on the basis of dictionary and internet usage. In "BSS" (C0000901341/1-BSS) on the other hand the sign was found to be a generic indication for "balanced salt solution" in the medical and pharmaceutical fields. See para.4–483 above.

4–498 The same approach should be adopted for the interpretation of art.12(2)(a) of the Directive. It referred "implicitly but necessarily, both to the perspective of the average consumer of the type of goods or services concerned and to that of persons in the trade who deal with the type of goods or services in question commercially".[828]

In this case the product had a widespread pattern of consumption and involved several successive intermediaries; accordingly, the views of the average consumer as well as of persons in the trade who deal with the type of product in question had to be taken into account. The *Windsurfing Chiemsee* judgment[829] on art.3(1)(c) and art.3(3) supported this view.

Considering art.3(1)(c) the Court had indicated that:

"geographical names which are liable to be used by undertakings must remain available to such undertakings as indications of the geographical origin of the category of goods concerned".[830]

"The Court was accordingly making it clear that the descriptive character of a trade mark (at the time of its registration) must be assessed globally, taking into account the perspective of all relevant classes of persons, that is to say both that of the average consumer of the type of goods concerned and of persons in the trade who deal with the type of goods concerned commercially."[831]

4–499 Since the "in the trade" concept appeared in both art.3(1)(c) and art.12(2)(a), it should be given the same meaning in terms of logic but also for reasons of legal certainty.

Regarding art.3(3) the Court had stated in even more clearer terms that the competent authority must make an overall assessment, taking inter alia into account statements from chambers of commerce and industry or other trade and professional associations. A.G. Léger referred to the Opinion of A.G. Cosmas who had underlined that the relevant class of persons comprises consumers of the relevant product as well as traders and manufacturers of similar products.[832] "The same should apply for the purposes of assessing the generic character of a trade mark once it has been registered."[833]

From the opposite perspective, A.G. Léger viewed distinctive character at the time of the application and distinctive character at the time of revocation as essentially the same issue: two sides of the same coin. He accepted that

---

[828] Point 62 of the Opinion of A.G. Léger.
[829] *Windsurfing Chiemsee Produktions–und Vertriebs GmbH* (C-108/97 & C-109/97) [1999] E.C.R. I-2779.
[830] Point 66 of the Opinion of A.G. Léger.
[831] Point 67 of the Opinion of A.G. Léger.
[832] Point 72 of *Windsurfing Chiemsee Produktions–und Vertriebs GmbH* (C-108/97 & C-109/97) [1999] E.C.R. I-2779.
[833] Point 73 of the Opinion of A.G. Léger.

8. ARTICLE 3(1)(d)—SIGNS OR INDICATIONS

revocation could have material consequences for the trade mark proprietor, for example loss of advertising investment. This called for a global approach.

Assessing distinctive character only from the perspective of other traders would be against the objectives of the Directive to guarantee the identity of the marked products to the consumer and thus contribute towards an environment of undistorted competition in which undertakings can develop customer loyalty based on the quality of their products[834]: "that objective might be undermined if it were sufficient to prove that a trade mark had become generic only amongst the persons in the trade who deal with the type of goods or services in question commercially, for the trade mark to be revoked. To adopt such an approach would mean opening the door to certain practices that might distort competition within the market",[835] for example, the abusive use of revocation proceedings.[836]

4–500

Such an approach would also affect the indication of origin function of a trade mark:

"it would be to misconstrue this essential function of a trade mark to base the assessment of its generic character on the perspective only of persons in the trade who deal with the goods or services concerned commercially, to the exclusion of that of consumers or end users of that type of goods or services".[837]

(b) The judgment of the Court

4–501

The Court of Justice appeared to choose a somewhat narrow perspective relying on the language of the question and focusing on products where intermediaries participate in their distribution to the consumer or end user; however it also stressed that answering the question depended "principally"[838] on the meaning of the expression "in the trade".

Regarding interpretive methods it chose the same stance with the Advocate General; in interpreting national laws courts had to follow the wording and purpose of relevant directives rather the travaux preparatoires

---

[834] The discussion of the objectives of the Directive focused on the First, Third, and Tenth Recitals of the Preamble and a number of cases balancing competition with the exclusive nature of trade mark rights: *SA CNL-SUCAL NV v Hag GF AG* (C-10/89) [1990] E.C.R. I-3711; *Frits Loendersloot* (C-349/95) [1997] E.C.R. I-6227; *Bayerische Motorenwerke AG and BMW Nederland BV v Deenik* (C-63/97) [1999] E.C.R. I-905; *Merz & Krell GmbH & Co* (C-517/99) [2001] E.C.R. I-6959.
[835] Point 81 of the Opinion of A.G. Léger.
[836] Again, the A.G. cited the approach of A.G. Cosmas in *Windsurfing Chiemsee Produktions- und Vertriebs GmbH* (C-108/97 & C-109/97) [1999] E.C.R. I-2779, point 72.
[837] Point 87 of the Opinion of A.G. Léger.
[838] *Procordia*, para.14.

for the national rule.⁸³⁹ It added that the provision must be uniformly interpreted and applied in the light of the versions existing in all the Community languages.⁸⁴⁰

The Court concurred with the Advocate General that in the majority of the Community the provision was not restricted to those in trade and that this was also supported by the general scheme and the objectives of the Directive. It also found that the requirement of distinctiveness, linked with the essential function of a trade mark, was substantiated, amongst others, by arts 3 and 12.

4–502 However the delineation of the Court appeared to be narrower than that of the Advocate General:

> "If the function of the trade mark as an indication of origin is of primary importance to the consumer or end user, it is also relevant to intermediaries who deal with the product commercially. As with consumers or end users, it will tend to influence their conduct in the market."⁸⁴¹

The Court continued:

> "the relevant classes of persons comprise principally consumers and end users. However, depending on the features of the product market concerned, the influence of intermediaries on decisions to purchase, and thus their perception of the trade mark, must also be taken into consideration".⁸⁴²

And then the wording of the final answer appeared to leave the door open for a broader interpretation in the future. It started by narrowing the scope of the judgment to products the distribution of which involved intermediaries and ended by involving in the assessment of distinctive character all those in the trade who deal with the relevant product commercially, potentially including competitors:

> "The answer to the question referred must therefore be that Article 12(2)(a) of the Directive should be interpreted as meaning that in cases

---

⁸³⁹ Citing *Marleasing v La Comercial Internacional de Alimentacion* (C-106/89) [1990] E.C.R. I-4135; [1992] 1 C.M.L.R. 305; *Henkel KGaA v Deutches Patent- und Markenamt* (C-218/01) [2004] E.C.R. I-1725.

⁸⁴⁰ *Bestuur der Sociale Verzekeringsbank v Van der Vecht* (19/67) [1967] E.C.R. 445; and *Ferriere Nord v Commission* (C-215/95 P) [1997] E.C.R. I-4411. In essence the approach is identical with that of the A.G., although the Court appears to be more assertive linking the linguistic differences with the application—and not only the interpretation—of the provision.

⁸⁴¹ *Procordia*, para.23. The role of the intermediaries was to detect and anticipate the demand of the product but also to increase and direct it.

⁸⁴² *Procordia*, para.25.

where intermediaries participate in the distribution to the consumer or the end user of a product which is the subject of a registered trade mark, the relevant classes of persons whose views fall to be taken into account in determining whether that trade mark has become the common name in the trade for the product in question comprise all consumers and end users and, depending on the features of the market concerned, all those in the trade who deal with that product commercially."[843]

9. ARTICLE 3(1)(e)—FUNCTIONAL SHAPES

(1) Philips—the overriding scope of article 3(1)(e)   4–503

In *Philips*[844] the English Court of Appeal referred to the Court of Justice a list of seven questions, primarily in order to clarify art.3(1)(e), the "functionality" provision of the Directive, but also to obtain a framework for determining distinctiveness and the scope of protection.

The fourth question was on functionality. Is the existence of other shapes that can obtain the same technical result relevant when we consider whether the sign "consists exclusively of the shape of goods which is necessary to achieve a technical result" for the purposes of art.3(1)(e)(ii)? What is the appropriate test for determining when the restriction applies?

(a) *The Opinion of the Advocate General*   4–504

As we have already mentioned above the analysis of A.G. Ruiz-Jarabo Colomer was influenced by the finding of the national court that the contested trade mark was nothing more than "a combination of technical features produced to achieve a good practical design".[845] As a result, he focused on art.3(1)(e)(ii) that he considered to be primarily relevant to the outcome of the case because it could raise an obstacle that would have to be surmounted before even considering distinctiveness.

(i) The legal nature and scope of article 3(1)(e). Article 3(1)(e)   4–505
according to the Advocate General possessed a legal nature that was distinct from the other grounds under art.3(1). The exclusion was not linked with distinctiveness; instead it reflected "the legitimate concern to prevent individuals from resorting to trade marks in order to extend exclusive rights over technical developments".[846]

---

[843] *Procordia*, para.26.
[844] *Koninklijke Philips Electronics NV* (C-299/99) [2002] E.C.R. I-5475.
[845] Point 10, see paras 4–086 et seq., above.
[846] Point 16 of the Opinion of A.G. Ruiz-Jarabo Colomer.

This is why the art.3(3) route was not available:

> "Natural, functional or ornamental shapes are incapable, by express intention of the legislature, of acquiring a distinctive character. It is altogether otiose—as well as contrary to the scheme of the Directive—to consider whether or not such shapes have acquired distinctiveness".[847]

In terms of scope art.3(1)(e) was closer to art.3(1)(f) on signs that were contrary to public policy and art.3(1)(g) on deceptive. All these provisions were not affected by any findings regarding distinctiveness.

So he would consider first and in detail the fourth question submitted by the English court.

4–506 **(ii) The relevance of alternatives—trade marks, patents, and designs.** From a literal perspective there was nothing in art.3(1)(e) that could suggest that a "merely functional shape"[848] could be registered if there was an alternative, in terms of result, shape. "It suffices that the signs of which the trade mark consists should comprise exclusively features which are necessary in order to achieve a particular technical result."[849]

From a teleological interpretive perspective the Advocate General turned immediately to the concurring existence of trade mark rights with other intellectual property rights, in this case patent and design rights. The scope of the provision was to prevent trade mark rights from extending the effect of other rights that the legislator has chosen to protect for limited periods of time.

> "Were it not for the existence of subparagraph (e) of Article 3(1), it would be easy to overturn the balance of public interest which must exist between rewarding innovation fairly, by granting exclusive protection, and encouraging industrial development, which entails placing time-limits on such protection, with the purpose of making the goods or the design freely available once the time-limit expires."[850]

The Community legislation on patents and designs provided for limited protection in terms of time and the exclusion from design protection of designs solely dictated by technical function.

4–507 Further, a comparison between the functionality provisions of the Community regimes on designs and trade marks showed that the level of functionality had to be higher in the context of design rights where the existence of alternative designs would be taken into account. On the other hand:

---

[847] Point 17 of the Opinion of A.G. Ruiz-Jarabo Colomer.
[848] Point 28 of the Opinion of A.G. Ruiz-Jarabo Colomer.
[849] Point 28 of the Opinion of A.G. Ruiz-Jarabo Colomer.
[850] Point 31 of the Opinion of A.G. Ruiz-Jarabo Colomer.

9. ARTICLE 3(1)(e)—FUNCTIONAL SHAPES

"in so far as the essential features of a shape are necessary in order to fulfil a function, trade mark protection must not be granted without investigating whether that function could also be achieved by other features".[851]

This was attributed to the difference between designs and trade marks in terms of function and scope of protection. Design rights protect the product; trade marks protect the identity of the origin of the product.

Accepting that alternatives should be taken into account would raise a number of problems.

First, it would be possible for a single undertaking to register all the alternatives.

4–508

Secondly, trade mark courts would have to examine whether all the alternatives were equivalent.

Thirdly, there would be a risk—however slight—"that trade mark rights might unduly encroach on the field of patents" and he could not "see why the public interest should tolerate such a risk, since there are other effective ways available to owners of a product to protect their commercial asset, such as adding arbitrary features".[852] Note here that the Advocate General appeared to accept that an arbitrary feature would be required in order to obtain trade mark protection for the shape of a product.

Philips' attempt to take into account the legislative history of the provision failed. The Advocate General discarded the angle from which Philips was approaching the provision, focusing on the availability of alternative effective designs, but also noted that its arguments could not "supplement the higher considerations"[853] that supported his own arguments. The history of a provision could not become an influential interpretive tool. "It is for the judicature to supplement legislation in compliance with the legislative purpose."[854]

(b) The judgment of the Court

4–509

The Court's answer to the fourth question contributed the first building blocks towards a European theory of functionality.

(i) Article 3(1)(e)—the legal framework—a preliminary obstacle.

4–510

Contextualising the provision in its legal framework, the Court first noted that the grounds for refusal in art.3(1)(e) targeted a particular type of signs, those consisting of the shape of the specified product. According to the Seventh Recital in the Preamble to the Directive these grounds have been listed in an exhaustive manner.

---

[851] Point 35 of the Opinion of A.G. Ruiz-Jarabo Colomer.
[852] Point 40 of the Opinion of A.G. Ruiz-Jarabo Colomer.
[853] Point 41 of the Opinion of A.G. Ruiz-Jarabo Colomer.
[854] Point 41 of the Opinion of A.G. Ruiz-Jarabo Colomer.

A sign failing art.3(1)(e) would never acquire distinctive character according to art.3(3).

This meant that article 3(1)(e) was a preliminary obstacle concerning signs that were not "such as to constitute trade marks".[855]

4–511 **(ii) Article 3(1)(e)—the public interest.** The provision according to the Court had to be interpreted according to its underlying public interest: to prevent the monopolisation through trade mark law of technical solutions or functional characteristics that a user is likely to seek. It was intended to prevent trade mark protection from being extended beyond signs which served to distinguish a product or service from those offered by competitors:

> "so as to form an obstacle preventing competitors from freely offering for sale products incorporating such technical solutions or functional characteristics in competition with the proprietor of the trade mark".[856]

4–512 **(iii) The aim of article 3(1)(e)(ii).** The aim of art.3(1)(e)(ii) in particular was to:

> "preclude the registration of shapes whose essential characteristics perform a technical function, with the result that the exclusivity inherent in the trade mark right would limit the possibility of competitors supplying a product incorporating such a function or at least limit their freedom of choice in regard to the technical solution they wish to adopt in order to incorporate such a function in their product".[857]

4–513 **(iv) The relevance of alternatives.** To respond to Philips' claim that the existence of alternatives should be taken into account the Court looked at the wording of the provision and ruled that there was nothing there to support it:

> "Where the essential functional characteristics of the shape of a product are attributable solely to the technical result, article 3(1)(e), second indent, precludes registration of a sign consisting of that shape, even if that technical result can be achieved by other shapes."[858]

(2) Benetton—attractiveness v distinctiveness

4–514 *Benetton*[859] was the first case in which the Court dealt with "aesthetic" functionality, albeit in a very limited context. The question referred to it did not require a full-scale interpretation of art.3(1)(e)(iii) of the Directive,

---

[855] *Philips*, para.76.
[856] *Philips*, para.78.
[857] *Philips*, para.79.
[858] *Philips*, para.83.
[859] *Benetton Group SpA /G-Star International BV (BENETTON)* (C-371/06) [2007 E.C.R. I-7709.

9. ARTICLE 3(1)(e) — FUNCTIONAL SHAPES

concerning rather the fine distinction between the aesthetic value inherent in a product shape and the value possibly added to it through promotion and advertising as a "distinctive" design of a given undertaking.

(a) The facts in the main proceedings 4–515

The reference concerned a dispute in The Netherlands between G-Star International BV ("G-Star"), a designer and manufacturer of clothing (in particular jeans), who markets its products under the homonymous trade mark, and Benetton Group SpA ("Benetton") a company managing textile trading undertakings and selling its products through franchisees.

G-Star was the proprietor of two shape marks registered in the Benelux in respect of clothing in Class 25 of the Nice Classification. Those marks covered in particular the following distinctive elements of the product's appearance (the so called "Elwood" design):

— sloping stitching from hip height to the crotch seam, kneepads, yoke on the seat of the trousers, horizontal stitching at knee height at the rear, band of a contrasting colour or of another material at the bottom of the trousers at the rear, all on one garment;

— seams, stitching and cuts on the kneepad of the trousers, slightly baggy kneepad.

G-Star brought an action against Benetton before the Rechtbank te Amsterdam (Amsterdam District Court) in order to preclude the manufacture and distribution of in The Netherlands of a specific design of the latter's trousers. G-Star maintained that Benetton had infringed the trade mark rights attached to its Elwood design by manufacturing and putting on the market trousers with, inter alia, an oval kneepad and two lines of sloping stitching from hip height to crotch height.

Benetton responded by bringing a counterclaim, seeking the annulment 4–516 of G-Star's trade marks under Benelux Law, on the ground that the registered shapes "determined the market value of the goods to a great extent" as a result of their beauty and originality.

The first instance court dismissed both G-Star's claims and Benetton's counterclaim. Both parties lodged appeals before the Gerechtshof te Amsterdam (Amsterdam Regional Court of Appeal), which allowed G-Star's appeal and dismissed Benetton's application for annulment.

The Gerechtshof found that the Elwood trousers were a great commercial success mainly owing to G-Star's intensive advertising campaigns, which drew particular attention to the trousers' distinctive characteristics and kneepad design. Accordingly, it held that the reputation of the Elwood trousers was largely attributable not to the aesthetic qualities of the shape as such, but rather to the attractiveness resulting from the recognition of that shape as a trade mark.

4–517   Benetton lodged an appeal before the Hoge Raad der Nederlanden (Supreme Court of the Netherlands) challenging that analysis. The Hoge Raad took the view that the Court's finding in *Philips* that signs which cannot be registered under art.3(1)(e) of the Directive cannot acquire a distinctive character through the use did not cover the situation where, prior to the application for registration, the attractiveness of the shape was a consequence of its recognition as a trade mark.

Accordingly, it decided to stay the proceedings and refer the following questions to the Court of Justice:

> "(1) Must Article 3(1)(e), third indent, [of the Directive] be interpreted as meaning that the prohibition contained therein permanently precludes the registration of a shape as a trade mark where the nature of the product is such that its appearance and shaping determine its market value entirely or substantially as a result of their beauty or original character, or does the prohibition not apply where, prior to the application for registration, the attractiveness of the relevant shape to the public has been determined predominantly by the recognition of it as a distinctive sign?
>
> (2) If the answer to Question 1 is to the latter effect, to what extent must this attractiveness have prevailed for the prohibition no longer to apply?"

4–518   *(b)   The judgment of the Court*

The Court found appropriate to proceed to judgment without an opinion from its Advocate General.

With regard to the first question, it took the view that the national court essentially asked whether a shape that gives substantial value to a product can nevertheless constitute a trade mark under art.3(3) of the Directive where, prior to the application for registration, it acquired "attractiveness" as a result of its recognition as a distinctive sign.

The Court therefore considered that the question actually involved a sign which *initially* consisted of a shape giving substantial value to the product and which, *subsequently* and prior to application for registration, acquired recognition through advertising, that is to say on account of the promotional use made of it.[860]

Thus, the Court held that, contrary to the perception of the Hoge Raad, the shape in question fell squarely under the *Philips* principles that if a sign is caught by art.3(1)(e), it can no longer be registered by virtue of art.3(3) of the Directive, and that art.3(1)(e) should accordingly be regarded as a "preliminary obstacle" which cannot be overridden by the distinctiveness that sign may have acquired through use.[861]

---

[860] *Benetton*, para.22.
[861] *Benetton*, paras 26–27.

10. ARTICLE 3(1)(g)—TRADE MARKS OF A DECEPTIVE NATURE

The Court's answer therefore was that the third indent of art.3(1)(e) of the Directive does not allow the shape which gives substantial value to a product to constitute a trade mark under art.3(3) where, prior to its filing, that shape acquired attractiveness as a result of its recognition as a distinctive sign following advertising campaigns promoting the specific characteristics of the product in question; moreover, in view of that answer, it held that there was no need to address the second question.[862]

4–519

It is worth noting that the national court considered that the promotion of the shape increased not only its distinctiveness, but also its "attractiveness". In practice, that meant that, when the shape was applied for as a trade mark, its economic value was not exclusively or substantially due to its aesthetic features, but also to the extra "appeal" and "reputation" it had acquired through use.

However, the Court was not impressed by that argument. It stressed that if the appearance of the shape is *inherently* so attractive as to determine the value of the goods to a substantial extent, it is immaterial whether *subsequently* more value was added to that sign through promotion and advertising. In other words, it was irrelevant whether the use of the sign further increased and already substantial aesthetic value.

By taking that view the Court effectively precluded considerations linked to the acquired distinctiveness of the sign to be re-introduced in the analysis of functionality through the back door, by consistently holding that whatever consequences the use of the sign may have on its attractive or distinctive value, these can be taken into account only in the context of art.3(3) of the Directive and not when assessing the "preliminary obstacle" of aesthetic functionality.

4–520

However, that also means that if the value of the shape is *principally* attributable not to its aesthetic features, but rather on the appeal resulting from its reputation as a "famous" shape, the shape is not caught by the prohibition of the third indent of art.3(1)(e) of the Directive.

10. ARTICLE 3(1)(g)—TRADE MARKS OF A DECEPTIVE NATURE

(1) Elizabeth Emanuel—trade mark assignments

Emanuel[863] is the first case where the Court considered the application of art.3(1)(g). It is also evidence of how unfair competition and trade mark law are inextricably linked.

4–521

Elizabeth Emanuel, a fashion designer, started using the trade name ELIZABETH EMANUEL in 1990. In 1996 she signed an agreement with Hamlet International Plc; in return of financial support she transferred

---

[862] *Benetton*, paras 28–29.
[863] *Elizabeth Florence Emanuel v Continental Shelf 128 Ltd* (C-259/04) [2006] E.C.R. I-3089.

to a co-owned company her business, together with its goodwill, and an application for a composite mark including her trade name. The mark was registered in 1997. Later in the same year, she assigned once again her business, together with its goodwill and the registered trade mark to another company, Frostprint Ltd, which became Elizabeth Emanuel International Ltd. Emanuel became an employee of that company, a relationship that lasted only for a month. Indeed, the management of the company instructed its employees to be circumspect when answering questions regarding Emanuel. The trade mark registration was assigned to another company which later applied for an amendment of the registration to a simpler version. Emanuel opposed the application and sought the revocation of the trade mark incorporating her name. By the time the joined cases reached the Appointed Person, on appeal, the trade mark registration had been transferred to yet another entity, Continental Shelf 128 Ltd.

The Appointed Person[864] referred a number of questions to the Court seeking in essence the clarification of the provisions relating to deceptive registrations.

4–522 He highlighted that prior to the assignment the trade mark indicated to a significant proportion of the relevant public that a particular person was involved in the design or creation of the relevant goods and that at the time of the application after the assignment a significant portion of the relevant public wrongly believed that use of the trade mark indicated that the particular person was still involved in the design or creation of the relevant goods, and this belief was likely to affect the purchasing behaviour of that part of the public:

"1. Is a trade mark of such a nature as to deceive the public and prohibited from registration under Article 3(1)(g) [of Directive 89/104] in the following circumstances:

  (a) the goodwill associated with the trade mark has been assigned together with the business of making the goods to which the mark relates;
  (b) prior to the assignment the trade mark indicated to a significant proportion of the relevant public that a particular person was involved in the design or creation of the goods in relation to which it was used;
  (c) after the assignment an application was made by the assignee to register the trade mark; and
  (d) at the time of the application a significant portion of the relevant public wrongly believed that use of the trade mark indicated that the particular person was still involved in the design or creation of the goods in relation to which the mark was used, and this belief was likely to affect the purchasing behaviour of that part of the public?

---

[864] David Kitchin QC, *Elizabeth Emanuel Trade Mark* [2004] R.P.C. 15.

10. ARTICLE 3(1)(g)—TRADE MARKS OF A DECEPTIVE NATURE

2. If the answer to question 1 is not unreservedly yes, what other matters must be taken into consideration in assessing whether a trade mark is of such a nature as to deceive the public and prohibited from registration under Article 3(1)(g) [of Directive 89/104] and, in particular, is it relevant that the risk of deception is likely to diminish over time?

3. Is a registered trade mark liable to mislead the public in consequence of the use made of it by the proprietor or with his consent and so liable to revocation under Article 12(2)(b) [of Directive 89/104] in the following circumstances:

(a) the registered trade mark and the goodwill associated with it have been assigned together with the business of making the goods to which the mark relates;
(b) prior to the assignment the trade mark indicated to a significant proportion of the relevant public that a particular person was involved in the design or creation of the goods in relation to which it was used;
(c) after the assignment an application was made to revoke the registered trade mark; and
(d) at the time of the application a significant portion of the relevant public wrongly believed that use of the trade mark indicated that the particular person was still involved with the design or creation of the goods in relation to which the mark was used, and this belief was likely to affect the purchasing behaviour of that part of the public?

4. If the answer to question 3 is not unreservedly yes, what other matters must be taken into consideration in assessing whether a registered trade mark is liable to mislead the public in consequence of the use made of it by the proprietor or with his consent and so liable to revocation under Article 12(2)(b) [of Directive 89/104] and, in particular, is it relevant that the risk of deception is likely to diminish over time?"[865]

Emanuel submitted before the Court that there was a genuine risk that use of the trade mark might mislead the average consumer of the specified goods or services as to their origin and influence purchasing decisions. This should suffice to trigger the application of art.3(1)(g). Whether the goodwill and the trade mark had been assigned to the undertaking using the mark should be irrelevant once that risk had been demonstrated.

CSL on the other hand argued that the only relevant criterion was whether objectively the trade mark was of such a nature as to deceive or be liable to mislead the public. This was not the case with the contested name; consumers were aware that a trade name could be assigned.

---

[865] Reproduced in para.13.

4-523 (a) The Opinion of the Advocate General

(i) Admissibility of the reference. Advocate General Ruiz-Jarabo Colomer started by considering an issue that had caused considerable debate in the corridors of English courts. Was the Appointed Person entitled to use the art.234 procedure?

Having stated his preference for a stricter definition of what constituted a court or tribunal the Advocate General went on to suggest that the post of the Appointed Person satisfied the criteria set by the Court since the post was part of the judicial system of the United Kingdom.

This was based on two lines of argument. The first related to the post itself: there was statutory provision for the post; there were only two appeal routes from the decisions of the Trade Mark Registry, one to the court the other to the Appointed Person; and there were provisions ensuring its independence. The second focused on the nature of the proceedings before the Appointed Person: it applied legal rules, it conducted inter partes proceedings, and delivered judicial decisions, often acting at last instance.

4-524

(ii) The commercialisation of trade marks. To prepare the ground for answering the questions the Advocate General started by a general analysis of the nature of a registered trade mark as an object of commerce—that could be exploited on its own[866]—noting that trade mark rights could be transferred in a variety of ways together with other assets of an undertaking or on their own.

The Directive left the management of this area to Member States; the Regulation however provided for the independence of the Community Trade Mark from the entity behind the marked products.[867]

In principle transactions involving trade marks should be viewed from the same perspective as any other contract. "The logical approach is to accept the consequences of an act of free disposal, provided that there are no grounds such as to justify recovery of what was disposed of."[868]

4-525

(iii) The functions of trade marks—deceptive use. In order to develop what constituted deceptive use the Advocate General looked first at the functions of a trade mark and the purpose of trade mark rights.

Citing his Opinion in *Robelco*[869] he codified the jurisprudence of the Court as an attempt to ensure the integrity of a message.

---

[866] The A.G. used a Spanish civil law term, "autonomy of intention" to express the idea that a trade mark constituted an entity that could be exploited on its own.
[867] Article 17; see also art.21 of TRIPs.
[868] Point 39 of the Opinion of A.G. Ruiz-Jarabo Colomer.
[869] *Robelco NV v Robeco Groep NV* (C-23/01) [2002] E.C.R. I-10913; the A.G. had revisited the same theme in *Arsenal Football Club Plc v Matthew Reed* (C-206/01) [2002] E.C.R. I-10273.

10. ARTICLE 3(1)(g)—TRADE MARKS OF A DECEPTIVE NATURE

The specific purpose of trade mark rights was "to safeguard the correctness of the information which the registered trade mark provides concerning the origin of certain property. . .".[870]

4–526

Accordingly deceptive use had to be determined in relation to use of the sign as an indicator of origin. Trade marks did serve other functions, however "consideration of the concept of deception, as used in the provisions under review, must relate only to the abovementioned essential function".[871]

Regarding the type of sign in this case the Advocate General had no doubt that, following *Nichols*,[872] personal names could function as trade marks and that the usual criteria of trade mark law should be applied.

(iv) The perspective for determining deception. The Advocate General suggested that deception should be determined according to the standard of the average, reasonably well-informed, and reasonably observant and circumspect consumer.[873] There should not be a need for experts' reports and consumer research polls; instead, courts and trade mark authorities should exercise their own powers of assessment.

4–527

(v) Interpreting article 3(1)(g). The meaning of "deceive" was the critical issue in this case.

4–528

There are three relevant factors that can be identified in the narrative of the Opinion.

First, the mark had to confuse the public by virtue of its qualities, or its intrinsic characteristics as suggested in the intervention of the UK Government.

Secondly, it had to contain incorrect information, which might prove deceptive.

4–529

Thirdly, deceptiveness should be determined "from an objective point of view; in other words, in every reasonably imaginable case its use must give rise to such deception".[874]

(vi) The application of article 3(1)(g). So, should a change in ownership of a trade mark comprising the name of its original owner be

4–530

---

[870] Point 43; amongst the "tangential purposes" (point 44) the Court has recognised was that of an indication of quality in *SA CNL-SUCAL NV v Hag GF AG* (C-10/89) [1990] E.C.R. I-3711; and that of a vehicle for advertising in *Parfums Christian Dior SA v Evora BV* (C-337/95) [1997] E.C.R. I-6013.
[871] Point 46; he noted that consumers were aware that the quality of a branded product may vary over time. The Commission had submitted that the public interest behind art.3(1)(g) was the protection against the registration and use of signs that might mislead the average consumer, having an impact on his purchasing decisions.
[872] *Nichols Plc v Registrar of Trade Marks* (C-404/02) [2004] E.C.R. I-8499.
[873] Citing *Güt Springenheide and Tusky v Oberkreisdirektor des Kreises Sterfurty Amt für Lebersmittelüberwachung* (C-210/96) [1998] E.C.R. I-4657.
[874] Point 57, referring to Bender, "Absolute Eintragungshindernisse–artikel 7" in Ekey, and Klippel, Markenrecht, (Heidelberg, 2003), p.912; Gastinel, E., "La marque communautaire" (L.G.D.J., Paris, 1998), pp.88-89; and the ORLWOOLA (deceptively suggesting that the product was made of wool) case from the United kingdom as an example of deceptive use, *Joseph Crosfield & Son Ltd's Application ("Perfection")* [1910] 1 Ch. 130.

considered deceptive? The Advocate General suggested that the answer should be negative, using the above factors as a background rather than applying them directly. Instead he relied on his earlier points on the commercialisation of trade marks and personal names.

First, he supported that the legislature had made a clear choice, in respect of the Community Trade Mark regime, that as an entity a Community Trade Mark could be transferred on its own, separately from the business behind it and that the licensing provisions of the Directive pointed towards the same direction.

If it had been thought that consumers "were completely remote and incapable of understanding the vicissitudes experienced by undertakings which affect, in particular, trade marks, like any other object of commerce"[875] transfers and licensing would be regulated in a more prescriptive way. To the contrary he believed consumers knew that individuals bearing a trade marked name would not necessarily be involved in the production of products marketed under that trade mark.

4-531 Secondly, there was no reason for granting additional protection to personal names since the Court had clearly indicated with its case law that personal names should be treated in the same way as any other sign under trade mark law.

Note that in his conclusion regarding the first question he chose to use the terminology of the question. The introduction of "goodwill" limited the broad scope of his arguments: "the answer to the first preliminary question must be that a trade mark made up, at least in part, of a proper name, which has been transferred together with the goodwill of which it formed part, is not liable to deceive the public, within the meaning of Article 3(1)(g) ... even though it may give the mistaken impression that that person is involved in the design and manufacture of the goods".[876]

Would the answer differ if the transfer was made without the goodwill of the business?

4-532 **(vii) Interpreting article 12(2)(b).** The remaining questions necessitated the interpretation of article 12(2)(b).[877]

The Advocate General cited *Gorgonzola*[878] where the court "opted ... for a restrictive interpretation of revocation, requiring the actual existence, or a sufficiently serious risk, of deceit of consumers".[879]

---

[875] Point 62 of the Opinion of A.G. Ruiz-Jarabo Colomer.
[876] Point 65 of the Opinion of A.G. Ruiz-Jarabo Colomer.
[877] In relation to art.15(1)(c) of Reg. No.40/94, he referred to von Mühlendahl, and Ohlgart, Die Gemeinschaftsmarke Verlag C.H. Beck and Verlag Stämpfli + Cie, Munich, 1998 p.173.
[878] *Consorzio per la tutela del formaggio Gorgonzola v Kaserei Champignon Hofmeister GmbH & Co KG and Eduard Bracharz GmbH* (C-87/97) [1999] E.C.R. I-1301 a case on free movement of goods and Regulation 2081/92 on the protection of geographical indications and designations of origin.
[879] Point 68 of the Opinion of A.G. Ruiz-Jarabo Colomer.

10. ARTICLE 3(1)(g)—TRADE MARKS OF A DECEPTIVE NATURE

Following his earlier reasoning he suggested the customer's conflicting perception did not deserve to be classified as a case of deceit; "the mere use of a registered trade mark consisting of a proper name, transferred together with the goodwill with which it is associated, does not lead to deception of the kind referred to in Article 12(2)(b)".[880] However he also stressed that the national authority had to consider the particular features of the case in evaluating the effect of the use of the contested mark.

(b) The judgment of the Court

4–533

(i) Procedural Considerations. The Court dealt first with two procedural issues.

First, it rejected the observations submitted by Ms Emmanuel following the Opinion of the Advocate General.[881]

Secondly, it found that the Appointed Person could refer questions to the Court as court or tribunal under art.234. The Appointed Person was a permanent body enjoying the same guarantees of independence as judges, making findings of law in inter partes proceedings, and taking binding decisions that were final subject exceptionally to an application for judicial review.[882]

(ii) The interpretation of article 3(1)(g). Again the function of the trade mark became the starting point for answering the question:

4–534

"for the trade mark to be able to fulfil its essential role in the system of undistorted competition which the Treaty seeks to establish and maintain, it must offer a guarantee that all the goods or services bearing it have been manufactured or supplied under the control of a single undertaking which is responsible for their quality".[883]

(iii) Article 3(1)(g)—the public interest—consumer protection. The Court then identified consumer protection as the public interest behind art.3(1)(g).

4–535

---

[880] Point 71 of the Opinion of A.G. Ruiz-Jarabo Colomer.
[881] Citing amongst others *Emesa Sugar Sugar (Free Zone) NV v Amba* (C-17/98) [2000] E.C.R. I-665; and *Swedish Match AB v Secretary of State for Health* (C-210/03) [2004] E.C.R. I-11893 it held that there was no room for the submission of such observations in the Statute of the Court of Justice and the Rules of Procedure, unless the Court wished to reopen the oral procedure, in accordance with art.61 of the Rules of Procedure, if it considered that it lacked sufficient information, or that a critical for the case argument had not been debated between the parties. The Court felt that these conditions were not present in this case.
[882] It satisfied all the requirements set by the Court in cases like *Vaassen-Göbbels v Management of the Beambtenfonds voor het Mijnbedrijf* (61/65) [1966] E.C.R. 261; *Dorsch Consult Ingenieurgesellschaft mbH v EU Council and EC Commission* (C-54/96) [1997] E.C.R. I-4961; and *Nour Eddline El-Yassini v Secretary of State for Home Depostment* (C-416/95) [1999] E.C.R. I-1209.
[883] *Emanuel*, para.44, citing *Arsenal Football Club Plc* (C-206/01) [2002] E.C.R. I-10783.

Following *Nichols*,[884] there was no question that a personal name could perform the role that the Court had described as the function of a trade mark.

4–536   **(iv) The application of article 3(1)(g).** The problem here was whether the risk that consumers might think that Elizabeth Emanuel, that originally personified the goods bearing the ELIZABETH EMANUEL mark, was still involved with the production of the garments qualified as deceit under art.3(1)(g).

The Court found that the trade mark would still function as a guarantee of quality despite the transfer; "even if the average consumer might be influenced in his act of purchasing a garment bearing the trade mark ELIZABETH EMANUEL by imagining that the appellant in the main proceedings was involved in the design of that garment, the characteristics and the qualities of that garment remain guaranteed by the undertaking which owns the trade mark".[885] Accordingly the name as such could not be regarded as being of such a nature as to deceive the public according to art.3(1)(g).

The Court however added that it remained in the jurisdiction of the national court to determine whether the trade mark applicant intended to make the consumer believe that Elizabeth Emanuel was still involved with the garments. This might amount to fraud but still it "could not be analysed as deception for the purposes of article 3".[886]

The Court concluded that "a trade mark corresponding to the name of the designer and first manufacturer of the goods bearing that mark may not, by reason of that particular feature alone, be refused registration on the ground that it would deceive the public, within the meaning of Article 3(1)(g) ..., in particular where the goodwill associated with that trade mark, previously registered in a different graphic form, has been assigned together with the business making the goods to which the mark relates".[887]

4–537   **(v) The application of article 12(2)(b).** The Court found that the conditions of art.3(1)(g) were mirrored in art.12(2)(b) and that the analysis of the Court covered both provisions.

The reply to the third and the fourth questions was that "a trade mark corresponding to the name of the designer and first manufacturer of the goods bearing that mark is not, by reason of that particular feature alone, liable to revocation on the ground that that mark would mislead the public, within the meaning of Article 12(2)(b) ... in particular where the goodwill

---

[884] *Nichols Plc* (C-404/02) [2004] E.C.R. I-8499.
[885] *Emanuel*, para.48.
[886] *Emanuel*, para.50.
[887] *Emanuel*, para.51.

10. ARTICLE 3(1)(g)—TRADE MARKS OF A DECEPTIVE NATURE

associated with that mark has been assigned together with the business making the goods to which the mark relates".[888]

(2) Free movement of goods and deceptive use   4–538

Further guidance regarding the scope of the provision can be obtained from four judgments that looked at aspects of deceptive use in a trade mark context. All four of them were resolved on the basis of free movement of goods rules but there are useful analogies.

(a) Pall—use of the symbol®   4–539

The first of those cases had to do with the use of the symbol ®. In *Pall v Dahlhausen*[889] a reference from the Landgericht (Regional Court) Munich I the Court considered whether the prohibition of use of that symbol in Germany in relation to a trade mark not registered in the jurisdiction constituted a barrier to intra Community trade.

Pall, a producer and marketer of blood filters in Germany, had started proceedings against Dahlhausen who imported blood filters from Italy bearing the trade mark "Miropore®". Relying on s.3 of the German Law against Unfair Competition that prohibited misleading statements regarding the origin or the source of specific goods[890] it claimed that consumers would be misled since the mark had not been registered in Germany and sought an injunction against the marketing of the imported filters.

The Landgericht Munich I decided that according to German law the injunction should have been granted, it queried however whether it would amount to a quantitative restriction according to art.28 and referred the following questions to the Court:

"(1) Is the prohibition laid down in the case-law of the courts of the Federal Republic of Germany founded on Paragraph 3 of the Gesetz gegen den unlauteren Wettbewerb (Law on Unfair Competition) on putting goods into circulation in the Federal Republic of Germany with the symbol ® added to the name of the product when there is not trade

---

[888] *Emanuel*, para.53.
[889] *Pall Corp v PJ Dahlhausen & Co* (C-238/89) [1990] E.C.R. I-4827.
[890] German Law against Unfair Competition s.3 was a general clause against the use of misleading information. Section 27 of the Law on Foodstuffs and Consumer Items prohibited the marketing of cosmetic products using misleading names or packaging and, in particular, the attribution to such products of properties that they did not possess. The Law against Unfair Competition had been amended in 1994 and 2004; in 1994 the role of trade associations like the one involved in this case was restricted whereas the most recent amendment codified further, and to a certain extent relaxed the criteria for determining whether a specific act constituted an act of unfair competition but retained a broad provision against misleading acts. A number of more detailed laws regulate specific product markets.

mark protection in the Federal Republic of Germany tantamount in its effect to a quantitative restriction prohibited by Article [28] of the EEC Treaty if it is also applied to cases in which there is trade–mark protection in another EEC country?

(2) In the particular circumstances of the case in question, is Paragraph 3 of the Gesetz gegen den unlauteren Wettbewerb applicable for the purpose of protecting the legal interests mentioned in Article [30] of the EEC Treaty?"[891]

4–540   **(i) The legislative context.** The Court noted that in the absence of a specific rule on use of the symbol in Germany it would only apply the free movement of goods rules and reminded that they applied to all national trading rules capable of hindering, directly or indirectly, actually or potentially, intra-Community trade.[892]

The latter could only be accepted if they applied to both domestic and imported products, they were justified as necessary in order to satisfy imperative requirements relating, inter alia, to consumer protection and fair trading, they were proportionate to the objective pursued, and that objective could not be achieved by measures which were less restrictive in respect of intra-Community trade.[893]

4–541   **(ii) The effect on trade and the scope of the prohibition.** The Court started with the effect of the prohibition on intra Community trade and found that it could function as a barrier to trade. It could force the proprietor of a trade mark registered in one Member State but not in another to change its presentation and set up distinct distribution channels according to its marketing destination.

Its scope was to prevent error as to the place of registration and was applicable to domestic and imported products alike. It aimed to protect consumers from being misled as to the place of registration.

Balancing the two, the Court decided that the prohibition could not be justified. It relied on five main arguments; two had to do with the meaning of the symbol, the remaining three with unfair competition.

4–542   **(iii) The meaning of ®—proportionality.** First, the Court held that it had not been established that in practice the symbol was used and understood as indicating that the trade mark was registered in the country in which the product was marketed, rather than simply as an indication of registration in some countries.

So, the starting point for justifying the prohibition was weak.

---

[891] Reproduced in para.5.
[892] Citing *Procureur du Roi v Dassonville* (8/74) [1974] E.C.R. 837.
[893] Citing *Rewe-Zertral AG v Bundesmonopolverwaltung fur Bramtwein* (C-120/78) [1979] E.C.R. 649.

10. ARTICLE 3(1)(g)—TRADE MARKS OF A DECEPTIVE NATURE

Secondly, using a proportionality type of argument, the Court noted that even if consumers might be misled regarding the place of registration, the risk would not justify the considerable effect of the prohibition because consumers were more interested in the qualities of a product than in the place of registration of its trade mark.

(iv) Free movement of goods—unfair competition. One of the arguments put forward was that use of the symbol in the absence of regulation should be viewed as an act of unfair competition against its competitors. 4–543

In parallel if registration in any Member State would be considered sufficient, then marketers would choose to register the sign in the Member State with the most liberal system of registration.

The Court found that a prudent economic operator would look at the public register in order to determine the status of the mark rather than rely on the proclamation of registration on the product.

As to the aim of registration it remarked that the principal aim of the proprietor was to obtain legal protection in the Member State where the mark was registered. Use of symbols indicating registration were of an ancillary or supplementary nature. 4–544

Finally, the Court rejected the argument supported by the German Government that the prohibition could be justifiable under the misleading advertising Directive.[894] Placing the Directive in its broader context it held that since the prohibition had been found not to be justified by imperative requirements relating to consumer protection or fair trading—note that this was in the context of free movement of goods—it could not find a basis in the Directive.

(b) Clinique—the meaning of Clinique for cosmetics 4–545

In *Clinique*[895] the Court provided further guidelines on misleading character. The case was decided in the context of free movement of goods but on the fundamental questions on whether a sign is misleading or not the Court appeared to take a restrictive approach.

The case came before the Court as a reference from the Landgericht (Regional Court) Berlin. A trade association had started proceedings against the subsidiaries of Estée Lauder in France and Germany under the German Law against Unfair Competition and the Law on Foodstuffs and Consumer Items[896] claiming that the marketing of cosmetic products under

---

[894] Council Directive 84/450/EEC Relating to the Approximation of the Laws, Regulations and Administrative Provisions of the Member States Concerning Misleading Advertising [1984] OJ L250/17.
[895] *Verband Sozialer Wettbewerb eV v Clinique Laboratoires SNC et Estée Lauder Cosmetics GmbH* (C-315/92) [1994] E.C.R. I-317.
[896] See paras 10–091 and following, below.

the name "Clinique" could mislead consumers, suggesting that the products had medicinal properties. Until then Estée Lauder had been marketing the products under "Clinique" in the rest of the world, whereas in Germany it had using the name "Linique". It decided to revert to "Clinique" in order to reduce its packaging and advertising costs.

The Landgericht decided that the outcome of the case could be affected from the determination of whether the ultimate prohibition of "Clinique" was found to be against the free movement of goods rules and referred to the Court the following question:

> "Are Articles [28] and [30] of the EEC Treaty to be interpreted as precluding the application of a national provision on unfair competition under which the importation and marketing of a cosmetic product which has been lawfully manufactured and/or lawfully marketed in another European country may be prohibited on the ground that consumers would be misled by the product name—Clinique—in that they would take it to be a medicinal product, where that product is lawfully marketed without any objection under that name in other countries of the European Community?"[897]

4-546　　**(i) Setting the Context.** In order to provide a framework for answering the question the Court looked at the broader picture of Community law. At the time there were two Directives that could prove relevant, one on misleading advertising[898] and the other on cosmetic products.[899]

The scope of the misleading advertising Directive was to provide partial harmonisation of national laws on misleading advertising by establishing minimum objective criteria for determining misleading character and the minimum requirements for protection against misleading advertising.[900]

The cosmetic products Directive aimed to harmonise national rules on the packaging and labelling of cosmetic products.[901]

4-547　　Setting the two Directives into the hierarchical context of Community law the Court repeated that all secondary legislation should be interpreted in the light of the free movement of goods rules.[902] The general rule of art.28 was applicable even if national rules that regulated marketing requirements as to designation, form, size, weight, composition, presentation, labelling, and packaging applied to locally produced and imported products alike. In

---

[897] Reproduced in para.6.
[898] Council Directive 84/450/EEC Relating to the Approximation of the Laws, Regulations and Administrative Provisions of the Member States Concerning Misleading Advertising [1984] OJ 250/17.
[899] Council Directive 76/768/EEC on the Approximation of the Laws of the Member States Relating to Cosmetic Products [1976] OJ L 262/169.
[900] Citing *Pall Corp v PJ Dahlhausen* (C-238/89) [1990] E.C.R. I-4827.
[901] Citing *Parfuemerie-Fabrik 4711 v Provide* (C-150/88) [1989] E.C.R. 3891.
[902] Citing *Delhaize and Le Lion v Promalvin and AGE Bodegas Unidas* (C-47/90) [1992] E.C.R. I-3669.

10. ARTICLE 3(1)(g)—TRADE MARKS OF A DECEPTIVE NATURE

order to tolerate the application of the national rules the Court required a public-interest objective that took precedence over the free movement of goods.[903]

Proportionality was the other general principle invoked by the Court: rules had to be proportionate to the goals pursued.[904]

(ii) Cosmetics and the public interest. The Court focused on art.6(2) of Directive 76/768[905]—the cosmetics Directive—looking for the underlying public interest in the light of proportionality. It required Member States to take "all measures necessary to ensure that in the labelling, presentation for sale and advertising of cosmetic products, the wording, use of names, trade marks, images or other signs, figurative or otherwise, suggesting a characteristic which the products in question do not possess, shall be prohibited". 4–548

Its scope was delineated by its wording, the broader aim of the Directive that was to ensure free trade in cosmetic products, and the case law of the Court of Justice. It:

> "defines the measures to be taken in the interests of consumer protection and fairness of commercial transactions, which are included among the imperative requirements specified in the case-law of the Court in the context of the application of Article [28] of the Treaty. It also pursues the objective of protecting the health of humans, within the meaning of Article [30] of the Treaty, in so far as misleading information as to the characteristics of such products may have an effect on public health".[906]

So, through the interpretation of the Community provision behind the national legislation, the court reached the conclusion that the application of the national legislation should be consistent with art.28 and art.30 as interpreted in the Court's case law.

(iii) Unfair competition and free movement of goods—effect and scope of the prohibition. In order to describe what could fall under s.3 of the Act against Unfair Competition but, still, be considered a derogation from the free movement of goods rules the Court referred directly to its case law in *Pall*.[907] 4–549

Similarly, it held that the prohibition of the distribution in Germany of cosmetic products under the same name as in other Member States constituted in principle an obstacle to intra-Community trade.

---

[903] Citing *Keck and Mithouard* (C-267/91 & C-268/91) [1993] E.C.R. I-6097.
[904] Citing *Buet v Ministere Public* (382/87) [1989] E.C.R. 1235.
[905] Article 6(2) had been introduced into German law through s.27 of the Law on Foodstuffs and Consumer Items.
[906] *Clinique*, para.16.
[907] *Pall Corp* (C-238/89) [1990] E.C.R. I-4827.

The scope of the prohibition would be to protect consumers or the health of humans.

4–550   On balance the Court found the prohibition to be unjustifiable; this time for a number of factual reasons.

In Germany the Clinique products were sold exclusively in perfumeries and the cosmetic sections of departments stores, not in pharmacies.

The products were presented as cosmetic products, not as medicinal products.

4–551   The presentation of the products, apart from the contested name, did comply with the rules applicable to cosmetic products.

There was no evidence that the marketing of cosmetic products under Clinique in other Member States had misled consumers.

On the basis of the above the Court found that the prohibition was not necessary for consumer protection and the health of humans.

4–552   *(c)   MARS—advertising messages*

In *Mars*[908] the Court showed again that it would take a restrictive approach towards deceptiveness. The case was a reference by the Landgericht Koeln (Regional Court, Cologne). This time the trade mark itself did not constitute the principal issue. One of the unfair competition associations in Germany challenged the marketing of Mars ice cream bars imported from France to Germany. The packaging of the disputed bars included the sign "+ 10%" to indicate that the quantity of the bar had been increased by 10 per cent as part of an advertising campaign effective throughout Europe.

The association claimed that this was misleading and that marketing of the bars should be prohibited under s.3 of the Law against Unfair Competition. It also claimed that it infringed art.15 of the Law on Restraints of Competition, the competition provision protecting the freedom of retail trade in terms of pricing.

The association used two main arguments. The first, based on both unfair competition and competition laws, was that consumers were bound to assume that the "+ 10%" sign indicated an increase in content at a constant price. In order not to mislead the retailer should maintain the same price it had been charging before the increase. The second, based on unfair competition, targeted the presentation of the product: the way it had been incorporated on the packaging of the bar through an introduction of a new colour could hint to the consumer that the product had been increased by a quantity matching the surface covered by the new colour, that covered considerably more than 10 per cent of the packaging.

4–553   The Landgericht Koeln granted an interim injunction, finding that the presentation of the packaging could mean to the consumer that a bigger

---

[908] *Verein gegen Unwesen in Handel und Gewerbe Koln eV v Mars GmbH* (C-470/93) [1995] E.C.R. I-1923.

size, albeit negligibly bigger in quantitative terms, was offered without an increase in price. This restricted freedom of retail trade in the matter of the fixing of prices. In order to rule on the substance of the case however it referred the following question to the Court:

"Is it compatible with the principles of the free movement of goods to prohibit the marketing in a Member State of ice-cream snacks in a particular presentation which are produced in another Member State and lawfully marketed there in that same presentation, which is described in the application, (1) on the ground that the (new) presentation is liable to give consumers the impression that the goods are offered for the same price as under the old presentation, (2) on the ground that the visual presentation of the new feature '+ 10% ice-cream' gives consumers the impression that either the volume or the weight of the product has been considerably increased?".[909]

(i) Article 28—effect and scope of the prohibition. According to the case law of the Court the prohibition constituted a barrier to trade because it might require from the marketer to match the presentation of the product with its marketing destination, incurring additional packaging and advertising costs.[910] It added that although it applied to all products without distinction, it would hinder by its nature intra-Community trade.

It could only be permitted to satisfy an overriding requirement relating, inter alia, to consumer protection and fair trading, provided it was proportionate to the objective pursued and that objective could not be achieved by less measures.[911]

Turning to the justification of the prohibition the Court found that there was no evidence that Mars had as a result of the advertising campaign increased its prices, or that retailers had increased prices:

"In any case, the mere possibility that importers and retailers might increase the price of the goods and that consequently consumers may be deceived is not sufficient to justify a general prohibition which may hinder intra-Community trade."[912]

In its usual balancing and cautious manner the Court added that that fact did not prevent the Member States from taking action against duly proven actions which had the effect of misleading consumers.

4–554

4–555

---

[909] Reproduced in para.10.
[910] Citing *Procureur du Roi v Dassonville* (8/74) [1974] E.C.R. 837; and *Keck and Mithouard* (C-267/91 & C-268/91) [1993] E.C.R. I-6097.
[911] Citing *Rewe-Zentral Bundesmonopolverwaltung fur Branntwein* (120/78) [1979] E.C.R. 649; *Pall Corp v PJ Dahlhausen & G* (C-238/89) [1990] E.C.R. I-4827; and *Schutzverband gegen Unwesen In der Wirtschaft v Yves Rocher* (C-126/91) [1993] E.C.R. I-2361.
[912] *Mars*, para.19.

Regarding price fixing it found that the constraint imposed on the retailer not to increase prices would actually favour consumers. There was no contractual stipulation imposed on retailers; it applied only during the advertising campaign; and the actual information conveyed by the "+10%" sign ensured that consumers would not be misled.

Finally, regarding the visual presentation of the sign the Court rejected the allegations about its misleading character.

It found that a reasonably circumspect consumer would know that there was not necessarily a link between the size of the signs on the packaging, advertising the increase in quantity, and the actual size of that increase.

4–556 *(d) Cotonelle—the meaning of Cotonelle*

In *Cotonelle*[913] the reference covered deceptive use of a sign, not only from the perspective of free movement of goods rules but also according to the Directive. The starting point of this case was a judgment of the Corte d' Appello di Milano (Court of Appeal, Milan) that ordered Scott to stop using in Italy the trade mark COTONELLE for toilet paper and disposable handkerchiefs and invalidated the national registration of the same mark because it found that the mark might mislead consumers into thinking that the two products were made of or contained cotton. Registrations of COTONELLE had also been challenged, without success, in France and Spain.

As a result of that judgment Scott stopped distributing COTONELLE products in Italy and Fratelli Graffione SNC (Graffione), a wholesaler dealing in Scott products, notified its own customers that it, too, would stop distributing these two products.

Graffione started proceedings against Ditta Fransa (Fransa), a supermarket selling imported COTONELLE products in Italy. It argued that this was against Italian unfair competition rules since Graffione could not obtain the products in Italy whereas Fransa did through parallel imports.

4–557 In its response, Fransa relied on the territorial nature of trade mark rights. The Corte d' Appello judgment concerned the products that were manufactured and marketed in Italy; its products were lawfully marketed in France where it obtained them. An injunction would be against art.28 EC.[914]

It also claimed that if art.12(2)(b) of the Directive the outcome before the Corte d' Appello would be different.

As a result the Tribunale di Chiavari referred the following questions to the Court:

> "(1) Are Articles [28] and [30] to be interpreted as precluding restrictive application of national legislation of a Member State which prohibits the

---

[913] *Fratelli Graffione SNC* (C-313/94) [1996] E.C.R. I-6039.
[914] Citing *Verband Sozialer Wettbewerb eV v Clinique Laboratoires SNC et Estée Lauder Cosmetics GmbH* (C-315/92) [1994] E.C.R. I-317.

10. ARTICLE 3(1)(g)—TRADE MARKS OF A DECEPTIVE NATURE

movement within its territory of a product from another Member State where that product has been lawfully manufactured and lawfully bears a trade mark?

(2) Is Article 12(2)(b) of Directive 89/104 to be interpreted as entailing harmonisation of the national provisions on revocation of trade mark rights, on the grounds therein indicated, in relation to products distributed at Community level?

(3) In circumstances such as those at issue here, is the provision referred to in Question 2 above to be interpreted, having regard inter alia to the principle of proportionality, as precluding restrictive application of national legislation of a Member State intended to prevent the movement in that Member State of a product lawfully manufactured and bearing a trade mark in, and coming from, another Member State?"[915]

(i) Article 28 EC—unfair competition—effect and scope of the provision. The Court considered first whether art.28 EC and art.30 EC precluded the application of a national provision on unfair competition that would block the marketing of a product lawfully marketed in another Member State.

4–558

The Court repeated that such an injunction would constitute a measure having equivalent effect to a quantitative restriction on imports.[916] The question was whether it could be justified in order, in this case, to satisfy an overriding requirements relating to consumer protection or fair trading.[917]

The Court noted that it was for the national court first of all to interpret the judgment of the Corte d' Appello as to whether it prevented third parties from marketing the contested products.

If it targeted exclusively the proprietor of the Italian trade mark then third parties would not be prevented from importing and marketing the products in Italy and the injunction sought by Graffione would not be justified.

4–559

If the marketing in Italy of all COTONELLE products were to be prohibited then the barrier would have to be justified. This remained an open question that the national court had to resolve; the Court provided the parameters:

"The possibility of allowing a prohibition of marketing on account of the misleading nature of a trade mark is not, in principle, precluded by the fact that the same trade mark is not considered to be misleading in other

---

[915] Reproduced in para.11.
[916] Citing *Procureur du Roi v Dassonville* (8/74) [1974] E.C.R. 837.
[917] Citing *Rewe-Zentral* (120/78) [1979] E.C.R. 649; *Pall v Dalhausen* (C-238/89) [1990] E.C.R. I-4827; *Schutzverband gegen Unwesen In der Wirtschaft v Yves Rocher* (126/91) [1993] E.C.R. I-2361; and *Verein gegen Unwesen In Handel und Gewerbe Kaln v Mars* (C-470/93) [1995] E.C.R. I-1923.

Member States ... it is possible that because of linguistic, cultural and social differences between the Member States a trade mark which is not liable to mislead a consumer in one Member State may be liable to do so in another."[918]

"However ... in order to be justified, the measure adopted to protect consumers must really be necessary for that purpose and proportionate to the objective pursued, which must not be capable of being achieved by measures which are less restrictive of intra-Community trade."[919]

Citing *Clinique*[920] and *Mars*[921] the Court reminded that "the risk of misleading consumers cannot override the requirements of the free movement of goods and so justify barriers to trade, unless that risk is sufficiently serious".[922]

4-560   **(ii) The early days of article 12(2)(b).** The Court found that art.12(2)(b) of the Directive was not relevant to the principal issue of the current case. The aim of the Directive was to achieve a partial, rather than complete, harmonisation of national trade mark laws. And, according to the Fifth Recital in the Preamble of the Directive, Member States remained free to determine the effects of revocation or invalidity of trade marks. Further, according to the Sixth Recital, the Directive did not affect the application of provisions relating to unfair competition, civil liability or consumer protection.

Based on the facts of the case the Court chose to focus on the effect rather than the cause and ruled that art.12(2) left it to national law to determine whether and to what extent the use of a revoked trade mark ought to be prohibited.

11. ARTICLE 3(1)(h)—STATE EMBLEMS

(1) Maple Leaf—applicability of article 6ter to services

4-561

Maple Leaf[923] is a good example of the Court's readiness to interpret the provisions of the CTMR broadly when this is necessary to plug gaps in the legislation that would otherwise result in patently absurd and inequitable situations.

That case concerned the interpretation of art.7(1)(h) CTMR (the equivalent provision of art.3(1)(h) of the Directive, in conjunction with art.6ter of

---

[918] *Cotonelle*, para.22.
[919] *Cotonelle*, para.23.
[920] *Verband Sozialer Wettbewerb eV v Clinique Laboratoires SNC et Estée Lauder Cosmetics GmbH* (C-315/92) [1994] E.C.R. I-317.
[921] *Verein gegen Unwesen In Handel und Gewerbe Kaln* (C-470/93) [1995] E.C.R. I-1923.
[922] *Cotonelle*, para.24.
[923] *American Clothing Associates NV/OHIM* (C-202/08 P and C-208/08 P) [2009] E.C.R. 000

11. ARTICLE 3(1)(h)—STATE EMBLEMS

the Paris Convention, dealing with the scope of the protection to be afforded to State emblems for the purposes of trade mark law.

(a) Legislative framework   4–562

Article 7(1)(h) CTMR provides that signs which have not been authorised by the competent authorities and are to be refused pursuant to art.6ter of the Paris Convention cannot be registered as Community trade marks.

Article 6ter (1) stipulates the following, insofar as is relevant to the case:

"(1) (a) The countries of the Union agree to refuse or to invalidate the registration ... without authorisation by the competent authorities, either as trademarks or as elements of trademarks, of armorial bearings, flags, and other State emblems, of the countries of the Union ... and any imitation from a heraldic point of view.

(b) The provisions of subparagraph (a), above, shall apply equally to armorial bearings, flags, other emblems, abbreviations, and names, of international intergovernmental organisations [...]

(c) The countries of the Union shall not be required to apply the said provisions when the use or registration ... is not of such a nature as to suggest to the public that a connection exists [with] the organisation concerned ... or if such use or registration is probably not of such a nature as to mislead the public as to the existence of a connection between the user and the organisation [...]"

Article 6sexies requires the countries of the Union to protect service marks, without however being obliged to also provide for their registration.

On the other hand, art.16 of the Trade Mark Law Treaty, adopted in Geneva on October 27, 1994, provides that the contracting parties shall register service marks and apply to them the provisions of the Paris Convention concerning trade marks.

(b) Background to the dispute   4–563

American Clothing Associates NV ("American Clothing") sought to register at OHIM as a Community trade mark a figurative sign consisting of a black and white image of a maple leaf with the letters "RW" below it, essentially in order to designate leather goods, clothing articles and tailoring services in Classes 18, 25 and 40 of the Nice Classification.

The Office refused the application in its entirety pursuant to art.7(1)(h) CTMR, stating that the mark was liable to give rise to an impression on the part of the public that it was linked to Canada, inasmuch as the maple leaf reproduced in the trade mark applied for was a copy of the national emblem of that country.

American Clothing filed a notice of appeal against the examiner's refusal which was dismissed by the Office's Boards of Appeal. American Clothing appealed that decision to the Court of First Instance.

4–564 *(c) The judgment of the Court of First Instance*

The Court of First Instance[924] annulled the Office's decision insofar as it related services in Class 40, on the ground that art.6ter(1)(a) of the Paris Convention, to which art.7(1)(h) CTMR directly refers, does not apply to service marks.

In doing so, the Court of First Instance applied art.6ter of the Paris Convention literally, effectively holding that the legal basis for the rejection and, by extension, the conditions for refusal, were to be found not in art.7(1)(h) CTMR, but rather in art.6ter directly.

Moreover, it held that it was precisely in order to extend to service marks the protection granted by the Paris Convention to trade marks that a specific provision was inserted in art.16 of the Trade Mark Law Treaty, which, however, had not been ratified by the European Community.[925]

The Court of First Instance also held that when adopting the CTMR, the Community legislature was aware of the economic importance of services and could have extended the protection granted by art.6ter also to service marks, had it considered appropriate to do so. Accordingly, it was not for the Community judicature to take the place of the legislature and apply an interpretation *contra legem* of those provisions, whose meaning is in no way ambiguous.[926]

4–565 As to the remainder, the Court of First Instance rejected the appeal, holding that registration was correctly refused in respect of the goods in Classes 18 and 25.

In reaching that conclusion, it observed that when assessing a complex mark for the purposes of art.6ter it was sufficient if any of its components corresponded to a State emblem or was an imitation thereof "from a heraldic point of view", which meant that it was the "heraldic description" of the emblem that had to be considered, rather than its "geometric description".[927]

Finally, it noted that the application of art.6ter is not subject to the existence of a possibility of error on the part of the public as regards the origin of the goods, or as regards the existence of a connection between the proprietor and the State whose emblem appears in the mark.[928]

---

[924] Judgment in *American Clothing Associates v OHIM (Representation of a maple leaf)* (T-215/06) [2008] E.C.R. II-303.
[925] Judgment of the CFI, para.31.
[926] Judgment of the CFI, para.32.
[927] Judgment of the CFI, para.72.
[928] Judgment of the CFI, para.77.

11. ARTICLE 3(1)(h)—STATE EMBLEMS

Both American Clothing and the Office appealed that judgment to the Court of Justice, to the extent that it adversely affected their respective positions.

(d) The opinion of the Advocate General 4–566

Advocate General Ruiz-Jarabo Colomer took the view that the Court of First Instance had correctly rejected the mark in respect of the goods applied for, but had erroneously accepted the application insofar as protection was sought for services.

(i) Emblems v trade marks: different functions. In the first place, he 4–567
observed that American Clothing could not rely on the argument that State emblems should be protected only insofar as their essential function was affected, by applying the same criteria as for trade mark protection by analogy. Unlike trade marks, emblems cannot be viewed as having a commercial function or as indicating origin, other than possibly identifying a country and its inhabitants, or representing its sovereignty.

Thus, even on the assumption that emblems had "essential functions", the role they fulfil is totally different from that of trade marks, which sufficed to render the drawing of analogies between the two entirely inappropriate. In fact, the contrast between the two situations would suffice to justify their different treatment in law.[929]

(ii) Emblems v trade marks: different scope. Then, the Advocate 4–568
General observed that the Paris Convention confers an absolute protection on emblems, at least in the following respects: first, art.6ter applies to all the products and, if the national law so provides, to all the services in the Nice classification; secondly, the protection is not conditional on the establishment of a link between the mark and the emblem; finally, various limitations characteristic of commercial symbols, like for instance invalidity and expiry, do not affect national emblems.[930]

Indeed, the second sentence of art.6ter(1)(c) allows the registration or use of a sign if it does not indicate a connection with the *intergovernmental organisation* which is the proprietor of the corresponding emblem; it may therefore be inferred, *a contrario sensu*, that the need for such a connection is not required for State emblems, but only for the insignia of international institutions.[931] Consequently, an exact replica or an imitation of the emblem is enough to unleash the protection afforded to national symbols by art.6ter.[932]

---

[929] Points 63 and 67 of the Opinion of A.G. Ruiz-Jarabo Colomer.
[930] Points 74 and 76 of the Opinion of A.G. Ruiz-Jarabo Colomer.
[931] Citing Bodenhausen, G.H.C., *Guide to the application of the Paris Convention for the Protection of Industrial Property*, BIRPI, 1969, p. 101.
[932] Point 75 of the Opinion of A.G. Ruiz-Jarabo Colomer.

4–569 **(iii) Imitation "from a heraldic point of view".** Next, the Advocate General dealt with the dichotomy between "heraldic" and "geometric" description. Although he recognised that the protection of emblems is subject to certain restrictions, in the sense that it does not cover the semantic content incorporated in the emblem but only its "heraldic expression", he did not accept that the applicability of art.6ter should be based on its geometric description. In fact, so detailed a comparison would practically negate the protection afforded to emblems, since the existence of any nuance or differentiation, however secondary, would be enough to deny the existence of identity between the respective representations.

Moreover, he took the view that the need for an "imitation" did not imply the existence of a likelihood of confusion. Rather, it is sufficient for refusing protection if the copy possesses the "heraldic connotations" which generally distinguish the emblem from other signs, as expressed in the descriptions which the States communicate to the International bureau.[933]

4–570 **(iv) Confusion as to endorsement.** As to the argument that the Court of First Instance disregarded the overall impression of the sign applied for, Advocate General Ruiz-Jarabo Colomer stressed that the wording of art.6ter expressly extends to situations in which national symbols are used "as elements of trademarks". Hence, that expression would become completely devoid of meaning if it were possible to circumvent the relevant prohibition by simply placing the emblem in a sign with more components.[934]

Furthermore, he pointed out that the application of art.6ter is not subject to the possibility of an error as regards the origin of the goods, or the existence of a connection between the proprietor of the sign and the State whose emblem it reproduces. Although it may be true that the ratio of art.6ter lies in the need to prevent the public from erroneously believing that there is an official approval or endorsement of the goods bearing the emblem by that State, the existence of such a link is not a specific condition for its application.[935]

4–571 **(v) Applicability of article 6ter to services.** Finally, the Advocate General took the view that the Court of First Instance had misinterpreted the aim of the Paris Convention and the reference made to it by art.7 CTMR.

As regards the correct interpretation of art.6ter, he recalled that the essential aim of the Paris Convention is to uphold the principle of national treatment, combining it with minimum rules for the protection of industrial property rights.

Accordingly, the Court of First Instance was wrong to seek in that provision the requirements for denying protection. Although, admittedly,

---

[933] Point 85 of the Opinion of A.G. Ruiz-Jarabo Colomer.
[934] Point 88 of the Opinion of A.G. Ruiz-Jarabo Colomer.
[935] Point 94 of the Opinion of A.G. Ruiz-Jarabo Colomer.

that provision does not extend to service marks, it does not concern itself with delimiting the scope of protection afforded to emblems either. Rather, it only requires the contracting States not to register trade marks containing national emblems, while leaving them free to extend protection to service marks should they so wish.[936]

Therefore, he considered that the question whether the corresponding absolute ground for refusal also applies to services depends on the interpretation of art.7(1)(h) CTMR. 4–572

In that regard, he noted that the seventh and ninth recitals in the preamble to the CTMR refer to both goods and services, as also does art.1(1), which defines Community trade marks as marks registered for either of them. Additionally, he observed that the CTMR contains no provision which effectively distinguishes between them in any meaningful way.[937]

Accordingly, the Advocate General concluded that, in view of the equal treatment reserved by the European legislature for both types of signs, the reference in art.7(1)(h) to the Paris Convention must be understood as only relating to the kind of sign to be protected and not to the scope of its actual protection.[938]

(e) Findings of the Court 4–573

(i) The meaning of "heraldic imitation". At the outset, the Court concurred with the Advocate General that both the functions State emblems perform and their treatment in Community and international law are clearly distinct from the role and protectable aspects of trade marks.

That is especially true with regard to likelihood of confusion which, unlike its importance for trade mark protection, is not required for the protection of an emblem, since art.6ter(1)(a) of the Paris Convention makes no reference to it. In particular, it is apparent from the second sentence of that provision that the protection of State emblems is not subject to there being a connection in the mind of the public between the trade mark and the emblem.[939]

The Court then turned to the interpretation of the expression "imitation from a heraldic point of view" observing that art.6ter prohibits the registration and use of a State emblem not only when it is filed as a trade mark as such, but also when it constitutes an element of a trade mark. Furthermore, that provision prohibits the imitation of the emblem in addition to precluding its exact replication.

However, the Court noted also that the prohibition applies only to imitations of the emblem from a heraldic perspective, that is to say, is limited to signs which contain heraldic connotations serving to distinguish the emblem from other signs. 4–574

---

[936] Point 107 of the Opinion of A.G. Ruiz-Jarabo Colomer.
[937] Point 111 of the Opinion of A.G. Ruiz-Jarabo Colomer.
[938] Point 113 of the Opinion of A.G. Ruiz-Jarabo Colomer.
[939] *Maple Leaf,* para.45.

Moreover, it agreed with the Advocate General that the protection against imitation from a heraldic point of view refers not to the subject-matter of the emblem as such, but rather to its heraldic expression. It is therefore necessary, in order to determine whether there is an imitation, to consider the heraldic description of the emblem at issue and not its geometric reproduction, as this would limit the protection only to cases of graphic equivalence, which is already prohibited by the first part of that provision.[940]

Accordingly, it is the perception of the average consumer as to whether an imitation in the above sense exists that should be taken into account. A difference detected by a specialist in heraldic art, will not necessarily be perceived by the average consumer who, in spite of differences at the level of certain heraldic details, can still see in the trade mark an imitation of the emblem in question.[941]

4-575 Furthermore, the Court observed that the heraldic description of the emblem normally contains only certain descriptive graphic elements, and does not necessarily concern itself with particular features of the artistic interpretation. Hence, it held that the Court of First Instance did not err in law by holding that a number of artistic interpretations of one and the same emblem were possible.

Lastly, the Court held in that connection that as art.6ter applies also to individual elements of complex trade marks, it is sufficient for a single component of the mark applied for to imitate such an emblem for that mark to be refused registration. As a result, to the extent the Court of First Instance had found that the maple leaf represented on the sign applied for is an imitation of the Canadian emblem, it did not need to examine the overall impression produced by that mark.[942]

4-576 **(ii) Application to service marks.** As regards the Court of First Instance's refusal to apply art.7(1)(h) CTMR, the Court again shared the view of Advocate General Ruiz-Jarabo Colomer that the Paris Convention provides for a minimum level of protection for elements falling within its scope, while leaving the contracting States free to extend the scope of its application beyond that bare minimum.

Consequently, it inferred that whilst art.6ter leaves the extension of the protection guaranteed to trade marks also to services to the discretion of the States party to the Convention, it cannot be interpreted as requiring those States to treat these types of marks differently.[943]

Moreover, it noted that, as a rule, the CTMR does not differentiate between goods and services and where it wanted to draw such a distinction, as for example in art.7(1)(e), (j) and (k), it did so expressly. Accordingly, art.7(1)(h) must be regarded as following the rule rather than the exception,

---

[940] *Maple Leaf*, paras 48–49.
[941] *Maple Leaf*, paras 50–51.
[942] *Maple Leaf*, para.59.
[943] *Maple Leaf*, para.73.

the more so since it does not contain any explicit restriction as to the type of mark covered by it.[944]

In addition, the Court held that this interpretation of art.7(1)(h) is further supported by art.7(1)(i) CTMR, the scope of which is analogous to that of subpara.(h), insofar as it concerns marks which include badges, emblems or escutcheons other than those covered by art.6ter.   4–577

Given that art.7(1)(i) applies without distinction to marks for both goods and services, it would be absurd to refuse registration to a service mark containing a badge and not to one imitating a State flag. Indeed, if the legislature wished to grant such protection to badges and escutcheons, it should be assumed that, a fortiori, it also intended to grant at least an equivalent level of protection to flags and other emblems of States.[945]

Consequently, the Court concluded that the judgment under appeal erred in finding that, by refusing registration of the trade mark applied for in respect of services, OHIM had infringed art.7(1)(h) CTMR in conjunction with art.6ter of the Paris Convention.

12. ARTICLE 3(2)(d)—BAD FAITH

(1) Lindt & Sprüngli—what is bad faith?   4–578

Lindt & Sprüngli[946] was the first case in which the Court was asked to provide guidance on the interpretation of the concept of bad faith for the purposes of Community trade mark law.

Although the order for reference concerned invalidity proceedings brought against a registered Community trade mark under art.51(1)(b) CTMR (new art.52), its findings are equally applicable in the context of art.3(2)(d) of the Directive.

(a) The facts in the main proceedings   4–579

The national proceedings arose out of a situation in which a number of competing undertakings originally marketed related products (chocolate Easter bunnies) in similar shapes and presentations. One of those undertakings then registered its own particular configuration as a three-dimensional trade mark and used it as a basis for preventing its competitors from marketing within the European Union resembling product shapes. Was that undertaking, however, acting in bad faith when applying for the mark in the knowledge of those circumstances?

---

[944] *Maple Leaf*, paras 76–77.
[945] *Maple Leaf*, paras 79–80.
[946] *Chocoladefabriken Lindt & Sprüngli AG/Franz Hauswirth GmbH* (C-529/07), not yet published.

The reference was made by the Austrian Oberster Gerichtshof in the course of a dispute between Chocoladefabriken Lindt & Sprüngli AG ("Lindt"), a Swiss company, and Franz Hauswirth GmbH ("Hauswirth"), a company established in Austria.

In 2000 Lindt obtained a Community trade mark registration, representing a gold-coloured chocolate bunny, in a sitting position, wearing a red ribbon and a bell and with the words "Lindt GOLDHASE" in brown lettering, essentially corresponding to the shape of a chocolate bunny it has marketed since the early 1950s.

4–580 Hauswirth has marketed chocolate bunnies since 1962. According to the order for reference, the shape of those bunnies is confusingly similar to the one covered by Lindt's trade mark, despite the fact that a different brand name is affixed on their packaging.

Following registration, Lindt brought infringement proceedings against Hauswirth, who counterclaimed that the registration had been made in bad faith and the trade mark should therefore be declared invalid.

At first instance, the Handelsgericht (Commercial Court) in Vienna dismissed the main claim and upheld the counterclaim. On appeal, the Oberlandesgericht (Higher Regional Court) partly quashed that judgment, rejecting both the action and the counterclaim. Both parties appealed to the Oberster Gerichtshof (Supreme Court).

4–581 The Oberster Gerichtshof stated that the decision on the counterclaim brought by Franz Hauswirth depends on whether Lindt was acting in bad faith when applying for registering the shape at issue as a trade mark and referred the following questions to the Court for a preliminary ruling:

"(1) Is art.51(1)(b) CTMR to be interpreted as meaning that an applicant for a Community trade mark is to be regarded as acting in bad faith where he knows, at the time of his application, that a competitor in (at least) one Member State is using the same sign, or one so similar as to be capable of being confused with it, for the same or similar goods or services, and he applies for the trade mark in order to be able to prevent that competitor from continuing to use the sign?

(2) If the first question is answered in the negative:

Is the applicant to be regarded as acting in bad faith if he applies for the trade mark in order to be able to prevent a competitor from continuing to use the sign, where, at the time he files his application, he knows or must know that by using an identical or similar sign for the same goods or services, or goods or services which are so similar as to be capable of being confused, the competitor has already acquired a 'valuable right' ('wertvollen Besitzstand')?

(3) If either the first or the second question is answered in the affirmative:

Is bad faith excluded if the applicant's sign has already obtained a reputation with the public and is therefore protected under competition law?"

(b) The Opinion of the Advocate General

4–582

Advocate General Sharpston started her analysis by observing that the relevant provisions of Community trade mark law do not contain a clear definition of bad faith, or otherwise describe that notion.

However, she inferred from the overall scheme of the legislation that bad faith appeared to be an inherent defect in the application (rather than in the trade mark itself), which fundamentally vitiates the registration regardless of other circumstances; that concept, moreover, should be given the same meaning under both the Regulation and the Directive and should apply equally to both Community and national trade marks.[947]

The Advocate General noted though that bad faith cannot be defined in the abstract or confined to a limited set of circumstances, such as the existence of a particular kind of prior right, a lack of intention to use the mark, or the actual or constructive knowledge of the existing use of a similar mark.

Rather, its nature seems to imply a subjective incentive on the part of the applicant in the form of a dishonest intention or other "sinister motive", which will normally follow from objective criteria, including, but not limited to, the ones listed by the referring court; in short, it involves conduct which departs from accepted principles of ethical behaviour or honest business practices, which can only be identified by reference to the specific facts of each case.[948]

4–583

Accordingly, she concluded that there is no simple, decisive test for establishing whether a trade mark application is made in bad faith, in particular since that notion involved a subjective state of mind linked to an intention incompatible with accepted standards of honest or ethical conduct, which is only ascertainable from objective evidence, and which must be assessed case by case.

Moreover, she noted that bad faith requires actual or constructive knowledge of the circumstances from which that incompatibility with the accepted standards of honest or ethical conduct may be deduced and that, in the absence of direct evidence to that effect, the existence of such knowledge may be determined by reference to the common state of knowledge in the economic sector concerned.

As regards, finally, the specific circumstances put forward in the order for reference, Advocate General Sharpston considered that:

4–584

— an intention to prevent others from using similar signs in respect of similar products may be incompatible with such standards if the applicant knew that others were already legitimately using those signs, particularly if that use was substantial and longstanding and enjoyed legal protection, and if the nature of the sign was dictated by technical or commercial constraints;

---

[947] Points 41–42 of the Opinion of A.G. Sharpston.
[948] Point 60 of the Opinion of A.G. Sharpston.

— however, such an intention would not be incompatible with those standards if the applicant's sign had enjoyed similar or greater legal protection and was used in such a way, to such an extent and over such a time, that the use of similar signs could derive unjustified benefit from the applicant's marks, and if third parties were not constrained in their ability to choose dissimilar signs.

4–585 *(c) The findings of the Court*

As a starting point, the Court observed that the relevant time for determining whether there is bad faith on the part of the applicant is the time of the filing of the application; furthermore, whether the applicant is acting in bad faith must be the subject of an overall assessment that takes account of all the factors relevant to the particular case.[949]

Turning to the questions referred, it held that a presumption of knowledge by the applicant that third parties use identical or similar signs may be deduced, among other facts, from general knowledge in the economic sector concerned, while that knowledge can be inferred, inter alia, from the duration of such use, in the sense that the more that use is long-standing, the stronger that presumption will be.

However, the fact that the applicant knows or must know that a third party has long been using an identical or similar sign is not of itself sufficient to conclude that the applicant is acting in bad faith; consequently, consideration must also be given to the applicant's intention at the time the application is filed.[950]

4–586 Then, the Court observed that insofar as that intention is, necessarily, a subjective factor, it will have to be determined by reference to objective indications, arising from the facts of the particular case.

In that regard, it noted that the intention to prevent other parties from marketing similar products may, in certain circumstances, be indicative of bad faith, in particular when subsequently it becomes apparent that the applicant applied for the mark without intending to use it in accordance with its essential funcion, his sole objective being to prevent third operators from entering the market.[951]

Equally, the fact that a third party has long used a similar sign is also a factor to be taken into consideration, since, in such a case, the applicant's sole aim in obtaining a registration might be to compete unfairly with a competitor whose sign has obtained some degree of legal protection because of characteristics of its own.[952]

4–587 Furthermore, the Court concurred with the Advocate General that the nature of the sign may also be relevant, in that the existence of bad faith might

---

[949] *Lindt & Sprüngli*, paras 34–35.
[950] *Lindt & Sprüngli*, paras 40–41.
[951] *Lindt & Sprüngli*, paras 43–45.
[952] *Lindt & Sprüngli*, paras 46–47.

more readily be established where the competitors' freedom to choose the shape of their products is limited by technical or commercial constraints, since, in such a case, the proprietor will be able to prevent not merely the use of identical or similar signs, but actually the marketing of comparable products.

However, it cannot be excluded that, even in such circumstances, the application may be in pursuit of a legitimate objective. That may in particular be the case where the applicant knows that a newcomer in the market is trying to take advantage of his sign by copying its presentation and seeks to register that sign precisely with a view to preventing such copying.[953]

Accordingly, consideration should also be given to the reputation the sign may have acquired by the time of its filing, as well as to the extent to which that reputation might justify the applicant's interest in ensuring a wider protection for his sign.[954]

Therefore, the Court ruled that, in order to determine whether the applicant is acting in bad faith, the national court must take into consideration all the factors relevant to the case and in particular:

4-588

— the fact that the applicant knows or must know that a third party is using an identical or similar sign capable of being confused with the sign for which registration is sought;

— the applicant's intention to prevent that third party from continuing to use such a sign; and

— the degree of legal protection enjoyed by the third party's sign and by the sign for which registration is sought.

Thus, in *Lindt & Sprüngli* the Court seems to be distinguishing between situations of long lasting and well-established use of similar signs by competitors, which cannot legitimately be discontinued by having recourse to trade mark protection, and parasitic use by newcomers with the sole purpose of exploiting the sign's reputation, which the owner may lawfully prevent by relying on its trade mark rights without acting in bad faith.

13. ARTICLE 3(3)—DISTINCTIVE CHARACTER ACQUIRED THROUGH USE

(1) Windsurfing Chiemsee—the test for assessing acquired to distinctive character

In the second part of *Windsurfing Chiemsee*[955] the Court established the test assessing distinctive character that had been acquired through use.

4-589

---
[953] *Lindt & Sprüngli*, paras 48–49.
[954] *Lindt & Sprüngli*, paras 51–52.
[955] *Windsurfing Chiemsee Produktions- und Vertriebs GmbH* (C-108/97 & C-109/97) [1999] E.C.R. I-2779.

The German court had indicated that the "need to leave free" (Freihaltebedürfnis) doctrine would also be relevant in the interpretation of art.3(3) because national legislation and the courts appeared to require "trade acceptance" together with consumer recognition.

Accordingly the Landgericht referred the following questions to the Court:

> "What requirements follow from [art.3(3)] for the registrability of a descriptive designation under Article 3(1)(c)?"
>
> "In particular, are the requirements the same in all cases, or are the requirements different according to the degree of the need to leave free?"
>
> "Is in particular the view hitherto taken in the German case-law, namely that in the case of descriptive designations which need to be left free, trade acceptance in more than 50% of the trade circles concerned is required and is to be demonstrated, compatible with that provision?"
>
> "Do requirements follow from this provision as to the manner in which descriptive character acquired by use is to be ascertained?"[956]

(a) The Opinion of the Advocate General

4–590 Both defendants had linked the distinctive character acquired through use, according to art.3(3), with the reference to "trade acceptance" included in s.8(3) of the Markengesetz. Huber viewed them as two sides of the same coin whereas Attenberger supported that the distinctive character under art.3(3) was akin to "trade acceptance" and differed from the concept of distinctive character under art.3(1)(b). The Commission rejected the applicability of the German doctrine as well as the reliance on set percentages.

Advocate General Cosmas dealt with the second set of questions briefly, having found that the contested sign should not require evidence of acquired distinctive character.

Without any reservation, he accepted the Commission's view that the "need to leave free" doctrine, in all its variations, should not be taken into account. Instead he suggested a number of criteria.

4–591 First, there should be use of the sign for a reasonably long period of time, testing the durability of the trade mark and giving the opportunity to those opposing registration to act.

Secondly, use of the sign should lead the relevant public to perceive the sign as distinguishing the goods or services of a particular undertaking. The relevant public comprised primarily the respective consumers; the views of traders and manufacturers of similar products should also count, however the motives behind the views of the trade should be a counterbalancing factor.

---

[956] Reproduced in para.17.

13. ARTICLE 3(3)—DISTINCTIVE CHARACTER ACQUIRED THROUGH USE

Thirdly, he accepted the usefulness of evaluating distinctive character on the basis of percentages and set the minimum limit at 50 per cent of the relevant public believing that the marked product is linked with a particular undertaking.

Finally, he provided some guidelines on the type of evidence that could show distinctiveness, stressing again that the link with a particular undertaking rather than the commercial success of the product had to be established. Accordingly information regarding advertising expenditure or the market share enjoyed by the marked product did not appear to be useful. The views of the relevant Chamber of Commerce or appropriate experts were more relevant. Courts could also use the findings of consumer surveys—but should not rely exclusively or predominantly on them—provided that they were conducted by a reliable pollster, using an appropriately constructed questionnaire and targeting the relevant segment of the population.

4–592

He concluded that a trade mark can acquire distinctive character if there is appropriate evidence that its use for a reasonable period of time made caused the public to believe that the marked product derives from a particular undertaking.

(b) The judgment of the Court

The Court distilled the second set of questions into being an enquiry about the requirements for acquiring distinctive character through use according to art.3(3) and whether the "need to leave free" doctrine affected them.

4–593

It saw art.3(3) as a major exception to the rule laid down in art.3(1)(b), art.3(1)(c) and art.3(1)(d). It was clear for the Court that the concept of distinctive character should be given the same meaning throughout art.3. The mark had to identify the marked product as originating from a particular undertaking.

The same rule applied to geographical indications.

"Where that is the case, the geographical designation has gained a new significance and its connotation, no longer purely descriptive, justifies its registration as a trade mark."[957] The German doctrine had no application on this process.

4–594

To make sure that art.3(3) was viewed as a self-existent provision the Court came up with a multifactor test for acquired distinctive character.

(i) The overall assessment of distinctive character. The Court used the overall assessment concept in order to describe the general tenor of the test: "the competent authority must make an overall assessment of the evidence that the mark has come to identify the product concerned as originating from a particular undertaking....".[958]

4–595

---

[957] *Windsurfing Chiemsee*, para.47.
[958] *Windsurfing Chiemsee*, para.49.

4–596   *A multi-factor test.* It then identified specific factors that had to be considered as part of the overall assessment.

First, the specific nature of the geographical name; a well-known geographical name would require long-standing and intensive use in order to acquire a new significance, even more so when the name is familiar in relation to the same category of goods.

The Court went on to identify seven more factors: the market share held by the mark; the intensity of use; the geographical spread of use; the longevity of use; the amount invested in promoting the mark; the proportion of the relevant class of persons who, because of the mark, identify goods as originating from a particular undertaking; and statements from chambers of commerce and industry or other trade and professional associations.

4–597   Note that the last factor could bring the views of competitors into the assessment, introducing a competition element to it.

The Court also described the desired outcome of that test: the relevant class of persons, or at least a significant proportion thereof, must identify the goods as originating from a particular undertaking because of the trade mark.

It rejected though the practice of relying solely on general, abstract data such as predetermined percentages. Opinion polls could be useful, where a national authority "has particular difficulty"[959] in establishing whether a contested sign has acquired the necessary distinctive character. The national authority would then have to rely on the conditions laid down by its own national law regarding the polls.

(2) Philips—reinforcing Windsurfing Chiemsee

4–598   The third question referred to the Court in *Philips*[960] targeted the conditions and the method in which distinctive character could be gained through use.

Where a trader had been the only supplier of a product, would extensive use of a sign that consisted of the shape of the product and did not incorporate a capricious addition be sufficient to render the sign distinctive for the purposes of art.3(3) when a substantial proportion of the relevant trade and public associated the shape with that trader and no other undertaking and believed that goods of that shape came from that trader unless there was a statement to the contrary?

Advocate General Ruiz-Jarabo Colomer found that the question could be answered by reference to his brief answer to the second question,[961] where he implied that shapes would require an arbitrary addition in order to become distinctive, and his analysis of art.3(1)(e), in particular the conclusion that it was not in any way connected with distinctiveness.

---

[959] *Windsurfing Chiemsee*, para.53.
[960] *Koninklijke Philips Electronics NV* (C-299/99) [2002] E.C.R. I-5475.
[961] See paras 4–087 and following, above.

13. ARTICLE 3(3)—DISTINCTIVE CHARACTER ACQUIRED THROUGH USE

(a) The judgment of the Court 4-599

For the Court, art.3(3) provided that through use a sign that failed art.3(1)(b), art.3(1)(c), or art.3(1)(d) could overcome the objection through evidence of acquired distinctive character. According to *Windsurfing Chiemsee*[962] this meant that the mark was able to identify the specified product as originating from a particular undertaking, and thus to distinguish that product from goods of other undertakings.

Philips had argued before the Court that the de facto monopoly described in the question should be seen as an advantage towards registration rather than an impediment. Remington on the other hand urged the Court to adopt a balanced approach and require evidence that the sign indeed functioned as an indicator of origin. And, whereas France and the Commission focused on the outcome rather than the circumstances of use, the United Kingdom supported that public recognition resulting from the monopoly rather than use of the mark should be discounted.

The Court chose the middle ground; it referred to the test and the criteria adopted in *Windsurfing Chiemsee* and reminded that art.3(3) would be irrelevant in relation to a sign that had been refused registration under art.3(1)(e).

(i) Indication of source—the requirement for specific and reliable date. The Court underlined three particular points. 4-600

First, it repeated that general, abstract data, such as predetermined percentages, would not be useful and added that in order to establish acquired distinctive character demanded specific and reliable data.

Secondly, it stressed that acquired distinctiveness should not be established outside the context delineated by the expectations of the consumer, following an easier route based on market conditions:

"the distinctive character of a sign consisting in the shape of a product, even that acquired by the use made of it, must be assessed in the light of the presumed expectations of an average consumer of the category of goods or services in question, who is reasonably well-informed and reasonably observant and circumspect".[963]

This was reinforced by the third point made by the Court: 4-601

"the identification, by the relevant class of persons, of the product as originating from a given undertaking must be as a result of the use of the

---

[962] *Windsurfing Chiemsee Produktions- und Vertriebs GmbH* (C-108/97 & C-109/97) [1999] E.C.R. I-2779.
[963] *Windsurfing Chiemsee*, para.63, citing *Güt Springenheide and Tusky v Oberkreisdirektor des Kreises Steinfurt-AMT für Lebensmittelüberwachung* (C-210/96) [1998] E.C.R. I-4657.

mark as a trade mark and thus as a result of the nature and effect of it, which make it capable of distinguishing the product concerned from those of other undertakings".[964]

So under the circumstances described above the type of use described by the referring court could generate the distinctive character that was necessary to satisfy art.3(3), provided that the three points made by the Court were satisfied. Verifying this remained in the jurisdiction of the national court.

(3) Kit-Kat—combined use

4–602   The *Kit-Kat* case[965] revisited slogans as trade marks from a different perspective. The reference from the English Court of Appeal enquired whether the distinctive character of a mark referred to in art.3(3) of the Directive could be acquired following or in consequence of the use of that mark as part of or in conjunction with another mark.

The sign in question was the slogan HAVE A BREAK that Nestlé applied to register as a trade mark in the United Kingdom. Nestlé was already the proprietor of the marks HAVE A BREAK... HAVE A KIT KAT and KIT KAT covering the same specification, chocolate, chocolate products, confectionery, candy and biscuits. Mars opposed the application claiming that the mark lacked distinctive character under art.3(1)(b).

On appeal the UK court found that the slogan as such was indeed devoid of distinctive character. Registration could be obtained only if Nestlé could prove that the sign had acquired distinctive character through use. The problem was that the expression HAVE A BREAK was used as part of the trade mark HAVE A BREAK... HAVE A KIT KAT rather than as an independent trade mark.

4–603   *(a)   The Opinion of the Advocate General*

Advocate General Kokott reiterated that following *Erpo Mobelwerk*[966] "the universally applicable concept of distinctive character"[967] precluded specific criteria from being applied in the case of specific types of trade marks.

She then distinguished between inherent and acquired distinctiveness. Article 3(1)(b) covered inherent distinctiveness, and as "a matter of principle that examination is to be conducted independently of use of the sign. It has regard only to whether the sign in itself has distinctive character".[968]

---

[964] *Windsurfing Chiemsee*, para.64.
[965] *Societe des Produits Nestlé v Mars UK Ltd* (C-353/03) [2005] E.C.R. I-6135.
[966] *Office for Harmonisation in the Internal Market v Erpo Möbelwerk* (C-64/02 P) [2004] E.C.R. I-10031.
[967] Point 16 of the Opinion of A.G. Kokott.
[968] Point 18 of the Opinion of A.G. Kokott.

13. ARTICLE 3(3)—DISTINCTIVE CHARACTER ACQUIRED THROUGH USE

Article 3(3) however diluted art.3(1)(b) allowing the registration of marks that had acquired distinctive character through use. Delineating the scope of her Opinion and the judgment of the Court she stressed that the role of the Court was to express a view on the interpretation of art.3(3) rather than decide whether HAVE A BREAK had acquired a distinctive character.

She rejected outright the argument submitted by Mars and supported by the Commission that art.3(3) use of the contested mark as an element of another mark should not be considered under that provision.

4–604

Following a literal interpretive path she noted that use of a mark meant both independent use of the sign and use as part of another composite trade mark. She supported that art.10(2)(a) pointed towards the same conclusion. If use of a mark as part of a composite sufficed to maintain the validity of the registration, it had to suffice for obtaining the same registration.

The Advocate General contrasted the concept of use in the context of art.5—where the Court had limited protection to cover instances that affect the function of a trade mark as a guarantee of origin—and in that of art.3(3) where, she claimed, it fulfilled a different function, to describe the manner in which a sign might acquire distinctive character through use.

The Court had considered this type of use in *Philips*.[969] It had to be used as a trade mark, but this did not preclude use of the relevant sign as part of a trade mark.

4–605

Use under art.3(3) had to "be construed from the perspective of the result. Any use which confers on a sign the distinctive character necessary for registration as a mark must be deemed to be use of a mark as a trade mark".[970]

She found the view of Mars, also adopted by the United Kingdom, that the risk of extending the protection of the principal mark to cover the derivative mark meant that stricter criteria had to be adopted when only one part of the principal mark was assessed because then a derivative of the derivative could be protected, to be illusory. "If a primary derivative mark possesses no sufficient distinctive character of its own but acquires distinctiveness only by way of the connection with the principal mark then it is unlikely that a secondary derivative mark will be able to acquire distinctive character on the basis of its connection with the primary derivative mark."[971]

---

[969] She cautioned that *Koninklijke Philips Electronics NV* (C299/99) [2002] E.C.R. I-5475 should be read keeping in mind that it dealt primarily with art.3(1)(e) of the Directive and that the Court did not have to interpret art.3(3) as well.

[970] Point 33 of the Opinion of A.G. Kokott. The reference in *Koninklijke Philips Electronics NV* (C-299/99) [2002] E.C.R. I-5475 to the nature and effect of a trade mark as the background of use required under art.3(3) strengthened the interpretive approach of the A.G.

[971] Point 36 of the Opinion of A.G. Kokott.

4–606   Advocate General Kokott also mentioned that so far the practice of the Court, the Court of First Instance, and the Community Trade Mark Office was not to refuse trade mark recognition to parts of a trade mark that had themselves acquired a distinctive character.[972]

Nevertheless, gathering evidence of distinctiveness acquired through use would not be an easy exercise. It would not be sufficient "for the purposes of demonstrating acquisition of distinctive character, as a result of use as a part of a composite mark, to provide documentary evidence of use of the overall mark. Rather it must also be demonstrated that the relevant consumer groups understand the element in question, if used separately, to designate a product as originating from a specific undertaking, thus distinguishing it from products of other undertakings".[973]

In practice it would be easier to find distinctive character for the essential elements of a primary mark whereas inessential elements would be less likely to develop a distinctive character.

4–607   *(b)   The judgment of the Court*

The Court reiterated the parameters of distinctive character.

Both inherent and acquired through use distinctive character had to be assessed in relation to the specified goods or services and the presumed expectations of the relevant class of persons. Acquired distinctive character had to be the result of use as a trade mark.[974] Article 3(3) did not indicate any further restriction. Identification of the specified product or service as originating from a given undertaking, "and thus acquisition of distinctive character, may be as a result both of the use, as part of a registered trade mark, of a component thereof and of the use of a separate mark in conjunction with a registered trade mark. In both cases it is sufficient that, in consequence of such use, the relevant class of persons actually perceive the product or service, designated exclusively by the mark applied for, as originating from a given undertaking".[975]

---

[972] Referring by way of example to *Windsurfing Chiemsee Produktions- und Vertriebs GmbH* (C-108/97 & C-109/97) [1999] E.C.R. I-2779; *Alcon Inc v Office for Harmonization in the Internal Market (Trade Marks and Designs)* (T-237/01) [2003] E.C.R. II-411, and the decision of the Second Board of Appeal in Case R 111/2000-2 *Ringling Bros–Barnum & Bailey combined shows Inc (The Greatest Show on Earth)*.
[973] Point 43. She accepted the submission of the UK Government that it would not be sufficient to show that consumers merely wondered whether the product or service originated from the owner of the primary mark; this, however, would be a consideration for assessing likelihood of confusion.
[974] Citing *Koninklijke Philips Electronics NV* (C-299/99) [2002] E.C.R. I-5475.
[975] *Kit Kat*, para.30.

13. ARTICLE 3(3)—DISTINCTIVE CHARACTER ACQUIRED THROUGH USE

(4) Storck I—article 7(3)—sales figures—amount spent on advertising   4–608

Part of the appeal in *Storck I*[976] challenged the findings of the Court of First Instance in relation to the evidence that is required for establishing that distinctive character has been acquired through use under art.7(3).

(a) The judgment of the Court of First Instance   4–609

The Court of First Instance had agreed with the Board of Appeal that the sign—the shape of a sweet—had not acquired distinctive character through use, finding that the evidence was insufficient. Sales figures and the amount spent on advertising to promote the product did not establish that the actual, three-dimensional, mark had become distinctive as a result of use.

Storck had argued that samples of plastic bags in which the sweets were sold bearing reproductions of the shape of the sweets constituted a "primary reference" point for the consumer and that they should be seen as evidence that the shape was the subject of the advertising as the mark of the product.

Responding to the argument the Board had stressed that it should not perform an abstract assessment but, instead, consider the probable way in which the average consumer perceived the representation of the sweets.

The consumer would first notice the name "Werther's Original" written in large print over almost half of the packet and surrounded by further details such as a small oval sign bearing the name Storck and the stylised picture of a small village below which might be perceived as a reference to "Traditional Werther's Quality". The lower half of the packet depicted a colour photograph of a pile of about 15 sweets and the statement "The classic candy made with real butter and fresh cream".   4–610

The Board found that the way the sweets were represented on the packaging served simply as an illustration of its contents rather than as an indication of source. It was a realistic picture of a pile of unwrapped sweets, rather than a representation of the mark applied for, that did not intend to emphasise the two potentially distinctive characteristics of the mark. It highlighted in particular the combination of the statement "The classic candy made with real butter and fresh cream" with the picture. They complemented each other in that the statement described the nature of the sweets and the picture depicted them.

The Board accepted that a product might simultaneously bear multiple marks but this general proposition did not mean that the particular representation on the packaging of the sweets functioned as a trade mark.

---

[976] *August Storck KG v Office for Harmonisation in the Internal Market (Trade Marks and Designs)* (C-24/05 P) [2006] E.C.R. I–5677.

4–611   As a result, the advertising expenditure could not be linked with the use of the mark applied for. The Board found that the surveys submitted to support the application proved that the sweets were sold on the basis of their name, not their shape, functioning as a trade mark.

The Court of First Instance added to the above that Storck had stated on the application form that the sweets were not sold loose; they were individually wrapped and sold in a packet. The average consumer would not be able to see the shape of the sweet prior to the sale of the product in order to perceive it as an indication of origin.

Before the Court of Justice, Storck had argued that the Court of First Instance had infringed art.7(3) of the Regulation in three ways: first, by making the relevant evidence subject to false requirements; secondly, by wrongly confirming the function of the representation of the mark on the packaging of the product; and, thirdly, by wrongly taking into consideration consumer perception at the time of the decision to buy.

(b)   The Opinion of the Advocate General

4–612   **(i) The application of article 7(3)—three-dimensional signs.** Advocate General Ruiz-Jarabo Colomer made it clear that he would deal only with those elements of the fourth ground that raised legal questions, not with those that involved the possible re-assessment of facts like the assertions regarding the impression of the sign on the wrapping.

He referred to *Nestlé*[977] where the Court held that the acquisition of distinctive character did not necessarily entail independent use of a sign. In the current case the Court of First Instance had not contradicted this, nor had it attempted to establish a general rule for three-dimensional signs; it had merely assessed the evidence in the case before it.

4–613   **(ii) The application of article 7(3)—the time for determining distinctiveness.** The Advocate General referred again to *Nestlé* and then to the *Picasso*[978] case.

His interpretation of the first case appeared to leave the question of the decisive moment for determining distinctive character unanswered since the Court had only indicated that it would be sufficient "that the relevant sectors perceive the product or service, designated exclusively by the mark applied for, as originating from a given undertaking".[979]

The second case also appeared to be, to say the least, inconclusive:

"Apart from my feeling that the present discussion would be more appropriate in the context of Article 8(1)(b) of Regulation No 40/94, it is worth

---

[977] *Societe des Produits Nestlé v Mars UK Ltd* (C-353/03) [2005] E.C.R. I-6135.
[978] *Ruiz-Picasso v Office for Harmonisation in the Internal Market (Trade Marks and Designs)* (C-316/04 P) [2006] E.C.R. I-643.
[979] Point 59 of the Opinion of A.G. Ruiz-Jarabo Colomer.

13. ARTICLE 3(3)—DISTINCTIVE CHARACTER ACQUIRED THROUGH USE

noting that in Ruiz-Picasso the Court of Justice endorsed the reasoning of the Court of First Instance on the likelihood of confusion, to the effect that the relevant public also perceives the products and the marks relating to them in circumstances unconnected with any act of purchase, although on such occasions displaying a lower level of attention, which does not prevent taking into account the particularly high level of attention which the average consumer pays when he prepares and makes his choice between different products in the same range."[980]

Expressing his own view on the point he veered towards the point of sale and the time of making the purchase at least in comparison with advertising: **4–614**

"In a system in which competition is not distorted ... it is plain that the protection for proprietors of the type of intellectual property right in question is concentrated in the culminating moment when the consumer makes his decision, the purchase of the product or the engagement of the service, whilst prior advertising is a measure intended to induce that consumer to opt for a particular acquisition, and it is therefore difficult to understand why it should be taken into account on an equal footing with the act of purchasing the product."[981]

The argument of the appellant based on the post sale effect of the mark at the time of consumption was rejected by the Advocate General as even less comprehensible.

(c) The judgment of the Court **4–615**

(i) Article 7(3)—three-dimensional signs. The Court divided the fourth ground of appeal into three parts.

The first part claimed that the Court of First Instance had wrongly held that a mark made up of the three-dimensional shape of the product concerned could not acquire distinctive character if accompanied by a word or figurative mark.

The second targeted the confirmation of the assessment of the Board that the representation of the product on the packaging showed merely its contents. The mark and the product were the same thing and accordingly its reproduction functioned as information regarding the contents of the packet but also an indication of origin.

The third part supported that the Court had wrongly discounted consumer perceptions before the point of sale, for example as a result of advertising, and, after the point of sale, when consuming the product.

---

[980] Point 60 of the Opinion of A.G. Ruiz-Jarabo Colomer.
[981] Point 61 of the Opinion of A.G. Ruiz-Jarabo Colomer.

4–616 **(ii) Three-dimensional marks—limiting the scope of Nestlé.** The Court accepted that following *Nestlé*[982] a three-dimensional mark might in certain circumstances acquire distinctive character through use even if it were used in conjunction with a word mark or a figurative mark. Its next statement though limited that possibility considerably:

> "However, it must be stressed that a three-dimensional mark is essentially different from its two-dimensional graphic representation. It follows that where, as in the present case, a picture of the product features on the packaging, consumers do not actually see the mark itself, being the mark consisting of the three-dimensional form of the product."[983]

And then, in the same paragraph the Court reduced the effect of the above statement by introducing a new consideration; a classic example of the, sometimes confusing, habit of the court to rely on balancing exercises:

> "It is possible, however, that the two-dimensional representation of such a mark may in certain circumstances facilitate awareness of the mark by the relevant public where it enables the essential elements of the three-dimensional shape of the product to be perceived."[984]

The Court then reverted to its sceptical original logic, by reminding that according to *Philips*[985] and *Nestlé*[986] the acquisition of distinctive character through use had to be the result of the use of the mark as a trade mark, i.e. use of the mark for the purposes of the identification by the relevant class of persons of the product or service as originating from a given undertaking.

Therefore, it added not every use of the mark, "a fortiori use of a two-dimensional representation of a three-dimensional mark, amounts necessarily to use as a mark".[987]

4–617 **(iii) The application of article 7(3).** It found that the Court of First Instance had not erred in law; following a factual assessment it had found that the representation related to the contents rather than the mark in question. In terms of law, though, it had accepted, by endorsing the relevant statement of the Board, that a product might bear several marks at the same time.

Accordingly the first two parts of the fourth ground were unfounded.

---

[982] *Societe des Produits Nestlé* (C-353/03) [2005] E.C.R. I-6135.
[983] *Storck I*, para.60.
[984] *Storck I*, para.60.
[985] *Koninklijke Philips Electronics NV* (C-299/99) [2002] E.C.R. I-5475.
[986] *Societe des Produits Nestlé* (C-353/03) [2005] E.C.R. I-6135.
[987] *Storck I*, para.62.

13. ARTICLE 3(3)—DISTINCTIVE CHARACTER ACQUIRED THROUGH USE

(iv) The timing for determining distinctive character. As to the third ground the Court accepted that distinctive character might be acquired "inter alia, after the normal process of familiarising the relevant public has taken place".[988]

4–618

This meant that "all the circumstances in which the relevant public may see that mark must be borne in mind. That means not only when the decision to purchase is made but also before that point, for example as a result of advertising, and when the product is consumed".[989]

But the critical time was the point when the average consumer made a choice:

"it is when making his choice between different products in the category concerned that the average consumer exhibits the highest level of attention[990] ... so that the question whether or not the average consumer sees the mark at the time of purchase is of particular importance for determining whether the mark has acquired distinctive character through use".[991]

It found that the Court of First Instance had not taken into account only the time when the decision to purchase was made. It had considered the effect of the packaging on the consumer "logically, with reference to the actual time of purchase".[992]

4–619

And, it had rightly found that the surveys failed to distinguish between the various circumstances in which consumers might have seen the mark, and accordingly could not furnish proof that the mark applied for was known.

Accordingly, the fourth ground was rejected as unfounded.

(5) Storck II—sales figures in abstract

4–620

In *Storck II*[993] the mark consisted of a gold-coloured sweet wrapper. The Court of First Instance agreed with the Board that the applicant had not established the mark had acquired distinctive character. The sales figures that had been provided failed to show the share it enjoyed in the market in the absence of any information regarding the total volume of the relevant product market. The same applied to advertising costs.

In addition the information provided was patchy and in some cases unpersuasive.

The Court of First Instance appeared to require strong data covering the entire Community because the trade mark should have become distinctive through use throughout its territory.

---

[988] *Storck I*, para.70, citing *Libertel Groep BV* (C-104/01) [2003] E.C.R. I-3793; and *Mag Instrument Inc* (C-132/02 P) [2004] E.C.R. I-9165.
[989] *Storck I*, para.71.
[990] Citing *Ruiz-Picasso* (C-361/04 P) [2006] E.C.R. I-643.
[991] *Storck I*, para.72.
[992] *Storck I*, para.74.
[993] *August Storck KG* (C-25/5 P) [2006] E.C.R. 000.

As to the surveys produced by the applicant the Court of First Instance found that they only proved that the sweets were sold because of their name rather than their wrappings.

4-621 *(a) The Opinion of the Advocate General*

The Advocate General divided his discussion of the art.7(3) ground of appeal into two parts. First he dealt with the evidence of use and then with its geographical extent.

4-622 **(i) Article 7(3)—evidence of use.** Storck had attacked the finding of the Board that the figures relating to sales and advertising expenditure had failed to establish that the mark had acquired distinctive character through use and the condition that additional information regarding the overall size of these markets should be produced.

To an extent Storck replayed the argument that the condition of the market was irrelevant. In the same way that the existence of similar packaging should be irrelevant for establishing distinctive character, the existence or absence of other well-known marks should be irrelevant for the acquisition of distinctive character.

The Advocate General reminded the factors the Court had established in *Windsurfing Chiemsee*[994] and *Philips*[995] and added that the applicability and evidential value of these factors remained in the jurisdiction of the Court of First Instance that had considered the appellant's assertions but still found that one of the factors, the share of the market in terms of sales, should be decisive.

Note that the share in the advertising market, an apparently new factor compared with those mentioned in *Windsurfing Chiemsee*, failed to attract any further discussion.

4-623 **(ii) Article 7(3)—geographical extent.** Finally, Storck argued that requiring evidence of use throughout the Member States went against two of the fundamental objectives of the Union: the abolition of national borders and the creation of a single market.

The appellant relied partly to art.142a(2) of Reg. No.40/94, one of the enlargement provisions.[996]

---

[994] *Windsurfing Chiemsee Produktions- und Vertriebs GmbH* (C-108/97 & C-109/97) [1999] E.C.R. I-2779.

[995] *Koninklijke Philips Electronics NV* (C-299/99) [2002] E.C.R. I-5475.

[996] Providing that the "registration of a Community trade mark which is under application at the date of accession may not be refused on the basis of any of the absolute grounds for refusal listed in Article 7(1) [of Reg. No. 40/94], if these grounds became applicable merely because of the accession of a new Member State". Article 7(1)(b) provides that "trade marks which are devoid of any distinctive character" shall not be registered whereas art.7(2) provides that art.7(1) "shall apply notwithstanding that the grounds of non-registrability obtain in only part of the Community" and art.7(3) that art.7(1)(b) shall not apply if the trade mark has become distinctive in relation to the goods or services for which registration is requested in consequence of the use which has been made of it.

13. ARTICLE 3(3)—DISTINCTIVE CHARACTER ACQUIRED THROUGH USE

The Advocate General followed the line suggested by the Office. Reading art.7(1)(b) together with art.7(2) meant that lack of distinctive character in part of the Union should lead to the rejection of the application for registration. Admittedly, art.7(3) did not refer to art.7(2). It would be illogical though to demand a lower geographical threshold under art.7(3).

He added that the later "political" enlargement provision should not affect the application of art.7(3).

(b) The judgment of the Court 4–624

The Court repeated the test it had established in its earlier case law.[997] All the facts should be taken into account including: the market share held by the mark; how intensive, geographically widespread and long-standing use of the mark had been; the amount invested by the undertaking in promoting the mark; the proportion of the relevant class of persons who, because of the mark, identified goods as originating from a particular undertaking; and statements from chambers of commerce and industry or other trade and professional associations.

(i) Article 7(3)—market share. The Court remarked that market share was one of the relevant factors: 4–625

"Such is the case, in particular, where ... a mark consisting of the appearance of the product in respect of which registration is sought appears to be devoid of any distinctive character because it does not depart significantly from the norm or customs of the sector. It is probable, in such a case, that such a mark is likely to acquire distinctive character only if, following the use which is made of it, the products which bear it have more than a negligible share of the market in the products at issue."[998]

The same reasoning applied to advertising expenditure.

In any case the relevance of that information for determining whether a mark had acquired distinctive character through use was part of the assessment of the facts of the case.

The first part of the fourth ground of appeal was rejected as unfounded.

(ii) Article 7(3)—geographical extent. The Court was unequivocal in its approach. Following the same reasoning with the Advocate General it ruled that "a mark can be registered under Article 7(3) of Regulation No 40/94 only if evidence is provided that it has acquired, through the use which 4–626

---

[997] *Windsurfing Chiemsee Produktions- und Vertriebs GmbH* (C-108/97 & C-109/97) [1999] E.C.R. I-2779; *Koninklijke Philips Electronics NV* (C-299/99) [2002] E.C.R. I-5475; and *Societe des Produits Nestlé* (C-353/03) [2005] E.C.R. I-6135.
[998] *Storck II*, para.76.

has been made of it, distinctive character in the part of the Community in which it did not, ab initio, have such character for the purposes of Article 7(1)(b). The part of the Community referred to in Article 7(2) may be comprised of a single Member State".[999]

The Act of Accession reinforced rather than weakened the Court's stance:

> "As they found it necessary to introduce an express provision to the effect that registration of a Community trade mark which is under application at the date of accession may not be refused on the basis of any of the absolute grounds for refusal listed in Article 7(1) of Regulation No 40/94, if these grounds became applicable merely because of the accession of a new Member State, the authors of the Act of Accession considered that, if that provision did not exist, such an application would have had to have been refused if the mark was devoid of any distinctive character in one of the new Member States."[1000]

The second part of the fourth ground was also rejected as unfounded.

4–627 **(6) Europolis—acquired distinctive character in the Benelux— linguistic and geographical considerations**

In *Europolis*[1001] the Court was asked to determine how a trade mark might acquire distinctive character through use, under art.3(3) of the Directive. The case had reached the Gerechtshof te 's-Gravenhage (Hague Regional Court of Appeal) as an appeal against the decision of the Benelux Trade Mark Office to reject the application of EUROPOLIS for "insurance, financial affairs, monetary affairs, real estate affairs, transport, packaging and storage of goods, and travel arrangements" for lack of distinctive character, despite evidence that the mark had been used for a 10-year period before the application.

The Dutch court considered that the mark had no "intrinsic distinctive character".[1002] As to whether the sign had acquired distinctiveness through use the Trade Mark Office required recognition of the sign as a trade mark throughout the Benelux whereas the applicant supported that it would be enough to be recognised as a trade mark by the relevant public in a substantial part of the Benelux.

Viewing the issue of acquired distinctiveness from a rather formalistic perspective the Hague Regional Court of Appeal referred to the Court of Justice a number of questions.

---

[999] *Storck II*, para.83.
[1000] *Storck II*, para.85.
[1001] *Bovemij Verzekeringen NV* (C-108/05) [2006] E.C.R. I–7605.
[1002] Point 20 of the Opinion of A.G. Sharpston.

13. ARTICLE 3(3)—DISTINCTIVE CHARACTER ACQUIRED THROUGH USE

4–628 First, whether art.3(3) necessitated the sign to be regarded as a trade mark throughout the Benelux.

Secondly, if the answer to the first question were negative, whether it would be enough to be regarded as a trade mark by the relevant section of the public in a substantial part of the Benelux, for example only in The Netherlands.

The third question had to do with distinctiveness of word marks in regions characterised by their language: the first part of the question enquired whether it was necessary to take into account the language regions—or linguistic communities as A.G. Sharpston put it—within the Benelux; the second, if it suffices to be regarded as a trade mark in a substantial part of the language region of the Benelux in which that language is an official language.

(a) The Opinion of the Advocate General

4–629 The delineation of the subject matter of the case by the Advocate General is quite interesting. Despite the fact that the first two questions referred to trade marks in general rather than word marks she narrowed the scope of the Opinion to cover only word marks by referring to the subject matter of the proceedings before the Dutch court.[1003]

And then having narrowed the overall scope of the Opinion down to word marks she broadened its legal subject matter by examining not only the issue of distinctiveness acquired through use, as requested by the national court, but also how word marks fit in the Directive and the jurisprudence of the Court, and the basis for determining that they are devoid of any distinctive character.

Looking at word marks the Advocate General repeated the position of the Court; "a word or combination of words may serve to designate some characteristic(s) of a product. Words used for that purpose are not registrable by virtue of Article 3(1)(c). They are similarly necessarily devoid of any distinctive character with regard to that product within the meaning of Article 3(1)(b), as the Court has already held."[1004]

4–630 On the other hand a word or a combination of words "may identify a product (whether or not in the process they also incidentally describe it). Such a word mark is registrable as a trade mark because it is not caught by either Article 3(1)(b) or Article 3(1)(c)".[1005]

Note that the Advocate General employed the term "identify" instead of "distinguish". It could be argued that the first term is broader.

She then referred to the public interest behind art.3(1)(c), "that all signs or indications which may serve to designate characteristics of the goods or

---

[1003] Contrast with her Opinion in *Boehringer II*, see paras 8–255 and following, below.
[1004] Point 28, citing *Koninklijke KPN Nederland NV* (C-363/99) [2004] E.C.R. I-1619, para.13.
[1005] Point 28 of the Opinion of A.G. Sharpston.

services for which registration is sought may be freely used by all",[1006] but focused in particular on word marks citing *Linde*[1007] and *Campina Melkunie*[1008]:

> "The public interest in not allowing a descriptive combination of words to be registered and protected as a trade mark is clear. Such registration prevents other undertakings (and hence potential competitors) from using obvious terms to describe their products to consumers, thus placing them at a competitive disadvantage."[1009]

4-631   This, she added, would be against the purpose of the Directive to remove disparities which may impede free movement and distort competition, referring to Recital 1.

Registrability under art.3(1)(b) and art.3(1)(c) should be assessed according to the perception of the "relevant class of person"[1010] in the Member State where registration is sought. The linguistic abilities of that class were critical because they ultimately determined registrability[1011]:

> "Put another way, words that convey meaning through their ability to describe goods or services may not be registered as marks, but where they fail to convey meaning because of linguistic differences, they cannot perform a descriptive function. There is therefore no bar to their registration arising from Article 3(1)."[1012]

To determine whether the sign had acquired distinctiveness the overall assessment test developed in *Windsurfing Chiemsee*[1013] should be applied, to establish whether the relevant class of persons, or at least a significant proportion—according to the Advocate General significant meant a considerable part but not necessarily the majority—thereof identify the

---

[1006] Citing *Campina Melkunie BV v Benelux-Merkenbureau* (C-265/00) [2004] E.C.R. I-1699; *Windsurfing Chiemsee Produktions- und Vertriebs GmbH* (C-108/97 & C-109/97) [1999] E.C.R. I-2779; and *Libertel Groep BV* (C-104/01) [2003] E.C.R. I-3793.

[1007] *Linde AG* (C-53/01), *Winward Industries Inc* (C-54/01) and *Rado Uhren AG* (C-55/01) [2003] E.C.R. I-3161.

[1008] *Campina Melkunie BV* (C-265/00) [2004] E.C.R. I-1699.

[1009] Point 29. He noted that the Court did not appear to distinguish between the public interest behind art.3(1)(b) and that behind art.3(1)(c); in *Koninklijke KPN Nederland NV* (C-363/99) [2004] E.C.R. I-1619 the Court assessed distinctiveness under art.3(1)(b) but referred to the public interest in terms of art.3(1)(c).

[1010] Citing *Windsurfing Chiemsee Produktions- und Vertriebs GmbH* (C-108/97 & C-109/97) [1999] E.C.R. I-2779; and *Koninklijke KPN Nederland NV* (C-363/99) [2004] E.C.R. I-1619.

[1011] See the Opinion of A.G. Jacobs in *Matrazen Concord AG* (C-421/04) [2006] E.C.R. I-2303, see paras 4–460 and following, above.

[1012] Point 32 of the Opinion of A.G. Sharpston.

[1013] *Windsurfing Chiemsee Produktions- und Vertriebs GmbH* (C-108/97 & C-109/97) [1999] E.C.R. I-2779. On how use can lead to distinctiveness he also cited *Libertel Groep BV* (C-104/01) [2003] E.C.R. I-3793 in particular paras 62–67.

13. ARTICLE 3(3)—DISTINCTIVE CHARACTER ACQUIRED THROUGH USE

products as originating from a particular undertaking because of the mark.[1014]

She also noted that the factors of this test related either to the actual use of the mark or its identification with the product. In essence art.3(3) requirements mirrored the assessment that had to be made under art.3(1)(b) and art.3(1)(c).[1015]

4–632

The relevance of the linguistic abilities of that class of persons depended on the original meaning of the words. "Where the fact that the words normally convey descriptive meaning to the relevant class was a bar to registration, it must then be relevant to examine whether, for those persons, the word mark has nevertheless acquired distinctive character through use and thus qualifies for registration under Article 3(3)."[1016] Article 3(3) had to be applied "within the same parameters as were used to identify the original lack of distinctiveness".[1017]

(i) The territorial scope of the assessment. After this general assessment she turned to the actual questions referred by the Dutch court. Regarding the territorial scope of assessment the Court had already held that the territory of the Benelux should be equated with the territory of a Member State for the purposes of art.5(2).[1018]

4–633

If it were enough to have a reputation in a substantial part of the Benelux, which may consist of a part of one of the Benelux countries for art.5(2), it should be similarly enough to acquire distinctive character through use in a substantial part of the Benelux for art.3(3).

(ii) Community and national trade marks. The Benelux Trade Mark Office's position that a trade mark should enjoy distinctiveness throughout the Benelux was wrongly based on *General Motors*.[1019] The latter concerned a Community Trade Mark—a new Community right rather than a harmonised national right—the unitary character of which made it reasonable to require evidence of distinctiveness over a wider area.

4–634

The Advocate General also highlighted the importance both of the existence of art.7(2) of the Community Trade Mark Regulation, providing that art.7(1) applies notwithstanding that the grounds of non registrability obtain in only part of the Community, and of the fact that there was no equivalent provision in the Directive:

[1014] *Koninklijke Philips Electronics NV* (C-299/99) [2002] E.C.R. I-5475.
[1015] Here the A.G. made a reference to a judgment of the Court of First Instance, *Ford Motor Co v OHIM* (Case T-91/99) [2000] E.C.R. II-1925, applying the corresponding provisions of the Regulation, art.7(1) and art.7(3). She noted however that there are different territorial considerations in the case of Community Trade Marks, because they are conceptually different from national trade marks.
[1016] Point 38 of the Opinion of A.G. Sharpston.
[1017] Point 39 of the Opinion of A.G. Sharpston.
[1018] *General Motors Corp v Yplon SA* (C-375/97) [1999] E.C.R. I-5421.
[1019] *General Motors Corp* (C-375/97) [1999] E.C.R. I-5421.

"Because the Community trade mark is a unitary mark which, if registered, will be effective throughout the territory of the Community, it is right to impose the condition contained in Article 7(2). Such a mark ought not to be registered if there exist, in any part of the Community, grounds for non-registration. The same considerations do not apply to the registration of national trade marks as harmonised by the Trade Marks Directive."[1020]

She agreed however with the Benelux Trade Mark Office that linguistic communities in a Member State or in the Benelux should be taken into account in assessing distinctive character acquired through use; this was linked with her earlier discussion on the relevant class of consumers. In this case the relevant class comprised Dutch speakers for whom EUROPOLIS lacked distinctive character. "It is therefore only within that linguistic community that distinctiveness must be acquired for registration purposes".[1021]

4-635 Finally, on the proportion of the relevant class that must conceive the sign—the Advocate General used the term mark—as a source identifier she once again started from art.3(1)(b) and art.3(1)(c). If the class that viewed the sign as lacking distinctiveness or being descriptive is reasonably large then "it is statistically likely that one will find some data that are at variance with the norm".[1022]

But one must look at the totality of the available data. If the class described above constituted a large proportion of the relevant consumers the authorities should require a significant proportion of that class to perceive the sign "as identifying, in a distinctive way, the origin of the goods or services to which it is applied".[1023] And registration should not be granted if only a small proportion of the same class perceive the sign as a trade mark.

Following the opposite approach would disregard the public interest behind art.3(1)(c)—note the absence of a reference to art.3(1)(b)—creating a situation in the marketplace where the sign would be protected although the majority of consumers still viewed it as descriptive. From an interpretive perspective it would imply that art.3(3) could be applied independently from art.3(1); this according to the Advocate General would create the paradox "that both provisions—which have opposite effects—could be satisfied at the same time in the same territory".[1024]

4-636 Note that the two provisions share the same aim, that only distinctive signs are registered, from two different perspectives, with use making the difference. They are inextricably linked.

[1020] Point 45 of the Opinion of A.G. Sharpston.
[1021] Point 50, and fn.30 citing para.30 of *Libertel Groep BV* (C-104/01) [2003] E.C.R. I-3793 requiring that the examination of registrability must be undertaken by reference to the actual situation rather than in the abstract.
[1022] Point 52 of the Opinion of A.G. Sharpston.
[1023] Point 52 of the Opinion of A.G. Sharpston.
[1024] Point 55 of the Opinion of A.G. Sharpston.

13. ARTICLE 3(3)—DISTINCTIVE CHARACTER ACQUIRED THROUGH USE

There was a Benelux peculiarity—not raised in the reference to the Court—that the Advocate General also took into account to support her approach. Article 13C(1) of the Uniform Benelux Law provided that the exclusive right to a trade mark expressed in one of the national or regional languages of the Benelux territory covers its translations in the other languages. This highlighted the "importance of not overriding the public interest aims of Article 3(1)(b) and Article 3(1)(c) save where acquisition of distinctive character through use is indeed solidly established".[1025]

So, the Advocate General required distinctiveness acquired through use throughout the linguistic community in the Member State. Otherwise there was a risk that registration could be obtained as a result of use in a sub-part of the linguistic community.

To demonstrate this she employed a useful geographical example. If the mark was descriptive in Dutch, distinctiveness acquired through use by Dutch speakers in Flanders should not be enough; the mark should have become distinctive for Dutch Speakers throughout the Benelux, covering at least The Netherlands and the bilingual region of Brussels.[1026]

(b) The judgment of the Court   4-637

In relation to the first two questions the Court[1027] reminded that according to its case law[1028] that the Benelux territory must be treated like the territory of a Member State according to art.1 of the Directive.

Article 3(3) constituted an exception to art.3(1)(b) to (d); accordingly its scope should be "be interpreted in light of those grounds for refusal".[1029] Following *Storck II*[1030] it held that "Article 3(3) of the Directive must be interpreted as meaning that the registration of a trade mark can be allowed on the basis of that provision only if it is proven that that trade mark has acquired distinctive character through use throughout the territory of the Member State or, in the case of Benelux, throughout the part of the territory of Benelux in which there exists a ground for refusal".[1031]

The answer to the third question followed the same logic: "to assess whether a mark has acquired distinctive character through use which would justify disregarding the grounds for refusal under art.3(3) of the Directive, it is necessary to take into account the part of Benelux where Dutch is spoken"[1032] since Dutch was one of the official languages of the

---

[1025] Point 56 of the Opinion of A.G. Sharpston.
[1026] The Commission had supported a similar interpretation, however it was based on *Ford Motor Co v OHIM* (T-91/99) [2000] E.C.R. II-1925 the relevance of which for this particular point had been rejected by the A.G.
[1027] Judgment of September 7, 2006, 2006 WL 2560433.
[1028] Citing *General Motors Corp* (C-375/97) [1999] E.C.R. I-5421.
[1029] *Europolis*, para.21.
[1030] *August Storck KG (Trade Marks and Designs)* (C-25/05 P) [2006] E.C.R. 000.
[1031] *Europolis*, para.23.
[1032] *Europolis*, para.26.

Benelux and the trade mark could be descriptive in that language. The competent authority would have to apply the *Windsurfing Chiemsee*[1033] test on the relevant class of persons.

It is noted that the Court focused on the official languages of, rather than the languages spoken at, the relevant Member State.

4-638 **(7) Pure Digital—the relevant point in time**

In *Pure Digital*[1034] the Court had the opportunity to clarify when the mark must have become distinctive for the purposes of art.7(3) CTMR.

It is worth noting at the outset, that art.7(3) CTMR is not worded in exactly the same way as the equivalent provision in the Directive. Indeed, the language of art.3(3) of the Directive seems to be more restrictive than its counterpart in the Regulation, but at the same time provides for exceptions.

Specifically, while art.3(3) of the Directive states that a trade mark "... shall not be refused registration or be declared invalid ... if, before the date of application ... it has acquired a distinctive character" and adds that "any Member State may in addition provide that this provision shall also apply where the distinctive character was acquired after the date of application ... or after the date of registration", art.7(3) CTMR merely provides that a mark shall not be refused registration "if [it] has become distinctive in relation to the goods or services for which registration is requested in consequence of the use which has been made of it", without clearly stating that this must have happened before the date of the application.

But is that discrepancy legally significant?

It should further be recalled that the CTMR also contains art.51(2) which, in respect of invalidity proceedings, stipulates that even where the Community trade mark has been registered in breach of art.7(1) (b), (c) or (d), "it may nevertheless not be declared invalid if [...] it has after registration acquired a distinctive character in relation to the goods or services for which it is registered".

4-639 *(a) Background to the dispute*

The matter was brought before the Court of Justice in the context of an appeal lodged by Imagination Technologies Ltd ("Imagination Technologies") against the judgment of the Court of First Instance[1035] that

---

[1033] *Windsurfing Chiemsee Produktions- und Vertriebs GmbH* (C-108/97 & C-109/97) [1999] E.C.R. I-2779.
[1034] *Imagination Technologies Ltd/OHIM (PURE DIGITAL)* (C-542/07P) [2001] E.C.R. 00.
[1035] *Imagination Technologies Ltd/OHIM (PURE DIGITAL)* (T-461/04)

had dismissed its action for annulment of the decision of the Second Board of Appeal of OHIM refusing registration to the word sign "PURE DIGITAL".

Imagination Technologies had sought to register that expression as a Community trade mark in respect of, essentially, electronic goods and telecommunication services, included respectively in Classes 9 and 38 of the Nice Classification. The Office rejected the application on the grounds that it was both descriptive and devoid of any distinctive character within the meaning of art.7(1)(b) and (c) CTMR. It also found that the submitted evidence of acquired distinctiveness was insufficient for the purposes of art.7(3).

That refusal was upheld both by the Boards of Appeal of the Office and by the Court of First Instance.

Imagination Technologies appealed only against the second limb of that refusal, pleading infringement of art.7(3) CTMR. It contended that the relevant point in time for assessing distinctiveness was not the time of the application, as erroneously held by the Court, but rather the time of the finalisation of the examination procedure by the Office.

(b)   The judgment of the Court of First Instance 4–640

The Court of First Instance rejected the applicant's evidence of use on the ground that it related to a date after the application had been filed, referring to its settled case law,[1036] that a mark must have become distinctive through use before the application was filed. According to the Court of First Instance, that interpretation is the only one compatible with the logic of the system of absolute and relative grounds for refusal, according to which the date of filing of the application for registration determines the priority of one mark over another; moreover it makes possible to avoid a situation in which the applicant may take undue advantage of the length of the registration procedure in order to prove that his mark has become distinctive subsequent to the filing of the application.[1037]

Moreover, the Court of First Instance dismissed the applicant's argument based on art.51(2) CTMR (new art.52), on the ground that even though that provision serves to safeguard the legitimate expectations of the proprietor and the investments made in the period which has elapsed since registration, there are no such expectations at the stage of a mere application for registration worthy of any protection.[1038]

[1036] *eCopy v OHIM(ECOPY)* (C-247/01) [2002] E.C.R. II-5301, para.36; *El Corte Inglés v OHIM—Pucci (EMILIO PUCCI)* (T-8/03) [2004] E.C.R. II-4297, paras 71 and 72; and *BIC v OHIM (Shape of a lighter)* (T-262/04) [2005] E.C.R. II-5959, para.66
[1037] Judgment of the CFI, para.77.
[1038] Judgment of the CFI, para.78.

4–641 *(c)   The judgment of the Court Justice*

Before the Court, Imagination Technologies principally relied on the following two lines of argument: firstly, it claimed that the very existence of art.51(2) CTMR (new art.52) meant that it was not incompatible with the "logic of the system" to take into account events subsequent to the date of the application, all the more so since that provision does not require that the relevant use should also take place after the registration of the mark. Secondly, it maintained that the proprietor of a mark registered erroneously cannot be said to entertain any "legitimate expectations", being perfectly aware of the fragility of its registration.

The Court did not agree with the appellant.

First, it pointed out that it is apparent from the very wording of art.7(3) CTMR (new art.7) and more particularly from the use of the verbs in the past tense in the phrases "the mark has become" and "in consequence of the use which has been made of it" that the mark must have acquired the requisite distinctiveness already at the time of filing of the application.[1039]

4–642 Secondly, it observed that, unlike the second sentence of art.3(3) of the Directive, art.7(3) CTMR does not provide for an option to apply that provision to trade marks which acquire distinctive character after the date of application or after the date of registration; this shows that the Community legislature intended to restrict the applicability of art.7(3) only to marks that have acquired distinctiveness prior to the date of application. Thus, the Court concluded that a literal interpretation of both art.7(3) CTMR and the first sentence of art.3(3) of the Directive clearly support the interpretation of the Court of First Instance.[1040]

Thirdly, the Court confirmed the view that such an interpretation is the only one compatible with the logic of the system of absolute and relative grounds for refusal, according to which the date of filing of the application determines the priority of one mark over another. It noted that if the appellant's view was followed, a trade mark which is devoid of any distinctive character at the time of the application could serve as a basis for an opposition or an invalidity action against a mark with a subsequent filing date, but which was distinctive from the outset. However, such a situation is particularly unacceptable when the second mark has reached the requisite levels of distinctiveness before the first one.[1041]

Fourthly, it rejected the argument ex art.51(2) CTMR on the ground that insofar as that provision establishes an exception to the absolute grounds for invalidity laid down by art.51(1) CTMR (new art.52), it should be interpreted

---

[1039] *Pure Digital*, para.42.
[1040] *Pure Digital*, para.42.
[1041] *Pure Digital*, paras 51–52.

restrictively and could therefore not serve as a basis for interpreting art.7(3) by analogy.[1042]

4–643 Fifthly, it concurred with the Court of First Instance that although the exception introduced by art.51(2) CTMR (new art.52) is justified by the legitimate expectations of the proprietor arising from the registration of its mark and by the investments he may have made in the meantime, such legitimate expectations cannot be said to exist at the time when the application is filed. In particular, it cannot be argued that each and every proprietor of a trade mark registered erroneously has acted in bad faith; if that was the case, art.51(1)(b) CTMR (new art.52), which establishes bad faith as an absolute ground for invalidity, would have to be applied in all cases where trade marks were registered erroneously, with the result that art.51(2) would be rendered meaningless.[1043]

Therefore, the Court of Justice upheld the interpretation of the Court of First Instance that the material point in time for assessing whether the mark has acquired distinctive character in consequence of the use that has been made of it is the time of application and rejected the appeal as ill-founded in law.

In view of the Court's reasoning, that conclusion is clearly transposable also to art.3(3) of the Directive in the sense that unless there is a clear exception to the contrary in the national law, the first sentence of that provision, requiring that the mark must have become distinctive before the date of the application, is to be taken literally.

4–644 Finally, it is also worth noting that, in another case,[1044] the Court of First Instance has interpreted art.51(1)(a) CTMR (new art.52), which states that a Community trade mark shall be declared invalid if registered contrary to art.7, to the effect that the only time to be taken into account for that assessment is the date of the application for registration.

Interestingly enough, that interpretation runs counter to the current practice of the Office, which, for the purposes of invalidity proceedings, requires that the mark should comply with art.7 *both* at the time of its filing *and* at the time of its registration. To defend its practice, the Office has appealed that judgment before the Court. Although, admittedly, the judgment in *Pure Digital* is not directly relevant to that case, it remains to be seen how the Court will interpret art.51(1)(a), so as to complete the puzzle relating to the date on which distinctiveness must have been acquired through use.

14. CONCLUSION

4–645 The Court has decided a large number of cases on absolute grounds in a relatively short period of time since it has to consider the same, in terms of

---

[1042] *Pure Digital*, para.54.
[1043] *Pure Digital*, paras 55–56.
[1044] Frosch Touristic GmbH/OHIM (FLUGBÖRSE) (T-189/07) (2009) E.C.R. 00.

substance, body of law both as an interpretive court, when it considers preliminary references regarding the Directive, and an appellate court, when it reviews challenges to the Community Trade Mark registration process and applies the Community Trade Mark Regulation.

Attempting to establish concrete interpretive principles the Court has rejected the application of broad doctrines and instead is looking for the public policy behind each specific provision of the law. Admittedly, in *Windsurfing Chiemsee*,[1045] the Court found that the public policy behind the provision that descriptive signs should not be protected as trade marks is the need to keep them free for other traders to use. A concept applied by German courts and rejected as a doctrine in the same case. Although it appears that the Court re-introduced the same principle through the back door it can also be argued that this time there is a narrower context, delineated by the wording of the provision, a specific test adopted by the Court and so on.

The Court is also attempting to internalise competition issues in the way it interprets absolute grounds. The discourse on what constitutes a sign, the graphical representation requirements, the concept of distinctiveness, or the functionality provision is evidence of the Court's awareness that more and broader rights will inevitably lead to more friction in the marketplace.

4–646 The Court has taken a cautious approach, probably recognising that defending against a weak right may prove more uncertain, and potentially much more costly, than attempting to enforce a weak right; in *Doublemint*[1046] it held that no sign is per se unregistrable and stressed that each provision should be considered against its public policy background. This means that examination must be thorough and concrete.

Admittedly, the Court itself has appeared to be too liberal in the application of its own guidelines, accepting for example that *Baby-Dry*[1047] is such an unusual syntactical combination of two otherwise descriptive words that the sign should be allowed to be registered for nappies.

But those who rushed to use *Baby-Dry* as an authority that almost everything can now be registered as a trade mark are confusing the reasoning with its application. The unusual syntactical juxtaposition of two words is a perfectly logical reasoning for accepting that two descriptive terms can be combined into a new distinctive whole. Whether this reasoning was correctly applied by the Court in *Baby-Dry* is a different, and really irrelevant, question.

[1045] *Windsurfing Chiemsee Produktions- und Vertriebs GmbH* (C-108/97 & C-109/97) [1999] E.C.R. I-2779.
[1046] *WM Wrigley Jr Co* (C-191/01 P) [2003] E.C.R. I-12447.
[1047] *Procter & Gamble Co* (C-383/99 P) [2001] E.C.R. I-6251

Chapter 5

RELATIVE GROUNDS

1. Introduction	5–001
2. The Provisions of the Directive and the Regulation	5–002
(1) The Trade Marks Directive	5–002
(2) The Community Trade Mark Regulation	5–003
3. LTJ Diffusion—Establishing Identity Between Marks	5–004
4. Confusion, Similarity, and Distinctiveness	5–010
(1) Sabel—confusion and association: alternative concepts?	5–011
(2) Canon—distinctiveness, confusion, and association	5–017
(3) Lloyd Schuhfabrik—properly substantiated and genuine confusion	5–020
(4) Marca Mode—revisiting Sabel—a positive finding on confusion	5–023
(5) Lloyd—the distinctiveness factors	5–028
(6) The average consumer	5–030
5. Establishing Confusion—Global Appreciation	5–031
(1) The three tests	5–031
(2) The test for confusion	5–032
(3) Canon—global appreciation in a wider context	5–035
(4) Vedial—cumulative similarity/identity conditions	5–038
(5) Sabel—comparing the marks	5–043
(6) Lloyd—aural similarity	5–045
(7) Mühlens—a challenge to Lloyd	5–048
(8) Matratzen I—similarity between a figurative and a word mark	5–056
(9) Flexi Air—distinctiveness as part of a multifactor assessment	5–066
(10) Comparing the goods or services	5–074
6. Levi Strauss—The Timing of the Assessment	5–078
7. Revisiting Global Appreciation	5–094
(1) Picasso/Picaro—the limitations of Arsenal	5–095
(2) Rossi—protection of surnames—global appreciation—the Community Trade mark registration process	5–106
(3) Medion—the importance of dominant elements	5–137
(4) Praktiker—a special case for retail services?	5–141
(5) Travatan—the mediation of professionals: pharmaceuticals	5–146
(6) Limoncello—Quicky—La Española: composite marks	5–152
(7) Armafoam—confusion in part of the Community	5–164

8. Marks with a Reputation	5–169
(1) General Motors—the factors for assessing reputation	5–169
(2) Fincas Tarragona—marks well known "in a Member State"	5–173
(3) Pago—reputation "in the Community"	5–180
(4) Davidoff v Gofkid—the scope of article 5(2)	5–191
(5) Fitnessworld—the interpretive limits of Davidoff v Gofkid	5–197
(6) Adidas v Fitnessworld—global appreciation in the context of article 5(2)	5–201
(7) Adidas v Fitnessworld—use as a trade mark	5–204
(8) Intel—proof of dilution: chasing the chimera?	5–207
(9) Bellure—unfair advantage	5–230
(10) Nasdaq—putting the Intel into perspective?	5–240
9. Conclusion	5–247

1. INTRODUCTION

5–001 This chapter considers the case law of the Court of Justice on conflicts with earlier rights. They are resolved by art.4 of the Harmonisation Directive and art.8 of the Community Trade Mark Regulation.

Conflict resolution is based on a general principle that the earlier right shall prevail and the application of three basic rules. When there is identity between the trade marks or signs on the one hand and between the respective goods or services on the other, resolution appears to be almost automatic. When similarity becomes part of the equation, the criterion is "likelihood of confusion on the part of the public, which includes the likelihood of association". Trade marks that have obtained "a reputation" reach another level; they can prevail against similar or identical signs for "goods or services which are not similar" where use of the later trade mark or sign "without due cause would take unfair advantage of, or be detrimental to, the distinctive character or the repute of the earlier trade mark".

The adoption of the last rule remained optional at the national level. Member States were free to determine its application in relation to their own national rights. The Community Trade Mark regime had chosen to apply it in the conflicts involving Community Trade Mark Rights. Another potentially differentiating factor is who can challenge a right. Member States are free to set the participation rules, provided that at least the owner of the earlier right would be able to obtain protection. The Community Trade Mark regime opted for enabling only the owners of earlier rights to challenge a Community Trade Mark on the basis of their respective rights.

This chapter too is structured around the provisions of the Directive and it explores both the opinions and the judgments for each case brought before the Court.

2. THE PROVISIONS OF THE DIRECTIVE AND THE REGULATION

(1) The Trade Marks Directive

Article 4—Further grounds for refusal or invalidity concerning conflicts with earlier rights 5–002

1. A trade mark shall not be registered or, if registered, shall be liable to be declared invalid:

   a. if it is identical with an earlier trade mark, and the goods or services for which the trade mark is applied for or is registered are identical with the goods or services for which the earlier trade mark is protected;

   b. if because of its identity with, or similarity to, the earlier trade mark and the identity or similarity of the goods or services covered by the trade marks, there exists a likelihood of confusion on the part of the public, which includes the likelihood of association with the earlier trade mark.

2. "Earlier trade marks" within the meaning of para.1 means:

   a. trade marks of the following kinds with a date of application for registration which is earlier than the date of application for registration of the trade mark, taking account, where appropriate, of the priorities claimed in respect of those trade marks;

      i. Community trade marks;
      ii. trade marks registered in the Member State or, in the case of Belgium, Luxembourg or the Netherlands, at the Benelux Trade Mark Office;
      iii. trade marks registered under international arrangements which have effect in the Member State;

   b. Community Trade Marks which validly claim seniority, in accordance with the Regulation on the Community Trade Mark, from a trade mark referred to in (a) (ii) and (iii), even when the latter trade mark has been surrendered or allowed to lapse;

   c. applications for the trade marks referred to in (a) and (b), subject to their registration;

   d. trade marks which, on the date of application for registration of the trade mark, or, where appropriate, of the priority claimed in respect of the application for registration of the trade mark, are well known in a Member State, in the sense in which the words "well known" are used in art.6bis of the Paris Convention.

3. A trade mark shall furthermore not be registered or, if registered, shall be liable to be declared invalid if it is identical with, or similar to, an

earlier Community trade mark within the meaning of para.2 and is to be, or has been, registered for goods or services which are not similar to those for which the earlier Community trade mark is registered, where the earlier Community trade mark has a reputation in the Community and where the use of the later trade mark without due cause would take unfair advantage of, or be detrimental to, the distinctive character or the repute of the earlier Community trade mark.

4. Any Member State may furthermore provide that a trade mark shall not be registered or, if registered, shall be liable to be declared invalid where, and to the extent that:

   a. the trade mark is identical with, or similar to, an earlier national trade mark within the meaning of para.2 and is to he, or has been, registered for goods or services which are not similar to those for which the earlier trade mark is registered, where the earlier trade mark has a reputation in the Member State concerned and where the use of the later trade mark without due cause would take unfair advantage of, or be detrimental to, the distinctive character or the repute of the earlier trade mark;

   b. rights to a non-registered trade mark or to another sign used in the course of trade were acquired prior to the date of application for registration of the subsequent trade mark, or the date of the priority claimed for the application for registration of the subsequent trade mark and that non-registered trade mark or other sign confers on its proprietor the right to prohibit the use of a subsequent trade mark;

   c. the use of the trade mark may be prohibited by virtue of an earlier right other than the rights referred to in paras 2 and 4(b) and in particular:
      i. a right to a name;
      ii. a right of personal portrayal:
      iii. a copyright;
      iv. an industrial property right;

   d. the trade mark is identical with, or similar to, an earlier collective trade mark conferring a right which expired within a period of a maximum of three years preceding application;

   e. the trade mark is identical with, or similar to, an earlier guarantee or certification mark conferring a right which expired within a period preceding application the length of which is fixed by the Member State;

   f. the trade mark is identical with, or similar to, an earlier trade mark which was registered for identical or similar goods or services and conferred on them a right which has expired for failure to renew

2. THE PROVISIONS OF THE DIRECTIVE AND THE REGULATION

within a period of a maximum of two years preceding application, unless the proprietor of the earlier trade mark gave his agreement for the registration of the later mark or did not use his trade mark;

g. the trade mark is liable to be confused with a mark which was in use abroad on the filing date of the application and which is still in use there, provided that at the date of the application the applicant was acting in bad faith?

5. The Member States may permit that in appropriate circumstances registration need not be refused or the trade mark need not be declared invalid where the proprietor of the earlier trade mark or other earlier right consents to the registration of the later trade mark.

6. Any Member State may provide that, by derogation from paras 1 to 5, the grounds for refusal of registration or invalidity in force in that state prior to the date on which the provisions necessary to comply with this Directive enter into force, shall apply to trade marks for which application has been made prior to that date.

(2) The Community Trade Mark Regulation

Article 8—Relative grounds for refusal 5–003

1. Upon opposition by the proprietor of an earlier trade mark, the trade mark applied for shall not be registered:

    (a) if it is identical with the earlier trade mark and the goods or services for which registration is applied for are identical with the goods or services for which the earlier trade mark is protected;

    (b) if because of its identity with or similarity to the earlier trade mark and the identity or similarity of the goods or services covered by the trade marks there exists a likelihood of confusion on the part of the public in the territory in which the earlier trade mark is protected; the likelihood of confusion includes the likelihood of association with the earlier trade mark.

2. For the purposes of para.1, "Earlier trade marks" means:

    (a) trade marks of the following kinds with a date of application for registration which is earlier than the date of application for registration of the Community trade mark, taking account, where appropriate, of the priorities claimed in respect of those trade marks:

    (i) Community trade marks;
    (ii) trade marks registered in a Member State, or, in the case of Belgium, the Netherlands or Luxembourg, at the Benelux Trade Mark Office;

- (iii) trade marks registered under international arrangements which have effect in a Member State;
- (iv) trade marks registered under international arrangements which have effect in the Community;

(b) applications for the trade marks referred to in subpara.(a), subject to their registration;

(c) trade marks which, on the date of application for registration of the Community trade mark, or, where appropriate, of the priority claimed in respect of the application for registration of the Community trade mark, are well known in a Member State, in the sense in which the words "well known" are used in art.6bis of the Paris Convention.

3. Upon opposition by the prorietor of the trade mark, a trade mark shall not be registered where an agent or representative of the proprietor of the trade mark applies for registration thereof in his own name without the proprietor's consent, unless the agent or representative justifies his action.

4. Upon opposition by the proprietor of a non-registered trade mark or of another sign used in the course of trade of more than mere local significance, the trade mark applied for shall not be registered where and to the extent that, pursuant to the Community legislation or the law of the Member State governing that sign:

   (a) rights to that sign were acquired prior to the date of application for registration of the Community trade mark, or the date of the priority claimed for the application for registration of the Community trade mark;

   (b) that sign confers on its proprietor the right to prohibit the use of a subsequent trade mark.

5. Furthermore, upon opposition by the proprietor of an earlier trade mark within the meaning of para.2, the trade mark applied for shall not be registered where it is identical with or similar to the earlier trade mark and is to be registered for goods or services which are not similar to those for which the earlier trade mark is registered, where in the case of an earlier Community trade mark the trade mark has a reputation in the Community and, in the case of an earlier national trade mark, the trade mark has a reputation in the Member State concerned and where the use without due cause of the trade mark applied for would take unfair advantage of, or be detrimental to, the distinctive character or the repute of the earlier trade mark.

3. LTJ DIFFUSION—ESTABLISHING IDENTITY BETWEEN MARKS

The Court considered the criteria for establishing identity between signs in **5–004**
LTJ Diffusion v Sadas.[1]

Under art.5(1)(a) of the Directive (new art.5(1)(a)) the proprietor of a registered trade mark may prevent third parties from using in the course of trade any sign which is identical with the trade mark in relation to goods or services identical with those for which it is registered. The case was a reference from the Tribunal de Grande Instance (Regional Court), Paris, and involved a comparison between a registered figurative trade mark, the name Arthur written in distinctive way and bearing a dot below the first letter A, and the word mark "Arthur et Félicie".[2]

The French Court enquired whether art.5(1)(a) covers only an identical reproduction, without addition or omission, of the earlier mark or it can also cover a reproduction of the distinctive element of an earlier mark or a full reproduction of the earlier mark but with the addition of new signs.

(a) The Opinion of the Advocate General

Advocate General Jacobs opted for a strict interpretation of the term "identical" because of its actual meaning—dictionary definitions in all the languages of the Community stressed the sameness of the compared elements—but also because of the scheme, history, and context of the provision. **5–005**

According to the Tenth Recital of the Preamble, identity conferred absolute, unconditional protection that "should clearly not be extended beyond those situations for which it was intended if the aim of ensuring freedom of trade and undistorted competition in the internal market is to be achieved".[3] He viewed this absolute protection as something exceptional because confusion constituted the theoretical and historical backbone of the Directive. The original proposal for the Directive did not include this type of protection.[4] He also looked at the provision from an international perspective: art.16(1) of the Agreement on Trade-Related Aspects of Intellectual Property Rights provides only for a presumption of confusion in the case of identity: "In case of the use of an identical sign for identical goods or services, a likelihood of confusion shall be presumed". According to the Advocate General confusion remained the key issue, however where "rigorously identical signs or marks are used in the course of trade for identical goods or services, it is difficult if not impossible to conceive of

---

[1] *LTJ Diffusion SA v Sadas Vertbaudet SA* (C-291/00) [2003] E.C.R. I-2799.
[2] Note that the Court of First Instance found that there would be likelihood of confusion between the signs in *Sadas SA v Office for Harmonisation in the Internal Market (Trade Marks and Designs)* (T-346/04) [2006] E.T.M.R. 27.
[3] Point 33 of the Opinion of A.G. Jacobs.
[4] [1980] OJ C351/1; for the amended proposal see [1985] OJ C351/4.

circumstances in which all likelihood of confusion could be ruled out. In such cases, it would be both redundant and extravagant to require proof of that likelihood".[5] Likelihood of confusion, he continued, in the case of identity between marks and products "can be presumed without further investigation".[6]

5–006   As to the boundaries between identity and similarity he suggested that absolute identity in every detail is required; "in principle, any difference, whether it might be viewed as adding, removing or modifying any element, must involve loss of identity".[7] He excluded, however, differences that are not noticeable.

In order to provide a test for determining identity he suggested a two step process.

First the national authority had to "identify what it is that is perceived by the average, reasonably well-informed, observant and circumspect consumer as the relevant marks, or the relevant mark and sign".[8]

5–007   Then it should perform the global assessment test, adopted by the Court in *Sabel*[9] and *Lloyd*,[10] focusing on the visual, aural, and conceptual elements of the two signs, the overall impression created by them, and their distinctive and dominant components: "a mark and a sign, or two marks, will always be identical where in the light of such an assessment any differences are minute and wholly insignificant, so that the average consumer would not find any noticeable difference between the two; otherwise, they can be regarded as no more than similar".[11]

Recognising that it remained for the national court to apply the test to the facts of the case he suggested that use of a different script and the addition of another name appeared to make the two signs similar rather than identical.

Note that the language of the French law differed from that of the Directive. Article L. 713-2 of the Code[12] prohibited the "reproduction, use or affixing of a mark, even with the addition of words such as: formula, style, system, imitation, type or method, or the use of a mark which has been reproduced, in respect of goods or services identical with those for which the mark is registered".

5–008   This provision according to French doctrine covered cases where a distinctive element of a composite mark is reproduced (contrefaçon partielle) or where a distinctive element of a composite mark is reproduced

---

[5] Point 37 of the Opinion of A.G. Jacobs.
[6] Point 39; contrast with para.6–024 below and following, above.
[7] Point 41 of the Opinion of A.G. Jacobs.
[8] Point 49; however for registered trade marks the starting point should be the mark as registered.
[9] *Sabel BV v Puma AG, Rudolf Dassler Sport* (C-251/95) [1997] E.C.R. I-6191.
[10] *Lloyd Schuhfabrik Meyer & Co GmbH* (C-342/97) [1999] E.C.R. I-3819.
[11] Point 47 of the Opinion of A.G. Jacobs.
[12] Book VII of the French Code de la propriété intellectuelle (Intellectual Property Code), JORF of July 3 1992, p.8801.

3. LTJ DIFFUSION—ESTABLISHING IDENTITY BETWEEN MARKS

together with additions that do not affect the identity of the mark (adjonction inopérante). This explains the way the French court expressed the questions posed to the Court.

The Advocate General noted that art.5(1)(a)—and its mirror art.4(1)(a) to which the same interpretation should be applied—are provisions aiming towards total rather than partial harmonisation and it was the language of the Directive that should delineate the scope of the national implementing provisions.

(b) The judgment of the Court

The Court stressed that both articles of the Directive should be interpreted in the same way. Its interpretive approach was based on the familiar theme expressed above in *Arsenal*[13] that the essential function of a trade mark is to guarantee the identity of origin of the marked goods or services to the consumer or end user by enabling him, without any possibility of confusion,[14] to distinguish the goods or services from others which have another origin. In order to ensure that guarantee the proprietor must be protected against "competitors wishing to take unfair advantage of the status and reputation of the trade mark by selling products illegally bearing it".[15]

5–009

Accordingly, and within limits,[16] art.5(1) provided that the proprietor is entitled to prevent all third parties from using his trade mark in the course of trade. And whereas art.5(1)(b) requires a likelihood of confusion, art.5(1)(a) "does not require evidence of such a likelihood in order to afford absolute protection in the case of identity of the sign and the trade mark and of the goods or services".[17]

Following the logic of the Advocate General the Court held that the criterion of identity of the sign and the trade mark must be interpreted strictly: "There is therefore identity between the sign and the trade mark where the former reproduces, without any modification or addition, all the elements constituting the latter."[18]

It also held that identity should be assessed globally from the perspective of the average consumer described in *Lloyd Schuhfabrik Meyer*.[19] It added however one further consideration to the global assessment test: "Since the perception of identity between the sign and the trade mark is not the result of a direct comparison of all the characteristics of the elements compared,

---

[13] See also *Medion AG v Thomson Multimedia Sales Germany & Austria GmbH* (C-120/04) [2005] E.C.R. I-8551, paras 5–137 and following, below.
[14] *Arsenal Football Club Plc* (C-206/01) [2002] E.C.R. I-10273.
[15] *LTJ Diffusion*, para.46.
[16] For example *Parfums Christian Dior SA v Evora BV* (C-337/95) [1997] E.C.R. I-6013.
[17] *LTJ Diffusion*, para.49.
[18] *LTJ Diffusion*, para.51.
[19] *Lloyd Schuhfabrik Meyer & Co GmbH v Klijsen Handel BV* (C-342/97) [1999] E.C.R. I-3819.

insignificant differences between the sign and the trade mark may go unnoticed by an average consumer."[20]

4. CONFUSION, SIMILARITY, AND DISTINCTIVENESS

5–010 The second scenario of trade mark conflicts covered by European trade mark law involves an element of similarity: similarity of signs and identity of goods or services, identity of signs and similarity of goods or services, or similarity of goods or services or similarity of both signs and goods or services. Here, likelihood of confusion becomes the essential condition for protection of the earlier sign.

The provision is somewhat awkwardly worded, but as it has already been hinted above confusion constitutes the justificatory core of trade mark protection. Advocate General Ruiz-Jarabo Colomer in *Arsenal*[21] appeared even to suggest that where the signs and the goods or services are both identical there is only a presumption of infringement that can be rebutted if there is no confusion.

(1) Sabel—confusion and association: alternative concepts?

5–011 *Sabel*[22] was the first case where the Court had to determine the meaning of confusion; it involved a comparison between a composite and a pictorial trade mark. Puma, the registered proprietor of two German trade marks depicting felines—both were abstract figures, the first a leaping big puma and the second a chasing puma—opposed Sabel's application for registration of a trade mark comprising the name "SABEL" underneath the figure of a spotted chasing feline, a cheetah. There was partial overlap between the product specifications.

The case reached the Bundesgerichtshof (Federal Court of Justice) which decided, provisionally, that according to the traditional principles of German trade mark law there was no likelihood confusion.

However, it stayed proceedings in order to ascertain from the Court of Justice the relevance of the common semantic content of the "chasing felines" signs, given the ambiguity of the language of art.4(1)(b) of the Directive providing that likelihood of confusion includes the likelihood of association:

"With reference to the interpretation of Article 4(1)(b) . . . is it sufficient for a finding that there is a likelihood (Gefahr: risk) of confusion between a sign composed of text and picture and a sign consisting merely of a

---

[20] *LTJ Diffusion*, para.53.
[21] *Arsenal Football Club Plc* (C-206/01) [2002] E.C.R. I-10273.
[22] *Sabel BV v Puma AG, Rudolf Dassler Sport* (C-251/95) [1997] E.C.R. I-6191.

picture, which is registered for identical and similar goods and is not especially well known to the public, that the two signs coincide as to their semantic content (in this case, a bounding feline)?

What is the significance in this connection of the wording of the Directive, in terms of which the likelihood (Gefahr: risk) of confusion includes the likelihood that a mark may be associated with an earlier mark?"[23]

Note the emphasis the national court placed on the facts of the case: it underlined that Sabel's sign was composed of a combination of a word and a picture whereas Puma's mark consisted only of a picture and was not especially well known to the public. In its provisional judgment it had also noted that Puma's mark consisted of an abstract representation of a common animal querying whether this should constitute a ground for opposing the registration of a mark comprising a similarly common representation.

(a) The Opinion of the Advocate General

Before the Court the Benelux Governments submitted that the term "likelihood of association" should be construed according to its Benelux interpretation because the inclusion of the term into the Directive was the result of their intervention that in turn aimed to give to the concept of confusion the meaning attributed by art.13a of the Uniform Benelux Law on Trade Marks that renders the scope of protection dependant on the resemblance between the marks rather than the likelihood of confusion.

5–012

The Commission and the Government of the United Kingdom opposed this sweeping approach. Based on the freedom of movement case law of the Court of Justice they argued that the scope of trade mark protection should be commensurate with the essential function of a trade mark as a guarantee of origin of the marked product.

In the Benelux likelihood of association could arise in the following situations: first, where the public confuses the sign and the mark in question (likelihood of direct confusion); secondly, where the public makes a connection between the proprietors of the sign and those of the mark and confuses them (likelihood of indirect confusion or association); and thirdly, where the public considers the sign to be similar to the mark and perception of the sign calls to mind the memory of the mark, although the two are not confused (likelihood of association in the strict sense).

Following a thorough analysis of the Benelux concept of association, Advocate General Jacobs supported that Benelux law went further than the trade mark laws of other Member States covering "non-origin association"[24]; the third type of association was not encountered in other Member States.

5–013

---

[23] Reproduced in para.10.
[24] Point 39 of the Opinion of A.G. Jacobs.

The Benelux countries failed to incorporate this type into the Directive as an optional expansion of the scope of protection or even as an alternative to "risk of confusion". They succeeded however as part of a compromise to obtain a mention of the term in "a likelihood of confusion on the part of the public, which includes the likelihood of association with the earlier trade mark". The Advocate General recounted the history of the inclusion of the term into the Directive, but doubted whether it was permissible to take it into account and whether, in any case, carried any relevance in interpreting the provision.

5–014 **(i) The language of the provision and the principles of the Directive.** Turning to the language of both the provision and the Tenth Recital he found it difficult to "see how association not involving confusion can be brought within the Directive when the Directive requires a likelihood of confusion which includes the likelihood of association". As Laddie J. neatly expressed the point in Wagamama, an English case on this very issue: it would be "unconventional use of language to provide that the smaller (i.e. likelihood of confusion) includes the larger (i.e. likelihood of association)".[25] The introduction into European trade mark law of a new—for the majority of the Member States—concept that also departed from the jurisprudence of the Court of Justice would have required much clearer and unambiguous language.

The inclusion of "likelihood of association" probably meant that confusion should be interpreted in a broad sense clearly covering mistaking one product for another but also making a connection between the entities behind the conflicting signs.

The Advocate General also accepted that the Benelux non-origin association went against two fundamental principles underlying the Directive. It would hinder rather than facilitate the free movement of goods within the internal market. And it would undermine the principle of co-existence not only between trade marks from different national systems by setting the common standard at a very high level but also between national systems and the Community Trade Mark system by raising a difficult to overcome national obstacle to registration at the Community level.

5–015 Finally, he noticed that association was not mentioned either in the Paris Convention or the World Trade Organisation's Agreement on Trade-Related Aspects of Intellectual Property Rights.

He concluded that "while the likelihood of association with an earlier mark is a factor to be taken into account, registration of a mark cannot be opposed unless it is established that there is a genuine and properly substantiated likelihood of confusion about the origin of the goods or services in question".[26]

---

[25] Point 44, referring to *Wagamama Ltd v City Centre Restaurants Plc* [1995] F.S.R. 713.
[26] Point 55 of the Opinion of A.G. Jacobs.

4. CONFUSION, SIMILARITY, AND DISTINCTIVENESS

(b) The judgment of the Court   5–016

The Court of Justice looked first at the language of the provision stating that the logical deduction would be that likelihood of association is not an alternative to likelihood of confusion but simply serves to define its scope: "The terms of the provision itself exclude its application where there is no likelihood of confusion on the part of the public."[27] This was also supported by a purposive analysis: the Tenth Recital setting out that the likelihood of confusion constitutes the specific condition of protection.

(2) Canon—distinctiveness, confusion, and association   5–017

In *Canon*[28] the Court reiterated that association and confusion were not distinct concepts.

Metro-Goldwyn-Mayer Inc had applied in Germany for registration of "CANNON" for "films recorded on video tape cassettes (video film cassettes); production, distribution and projection of films for cinemas and television organisations". Canon Kabushiki Kaisha (CKK) opposed the application based on its earlier registration of "Canon" for "still and motion picture cameras and projectors; television filming and recording devices, television retransmission devices, television receiving and reproduction devices, including tape and disc devices for television recording and reproduction". The evidence showed that there was no overlap between manufacturers of video recorders and video tape producers and consumers were aware that video recorders and video tapes ordinarily came from different sources; it also established that "Canon" enjoyed a reputation in Germany.

The case reached the Bundesgerichtshof (Federal Court of Justice) which sought from the Court of Justice to ascertain whether in assessing product similarity the relevant authority should take into account the distinctiveness of the earlier mark, in particular the distinctiveness that is the result of its reputation.

(a) The Opinion of the Advocate General   5–018

Advocate General Jacobs started by looking again at the meaning of confusion. He supported that in principle if "there is no likelihood of the public assuming that there is any sort of trade connection between the marks 'Canon' and 'CANNON', there is no likelihood of confusion within the meaning of Article 4(1)(b) of the Directive".[29] Elaborating on the importance of the "place of origin" he noted that "it is not sufficient to show simply that there is no likelihood of the public being confused as to the place in

---

[27] *Sabel*, para.18.
[28] *Canon Kabushiki Kaisha* (C-39/97) [1998] E.C.R. I-5507.
[29] *Canon*, para.30.

which the goods are manufactured or the services performed: if, despite recognising that the goods or services have different places of origin, the public is likely to believe that there is a link between the two concerns, there will be a likelihood of confusion within the meaning of the Directive".[30]

5–019 *(b) The judgment of the Court*

The Court of Justice dealt first with product similarity and the importance of reputation.[31] Then, based on the positive distinctiveness requirements of the Directive and its own case law in *Hag II*,[32] it considered the concept of confusion, holding that there "is a likelihood of confusion within the meaning of Article 4(1)(b) of the Directive where the public can be mistaken as to the origin of the goods or services in question".[33] The Court referred directly to the suggestion of the Advocate General[34] and held that there is a likelihood of confusion if there is a risk that the "public might believe that the goods or services in question come from the same undertaking or, as the case may be, from economically-linked undertakings".[35]

5–020 **(3) Lloyd Schuhfabrik—properly substantiated and genuine confusion**

In *Lloyd Schuhfabrik*[36] the Landgericht Munchen I (Munich I Regional Court) requested further clarifications on the concept of likelihood of confusion. Lloyd Schuhfabrik, the registered proprietor of "Lloyd" for footwear, claimed that Klijsen's use of "Loint's" constituted trade mark infringement.

The German court sought some guidance regarding similarity between the two signs but also regarding the concept of confusion. It submitted a number of detailed questions, some very closely linked with the facts of the case.

> "1. Does it suffice, for there to be a likelihood of confusion because of similarity between the sign and the trade mark and identity of the goods or services covered by the sign and the mark, that the mark and the sign each consist of a single syllable only, are identical in sound both at the beginning and as regards the only combination of vowels and the— single—final consonant of the mark recurs in the sign in similar form ('t' instead of 'd') in a consonant cluster of three consonants including 's'; specifically, do the designations 'loyd' and 'Loint's' for shoes conflict?

---

[30] *Canon*, para.30
[31] See paras 5–169 and following, below.
[32] *SA CNL-SUCAL NV v Hag GF AG* (C-10/89) [1990] E.C.R. I-3711.
[33] *Canon*, para.26.
[34] See point 30.
[35] *Canon*, para.29.
[36] *Lloyd Schuhfabrik Meyer & Co GmbH* (C-342/97) [1999] E.C.R. I-3819.

4. CONFUSION, SIMILARITY, AND DISTINCTIVENESS

2. What is the significance in this connection of the wording of the Directive which provides that the likelihood of confusion includes the likelihood of association between the sign and the trade mark?

3. Must a special distinctive character, and hence an extended material scope of protection of a distinguishing sign, already be taken to exist where there is a degree of recognition of 10 per cent in the relevant section of the public? Would that be the case with a degree of recognition of 36 per cent?

Would such an extension of the scope of protection lead to a different answer to Question 1, if that question were to be answered by the Court of Justice in the negative?

4. Is a trade mark to be taken to have an enhanced distinctive character simply because it has no descriptive elements?"[37]

(a)   The Opinion of the Advocate General   5–021

Advocate General Jacobs made a specific to this issue point conceding that the Court had "on occasions at the prompting of national courts given rulings tied closely to the facts of particular cases. The distinction between interpretation and application is not clear-cut—indeed interpretation may be considered an integral part of the process of applying a legal rule. Almost any question, however specific to a particular set of facts, can be formulated in the guise of an abstract question of interpretation".[38] However, it is for the Court of Justice to interpret the law and for the national court to decide, according to the facts of the case and applying the law as interpreted by the Court of Justice, whether there is a likelihood of confusion.

Regarding the concept of confusion the Advocate General repeated the relevant parts of the Court's judgment in *Sabel*.[39] He added that in assessing the likelihood of confusion the national court will apply national rules of evidence, however the "standard and criteria to be applied ... in making that assessment are a matter of Community law".[40] Accordingly, the "likelihood of confusion must be properly substantiated and genuine—it must not be merely hypothetical or remote".[41]

(b)   The judgment of the Court   5–022

The Court of Justice concurred with the Advocate General regarding its own role: it "is limited to providing the national court with the guidance on interpretation necessary to resolve the case before it, while it is for the national

---

[37] Reproduce in para.10.
[38] Point 9. An interpretive issue that is almost always relevant in trade mark cases.
[39] *Sabel BV v Puma AG, Rudolf Dassler Sport* (C-251/95) [1997] E.C.R. I-6191.
[40] Point 20 of the Opinion of A.G. Jacobs.
[41] Point 21 of the Opinion of A.G. Jacobs.

court to apply the rules of Community law, as interpreted by the Court, to the facts of the case under consideration".[42]

Albeit, it did not also take up—at least directly—the point made by the Advocate General regarding the Community standard of likelihood of confusion. Instead it chose to answer the questions on similarity.

The reader is reminded that in *Sabel*[43] the Court of Justice, discussing a judgment of the Benelux Court,[44] noted that it was based on the idea that, where a sign is likely to give rise to association with a mark, the public makes a connection between the sign and the mark that may be detrimental either if it leads to confusion as to origin or it results in the goodwill attached to the earlier mark being transferred to the sign and the dilution of its image. Now that the confusion tests devised by the Court of Justice took into account the reputation of the earlier mark the supporters of non-origin association sensed an opportunity to introduce the concept through the backdoor by utilising the concept of reputation.

(4) Marca Mode—revisiting Sabel—a positive finding on confusion

5–023 In *Marca Mode*[45] the Supreme Court of The Netherlands attempted to stretch the limits of confusion.[46] Adidas, the proprietor in the Benelux of the three stripes trade mark started infringement proceedings against Marca Mode a company marketing sports clothes with two parallel stripes running along their length and a white and orange t-shirt bearing three black vertical stripes running in parallel down its entire length, broken up by a medallion comprising a picture of a cat and the word TIM. The case reached the Dutch Supreme Court where Marca Mode argued that after *Sabel* it was necessary to establish a likelihood of confusion rather than a likelihood of association.

The Advocate General of the Dutch court—A.G. Bakels—conceded that as a result of the Directive and the case law of the Court of Justice the law has changed and indicated that Benelux courts should apply the new law even if they would have preferred that case law to have gone the other way. The Dutch Supreme Court did not follow his recommendations; to the contrary it interpreted SABEL as appearing to indicate that the existence of a risk of association is sufficient when the earlier mark has a particularly distinctive character either per se or as a result of its reputation, since the possibility that the association arising from some semantic or other similarity may create confusion cannot be ruled out and sought from the Court of Justice to confirm whether its reading had been correct.

---

[42] *Lloyd Schuhfabrik*, para.11, citing *Staatssecretaris van Financien v Shipping and Forwarding Enterprise SAFE BV* (C-320/88) [1990] E.C.R. I-285.
[43] *Sabel BV* (C-251/95) [1997] E.C.R. I-6191.
[44] *Jullien v Verschuere* [1983] Jur. Vol. 4, p.36.
[45] *Marca Mode CV v Adidas AG Adidas Benelux BV* (C-425/98) [2000] E.C.R. I-4861.
[46] *Marca Mode v Adidas AG and Adidas Benelux BV* [1999] E.T.M.R. 791 HR (NL).

4. CONFUSION, SIMILARITY, AND DISTINCTIVENESS

(a) The Opinion of the Advocate General

Advocate General Jacobs reiterated the arguments against a broad interpretation of association that he had already developed in *Sabel* and reviewed the Court's tests for establishing confusion that in *Sabel* and *Canon*[47] had declined to expand the scope of protection beyond confusion. He noted that "the Hoge Raad is in effect asking the Court to reverse the terms of the Directive: confusion ... which includes the likelihood of association in Article 5(1)(b) means, in its view, association ... which includes the likelihood of confusion. The Court has already considered and expressly rejected that view in SABEL".[48]

5–024

Expanding the scope of his Opinion he then explored a number of corroborating reasons of principle. First, a broad interpretation of the scope of confusion would hinder the internal market, derogating from the free movement of goods principle and going against the jurisprudence of the Court. Secondly, it would hinder the application of the Community Trade Mark Regulation, enabling more national marks to be raised as obstacles to Community Trade Mark applications without a genuine and properly substantiated risk of confusion. Thirdly, it would be against the spirit of the Paris Convention and the Agreement on Trade-Related Aspects of Intellectual Property Rights; both linked trade mark protection with likelihood of confusion. Fourthly, the language adopted by national legislators in implementing the Directive favoured a narrow approach. The United Kingdom referred to likelihood of confusion whilst all the other versions, except the Dutch, referred to risk or danger of confusion. The Dutch, more open ended, approach focused on circumstances in which confusion can arise, including the risk of association; this, to an extent, explained the conceptually diversified translation of *Sabel* in The Netherlands.

Focusing on distinctiveness he supported that, according to the jurisprudence of the Court, "the fact that the earlier mark is distinctive will often be relevant for determining whether there is in fact a likelihood of confusion".[49]

However, likelihood of confusion had to be proven rather than assumed; distinctiveness and reputation simply constituted factors that courts had to consider. Looking at the overall scheme of protection and taking into account the protection afforded by art.5(2) he noted: "Granting yet further protection to marks with a reputation in the absence of confusion would amount to granting protection against dilution, namely the blurring of the distinctiveness of a mark such that it is no longer capable of

5–025

---

[47] *Sabel BV* (C-251/95) [1997] E.C.R. I-6191; *Canon Kabushiki Kaisha* (C-39/97) [1998] E.C.R. I-5507.
[48] Point 31 of the Opinion of A.G. Jacobs.
[49] Point 42 of the Opinion of A.G. Jacobs.

arousing immediate association with the goods for which it is registered and used. To do so by a creative interpretation of Article 5(1)(b) would run counter to the scheme of the Directive, which clearly envisages that such additional protection should be conferred, if at all, by virtue of Articles 4(4)(a) and 5(2) at Member States' option: see the ninth recital in the preamble".[50]

He added that the Hoge Raad had not sought a ruling as to whether art.5(2) should cover similar as well as dissimilar products, as supported by Adidas and urged the Court to consider this at a later more appropriate instance following a more extensive and open debate.

5–026 *(b) The judgment of the Court*

The Court concurred with the Advocate General; it considered only the questions referred to it, holding that art.5(1)(b) requires a positive finding on likelihood of confusion even where the protected mark enjoys a particularly distinctive character.

It stressed from "the outset that, even in particular circumstances such as those outlined by the Hoge Raad in its order for reference, a likelihood of confusion cannot be presumed".[51]

Clarifying its judgment in *Sabel* it repeated that the particularly distinctive character of the earlier mark might increase the likelihood of confusion and that the conjunction of conceptual similarity between the earlier mark and the sign with the fact that the mark possessed a particularly distinctive character might contribute to proving likelihood of confusion.

5–027 But this did not imply a presumption of likelihood of confusion resulting from the existence of a likelihood of association in the strict sense. Likelihood of confusion had to be proven in a positive way: in *Sabel* "the Court referred by implication to the assessment of evidence which the national court must undertake in each case pending before it. It did not excuse the national court from the necessary positive finding of the existence of a likelihood of confusion which constitutes the matter to be proved".[52]

The reputation of a mark was one of the elements courts should examine in their global assessment of likelihood of confusion and according to *Canon* "marks with a highly distinctive character, in particular because of their reputation, enjoy broader protection than marks with a less distinctive character... Nevertheless, the reputation of a mark does not give grounds for presuming the existence of a likelihood of confusion simply because of the existence of a likelihood of association in the strict sense".[53]

---

[50] Point 44 of the Opinion of A.G. Jacobs.
[51] *Marca Mode*, para.33.
[52] *Marca Mode*, para.39.
[53] *Marca Mode*, para.41.

4. CONFUSION, SIMILARITY, AND DISTINCTIVENESS

(5) Lloyd—the distinctiveness factors

(a) The Opinion of the Advocate General 5–028

In *Lloyd Schuhfabrik*[54] Advocate General Jacobs considered what contributed distinctiveness to a trade mark for the purposes of expanding the scope of protection. He justified this expansion by noting that, although it appeared that distinctiveness of a trade mark would make confusion less rather than more likely, the similarity between the distinctive elements of a mark and a sign makes them both distinguishable from other signs but increases the risk of confusion between themselves. As to distinctiveness, market recognition was one of the factors to be taken into account but there was a "specific threshold beyond which it should be given decisive weight".[55]

In terms of inherent distinctiveness he suggested that "there must be certain aural, visual or conceptual features which particularly distinguish it from other signs".[56] He added that the absence of descriptive elements may be a factor in assessing the distinctiveness of a mark but it will not necessarily render the mark distinctive, "despite the absence of descriptive elements, a mark may still lack original features or be commonplace...".[57]

(b) The judgment of the Court 5–029

The Court followed the Advocate General. Citing *Windsurfing Chiemsee*,[58] it repeated that it is not possible to state in general terms when a mark has a strong distinctive character. Instead, it is necessary to make "an overall assessment of the greater or lesser capacity of the mark to identify the goods or services for which it has been registered as coming from a particular undertaking, and thus to distinguish those goods or services from those of other undertakings",[59] applying the same criteria: account should be taken in particular of the "inherent characteristics of the mark, including the fact that it does or does not contain an element descriptive of the goods or services for which it has been registered; the market share held by the mark; how intensive, geographically widespread and long-standing use of the mark has been; the amount invested by the undertaking in promoting the mark; the proportion of the relevant section of the public which, because of the mark, identifies the goods or services as originating from a

---

[54] *Lloyd Schuhfabrik Meyer & Co GmbH* (C-342/97) [1999] E.C.R. I-3819.
[55] Point 21 of the Opinion of A.G. Jacobs.
[56] Point 22 of the Opinion of A.G. Jacobs.
[57] Point 23 of the Opinion of A.G. Jacobs.
[58] *Windsurfing Chiemsee Produktions- und Vertriebs GmbH* (C-108/97 & C-109/97) [1999] E.C.R. I-2779.
[59] *Lloyd*, para.22.

particular undertaking; and statements from chambers of commerce and industry or other trade and professional associations".[60]

5–030 (6) The average consumer

In *Lloyd Schuhfabrik* the Court adopted the perspective of the average consumer of the products covered by the trade mark as the most relevant for determining whether there is likelihood of confusion. Citing earlier case law[61] the Court held:

> "For the purposes of that global appreciation, the average consumer of the category of products concerned is deemed to be reasonably well-informed and reasonably observant and circumspect. However, account should be taken of the fact that the average consumer only rarely has the chance to make a direct comparison between the different marks but must place his trust in the imperfect picture of them that he has kept in his mind. It should also be borne in mind that the average consumer's level of attention is likely to vary according to the category of goods or services in question."[62]

5. ESTABLISHING CONFUSION—GLOBAL APPRECIATION

5–031 (1) The three tests

Regarding confusion the Court has developed and applied three distinct tests. In essence the first test, the test for establishing confusion, comprises the other two tests that in turn provide the factors courts have to consider for determining whether the conflicting trade marks and the goods or services covered by them are respectively similar with each other.

(2) The test for confusion

5–032 *(a) Sabel—global appreciation—a test for confusion*

In *Sabel*[63] once the Court dealt with the relationship between confusion and association it turned its attention to formulating a test for establishing whether there is a likelihood of confusion.

---

[60] *Lloyd*, para.23.
[61] *Gut Springenheide GmbH and Tusky v Oberkreisdirektor des Kreises Steinfurt–AMT für Lebensmittelüberwachung, Oberundesanwalt Beim Bundesverwaltungsgericht* (C-210/96) [1998] E.C.R. I-4657.
[62] *Lloyd Schuhfabrik Meyer & Co GmbH* (C-342/97) [1999] E.C.R. I-3819, para.26.
[63] *Sabel BV* (C-251/95) [1997] E.C.R. I-6191.

5. ESTABLISHING CONFUSION—GLOBAL APPRECIATION

(b) The Opinion of the Advocate General

Linking the case with the earlier pre-harmonisation jurisprudence of the Court A.G. Jacobs referred to its free movement of goods case law developed in *Terrapin Terranova*,[64] *Hag II*,[65] *Ideal Standard*,[66] and *Renault v Audi*.[67] In all these cases the risk of confusion served as the justification behind the exercise of national trade mark rights, linking the specific subject matter of rights and the essential function of a trade mark as a guarantee of the identity of the origin of the marked product.[68] The risk of confusion however had to be genuine rather than the pretext for arbitrary discriminations or a disguised restriction on intra-Community trade.

5–033

This review assisted the Advocate General first in rejecting a broad definition of confusion[69] but also in suggesting a narrow test for proving confusion, a test that would enhance the principle of coexistence: "the Directive must be read as laying down a common standard on the basis of which trade marks from different national systems are enabled to co-exist. The standard should not therefore be set at too high a level. In that respect the Directive is perhaps different from harmonising measures in other sectors, where a high level of protection may be desirable in the general interest and where what is essential to ensure free trade is merely that the same standard should be set for all Member States. The Trade Marks Directive, if interpreted too stringently, would have the effect of insulating the national markets. In the absence of a clear intention to that effect, the Directive should accordingly not be read as imposing the most restrictive standard found in the laws of Member States".[70]

However, his attention shifted to the issue of similarity of marks rather than an overall test for confusion.[71] To an extent this was inevitable because according to the facts of the case there was at least a partial overlap between the goods covered by the two signs and both the Advocate General and the Court concentrated on the relevance the similarity of signs had for the overall finding of confusion.

(c) The judgment of the Court

The Court's examination of art.4(1)(b) of the Directive resulted first in the obvious statement that "Article 4(1)(b) of the Directive ... provides that a trade mark conflicts with an earlier trade mark if, because of the identity or

5–034

---

[64] *Terrapin (Overseas) Ltd v Terranova Industrie CA Kapferer and Co* (119/75) [1976] E.C.R. 1039.
[65] *SA CNL-SUCAL NV* (C-10/89) [1990] E.C.R. I-3711.
[66] *HT Internationale Heiztechnik v Ideal Standard* (C-9/93) [1994] E.C.R. I-2789.
[67] *Deutsche Renault v AUDI* (C-317/91) [1993] E.C.R. I-6227.
[68] *Hoffmann-la Roche & Co AG and Hoffmann-la Roche AG v Centrafarm Vertriebsgesellschaft Pharmazeutischer Erzeugnisse mbH* (102/77) [1978] E.C.R. 1139.
[69] See paras 5–012, and following, above.
[70] Point 51 of the Opinion of A.G. Jacobs.
[71] See paras 5–043, and following, below.

similarity of both the trade marks and the goods or services covered, there exists a likelihood of confusion...".[72]

Citing the Tenth Recital and the reference therein to "numerous elements" on which confusion depends the Court came up with a new term: the "likelihood of confusion must therefore be appreciated globally, taking into account all factors relevant to the circumstances of the case".[73]

The wider importance of "global appreciation" outside the factual context of *Sabel* that concerned only the similarity of signs became apparent in *Canon*.

(3) Canon—global appreciation in a wider context

5–035 *(a) The Opinion of the Advocate General*

In *Canon*[74] A.G. Jacobs stated that according to the tenth recital a number of factors, including the recognition of the mark, had to be taken into account before deciding whether there is sufficient similarity of goods or services to give rise to a likelihood of confusion and took the reference of the Court to global appreciation in *Sabel* to confirm his statement.

He attributed to global appreciation a wider significance: "It is true that that statement was made in a different context: the Court was there considering the question whether conceptual similarity of the marks alone could give rise to confusion within the meaning of Article 4(1)(b), in a situation in which the goods in question were clearly the same. However the statement is one of general application".[75]

But his attention shifted once again to the more specific test for establishing similarity between the respective goods or services.[76]

5–036 *(b) The judgment of the Court*

This time the Court appeared to be more systematic.

First, it confirmed that "the likelihood of confusion on the part of the public, in the absence of which Article 4(1)(b) of the Directive does not apply, must be appreciated globally, taking into account all factors relevant to the circumstances of the case".[77]

Secondly, it elaborated on the meaning of global appreciation or assessment, based on the Tenth Recital:

"A global assessment of the likelihood of confusion implies some interdependence between the relevant factors, and in particular a similarity

---

[72] *Sabel*, para.12.
[73] *Sabel*, para.22.
[74] *Canon Kabushiki Kaisha* (C-39/97) [1998] E.C.R. I-5507.
[75] Point 40 of the Opinion of A.G. Jacobs.
[76] See paras 5–074 and following, below.
[77] *Canon*, para.16, citing *Sabel BV* (C-251/95) [1997] E.C.R. I-6191.

5. ESTABLISHING CONFUSION—GLOBAL APPRECIATION

between the trade marks and between these goods or services. Accordingly, a lesser degree of similarity between these goods or services may be offset by a greater degree of similarity between the marks, and vice versa. The interdependence of these factors is expressly mentioned in the tenth recital of the preamble to the Directive, which states that it is indispensable to give an interpretation of the concept of similarity in relation to the likelihood of confusion, the appreciation of which depends, in particular, on the recognition of the trade mark on the market and the degree of similarity between the mark and the sign and between the goods or services identified."[78]

Thirdly, as we have already seen above, it confronted the issue of the relevance of distinctiveness in determining confusion: "marks with a highly distinctive character, either per se or because of the reputation they possess on the market, enjoy broader protection than marks with a less distinctive character".[79]

5–037

What the Court failed to do however is provide a definitive interpretation of global appreciation or assessment; its conclusion was narrowed to conform with the terms of the reference: "It follows that, for the purposes of Article 4(1)(b) of the Directive, registration of a trade mark may have to be refused, despite a lesser degree of similarity between the goods or services covered, where the marks are very similar and the earlier mark, in particular its reputation, is highly distinctive".[80]

(4) Vedial—cumulative similarity/identity conditions

5–038

In *Vedial*[81] the Court reconfirmed that the two similarity/identity requirements are cumulative.

The case involved opposition proceedings against the application for registration of a composite mark, incorporating the word HUBERT combined with the bust of a chef, for amongst others "milk and milk products" and "vinegar and sauces". The opposition was based on an earlier registration in France of the word mark SAINT-HUBERT 41 for "butters, edible fats, cheeses and all dairy products". The opposition was rejected by the Opposition Division and the Board of Appeal.[82]

The Court of First Instance found "dairy products" and "edible fats" were identical with "milk and milk products" and similar to "vinegar and sauces". However, the two marks were not found to be similar. It held that even

---

[78] *Canon*, para.17.
[79] *Canon*, para.18.
[80] *Canon*, para.19.
[81] *Vedial SA v Office for Harmonisation in the Internal Market (Trade Marks and Designs)* (C-106/03 P) [2004] E.C.R. I-9573, an appeal against the decision of the Court of First Instance in *Vedial SA v Office for Harmonisation in the Internal Market (Trade Marks and Designs)* (T-110/01) [2002] E.C.R. II-5275.
[82] Case R 127/2000-1, March 9, 2001.

though there was identity and similarity between the goods covered by the conflicting marks, the visual, aural and conceptual differences between the two marks meant that there would be no likelihood of confusion in the mind of the targeted public.

5–039　The first ground of appeal was based on the Office's admission before the Court of First Instance that there was phonetic similarity between the marks. Vedial claimed that the Court of First Instance had thus infringed the general principle of Community law that the parties delimit the subject-matter of a case.[83] The Court of First Instance, it claimed, had infringed that principle by finding that the conflicting marks displayed no similarities. The Office refuted the claim; the principle relied upon by Vedial applied in civil law but not to predominantly administrative law disputes like those concerning the Community Trade Mark. In any case, the Office had no locus standi of its own; it was not a party to the proceedings before the Board of Appeal; it noted that France Distribution, the other party to those proceedings, had not in any way agreed with Vedial's claims. Further, the role of the Court of First Instance was to determine whether the Board had correctly applied the law.

Vedial also contended that the Court of First Instance had misapplied the likelihood of confusion test by third ground of appeal by finding that there was no likelihood of confusion without establishing whether there was a risk that the public might believe that the respective goods or services originated from economically linked undertakings.

5–040　*(a)　The Opinion of the Advocate General*

Delimiting the dispute. Advocate General Ruiz-Jarabo Colomer suggested that the claim should be rejected, not because the proceedings were of an administrative nature, but because it would also need to be established that the litigant was "dominus litis"—that it could claim ownership of the contested asset—and that the subject-matter of the proceedings might be freely availed of.[84] Based on the functions of a trade mark he suggested that in trade mark proceedings there were wider interests that courts had to take into account. There was a public interest, primarily protecting consumers, distinct from the interest of the proprietor. Still, in the case of conflicts with earlier rights, and for reasons of efficiency, the legislator had entrusted their owners with protecting that public interest together with their own. The owner of an earlier right remained free to exercise it and institute opposition proceedings. The Office's capacity on the other hand as defendant "is limited to defending the legality of the decision of one of its bodies, namely, the Board of Appeal concerned",[85] it lacked the capacity of "dominus litis".

---

[83] Citing *van Schijndel and Johannes Nicolaas Cornelis van Veen v Stichting Pensioenfonds voor Fysiotherapeuten* (C-430/93 and C-431/93) [1995] E.C.R. I-4705.
[84] Citing Ramos Méndez, *Derecho Procesal Civil* (Bosch, 1986).
[85] Point 50 of the Opinion of A.G. Ruiz-Jarabo Colomer.

5. ESTABLISHING CONFUSION—GLOBAL APPRECIATION

The likelihood of confusion test. The Advocate General considered the similarity tests as cumulative but distinct from each other:

5–041

"From the moment that the Court of First Instance reached the conclusion ... that the signs were not similar to each other ... there is neither the likelihood of confusion nor the likelihood of association to which the appellant refers. In the absence of such similarity, it is pointless to wonder whether the public would think that products identified by the new mark originate from an undertaking which is economically linked to the proprietor of the earlier mark."[86]

(b) The judgment of the Court

5–042

Delimiting the dispute. The Court dismissed this ground by focusing on the role of the Court of First Instance; even if the parties were in agreement and shared a particular view "the Court of First Instance was in no way bound by that view, but had a duty to determine whether, by finding that there was no similarity between the two marks, the Board of Appeal had infringed Regulation No 40/94 in the contested decision".[87]

The likelihood of confusion test. The Court revisited its jurisprudence[88] and held that "likelihood of confusion presupposes both that the mark applied for and the earlier mark are identical or similar, and that the goods or services covered in the application for registration are identical or similar to those in respect of which the earlier mark is registered. Those conditions are cumulative".[89] Having found that the marks were not similar the Court of First Instance had correctly concluded that there was no likelihood of confusion.

Comparing the marks. The test for comparing conflicting marks focuses on their visual, aural, and conceptual similarities. Still, it remains an open ended test with the Court stressing that all the relevant factors should be taken into account.

(5) Sabel—comparing the marks

(a) The Opinion of the Advocate General

5–043

In *Sabel*[90] A.G. Jacobs reviewed the criteria employed by the Bundesgerichtshof for comparing the two marks. The overall impression

---

[86] Point 59 of the Opinion of A.G. Ruiz-Jarabo Colomer.
[87] *Vedial*, para.42.
[88] *Canon Kabushiki Kaisha* (C-39/97) [1998] E.C.R. I-5507.
[89] *Vedial*, para.51.
[90] *Sabel BV* (C-215/95) [1997] E.C.R. I-6191.

made by the marks should form the basis of the comparison. However, two additional elements could shift the balance. First, the characterising force of the sign seeking protection should also be taken into account as a positively correlative factor; this characterising force could be either intrinsic or the result of the mark's commercial standing. On the other hand descriptive signs with little imaginative content should face a stricter test of similarity. These criteria influenced his analysis.

He supported that reliance to the overall impression of the sign is "perhaps self-evident. Given that the essential criterion is the likelihood of confusion, the Bundesgerichtshof must be correct in considering that what is important is the overall impression conveyed by the mark".[91] Considering the relevance of the addition of a textual element to a pictorial sign he suggested that this was essentially a question of fact for the national court.

So from the very beginning it becomes apparent that the application of automated rules is discouraged.

Turning to the relevance of the shared signification of the two signs he supported that it should be taken into account and may even become the deciding factor, however he also suggested that it would be "difficult to establish the likelihood of confusion on the basis of conceptual similarity alone in circumstances in which the earlier mark is not well known, particularly when, as here, the image in question is not particularly creative or unusual".[92] For the Advocate General the critical issue was to establish a genuine and properly substantiated likelihood of confusion as to origin.[93]

5–044   *(b)   The judgment of the Court*

The Court attempted to provide a systematic test. Similarity of signs must be decided following a global appreciation. "That global appreciation of the visual, aural or conceptual similarity of the marks in question, must be based on the overall impression given by the marks, bearing in mind, in particular, their distinctive and dominant components. The wording of art.4(1)(b) of the Directive—"... there exists a likelihood of confusion on the part of the public..."—shows that the perception of marks in the mind of the average consumer of the type of goods or services in question plays a decisive role in the global appreciation of the likelihood of confusion. The average consumer normally perceives a mark as a whole and does not proceed to analyse its various details".[94]

---

[91] Point 59 of the Opinion of A.G. Jacobs.
[92] Point 62 of the Opinion of A.G. Jacobs.
[93] Repeating a point he had already made, see para.5–021, above; to reinforce its importance his perspective on similarity tests had become narrower.
[94] *Sabel*, para.23.

5. ESTABLISHING CONFUSION—GLOBAL APPRECIATION

It went on to hold that the more distinctive the earlier mark, the greater will be the likelihood of confusion and that conceptual similarity "resulting from the fact that two marks use images with analogous semantic content may give rise to a likelihood of confusion where the earlier mark has a particularly distinctive character, either per se or because of the reputation it enjoys with the public".[95]

Turning to the actual circumstances of the case it found that, since the earlier mark was not especially well known and possessed little imaginative content, conceptual similarity would not be enough to give rise to a likelihood of confusion.

(6) Lloyd—aural similarity 5–045

The test was developed further in *Lloyd Schuhfabrik*.[96] As you recall, the case involved the marks "Lloyd" and "Loint's".

(a) The Opinion of the Advocate General 5–046

Advocate General Jacobs repeated *Sabel*'s main points and introduced into the comparison the nature of the goods by adding that as part of the global assessment exercise:

> "it may ... be relevant ... to consider not only the degree of aural similarity of the mark and the sign but also the degree (or absence) of visual and conceptual similarity. In the absence of visual or conceptual similarity it would be necessary to consider whether, having regard to all the circumstances including the nature of the goods and the conditions in which they were marketed, the degree of any aural similarity would of itself be likely to give rise to confusion".[97]

(b) The judgment of the Court 5–047

The Court followed the Opinion of the Advocate General. The global appreciation must be based on the overall impression created by the marks "bearing in mind, in particular, their distinctive and dominant components ... The average consumer normally perceives a mark as a whole and does not proceed to analyse its various details".[98] It added that the importance attributed to each one of the elements of the similarity test must be evaluated, where appropriate, "taking account of the category of goods or

---

[95] *Sabel*, para.24. see also *Levi Strauss & Co v Casucci SpA* (C-145/05) [2006] E.C.R. 0000, [2006] E.T.M.R. 71.
[96] *Lloyd Schuhfabrik Meyer & Co GmbH* (C-342/97) [1999] E.C.R. I-3819.
[97] Point 18 of the Opinion of A.G. Jacobs.
[98] *Lloyd*, para.25.

services in question and the circumstances in which they are marketed"[99]; there may be cases where mere aural similarity might cause confusion.

5-048 **(7) Mühlens—a challenge to Lloyd**

Mühlens[100] challenged the relevance of the three specific factors courts had to examine in order to assess trade mark similarity. The case also exemplifies that under the architecture of co-existence sometimes courts facing identical facts would reach contrasting conclusions.

It came before the Court of Justice as an appeal against a judgment of the Court of First Instance[101] dismissing the action for annulment against a decision of the Second Board of Appeal that had in turn dismissed the opposition by Mühlens, the owner of a figurative Community Trade Mark incorporating the word "Sir" and a heraldic figure for goods in Class 3 ("Perfumery, essential oils, cosmetics, hair lotions, dentifrices, soaps"), against the word mark "Zirh" for goods and services in Classes 3, 5, and 42.

5-049 *(a) The judgment of the Court of First Instance*

The Court of First Instance conducted the global assessment test and found that visually and conceptually the signs were not similar. Phonetically there were similarities, in particular concerning the way the marks would be pronounced in English-speaking countries and Spain. Following *Lloyd*[102] the Court of First Instance accepted that phonetic similarity alone could lead to a finding of similarity, however according to its own case law "phonetic similarities may be counteracted by the conceptual differences between the trade marks in question. For there to be such a counteraction, at least one of the marks at issue must have, from the point of view of the relevant public, a clear and specific meaning so that the public is capable of grasping it immediately".[103]

---

[99] *Lloyd*, para.27.
[100] *Mühlens GmbH & Co KG v Office for Harmonisation in the Internal Market (Trade Marks and Designs)* (C-206/04 P) [2006] E.C.R. I-271.
[101] *Mühlens v Office for Harmonisation in the Internal Market (Trade Marks and Designs)* (T-355/02) [2004] E.C.R. II-791.
[102] *Lloyd Schuhfabrik Meyer & Co GmbH* (C-342/97) [1999] E.C.R. I-3819; and *Mystery Drinks v Office for Harmonisation in the Internal Market (Trade Marks and Designs)* (T-99/01) [2003] E.C.R. II-43.
[103] *Mühlens*, para.49, citing *Phillips-Van Heusen v Office for Harmonisation in the Internal Market (Trade Marks and Designs)* (T-292/01) [2003] E.C.R. II-4335. The case involved an opposition against the registration of the word mark BASS as a Community Trade Mark for footwear and clothing based on the registration in Germany of the trade mark PASH for identical and similar goods. The Third Board of Appeal had found that the marks where visually similar and phonetically similar, in particular in some regions in Germany where the consonants B and P were pronounced in a very similar manner. In terms of conceptual similarity the Board had held that neither of the two signs had a settled meaning in relation to the products concerned—BASS would be understood by the average German consumer to be a reference to the voice of a singer or a musical instrument whereas PASH was a term

5. ESTABLISHING CONFUSION—GLOBAL APPRECIATION

In this case the word "Sir" had an obvious meaning understood by the public despite the fact that it had no link with the product. It also accepted the Office's argument that phonetic similarity is less important when at the time of purchase the relevant public sees the marks. The submission that the products covered by the earlier mark were also sold through other channels, for example beauty salons, did not alter the Court of First Instance's conclusion that the conflicting signs were not sufficiently similar for establishing confusion.

Before the Court of Justice Mühlens claimed that the Court of First Instance had misconstrued the concept of likelihood of confusion in two ways. First, phonetic similarity should lead to a finding of likelihood of confusion, in particular given the methods of marketing for the specified goods and services. Secondly, phonetic similarity should not be counteracted by conceptual considerations.

(b) The Opinion of the Advocate General 5–050

(i) Balancing the factors. Advocate General Ruiz-Jarabo Colomer was tempted to consider the first part of the plea as inadmissible because it challenged factual findings made by the Court of First Instance. He chose though to examine it applying the "interpretative principle in dubio pro actione".[104] This is a typical example of the transformation of the functioning

---

used in a German dice game—so there would be no conceptual similarity. Still it found that there was a likelihood of confusion as a result, in particular, of phonetic similarity. The Court of First Instance found that there was limited visual similarity, relying less than the Board of Appeal on the similarity between the letters B and P. On phonetic similarity it agreed with the Board on the pronunciation of the letters B and P but found that the ending syllables would not be pronounced in the same way. On the semantic level it found that there was no similarity between the two signs. It also held however that the conceptual differences were such as to counteract the visual or phonetic similarities: (para.54) "Next, it must be held that the conceptual differences which distinguish the marks at issue are such as to counteract to a large extent the visual and aural similarities . . . For there to be such a counteraction, at least one of the marks at issue must have, from the point of view of the relevant public, a clear and specific meaning so that the public is capable of grasping it immediately. In this case that is the position in relation to the word mark BASS, as has just been pointed out in the previous paragraph. Contrary to the findings of the Board of Appeal . . . that view is not invalidated by the fact that that word mark does not refer to any characteristic of the goods in respect of which the registration of the marks in question has been made. That fact does not prevent the relevant public from immediately grasping the meaning of that word mark. It is also irrelevant that, since the dice game Pasch is not generally known, it is not certain that the word mark PASH has, from the point of view of the relevant public, a clear and specific meaning in the sense referred to above. The fact that one of the marks at issue has such a meaning is sufficient—where the other mark does not have such a meaning or only a totally different meaning—to counteract to a large extent the visual and aural similarities between the two marks."

It also noted that phonetic similarity is less important in the case of goods sold in such circumstances where the consumer perceives the sign visually.

Taking into account all these factors in its global appreciation test it found that there was no likelihood of confusion.

[104] Point 35 of the Opinion of Ruiz-Jarabo Colomer.

of the Court from an interpretive court to a court that is part of an appeals system; the principle aimed for effective judicial protection and called for continuation of the proceedings until a decision on the substance is reached.

Mühlens relied on a German theory to read *Lloyd* as setting a doctrine that phonetic similarity should be sufficient for the purposes of a confusion test; consumers did not always have the marked products in front of them at the time of purchase; gifts, mail-order and telephone sales, and recommendations were verbal rather than visual. This made sense, according to the Office, but only in specific factual scenarios. Indeed *Lloyd* recognised the possibility that phonetic similarity might suffice, but nevertheless required an overall assessment of all the relevant factors before reaching a conclusion; after all the Court of Justice was trying to give general rulings.

The Advocate General agreed that *Lloyd* did not rule out the possibility that phonetic similarity might suffice; it did not render phonetic similarity the ultimate confusion arbiter. "From the logical and linguistic point of view, where 'the possibility is not excluded' that something may happen, it is recognised that it is not very probable and, implicitly, that such an event is unusual. In any case, that statement provides no basis for inferring a general rule according to which it is doubtful that a specific case will arise."[105]

5–051　Regarding the importance that channels of trade might give to phonetic similarity he remarked that the Court of First Instance had not overlooked this issue; it found the evidence submitted by Mühlens insufficient. Whether its assessment was right or not was outside the jurisdiction of the Court of Justice according to art.225 EC and art.58 of the Statute of the Court of Justice.[106]

The second part of the plea challenged the concept, and its application, of the balancing suggested by the Court of First Instance and the counteraction of phonetic by conceptual similarity. Advocate General Ruiz-Jarabo Colomer found that the jurisprudence of the Court demanded an overall assessment that took into account all the relevant factors so as a concept the approach of the Court of First Instance was correct. Its specific application was, again, a question of assessing evidence.

On the legality of the "counteraction" rule he repeated his position expressed in *Picasso*[107] that the Court of Justice could only review it "where the contested rule was relied on in an absolute and a priori manner without prior individual analysis of the various components, resulting in its automatic application in a way that conflicted with . . . the case-law of the Court of Justice. Of course, it would also be necessary for the appellant to allege

---

[105] Point 45. To reinforce his reading of *Lloyd Schuhfabrik Meyer & Co GmbH* (C-342/97) [1999] E.C.R. I-3819 he looked at the translations of the contested para.28 in a number of languages; all led to the same conclusion.

[106] Citing *Commission v Camar and Tico* (C-312/00 P) [2002] E.C.R. I-11355.

[107] See the Opinion of the A.G. in *Claude Ruiz-Picasso v Office for Harmonisation in the Internal Market (Trade Marks and Designs)* (C-361/04 P) [2006] E.C.R. I-643.

distortion of the facts,[108] a possibility not to be taken into account here since no such allegation was made."[109]

The Court of First Instance had examined all the factors and considered that the conceptual aspect was decisive. There was nothing wrong with the process it followed.

(ii) The "cohabitation" between the Community Trade Mark and national rights. The Advocate General then discussed in some detail a judgment of the Landgericht Hamburg[110] that Mühlens had submitted in order to boost the first part of the appeal. The parties, contested signs, and products were the same; still the German court held that there was a likelihood of confusion. According to the Advocate General this was the result of the cohabitation, rather than coexistence, between the Community Trade Mark system and national rights.

5–052

The "correspondence with national law is reflected in cases of infringement of Community trade marks, a field governed by Community law and, on an ancillary basis, the laws of the Member States, as if the principle of subsidiarity had been inverted".[111] He went through the main points of the enforcement process.

The national courts that have taken the role of Community Courts regarding the enforcement of Community Trade Marks decide whether they have jurisdiction in accordance with arts 93 and 94 of the Regulation, and assume responsibility, under art.97(3), "for applying the provisions in force for actions of that kind within the legal system of the country in which they are located, without prejudice to the specific provisions of the regulation, which are in fact scant and diffuse, despite the unitary and independent orientation which the legislature sought to attribute to them".[112]

"From the substantive point of view, Regulation No 40/94 merely grants the proprietor, in Article 9(1) and (2), a ius prohibendi and a right to compensation which is 'reasonable' (sic) for events subsequent to publication of the Community trade mark application which, after due publication of registration of the mark, are prohibited. To this must be added the right to ask that a trade mark reproduced in a dictionary, encyclopaedia or any other reference work should be accompanied by an indication that it is a registered trade mark [Article 10 of the Regulation]. In such cases,

---

[108] Citing *Hilti AG v Commission* (C-53/92) [1994] E.C.R. I-667.
[109] Point 55 of the Opinion of Ruiz-Jarabo Colomer.
[110] *Mühlens GmbH & Co KG v Zirh International Corp* [2005] E.T.M.R. 55; this was a Community Trade Mark infringement action between the same parties. The German court rejected the Court of First Instance's interpretation of *Lloyd Schuhfabrik Meyer & Co GmbH* (C-342/97) [1999] E.C.R. I-3819 and, instead, applied a theory developed by the case law of the Bundesgerichtshof (German Supreme Court) that relied primarily on phonetic similarity.
[111] According to art.14 of the Community Trade Mark Regulation. He cited Gastinel, La Marque Communautaire (L.G.D.J., 1998) p.197, as the original source of this succinct remark.
[112] Point 63 of the Opinion of Ruiz-Jarabo Colomer.

there is no mention of the applicable law: the ius and the forum coincide, so that the competent court relies on its own law, which in this case acquires the status of Community law."[113]

"On the other hand, other rights of action, in particular actions for compensation, are governed by the law of the Member State in which the infringements have occurred (lex loci commissi delictii), pursuant to Article 98(2) of Regulation No 40/94, with the consequence that the Community trade mark courts are being progressively called on to have recourse to foreign law, thereby detracting from the unitary approach which was intended for industrial property of this kind.[114] Thus, legal provisions and case-law regarding liability for damage vary from one Member State to another, and this has repercussions on the sum which the proprietor of a Community trade mark whose rights have been infringed will obtain by way of compensation in one forum or another,[115] depending on the criteria used to evaluate the loss suffered and the level of compensation."[116]

"For their part, provisional and precautionary measures adopted by the Community trade mark courts are subject to the lex fori, in accordance with Article 99 of Regulation No 40/94. Their scope depends, however, on the origin of their jurisdiction: if it derives from paragraphs 1, 2, 3 or 4 of Article 93, they may be enforced in any Member State; in contrast, those adopted by the Community trade mark court of the place where the harmful event was committed will only take effect in the Member State of that judicial authority."[117]

5–053 In order to avoid conflicting judgments the Community Trade Mark Regulation includes provisions on related actions (art.100), cases involving circumstances similar to litispendency (art.105), and counterclaims (art.96(7)).[118] The essence is that these "provisions contemplate the possible suspension of proceedings that are pending or inadmissibility of the originating application, declared either by the Community trade mark court or by another national judicial authority, the sole justification for this being the avoidance of conflicting decisions . . .".[119]

---

[113] Point 64; citing Lobato García-Miján, *La Marca Comunitaria–Aspectos Procesales y de Derecho Internacional Privado del Reglamento sobre la Marca Comunitaria* (Publicaciones del Real Colegio de España, 1997), p.183.
[114] Von Mühlendahl and Ohlgart, *Die Gemeinschaftsmarke* (C.H. Beck and Stämpfli & Cie AG Munich, 1998), pp.213–214.
[115] Lobato García-Miján, *La Marca Comunitaria—Aspectos Procesales y de Derecho Internacional Privado del Reglamento sobre la Marca Comunitaria* (Publicaciones del Real Colegio de España, Bologna, 1997), p.187.
[116] Point 65 of the Opinion of Ruiz-Jarabo Colomer.
[117] Point 66, citing Bumiller, *Durchsetzung der Gemeinschaftsmarke in der Europäischen Union* (C.H. Beck, 1997), p.21.
[118] Recital 16 states that ". . . contradictory judgments should be avoided in actions which involve the same acts and the same parties and which are brought on the basis of a Community trade mark and parallel national trade marks . . .".
[119] Point 69 of the Opinion of Ruiz-Jarabo Colomer.

5. ESTABLISHING CONFUSION—GLOBAL APPRECIATION

The Advocate General accepted that these provisions did not cover the facts of the case before the German court. However, he invoked the general principles of the Community legal order—first, the principle of judicial cooperation between national courts and the Court of Justice; secondly, the principle of effectiveness of Community law; and, thirdly, the principle requiring sincere cooperation under art.10 EC—to support the application of Community law as interpreted by the Court of Justice. If in doubt the national court should use the preliminary ruling mechanism, rather than apply a Community provision "in a manner that openly conflicts with the case-law of the Court of First Instance of the European Communities".[120] The Advocate General urged German courts to test the validity of their interpretation of the global appreciation test through a reference to the Court of Justice.

(c)   The judgment of the Court   5–054

The Court in its analysis of Lloyd stressed that "it is conceivable that the marks' phonetic similarity alone could create a likelihood of confusion... However, it must be noted that the existence of such a likelihood must be established as part of a global assessment as regards the conceptual, visual and aural similarities between the signs at issue. In that regard, the assessment of any aural similarity is but one of the relevant factors for the purpose of that global assessment".[121] It added that "one cannot deduce from paragraph 28 of the judgment in Lloyd Schuhfabrik Meyer that there is necessarily a likelihood of confusion each time that mere phonetic similarity between two signs is established".[122]

Having rejected the theoretical background of the first part of the appeal and without considering the methodology of the Court of First Instance in detail it ruled that it had correctly considered the overall impression created by the two signs at issue for the purpose of the global assessment of the likelihood of confusion.

As to the link between phonetic similarity and channels of trade or methods of marketing it ruled that the Court of First Instance had exclusive jurisdiction to find and appraise the relevant facts and to assess the evidence. Unless there was a distortion of the facts or evidence the Court had no jurisdiction to reconsider them[123]; and there was no such claim in this case.

The methodology of the Court of First Instance regarding the counteraction of aural similarity was approved by the Court in its consideration of the second part of the appeal. Citing *Picasso*,[124] it repeated that "global   5–055

---

[120] Point 74 of the Opinion of Ruiz-Jarabo Colomer.
[121] *Mühlens*, para.21.
[122] *Mühlens*, para.22.
[123] Distinguishing *BioID AG* (C-37/03 P) [2005] E.C.R. I-7975.
[124] *Claude Ruiz-Picasso and Others v Office for Harmonisation in the Internal Market (Trade Marks and Designs)* (C-361/04 P) [2006] E.C.R. I-643.

assessment means that conceptual and visual differences between two signs may counteract aural similarities between them, provided that at least one of those signs has, from the point of view of the relevant public, a clear and specific meaning, so that the public is capable of grasping it immediately".[125]

The Court finally looked at the application of this balancing exercise on the facts of the case, and in particular the claim that the Court of First Instance had wrongly found that the word "SIR" had a clear and specific meaning and that it had such a meaning only if the word were pronounced in the English way. Again, the Court ruled that this was a finding of fact outside the jurisdiction of the Court of Justice since there was no distortion of fact or evidence.

5–056 **(8) Matratzen I—similarity between a figurative and a word mark**

In *Matratzen I*[126] the Court considered the similarity between two marks, a figurative mark including the word MATRATZEN and the word mark MATRATZEN. It also touched the issue of coexistence. Matratzen had applied to register as a Community Trade Mark a sign combining the slogan "MATRATZEN Markt CONCORD" with a drawing of a human figure carrying a mattress.

The specification included "cushions; pillows; mattresses; air cushions and beds for medical purposes" in Class 10; "mattresses; air beds; beds; duckboards, not of metal; loose covers; bedding" in Class 20; and "bed blankets; pillow shams; bed linen; eiderdowns [down coverlets]; cambric covers; mattress covers; sleeping bags" in Class 24.

Hukla opposed the application, based on its earlier registration in Spain of the word mark "Matratzen" for "All kinds of furniture and, particularly, rest furniture, such as beds, studio couches, camp beds, cradles, couches, hammocks, bunks and carrycots; transformable furniture; wheels for beds and furniture; bedside tables; chairs, armchairs; spring mattresses, straw mattresses, mattresses and pillows" in Class 20.

The Opposition Division rejected the opposition in respect of the Class 10 goods and upheld it in respect of the goods in Classes 20 and 24. Both parties appealed to the Board of Appeal that found that the two marks would be considered similar in Spain and that the products covered by the marks were either identical or similar and concluded that there would be a likelihood of confusion in respect of all the goods specified in the application.

---

[125] *Mühlens*, para.35.
[126] *Matratzen Concord GmbH (Trade Marks and Designs)* (C-3/03 P) [2004] E.C.R. I-3657 an appeal against the judgment of the Court of First Instance (Fourth Chamber) in *Matratzen Concord GmbH* (T-6/01) [2002] E.C.R. II-4335, which in turn had dismissed the action against the decisions of the Second Board of Appeal in Joined Cases R 728/1999-2 and R 792/1999-2 October 31, 2000.

5. ESTABLISHING CONFUSION—GLOBAL APPRECIATION

(a)   The judgment of the Court of First Instance   5–057

The Court of First Instance made a general point on similarity between the marks, "... two marks are similar when, from the point of view of the relevant public, they are at least partially identical as regards one or more relevant aspects".[127]

The existence of "Matratzen" in both trade marks meant for the Court of First Instance that the earlier trade mark was identical to one of the signs making up the trade mark applied for from a visual and phonetic perspective.

It added that similarity between some elements of the mark would not suffice; the assessment of similarity should be based on the overall impression created by the marks, taking account of their distinctive and dominant components that in some cases might dominate the overall impression conveyed by a mark.

Following an analysis of the components of the trade mark applied for it   5–058
found that the word "Matratzen" was its dominant element.

Despite its meaning in German—mattress—the Court of First Instance found that there was no evidence that a significant number of consumers in Spain would understand its German meaning. There was no evidence that a significant part of the relevant public in Spain had sufficient knowledge of German; it did not resemble "colchón", the Spanish word for mattress; and although it was similar to the English word "mattresses" the Court of First Instance found that it was not part of the basic vocabulary of English in order to be understood widely in its descriptive meaning. Because of its placement in the figurative mark and the fact that it was characterised by a preponderance of consonants with hard pronunciation it appeared more likely to be kept in mind by the relevant public.

It held "that considered cumulatively, the degree of similarity between the trade marks in question and the degree of similarity between the goods covered by them are sufficiently high".[128]

Matratzen had also argued that the considerations expressed in art.12(b)   5–059
of the Regulation should be taken into account. The Court of First Instance found that even if art.12(b) were to have an effect on the registration procedure that effect should be limited; and, following the analysis regarding the meaning of the word, "Matratzen" was not descriptive in Spain.

Finally, an argument based on free movement of goods principles and the descriptive nature of the earlier trade mark in German was rejected on two grounds. The first had to do with the architecture of coexistence between Community and national trade mark rights:

"It is clear from Article 106(1) of Regulation No 40/94 that the regulation does not affect the right existing under the laws of the Member States to

---

[127] *Matratzen Concord Gmbh* (T-6/01) [2002] E.C.R. II-4335, para.30.
[128] *Matratzen I*, para.38.

bring claims for infringement of earlier rights in relation to the use of a later Community trade mark. Consequently, if, in a specific case, there exists a likelihood of confusion between an earlier national trade mark and a sign for which an application for registration as a Community trade mark has been made, the use of that sign may be prohibited by the national courts in infringement proceedings. No distinction is made, in that regard, according to whether or not that sign has actually been registered as a Community trade mark. Accordingly, neither the registration of a sign as a Community trade mark nor the refusal of such registration have any effect on the possibility for an applicant for a Community trade mark of marketing his goods under that sign in the Member State in which the earlier trade mark is registered."[129]

And, secondly, because, under art.30 EC, the exercise of the national right was justified. "The right attributed to a trade-mark proprietor of preventing any use of the trade mark which is likely to impair the guarantee of origin so understood is part of the specific subject-matter of the trade-mark rights."[130]

Before the Court of Justice Matratzen raised two pleas, based on art.8(1)(b) and the free movement of goods rules.

5-060   *(b)   The reasoned order of the Court of Justice*

The Court found the appeal to be clearly unfounded and rejected it by reasoned order under art.119 of the Rules of Procedure.[131]

5-061   **(i) Global appreciation—dominant elements.** Matratzen claimed that the Court of First Instance had failed to conduct a proper global appreciation by focusing on similarities between specific elements of the marks.

It also claimed that the Court of First Instance had erred in law in its assessment of the factual circumstances by holding that the word "Matratzen" dominated in the trade mark applied for. Instead it should have found the word "Concord" to be the dominant element. It was a more familiar word for Spanish speakers, and would remain more clearly and easily fixed in the memory for consumers.

In addition it alleged that the principles on the limitation of the effects of a trade mark should be applied by analogy, and "Matratzen" should not be relied on against the application of a composite mark.

5-062   The Office argued that Matratzen's arguments should be rejected as inadmissible since they involved exclusively findings and assessments of fact.

The Court repeated the main points of its case law on likelihood of confusion that was the essential condition for the application of art.8(1)(b).

---

[129] *Matratzen I*, para.57.
[130] *Matratzen I*, para.58.
[131] *Matratzen Concord GmbH* (C-3/03 P) [2004] E.C.R. I-3657.

5. ESTABLISHING CONFUSION—GLOBAL APPRECIATION

Regarding the global assessment part of the claim it held that the Court of First Instance had rightly pointed out that "the assessment of the similarity between two marks does not amount to taking into consideration only one component of a complex trade mark and comparing it with another mark".[132] Instead it had considered each mark as a whole and had held that this did not mean that the overall impression "created in the mind of the relevant public by a complex trade mark may not, in certain circumstances, be dominated by one or more of its components".[133]

The Court of First Instance had taken all the necessary steps to complete the global appreciation test, and the first part of the plea was rejected as unfounded.

5–063

The second part of the first plea, that challenged the interpretation of the facts of the case regarding the dominant characteristics of the mark applied for, was rejected as inadmissible because it merely challenged the appraisal of the facts without alleging any distortion of the evidence.[134]

Finally, regarding the third part of the plea the Court agreed with the Court of First Instance that art.12(b) was irrelevant. Article 12(b) "concerns the limitation of the effects of the Community trade mark itself... It does not concern the status of an earlier trade mark, within the meaning of Article 8(2) of Regulation No 40/94".[135]

(ii) The exercise of trade mark rights and free movement of goods. Matratzen had argued that the exercise of the Spanish trade mark rights in relation to a term that would be descriptive in Germany was against the second sentence of art.30 EC.

5–064

The Office responded that in opposition proceedings it should not be possible to challenge an earlier national trade mark.

It added that according to the principle of coexistence, registrability at the Community Trade Mark level and at the level of different Member States should be assessed according to the same legal criteria; however, the outcome of the assessment might vary in each individual case because it had to be conducted from the perspective of the respective relevant public. Accordingly, a term that was descriptive in one language could very well be registered in a Member State with another language.[136]

The Court focused on the free movement of goods issue. It reminded us that the EC Treaty did not affect the existence of national intellectual

5–065

---

[132] *Matratzen I*, para.32.
[133] *Matratzen I*, para.32.
[134] Citing *DKV Deutsche Krankenversicherung AG* (C-104/00 P) [2002] E.C.R. I-7561; *Telefon & Buch* (C-326/01 P) [2004] E.C.R. I-1371; and *Streamserve Inc v OHIM* (C-150/02 P) [2004] E.C.R I-1461.
[135] *Matratzen I*, para.35.
[136] Compare with the position on absolute grounds; see for example paras 4–347 and following, and 4–366 and following, above.

property rights but could restrict their exercise.[137] Article 30 allowed derogations to the fundamental principle provided that they were justified in order to safeguard the specific subject-matter of the relevant right. It referred to the essential function of trade marks as guarantees of origin and concluded that the right of preventing any use of the trade mark which was likely to impair the guarantee of origin was part of the specific subject-matter of the trade mark rights.[138]

The Court of First Instance had rightly followed the objectives and propositions developed by the jurisprudence of the Court of Justice by holding that the principle of the free movement of goods did not prohibit either a Member State from registering, as a national trade mark, a sign which, in the language of another Member State, was descriptive of the specified goods or services, or the proprietor of such a trade mark from opposing a later Community Trade Mark application.

5–066 **(9) Flexi Air—distinctiveness as part of a multifactor assessment**

In *Flexi Air*[139] the Court looked at the relevance of distinctiveness for assessing likelihood of confusion. The case was an appeal against a judgment of the Court of First Instance dismissing an action against a decision of the Board of Appeal.[140]

L'Oréal filed an application for registration of FLEXI AIR as a Community Trade Mark for "shampoos; gels, mousses and balms, preparations in aerosol form for hairdressing and hair care; hair lacquers; hair-colouring and hair-decolorising preparations; permanent waving and curling preparations; essential oils" in Class 3. Revlon filed a notice of opposition based on registrations of the FLEX in France, Sweden, and the United Kingdom. The specifications of the earlier registrations covered "bleaching preparations and other substances for laundry use; cleaning, polishing, scouring and abrasive preparations; soaps; perfumery, essential oils, cosmetics, hair lotions; dentifrices" in Class 3 and "tobacco (raw or manufactured); smokers' articles; matches' in Class 34 in France; "shampoos; hair balsam, mousse, hair spray and hair gel" in Class 3 in Sweden; and "shampoos and conditioning preparations, all for hair" in Class 3 in the United Kingdom.

---

[137] Citing *Terrapin (Overseas) Ltd* (119/75) [1976] E.C.R. 1039; and *Dansk Supermarked A/S v A/S Imerco* (58/80) [1981] E.C.R. 181.
[138] Citing *Bristol-Myers Squibb v Paranova A/S* (C-427/93) and *CH Boehringer Sohn, Boehringer Ingelheim KG and Boehringer Ingelheim A/S v Paranova A/S* (C-429/93) and *Bayer Aktiengesellschaft and Bayer Danmark A/S v Paranova A/S* (C-436/93) [1996] E.C.R. I-3457; and *Boehringer Ingelheim Pharma KG v Swingward Ltd* (C-143/00) [2002] E.C.R. I-3759.
[139] *L'Oréal SA v Office for Harmonisation in the Internal Market (Trade Marks and Designs)* (C-235/05 P) Reasoned Order, August 20, 2005.
[140] *L'Oréal v Office for Harmonisation in the Internal Market (Trade Marks and Designs)* (T-112/03) [2005] E.C.R. II-949 dismissing the action against the decision of the Board of Appeal in Case R 396/2001-4, January 15, 2003.

5. ESTABLISHING CONFUSION—GLOBAL APPRECIATION

The Opposition Division of the Office accepted the opposition and rejected L'Oréal's application for registration on the ground that there was a likelihood of confusion between its trade mark applied and the earlier trade mark registered in the United Kingdom. The Board of Appeal concurred with the Opposition Division. It found that the earlier mark was weak in terms of distinctive character, however, and given the similarities between the two marks, the risk of confusion could not be excluded.

(a) The judgment of the Court of First Instance 5–067

L'Oréal relied on three grounds in order to challenge the decision of the Board. The first had to do with the proof of genuine use in respect of the Revlon mark. This was rejected on the basis of a number of procedural failures on behalf of L'Oréal. The third claimed that the Board had granted broader protection to the United Kingdom than the protection it would enjoy in the jurisdiction because it had failed to examine the validity of the national right. This was rejected because there was no provision in the Regulation requiring or even allowing the examination of the validity of the national right that formed the basis of the opposition.

With the second ground L'Oréal claimed that the Board had infringed art.8(1)(b). One of the main arguments supporting this claim was that because the earlier mark was weak in terms of distinctive character only a complete reproduction of that mark could give rise to a likelihood of confusion.

The Court of First Instance rejected this general proposition:

> "That argument must be rejected. Although the distinctive character of the earlier mark must be taken into account when assessing the likelihood of confusion ... it is only one factor among others involved in that assessment. Thus, even in a case involving an earlier mark of weak distinctive character, on the one hand, and a trade mark applied for which is not a complete reproduction of it, on the other, there may be a likelihood of confusion on account, in particular, of a similarity between the signs and between the goods or services covered."[141]

The Court of First Instance started its analysis from the comparison between the products. Inevitably, it found that they were either identical or very similar. 5–068

Regarding the visual similarity between the marks it found that "FLEX" was the dominant element in the later mark, agreeing with the Board of Appeal:

---

[141] *Flexi Air*, para.61, citing *Canon Kabushiki Kaisha v Metro-Goldwyn-Mayer Inc* (C-39/97) [1998] E.C.R. I-5507.

"On the visual level, the Board of Appeal took the view that the sign FLEXI AIR consists essentially of the word 'flex'. In addition, being placed at the beginning, the element 'flex' is likely to have a greater impact than the rest of the sign applied for. The word 'air' is in the secondary position and is shorter. Consumers generally take more note of a mark's beginning than of its ending. The dominant character of the element 'flex' is not substantially altered by the addition of the letter 'i'. The Board of Appeal therefore concluded that the signs are visually similar."[142]

It then rejected the argument that two words by definition could not be visually similar to one word, "... it must be pointed out, firstly, that there is no reason why a sign consisting of two words and a sign consisting of a single word may not be visually similar. Secondly, in this case, neither the fact that neither of the two words in the sign applied for is identical to the earlier sign nor the fact that the latter is short is capable of invalidating the visual similarity created by the coincidence of four letters of the sign applied for out of eight, placed in the same order and at the beginning of both signs".[143]

5–069   Phonetically, the signs were also similar. The addition of "I" and the word "AIR" played an insignificant role.

Conceptually, both signs were founded on a common meaning in English:

"The arguments regarding, respectively, the lack of distinctive character of the earlier sign, the fact that the word 'flexi' does not exist in the English language and the fact the sign FLEXI AIR is a fanciful name must also be rejected, since they are not such as to overcome the fact that the words 'flex' and 'flexi' both refer, in English, to flexibility ..."[144]

The Court of First Instance then went on to assess whether on the basis of the above the Board was correct in finding that there was a likelihood of confusion: "there is a likelihood that consumers will believe that the slight difference between the signs reflects a variation in the nature of the goods or stems from marketing considerations, and not that that difference denotes goods from different traders".[145]

Before the Court of Justice L'Oréal argued that the Court of First Instance had infringed art.8(1)(b) and art.36 and art.53 of the Statute of the Court of Justice. The Court found the appeal to be manifestly unfounded and rejected it by issuing a reasoned order.

---

[142] *Flexi Air*, para.64.
[143] *Flexi Air*, para.66.
[144] *Flexi Air*, para.78, citing *Koubi v Office for Harmonisation in the Internal Market (Trade Marks and Designs)* (T-10/03) [2004] E.C.R. II-719.
[145] *Flexi Air*, para.81.

5. ESTABLISHING CONFUSION—GLOBAL APPRECIATION

(b) The reasoned order of the Court 5–070

With the art.8(1)(b) claim the appellant argued that whilst the Court of First Instance considered the weak distinctive character of the earlier mark when it assessed likelihood of confusion between the marks at issue but not when assessing similarity between the two signs.

First, it supported that the term FLEX has been given disproportionate weight in assessing similarity; secondly, the assessment method used by the Court of First Instance went against earlier judgments where non-distinctive elements had been discounted from being the dominating elements of composite trade marks.[146]

The Office responded that this plea was based on an incorrect interpretation of the judgment. The Court of First Instance had taken into account the weak distinctive character of the earlier mark, but had not attributed to it the significance claimed by the appellant.

In terms of substance it argued that the assessment of likelihood of confusion involved a number of factors, including the degree of similarity of the marks in question and that of the goods or services covered. The assessment of similarity was based on the perception of the relevant public. The role of the distinctive character of the earlier mark was different: it was the most important factor in defining the framework delimiting the extent of protection.

Further, it supported that the degree of distinctiveness of each one of the 5–071
elements of a composite mark was a relative issue. A weak element might still dominate amongst other weaker elements. The Court repeated the main points of its case law regarding likelihood of confusion and its global assessment.

The principle that "as the more distinctive the earlier mark, the greater the risk of confusion . . ., marks with a highly distinctive character, either per se or because of the reputation they possess on the market, enjoy broader protection than marks with a less distinctive character"[147] formed part of the wider principle that there was some interdependence between the factors of the global assessment.

The Court of First Instance made a finding about the distinctive character 5–072
of the earlier mark, compared the products and the signs following the guidelines of the Court, and concluded that there was a likelihood of confusion:

"In that regard, the Court of First Instance cannot be criticised for not having disregarded, in its examination of the similarity of the signs in

---

[146] Citing amongst others *Matratzen Concord GmbH* (T-6/01) [2002] E.C.R. II-4335.
[147] *Flexi Air*, para.36, citing *Sabel BV v Puma AG, Rudolf Dassler Sport* (C-251/95) [1997] E.C.R. I-6191; *Canon Kabushiki Kaisha* (C-39/97) [1998] E.C.R. I-5507; and *Lloyd Schuhfabrik Meyer & Co GmbH* (C-342/97) [1999] E.C.R. I-3819.

question, the element 'FLEX', which is common to the marks, on the ground that the earlier mark is only of weak distinctive character."[148]

The Court, functioning more as an interpretive rather than an appeal court, went on to reject the logic behind the argument of the appellant that rendered distinctive character the decisive factor:

"The result would be that where the earlier mark is only of weak distinctive character a likelihood of confusion would exist only where there was a complete reproduction of that mark by the mark applied for, whatever the degree of similarity between the marks in question. If that were the case, it would be possible to register a complex mark, one of the elements of which was identical with or similar to those of an earlier mark with a weak distinctive character, even where the other elements of that complex mark were still less distinctive than the common element and notwithstanding a likelihood that consumers would believe that the slight difference between the signs reflected a variation in the nature of the products or stemmed from marketing considerations and not that that difference denoted goods from different traders."[149]

Finally, it repeated the point made in *Matratzen*[150] that a comparison between two marks can only be made by considering each one as a whole.

5-073 The Court raised another ground for rejecting the appeal; the appraisal requested by L'Oreal would require a review of the facts of the case, not of a point of law.[151] Note that the final ground for rejecting the appeal was mentioned at the end of the discussion of the first plea; the Court discussed the substance of the plea and then added that in any case the plea would be inadmissible.

The second plea was also rejected by the Court. It was obvious from the analysis of the first plea that the Court of First Instance had carried an assessment of the likelihood of confusion between the two marks describing throughout the judgment the reasons for its stance.

5-074 **(10) Comparing the goods or services**

In *Canon*[152] the Court came up with a test for determining whether goods or services are similar.

---

[148] *Flexi Air*, para.39.
[149] *Flexi Air*, para.45.
[150] *Matratzen Concord GmbH* (C-3/03 P) [2004] E.C.R. I-3657.
[151] Citing *DKV Deutsche Krankenversicherung AG* (C-104/00 P) [2002] E.C.R. I-7561; *Telefon & Buch* (C-326/01 P) [2004] E.C.R. I-1371; and the order in *Matratzen Concord GmbH* (C-3/03 P) [2004] E.C.R. I-3657.
[152] *Canon Kabushiki Kaisha* (C-39/97) [1998] E.C.R. I-5507.

5. ESTABLISHING CONFUSION—GLOBAL APPRECIATION

(a) The Opinion of the Advocate General

According to A.G. Jacobs the gist was whether "it is permissible to consider goods or services to be similar in relation to particularly distinctive marks when such goods or services would not be considered to be similar in relation to other, less distinctive marks? Or should the test for assessing the similarity of goods or services be objective (i.e. unrelated to the nature of the marks in question)?"[153]

He described distinctiveness as a matter of degree, attributed to the fact that a mark is well known or possesses an unusual character, and noted that, according to *Sabel*, the "more well known or unusual a trade mark, the more likely it is that consumers might be confused into believing there to be trade connection between goods or services bearing the same or a similar mark".[154]

The contrasting positions supported before the Court were both based on the Tenth Recital of the Preamble of the Directive stating that:

5–075

> "whereas it is indispensable to give an interpretation of the concept of similarity in relation to the likelihood of confusion; whereas the likelihood of confusion, the appreciation of which depends on numerous elements and, in particular, on the recognition of the trade mark on the market, [on] the association which can be made with the used or registered sign, on the degree of similarity between the trade mark and the sign and between the goods or services identified, constitutes the specific condition for such protection; whereas the ways in which likelihood of confusion may be established, and in particular the onus of proof, are a matter for national procedural rules which are not prejudiced by the Directive".

One view was that the similarity of goods or services test could not be an objective test, according to the statement that "it is indispensable to give an interpretation of the concept of similarity in relation to the likelihood of confusion". The other, that the test had to be an objective test, without looking at the nature or reputation of the earlier mark, because taking into account the reputation of an earlier mark at the examination stage would make the process of registration lengthier, more burdensome, and legally uncertain.

The Advocate General noted that the Recital did refer to the recognition of the mark as an important element in determining likelihood of confusion which in turn had to be taken into account in assessing the similarity of goods or services. Objections based on practical problems would not alter

---

[153] Point 31 of the Opinion of A.G. Jacobs.
[154] Point 32 of the Opinion of A.G. Jacobs.

the Advocate General's conceptual analysis. To resolve them he suggested a balancing exercise: "although in my view the degree of recognition of the mark must be taken into account in deciding whether there is sufficient similarity to give rise to confusion, the requirement of similarity must be given full weight, both in assessing the similarity of the marks and in assessing the similarity of the goods or services in question".[155]

5-076   So a similarity of goods or services should be applied in each and every case. "Objective factors", viewed approvingly by the Advocate General, for such a test had been suggested by the UK and the French Governments.

The UK proposal suggested the following non-exhaustive list of factors, all linked with the goods or services themselves: the uses of the respective goods or services; the users of the respective goods or services; the physical nature of the goods or acts of service; the trade channels through which the goods or services reach the market; in the case of self-serve consumer items, where in practice they are respectively found or likely to be found in supermarkets and in particular whether they are, or are likely to be, found on the same or different shelves; and, the extent to which the respective goods or services are in competition with each other: that inquiry may take into account how those in trade classify goods, for instance whether market research companies, put the goods or services in the same or different sectors.[156]

The French proposal focused on the nature of the goods or services, their intended destination and clientele, their normal use and the usual manner of their distribution.

5-077   *(b)   The judgment of the Court*

The Court of Justice referred to the global assessment of the likelihood of confusion and the interdependence and balancing between the relevant factors. It accepted that the distinctive character of the earlier trade mark "and in particular its reputation, must be taken into account when determining whether the similarity between the goods or services covered by the two trade marks is sufficient to give rise to the likelihood of confusion".[157] In assessing similarity of goods or services it added "all the relevant factors relating to those goods or services themselves should be taken into account. Those factors include, inter alia, their nature, their end users and their method of use and whether they are in competition with each other or are complementary".[158]

---

[155] Point 44 of the Opinion of A.G. Jacobs.
[156] Originally developed by Jacob J. in *British Sugar Plc v James Robertson & Sons Ltd* [1996] R.P.C. 281.
[157] *Canon*, para.24.
[158] *Canon*, para.23.

6. LEVI STRAUSS—THE TIMING OF THE ASSESSMENT

5–078 In *Levi Strauss v Casucci*[159] the Court ruled on two issues: the relevant time for assessing likelihood of confusion; it also elaborated on the significance of distinctive character for the purposes of assessing likelihood of confusion.

Levi Strauss was a reference from the Belgian Cour de Cassation. Levi Strauss, the proprietor of a graphic mark for clothing described as the "mouette" (seagull) pocket design, had started infringement proceedings against Casucci who marketed jeans applying a somewhat similar design on the pockets.

Levi Strauss was unsuccessful at first instance. Before the Brussels Cour d'Appel (Court of Appeal) it argued that a significant factor in the global assessment of the likelihood of confusion should be the highly distinctive character of its trade mark based on its imaginative content and long and widespread use. The court found that there was little similarity between the two signs.

5–079 It also found that the mark had lost its highly distinctive character, because its components had become common in the clothing market.

Levi Strauss appealed further to the Cour de Cassation (Court of Cassation) and supported that the distinctive character of a mark should be judged at the time when the allegedly infringing sign had come into use and not, as the the Cour d'Appel did, at the time of the ruling.

Levi Strauss added that the Cour d'Appel had not attributed the weakening of distinctive character to Levi Strauss.

5–080 Based on those two arguments it argued that the Cour d'Appel was not entitled to hold that the "mouette" mark was no longer highly distinctive.

The Cour de Cassation stayed proceedings and referred the following questions to the Court of Justice:

> "(1) For the purposes of determining the scope of protection of a trade mark which has been lawfully acquired on the basis of its distinctive character, in accordance with Article 5(1) of Directive 89/104, must the court take into account the perception of the public concerned at the time when use was commenced of the mark or similar sign which allegedly infringes the trade mark?
>
> (2) If not, may the court take into account the perception of the public concerned at any time after the commencement of the use complained of? Is the court entitled in particular to take into account the perception of the public concerned at the time it delivers the ruling?
>
> (3) Where, in application of the criterion referred to in the first question, the court finds that the trade mark has been infringed, is it entitled, as a general rule, to order cessation of the infringing use of the sign?

---

[159] *Levi Strauss & Co v Casucci SpA* (C-145/05) [2006] E.C.R.0000; [2006] E.T.M.R.710.

(4) Can the position be different if the claimant's trade mark has lost its distinctive character wholly or in part after commencement of the unlawful use, but solely where that loss is due wholly or in part to an act or omission by the proprietor of that trade mark?"[160]

5-081 *(a) The Opinion of the Advocate General*

Advocate General Ruiz-Jarabo Colomer delivered his Opinion on January 17, 2006.[161] He started by noting that, formally, trade mark protection could be perpetuated; however trade marks were not immune from competition and the changing circumstances at the marketplace that could divest them from their reason for existence, to distinguish the products of one undertaking from those of others. Consumer perception belonged to those circumstances and its timing was critical for the outcome of this case.

As to the economic significance of the case he remarked that it would suffice to observe casually the number of people wearing jeans at anyone time.[162]

5-082 **(i) The relevant time for assessing confusion.** The Advocate General considered the first two questions jointly as essentially asking whether confusion should be determined at the time when use of the allegedly infringing sign first started, at some other time thereafter, or at the time of the relevant ruling.

He reminded the Court's jurisprudence on the function of a trade mark[163] and pointed out that only a trade mark that possessed distinctive character could fulfil that function.[164]

Trade mark rights commenced at the time of filing and their publication in the relevant trade mark journal and it would be reasonable to assume that they could be exercised throughout the time they remained effective.

5-083 He concurred with the Commission that, after *Sabel*,[165] the relevant consumer's perception of the trade mark had become a critical factor for determining likelihood confusion, being the most relevant criterion for

---

[160] Reproduced in para.12.
[161] Comment based on the Greek text available at *http://www.curia.eu*.
[162] The A.G. made a number of references to diverse sources, from http://www.wikipedia.org and Encyclopedia Britannica, stressing the European origin of the fabric back to the sailors of Genova (Gênes, jeans) and the city of Nimes (serge de Nîmes, denim) to the work of an Afghan novelist, Hosseini, *The Kite Runner* (Riverhead Books, 2003), on the symbolisms of the "American" way of dressing in 1970s' Kabul.
[163] Citing *Hoffmann-La Roche & Co AG and Hoffmann-la Roche AG* (C-102/77) [1978] E.C.R. 1139; *Koninklijke Philips Electronics NV* (C-299/99) [2002] E.C.R. I-5475; and *BioID AG* (C-37/03 P) [2005] E.C.R. I-7975.
[164] Citing *SAT.1 SatellitenFernsehen GmbH* (C-329/02 P) [2004] E.C.R. I-8317; and *BioID AG* (C-37/03 P) [2005] E.C.R. I-7975.
[165] *Sabel BV* (C-251/95) [1997] E.C.R. I-6191.

determining its distinctive character. That perception could change with time, influenced, in particular, by the behaviour of other competitors. Advocate General Ruiz-Jarabo Colomer underlined that trade mark rights under art.5 would be fully operative only if they provided ipso facto protection to their owner through an action in case of infringement. And infringement would start at the time the products bearing the infringing sign were put on the market and last until such products ceased to exist.

Accordingly the national court should not take as a reference point for determining confusion any time later than the time the infringing act commenced because otherwise it would be restricting the scope of trade mark protection.

At the same time protection should not extend beyond the point of time that the owner of the rights had ceased to enjoy those rights. Determining that point would be essential for determining the period for which compensation might be sought when the trade mark had lost its distinctive character at the time of the trial.

Concluding, Advocate General Ruiz-Jarabo Colomer suggested that the answer to the first two questions should be that national courts had to take into account the relevant public's perception of the trade mark at the point of time that use of the other sign had started.

(ii) The scope of the right. The Advocate General noted that the Directive did not aim to approximate national laws at the procedural level. 5–084

Still, the introduction of a directive into the legal order of a Member State should follow the principle of cooperation, provided by art.10 EC, and the case law of the Court requiring genuine and effective protection of the rights envisaged in the directive.

Article 5(3) of the Directive suggested that cessation of use of an infringing sign would be an effective measure.[166]

It remained for the national court to decide whether cessation was indeed the appropriate measure in the current case.

(iii) The scope of the right—loss of distinctive character. The Advocate General viewed the fourth question as a variation on the same theme. 5–085

The Commission had suggested taking a strict approach. Since the assessment of distinctive character was based on objective criteria its loss could not be the result of the behaviour of the owner of the right. The latter would be relevant only for the application of art.9 on acquiescence and art.12 on revocation and invalidity.

---

[166] Article 5(3) provides: The following, inter alia, may be prohibited under paras 1 and 2: a. affixing the sign to the goods or to the packaging thereof; b. offering the goods, or putting them on the market or stocking them for these purposes under that sign, or offering or supplying services thereunder; c. importing or exporting the goods under the sign; d. using the sign on business papers and in advertising.

Otherwise the scope of protection would be undermined because an undertaking that had put on the market infringing products would be able to benefit from its activities whilst defending its infringing acts. Competitors, according to the Commission, should instead rely on the provisions on revocation and invalidity for attacking a trade mark registration.

5-086 The Advocate General, however, suggested that there could be instances where loss of the distinctive character of a trade mark could be attributed to factors related to its use by the trade mark owner, its extensive copying by third parties, or consumer behaviour.

The example provided by the Advocate General referred to a mark becoming generic as the result of its widespread use combined with the inactions of its owner.[167]

He agreed with the Commission to the extent that the loss of distinctive character should not be relevant were it to result from the actions of third parties. However, if it were the result of the abuse of the mark by its owner or a shift in consumer perception then competing undertakings would have the option to seek the invalidation or revocation of the registration according to art.3(1)(b) or art.12 respectively.

Concluding, he suggested that the national court should refrain from granting a cessation order only when third parties rely on the widespread use of the trade mark for reasons unrelated to the use of their own signs, and provided that they have sought the invalidation or revocation of the registration of the trade mark.

5-087 *(b) The judgment of the Court*

This time the style of the judgment of the Court was less verbose than usual. Compared with the almost contemporaneous judgments in the *Storck* cases[168] the difference was striking. It answered the questions without even describing the arguments of the parties.

5-088 **(i) The relevant time for assessing confusion.** The Court took the rights of the trade mark proprietor as its starting point. In order to ensure the essential function of a trade mark "the proprietor must be protected against competitors wishing to take unfair advantage of the status and reputation of the trade mark by selling products illegally bearing that mark".[169] Only then did the Court refer to likelihood of confusion. "That must also be the case where, on the basis of a similarity between the signs and the mark in question, there is a likelihood of confusion between them."[170]

---

[167] However, the Greek and French translations of the original Spanish text were not entirely clear.
[168] *August Storck KG* (C-24/05 P) [2006] E.C.R. I-5677; and *August Storck KG* (C-25/05 P) [2006] E.C.R. 000.
[169] *Levi Strauss*, para.15, citing *Frits Loendersloot* (C-349/95) [1997] E.C.R.I-6227; and *Arsenal Football Club Plc* (C-206/01) [2002] E.C.R.I-10273.
[170] *Levi Strauss*, para.15.

6. LEVI STRAUSS—THE TIMING OF THE ASSESSMENT

Having described the aim of the Directive it reminded that Member States should ensure that the rights conferred by it could be effectively relied upon before the national courts, and ruled that the "proprietor's right to protection of his mark from infringement is neither genuine nor effective if account may not be taken of the perception of the public concerned at the time when the sign, the use of which infringes the mark in question, began to be used".[171]

Assessing the likelihood of confusion at a later time might give the user of the sign an undue advantage, resulting from his own unlawful behaviour "by alleging that the product had become less renowned, a matter for which he himself was responsible or to which he himself contributed".[172]

The Court then looked at the same picture from the perspective of the competitors of the trade mark proprietor. Their interests were protected by art.12(2)(a):

5–089

"Thus, by balancing the interests of the proprietor against those of his competitors in the availability of signs, the legislator considered, in adopting this provision, that the loss of that mark's distinctive character can be relied on against the proprietor thereof only where that loss is due to his action or inaction. Therefore, as long as this is not the case, and particularly when the loss of the distinctive character is linked to the activity of a third party using a sign which infringes the mark, the proprietor must continue to enjoy protection."[173]

It concluded that art.5(1) "must be interpreted as meaning that, in order to determine the scope of protection of a trade mark which has been lawfully acquired on the basis of its distinctive character, the national court must take into account the perception of the public concerned at the time when the sign, the use of which infringes that trade mark, began to be used".[174]

(ii) **The scope of protection.** The Court was more forceful in its approach than the Advocate General.

5–090

It emphasised that where there was a likelihood of confusion the proprietor should be entitled to prevent all third parties not having its consent from using that sign in the course of trade.

To achieve this aim, art.5(3) provided a non-exhaustive list of measures but did not require them to take a particular form; national authorities retained a degree of discretion.

In addition the requirement of genuine and effective protection required national courts to take the most appropriate for each particular case measures

---

[171] *Levi Strauss*, para.17.
[172] *Levi Strauss*, para.18.
[173] *Levi Strauss*, para.19.
[174] *Levi Strauss*, para.20.

in order to safeguard the proprietor's rights and remedy infringements of its mark. An order to cease use of the infringing sign was clearly seen by the Court as a measure which could genuinely and effectively safeguards those rights.

It concluded that:

> "where the competent national court finds that the sign in question constituted an infringement of the mark at the time when the sign began to be used, it is for that court to take such measures as prove to be the most appropriate in the light of the circumstances of the case in order to safeguard the proprietor's rights deriving from Article 5(1) ...; such measures may include, in particular, an order to cease use of that sign".[175]

5-091 **(iii) Scope of protection—the requirement of vigilant conduct.** The Court referred again to the balancing exercise[176] attempted by the Directive and looked at the provisions where the behaviour of the trade mark proprietor played a role.

Article 9(1) covered acquiescence in the use of a trade mark registered at a later date; art.10 provided for sanctions in the case of non use of a registered trade mark; and, art.12(1) and art.12(2) rendered a trade mark that had not been put to genuine use liable to revocation.

The Court inferred that protection of trade mark rights was not unconditional; rather it "is limited in particular to those cases in which the proprietor shows himself to be sufficiently vigilant by opposing the use of signs by other operators likely to infringe his mark".[177]

5-092 Indeed the Court widened the scope of the above statement to become a general principle. "The requirement of vigilant conduct is not confined to trade mark protection, in fact, and may apply in other fields of Community law where an individual seeks to benefit from a right deriving from that legal order."[178]

Re-focusing on the application of this principle to trade mark law it referred to art.12(2). The Court added that inactivity might also take the form of a failure on the part of the proprietor to utilise art.5 in due time.

Establishing the grounds for revocation remained in the jurisdiction of the national court: "it is for the competent national court to establish revocation, if appropriate, linked in particular to such a failure, including in the context of proceedings seeking protection of the exclusive rights conferred

---

[175] *Levi Strauss*, para.25.
[176] Referring to *Libertel Group BV* (C-104/01) [2003] E.C.R.I-3793 as an example of the balancing between the interests of different actors attempted by the Court.
[177] *Levi Strauss*, para.30.
[178] *Levi Strauss*, para.31.

by Article 5 . . ., and which may have been brought late by the proprietor of the mark".[179]

However, national courts would have to follow the above guidelines because otherwise the objective of the "same protection under the legal systems of all the Member States"[180] would be undermined. Once revocation had been established national courts should not issue such an order, even if there was a likelihood of confusion at the time that use of the sign had began.

5–093

Concluding, it held that:

"the answer to the fourth question must be that it is not appropriate to order cessation of the use of the sign in question if it has been established that the trade mark has lost its distinctive character, in consequence of acts or inactivity of the proprietor, so that it has become a common name within the meaning of Article 12(2) . . . and the trade mark has therefore been revoked".[181]

7. REVISITING GLOBAL APPRECIATION

Once the Court established the basic tests, national courts start referring special cases challenging aspects of the global appreciation approach.

5–094

One of the areas that remained unexplored was the effect of confusion away from the point of sale. To what extent would post-sale confusion, in particular, be considered actionable? Global appreciation would also have to be fine-tuned in relation to particular types of sign, for example, surnames or composite marks.

The Court would also have to elaborate on the scope of protection of a trade mark for retail services.

(1) Picasso/Picaro—the limitations of Arsenal

5–095

The *Picasso/Picaro*[182] case came before the Court in the form of an appeal against a judgment of the Court of First Instance[183] that had dismissed an action for annulment of a decision of the Office's Third Board of Appeal[184] rejecting the opposition by the proprietors of the Community

---

[179] *Levi Strauss*, para.35.
[180] Set out in the Ninth Recital; the Court referred here to *Class International BV v Colgate-Palmolive Co, Unilever NV, SmithKline Beecham Plc and Beecham Group Plc* (C-405/03) [2005] E.C.R. I-8735 in relation to the onus of proving infringement of the proprietor's exclusive rights.
[181] *Levi Strauss*, para.37.
[182] *Claude Ruiz-Picasso v Office for Harmonisation in the Internal Market (Trade Marks and Designs)* (C-361/04 P) [2006] E.C.R. I-643.
[183] *Claude Ruiz-Picasso* (T-185/02) [2004] E.C.R. II-1739.
[184] Case R-247/2001–3 March 18, 2002.

Trade Mark PICASSO for "vehicles; apparatus for locomotion by land, air or water, motor cars, motor coaches, trucks, vans, caravans, trailers" against DaimlerChrysler AG's application for registration of the word PICARO for "vehicles and parts therefor; omnibuses". The Picasso estate—comprising members of the artist's family—was the proprietor of the PICASSO mark.

5–096 (a) *The judgment of the Court of First Instance*

The Court of First Instance had found that the signs were visually and, to a lesser degree, phonetically similar. However, it also held that the marks were conceptually dissimilar. PICASSO was overwhelmingly linked with the artist whereas PICARO had no meaning outside the Spanish language; in Spanish "pícaro" means a cheeky, roguish, comical, low-life character, featuring in "picaresque", a particular genre of Spanish literature.[185]

Note the attention that the Court of First Instance paid to the meaning of PICASSO for the average consumer:

"The word sign PICASSO has a clear and specific semantic content for the relevant public. Contrary to the applicants' submissions, the relevance of the meaning of the sign for the purposes of assessing the likelihood of confusion is not affected in the present case by the fact that that meaning has no connection with the goods concerned. The reputation of the painter Pablo Picasso is such that it is not plausible to consider, in the absence of specific evidence to the contrary, that the sign PICASSO as a mark for motor vehicles may, in the perception of the average consumer, override the name of the painter so that that consumer, confronted with the sign PICASSO in the context of the goods concerned, will henceforth disregard the meaning of the sign as the name of the painter and perceive it principally as a mark, among other marks, of motor vehicles."[186]

The Court of First Instance also rejected the argument that the name PICASSO was well known and deserved broader protection; it held that the fact that the artist behind the name is well known does not automatically mean that there is a stronger likelihood of confusion in respect of the relevant goods. In particular since the relevant public would pay significant attention to the product at the time of purchase because of its nature, price, and characteristics. The Court of First Instance however did not take into account the perception of the public away from the time and point of sale:

---

[185] In fn.11 of the Opinion, A.G. Ruiz-Jarabo Colomer also mentions Hergé's use of the word in Tintin and the Picaros (Casterman, Tourai, 1976) describing a band of guerrillas led by Geneal Alcázar.
[186] *Claude Ruiz-Picasso* (T-185/02) [2004] E.C.R. II-1739, para.57.

"A refusal to register a trade mark because of the likelihood of confusion with an earlier mark is justified on the ground that such confusion is liable to have an undue influence on the consumers concerned when they make a choice with respect to the goods or services in question. It follows that account must be taken, for the purposes of assessing the likelihood of confusion, of the level of attention of the average consumer at the time when he prepares and makes his choice between different goods or services within the category for which the mark is registered".[187]

"It should be added that the question of the degree of attention of the relevant public to be taken into account for assessing the likelihood of confusion is different from the question whether circumstances subsequent to the purchase situation may be relevant for assessing whether there has been a breach of trade mark rights . . ."[188]

(b) The Opinion of the Advocate General

5-097

Advocate General Ruiz-Jarabo Colomer[189] started by expressing his surprise that the name of Picasso would become the subject matter of mundane litigation: ". . . it is perfectly legitimate to protect such a name against harmful attacks, but its widespread use for purely commercial ends outside the field in which gained its renown could be detrimental to the respect which his extraordinary personality deserves".[190]

His analysis followed the pattern of the appeal that was divided in four parts.

(i) Conceptual similarity. The first part targeted the approach of the Court of First Instance regarding conceptual similarity and the weight it gave to the fact that the name had a meaning outside the context of the specified goods. The Advocate General restated the established tests of the Court and noted that the assessment of the graphic, phonetic, or conceptual components that are considered to be dominant is a matter for the court before which proceedings have been brought. He added that the Court of Justice did not have the authority to review questions of fact. He repeated however his position that the Court of Justice in this area should function as the highest interpreter of the law.[191]

5-098

He supported that in this case the Court of First Instance appeared to consider all the elements of the comparison before focusing on the conceptual element that it considered to be particularly relevant. In making the

---

[187] *Claude Ruiz-Picasso* (T-185/02) [2004] E.C.R. II-1739, para.59.
[188] *Claude Ruiz-Picasso* (T-185/02) [2004] E.C.R. II-1739, para.60.
[189] *Claude Ruiz-Picasso* (C-361/04 P) [2006] E.C.R. I-643.
[190] Point 3 of the Opinion of A.G. Ruiz-Jarabo Colomer.
[191] Originally expressed in his Opinion on *DKV Deutsche Krankenversicherung AG* (C-104/00 P) [2002] E.C.R. I-7561, paras 58–60.

comparison it did not take the further step of considering the goods and the market because there was not enough similarity in the first place, and this was indeed what, according to the Advocate General, the Court had demanded in *Lloyd Schuhfabrik*.[192]

5–099 **(ii) The distinctiveness of PICASSO.** The second part of the appeal focused on the distinctiveness of PICASSO and claimed that the Court of First Instance had not followed the Court's jurisprudence expressed in *Sabel*[193] and *Lloyd Schuhfabrik*[194] that there is a higher risk of confusion when the earlier mark has a higher degree of distinctiveness.

The Advocate General though stressed that the Court of First Instance had found that PICASSO had not obtained such distinctiveness as a mark for vehicles.

5–100 **(iii) The post-sale effect of the trade mark.** The third ground of appeal focused on the post-sale effect of the mark, mentioned in *Arsenal*,[195] that the Court of First Instance did not take into account.

Here the Advocate General turned his attention to the *Arsenal* judgment:

"Paragraph 57 admits the possibility that some consumers may interpret the sign as designating Arsenal FC as the undertaking of origin of the goods, particularly once the goods have been sold by Mr Reed and are no longer on the stall where the notice stating that they are not officially endorsed by the club is displayed. Beyond that it does not establish any general rule that the purpose of a trade mark continues after the sale of the items of which it forms part."[196]

According to the Advocate General the post-sale confusion argument simply confirmed that there was a breach of trade mark rights. He went on to support that most writers do not accept that post-sale confusion is relevant for determining likelihood of confusion.

5–101 **(iv) Post-sale confusion.** Finally, the fourth part of the appeal challenged the distinction drawn by the Court of First Instance between opposition and infringement proceedings regarding the role of post-sale confusion in determining likelihood of confusion. According to the appellants post-sale confusion should be relevant in both cases in particular in the case of goods which are permanently on public view.

The Advocate General though read the judgment of the Court of First Instance under a different light:

---

[192] *Lloyd Schuhfabrik Meyer & Co GmbH* (C-342/97) [1999] E.C.R. I-3819.
[193] *Sabel BV* (C-251/95) [1997] E.C.R. I-6191.
[194] *Lloyd Schuhfabrik Meyer & Co GmbH* (C-342/97) [1999] E.C.R. I-3819.
[195] *Arsenal Football Club Plc* (C-206/01) [2002] E.C.R. I-10273.
[196] *Picasso/Picaro*, para.53.

7. REVISITING GLOBAL APPRECIATION

"that statement [see para.60 of the judgment of the Court of First Instance cited above] only highlights the distinction between, on the one hand, gauging the degree of attention of the public in order to assess the likelihood of confusion between two signs which are inevitably similar, because if they were identical it would be a case of breach of trade mark rights, and, on the other hand, weighing up the importance of particular circumstances subsequent to sale with a view to ascertaining whether there has been a breach of the industrial property right in question. Paragraph 60 shows that at no time did the Court of First Instance refer to any difference in the analysis of the likelihood of confusion depending on whether the context involves opposition proceedings or infringement proceedings".[197]

(v) **Concluding remarks.** The Advocate General concluded with two general comments. First, where a name such as Picasso is used in a completely different to its original context it will not automatically carry with it its distinctiveness; without use it is doubtful whether the name conveys information regarding the source of the product. Secondly, there is a general interest in protecting the names of great artists from commercialisation. 5–102

(c) The judgment of the Court 5–103

The Court of Justice followed a similar approach.

The Court confirmed that the conceptual differences between two signs may counteract their visual and phonetic similarities. Turning to the contested judgment the Court noted that the Court of First Instance considered that facing the word PICASSO the relevant public would see it as a reference to the artist; this would greatly "reduce the resonance with which, in this case, the sign is endowed as a mark, among others, of motor vehicles".[198]

It also found that the Court of First Instance had considered the degree of distinctiveness of PICASSO and found it devoid of any highly distinctive character in relation to motor vehicles.

The Court examined together the two parts of the appeal based on the post-sale effect of the sign. It found that the Court of First Instance was entitled to take into account the high level of consumer attention at the time of purchase: 5–104

"Where it is established in fact that the objective characteristics of a given product mean that the average consumer purchases it only after a

---
[197] *Picasso/Picaro*, para.61.
[198] *Picasso/Picaro*, para.27.

particularly careful examination, it is important in law to take into account that such a fact may reduce the likelihood of confusion between marks relating to such goods at the crucial moment when the choice between those goods and marks is made."[199]

On the post-sale effects of the mark the Court found that the Court of First Instance was also entitled to observe that these do not "prevent the taking into account of the particularly high level of attention exhibited by the average consumer when he prepares and makes his choice between different goods in the category concerned".[200]

The Court acknowledged that there will be situations where the public will pay a low degree of attention, however taking into account the lowest degree of attention "would amount to denying all relevance, for the purpose of an assessment of the likelihood of confusion, to the criterion relating to the variable level of attention according to the category of goods".[201] And, it would be unreasonable to require from the authority assessing likelihood of confusion to determine for each product the average amount of consumer attention subtracting from the level of attention shown in different situations.

5–105   Turning its attention to *Arsenal*[202] it noted that the case involved the application of a sign that was identical to the registered trade mark on identical goods. This should be precluded according to art.5(1)(a). The Court had referred to the post-sale effect of the sign in order to assert that the message conveyed at the point of sale—regarding the source of the product—did not alter its interpretation. In a re-balancing exercise the Court combined the factual background of the earlier case with the legal findings of its current case in order to negate a broad reading of *Arsenal* on post-sale confusion. Almost defensively the Court states: "In doing so, the Court did not in any way express a general rule from which it could be inferred that, for the purposes of an assessment of the likelihood of confusion ... there is no need to refer specifically to the particularly high level of attention displayed by consumers when purchasing a certain category of goods".[203]

Finally, it accepted that the Court of First Instance had not held that likelihood of confusion had to be interpreted differently for the purposes of infringement than for the purposes of opposition. It had only asserted that the degree of attention of the relevant public had to be taken into account.

---

[199] *Picasso/Picaro*, para.40.
[200] *Picasso/Picaro*, para.41.
[201] *Picasso/Picaro*, para.42.
[202] *Arsenal Football Club Plc* (C-206/01) [2002] E.C.R. I-10273.
[203] *Picasso/Picaro*, para.47.

7. REVISITING GLOBAL APPRECIATION

(2) Rossi—protection of surnames—global appreciation— the Community Trade Mark registration process

5-106

The scope of the registration of a surname as a trade mark was challenged in *Sergio Rossi*,[204] an appeal against a judgment of the Court of First Instance[205] dismissing an action for annulment of the decision of the First Board of Appeal.[206] The case is also an excellent example of how the global appreciation test is applied in practice. At the same time it gave the Court the opportunity to look at the Community Trade Mark registration process and limit the opportunities for challenging the decisions of the Boards.

Sissi Rossi Srl (Sissi Rossi) had applied for the registration of the word mark SISSI ROSSI as a Community Trade Mark for "leather and imitations of leather, and goods made of these materials and not included in other classes; animal skins, hides; trunks and travelling bags; umbrellas, parasols and walking sticks; whips, harness and saddlery" in Class 18.

Calzaturificio Rossi SpA, a company that at a later stage was acquired through merger by Sergio Rossi SpA (Sergio Rossi), opposed the application for registration on the basis of earlier registrations, in Italy as a national trade mark registration and in France as an international trade mark registration, of the mark MISS ROSSI for "footwear" in Class 25. The opposition related to "leather and imitations of leather, and goods made of these materials and not included in other classes; animal skins, hides; trunks and travelling bags".

The Opposition Division accepted the opposition and refused the application for registration. The Board of Appeal annulled that decision finding, first, that the marks were only vaguely similar and, secondly, that, on balance, the differences between the goods outweighed their commonalities, and accordingly there was no likelihood of confusion.

5-107

Looking at the two products that appeared to be closer than the rest, "women's footwear" and "women's bags" it held that they were complementary but still not similar. Sergio Rossi brought an action before the Court of First Instance seeking the annulment of the decision however its arguments targeted the particular part of the decision regarding footwear and bags.

(a) The judgment of the Court of First Instance

5-108

The Court of First Instance decided, first, to refuse to take into account new evidence submitted by Sergio Rossi. Secondly, to examine only that part of the appeal that related to women's footwear and bags since Sergio Rossi had failed to produce any argument against the findings of the Board regarding the remaining goods. Thirdly, that a general reference to the entirety of the

---

[204] *Sergio Rossi SpA* (C-214/05 P) [2006] WL 644778; [2006] WL 1911362.
[205] *Sergio Rossi* (T-169/03) [2005] E.C.R. II-685.
[206] Case R-569/2002–1, February 28, 2003.

submissions Sergio Rossi had argued in the proceedings before the Office was not enough to cover the lack of argument in the application before the Court of First Instance. Fourthly, that the claim that all the goods were sold through the same channels and made of the same raw material was inadmissible because it had not been argued before the Office. Fifthly, it looked at the substance of the case and found that there was no likelihood of confusion.

It is worth covering in more detail how it reached its decision on likelihood of confusion, since, as we will see below, the Court of Justice found that the assessment of the facts belonged to the jurisdiction of the Court of First Instance.

5–109 **(i) The arguments of the parties.** Regarding the issue of similarity between products Sergio Rossi had argued that goods such as "women's footwear" and goods covered in the specification of the trade mark application such as "leather and imitations of leather, and goods made of these materials and not included in other classes; animal skins, hides; trunks and travelling bags" and "women's bags" in particular were similar.

It relied on three lines of argument. The first concerned the complementary character of the two products: shoes and handbags fulfilled an aesthetic function; consumers in Italy and France often viewed the two products as parts of a set. The second focused on the fact that the products were made of the same material. The third supported that both the channels of trade and the end consumers were identical.

The Office conceded that according to a practice adopted by its Opposition Divisions "clothing" and "footwear" were regarded as complementary to "goods made of leather and imitation leather and bags", "handbags" in particular.

5–110 However, this should not lead to an automatic conclusion that the products were similar. The fact that consumers were looking for shoes to match the bag did not show that the two were similar.

Regarding similarity between the marks Sergio Rossi had supported that the degree of similarity between the marks should be regarded as considerable and not slight. The commonness of "Rossi" as a surname did not preclude MISS ROSSI from being distinctive. It added that the Board of Appeal had wrongly found that the Miss and Sissi were the dominant parts of the two marks.

The Office adopted the finding of the Board of Appeal that the degree of similarity was low.

5–111 The intervener, Sissi Rossi, supported that MISS ROSSI and SISSI ROSSI were not similar. MISS ROSSI was not highly distinctive; accordingly the assessment of similarity should concentrate on the respective first words of the two marks that were sufficiently different, in particular in terms of their respective conceptual content.

7. REVISITING GLOBAL APPRECIATION

As to likelihood of confusion Sergio Rossi had supported that there was a likelihood of association, in particular in the market for bags in France where Sergio Rossi had an active presence.

(ii) The targeted public. The Court of First Instance started its analysis by limiting the scope of the dispute. The arguments of Sergio Rossi focused exclusively on the similarity between "women's footwear" and "women's bags". Accordingly, it would reject the principal head of claim, seeking annulment of the contested decision in its entirety and consider only the alternative claim, seeking partial annulment of the contested decision in respect of "women's bags".

5–112

It then described the relevant public. Both products were for everyday consumption and intended for a female public; "the target public is, essentially, composed of average female consumers",[207] in principle French and Italian since the earlier registrations covered France and Italy.

(iii) Similarity between the products. The Court of First Instance stressed that similarity between the goods or services was an essential requirement for the application of art.8(1)(b) and that similarity should be assessed according to the test adopted by the Court of Justice in *Canon*.[208]

5–113

It accepted that the fact that both products were often made of the same raw material, leather or imitation leather, was a factor that should be taken into account. However, on its own it would not suffice to establish similarity because a large number of goods were made of leather or imitation leather.

The Court of First Instance then followed a narrow approach regarding the consideration of the end consumers as a relevant factor. It noted that the Court in its *Canon* test had expressly referred to the intended purpose of the goods, rather than the end consumers. "Accordingly, the fact that the end consumers of the goods are identical cannot be regarded as a significant factor in assessing the similarity between the goods."[209]

It appeared to follow a mechanistic approach, overlooking the statement in *Canon*[210] that all the relevant factors should be taken into account; the factors listed therein would be commonly relevant in most cases but should not exclude the applicability of other relevant factors.

5–114

As to the intended purpose of the goods it accepted that the intended purposes of the goods were different; shoes were used to dress feet and bags to carry objects. The goods were not interchangeable and, therefore, not in competition.

---

[207] *Rossi*, para.49.
[208] Citing *Canon Kabushiki Kaisha* (C-39/97) [1998] E.C.R. I-5507, and in respect of the Regulation, *Pedro Díaz SA v Office for Harmonisation in the Internal Market (Trade Marks and Designs)* (T-85/02) [2003] E.C.R. II-4835.
[209] *Rossi*, para.56.
[210] *Canon Kabushiki Kaisha* (C-39/97) [1998] E.C.R. I-5507.

It rejected the "aesthetic function" argument for two reasons. It found that it carried limited value in relation in the clothing and fashion sector, but this alone could not lead the consumer to believe that those two products originated from the same undertaking or from economically linked undertakings; the factor was too general to permit a finding that the goods were similar. In addition, it underlined that women's shoes and bags were not merely luxury items with a primarily decorative function. Their primary function remained the dressing of feet and the carrying of objects, respectively.

5–115　Again, without necessarily questioning the outcome of the judgment, it can be argued that, the Court of First Instance did not follow the liberal spirit of *Canon* requiring all the relevant factors to be taken into account for determining similarity. Individually, each one of them on its own might not lead to a finding of similarity. Jointly, however, they might contribute to such a finding. Note though, the point of the Advocate General regarding the role of the Court of First Instance.

As to the complementary character of the goods, the Court of First Instance adopted the definition of the Office's Opposition Guidelines[211]: "complementary goods are goods which are closely connected in the sense that one is indispensable or important for the use of the other so that consumers may think that the same undertaking is responsible for the production of both goods".

Sergio Rossi had failed according to the Court of First Instance to establish that the goods were complementary in this way in terms of their function.

5–116　Aesthetic complementarity was subjective, "determined by the habits and preferences of consumers to which producers' marketing strategies or even simple fashion trends may give rise".[212] The Court of First Instance seemed open to accepting that this aesthetic or subjective complementary nature might be relevant once it had reached the stage of a true aesthetic "necessity", when consumers would think it unusual or shocking to carry a bag which did not perfectly match their shoes. However the simple search for aesthetic harmony was considered to be too general a factor to satisfy by itself a finding that all the goods concerned were complementary and, thus, similar.

In addition, the Court of First Instance doubted whether consumers would necessarily perceive a product that functioned as a complement of or accessory to another to have the same commercial origin with that other product.

Here, the Court of First Instance showed signs of a less rigid stance. "For that to be the case, consumers would also have to consider it usual for those products to be sold under the same trade mark, which normally implies that a large number of the producers or distributors of the goods are the same".[213] Albeit, the applicant had failed to produce evidence showing that

---

[211] OHIM, Opposition Guidelines Pt II Ch.2 para.2.6.1.
[212] *Rossi*, para.61.
[213] *Rossi*, para.63.

in the minds of the relevant public, producers of shoes and of bags were usually the same; general assertions were not enough.

It is suggested, though, that this discussion could be better placed as part of the global assessment of the likelihood of confusion than as a factor for determining product similarity. 5–117

The next step of the Court of First Instance was to consider the channels of distribution. Here, adopting the analysis of the Board of Appeal, the Court of First Instance appeared to accept that all the factors should be viewed jointly, as combined and interacting factors of one test, rather than a combination of mini tests. Albeit, it did this in order to juxtapose the only factor it accepted as evidence of similarity with the offsetting findings:

"... with respect to the channels of distribution, the Board of Appeal made the relevant point that the goods in question are sometimes, but not always and not necessarily, sold in the same shops. It also acknowledged that, whilst that fact was indeed an indication that the goods in question were similar, it did not suffice to cancel out the differences between those goods."[214]

It found that Sergio Rossi had failed to establish three things that could have helped its case: that the goods in question were normally sold in the same places; or, that consumers necessarily expected to find in shoe shops a wide choice of women's bags and vice versa; or, that consumers generally expected producers of shoes to sell bags under the same trade mark or vice versa.

Concluding, the Court of First Instance accepted that the goods did have some in common, in particular the fact that they were sometimes sold through the same outlets. This time it viewed the differences as not so sufficient to rule out, by themselves, the possibility of a likelihood of confusion, particularly where the mark applied for was identical to an earlier mark which was distinctive to a particularly high degree.

This meant that it would also have to examine the similarity between the two marks.

(iv) Similarity between the marks. The Court of First Instance referred to the test for determining similarity, appearing to mix it up with the global appreciation of the likelihood of confusion. "It is settled case-law that, in so far as the visual, aural or conceptual similarity of the marks in question is concerned, the comprehensive assessment of the likelihood of confusion must be based on the impression given by the marks as a whole, account being taken of, inter alia, their distinctive and dominant components".[215] 5–118

---

[214] *Rossi*, para.65.
[215] *Rossi*, para.69; citing *Phillips-Van Heusen v Office for Harmonisation in the Internal Market (Trade Marks and Designs)* (T-292/01) [2003] E.C.R. II-4335 and the case law cited therein.

Despite the fact that the Court of First Instance had clearly divided the judgment into three parts it succumbed to the temptation of making early references to confusion, that could clutter the judgment and undermine its outcome.

In any case, the Court of First Instance went on to examine the factors adopted by the Court of Justice in *Sabel*.[216]

5–119 Visually, the second word of the two marks was identical, whereas the first words shared the three letters "iss". However, "Sissi" was a longer word than "Miss" and the respective initial, "s" and "m", and final, "i" and "s", letters were visually different.

Phonetically, the first words of both marks were characterised by the strong sound of the double "s" and by the presence of the sole vowel "i". However, the two words had a different number of syllables and in French, unlike in Italian, the stress will be placed on the last syllable.

Conceptually, Italian and French consumers alike would perceive the word "Rossi" as a surname of Italian origin and "Sissi" as a female forename; the targeted consumers targeted would also understand the word "Miss" in its English meaning. Sergio Rossi had supported that both marks would create the impression of a woman with the surname "Rossi"; the Court of First Instance noted however that there was, still, a conceptual difference between the word "Miss" and a specific forename.

5–120 The result of these comparisons was inconclusive; the marks resembled each other in some respects but differed in others. Accordingly, the degree of similarity depended on whether "Rossi", the common element, constituted the distinctive and dominant element of the two marks.

The Court of First Instance highlighted that "Rossi" occupied the second part of the two marks without being prominent in any way and underlined that this had not been disputed by Sergio Rossi, that only claimed that the Board had wrongly found that that the "Miss" and "Sissi" were the dominant elements.

It concluded that even if the two first words were not the dominant elements but instead had respectively the same impact as "Rossi", the degree of similarity would only be raised to average from low; it would not become considerable as argued by Sergio Rossi.

5–121 **(v) Likelihood of confusion.** The Court of First Instance defined likelihood of confusion as:

> "the likelihood that the public might believe that the goods or services in question originate from the same undertaking or, as the case may be, economically linked undertakings. The likelihood of confusion as to the commercial origin of the goods must be assessed comprehensively, by

---

[216] *Sabel BV* (C-251/95) [1997] E.C.R. I-6191.

reference to the perception by the relevant public of the marks and goods in question and taking account of all the factors relevant to the case, in particular the interdependence between the similarity of the trade marks and that of the goods or services".[217]

It added that the more distinctive the earlier mark, the greater the likelihood of confusion would be.[218] In this case the earlier marks were not highly distinctive. "Therefore, it need only be examined whether the similarities between the marks are sufficient to outweigh the differences between the goods in question and to give rise to a likelihood of confusion on the part of the target public."[219]

Balancing the two the Court of First Instance held that there was no likelihood of confusion between the two marks. It did not elaborate on the mechanics of this balancing exercise; it reached its conclusion by simply referring to the paragraphs of its judgment where the differences between the goods and the differences between the marks were established.

(vi) "Likelihood of association". The Court of First Instance examined separately the claim of Sergio Rossi that there was a likelihood of association "in so far as the consumer might believe that the goods sold under the marks in question originate from the same undertaking or from economically linked undertakings".[220] In essence, the reference to likelihood of association was nothing more than an invitation to the Court of First Instance to reconsider likelihood of confusion. Regarding this argument the applicant had concentrated on the French market in particular.

5–122

The Court of First Instance observed that Sergio Rossi had not challenged the Board of Appeal's finding that the surname "Rossi" was seen as a very common Italian surname by both Italian and French consumers.

It also found that in the clothing and fashion market "surname" marks were quite common; accordingly "it may be assumed, as a general rule, that a very common name will appear more frequently than a rare name".[221]

(vii) The starting point for determining likelihood of confusion. Finally, the argument of Sergio Rossi that it was active in the sector of handbag production served a welcome reminder about what registered trade mark law is all about: protection of trade marks in relation to the specification of the registration:

5–123

---

[217] *Rossi*, para.77; citing *Laboratorios RTB v Office for Harmonisation in the Internal Market (Trade Marks and Designs) (BASS)* (T-162/01) [2003] E.C.R. II-2821.
[218] Citing *Canon Kabushiki Kaisha* (C-39/97) [1998] E.C.R. I-5507; and *Lloyd Schuhfabrik Meyer & Co GmbH* [1999] E.C.R. I-3819.
[219] *Rossi*, para.79.
[220] *Rossi*, para.81.
[221] *Rossi*, para.83.

"[T]he the fact that the applicant is also active in the sector of handbag production is irrelevant to the assessment of the likelihood of confusion between the earlier marks and the mark applied for. The goods designated by the marks in question must be examined as they are protected by those marks. The earlier marks are not registered for 'goods made of leather or imitation leather not included in other classes' but are regarded as registered in respect of 'women's footwear' only. It follows that the applicant is not entitled to rely on the marks in order to protect the line in handbags produced by him."[222]

5-124   *(b)   The challenge before the Court of Justice*

Before the Court Sergio Rossi claimed that the Court of First Instance had misapplied its Rules of Procedure and, also, infringed art.8(1)(b) of Regulation.

5-125   *(c)   The Opinion of the Advocate General*

Advocate General Kokott divided the case into four parts. She started with Sergio Rossi's two procedural points and then looked at the claims based on art.8(1)(b) of the Regulation regarding the similarity between the two marks and the respective products.

5-126   **(i) Limiting the scope of the appeal.** The first procedural point regarded the decision of the Court of First Instance to reject in an outright manner the principal head of the claim that covered the broader categories of goods and focus exclusively on the part of the action appeal that related to women's shoes and bags, arguing that it had infringed art.81 of its Rules of Procedure[223] because the judgment gave no reasons for dismissing the principal head of claim.

The appellant accepted that the arguments in support of the action before the Court of First Instance related almost exclusively to the similarity between shoes and bags however it argued that the similarity between all of the goods covered by the two marks was referred to several times in the application submitted to the Court of First Instance.

In addition, it supported that the arguments, on the channels of trade and raw materials, relied upon during the hearing should not be held to be inadmissible under art.48(2) of the Rules of Procedure[224] as new pleas in law since they were simply additional arguments.

---

[222] *Rossi*, para.84.
[223] Article 81 requires the Court of First Instance to indicate in the judgment the grounds for its decision.
[224] Article 48(2) provides: "No new plea in law may be introduced in the course of proceedings unless it is based on matters of law or of fact which come to light in the course of the procedure."

7. REVISITING GLOBAL APPRECIATION

5–127 Sissi Rossi and the Office argued that the Court of First Instance could not substitute itself for the parties and assess an issue in the dispute that the parties had failed to raise.

The Advocate General found that the Court of First Instance had clearly indicated why it had rejected the principal head of the claim. The limitation was justified according to art.41(c) of the Rules of Procedure.[225] The summary of the pleas had to be sufficiently clear and precise in order to allow the defending party to prepare its defence and the Court of First Instance to exercise its power. The facts and the points of law had to be presented in a coherent and comprehensible way.

Sergio Rossi had focused both in terms of factual evidence and points of law on the similarity between women's shoes and bags. These arguments could not be transposed to the other products.

She also believed that the additional arguments presented before the Court of First Instance in essence constituted a new claim broadening the scope of the case.

5–128 **(ii) Rejecting new evidence.** The appellant supported that the Court of First Instance by failing to take into account the evidence it had submitted had infringed art.44(1)(e) of its Rules of Procedure.[226] It claimed that the current case diverged from the established case law of the Court of First Instance that covered cases where the applicants had had their arguments initially rejected by the Office. Here Sergio Rossi could not have challenged the arguments of the Board because the Board had decided in favour of the original appellant; its arguments were expressed for the first time in its decision.

Sergio Rossi also argued that the art.73 of the Regulation[227] had been infringed since it had not been given the opportunity to present its views before the Board of Appeal on whether there was similarity between the goods concerned. The Court of First Instance should have either allowed the evidence to be presented or annulled the contested decision and refer the case back to the Board for the evidence to be presented there.

Advocate General Kokott noted that according to art.63 of the Regulation the Court of First Instance had the jurisdiction to review only the legality of the decisions of the Boards. According to art.74(1) of the Regulation[228] the

---

[225] Article 44(1) of the Rules of Procedure of the Court of First Instance provides: "An application of the kind referred to in Art.21 of the Statute of the Court of Justice shall state: ... (c) the subject-matter of the proceedings and a summary of the pleas in law on which the application is based; (d) the form of order sought by the applicant; (e) where appropriate, the nature of any evidence offered in support".

[226] Rules of Procedure art.44(1).

[227] Article 73 provides: "Decisions of the Office shall state the reasons on which they are based. They shall be based only on reasons or evidence on which the parties concerned have had on opportunity to present their comments".

[228] Article 74(1) provides: "In proceedings before it the Office shall examine the facts of its own motion; however, in proceedings relating to relative grounds for refusal of registration, the Office shall be restricted in this examination to the facts, evidence and arguments provided by the parties and the relief sought".

5–129
Office could only consider the evidence and the arguments presented by the parties in relation to relative grounds. Accordingly facts that had not been presented before the Office could not be employed to challenge the legality of the decisions of the Board.[229]

She upheld the jurisprudence of the Court of First Instance that the legality of the decision could only be reviewed by the Court of First Instance on the basis of facts that were known and the law that was effective at the date of the decision.[230]

Sergio Rossi had the opportunity to present all the pertinent evidence; if the Office throughout the registration process had violated its procedural rights the particular violation as such should have been raised. This however, would not alter the evidentiary framework of the Court of First Instance.

She concluded that this claim should be rejected.

The subsidiary claim regarding the right to be heard should also be rejected following the same analysis but also because it had been put forward at a late stage.

5–130
(iii) Article 8(1)(b) considerations. The Advocate General reminded that the competence for assessing the facts belonged to the Court of First Instance; the Court could review that assessment only if the Court of First Instance had distorted the evidence submitted to it. Accordingly claims that referred only to the appreciation of the facts by the Board should be inadmissible.

Sergio Rossi had argued that the Board had failed to take sufficiently into account the fact that for women the compatibility between their shoes and their handbags constituted an important issue.

Regarding the similarity between the two signs Sergio Rossi claimed that the Court of First Instance made an incorrect assessment. In particular it argued that the finding that "Rossi" was a very well-known surname to French consumers had not been supported by objective evidence. Even if it were, it added, this should not preclude that it could function as an indication of origin.

According to the apportionment of competences before the Court of First Instance and the Court of Justice she found both claims to be inadmissible.

---

[229] Citing a number of decisions of the Court of First Instance: *eCopy Inc v Office for Harmonisation in the Internal Market (Trade Marks and Designs)* (T-247/01) [2002] E.C.R. II-5301; *DaimlerChrysler Corp v Office for Harmonisation in the Internal Market (Trade Marks and Designs)* (T-128/01) [2003] E.C.R. II-701; *Samar SpA v Office for Harmonisation in the Internal Market (Trade Marks and Designs)* (T-115/03) [2004] WL 59046.

[230] Citing *eCopy Inc* (T-247/01) [2002] E.C.R. II-5301; *Salomon SA v Commission* (T-123/97) [1999] E.C.R. II-2925, *Graphischer Maschinenbau v Commission* (T-126/99) [2002] E.C.R. II-2427; and *SAM Schiffahrt et Stapf v Germany* (C-249/95) [1997] E.C.R. I-4475, from the perspective of the Court of Justice as well as a number of judgments dealing with State aid like *Spain v Commission* (C-276/02) [2004] E.C.R. I-8091.

7. REVISITING GLOBAL APPRECIATION

(d) The judgment of the Court   5–131

(i) Article 8(1)(b). The Court started by considering art.8(1)(b), the substantive part of the appeal. Following the proposal of the Advocate General it found that both claims should be rejected as inadmissible.

The Court of First Instance alone had the competence to assess the value that should be attached to the evidence. The only obligation imposed on it was to provide reasons that would allow the Court to exercise its judicial review, in particular whether there had been any distortion of the evidence.[231]

Assessing the relevance of the fact that a party had refrained from relying on certain facts constituted clearly a part of its competence.

In this case the Court of First Instance had conducted an overall assess- 5–132
ment of the likelihood of confusion and provided sufficient reasons for its findings.

Regarding the outcome of the assessment the Court of Justice could not substitute its own assessment of the facts for that of the Court of First Instance.[232]

(ii) Limiting the scope of the appeal. The Court noted that in reality 5–133
the first ground of appeal challenged the validity of the rejection of the principal head of claim by the Court of First Instance because Sergio Rossi had not included any argument to support it in the application itself.

Following again the line of the Advocate General it noted that the Court had already ruled that the statement required under the identical provisions in art.44(1)(c) of the Rules of Procedure of the Court of First Instance and art.38(1) of the Rules of Procedure of the Court of Justice—both reiterating a requirement set by art.21 of the Rules of Procedure of the Court of Justice—should be sufficiently clear and precise to enable the defendant to prepare its defence and the Court to exercise its power of review and that was necessary for the essential matters of law and of fact on which an action was based to be indicated coherently and intelligibly in the application itself.[233]

The Court of First Instance had rejected the principal claim because the argument put forward in the application referred only to "women's bags" and "women's footwear". And the Court added that the appellant had failed to put forward any genuine argument before the Court of Justice to demonstrate that the application brought before the Court of First Instance did refer to matters of law and of fact in support of that claim.

Further streamlining and tightening the process of challenging decisions of the Boards of Appeal the Court added:

---

[231] *Commission v CEVA and Pfizer* (C-198/03 P) [2005] E.C.R. I-6357.
[232] *DKV Deutsche Krankenversicherung AG* (C-104/00 P) [2002] E.C.R. I-7561; and *BioID AG* (C-37/03 P) [2005] E.C.R. I-7975.
[233] *Italy v Commission* (C-178/00) [2003] E.C.R. I-303; and *Ireland v Commission* (C-199/03) [2005] E.C.R. I-8027.

"Since that claim was inadmissible, it is apparent that the appellant was, in reality, putting forward a new plea by relying on matters of law or of fact at the hearing which had the same purpose as that claim. Under Art.48(2) of the Rules of Procedure of the Court of First Instance, no new plea in law may be introduced in the course of proceedings unless it is based on matters of law or of fact which come to light in the course of the procedure. As the appellant has not alleged that that was the case, the Court of First Instance rightly rejected that plea on the ground that those matters were submitted out of time."[234]

5–134 **(iii) The second ground of appeal.** Here too, the Court upheld the view of the Advocate General.

It looked first at the claim of infringement of art.44(1)(e) of the Rules of Procedure of the Court of First Instance.

It stressed that under art.63 of the Regulation decisions of the Boards of Appeal could be annulled or altered only on a number of specific grounds: lack of competence, infringement of an essential procedural requirement, failure to comply with the EC Treaty, of Reg.40/94 or of any rule of law relating to their application, or misuse of power.

5–135 Accordingly, the scope of the review of their decisions by the Community Courts was limited to grounds of legality; it was not intended to re-examine the facts that had been assessed during the process before the Office.

It then repeated that under art.74(1) of the Regulation in proceedings relating to refusal of registration the Office was restricted in its examination to the facts, evidence, and arguments provided by the parties and the relief sought.

Accordingly, the lawfulness of its decisions could not be challenged on the basis of facts that were not relied upon by the parties and the Court of First Instance could take into account evidence intended to prove those facts.

5–136 The Court again strengthened the role of the Boards and tightened the registration process. "Contrary to what the appellant maintains, the fact that the Board of Appeal relied on evidence adduced before OHIM to draw conclusions different from those reached by the Opposition Division is irrelevant in this respect, because the appraisal of the evidence conducted by that Board could, in any event, be challenged before the Court of First Instance."[235]

So, if the appellant believed that the Board of Appeal had deprived it of the opportunity to present specific evidence in a timely manner it should have put forward a plea based on the second sentence of art.73 of the Regulation:

---

[234] *Rossi*, para.40.
[235] *Rossi*, para.53.

7. REVISITING GLOBAL APPRECIATION

"However, any infringement by the Board of Appeal of the appellant's right to present its comments does not mean that the Court of First Instance is obliged to proceed with its own assessment of facts and evidence which were not put forward previously before OHIM."[236]

Finally, the Court dismissed the art.73 claim. It found that according to art.48(2) of the Rules of Procedure of the Court of First Instance no new plea in law could be introduced in the course of proceedings unless it was based on matters of law or of fact which came to light in the course of those proceedings.

The appellant itself had accepted that in the application to the Court of First Instance it did not allege that the Board had infringed art.73. The complaint was raised for the first time at the hearing although, as Sergio Rossi had also accepted, relevant evidence had been known by and made available to it at the time of lodging its application at the Court of First Instance.

(3) Medion—the importance of dominant elements   5–137

In *Medion*,[237] a reference from the Oberlandesgericht (Higher Regional Court) of Dusseldorf, the Court of Justice reconsidered the global appreciation test. Medion, the registered proprietor of LIFE for electronic entertainment goods in Germany, brought an infringement action against Thomson which applied on identical products the sign THOMSON LIFE.

In determining whether there was likelihood of confusion in cases of conflicting marks that comprised identical components, German courts applied a technique known as the Pragetheorie. The decisive criterion was the overall impression conveyed by the marks; in particular courts had to examine whether the common component dominates in the composite mark whereas the remaining components play a minor role in the overall impression.

If the common component merely contributed to the overall impression there would be no likelihood of confusion, even if the earlier sign that had been incorporated in the composite mark retained an independent distinctive presence.

Another aspect of the Pragetheorie was the recognition that individual   5–138
components of the overall presentation of a product could have a specific function, independent of the distinguishing function of other components. So, a component that designated the undertaking behind the product rather than the product itself was considered to be a secondary rather than a dominant component of the composite sign.

---

[236] *Rossi*, para.54.
[237] *Medion AG* (C-120/04) [2005] E.C.R. I-8551.

Counterbalancing this assumption courts also had to take into account the peculiarities of each product market; the name of the manufacturer was particularly relevant for fashion products for example. Accordingly, if such a name formed part of a composite mark it would be considered a dominant or characterising element. In such cases courts would also weigh the distinctiveness of each element. For example if the other components were "normally distinctive" the dominance of the earlier mark would not be challenged; but, if the earlier mark was particularly distinctive then its dominance would be even stronger.

Applying this technique on the facts of the case there would be no likelihood of confusion. In the relevant product market the name of the manufacturer was considered to be particularly important; it characterised the overall designation. However, it was also argued before the German court that the two elements of the composite sign, THOMSON and LIFE, retained their individualistic distinctiveness and autonomy and that there could be a likelihood of confusion since some consumers might think that these were LIFE products originating from THOMSON; the "goods designated by the composite sign may be construed as LIFE products from the THOMSON stable; that may give rise to the misconception that the products designated by the applicant with the LIFE tag alone originate from the defendant".[238]

For the German court what differentiated this case from *Sabel*[239] was the possibility that LIFE, the name of the applicant, would be appropriated by the defendant. Accordingly it referred to the Court of Justice the following question:

> "Is Article 5(1)(b) of the Directive to be interpreted as meaning that where the goods or services covered by competing signs are identical there is also a likelihood of confusion on the part of the public where an earlier word mark with normal distinctiveness is reproduced in a later composite word sign belonging to a third party, or in a word sign or figurative sign belonging to a third party that is characterised by word elements, in such a way that the third party's company name is placed before the earlier mark and the latter, though not alone determining the overall impression conveyed by the composite sign, has an independent distinctive role within the composite sign?"

5-139   *(a)*   *The Opinion of the Advocate General*

Advocate General Jacobs rejected the basic idea that that there was a need for a specific theory "which formally articulates a set of rules to apply automatically in certain cases"[240]; he supported that it would be preferable to

---

[238] Point 12 of the Opinion of the German court.
[239] *Sabel BV* (C-251/95) [1997] E.C.R. I-6191.
[240] Point 18 of the Opinion of A.G. Jacobs.

7. REVISITING GLOBAL APPRECIATION

rely on the global appreciation principles established by the Court. However he was drawn into a discussion of the German Pragetheorie because he also recognised that such theories could provide guidance on how to apply the basic principles.

He repeated the by now familiar position that similarity between the respective marks is "a necessary but not a sufficient condition"[241]; it is one of a number of interdependent factors. Particularly relevant in this case would be four factors. First, that when the goods are identical, "less similarity between the marks may give rise to a likelihood of confusion"[242]; secondly, that the more distinctive the earlier mark, the greater will be the likelihood of confusion; thirdly, that the average consumer perceives the mark as a whole; and fourthly, that the attention of the average consumer varies.[243] Regarding the fourth factor in particular, the Advocate General made a novel assumption triggered by the factual findings of the German court: the average consumer's level of attention will tend to be lower because in the market for electronic entertainment goods customers pay particular attention to the designation of the manufacturer.

He also noted that the Court had by reasoned order dismissed an appeal against a judgment of the Court of First Instance[244] that dealt with similar issues:

"The Court [of First Instance] rightly pointed out ... that the assessment of the similarity between two marks does not amount to taking into consideration only one component of a complex trade mark and comparing it with another mark. On the contrary, such a comparison must be made by examining the marks in question, each considered as a whole. It also held that that does not mean that the overall impression created in the mind of the relevant public by a complex trade mark may not, in certain circumstances, be dominated by one or more of its components."[245]

"Furthermore, ... the Court [of First Instance] ... devoted a significant part of its reasoning to an appreciation of their distinctive and dominant elements and of the likelihood of confusion on the part of the public, a likelihood which it appreciated globally, taking into account all the factors relevant to the circumstances of the case."[246]

According to the Advocate General the Court, as expected within the global appreciation context, had endorsed an approach similar to the Pragetheorie. "The Court's statement ... that the overall impression of a composite mark

---

[241] Point 21 of the Opinion of A.G. Jacobs.
[242] Point 25 of the Opinion of A.G. Jacobs.
[243] Some of these factors made confusion more likely, others less likely.
[244] *Matratzen Concord GmbH* (C-3/03 P) [2004] E.C.R. I-3657.
[245] *Medion*, para.32.
[246] *Medion*, para.33.

may, in certain circumstances, be dominated by one or more of its components reflects that proposition. The extent to which the overall impression is so dominated is a question of fact for the national court."[247]

Advocate General Jacobs concluded that in case like the current the assessment must be based "on the overall impression given by each mark, bearing in mind, in particular, their distinctive and dominant components, the nature of the public concerned, the category of goods or services in question and the circumstances in which they are marketed".[248] The concern of the national court that "a third party can usurp an earlier sign by adding a company name"[249] should be reviewed within the context of unfair competition rather than trade mark law.

5–140 *(b) The judgment of the Court*

The Court started its analysis by repeating that the essential function of a trade mark is to guarantee the identity of the origin of a product by enabling consumers, without any possibility of confusion, to distinguish it from products which have another origin. This is the reason behind art.5(1)(b). It then reviewed its jurisprudence on global appreciation highlighting the point made in *Matratzen*[250] that the comparison between the two conflicting signs "must be made by examining each of the marks in question as a whole, which does not mean that the overall impression conveyed to the relevant public by a composite trade mark may not, in certain circumstances, be dominated by one or more of its components".[251]

However, the Court also added that in some cases an earlier mark that had become part of an unconnected, later, composite mark might have an independent distinctive role in the composite mark, without being the dominant component, leading the public to believe that there is an economic link between the two undertakings behind the two marks. Imposing a condition that the earlier mark becomes the dominant component would deprive the owner of the earlier mark of its exclusive right in such a case where the overall impression of the composite sign is not dominated by the earlier mark but might still cause confusion. By way of example the Court

---

[247] Point 33. The Advocate General referred to another similar case decided by the Court of First Instance, *Reemark Gesellschaft fur Markenkooperation mbH v Office for Harmonisation in the Internal Market (Trade Marks and Designs)* (T-22/04) [2005] E.C.R. II-1559 which found that there would be confusion between WEST and WESTLIFE; however he reminded that the Court of First Instance is reviewing the application of established legal principles by the Board of Appeal whereas the Court of Justice is answering questions of law. So a judgment of the Court of First Instance should not precipitate a preliminary ruling by the Court of Justice.
[248] Point 39 of the Opinion of A.G. Jacobs.
[249] Point 40. Note that the term "usurp" rather than the more controversial "misappropriate" has been used.
[250] *Matratzen Concord GmbH* (C-3/03 P) [2004] E.C.R. I-3657.
[251] *Medion*, para.29

concocted the scenario of an owner of a widely-known mark combining it with another unconnected earlier mark in a new composite sign:

> "It must therefore be accepted that, in order to establish the likelihood of confusion, it suffices that, because the earlier mark still has an independent distinctive role, the origin of the goods or services covered by the composite sign is attributed by the public also to the owner of that mark."[252]

Article 51(b) should "be interpreted as meaning that where the goods or services are identical there may be a likelihood of confusion on the part of the public where the contested sign is composed by juxtaposing the company name of another party and a registered mark which has normal distinctiveness and which, without alone determining the overall impression conveyed by the composite sign, still has an independent distinctive role therein".[253]

(4) Praktiker—a special case for retail services?

In this case[254] the Court confirmed that a trade mark could be registered for retail services but also considered whether a special, stricter, test had to be applied in the case of trade marks registered for retail services.

5–141

The first question concerned the registrability of services. The second and the third question referred by the Bundespatentgericht sought clarifications regarding the scope of protection:

> "2. To what extent must the content of such services provided by a retailer be specified in order to guarantee the certainty of the subject-matter of trade-mark protection that is required in order to (a) fulfil the function of the trade mark, as defined in Article 2 of the Directive, namely, to distinguish the goods or services of one undertaking from those of other undertakings, and (b) define the scope of protection of such a trade mark in the event of a conflict?
> 3. To what extent is it necessary to define the scope of similarity (Article 4(1)(b) and Article 5(1)(b) of the Directive) between such services provided by a retailer and (a) other services provided in connection with the distribution of goods, or (b) the goods sold by that retailer?"[255]

---

[252] *Medion*, para.36.
[253] *Medion*, para.37.
[254] *Praktiker Bau- und Heimwerkermärkte AG v Deutsches Patent-und Markenant* (C-418/02) [2005] E.C.R. I-5873.
[255] Reproduced in point 22.

5-142   *(a)   The Opinion of the Advocate General*

> Advocate General Léger first clarified that retailers do not differ from manufacturers who sell their products themselves; they, too, should be able to distinguish themselves from their competitors.
>
> The essential function of a trade mark became the starting point for his analysis:

"... in so far as the purpose of a service mark is to enable consumers to identify the enterprise supplying the service, the registration of the mark implies that the service which it is intended to designate is itself identifiable as such, by means of a mark. In other words, it must be possible for consumers to perceive the activity, as such, for which applicant is seeking the registration of a mark as constituting a service. This requirement follows from the very function of the mark and its corollary, the principle of speciality, which means that the rights which it confers can be exactly determined. A mark cannot be registered for a service which cannot be perceived as such by consumers, with the result that the scope of protection could not be ascertained".[256]

> He admitted that ascertaining some services related with the sale of products, for example bringing them together for the purposes of selling them, could be difficult. However, developments in marketing meant that "the conditions under which the act of sale itself takes place may constitute, in the relationship between retailer and consumer, a reason for buying which is just as important as the quality and price of the goods sold".[257] Looking at the two extremes he referred to the advice a consumer can get from a specialist at a wine shop or the selection of products for sale at a bargain store, according to a certain quality standard in the specific price range. In both cases it was the selection of goods that attracted consumers rather than the presence of any particular product brand. The same criterion could be applied to the shop that, as in this case, was selling building, home improvement and gardening goods.[258] He agreed with the decision of the Board of Appeal in *Giacomelli Sport*,[259] that a service supplied in connection with retail trading may constitute a service for which a trade mark can be registered.

5-143   Regarding the required degree of detail in the specification of retail services he supported that for reasons of legal certainty and sound administration a common standard should be adopted throughout the Union. He

---

[256] Point 47 of the Opinion of A.G. Léger.
[257] Point 50 of the Opinion of A.G. Léger.
[258] Referring to Grabrucker, "Marks for Retail Services—An Example for Harmonising Trade Mark Laws", 34 IIC 503 (2003) for a review of national practices relating to retail services.
[259] Case R 46/1998-2, December 17, 1999.

7. REVISITING GLOBAL APPRECIATION

suggested that the "registration of a mark for services supplied in connection with the retail sale of goods should clearly indicate both the specific nature of those services and the goods or types of goods to which they relate ... this dual requirement is justified, in the light of the scheme and purpose of the Directive, by the particular nature of the services supplied in connection with retail trading".[260]

Advocate General Léger opted for this stricter approach because of the balancing act that trade mark law is asked to perform:

> "trade-mark law is somewhat paradoxical in conferring upon one retailer in particular exclusive rights in marks which serve the marketing of goods or services in order to promote the free movement of those goods and services. To reconcile the interests of the protection afforded by the mark and free movement, in the trade-mark law registration system the applicant must, in consideration of the exclusive rights which he claims, indicate exactly the mark and the goods and services to which those rights relate."[261]

Regarding the third question, he accepted that trade mark law should avoid giving retailers extensive protection "that cover other services that might be offered in connection with selling goods, as well as all the goods sold by such proprietor. Like the national court, I consider that recognition of the possibility of registering such marks should not have the consequence of permitting them to replace goods marks or of impairing the advantages attaching to them".[262]

However, he was against adopting exceptional set criteria for delimiting 5–144
the area of similarity between services supplied in connection with the retail sale of goods and the other services which may be offered in the course of marketing in general or the actual goods. The global appreciation test and the interdependence between the factors of the test provided the flexibility that was necessary to deal with this problem. He noted that according to the jurisprudence of the Court likelihood of confusion had to be established for each individual case and could not be presumed.

(b) The judgment of the Court   5–145

The Court agreed that the concept of "services" should be interpreted in the same way throughout the Union, otherwise conditions for the registration of "service trade marks"[263] could vary according to the laws of each Member State.

---

[260] Point 71 of the Opinion of A.G. Léger.
[261] Point 79 of the Opinion of A.G. Léger.
[262] Point 89 of the Opinion of A.G. Léger.
[263] *Praktiker*, para.32.

It described the objective of retail trade as the sale of goods to consumers that "includes, in addition to the legal sales transaction, all activity carried out by the trader for the purpose of encouraging the conclusion of such a transaction. That activity consists, inter alia, in selecting an assortment of goods offered for sale and in offering a variety of services aimed at inducing the consumer to conclude the above-mentioned transaction with the trader in question rather than with a competitor".[264]

The Court found that there was no overriding reason based on the Directive or on general principles of Community law precluding the above services from being covered by the concept of "services" within the meaning of the Directive. In relation to the Regulation it reminded us that the Office had accepted the principle of registration of Community Trade Marks for retail services.

It then rejected the argument that a more restrictive specification of retail services would be required. It accepted that a restrictive approach would "reduce the protection afforded to the proprietor of the trade mark, so that questions concerning the application of Articles 4(1) and 5(1) of the Directive would arise less often",[265] however this would not be adequate justification.

Being more permissive from the Advocate General the Court held that the applicant should only "be required to specify the goods or types of goods to which those services relate".[266]

The Court found the third question to be speculative, there was no indication in the reference that the referring court could find it necessary to rule on the concept of "similarity" in connection with "likelihood of confusion". Accordingly it declined to answer the question. "The Court of Justice has no jurisdiction to answer questions referred for a preliminary ruling where it is obvious that the interpretation of Community law sought bears no relation to the actual facts of the main proceedings or to their purpose, where the problem is hypothetical, or where the court does not have before it the factual or legal material necessary to give a useful answer to the questions submitted."[267]

5–146 **(5) Travatan—the mediation of professionals: pharmaceuticals**

(a) The attentiveness variable

As we have already seen, in *Lloyd Schuhfabrik* the Court reaffirmed the general principle that "for the purposes of the global assessment the average consumer of the category of products concerned is deemed to be reasonably well-informed, observant and circumspect". However, those qualities do not

---

[264] *Praktiker*, para.34.
[265] *Praktiker*, para.46.
[266] *Praktiker*, para.50.
[267] *Praktiker*, para.57, citing *Traunfellner GmbH v österreichische Autobahnen-und SchnellstraCen-Finanzierungs-AG* (T-421/01) [2003] E.C.R. I-11941.

make the average consumer impervious to confusion, especially since he "only rarely has the chance to make a direct comparison between the different marks, but must place his trust in the imperfect picture of them that he has kept in his mind". Moreover, the Court stressed that this "average" level of attentiveness may fluctuate depending on the circumstances, since "the average consumer's level of attention is likely to vary according to the category of goods or services in question and the way they are marketed".[268]

That definition of the relevant consumer profile and levels of attentiveness provides a remarkably flexible tool for adapting the threshold of confusion to the particularities of each situation and stresses even further the need for a case by case approach in assessing the relevant risk.

In *Picasso*, the Court elaborated further on the above principles, by noting that for the purposes of the assessment of confusion "account must be taken of the fact that, in view of the nature of the goods concerned and in particular their price and their highly technological character, the average consumer displays a particularly high level of attention at the time of purchase of such goods" and that "where it is established in fact that the objective characteristics of a given product mean that the average consumer purchases it only after a particularly careful examination, it is important in law to take into account that such a fact may reduce the likelihood of confusion between marks relating to such goods at the crucial moment when the choice between those goods and marks is made".[269]

Even though, admittedly, that view has the result of making the enforcement of trade mark rights in specific market sectors subject to stricter conditions, its economic justification is immediately obvious: if in relation to certain products confusion is indeed less likely to occur, it is only natural that trade mark owners in those fields should not be overprotected and that the corresponding rights should be enforced only to the extent that they are actually threatened.

(b) The special case of pharmaceuticals 5–147

Applying that principle to pharmaceutical preparations, the Court of First Instance has consistently held that if the substance concerned is not entirely harmless, but may have relatively important implications for the consumer's health, the attentiveness of the public tends to be higher, and this is irrespective of whether in the particular case the patient is assisted by qualified professionals.[270]

The reference to "professionals" show that it is also necessary to consider the sophistication of the relevant consumer, which again depends on the

---

[268] *Lloyd Schuhfabrik Meyer* (C-342/97) [1999] E.C.R. I-3819, para.26.
[269] *Ruiz-Picasso v OHIM* (C-361/04 P) [2006] E.C.R. I-643, paras 39–43.
[270] See the judgment of February 13, 2008, *Sanofi-Aventis SA v OHIM* (ATURION/URION) (T-146/06), not yet published, para.27.

characteristics of the goods and which can be particularly important when addressing the semantic content of a mark, as for example when determining the ease with which specialised terms are likely to be understood by professionals, as compared to their perception by the general public.

A good example of the interaction of those concepts is the sector of prescription pharmaceuticals, with which the Court was confronted in *Travatan*,[271] an appeal dealing with the impact of the mediation of professionals on the definition of the relevant consumer profile and the levels of attentiveness likely to be displayed.

5–148 That interaction gave rise to two interrelated questions: the first one was who is the relevant consumer, given that in the case of prescription pharmaceuticals the choice of the appropriate substance is usually made by the physician, rather than the patient; the second was how far does the assistance of medical professionals affect the already high levels of attentiveness ordinary consumers are likely to display, when confronted with potentially hazardous substances.

As regards the first point, the Court of First Instance[272] followed its well-established case law[273] that in the case of prescription pharmaceuticals there are more than one consumer circles involved, that is, the relevant public comprises both the medical professionals who prescribe the remedy and the end consumer who ultimately purchases it. When assessing confusion, however, it did not make a clear distinction between the perception of the respective consumer circles, holding rather that the marks "TRAVATAN" and "TRIVASTAN" are likely to be confused by the "public".

5–149 *(c) The Opinion of the Advocate General*

Advocate General Kokott disagreed with the position taken by the Court of First Instance as regards prescription pharmaceuticals, observing that:

> "[Even if regard is had] to patients too, because [. . .] they can influence a doctor's prescription, in the case of medicinal products available only on prescription their influence has very little significance when compared with the doctor's responsibility for the decision.
>
> In particular, the possible influence exerted by patients cannot mean that the patient is regarded as the reasonably well-informed and reasonably observant and circumspect consumer of those products. The average consumer must rather be determined by reference to the group that largely determines decisions on the acquisition of medicinal products

---

[271] Cite *Alcon Inc v OHIM* (C-412/05 P).
[272] Cite Case *Alcon v OHIM—Biofarma* (TRAVATAN) (T-130/03).
[273] See judgments of February 13, 2007, *Mundipharma AG v OHIM* (RESPICUR/RESPICORT) (T-265/04) ECR II-449, para.57; and of February 13, 2007, *Ontex NV v OHIM* (CURON/EURON) (T-353/04) ECR II-10*, para.55–58.

available only on prescription that is to say by reference to prescribing doctors.

The risk [of confusion] on the part of a patient who, independently of prescription, is confronted with the mark, is also of little significance, under trade mark law at any rate. In the Picasso judgment, the Court of Justice regarded the moment when the choice between the goods and marks is made as crucial for assessing the likelihood of confusion. Other points in time, at which confusion on the part of consumers might be more likely because they display a lesser level of attention, are by contrast of secondary importance."[274]

(d) Findings of the Court   **5–150**

Notwithstanding, the Court concurred with the Court of First Instance that the relevant public consists both of professionals in the medical field and of the end-users of the substances concerned, stressing that even though prescription drugs are obtained through intermediaries such as healthcare professionals, who are liable to influence, or even to determine, the choice made by the end-users, this fact is not of itself capable of excluding all likelihood of confusion on the part of the final consumer. This is because end-users will "eventually be faced with those products, even if that takes place during separate purchasing transactions for each of those individual products, at various times".[275]

The Court also observed that since it is undisputed that the whole process of marketing the goods at issue is aimed at the end-user's acquisition of them, the role played by healthcare professionals "must be in part balanced against the high degree of attentiveness which may be shown by those users when such goods are prescribed and, consequently, against those users' ability to make those professionals take into account their perception of the trade marks and, in particular, their requirements or preferences".[276]

One exception the Court seems to be accepting in this context, however, is when the trade mark relates not to prescription pharmaceuticals sold to end-users through the ordinary distribution channels, but rather to substances directly administered by the doctor, for example substances for use in surgery, in respect of which the relevant public only consists of medical specialists.[277]

Moreover, in order to dispel the uncertainty arising from contradictory decisions in the matter and give more authority to its findings, the Court

---

[274] Points 49–51 of the Opinion of A.G. Kokott.
[275] *Travatan*, paras 57–58.
[276] *Travatan*, para.61.
[277] See *Travatan*, para.66; as well as *Alcon Inc v OHIM* (BSS/BSS) (T-273/01) ECR II-411, para.42, confirmed by the Order of the Court of Justice of October 5, 2004; *Alcon Inc v OHIM* (BSS) (C-192/03 P) ECR I-8993, para.30.

explicitly stressed that the above interpretation is "the only correct one, and that it cannot be called into question by arguments derived either from decisions of the Boards of Appeal, or from the previous case-law of the Community Courts".[278].

5–151 As regards the outcome, the Court held that although the Court of First Instance had committed an error of law in not distinguishing between the respective consumer profiles when assessing confusion, its decision could nevertheless stand, considering that even if only end-users are finally confused, this is sufficient to trigger the consequences of art.8(1)(b) CTMR.

The judgment in *Travatan* has therefore shed light on a number of questions arising from professional assistance in the acquisition of pharmaceutical products, by clarifying that (a) as regards prescription drugs the relevant public consists of both physicians and patients; (b) the mediation of professionals cannot in itself exclude all likelihood of confusion on the part of end-users; (c) those users are likely to be more attentive when dealing with potentially hazardous substances[279]; and (d) in any event, account must also be taken of the end-user's imperfect recollection, especially since confusion may arise during separate transactions, occurring at different points in time.

5–152 **(6) Limoncello—Quicky—La Española: composite marks**

In *Limoncello*,[280], *Quicky*[281] and *La Española*[282] the Court dealt with the importance to be attached to the figurative elements of composite signs in conflicts with other complex marks, or with signs consisting only of verbal elements. A comparative reading of those judgments shows that the impact of the figurative components on the assessment of likelihood of confusion depends less on their prominence in terms of size and position, and more on the interaction of the various components between them, as determined by their relative distinctiveness.

In the end, the pivotal question is whether any of the components forming-up the signs can be regarded as negligible, in which case the comparison can legitimately focus only on the other elements, or if, conversely, none of them can be discarded as unimportant, in which case

---

[278] *Travatan*, para.64.
[279] Apparently in the sense that the more dangerous the substance, or the more serious the disease, the higher the degree of attentiveness likely to be employed by the public. That the degree of attentiveness should be proportional to the specific properties of the product concerned follows not only from the conditional formulation in *Travatan*, that consumers "*may* be more attentive", but also from the statement in *Picasso* that "the average consumer displays a particularly high level of attention [...] where it is established in fact that the *objective characteristics* of a given product mean that the average consumer purchases it only after a particularly careful examination...".
[280] *Shaker di L Laudato & C Sas v OHIM* (LIMONCELLO) (C-334/05 P).
[281] *Société des Produits Nestlé v OHIM* (QUICKY) (C-193/06 P).
[282] *Aceites del Sur-Coosur SA v Koipe Corporación* (LA ESPAÑOLA) (C-498/07 P).

the comparison must per force be based on all the components of the marks, since they are all deemed to influence, to a greater or lesser extent, the impression given by the signs as a whole.

(a)   Limoncello—non-negligible word elements cannot be ignored   5–153

Limoncello concerned an opposition based on the Spanish word mark "LIMONCHELO", against the registration of a sign composed of the words "Limoncello della Costiera Amalfitana—Shaker", coupled with the device of an elaborate disk decorated with lemons. Both marks essentially covered alcoholic drinks, in Class 33 of the Nice Classification.

Both the opposition division and the Boards of Appeal of the Office upheld the opposition, on the grounds that the dominant element of the mark applied for was the word "Limoncello", which was visually and phonetically similar to the earlier word mark.

The Court of First Instance[283] annulled the decision of the Board holding the following as regards the comparison of the signs:

"[T]he Board of Appeal had to consider which component of the trade mark claimed was apt, by virtue of its visual, phonetic or conceptual characteristics, to convey, by itself, an impression of that mark which the relevant public keeps in mind, with the result that all the other components of the mark are negligible in that respect. . . .

However, if the trade mark claimed is a complex mark which is visual in nature, the assessment of the overall impression created by that mark and the determination as to whether there is any dominant element must be carried out on the basis of a visual analysis. Accordingly, in such a case, it is only to the extent to which a potentially dominant element includes non-visual semantic aspects that it may become necessary to compare that element with the earlier mark, also taking into account those other semantic aspects, such as for example phonetic factors or relevant abstract concepts."

Following that approach, the Court of First Instance held that the representation of the round dish decorated with lemons was clearly the dominant component of the mark applied for and that, since the word elements of that mark were not dominant on a visual level, there was no need to analyse the phonetic and conceptual characteristics of those elements, or to adjudicate on the distinctiveness of the earlier mark.   5–154

In doing so, the Court of First Instance essentially took the view that, in the case of combined word and device marks, the visual prominence of the various elements takes precedence over the assessment of their

---

[283] *Shaker v OHIM—Limiñana y Botella (Limoncello della Costiera Amalfitana shaker)* (T-7/04) [2005] E.C.R. II-2305, paras 53–54, 59 and 68.

distinctiveness. In other words, if a part of the sign is visually less striking than others, it automatically becomes negligible and its impact on confusion need not be explored any further.

The Court of Justice disagreed with that analysis. It held that that the Court of First Instance had merely paid lip-service to the principle that the global appreciation of the likelihood of confusion must be based on the overall impression created by the signs, but not effectively applied it in practice.

Referring to the principles established in *Matratzen* and *Medion*, it reminded that the assessment of the similarity between two marks means more than taking just one component of a composite trade mark and comparing it with the other and that the comparison must be made by examining each of the marks in question as a whole.[284]

Thus, it held that although in certain circumstances the overall impression conveyed by a composite trade mark may be dominated by one or more of its components, this does not mean that the other elements of the sign can simply be disregarded, without even addressing their possible impact on that impression, not only visually, but also phonetically and semantically.

5–155 *(b) Quicky—unclear dominance: all elements count*

In *Quicky*,[285] another opposition case, Nestlé applied to register as a Community Trade Mark a sign consisting of the stylised word "QUICKY", combined with a larger, stylised bunny device. Quick restaurants opposed based on its earlier French and Benelux registrations of the words "QUICK" and "QUICKIES".

The Office upheld the opposition. On appeal, the Board confirmed the rejection of the application holding that, despite the substantial visual differences contributed by the bunny device, the strong phonetic similarities between the words "QUICKY" and "QUICKIES" were sufficient to give rise to a likelihood of confusion between the signs, within the meaning of art.8(1)(b) CTMR.

The Court of First Instance[286] shared that conclusion. It took the view that to the extent that the verbal elements of the signs were both visually and phonetically similar, the figurative element could only offset that similarity if it was capable of dominating on its own the image kept in the consumer's memory; that, however, could not happen if the visual impact of the device was of equal or inferior "intensity" to that of the verbal components.

5–156 The Court also remarked that insofar as words are, as a rule, more distinctive than images and the verbal element in the application is at least as prominent as the bunny device, the latter could not overshadow the similarity between the words, or lead to the conclusion that those

---

[284] *Limoncello*, paras 37–43.
[285] Cite *Société des Produits Nestlé v OHIM* (QUICKY) (C-193/06 P).
[286] *Société des Produits Nestlé* (T-074/04), paras 47–59.

elements are in fact negligible. Besides, the widespread use of animal characters on foodstuffs rendered the pictorial element quite banal, reducing thus further its relative impact on the overall impression given by the signs.

The Court of Justice disagreed with the mechanics of that analysis.

It stressed that it could not be sustained in law that every time two marks coincide in their verbal elements, which are more than negligible, there is a likelihood of confusion, since such a view effectively ignores the possible impact of the figurative element on the visual impression given by the signs as a whole.[287]

5–157

Specifically, the Court held that although the Court of First Instance had rightly examined the relative importance of the bunny device as compared to the significance of the other elements in the application, it could not simply disregard that device when comparing the signs as a whole, solely on the ground that it was not dominant.[288]

It observed also that the mere fact that a component is not dominant does not necessarily imply that it is insignificant, or that it should be overlooked for the purposes of the comparison. Actually, such a conclusion can only be reached if it is first established that the element in question is indeed negligible, in an independent and positive manner, something that the Court of First Instance had not done in the case at hand.[289]

Accordingly, the Court of Justice set aside the judgment under appeal and remitted the case to the Court of First Instance for further prosecution.

Quicky in fact teaches us that it is not appropriate to single out an element of a composite mark and treat it as dominant, if the other components are not clearly subordinate to it in terms of prominence and distinctiveness. On the contrary, if all the parts of a complex mark are of more or less equal significance, their collective impact on the overall impression conveyed to the consumer must carefully be assessed, before deciding whether there is a likelihood of confusion.

5–158

At the same time, *Quicky* points once more against the use of aprioristic axioms in trade mark examination, like the abstract generalisation that word elements are by definition more distinctive than devices, or that animal motifs as a whole are banal in respect of food products. Rather, such findings are only justified if properly substantiated and their application to the case properly explained.

(c) La Española—dominant figurative elements: get-up imitation

In *La Española*[290] the Court dealt with the similarity between bottle labels for olive oil. The case concerned two quite successful brands of olive oil,

5–159

---

[287] *Quicky*, para.37.
[288] *Quicky*, para.41.
[289] *Quicky*, para.44.
[290] *Aceites del Sur-Coosur SA v Koipe Corporación* (LA ESPAÑOLA) (C-498/07 P).

already present on the Spanish market for some time. When one of those marks was applied for as a Community Trade Mark, the owner of the other opposed that application on the basis of both its Community and Spanish trade marks.

Both marks were composite trade marks containing pictorial elements that represented essentially the same theme: a woman dressed in a traditional Spanish costume, sitting in a certain manner, close to an olive branch with an olive grove in the background. Moreover, the respective images did not merely borrow on the same subject, but rather consisted of an almost identical arrangement of spaces, colours, positions for brand names, and style of lettering. The only substantial difference between them lay in the different word elements used in each mark. The brand name of the applicant was "La Española", whereas the opponent was using the name "Carbonell".

Thus, the overall setting was reminiscent of a classic get-up imitation case, apart from the fact that the applicant was not a newcomer to the market, but rather a prominent player in the sector with a reputation of his own. Moreover, the opponent's Community Trade Mark could not validly be relied on because it was filed later than the contested sign.

5–160 The opposition division and the Boards of Appeal of the Office dismissed the opposition under both art.8(1)(b) and (5) CTMR (new art.8), taking the view that the different names were sufficient to render the marks visually and phonetically distinguishable from each other and, thus, dissimilar as a whole. The opponent appealed to the CFI.

The Court of First Instance[291] annulled the Board's decision, holding that the quasi-identical figurative elements of the signs sufficed to render them confusingly similar overall. Specifically, it found that "the elements common to the two marks at issue, seen as a whole, produce an overall visual impression of great similarity, since the mark applied for reproduces very precisely the essence of the message and the visual impression given by the earlier mark" which was not diminished by the use of different brand names, since the expression "La Española" merely refers to the geographical origin of the goods and, accordingly, has a very weak distinctive character.

Having thus established that the verbal component of the application was in fact negligible, the Court of First instance refrained from comparing the marks aurally, or from further exploring the impact the differences between the word elements had on the perception of the consumer. The Court justified that approach by stressing that, as regards consumer goods sold in supermarkets, it is the visual impression that primarily determines the consumer's choice.

5–161 The applicant appealed to the Court of Justice raising a number of points: first, it claimed that the judgment under appeal had failed to differentiate

---

[291] *Koipe v OHIM—Aceites del Sur* (LA ESPAÑOLA) (T-363/04), paras 103–105.

7. REVISITING GLOBAL APPRECIATION

between the various Community and Spanish marks relied on by the opponent, taking thus into account marks which were not actually earlier. Secondly, it argued that by exclusively relying on the of the device components the Court of First Instance failed to examine the marks in their entirety, its examination being partial and selective. Finally, it contended that the Court had unduly disregarded the coexistence of the marks on the market and the independent reputation of the sign applied for, while also defining the average consumer as extremely careless.

The Court of Justice dismissed the appeal, holding that the Court of First Instance had not committed any error of law justifying the annulment of its judgment.

As to the first point, it held that to the extent that the opposition was also based on a number of earlier Spanish registrations which were identical with the Community Trade Mark complained of, the omission to clearly differentiate between those rights was not material for the result of the appeal. In particular, insofar as the findings of the Court of First Instance clearly referred to the situation on the Spanish market and were based on the perception of the marks by Spanish consumers, that omission did not materially affect the definition of the relevant public, or changed anything in the analysis.[292]

5–162

As regards the alleged infringement of art.8(1)(b) CTMR, it held that the Court of First Instance had not altogether disregarded the impact of the word elements on the assessment of the likelihood of confusion. On the contrary, it is precisely in the context of that appraisal that the judgment under appeal described the element in question as negligible, by holding that, on account of its weak distinctiveness it could not invalidate the conclusion that the signs were visually similar.[293]

Moreover, it held that as olive oil is a very common product in Spain and is mostly purchased in establishments where goods are arranged on shelves, the Court of First Instance correctly found that the relevant consumer is guided more by the visual impact of the mark he is looking for and that, accordingly, the figurative element of the marks acquires a greater importance, which substantially increases the likelihood of confusion.[294]

The Court also observed that the coexistence of two marks on the same market may diminish the likelihood of confusion only if it is "peaceful", which was not the case here. On the contrary, the evidence on file showed that the matter of the similarity between the two signs had been at issue between the undertakings concerned before the national courts for a number of years.[295]

5–163

Finally, the Court dismissed the arguments concerning the relevant public and the reputation of the applicant's mark, holding, first, that the find-

---

[292] *La Española*, paras 43–45.
[293] *La Española*, paras 69–72.
[294] *La Española*, paras 74–76.
[295] *La Española*, paras 80–83.

ings of the Court of First Instance as regards the attention of the consumer were factual in nature and, secondly, that the reliance on the well-known character of the application was irrelevant in law, as being contrary to the principle that the scope of protection of the earlier mark should be determined by reference to its own distinctiveness.

Of course, the result in *La Española* is not easily transposable to all kinds of get-up imitation cases. What characterised that case was the very weak distinctive character of the word component as compared to the elaborate and prominent device, a fact that is not likely to be present in similar settings. Notwithstanding, the focus on the strong visual similarity as a factor that substantially increases the risk of confusion suggests that it will not always be so easy for infringers to escape the consequences of their actions by merely adding a different brand name to an otherwise very similar packaging.

(7) Armafoam—confusion in part of the Community

5–164 *(a) Linguistic considerations*

In *Armafoam*[296] the Court dealt with the impact of possible variations in the understanding of a Community Trade Mark in different parts of the Community and its impact on the assessment of likelihood of confusion. The linguistic diversity of the European Union inevitably leads to fluctuations in the perception of the same term by consumers in different Member States, which become particularly relevant when dealing with the conceptual comparison of the signs, or when assessing which is the dominant or distinctive element of a complex mark in the context of relative grounds for refusal.

The case concerned an opposition against the registration of the sign "ARMAFOAM", by the owner of earlier Community Trade Mark "NOMAFOAM". OHIM had found the signs to be confusingly similar, in particular for European consumers who do not understand English and, thus, are not in a position to grasp the descriptive connotations of the word "FOAM" in relation to the goods concerned.

Referring to its settled case law in the matter,[297] the Court of First Instance concurred with the Board of Appeal that a risk of confusion does not have to be present throughout the entire territory of the European Union and that it suffices if it exists only in part of the Community, transposing thus into the context of relative grounds the rule reflected by art.7(2) CTMR that an absolute ground of refusal applies even if its effects are limited only to part of the relevant territory.[298]

---

[296] *Armacell Enterprise GmbH v OHIM* (ARMAFOAM) (C-514/06 P).
[297] See *Gateway, Inc v OHIM* (ACTIVY MEDIA GATEWAY) (T-434/05), para.47, and the case law cited.
[298] *Armacell v OHIM—nmc (ARMAFOAM)* (T-172/05) [2006] E.C.R. II-4061, para.33.

7. REVISITING GLOBAL APPRECIATION

Applying that principle to the conceptual comparison, the Court of First Instance noted that, when considered in their entirety, the marks were fanciful constructions that did not convey any coherent meaning and that only English-speaking consumers were likely automatically to perceive the suffix "foam" as a meaningful term. Accordingly, it held that at least as far as non-English-speaking consumers were concerned the marks were visually and phonetically similar and that this overall impression of similarity could not be offset by conceptual considerations.

(b) The unitary character of Community Trade Marks   5–165

The Court of Justice confirmed that view, holding that it was compatible with the unitary character of Community Trade Marks. It explained that:

> "[According to] Article 1(2) CTMR a Community trade mark has a unitary character. Subject to the exceptions of Article 106, on the prohibition of use, and of Article 107, on prior rights applicable to particular localities, the Community trade mark 'shall have equal effect throughout the Community: it shall not be registered, transferred or surrendered or be the subject of a decision revoking the rights of the proprietor or declaring it invalid, nor shall its use be prohibited, save in respect of the whole Community.[299]
>
> Under Article 8(1)(b) and (2) [of the Regulation] where the earlier mark relied on in support of opposition proceedings is a Community trade mark, the trade mark in respect of which registration is sought will not be registered if there exists a likelihood of confusion on the part of the public in the Community territory.
>
> It does not follow from Article 8(1)(b) that, for a Community trade mark to be refused registration under that provision, the likelihood of confusion must exist in all Member States and in all linguistic areas of the Community.
>
> In fact, the unitary character of the Community trade mark means that an earlier mark can be relied on in opposition proceedings against any application for registration of a Community trade mark which would adversely affect the protection of the first mark, even if only in relation to the perception of consumers in part of the Community".[300]

It follows that the expression "equal effects" used to describe the nature of the unitary character of the Community Trade Mark does not actually mean that the mark should be enforced in a "uniform" manner. In reality, the Court has indirectly but clearly reaffirmed the rule in *Matratzen* that the application of trade mark law in the internal market is still under the influence of "linguistic", even "cultural" barriers, if not legal ones.

---

[299] *IHT Internationale Heiztechnik and Danzinger* (C-9/93) [1994] E.C.R. I-2789, para.55.
[300] *Armafoam*, paras 54–57.

In practice, that means that if the weakness of a term points against the existence of a likelihood of confusion, that factor must be present throughout the Community for confusion to be safely excluded. By contrast, if the specific meaning of a term enhances that risk, it suffices that this meaning is clear to consumers in any part of the Community for the corresponding consequences to be triggered.[301]

5-166 Accordingly, the conceptual comparison should not be carried out in the abstract, or by reference to artificial averages. Rather, it must adapt to the linguistic and cultural diversity of the European Union, taking into account the real understanding of the term concerned in the various Member States. Helpfully enough, the Courts have mitigated the practical complexity of that approach, by considering that the extent to which a language is spoken or understood in a given territory is a well-known fact that can be relied on by the competent authority even in the absence of specific evidence or arguments.[302]

Note also that in *Zipcar*[303] the Court explicitly confirmed that the above rule applies equally to national marks, in the sense that if in a Member State there are various linguistic zones, or if the understanding of foreign languages varies from one area to another, it suffices if there is a likelihood of confusion in any part of the relevant territory. It stressed, however, that this should not be interpreted as establishing an inflexible rule of law, whereby the average consumer is always deemed to have as his mother tongue the language that is predominant in the Member State concerned, or to have no particular knowledge of other languages.[304]

5-167 *(c) The impact on conversion*

Next, the Court addressed the argument that the Court of First Instance should have also compared the marks from the point of view of English-speaking consumers, in order to determine whether the application could at least be converted into national trade marks in territories that were not affected by the rejection.

Although the Court admitted in that connection that according to art.108(2)(b) CTMR the grounds on which a Community Trade Mark is rejected also determine the scope of its possible conversion, it held, nevertheless, that the Court of First Instance was not required to extend its examination to the whole of the European Union, since the purpose of opposition proceedings is "to provide undertakings with an opportunity to oppose, by

---

[301] See in that direction the judgment of October 6, 2004 in *New Look Ltd v OHIM (NL SPORT, NL JEANS, NL ACTIVE, NL COLLECTION)* (T-117/03, T-118/03, T-119/03 & T-171/03) [2005] ECR II-3471.
[302] See in that connection the analysis of the Court of First Instance in *New Look Ltd v OHIM (NEW LOOK)* (T-435/07), paras 22–25.
[303] *Zipcar, Inc v OHIM* (ZIPCAR) (C-394/08 P).
[304] See *Zipcar*, paras 49–51.

way of a single procedure, applications which might give rise to a likelihood of confusion" with their earlier marks, and not "to resolve in advance possible conflicts at national level".[305]

Moreover, it observed that insofar as the Court of First Instance had upheld the decision rejecting the mark only with regard to non-English speakers, its judgment did not prevent the appellant from requesting the conversion of its Community Trade Mark application into national trade marks in English-speaking countries.[306]

It is worth noting, however, that this last statement of the Court is contrary to the practice of the OHIM to refuse conversion in cases where the rejection is based on an earlier Community Trade Mark, on the assumption that, due to the unitary character of that right, the ground of rejection extends, as a matter of legal fiction, to the whole of the Community territory, even if in practice there is a likelihood of confusion only in respect of certain languages.

5–168

Although, admittedly, that statement of the Court qualifies as obiter dicta to the extent that the case did not directly concern the conversion of the application at issue into national marks, it is nonetheless interesting to see whether the Court will maintain the same view also in the future, as well as the impact such an approach may ultimately have on the current practice of the Office.

8. MARKS WITH A REPUTATION

(1) General Motors—the factors for assessing reputation

5–169

The first case that tested the requirements for obtaining this new type of protection was *General Motors Corp v Yplon SA*.[307]

The case came as a reference from the Belgian Tribunal de Commerce, Tournai. General Motors, the proprietor of the trade mark "Chevy" for motor vehicles sought an injunction against Yplon's use of the same sign for cleaning products. The Belgian court wanted to know the extent of reputation required in order to benefit from art.5(2) of the Directive; in particular whether reputation within one of the Benelux countries or a part thereof would suffice.

(a) The Opinion of the Advocate General

5–170

Advocate General Jacobs considered first the relationship between "marks with a reputation", under art.4(4)(a) and art.5(2) of the Directive, and "well-known" marks, according to art.6bis of the Paris Convention and art.16(3) of

---

[305] *Armafoam*, paras 60–61.
[306] *Armafoam*, para.62.
[307] *General Motors Corp v Yplon SA* [1999] E.C.R. I-5421.

TRIPs. He noted the exceptional character of the protection of "well-known" marks that extended even to unregistered marks and suggested that a relatively high standard should be required for marks enjoying such protection. Indeed, all national laws employed different terms for these two concepts.[308] A mark with a "reputation" he argued "need not be as well known as a well-known mark".[309] He supported that a mark with a reputation had to be known to a significant part of the relevant sectors of the public but advocated against setting fixed criteria. Fixed criteria were potentially arbitrary; instead courts should apply a variety of criteria including the degree of knowledge or recognition of the mark in the relevant sectors of the public; the duration, extent and geographical area of use of the mark; and the scale and scope of investment in promoting the mark.

Turning to the peculiarities of the Benelux trade mark system that brought protection in three national jurisdictions under the same umbrella, he agreed with the position taken by the Commission that for the purposes of art.5(2) the Benelux territory should be assimilated to the territory of a single Member State. It would then be sufficient to have a reputation in a substantial part of the Benelux territory which could be part only of one of the Benelux countries. "That is the sole method of recognising the cultural and linguistic differences which may exist within a Member State; thus a mark may have a regional reputation, for example in the Dutch-speaking part of Belgium".[310]

5–171   *(b)   The judgment of the Court*

The Court of Justice identified a conceptual linguistic difference regarding the terms "known" and "reputation". The German, Dutch, and Swedish versions used words closer to the first term without indicating the extent of knowledge required, whereas the other versions used expressions closer to "reputation" implying, "at a quantitative level a certain degree of knowledge amongst the public".[311] This was viewed as simply a nuance since, in the context of a uniform interpretation of Community law and the general scheme of the Directive, "a knowledge threshold requirement emerges from a comparison of all the language versions of the Directive".[312]

Note the language used by the Court in order to indicate the relationship that must be established between the earlier mark and the later sign in order to trigger the application of art.5(2) and how this relationship is linked with the reputation requirement and the damage envisaged in the provision. The

---

[308] On the other hand the Advocate General also noted that reference to "reputation" in English could involve qualitative criteria; the same applied to the French term. See Annette Kur, "Well-known marks, highly renowned marks and marks having a (high) reputation—what's it all about?" (1992) 23 I.I.C. 218.
[309] Point 37 of the Opinion of A.G. Jacobs.
[310] Point 47 of the Opinion of A.G. Jacobs.
[311] *General Motors*, para.21.
[312] *General Motors*, para.22.

8. MARKS WITH A REPUTATION

Court uses the term "association" and at the same time requires a certain degree of knowledge. This degree of knowledge is pivotal because it is considered as a condition for making the association and the reason for the damage suffered by the earlier mark. Later in the judgment the Court also observed that "the stronger the earlier mark's distinctive character and reputation the easier it will be to accept that detriment has been caused to it".[313]

"Such a requirement is also indicated by the general scheme and purpose of the Directive. In so far as Article 5(2) of the Directive, unlike Article 5(1), protects trade marks registered for non-similar products or services, its first condition implies a certain degree of knowledge of the earlier trade mark among the public. It is only where there is a sufficient degree of knowledge of that mark that the public, when confronted by the later trade mark, may possibly make an association between the two trade marks, even when used for non-similar products or services, and that the earlier trade mark may consequently be damaged".[314]

The Court then identified the public in relation to which reputation should be considered as the public "concerned by that trade mark, that is to say, depending on the product or service marketed, either the public at large or a more specialised public, for example traders in a specific sector".[315]

5-172

It rejected the adoption of fixed percentages but required that the mark must be "known by a significant part of the public concerned by the products or services covered by that trade mark".[316] This should be determined by taking into consideration "all of the relevant facts of the case, in particular the market share held by the trade mark, the intensity, geographical extent and duration of its use, and the size of the investment made by the undertaking in promoting it".[317]

In terms of territorial coverage the Court held that it would be sufficient to have a reputation in "a substantial part"[318] of the relevant Member State, and in this case this substantial part could be a part of one of the Benelux countries.

(2) Fincas Tarragona—marks well known "in a Member State"

(a) Well-known v reputed marks

5-173

In *Fincas*[319] the question referred to the Court did not relate to the notion of "reputation", but rather to the specific protection afforded to trade marks

---
[313] *General Motors*, para.30.
[314] *General Motors*, para.23.
[315] *General Motors*, para.24.
[316] *General Motors*, para.26.
[317] *General Motors*, para.27.
[318] *General Motors*, para.28.
[319] *Alfredo Nieto Nuño v Leonci Monlleó Franquet* (FINCAS TARRAGONA) (C-328/06) [2007] E.C.R. I-40093.

which are "well-known in a Member State, in the sense in which the words 'well-known' are used in Article 6bis of the Paris Convention", within the meaning of art.4(2)(b) of the Directive.

So far, the relationship between "reputed" and "well-known" marks has not been fully explored by the Court of Justice. Although in *General Motors*[320] and *Nasdaq*[321] the Court briefly addressed specific facets of the interrelation between them, it refrained from carrying out a full-scale comparison of the relevant provisions of the Directive and the CTMR,[322] on the grounds that such a comparative analysis was not strictly necessary for the purposes of those cases.

On the other hand, the Court seems to be accepting, at least indirectly, that the notions of "reputation" and "well-known character" present a number of similar traits which approximate them to a significant extent. This follows from the statements of the Court that these notions are "kindred concepts"[323] that imply a "knowledge threshold requirement"[324] and is further stressed by its frequent reference to "well-known" marks in the context of provisions actually dealing with trade marks with a reputation.[325]

5–174 In that regard, the Court of First Instance seems to have taken a further step towards the full assimilation of "well-known" and "reputed" marks by taking the view that the underlying requirements of "reputation" and "well-known" character are overlapping, at least insofar as the conditions for the acquisition of the relevant rights are concerned. This can be inferred from the position it adopted in *Tosca Blu*[326] that art.8(5) CTMR also applies to "well–known" marks within the meaning of art.8(2)(c) of that regulation, on the sole condition that the latter have been registered, as also suggested by art.16(3) of the TRIPs Agreement.

That is also the practice of OHIM, which although recognises that the function and scope of the above provisions are different, it nevertheless applies essentially the same criteria in terms of market recognition and brand awareness when determining whether the substantive requirements laid down by them have been met.[327]

This is further attested if the wording used by the Court in *General Motors* for marking the requisite threshold for reputation, namely that the

---

[320] *General Motors*, paras 13–23.
[321] *Nasdaq*, para.51.
[322] These are arts 4(2)(b) of the Directive and 8(2)(c) CTMR in respect of well-known marks and arts 4(4)(a) and 5(2) of the Directive and 8(5) and 9(1)(c) CTMR in respect of trade marks with a reputation.
[323] *Fincas*, para.17.
[324] *General Motors*, para.22.
[325] cf. the English version of the judgment in *Gofkid*.
[326] See the judgment of the Court of First Instance in *Tosca Blu* (T-150/04) (cite), paras 49–61.
[327] See Guidelines Concerning Procedures before the Office for Harmonisation in the Internal Market (Trade Marks and Designs), Pt C: Opposition Guidelines Pt 5: Trade marks with reputation—art.8 (5) CTMR Ch.III s.3.2, pp.375–376, available on the website of the Office, http://oami.europa.eu.

mark must be "known by a significant part of the [relevant] public"[328] is compared to the very similar expression used by the WIPO Recommendations on the Protection of Well-Known marks, i.e. that a trade mark is well known if it is "known in the relevant sector" of the market.[329]

(b)   The facts in the main proceedings   5–175

In *Fincas* the reference concerned a dispute between Mr Nieto Nuño, proprietor in Spain of the word mark "FINCAS TARRAGONA", covering "management of property in sole or joint ownership, letting of property, sale of property, legal advice and property development" in Class 36 of the Nice Classification, and Mr Monlleó Franquet, an estate agent in the city of Tarragona, who had used, over a period of several years, the expression "FINCAS TARRAGONA", in Spanish, or "FINQUES TARRAGONA", in Catalán, for the purpose of designating his business.

Mr Nieto Nuño brought proceedings under Spanish trade mark law before the Juzgado de lo Mercantil 3 de Barcelona against Mr Monlleó Franquet, arguing that the latter had infringed his registered trade mark.

Mr Monlleó Franquet maintained in his defence that the name under which he conducted his business was an earlier well-known trade mark, which he had been using prior to the filing of Mr Nieto Nuño's mark and put forward a counter-claim seeking the annulment of that registration.

The national court observed that the defendant in the main proceedings   5–176
used his non-registered mark only in the city of Tarragona and its surrounding area, meaning that the relevant public, consisting of Mr Monlleó Franquet's clientele, customers and competitors, was limited to that territory and, thus, extended neither to the whole of Spain, nor to a significant part of it.

Against that background, the Juzgado de lo Mercantil 3 de Barcelona decided to stay the proceedings and to refer the following question to the Court of Justice for a preliminary ruling:

"Must the concept of trade marks which are 'well known' in a Member State, referred to in Article 4 of [the Directive] be taken to indicate solely and exclusively the degree of knowledge and establishment in a Member State or in a significant part of the territory of that State, or may the determination of whether a mark is well known be linked to a territorial scope which does not coincide with that of the territory of a State but rather with an autonomous community, region, district or city, depending on the goods or services which the mark covers and the persons to whom the

---

[328] *General Motors*, para.26.
[329] See art.2(2)(c) of the WIPO Recommendations [1999] concerning Provisions on the Protection of Well-Known Marks, available following the links at *http://www.wipo.int*.

mark is actually addressed, in short, depending on the market in which the mark is used?"

5–177 *(c) The Opinion of the Advocate General*

Advocate General Mengozzi started his examination by making an extensive analysis of the relevant provisions of the Directive against the backdrop of the Paris Convention and its derivative Treaties, in order to determine the purpose and function of the corresponding provisions under Spanish Law.

In particular, he observed that art.6bis of the Paris Convention, at least within the scope attributed to it by art.16(2) of the TRIPs Agreement, applies both where the mark has become well known following its use in the territory of the State where protection is sought and where it has become well known without being used there in the strict sense, but rather as a result of the spill-over effect of promotional campaigns and advertising carried out in that State or even outside its territory.[330]

He then suggested that the trade mark rights acquired by virtue of such use are in fact covered both by art.4(2)(b) and by art.4(4)(b) of the Directive, respectively relating to well-known and de facto trade marks, and that Member States were free not only to grant protection to unregistered trade marks, thus recognising that the mere use of a sign gives rise to an exclusive right, but also to define the conditions and scope of that protection.[331]

Based on the premise that such a protection may be available not only where the knowledge of the mark has achieved a particular geographical dimension, but also without any specific requirement as to a minimum awareness of the sign on the part of the public or the territorial extent of its use,[332] Advocate General Mengozzi proposed to answer the question referred to the Court to the effect that art.4 of the Directive did not preclude the cancellation of a later trade mark on the basis of an earlier unregistered trade mark which is well known not throughout the territory of the State concerned, or a substantial part of it, but only in a more limited geographical area.

5–178 *(d) The judgment of the Court*

The Court did not share the view put forward by the Advocate General.

First, it noted that that the question referred to it was limited to the geographical area in which the mark must be known and not to the overall criteria for assessing whether it is indeed well known, considered in terms of the degree of knowledge of the mark among the public. Secondly, it observed that, according to the facts in the main proceedings, the mark at

---

[330] Point 41 of the Opinion of A.G. Mengozzi.
[331] Points 42–45 of the Opinion of A.G. Mengozzi.
[332] Point 46 of the Opinion of A.G. Mengozzi.

issue was not known throughout the territory of the Member State of protection, or in a substantial part of it, but was merely well known in a city and its surrounding area.

Moreover, it pointed out that although the provision under interpretation lacked a definition in that regard, a trade mark could not be required to be well known "throughout" the territory of the Member State, being sufficient for it to be well known in a substantial part of it,[333] by analogy to what applied to the kindred concept of "reputation", which, for the purposes of art.5(2) of the Directive had also to be assessed "in the Member State" concerned.[334]

The Court stressed, however, that the customary meaning of the expression "in a Member State" precluded the application of that provision to a situation where the well-known status of the mark is limited to a city and to its surrounding area which, together, do not constitute a substantial part of the Member State.[335]   5–179

Notwithstanding, this did not preclude the possibility to protect unregistered signs with a local repute pursuant to art.4(4)(b) of the Directive, covering de facto trade marks, or under art.6(2) thereof, governing the protection of rights that only apply to in a particular locality.

Accordingly, the Court interpreted art.4(2)(d) of the Directive as meaning that the earlier trade mark must be well known throughout the territory of the Member State of protection or in a substantial part of it and that local knowledge, such as the one limited to a city and to its surrounding area, was not enough if that area does not constitute a substantial part of the Member State in issue.

Furthermore, apart from clarifying the territorial scope of the expression "in a Member State" by using the same criteria as those applicable to reputed marks, the judgment in *Fincas* is also important because it clarified that although the mark must be known in the territory of a Member State, the concept of a "well-known" trade mark under the Directive and the conditions for its protection must be interpreted not according to the legislation of that State, but in a uniform manner throughout the Community, being a notion of European rather than national law.

(3) Pago—reputation "in the Community"   5–180

Pago[336] is the necessary complement to *General Motors* with regard to the territorial scope of reputation; while in *General Motors*[337] and *Fincas*[338] the

---

[333] *Fincas*, para.17.
[334] As held in *General Motors*, para.28.
[335] *Fincas*, paras 18–21.
[336] *PAGO International GmbH v Tirol Milch registrierte Genossenschaft mbH* (PAGO) (C-301/07).
[337] *General Motors*.
[338] *Alfredo Nieto Nuño v Leonci Monlleó Franquet* (FINCAS TARRAGONA) (C-328/06) [2007] E.C.R. I-40093.

Court dealt with the geographical extent of the knowledge required for a sign to qualify as a mark with reputation or as a mark well known "in a Member State", in *Pago* the question was about the meaning of the expression reputation "in the Community", within the meaning of art.9(1)(c) CTMR.

5–181   *(a)   The facts in the main proceedings*

In *Pago* the order reference was made in the context of a dispute between PAGO International GmbH ("Pago GmbH") and Tirol Milch registrierte Genossenschaft mbH ("Tirol Milch").

Pago GmbH is the proprietor of a Community Trade Mark, registered in respect of, inter alia, fruit drinks and fruit juices. Its mark essentially consists of the representation of a green glass bottle, used by Pago for a number of years in marketing next to a distinctive label and cap reproducing a device of a full glass of fruit drink and the word "pago" in large characters.

Tirol Milch markets in Austria a fruit and whey drink called "Lattella", packaged in glass bottles whose design resembles in several respects (shape, colour, label, cap) the one depicted in the Community Trade Mark of Pago GmbH. In the advertising for its drink Tirol Milch uses a representation which also shows a bottle next to a full glass.

5–182   From the facts set out in the order for reference it appeared that there is no likelihood of confusion between the signs, since the bottle labels used by Pago GmbH and Tirol Milch bear the names "Pago" and "Lattella" respectively and both names are widely known in Austria. Rather, the parties to the main action proceeded on the basis that the conditions of art.9(1)(c) CTMR have been met in as much as, first, the sign in dispute is similar to the earlier Community Trade Mark of Pago GmbH, and secondly, the drink marketed by Tirol Milch is not similar to the juice marketed by Pago.

Pago GmbH sought an injunction before the Handelsgericht Wien prohibiting Tirol Milch from (i) promoting, offering for sale, marketing or otherwise using its drink in the bottles at issue; and (ii) advertising a representation of the bottles together with a full glass. That court granted the injunction but its decision was reversed by the Landesgericht Wien. Pago appealed to the Oberster Gerichtshof.

The Oberster Gerichtshof took the view that the question whether there has been an infringement of Pago's Community Trade Mark was to be assessed solely in accordance with the CTMR. However, since Pago's trade mark is widely known in Austria but not necessarily in other Member States, the Oberster Gerichtshof considered that it required guidance as to how the phrase "[has] a reputation in the Community" in art.9(1)(c) of the Regulation should be construed, and referred the following questions for a preliminary ruling:

8. MARKS WITH A REPUTATION

(1) Is a Community Trade Mark protected in the whole of the Community as a "trade mark with a reputation" for the purposes of art.9(1)(c) of the Regulation if it has a "reputation" only in one Member State?

(2) If the answer to the first question is in the negative: is a mark which has a "reputation" only in one Member State protected in that Member State under art.9(1)(c) of the Regulation, so that a prohibition limited to that Member State may be issued?

(b)   The Opinion of the Advocate General

(i) Reputation "in the Community": should General Motors apply by analogy? Advocate General Sharpston observed at the outset of her Opinion that even though the first question is put in a way suggesting that the answer should be either "yes" or "no", implying that whichever answer is given will be equally applicable in every case in which the mark has a reputation in a single Member State, it was necessary to approach the issue in a more flexible manner.   5–183

In any event, she agreed with the parties that *General Motors* provided the starting point for the analysis, to the extent that it had already established that, as a matter of principle, a national trade mark need not have a reputation throughout the territory of the Member State where it is registered and that, accordingly, it is sufficient for a Benelux trade mark to have a reputation in a substantial part of the Benelux territory, which might consist of a part of one of the Benelux countries.[339]

However, although she remarked that the first part of that finding was necessarily transposable to the question at issue, she did not agree that asking whether one Member State could be considered as a "substantial part" of the Community was the right way of approaching the question.

The Advocate General stressed that the CTMR is based on the premise that the Community Trade Mark is unitary in character and that an approach which focused on Member State boundaries when seeking to establish the extent of a Community Trade Mark's reputation was, in consequence, fundamentally misconceived. Rather, the starting point must be the territory of the Community regardless of frontiers, as a single and indivisible whole. As a corollary, it is irrelevant whether a reputation exists in one Member State, or any given number of Member States. It is likewise irrelevant whether those Member States are "big", "medium-sized" or "small" (on whatever basis those terms are defined).[340]   5–184

Instead, the Advocate General proposed the following alternative test:

As a starting point, it is necessary for the national court to establish whether the trade mark has a "reputation"; in doing so, it must first identify

---
[339] *General Motors*, paras 28–29.
[340] Point 29 of the Opinion of A.G. Sharpston.

the public concerned by the trade mark in the context of the Community as a whole, without regard to national borders; second, it should proceed to determine whether the reputation exists amongst a significant part of the public concerned. Then, the national court must determine whether the trade mark indeed has a reputation "in the Community", bearing in mind that the trade mark proprietor need not demonstrate that the trade mark has a reputation throughout the Community, but only in a "substantial part" of it.[341]

5–185 Next, the Advocate General recalled that, in *Fincas*, the Court had established in relation to the kindred concept of "well-known" marks, what is not a "substantial part" of the relevant territory, by holding that the city of Tarragona and its surrounding area within Spain were not a substantial part of that Member State. She went on to note that if that reasoning is applied by analogy to the question sub judice, it follows that where the "part" concerned is, in terms of its size and economic weight, paltry in comparison with the entire Community and where the relevant public is more widely spread, that part cannot be deemed to constitute a "substantial part" of the Community as a whole. She moreover observed that this conclusion is further supported by the ordinary meaning of the term "substantial" and also accords with common sense.

Thus, Advocate General Sharpston concluded that, as with the concept of relevant public, the territorial aspect of "reputation" cannot be defined by reference to an abstract figure or a particular number of Member States. The national court will have to evaluate a number of factors to determine whether a particular trade mark enjoys a reputation in a substantial part of the Community. Such factors will include, but not be limited to, the economic significance of the territory within the Community, the geographical extent of the area where the trade mark has a reputation and the demographics of the public concerned.

Finally, the Advocate General dismissed the ex art.50(1)(a) CTMR (new art.51) argument put forward by Pago GmbH that if use in one Member State is sufficient to preserve the rights relating to a Community Trade Mark, reputation in that State should, by analogy, be sufficient to trigger the protection conferred by art.9(1)(c), by noting that the different subject matter of the two provisions rendered the drawing of analogies between them quite inappropriate.

5–186 Thus, the main steps of the Advocate General's reasoning can be summed-up as follows[342]:

(a) it is not possible to establish whether a Community Trade Mark has a reputation in the Community on the basis of whether that trade mark has a reputation in any one Member State;

---

[341] Points 30–31 of the Opinion of A.G. Sharpston.
[342] Point 40 of the Opinion of A.G. Sharpston.

(b) it follows from the unitary character of the Community Trade Mark that the Community territory should be considered as a whole;

(c) *General Motors* should be applied by analogy to establish what constitutes a substantial part of the Community;

(d) this must be determined in any particular case by taking account of the public concerned by the products or services covered by the trade mark and the importance of the area where the reputation exists, as defined by factors such as its geographical extent, population and economic significance.

Advocate General Sharpston therefore proposed to answer the first question to the effect that a trade mark has a "reputation in the Community" within the meaning of art.9(1)(c) CTMR if it has a reputation in a substantial part of the Community, adding that what constitutes a substantial part of the Community for that purpose should not be dependent on national boundaries but must be determined by an assessment of all the relevant circumstances of the case, taking account, in particular, of (i) the public concerned by the products or services covered by the trade mark and the proportion of that public which knows of the mark; and (ii) the importance of the area in which the reputation exists, as defined by factors such as its geographical extent, population and economic significance.

(ii) Is a local reputation sufficient for obtaining an injunction? In dealing with the second question, the Advocate General observed that the core of the matter is whether a Community Trade Mark which has a reputation only in one Member State and thus cannot be said to have a reputation in the Community, is nonetheless protected in that Member State, so that a prohibition against infringement limited to that Member State may be issued.

5–187

In that connection, she considered that it was implicit in the answer to the first question that a trade mark which has a reputation in only one Member State does not qualify as a trade mark with a "reputation in the Community". Given that the existence of a "reputation in the Community" is the specific condition required to trigger art.9(1)(c), the answer to the second question is obvious: if that condition is not satisfied, no right to protection arises and the national court should not grant relief to enforce a legal right that does not exist.[343]

Moreover, she dismissed the argument that, if such limited protection did not exist, the Community Trade Mark would not be a viable alternative to national trade marks, because its proprietor would be unable to protect his interests in that Member State without also owning a national trade mark.

5–188

---

[343] Point 44 of the Opinion of A.G. Sharpston.

First, she noted that although it is true that Community and national trade marks have similar purposes, in as much as the objective of both art.9(1)(c) CTMR and art.5(2) of the Directive is to provide protection against damage to reputation, they reach that objective by different routes and operate in different contexts. Contrary to national trade marks, the unitary nature of the Community Trade Mark means that it is effectively protected throughout the Community and not merely in the part where it was found to have a reputation. Thus, it is precisely because the protection afforded to a Community Trade Mark is so extensive that the conditions laid down in the Regulation must be satisfied in full before it is triggered.

Secondly, even though she admitted that where a Community Trade Mark has a reputation in a Member State but not in a substantial part of the Community, national registration in that Member State will be necessary in order to protect the reputation of the mark in that territory, she found this to be generally consistent with the concept that the Community Trade Mark and national trade marks operate at different levels, but in parallel.

Accordingly, Advocate General Sharpston suggested that the second question should be answered to the effect that a Community Trade Mark which has a reputation in an area which is not a substantial part of the Community does not enjoy, under art.9(1)(c) CTMR, protection limited to that area. Consequently, a prohibition against infringement limited to that area may not be issued.

5–189 *(c) Consequences*

With regard to the second question the Advocate General seems to be taking an "all or nothing" approach: based on the notion of unitary character, she considers that Community Trade Marks are protected throughout the Community and not merely in the part where they have a reputation, in what could be described as a "maximalist" approach. Although the argument that this conclusion necessarily follows from the answer to the first question is indeed compelling, it may nevertheless lead to the following complications:

First, the view that the reputation of a Community Trade Mark may be protected also in territories where that mark is not actually reputed, does not sit comfortably within the context of art.4(3) of the Directive. According to that interpretation, that provision would effectively allow the proprietors of reputed Community Trade Marks to prevent the registration of national marks by way of a legal "fiction", namely that the Community Trade Mark invoked as a basis of the opposition is "assumed" to be reputed in the Member State at issue, even if this is not the case in practice.

However, even if in those cases the condition of reputation is presumed to be fulfilled, it is doubtful whether that "fictitious" reputation can ever be harmed by the use of the later mark. This is all the more questionable in view of the statements of the Court in *Intel*, first, that there can be no link between the marks if the public targeted by one of the two is never confronted with the other,[344] and, secondly, that detriment requires evidence of a change in the economic behaviour of the consumer consequent of the use of the later mark, or a serious likelihood that such will be the case in the future.[345] In other words, in view of the high standard of proof laid down in *Intel* as regards detriment it serves nothing to assume that reputation exists, if that assumption cannot subsequently be used for a specific, *in concreto* assessment of detriment.

Secondly, there is also a problem with the reverse side of that coin, namely the proposition that unitary character effectively means that a Community Trade Mark is protected in a uniform way throughout the Community and, by extension, a local reputation cannot enhance the protection of the earlier mark in the limited territory where that reputation actually exists. 5–190

In fact, that view seems to run contrary to the findings of the Court in *Armacell*, that the effect of unitary character is that "a Community trade mark can be relied on against any [subsequent] trade mark which would adversely affect the protection of the first mark, even if only in relation to the perception of consumers in part of the Community".[346] Although that statement was made in the context of likelihood of confusion, there is nothing to prevent its application also in the framework of reputed marks, or in infringement proceedings.

Otherwise, the notion of unitary character would finally result in having different effects depending on the context in which it operates, a solution which is not "unitary" at all. Equally, it would lead to the paradox of the concept of reputation having a wider scope of application when serving as a means of enhancing the likelihood of confusion, than when it comes to the protection of its own economic value. That paradox can only be avoided by a holistic approach, that is, by always interpreting reputation in relation to detriment, which ultimately provides the specific reason for its protection.

(4) Davidoff v Gofkid—the scope of article 5(2) 5–191

Despite the fact that the language of the provision is clear, in *Davidoff v Gofkid*[347] the Court was asked to consider whether art.5(2) and art.4(4) also covered identical or similar goods or services.

Gofkid is a peculiar case. First, the Court appears to forego the distinction between marks with a reputation and well-known marks referring only to well-known marks. Apparently, this was the result of a translational breakdown. Still, the fact that it went unnoticed is perhaps evidence of the

---

[344] *Intel*, para.48.
[345] *Intel*, para.77.
[346] *Armacell Enterprise GmbH* (C-514/06 P), para.57.
[347] *Davidoff & Cie SA and Zino Davidoff SA* (C-292/00) [2003] E.C.R. I-389.

conceptual uncertainties trade mark law is facing: do we use a new language but think in old terms or is it the other way round? Secondly, the Court did not follow the path indicated by the Advocate General; this is not unusual as such but the Court also avoided a textual analysis of the provision that would be consistent with its interpretive approach in *Sabel*.[348] And, finally, it demonstrates how difficult it is for the Court to reach an overall reasonable decision by looking only at aspects of the case.

The case was referred to the Court of Justice by the German Bundesgerichtshof (Federal Court of Justice). Davidoff was the owner of the homonymous trade mark for, inter alia, goods in Classes 14 ("precious metals and their alloys and goods in precious metals or coated therewith, not included in other classes; jewellery, precious stones; horological and chronometric instruments") and 34 ("tobacco; smokers' articles; matches"). It started proceedings against use by Gofkid of the later trade mark "Durffee" registered in a particular script (the "D" and "ff" elements in "Durffee" were similar to those in "Davidoff") for goods in Classes 14 and 34.

The German Court decided that the outcome of the case relied, first, on whether protection of marks with a reputation covered cases where the relevant goods or services are identical or similar, but there is no likelihood of confusion[349] and, secondly, on whether the additional protection may be granted only in cases where the use of the sign would take unfair advantage of, or be detrimental to, the distinctive character or repute of the earlier mark, or whether other national rules may also be applied. Both questions were triggered by the finding that before the adoption of the new national law in 1995,[350] that transposed the Directive, trade mark law in conjunction with the Law Prohibiting Unfair Competition[351] would prevent use of a sign similar to a well-known mark that possessed particular reputation and prestige value if the sign deliberately and without any overriding necessity resembled the earlier mark.

5-192   *(a)   The Opinion of the Advocate General*

The Advocate General recognised that the literal terms of the Directive appeared to leave a gap regarding the protection of marks with a reputation, that could be filled by the proposition that since art.4(4)(a) and art.5(2)

---

[348] *Sabel BV* (C-251/95) [1997] E.C.R. I-6191.
[349] Note that the wording of the first question was, perhaps, wider, however both the Advocate General and the Court of Justice were satisfied that this is what in essence the German Court wanted to know. The actual question was: "Are the provisions of Art.4(4)(a) and Art.5(2) to be interpreted (and where appropriate applied) as also entitling the Member States to provide more extensive protection for marks with a reputation in cases where the later mark is used or to be used for goods or services identical with or similar to those in respect of which the earlier mark is registered?"
[350] See Fammler, "The New German Act on Marks: EC Harmonisation and Comprehensive Reform" [1995] E.I.P.R. 22.
[351] See, for example *Shell* [1996] E.I.P.R. D45.

enable protection against use on dissimilar products they must, a fortiori, enable such protection where the products are similar.

(i) The Ambiguities of Sabel and General Motors. In a passage that is particularly important from an interpretive as well as trade mark law perspective for showing how contradictory meanings can be attributed to the same judgment Advocate General Jacobs noted that according to one reading of *Sabel*[352] and General Motors[353] the Court had accepted that protection under art.4(4)(a) and art.5(2) was an extension of "a comparable protection available where [the marks] are similar"[354]; the Court had stated that protection of a mark with a reputation can be achieved "even where" or "when" the later signs are used on non-similar products.

5–193

On another reading however, "even where/when"... need not necessarily be taken to mean "including cases where", that is to say "in cases where products are similar and also in cases where they are not". It might also be seen as stressing the difference which was highlighted by the Court in *Canon*[355]: "In contrast to Art.4(4)(a), which expressly refers to the situation in which the goods or services are not similar, Art.4(1)(b) provides that the likelihood of confusion presupposes that the goods or services covered are identical or similar." Moreover, those statements were not findings of law underpinning the rulings in the two cases in question but rather commentaries on related points; in neither case was the use of the word "even" by the Court germane to the matter under consideration.[356]

Accordingly the Court had to look at the provision from the very beginning.

(ii) A literal interpretation. The linguistic clarity of the provision was compelling for the Advocate General:

5–194

> "Where a legislative provision is clear, it is in principle unnecessary and undesirable to look behind the terms adopted. That having been said, however, in the present case the drafting history of the Directive—which is closely linked to that of the Regulation—tends to support a literal interpretation."[357]

In the preamble to the Directive there was no indication that protection of marks with a reputation should encompass similar or identical products. Placing the provision in its historical context he noted that in the original proposal for the Directive protection was limited against use on identical or similar products. The extended protection was the result of the adoption of

---

[352] Referring to para.20 of *Sabel BV* (C-251/95) [1997] E.C.R. I-6191.
[353] Referring to para. 23 of *General Motors Corp* (C-375/97) [1999] E.C.R. I-5421.
[354] Point 30 of the Opinion of A.G. Jacobs.
[355] *Canon Kabushiki Kaisha* (C-39/97) [1998] E.C.R. I-5507, para.22.
[356] Point 31 of the Opinion of A.G. Jacobs.
[357] Point 34 of the Opinion of A.G. Jacobs.

a provision on marks with a reputation by the Community Trade Mark Regulation; this was intended to be an advantage of the Community Trade Mark system as opposed to national trade mark systems.[358] In addition, the wording of the Directive was deliberately chosen despite the suggestion "that the protection in question should extend to use for both similar and dissimilar goods, the legislature chose a form of words which referred to dissimilar products alone".[359]

5–195 **(iii) The protection gap.** Considering the argumentation for an interpretation to the contrary he found it to be not compelling. Citing *Marca Mode*,[360] he stated that confusion cannot be inferred from reputation alone. So, a gap might exist where use of a similar sign makes a link with an earlier mark with a reputation but additional information explicitly denies the connection required for establishing confusion.[361] He suggested that even in such cases there may be at the end a likelihood of confusion.

But even if there was no confusion the earlier mark could still be protected according to his interpretation of art.4(1) and art.5(1), on the one hand, and art.4(4)(a) and art.5(2), on the other. The importance of distinctiveness for establishing confusion, recognised by the Court in *Sabel*[362] and *Canon*[363] provided the key for this continuum of protection. The starting point was that marks "having a reputation thus do not enjoy a separate and independent system of protection but rather the same general protection as is afforded to all marks, together with a specific, supplementary and optional protection",[364] dependant on specific and distinct from confusion criteria. However, a particularly distinctive character, that could be either inherent or the result of reputation, would assist in bridging the gap in the global appreciation of confusion test:

> "Thus, although there may be an area in which a trade mark having a reputation is not protected against the use of identical or similar marks or signs—namely where the products in question are similar and there is no likelihood of confusion—the very definition of that area means that it is likely to be insignificant in practice, and its extent is still further limited by the Court's case law. In deliberately not providing for that area, moreover, the legislature may well have been expressing its intention that likelihood of confusion should be the normal criterion for protection. It may

---

[358] See Bulletin of the European Communities, 1980 Supplement 5/80, p.13.
[359] Point 36, citing the Opinion of the Economic and Social Committee, [1981] OJ C310/22, recommending that the Directive should follow the Regulation in specifying that signs similar to well-known marks "may not be used for dissimilar goods either".
[360] *Marca Mode CV v Adidas AG & Adidas Benelux BV* (C-425/98) [2000] E.C.R. I-4861.
[361] He referred to *Arsenal Football Club Plc* (C-206/01) [2002] E.C.R. I-10273 that was, then, pending before the Court as an example.
[362] *Sabel BV* (C-251/95) [1997] E.C.R. I-6191.
[363] *Canon Kabushiki Kaisha* (C-39/97) [1998] E.C.R. I-5507.
[364] Point 46 of the Opinion of A.G. Jacobs.

8. MARKS WITH A REPUTATION

also have had in mind that the area of dissimilar products is one in which dishonest operators might well take unfair advantage of a well known mark unless extra protection is granted, whereas it would be considerably more difficult to take such advantage in the area of similar products without giving rise to a likelihood of confusion."[365]

He concluded that an interpretation to the contrary would cause legal uncertainty and would limit the pool of potential Community Trade Marks, since more national trade mark rights could be raised as obstacles according to art.8(5) of the Regulation. This would be against the objective of art.14 of the EC Treaty—the achievement of an internal market—that underlined the Directive.

(b) The judgment of the Court 5–196

The Advocate General had built up an almost foolproof case for a literal interpretation. Confusion as to origin constituted the legitimising backbone of the Directive and the consistent mantra of the earlier jurisprudence of the Court of Justice. Derogations from the mantra should be interpreted strictly. Albeit, this time, the Court chose a different and much shorter route; it started by observing that art.5(2)—and, mutatis mutandis, art.4(4)—must be interpreted in the light "of the overall scheme and objectives of the system of which it is a part"[366] rather than in an exclusively literal manner.

Hostage to the argument that art.5(2) provided more rather than different protection compared with art.5(1), the Court held that it "cannot be given an interpretation which would lead to marks with a reputation having less protection where a sign is used for identical or similar goods or services than where a sign is used for non-similar goods or services".[367]

Linking the scope of protection under the two articles the Court noted that in the absence of confusion, art.5(1)(b) "could not be relied on by the proprietor of a mark with a reputation to protect himself against impairment of the distinctive character or repute of the mark".[368] Accordingly, art.4(4) and art.5(2) entitled Member States to provide specific protection for registered trade marks with a reputation against use of similar marks on signs on identical or similar goods or services.

(5) Fitnessworld—the interpretive limits of Davidoff v Gofkid 5–197

In *Adidas v Fitnessworld*[369] the Court looked at three questions referred to it by the Hoge Raad: first, whether art.5(2) covered identical and similar as well

---

[365] Point 51 of the Opinion of A.G. Jacobs.
[366] *Davidoff*, para.24.
[367] *Davidoff*, para.25.
[368] *Davidoff*, para.29.
[369] *Adidas-Salomon AG and Adidas Benelux BV* (C-408/01) [2003] E.C.R. I-12537.

as dissimilar goods or services and, following the intervention of the United Kingdom, the extent of freedom that national courts enjoyed, following the Court's interpretation of art.5(2) in *Gofkid*[370]; secondly, whether there was a distinct, from *Sabel*,[371] test for determining similarity between marks for the purposes of art.5(2); and, thirdly, whether use of a sign as an embellishment constitutes infringement of an earlier similar trade mark.

Adidas, based on its registration of the "three stripes" device mark in the Benelux—a mark that was found to be strong and enjoying general recognition—started trade mark infringement proceedings against Fitnessworld which marketed clothing garments bearing a "two stripes" motif, applied to the side seams of the garment. Fitnessworld's stripes were running in parallel and in terms of colour were in contrast with the background colour of the garment.

The Gerechtshof held that there was no trade mark infringement, since there was no likelihood of confusion, and that Fitnessworld used its sign as an embellishment. On appeal Adidas claimed before the Hoge Raad that the case fell under art.5(2).

The answer to the first question—whether art.5(2) covered identical and similar as well as dissimilar good or services—had to conform to *Gofkid*. However, the United Kingdom, testing the limits of the judgment, supported that the Court ruled that Member States may extend protection to identical and similar goods rather than that they are obliged to do so. Member States remained free to follow a literary interpretation of the provision. Since adoption of the provision remained optional, the degree of its implementation should also remain optional.

5–198 *(a) The Opinion of the Advocate General*

Advocate General Jacobs, despite his doctrinal disagreement with the Court in *Gofkid*, did not support this line of argument.

First because the Court had clearly stated that "art.5(2) cannot be given an interpretation which would lead to well-known marks having less protection where a sign is used for identical or similar goods or services than where a sign is used for non-similar goods or services".[372]

Secondly, because the seventh Recital of the Preamble stated that "the grounds for refusal or invalidity concerning the trade mark itself ... or concerning conflicts between the trade mark and earlier rights, are to be listed in an exhaustive manner, even if some of these grounds are listed as an option for the Member States which will therefore be able to maintain or introduce those grounds in their legislation".

---

[370] *Davidoff & Cie SA and Zino Davidoff SA* (C-292/00) [2003] E.C.R. I-389.
[371] *Sabel BV* (C-251/95) [1997] E.C.R. I-6191.
[372] *Davidoff & Cie SA and Zino Davidoff SA* (C-292/00) [2003] E.C.R. I-389, para.25.

8. MARKS WITH A REPUTATION

Thirdly, because the Court had already held that art.5, art.6, and art.7 are provisions that require complete harmonisation.[373]   **5–199**

Finally, since the national legislation challenged in *Gofkid* followed the same wording with art.5(2), it was unlikely that the Court had simply issued a permissive rather than an obligatory judgment.

(b) The judgment of the Court   **5–200**

The Court indeed referred to its earlier judgment in a non permissive way. It broadened, however, the scope of the question in order to deal with the challenge of the United Kingdom.

> "In that regard, it should be noted that where a Member State exercises the option provided by Art.5(2) of the Directive, it must grant to the proprietors of marks with a reputation a form of protection in accordance with that provision."[374]

It followed the Opinion of the Advocate General and ruled that if the Member State "transposes Art.5(2) ... [it] must therefore grant protection which is at least as extensive for identical or similar goods or services as for non-similar goods or services. The Member State's option thus relates to the principle itself of granting greater protection to marks with a reputation, but not to the situations covered by that protection when the Member State grants it".[375]

In essence, the Court confirmed that national courts are required to interpret national provisions transposing a directive according to the wording and the purpose of the directive.[376]

(6) Adidas v Fitnessworld—global appreciation in the context of article 5(2)   **5–201**

One of the questions in *Fitnessworld*[377] was whether the criteria of similarity between an earlier mark and a later mark or sign under art.5(2) are the same with those under art.5(1).

---

[373] *Levi Strauss & Co and Levi Strauss (UK) Ltd v Tesco Stores, Tesco Plc* (C-414/99) and *Costco Wholesale UK Ltd* (C-415/99) and *Zino Davidoff SA v A&G Imports Ltd* (C-416/99) [2001] E.C.R. I-8691; and *Robelco NV* (C-23/01) [2002] E.C.R. I-1093.
[374] *Fitnessworld*, para.18.
[375] *Fitnessworld*, para.20.
[376] *Von Colson and Kamann v Land Nordhein-Westfalen* (C-14/83) [1984] E.C.R. 1891; *Dorit Harz v Deutsche Tradax GmbH* (C-79/83) [1984] E.C.R. 1921; and *Coote v Granada Hospitality Ltd* (C-185/97) [1998] E.C.R. I-5199.
[377] *Adidas-Salomon AG and Adidas Benelux BV v Fitnessworld Trading Ltd* (C-408/01) [2003] E.C.R. I-12537.

5–202   *(a)   The Opinion of the Advocate General*

Advocate General Jacobs supported that the test elaborated in *Sabel*[378] and *Lloyd*[379] should also be applied here. The difference was that it would not be necessary to show that the similarity gives rise to a likelihood of confusion. The Court had already clearly stated in *Marca Mode*[380] that art.5(2) did not require the existence of a likelihood of confusion. He suggested that the provision should be linked with the effect of the use complained of rather than with a particular state of mind on the part of consumers. Unless the later sign brought the earlier mark to the mind of the relevant public it would not affect the earlier mark in any way.

In his general analysis of the provision he had identified three types of effect that could possibly fall under art.5(2): dilution, degradation, or free riding. Preferring to use the term connection rather than association—note that the Commission had submitted that a likelihood of association would be sufficient—he referred to the Court's ruling in General Motors[381]:

> "It seems obvious that use of a sign cannot have such an effect unless the sign brings the mark in some way to the mind of the relevant public. Thus, considering in the light of the general scheme and purpose of the Directive the requirement in Art.5(2) that the trade mark have a reputation, the Court has stated that it is only where there is a sufficient degree of knowledge of the mark that the public, when confronted by the sign, may possibly make a connection between the two and that the mark may consequently be damaged."[382]

He believed that specifying the criteria in detail would not be helpful. National courts would be able to decide whether as a result of sensory or conceptual similarity between the two signs the use complained of take unfair advantage of, or be detrimental to, the distinctive character or the repute of the mark.

5–203   *(b)   The judgment of the Court*

The Court cited the same cases with the Advocate General and ruled that "[T]he condition of similarity between the mark and the sign, referred to in art.5(2) of the Directive, requires the existence, in particular, of elements of visual, aural or conceptual similarity".[383]

---

[378] *Sabel BV* (C-251/95) [1997] E.C.R. I-6191.
[379] *Lloyd Schuhfabrik Meyer & Co GmbH* (C-342/97) [1999] E.C.R. I-3819.
[380] *Marca Mode CV v Adidas AG & Adidas Benelux BV* (C-425/98) [2000] E.C.R. I-4861.
[381] *General Motors Corp* (C-375/97) [1999] E.C.R. I-5421.
[382] *General Motors*, para.49.
[383] *Fitnessworld*, para.28.

8. MARKS WITH A REPUTATION

It too preferred to use the term connection rather than association; the public must make a connection between the sign and the mark, establish a link between them "even though it does not confuse them".[384] The existence of such a link must be appreciated globally taking into account all the factors relevant to the circumstances of the case.

In essence the similarity test is the same under both art.5(1)(b) and art.5(2), however in *Fitnessworld* the language of the Court appears to be less detailed and more abstract; there is perhaps a hint that the Court is moving away from the multi-factor tests expressed in *Sabel*[385] and *Canon*[386] towards a more conceptual approach.

(7) Adidas v Fitnessworld—use as a trade mark 5–204

The third question in *Fitnessworld*[387] dealt with a wider issue of use. The Hoge Raad asked the Court of Justice whether the fact that the later sign is viewed as an embellishment is relevant in assessing the similarity between the mark and the sign. The question was in the context of art.5(2), however the ruling should also be relevant for the purposes of art.5(1).

(a) The Opinion of the Advocate General 5–205

Advocate General Jacobs considered that whether the sign was viewed as an embellishment did not assist in the assessment of similarity.

It would be relevant however in the overall assessment of the applicability of art.5(2). He rejected a broad claim that a sign that is viewed as a decoration cannot cause a connection with a trade mark. He noted that some trade marks were based on common shapes, patterns, or even colours,[388] and so even merely decorative use of a similar shape, pattern, or colour could remind the public of the earlier trade mark.

He added that, from a literal perspective, art.5(2) did not refer to whether the sign must be viewed as a mark; he found the Commission's claim that art.5(5)[389] should lead to such an interpretation as unpersuasive since art.5(5) targets provisions outside trade mark law. However, he believed that if the "the relevant section of the public perceives a given sign as doing no more than embellishing goods, and in no way as identifying their origin,

---

[384] *Fitnessworld*, para.29.
[385] *Sabel BV* (C-251.95) [1997] E.C.R. I-6191.
[386] *Canon Kabushiki Kaisha* (C-39/97) [1998] E.C.R. I-5507.
[387] *Adidas-Salomon AG and Adidas Benelux BV* (C-408/01) [2003] E.C.R. I-12537.
[388] The A.G. referred in particular to *Libertel Groep BV* (C-104/01) [2003] E.C.R. I-3793; earlier in his examination of the second question he had referred to *Sieckmann* (C-273/00) [2002] E.C.R. I-11737. This recurring link between what is registered with its scope of protection can become particularly relevant when the enforcement limits of some types of signs are tested in practice.
[389] *Robelco NV* (C-23/01) [2002] E.C.R. I-1093.

that sign cannot be regarded as used for the purpose of distinguishing those goods".[390] A sign that functions purely as an embellishment or decoration would not be perceived as a badge of origin. Distinguishing *Fitnessworld* from *Arsenal*[391] he underlined that the latter was an art.5(1)(a) case. "In that context the unauthorised use by a third party of the identical mark on identical goods was plainly trade mark use, notwithstanding that perception."[392] So, use of the later sign as a trade mark was an implied condition of art.5(2).

To support further his position he referred to the "public interest" the Court has applied in its interpretation of art.3(1)(c) and art.3(1)(e). By analogy, it would be unjustified to employ trade mark law in order block use of common decorations, motifs, or colours, by competitors.

5-206 (b) *The judgment of the Court*

The Court followed a much less analytical route to reach the same outcome. It viewed the establishment of the connection between the earlier trade mark and the later sign as the decisive factor. If the sign establishes a link then the fact that it is viewed as an embellishment is not, "in itself, an obstacle to the protection conferred by art.5(2)".[393] However, where the relevant public views the sign purely as an embellishment "it necessarily does not establish any link with a registered mark. That therefore means that the degree of similarity between the sign and the mark is not sufficient for such a link to be established".[394]

5-207 (8) **Intel—proof of dilution: chasing the chimera?**

Intel[395] was an ambitious attempt to settle all the outstanding questions surrounding the condition of "detriment to the distinctiveness" of a reputed mark with a single stroke. While *General Motors*[396] and *Fitnessworld*[397] had respectively settled the concepts of reputation and similarity and had briefly touched upon the notions and mechanics of detriment and/or unfair advantage, the specific requirements for proving such detriment largely remained uncharted territory.

---

[390] *Fitnessworld*, para.60. He referred once again to *Libertel Groep BV v Benelux-Merkenbureau* (C-104/01) [2003] E.C.R. I-3793 where the Court stated that a trade mark must distinguish the goods or services concerned as originating from a particular undertaking. This was the essential function of a trade mark, to act as a badge of origin.
[391] *Arsenal Football Club Plc* (C-206/01) [2002] E.C.R. I-10273.
[392] Point 62 of the Opinion of A.G. Jacobs.
[393] *Fitnessworld*, para.39.
[394] *Fitnessworld*, para.40.
[395] *Intel Corp Inc v CPM United Kingdom Ltd* (INTEL) (C-252/07), not yet published.
[396] *General Motors* (CHEVY) (C-375/97) [1999] E.C.R. I-5421.
[397] *Adidas-Salomon AG and Adidas Benelux BV* (C-408/01) [2003] E.C.R. I-12537.

8. MARKS WITH A REPUTATION

(a) The facts in the main proceedings 5–208

Intel Corp Inc ("Intel") is the proprietor in the United Kingdom of the word mark "INTEL", as well as of various other national and Community Trade Marks consisting of or including that word. Those marks essentially cover computers and computer-related goods and services in Classes 9, 16, 38 and 42 of the Nice Classification. According to the facts, the word "INTEL" moreover has a "huge" reputation in the United Kingdom for microprocessor products (chips and peripherals), multimedia and business software.

CPM United Kingdom Ltd ("CPM") is the proprietor of the word mark "INTELMARK", registered in the United Kingdom for "marketing and telemarketing services" in Class 35 of the Nice Classification.

Intel lodged an application for a declaration of invalidity against CPM's registration, claiming that the use of that mark would take unfair advantage of, or be detrimental to, the distinctive character or the repute of its earlier trade mark within the meaning of s.5(3) of the Trade Marks Act.

Its application was dismissed both by the Hearing Officer and the High Court. Intel appealed to the Court of Appeal (England and Wales) (Civil Division).

Intel argued that both art.4(4)(a) and art.5(2) of the Directive seek to 5–209 protect a trade mark with a reputation against dilution. Relying on *Fitnessworld*, it maintained that any link between the earlier reputed mark and the later sign in the perception of the public was enough to cause detriment. Moreover, by referring to *General Motors*, it submitted that, where the earlier mark is unique and has a strong distinctive character, detriment will be caused to it by virtually any use for other goods or services and that, unless encroachment was stopped at the outset, that mark would suffer a death "by a thousand cuts".

In its statement of the facts, the referring Court found, first, that the mark "INTEL" consists of an invented word and is highly reputed and unique, in the sense that it has not been used by anyone for any other goods or services, secondly, that the marks at issue are similar, but not confusingly so and, thirdly, that the respective goods and services are dissimilar "to a substantial degree".

However, the Court of Appeal was uncertain whether, in such factual circumstances, the proprietor of an earlier reputed mark is entitled to the protection of art.4(4)(a) of the Directive. Accordingly, it decided to stay proceedings refer the following questions to the Court:

"(1) For the purposes of Article 4(4)(a) of the [Directive], where:

(a) the earlier mark has a huge reputation for certain specific types of goods or services,
(b) those goods or services are dissimilar or dissimilar to a substantial degree to the goods or services of the later mark,

(c) the earlier mark is unique in respect of any goods or services,
(d) the earlier mark would be brought to mind by the average consumer when he or she encounters the later mark used for the services of the later mark,

are those facts sufficient in themselves to establish (i) 'a link' within the meaning of paragraphs 29 and 30 of [Adidas-Salomon and Adidas Benelux], and/or (ii) unfair advantage and/or detriment within the meaning of that Article?

(2) If no, what factors is the national court to take into account in deciding whether such is sufficient? Specifically, in the global appreciation to determine whether there is a 'link', what significance is to be attached to the goods or services in the specification of the later mark?

(3) In the context of Article 4(4)(a) [of the Directive], what is required in order to satisfy the condition of detriment to distinctive character? Specifically, (i) does the earlier mark have to be unique, (ii) is a first conflicting use sufficient to establish detriment to distinctive character and (iii) does the element of detriment to distinctive character of the earlier mark require an effect on the economic behaviour of the consumer?"

5–210 *(c) The Opinion of the Advocate General*

Advocate General Sharpston provided the context for her analysis by referring to the genesis of the dilution doctrine[398] and to the detailed description of that notion by Advocate General Jacobs in *Fitnessworld*.[399]

She stressed, however, that the Court's task was not to define dilution in the abstract, but to interpret the relevant provisions of the Directive, with a view to drawing a fair balance between the interests of the owners of famous marks and the need to avoid such rights from being used abusively to the detriment of other, weaker market operators.

She also observed that the questions referred to the Court overlapped to a substantial degree and that, taken together, they ask, essentially what factors are to be taken into account and to which extent those factors must be present, in order to establish (i) a "link" between the signs in the mind of the public; (ii) free riding; (iii) detriment to distinctiveness (blurring); and (iv) detriment to repute (tarnishment).

5–211 **(i) Relationship between link and infringement.** The Advocate General recalled that, according to the case law, the establishment of a link in the mind of the public is a necessary condition for the existence of an infringement and that such a link is mainly the consequence of a degree of

---

[398] Citing Frank Schechter "The rational basis of trademark protection" [1927] *Harvard Law Review* 813.
[399] See in particular paras 36–39 of the Advocate General's opinion in *Adidas Fitnessworld*

similarity between the mark and the sign.[400] Moreover, as is clear from the same case law, the existence of such a link must be appreciated globally, that is, by having regard to all the factors relevant to the particular case.[401]

However, she considered that even though the factors that are relevant for the assessment of a possible link will also be pertinent when appraising infringement, the mere existence of such a link was not sufficient of itself to prove the existence of detriment or unfair advantage. In other words, not every link is detrimental, in the same manner that not any association between the marks can give rise to a likelihood of confusion.[402]

Accordingly, the Advocate General took the view that the fact that the earlier mark would be "brought to mind" by the consumer when encountering the later sign, is tantamount to the existence of a "link", "association" or "connection" within the meaning of the case law; those terms are in fact equivalent, to the extent that they all imply a mental process above the threshold of "consciousness" that is, something more than a "vague, ephemeral, indefinable feeling or subliminal influence".[403]

She remarked, nevertheless, that such a link must be of a "reasonably substantial nature" since it must be made by a substantial part of the relevant public (apparently in view of the fact that there must be a tangible risk of detriment for protection to be triggered, that is, something more than a remote possibility, confined to a limited number of cases).

Moreover, the Advocate General referred to the equivalent provision of US law[404] as giving a useful example of the kind of factors that may be taken into account in assessing detriment. According to that provision, in determining whether a mark is likely to cause dilution by blurring, the court may consider all relevant factors, including the degree of similarity between the marks, the degree of inherent or acquired distinctiveness of the famous mark, the extent to which the owner of the famous mark is engaging in substantially exclusive use of the mark, the degree of recognition of the famous mark and any actual association between the marks.

Although she observed that that provision naturally has no force in Community law and the factors it enumerates are to be considered when assessing the likelihood of dilution itself, rather than the existence of a link in the mind of the public (which is not an explicit condition in the American legislation), they still seem relevant to establishing whether such a link exists, all the more so since they largely coincide with the test applied by the Court to the assessment of likelihood of confusion.[405]

5–212

---

[400] *Fitnessworld*, para.29.
[401] *Fitnessworld*, para.30.
[402] Point 43 of the Opinion of A.G. Sharpston.
[403] Point 46 of the Opinion of A.G. Sharpston.
[404] United States Trade Mark Act of 1946 s.43(c), as amended by the Trademark Dilution Revision Act of 2006 (15 U.S.C. 1051 et seq).
[405] Point 57 of the Opinion of A.G. Sharpston.

5–213 Turning, lastly, to the significance of the goods and services concerned for the establishment of a link, she took the view that it was not necessary that their nature should imply an economic connection between the owners of the two marks, as the referring Court seemed to be suggesting. Besides, such a view would practically efface the distinction between the respective conditions under which the basic protection against likelihood of confusion and the extensive protection afforded to famous marks are available.

Notwithstanding, the Advocate General accepted that the nature of the goods is important, in particular in one respect: if the goods in conflict are so far apart that the respective consumer circles do not overlap, it is highly unlikely that an association will ever take place. Conversely, where either mark is used for goods or services targeting the general public, or where both are used for related products, the likelihood of an association on the part of the public is correspondingly much stronger.[406]

5–214 **(ii) Free riding.** Advocate General Sharpston then observed that the concept of unfair advantage focuses on benefit to the later sign, rather than harm to the reputed mark. That implies some sort of boost given to the later sign by way of its association with the earlier mark. She considered, though, that the facts set out in the first question seemed too flimsy on their own to support a finding of free-riding.[407]

In general, it would seem that as the reputation of the earlier mark and the similarity of the goods and services covered by the respective marks increase, so will the likelihood that the later sign will derive advantage from its connection with the reputed mark. But usually more will be needed. If the later sign is to derive such advantage, its association with earlier mark must be such as to enhance its performance.[408]

Thus, what is finally decisive is the relationship between the prestigious connotations of the earlier mark and the context in which the later mark is used, in the sense that the image and appeal of the reputed mark must somehow be transferable to the latter.

5–215 **(iii) Blurring.** Turning to the third question, the Advocate General stressed that, unlike free-riding, the notion of blurring focuses on harm to the earlier mark, necessarily implying a lessening of its distinctiveness. Again, she considered the factors listed in the first question to be insufficient, on their own, to support a finding of dilution, although she admitted that they were in no way inconsistent with such a finding.[409]

In that connection she found that, like all other relevant factors, "uniqueness" is not essential of itself to lead to dilution. Terms such as "truly

---
[406] Point 60 of the Opinion of A.G. Sharpston.
[407] Points 62–63 of the Opinion of A.G. Sharpston.
[408] Points 65–66 of the Opinion of A.G. Sharpston.
[409] Points 68–69 of the Opinion of A.G. Sharpston.

unique" and "substantially unique" were not only difficult to define but also impractical in their application. What counts in the end, is that the more distinctive a mark is, the more likely it becomes that its distinctiveness will be impaired by the presence of other marks.[410]

As regards the standard of proof, she considered that the question whether "a first conflicting use" is enough, was in reality misconceived, since, as a matter of definition, a first conflicting use may not in itself cause detriment, given that the very point of both art.4(4)(a) and art.5(2) is to prevent or pre-empt repeated conflicting use which would dilute the earlier mark; as is obvious, a first use cannot produce such an effect on its own, but the likelihood of that being caused by repeated use may still be extrapolated from the overall circumstances.[411]

Lastly, as to the question whether an effect on consumers' economic behaviour is required, she expressed the opinion that detriment to distinctiveness need not necessarily involve actual pecuniary damage, so that a change in economic behaviour is not essential. Surely, however, any evidence of actual negative change in consumer behaviour would buttress the case for dilution.[412]

5–216

Consequently, the Advocate General supported a holistic approach, refusing to clearly favour any specific factor over the others, all the more so since blurring will usually be the result of the combined effect of various circumstances and thus can only be evaluated by taking a case by case approach.

(iv) Tarnishment. Finally, the Advocate General dealt briefly with tarnishment. She observed that that type of infringement again concerns harm to the earlier mark, in the form of detriment to its repute. That form of damage appears to be a step beyond blurring, in that the mark is not merely weakened but actually degraded by the link which the public makes with the later mark. Accordingly, the most important factor in this regard should be whether the connotations of the later mark are indeed such as to harm the repute of the earlier mark. Thus, in cases of alleged tarnishment, it will be necessary to compare the connotations of each mark, in relation either to the goods or services covered or to the broader message which they convey, and to evaluate the damage entailed.

5–217

(d) The judgment of the Court

5–218

(i) Detriment in the form of dilution by blurring. The Court started its analysis by noting that the condition of detriment or unfair advantage is the specific condition of the protection conferred by arts 4(4)(a) and 5(2) of the

---

[410] Point 72 of the Opinion of A.G. Sharpston.
[411] Point 73 of the Opinion of A.G. Sharpston.
[412] Point 74 of the Opinion of A.G. Sharpston.

Directive[413] and that any of the three types of injury stipulated in those provisions suffices to trigger that form of protection.

As regards, in particular, the detriment to the distinctive character of the earlier mark, which the Court also described as "dilution", "whittling away" or "blurring", it concurred with the generally accepted view that such detriment is caused when that mark's ability to identify the goods or services for which it is registered as coming from the proprietor of that mark is weakened by the use of the later sign, which leads to the dispersion of its identity and hold upon the public mind. It also confirmed that this is notably the case when a mark, which used to arouse immediate association with the goods and services for which it is registered, is no longer capable of doing so.[414]

The Court moreover reiterated that the types of injury referred to in art.4(4)(a) of the Directive, where they occur, are the consequence of a certain degree of similarity between the marks, by virtue of which the relevant section of the public makes a connection between the two marks, that is to say, establishes a link between them even though it does not confuse them.[415]

It also concurred with the view of the Advocate General that the existence of such a link is not sufficient, in itself, to establish that there is one of the types of injury referred to in art.4(4)(a) of the Directive.

5-219 **(ii) The relevant public.** Then, the Court observed that the public to be taken into account for the purposes of art.4(4)(a) varies depending on the type of injury claimed each time and proposed a two-fold test for its definition:

In the first place, the mark's reputation must be assessed, by reference to the perception of the relevant public, which consists of average consumers of the goods or services for which that mark is registered, who are reasonably well informed and reasonably observant and circumspect.[416]

Secondly, if what has been claimed is detriment to the distinctive character or the repute of the earlier mark, it is the average consumers of the goods and services for which that mark is registered, who must be taken into account; conversely, in cases of unfair advantage, its existence must be assessed by reference to the average consumers of the goods or services for which the later mark is registered and/or used.[417]

5-220 **(iii) Standard and burden of proof.** Next, the Court noted that the burden of proving detriment or unfair advantage falls on the proprietor of the earlier mark, who must adduce appropriate evidence to that effect.

---

[413] Citing, among others, *Marca Mode*, para.36 and *Fitnessworld*, para.36.
[414] *Intel*, para.29.
[415] *General Motors*, para.23, *Fitnessworld*, para.29.
[416] *General Motors*, para.24.
[417] *Intel*, paras 35–36.

It stressed though, that the proprietor is not required to demonstrate actual and present injury to its mark for the purposes of art.4(4)(a), since, when it is foreseeable that such injury will ensue from the use of the later mark, he cannot be expected to wait for it actually to occur in order to be able to prohibit that use; in any event, however, he must at least establish that there is a serious risk that such an injury will occur in the future.[418]

Then, the Court proceeded to apply these general principles to the questions pending before it.

(iv) The existence of a link. After recalling that the possible existence of a link between the marks must be assessed globally, by taking into account all relevant facts and circumstances,[419] it went on to address the significance of the factors specifically singled out by the referring Court. 5–221

As regards the degree of similarity between the marks, it noted that the more similar they are, the more likely it is that the later mark will bring the earlier mark to mind. That is particularly the case where the marks are identical. However, even that fact is not sufficient for concluding that a link will be positively established.

Likewise, the stronger the distinctive character of the earlier mark, whether inherent or acquired through use, the more likely it is that such a link will occur. Accordingly, insofar as the marks ability to identify the goods or services for which it is registered and, therefore, its distinctive character are all the stronger if that mark is unique, it is particularly relevant to ascertain whether the earlier mark is "unique" or "essentially unique".[420]

The Court also pointed out that the goods and services of the conflicting marks are directly relevant for the mechanics of association, especially inasmuch as they determine the kind of public to which the earlier mark is known. 5–222

In that regard, it recalled that the reputation of the earlier mark may extend to either the public at large or a more specialised public.[421]

Accordingly, the following situations can be envisaged[422]:

First, it is possible that the section of the public concerned by the goods or services of the earlier mark is completely distinct from the public targeted by the later mark, which means that the earlier mark may not be known to the customers of the later mark, despite its reputation. In such a case, the public targeted by each mark may never be confronted with the other so as to establish a link between the two. 5–223

Secondly, even if the relevant consumer circles are the same or overlap to some extent, those goods or services may be so dissimilar that the later

---

[418] *Intel*, para.38.
[419] Citing *Fitnessworld*, para.30.
[420] *Intel*, para.38.
[421] Citing *General Motors*, para.24.
[422] *Intel*, paras 48–53.

mark is unlikely to bring the earlier mark to the mind of the relevant public, if that sign is seen in an entirely different context.

Thirdly, the reputation of the earlier mark may have spilled-over beyond its natural consumer circles either to the general public or, at least, to the customers of the later mark. In such a case, an association cannot be excluded even if the respective sectors are in theory distinct.

Thus, the Court answered point (i) of the first question and the second question by holding that the existence of a link must be assessed globally and that the fact that the later mark calls the earlier reputed mark to mind is tantamount to the existence of such a link.

5–224   **(v) The assessment of detriment.** As regards the relationship between association and damage, the Court held that, just like the appraisal of a possible a link between the marks, the existence of detriment must be assessed globally, taking into account all factors relevant to the circumstances of the case.

Thus, the mere existence of such a link does not dispense the proprietor of the earlier trade mark from having to prove an actual and present injury to its mark, or a serious likelihood that such an injury will occur in the future. For the same reason, the circumstances referred to by the national Court are not necessarily sufficient to trigger the application of art.4(4)(a) of the Directive.

However, the Court noted also that the more immediately and strongly the earlier mark is brought to mind by the later sign, the greater the likelihood that detriment or unfair advantage will occur. Similarly, the stronger the earlier mark's distinctive character and reputation the easier it will be to accept that detriment has been caused to it.

5–225   As regards in particular dilution, it is not necessary for the earlier mark to be unique in order to establish such injury or a serious likelihood that it will occur in the future. A trade mark with a reputation necessarily has distinctive character, at the very least acquired through use; therefore, even if that mark is not unique, the use of a later identical or similar mark may still be such as to weaken its distinctive character. However, the more "unique" the earlier mark appears, the greater the likelihood that the use of a later identical or similar mark will be detrimental to its distinctive character.[423]

Finally, the Court held that a first use of an identical or similar mark may suffice, in some circumstances, to cause detriment or to give rise to a serious likelihood that such detriment will occur in the future.[424]

Moreover, considering that blurring is caused when the mark's ability to identify the goods or services for which it is registered is weakened because the use of the later mark leads to dispersion its identity and hold upon the public mind, the proof of dilution requires evidence of a change in the

---

[423] *Intel*, paras 72–74.
[424] *Intel*, para.75.

economic behaviour of the consumer consequent on the use of the later mark, or at least a serious likelihood that such a change will occur in the future.[425]

(e) Repercussions   5–226

The core issue in *Intel* is the approach it has taken as regards the evidential standard for proving detriment and, in particular, its statement as regards the need for a change in the "economic" behaviour of the consumer.

A number of questions arise in that connection:

First, is this standard applicable by analogy also in cases of unfair advantage, or does it only concern detriment, given that the public involved in either case is different[426]?

Secondly, does that change in fact mean that the consumer must appear less inclined to buy the designated goods in the future, or does it suffice if he is less capable of immediately recognising the mark than before? In other words, does the owner of the reputed mark have to prove tangible pecuniary damage in the form of loss of sales, or can he merely rely on a decline of the value inherent in the mark, however imperceptible? The latter surely seems to be more in line with the dilution doctrine which focuses on the "aura" of the mark, rather than its actual contribution to the selling of the products it distinguishes.   5–227

On the other hand, it is sufficiently clear that the distinction between proof of "actual" and "future" detriment does not follow from the difference in the nature of registration and infringement proceedings (compare the conditional wording "would be detrimental", in arts 8(5) CTMR and 4(4)(a) of the Directive, to the positive formulation "is detrimental" in arts 9(1)(c) and 5(2) respectively).

This is apparent from the statement of the Court that "when injury is foreseeable the proprietor of the earlier mark cannot be required to wait for it actually to occur"[427] and that "a first conflicting use may suffice, in some circumstances" to cause *actual* detriment or to give rise to a serious likelihood that such detriment will occur in the future.[428]   5–228

Moreover, if the notion of a "death by a thousand cuts" is to have any meaning, the likelihood of detriment cannot be required to be perceptible in economic terms before it becomes actionable. In that sense, *Intel* should not be read in an over-restrictive manner. Rather, the pivotal question seems to be whether the detriment can be regarded as foreseeable, in view of the overall circumstances of the case.

---

[425] *Intel*, para.76.
[426] See also in that regard the statement in para.78.
[427] *Intel*, para.38.
[428] *Intel*, para.75.

5-229   Another interesting issue is the one raised by the Advocate General in her concluding remarks[429] as regards the standard used by the Court of First Instance in the context of art.8(5) CTMR, namely that the proprietor "is not required to prove actual and present harm, but only to adduce prima facie evidence of a future risk which is not hypothetical".[430]

Is that formulation compatible with the standard set out in *Intel*, even though it does not specifically require a change in the economic behaviour of the consumer? At first sight, it would seem that requiring proof of a "serious likelihood" is not quite the same as establishing a risk which is "not merely hypothetical". In fact, the first formulation seems to be closer to the wording of the law, which clearly requires a probability rather than a remote possibility (in the sense that the detriment cannot "merely be excluded").

Moreover, the even less restrictive view taken by the Court of First Instance in certain cases[431] that "if the mark applied for does not, *at first sight*, appear capable of giving rise to one of the three types of risk covered by Article 8 (5) CTMR [...], the opposition must be rejected unless a non-hypothetical, future risk of detriment or unfair advantage can be established by other evidence" does not seem to be viable any longer. Inasmuch as the Court did not refer to any such exceptional circumstances where detriment would appear immediately obvious, the need to prove the injury claimed is a task that cannot be side-stepped.

It is also worth noting that even though so far the Court of First Instance has not upheld any opposition purely on the basis of blurring, it has nevertheless accepted the application of art.8(5) in a number of cases,[432] mainly involving unfair advantage, without actually analysing in detail the economic benefit gained by the infringing sign.

It is therefore interesting to see whether and to which extent the Court of First Instance will maintain its current practice also in the future, or whether it will move towards a more stringent approach in view of the Court's judgment in *Intel*.[433]

5-230   **(9)   Bellure—unfair advantage**

Bellure[434] was another reference for a preliminary ruling from the Court of Appeal of England and Wales (Civil Division), this time dealing, inter alia,

---

[429] See Point 85 of the Opinion of A.G. Sharpston.
[430] See, among others, *Citigroup v OHIM* (T-181/05), para.77 and the case law cited therein.
[431] See in particular *SIGLA v OHIM—Elleni Holding (VIPS)* (T-215/03) [2007] E.C.R. II-711, para.48.
[432] *Aktieselskabet af 21 november 2001 v OHIM* (TDK) (T-477/04); *Citigroup* (CITIBANK) (T-181/05); *Antartica Srl v OHIM* (NASDAQ) (T-47/06); *Mülhens v OHIM—Spa Monopole* (MINERAL SPA) (T-93/06); *L'Oreal v OHIM* (SPALINE) (T-21/07).
[433] In that connection, see also the discussion of the judgment in *Antartica Srl v OHIM (NASDAQ)* (C-320/01 P), below para.5-240.
[434] *L'Oréal SA, Lancôme parfums et beauté & Cie SNC, Laboratoire Garnier & Cie v Bellure NV, Malaika Investments Ltd, Starion International Ltd* (BELLURE).

with the concept of unfair advantage within the meaning of art.5(2) of the Directive.

(a)   The facts in the main proceedings and the question referred   **5–231**

The reference was made in the context of a dispute between L'Oréal SA, Lancôme parfums et beauté & Cie SNC and Laboratoire Garnier & Cie, against Bellure NV, Malaika Investments Ltd, and Starion International Ltd.

The claimants are members of the L'Oréal group, which produces and markets fine fragrances. In the United Kingdom, they are proprietors of a number of well-known trade marks for perfumes. Some of the trade marks consist of the commercial names of those products, while others consist of a representation of the perfume bottles or packaging together with the name of the fragrance concerned.

The defendants market in the UK imitations of fine fragrances bearing different commercial names but sold in bottles and packaging generally similar in appearance to those of the corresponding products of the claimants. They also make "comparison lists" available to their retailers, which indicate the fine fragrance to which the specific imitation corresponds by making reference to its trade mark.

The claimants brought proceedings before the High Court against the   **5–232**
defendants alleging infringement of their trade mark rights. They argued that the reproduction of their marks infringed s.10(1) of the Trade Marks Act (which essentially corresponds to art.5(1)(a) of the Directive, while the use of similar bottles and packaging was contrary to s.10(3) of the same Act (corresponding to art.5(2) of the Directive.

The High Court granted the application fully insofar as it was based on s.10(1) and partly inasmuch as it relied on s.10(3). The defendants appealed to the Court of Appeal, which decided to stay the proceedings and refer a number of questions to the Court for a preliminary ruling.

As regards the use of the comparison lists reproducing the word marks of the claimants, the referring Court was uncertain whether use in comparative advertising within the meaning of Directive 84/450 may be prevented under art.5(1)(a), or permitted under art.6(1)(b), of Directive 89/104.[435]

With regard to the use of packaging and bottles similar to those of the fragrances of the plaintiffs, the referring court sought clarification of the concept of "unfair advantage" within the meaning of art.5(2) of the Directive, in the following terms:

"(5) Where a trader uses a sign which is similar to a registered trade mark which has a reputation, and that sign is not confusingly similar to the trade mark, in such a way that:

---

[435] For more about the first to fourth questions in that reference see paras 10–065 and following.

(a) the essential function of the registered trade mark of providing a guarantee of origin is not impaired or put at risk;
(b) there is no tarnishing or blurring of the registered trade mark or its reputation or any risk of either of these;
(c) the trade mark owner's sales are not impaired; and
(d) the trade mark owner is not deprived of any of the reward for promotion, maintenance or enhancement of his trade mark;
(e) but the trader gets a commercial advantage from the use of his sign by reason of its similarity to the registered mark,

does that use amount to the taking of an 'unfair advantage' of the reputation of the registered mark within the meaning of Article 5(2) of the Directive?"

5–233 *(b) The Opinion of the Advocate General*

In the first place, A.G. Mengozzi noted that the referring court was taking the view that, to conclude that there is an unfair advantage where the use of the later mark is not liable to affect the origin function of the earlier mark, does not tarnish, degrade or blur its reputation, and does not have a negative impact on the owner's sales or investment, but still confers a commercial advantage on the third party, would effectively deprive the word "unfair" of any meaning.

Then, he recalled that, according to the case law, the protection conferred by art.5(2) also covers situations involving the use of a sign that is similar to the reputed mark for goods that are identical or similar and is not designed to combat only the likelihood of confusion on the part of the public. Rather, it presupposes that the similarity between the well-known mark and the sign enables the public to make a connection between them, in a way that is detrimental to the earlier mark or confers benefit of the later sign. Those conditions, however, are independent from each other, in the sense that each of either of them may justify of itself the corresponding type of protection.

Thus, A.G. Mengozzi concluded that it could not be ruled out on the basis of the circumstances referred to by the national court that the advantage gained from the use of a sign that is similar to another person's well-known mark may be classified as unfair, within the meaning of art.5(2) of the Directive.[436]

5–234 Next, the Advocate General turned to the case law of the Court of First Instance on the interpretation of art.8(5) CTMR[437] that the taking of unfair advantage relates to the risk that the image of the mark with a reputation or the characteristics which it projects are transferred to the goods covered by

---

[436] Point 97 of the Opinion of A.G. Mengozzi.
[437] *SIGLA v OHIM—Elleni Holding (VIPS)* (T-215/03) [2007] E.C.R. II-711, paras 40–42; *Japan Tobacco v OHIM—Torrefacçao Camelo (CAMELO)* (T-128/06), paras 46 and 65; and *Mülhens v OHIM—Spa Monopole (MINERAL SPA)* (T-93/06), paras 38–40.

the mark applied for, with the result that the marketing of those goods is made easier by that association, and that there is such advantage also where the consumer, without necessarily confusing the commercial origin of the respective products, is attracted by the mark applied for and buys the products covered by it on the ground that they bear a mark which is identical or similar to a mark with a reputation.

The Advocate General observed though that those two situations were not equivalent: it is one thing to say that the effect of the reputed mark's image on the products identified by the later mark is that the marketing of those goods is made easier, and quite another, that it is solely as a result of that effect that the consumer is induced to buy such products in preference to others. He found the latter view to be too restrictive, since it practically means that a reputed mark is protected against free-riding only where it can be demonstrated that consumers would not buy the products in question if they didn't bear the specific sign.[438]

Accordingly, he concurred with the view taken by A.G. Sharpston in *Intel* that what must actually be established is some sort of boost given to the later sign by its link with the reputed mark.[439] To that effect, it should be sufficient to demonstrate that the later sign carries a particular attraction for the consumer due to its association with the positive qualities projected by the reputation of the earlier mark in such a way as to induce him to buy the products bearing that sign.

But is this sufficient for concluding that the advantage is unfair?

5–235

To solve that riddle, the Advocate General had recourse to the additional condition in the relevant provisions that protection is not triggered if the defendant can show "due cause" justifying the advantage. From the very juxtaposition of this redeeming condition to the need for the advantage to be unfair, he inferred that where due cause cannot be shown, such an advantage must be deemed to be unfair. In other words, he considered that where the only apparent purpose of using a sign that is similar a well-known mark is to exploit its reputation or particular image, the advantage derived by that use is presumed to be unfair; however, that presumption may be rebutted by demonstrating that there is a due cause, capable of justifying such use.[440]

(c) The judgment of the Court

5–236

As a preliminary point the Court noted that it had no jurisdiction to review the legal and factual context of the case, which fell to be determined by the referring court,[441] even if "it may appear prima facie unlikely" that use by a third party of a sign similar to a trade mark, in order to market goods which

---

[438] Point 101 of the Opinion of A.G. Mengozzi.
[439] Point 62 of her opinion in *Intel*.
[440] Points 108–109 of the Opinion of A.G. Mengozzi.
[441] *Neri* (C-153/02) paras 34 and 35; and *ASM Brescia* (C-347/06), para.28.

imitate those for which that mark is registered, will benefit of its repute without concomitantly causing harm to the image or the marketing of the goods bearing that mark.

It also recalled, referring to *Gofkid* and *Fitnessworld*, that art.5(2) of the Directive also applies in relation to goods and services identical with or similar to those in respect of which the earlier mark is registered[442] and that the degree of similarity between the signs need not be such as to cause a likelihood of confusion on the part of the public, being generally sufficient that such similarity causes the public to establish a link between the sign and the mark.[443]

Then, the Court proceeded to analyse the notions of "detriment to repute" and "unfair advantage", which had not formed part of the dispute in *Intel*.

5–237 It defined the former as the "tarnishment" or "degradation" of the earlier mark, caused when the goods or services of the later sign are perceived by the public in such a way that the earlier mark's power of attraction is reduced. It also pointed out that such detriment may arise in particular from the fact that the goods or services of the later mark possess a characteristic or quality which is liable to have a negative impact on the image of the reputed mark.[444]

With regard to the concept of "unfair advantage", also referred to as "parasitism" or "free-riding", it held that it relates to the advantage taken by a third party as a result of the use of an identical or similar sign and that it covers, in particular, cases where there is clear exploitation on the coat-tails of the reputed mark, by reason of a transfer of the image embedded in that mark, or of the characteristics which it projects, to the goods designated by the later sign.[445]

As regards, next, the appreciation of unfair advantage, the Court referred to the principles laid down in *Intel* and, in particular, to the need for an overall assessment of all the relevant factors.[446] It added, moreover, that although advantage may generally be taken even if the use of the later sign is not detrimental, the fact that there is a likelihood of dilution or tarnishment is a factor that should also be taken into account for the purposes of that global assessment.

5–238 Turning to the facts of the case, it noted that the referring court had established that the defendants used a similar product get-up in order to market "downmarket" imitations of the luxury fragrances sold by the claimants and that the public was expected to establish a link between the respective packagings likely to confer a commercial advantage on the defendants; moreover, the similarity between the products and their packaging was created intentionally, with the aim of facilitating the marketing of the defendants' imitations.

---

[442] *Gofkid*, para.30.
[443] *Fitnessworld*, paras 29 and 31.
[444] *Bellure*, para.40.
[445] *Bellure*, para.41.
[446] *Intel*, paras 67–69.

8. MARKS WITH A REPUTATION

On the basis of those findings, it stressed that the fact that the marketing strategies of the defendants were intended to take advantage, for promotional purposes, of the repute of the earlier marks should be given particular weight in assessing whether that advantage was unfair.[447]

Finally, it observed that where a third party attempts to benefit from the power of attraction, the reputation or the prestige of the earlier mark, and to exploit, without paying any financial compensation and without making any efforts of his own, the marketing expenditure of the proprietor of that mark, the advantage resulting from such use must be considered to have been unfairly taken.[448]

(d) Applying Gofkid to get-up imitation   5–239

Apart from giving a detailed definition of the concept of unfair advantage, the judgment in *Bellure* is also significant because it provides a good example of how the provisions on reputed marks can be used in conflicts involving identical or similar goods.

Indeed, in cases of get-up imitation the principles developed by the Court in *Gofkid*[449] and *Fitnessworld*[450] seem to find their natural field of application, since, most of the time, the use of a different brand name on a similar product packaging will considerably reduce, if not altogether exclude, the likelihood of confusion. *Bellure*, however, shows that trade mark owners can still have recourse to the provisions on reputed marks, as an alternative means of redress against the slavish copying of their product get-up.

On the other hand, the fact that in the order for reference the commercial advantage taken by the defendants was taken for granted deprived the Court of the opportunity to address in more detail the standard of proof applicable in cases of unfair advantage, as it did in *Intel* with regard to detriment.

Notwithstanding, the statement that an intentional imitation aimed at dispensing the defendant from the need to independently promote its products is a strong presumption of unfair advantage is particularly useful, insofar as it actually suggests that the economic benefit the infringer hopes to derive from the copying is significant enough to worth the attempt and not just "hypothetical".

(10) Nasdaq—putting Intel into perspective?   5–240

Nasdaq[451] concerned an appeal from a judgment of the Court of First Instance in a dispute that arose in the context of an opposition brought by

---

[447] *Bellure*, para.48.
[448] *Bellure*, para.49.
[449] *Davidoff & Cie SA and Zino Davidoff SA* (C-292/00) [2003] E.C.R. I-389.
[450] *Adidas-Salomon AG and Adidas Benelux BV* (C-408/01) [2003] E.C.R. I-12537.
[451] *Antartica Srl v OHIM* (NASDAQ) (C-320/07 P).

The Nasdaq Stock Market, Inc ("Nasdaq Stock Market") against Antartica Srl ("Antarctica") under art.8(5) CTMR.

Antartica had sought to register as Community Trade Mark a figurative sign essentially consisting of the stylised word "nasdaq" for a range of goods in Classes 9, 12, 14, 25 and 28 of the Nice Classification.

Nasdaq Stock Market opposed the application based on its earlier Community word mark "NASDAQ", on the grounds that the use of the mark applied without due cause would take unfair advantage of the distinctive character and repute its earlier mark had acquired in respect of, inter alia, stock exchange price quotation and financial services.

5-241 The Opposition Division of OHIM had rejected the opposition, on the grounds that the reputation of the earlier mark had not been properly substantiated. The Office's Boards of Appeal annulled the decision of the Opposition Division on the grounds that both reputation and unfair advantage had been proved.

Antartica brought an application for the annulment of that decision before the Court of First Instance, which held that art.8(5) was indeed applicable to the case and dismissed the action as unfounded.

Antarctica appealed to the Court of Justice arguing, first, that the Court of First Instance had defined the relevant public wrongly and, secondly, that it had misapplied the factors to be taken into account when assessing the existence of unfair advantage.

5-242 (a) *The judgment of the Court of First Instance*[452]

It is useful to take a look at the assessment of unfair advantage made by the Court of First Instance and compare it to the principles laid down in *Intel* as regards proof of detriment, as both A.G.s Sharpston and Mengozzi also did in *Intel*[453] and *Bellure*[454] respectively.

First, the Court of First Instance held that the reputation of the earlier mark had been established in respect of financial and stock exchange price quotation services not only among the professional public, but also with regard to an important sub-section of the general public interested in the financial indices on account of their current or future investments.[455] That finding was further supported by the inherently very distinctive nature of the earlier mark, its omnipresence not only in specialist publications but also in the general press, as well as the interest shown by a large part of the general public in developments in the financial markets.[456]

Then, the Court recalled that the proprietor of the earlier mark is not required to demonstrate actual and present harm to his mark, but merely

---

[452] Antartica Srl/OHIM (NASDAQ) (T-47/06).
[453] See Point 85 of the Opinion of A.G. Sharpston in *Intel*.
[454] See Points 99–100 of the Opinion of A.G. Mengozzi in *Bellure*.
[455] Judgment of the Court of First Instance para.51.
[456] Judgment of the Court of First Instance para.58.

adduce prima facie evidence of a future risk, which is not hypothetical, of either unfair advantage or detriment. Interestingly enough, it added that such a conclusion may be established, in particular, on the basis of "logical deductions" resulting from an analysis of the probabilities following from the usual practices in the relevant commercial sector, as well as all the other circumstances relevant to the case.[457]

Then, the Court held that it could be derived from the minutes of the ordinary meeting of Antartica's shareholders that approved the adoption of the sign at issue as its brand name, first, that its shareholders were aware that the term "nasdaq" designated "the American online stock market", and secondly that the word had been chosen because it was regarded as denoting Antartica's main activity, which consisted in the design, manufacture and sale of high-tech materials and sports equipment. Therefore, it considered that the high-tech stocks listed on the Nasdaq Stock Market imbued the earlier mark with a certain image of modernity, which was transferrable to the high-tech composite materials marketed by Antartica.[458]

5-243

Accordingly, the Court of First Instance ruled that there was enough prima facie evidence to establish the existence of a future risk, which was not hypothetical and that Antartica had not proved the existence of a due cause by arguing that the choice of its mark was due to the fact that it constituted an acronym for the expression "Nuovi Articoli Sportivi Di Alta Qualità" (New High Quality Sporting Articles).

(b) Findings of the Court

5-244

As regards the part of the plea dealing with the definition of the relevant public, the Court referred to its findings in *Intel* that the public will vary according to the type of injury alleged each time and that with regard to unfair advantage the public to be taken into consideration consisted of the customers of the goods or services designated by the later mark.[459]

Thus, it concluded that insofar as the Court of First Instance had held that the reputation of the earlier mark reaches further than the professional public specialising in financial information, it had "implicitly, but clearly" included in its examination the average customer of the goods for which the later mark had been applied for.[460]

Finally, the Court dismissed Antartica's arguments as to the existence of unfair advantage by observing that the findings of the Court of First Instance concerned an assessment of a factual nature that was not subject to the Court's review.[461]

---

[457] Judgment of the Court of First Instance para.54.
[458] Judgment of the Court of First Instance para.60.
[459] *Intel*, para.60.
[460] *Nasdaq*, paras 49–50.
[461] *Nasdaq*, para.53.

5-245 *(c) Applying Intel in practice*

Nasdaq is particularly interesting as regards the degree of freedom it allowed to the Court of First Instance in assessing whether detriment or unfair advantage are likely to occur.

It is worth noting that the Court of First Instance implied the existence of a detrimental link by reference to circumstantial evidence rather than hard facts.

First, its findings in relation to reputation were mostly based on indirect indications suggesting a spill-over beyond the financial sector; secondly, its inferences as to the transferability of Nasdaq's image to the clothing market did not extend to the question whether consumers would actually consider the garments bearing the later sign more attractive, or whether their economic behaviour would be affected, to use the terminology in *Intel*.

5-246 That is not to say that its analysis is not convincing. On the contrary, even if the reference to the Nasdaq stock exchange is not seen as directly indicating clothing made of high-tech materials, its association with the defendant's sign certainly makes it easier to remember and recognise; in that sense, even if the later mark cannot be regarded as benefiting from Nasdaq's image or repute, it surely exploits its attractive powers, that is, its distinctiveness.

Notwithstanding, the fact remains that the Court of First Instance relied more on the (fully proved) fact that the imitation was intentional and less on its economic repercussions. In that sense, its findings are closer to *Bellure* than to *Intel*.

However, the Court of Justice did not take issue with that assessment. Although all it said was that the task of assessing the facts fell on the Court of First Instance, it still agreed, at least implicitly, with the legal framework within which that assessment was made, including the statement that the overall evaluation of detriment may be based on "logical deductions resulting from probabilities" instead of direct proof.

If the Court maintains that approach also in future cases, it may finally become apparent that, after all, the evidential standard proposed in *Intel* was not set as high as it seems at first sight.

9. CONCLUSION

5-247 This chapter has explored the three layers of trade mark conflicts; the first two are based on confusion, the third on reputation.

In the first case where there is total identity there is at least a presumption of confusion. What the Court needs to settle is whether this presumption can be rebutted.

In the case of similarity the Court founded its case law on the concept of confusion. The standard appears to be rigorous: confusion must be genuine and properly substantiated. At the same time the Court has highlighted the link between the function of a trade mark, that continues to serve as the

9. CONCLUSION

justification behind protection, with the interests of the trade mark proprietor. Conceptually that is a logical consequence, however in terms of semantics it is a telling detail that the trade mark proprietor and appears to be a new starting point in the reasoning of the Court. This will be explored further in Ch.6.

The test for establishing confusion is a multifactor open-ended test, with trade mark and product similarity being cumulative conditions. The Court has also established that stronger marks, either because they are inherently distinctive or because they have grown in terms of distinctiveness through use, will inevitable enjoy a wider scope of protection; without this meaning that product similarity will become redundant in the case of very strong trade marks. A positive finding on likelihood of confusion will always be required. 5–248

To assess distinctiveness and reputation the Court has suggested a number of factors that must be considered and insisted that there is no need to set specific targets in terms of consumer recognition that a highly distinctive trade mark or a trade mark with a reputation must reach. What needs to be established however is that the trade mark has become distinctive or gained reputation in respect of the particular product rather than as a name in abstract.

What the Court is still uncertain about is whether the concept of confusion encompasses confusion away from the point of sale; would, for example, post-sale confusion suffice when as a result the behaviour of the consumer is affected at the point of sale, subsequent to and as a result of the post-sale confusion?

The partial tests for determining trade mark and product similarity comprise a broad number of questions with the Court underlining that all the facts of each individual case must be taken into account. Indeed, the trade mark similarity test is applied in respect of all three layers of protection. 5–249

In terms of marks with a reputation note that the Court has looked for the purpose of the provision in order to interpret it and gone against a strict literal interpretation. This area of trade mark law, though, remains largely uncharted with the Court giving contradictory signs.

The angle that all these questions are examined from is that of the average consumer of the relevant product.

CHAPTER 6

SCOPE OF PROTECTION, LIMITATIONS AND ENFORCEMENT

1. Introduction	6–001
2. The Provisions of the Directive and the Regulation	6–002
(1) The Trade Marks Directive	6–002
(2) The Community Trade Mark Regulation	6–004
3. Identical Signs and Goods or Services—The Scope of Protection	6–008
(1) Hölterhoff—limiting the scope of protection	6–009
(2) Arsenal—a counterbalancing exercise	6–014
(3) Adam Opel—challenging the limits of protection	6–024
(4) Marca II—availability and scope of protection	6–040
(5) Smirnoff—use by intermediaries	6–051
(6) Bellure—broadening the scope of protection	6–056
(7) Google—taking a step back—the relevance of context	6–066
4. The Conflict between Trade Marks and Trade Names	6–080
(1) Robelco—trade marks and trade names	6–080
(2) Céline—trade names performing a distinguishing function	6–084
5. Limitations to Trade Mark Rights	6–094
(1) BMW—setting the principles	6–094
(2) Gerolsteiner Brunnen—the scope of article 6(1)(b)	6–116
(3) Gillette—indicating compatibility	6–125
(4) Adam Opel	6–139
6. Enforcing the Community Trade Mark	6–141
(1) Nokia—adequate enforcement	6–141
(2) Davidoff III—seizure of infringing goods	6–151
7. Conclusion	6–157

1. INTRODUCTION

This chapter explores the scope of protection and considers trade mark conflicts from the perspective of trade mark infringement and enforcement. **6–001**

It also considers conflicts between trade mark and other types of rights over commercial indicia. For the relationship and conflicts between trade marks and geographical indications the reader should also consider Ch.10.

The concepts of use, confusion, dilution and so on and the tests for determining infringement are similar to those developed in Ch.5. Here though the conflicts and the comparisons courts have to make become more concrete. The context and the background of each case become even more relevant.

This chapter also examines the balancing exercise attempted by the Court between the scope of essentially exclusionary rights and the limitations that are necessary for a competitive market to function.

Finally, issues specific to the enforcement of the Community Trade Mark are considered at the end of this chapter.

2. THE PROVISIONS OF THE DIRECTIVE AND THE REGULATION

6–002 **(1) The Trade Marks Directive**

(a) Article 5—rights conferred by a trade mark

1. The registered trade mark shall confer on the proprietor exclusive rights therein. The proprietor shall be entitled to prevent all third parties not having his consent from using in the course of trade:

   a. any sign which is identical with the trade mark in relation to goods or services which are identical with those for which the trade mark is registered;

   b. any sign where, because of its identity with, or similarity to, the trade mark and the identity or similarity of the goods or services covered by the trade mark and the sign, there exists a likelihood of confusion on the part of the public, which includes the likelihood of association between the sign and the trade mark.

2. Any Member State may also provide that the proprietor shall be entitled to prevent all third parties not having his consent from using in the course of trade any sign which is identical with, or similar to, the trade mark in relation to goods or services which are not similar to those for which the trade mark is registered, where the latter has a reputation in the Member State and where use of that sign without due cause takes unfair advantage of, or is detrimental to, the distinctive character or the repute of the trade mark.

3. The following, inter alia, may be prohibited under paras 1 and 2:

   a. affixing the sign to the goods or to the packaging thereof;

   b. offering the goods, or putting them on the market or stocking them for these purposes under that sign, or offering or supplying services thereunder;

2. THE PROVISIONS OF THE DIRECTIVE AND THE REGULATION

    c. importing or exporting the goods under the sign;

    d. using the sign on business papers and in advertising.

4. Where, under the law of the Member State, the use of a sign under the conditions referred to in 1(b) or 2 could not be prohibited before the date on which the provisions necessary to comply with this Directive entered into force in the Member State concerned, the rights conferred by the trade mark may not be relied on to prevent the continued use of the sign.

5. Paragraphs 1 to 4 shall not affect provisions in any Member State relating to the protection against the use of a sign other than for the purposes of distinguishing goods or services, where use of that sign without due cause takes unfair advantage of, or is detrimental to, the distinctive character or the repute of the trade mark.

(b) *Article 6—limitation of the effects of a trade mark*   6–003

1. The trade mark shall not entitle the proprietor to prohibit a third party from using, in the course of trade,

    a. his own name or address;

    b. indications concerning the kind, quality, quantity, intended purpose, value, geographical origin, the time of production of goods or of rendering of the service, or other characteristics of goods or services;

    c. the trade mark where it is necessary to indicate the intended purpose of a product or service, in particular as accessories or spare parts; provided he uses them in accordance with honest practices in industrial or commercial matters.

2. The trade mark shall not entitle the proprietor to prohibit a third party from using, in the course of trade, an earlier right which only applies in a particular locality if that right is recognised by the laws of the Member State in question and within the limits of the territory in which it is recognised.

(2) The Community Trade Mark Regulation

(a) *Article 9—rights conferred by a Community Trade Mark*   6–004

1. A Community trade mark shall confer on the proprietor exclusive rights therein. The proprietor shall be entitled to prevent all third parties not having his consent from using in the course of trade:

(a) any sign which is identical with the Community trade mark in relation to goods or services which are identical with those for which the Community trade mark is registered;

(b) any sign where, because of its identity with or similarity to the Community trade mark and the identity or similarity of the goods or services covered by the Community trade mark and the sign, there exists a likelihood of confusion on the part of the public; the likelihood of confusion includes the likelihood of association between the sign and the trade mark;

(c) any sign which is identical with or similar to the Community trade mark in relation to goods or services which are not similar to those for which the Community trade mark is registered, where the latter has a reputation in the Community and where use of that sign without due cause takes unfair advantage of, or is detrimental to, the distinctive character or the repute of the Community trade mark.

2. The following, inter alia, may be prohibited under para.1:

(a) affixing the sign to the goods or to the packaging thereof;

(b) offering the goods, putting them on the market or stocking them for these purposes under that sign, or offering or supplying services thereunder;

(c) importing or exporting the goods under that sign;

(d) using the sign on business papers and in advertising.

3. The rights conferred by a Community trade mark shall prevail against third parties from the date of publication of registration of the trade mark. Reasonable compensation may, however, be claimed in respect of matters arising after the date of publication of a Community trade mark application, which matters would, after publication of the registration of the trade mark, be prohibited by virtue of that publication. The court seized of the case may not decide upon the merits of the case until the registration has been published.

6–005 *(b) Article 10—reproduction of Community Trade Marks in dictionaries*

If the reproduction of a Community trade mark in a dictionary, encyclopaedia or similar reference work gives the impression that it constitutes the generic name of the goods or services for which the trade mark is registered, the publisher of the work shall, at the request of the proprietor of the Community trade mark, ensure that the reproduction of the trade mark at the latest in the next edition of the publication is accompanied by an indication that it is a registered trade mark.

3. IDENTICAL SIGNS AND GOODS OR SERVICES

(c) Article 11—*prohibition on the use of a Community Trade Mark registered in the name of an agent or representative*   6-006

Where a Community trade mark is registered in the name of the agent or representative of a person who is the proprietor of that trade mark, without the proprietor's authorisation, the latter shall be entitled to oppose the use of his mark by his agent or representative if he has not authorised such use, unless the agent or representative justifies his action.

(d) Article 12—*limitation of the effects of a Community Trade Mark*   6-007

A Community trade mark shall not entitle the proprietor to prohibit a third party from using in the course of trade:

(a) his own name or address;

(b) indications concerning the kind, quality, quantity, intended purpose, value, geographical origin, the time of production of the goods or of rendering of the service, or other characteristics of the goods or service;

(c) the trade mark where it is necessary to indicate the intended purpose of a product or service, in particular as accessories or spare parts, provided he uses them in accordance with honest practices in industrial or commercial matters.

3. IDENTICAL SIGNS AND GOODS OR SERVICES—THE SCOPE OF PROTECTION

The scope of trade mark protection in the case of identical signs and identical goods or services was considered by the Court in *Hölterhoff*[1] and *Arsenal*.[2] The Court applied analogous principles in both cases. However their outcomes appear contradictory, perhaps because although both cases were characterised by their facts the Court of Justice could only look at the snippets referred to it by the national courts.   6-008

(1) Hölterhoff—limiting the scope of protection   6-009

In *Hölterhoff* Freiesleben was the proprietor of two trade marks in Germany—Spirit Sun and Context Cut—covering respectively diamonds and precious stones for further processing as jewellery and precious stones

---

[1] *Michael Hölterhoff v Ulrich Freiesleben* (C-2/00) [2002] E.C.R. I-4187.
[2] *Arsenal Football Club Plc* (C-206/01) [2002] E.C.R. I-10273.

for further processing as jewellery. In reality both signs were weak trade marks because in addition to the information as to product origin they conveyed information regarding product characteristics. The products were characterised by distinctive cuts, protected by patents; the Spirit Sun trade mark referred to a round cut with facets radiating from the centre and the Context Cut trade mark to a square cut with a tapering diagonal cross. This weakness was not an issue before the referring German court and could not become one before the Court of Justice.

Hölterhoff, a dealer in precious stones, offered for sale to a jeweller stones that he described by using the names Spirit Sun and Context Cut. Indeed the jeweller ordered two stones in the Spirit Sun cut. However, on the sales invoice and the delivery note the stones were described as rhodolites; their packaging and all related documentation made no reference to the Spirit Sun and the Context Cut trade marks.

Freiesleben started trade mark infringement proceedings. The case reached the Oberlandesgericht Düsseldorf on appeal that referred to the Court of Justice the following question:

"Does an infringement of a trade mark in the sense contemplated in Article 5(1)(a) and (b) of Directive 89/104/EEC occur where the defendant reveals the origin of goods which he has produced himself and uses the sign in respect of which the plaintiff enjoys protection solely to denote the particular characteristics of the goods he is offering for sale so that there can be no question of the trade mark used being perceived in trade as a sign indicative of the firm of origin?"[3]

6-010 Note that the German court had established that Hölterhoff had used the trade marks in order to describe the cut of the stones. There was no question regarding the source of the stones; the source was Hölterhoff. Also, there was no suggestion of a link between the product and Freiesleben.

According to the court in Germany there were two views on the effect of use of a sign that is identical to a registered trade mark. Some argued that it would constitute infringement only where the sign is used as a means of distinction. Others argued that any use in trade should suffice.

France and the United Kingdom intervened from diametrically opposed positions. The French Government argued that the list of uses in art.6 should be deemed to be exhaustive and that the use described by the German court involved use of an identical sign on identical products, rather than use of words that were necessary to describe a particular cut. The UK Government supported that the factual scenario typified art.6(1)(b). A competitor indicates that its goods have the same characteristics as those of the trade mark proprietor making it clear that its goods do not originate from the trade mark proprietor.

---

[3] Reproduced in para.11 of the judgment.

3. IDENTICAL SIGNS AND GOODS OR SERVICES

To exemplify the fluidity of the situation the Commission initially supported that it should be possible for a trade mark proprietor to prohibit any use of an infringing sign under art.5, unless art.6 becomes applicable. But, it changed its position at the hearing of the case, supporting that art.5(1) conferred an entitlement to prevent use of a sign as a trade origin indicator; art.6(1) simply elucidated the limitation of art.5(1). Would registration of a question mark for magazines allow the proprietor to stop other publishers asking questions on their first pages? A provocative question asked by way of example by the Commission, attempting to justify its radical change of mind.

(a) The Opinion of the Advocate General   6–011

Advocate General Jacobs viewed the question from a wider perspective taking into account art.5(1)(a) within the scheme of art.5 but also the limitations to its application introduced by art.6(1).

He linked the negative exclusionary rights expressed in art.5(1) with the positive rights arising from ownership: "[a] trader registers or acquires a trade mark primarily not in order to prevent others from using it but in order to use it himself".[4] Since the two aspects were inseparably linked the exclusive aspect covered use by other parties of the protected trade mark to identify their goods or services, negating the essential function of a trade mark.

He combined art.5(5) with *BMW*[5] to support that only use for the purposes of distinguishing goods or services falls under art.5(1) and (2). Turning to the actual case he repeated the factual findings of the German court and noted that, although the list was not exhaustive, the contested use was not included in the list of art.5(3). "Use of that kind is ... simply too far removed from the essential function of a trade mark to entitle a trade mark proprietor to prevent it under Article 5(1)."[6]

Concluding his analysis on art.5(1) he stressed that other factual circumstances—attaching the sign to the goods for example, like the factual scenario of Arsenal[7]—could open a different approach, making it clear that he did not wish to express a broader than necessary view.

(i) The influence of the Comparative Advertising Directive. His   6–012
analysis of art.6(1) was based on *BMW*.[8] It is worth referring though to his

---

[4] Point 34 of the Opinion of A.G. Jacobs.
[5] *Bayerische Motorenwerke AG and BMW Nederland BV v Deenik* (C-63/97) [1999] E.C.R. I-905; see para.6–094, below.
[6] *Hölterhoff*, para.39.
[7] *Arsenal Football Club Plc* (C-206/01) [2002] E.C.R. I-10273.
[8] See the Opinion of the A.G. in *Bayerische Motorenwerke AG and BMW Nederland BV* (C-63/97) [1999] E.C.R. I-905.

parallel analysis based on the Advertising Directive.[9] The reference to the Trade Marks Directive in the preamble to the Advertising Directive facilitated the development of his thesis. Recitals 13–15 stated that the two would coexist and that comparative advertising condoned by the Advertising Directive would not constitute a breach of the exclusive trade mark rights established by the Trade Marks Directive.

Under art.2(2)(a) of the Advertising Directive comparative advertising is any advertising which explicitly or by implication identifies a competitor or goods or services offered by a competitor. This, indeed, was what Mr Hölterhoff was doing; he was entitled to do so, provided his actions did not fall under art.3a of the Advertising Directive in the same way that they should not fall under the proviso in art.6(1) of the Trade Marks Directive.

He underlined that Directive 97/55 had not amended the Trade Marks Directive, inferring that the latter must have permitted such comparative advertising unless the two directives were incompatible. It would be absurd for a legislator to adopt two directives with contradictory provisions.

6–013 *(b) The judgment of the Court*

The analysis of the Court was very much linked with the facts. Seeking the substance of the referred question it stated that it sought "to ascertain whether, pursuant to Article 5(1) of the Directive, the proprietor of the trade mark may prevent a third party from using the trade mark in a factual situation such as that which the national court describes in detail".[10]

The answer to the question was also based on the facts:

"In that regard, it is sufficient to state that, in a situation such as that described by the national court, the use of the trade mark does not infringe any of the interests which art.5(1) is intended to protect. Those interests are not affected by a situation in which:

— the third party refers to the trade mark in the course of commercial negotiations with a potential customer, who is a professional jeweller,
— the reference is made for purely descriptive purposes, namely in order to reveal the characteristics of the product offered for sale to the potential customer, who is familiar with the characteristics of the products covered by the trade mark concerned,
— the reference to the trade mark cannot be interpreted by the potential customer as indicating the origin of the product."[11]

---

[9] Directive 84/450 relating to the approximation of the laws, regulations and administrative provisions of the Member States concerning misleading advertising [1984] OJ L250/17, as amended by Directive 97/55 amending Directive 84/450 concerning misleading advertising so as to include comparative advertising [1997] OJ L290/18: see the discussion in Ch.9 below.
[10] *Hölterhoff*, para.13.
[11] *Hölterhoff*, para.16.

3. IDENTICAL SIGNS AND GOODS OR SERVICES

The Court concluded that it was not necessary to consider further what constitutes use of a trade mark under art.5(1)(a) and (b) and that "where a third party, in the course of commercial negotiations, reveals the origin of goods which he has produced himself and uses the sign in question solely to denote the particular characteristics of the goods he is offering for sale so that there can be no question of the trade mark used being perceived as a sign indicative of the undertaking of origin".[12]

(2) Arsenal—a counterbalancing exercise 6–014

In parallel with *Hölterhoff* the Court considered the same issue in *Arsenal*.[13]

Arsenal involved the sale by Reed of unofficial football merchandise products. At the point of sale a sign informed prospective customers about their unauthorised nature:

> "The word or logo(s) on the goods offered for sale, are used solely to adorn the product and does not imply or indicate any affiliation or relationship with the manufacturers or distributors of any other product, only goods with official Arsenal merchandise tags are official Arsenal merchandise."

Arsenal had registered the relevant insignia as trade marks for clothing; it claimed passing off and registered trade mark infringement.

The passing off claim failed because there was insufficient evidence regarding deception and damage. Looking at the trade mark infringement claim Laddie J. linked the absence of evidence of confusion with the function of the unauthorised signs: there was no evidence of confusion because the signs did not indicate trade origin; they were badges of support, loyalty, and affiliation rather than badges of origin.

Accordingly he sought clarifications from the Court of Justice as to: (i) whether use that does not indicate trade origin, and at the same time does not fall within the scope of art.6(1) of the Directive, constitutes an infringement; and (ii) whether use that could be perceived as a badge of support, loyalty or affiliation constitutes use indicating trade origin.[14]

(a) The Opinion of the Advocate General 6–015

The analysis of art.5 by A.G. Ruiz-Jarabo Colomer focused on two points: first the uses that fell under art.5(1); and secondly the protectable interests of the registered proprietor:

---

[12] *Hölterhoff*, para.17.
[13] *Arsenal Football Club Plc* (C-206/01) [2002] E.C.R. 1-10273.
[14] *Arsenal Football Club Plc* [2001] R.P.C. 46.

SCOPE OF PROTECTION, LIMITATIONS AND ENFORCEMENT

"[A]ccording to Article 5(1) and (2), the proprietor of a trade mark may not prevent any use of a sign, but only uses whose purpose is to distinguish the goods or services to which it relates from those of other undertakings. Otherwise, Article 5(5) would have no raison d'être.[15] In other words, Article 5(1) protects the accuracy of the information which the registered sign provides on the goods or services which it represents and, thus, their identification[16] ... the proprietor may object to the use by a third party of his trade mark as such."[17]

6–016 **(i) The concept of use.** Noting that the Court had refrained from providing a definition in *Hölterhoff*,[18] the Advocate General elaborated on the concept of use and stated that use leading to misleading indications as to origin, provenance, quality, or reputation fell within the scope of art.5(1) and (2). Insisting strictly on origin, he claimed, would be a "simplistic reductionism".[19] After all, consumers are often unaware of who is the actual producer; it is enough that the product carries a trade mark that conveys an autonomous message. Note that at the hearing the Commission in order to resolve the conceptual difficulties surrounding use supported that to the extent that trade mark use was relevant in the case of identity it should be construed as referring to uses which serve to distinguish products rather than to indicate their origin and uses which affect the interests of the proprietor, for example tarnishing the reputation surrounding the product.

What is interesting however is that the Advocate General also provided a defence: "anyone who uses another's trade mark may claim in defence to the proprietor's objection that his use of it does not indicate the origin of the goods or of the services or give rise to confusion over their quality and reputation".[20] So, protection should not be automatic. On the same theme he repeated that there is a presumption of likelihood of confusion in the case of identity; but that presumption may be rebutted, "there is a possibility, however remote it may be, that in a specific case use of a sign identical with another registered as a trade mark may not be prevented by the proprietor on the basis of Article 5(1)(a)".[21] In cases of identity between signs and products there is a "presumption iuris tantum that the use by a third party of the trade mark is use thereof as such".[22]

Providing guidelines on the uses described by the High Court—that had to determine according to the evidence whether they were in or outside trade—first he identified uses that were unrelated to the protectable

---

[15] Point 38 of the Opinion of A.G. Ruiz-Jarabo Colomer.
[16] Point 39 of the Opinion of A.G. Ruiz-Jarabo Colomer.
[17] Point 40 of the Opinion of A.G. Ruiz-Jarabo Colomer.
[18] *Michael Hölterhoff v Ulrich Freiesleben* (C-2/00) [2002] E.C.R. I-4187.
[19] Point 46 of the Opinion of A.G. Ruiz-Jarabo Colomer.
[20] Point 50 of the Opinion of A.G. Ruiz-Jarabo Colomer.
[21] Point 52 of the Opinion of A.G. Ruiz-Jarabo Colomer.
[22] Point 88 of the Opinion of A.G. Ruiz-Jarabo Colomer.

3. IDENTICAL SIGNS AND GOODS OR SERVICES

functions of a trade mark. Trade mark rights did not cover use "outside the course of trade, that is, outside any commercial activity involving the production and supply of goods and services on the market".[23]

Then, he attempted to define use in trade from a positive perspective. Trade according to the Advocate General was narrower than economic activity of some sort: "The use which the proprietor of the trade mark may prevent is not any that might constitute a material advantage for the user, or even a use which is capable of being expressed in economic terms, but only, as expressed more precisely in all the language versions other than the Spanish, use which occurs in the world of business, in trade, the subject of which is, precisely, the distribution of goods and services in the market. In short, use in trade."[24] Examples of use outside trade for the purposes of trade mark law would be the private use of the BMW mark on a key ring, Warhol's use of the Campbell brand in his paintings, or use for educational purposes. 6–017

He supported however that expressing support, loyalty, or affiliation to the club did signify a connection between the goods and the football club. The nature of the link was irrelevant, it sufficed that it influenced consumers to buy the product: "the decisive factor is not the feelings which the consumer who buys the goods which the trade mark represents, or even the third party using it, harbour towards the registered proprietor, but the fact that they are acquired because, by bearing the sign, the goods identify the product with the trade mark—irrespective of what the consumer thinks of the mark—or even, as the case may be, with the proprietor".[25]

(ii) The interests of the trade mark proprietor. Pointing towards a significant shift in the balances inherent to trade mark law he proclaimed: 6–018

"The debate must be moved on to a different ground. Given that, where there is identity, the consumer purchases the goods because they bear the sign, the base from which the answer ... must be provide is that of the person exploiting it without being the proprietor. It is not the reason for which a person buys goods or uses services that I must examine but the reason which has led the person who is not the proprietor of the trade mark to place the goods on the market or to provide the service using the same distinctive sign. If, regardless of the reason which motivates him, he attempts to exploit it commercially, then he can be said to be using it as a trade mark and the proprietor will be entitled to object, within the limits and to the extent allowed under Article 5 of the Directive."[26]

---

[23] Point 59 of the Opinion of A.G. Ruiz-Jarabo Colomer.
[24] Point 62 of the Opinion of A.G. Ruiz-Jarabo Colomer.
[25] *Arsenal*, para.67.
[26] *Arsenal*, para.69.

Closing the circle he turned his attention to the football club and the reasons behind registering its crests as trade marks. Their commercial exploitability proved critical. Clubs register their signs in order to exploit them through merchandising that has become a lifeline for them; they should be entitled to object to third parties exploiting identical signs. The signs have become their intangible property.

6–019   (b) *The judgment of the Court*

The Court of Justice[27] accepted that Mr Reed's unauthorised use constituted use in the course of trade: "the use of the sign identical to the mark is indeed use in the course of trade, since it takes place in the context of commercial activity with a view to economic advantage and not as a private matter".[28]

The position of the trade mark proprietor and the function of a trade mark were pivotal in the Court's analysis. The essential function of a trade mark was that of a guarantee of origin, to ensure that guarantee "the proprietor must be protected against competitors wishing to take unfair advantage of the status and reputation of the trade mark by selling products illegally bearing it".[29] The Court referred to its judgments in *Hoffmann-La Roche*[30] and *Loendersloot*,[31] however it is the first time that the link was expressed in such strong terms, albeit in a cyclical way.

6–020   **(i) The interests of the trade mark proprietor**

"It follows that the exclusive right under Article 5(1)(a) of the Directive was conferred in order to enable the trade mark proprietor to protect his specific interests as proprietor, that is, to ensure that the trade mark can fulfil its functions. The exercise of that right must therefore be reserved to cases in which a third party's use of the sign affects or is liable to affect the functions of the trade mark, in particular its essential function of guaranteeing to consumers the origin of the goods."[32]

The mirror argument was that the proprietor might not prohibit uses that could not affect its "own interests as proprietor of the mark, having regard to its functions".[33] Referring to *Hölterhoff*, the Court noted that uses for purely descriptive purposes are excluded from the scope of art.5(1)

[27] *Arsenal Football Club Plc* (C-206/01) [2002] E.C.R. I-10273.
[28] *Arsenal*, para.40.
[29] *Arsenal*, para.50.
[30] *Hoffmann-la Roche & Co AG and Hoffmann-la Roche AG* (102/77) [1978] E.C.R. 1139.
[31] *Frits Loendersloot* (C-349/95) [1997] E.C.R. I-6227.
[32] *Arsenal*, para.51.
[33] *Arsenal*, para.54.

3. IDENTICAL SIGNS AND GOODS OR SERVICES

"because they do not affect any of the interests which that provision aims to protect, and do not therefore fall within the concept of use within the meaning of that provision".[34]

In this case the signs were used in such a way as to create the impression of a material link in the course of trade between the unauthorised goods and the club as proprietor of the trade mark. The presence of the notice at the point of sale made no difference because, even if those who were aware of it would not be confused, there was a possibility that others who came across the goods after their sale and away from the stall might perceive the signs as designating the club as the undertaking from which the goods originated: "there is a clear possibility in the present case that some consumers, in particular if they come across the goods after they have been sold by Mr Reed and taken away from the stall where the notice appears, may interpret the sign as designating Arsenal FC as the undertaking of origin of the goods".[35]

(ii) Protecting the consumer. In order to justify its judgment from the consumer's perspective, the Court added that under these circumstances the guarantee that all goods bearing the same "trade mark have been manufactured or supplied under the control of a single undertaking which is responsible for their quality"[36] would be impaired. Indeed, Mr Reed's products did not come from Arsenal. Following this line of reasoning, the fact that the sign was perceived as a badge of support for or loyalty or affiliation to the proprietor of the mark had become immaterial.

6–021

(c) Back to the national Court

6–022

The judgment of the European Court of Justice was not welcomed by the referring judge. Back to the High Court, Laddie J. interpreted it as holding that where the respondent's use is not intended by him, or understood by the public, to be a designation of origin, there can be no infringement because such use does not prejudice the essential function of the registered mark. The holding that, in the circumstances of the case, the claimant should succeed, was a finding of fact rather than law which exceeded the jurisdiction of the Court of Justice. Applying the law, as interpreted by the Court in the part of the judgment he found binding, he concluded that there was no trade mark infringement.[37]

Arsenal appealed and, at the Court of Appeal,[38] Aldous L.J. stated that Laddie J. would be entitled to disregard the Court's conclusions to the

---

[34] *Arsenal*, para.54.
[35] *Arsenal*, para.57.
[36] *Arsenal*, para.58.
[37] *Arsenal Football Club Plc* [2002] EWHC 2695.
[38] *Arsenal Football Club Plc* [2003] EWCA Civ 696.

extent that they were based upon an inconsistent with his judgment factual background. Only the ruling upon interpretation was binding.

Summarising the position of the Court of Justice he stated: "registration of a trade mark gave to the proprietor a property right.... The relevant consideration was whether the use complained about was likely to damage that property right or, as the [Court of Justice] put it, is likely to affect or jeopardise the guarantee of origin which constitutes the essential function of the mark. That did not depend on whether the use complained of was trade mark use".[39]

6–023 He added that the Court of Justice looked at the interest of the proprietor, and considered whether that interest is liable to be affected, and not at the type of the allegedly infringing use. The "consideration is whether the third party's use affects or is likely to affect the functions of the trade mark. An instance of where that will occur is given, namely where a competitor wishes to take unfair advantage of the reputation of the trade mark by selling products illegally bearing the mark. That would happen whether or not the third party's use was trade mark use or whether there was confusion".[40]

According to his interpretation the Court of Justice had relied on whether the right given by registration is likely to be affected by a third party's use rather than whether Mr Reed's use was such that it would be perceived by some customers or users as a designation of origin.

He concurred with the Court that in the circumstances use by Mr Reed was liable to jeopardise the guarantee of origin function of the trade mark: "The trade marks, when applied to the goods, were purchased and worn as badges of support, loyalty and affiliation to Arsenal, but that did not mean that the use by a third party would not be liable to jeopardise the functions of the trade marks, namely the ability to guarantee origin. To the contrary, the wider and more extensive the use, the less likely the trade marks would be able to perform their function."[41]

6–024 **(3) Adam Opel—challenging the limits of protection**

Adam Opel[42] was a reference by the Landgericht Nürnberg-Fürth (Germany).

Adam Opel AG (Opel) was the registered proprietor in Germany of a figurative mark, known as the "Opel Blitz", for a number of products including "toys". AUTEC AG (Autec) was a marketer of remote controlled model cars, sold under the brand "Cartronic".

---

[39] *Arsenal Football Club Plc* [2003] EWCA Civ 696, para.33.
[40] *Arsenal Football Club Plc* [2003] EWCA Civ 696, para.37.
[41] *Arsenal Football Club Plc* [2003] EWCA Civ 696, para.48. Note that according to the judge the emphasis is on the trade mark rather than the product to which the trade mark is applied.
[42] *Adam Opel AG v Autec AG* (C-48/05), Opinion of the Advocate General, March 7, 2006.

3. IDENTICAL SIGNS AND GOODS OR SERVICES

Opel started trade mark infringement proceedings in Germany targeting the use of its registered trade mark on the grille of a replica (on a scale of 1:24) of one of Opel's original models, the Opel Astra V8 Coupé. On the packaging, the instructions, and the remote control there were various indications linking the product with Autec; for example the instructions of use and the front of the remote control bore the signs "Cartonic ®" whereas "AUTEC ® AG" appeared on the back page of the instructions and the on the reverse of the control there was a sticker incorporating the "AUTEC ® AG D 90441 Nürnberg".

The Landgericht Nürnberg-Fürth referred the following questions to the Court:

"1. Does the use of a protected trade mark, including as a 'toy', constitute use as a trade mark under Article 5(1)(a) when the manufacturer of toy-scale cars produces a scale model of a car that actually exists, including the sign placed on the model of the owner of the brand, and markets this scale model?

2. If the answer to question 1 is yes: Does the means of use of the brand described in question 1 constitute a mention relating to the type or quality of the scale-model of the vehicle under the terms of Article 6(1)(a) of the Directive?

3. If the answer to the question under two is yes: What are, in a case of this type, the determining criteria for evaluating whether use of the brand constitutes honest use in commercial or industrial practices? Is there a specific link with such use when the manufacturer of the scale model places on the packaging and on an accessory necessary for the use of the scale model a recognizable sign of its own brand for the public along with an indication of the offices of the company?"[43]

(a) The Opinion of the Advocate General 6–025

Advocate General Ruiz-Jarabo Colomer at the very beginning of his Opinion noted that a basic characteristic of toys was that they constituted the representation of something else.[44] Having cited a couple of historical examples of toys imitating reality, he added, setting the parameters of the current case, that it would be useful to analyse whether the copying of a brand—also registered for toys—in order to imitate reality infringed trade mark rights or whether it might be considered as lying outside the limits of trade mark protection.

The first question concerned whether use of the Opel logo constituted use as a trade mark, accordingly he intended to focus on two aspects: use of the sign as a trade mark and use of the sign for other purposes.

---

[43] Point 14. See also para.6–139, below for the answers to questions 2 and 3.
[44] Citing the Opinion of A.G. Jacobs in *Office for Harmonisation in the Internal Market (Trade Marks and Designs) v Zapf Creation AG* (C-498/01 P) [2004] E.C.R. I-11349.

6-026   **(i) Use of a sign as a registered trade mark.** The Advocate General took as a starting point for his analysis the ruling in *BMW*[45] on the scope of trade mark rights under art.5(1)(a). Elaborating on this theme he referred to his Opinion in *Arsenal*[46] where he supported that absolute protection meant that there was a iuris tantum presumption of infringement rather than protection in respect of all parties and in all circumstances.[47]

And, according to his interpretation, in *Arsenal*[48] the Court had followed a similar teleological approach by linking the exclusive right with the function of a trade mark[49] and holding that use that did not harm the rights of the proprietor fell outside the scope of the protection.

In this case the national court had to conduct a similar evaluation, recognising the fact that the Opel logo appeared on the body of the toy cars independently of whether the manufacturer was a licensee or a third party.

6-027   **(ii) Other uses of a sign.** The Advocate General continued with the analysis of the relevant jurisprudence of the Court. The use of a sign described in *BMW*[50] was the only one that clearly fell outside the scope of protection under art.5(1)(a).

Regarding the exceptions under art.6(1)(b) he noted that they applied when third parties for reasons dictated by the public interest were allowed to benefit from the advantages deriving from use of the sign as a trade mark.

Citing *Hölterhoff*[51] he added that references for purely descriptive purposes did not constitute use as a trade mark because, in these conditions, there was no harm done to the interests that art.5(1) aimed to protect.

6-028   And he referred to his Opinion in *Arsenal*[52] where he had included to non-infringing uses private use, use of symbols that failed to satisfy the requirements for their registration, and uses for educational purposes. He had also stated there that the national judge had to take additional factors into account, like the nature of the goods, the structure of the market, and the penetration of the brand.

Concluding, he stated that uses outside of the essential function of a trade mark would have to be assessed progressively, on a case by case basis. Looking at them from a broader theoretical and justificatory perspective he remarked that, unlike the cases falling under art.6(1), they did not require

---

[45] *Bayerische Motorenwerke AG and BMW Nederland BV* (C-63/97) [1999] E.C.R. I-905.
[46] *Arsenal Football Club Plc* (C-206/01) [2002] E.C.R. I-10273.
[47] See paras 6–015 and following, above.
[48] See paras 6–019 and following, above.
[49] On the protectable function of a trade mark he cited *Hoffmann-la Roche & Co AG and Hoffmann-la Roche AG* (102/77) [1978] E.C.R. 1139; *Koninklijke Philips Electronics NV* (C-299/99) [2002] E.C.R. I-5475; and *Ansul BV v Ajax Brandbeveiliging BV* (C-40/01) [2003] E.C.R. I-2439.
[50] *Bayerische Motorenwerke AG and BMW Nederland BV* (C-63/97) [1999] E.C.R. I-905.
[51] *Michael Hölterhoff v Ulrich Freiesleben* (C-2/00) [2002] E.C.R. I-4187.
[52] *Arsenal Football Club Plc* (C-206/01) [2002] E.C.R. I-10273.

3. IDENTICAL SIGNS AND GOODS OR SERVICES

a restrictive interpretation, because they did not constitute derogations, but rather limitations on the use of ius prohibendi.

(iii) Application to the facts—article 5(1)(a). Having set the background—"the jurisprudential panorama"[53]—he went on to examine how the facts of the case fitted into it. 6–029

He found that the application of the logo on the toy cars should not be linked with the function of a trade mark for two reasons: first, because of the nature of the product and, secondly, because of consumer perception.

Looking at the product market he noted that miniature cars, trains, ships and aeroplanes, had been marketed widely since 1898; little cars were the "Proustian madeleine" of adults reliving their childhood experiences. The audience for the product comprised children of different ages but also adult collectors. To satisfy demand the toys had to replicate even the tiniest details of the original car, including the signs appearing on them. The car industry had only recently been involved in this market, primarily in order to build customer loyalty though merchandising and advertising.

As a result of that "product market" analysis he concluded that it would be difficult to imagine that the public would automatically associate the signs appearing on the toy cars with the manufacturer. 6–030

A monopoly over the use of the signs on toy cars, following a too rigorous interpretation of the jus prohibendi, would threaten the existence of the car toy market. The licensees of the car manufacturers "would be the only ones authorized to provide detailed replicas of the authentic vehicles, thereby unjustifiably restricting the freedom of competitors to conduct their business".[54]

The Advocate General started his discussion of consumer perception with a reference to *Anheuser-Busch*.[55] In that case the Court had ruled that the identification of possible harm caused by a third party's use depended on the perception of a material link in the course of trade between the third party's products and those of the trade mark proprietor. So, what courts had to do was assess whether the relevant consumers perceived the sign as designating the trade mark proprietor.

The referring Court had examined the link created by the sign and found that, as intended by the nature of the product, it established a link between the miniature prototype and the real car, but not with the toy models manufactured by Opel's licensees. This should not constitute trade mark infringement: "This would only be the case if the consumer associated the Opel sign on the toy cars of third parties with the one figuring on the toy cars marketed by Opel."[56] 6–031

---

[53] Point 35 of the Opinion of A.G. Ruiz-Jarabo Colomer.
[54] Point 41 of the Opinion of A.G. Ruiz-Jarabo Colomer.
[55] *Anheuser-Busch Inc v Budejovicky Budvar, narodni podnik* (C-245/02) [2004] E.C.R. I-10989, see para.10–133, below.
[56] Point 44 of the Opinion of A.G. Ruiz-Jarabo Colomer.

SCOPE OF PROTECTION, LIMITATIONS AND ENFORCEMENT

The next remark of the Advocate General was that the toy car and the original car did not belong to the same category of goods, thus they did not constitute identical goods under art.5(1)(a).

Note though that, as mentioned above, Opel had been trying to exercise its rights based on the registration of its trade mark for toys, not for cars.

6–032 In his concluding suggestion on how the first question should be answered the Advocate General refocused on the importance of use as a trade mark. Use of a registered sign on toys should not constitute use as a trade mark under the terms of art.5(1)(a) when the manufacturer of a model car reproduced on a smaller scale and marketed a replica of an actual existing model bearing the trade mark of the owner.

Advocate General Ruiz Zarabo decided to look briefly at the remaining two questions, in the hypothetical scenario of a negative answer to the first question, finding that art.6 would also cover the use made by the toy manufacturer.[57]

(b) The judgment of the Court

6–033 **(i) Use in relation to toys.** The Court observed at the outset that it was not disputed in the main proceedings that the sign was used with a view to economic advantage and not as a private matter, without the consent of the trade mark proprietor and, in so far as the Opel logo has been registered for toys, that the use was in respect of identical goods, as envisaged in art.5(1)(a) of the Directive.

Moreover, it noted that the use is "in relation to goods" within the meaning of that provision, since it concerns the affixing of the sign onto goods and the offering of those goods for sale, by putting them on the market or stocking them for the purposes of art.5(3)(a) and (b) of the Directive.[58]

Notwithstanding, it held that the above were not enough to trigger the absolute protection provided for in art.5(1)(a), insisting on a narrow interpretation of its preventive scope. Following *Arsenal*[59] and *Anheuser-Busch*[60] it stressed that the exclusive right afforded by that provision had the purpose to enable the trade mark proprietor to protect his specific interests, that is, to ensure that the mark can fulfil its functions and that, accordingly, the exercise of its rights must be limited to cases where the essential function of the mark was endangered.

6–034 On that premise, the Court concluded that the affixing of a sign identical to a trade mark registered for toys on scale models of vehicles cannot be

---

[57] Paras 6–139 and following, below.
[58] Citing *Arsenal*, paras 40–41.
[59] *Arsenal*, para.51.
[60] *Anheuser-Busch*, para.59.

3. IDENTICAL SIGNS AND GOODS OR SERVICES

prohibited under art.5(1)(a) of the Directive, unless it affects, or is liable to affect, the functions of that mark.[61]

The Court also took notice that, according to the facts stated in the order for reference, the average consumer of toy cars in Germany is used to scale models being based on real products and even accords great importance to absolute fidelity to the original, so that he would take the Opel logo appearing on the miniatures as a mere indication that the toy is a reduced-scale reproduction of a real Opel car.

On this point, the Court remarked that if by that explanation the referring court implied that the relevant public does not perceive the Opel logo appearing on the scale models as an indication of their origin, it would have to conclude that the use at issue does not affect the essential function of Opel's trade mark for toys.[62]

However, it stressed that it was for the referring court to determine, by reference to the perception of the average consumer of toys in Germany, whether the use at issue was likely to affect the functions of Opel's logo, noting also in that connection that Opel did not appear to have claimed that said use affected the other functions of its trade mark. 6–035

The Court then assessed the same question in relation to the registration of Opel's mark for motor vehicles. In that regard, it admitted that its judgment in *BMW*,[63] where the services of repair of vehicles of a particular make had been found to be identical with the cars so repaired, was quite exceptional and could not be applied to the case at issue; to the extent that Autec sells toys and not vehicles, the use of the Opel logo in the present instance cannot be said to cover identical goods, within the meaning of art.5(1)(a) of the Directive.[64]

(ii) Possible threat to other functions. Despite the fact that Opel had not specifically argued that any of the other functions of its trade mark were liable to be affected by Autec's use, the Court went on to also examine the applicability of art.5(2) to the facts, pointing out that it is for the Court to provide the national court with all those elements for the interpretation of Community law which may be of assistance in adjudicating on the case.[65] 6–036

After observing that Germany had implemented in its national law the optional provision of art.5(2), the Court also noted: (a) that the Opel logo is also registered for motor vehicles; (b) that, subject to verification by the referring court, it is a well-known mark in Germany for that kind of products; and (c) that a motor vehicle and a scale model of that vehicle are not similar products.

---

[61] *Opel*, para.22.
[62] *Opel*, para.24.
[63] *Bayerische Motorenwerke AG and BMW Nederland BV* (C-63/97) [1999] E.C.R. I-905.
[64] *Opel*, paras 27–30.
[65] Citing *Trojani* (C-456/02), para.38; and *Ioannidis* (C-258/04), para.20.

Thus, it considered that, at least prima facie, the circumstances of the case did not preclude the application of art.5(2), provided that it could be established that the use at issue was likely to take unfair advantage of, or be detrimental to, the distinctive character or the repute of Opel's registration for motor vehicles.[66]

All the more so, since Opel had argued at the hearing that it has an interest in the quality of scale models of vehicles bearing its trade mark being good, and in those models being absolutely up to date, as otherwise the reputation of its trade mark for motor vehicles would be damaged.

6–037   **(iii) Can a specific toy model be described by reference to the original product?** As regards the question whether the use in issue could be allowed by virtue of art.6 of the Directive, the Court held, as a preliminary point, that the affixing of Opel's trade mark on scale models could not be authorised on the basis of art.6(1)(c), because it was not meant to indicate the intended purpose of the toys concerned.[67]

Then, it turned to the main issue under the second question, namely the applicability to the case of the exception included in art.6(1)(b). In that regard, it held that, although this provision is primarily designed to prevent the trade mark proprietor from prohibiting the use by competitors of descriptive terms forming part of his mark in order to indicate certain characteristics of their products,[68] its wording is in no way specific to such a situation.

Thus, it cannot be excluded a priori that a trade mark may be used for descriptive purposes, if its use merely consists in giving indications about the kind, quality or other characteristics of the relevant products and provided that it is made in accordance with honest practices in industrial or commercial matters.[69]

6–038   In that connection, the Commission had argued that, in specific circumstances, the identical reproduction of each and every detail of the original product, including the copying of its trade mark, might constitute an essential characteristic of the reduced replica, so that art.6(1)(b) of the Directive could apply, as for example when the scale models were intended for collectors.

However, the Court took the view that the facts of the case did not support such a scenario. Accordingly, it disagreed with the approach of Advocate General and held that the affixing of a sign identical to a trade mark for motor vehicles to toy scale models, in order to reproduce the original faithfully, is not intended to provide an indication as to a characteristic

---

[66] *Opel*, para.34.
[67] *Opel*, para.39.
[68] Citing *Windsurfing Chiemsee* (C-180/97 & C-109/97) [1999] E.C.R. I-2779, para.28.
[69] *Opel*, para.43.

of those models, but is merely an element in the faithful reproduction of the real product.[70]

In short, the judgment in *Adam Opel* seems to be suggesting that the reproduction of the mark of the original product on toy models does not fall within the scope of art.5(1)(a) of the Directive, even if the proprietor holds a registration in respect of those goods, on the assumption that in such cases the public will not see the sign as designating origin; nevertheless, such use might still be covered by art.5(2), to the extent that it takes unfair advantage of the reputation of the trade mark.

However, the assumption that in the situation *in casu* there is no likelihood of confusion seems to have been made bearing in mind more the real business of the plaintiff and less his registration for toys, since it is difficult to imagine how that conclusion could be escaped if Opel's logo had actually been used for distinguishing toys. In that sense, the Court seems to have interpreted the absolute prohibition contained in art.5(1)(a) of the Directive in a quite restrictive manner, in that it did not give sufficient weight to possible future uses of the mark squarely falling within the confines of the registration.

6–039

At the same time, *Adam Opel* seems to be taking a similarly restrictive approach as regards the exception in art.6(1)(b), at least insofar as it refuses to concede that traders in the toy industry act in accordance with honest practices, apparently on the assumption that toys do not necessarily need to imitate known products without the consent of their manufacturer.

Is this view justified, however, even if in the relevant industry the identification of the type of plaything concerned is traditionally made by reference to the original, as the order for reference seems to imply? Moreover, that approach does not adequately explain how the public will actually perceive the reproduction of the mark on the toy, if it sees it neither as indication of origin, nor as an identification of the type of toy concerned.[71]

Of course, the Court left open the possibility to apply the exception in sectors where the reproduction of the mark on the replica is somehow inevitable, but the fact remains that in this way a substantial part of the toy industry is made subject to the owner's control, so that the marketing of "undesired" imitations is effectively avoided. However, it is difficult to see how the cut-off point between "honest" and "dishonest" practices is to be drawn in similar situations, if not by reference to the established practices in the relevant sector.

---

[70] *Opel*, para.44.
[71] For instance, that view seems to be stricter than the approach taken by the Advocate General in *OHIM v Zapf Creation AG* (NEW BORN BABY) (C-473/01 P).

6-040 **(4) Marca II—availability and scope of protection**

Marca II[72] is in a way the sequel of *Marca Mode*,[73] albeit in a different context. Once again, Adidas challenged on the basis of its well-known three-stripe trade mark the use by competitors of signs consisting of a double stripe in contrasting colours to conceal and strengthen the seams of their garments. The question concerned the application of the requirement of availability for the purposes of defining the scope of trade mark rights.

6-041 *(a) The facts in the main proceedings and the order for reference*

The dispute arose in the context of proceedings between Adidas AG and its Benelux subsidiary (together "Adidas"), on the one hand, and Marca Mode CV, C&A Nederland CV, H&M Hennes & Mauritz Netherlands BV and Vendex KBB Nederland BV ("the defendants"), on the other.

Adidas owns in the Benelux a number of figurative trade mark registrations for sports and leisure clothing, composed of three vertical, parallel stripes of equal width, running the length of the sides, shoulders, sleeves, legs and side seams of a garment, in contrasting colours.

Having found that some of the defendants had begun to market leisure clothing featuring two parallel stripes, in shades contrasting with the basic colour of the garment, Adidas brought interlocutory proceedings before the Rechtbank te Breda (local court of Breda) seeking to prohibit the use of any sign consisting of its registered three-stripe logo or a motif similar to it. For their part, the defendants brought applications for a declaration that they are free to place two stripes on their sports and leisure garments for decorative purposes.

Rechtbank te Breda granted the relief sought by Adidas. On appeal, however, the Gerechtshof te 's-Hertogenbosch set aside that judgment, rejecting both the application of Adidas and those of the defendants. It held, essentially, that the three-stripe motif registered by Adidas is not very distinctive per se but that, owing to intensive advertising, it had acquired considerable distinctive character and become well known. However, given that simple stripe logos must, generally, remain available, they cannot be invoked against the use of two-stripe motifs.

6-042 Adidas appealed to the Hoge Raad (Supreme Court of the Netherlands), taking the view that the requirement of availability must be taken into account only when examining the application of the grounds for refusal or invalidity provided for in art.3 of the Directive. The Hoge Raad decided to

---

[72] *Adidas AG and Adidas Benelux BV/Marca Mode CV, C&A Nederland, H&M Hennes & Mauritz Netherlands BV and Vendex KBB Nederland BV* (MARCA II) (C-102/07) [2008] E.C.R. I-2439.
[73] *Marca Mode CV v Adidas AG* (C-425/98) [2000] E.C.R. I-4681.

3. IDENTICAL SIGNS AND GOODS OR SERVICES

stay the proceedings and refer the following questions to the Court for a preliminary ruling:

"1. In the determination of the extent to which protection should be given to a trade mark formed by a sign which does not in itself have any distinctive character or by a designation which corresponds to the description in Article 3(1)(c) of the Directive ... but which has become a trade mark through the process of becoming customary ('inburgering') and has been registered, should account be taken of the general interest in ensuring that the availability of given signs is not unduly restricted for other traders offering the goods or services concerned ('Freihaltebedürfnis')?

2. If the answer to Question 1 is in the affirmative: does it make any difference whether the signs which are referred to therein and which are to be held available are seen by the relevant public as being signs used to distinguish goods or merely to embellish them?

3. If the answer to Question 1 is in the affirmative: does it, further, make any difference whether the sign contested by the holder of a trade mark is devoid of distinctive character, within the terms of Article 3(1)(b) of the Directive ... or contains a designation, within the terms of Article 3(1)(c) of the Directive?"

(b) The Opinion of the Advocate General 6-043

After considering the origins of the Freihaltebedürfnis principle in German case law under the regime preceding the Directive and recalling that it concerned a real, current and serious risk to the availability of signs that ought to remain free for the use of competitors, A.G. Ruiz-Jarabo Colomer referred to its treatment under Community law.

In that regard, he reminded the Court that although in *Windsurfing Chiemsee* the Court stated that "the application of Article 3(1)(c) of the Directive does not depend on there being a real, current or serious need to leave [a sign or indication] free",[74] it nevertheless acknowledged the link between that principle and the general interest underlying that provision.[75]

Moreover, he observed that, since then, the Court has repeatedly drawn attention to the need to apply the principle of when deciding whether a sign is eligible for registration[76] and has also extended its application to art.3(1)(b) and (e) of the Directive.[77]

---

[74] *Windsurfing Chiemsee*, para.35.
[75] *Windsurfing Chiemsee*, paras 26–27.
[76] Citing *LibertelGroep BV* (C-104/01) [2003] E.C.R. I-3793, para.52; and *Henke KGaA* (C-218/01) [2004] E.C.R. I-1725, paras 40–41.
[77] Citing *SAT.1 Satellitenfernsehen GmbH* (C-329/02 P) [2004] E.C.R. I-8317, paras 26–27; and *Koninklijke Philips Electronics NV* (C-299/99) [2002] E.C.R. I-5475, para.80.

6-044   The Advocate General then moved on to examine whether it was appropriate to apply the principle of availability in the context of arts 5 and 6 of the Directive.

With regard to art.5, he advanced two arguments militating against its application when determining the scope of protection: the first, related to the origin of the Freihaltebedürfnis principle, which is clearly linked to the registration of signs rather than to the exercise of the rights conferred on the holder of the mark. The second was drawn from the overall scheme of the Directive, which places the limitations of those rights under art.6; thus, allowing the principle of availability to be taken into account in the framework of art.5 would entail the addition of an unwritten condition, which would be contrary to the principle of legal certainty and to the spirit of the relevant provisions.[78]

Next, he turned to art.6(1) of the Directive, noting the similarities in the structure between art.3(1)(c) on the one hand and art.6(1)(b), on the other, which advocates in favour of a comparative analysis of the respective provisions. He also pointed out that the Court has not ruled out the use of the requirement of availability as a criterion for the interpretation of art.6 and, by extension, as a factor to be taken into account when assessing the limitation of the rights of trade mark proprietors under that provision.[79]

6-045   Based on the similar wording and purpose pursued by arts 3(1)(c) and 6(1)(b), he concluded that it is necessary to consider the requirement of availability when establishing the scope of protection of a mark composed of one of the indications referred to in art.3(1)(c) of the Directive, which has been registered on account of the distinctive character it acquired through use, but that it is not appropriate to rely on that principle where a sign inherently devoid of distinctive character, within the meaning of art.3(1)(b), subsequently acquired such distinctiveness by use.[80]

Finally, in reply to the second question he considered that the perception by the public of a sign subject to the requirement of availability has only limited relevance in the above circumstances: if the average consumer regards the sign as having a merely decorative purpose, he will not identify it as a badge of origin, from which it follows that the sign will not be suitable for performing its essential function and, thus, its scope of protection will have to be diminished accordingly; otherwise, the contrary should apply.[81]

(c) The judgment of the Court

6-046   **(i) The impact of the requirement of availability on the scope of protection.** In the first place, the Court formally recognised the

---

[78] Point 48 of the Opinion of A.G. Ruiz-Jarabo Colomer.
[79] Point 69 of the Opinion of A.G. Ruiz-Jarabo Colomer.
[80] Point 80 of the Opinion of A.G. Ruiz-Jarabo Colomer.
[81] Points 81–82 of the Opinion of A.G. Ruiz-Jarabo Colomer.

3. IDENTICAL SIGNS AND GOODS OR SERVICES

significance of the principle of availability in the system of European trade mark law, by confirming that there are public interest considerations, connected in particular with the need for undistorted competition, which require that certain signs should be used freely by all economic operators.[82]

Specifically, the Court recalled that the requirement of availability is both the reason underlying certain of the grounds for refusal set out in art.3 of the Directive and the justification for the sanction set out in art.12(2)(a), according to which a trade mark is liable to revocation if it has become generic in the relevant sector. In substance, by those provisions the Community legislator sought to balance the legitimate interests of trade mark proprietors against those of competitors in the availability of signs.

It observed, however, that the case at issue fell outside that framework, since it only raised the question whether the requirement of availability constitutes a relevant criterion for the purposes of defining the protection to be afforded to trade mark proprietors. As was clear from the facts, the defendants did not seek to have the mark of Adidas either revoked or declared invalid, but merely a declaration that they were entitled to use motifs other than the one registered by the trade mark owner, without the consent of the latter.[83]

In that sense, the relevance of that argument had to be examined exclusively in the light of arts 5 and 6(1)(b) of the Directive, which specifically delimit the scope of trade mark protection, without having recourse to the purpose and function of arts 3 and 12.

6–047

As regards, first, art.5(1)(b), the Court pointed out once more that the protection conferred by it is subject to the existence of a likelihood of confusion, the assessment of which depends on all relevant factors, as set out in the 10th Recital of the Preamble to the Directive.

It stressed, however, that the need for the sign to remain available for other economic operators cannot be one of those factors. Rather, the answer to the question as to whether there is a likelihood of confusion must be based on the perception by the relevant public as to origin and not on considerations extraneous to that perception. If a third party could rely on the requirement of availability to use a sign which is nevertheless similar to an earlier mark, without the proprietor of the latter being able to oppose that use, the effective application of art.5(1) of the Directive would be seriously undermined.[84]

The Court also underlined that those considerations apply in particular to stripe motifs. Such motifs are widely available and may be placed in a vast number of ways on sports garments by all operators. Nonetheless, competitors cannot rely on the requirement of availability in order to place on their garments motifs which are so similar to that registered by the trade

6–048

---

[82] *Marca II*, para.22.
[83] *Marca II*, para.25.
[84] *Marca II*, paras 30–31.

mark owner, that give rise to a likelihood of confusion in the mind of the public.

For much the same reasons, the Court held that the perception of the sign as mere decoration cannot constitute a restriction on the protection conferred by art.5(1)(b) when, despite its decorative nature, that sign is so similar to the registered trade mark that the public is likely to believe that the respective goods have the same commercial origin.[85]

Accordingly, the national Court would have to determine whether the consumer, when confronted with garments featuring stripe motifs in the same places and with similar characteristics as the logo registered by Adidas, except for the fact that they consist of two rather than three stripes, may be mistaken as to the origin of those goods.

6–049 As is moreover clear from the 10th Recital in the Preamble to the Directive, that appreciation depends not solely on the degree of similarity of the signs, but also on the ease with which the sign may be associated with the mark, having regard, in particular, to the recognition of the latter on the market.

Finally, the Court held that the same line of reasoning applied also to art.5(2) of the Directive (new art.5(2)), with the result that the requirement of availability could not influence the assessment whether the use of the sign takes unfair advantage of, or is detrimental to, the distinctive character or the repute of the trade mark either.[86]

6–050 **(ii) The requirement of availability as a limiting factor.** As regards the interpretation of art.6(1)(b) of the Directive, the Court concurred with the Advocate General that insofar as that provision seeks to ensure that all economic operators remain free to use descriptive indications in a fair manner, it essentially constitutes an expression of the requirement of availability.

However, it observed at the same time that the requirement of availability cannot constitute an independent restriction of the effects of the trade mark, in addition to those expressly provided for in art.6(1)(b). At any rate, in order for a third party to invoke the exceptions included in that provision, the indication used by it must necessarily relate to one of the characteristics of the goods or services concerned and not merely on its purely decorative nature.[87]

Consequently, the Court concluded that to the extent that the two-stripe motifs at issue were not meant as an indication of any of characteristics of the garments on which they were placed, but merely served ornamental purposes, the defendants in the main proceedings could not rely on art.6(1)(b) of the Directive to justify their use.

---

[85] *Marca II*, para.34.
[86] *Marca II*, para.43.
[87] *Marca II*, paras 47–48.

3. IDENTICAL SIGNS AND GOODS OR SERVICES

(5) Smirnoff—use by intermediaries 6–051

In *Smirnoff*[88] the Court dealt with the right of the trade mark proprietor to prevent the use of an identical sign within the context of art.9(1)(a) and (2)(d) CTMR, the equivalent provisions to arts 5(1)(a) and 5(3)(d) of the Directive.

(a) The facts in the main proceedings 6–052

The question arose in the context of a dispute between UDV, proprietor of the Community Trade Mark "Smirnoff Ice", registered for, inter alia, "alcoholic beverages", in Class 33 of the Nice Classification, and Brandtraders, a company operating a website on which companies can anonymously place advertisements and negotiate their transactions. In accordance with the relevant terms and conditions, as soon as Brandtraders is informed of an agreement, it concludes with the purchaser a contract of sale for commission, acting as the vendor's broker, that is to say, in its own name but on behalf of the vendor.

Following the sale in that manner of a quantity of goods bearing the mark "SMIRNOFF ICE", UDV sought to obtain an injunction against Brandtraders which was accepted by the competent Belgian Court, which held that Brandtraders had infringed art.9(1) and (2) CTMR on account of the fact that it advertised, purchased and resold the goods in question.

On appeal, the hof van beroep te Brussel (Court of Appeal, Brussels) annulled the order and dismissed as unfounded UDV's application on the grounds that, inter alia, Brandtraders had not placed the allegedly infringing references on the website itself and had not used the sign in relation to trade in goods in which it was itself a contractual party, given that it was merely acting on behalf of a third party; in that sense it had not made use of the for the purposes of art.9(1) and (2) CTMR.

UDV brought an appeal before the Hof van Cassatie (Court of Cassation) 6–053 against that judgment claiming that it is not necessary, for the application of art.9(1)(a) and (2)(d) CTMR, that the third party concerned act on its own behalf and/or use the sign at issue as an interested party in relation to the sale of goods in which it is itself a contractual party. The Hof van Cassatie decided to stay the proceedings and to refer the following questions to the Court for a preliminary ruling:

"(1) For there to be use of the sign within the meaning of Article 9(1)(a) and (2)(d) [CTMR], is it necessary that a third party, within the meaning of Article 9(1)(a) of [that] regulation:

---

[88] *UDV North America Inc v Brandtraders NV* (SMIRNOFF ICE) (C-62/08), not yet published.

(a) uses the sign on his own behalf?

(b) uses the sign as an interested party in relation to trade in goods in which he is himself a contractual party?

(2) Can a trade intermediary who acts in his own name, but not on his own behalf, be regarded as a third party who uses the sign within the meaning of Article 9(1)(a) and (2)(d)?"

6–054   (b)   *The reasoned order of the Court*

Considering that the answer to the questions referred raised no reasonable doubt, the Court decided, in accordance with art.104(3) of its Rules of Procedure, to its decision by reasoned order.

Before the Court, Brandtraders remarked that, under Belgian law, a broker acts in his own name but on behalf of a third principal, in this case the vendor, meaning that he does not actually acquire title to the goods when a sales contract is concluded. As a result, it claimed that the use by a third party of a sign which is identical with a registered mark must relate to that third party's own goods in order for that use to be prevented.

The Court rejected that argument, noting that all the conditions set out in its case law with regard to the concept of "use" within the meaning of art.5(1) of the Directive, had been fulfilled and that, consequently, the fact that the party at issue used a sign which is identical with a registered mark in relation to goods which are not its own, in that it does not have title to them, is not relevant and can therefore not mean by itself that the use made in this case does not fall under the definition of art.9(1) CTMR.[89]

More specifically, it held that the use at issue is clearly in the context of a commercial activity with a view to economic advantage, since Brandtraders acted in the context of a sales contract and received remuneration for that action; the fact that the broker acted on behalf of a third vendor is in that regard irrelevant.[90]

6–055   In addition, it is clear that said use is in relation to goods since, even though it is not a case of affixing the sign to the goods, there is use "in relation to goods" in the form of the using the sign at issue on business papers. Inasmuch as such a link is established, it is irrelevant that the third party uses a sign for the marketing of goods which are not its own, in the sense that it does not acquire title thereto.[91]

Lastly, the Court held that the use of the sign is likely to create the impression that there is a material link in trade between the goods on which they are affixed and the undertaking from which they originate; indeed, by making such use, the third party "assumes de facto the essential prerogative

---

[89] *Smirnoff*, para.43.
[90] *Smirnoff*, paras 45–46.
[91] *Smirnoff*, paras 47–48.

3. IDENTICAL SIGNS AND GOODS OR SERVICES

that is granted to the proprietor of a mark, namely the exclusive power to use the sign at issue so as to distinguish goods'", that is, clearly makes use of the sign as a trade mark.[92]

(6) Bellure—broadening the scope of protection 6–056

In *Bellure*,[93] the Court took a decisive step towards relaxing the criteria imposed by its previous case law on the application of art.5(1)(a) of the Directive, by clearly including in the protected subject-matter of that provision functions of the mark other than its essential one.

The first and second questions in that judgment concerned the use by manufacturers of smell-alike perfumes of "comparison lists", indicating the fine fragrances to which the specific imitations correspond by referring to their registered trade marks.[94]

By the first question, the referring court asked whether art.5(1)(a) or (b) of the Directive must be interpreted as meaning that the trade mark proprietor is entitled to prevent the use by a third party in comparative advertising of a sign identical with its mark in relation to identical goods, where such use is not capable of jeopardising the essential function of the mark.

By the second question, it asked whether the proprietor of a well-known mark can oppose such use under art.5(1)(a), even where that use is not capable of jeopardising the function of the mark as a guarantee of origin, or harm its reputation, whether by tarnishment or dilution or in any other way, but none the less plays a significant role in the promotion of the goods of the third party.

(a) The Opinion of the Advocate General 6–057

In drawing up the framework for his analysis, A.G. Mengozzi observed that even though the first question presented similar traits with the ruling in *O2*,[95] the respective cases differed in an important aspect, namely that, unlike in O2, the facts at issue concerned the use of identical and not merely similar signs.

That observation gave him the opportunity to focus from the outset to the question whether the existence of a likelihood of confusion, which is undisputedly a conditio sine qua non for the application of art.5(1)(b) of the Directive, is really an implicit condition also for the application of art.5(1)(a).

---

[92] *Smirnoff*, paras 49–51.
[93] L'Oréal SA, Lancôme parfums et beauté & Cie SNC, Laboratoire Garnier & Cie / Bellure NV, Malaika Investments Ltd, Starion International Ltd (BELLURE) (C-487/07) E.C.R. [2009] E.C.R. 0.
[94] For a more detailed account of the facts of that case see para.5–230, above. For the part concerning comparative advertising see para.10–065 and following.
[95] *O2*.

SCOPE OF PROTECTION, LIMITATIONS AND ENFORCEMENT

Referring to the 9th Recital in the Preamble to the Directive, he noted, first of all, that the scope of the harmonised protection afforded to trade marks by Community law, as prescribed by the Directive, derives essentially from art.5(1) and (3) thereof, whereas art.5(2) simply permits Member States to introduce into their laws the more extensive protection provided for in that provision. Thus, where that optional rule has been implemented, the two types of right coexist as complementary layers of protection.

6–058 That, however, cannot give of itself an outright answer to the question whether the protection conferred by art.5(1)(a) extends beyond the essential function of the mark as an origin indicator, since it does not actually solve the problem whether the two types of protection are clearly distinct, or rather merely overlapping.

Nor can the answer to that question be unambiguously derived from the wording of the 10th Recital to the Directive. That Recital, which deals with the "protection afforded by the registered trade mark" in general terms, clearly does not refer only to situations involving similarity, when it states that "the likelihood of confusion constitutes the specific condition for such protection". Moreover, the fact that it further specifies that the protection "is absolute in the case of identity" is not decisive either, since it could simply mean that, in such a case, the proprietor of the mark is not required to *prove* a likelihood of confusion, in that this is presumed to be the case, and not necessarily that use of the mark may be prohibited also where there is no such likelihood. On the other hand, it also states that the function of the protection in question "is *in particular* to guarantee the trade mark as an indication of origin".[96]

In view of that uncertainty in the text of law, A.G. Mengozzi moved on to examine the evolution of the Court's case law in the matter, finding particularly helpful in that regard the judgments in *Arsenal* and *Adam Opel*.

6–059 In that regard, he pointed out that the Court stated for the first time in *Arsenal* that the exercise of the exclusive right afforded by art.5(1)(a) is reserved to cases where the use of the sign is liable to affect the *functions* of the trade mark, *in particular* its essential function of guaranteeing origin,[97] making thus the existence of an impact on the functions of the mark a prerequisite for the enforceability of that right. That, however, does not necessarily mean that the prohibition is triggered where *any* of the functions of the trade mark are liable to be affected or, in other words, that *all* the functions which the trade mark may fulfil are *equally protectable* in law.[98]

Next, he observed that in *Adam Opel* the Court took a further step towards recognising that protection is to be afforded not only in respect of a trade mark's essential function but also in respect of other functions, when

---

[96] Point 38 of the Opinion of A.G. Mengozzi.
[97] *Arsenal*, para.51.
[98] Point 45 of the Opinion of A.G. Mengozzi.

3. IDENTICAL SIGNS AND GOODS OR SERVICES

it stated that the trade mark proprietor is entitled to prevent the use of its mark by third parties "*if* that use affects ... *the functions* of the trade mark".[99] From that formulation, the Advocate General inferred that that what is ultimately necessary for activating the protection conferred by art.5(1)(a) is that there must be an adverse effect on *any* of the functions of the mark, in the sense there is protection if *whichever* of the functions of the mark is liable to be affected.

Nevertheless, he noted that the gradual development in the Court's case law towards the protection of trade mark functions other than as a guarantee of origin did not entirely settle the issue, especially insofar as it left open the question of the identification of those other functions, as well as the question of ascertaining how such protection may be reconciled with the protection of well-known marks under art.5(2) of the Directive.

With regard to the first of those questions, he pointed out that neither the Directive nor the case law of the Court have provided a list or a description of the other functions a trade mark performs, other than the one included in the opinion of A.G. Jacobs in *Parfums Christian Dior*[100] and the statements of A.G. Ruiz-Jarabo Colomer in *Arsenal*[101] that it would be "simplistic reductionism to limit the function of the trade mark to an indication of trade origin" and that a trade mark "acquires a life of its own, making a statement ... about quality, reputation and even, in certain cases, a way of seeing life".

6–060

Then, he had a closer look at the way trade marks function on the market, focusing in particular on the quality and communication functions. He defined the former as the guarantee the trade mark provides as to the consistency (or uniformity) in the quality of products identified by it[102] and the latter as "a vehicle for providing consumers with various kinds of information on the goods", be it information communicated directly by the sign which the mark consists of (for example, information on the product's physical characteristics) or, "accumulated" information relating to non-physical characteristics thereof (for instance, quality, trustworthiness, reliability, luxury, strength, etc.).[103]

He noted however that, while such cases confirm that the protection which the trade mark enjoys by virtue of art.5 of Directive goes beyond the need to protect the its function as guarantee of origin, the question nevertheless remains open as to what extent that protection ought to be conferred by art.5(1)(a), or covered by the optional provision of art.5(2) of the Directive, which, as confirmed by the judgment in *Gofkid*, also applies to identical or similar goods.

---

[99] *Adam Opel*, para.37.
[100] See the opinion of A.G. Jacobs in *Parfums Christian Dior SA v Tuk Consultancy BV* (C-300/98), in particular points 39, 41 and 42.
[101] See the opinion of A.G. Ruiz-Jarabo Colomer in *Arsenal*, points 46 and 47.
[102] Point 53 of the Opinion of A.G. Mengozzi.
[103] Point 54 of the Opinion of A.G. Mengozzi.

6–061   Notwithstanding, he pointed out that the circumstances of the case rendered it unnecessary to undertake an exhaustive description of the trade mark functions that could be protected under art.5(1)(a), since the questions referred were based on the finding that the use made by the defendants do not have any effect on the reputation of the earlier marks and, accordingly, on the communication functions carried out by them.

Moreover, the mere fact that the use complained of enables the defendants to take unfair advantage of that reputation does not mean that such a use is liable to undermine the functions which the marks in question perform as a result of that reputation.

(b) Findings of the Court

6–062   Before addressing the substantive issues relating to the first and second questions, the Court noted that, insofar as the comparison lists used by the defendants were aimed at promoting the supply of goods and explicitly identified the products of a competitor, they fell within the ambit of arts 2(1) and 2(2a) of Directive 84/450 and, thus, constituted comparative advertising.

Citing *O2 Holdings*, it also recalled that the use of a sign identical with the mark of a competitor in that manner was to be regarded as use for the advertiser's own goods and services and could therefore be prevented by virtue of art.5(1) and (2) of the Directive, unless it satisfied all the conditions laid down in art.3a(1) of Directive 84/450, under which comparative advertising is permitted.

Moreover, it observed that insofar as the use at issue was for identical signs and concerned identical goods, it fell within the scope of art.5(1)(a) of the Directive and not that of art.5(1)(b).

6–063   The Court then reiterated its statements in *Arsenal* and *Adam Opel* that the exercise of the rights conferred by art.5(1)(a) is reserved to cases in which the functions of the trade mark are likely to be affected, adding however that "these functions include not only the essential function of the trade mark, but also its other functions, in particular that of guaranteeing the quality of the goods or services in question and those of communication, investment or advertising".[104]

In addition, it explicitly clarified that the protection conferred by art.5(1)(a) is broader than that provided by art.5(1)(b), the application of which requires a likelihood of confusion, noting that this was also attested by the 10th Recital to the Directive, which states that in case of identity the protection afforded by the registered trade mark is absolute, whereas in case of mere similarity the existence of a likelihood of confusion constitutes the specific condition for such protection.[105]

---

[104] *Bellure*, para.58.
[105] *Bellure*, para.59.

3. IDENTICAL SIGNS AND GOODS OR SERVICES

Notwithstanding, the Court underlined that "absolute" protection under that provision does not mean unlimited protection, by stressing that a trade mark proprietor cannot oppose the use of an identical sign if that use is not liable to cause detriment to any of the functions of his mark.[106]

6–064

To make this point even clearer, it referred by way of example to its judgment in *Hölterhoff* where the use served purely descriptive purposes and thus was held not to constitute "use" for the purposes of art.5(1)(a). It observed, however, that the situation in the main proceedings was fundamentally different from the facts in *Hölterhoff*, in that the marks reproduced in the comparison lists were used for advertising and not merely for descriptive purposes.

Accordingly, it stated that it was for the referring court to determine whether the use made by the defendants was liable to affect one of the functions of the earlier marks and, in particular, their functions of communication, investment or advertising. In the negative, and insofar as the case concerned reputed marks, the national court would also have to examine whether the use complained of was caught by art.5(2), the applicability of which does not necessarily require a likelihood of detriment, provided of course that an unfair advantage to the repute of that mark could be established.

Undoubtedly, the judgment in *Bellure* is a further step in the "gradual development" of the case law of the Court—to use the expression of A.G. Mengozzi—towards a broader and more rational trade mark protection.

6–065

Although the Court refrained from defining in detail, at least for now, the functions of "guaranteeing the quality of the goods or services" and of "communication, investment or advertising" performed by trade marks, it is still important that it formally recognised their existence, as well as the fact that they form part of the protectable subject-matter under art.5(1)(a) of the Directive.

Moreover, by accepting that those further functions are protected by art.5(1)(a) of the Directive (new art.5(1)(a)), the Court seems to be suggesting that trade mark proprietors can invoke them even where the earlier mark does not have a reputation. Although it may be true that in the specific case the earlier mark was well known, that conclusion can none the less be inferred, first, by the absence of any reference by the Court to the need for the earlier mark to be reputed when generally defining the scope of art.5(1)(a) and, secondly, *a contrario sensu* from its statement that "furthermore, insofar as [the earlier marks] have a reputation, their use ... can also be prevented under Article 5(2)".[107]

In doing so, the Court actually went one step beyond what was suggested by the Advocate General in the direction of delimiting the relationship between arts 5(1) and 5(2) of the Directive, by recognising in essence that,

---

[106] Citing *Arsenal*, para.54, and *Adam Opel*, para.22.
[107] *Bellure*, para.64.

at least where the signs and the goods are identical, these provisions partly overlap, differing only inasmuch as that the latter also covers instances where the use of the later sign draws unfair advantage of the repute of the earlier well-known mark.

That "rapprochement" of the scopes of the respective provisions is particularly significant in view of the optional character of art.5(2), since it caters for protection against detriment unrelated to a likelihood of confusion and this regardless of whether the earlier mark has a reputation or not.

(7) Google—taking a step back—the relevance of context

6–066 The three joined *Google* cases[108] were the first encounter between trade mark law and the world wide web before the Court. All three cases evolved around the use of trade marks, registered in France and/or as Community Trade Marks, as keywords that triggered third parties' advertisements whenever they were entered into Google's search engine, a function of Google's AdWords tool. The advertisements appeared next to the original results of the search for the trade marked term. AdWords facilitated the communication and interaction between Google and advertisers.

Advocate General Poiares Maduro started by noting that the case required the interpretation of Directive 89/104, Regulation No.40/94, but also of 2000/31, on information society services.[109]

6–067 *(a) The Factual Context*

According to the facts of the first case sites that were offering counterfeits of Louis Vuitton (LV) products and Google had been offering to potential advertisers keywords that combined LV's trade marks with terms like "replica" and "imitation". Google was found to infringe LV's registered trade mark rights.

In the second case the advertising sites belonged to genuine competitors of the proprietors of the trade marks "bourse des vols", "bourse des voyages" and "BDV". Google was found to infringe and, on appeal, to be an accessory to trade mark infringement.

The third case also concerned advertisements by competitors of the proprietor of the trade mark "Eurochallenges". The French Court referred the following questions to the Court.

---

[108] *Google France Google Inc v Louis Vuitton Malletier* (C-236/08), *Google France v Viaticum Luteciel* (C-237/08), and *Google France v CNRRH Others* (C-238/08); the Opinion of the Advocate General was delivered on September 22, 2009.

[109] Directive 2000/31 on certain legal aspects of information society services, in particular electronic commerce, in the internal market ("Directive on electronic commerce") [2000] OJ L178/1.

3. IDENTICAL SIGNS AND GOODS OR SERVICES

(b)   The Opinion of the Advocate General   6–068

In all three cases the French court referred a number of questions (eight overall)[110] to the Court, however the Advocate General considered that all eight questions posed the same basic question:

"[D]oes the use by Google, in its AdWords advertising system, of keywords corresponding to trade marks constitute an infringement of those trade marks? Although the references are formulated somewhat differently, they all ask for an interpretation of Article 5(1) of Directive 89/104 and therefore concern that basic question of whether Google has committed a trade mark infringement."[111]

Turning to the substance of the questions the Advocate General distinguished between use by Google and use by advertisers.

(i) Contributory infringement v liability. The references concerned   6–069
"the use in AdWords of keywords which correspond to trade marks; this use, as described, consists in the selection of those words so that ads are presented as results and in the display of ads alongside the natural results provided for those words".[112] This set the parameters of the case; it did not concern use of trade marks on the advertisers' sites, the products sold on those sites, or in the text of the advertisements.

Indeed he suggested that trade mark proprietors were attempting to connect the use of keywords partly because of the suggestive power of the argument: "The goal of trade mark proprietors is to extend the scope of trade mark protection to cover actions by a party that may contribute to a trade mark infringement by a third party."[113] He found the concept of contributory infringement, as it is known in the United States, to be foreign to European trade mark jurisprudence where infringement was covered under the legal concept of liability.[114] The Advocate General added that trade mark proprietors had gone even further arguing that even the possibility that a system like AdWords might be used to infringe constitutes in itself an infringement.

Advocate General Maduro dismissed from the outset the argument that use of the keywords did not constitute use of the relevant trade marks. Keyword use constituted use of a sign representing a trade mark and should be construed as use of that trade mark.

---

[110] Reproduced in Points 20, 24, and 28.
[111] Point 38 of the Opinion of A.G. Maduro.
[112] Point 46 of the Opinion of A.G. Maduro.
[113] Point 48 of the Opinion of A.G. Maduro.
[114] Citing *Inwood Laboratories, Inc v Ives Laboratories, Inc*, 456 US 844 (S. Ct 1982); and *Optimum Technologies, Inc v Henkel Consumer Adhesives, Inc*, 496 F.3d 1231, 1245 (11th Cir. 2007); *Rolex Watch USA v Meece*, 158 F.3d 816 (5th Cir. 1998); *Hard Rock Cafe Licensing Corp v Concessions Services, Inc*, 955 F.2d 1143 (7th Cir. 1992). *Optimum Technologies* was cited in particular for the additional conditions the Court required.

SCOPE OF PROTECTION, LIMITATIONS AND ENFORCEMENT

Here there was clearly unauthorised use by third parties. He had to ascertain whether three additional requirements were satisfied[115] in relation to the two uses of the keywords by Google: (i) the use that allowed advertisers to select keywords; and (ii) the display of the advertisements next to the search results that contained the trade mark. The two were linked but distinct according to timing (selecting and displaying respectively), target audience (advertisers and internet users), and product (Google's service and advertised goods or services).

6–070   **(ii) Google's "selection" use.** Advocate General Maduro noted that only use as part of a "commercial activity with a view to a gain"; as opposed to private use, constituted infringing use.[116] This condition was clearly satisfied; Google was being remunerated, albeit not at the point of selection but at the point where the internet user was making the click to get into the advertiser's site.

The second condition required use in relation to goods or services that were identical or similar to those covered by the specification. He noted that the list of art.5(3) of Directive 89/104 referred to use "in advertising". He viewed this however as use as part of an advertisement, different from use as a keyword: "The artificial categorisation of all Google's activities in AdWords as uses 'in advertising' would obscure what this condition seeks to determine: to which goods or services each use relates. This, of course, may vary according to the use."[117]

The Court had required use "in such a way that a link is established between the sign ... and the goods marketed or the services provided".[118] Here however use was internal to AdWords and concerned only Google and the advertisers. Accordingly, the second condition was not satisfied.

The third condition was whether this type of use was liable to affect the essential function of the trade mark, "by reason of a likelihood of confusion on the part of the public".[119] Here the Advocate General linked this condition with what we have discussed above. He reminded the Court that the four conditions had to be applied cumulatively but also that in most cases where the preceding question was found not to infringe the current question followed the same route.

6–071   **(iii) Google's display use.** Advocate General Maduro noted that although this was a distinct type of use there was "no substantial difference

---

[115] Citing *O2Holdings and O2 (UK)* (C-533/06) [2008] E.C.R. I-4231; *Arsenal Football Club* (C-206/01) [2002] E.C.R. I-10273; *Anheuser-Busch* (C-245/02) [2004] E.C.R. I-10989; *Medion* (C-120/04) [2005] E.C.R. I-8551; *Adam Opel* (C-48/05) [2007] E.C.R. I-1017; and *Céline* (C-17/06) [2007] E.C.R. I-7041.
[116] Citing *Celine* and *Arsenal*.
[117] Point 64 of the Opinion of A.G. Maduro.
[118] Citing *Céline*, para.23.
[119] Point 67 of the Opinion of A.G. Maduro.

3. IDENTICAL SIGNS AND GOODS OR SERVICES

between the use that Google, itself, makes of the keywords in its search engine and the use that it makes of them in AdWords: it displays certain content in response to those keywords".[120] He added that the advertised sites, even the counterfeit ones, could feature among the natural search results; in any case natural results had very similar characteristics with the advertisements, both incorporated a short message and a link. The difference was simply the degree of exposure.

He found it difficult to argue for a distinction between the two, in terms of trade mark protection, albeit he accepted that this did not mean that the display use might not be found to infringe.

Turning to the three conditions he found that the display use was a commercial activity with a view to a gain since it operated in the same context, "Google gets nothing directly from this use, it obviously lies at the root of the income that Google obtains from AdWords, which in turn allows it to support its search engine. As such, the display of natural results in Google's search engine also satisfies this condition".[121]

Regarding the second condition he suggested that this was exactly what Google was doing "it establishes a link between those keywords and the sites advertised, including the goods or services sold via those sites. Even though the keywords do not feature in the ads themselves, this use falls under the notion of use 'in advertising' as referred to in Article 5(3)(d) of Directive 89/104: the link established is between the trade mark and the goods or services advertised".[122]

6–072

On the essential function of a trade mark he reminded that the questions referred to the Court concerned exclusively Google's, but not the advertisers, use.

Despite the link established between the keywords and the advertised products he supported that whether the link led to confusion should not be presumed, to the contrary it had to be positively established.[123]

The evaluation of factual scenarios did not fall within the jurisdiction of the Court but made the broader point that by "comparing ads with natural results, the parties assume that natural results are a proxy for 'true' results—that is to say, that they originate from the trade mark proprietors themselves. But they do not. Like the ads displayed, natural results are just information that Google, on the basis of certain criteria, displays in response to the keywords. Many of the sites displayed do not in fact correspond to the sites of the trade mark proprietors".[124] He added that internet users were sophisticated and would sift through the results of the search; Google's search engine was simply a tool and the link it established was not enough to lead to confusion. Internet users would only decide on the origin

6–073

---

[120] Point 71 of the Opinion of A.G. Maduro.
[121] Point 77 of the Opinion of A.G. Maduro.
[122] Point 79 of the Opinion of A.G. Maduro.
[123] Citing *Marca Mode* (C-425/98) [2000] E.C.R. I-4861.
[124] Point 87 of the Opinion of A.G. Maduro.

of the goods or services offered on the sites by leaving Google and entering those sites.

Turning to the advertisements he believed that Internet users processed them in the same in the same way:

> "As with natural results, internet users will only make an assessment as to the origin of the goods or services advertised on the basis of the content of the ad and by visiting the advertised sites; no assessment will be based solely on the fact that the ads are displayed in response to keywords corresponding to trade marks. The risk of confusion lies in the ad and in the advertised sites, but, as has already been pointed out, the Court is not being asked about such uses by third parties: it is being asked only about the use by Google of keywords which correspond to trade marks."[125]

Accordingly, neither the display of ads nor the display of natural results might lead to a risk of confusion as to the origin of goods and services.

6–074   **(iv) The relevance of reputation.** The protection trade marks with a reputation enjoyed, according to the Advocate General, was independent of the essential function of the trade mark of guaranteeing the origin of the goods or services, and related to other functions. Citing *L'Oréal*[126] he added that "such other functions of the trade mark include guaranteeing the quality of goods or services and those of communication, investment or advertising; it has also stated that such functions are not limited to trade marks which have a reputation but apply in the case of all trade marks".[127] These functions were linked with innovation and commercial investment and were not protected in the same absolute way with confusion as to origin but according to a sliding scale, with art.5(2) of Directive 89/104 at the top. Article 5(1)(a) was at the middle; the trade mark proprietor could prevent uses that affected the functions of guaranteeing the quality of the goods or services in question and those of communication, investment or advertising. Article 5(1)(b) was at the bottom of the scale: "This protection, the Court has stated, is not the same as the protection under Article 5(1)(a): since mere similarity between goods or services is at issue, 'the likelihood of confusion constitutes the specific condition for such protection'. Accordingly, the other functions of the trade mark can be affected only in very specific cases, yet to be defined by the Court."[128]

Contextualising trade mark protection he stressed "whatever the protection afforded to innovation and investment, it is never absolute. It must

---

[125] Point 91 of the Opinion of A.G. Maduro.
[126] *L'Oréal* (C-487/07) [2009] E.C.R. I-0000.
[127] Point 95 of the Opinion of A.G. Maduro.
[128] Point 100, citing *L'Oréal*, para.59.

3. IDENTICAL SIGNS AND GOODS OR SERVICES

always be balanced against other interests, in the same way as trade mark protection itself is balanced against them. I believe that the present cases call for such a balance as regards freedom of expression and freedom of commerce".[129] In this particular context he added that the promotion of innovation and investment also required competition and open access to ideas, words, and signs:

> "That promotion is always the product of a balance that has been struck between incentives, in the form of private goods given to those who innovate and invest, and the public character of the goods necessary to support and sustain the innovation and investment. That balance is at the heart of trade mark protection. Accordingly, despite being linked to the interests of the trade mark proprietor, trade mark rights cannot be construed as classic property rights enabling the trade mark proprietor to exclude any other use."[130]

The transformation of public into private goods was a product of the law and appropriately limited to the legitimate interests that the law deemed worthy of protection, accordingly protection would cover only some types of use. Others, like use for purely descriptive purposes[131] or use in comparative advertising, could fall outside the scope of protection.

Following a parallel path he concluded that "given the lack of any risk of confusion, trade mark proprietors have no general right to prevent those uses".[132] Otherwise, trade mark proprietors could establish an absolute right of control over the use of their trade marks as keywords: "Such an absolute right of control would cover, de facto, whatever could be shown and said in cyberspace with respect to the good or service associated with the trade mark."[133] Keywords were at the heart of the internet's architecture, they should be seen as content-neutral in themselves, and freely accessed in the context of lawful activities.

He concluded that:

6–075

> "[T]he uses by Google, in AdWords, of keywords which correspond to trade marks do not affect the other functions of the trade mark, namely guaranteeing the quality of the goods or services or those of communication, investment or advertising. Trade marks which have a reputation are entitled to special protection because of those functions but, even so, such functions should not be considered to be affected. Thus, the uses by

---

[129] Point 102, citing *Karner* (C-71/02) [2004] E.C.R. I-3025; and *Booker Aquaculture and Hydro Seafood* (C-20/00 & C-64/00) [2003] E.C.R. I-7411 as examples where the Court has dealt with the same issues in a different context.
[130] Point 103 of the Opinion of A.G. Maduro.
[131] Citing *Hölterhoff* (C-2/00) [2002] E.C.R. I-4187.
[132] Point 107 of the Opinion of A.G. Maduro.
[133] Point 108 of the Opinion of A.G. Maduro.

SCOPE OF PROTECTION, LIMITATIONS AND ENFORCEMENT

Google may not be prevented even if they involve trade marks which have a reputation."[134]

6-076 **(v) Introducing use by third parties.** Advocate General Maduro went on to examine whether Google's possible contribution, through AdWords, to trade mark infringement by third parties constituted, in itself, trade mark infringement. He acknowledged that trade mark proprietors faced considerable practical difficulties in dealing with sites with counterfeit products but added that that in this case they were trying to stop the message by stopping the messenger.

The argument for contributory infringement would involve a significant expansion of the scope of protection, novel to most Member States, and "alien to the case-law of the Court, which has so far focused on separate, individual uses".[135]

Turning back to the point regarding the messenger he rejected the concept of contributory infringement also because of the risks in restricting a system that facilitate access to and delivery of information. Putting the internet in a historical context he added that similar problems were encountered by the invention of printing and the introduction of other innovative products.[136]

Instead of transforming trade mark law into a blunt tool for addressing the trade mark proprietors' concerns he supported the option of properly delineated areas of protection. This could cover some of Google's activities, for example the information Google provided advertisers allowing them to maximise exposure, in particular when this information was provided to counterfeit sites or the keywords comprised words conceptually linked with counterfeiting.

6-077 **(vi) The liability exemption for hosting.** The next step was to consider whether the liability exemption for hosting applied to the content featured by Google in AdWords under art.14 of Directive 2000/31.[137]

---

[134] Point 113 of the Opinion of A.G. Maduro.
[135] Point 117 of the Opinion of A.G. Maduro.
[136] Interestingly citing a judgment of the US Supreme Court, *Sony Corp of America v Universal City Studios, Inc*, 464 US 417 (1984).
[137] Providing amongst others that: "1. Where an information society service is provided that consists of the storage of information provided by a recipient of the service, Member States shall ensure that the service provider is not liable for the information stored at the request of a recipient of the service, on condition that:

(a) the provider does not have actual knowledge of illegal activity or information and, as regards claims for damages, is not aware of facts or circumstances from which the illegal activity or information is apparent; or
(b) the provider, upon obtaining such knowledge or awareness, acts expeditiously to remove or to disable access to the information.

...

3. This Article shall not affect the possibility for a court or administrative authority, in accordance with Member States' legal systems, of requiring the service provider to terminate or prevent an infringement, nor does it affect the possibility for Member States of establishing procedures governing the removal or disabling of access to information."

3. IDENTICAL SIGNS AND GOODS OR SERVICES

Briefly, he supported that the provision of hyperlink services and search engines fell squarely within the notion of information society services and was consistent with the aim pursued by Directive 2000/31 to create a free and open public domain on the internet.

Article 15 of Directive 2000/31 was viewed by the Advocate General "not merely as imposing a negative obligation on Member States, but as the very expression of the principle that service providers which seek to benefit from a liability exemption should remain neutral as regards the information they carry or host".[138] This was:

"[B]est illustrated by comparison with Google's search engine, which is neutral as regards the information it carries [fn. omitted]. Its natural results are a product of automatic algorithms that apply objective criteria in order to generate sites likely to be of interest to the internet user. The presentation of those sites and the order in which they are ranked depends on their relevance to the keywords entered, and not on Google's interest in or relationship with any particular site. Admittedly, Google has an interest—even a pecuniary interest—in displaying the more relevant sites to the internet user; however, it does not have an interest in bringing any specific site to the internet user's attention."[139]

However, the position regarding the content featured in AdWords was different. Google's display of ads stemmed from its relationship with the advertisers. It could not be seen as a neutral information vehicle and should not be covered by the liability exemption.

(vii) Use by the advertisers. The final point examined by A.G. Maduro was whether trade mark proprietors could prevent the use by advertisers, in AdWords, of keywords corresponding to their trade marks. **6-078**

First, he found the selection process to constitute private use rather than a commercial activity. They were the consumers of Google's services and if what Google was selling was lawful their purchase should be equally lawful. Indeed it could be part of straightforward legitimate activities like descriptive uses, comparative advertising, and product reviews.

Article 15 1 provided that:
"Member States shall not impose a general obligation on providers, when providing the services covered by Articles 12, 13 and 14, to monitor the information which they transmit or store, nor a general obligation actively to seek facts or circumstances indicating illegal activity.
2. Member States may establish obligations for information society service providers promptly to inform the competent public authorities of alleged illegal activities undertaken or information provided by recipients of their service or obligations to communicate to the competent authorities, at their request, information enabling the identification of recipients of their service with whom they have storage agreements."
[138] Point 143 of the Opinion of A.G. Maduro.
[139] Point 144 of the Opinion of A.G. Maduro.

Trade mark proprietors could intervene at the time their trade marks appeared in the advertisement.

6–079 **(viii) Answering the questions.** Concluding A.G. Maduro suggested the following:

"(1) The selection by an economic operator, by means of an agreement on paid internet referencing, of a keyword which will trigger, in the event of a request using that word, the display of a link proposing connection to a site operated by that economic operator for the purposes of offering for sale goods or services, and which reproduces or imitates a trade mark registered by a third party and covering identical or similar goods, without the authorisation of the proprietor of that trade mark, does not constitute in itself an infringement of the exclusive right guaranteed to the latter under Article 5 of First Council Directive 89/104/EEC of 21 December 1988 to approximate the laws of the Member States relating to trade marks.

(2) Article 5(1)(a) and (b) of Directive 89/104 and Article 9(1)(a) and (b) of Council Regulation (EC) No 40/94 of 20 December 1993 on the Community trade mark must be interpreted as meaning that a trade mark proprietor may not prevent the provider of a paid referencing service from making available to advertisers keywords which reproduce or imitate registered trade marks or from arranging under the referencing agreement for advertising links to sites to be created and favourably displayed, on the basis of those keywords.

(3) In the event that the trade marks have a reputation, the trade mark proprietor may not oppose such use under Article 5(2) of Directive 89/104 and Article 9(1)(c) of Regulation No 40/94.

(4) The provider of the paid referencing service cannot be regarded as providing an information society service consisting in the storage of information provided by the recipient of the service within the meaning of Article 14 of Directive 2000/31/EC of the European Parliament and of the Council of 8 June 2000 on certain legal aspects of information society services, in particular electronic commerce, in the internal market ('Directive on electronic commerce')."[140]

4. THE CONFLICT BETWEEN TRADE MARKS AND TRADE NAMES

6–080 **(1) Robelco—trade marks and trade names**

Robelco[141] was the first case that the Court looked at the meaning of art.5(5). Robeco, an asset management company that owned the Benelux

---

[140] Point 155 of the Opinion of A.G. Maduro.
[141] *Robelco NV v Robeco Groep NV* (C-23/01) [2002] E.C.R. I-1093; see also *Anheuser-Busch v Budejovicky Budvar Narodni Podnik* (C-245/02) [2004] E.C.R. I-10989, paras 10–133 and following, below.

4. THE CONFLICT BETWEEN TRADE MARKS AND TRADE NAMES

trade mark Robeco, started trade mark infringement proceedings against Robelco, a business park property developer, seeking a restraining order against use of the sign Robelco, or any other similar to Robeco sign, as a trade name or company name.

The case reached the Hof van Beroep (Court of Appeal), Brussels, that referred two questions to the Court of Justice regarding the interpretation of art.5(5): (i) does the provision cover signs that are similar as well as identical to an earlier trade mark?; (ii) if the answer is yes, then is there a likelihood of confusion requirement or would likelihood of association suffice?[142]

The parties agreed that art.5(5) was not a trade-mark law provision. Robeco supported that the term sign covered identical as well as similar signs and that whether there is a likelihood of confusion or association is irrelevant according to the provision. Robelco, on the other hand, contended that there must be identity between the trade mark and the sign, otherwise it would be necessary to assess in each case whether there exists a likelihood of confusion. The Commission submitted that art.5(5) was not a harmonisation provision; its purpose was to exclude this area of law from

---

[142] The national court highlighted the difference between art.13A(1)(d) of the Uniform Benelux Law and art.5(5) of the Directive. Article 13A(1)(d) explicitly covered similar signs. So it questioned whether the two provisions were consistent with each other. Article 5(5) of the Directive provides: "Paragraphs 1 to 4 shall not affect provisions in any Member State relating to the protection against the use of a sign other than for the purposes of distinguishing goods or services, where use of that sign without due cause takes unfair advantage of, or is detrimental to, the distinctive character or the repute of the trade mark." Article 13A(1) of the Uniform Benelux Law as amended in 1996 following the transposition of the Directive provides:

"Without prejudice to any application of the ordinary law governing civil liability, the exclusive rights in a trade mark shall entitle the proprietor to oppose:

(a) any use, in the course of trade, of the mark in respect of the goods for which the mark is registered;
(b) any use, in the course of trade, of the mark or a similar sign in respect of the goods for which the mark is registered or similar goods where there exists a risk of association on the part of the public between the sign and the mark;
(c) any use, in the course of trade and without due cause, of a trade mark which has a reputation in the Benelux countries or of a similar sign for goods which are not similar to those for which the trade mark is registered, where use of that sign would take unfair advantage of, or would be detrimental to, the distinctive character or the repute of the trade mark;
(d) any use, in the course of trade and without due cause, of a trade mark or of a similar sign other than for the purposes of distinguishing goods, where use of that sign without due cause takes unfair advantage of, or is detrimental to, the distinctive character or the repute of the trade mark."

The Commission suggested and the A.G. appeared to accept that art.5(5) was adopted to accommodate the original art.13(A)(1) that prior to the Directive provided:

"Without prejudice to any application of the ordinary law governing civil liability, the exclusive rights in a trade mark shall entitle the proprietor to oppose:

1. any use of the trade mark or a similar sign in respect of the goods for which the mark is registered or similar goods;
2. any other use of the trade mark or a similar sign in the course of trade and without due cause which would be liable to be detrimental to the owner of the trade mark."

The amended version is closer to the language used in the Directive.

SCOPE OF PROTECTION, LIMITATIONS AND ENFORCEMENT

harmonisation. The national court had correctly established that art.5(5) was applicable on the facts of the case and it was free to decide how the national provision should be interpreted.

6–081 *(a) The Opinion of the Advocate General*

Advocate General Ruiz-Jarabo Colomer considered that the critical question was whether art.5(5) is a provision that falls under the scope of Community law or national law rather than whether it is a trade mark law provision or not.

Regarding the second issue he noted that "although it may be appropriate to consider that trade mark law covers only those matters which relate essentially to the distinguishing function of trade marks, it is not unreasonable to imagine a wider category which encompasses the whole range of conflicts which might arise in relation to a trade mark".[143]

According to his first distinction he described art.5 as establishing two boundaries, one positive and one negative:

> "In the positive sense, the right to prohibit use of identical or similar signs for identical or similar products, where there is a likelihood of confusion, is a harmonised right of trade mark proprietors. In the negative sense, the strengthened protection of the distinctive character and goodwill of trade marks which have a reputation and the rules relating to use of a sign in a way which is not designed to identify the origin of goods or services are not subject to approximation at Community level."[144]

6–082 The Advocate General found the language of art.5(5) puzzling: "Where a sign is not used, directly or indirectly, subliminally or unintentionally, to identify goods or services, I fail to see what relevance it can have to trade for the purposes of trade mark law."[145] Unless, the provision covered signs that are not used as trade marks in the formal sense. Indeed, this is how the national court and the parties viewed the provision, and the Advocate General, somewhat reluctantly, adopted the same perspective.

He noted that he had no evidence at his disposal that could lead him to an alternative view and the analysis of the questions referred did not force him to conclude otherwise.[146] So the:

> "[S]ituation where a sign is used otherwise than for the purpose of distinguishing the origin of goods or services is not covered by Article 5(1), which refers to the identification of goods and services, and is instead

---

[143] Point 29 of the Opinion of Ruiz-Jarabo Colomer.
[144] Point 31 of the Opinion of Ruiz-Jarabo Colomer.
[145] Point 32 of the Opinion of Ruiz-Jarabo Colomer.
[146] Point 33 is particularly interesting for identifying ways that would allow the Advocate General to ignore the submissions of the parties and interveners and the position of the referring court and look at a case from a new angle.

4. THE CONFLICT BETWEEN TRADE MARKS AND TRADE NAMES

specifically caught by the reservation in favour of the legislatures of the Member States laid down in Article 5(5). That area is outside the scope of the Directive, which, furthermore, and for the avoidance of any doubt, confers on the Member States the power to legislate on such matters."[147]

Accordingly Member States were free to legislate as they wished in this area. Imposing restrictions would lead to an unjustified restriction of the freedom of action they enjoy in areas such as unfair competition, consumer protection and civil liability. From a trade mark law perspective, art.5(1) and art.5(2) and all the similarity requirements therein were linked with the function of a trade mark as distinguishing signs; this function was not relevant in the case of art.5(5). And looking at the relevant Benelux provision he noted that the Benelux legislature did not appear to exceed its powers under Community law.

(b) The judgment of the Court 6–083

The Court accepted the core of the Commission's submission: "it is clear from Article 5(5) of the Directive that the harmonisation brought about by Article 5(1) to (4) does not affect national provisions relating to the protection of a sign against use other than for the purpose of distinguishing goods or services, where such use without due cause takes unfair advantage of, or is detrimental to, the distinctive character or the repute of the trade mark".[148] The third Recital confirmed this.

Member States "may adopt no legislation in this area or they may, subject to such conditions as they may determine, require that the sign and the trade mark be either identical or similar, or that there be some other connection between them".[149]

(2) Céline—trade names performing a distinguishing function 6–084

In *Céline*[150] the Court dealt with trade names not from the perspective of art.5(5) of the Directive, as in *Robelco*, but under art.5(1)(a). The novel element was whether a company name is capable of being used in relation to goods or services within the meaning of that provision, opening thus new possibilities as regards the protection against signs performing a trade mark like function.

Céline SA, a high-end clothing and fashion accessories manufacturer, is the owner of the word mark "CÉLINE", registered in France in respect of, inter alia, "clothes and shoes". Mr Grynfogel, another French trader,

---

[147] Point 34. The Third Recital of the Preamble to the Directive is clear about approximation.
[148] *Robelco*, para.30.
[149] *Robelco*, para.35.
[150] *Céline SARL v Céline SA* (C-17/06) [2007] E.C.R. I-7041.

517

operated in Nancy a ready-to-wear garments business, trading as "Céline", which was subsequently transferred to Céline SARL. Upon being alerted to that state of affairs, Céline SA brought proceedings against Céline SARL, seeking an order prohibiting it from infringing its trade mark by using the company name and shop title "Céline".

The Tribunal de Grande Instance de Nancy (Nancy Regional Court) granted the relief sought and prohibited Céline SARL from using the term "Céline" either on its own or in conjunction with other terms and ordered it to change its company name to one incapable of being confused with the plaintiff's mark.

6–085   Céline SARL brought an appeal against that judgment before the Cour d'appel de Nancy (Nancy Court of Appeal), arguing that the use of its sign did not amount to infringing conduct, since it is not the function of either a company or a shop title to distinguish goods or services and that, in any event, there could be no confusion as to origin, as Céline SA operated exclusively in the luxury market.

The Cour d'appel de Nancy decided to stay the proceedings and to refer the following question to the Court for a preliminary ruling:

> "Must Article 5(1) of [the directive] ... be interpreted as meaning that the adoption, by a third party without authorisation, of a registered word mark, as a company, trade or shop name in connection with the marketing of identical goods, amounts to use of that mark in the course of trade which the proprietor is entitled to stop by reason of his exclusive rights?"

6–086   *(a)   The Opinion of the Advocate General*

Advocate General Sharpston started her analysis by pertinently observing that to the extent that the referring court was asking whether the adoption of a company or trade name can constitute use within the meaning of art.5(1) of the Directive, it was necessary to distinguish between the formal adoption of such a name and the way in which it is subsequently used in the course of trade.

After noting that according to the case law,[151] the application of art.5(1) (a) requires that the sign must be used to distinguish goods and that its use must be likely to affect the trade mark's essential function, in particular by creating the impression that there is a material link in trade between the trade mark proprietor and the goods so distinguished, she moved on to apply those principles to the usual function of company names.

In that regard, she agreed that although the adoption and use of a company and/or trade name was in principle capable of constituting "use"

---

[151] Citing the judgments in *Bayerische Motorenwerke AG and BMW Nederland BV* (C-63/97) [1999] E.C.R. I-905; *Arsenal Football Club Plc* (C-206/01) [2002] E.C.R. I-10273; and *Busch Inc v Budejovicky Budvar, narodni podnik* (C-245/02) [2004] E.C.R. I-10989.

4. THE CONFLICT BETWEEN TRADE MARKS AND TRADE NAMES

within the meaning of art.5(1) of the Directive, this would not "necessarily and automatically" be true in all cases.[152]

6–087 Specifically, she remarked that a company name need not necessarily be used "in relation to" goods or services which the company supplies, in particular since its use may be confined to more formal circumstances, as when for instance the company is actually trading under one or more other names. And even where the company name is used in some relation to goods, that use will not necessarily be such as to distinguish those goods by designating their origin. A fortiori, this means that the mere registration of a company name must normally fall outside the scope of art.5(1), even though it is quite unlikely that the adoption of a trade name will not also be followed by actual use "in the course of trade".[153]

Moreover, the existence of a non-exhaustive list, in art.5(3), of types of conduct which may be prohibited under art.5(1) and (2) does not imply that all instances of such conduct will always fall within the scope of those provisions. It will always be necessary to ascertain, in addition, whether the particular conduct meets the specific requirements triggering that type of prohibition.

The Advocate General therefore suggested to answer the question referred to the effect that the mere adoption of a company or trade name does not normally constitute use within the meaning of art.5(1) of the Directive and that the subsequent use of such a name in the course of trade must be assessed by the competent court on the facts of each case, in order to determine whether it constitutes use in relation to goods or services for the purposes of that provision.

6–088 However, she noted also that insofar as the right which Céline SA seeks to assert derives from trade mark law and from its status as trade mark proprietor, it was further necessary to address the possible impact on the case of the limitation in art.6(1)(a), under which the proprietor may not prevent another person from using his own name in the course of trade, if that use is in accordance with honest practices in industrial or commercial matters.

Citing *Anheuser Busch*[154] and *BMW*,[155] she recalled in this context that art.6(1)(a) is not confined to names of natural persons and that the condition of honest practices implies a duty to act fairly in relation to the legitimate interests of the trade mark owner.

Furthermore, she noted that what was at stake in the main proceedings was whether the adoption of the company name after the registration of the trade mark and its possible use in relation to goods, is in accordance with honest practices; indeed, even if the name had been adopted before registration, the "honest practices" condition could only become relevant

---

[152] Point 34 of the Opinion of A.G. Sharpston.
[153] Point 35 of the Opinion of A.G. Sharpston.
[154] *Anheuser Busch*, paras 77–80.
[155] *BMW*, para.61.

after that registration, although in such a case its relevance would obviously be affected by the relative timing.

6–089   At all events, she stressed that the question of knowledge is crucial in that connection, since a person cannot normally be said to be acting in accordance with honest commercial practices if he adopts a name which he knows to be identical or similar to an existing trade mark.[156]

However, mere ignorance of the existence of the trade mark cannot be sufficient to exonerate that person of all responsibility. In fact, honest practice in the choice of a name implies a reasonable diligence in ascertaining that the name chosen does not conflict with prior trade-mark rights, and thus in verifying the existence of any such marks, all the more so since a search in national and Community Trade Mark registers is not normally particularly difficult or burdensome.[157]

On the other hand, if the search reveals the existence of similar or identical trade marks, the applicability of the prohibition should depend on the user's subsequent conduct, given that the compliance with honest practices would presumably imply at least contacting the trade mark proprietor and seeking his approval. Such a course of action may relieve the user of all possible responsibility not only if an approval is actually given, but also when it results in acquiescence on the part of the owner, which, depending on the circumstances, may be equalled to his (tacit) consent, within the meaning of art.51 of the Directive.[158]

6–090   *(b)   The judgment of the Court*

The Court followed the example of the Advocate General and examined the question referred as regards both the rule contained in art.5 and the corresponding exception included in art.6(1)(a) of the Directive.

6–091   **(i) The function of company names.** With regard to the former, it stressed that, as follows from the scheme of that provision, use of the sign in relation to goods or services within the meaning of ss.5(1) and 5(2) is use for the purpose of distinguishing those goods and services, whereas s.5(5) dealt with use for other purposes.

Then, it referred to its judgment in *Robelco* that the purpose of a company, trade or shop name is not, of itself, to distinguish goods and services. Rather, the purpose of a company name is to identify a company, while that of a trade or shop name is to designate a business or the establishment where it is carried out. Accordingly, where the use is limited to those purposes, it cannot be considered as being "in relation to goods" within the meaning of art.5(1) of the Directive.[159]

---

[156] Points 53–54 of the Opinion of A.G. Sharpston.
[157] Point 55 of the Opinion of A.G. Sharpston.
[158] Points 57–58 of the Opinion of A.G. Sharpston.
[159] *Céline*, para.21.

4. THE CONFLICT BETWEEN TRADE MARKS AND TRADE NAMES

Conversely, it held that there is use "in relation to goods" where a third party either affixes the sign constituting his company, trade or shop name to goods or, even where the sign is not so affixed, where it is used in a way that a link is established between that sign and the goods or services marketed or provided by the third party.[160]

Finally, it left it up to the national court to determine whether the facts of the specific case actually corresponded to such use, or whether the use made of the sign was liable of affecting the essential function of the registered trade mark.

It is worth noting, however, that even if the criterion of use "in relation to goods" is satisfied in the above sense, it is questionable whether the activities carried out under a company or, in particular, shop name will ever be "identical" with the goods for which the trade mark is protected in the sense of art.5(1)(a) of the Directive, unless of course the company name is also used as a trade mark in the strict sense by being actually affixed on goods, as a "house" mark.

6–092

In a traditional analysis under the Nice Classification, activities more indirectly linked to goods would most likely classify as retail services falling under Class 35 of the Nice Agreement, within the meaning of the Court's judgment in *Praktiker*.[161] Thus, however close the link between those activities and the goods to which they relate, it will be very difficult to ignore the fact that the comparison still concerns goods on the one hand, and services on the other, which although on occasion may display similarities, cannot be regarded as being identical.[162]

Unless of course one skips the question altogether and only focuses on the nature of the goods to which the use "relates" one way or another.

(ii) The "honest practices" exception. Next, the Court noted that it is for the Court to provide the national court with all the elements for the interpretation of Community law which may be of assistance in adjudicating on the case pending before it, whether or not that court has specifically referred to them in its questions.

6–093

Consequently, it went on to examine the impact of the exception provided for in art.6(1)(a) to the facts, pointing out that the condition of complying with "honest practices in industrial or commercial matters" stated in that provision basically constitutes an expression of the duty to act fairly in relation to the legitimate interests of the trade mark proprietor.[163]

---

[160] *Céline*, paras 22–23.
[161] *Praktiker Bau und Heimwerkermärkte* (C-418/02) [2005] E.C.R. I-5873.
[162] That was the approach taken by the Court of First Instance in *Oakley, Inc v OHIM* (THE O STORE) (T-116/06) when comparing the retailing of all sorts of clothing to the garments themselves, by stressing the different nature and purpose of goods as compared to services.
[163] Citing *Anheuser-Busch*, para.82.

In that regard, it held that, in assessing whether the condition of honest practice is satisfied, account must be taken, first, of the extent to which the use of the name is understood by at least a significant section of the public, as indicating a link between the third party's goods or services and the trade-mark proprietor, and, secondly, of the extent to which the third party ought to have been aware of that. Another factor to be taken into account is whether the trade mark enjoys a reputation in the Member State in which it is registered, from which the third party might profit.[164]

Note that in relation to honest practices the Court focused primarily on objective factors, like the perception of the relevant public and the possible reputation of the earlier mark,[165] rather than on the more subjective criteria linked to the knowledge of the third party as to the existence of the earlier mark and the diligence displayed in ascertaining whether such conflicting prior rights actually exist, suggested by the Advocate General.

5. LIMITATIONS TO TRADE MARK RIGHTS

6-094 **(1) BMW—setting the principles**

BMW[166] was the first case that came before the Court seeking the interpretation of art.6. It was a reference from the Hoge Raad (Supreme Court) of the Netherlands.

BMW was the registered proprietor of the BMW trade marks—the BMW acronym as such and two figurative trade marks—in the Benelux. The specification covered motor vehicles, engines, spare parts and accessories. BMW cars were marketed through a network of dealers that were required to meet the standards set by BMW. Deenik run a garage; he specialised in repairing BMW cars and was also trading second-hand BMWs.

BMW claimed before the Dutch courts that use of its marks in Deenik's advertisements constituted trade mark infringement. The Arrondissementsrechtbank te Zwolle (Tribunal of Zwolle) decided, that although a number of statements made by Deenik in advertisements of his business constituted unauthorised use of the BMW marks insofar as they might create the impression that he was part of the BMW's dealer network, Deenik remained free to use in advertisements statements such as "Repairs and maintenance of BMWs" since it was clear that that statement referred only to products bearing the BMW mark. He could also use statements such as "Specialist in BMWs". The decision was confirmed by the Gerechtshof (Court of Appeal), Arnhem.

---

[164] *Céline*, para.34.
[165] Citing *Anheuser-Busch*, para.83.
[166] *Bayerische Motorenwerke AG and BMW Nederlard BV* (C-63/97) [1999] E.C.R. I-905.

5. LIMITATIONS TO TRADE MARK RIGHTS

The case reached the Hoge Raad that stayed proceedings and referred the following questions to the Court:

"(1) In view of the fact that, with regard to the rights associated with a trade mark, the Directive contains a transitional legal provision only for the purpose of the case described in Article 5(4), are Member States otherwise free to lay down rules on the matter, or does Community law in general, or the objective and tenor of Directive 89/104 in particular, have the effect that Member States are not entirely free in that regard but must comply with specific restrictions, and if so which?

(2) If someone, without the authorisation of the trade mark proprietor, makes use of that proprietor's trade mark, registered exclusively for specified goods, for the purpose of announcing to the public that he;

 (a) carries out repair and maintenance work on the goods which have been placed on the market under that trade mark by the proprietor or with his consent, or that he;
 (b) is a specialist or is specialised with regard to such goods, does this, under the scheme of Article 5 of the Directive, involve:
   (i) use of the trade mark in relation to goods which are identical to those for which it was registered, as referred to in Article 5(1)(a);
   (ii) use of that trade mark in relation to services which must be deemed to constitute use of the trade mark within the meaning of Article 5(1)(a) or use of the trade mark as referred to in Article 5(1)(b), on the assumption that it can be stated that there is an identity between those services and the goods for which the trade mark was registered;
   (iii) use of the trade mark as referred to in Article 5(2); or
   (iv) use of the trade mark as referred to in Article 5(5)?

(3) For the purpose of answering Question 2, does it make any difference whether announcement (a) or announcement (b) is involved?

(4) In the light of the provision in Article 7 of the Directive, does it make any difference, with regard to the question whether the proprietor of the trade mark can prevent use of his trade mark registered exclusively for specified goods, whether the use referred to in Question 2 is that under (i), (ii), (iii) or (iv)?

(5) On the assumption that both or one of the cases described at the start of Question 2 involve the use of the proprietor's trade mark within the meaning of Article 5(1), whether under Article 5(1)(a) or (b), can the proprietor prevent that use only where the person thus using the trade mark thereby creates the impression that his undertaking is affiliated to the trade-mark proprietor's network, or can he also prevent that use where there is a good chance that the manner in which the trade mark is used for those announcements may create an impression among the

6–095

public that the trade mark is in that regard being used to an appreciable extent for the purpose of advertising his own business as such by creating a specific suggestion of quality?"[167]

(a) The Opinion of the Advocate General

6–096   **(i) The effect of the Directive.** Advocate General Jacobs dealt first with the effect of the Directive. The Benelux law was amended according to the Directive in January 1, 1996 whereas the deadline for its implementation was December 31, 1992. The Directive incorporated specific transitional provisions: art.5(4) provided that where, under the law of the Member State, the use of a sign under the conditions referred to in art.5(1)(b) or art.5(2) could not be prohibited before the date on which the provisions necessary to comply with the Directive entered into force in the Member State concerned, the rights conferred by the trade mark could not be relied on to prevent the continued use of the sign; art.3(4) and art.4(6) stated that Member State might provide that the grounds of refusal of registration or invalidity in force in that state prior to the date on which the provisions necessary to comply with the Directive entered into force should apply to trade marks for which application was made prior to that date. There was no provision dealing with which national law should be applied, the one effective prior to the adoption of the Directive or that following its adoption, in respect of litigation on use of a sign which commenced before the date that the Directive came into force and was still continuing.

Citing *Marleasing*[168] the Advocate General suggested that in respect of the continued use of the sign after the date by which the Directive should have been implemented, the rights under art.5 should be enforced, unless the case fell under art.5(4): "With effect from that date, whether or not the Directive has been transposed into national law, all provisions of national law must be interpreted as far as possible in accordance with the Directive."[169]

If the Directive had not been properly implemented, the question would be whether it could have direct effect in proceedings brought against individuals. In this case, use of the marks during the period before the date for implementing the Directive had passed would be covered under the previous national law. Substantive rules could be interpreted as applying to situations existing before their entry into force only insofar as it clearly followed from their terms, objectives or general scheme that such an effect should be given to them; but there was no such need in this case.[170]

---

[167] Reproduced in para.12.
[168] *Marleasing v La Comercial Internacional de Alimentacion* (C-106/89) [1990] E.C.R. I-4135.
[169] Point 28 of the Opinion of A.G. Jacobs.
[170] He cited *Marshall v Southampton and South-West Hampshire Area Health Authority* (152/84) [1986] E.C.R. 723; and *Faccini Dori v Recreb Srl* (C-91/92) [1994] E.C.R. I-3325; and *Amministrazione delle Finanze dello Stato v Salumi* (212/80 to 217/80) [1981] E.C.R. 2735 for the specific proposition. The latter was also supported by *Ct Control and Jct Benelux v Commission* (C-121/91 & C-122/91) [1993] E.C.R. I-3873; and *Conserchimica v Amministrazione delle Finanze dello Stato* (C-261/96) [1997] E.C.R. I-6177.

5. LIMITATIONS TO TRADE MARK RIGHTS

He concluded that, when implementing the Directive in national law, Member States were not free to adopt any transitional provisions other than those expressly provided for by the Directive insofar as such transitional provisions would prejudice the complete and correct transposition of the Directive.

(ii) The role of the Court. Before turning to the substantive trade mark issues A.G. Jacobs noted that BMW's registrations covered motor vehicles and their parts and accessories but not services relating thereto. In his Opinion he considered Deenik's use first in relation to goods and second in relation to services. 6–097

Further, he suggested that it would not be appropriate for the Court to seek to give guidance on the specific forms of words which were an issue in the national proceedings. Instead, the Court should give guidance on the applicable principles.

(iii) Use of the mark in relation to goods 6–098

Article 5(1) (a) He found the advertisements regarding the sale of second-hand BMWs to fall within art.5(1)(a) since they concerned use of the mark in relation to the genuine article:

> "Indeed, even the advertisement of the repairs and maintenance services falls within that provision in so far as it can be read as meaning simply that Mr Deenik's garage is capable of servicing BMW cars and not that the servicing provided there is authorised by BMW ... in that case the mark is being used to describe what can be repaired and serviced and is thus being used 'in relation to' the cars, rather than Mr Deenik's services."[171]

Exhaustion of rights However, since the cars had already been put on the market in the Community by the proprietor or with his consent, he found that BMW's trade marks rights had been exhausted under art.7(1). 6–099

As to the applicability of art.7(2) he referred to *Dior*[172] where the Court held that a reseller was free to make use of the trade mark in order to bring to the public's attention the further commercialisation of the marked goods and that the trade mark owner might object to such use only if it were to seriously damage the reputation of the mark.

He believed that the same principle should cover the case where "there is a genuine and properly substantiated likelihood of advertising leading the public to believe that the reseller is an authorised distributor ... in order to prevent the public being misled in that way, even if, because the

---

[171] Point 35 of the Opinion of A.G. Jacobs.
[172] *Parfums Christian Dior SA v Evora BV* (C-337/95) [1997] E.C.R. I-6013.

undertaking in question is competent and respectable, there is thereby no damage to his reputation".[173]

It was the national court that had to carry out the assessment of that likelihood.

6-100 *The aura of quality* Regarding the last question raised by the Hoge Raad A.G. Jacobs remarked:

> "[I]f there is no likelihood of the public being confused into believing that there is some sort of trade connection between the reseller and the trade-mark owner, the mere fact that the reseller obtains an advantage by the use of the trade mark because the sale of the trade-marked goods gives his own business an aura of quality is not... a legitimate reason within the meaning of Article 7(2) of the Directive for a trade-mark owner to object to the advertising of his own goods. Otherwise it would be unduly difficult for the trader effectively to inform the public of the business in which he is engaged."[174]

6-101 **(iv) Use of the mark in relation to services**

Article 5(1)(b) Use of the mark in relation to the repairs and maintenance could fall under art.5(1)(b), since goods and services could not be identical to each other. The national court would have to assess the likelihood of confusion according to the relevant case law of the Court[175]; he stressed that "with reference to the last question raised by the Hoge Raad, it is accordingly clearly not sufficient for the application of Article 5(1)(b), in the absence of any such confusion, to show simply that the reseller derives advantage from the mere fact that he deals in the trade-marked goods because the trade mark's aura of quality rubs off to some extent, giving his own business a high quality image".[176]

6-102 *Article 5(2)* He also left open the possibility of applying art.5(2). Again the applicability of that provision to the facts of the case was an issue the national court had to determine. He agreed though with the submission of the Commission and the Government of the United Kingdom that it seemed unlikely. It would be difficult to hold that advertising legitimate economic activities could be regarded as use without due cause or that it would be detrimental. "Any detriment to BMW is perhaps caused primarily, as the Commission suggests, by the competition offered by independent garages

---

[173] Point 39 of the Opinion of A.G. Jacobs.
[174] Point 42 of the Opinion of A.G. Jacobs.
[175] He cited *Sabel BV* (C-251/95) [1997] E.C.R. I-6191; and his Opinion in *Canon Kabushiki Kaisha* (C-39/97) [1998] E.C.R. I-5507; [1998] 1 C.M.L.R. 445.
[176] Point 45 of the Opinion of A.G. Jacobs.

5. LIMITATIONS TO TRADE MARK RIGHTS

to BMW's authorised distributors. Such detriment is not material from the point of view of trade-mark protection."[177]

Article 5(5) Similarly, the applicability of art.5(5) appeared unlikely, because it required the use to be "without due cause". 6–103

The application of article 6 Despite the fact that the national court had failed to refer directly to art.6 in its questions the Advocate General discussed its potential application in relation to the provision of services by an independent trader since it had been raised by the United Kingdom Government in its written observations and by BMW, the Italian Government and the Commission in response to a question posed by the Court. 6–104

BMW based its observations on the inclusion of "necessary" in the wording of art.6(1)(c) arguing that there was no necessity for Deenik to use the marks.

The issue would have to be decided by the national court; however, the Advocate General discussed the principles behind the provision.

He characterised BMW's suggestion that Deenik could offer the services of car maintenance and repair without the need to name any specific make of car as unrealistic. He accepted the argument of the United Kingdom Government that if Deenik did in fact specialise in maintaining and repairing BMW cars it was difficult to see how he could effectively communicate that fact to his customers without using the BMW signs, "whether there is any benefit to Mr Deenik is not the key issue. The issue is the extent to which a trader in his position should be free to describe the nature of the services he is offering".[178] 6–105

According to the Advocate General art.6(1) precluded the owner of a trade mark from preventing the use of the mark by an independent trader to advertise repair and servicing of the goods covered by the mark, provided that the independent trader did so "in accordance with honest practices in industrial or commercial matters".

Enabling the trade mark proprietor to prevent such use would be an undue restriction on the trader's freedom, unless the advertising was designed to lead the public to believe that the reseller was authorised by the trade mark proprietor or to damage seriously the reputation of the trade mark. It would not, however, be contrary to honest practices within the meaning of art.6(1) merely to derive advantage from the use of a mark.

He stressed again that the national court should take into account the need to ensure that the concept of "honest practices in industrial or commercial matters" would not be interpreted so broadly as to constitute an unjustified impediment to trade or to fair competition.

---

[177] Point 47 of the Opinion of A.G. Jacobs.
[178] Point 54 of the Opinion of A.G. Jacobs.

SCOPE OF PROTECTION, LIMITATIONS AND ENFORCEMENT

6–106   *(b)   The judgment of the Court*

6–107   **(i) The effect of the Directive.** The Court remarked that the transitional problem actually facing the Hoge Raad was different from that governed by art.5(4) and that the Directive did not provide a rule for determining the national law applicable in such a situation.

It accepted that there was no reason, based on the effectiveness of Community law in general or of the Directive in particular, to opt for any given solution; accordingly the national court should determine in the light of the applicable national rules the law that should be applied.[179]

In any case the applicable national law should be interpreted, as far as possible, in the light of the wording and purpose of the Directive in order to achieve the result pursued by it and comply with the third paragraph of art.189 EC.[180] That obligation covered transitional rules as well.

6–108   **(ii) The legislative framework.** Before considering the questions referred to it the Court described the legislative framework. It presented the main points of art.5, art.6 and art.7, and concluded that "it must be emphasised that classifying the mark as falling under one specific provision or another of Article 5, as the case may be, is not necessarily determinant as regards the assessment as to whether the use in question is permissible".[181]

6–109   **(iii) Unauthorised use to inform the public and article 5.** The Court looked together at the second and the third question. It did not follow the distinction of the Advocate General between use in relation to goods and use in relation to services; instead it ruled that use for the purpose of informing the public that another undertaking carries out the repair and maintenance of goods covered by that mark or that it has specialised or is a specialist in such goods constitutes, in circumstances such as those described in the judgment making the reference, use of the mark within the meaning of art.5(1)(a) of the Directive.

To reach that conclusion it looked, first, at the applicability of art.5(5) and underlined that the scope of application of art.5(1) and art.5(2) of the Directive, on the one hand, and art.5(5), on the other, depended on whether the trade mark was used for the purpose of distinguishing the relevant goods or services as originating from a particular undertaking—as a trade mark as such—or whether it was used for other purposes.

Now, in a situation such as that described in the reference use of the trade mark intended to distinguish the goods in question as the subject of the

---

[179] *Frits Loendersloot* (C-349/95) [1997] E.C.R. I-6227.
[180] *Marleasing v La Comercial Internacional de Alimentacion* (C-106/89) [1990] E.C.R. I-4135; and *Faccini Dori v RE.C.R.eb Srl* (C-91/92) [1994] E.C.R. I-3325.
[181] *BMW*, para.30.

5. LIMITATIONS TO TRADE MARK RIGHTS

services provided by the advertiser. The advertiser would use the BMW marks in order to identify the source of the goods in respect of which the services were supplied, and thus to distinguish those goods from any others in respect of which the same services might have been provided.

At the same time the Court found that sale of goods constituted a service: **6–110**

"If the use of the trade mark in advertisements for the service which consists of selling second-hand BMW cars is undoubtedly intended to distinguish the subject of the services provided, it is not necessary to treat any differently the advertisements for the service consisting of repair and maintenance of BMW cars. In that case, too, the mark is used to identify the source of the goods which are the subject of the service."[182]

The Court also clarified the purpose of the references to unfair advantage and detriment to the distinctive character or repute of the mark in art.5(2) and art.5(5). It stressed that they should be taken into account only in relation to those two provisions: "Those matters are ... to be taken into account, not when classifying use under Article 5, but when assessing the legality of that use in the situations covered by Article 5(2) or (5)."[183]

Finally, it found the contested use to be "in the course of trade", noting that art.5(3) expressly mentioned use of the sign in advertising as an example of use that might be prohibited.

(iv) The limitations to the exercise of trade mark rights. The Court **6–111** noted that since use in the advertisements fell within the scope of art.5(1)(a), it should be prohibited unless art.6 or art.7 were applicable. To consider this question it did distinguish between the advertisements for the sale of second-hand cars and the advertisements for the repair and maintenance of cars.

The sale of second-hand BMWs advertisements Here the Court applied **6–112** its case law developed in *Dior*.[184] It held that it would be contrary to art.7 of the Directive for the proprietor of the BMW mark to prohibit the use of its mark by another person for the purpose of informing the public that he had specialised or is a specialist in the sale of second-hand BMWs, provided that the advertising concerned cars that had been put on the Community market under that mark by the proprietor or with its consent and that the way in which the mark is used in that advertising did not go against art.7(2).

It accepted that giving the impression of a commercial connection between the reseller and the trade mark proprietor, in particular that the

---

[182] *BMW*, para.39.
[183] *BMW*, para.40.
[184] *Parfums Christian Dior SA* (C-337/95) [1997] E.C.R. I-6013.

reseller was part of the trade mark proprietor's distribution network or that there was a special relationship between the two undertakings, might constitute a legitimate reason within the meaning of art.7(2).

This was based on a number of arguments: first, such advertising was not essential to the purpose of the exhaustion rule; secondly, it would be contrary to the art.7 obligation to act fairly in relation to the legitimate interests of the trade mark owner and it would affect the value of the trade mark by taking unfair advantage of its distinctive character or repute; thirdly, it was incompatible with the specific object of a trade mark, described as the protection of the proprietor against competitors wishing to take advantage of the status and reputation of the trade mark.[185]

6–113 On the other hand, "the mere fact that the reseller derives an advantage from using the trade mark in that advertisements for the sale of goods covered by the mark, which are in other respects honest and fair, lend an aura of quality to his own business does not constitute a legitimate reason within the meaning of Article 7(2) of the Directive".[186]

Inevitably looking at the facts of the case the Court stated that a reseller who sold second-hand BMWs cars and who had genuinely become a specialist in that market would be unable to communicate this to his customers without using the BMW marks:

> "In consequence, such an informative use of the BMW mark is necessary to guarantee the right of resale under Article 7 of the Directive and does not take unfair advantage of the distinctive character or repute of that trade mark."[187]

6–114 *The repair and maintenance of BMWs* The Court found that in respect of the repair and maintenance of BMWs the rights of the trade mark proprietor were not exhausted; advertisements relating to car repair and maintenance did not affect further commercialisation of the cars in question.

However, here the Court had to consider whether use of the trade mark might be legitimate under art.6(1)(c). The example chosen by the Court showed its willingness to expand the scope of the provision:

> "Like the use of a trade mark intended to identify the vehicles which a non-original spare part will fit, the use in question is intended to identify the goods in respect of which the service is provided."[188]

Regarding the necessity condition it endorsed the view of the Advocate General that if an independent trader carried out the maintenance and

---

[185] *SA CNL-SUCAL NV v Hag GF AG* (C-10/89) [1990] E.C.R. I-3711.
[186] *BMW*, para.53.
[187] *BMW*, para.54.
[188] *BMW*, para.59.

repair of BMWs or was in fact a specialist in that field, that fact could not in practice be communicated to his customers without using the BMW marks.

6–115 Finally, the condition requiring use of the trade mark to be in accordance with honest practices in industrial or commercial matters should be regarded as constituting in substance the expression of a duty to act fairly in relation to the legitimate interests of the trade mark owner. Using another analogy the Court found this to be similar to the duty imposed on a reseller using another's trade mark to advertise the resale of products covered by that mark.[189]

The Court saw art.6 as sharing a common scope with art.7: to reconcile the fundamental interests of trade mark protection with those of free movement of goods and freedom to provide services in the Common Market in such a way that trade mark rights would be able to fulfil their essential role in the system of undistorted competition which the Treaty sought to establish and maintain. As a result the application of the two provisions would follow a similar reasoning: "the use of another's trade mark for the purpose of informing the public of the repair and maintenance of goods covered by that mark is authorised on the same conditions as those applying where the mark is used for the purpose of informing the public of the resale of goods covered by that mark".[190]

(2) Gerolsteiner Brunnen—the scope of article 6(1)(b)   6–116

In *Gerolsteiner Brunnen*[191] the Court considered the same provision from a different angle. Since 1985 Gerolsteiner Brunnen (Gerolsteiner) was the registered proprietor of the word mark GERRI and of a number of figurative marks incorporating the word GERRI in Germany; the specification covered mineral water, non-alcoholic beverages, fruit-juice based drinks, and lemonades. Indeed Gerolsteiner marketed mineral water and soft drinks with a mineral water base.

Putsch had been marketing in Germany since the mid 1990s soft drinks with the KERRY SPRING appearing on their labels. The soft drinks were manufactured and bottled in Ballyferriter in County Kerry, Ireland, by Kerry Spring Water, an Irish company using water from a spring called Kerry Spring.

Gerolsteiner claimed that this constituted trade mark infringement. Putsch retorted that the contested had always been used as an indicator of geographical origin. The case reached the Bundesgerichtshof that stayed proceedings and referred the following questions to the Court:

---

[189] Citing *SA CNL-SUCAL NV v Hag GF AG* (C-10/89) [1990] E.C.R. I-3711.
[190] *BMW*, para.63.
[191] *Gerolsteiner Brunnen GmbH & Co v Putsch GmbH* (C-100/01) [2004] E.C.R. I-691.

"1. Is Article 6(1) (b) of the First Trade Mark Directive also applicable if a third party uses the indications referred to therein as a trade mark (markenmässig)?

2. If so, must that use as a trade mark be taken into account when considering, pursuant to the final clause of Article 6(1) of the First Trade Mark Directive, whether use has been in accordance with honest practices in industrial or commercial matters?"[192]

6–117 *(a) The Opinion of the Advocate General*

Advocate General Stix-Hackl started her legal analysis by identifying the main disputed point: "What is at issue is whether [Article 6] also applies if the use is intended not, or not only, to describe the goods or service, but also to differentiate them from competitors' goods or services."[193]

6–118 **(i) The wording and context of article 6(1)(b).** In her textual analysis of the provision she underlined that art.6(1) (b) did not distinguish between types of use. It referred simply to "indications" of geographical origin. The wording was inconclusive since indications of geographical indications could also be protected as trade marks.

She added that the Directive also failed to indicate circumstances where a sign was "used as a trade mark": "Making the application of Article 6(1) (b) dependent on the type of use made of a sign distinguishing between descriptive use and use as a trade mark is tantamount to making that application dependent on an unwritten factual ingredient."[194]

The historical context of the provision supported her interpretation. The original proposal provided that the limitation of trade mark rights would apply only where the descriptive indication was not used as a trade mark; however, in the amended proposal the provision was amended to its current version: "The Community legislature thus deliberately refrained from drawing a distinction according to type of use."[195]

Finally, she conceded that the corresponding provisions in Greece, Italy, and Spain provided that a sign might not be used as a trade mark but only in a descriptive manner, however this should not be seen as decisive.

6–119 **(ii) The "schematic" classification.** The next step was to consider the provision against its broader legislative context.

The link between art.5 and art.6 required that the use in question should also be covered by art.5. Otherwise, she agreed with the Commission and

---

[192] Reproduced in para.10.
[193] Point 34 of the Opinion of A.G. Stix-Hackl.
[194] Point 36 of the Opinion of A.G. Stix-Hackl.
[195] Point 40 of the Opinion of A.G. Stix-Hackl.

Putsch, "reliance on Article 6 would be meaningless if the use in question did not in any case come under Article 5".[196]

Advocate General Stix-Hackl found further support in the case law of the Court on art.5. According to her reading, *Hölterhoff*[197] and *Arsenal*,[198] combined with the essential function of a trade mark established in *Hoffman-la Roche*,[199] made it clear that the "admissibility of using a sign for purposes other than to distinguish the goods or services of one undertaking from those of another cannot be inferred from Article 6 of the Trade Mark Directive, because such a use does not fall within the protective scope of Article 5".[200]

She also rejected the argument submitted by the Government of the United Kingdom on the potential interpretive inconsistency between art.3(1)(c) and art.6(1)(b). She reminded what the Court had held in *Windsurfing Chiemsee*[201] and noted that only registration would be prohibited, not the simple use of the indication of geographical origin.

6–120

In any case *Windsurfing Chiemsee* concerned the trade mark registrability criteria for geographical names; here the trade mark for which protection had been sought consisted of an imaginary name.

(iii) A teleological analysis of article 6(1)(b). The Advocate General then looked for the scope and purpose of the provision. She repeated that art.6 served as a balancing mechanism between trade mark rights and free movement of goods[202]: "As a sort of regulating device, therefore, Article 6 ... is closely linked to the exclusive rights set out in Article 5."[203] She also remarked that the reference to "honest practices in industrial or commercial matters" ensured that the protective function of the trade mark would not be jeopardised.

6–121

The weighing up of the interests of the trade mark proprietor with those of the third party in each specific case rather than create legal uncertainty would allow the proper balance of interests to be struck, as required by Community law.

Accordingly she concluded use of a sign as a trade mark did not constitute a ground for precluding the application of art.6(1)(b) as a matter of principle.

(iv) Use in accordance with honest practices. The Advocate General reminded the Court that in *BMW*[204] the Court had described this condition as a duty to act fairly in relation to the legitimate interests of the trade mark

6–122

---

[196] Point 43 of the Opinion of A.G. Stix-Hackl.
[197] *Michael Hölterhoff v Ulrich Freiesleben* (C-2/00) [2002] E.C.R. I-4187.
[198] *Arsenal Football Club Plc* (C-206/01) [2002] E.C.R. I-10273.
[199] *Hoffmann-la Roche & Co AG and Hoffmann-la Roche AG* (C-102/77) [1978] E.C.R. 1139.
[200] Point 45 of the Opinion of A.G. Stix-Hackl.
[201] *Windsurfing Chiemsee Produktions- und Vertriebs GmbH* (C-108/97 & C-109/97) [1999] E.C.R. I-2779.
[202] *Bayerische Motorenwerke AG and BMW Nederland BV* (C-63/97) [1999] E.C.R. I-905.
[203] Point 49 of the Opinion of A.G. Stix-Hackl.
[204] *Bayerische Motorenwerke AG and BMW Nederland BV* (C-63/97) [1999] E.C.R. I-905.

owner. Accordingly, the use as a trade mark should be taken into account in the assessment of the condition.

She supported, once again, that the circumstances and interests of the parties should be given particular consideration and suggested a number of factors that should be taken into account either with regard to the registered trade mark or the way the indications would be used.

First, she identified the distinctive character and the repute of the registered trade mark. Secondly, deliberately deceiving the public would not accord with honest practices; it appears that the intention of the third party as well as the perception of the public could influence the finding on this factor. Thirdly, the way the sign was used could also be decisive; she suggested that there was a close link between the way the indication was used and the purpose for which it could be used. Amongst, the additional factors that should be considered here were the degree of similarity of the indication with the registered mark, the degree of emphasis of the indication, including where this went beyond what might be required under Community law, and the public perception of the indication as a trade mark.

She noted that in relation to mineral waters there were specific rules at the Community level[205] however the simple use of the name of the spring did not allow any conclusions to be drawn about the purpose of that indication.

6–123   (b)   *The judgment of the Court*

The Court repeated its findings in *BMW*[206] which formed the background for its analysis.

It agreed with the Advocate General that the provision did not distinguish between the possible uses of the indications referred to in art.6(1)(b): "For such an indication to fall within the scope of that article, it suffices that it is an indication concerning one of the characteristics set out therein, like geographical origin."[207]

The Court underlined that the trade mark GERRI had no geographical connotation whereas the sign KERRY SPRING referred to the geographical origin of the water, the place where the product was bottled, and the place where the producer was established, noting that the Commission emphasised the geographical nature of the expression KERRY SPRING, and that Kerry Spring was included in the list of mineral waters recognised by Ireland for the purposes of Council Directive 80/777.

6–124   On the other hand the referring court had found that there was a likelihood of aural confusion between GERRI and KERRY, accepting that consumers were shortening KERRY SPRING to KERRY.

---

[205] Council Directive 80/777 on the approximation of the laws of the Member States relating to the exploitation and marketing of natural mineral waters [1980] OJ L229/1.
[206] *Bayerische Motorenwerke AG and BMW Nederland BV* (C-63/97) [1999] E.C.R. I-905.
[207] *Gerolsteiner Brunner*, para.19.

5. LIMITATIONS TO TRADE MARK RIGHTS

So, the critical question was whether art.5(1)(b) allowed the trade mark proprietor to prevent a third party from using the indication of geographical origin. Article 6(1) had to be considered, and the only test it provided for was assessing that the indication of geographical origin was used in accordance with honest practices in industrial or commercial matters. This, according to *BMW*,[208] meant that there was a duty to act fairly in relation to the legitimate interests of the trade mark owner.

It concluded that art.6(1)(b) should be interpreted as meaning that, where there existed a likelihood of aural confusion between a word mark registered in one Member State and an indication, in the course of trade, of the geographical origin of a product originating in another Member State, the proprietor of the trade mark might prevent the use of the indication of geographical origin only if that use were not in accordance with honest practices in industrial or commercial matters. This was an issue for the national court to decide, following an overall assessment of all the circumstances of the particular case in that regard.

Still, the Court held that:

> "[T]he mere fact that there exists a likelihood of aural confusion between a word mark registered in one Member State and an indication of geographical origin from another Member State is ... insufficient to conclude that the use of that indication in the course of trade is not in accordance with honest practices. In a Community of 15 Member States, with great linguistic diversity, the chance that there exists some phonetic similarity between a trade mark registered in one Member State and an indication of geographical origin from another Member State is already substantial and will be even greater after the impending enlargement."[209]

(3) Gillette—indicating compatibility 6–125

Gillette[210] was a classic case testing the extent that a trade mark can be used in order to indicate compatibility with the trade marked product. The case was a reference from the Korkein Oikeus (Supreme Court) of Finland.

Gillette was the registered proprietor of the trade marks "Gillette" and "Sensor" in Finland; the specification included razors. The actual product put on the market was a razor that consisted of a handle and a blade that could be attached on the handle; the blades were also sold on their own to be used as replacements. LA-Laboratories (LA) marketed its own razor, also consisting of a handle and a blade under the trade mark "Parason Flexor". Its blades were similar to Gillette's and they too were sold on their own; on the packaging of the blades there was a sticker with the message

---

[208] *Bayerische Motorenwerke AG and BMW Nederland BV* (C-63/97) [1999] E.C.R. I-905.
[209] *Gerolsteiner Brunner*, para.25.
[210] *The Gillette Company v LA-Laboratories Ltd Oy* (C-228/03) [2005] E.C.R. I-2337.

"All Parason Flexor and Gillette Sensor handles are compatible with this blade".

Gillette claimed before the Finnish courts that this constituted trade mark infringement. It argued that LA's use created a link between the two products or at least gave the impression that it was licensed or otherwise authorised by Gillette. LA claimed that it fell under art.6(1)(c) of the Directive:

"When applying Article 6(1)(c) of the First Council Directive 89/104/EEC to approximate the laws of the Member States relating to trade marks:

1) What are the criteria
   a) on the basis of which the question of regarding a product as a spare part or accessory is to be decided, and
   b) on the basis of which those products to be regarded as other than spare parts and accessories which can also fall within the scope of the said subparagraph are to be determined?
2) Is the permissibility of the use of a third party's trade mark to be assessed differently, depending on whether the product is like a spare part or accessory or whether it is a product which can fall within the scope of the said subparagraph on another basis?
3) How should the requirement that the use must be 'necessary' to indicate the intended purpose of a product be interpreted? Can the criterion of necessity be satisfied even though it would in itself be possible to state the intended purpose without an express reference to the third party's trade mark, by merely mentioning only for instance the technical principle of functioning of the product? What significance does it have in that case that the statement may be more difficult for consumers to understand if there is no express reference to the third party's trade mark?
4) What factors should be taken into account when assessing use in accordance with honest commercial practice? Does mentioning a third party's trade mark in connection with the marketing of one's own product constitute a reference to the fact that the marketer's own product corresponds, in quality and technically or as regards its other properties, to the product designated by the third party's trade mark?
5) Does it affect the permissibility of the use of a third party's trade mark that the economic operator who refers to the third party's trade mark also markets, in addition to a spare part or accessory, a product of his own with which that spare part or accessory is intended to be used with?"[211]

---

[211] Reproduced in para.23.

5. LIMITATIONS TO TRADE MARK RIGHTS

(a) The Opinion of the Advocate General

(i) The context for the interpretation of article 6. Advocate General 6–126
Tizzano started his analysis by the essential function of a trade mark as a guarantee of the origin of the marked product.[212] This led to the exclusive right that covered protection against unauthorised use likely to cause confusion. Article 6 imposed limitations to the rights of trade mark proprietors, in order to reconcile the fundamental interests of trade mark protection with the principles of free movement of goods and freedom to provide services in the system of undistorted competition envisaged by the Treaty[213]:

> "It can therefore be said that, in limiting the exclusive right provided for under Article 5, Article 6(1) (c) of Directive 89/104 seeks to balance the owner's interest in the trade mark being able to perform to the full its function of guaranteeing the product's origin against the interest of other traders in having full access to the market, but leaving the door open—as would appear borne out by the broad reference to free movement in the Court's statement quoted above and as we will see below—for other interests too to come into play."[214]

(ii) The fundamental criterion for the application of article 6(1)(c). 6–127
Advocate General Tizzano identified the function of the trade mark as an indicator of the intended purpose rather than the origin of the product as the main condition that had to be satisfied in order for a third party's trade mark to be lawfully placed on a product. This would arise in the case of accessories and spare parts but also in that of products capable of being used together, using the example of a computer and its operating programme to illustrate the second scenario.

This meant that art.6(1)(c) should cover use in respect of any product if that use would be necessary to indicate its intended purpose.

The history and wording of the provision supported this interpretation. The original proposal referred specifically to accessories or spare parts whereas the adopted version widened its scope by including the words "in particular".[215] In addition it referred to services, for which it would be less likely to need to refer to spare parts or accessories, as well as goods.

So, "the fundamental factor in all cases is whether the use of the third 6–128
party's trade mark is necessary in order to indicate the intended purpose of

---

[212] Citing the 10th Recital to the Preamble and, indicatively, *Hoffmann-la Roche & Co AG and Hoffmann-la Roche AG* (102/77) [1978] E.C.R. 1139; *Arsenal Football Club Plc* (C-206/01) [2002] E.C.R. I-10273; *Ansul BV v Ajax Brandbeveiliging BV* (C-40/01) [2003] E.C.R. I-2439.
[213] Citing *Gerolsteiner Brunnen GmbH & Co v Putsch GmbH* (C-100/02) [2004] E.C.R. I-691.
[214] Point 30 of the Opinion of A.G. Tizzano.
[215] For the original proposal see Proposal for a First Council Directive to approximate the laws of the Member States relating to trade mark [1980] OJ C351/1.

the product (or service) and does not give rise to confusion as to its origin".[216]

The Advocate General supported that this was all that the Court had to hold in response to the first two questions, since there was no need to distinguish main products from accessories and spare parts.

6–129 **(iii) The factors for assessing whether the use was necessary.** The Advocate General acknowledged that delineating the scope of the provision would be a difficult exercise. The history and the wording of the provision pointed towards a stricter interpretation, the context of the provision opened the door to a wider set of interests, whereas the case law of the Court appeared to favour a broader interpretation:

> "For my part, I have no difficulty accepting that the approach proposed by Gillette appears more in keeping with the letter of Article 6(1)(c) of the directive, which refers to the use of the third party's trade mark not as 'efficient' but as 'necessary', and needless to say the two are not synonymous."[217]

Again he sought support from the legislative history of the provision, this time though for limiting its scope. The original proposal covered use "for the purpose of indicating the intended purpose of accessories or spare parts", the final use "where it is necessary to indicate the intended purpose".

He accepted though that the provision could not be interpreted solely on that basis, "in fact ... that provision opens the door also to other [other than the trade mark proprietor's] values and interests which it does not expressly mention but which in the broader perspective it would be difficult to ignore"[218]; *BMW*[219] was an attempt to reconcile different interests. Still, those interests were directed towards a common purpose: ensuring a system of undistorted competition and the right of consumers to choose from a variety of interchangeable products.

6–130 Note that he chose to focus on the interests of the trade mark proprietor and consumers but not on those of the competitors of the trade mark proprietor. *BMW*[220] according to the Advocate General "did indeed reconcile the requirement of protecting the trade mark owner with that of protecting the consumer even in terms of maximising competition and providing complete information".[221] His understanding was that the Court instead of considering

---

[216] Point 39 of the Opinion of A.G. Tizzano.
[217] Point 51 of the Opinion of A.G. Tizzano.
[218] Point 55 of the Opinion of A.G. Tizzano.
[219] *Bayerische Motorenwerke AG and BMW Nederland BV* (C-63/97) [1999] E.C.R. I-905.
[220] *Bayerische Motorenwerke AG and BMW Nederland BV* (C-63/97) [1999] E.C.R. I-905.
[221] Point 58 of the Opinion of A.G. Tizzano.

5. LIMITATIONS TO TRADE MARK RIGHTS

whether the garage owner's business would be commercially viable it focused solely on the need to provide prospective customers with the fullest possible information. The Court appeared to be satisfied simply by the fact that the use of a third party's trade mark was the only effective means of extending the range of products from which the prospective purchaser could choose.

If the Court would follow the same approach, use of the Gillette trade marks should be considered necessary if it were the only means of providing the information that LA's blades fitted Gillette handles.

Inevitably there was some uncertainty regarding the test of necessity; this, he suggested, could be resolved at the stage of examining the circumstances and manner of use of the trade mark according to art.6(1): "The less rigorous [the interpretation of necessity] may be, the more stringent will be the scrutiny of the manner of use. At the same time, it is precisely on the more solid ground of that scrutiny that the actual 'necessity' of the use of the mark can be better assessed and such doubts as may always arise in the abstract in that regard dispelled."[222]

Indeed he believed that the Court had adopted a unitary approach, tilting the balance towards compliance with honest practices rather than the condition of necessity.

6–131

Subject to the above qualifications he proposed that "the Court should answer the third question to the effect that the use of a third party's trade mark is 'necessary' to indicate the intended purpose of a product if it constitutes the only means of providing consumers with complete information as to the possible uses of the product in question".[223]

(iv) The concept of "honest practices in industrial and commercial matters". According to *BMW*,[224] the condition of "honest practices in industrial and commercial matters" was interpreted as a duty to act fairly in relation to the legitimate interests of the trade mark owner.

6–132

Following *BMW* and *Gerolsteiner Brunnen*[225] he delineated the scope of that duty by combining the case law of the Court with the Preamble to Directive 97/55, providing that the exclusive trade mark right would not be infringed where a third party uses the trade mark in compliance with the conditions laid down by that Directive.

Accordingly he found that there were two conditions that had to be satisfied. The advertisement should not create confusion in the market place or seek to take unfair advantage of the reputation of a trade mark of a competitor. Based on the analogies between trade mark law and comparative

---

[222] Point 69 of the Opinion of A.G. Tizzano.
[223] Point 71 of the Opinion of A.G. Tizzano.
[224] *Bayerische Motorenwerke AG and BMW Nederland BV* (C-63/97) [1999] E.C.R. I-905.
[225] *Gerolsteiner Brunnen GmbH & Co v Putsch GmbH* (C-100/01) [2004] E.C.R. I-691.

SCOPE OF PROTECTION, LIMITATIONS AND ENFORCEMENT

advertising that the Court had indicated in *Toshiba*[226] he supported that in order to assess the applicability of the two conditions on a particular case, national courts should follow the "global assessment" route taking into account all the factors that could be relevant to the circumstances of the case.[227]

6-133   **(v) The activities of the advertiser.** Advocate General Tizzano found that the fifth question, in essence, enquired whether the assessment of the lawfulness of a comparative advertisement relied on the fact that the advertiser also sold the type of product that the advertised product was intended to be used with.

He found that this should not be considered as a new criterion although it could be one of the factors courts had to take into account in their assessment of the two conditions mentioned above.

6-134   *(b)   The judgment of the Court*

(i) The criteria that make use necessary. The Court looked at the first three questions together, as essentially seeking the criteria that for interpreting the requirement of necessity under art.6(1)(c).

It started its analysis by reminding the court briefly its case law on the rights of the proprietor and the essential function of a trade mark.[228] On the limitations imposed by art.6(1) it referred to the principles established in *BMW*[229] and *Gerolsteiner Brunnen*.[230] Article 6 sought "to reconcile the fundamental interests of trade mark protection with those of free movement of goods and freedom to provide services in the common market in such a way that trade mark rights are able to fulfil their essential role in the system of undistorted competition which the Treaty seeks to establish and maintain".[231]

The Court noted that art.6(1)(c) did not lay down criteria for determining whether a given intended purpose of a product fell within its scope, but merely required that use of the trade mark be necessary in order to indicate such a purpose and that the intended purpose of the products as accessories or spare parts was cited only by way of example.

---

[226] *Toshiba Europe GmbH v Katun Germany GmbH* (C-112/99) [2001] E.C.R. I-7945; see para.10–005, below.
[227] See *Sabel BV* (C-251/95) [1997] E.C.R. I-6191.
[228] Citing *SA CNL-SUCAL NV v Hag GF AG* (C-10/89) [1990] E.C.R. I-3711; *Merz&Krell GmbH & Co v Deutches Patent-und Markenamt* (C-517/99) [2001] E.C.R. I-6959; *Arsenal Football Club Plc v Matthew Reed* (C-206/01) [2002] E.C.R. I-10273; *Hoffmann-la Roche & Co AG and Hoffmann-la Roche AG* (102/77) [1978] E.C.R. 1139; and *Koninklijke Philips Electronics NV* (C-299/99) [2002] E.C.R. I-5475.
[229] *Bayerische Motorenwerke AG and BMW Nederland BV* (C-63/97) [1999] E.C.R. I-905.
[230] *Gerolsteiner Brunnen GmbH & Co v Putsch GmbH* (C-100/01) [2004] E.C.R. I-691.
[231] *Gillette*, para.29.

5. LIMITATIONS TO TRADE MARK RIGHTS

Accordingly the provision clearly went beyond the distinction between accessories and spare parts and it was not necessary to determine whether a product should be regarded as an accessory or a spare part.

6–135

It then held that its holdings in *BMW*[232] were equally valid in the case. The Court had held that use of a trade mark to inform the public that the advertiser was specialised in the sale, or that he carried out the repair and maintenance, of products bearing that trade mark constituted a use indicating the intended purpose of a product: "That information is necessary in order to preserve the system of undistorted competition in the market for that product or service."[233] In the case in the main proceedings, the Gillette marks were being used by a third party in order to provide the public with comprehensible and complete information as to the intended purpose of the product, in other words its compatibility with the product bearing those trade marks.

According to *BMW* such use would be necessary in cases where the information could not in practice be communicated to the public without using the relevant trade marks. This meant that "use must in practice be the only means of providing such information"[234]:

"In that respect, in order to determine whether other means of providing such information may be used, it is necessary to take into consideration, for example, the possible existence of technical standards or norms generally used for the type of product marketed by the third party and known to the public for which that type of product is intended. Those norms, or other characteristics, must be capable of providing that public with comprehensible and full information on the intended purpose of the product marketed by that third party in order to preserve the system of undistorted competition on the market for that product."[235]

This was an issue that the national court had to determine according to the above requirements but also taking account of the nature of the public for which the product marketed by LA was intended.

6–136

Finally, since art.6(1)(c) made no distinction between the possible intended purposes of products the criteria would be the same for all the possible intended purposes.

(ii) The interpretation of "honest practices". The Court cited its holdings in *BMW*[236] and *Gerolsteiner Brunnen*[237] that the condition of

6–137

---

[232] *Bayerische Motorenwerke AG and BMW Nederland BV* (C-63/97) [1999] E.C.R. I-905.
[233] *Gillette*, para.33.
[234] *Gillette*, para.35.
[235] *Gillette*, para.36.
[236] *Bayerische Motorenwerke AG and BMW Nederland BV* (C-63/97) [1999] E.C.R. I-905.
[237] *Gerolsteiner Brunnen GmbH & Co v Putsch GmbH* (C-100/01) [2004] E.C.R. I-691.

"honest use" required to act fairly in relation to the legitimate interests of the trade mark proprietor. Citing Dior it added that such an obligation was similar to that imposed on resellers using another's trade mark to advertise the resale of products covered by that mark.

The Court identified four instances that use of a trade mark would not comply with honest practices in industrial or commercial matters:

- first, where use might give the impression of a commercial connection between the reseller and the trade mark proprietor;
- secondly, where it might affect the value of the trade mark by taking unfair advantage of its distinctive character or repute;
- thirdly, where it might discredit or denigrate that mark; and
- fourthly, where the third party presented its product as an imitation or replica of the product bearing the trade mark.

The outcome remained in the jurisdiction of the national court to determine, taking account of:

> "[T]he overall presentation of the product marketed by the third party, particularly the circumstances in which the mark of which the third party is not the owner is displayed in that presentation, the circumstances in which a distinction is made between that mark and the mark or sign of the third party, and the effort made by that third party to ensure that consumers distinguish its products from those of which it is not the trade mark owner."[238]

6–138 There were two outstanding points the Court had to deal with.

First, the fact that a third party used a trade mark in order to indicate the intended purpose of its product did not necessarily mean that it was presenting that product as being of the same quality as, or having equivalent properties to, those of the product bearing the trade mark. Resolution of these questions depended on the facts of the case.

Secondly, the fact that the product marketed by the third party had been represented as being of the same quality as, or having equivalent properties to, the product whose trade mark was used was one of the factors the national court had to take into account.

Finally the Court held that on its own the fact that the third party marketed not only a spare part or accessory but also the product itself with which the spare part or accessory was intended to be used was not relevant, provided that use of the trade mark satisfied the other requirements.

---

[238] *Gillette*, para.46.

5. LIMITATIONS TO TRADE MARK RIGHTS

(4) Adam Opel 6–139

(a) The Opinion of the Advocate General

(i) Application to the facts—article 6(1). Advocate General Ruiz-Jarabo Colomer[239] decided to look briefly at the remaining two questions, in the hypothetical scenario of a negative answer to the first question. The aim of art.6(1) was to balance between the interests of the trade mark proprietor on the one hand and those of its competitors on the other, seeking to secure the availability of descriptive signs. But, since it constituted an exception to the general rules on protection under art.5 he accepted it had to be interpreted narrowly.

Accordingly, he found it difficult to argue that the reproduction of the sign on the toy car qualified as an indication of the type or quality of the product. However since the nature of a model necessitated the accurate and detailed copy of the original, the sign should be considered as falling within the scope of art.6(1)(b) as describing other characteristics of the product because it achieved two objectives: it enhanced the information conveyed to consumers and ensured that the operators in the same product market competed under the same conditions.

In essence what the Advocate General suggested was considering the market for each replica as a distinct product market.

The third question covered the remaining consideration for the application of art.6(1)(b), had the sign been used in accordance with honest commercial or industrial practices? 6–140

To answer that question he went back to the jurisprudence of the Court in *Gillette*. The most relevant of the uses mentioned therein would be where the third party presented its product as an imitation or reproduction of the marked product. This would not however cover miniature toys because they did not imitate the miniatures manufactured by Opel licensees but the actual car manufactured by Opel.

According to the Advocate General compliance with the condition of honest practices should be determined according to *Anheuser-Busch*[240] by making an overall assessment of the facts of the case and taking into account three particular factors: the extent that use of a commercial name would be understood by the relevant public as indicating a link between the third party's products and the trade mark proprietor; the extent that the third party should have been aware of this; and whether it possessed a reputation from which the third party could benefit in order to market its own products.

The way AUTEC presented its products warranted the application of art.6(1)(b); the inclusion of its own trade marks and indications was evidence of honest behaviour in compliance with commercial practice.

---

[239] See para.6–024, above.
[240] *Anheuser-Busch Inc* (C-245/02) [2004] E.C.R. I-10989.

(b) The judgment of the Court

The Court found that the question really concerned art.6(1)(b). The provision was primarily designed to prevent the proprietor of a trade mark from prohibiting other parties from using the descriptive terms that formed part of the trade mark in order to indicate certain characteristics of their own products. However, the wording of the provision was broader and should not be seen as specific to such a situation. Turning to the facts of the case the Court found that the affixing of the sign was not intended to provide an indication as to the characteristics of the scale models, but was merely an element in the faithful reproduction of the original vehicle and fell outside art.6(1)(b).

6. ENFORCING THE COMMUNITY TRADE MARK

6–141 **(1) Nokia—adequate enforcement**

The enforcement perspective of the Community Trade Mark is being considered by the Court in *Nokia*,[241] a reference from the Swedish Högsta Domstolen (Supreme Court).

Nokia had brought a trade-mark infringement action, based on its Community Trade Mark registration of NOKIA for mobile telephones, against Joacim Wärdell for importing into Sweden adhesive stickers bearing the sign NOKIA.

The Stockholms Tingsrätten (Stockholm District Court) found that Wärdell's acts constituted objective acts of infringement and, because there was a risk of repetition, issued a prohibition on continuing infringement. Wärdell appealed to the Svea Hovrätten (Court of Appeal, Svea) claiming that use of the trade mark NOKIA had not been deliberate or negligent and that there was no risk of repetition.

6–142 Svea Hovrätten found that the importation of the stickers should not be seen as part of a continuing trade mark infringement, given his history and the fact that he could only be accused of being careless. And, although it accepted that the risk of repetition could not be eliminated, it varied the judgment of the Stockholms Tingsrätten on that point. Nokia appealed to the Högsta Domstolen that stayed proceedings and referred four questions regarding the interpretation of art.98(1) of the Regulation[242]

---

[241] *Nokia Corp v Joacim Wärdell* (C-316/05) [2007] 1 C.M.L.R. 37; [2006] WL 1911371.
[242] Article 98(1) provides: "Where a Community trade mark court finds that the defendant has infringed or threatened to infringe a Community trade mark, it shall, unless there are special reasons for not doing so, issue an order prohibiting the defendant from proceeding with the acts which infringed or would infringe the Community trade mark. It shall also take such measures in accordance with its national law as are aimed at ensuring that this prohibition is complied with."

and whether it went beyond the parallel provision of the Swedish Trade Mark Law[243]:

"(1) Is the condition relating to special reasons in the first sentence of Article 98(1) of Council Regulation (EC) No 40/94 of 20 December 1993 on the Community trade mark to be interpreted as meaning that a court which finds that the defendant has infringed a Community trade mark may, irrespective of the other circumstances, refrain from issuing a specific prohibition of further infringement if the court considers that the risk of further infringement is not obvious or is otherwise merely limited?

(2) Is the condition relating to special reasons in the first sentence of Article 98(1) of the Regulation on the Community trade mark to be interpreted as meaning that a court which finds that the defendant has infringed a Community trade mark may, even if there is no such ground for refraining from issuing a prohibition of further infringement as contemplated in Question 1, refrain from issuing such a prohibition on the grounds that it is clear that a further infringement is covered by a statutory general prohibition of infringement under national law and that a penalty may be imposed on the defendant if he commits a further infringement intentionally or with gross negligence?

(3) If the answer to Question 2 is no, must specific measures, by which a prohibition is for example coupled with a penalty, be taken in such a case to ensure that the prohibition is complied with, even where it is clear that a further infringement is covered by a statutory general prohibition of infringement under national law and that a penalty may be imposed on the defendant if he commits a further infringement intentionally or with gross negligence?

(4) If the answer to Question 3 is yes, does this apply even where the conditions for adopting such a specific measure in the case of a corresponding infringement of a national trade mark would not be regarded as fulfilled?"[244]

(a) The Opinion of the Advocate General 6–143

Advocate General Sharpston divided her Opinion into three parts. First, she considered the meaning of "special reasons" in art.98(1); then, whether national provisions could fit into those "special reasons"; and thirdly, the adequacy of specific measures arising from national provisions the scope of which was to ensure compliance with a prohibition.

---

[243] Section 37 provides that a trade mark infringement that has been committed deliberately or with gross negligence is punishable by a fine or imprisonment; s.37a provides that the court may, on application by the proprietor of the trade mark, prohibit the infringer, under penalty of a fine, from continuing the infringement.
[244] Reproduced in point 17.

6-144 **(i) Article 98(1)—the "special reasons" condition.** The analysis of the Advocate General started with the wording of the provision, expressed in mandatory terms: "the court shall issue a prohibition order". It reflected the fundamental right of a trade mark proprietor to prohibit infringement, according to art.9(1) of the Regulation.

This led her to support that the general rule was to prohibit continued infringement; the concept of "special reasons" was a derogation to that principle, and, accordingly, should be interpreted narrowly.

She then considered the scheme of the Regulation. The 15th Recital of the Preamble to the Regulation provided the context for interpreting the provision stating that "decisions regarding the validity and infringement of Community trade marks must have effect and cover the entire area of the Community, as this is the only way of preventing inconsistent decisions on the part of the courts and the Office and of ensuring that the unitary character of Community trade marks is not undermined".

6-145 She concurred with the Commission that achieving those aims necessitated a uniform interpretation of art.98(1) and suggested that leaving Member States leeway to assess the risk of continuation of infringement would lead to different results in different Member States. This would go against the fundamental principle that a Community Trade Mark should enjoy the same protection throughout the Union.

Nevertheless, the concept of "special reasons" was included in the provision; the Advocate General had to find a purpose for it. She remarked that it would not be appropriate to discuss this in detail, since the national court had not asked for examples of what might constitute "special reasons" and the pleadings before the Court had not considered that question. But she felt she had to set some sort of parameters for the current case by stressing the exceptional nature of "special reasons" and the limitations imposed by the referring court:

> "It may be that in exceptional cases the degree of risk of further infringement is one of a number of circumstances which, taken as a whole, are indeed capable of constituting 'special reasons' within the meaning of Article 98(1). However, the national court's question specifically concerns only the degree of risk of further infringement 'irrespective of the other circumstances'."[245]

Surveying the greater picture, the background behind the development of trade mark law in Europe, the Advocate General rejected Wärdell's argument that this line of interpretation would be against the free movement of goods rules. On the contrary, such protection required that infringement should as a general rule be prohibited.

---

[245] Point 25 of the Opinion of A.G. Sharpston.

6. ENFORCING THE COMMUNITY TRADE MARK

The final point was probably the strongest. This case involved an identical sign used in relation to identical goods: "In such circumstances the derogation should in principle not apply at all. At the very most, it might perhaps apply where it is materially impossible for the defendant to repeat the infringement, for example (to borrow the illustrations given by Nokia) if the defendant is a company which has been wound up or if the mark in question has expired."[246]

6-146

She concluded that the condition relating to "special reasons" would not be satisfied if a court which found that the defendant had infringed a Community Trade Mark refrained from issuing a specific prohibition of further infringement solely on the ground that it considered that the risk of further infringement was not obvious or was otherwise merely limited.

(ii) "Special reasons" and national provisions. The second question focused on the relationship between national law and art.98(1). Assuming that a national court had found infringement of a Community Trade Mark and that there was no exceptional case for not issuing a prohibition of further infringement, could it still refrain from issuing such a prohibition on the grounds that a further infringement would be covered by a statutory general prohibition of infringement under national law and that a penalty might be imposed on the defendant that committed a further infringement intentionally or with gross negligence?

6-147

Advocate General Sharpston followed again a strict approach based on the language, context, and scope of the provision.

First, a general provision of national legislation could not by definition be a "special" reason because on a natural reading the term implied that the reason should be special to a particular case, normally relating to facts rather than law.[247] Further, art.98(1) explicitly required that an order prohibiting further infringement should be the standard measure against infringement.

Secondly, in terms of context, refusing to order prohibition under art.98(1) because of the existence of a national general prohibition of further infringement would make application of Community law rules dependent on national law, against the primacy of Community law principle and the unitary character of the Regulation.

6-148

Thirdly, it would in effect deprive art.98(1) of all meaning, in particular since such an order might often be more effective than a general prohibition on infringement.[248]

---

[246] Point 27 of the Opinion of A.G. Sharpston.
[247] She reminded the Court that TRIPs required Member States under art.44(1) and art.61 to provide for civil and criminal sanctions, including prohibition, for infringement of intellectual property rights. So, the existence of national law sanctions could not therefore be a special reason not to order prohibition under art.98(1).
[248] She referred, for example, to the advantages that such a prohibition would give under French law where specific measures could be taken without the need to institute fresh proceedings.

SCOPE OF PROTECTION, LIMITATIONS AND ENFORCEMENT

Indeed, art.37a of the Swedish law appeared to be quite cumbersome compared with art.98(1), requiring a separate application to the court and proof that the infringement was intentional or the result of serious negligence.

Inevitably, she suggested that the answer to the Swedish court should be in the negative.

6–149   (iii) **The adequacy of "national" measures.** The remaining two questions were examined jointly by the Advocate General.

Wärdell's argument against an affirmative response was based on art.14(1) of the Regulation which stated that "infringement of a Community trade mark shall be governed by the national law relating to infringement of a national trade mark". He supported that a provision in the national law for a general prohibition of infringement with the possibility of a penal sanction would suffice to fulfil the art.98(1) requirement.

Again the analysis of the Advocate General started with a textual analysis stressing that the same provision concluded with "in accordance with the provisions of Title X" and that Title X included art.98(1), a mandatory provision according to her earlier findings.

6–150   The "formulation" of art.98(1) required that "national law should make available specific measures to back up such a prohibition and thus ensure that it is complied with".[249] A general statutory prohibition on infringement under national law would not be sufficient. Even more so when the penalty required three additional steps, it could be imposed: "(i) at the national court's option; (ii) on application by the trade mark holder; and (iii) to a defendant who commits a further infringement intentionally or with negligence, is insufficient to satisfy the requirement".[250]

The general requirement was that national should provide for specific and effective measures for the purposes of art.98(1). The competence of domestic legal system covered only the detailed procedural rules governing court actions for safeguarding Community Trade Mark rights with the limitation that these rules should not be less favourable than those governing similar domestic actions, according to the principle of equivalence, and should not render virtually impossible or excessively difficult the exercise of Community Trade Mark rights, according to the principle of effectiveness.[251]

She added that these two principles did not necessarily imply some additional sanction or penalty: "Rather, the consequences of breaching the prohibition must be clearly laid down, either specifically by the national court in question or more generally by national law."[252]

Finally, A.G. Sharpston suggested that whether the infringement provisions regarding registered trade marks at the national level corresponded to

---

[249] Point 41 of the Opinion of A.G. Sharpston.
[250] Point 41 of the Opinion of A.G. Sharpston.
[251] Citing *Clean Car Autoservice GmbH v Stadt Wien and Republik Österreich* (C-472/99) [2001] E.C.R. I-9687 as an authority for the broader principle.
[252] Point 42.

standard set by art.98(1) should make no difference to the analysis: "The principle of equivalence does not require that where Community law confers a high level of protection on a right derived from Community law, equivalent rights derived from national law (even harmonised national law) necessarily enjoy the same level of protection."[253]

(2) Davidoff III—seizure of infringing goods   6–151

Davidoff III[254] dealt with a specific interpretation problem as regards the enforcement of Community Trade Marks, which arose with the accession of the Community to the Protocol relating to the Madrid Agreement concerning the international registration of marks adopted at Madrid on June 27, 1989 ("the Protocol")[255].

The issue related to the application of Regulation 1383/2003,[256] concerning customs action against goods suspected of infringing intellectual property rights, to international registrations designating the European Community within the meaning of art.146 CTMR (new art.151).[257]

Article 2 of Regulation 1383/2003 defines infringing goods as, inter alia, counterfeit goods that infringe rights acquired "under Community law, as provided for by the CTMR or the law of the Member State in which the application for action by the customs authorities is made".

By virtue of art.5(1) and (4) of said Regulation, a right-holder may apply in   6–152
writing to the competent customs department of the Member State for action; where the applicant is the holder of a Community Trade Mark he may, in addition, request action by the authorities of one or more other Member States.

(a) The facts in the main proceedings   6–153

The dispute arose in the course of proceedings between Zino Davidoff SA ("Davidoff") and the Bundesfinanzdirektion Südost (South Eastern Federal Revenue Office), when Davidoff lodged an application with the latter under art.5(4) of Regulation 1383/2003, for border seizure of goods suspected of infringing 12 internationally registered trade marks, of which Davidoff is holder.

Bundesfinanzdirektion Südost dismissed the action on the grounds that art.5(4) of Regulation 1383/2003, which extends only to "right-holders of a

---

[253] Point 43 of the Opinion of A.G. Sharpston.
[254] *Zino Davidoff SA v Bundesfinanzdirektion Südost* (DAVIDOFF III) (C-302/08).
[255] The Community acceded to the Madrid Protocol with effect from October 1, 2004 by virtue of Council Decision 2003/793 [2003] OJ L296/20.
[256] Regulation 1383/2003 concerning customs action against goods suspected of infringing certain intellectual property rights and the measures to be taken against goods found to have infringed such rights [2003] OJ L296/7.
[257] Article 146 is included in Title XIII, containing provisions specifically relating to the International Registration of marks, which was added to the CTMR by Regulation 1992/2003 [2003] OJ L296/1.

Community trademark", was not amended by the Community legislature despite the Community's accession to the Protocol. Thus, it took the view that that the wording of that provision does not cover the owners of internationally registered trade marks.

Davidoff brought an appeal against that decision before the Finanazgericht München, which considered that the provisions at issue pose problems relating to the interpretation of Community law. Accordingly, it stayed the proceedings and referred the following question to the Court for a preliminary ruling:

"In the light of the accession of the Community to the [Protocol], is Article 5(4) of Regulation [No 1383/2003] to be interpreted as meaning that, despite the use of the term 'Community trademark', marks with international registrations within the meaning of Article 146 et seq. of Regulation [No 40/94], are also covered?"

6–154   *(b) The judgment of the Court*

The Court decided to proceed to judgment without an Advocate General's opinion.

The first point it considered to be of relevance in resolving the question whether the holder of an internationally registered trade mark is entitled to secure action by the customs authorities in the same manner like proprietors of Community Trade Marks, was that Regulation 1383/2003 had been adopted prior to the accession of the Community to the Madrid Protocol.

Accordingly, it turned for its interpretation to the provisions of the Protocol itself and to Regulation No.1992/2003, which, according to the Sixth and Eighth Recitals in its Preamble, introduces measures which are necessary to give effect to the accession of the Community to the Protocol and, in particular, to allow holders of international registrations to apply for protection under the Community Trade Mark system.

6–155   In that regard, it observed that art.4(1) of the Protocol provides that the protection of the mark in each of the designated countries is to be the same as if the mark had been filed directly with the trade mark office of that state.

Moreover, art.146(2), inserted to the CTMR by Regulation No.1992/2003, stipulates that the international registration of a trade mark designating the European Community is to have the same effect as a Community Trade Mark.

The Court therefore considered it to be apparent that the Community legislature intended, so far as their practical effects are concerned, to treat internationally registered marks in the same way as Community Trade Marks.

6–156   Next, it noted that, according to its wording, art.5(4) of Regulation 1383/2003 only implements a specific procedure for the protection

Community Trade Marks, that is, merely deals with their effects and not with their definition.[258]

Thus, in view of the full assimilation of the two types of marks brought about by the above provisions, the Court concluded that art.5(4) of Regulation No.1383/2003 allowed the holders of International Registrations with effect in the Community to secure action by the customs authorities of one or more Member States, just like the proprietor of a Community Trade Mark.[259]

7. CONCLUSION

It would be misleading to draw broad conclusions on the scope of protection from the relevant case law of the Court of Justice. **6–157**

Its approach seems to change from case to case, sometimes hinting to broadening the scope of protection, other times appearing to deny protection even in cases where infringement would appear to be an automatic presumption and being permissive in its approach towards limitations. The Court is often getting involved with the facts of the case and allows factual contexts to delimit its interpretive rulings. It is difficult to identify strict, easily applicable criteria.

Still, the Court's consistently pragmatic approach must also be acknowledged and appreciated. The Court recognises that trade marks are tools used by marketers, their competitors, and consumers in a market place that evolves constantly. Trade marks must be protected in order to fulfil their function as a carrier of information; at the same time markets must remain open and competitive. Hence, the Court has so far avoided a doctrinal, macroscopic, interpretive approach. Instead it chooses to focus on the area of protection that is relevant and specific to each individual case. It takes into account the factual and market contexts and views trade mark law as one piece of a bigger market regulation picture.

After all, context is everything in the interpretation and application of trade mark law. Accepting this more explicitly would allow the Court to reconcile what appear to be inconsistencies in its trade mark jurisprudence.

---

[258] *Davidoff III*, paras 23–24.
[259] *Davidoff III*, para.26.

Chapter 7

CHALLENGING OR MAINTAINING THE REGISTRATION

1. Introduction	7–001
2. The Legislative Context	7–002
(1) The provisions of the Directive	7–002
3. The Case law of the Court	7–007
(1) Ansul—the concept of "genuine use"	7–007
(2) Laboratoire de la Mer—subjective and objective perspectives	7–024
(3) Radetzky—use in respect of non-profitable activities	7–030
(4) Silberquelle—use on promotional items	7–038
(5) Nasdaq—complementary services offered free of charge	7–049
(6) Lidl—start of the use requirement and proper reasons for non-use	7–054
(7) Bainbridge—defensive registrations	7–066
4. Challenging a Community Trade Mark	7–074
(1) Sunrider—evidence of use; the burden of proof	7–074
5. Conclusion	7–089

1. INTRODUCTION

Using the trade mark is the main requirement that the proprietor of a trade mark right needs to satisfy. A trade mark registration can also be challenged on the basis of earlier rights or absolute grounds covered in Chs 4 and 5 respectively. **7–001**

Note that the principle of "use" for the purposes of maintaining a registration is also being developed by the Court in cases where the owner of an earlier right must establish use in order to attack a Community Trade Mark application or registration.[1]

The Eighth Recital states:

"Whereas in order to reduce the total number of trade marks registered and protected in the Community and, consequently, the number of

---

[1] See *The Sunrider Corp v Office for Harmonisation in the Internal Market (Trade Marks and Designs)* (C-416/04 P) 2006 WL 1275044.

conflicts which arise between them, it is essential to require that registered trade marks must actually be used or, if not used, be subject to revocation; whereas it is necessary to provide that a trade mark cannot be invalidated on the basis of the existence of a non-used earlier trade mark, while the Member States remain free to apply the same principle in respect of the registration of a trade mark or to provide that a trade mark may not be successfully invoked in infringement proceedings if it is established as a result of a plea that the trade mark could be revoked; whereas in all these cases it is up to the Member States to establish the applicable rules of procedure."

2. THE LEGISLATIVE CONTEXT

(1) The provisions of the Directive

7–002 *(a) Article 10—use of trade marks*

1. If, within a period of five years following the date of the completion of the registration procedure, the proprietor has not put the trade mark to genuine use in the Member State in connection with the goods or services in respect of which it is registered, or if such use has been suspended during an uninterrupted period of five years, the trade mark shall be subject to the sanctions provided for in this Directive, unless there are proper reasons for non-use.
2. The following shall also constitute use within the meaning of para.1:

(a) use of the trade mark in a form differing in elements which do not alter the distinctive character of the mark in the form in which it was registered;

(b) affixing of the trade mark to goods or to the packaging thereof in the Member State concerned solely for export purposes.

3. Use of the trade mark with the consent of the proprietor or by any person who has authority to use a collective mark or a guarantee or certification mark shall be deemed to constitute use by the proprietor.
4. In relation to trade marks registered before the date on which the provisions necessary to comply with this Directive enter into force in the Member State concerned:

(a) where a provision in force prior to that date attaches sanctions to non-use of a trade mark during an uninterrupted period, the relevant period of five years mentioned in para.1 shall be deemed to have begun to run at the same time as any period of non-use which is already running at that date;

2. THE LEGISLATIVE CONTEXT

(b) where there is no use provision in force prior to that date, the periods of five years mentioned in para.1 shall be deemed to run from that date at the earliest.

(b) Article 11—sanctions for non use of a trade mark in legal or administrative proceedings

7–003

1. A trade mark may not be declared invalid on the ground that there is an earlier conflicting trade mark if the latter does not fulfil the requirements of use set out in art.10(1), (2) and (3) or in art.10(4), as the case may be.

2. Any Member State may provide that registration of a trade mark may not be refused on the ground that there is an earlier conflicting trade mark if the latter does not fulfil the requirements of use set out in art.10(1), (2) and (3) or in art.10(4), as the case may be.

3. Without prejudice to the application of art.12, where a counter-claim for revocation is made, any Member State may provide that a trade mark may not be successfully invoked in infringement proceedings if it is established as a result of a plea that the trade mark could be revoked pursuant to art.12(1).

4. If the earlier trade mark has been used in relation to part only of the goods or services for which it is registered, it shall, for purposes of applying paras 1, 2 and 3, be deemed to be registered in respect only of that part of the goods or services.

(c) Article 12—grounds for revocation

7–004

1. A trade mark shall be liable to revocation if, within a continuous period of five years, it has not been put to genuine use in the Member State in connection with the goods or services in respect of which it is registered, and there are no proper reasons for non-use; however, no person may claim that the proprietor's rights in a trade mark should be revoked where, during the interval between expiry of the five-year period and filing of the application for revocation, genuine use of the trade mark has been started or resumed; the commencement or resumption of use within a period of three months preceding the filing of the application for revocation which began at the earliest on expiry of the continuous period of five years of non-use, shall, however, be disregarded where preparations for the commencement or resumption occur only after the proprietor becomes aware that the application for revocation may be filed.

2. A trade mark shall also be liable to revocation if, after the date on which it was registered:

(a) in consequence of acts or inactivity of the proprietor, it has become the common name in the trade for a product or service in respect of which it is registered;

(b) in consequence of the use made of it by the proprietor of the trade mark or with his consent in respect of the goods or services for which it is registered, it is liable to mislead the public, particularly as to the nature, quality or geographical origin of those goods or services.

7-005 *(d) Article 13—grounds for refusal or revocation or invalidity relating to only some of the goods or services*

Where grounds for refusal of registration or for revocation or invalidity of a trade mark exist in respect of only some of the goods or services for which that trade mark has been applied for or registered, refusal of registration or revocation or invalidity shall cover those goods or services only.

7-006 *(e) Article 14—establishment a posteriori of invalidity or revocation of a trade mark*

Where the seniority of an earlier trade mark which has been surrendered or allowed to lapse, is claimed for a Community Trade Mark, the invalidity or revocation of the earlier trade mark may be established a posteriori.

The Regulation provisions on surrender, revocation, and invalidity are found under Title Pt VI of the Regulation (arts 49–56).

3. THE CASE LAW OF THE COURT

(1) Ansul—the concept of "genuine use"

7-007 *Ansul*[2] was the first case where the Court considered the concept of use for the purposes of art.10 and art.12 of the Directive.

Ansul was the proprietor of the trade mark Minimax in the Benelux, since 1971; the specification covered fire extinguishers and associated products. The special marketing authorisation required for fire extinguishers expired in 1988 and Ansul stopped marketing fire extinguishers in 1989. However, it continued selling component parts and extinguishing substances for Minimax fire extinguishers to undertakings that were responsible for maintaining them. It also continued itself checking, maintaining, and repairing Minimax products. As a result Minimax had been used on invoices, stickers, and strips with the statement Gebruiksklaar Minimax (Ready for use Minimax).

Ajax, the subsidiary of the German manufacturer of fire extinguishers Minimax GmbH, was the proprietor of a composite mark incorporating the

---

[2] *Ansul BV v Ajax Brandbeveiliging BV* (C-40/01) [2003] E.C.R. I-2439.

3. THE CASE LAW OF THE COURT

word Minimax in the Benelux since 1992; the registration covered fire extinguishers and extinguishing substances, and for the installation, repair, maintenance and refilling of fire extinguishers. When Ajax started using the mark in 1994 Ansul objected by a letter and successfully filed an application for Minimax for certain services, including the maintenance and repair of fire extinguishers. Originally the trade mark Minimax was owned by the same German entity in Germany and The Netherlands; it was expropriated after the Second World War and the Dutch registration became Ansul's Benelux registration whereas the German registration passed to Minimax GmbH.

Ajax attacked both of Ansul's registrations, the first on the basis of non-use and the second on the ground that the application had been filed in bad faith. Ansul resisted the applications and at the same time sought an injunction against use of the Minimax mark in the Benelux.

7–008

The case reached the Hoge Raad (Supreme Court) of the Netherlands. The Dutch court held that in assessing whether the use to which a trade mark is put is normal, all the particular facts and circumstances of each case had to be taken into account in order to show whether the aim of the use was to preserve an outlet for the marked products rather than maintain the trade mark rights, having regard to what would be considered to be usual and commercially justified in the relevant business sector. Referring to the relevant jurisprudence of the Benelux Court of Justice, it added that as a rule account should be taken of the kind, extent, frequency, regularity and duration of the use, of the kind of relevant goods or service, and the kind and size of the undertaking.[3]

However the Hoge Raad also held that the interpretation of the relevant provision of the Uniform Benelux Law had to conform to the interpretation of art.12(1). Accordingly it decided to stay proceedings and to refer the following questions to the Court for a preliminary ruling:

"1. Must the words put to genuine use in Article 12(1) of Directive 89/104 be interpreted in the manner [set out above] and, if the answer is in the negative, on the basis of which (other) criterion must the meaning of genuine use be determined?

2. Can there be genuine use as referred to above also where no new goods are traded under the trade mark but other activities are engaged in as set out [above]?"[4]

(a) The Opinion of the Advocate General

7–009

(i) The legislative framework. Advocate General Ruiz-Jarabo Colomer started his analysis with an overview of the legislative concepts of the use

---
[3] *Turmac v Reynolds* (A80/1) [1981] E.C.C. 346.
[4] Reproduced in para.22.

requirement. He noted that at the international level the Paris Convention adopted art.5C[5] in 1925 at the revision of The Hague; and that TRIPs art.2(1) provided that WTO members had to comply with, amongst others, art.5C. He also mentioned art.19 of the Trademark Law Treaty.

At the Community level the Eighth Recital in the Preamble to the Directive stated that it was essential to introduce a use requirement in order to reduce the total number of trade marks registered and protected in the Community and the number of conflicts potentially arising between them. The Regulation followed the same approach through the Ninth Recital and art.15, art.43, art.50 and art.56.

The Uniform Benelux law provided in its original version prior to the amendments introduced as a result of the Directive for a three-year period of non-use immediately following filing or for a five-year period at any other stage.[6] Article 5 in its amended version provided for a five-year interruption period of normal use and that the court might allocate all or part of the burden of proving use to the trade mark proprietor.

He viewed the Uniform Benelux Law as a reference point but he stressed that the definitive answer could only be provided by Community provisions. "Since trade mark proprietors are intended to enjoy the same level of protection in all the Member States, the reply must be framed according to the law of the European Union"[7] interpreted in an integrationist manner.[8]

7–010 **(ii) Interpreting use.** Advocate General Ruiz-Jarabo Colomer stressed that a trade mark register should reflect the reality of the market place. He agreed with the Commission that "[o]nly marks that are used in commercial life should be registered by offices with responsibility for industrial property matters ... defensive and strategic registrations must be refused".[9]

Use and the manner of use justified the exclusive character of trade mark rights but also reconciled the objectives of trade mark law with those of

---

[5] Article 5C provides: "(1) If, in any country, use of the registered mark is compulsory, the registration may be cancelled only after a reasonable period, and then only if the person concerned does not justify his inaction. (2) Use of a trademark by the proprietor in a form differing in elements which do not alter the distinctive character of the mark in the form in which it was registered in one of the countries of the Union shall not entail invalidation of the registration and shall not diminish the protection granted to the mark. (3) Concurrent use of the same mark on identical or similar goods by industrial or commercial establishments considered as co-proprietors of the mark according to the provisions of the domestic law of the country where protection is claimed shall not prevent registration or diminish in any way the protection granted to the said mark in any country of the Union, provided that such use does not result in misleading the public and is not contrary to the public interest."

[6] The original provision, also provided that the court might allocate all or part of the burden of proving use to the trade mark proprietor; however non use at a time that predated the action by more than six years had to be proved by the person claiming non-use.

[7] Point 38, citing para.42 of *Levi Strauss & Co and Levi Strauss (UK) Ltd* (C-414/99) and *Costco Wholesale UK Ltd* (C-415/99) and *Zino Davidoff SA* (C-416/99) [2001] E.C.R. I-8691.

[8] Repeating a point he had made in *Merz&Krell GmbH & Co* (C-517/99) [2001] E.C.R. I-6959; and *Koninklijke KPN Nederland NV* (C-363/99) [2004] E.C.R. I-1619.

[9] Point 42 of the Opinion of A.G. Ruiz-Jarabo Colomer.

3. THE CASE LAW OF THE COURT

competition, "it is necessary to reiterate that the relationship between the rights a trade mark confers on its proprietor and the mark itself is fundamental: the purpose of the legal benefits it carries with it is to enable the consumer to distinguish the goods or service identified, so that the ability to discriminate, on which freedom of choice depends, might lead to the establishment of a system of open competition in the internal market".[10]

He added that use was also critical from the contrasting perspective of the alleged infringer, citing *Arsenal*[11] where the Court had to ascertain the circumstances in which a third party was using a distinctive sign as a trade mark, in order to determine the circumstances in which the proprietor could prohibit him from doing so.

He supported that the concept of use should mean the same thing in both situations. Accordingly, he followed the path he had indicated in *Arsenal*.

7–011

First, use had to be commercial use, or as the Directive put use in the course of trade. Secondly, use should be "for the purpose of distinguishing the goods or services by their origin or source, by their quality or by their reputation".[12]

The "genuine" requirement The first introductory point he made was that genuine meant not token. Elaborating further on this he considered first what did not constitute genuine use: "Where use is a mere sham, is formalistic or notional, where it is empty of substance and directed solely at avoiding revocation and does not serve to carve out an opening in the market for the goods and services to which it relates, that use does not constitute genuine use."[13]

7–012

A positive definition was more difficult. He examined the linguistic variations on the theme of genuineness—some Member States referred to normal use, others to serious, genuine, or effective—and concluded "the kind of use intended by the Community legislature is what may be described as sufficient in relation to the function performed by a trade mark".[14]

Following a purposive interpretation he added that use had to be sufficient or appropriate to distinguish the proprietor's goods or services in the market "so as to create an outlet by free, open and fair competition".[15]

He then suggested a number of factors for proving that the use was indeed genuine.

7–013

First, it should involve use of the sign in relation to the goods and services for which the mark was registered.

Secondly, it had to be use of the sign exactly as it was granted and registered with all its components; exceptionally, it could also cover use with

---

[10] Point 44 of the Opinion of A.G. Ruiz-Jarabo Colomer.
[11] *Arsenal Football Club Plc* (C-206/01) [2002] E.C.R. I-10273.
[12] Point 48 of the Opinion of A.G. Ruiz-Jarabo Colomer.
[13] Point 50 of the Opinion of A.G. Ruiz-Jarabo Colomer.
[14] Point 52 of the Opinion of A.G. Ruiz-Jarabo Colomer.
[15] Point 53 of the Opinion of A.G. Ruiz-Jarabo Colomer.

CHALLENGING OR MAINTAINING THE REGISTRATION

differences affecting elements that did not alter the distinctive character of the mark in the form in which it was registered.

7-014 Thirdly, it would have to be "public and external, directed at the outside world. . . . Accordingly there will be genuine use not only where the goods are being sold or the services supplied, but also where the trade mark is being used for advertising with a view to those goods or services being launched in the market".[16]

On the other hand this also meant that private use that did not extend beyond the internal province of the proprietor's undertaking should not be considered sufficient: "Preparations for the marketing of goods or services do not, therefore, constitute sufficient or effective use, nor does getting them shop-ready or storing them where they do not leave the undertaking's premises."[17]

Affixing the mark to the goods or their packaging for export purposes would be sufficient in exceptional circumstances only, in order to protect undertakings whose main activity would be export trade.

7-015 Fourthly, it had to be appropriate to the aims of a trade mark. On the one hand, use with the sole aim of preventing revocation would not be genuine. On the other, it introduced an element of objectivity into the assessment. Even where the aim would be other than to prevent revocation use should be appropriate at least to a minimum degree for fulfilling the functions ascribed to trade marks by the law. This should be determined on the basis of the circumstances of each case[18] and it would be for the national court to decide, taking into account the following criteria.

The starting point should be the sale or supply of the goods or services under the trade mark: "The point beyond which commercial use of the trade mark may be considered appropriate and genuine is directly related to the type of goods or category of service."[19]

Irrespective of volume of sales or size of the proprietor's undertaking, use had to be consistent rather than sporadic or occasional. He added that the structure and limits of the relevant market and the average consumer's perception of the product in question should also be taken into account together with the nature of the product.

Having described the factors the national court would have to take into account he noted that their application on the circumstances surrounding

---

[16] Point 56, citing his Opinion in *Sieckmann* (C-273/00) [2002] E.C.R. I-11737 on the advertising function of a trade mark.

[17] Point 57, citing Fernández-Novoa, *Derecho de Marcas* (Montecorvo SA, 1990), pp.253–254.

[18] He also referred to r.22(2) of Commission Regulation 2868/95 implementing Council Regulation 40/94 [1995] OJ L303/1, providing that the proof of use was to consist of indications concerning the place, time, extent and nature of use of the opposing trade mark for the goods and services in respect of which it was registered; r.22(3) added that the evidence would comprise supporting documents and items such as packages, labels, price lists, catalogues, invoices, photographs, newspaper advertisements, and statements in writing. See also *The Sunrider Corp v Office for Harmonisation in the Internal Market (Trade Marks and Designs)* (C-416/04 P) 2006 WL 1275044.

[19] Point 61 of the Opinion of A.G. Ruiz-Jarabo Colomer.

3. THE CASE LAW OF THE COURT

use of the Minimax trade mark fell under the competence of the referring national court.

(b) The judgment of the Court 7–016

The Court started its analysis by one of the facts of the case: the reason behind the first question was the fact that Ansul had not put on the market any new fire extinguishers under the mark but was inspecting used equipment that had already been sold. It then went on to determine whether the concept of genuine use had to be interpreted in a uniform manner within the Community legal order.

(i) Uniform interpretation. The Court referred to the requirements of 7–017 the uniform application of Community law and the principle of equality as setting that "the terms of a provision of Community law which make no express reference to the law of the Member States for the purpose of determining its meaning and scope must normally be given an autonomous and uniform interpretation throughout the Community; that interpretation must take into account the context of the provision and the purpose of the legislation in question".[20]

In the absence of earlier case law the Court referred in detail to the Preamble to the Directive. The Directive did not aim to harmonise fully the laws of the Member States; however, the provisions which most directly affected the functioning of the internal market should be harmonised, and the Third Recital in particular did not preclude the complete harmonisation of those provisions.[21] The Seventh Recital indicated that the conditions for obtaining and continuing to hold a registered trade mark should, in general, be identical in all Member States. The use requirement was introduced by the Eighth Recital; its purpose was to reduce the number of conflicts arising between trade marks. The Ninth Recital stated that it was fundamental, in order to facilitate the free circulation of goods and services, to ensure that registered trade marks enjoyed the same protection under the legal systems of all the Member States. The 12th Recital provided that the Directive had to be consistent with the Paris Convention.

The concept of use was covered in arts 10–15 of the Directive and art.15 7–018 and art.50 of the Regulation in the context of maintaining but also challenging trade mark rights.[22]

So, according to the Court, the Community legislature intended to subject the maintenance of trade mark rights to the same condition regarding

---

[20] *Ansul*, para.26, citing case *Luxembourg v Linster* (C-287/98) [2000] E.C.R. I-6917.
[21] Citing *Silhouette International Schmied GmbH & Co KG v Hartlaver Handelsgesellschaft mbH* (C-355/96) [1998] E.C.R. I-4799.
[22] For example *The Sunrider Corp v Office for Harmonisation in the Internal Market (Trade Marks and Designs)* (C-416/04 P) [2006] E.C.R. 000.

genuine use throughout the Union[23]; in turn the concept of genuine use should be given the same interpretation in art.10 and art.12 of the Directive.

7–019 **(ii) The concept of genuine use.** The Court found that the Paris Convention failed to provide the necessary guidance for defining the concept of genuine use; therefore it had to be determined according to the provisions of the Directive.

The first requirement set by the Court was that according to the Eighth Recital genuine use meant actual use of the mark. The wording used in some national provisions—including the Dutch, Spanish, Italian, and English version—that referred to effective and genuine use supported that approach.

The second requirement was that use should not be merely token, serving solely to preserve the rights conferred by the mark. It had to be consistent with the essential function of a trade mark as a guarantee of the identity of the origin of goods or services.

7–020 This meant that the:

> "[P]rotection the mark confers and the consequences of registering it in terms of enforceability vis-à-vis third parties cannot continue to operate if the mark loses its commercial raison d'être, which is to create or preserve an outlet for the goods or services that bear the sign of which it is composed, as distinct from the goods or services of other undertakings. Use of the mark must therefore relate to goods or services already marketed or about to be marketed and for which preparations by the undertaking to secure customers are under way, particularly in the form of advertising campaigns."[24]

Such use, however, could be either by the trade mark proprietor or by a third party with authority to use the mark, according to art.10(3).

The third requirement was that the assessment of genuine use should take account of all the relevant facts and circumstances, "in particular whether such use is viewed as warranted in the economic sector concerned to maintain or create a share in the market for the goods or services protected by the mark".[25]

Those included the nature of the goods or service at issue, the characteristics of the market concerned and the scale and frequency of use of the mark. The Court appeared to indicate that the quantitative dimension of use could also be relevant, albeit not determinative; it should always be seen in correlation with the remaining factors: "Use of the mark need not, therefore, always be quantitatively significant for it to be deemed genuine, as that

---

[23] Citing *Levi Strauss & Co and Levi Strauss (UK) Ltd* (C-414/99) and *Costco Wholesale UK Ltd* (C-415/99) and *Zino Davidoff SA* (C-416/99) [2001] E.C.R. I-8691, paras 41–42.
[24] *Ansul*, para.37.
[25] *Ansul*, para.38.

3. THE CASE LAW OF THE COURT

depends on the characteristics of the goods or service concerned on the corresponding market."[26]

Use in respect of "integral parts" Turning to the circumstances of the case the Court held that the use might also be genuine for goods that were no longer available: 7–021

> "That applies, inter alia, where the proprietor of the trade mark under which such goods were put on the market sells parts which are integral to the make-up or structure of the goods previously sold, and for which he makes actual use of the same mark under the conditions described [above]."[27]

Use in respect of directly related goods and services The same principle applied to goods and services which were directly related to those goods and intended to meet the needs of their customers: "That may apply to after-sales services, such as the sale of accessories or related parts, or the supply of maintenance and repair services."[28]   7–022

(iii) The competence of the national Court. Following the above analysis in respect of the first question, the Court noted that the assessment of the circumstances of the case belonged to the national court under the division of functions provided for by art.234 EC,[29] to apply the rules of Community law, as interpreted by the Court, to the individual case before it.   7–023

(2) Laboratoire de la Mer—subjective and objective perspectives   7–024

In *Laboratoire de la Mer*[30] the Court reconfirmed the approach it had taken in *Ansul*.[31] Laboratoires Goemar, a French company specialising in seaweed products, was the proprietor of the trade mark "Laboratoire de la Mer" in the United Kingdom, registered in 1988 in respect of pharmaceutical, veterinary and sanitary products, dietetic products for medical use all containing marine products, included in class 5 and in 1989, in respect of perfumes and cosmetics containing marine products included in class 3.

La Mer Technology sought the revocation of those registrations for non-use. At the Trade Mark Registry the marks were revoked only for

---

[26] *Ansul*, para.39.
[27] *Ansul*, para.41.
[28] *Ansul*, para.42.
[29] *Staatssecretaris van Financien v Shipping and Forwarding Enterprise Safe BV* (C-320/88) [1990] E.C.R. I-285.
[30] *La Mer Technology Inc v Laboratoires Goëmar SA* (C-259/02) [2004] E.C.R. I-1159.
[31] *Ansul BV* (C-40/01) [2003] E.C.R. I-2439.

perfumes in class 3 and pharmaceutical, veterinary and sanitary products in Class 5.

La Mer Technology challenged the part of the decision rejecting its application before the High Court. The High Court accepted the appeal in relation to the remaining products in class 5; for cosmetics containing marine products in class 3 it found that Laboratoires Goemar had appointed a Scottish company to distribute its products in the United Kingdom and that the low turnover reflected a commercial failure rather that the intention of the Laboratoires Goemar to use the trade mark for maintaining its registration. Indeed the company was taking measures to reverse that failure. Accordingly it stayed proceedings and referred the following questions to the Court:

"1. What factors should be taken into account when deciding whether a mark has been put to genuine use in a Member State within the meaning of Arts 10(1) and 12(1) of [the Directive]?
In particular:
2. Should the extent of use of the mark in relation to the goods or services for which the mark is registered in the Member State be taken into account?
3. Is any amount of use, however small, sufficient if it was made with no purpose other than commercially dealing in the goods or providing the service concerned?
4. If the answer to the foregoing question is no, what is the test for determining how much use is sufficient, and in particular does that test include a consideration of the nature and size of the business of the registered proprietor?
5. Is token or sham use to be disregarded, and in particular is use whose sole or predominant purpose is defeating a potential claim for revocation to be disregarded?
6. What types of use can be considered, and in particular is it necessary to show that the mark has been used in the course of trade in the Member State concerned and, in further particular, would importation by a single customer into that Member State be sufficient?
7. Is it necessary to disregard use occurring after the filing of the application for revocation even for the purpose of testing whether use during the relevant period was genuine?"

7–025   *(a) The reasoned order of the Court*

The Court informed the national court that it found that the answers to the first six questions could be deduced from its judgment in *Ansul*[32] and that the answer to the seventh question could be given according to art.104(3)

---

[32] *Ansul BV* (C-40/01) [2003] E.C.R. I-2439.

3. THE CASE LAW OF THE COURT

of its Rules of Procedure[33] by reasoned order. The national court withdrew the fifth question but insisted on the remaining questions.

The Court decided to respond to all the remaining questions by reasoned order.

(i) Genuine use: the criteria and types of use. The Court repeated that genuine use meant actual use, use that was not merely token serving solely to preserve the rights conferred by the mark. The use had to be consistent with the essential function of a trade mark. Genuine use entailed use of the mark on the market for the goods or services protected by that mark and not just internal use by the undertaking concerned. It should relate to goods or services already marketed or about to be marketed and for which preparations by the undertaking to secure customers were under way, particularly in the form of advertising campaigns. Such use might be either by the trade mark proprietor or by a third party with authority to use the mark. And finally, the assessment of genuine use should consider all the relevant facts and circumstances.

7–026

The application of the principles From all the above the Court concluded that "the preservation by a trade mark proprietor of his rights is predicated on the mark being put to genuine use in the course of trade, on the market for the goods or services for which it was registered in the Member State concerned".[34]

7–027

In some cases, it added, use that was not quantitatively significant might be sufficient to establish genuine use: "Even minimal use can therefore be sufficient to qualify as genuine, on condition that it is deemed to be justified, in the economic sector concerned, for the purpose of preserving or creating market share for the goods or services protected by the mark."[35]

It reminded that the question whether the relevant use was sufficient to preserve or create a share in the relevant product market depended on the assessment of each individual case by the national court: "The characteristics of those products and services, the frequency or regularity of the use of the mark, whether the mark is used for the purpose of marketing all the identical products or services of the proprietor or merely some of them, or evidence which the proprietor is able to provide, are among the factors which may be taken into account."[36] Similarly, the characteristics of the relevant market should also be taken into account.

---

[33] The possibility "for the Court, in simplified proceedings, to give its decision on a question referred for a preliminary ruling by reasoned order, means that the Court now has available to it a 'filter system' "; this is how A.G. Stix-Hackl had described the effect of art.104(3) in *Intermodal Transports BV v Staatssecretaris van Financien* (C-495/03) [2005] E.C.R. I-8151.
[34] *Laboratoire de la Mer*, para.20.
[35] *Laboratoire de la Mer*, para.21.
[36] *Laboratoire de la Mer*, para.22.

7-028   The Court found use of the mark by a single client which imported the marked products could be sufficient, provided that the importation had a genuine commercial justification for the trade mark proprietor.

Accordingly it held that it was not possible to determine a priori, and in the abstract, a quantitative threshold. The Court insisted that the national court should appraise all the circumstances of the case rather than apply a prescriptive de minimis rule.

The Court also held that where use of the mark did not have as its essential aim the preservation or creation of market share for the specified goods or services it should not be considered genuine.

7-029   **(ii) Use after the filing of the application for revocation.** The Court stressed that art.12(1) made it clear that the mark should be put to genuine use prior to the filing of an application for revocation; in addition the commencement or resumption of use of the mark before the filing of an application for revocation would not suffice if it appeared that it occurred only after the proprietor had become aware that an application for revocation might be filed:

> "Nevertheless, the Directive does not expressly preclude in assessing the genuineness of use during the relevant period, account being taken, where appropriate, of any circumstances subsequent to that filing. Such circumstances may make it possible to confirm or better assess the extent to which the trade mark was used during the relevant period and the real intentions of the proprietor during that time."[37]

Where the particular evidence of use should lie remained a question that the national court had to answer.

7-030   **(3)   Radetzky—use in respect of non-profitable activities**

(a)   The facts in the main proceedings and the order for reference

In *Radetzky*[38] the Court was asked to clarify whether the use a non-profit-making association makes of its trade marks in promoting its activities and in fund raising constitutes genuine use within the meaning of art.12(1) of the Directive.

The reference was made in the context of a dispute between the Verein Radetzky-Orden ("Radetzky Orden") and the Bundesvereinigung Kameradschaft "Feldmarschall Radetzky" ("BKFR") concerning the revocation of the latter's trade marks on the grounds of non-use.

---

[37] *Laboratoire de la Mer*, para.31.
[38] *Verein Radetzky-Orden v Bundesvereinigung Kameradschaft "Feldmarschall Radetzky"* (C-442/07), not yet published.

3. THE CASE LAW OF THE COURT

The BKFR is a non-profit-making association, which does not sell any goods or provides any services for remuneration. Its activity consists, on the one hand, in the preservation of military traditions, such as the organisation of memorial services for members of the armed forces who have fallen in combat, remembrance services, military reunions and the upkeep of war memorials and, on the other, in charitable work, such as the collection of money and donations in kind and their subsequent distribution to the needy.

The BKFR is the proprietor of various word and figurative trade marks, representing essentially badges of honour, entered in the register of the Austrian Patent Office in respect of the following services, in classes 37, 41 and 45 of the Nice Classification: upkeep of war memorials (class 37); entertainment, sporting and cultural activities, organisation of military reunions (class 41); charitable work for the needy (class 45). BKFR awards orders and decorations corresponding to its marks, which its members wear at various events and when collecting and distributing donations. The marks are also printed on invitations to forthcoming events, on stationery and on the association's promotional material.

7–031

The Radetzky-Orden sought to have BKFR's trade marks cancelled on grounds of non-use pursuant to the relevant provisions of Austrian law.[39] It claimed that the BKFR had not used its trade marks commercially over the course of the previous five years.

The Austrian Patent Office granted Radetzky-Orden's application and cancelled BKFR's trade marks. The BKFR appealed against that decision to the Oberster Patent-und Markensamt, which decided to stay the proceedings and refer the following question to the Court for a preliminary ruling:

"Is Article 12 (1) of the Directive to be construed as meaning that a trade mark is put to (genuine) use to distinguish goods and services of one undertaking from those of other undertakings in the case where a non-profit-making association uses the trade mark in announcements for events, on business papers and on advertising material and that trade mark is used by the association's members when collecting and distributing donations inasmuch as those members wear badges featuring that trade mark?"

(b) The respective arguments

7–032

The Radetzky-Orden claimed that according to art.5 of the Directive trade mark protection is closely linked to the supply of goods and services in the course of trade and that trade mark use thus implies a supply for consideration. Accordingly, the term "genuine use" in art.12 of the Directive only applies to commercial or entrepreneurial activity carried out for profit. Conversely, activities which are exclusively non-profit-making fall outside the scope of trade mark protection.

---

[39] Paragraph 33a of the Markenschutzgesetz 1970, BGBl. 260/1970; "the MSchG".

The BKFR countered that although charitable organisations are non-profit-making associations, they compete against each other in their particular field of activity and thus act like entrepreneurs in any other sector, even where their proceeds are not kept as profit, but made available to the needy. Insofar as the signs used for that purpose, such as marks, decorations, insignia and coats of arms, indicate the origin of their services and allow the public to distinguish them from those of other organisations, they are put to genuine trade mark use. In fact, the award of decorations and distinctions containing the mark to persons outside the organisation is a form of advertising or merchandising that actually serves to promote the association's core activities.

7–033   *(c)   The Opinion of the Advocate General*

Advocate General Mazák started his analysis by referring to the Court's statements in *Ansul*[40] and *La Mer*[41] that the question of genuine use must be examined by taking into consideration all the relevant circumstances of the case and in particular the nature and characteristics of the market in which the trade mark is used, especially insofar as those characteristics may directly affect the marketing strategy of the proprietor of the mark.

Accordingly, he stressed the need to examine the question of genuine use of a trade mark by non-profit-making associations by reference to the purpose and nature of their activities and by taking into account the manner in which such organisations generally supply goods and services.[42]

Next, the Advocate General observed that when raising funds and distributing donations, non-profit-making associations actually compete with each other in order to attract donations from the public and, thus, engage in business or in commercial activity, in the wider sense of those terms. Thus, he concluded that non-profit-making associations are, in principle, market players which acquire and provide goods and services in conformity with the norms prevailing in the relevant sector. Conversely, completely ignoring the commercial or business environment in which such organisations operate would be unrealistic and could potentially undermine their activities.[43]

7–034   Moreover, he noted that art.5 of the Directive, which enumerates the rights conferred by a trade mark, does not require that goods and services actually be supplied for profit or indeed for consideration. The question of whether the proprietor uses the trade mark for the purposes of personal enrichment is thus not relevant when assessing whether the trade mark is being put to genuine use within the meaning of art.12(1) of the Directive.[44]

---

[40] *Ansul*, paras 38–39.
[41] *La Mer*, paras 22–23.
[42] Point 25 of the Opinion of A.G. Mazák.
[43] Point 27 of the Opinion of A.G. Mazák.
[44] Point 28 of the Opinion of A.G. Mazák.

3. THE CASE LAW OF THE COURT

Accordingly, the Advocate General considered that the use of the sign in fund raising serves as an indication to donors of the identity of the association in question and the purposes for which the funds are collected and thus constitutes genuine use of the trade mark.[45] However, when the sign is used for the announcement or advertisement of purely private ceremonies or events, principally involving existing members of the association, the use is merely internal and thus cannot qualify as genuine for the purposes of art.12(1) of the Directive.[46]

Advocate General Mazák therefore proposed to answer the question in the affirmative, but only insofar as the non-profit-making association uses the trade mark in announcements for public fund-raising events, or when the sign is used on business papers addressed to members of the public and on advertising material soliciting donations from the public, while leaving it up to the national Court to assess whether the facts in the main proceedings corresponded to such use.

(d) The judgment of the Court   7–035

In establishing the framework for its analysis, the Court referred to its statements in *Ansul* that the use made of the sign is "genuine" within the meaning of art.12(1) of the Directive when it is consistent with the essential function of a trade mark, which is to guarantee the identity of the origin of goods or services to the consumer and that it entails use of the mark on the market for the designated goods or services and not just internal use within the undertaking concerned. It also recalled, that the protection conferred by the mark and its enforceability vis-à-vis third parties cannot continue to operate if the mark loses its commercial raison d'être, which is to create or preserve an outlet for the goods or services that bear the sign, as distinct from those of other undertakings.[47]

As regards the case at issue, the Court noted that although the financial implications of marks and their use on the market are apparent from the Paris Convention, which refers to them as "trade marks", the fact that goods or services are offered on a non-profit-making basis is not decisive in itself for ascertaining whether the use is indeed genuine, in the sense that the fact that a charitable association does not seek to make profit does not mean that its objective cannot be to create and, later, to preserve an outlet for its goods or services.[48]

In that connection, the Court also observed that, in modern economy, various types of non-profit-making associations have sprung up which, at first sight, offer their services free but which, in reality, are financed through subsidies or receive payment in various forms.

---

[45] Point 29 of the Opinion of A.G. Mazák.
[46] Point 30 of the Opinion of A.G. Mazák.
[47] *Ansul*, paras 35–37.
[48] *Radetzky*, paras 15–17.

7-036   Consequently, trade marks registered by such organisations may have a raison d'être, in that they protect the association against the possible use in business of identical or similar signs by third entities. Thus, as long as the mark is used in order to identify and promote the goods or services for which it has been registered, there is nothing to prevent such use from being regarded as "genuine" within the meaning of art.12(1) of the Directive.[49]

Moreover, the Court concurred with the view taken by the Advocate General[50] that, use in purely private ceremonies or events, or for the advertisement or announcement of such ceremonies or events, constitutes merely internal use of the mark and not "genuine use" for the purposes of art.12(1) of the Directive.[51]

Thus, the Court concluded that where a non-profit-making association uses the mark in its relations with the public, such as in the course of announcements of forthcoming events, on business papers and on advertising material, or where its members wear badges featuring that mark when collecting donations, it makes genuine use of its registered trade mark.

However, it noted that it was for the national Court to ascertain whether the marks in the main proceedings were actually used to identify and promote services offered to the general public, or whether the use made of them was merely internal.

7-037   In *Radetzky* the Court seems to be taking the broad view that a real and effective exploitation of the mark is not necessarily incompatible with its use in non-profitable activities or with the rendering of services free of charge, provided, first, that such use is outward and external and, secondly, that the use of the mark in this manner complies with the established norms and characteristics of the relevant market sector.

On the other hand, its view with regard to internal use seems to be quite restrictive, at least insofar as many non-profit making associations, like e.g. mutual assistance funds and other professional organisations, actually depend for the financing of their activities on the subscription fees and donations collected from its members, who are in reality its "customers". Moreover, the very purpose of such associations is to offer a variety of services to its members, often on a non-profit making basis. It is therefore questionable whether the use of an association's marks in its relations with its members should always be regarded as an internal affair, or whether this should depend on the facts of the particular case.

7-038   **(4)   Silberquelle—use on promotional items**

Silberquelle[52] was another reference from the Austrian Oberster Patent-und Markensamt concerning non-profitable use. This time, however, the Court

---

[49] *Radetzky*, paras 18–21.
[50] At point 30 of his Opinion.
[51] *Radetzky*, para.22.
[52] *Silberquelle GmbH v Maselli Strickmode GmbH* (C-495/07), not yet published.

had to deal not with use in the course of activities which, by nature, are non profitable, but rather with the offer of promotional items free of charge as a means of enhancing the sales of other goods.

(a) The facts in the main proceedings and the order for reference   7–039

The reference was made in the context of an action brought by Silberquelle GmbH ("Silberquelle") against Maselli-Strickmode GmbH ("Maselli") in respect of the partial revocation of the latter's mark for lack of genuine use.

Maselli is a manufacturer and seller of clothing. It is the owner, in Austria, of the word mark "WELLNESS", registered in respect of, inter alia, the following goods, in classes 16, 25 and 32 of the Nice Classification: printed matter (class 16); clothing (class 25); and alcohol-free drinks (class 32).

In the context of the sale of its clothing, Maselli used its mark to designate an alcohol-free drink which was handed out as a gift in bottles marked "WELLNESS-DRINK", along with the clothing sold. In its promotional documents, Maselli made reference to the free gifts labelled with the WELLNESS mark, but has not used its mark for drinks sold separately.

Silberquelle, an undertaking which sells alcohol-free drinks, applied for   7–040
cancellation of the WELLNESS mark in respect of class 32 products, on grounds of non-use. The Austrian Patent Office accepted Silberquelle's request and cancelled the mark for that class. Maselli brought an action against that decision before the Oberster Patent-und Markensamt.

The Oberster Patent- und Markensamt took the view that the resolution of the dispute turns on the interpretation of Directive 89/104 and decided to refer the following question to the Court of Justice:

> "Are Articles 10(1) and 12(1) of the Directive to be interpreted as meaning that a trade mark is being put to genuine use if it is used for goods which the proprietor of the trade mark gives, free of charge, to purchasers of his other goods after conclusion of the purchase contract?"

(b) The principal arguments   7–041

Silberquelle argued that the decision of the Austrian Office to cancel Maselli's registration is correct and should be upheld. Silberquelle based its claim on a comparative analysis of arts 5 and 10 of the Directive, pointing out that the latter provision does not mention advertising as a method of using a trade mark.

Silberquelle also put forward that by repeatedly emphasising, in *Ansul*, that the use of the trade mark must increase the presence on the market of goods bearing that mark, the Court tacitly denied that there is genuine use where the use of the mark increases the sales of other products. Thus, the offer of the WELLNESS soft drink as a free gift following the purchase of garments did not create any market share for that drink, which was only obtained by consumers by indirect means.

7-042 Maselli, on the other hand, contended that it had made sufficient use of the mark, albeit with a "secondary function". The distribution of the drink without charge leads to that product indirectly entering the relevant market, that is, the market for non-alcoholic drinks, thereby resulting in the acquisition of a market share in that sector.

Maselli moreover maintained that its use of the mark complied with the essential function of the mark as a guarantee of origin, since the mark in fact indicates that the soft drink comes from the same undertaking as the clothing.

Finally, Maselli referred to the damage it would suffer if its mark is revoked, since the subsequent registration of its mark by a competitor would require it to amend its advertising strategy, making a mockery of its marketing system in general.

7-043 *(c) The Opinion of the Advocate General*

Advocate General Ruíz-Jarabo Colomer tackled the issue from three interrelated perspectives, pointing out that it was essential to interpret the principles laid down by the Court in *Ansul* in the light of the aims pursued by the Directive.

7-044 **(i) Use as a guarantee of origin.** First, he observed that the Directive contains two categories of provisions, namely those relating to the organisation of national trade mark registrations (arts 2, 3, 4 and 10 to 14) and those relating to the rights conferred by the trade mark (arts 5 to 9). He further noted that the function of a trade mark as a guarantee of origin, on which Maselli essentially relied, is connected with the second group of provisions, and, in particular, with arts 4(1) and 5(1) which are closely linked to the likelihood of confusion.[53]

He also stressed that although, in *Ansul*, the Court required that the use of the mark must always be geared to its essential function,[54] that requirement was in fact secondary to the need to use the mark "in order to create or preserve an outlet for those goods or services". Moreover, it is equally clear from *Ansul* that the essential function of a trade mark is to enable, without any possibility of confusion, a particular product or service to be distinguished from others which have another origin,[55] which draws attention to the connection between the function as a guarantee of origin and the likelihood of confusion.[56]

---

[53] Points 34–35 of the Opinion of A.G. Ruiz-Jarabo Colomer.
[54] *Ansul*, para.43.
[55] *Ansul*, para.36.
[56] Points 36–39 of the Opinion of A.G. Ruiz-Jarabo Colomer.

3. THE CASE LAW OF THE COURT

Then, the Advocate General pointed out that the likelihood of confusion only arises where a consumer discovers similar marks at the crucial moment when he chooses between competing goods. To the extent, however, that the drinks which Maselli hands out are not made available to the public in the usual soft-drink retail establishments, any such comparison is impossible and, therefore, any possibility of confusion on the part of the relevant customers is excluded. Accordingly, Maselli cannot rely on the need to protect its advertising strategies, if those strategies do not comply with the essential function of the mark, properly understood.[57]

(ii) The importance of using the mark in the reference market. 7–045
Secondly, the Advocate General considered that the position taken by Maselli is not compatible with the overall scheme of the Directive, as expressed in its Eighth Recital, which refers to the obligation to provide evidence of the use as a means of reducing the total number of marks registered in the Community and, ultimately, as serving the objective of protecting freedom of competition.[58]

Thus, the transparency which must prevail both in the market and on the registry explains why competitors have the capacity to cancel inactive registrations which do not fulfil the essential function of trade marks, since if the goods are not offered for sale, the mark does not generate any type of economic benefit. Accordingly, a trade mark proprietor must place the goods bearing the mark on the relevant market for those goods, which, in the main proceedings, is the non-alcoholic drinks market; if trade mark proprietors did not act in that manner, their goods would not be distinguishable from others.[59]

In fact, by receiving the WELLNESS drink as a free gift when purchasing clothing, the consumer does not perform any conscious act of acquiring the drink by comparing it with other similar products and, hence, the trade mark is not strengthened vis-à-vis competitors' marks because of the customer's preference. In practice, however, this means that the trade mark remains outside the reference market and, therefore, does not compete with other marks, since it appears unlikely that someone who takes a liking to the drink would be prepared to spend more money on clothes, simply to receive the drink.[60]

(iii) Use in advertising. Lastly, the Advocate General pointed out that 7–046
although the Court has accepted that use of the mark in advertising qualifies as genuine use, as does use in relation to goods and services which are about to be marketed and for which preparations to secure customers

---

[57] Points 40–43 of the Opinion of A.G. Ruiz-Jarabo Colomer.
[58] Point 44 of the Opinion of A.G. Ruiz-Jarabo Colomer.
[59] Points 47–48 of the Opinion of A.G. Ruiz-Jarabo Colomer.
[60] Point 49 of the Opinion of A.G. Ruiz-Jarabo Colomer.

are under way,[61] such circumstances are distinguishable from the "abstract" use of a trade mark, that is, where its use has no specific connection with the market for the goods on which it is fixed.[62]

He also remarked that this was precisely the case with the WELLNESS-DRINK mark, since, in the absence of any effective link with the soft drinks market, the beverage bearing the WELLNESS mark becomes a mere advertising tool which is completely unconnected with the sale of soft drinks, or with the acquisition of a market share in that sector.[63]

Consequently, the Advocate General concluded that a trade mark which does not compete on the market for the goods for which it was registered is not put to genuine use within the meaning of the Directive, even where the goods bearing the mark are an advertisement to promote the sales of other products bearing the same mark.[64]

On those grounds, he proposed to answer the question referred to the Court in the negative.

7–047   (d)   *The judgment of the Court*

The Court noted at the outset that the case concerned by the order for reference was different from one in which the proprietor of a mark sells promotional items in the form of souvenirs or other derivative products. In addition, the revocation proceedings only concerned class 32, which covers the promotional items at issue, and not class 25, encompassing the goods actually sold by the trade mark owner, namely clothing.

The Court then referred to its judgments in *Ansul* and *Radetzky* and recalled once more that "genuine use" within the meaning of the Directive must be understood to denote actual use and that, in view of the number of marks that are registered and the conflicts that are likely to arise between them, it is essential to maintain the rights conferred by a mark for a given class of goods or services only where that mark has been used on the market for goods or services belonging to that class.[65]

The Court however considered that those conditions are not fulfilled where promotional items are merely handed out as a reward for the purchase of other goods, that is, in order to promote the sale of the latter, since, in such a situation, those items are not at all distributed with the aim of penetrating the market for goods in the same class. In fact, using the mark in this manner does not contribute to creating an outlet for the designated goods or to distinguishing, in the interest of the customer, those items from the goods of other undertakings.[66]

---

[61] *Ansul*, para.37; *La Mer* para.19.
[62] Points 51–52 of the Opinion of A.G. Ruiz-Jarabo Colomer.
[63] Point 53 of the Opinion of A.G. Ruiz-Jarabo Colomer.
[64] Point 56 of the Opinion of A.G. Ruiz-Jarabo Colomer.
[65] *Ansul*, paras 35–37; *Radetzky*, paras 13–14.
[66] *Silberquelle*, paras 20–21.

3. THE CASE LAW OF THE COURT

In the light of those considerations, the Court held that the answer to the question referred should be that arts 10(1) and 12(1) of the Directive must be interpreted as meaning that, where the proprietor of a mark affixes that mark to items that it gives, free of charge, to purchasers of its goods, it does not make genuine use of that mark in respect of the class covering those items.

In reaching this conclusion the Court in substance qualified its judgment in *Ansul* in two important respects:

7–048

First, it clarified that the use of the trade mark in advertising cannot be regarded as genuine if it relates to the promotion of goods other than those covered by the registration, since in such a case the use does not concern the marketing of the goods actually sold, or of goods which are about to be marketed and for which preparations to secure customers are under way, as required by *Ansul*.[67]

Secondly, it effectively denied that the use of the trade mark in respect of promotional items free of charge concerns goods which are "directly related" to the goods actually marketed by the proprietor within the meaning of that judgment, unlike the offering of after-sale services or the sale of accessories and spare parts.[68]

(5) Nasdaq—complementary services offered free of charge

7–049

Soon after *Radetzky* and *Silberquelle*, the Court had the opportunity to further explore the notion of genuine use in connection with the free offer of services in *Nasdaq*,[69] a case brought before it on appeal from a judgment of the Court of First Instance.[70]

Nasdaq concerned a dispute that arose in the context of an opposition brought by The Nasdaq Stock Market Inc ("Nasdaq Stock Market") against Antartica Srl ("Antarctica") pursuant to art.8(5) CTMR.[71]

Antartica had sought to register as Community Trade Mark a figurative sign essentially consisting of the stylised word "nasdaq" in respect of a range of goods in classes 9, 12, 14, 25 and 28 of the Nice Classification.

Nasdaq Stock Market opposed the application based on its earlier Community word mark "NASDAQ", on the grounds that the use of Antartica's mark without due cause would take unfair advantage of, or be detrimental to, the distinctive character and repute its earlier mark enjoyed in respect of, inter alia, "stock exchange price quotation services; listings of securities for quotations for sale or information purposes" and "financial services, amongst others, providing and updating an index of security values", in classes 35 and 36 of the Nice Classification.

7–050

---

[67] See *Ansul*, para.37.
[68] See *Ansul*, para.42.
[69] *Antartica Srl v OHIM* (NASDAQ) (C-320/07 P) [2009] E.C.R. 00.
[70] *Antartica Srl v OHIM* (NASDAQ) (T-047/06).
[71] Although that case is not concerned with the obligation to use the mark as a means of maintaining the registration, it is relevant here insofar as it deals with the notion of genuine use in general.

The Opposition Division of OHIM rejected the opposition, holding that the reputation of the earlier mark had not been properly substantiated, since the mark "NASDAQ" had not been used in the Community to the requisite standard. Nasdaq Stock Market appealed to the Boards of Appeal of OHIM, which annulled the Opposition Division's decision on the ground that the latter had wrongly considered that the conditions for the application of art.8(5) CTMR had not been fulfilled.

Antartica brought an action for the annulment of that decision before the Court of First Instance contending, for the first time at that stage, that the mere references made to the Nasdaq indices in the Community do not constitute "genuine use" of the mark NASDAQ and that, as a result, they cannot support the alleged reputation of the earlier mark.

7–051 Although the Court of First Instance recalled that, according to art.135(4) of its Rules of Procedure, the parties' pleadings may not change the subject-matter of the proceedings before the Board of Appeal, it nevertheless observed that, according to the case law, the reputation of the earlier mark must be determined by the intensity, geographical extent and duration of its use and that, in order to ascertain whether art.8(5) CTMR applied to the case, the Board of Appeal was obliged, before determining whether the mark "NASDAQ" was reputed, to assess first whether that mark had been used at all.

Accordingly, it considered that Antartica's claim did not unduly modify the subject matter of the dispute before the Board of Appeal, taking in substance the view that a plea based on art.8(5) CTMR tacitly raises, as an additional preliminary issue, the question of whether the mark has been put to genuine use in the first place.[72]

Moreover, the Court of First Instance found that, insofar as the references to the Nasdaq indices related to the stock exchange price quotation and financial services for which the earlier mark was registered in classes 35 and 36, they constituted genuine use of that mark and this regardless of the fact that the corresponding information was offered free of charge.[73] Furthermore, the Court of First Instance held that art.8(5) was applicable to the case and dismissed the action as unfounded.

7–052 Antartica appealed, requesting the Court of Justice to set aside the contested judgment on both counts. As regards proof of use, it claimed, essentially, that genuine use can take place only if the mark is used in connection with the sale of goods or services; contrary to that rule, however, Nasdaq Stock Market's indices are available free of charge in the press and on television, while no evidence has been adduced to the effect that those indices are offered for consideration within the Community.

---

[72] That view of the Court of First Instance seems to be much more generous than the approach it took in *AMS Advanced Medical Services GmbH v OHIM* (T-425/03), where it held that the CTM applicant's proof of use defence must be raised at the latest during the proceedings before the Opposition Division.

[73] See para.45 of the judgment of the Court of First Instance.

3. THE CASE LAW OF THE COURT

The Nasdaq Stock Market countered that its financial and stock market services are not offered gratis and that only certain ancillary services, such as those relating to information, were provided to the general public free of charge, following the rule that advertising of this kind is always offered to the public free of charge.

The Court, however, did not agree with Antarctica's view that, as a matter of principle, the concept of genuine use cannot extend to services offered on a non-profit-making basis, or that it is based on the premise that the goods or services for which the trade mark is used are always paid for.[74] Conversely, it noted that, even if part of the services for which the earlier mark is registered are offered free of charge, that does not of itself mean that Nasdaq Stock Market will not seek, by such use of its trade mark, to create or maintain an outlet for those services in the Community, as against the services of other undertakings.[75]

Thus, the Court concurred with the judgment under appeal that, inasmuch as the Nasdaq indices refer to the stock exchange price quotation and financial services principally provided by Nasdaq Stock Market, the earlier mark had been put to genuine use in respect of all the services for which it was registered.

Although the Court did not say so expressly, the decisive factor for considering Nasdaq Stock Market's use of its mark in respect of free information services as genuine was the direct link of those services to its main financial activities and their complementary relationship with them, within the meaning of the Court's findings in *Ansul*.[76]

7–053

In that regard, *Nasdaq* must be distinguished from the judgment in *Silberquelle*. Unlike that case, where the mark was used for goods the sole purpose of which was to promote a different product, *Nasdaq* concerned the free offer of ancillary services that were functionally related to the owner's main activity, in the sense that those services were indispensable for the proprietor's principal business.

In that sense, *Nasdaq* is closer to the principles laid down in *Radetzky*, at least to the extent that it held that it is in the *nature* of stock index information services to be offered free of charge to investors, so as to enable them to effectively follow-up their investments and judge whether the time is opportune to enter or leave the market.

(6) Lidl—start of the use requirement and proper reasons for non-use

7–054

In *Lidl*[77] the Court dealt with the date on which, pursuant to art.10(1) of the Directive, the five-year period for putting the mark to genuine use starts

---

[74] *Nasdaq*, para.28.
[75] *Nasdaq*, para.29.
[76] See *Ansul*, para.42.
[77] *Armin Häupl v Lidl Stiftung & Co KG* (LE CHEF DE CUISINE) (C-246/05) [2007] E.C.R. I-4673.

577

counting as well as with the meaning of the expression "proper reasons for non-use" in art.12(1) of the Directive.

7–055 *(a) The facts in the main proceedings and the order for reference*

The reference was made in the context of a dispute between Mr Häupl and Lidl Stiftung & Co KG ("Lidl") concerning the cancellation of Lidl's Austrian part of the international trade mark "Le Chef DE CUISINE", on the grounds of non-use.

Lidl was the proprietor of the figurative mark "Le Chef DE CUISINE" in Germany. The effects of that registration were extended to Austria by virtue of art.3(4) of the Madrid Agreement. The international registration was published on December 2, 1993, but produced its effects as of the date of its filing, namely October 12, 1993.

Lidl operates a supermarket chain established in Germany. It extended its business in Austria by opening its first supermarket there on November 5, 1998. Before that date, Lidl began to store goods bearing the mark which had already been delivered to it, but the actual opening of its Austrian outlets had been delayed by "bureaucratic obstacles", in particular delays in the issue of the operating licenses.

7–056 On October 13, 1998, Mr Häupl sought to have that mark cancelled for the territory of the Republic of Austria on the ground of non-use. In his view, the five-year period provided for in the relevant provisions of Austrian law[78] began to run from the beginning of the protection period, namely on October 12, 1993. Lidl countered that that period only began to run on December 2, 1993, with the result that it did not expire until December 2, 1998. On that date, however, it was already displaying for sale goods bearing the mark at issue in its first Austrian supermarket.

The Austrian Patent Office upheld the request and declared the mark invalid as of October 12, 1998. Lidl lodged an appeal against that decision with the Oberster Patent- und Markensamt, which decided to stay proceedings and refer the following questions to the Court for a preliminary ruling:

"1. Is Article 10(1) of the Directive to be interpreted as meaning that the 'date of the completion of the registration procedure' means the start of the period of protection?

2. Is Article 12(1) of the Directive to be interpreted as meaning that there are proper reasons for non-use of a mark if the implementation of the corporate strategy being pursued by the trade mark proprietor is delayed for reasons outside the control of the undertaking, or is the trade mark proprietor obliged to change his corporate strategy in order to be able to use the mark in good time?"

---

[78] Paragraph 33a of the Markenschutzgesetz 1970, BGBl. 260/1970; "the MSchG".

3. THE CASE LAW OF THE COURT

(b) The Opinion of the Advocate General 7–057

First, A.G. Ruiz-Jarabo Colomer deduced from the way the order for reference was formulated that the second question was in fact subsidiary to the first one, since if the answer to the former was in the favour of the trade mark owner, the latter would automatically become devoid of purpose.

Moreover, he remarked that it was not appropriate to link, for the purposes of the discussion, the "end of the registration procedure" to the "start of the protection period". In that regard, he pointed out that there is a wide variety of registration systems in the Community, the procedural particularities of which are not fully aligned.

Despite the fact, however, that the registration formalities are not entirely covered by the scope of the Directive, there is always a common feature in all registration systems, at least insofar as the relevant procedure is concluded each time by the granting of the registration, usually by virtue of an administrative decision of the competent trade mark authorities, which is communicated to the applicant and published for the information of third parties.[79]

Nevertheless, to the extent that the Directive does not contain an all-encompassing definition of the precise moment when the registration procedure comes to an end, it is up to the legislation of the Member States to determine when that procedure is deemed to be concluded.[80] 7–058

Next, he turned to the specificities of International Registrations stressing that although in accordance with the Madrid Agreement the protection starts from the date of registration, which actually coincides with the date of either the international application or the national application on which the international mark is based, that protection is subject to the expiry of the term of one year within which national trade mark offices may inform the Bureau of their decision to refuse protection in their territory. Notwithstanding, he considered that the only workable date for the purposes of art.10(1) of the Directive, is the date the international mark is entered in the register.[81]

Therefore, A.G. Ruiz-Jarabo Colomer's answer to the first question was that the expression "date of completion of the registration procedure" in art.10(1) of the Directive does not refer to the start of the period of protection, with which it may coincide, but rather to the moment when the competent authority, in accordance with national rules, concludes the registration procedure, or, in the case of an international mark, when that procedure is completed by the International Bureau.

Although the proposed answer to the first question rendered unnecessary the discussion of the second one, the Advocate General decided to also 7–059

---

[79] Point 44 of the Opinion of A.G. Ruiz-Jarabo Colomer.
[80] Point 45 of the Opinion of A.G. Ruiz-Jarabo Colomer.
[81] Point 66 of the Opinion of A.G. Ruiz-Jarabo Colomer.

address art.12(1) of the Directive, in case the Court took a different view on the interpretation of art.10(1).

In that connection, he observed that art.12(1) merely refers to "proper reasons for non-use", without however giving any example of any such reasons. He therefore turned to art.19 of TRIPs which is more explicit in that regard, by stating that only circumstances which are independent of the will of the proprietor and which constitute an obstacle to the use of the mark, as for example import restrictions, are valid reasons for non-use.[82]

He also observed that the administrative procedures invoked by Lidl merely concerned its own commercial decision to sell the goods bearing the mark exclusively in its own supermarkets and, to that extent, did not directly relate to the use of the mark as such. In that sense, the delays in issuing the construction licenses for Lidl's outlets were not in the same league as, e.g. setbacks in the sanitary clearance of the foodstuffs bearing the mark, or delays in the approval of a pharmaceutical product by the competent authorities. For instance, Lidl could have launched its products on the market notwithstanding the above delays by granting licenses to third parties or by distributing its wares through ordinary food-stores.[83]

Accordingly, the Advocate General proposed that art.12(1) of the Directive should be interpreted as meaning that the reasons justifying the lack of use must be independent of the will of the trade mark owner and must constitute an obstacle to the use of the sign. If these two requirements are met, the bureaucratic formalities fall under the above exception; however, this is not the case when they obstruct the implementation of a corporate strategy, since in such a situation the undertaking conserves the power to adapt its strategy to the administrative requirements.

7–060 *(c) The judgment of the Court*

Before answering the questions referred to it, the Court had to determine whether the Oberster Patent- und Markensamt is a court or tribunal within the meaning of art.234 EC and whether the Court therefore has jurisdiction to rule on questions referred to it by that body.

In doing so, it recalled that the question of whether the body making a reference is a court or tribunal for the purposes of art.234 EC is a question governed by Community law alone and that, in answering that question, the Court must take account of a number of factors, such as whether the body is established by law, whether it is permanent, whether its jurisdiction is compulsory, whether its procedure is inter partes, whether it applies rules of law and whether it is independent.[84]

---

[82] Point 78 of the Opinion of A.G. Ruiz-Jarabo Colomer.
[83] Point 79 of the Opinion of A.G. Ruiz-Jarabo Colomer.
[84] *Dorsch Consult* (C-54/96) [1997] E.C.R. I-4961, para.23; and *Syfait* (C-53/03) [2005] E.C.R. I-4609, para.29.

3. THE CASE LAW OF THE COURT

Following a detailed examination of the relevant provisions of the Austrian Law on Patents,[85] which is the instrument establishing the Oberster Patent- und Markensamt and governing its function, it concluded that said body was a court or tribunal within the meaning of art.234 EC and that the Court therefore had jurisdiction to answer the questions submitted to it by that body.

(i) The start of the five-year period. With regard to the first question, the Court first of all pointed out that several legal systems are involved when a trade mark is registered internationally: both the provisions of the Madrid Agreement, which establishes the part of the registration taking place before the International Bureau, and national legal provisions apply. In addition, the latter must also comply with Community law, as also attested by art.1 of the Directive, which provides that it "shall apply to every trade mark ... which is the subject of ... an international registration having effect in a Member State".[86]

7–061

Further, the Court stressed that for the purpose of interpreting art.10(1) of the Directive, particular account must be taken of its Third and Fifth Recitals, respectively stating that the Directive is not intended to approximate fully the trade mark laws of the Member States and that the latter remain free to fix the procedural provisions concerning trade mark registration. Moreover, it noted that the art.10(1) does not determine in an unambiguous manner the starting point of the five-year period for which it provides, its wording merely defining that starting point in relation to the registration procedure, that is, by reference to an area which is outside the harmonising scope of the Directive.[87]

Thus, it took the view that the wording of art.10(1) actually implied that the Member States are entitled to organise their registration procedure as they deem fit and, in consequence, they can freely decide when that procedure is to be regarded as having been completed.[88]

Accordingly, the Court answered the first question to the effect that the "date of the completion of the registration procedure" within the meaning of art.10(1) of the Directive must be determined in each Member State in accordance with the procedural rules on registration in force in that State.

(ii) The "proper reasons" defence. With regard to the second question, the Court noted that, according to the order for reference, the deferment of the sale on the Austrian market of the goods bearing the mark at issue resulted, first, from Lidl's strategy of selling those goods only in its own outlets and, secondly, from the fact that the opening of its first Austrian supermarket was delayed by "bureaucratic obstacles".

7–062

---

[85] Patentgesetz 1970, BGBl. 259/1970.
[86] *Lidl*, para.25.
[87] *Lidl*, paras 26–27.
[88] *Lidl*, para.28.

It then defined the subject matter of the question as being whether there are proper reasons for non-use of if the implementation of the corporate strategy pursued by the trade mark proprietor is delayed for reasons outside its control, or whether the trade mark proprietor is obliged, in such a case, to change that strategy so as to be able to use the mark in good time.

The Court started its analysis by asking whether the term "proper reasons" within the meaning of art.12(1) should be given a uniform interpretation at all.

7–063   In that respect, it recalled that the need for uniform application of Community law and the principle of equality require that the terms of a provision of Community law which makes no express reference to the law of the Member States for the purpose of determining its meaning and scope must normally be given an autonomous and uniform interpretation throughout the European Community.[89]

Next, the Court referred to its judgment in *Ansul* where it was established that the concept of "genuine use" must be given a uniform interpretation and reiterated that arts 10–15 of the Directive and the Seventh, Eighth and Ninth recitals in its Preamble actually show that it was the legislature's intention that the maintenance of rights in a trade mark be subject to the same conditions in all Member States, so that the level of protection enjoyed by a trade mark does not fluctuate according to the legal system concerned.[90]

Accordingly, it concluded that since the objective of proper reasons is to justify situations in which there is no genuine use, so as to avoid the revocation of the mark, it was obvious that their function is closely linked to that of genuine use and that, as a result, the concept of "proper reasons" is subject to the same need for a uniform interpretation as the concept of "genuine use".

7–064   The Court went on to note, however, that art.12(1) does not contain any indication of the nature and characteristics of the "proper reasons" to which it refers and concurred with the Advocate General that the definition in art.19(1) of the TRIPs Agreement may therefore constitute a factor in the interpretation of the similar concept of proper reasons used in the Directive.

Thus, the Court found appropriate to determine what kind of circumstances constitute an obstacle to the use of the trade mark within the meaning of that provision, noting that although, quite often, circumstances arising independently of the will of the owner are likely at some point to hinder the preparations for the use of the mark, those difficulties can be overcome in a good many cases.

For that reason and in view also of the principle in the Eighth Recital to the Directive that registered trade marks must actually be used, the Court stated that it would be contrary to the scheme of art.12(1) to confer too broad a scope on the concept of proper reasons for non-use; in fact, the

---

[89] *Linster* (C-287/98) [2000] E.C.R. I-6917, para.43.
[90] *Ansul*, paras 27–31.

objective set out in that recital would be jeopardised if any obstacle, however minimal, were sufficient to justify the non-use of the mark, even if it arose independently of the proprietor's will.[91]

Therefore, the Court held that the obstacles in question should not only be beyond the control of the trade mark proprietor but must, moreover, have a direct relationship with the mark. It considered, however, that the obstacle concerned need not necessarily make the use of the sign "impossible" in order to be regarded as having a sufficiently direct relationship with the trade mark; it sufficed if it made the use of that sign "unreasonable", as for example where the proprietor of a trade mark is required to sell its goods in the outlets of its competitors, since in such a case, it does not appear reasonable to require the proprietor to change its corporate strategy merely in order to make the use of the mark possible.[92]

7–065

Accordingly, it found that only obstacles having a sufficiently direct relationship with a trade mark by making its use impossible or unreasonable and arise independently of the will of the proprietor may be described as "proper reasons for non-use", while stressing that it must be assessed on a case-by-case basis whether a change in the strategy of the undertaking to circumvent the obstacle in question would indeed make the use of that mark unreasonable.[93]

Consequently, the Court ruled that art.12(1) of the Directive must be interpreted as meaning that obstacles having a direct relationship with a trade mark which make its use impossible or unreasonable and which are independent of the will of the proprietor constitute "proper reasons for non-use" of that mark and that it was for the referring Instance to assess the facts in the main proceedings in the light of that guidance.

(7) Bainbridge—defensive registrations

7–066

(a) The facts

In *Bainbridge*[94] the Court was confronted with the question whether the use of a given sign can constitute genuine use also in respect of another very similar mark belonging to the same owner, as well as with the related issue whether the existence of national provisions allowing for "defensive registrations" amounted to proper reasons for non-use under Community law.

The case concerned an opposition to the registration of the CTM application "BAINBRIDGE", based on a number of earlier Italian registrations consisting of word and figurative versions of the signs "BRIGDE", "THE BRIDGE", "OLD BRIDGE", "THE BRIDGE BASKET", "FOOTBRIDGE",

---

[91] *Lidl*, para.51.
[92] *Lidl*, para.53.
[93] *Lidl*, para.54.
[94] *Il Ponte Finanziaria Spa v OHIM* (BAINBRIDGE) (C-234/06 P) [2007] E.C.R. I-7333.

"THE BRIDGE WAYFARER" and "OVER THE BRIDGE" which the opponent claimed to have used as a "family" of marks. The respective marks were filed in respect of identical or similar goods, namely leather products and articles of clothing in classes 18 and 25 of the Nice Classification.

The Office rejected the opposition taking the view that the aural and visual dissimilarities of the marks sufficed to rule out any likelihood of confusion. The Board of Appeal confirmed that view. First, it excluded from its assessment 5 of the 11 earlier registrations on the ground that their use had not been established. Secondly, it refused to classify the six remaining registrations as marks "in a series" since the number of them that were used in that manner was not sufficient for that purpose. Finally, it confirmed that there was no likelihood of confusion between the marks considered individually, in view of the absence of the minimum degree of similarity required in order to justify the application of the principle of interdependence.

7-067   *(b)   The judgment of the Court of First Instance*

In the first place, the Court of First Instance[95] held that the six earlier marks that were not subject to the user requirement within the meaning of art.43 CTMR (new art.42), because the five-year period following their registration had not yet elapsed, had to be taken into consideration for the purpose of assessing the existence of a likelihood of confusion. However, it also observed that only the two of those marks that had actually been used could be taken into account when assessing the existence of a "family of marks".

Secondly, the Court held that the opponent had failed to prove that the earlier registration "THE BRIDGE" had been used at all, in the sense that it was objectively present on the Italian market in a manner that was effective, consistent over time and stable in terms of the configuration of the sign. Moreover, with regard to whether the trade mark "BRIDGE" could be regarded as broadly equivalent to the mark "THE BRIDGE", and thus serve as proof of genuine use of the latter, the Court pointed out that art.15(2)(a) CTMR does not allow the proprietor of a registered trade mark to demonstrate use of that mark by relying on the use of a similar mark, covered by a separate registration.

Thirdly, with regard to the four earlier trade marks which were not taken into account for the purposes of assessing the likelihood of confusion on account of lack of use, the Court of First Instance confirmed that the Board of Appeal was right in rejecting the "defensive" registrations of those marks as incompatible with Community law.

As regards, lastly, the alleged infringement of art.8(1)(b) CTMR, the Court of First Instance found that although the respective goods were identical, the conflicting signs display some similarities only aurally and not visually or

---

[95] *Il Ponte Finanziaria v OHIM—Marine Enterprise Projects* (BAINBRIDGE) (T-194/03) [2006] E.C.R. II-00445.

conceptually. Accordingly, it considered that the Board of Appeal did not make any errors of assessment in concluding that there was no likelihood of confusion between the trade mark applied for and each of the six earlier marks considered individually. Moreover, it rejected the argument that those marks constituted a "family of marks" or "marks in a series", owing to the absence of evidence of use of all of the marks allegedly belonging to that "family" or, at the very least, of a sufficient number of marks capable of constituting such a "series".

(c) Findings of the Court 7–068

(i) Use in respect of a "family" of marks. The Court dealt first with the ground referring to the existence of a "series" or "family" of marks, noting at the outset that under arts 4–6 CTMR a trade mark "may be registered only individually" and that "the minimum five-year protection afforded by such registration is conferred on it only as an individual trade mark, even where several signs having one or more common and distinctive elements are registered at the same time".[96]

Then, it went on to analyse the doctrine of "family" of marks, observing that while it is true that, in the case of an opposition to the registration of a Community Trade Mark based on only one earlier trade mark that is not yet subject to the obligation of use, the assessment of the likelihood of confusion is to be carried out by comparing the marks as registered, the same does not apply where the opposition is based on several marks possessing common characteristics which make it possible for them to be regarded as part of a "family" or "series" of marks. In that regard, it explained that:

"Where there is a 'family' or 'series' of trade marks, the likelihood of confusion results more specifically from the possibility that the consumer may be mistaken as to the provenance or origin of goods or services covered by the trade mark applied for or considers erroneously that that trade mark is part of that family or series of marks.

[Therefore] no consumer can be expected, in the absence of use of a sufficient number of trade marks capable of constituting a family or a series, to detect a common element in such a family or series and/or to associate with that family or series another trade mark containing the same common element. Accordingly, in order for there to be a likelihood that the public may be mistaken as to whether the trade mark applied for belongs to a 'family' or 'series', the earlier trade marks which are part of that 'family' or 'series' must be present on the market."[97]

---

[96] *Bainbridge*, para.61.
[97] *Bainbridge*, paras 63–64.

Based on those considerations, the Court upheld the analysis of the Court of First Instance, pointing out that the latter had not required proof of use as such of the earlier marks, that is, use within the meaning of art.43 CTMR (new art.42), but only use of a sufficient number of them "as to be capable of constituting a family of marks and therefore of demonstrating that such a family or series exists for the purposes of the assessment of the likelihood of confusion".

7–069   **(ii) The value of "defensive" registrations.** Secondly, the Court confirmed that the appellant could not rely on the defensive nature, under Italian trade mark law, of certain of the registrations on which the opposition was based and that the Court of First Instance had rightly disregarded those marks for the purposes of the examination.

In that connection, it recalled that under arts 43 and 56(2) CTMR (new arts 42 and 57) the proprietor of the mark is required, both in opposition and invalidity proceedings, to furnish proof that the earlier trade mark has been put to genuine use if the defendant so requests, and that he cannot to shake off the burden placed upon him by relying on "national provisions which allow the registration of signs not intended to be used in trade, on account of their purely defensive function in relation to another sign which is being commercially exploited".[98]

Furthermore, it pointed out that the concept of "proper reasons" mentioned in those provisions refers essentially to circumstances preventing the use of the mark which are independent of the proprietor's will, rather than "to national legislation which makes an exception to the rule that a trade mark that has not been used for a period of five years must be revoked, even where such lack of use is intentional on the part of the proprietor of the trade mark" and that, accordingly, such "defensive registrations" were incompatible with Community Trade Mark law.[99]

7–070   **(iii) Simultaneous use of similar marks.** In the third place, the Court dealt with the exclusion from the assessment of the earlier mark "THE BRIDGE" on account of its non-use.

As regards the argument that, in rejecting the evidence submitted by the owner as insufficient, the Court of First Instance had in fact required proof of "continuous" use throughout the five-year period, the Court recalled that among the factors to be taken into account in ascertaining whether the use is sufficient to maintain or create a market share for the goods or services protected by the mark, were also the frequency or regularity of such use.

Thus, by holding that the evidence was very limited with regard to the first year and non-existent for the rest of the period, the Court of First

---

[98] *Bainbridge*, para.101.
[99] *Bainbridge*, paras 102–103.

3. THE CASE LAW OF THE COURT

Instance did not in any way require the appellant to establish "continuous" use, but rather merely appraised whether the scale and frequency of use were capable of demonstrating that the mark was present on the market in a manner that was effective, consistent over time and stable in terms of the configuration of the sign.

Next, the Court found that although under art.15(2)(a) CTMR (which corresponds to art.10(2)(a) of Directive) use of the Community Trade Mark "in a form differing in elements which do not alter the distinctive character of the mark in the form in which it was registered" also constitutes use within the meaning of that provision, the appellant could not rely on the use of the mark "BRIDGE" for the purpose of demonstrating use of the trade mark "THE BRIDGE", explaining that:

7–071

"[While] it is possible, as a result of [art.15(2)(a) CTMR], to consider a registered trade mark as used where proof is provided of use of that mark in a slightly different form from that in which it was registered, it is not possible to extend, by means of proof of use, the protection enjoyed by a registered trade mark to another registered mark, the use of which has not been established, on the ground that the latter is merely a slight variation on the former".[100]

That statement of the Court is rather peculiar, especially insofar as it is not backed up by any reference to any rule or principle of law that could justify such a drastic restriction of the scope of art.15(2)(a) CTMR. Nor did the Court refer to any overriding commercial considerations that could perhaps provide a valid reason for discriminating against owners of registered trade marks, as compared to traders who have not catered for the registration of all the variations of their marks.

7–072

In addition, that position of the Court seems to be at odds with its previous case law in the context of comparable, if not analogous, situations.

It should be recalled, that in *Kit-Kat*[101] the Court took a much more generous approach with regard to use under art.3(3) of the Directive, holding that "the acquisition of a distinctive character by a mark may also be the result of its use as part of another *registered* trade mark", as it is "sufficient that, in consequence of such use, the relevant class of persons actually perceives the product or service, designated by the mark, as originating from a given undertaking".

The Court elaborated further on that principle in *Aire Limpio*,[102] where it held that "that finding of general application" also applied when establishing whether an earlier mark has become particularly distinctive through use, for the purpose of ascertaining whether there is a likelihood of confusion

---

[100] *Bainbridge*, para.86.
[101] *Société Produits Nestlé v Mars* (C-353/04).
[102] *P L & D, S.A. v OHIM* (AIRE LIMPIO) (C-488/06) [2006] E.C.R. I-5725.

within the meaning of art.8(1)(b) CTMR, and this despite of the different "factual and procedural" setting of that case, as compared to the facts in *Kit-Kat*.

Accordingly, it confirmed that it was perfectly possible in law to establish the highly distinctive character of a mark on the basis of evidence relating to the use and well-known nature of another registered trade mark. Moreover, it would seem that, for the identity of reason, that rule should also include proof of reputation, since the circumstances relevant in such a case do not justify any difference of approach in that respect.

7-073   Although, admittedly, the judgments in *Kit-Kat* and *Aire Limpio* concerned different circumstances, there was nothing in the relevant legal provisions that compelled the Court to take such a generous approach. Conversely, arts 10 and 15 of the Directive and the Regulation, explicitly refer to the acceptability of use in a different form, if that use does not "alter" the distinctiveness of the mark as registered.

Finally, the practical implications of that statement may prove to be over-reaching, considering that in *Nasdaq*[103] the Court implicitly endorsed the position of the Court of First Instance that insofar as the reputed character of a trade mark is to be determined by reference to the intensity, geographical extent and duration of its use, it is necessary, before determining whether that mark is reputed, to assess whether it has been used at all.

In practice, that means that the different treatment of genuine use and enhanced distinctiveness risks to render the rule in *Aire Limpio* devoid of meaning, as trade mark owners will not be able to rely on the reputation of another registration in order to prove the well-known character of their marks, if they cannot prove in the same manner that the mark at issue has been genuinely used in the first place.

4. CHALLENGING A COMMUNITY TRADE MARK

7-074   **(1) Sunrider—evidence of use; the burden of proof**

In order to facilitate the establishment of the Community Trade Mark System the Regulation provides in art.43(2) and (3) that the owners of earlier national trade mark or Community Trade Mark rights opposing an application for registration of a Community Trade Mark might be challenged by the applicant and be required to furnish poof that during the period of five years preceding the date of publication of the Community Trade Mark application, the earlier trade mark has been put to genuine use in the Community or the relevant Member State in connection with the goods or services in respect of which it is registered and which the party opposing the application cites as justification for the opposition, or that there

---

[103] *Antartica v OHIM* (C-320/07 P) [2009] E.C.R. 00.

4. CHALLENGING A COMMUNITY TRADE MARK

are proper reasons for non-use, provided the earlier trade mark has at that date been registered for not less than five years.

In the absence of such proof the opposition shall be rejected.

Article 56(2) and (3) introduce the same principle for challenging a Community Trade Mark once it has been registered in revocation or invalidity proceedings on the basis of an earlier right.

7-075 *Sunrider*[104] was the first relevant case that reached the Court. It was an appeal against the judgment of the Court of First Instance dismissing the action for annulment of the Board of Appeal rejecting the application for registration of the mark VITAFRUIT as a Community Trade Mark for goods in classes 5, 29 and 32 of the Nice Agreement; critical was the specification under class 32 that covered "beers; mineral and aerated waters and other non-alcoholic drinks; fruit and vegetable drinks, fruit juices; syrups and other preparations for making beverages; herbal and vitamin beverages".[105]

The application was originally rejected by the Opposition Division following proceedings based on the registration of the mark VITAFRUT as a national trade mark in Spain for "non-alcoholic and non-therapeutic carbonic drinks, non-therapeutical cold beverages of all kinds, gaseous, granulated effervescent; fruit and vegetable juices without fermentation (except must), lemonades, orangeades, cold beverages (except orgeat), soda water, Seidlitz water and artificial ice", in classes 30 and 32. The evidence of use submitted by the proprietor of the earlier trade mark, Mr Espadafor Caba, opposing the application consisted of six bottle labels and ten invoices with a date earlier than the contested mark's filing date.

(a) The judgment of the Court of First Instance 7-076

The Court of First Instance rejected the action for annulment.

It found, first, that although use of the earlier trade mark had been under the company name Industrias Espadafor SA the Board of Appeal had been entitled to rely on the presumption that it had taken place with the consent of the proprietor and that the appellant had not disputed this point before the Board.

Secondly, that there was sufficient evidence for deciding that the earlier use had been genuine. It admitted that it might be preferable to have more evidence regarding the nature of use but nevertheless accepted that proof of sales during the period from May 1996 to May 1997 of around 300 cases of 12 items each of concentrated juices of various fruits representing sales of approximately 4,800 sufficed. Note, that the Board of Appeal had highlighted that the evidence of use concerned exclusively concentrated juices.

---

[104] *The Sunrider Corp v Office for Harmonisation in the Internal Market (Trade Marks and Designs)* (C-416/04 P) [2006] E.C.R. I-4237.

[105] *Sunrider v Office for Harmonisation in the Internal Market (Trade Marks and Designs)* (T-203/02) [2005] E.C.R. II-2793.

7-077 Thirdly, that the concentrated juices were destined for end-consumers and not for fruit juice manufacturers. Accordingly, the products of both parties targeted the same market.

Fourthly, that herbal and vitamin beverages and concentrated fruit juices were similar, based primarily on the argument that they were interchangeable because they shared the same purpose; they were competing non-alcoholic beverages, normally drunk cold, aiming to quench thirst. The fact that their ingredients differed did not alter this finding.

7-078 *(b) The judgment of the Court*

Before the Court the appellant pursued four lines of appeal: that the Court of First Instance had misinterpreted the rules on the burden of proof regarding earlier use; had misinterpreted the rules regarding proof of use; had misinterpreted the concept of genuine use; and, had misapplied the rules regarding product similarity.

Further, it challenged the admissibility of the Office's response.

7-079 **(i) The admissibility of the Office's response—article 116(1).** Sunrider claimed that the Office's response—a request to dismiss the appeal and order the appellant to pay the costs—was inadmissible because it sought a different form of order from that sought at first instance, based on art.116(1) of the Rules of Procedure of the Court of Justice.[106]

The Court rejected the inadmissibility claim based on two grounds.

First, it held that when the Court of First Instance does not grant the form of order sought by a party, or grants it only in part, then that party may choose not to seek that form of order from the Court of Justice when the latter hears an appeal against the judgment of the Court of First Instance. Even more so when it has obtained full satisfaction before the Court of First Instance and, in its response before the Court of Justice, seeks to have the appeal dismissed in its entirety.

Secondly, it noted that if the Court of Justice allowed the appeal and decided according to art.61 of the Statute of the Court of Justice to give itself final judgment it would be required to take account of that form of order, either to grant it again, in whole or in part, or to dismiss it.

7-080 **(ii) Dealing with new grounds.** The appellant argued that, whilst dealing with the plea relying on earlier use, the Court of First Instance had committed an error of law by not considering whether it could lawfully adopt a new decision with the same operative part as the contested decision,

---

[106] Article 116(1) provides: "A response may seek:—to dismiss, in whole or in part, the appeal or to set aside, in whole or in part, the decision of the Court of First Instance;—the same form of order, in whole or in part, as that sought at first instance and shall not seek a different form of order."

4. CHALLENGING A COMMUNITY TRADE MARK

relying on an earlier judgment of the Court of First Instance that appeared to require this from the Board of Appeal.[107]

The Court rejected the claim as unfounded according to its interpretation of *Henkel*.[108]

It ruled that under art.63 of the Regulation, the Court of First Instance had the jurisdiction to annul or alter a decision of a Board of Appeal for a limited number of grounds: lack of competence; infringement of an essential procedural requirement; infringement of the Treaty; infringement of the Regulation or of any rule of law relating to its application; and, misuse of power.

It clearly did not allow the Court of First Instance to annul or alter that decision on grounds which come into existence subsequent to its adoption.

7–081

What the Court of First Instance had decided in *Henkel* was that the Boards of Appeal were required to ascertain whether, at the time they ruled on an appeal against a decision of the Office, they might lawfully adopt a new decision with the same operative part as the decision appealed against. This was based on the principle of continuity, between the Office's adjudicating bodies—examiners, the Opposition Division and the Cancellation Division—and the Boards of Appeal.

(iii) The burden of proof regarding genuine prior use. The applicant claimed that the Court of First Instance should not rely on probabilities or presumptions regarding use of the earlier trade mark or require from the applicant to prove lack of consent when the use was made by a third party. The proprietor of the earlier trade mark had not produced any evidence that he had consented to use by the company Industrias Espadafor SA. The Board and the Court of First Instance had relied on a presumption of consent.

7–082

The Office responded that the presumption had been justified for a number of specific reasons.

The Court described the whole process step by step.

Article 43(2) and (3) provided that the applicant for a Community Trade Mark registration might request that the proprietor of an earlier trade mark opposing the registration produces proof that the trade mark had been put to genuine use.

7–083

Article 15(3) required genuine use to be made by the proprietor or with the proprietor's consent.

The proprietor of the earlier trade mark carried the burden of proving it consented to the use of the mark by a third party.

The Court found that the Court of First Instance had followed the process described above. Relying on the material adduced by the opposing party it had found that his consent had been proved. Part of his name was incorporated in the name of the company using the mark and he himself produced

7–084

---

[107] *Henkel KGaA* (T-308/01) [2003] E.C.R. II-3253.
[108] *Henkel KGaA* (T-308/01) [2003] E.C.R. II-3253.

the proof of use before the Opposition Division and the Board of Appeal. Had he not consented to that use it would be unlikely that he would be able to produce the actual proof.

Deciding whether the evidence actually proved his consent constituted an assessment of facts and remained in the jurisdiction of the Court of First Instance.[109]

7-085 **(iv) Evidence of genuine use.** The appellant submitted that the undated labels did not amount to proof of use.

The Court however saw the labels as part of the wider evidence submitted by the proprietor of the earlier trade mark. It noted that the findings of the Court of First Instance regarding sales based on the invoices remained unchallenged.

Accordingly the allegation that the labels in themselves failed to prove earlier use was not enough to set aside the judgment under appeal and was rejected as ineffective.

7-086 **(v) The concept of genuine use.** Sunrider argued that the evidence had shown only token use of the earlier mark that should not satisfy "genuine use" requirements, in particular after *Ansul*,[110] focusing on the limited nature, number, and geographical coverage of the transactions involving the trade mark and the character of the goods in question. It characterised the use as at most only sporadic and occasional rather than continuous, actual and stable.

The Office supported that in principle this ground of appeal was inadmissible, seeking in essence a reassessment of the evidence. In any case, the Court of First Instance was right in its evaluation, counterbalancing the small scale of the use and the fact that it related to a single customer, on the one hand, with the relatively short period of time in which they occurred, on the other.

The Court repeated its rulings in *Ansul* and *La Mer Technology*[111] that for assessing the genuine character of the use of the earlier trade mark regard must be had to all the facts and circumstances relevant to establishing whether the commercial exploitation of the mark in the course of trade was real, particularly whether such use was viewed as warranted in the economic sector concerned to maintain or create a share in the market for the goods or services protected by the mark, the nature of those goods or services, the characteristics of the market and the scale and frequency of use of the mark; there were no de minimis rules.

7-087 It found that the Court of First Instance had followed the assessment path described by the Court in the above cases.

---

[109] *BioID AG* (C-37/03 P) [2005] E.C.R. I-7975.
[110] *Ansul BV* (C-40/01) [2003] E.C.R. I-2439.
[111] *La Mer Technology Inc v Laboratoires Goemar SA* (C-259/02) [2004] E.C.R. I-1159.

5. CONCLUSION

First, it had analysed the place, time, extent and nature of that use.

And, secondly, it had sought to determine whether the trade mark had been used in order to create or preserve an outlet for "concentrated fruit juices" or had to be regarded as token.

The Court rejected the claim that the fact that use was linked with only one customer should a priori negate its genuine character; the territorial scope of the use was only one of several factors that had to be taken into account. Instead, it stressed that for each individual case all the relevant factors should be considered; accordingly volumes of sales that would suffice in one particular case could be insufficient in another.

(vi) The product comparison. This claim targeted the emphasis that the Court of First Instance had apparently given to the fact that the two products aimed at the same potential consumers. 7–088

The Court, however, ruled that the Court of First Instance had again considered all the relevant factors including their nature and method of use.

5. CONCLUSION

So far the approach of the Court has been pragmatic. It has rejected de minimis rules and rigid definitions and time limitations. The Court has provided the elements of a multi-factor test and insisted that the characteristics of the product and the relevant product market should be assessed as part of that test. 7–089

As the system matures the Court is increasingly dealing with variations on the same themes. It still remains to be seen whether it will get drawn into the factual details of the questions or persist that national courts have to decipher what the actual evidence is telling them.

Chapter 8

PARALLEL IMPORTS

1. Introduction	8–001
2. The General Principles	8–002
(1) The legislative framework	8–002
(2) Duties and taxes	8–006
(3) Quantitative restrictions	8–011
(4) The equality proviso	8–028
(5) Public policy considerations	8–030
(6) Protection of health and life of humans	8–036
(7) Codacons—labelling requirements—the residual power of the free movement of goods rationale	8–040
(8) Commission v Ireland—hallmarks and public interest	8–045
3. Free Movement of Goods and Intellectual Property	8–047
(1) The existence–exercise dichotomy	8–051
(2) The specific subject-matter of the right	8–053
(3) "Independent" rights	8–054
4. Free Movement of Goods and Trade Mark Law	8–056
(1) The early days—the essential function and the specific subject-matter of trade marks	8–056
(2) Developing the concept of consent	8–058
(3) Hag I—a restrictive approach	8–059
(4) Terrapin—consent and independent rights	8–061
(5) Merck v Stephar—lack of protection	8–062
(6) Pharmon v Hoechst—compulsory licence	8–063
(7) Centrafarm v American Home Products—changing direction	8–065
(8) HAG II—the concept of consent, the role and function of trade marks	8–067
(9) Ideal Standard—voluntary assignment	8–071
(10) Repackaging and parallel imports—Hoffmann-La Roche—setting the principles	8–075
5. Free Movement of Goods and the New Trade Mark Regime	8–089
(1) Bristol Myers Squibb and the related cases–article 7 of the Directive and the free movement of goods rules–the fifth repackaging condition	8–089
6. Pharmacia & Upjohn—Replacing The Trade Mark—The Requirement of Necessity	8–142
7. Boehringer—Revisiting Repackaging	8–155

595

8. Ballantine—Trade Mark Infringement and Policing Channels Of Trade	8–170
9. Dior—Beyond the Origin Function	8–190
10. Silhouette—the Territorial Scope of Exhaustion	8–209
11. Sebago—"Specific" Consent	8–223
12. Davidoff—"Clear" Consent	8–228
13. Peak Holding—The Concept of "Putting Goods on The Market"	8–243
14. Class International—Goods in Transit	8–247
15. Boehringer II—Revisiting Repackaging, Overstickering and Reboxing	8–253
16. Wellcome v Paranova—Is There a Requirement of Minimum Intervention?—The Extent Of Disclosure	8–282
17. Conclusion	8–290

1. INTRODUCTION

8–001 Free movement of goods constitutes one of the "four freedoms"[1] covered in the EC Treaty. It is a fundamental principle with a dual purpose.

The first is purely economic; a customs union and common market comprising individual Member States cannot be established unless goods from all the Member States are sold freely and compete effectively; if there is to be a single common market then goods must flow freely within its borders. The effect of national measures that block the importation of goods from one Member State to another, make their marketing more difficult, or raise their price, is the distortion of the free flow of goods and competition. Inevitably, in a single market such measures have to be eliminated.[2]

The second is socio-political and is linked with the power of consumption. To an extent we are all influenced by what we consume. By breaking down the barriers of consumption national consumers are gradually transformed into European consumers. "Foreign", but still European, trade marks

---

[1] The other three are free movement of persons, services, and capital.
[2] D. Swann, in *The Economics of the Common Market* 7th edn (Penguin, 1992), pp.11–12, provides the classic description of the steps towards economic union: "The free trade area is the least onerous in terms of involvement. It consists in an arrangement between states in which they agree to remove all customs duties (and quotas) on trade passing between them. Each party is free, however, to determine unilaterally the level of customs duty on imports coming from outside the area. The next stage is the customs union. Here tariffs and quotas on trade between members are also removed but members agree to apply a common level of tariff on goods entering the union from without. The latter is called the common customs, or common external, tariff. Next comes the common market and this technical term implies that to the free movement of goods within the customs union is added the free movement of the factors of production–labour, capital and enterprise. Finally there is the economic union. This is a common market in which there is also a complete unification of monetary and fiscal policy. There would be a common currency which would be controlled by a central authority and in effect the member states would become regions within the union."

2. THE GENERAL PRINCIPLES

signify the varied sources of goods but they also function as signposts of a European market place; they are evidence of an economic union.

2. THE GENERAL PRINCIPLES

(1) The legislative framework

The principle of free movement of goods has two sides. The first covers duties, charges, and taxes; the second, quantitative import and export restrictions.
Article 23 provides for the elimination of duties and charges.
Article 23(1) states that:

8-002

"The Community shall be based upon a customs union which shall cover all trade in goods and which shall involve the prohibition between Member States of customs duties on imports and exports and of all charges having an equivalent effect, and the adoption of a common customs tariff in their relation with third countries."

Article 23(2) describes the goods covered by the arts 23–25 and 28–31, the provisions apply "to products originating in Member States and to products coming from third countries which are in free circulation in Member States".
According to art.24 goods coming from a third country "shall be considered to be in free circulation in a Member State if the import formalities have been complied with and any customs duties or charges having equivalent effect which are payable have been levied in that Member State, and if they have not benefited from a total or partial drawback of such duties or charges".
Article 25 is the core provision on the Customs Union providing that:

8-003

"Customs duties on imports and exports and charges having equivalent effect shall be prohibited between Member States. This prohibition shall also apply to customs duties of a fiscal nature".[3]

---

[3] A comparison with the text of the old arts 9, 12, and 13 that have been repealed by arts 23 and 25 evidences the development and incremental federalisation of Community law that occurred in parallel with the establishment of a unified market. Article 12 considered new customs duties and art.13 existing duties. Following their consistent application the distinction has become redundant and been dropped. Article 26 sets that common Customs Tariff duties shall be fixed by the Council, acting by a qualified majority, following a proposal from the Commission. And according to art.27 the Commission shall be guided by: "(a) the need to promote trade between Member States and third countries; (b) developments in conditions of competition within the Community in so far as they lead to an improvement in the competitive capacity of undertakings; (c) the requirements of the Community as regards the supply of raw materials and semi-finished goods; in this connection the Commission shall take care to avoid distorting conditions of competition between Member States in respect of finished goods; (d) the need to avoid serious disturbances in the economies of Member States and to ensure rational development of production and an expansion of consumption within the Community". For an overview of the development of the law on the free movement of goods see for example Leidenmühler, "The Free Movement of Goods within an EC-Wide Market: Still a Work in Progress" (2004) 12 Cardozo J. Int'l & Comp. L. 163.

8–004 The second side of the free movement of goods principle is found in arts 28–31.
Article 28 focuses on imports:

"Quantitative restrictions on imports and all measures having equivalent effect shall be prohibited between Member States."

Article 29 covers export restrictions in an identical manner.

8–005 Possible exemptions to arts 28 and 29 can be based on art.30; prohibitions or restrictions on imports, exports or goods in transit can be justified on grounds of:

- public morality, public policy or public security;
- the protection of health and life of humans, animals or plants;
- the protection of national treasures possessing artistic, historic or archaeological value; or
- the protection of industrial and commercial property.

Article 30 also includes a proviso that such "prohibitions or restrictions shall not, however, constitute a means of arbitrary discrimination or a disguised restriction on trade between Member States".

Article 31(1) provides that Member States shall "adjust any State monopolies of a commercial character so as to ensure that no discrimination regarding the conditions under which goods are procured and marketed exists between nationals of Member States".[4]

Article 31(3) affords special mention and treatment to agricultural products:

"If a State monopoly of a commercial character has rules which are designed to make it easier to dispose of agricultural products or obtain for them the best return, steps should be taken in applying the rules contained in this article to ensure equivalent safeguards for the employment and standard of living of the producers concerned."

8–006 **(2) Duties and taxes**

Free movement of goods lies at the foundation of the European Union. Considering the first side of the principle the Court of Justice noted that "the prohibition of new customs duties or charges having equivalent effect, linked to the principle of the free movement of goods, constitutes a

---

[4] Article 31(2) ensures that the provision catches "any body through which a Member State, in law or in fact, either directly or indirectly supervises, determines or appreciably influences imports or exports between Member States" as well as "monopolies delegated by the State to others".

Member States must also refrain from introducing any new measure which is contrary to the principles laid down in art.31(1) or restricts the scope of the articles dealing with the prohibition of customs duties and quantitative restrictions.

2. THE GENERAL PRINCIPLES

fundamental rule which, without prejudice to the other provisions of the Treaty, does not permit of any exceptions".[5]

Following a purposive analysis the Court of Justice made clear from the beginning that the criterion for determining the compatibility of a national measure with the principle of free movement of goods is the effect rather than the purpose of the national measure. After all, the provision does refer to charges having an equivalent effect.[6]

Considering the applicability of art.25 (then art.16) it noted that it was not necessary to analyse the concept of the nature of the disputed fiscal system. "The disputed tax falls within Article [25] by reason of the fact that export trade in the goods in question is hindered by the pecuniary burden which it imposes on the price of the exported articles".[7]

(a) The product similarity issue   8–007

Indeed art.90(1) provides that Member States must not impose directly or indirectly on the products of other Member States any internal taxation that is in excess of that imposed on similar domestic products.[8] And irrespective

---

[5] *Commission v Italy* (24/68) [1969] E.C.R. 193, para.10. Later, the Court, without introducing exceptions to the general rule, acknowledged that a charge "escapes that classification if it relates to a general system of internal dues applied systematically and in accordance with the same criteria to domestic products and imported products alike ... if it constitutes payment for a service in fact rendered to the economic operator of a sum in proportion to the service, or again subject to fulfil obligations imposed by Community law"; *Commission v Germany* (18/87) [1988] E.C.R. 5427, at para.6. The Court treats similarly measures under obligations arising from international agreements covering all Member States; *Commission v Netherlands* (89/76) [1977] E.C.R. 1355. Note the relevance of the nature of the obligation under either Community law or international agreement, if the Member State is allowed but not mandated to take the measure the Court is reluctant to accept it; *Commission v Belgium* (314/82) [1984] E.C.R. 1543, para.8. For a review see O'Brien, "Company Taxation, State Aid and Fundamental Freedoms: Is the Next Step Enhanced Cooperation" (2005) 35 E.L. Rev. 209.

[6] In *Commission v Italy* (24/68) [1969] E.C.R. 193, the Court stressed that any pecuniary charge, irrespective of its size, designation, and mode of application which is imposed unilaterally on domestic or foreign goods because they cross a frontier constitutes a charge having equivalent effect. The Court was willing to consider the argument that the charge constituted consideration for a service provided by the authorities of the Member State; but it required a concrete service that would lead to a measurable, rather than general and difficult to assess, benefit for the recipient of the service. See also *Bresciani v Amministrazione Italiana delle Finanze* (87/75) [1976] E.C.R. 129 requiring that even where a measure is considered to constitute a service and a charge for this measure is imposed on domestic as well as imported produce, the charge will have to be applied in both cases according to the same criteria and at the same stage of production.

[7] *Commission v Italy* (7/68) [1968] E.C.R. 423 at 429. See also *Michailidis AE v IKA* (C-441/98 & C-442/98) [2000] E.C.R. I-7145 confirming the Court's approach; contributions to workers' insurance funds can be caught by art.25 according to their effect rather than their nature or intended purpose.

[8] Article 90 mentions any direct or indirect internal taxation of any kind. The Court, once again, has taken a purposive approach in interpreting the provision, see for example *Commission v Belgium* (2/62) [1962] E.C.R. 425; and *Humblot v Directeur des Services Fiscaux* (112/84) [1985] E.C.R. 1367 where it found that a punitively higher national French tax imposed on powerful cars was discriminatory because at the time there were no French manufactured cars falling inside the relevant category and as a result the tax was imposed only on imported cars.

of product similarity, according to art.90(2) Member States must not impose any internal taxation affording indirect protection to other products.[9] Article 90(2) appears to cover competing but not necessarily similar products. The distinction is a difficult one.[10]

8–008 *(b) Competition and substitution*

From a trade mark lawyer's perspective this line of cases reveals a fascinating analogy: a test for determining similarity between products from a different perspective. In *Commission v France*[11] the Court examined the market for spirits in order to determine whether it functioned as a single market or an umbrella for more specific drinks' markets. Following an analysis of the market it drew two conclusions:

"... First, there is, in the case of spirits considered as a whole, an indeterminate number of beverages which must be classified as 'similar products' within the meaning of Article [90], although it may be difficult to decide this in specific cases, in view of the nature of the factors implied by distinguishing criteria such as flavour and consumer habits. Secondly, even in cases in which it is impossible to recognize a sufficient degree of similarity between the products concerned, there are nevertheless, in the case of all spirits, common characteristics which are sufficiently pronounced to accept that in all cases there is at least partial or potential competition. It follows that the application of the second paragraph of Article [90] may come into consideration in cases in which the relationship of similarity between the specific varieties of spirits remains doubtful or contested."[12]

The Court relied on the competitive and substitution relation between products obtained from distillation. The process of distillation provided the decisive factor for determining similarity, rather than taste, type of use, and distinction according to whether the spirit was obtained from vines or cereals.

8–009 *(c) Comparing beer with wine*

A classic similarity scenario is the one comparing beer with wine. In *Commission v United Kingdom*[13] the Court found that there was a degree of

---

[9] "Furthermore, no Member State shall impose on the products of other Member States any internal taxation of such a nature as to afford indirect protection to other products."
[10] Indeed, cross elasticity of demand is an issue that is also relevant in competition law, see for example paras 9–081 and 9–083; elements of these questions resurface in the assessment of product similarity, see for example para.5–076.
[11] *Commission v France* (168/78) [1980] E.C.R. 347; see also *Commission v Denmark* (106/84) [1986] E.C.R. 833.
[12] *Commission v France* (168/78) [1980] E.C.R.347, para.12.
[13] *Commission v United Kingdom* (170/78) [1983] E.C.R. 2265.

2. THE GENERAL PRINCIPLES

substitution between them. It also noted that, for measuring the degree attention "should not be confined to consumer habits in a Member State or in a given region. Those habits, which were essentially variable in time and space, could not be considered to be immutable; the tax policy of a Member State must not therefore crystallize given consumer habits so as to consolidate an advantage acquired by national industries concerned to respond to them".[14]

At the same time it acknowledged the significant differences between the two products, like manufacturing processes and natural properties. The Court examined a number of criteria submitted before it: the Commission supported volume and alcohol content, the United Kingdom focused on product price excluding tax, whereas Italy looked at the issue from a negative perspective, considering the types of wine with which a comparison could not be drawn. It was Italy's approach that it found more pertinent:

"In view of the substantial differences in the quality and, therefore, in the price of wines, the decisive competitive relationship between beer, a popular and widely consumed beverage, and wine must be established by reference to those wines which are the most accessible to the public at large, that is to say, generally speaking the lightest and cheapest varieties".[15]

At the end, the Court made an overall assessment, and looked at all the criteria. It found that the submission of the United Kingdom—price net of tax—was difficult to follow because of the lack of evidence; all the other criteria, however, indicated to differing degrees that the United Kingdom subjected imported wine to a higher tax burden:

"Since such protection is most marked in the case of the most popular wines, the effect of the United Kingdom tax system is to stamp wine with the hallmarks of a luxury product which, in view of the tax burden which it bears, can scarcely constitute in the eyes of the consumer a genuine alternative to the typically produced domestic beverage".[16]

Concluding, the Court repeated that it is the discrimination against still light wines made from fresh grapes that made it decide that the United Kingdom had failed to fulfill its obligations under art.90(2).

---

[14] *Commission v United Kingdom* (170/78) [1983] E.C.R. 2265, para.8.
[15] *Commission v United Kingdom* (170/78) [1983] E.C.R. 2265, para.12.
[16] *Commission v United Kingdom* (170/78) [1983] E.C.R. 2265, para.27.

8-010   (d)   *Comparing whisky with liqueurs, and bananas with other fruits*

In *John Walker v Ministeriet for Skatter*[17] the Court followed a similar but more inclusive route. This time the decisive criteria, for deciding that liqueur fruit wine and whisky were not similar, were alcohol content and method of manufacture. Turning to a "healthier" market, the Court considered similarities between types of fruit in *Commission v Italy*.[18] Again following an analysis of the objective characteristics of bananas on the one hand and other fruits on the other it decided that they were not similar products because of their organoleptic properties and the distinct consumer needs they satisfied, bananas had low water content, and as a result did not quench thirst, but high nutritional value. Still, it found that the disproportionate consumption tax imposed on bananas constituted a protectionist measure.

8-011   (3)   **Quantitative restrictions**

Import and export quantitative restrictions and measures having an equivalent effect are prohibited according to arts 28 and 29. As expected, the Court defined both concepts in broad terms and on the basis of their effect rather than original scope.

8-012   (a)   *The broad principle*

Quantitative restrictions covered "measures which amount to a total or partial restraint of, according to the circumstances, imports, exports or goods in transit".[19]

Whereas, "[a]ll trading rules enacted by Member States which are capable of hindering directly or indirectly, actually or potentially, intra-Community trade are to be considered as measures having an effect equivalent to quantitative restrictions".[20] The Court introduced some flexibility into the system by noting that in the absence of a Community regulatory regime, in other words positive harmonisation which in this case meant lack of a system guaranteeing for consumers the authenticity of a product's designation of origin, a Member State may take measures to prevent unfair practices, "it is however subject to the condition that these measures should be reasonable and that the means of proof required should not act as a hindrance to trade between Member States and should, in consequence, be accessible to all Community nationals".[21] It accepted that some measures might be justified in principle, but still demanded that such measures

---

[17] *John Walker v Ministeriet for Skatter og Afgifter* (243/84) [1986] E.C.R. 875.
[18] *Commission v Italy* (184/85) [1987] E.C.R. 2013.
[19] *Geddo v Ente Nazionale Risi* (2/73) [1973] E.C.R. 865, para.7.
[20] *Procureur du Roi v Dassonville* (8/74) [1974] E.C.R. 837, para.5.
[21] *Procureur du Roi* (8/74) [1974] E.C.R. 837, para.6.

2. THE GENERAL PRINCIPLES

should not be applied in a discriminatory way or as a disguised restriction on trade between Member States.[22]

Dassonville also introduces into the picture the figure of the "parallel importer", the trader who ignores national barriers, buys where it is cheap, offers more choice to the consumer, and undercuts traditional channels of trade. When challenged by national regulations it uses European integration as a defense mechanism.[23]

(b) The principle, the exception, and the exception to the exception   8–013

In order to police the "borderline between legitimate and illegitimate national regulation"[24] the Court followed the trusted route of setting a wide principle with a narrow exception, and then introducing an exception to the exception that brings us back into the wide principle.

Or from an integrationist's perspective, it adopted a negative, in terms of harmonisation, position aiming to break down barriers. The absence of positive harmonisation justified exceptions. It then qualified these exceptions by requiring them to be reasonable, a positive requirement, and non-discriminatory, a negative requirement.[25] The Court consistently applied negative harmonisation in a way that broadened the scope of the free movement of goods principle.

Using the same tools it excluded from the scope of the principle cases where a difference in treatment between imported and domestic goods was not capable of restricting imports or of prejudicing the marketing of imported goods. According to the Court the aim of art.28 EC, again from a

---

[22] The Commission had already indicated in art.2(3) of Directive 70/50, [1970] OJ L13/29, that the following could constitute a measure having an equivalent effect: setting minimum or maximum prices for imported products; setting less favourable prices for imported products; reducing the intrinsic value of imported products; increasing the costs of imported products; setting payment conditions for imported products that differ from those for domestic products; setting specific for imported products, or different from those for domestic products, conditions regarding packaging, composition, identification, size, weight, etc; giving a preference to the purchase of domestic goods or otherwise hindering the purchase of imports; limiting publicity in respect of imported goods; setting for imported products stocking requirements that are different from those which apply to domestic goods; and mandating from importers of goods to have an agent in the territory of the importing Member State.

[23] Belgian law required for products with a "designation of origin" a certificate, issued by the authorities of the exporting country, that the product lawfully bore the designation. A parallel trader bought Scotch whisky lawfully marketed in France and imported it to Belgium without such a certificate from the United Kingdom. When prosecuted the parallel trader argued that the Belgian regulation constituted a measure equivalent to a quantitative restriction.

[24] W.P.J. Wills, "The Search for the Rule in Article 30 EEC: Much Ado About Nothing"? (1993) 18 E.L.Rev. 475 at 478.

[25] W.P.J. Wills, "The Search for the Rule in Article 30 EEC: Much Ado About Nothing" (1993) 18 E.L.Rev. 475 at 476: "Integration can be looked at from the negative side. The Community's efforts to integrate national markets are basically attempts to limit the influence of national governments on production and consumption activities throughout the Community. The desire ... stems from economic as well as political concerns."

negative harmonisation viewpoint, was to "eliminate obstacles to the importation of goods and not to ensure that goods of national origin always enjoy the same treatment as imported or reimported goods".[26]

8–014   *(c)   Intra-Community and intra-State trade*

Indicative of the Court's conviction and development in thinking regarding the creation of a truly internal European market was the answer to the question whether free movement of goods rules applied against national measures preventing trade within the territory of a single Member State.

In *Bluhme*[27] the Court held that such a restriction can violate the free movement of goods principle. Bluhme was accused of keeping on a Danish island a swarm of bees of a species other than the one specified by the Danish Government. The Court found this to be a measure equivalent to a quantitative restriction, albeit a justifiable one. It accepted A.G. Fennely's point that the contested measure prohibited the importation of bees from other Member States to a part of Danish territory and had a direct and immediate impact on trade. He stated that the Court, in its earlier case law:

> "was simply not prepared to accept that national rules on discharges from ships into the sea, on planning authorisation and licensing of shops, on the seizure of goods in the possession of tax defaulters and on the provision of information in good faith when concluding contracts were liable to have a discernible effect on trade. On the other hand, the impact on trade of the Decision at issue in the present case is direct and immediate. The import of bees from other Member States to a part of Danish territory is directly prohibited. In such a case, the scale of the effect on intra-Community trade is, as already stated, irrelevant."[28]

In a later case A.G. Léger considered *Bluhme* as covering circumstances "where local rules that applied to only part of the territory of a Member State affected trade in goods between that part of the national territory and the other Member States and also trade between that part of the national territory and the other parts of the territory of the same Member State".[29]

The Court reconfirmed that a charge proportional to their customs value, levied by a Member State on all goods entering a region in that State constitutes a charge having equivalent effect even if levied on goods originating from another part of the same State.[30]

---

[26] *Cognet* (355/85) [1986] E.C.R. 3231, para.10.
[27] See *Commission v Belgium* (C-2/90) [1992] E.C.R. I-4431; and *Ditlev Bluhme* (C-67/97) [1998] E.C.R. I-8033; [1999] 1 C.M.L.R. 612.
[28] [1999] 1 C.M.L.R. 612, point 19.
[29] *Jersey Produce Marketing Organisation Ltd v Jersey* (C-293/02), para.85.
[30] Citing *René Lancry SA v Direction Générale des Douanes* (C-363/93) [1994] E.C.R. I-3957 for "imports"; and *Simitzi v Municipality of Kos* (C-485/93) [1995] E.C.R. I-2655 for "exports".

2. THE GENERAL PRINCIPLES

(d)   The effect and scope of the measure   8–015

The Court had been interpreting the provisions on quantitative restrictions in an expansive and purposive way. It considered the effect the targeted measure had on the market rather than its stated objective in order to determine whether it constituted a quantitative restriction. The objectives of national measures became relevant when the Court examined whether they could be regarded as public policy considerations justifying their adoption. The Court appeared particularly forceful whenever there was an element of discrimination. In such instances, where the objective was discriminatory, even ineffective measures would be caught.[31]

For example, public procurement schemes favouring domestic products,[32] special phyto-sanitary controls and inspections targeting exclusively imported plant products,[33] as well as additional quality controls provided only for watches destined to be exported[34] were caught by art.28 EC or art.29 EC.

(e)   Discrimination based on origin   8–016

Similarly the Court viewed national campaigns supporting domestic products as "a reflection of the [relevant] government's considered intention to substitute domestic products for imported products on the [national] market and thereby to check the flow of imports from other Member States", rather than an advertising campaign.[35]

The Court accepted that the campaign did not amount to a binding measure but noted that even measures that do not have binding effect may be capable of influencing the behavior of consumers and traders in the Member State. It is the effect of the measure that counts rather than its form.

But, because in practice the targeted campaign has not been particularly effective, the Court turned back to examine its nature and context: "it is not possible to overlook the fact that, regardless of their efficacy, those two activities form part of a government programme which is designed to

---

[31] See below para.8–016.
[32] See for example: *Campus Oil Ltd v Minister for Industry and Energy* (72/83) [1984] E.C.R. 2727; *Du Pont de Nemours Italiana SpA v Unita Sanitaria Locale No.2 Di Carrara* (C-21/88) [1990] E.C.R. I-889.
[33] *Rewe-Zentrafinanz v Lanwirtschaftskammer* (4/75) [1975] E.C.R. 843.
[34] *Procureur de la République Besançon v Bouhelier* (53/76) [1977] E.C.R. 197.
[35] *Commission v Ireland* (249/81) [1982] E.C.R. 4005, para.23. The campaign consisted of a "Buy Irish" sign that the Irish government encouraged traders to use on goods made in Ireland and an advertising campaign organised by the Irish Goods Council. Two other elements of the campaign, a service informing consumers about goods made in Ireland and retailers stocking them and the organisation of exhibitions for Irish goods have been dropped. As to the fact that the Irish Goods Council was not a governmental organisation the Court noted that the Irish government could not escape liability because it appointed the members of its Management Committee, granted it public subsidies, and defined the aims and outline of its campaign.

8–017   Such broad campaigns must be distinguished from those that appeared to be more targeted and objective. In *Apple and Pear Development* the promotional campaigns of a "national development organization" for certain fruit varieties were considered compatible with the free movement of goods rules despite the fact that they were typical of national production; the Court noted, however, that disparaging the purchase of fruits produced in other Member States or encouraging consumers to choose exclusively according to national origin would not be accepted.[37] Another element of the case is the distinction between recommendations regarding product quality and presentation and the imposition of quality standards; the second would be against the free movement of goods provisions, given the state of positive integration in the field of agriculture. The European Union had already developed a system of common quality standards.

The Court also dealt with "origin-marking" national rules. Legislation requiring retail goods to be marked with their country of origin can cover both domestic and imported goods, however "... it has to be recognized that the purpose of indications of origin or origin-marking is to enable consumers to distinguish between domestic and imported products and that this enables them to assert any prejudices which they may have against foreign products".[38] The United Kingdom argued that indications of origin conveyed to consumers information regarding product quality. Balancing between the informational value of the scheme and its adverse effect on the unification of national markets and economic interpenetration in Europe the Court found that it violated art.28.

8–018   *(f)   The concept of "origin"*

From a trade mark law perspective, the added interest of these cases is that they deal with the concept of "origin".

The Court had tolerated "indication of origin" marking schemes when origin constituted one of the elements of the product, either because it indicated a specific and concrete quality or characteristic or because it encapsulated a socio-cultural value that is linked with a particular region. The Court noted in the United Kingdom case that if the "national origin of goods brings certain qualities to the minds of consumers, it is in manufacturers' interests to indicate it themselves on the goods or on their packaging and it is not necessary to compel them to do so. In that case, the protection of

---

[36] *Commission v Ireland* (249/81) [1982] E.C.R. 4005, para.25.
[37] *Apple and Pear Development Council v KJ Lewis Ltd* (222/82) [1983] E.C.R. 4083; the fruits in question were English and Welsh apple and pear varieties.
[38] *Commission v United Kingdom* (207/83) [1985] E.C.R. 1201, para.17. The measure covered clothing and textile goods, domestic electrical appliances, footwear, and cutlery.

2. THE GENERAL PRINCIPLES

consumers is sufficiently guaranteed by rules which enable the use of false indications of origin to be prohibited".[39]

The Court had already dealt with the significance of origin in *Commission v Ireland*.[40] The contested legislation were two Irish "Merchandise Marks Orders" requiring imported souvenir jewellery—i.e. jewellery invoking Irishness, like depictions of Irish characters, scenes, shamrocks, etc.—to bear an indication of origin or the word "foreign". Ireland maintained that the measures were restrictive but justified in the interests of consumer protection and fairness in commercial transactions between producers.

The Court looked at the argument from two different perspectives.

8–019

First, it considered the defensive position under art.36 (now art.30), repeating its finding that free movement of goods constituted a basic rule and that art.30 was a derogation that had to be interpreted strictly, "the exceptions therein cannot be extended to cases other than those specifically laid down".[41] Consumer protection and fairness of commercial transactions were not listed in art.30 and, as a result, did not constitute exceptions.

Then, it asked a more fundamental question regarding the nature of measures equivalent to quantitative restrictions. Would the argumentation of the Irish government bring the Orders outside the scope of art.28? The Court revisited the positive versus negative integration scenario.

The starting point was the relevant product market. In the absence of positive integration regarding the production and marketing of the relevant product it remained in the competence of Member States to regulate all matters relating to its production, distribution and consumption. This, however, was subject to the negative integration condition that national regulation should not present an obstacle to intra-Community trade:

8–020

> "It is only where national rules, which apply without discrimination to both domestic and imported products, may be justified as being necessary in order to satisfy imperative requirements relating in particular ... to the fairness of commercial transactions and the defence of the consumer that they may constitute an exception to the requirements arising under Article [28]".[42]

In this case the Orders fell at the discrimination hurdle, since they applied only to imported products. The Irish government responded to this by focusing on the product market: the appeal of the products in question was owed to their origin, "essentially ... the fact of their being manufactured in the place of where they are purchased and they bear in themselves an

---

[39] *Commission v United Kingdom* (207/83) [1985] E.C.R. 1201, para.21.
[40] *Commission v Ireland* (113/80) [1981] E.C.R. 1625.
[41] *Commission v United Kingdom* (207/83) [1985] E.C.R. 1201, para.7. It referred to *Bauhuis v Netherlands* (46/76) [1977] E.C.R. 5.
[42] *Commission v Ireland* (113/80) [1981] E.C.R. 1625, para.10. The Court referred to *Rewe-Zentrale AG v Bundesmonopolverwaltung für Branntwein* (120/78) [1979] E.C.R. 649.

implied indication of their Irish origin", a purchaser would be misled if the souvenir bought in Ireland was manufactured elsewhere.[43]

The counter-argument of the Commission was that it was unnecessary for the consumer to know a product is of a particular origin, unless the origin implies a certain quality, basic materials or process of manufacture, or a particular place in the folklore or tradition of the region in question.

8–021   The Court was not persuaded by the approach of the Irish government. The products were articles of ornamentation, reminiscent of Irish indications, and of little commercial value. Their real value was that tourists would buy them on the spot, their "essential characteristic ... is that they constitute a pictorial reminder of the place visited, which does not by itself mean that a souvenir ... must necessarily be manufactured in the country of origin".[44] The Court added that local manufacturers could, if they wished, affix their own mark of origin but it remained unnecessary to impose a discriminatory burden on imported products.

In *Kohl v Ringelhan*,[45] the Court added that an unfair competition provision should not be applied in such a way "that it becomes possible to prohibit the use of a distinctive symbol for the sole reason that the public may be misled as to the domestic or foreign origin of the goods, without it being necessary to adduce evidence of other specific factors establishing the existence of unfair competition. In such a case, the provision in question in fact applies only to the marketing of imported products".[46] A national provision that was applied in that way could not be perceived as legislation applied in a uniform manner to the marketing of domestic and imported products.

8–022   *(g) Discrimination based on product characteristics*

Regarding the subject of discrimination the Court applied criteria analogous to those chosen by the Commission.[47]

In *Cassis de Dijon* it made clear that measures that discriminated between products on the basis of their characteristics rather than their origin could be caught by art.28.[48] The Court considered the effect of German laws governing the marketing of alcoholic beverages. The authorities had blocked the importation of Cassis de Dijon liqueur from France to Germany because its alcoholic strength was lower than the 25 per cent required for such liqueurs.

---

[43] *Commission v Ireland* (113/80) [1981] E.C.R. 1625, para.12.
[44] *Commission v Ireland* (113/80) [1982] E.C.R. 1625, para.15.
[45] *Theodor Kohl KG v Ringelhan & Rennett SA and Ringelhan Einrichtungs GmBH* (177/83) [1984] E.C.R. 3651.
[46] *Theodor Kohl KG v Ringelhan & Rennett SA and Ringelhan Einrichtungs GmBH* (177/83) [1984] E.C.R. 3651, para.15.
[47] See fn.22, above
[48] *Rewe-Zentrale AG* (120/78) [1979] E.C.R. 649.

2. THE GENERAL PRINCIPLES

The Court conceded that in the absence of common rules relating to the production and marketing of alcohol it was for the Member States to regulate the production and marketing of alcohol and alcoholic beverages at the national level. Disparities in regulation could lead to intra-Community trade obstacles that "must be accepted in so far as those provisions may be recognised as being necessary in order to satisfy mandatory requirements relating in particular to the effectiveness of fiscal supervision, the protection of public health, the fairness of commercial transactions and the defence of the consumer".[49]

The German Government argued that there were public health and consumer protection considerations.

8–023

The public health consideration was that the proliferation of alcoholic beverages with low alcohol content could have adverse effects on public health by increasing consumer tolerance to alcohol. The Court found the argument not decisive, given the extremely wide range of weak alcoholic products on the market.

The consumer protection argument was based on the consideration that the lowering of alcohol content could secure a competitive advantage in relation to beverages with higher alcohol content, since alcohol was the most expensive ingredient because of its high rate of tax. The Court found the mandatory fixing of minimum alcohol contents excessive, since "it is a simple matter to ensure that suitable information is conveyed to the purchaser by requiring the display of an indication of origin and of the alcohol content on the packaging of products".[50]

(h) Selling arrangements

8–024

The Court reconsidered its position on what is covered under the free movement of goods rules in *Keck*.[51] Two "hypermarket" managers were prosecuted under French laws prohibiting the resale of products at a loss— loss-leaders—in order to undercut competition. The national court recognised the potential applicability of art.28 but noted that traders were increasingly using the provision as a blind weapon against trade regulation at the national level.

It asked the Court of Justice to look again at whether measures restricting or prohibiting certain selling arrangements affect trade within the scope of art.28. In this case the "hypermarkets" supported that the national law was incompatible with the free movement of goods rules because it targeted exclusively resale, and not sale by a manufacturer, at a loss.

Advocate General Van Gerven characterised sale at a loss a sales promotional method and supported that legislation which restricted or

---

[49] *Rewe-Zentrale AG* (120/78) [1979] E.C.R. 649, para.8.
[50] *Cassis de Dijon*, para.13.
[51] *Keck and Mithouard* (C-267/91 & C-268/91) [1993] E.C.R. I-6907.

prohibited advertising and sales promotions might at least affect marketing opportunities for imported products even if it applied both to domestic and imported products.[52] In this case, for example, an importer might not be able to compete effectively with a domestic producer who could sell his product at a loss.

8–025 He accepted however that national regulation of sales at a loss was in principle justified in order to ensure fair trading and consumer protection. Sales at a loss could eliminate competitors or function as a decoy inducing consumers to buy products marked at higher prices.

Balancing between the restrictive nature of the legislation and its justification he required it to be expressed in a sufficiently precise way targeting specific types of sale rather than in the form of a blanket prohibition. Sale at a loss in order to introduce a new product or to dispose of excessive stocks would still be legitimate.

Interestingly, the Advocate General delivered a second Opinion commenting on the responses that the parties gave to questions submitted by the Court. The most significant targeted the nature of the practice of resale at a loss. Did the prohibition of resale at a loss constitute an instrument for the suppression of a sales promotion method or did it form part of a national price control system? A non-discriminatory price control system would not be caught by art.28.[53]

8–026 The response of the French Government was that price controls had been abolished; still, it argued, the relevant legislation should be viewed as a measure against unfair competition between distributors rather than a promotion sales method.

The Advocate General found that the French argument focused exclusively on the condition of the French market. This did not alter the fact that sales at a loss also constituted a sales technique.

The Court followed a pragmatic approach taking into account how its jurisprudence functioned in the market place. "In view of the increasing tendency of traders to invoke Article [28] of the Treaty as a means of challenging any rules whose effect is to limit their commercial freedom even where such rules are not aimed at products from other Member States, the Court considers it necessary to re-examine and clarify its case law on this matter".[54]

8–027 It confirmed its *Cassis de Dijon* principles but added that:

> "contrary to what has previously been decided, the application to products from other Member States of national provisions restricting or prohibiting certain selling arrangements is not such as to hinder directly or indirectly, actually or potentially, trade between Member States within

---

[52] He cited *Oosthoek* (286/81) [1982] E.C.R. 4575 in particular.
[53] *EC Commission v Italy* (78/82) [1983] E.C.R. 1955.
[54] *Keck and Mithouard* (C-267/91 & C-268/91) [1993] E.C.R. I-6907, para.14.

the meaning of Dassonville[55] so long as those provisions apply to all relevant traders operating within the national territory and so long as they affect in the same manner, in law and in fact, the marketing of domestic products and of those from other Member States".[56]

Provided that the above conditions were fulfilled, the national provisions would fall outside the scope of art.28.

(4) The equality proviso

8–028

The Court had proven similarly pragmatic in applying its equality proviso exploiting the flexibility that the balancing of different factors offers to it. When the Court finds that the factual effect of such a national provision is to protect domestic established market players it simply chooses not to apply the proviso, whilst repeating that the principle of *Keck* was retained.

In *Punto Casa* Italian legislation restricting retail trading on Sundays was found to apply to all traders operating in Italy; accordingly it did not impede access of imported products to the domestic market compared with access of domestic products.[57]

In *Commission v Greece* the Court held that a domestic regulation providing for processed milk for infants to be sold exclusively by pharmacies was applied without distinction according to origin and satisfied the equality requirement set in *Keck*. The fact that Greece did not produce processed milk for infants was found to be irrelevant.[58]

In *Gourmet International* the Court applied *Keck* but held that a general prohibition on advertising for alcoholic beverages in the Swedish press, radio, and television would have a discriminatory effect in fact rather than in law. Alcohol consumption was rooted in traditional social practices; consumers were not familiar with non-domestic products and without advertising imported products would be at a comparative disadvantage.[59]

8–029

The application of such a flexible rule had inevitably led to criticisms that mirror the development of the Court's jurisprudence. Weatherill has highlighted the Court's obsession with formalism[60]; Gormley on the other hand criticises the reasoning behind *Keck*,[61] whereas Koutrakos notes that the Court has itself diminished the relevance of *Keck* with its more recent case

---

[55] *Procureur du Roi v Dassonville* (8/74) [1974] E.C.R. 837, see para.8–012.
[56] *Keck and Mithouard* (C-267/91 & C-268/91) [1993] E.C.R. I-6907, para.16.
[57] *Punto Casa SpA v Sindaco Del Commune di Capena* (C-69/93) [1994] E.C.R. I-2355.
[58] See, for example *Commission v Greece* (C-391/92) [1995] E.C.R. I-1621.
[59] *Konsumentombudsmannen v Gourmet International Products* (C-405/98) [2001] E.C.R. I-1795.
[60] Weatherill, "After Keck: Some Thoughts on how to Clarify the Clarification" (1996) 33 C.M.L. Rev. 49.
[61] Gormley, "Reasoning Renounced: the Remarkable Judgment in Keck and Mithouard" [1994] E.B.L. Rev. 63.

law that concentrates on the factual effect of national measures.[62] Davis, in a comprehensive review of the post-*Keck* case law, notes that the Court's repeated citation of *Keck* has been inevitable in order "to prevent Article 28 becoming a general competence to supervise national law for proportionality".[63] His conclusion reinforces "the Community law way": "[t]he important thing is to stay focused on purpose".[64]

8–030 **(5) Public policy considerations**

In the *Irish Souvenirs* case the Court of Justice described art.30 as an exception to a basic principle.[65] Articles 28 and 29 described the principle that had been broadly delineated by the Court. Article 30 provided the strictly interpreted exceptions that the Member State could use to justify the contested measures.[66] The list was exhaustive; only what was covered in the provision could form the justificatory basis for an exception. The proviso of art.30 opened up the sliding route that led back from the exceptions to the basic principle.

8–031 *(a) Public morality*

Public morality is the first ground. In *Henn and Darby* the Court accepted that public morality standards vary throughout Europe and it is for each Member State to determine the standards that are applied in its jurisdiction.[67]

Accordingly UK customs laws could be used in order to stop the importation of indecent and obscene articles despite the fact that there was a discrepancy between national criminal laws on possession of pornography, against which there was no absolute ban, and importation of pornography, against which an absolute ban was imposed.

The Court accepted the possibility of variations at the national level. "Each member state is entitled to impose prohibitions on imports justified on grounds of public morality for the whole of its territory ... The fact that certain differences exist between the laws enforced in the different constituent parts of a member state does not thereby prevent that state from applying a unitary concept in regard to prohibitions on imports imposed, on grounds of public morality, on trade with other member states."[68]

---

[62] Koutrakos, "On Groceries, Alcohol and Olive Oil: More on Free Movement of Goods" (2001) 26 E.L. Rev. 391.
[63] Gareth Davies, "Can Selling Arrangements Be Harmonised" [2005] E.R. Rev. 371 at 372.
[64] Gareth Davies, "Can Selling Arrangements Be Harmonised" [2005] E.R. Rev. 371 at 385.
[65] *Commission v Ireland* (113/80) [1981] E.C.R. 1625.
[66] Member States carry the burden of proof; *Openbaar Ministerie v Van der Veldt* (C-17/93) [1994] E.C.R. I-3537.
[67] *R. v Henn and Darby* (34/79) [1979] E.C.R. 3795. The products were imported from The Netherlands to the United Kingdom.
[68] *R. v Henn and Darby* (34/79) [1979] E.C.R. 3795, para.16.

2. THE GENERAL PRINCIPLES

The purpose of domestic law as a whole was to restrain the creation and marketing of pornography. So, "if a prohibition on the importation of goods is justifiable on grounds of public morality and if it is imposed with that purpose the enforcement of that prohibition cannot, in the absence within the member state concerned of a lawful trade in the same goods, constitute a means of arbitrary discrimination or a disguised restriction on trade contrary to article [30]".[69]

(b) The relevance of the domestic product market 8–032

The existence or not of the relevant domestic product market proved critical in a subsequent public morality case. In *Conegate* the seized products were inflatable dolls imported from Germany to the United Kingdom. The crucial difference with *Henn and Darby* was that there was no ban regarding the manufacture or marketing of inflatable dolls within the United Kingdom.[70]

The Court was clear in the pronouncement of a general interpretive rule. A "member state may not rely on grounds of public morality to prohibit the importation of goods from other Member States when its legislation contains no prohibition on the manufacture or marketing of the same goods on its territory".[71]

And given its tolerant, regarding domestic legal discrepancies, approach in *Henn and Darby* here the Court appeared more demanding. "Although it is not necessary ... that the manufacture and marketing of the products whose importation has been prohibited in the territory of all the constituent parts, it must at least be possible to conclude from the applicable rules, taken as a whole, that their purpose is, in substance to prohibit the manufacture and marketing of those products."[72] In this case the domestic restrictions imposed on sale of the relevant products did not amount in substance to a prohibition.

(c) Public policy 8–033

Potentially public policy constitutes a much broader ground for an exception under art.30. And from a trade mark lawyer's perspective the concept of public policy is particularly challenging because it keeps on resurfacing in the trade mark jurisprudence of the Court of Justice.

In the free movement of goods context the Court has been wary in its demarcation of the term. Public policy cannot be used as the fiat for introducing into art.30 grounds that are not specifically enlisted therein. We have seen for example in *Irish Souvenirs* that public policy does not cover

---

[69] *R. v Henn and Darby* (34/79) [1979] E.C.R. 3795, para.22.
[70] *Conegate v Commissioners of Customs and Excise* (121/85) [1986] E.C.R. 1007.
[71] *Henn and Darby* [1979] E.C.R. 3795, para.16.
[72] *Henn and Darby* (34/79) [1979] E.C.R. 3795, para.17.

consumer protection or fairness in commercial transactions.[73] This was reinforced in *Kohl v Ringelhan*[74] where the Court stressed that whatever "interpretation is to be given to the term 'public policy', it cannot be extended so as to include considerations of consumer protection"[75] for the purposes of art.30. Such considerations may be taken into account in order to determine whether the national measure falls within the scope of art.28, but not in order to exclude it under art.30.

In *Leclerc v Au Blé Vert*[76] the Court added to the list, of what does not constitute public policy, the protection of creativity and cultural diversity. Leclerc, a retailer expanding in new product markets in France, started undercutting book prices, against national legislation requiring book retailers to abide by the retail prices fixed by the publisher or importer. Prices for imported books were set by the importer, but if the imported book was published in France the price should not be lower than the price set by the publisher. Leclerc supported that in essence the law established a collective system of price maintenance that undertakings are precluded from establishing under art.81 of the Treaty. The French Government argued that art.81 applies to specific practices between undertakings and should not be construed as prohibiting Member States from adopting measures which might have an effect on competition. The only relevant to the case provision would be art.28.

8–034 The Court accepted that at the then current stage of development of competition policy in European law the market for books had not been regulated at the Community level. Accordingly Member States could enact such legislation, provided that it was consonant with the free movement of goods provisions. The national law failed because it created separate rules for imported books that made intra-Community trade more difficult. For example, the first importer of a book would gain the advantage of setting the retail price. The Court went on to deny justification under art.30 based on the need to protect books as cultural media. It reinforced what, by then, has become a mantra:

"Since it derogates from a fundamental rule of the Treaty, Article [30] must be interpreted strictly and cannot be extended to cover objectives not expressly enumerated therein. Neither the safeguarding of consumers' interests nor the protection of creativity and cultural diversity in the realm of publishing is mentioned in Article [30]. It follows that the justification put forward by the French government cannot be accepted."[77]

---

[73] *Commission v Ireland* (113/80) [1981] E.C.R. 1625.
[74] *Theodor Kohl KG v Ringelhan & Rennett SA and Ringelhan Einrichtungs GmBH* (177/83) [1984] E.C.R. 3651.
[75] *Theodor Kohl KG* (177/83) [1984] E.C.R. 3651, para.19.
[76] *Leclerc v Au Blé Vert* (229/83) [1985] E.C.R. 1.
[77] *Leclerc* (229/83) [1985] E.C.R. 1, para.30.

2. THE GENERAL PRINCIPLES

A case that evidences the diffidence of the Court in positively describing what constitutes public policy is *Cullet v Centre Leclerc*.[78] The case involved a French scheme imposing minimum retail prices for fuel on the basis of refinery prices and costs existing in France. This meant that the pricing of imported fuel started from a potentially higher minimum price than the price that could be afforded on the basis of the costs existing in the country of origin. The Court found that this was a measure equivalent to a quantitative restriction. The French Government introduced an ordre public argument. It claimed that the nature of the product demanded pricing controls; in their absence there could be public discontent raised by retailers affected by unrestricted competition leading to disturbances to law and order.

Advocate General Van Themaat was more forthright than the Court in condemning the argument:

> "If roadblocks and other effective weapons of interest groups which feel threatened by the importation and sale at competitive prices of certain cheap products or services, or by immigrant workers or foreign businesses were accepted as justification, the existence of the four fundamental freedoms of the Treaty could no longer be relied upon. Private interest groups would then, in the place of the Treaty and the Community (and, within the limits laid down by the Treaty, national) institutions, determine the scope of those freedoms. In such cases, the concept of public policy requires, rather, effective action on the part of the authorities to deal with such disturbances."[79]

The Court was more cautious and focused on the facts of the case. The basis of the claim was described as "disturbances to law and order (ordre public) and public security".[80] Instead of outright rejection, the Court chose proportionality and insufficient argumentation as the basis of its rejection of the point raised by the French government, stating "it is sufficient to observe that the French Government has not shown that an amendment of the regulations in question in conformity with the [free movement of goods'] principles ... would have consequences for law and order (ordre public) and public security which the French Government would be unable to meet with the resources available to it".[81]

---

[78] *Cullet v Centre Leclerc* (231/83) [1985] E.C.R. 305.
[79] *Cullet* (231/83) [1985] 2 C.M.L.R. 524 at 534. Note that the A.G. distinguished *Centre Leclerc* from *Campus Oil Ltd v Minister for Industry and Energy* (72/83) [1984] E.C.R. 2727. This is a good example of how the Opinion of the A.G. can influence the final outcome of the case without the Court necessarily following the same judicial path in its thinking. The comparison between the two cases also reveals how the Court's appreciation of a factual situation can alter its reasoning and affect its judgments.
[80] *Cullet* (231/83) [1985] E.C.R. 305, para.32.
[81] *Cullet* (231/83) [1985] E.C.R. 305, para.33.

8–035 (d) *Public security*

The idea of *ordre public* links public policy with the narrower, and more easily definable, concept of public security. In *Campus Oil*, a case involving an Irish law requiring petrol importers to purchase 35 per cent of the overall quantity of petrol they traded in at fixed prices from a state-owned refinery, the Court commented on the "public security" defence raised by the Irish Government.

Given the lack of a comprehensive and effective network of Community measures that would protect petrol supplies at the national level for each Member State national measures could be tolerated: "... petroleum products, because of their exceptional importance as an energy source in the modern economy, are of fundamental importance for a country's existence since not only its economy but above all its institutions, its essential public services and even the survival of the inhabitants depend upon them. An interruption of supplies of petroleum products, with the resultant dangers for the country's existence, could therefore seriously affect the public security that Article [30] allows States to protect".[82]

It then narrowed the coverage and applicability of "public security" both from a negative and a positive perspective. It held that pleading the "economic difficulties" that the elimination of trade barriers would cause would not as such justify national measures. It then went on to require that even a measure excepted under "public security" must be "justified by objective circumstances corresponding to the needs of public security"[83] and "must not create obstacles to imports which are disproportionate to those objectives".[84]

Note that national security measures can also be taken following arts 296–298.

8–36 **(6) Protection of health and life of humans**

In *Commission v France*[85] the Court considered advertising restrictions in respect of alcoholic beverages. It found that such restrictions could impede imports, because they would affect more directly imported products.

The legitimisation of the restriction becomes even more problematic if it discriminates against products originating in other Member States.

The relevant French legislation had regulated advertising exposure of alcoholic beverages following a codification according to type. The Court found that there were instances of discrimination:

---

[82] *Campus Oil Ltd v Minister for Industry and Energy* (72/83) [1984] E.C.R. 2727, para.34.
[83] *Cullet* (231/83) [1985] E.C.R. 305, para.36.
[84] *Cullet* (231/83) [1985] E.C.R. 305, para.37.
[85] [1980] E.C.R. 2299.

2. THE GENERAL PRINCIPLES

"It is apparent... that even though it is conceded that an appreciable number of national products are subject to the prohibitions and restrictions on advertising... nevertheless the fact remains that the classifications which determine the application of those provisions put products imported from other Member States at a disadvantage compared to national products and consequently constitute a measure having an effect equivalent to a quantitative restriction".[86]

The Court recognised the link between advertising and alcohol consumption and accepted the potential applicability of art.30, however it stressed that the restrictions should not constitute a means of arbitrary discrimination or a disguised restriction on trade between Member States.

In *Gourmet International Products*[87] the Court accepted that in principle advertising restrictions regarding alcoholic beverages could be tolerated provided they were proportionate to the objective pursued and did not constitute either a means of arbitrary discrimination or a disguised restriction on trade between Member States.

The contested national provision was quite restrictive:

8–037

"In view of the health risks involved in alcohol consumption, alcoholic beverages should be marketed with particular moderation. In particular, advertisements or other marketing measures must not be insistent, involve unsolicited approaches or encourage alcohol consumption. Advertising may not be used to market alcoholic beverages on radio or television. The same prohibition applies to satellite broadcasts subject to Law 1996:844 on Radio and Television. Advertising may not be used to market spirits, wines or strong beers either in periodicals or in other publications subject to the Regulation on Press Freedom and comparable to periodicals by reasons of their publication schedule. That prohibition does not however apply to publications distributed solely at the point of sale of such beverages."[88]

The Court found that an absolute prohibition would impede the marketing of imported products more, compared with domestic products that have gained a position in the market place.

It accepted though that such a prohibition could fall under art.30 EC since there was a direct link between advertising and alcohol consumption.

8–038

The assessment of proportionality required an examination of the national provisions and the facts that only the national court conduct. The

---

[86] *Commission v France*, para.14.
[87] *Konsumentombudsmannen (KO) v Gourmet International Products (GIP)* [2001] E.C.R. I-1795.
[88] Reproduced in para.4.

Court noted that there was "no evidence before the court to suggest that the public health grounds on which the Swedish authorities rely have been diverted from their purpose and used in such a way as to discriminate against goods originating in other Member States or to protect certain national products indirectly".[89]

8-039 Accordingly, it held that art.28 and art.30 "do not preclude a prohibition on the advertising of alcoholic beverages such as that [described in the national legislation] unless it is apparent that, in the circumstances of law and of fact which characterise the situation in the Member State concerned, the protection of public health against the harmful effects of alcohol can be ensured by measures having less effect on intra-Community trade."[90]

Another, more recent, example was *Douwe Egberts*.[91] The case involved labelling information that incorporated slimming and medical recommendations; this would infringe national laws on advertising and labelling of foodstuffs.

8-040 The Court found that the challenged advertising and labelling prohibitions constituted an obstacle to imports and held that art.28 and art.30 precluded national legislation prohibiting references in the advertising of foodstuffs imported from other Member States to "slimming" and to "medical recommendations, attestations, declarations or statements of approval".

(7) Codacons—labelling requirements—the residual power of the free movement of goods rationale

A reference from the Italian Council of State, *Codacons*[92] dealt with another sensitive, in terms of substance, and heatedly debated, in terms of politics, health-related issue. Codacons, the Coordination of the Associations for the Protection of the Environment and of Users' and Consumers' Rights, launched an application for the annulment of an Italian Decree implementing community legislation setting that the presence of genetically modified organisms ("GMOs") in a proportion not exceeding 1 per cent of the ingredients making up baby foods and follow-on formulae, caused by adventitious contamination, need not be indicated on the labelling of those products.

---

[89] *Gourmet International Products*, para.32, citing *R. v Henn and Darby* (34/79) [1979] E.C.R. 3795; and *Aragonesa de Publicidad Exterior SA and Publivia SAE v Departmento de Sanidad y Seguridad Social de la Generalitat de Cataluña* (C-1/90) [1991] E.C.R. I-4151.
[90] *Gourmet International Products*, para.34.
[91] *Douwe Egberts NV v Westrom Pharma NV, FICS-World BVBA* (C-239/02) [2004] E.C.R. I-7007.
[92] *Ministero della Salute v Coordinamento delle Associazioni per la Difesa dell'Ambiente e dei Diritti degli Utenti e dei Consumatori (Codacons)* (C-123/03) [2005] E.C.R. I-4167.

The question referred to the Court focused on whether the labelling exemption provided by art.2(2)(b) of Regulation 1139/98 applied to foodstuffs for infants and young children.[93]

(a) The judgment of the Court 8–041

The judgment of the Court shows the residual power of free movement of goods rules. The first part investigated which one of a number of Community legal provisions was applicable in the particular case; the considerations included a contrast between provisions covering a specific product in a vertical sense and provisions covering a type of product in respect of specific consumers. The second part showed how free movement of goods principles could act as a catalyst in assessing the applicability of the principle of precaution developed by the Court in cases involving to risks to human health.

(i) Contextualising the provision—vertical application. Typically, 8–042 the Court started its analysis by contextualising the provision within the broader Community legislation that was relevant. First it referred to art.4(2) of Directive 79/112,[94] by virtue of which the Community provisions applicable to certain specified foodstuffs and not to foodstuffs in general might introduce other compulsory particulars in addition to those listed in art.3 of the Directive.

Regulation No.1139/98, on the other hand, included provisions on labelling which were of a specific nature and applied vertically only to particular foodstuffs: those obtained wholly or in part from certain genetically modified soya beans or certain genetically modified types of maize, referred to in art.1(1) of the Regulation.

According to art.4 of Directive 89/398 the Commission was responsible for adopting specific directives regarding the labelling, presentation and advertising of certain products including infant formulae, follow-up milk and other follow-up foods, and baby foods. As a result Directives 91/321 and 96/5 were adopted, determining the rules on the composition and labelling

---

[93] Reg.1139/98 [2000] OJ L6/13, requires the indication "produced from genetically modified soya" or "produced from genetically modified maize" to be added to the labelling of relevant products. Art.2(2)(b) provides for an exception when the presence of GMOs is adventitious and does not exceed a de minimis threshold: "The specified foodstuffs shall not be subject to the additional specific labelling requirements where: ... (b) material derived from the [GMOs] referred to in Article 1(1), together with any material placed on the market pursuant to Regulation (EC) No 258/97 derived from other [GMOs], is present in their food ingredients or the food comprising a single ingredient in a proportion no higher than 1% of the food ingredients individually considered or food comprising a single ingredient, provided this presence is adventitious. In order to establish that the presence of this material is adventitious, operators must be in a position to supply evidence to satisfy the competent authorities that they have taken appropriate steps to avoid using the [GMOs] (or produce thereof) referred to in the previous paragraph as a source."
[94] [1979] OJ L33/1.

of infant formulae and follow-on formulae intended for use by infants in good health and processed cereal-based foods and baby foods for infants and young children.

8–043   **(ii) The interrelationship between layers of Community law.** Here, the question was how the Regulation and the Directives that covered advertising for those types of products interrelated:

> "The question therefore arises as to whether the specific labelling requirements of Regulation No 1139/98 also apply to foodstuffs intended for the particular nutritional use of infants and young children".[95]

Reading art.7(1) and (4) of Directive 89/398 under the Preamble's interpretive light the Court found that labelling requirements such as those laid down by Regulation 1139/98 applied in principle to foodstuffs intended for nutritional uses within the scope of the Directive unless it was necessary to provide for a derogation from those requirements in order to ensure that the particular nutritional purpose in question was attained.[96] And Directives 91/321 and 96/5 did not contain any specific labelling requirements relating to the presence of material derived from GMOs that derogated from the provisions of Regulation 1139/98.

The conclusion reached by the Court was that such requirements had not, at least yet, been deemed necessary and art.2(2)(b) of Regulation 1139/98 had to be interpreted as meaning that the exemption also applied to foodstuffs intended for the particular nutritional use of infants and young children.

8–044   **(iii) The free movement of goods rationale.** The Court also found that this interpretation was consistent with the precautionary principle, developed by the Court for cases involving uncertainty as to the existence or extent of risks to human health.[97]

Here the free movement of goods principle acted as a catalyst. The Court remarked that Regulation 1139/98 had a dual purpose: first, to remove potential obstacles to the free movement of products containing genetically modified soya and maize, and, secondly, to provide the final consumer with information.[98] The Regulation introduced additional labelling requirements to those imposed by Directive 79/112[99] and the Preamble to the Regulation noted that these requirements were intended to ensure that the final

---

[95] *Codacons*, para.52.
[96] *Union Deutsche Lebensmittelwerke GmbH v Schutzverband gegen Unwesen in der Wirtschaft eV* (C-101/98) [1999] E.C.R. I-8841.
[97] *Monsanto Agricoltura Italia SpA v Presidenza del Consiglio dei Ministri* (C-236/01) [2003] E.C.R. I-8105.
[98] *Eva Glawischnig v Bundesminister fur soziale Sicherheit und Generationen* (C-316/01) [2003] E.C.R. I-5995.
[99] [1979] OJ L33/1.

2. THE GENERAL PRINCIPLES

consumer was properly informed in relation to products that, as the Court underlined, had been placed on the market being considered safe for human health following the procedures of Directive 90/220[100] and Regulation 258/97[101]; it was to those procedures that the precautionary principle should be applied. Once the authorisation process had been completed the free movement of goods rationale should prevail.

(8) Commission v Ireland—hallmarks and public interest   8–045

In *Commission v Ireland*[102] the Irish Government had imposed extra obligations on the marketing of imported precious metal articles that were lawfully marketed, marked with hallmarks, in other Member States but did not comply with the Irish marking requirements concerning standards of fineness.

The importers had to replace the hallmarks with Irish marks certifying the official—lower—Irish standard. They also had to apply to the products a "sponsor's mark", indicating the relevant maker, worker, or dealer registered with the Irish authorities even when the products had already been marked with the equivalent mark conforming with the legislation of the Member State of origin. In addition the Irish authorities had adopted different hallmarks for products manufactured in Ireland and for products imported from other Member States.

(a) The judgment of the Court   8–046

The Court started its analysis by noting that at that stage the Community had not adopted common standards of fineness. But, even in the absence of harmonisation, obstacles to free movement resulting from rules targeting goods imported from other Member States where they were lawfully put on the market violate art.28 unless justified by a public interest objective.

On the balancing exercise between free movement of goods and effective consumer protection through the application of hallmarks the Court referred to its earlier jurisprudence that a Member State cannot require a fresh hallmark to be struck on products imported from other Member States when equivalent information is conveyed by the existing hallmark.[103]

The Court found that there was no justification for the hallmarking requirements imposed by Ireland. The same applied to the "sponsor's mark" requirement. The requirement could be justified only if the product did not bear a hallmark from the Member State of origin. Inevitably, applying different hallmarks according to origin was also found to be against art.28.

---

[100] [1996] OJ L107/10.
[101] [1997] OJ L43/1.
[102] *Commission v Ireland* (C-30/99) [2001] E.C.R. I-4619.
[103] *Rewe-Zentrale AG* (120/78) [1979] E.C.R. 649; *Houtwipper* (C-293/93) [1994] E.C.R. I-4249; *Robertson* (C-220/81) [1982] E.C.R. 2349.

3. FREE MOVEMENT OF GOODS AND INTELLECTUAL PROPERTY

8–047 There are four characteristics of intellectual property that are particularly relevant when we consider the links between free movement of goods and intellectual property.

The first is the exclusionary essence of intellectual property rights. They allow their owners to stop third parties from acts prescribed in the law that created them. Third parties require the licence of the right owner.

The second is its territorial existence. Intellectual property rights exist within the borders of the jurisdiction where they arise. Their potential effect outside their territory is the result of international agreements.

8–048 The third is the independence of intellectual property rights. A trade mark right in France for Apples for the "provision of communication services" is independent from the UK right for Apples for the "provision of communication services" irrespective of who is the owner of each right. The French right over Apples exists in France; the UK right over Apples exists in the United Kingdom.

For trade marks there is an additional independence dimension. A trade mark right in Germany for Apples for the "provision of communication services" might be independent from another German right covering Apples for "motor cars".

The fourth characteristic is its property nature. We cannot escape from the fact that intellectual property is property, whatever the justification behind its recognition as a property right. And in Europe property is considered to be a fundamental right that is left to the authority and control of Member States. Article 295 is clear; the Treaty shall in no way prejudice the rules of Member States governing the system of property ownership.

8–049 The combination of the four characteristics creates two fundamental problems for the free movement of goods. First, the owner of an intellectual property right in a Member State can stop the importation or marketing of products from other Member States that infringe its right. Secondly, a multi-jurisdictional owner of rights can, in principle, compartmentalise the European market into national markets. If the owner of the French Apples and the UK Apples is the same entity it can exercise its French right to stop the importation of products bearing the UK Apples.

How the law deals with this, is linked with the first characteristic of intellectual property mentioned above: its exclusionary essence. Intellectual property rights are not absolute rights. Each intellectual property law that creates a right has to settle at which stage in the chain of production and distribution a third party does not require a licence from the owner of the right in order to perform the prescribed acts. Or, from a positive perspective, for each law it "is necessary to decide which steps in the chain of production and distribution of goods require the licence of the right owner: manufacture, first sale of the manufacturer, subsequent sales and other

3. FREE MOVEMENT OF GOODS AND INTELLECTUAL PROPERTY

dealings, export and import, use"?[104] In most cases the intellectual property right is exhausted after the first sale of the product covered by the right by the right owner or with its consent.

But the problem remains in a world where products cross national borders. Where must the first sale occur in order for the right to be exhausted? Anywhere in the world or in the jurisdiction where the right exists? In the first case the law would opt for international exhaustion, in the second case for domestic exhaustion.

In the absence of complete European harmonisation in the field of intellectual property, that would involve the abolition of national rights and the adoption in their place of unitary European rights and, given the recognition by the Treaty of Member States' primacy regarding systems of property, free movement of goods rules have been adapted to accommodate intellectual property.

8–050

Article 30 includes intellectual property in the list of grounds that justify prohibitions on imports or exports, subject to the proviso that they do not constitute a means of arbitrary discrimination or a disguised restriction on trade between Member States.

Once again, the Court would have to interpret a provision balancing between positive and negative integration; between a general rule, a proviso, and a caveat to the proviso.

(1) The existence–exercise dichotomy

8–051

At first the Court tilted the balance aggressively towards the free movement of goods principle by making, in *Deutsche Grammophon*,[105] an apparently artificial distinction between the existence and the exercise of an intellectual property right. Deutsche Grammophon relied on its exclusive right of distribution in Germany, deriving from copyright, in order to stop in Germany the marketing of recordings that it had itself supplied to its French subsidiary.

The question referred from the German courts focused on the competition provisions of the Treaty.[106] However, the Court widened the scope of the question, linked competition with free movement, and exported the distinction between existence and exercise of a right from the field of competition to that of free movement of goods.

If the exercise of the right did not exhibit the elements of contract or concerted practice required by art.81 it was then necessary to consider its

---

[104] Cornish, *Intellectual Property* (London: Sweet and Maxwell, 1999), p.41.
[105] *Deutsche Grammophon v Metro* (78/70) [1971] E.C.R. 487
[106] Article 5 (now art.10) states that Member States must "abstain from any measure which could jeopardize the attainment of the objective of this Treaty", whereas art.85 (1) provides that "all agreements between undertakings, decisions by associations of undertakings and concerted practices which may affect trade between Member States and which have as their object or effect the prevention, restriction or distortion of competition within the common market".

8–052 compatibility with the other provisions of the Treaty, in particular those relating to the free movement of goods.

The attainment of a single market provided the legitimising background for linking competition with free movement. The creation of a single market necessitated both the free movement of goods within the borders of the Community and the establishment of rules ensuring that competition was not distorted.

Moving to art.30 the Court first accepted that a right related to copyright was covered by the term "industrial and commercial property", but added that it is:

> "clear from... Article [30] that, although the Treaty does not affect the existence of rights recognized by the legislation of a Member State with regard to industrial and commercial property, the exercise of such rights may nevertheless fall within the prohibitions laid down by the Treaty. Although it permits prohibitions or restrictions on the free movement of products, which are justified for the purpose of protecting industrial and commercial property, Article [30] only admits derogations from that freedom to the extent to which they are justified for the purpose of safeguarding rights which constitute the specific subject-matter of such property".[107]

Without examining the specific subject-matter of copyright the Court undermined the effectiveness of the right almost in its entirety. It juxtaposed its exclusive character with the essential purpose of the Treaty—the creation of a single market—and described as repugnant a prohibition that would legitimise the isolation of national markets on the ground that the distribution of the protected product occurred with the consent of the holder of the right, albeit in another Member State. The Court appeared to equate the exercise of the right with an arbitrary discrimination or disguised restriction on trade.

It concluded that:

> "it would be in conflict with the provisions prescribing the free movement of products within the common market for a manufacturer of sound recordings to exercise the exclusive right to distribute the protected Articles, conferred upon him by the legislation of a Member State, in such a way as to prohibit the sale in that state of products placed on the market by him or with his consent in another Member State solely because such distribution did not occur within the territory of the first Member State."[108]

---

[107] *Deutsche Grammophon* (78/70) [1971] E.C.R. 487, para.11.
[108] *Deutsche Grammophon* (78/70) [1971] E.C.R. 487, para.13.

3. FREE MOVEMENT OF GOODS AND INTELLECTUAL PROPERTY

(2) The specific subject-matter of the right   8–053

The Court transformed the dichotomy between existence and exercise into a more elaborate and nuanced principle in a patent case, *Centrafarm BV v Sterling Drug Inc.*[109]

Centrafarm bought a pharmaceutical product in the United Kingdom and imported it to The Netherlands. The product was protected in both jurisdictions by patents held by Sterling Drug, a subsidiary of which had been marketing the product in the United Kingdom. According to Dutch law Sterling Drug could block the marketing of the drug in The Netherlands by enforcing its patent. The Court of Justice had to decide whether this conformed to the free movement of goods rules. The Court found that it "is clear from ... Article [30] ... in particular its second sentence, as well as from the context, that whilst the Treaty does not affect the existence of rights recognized by the legislation of a Member State in matters of industrial and commercial property, yet the exercise of these rights may nevertheless ... be affected by the prohibitions of the Treaty".[110]

The Court applied the "derogation from a fundamental rule" analysis; exceptions are admitted "in fact only ... where such derogations are justified for the purpose of safeguarding rights which constitute the specific subject matter of this property".[111]

But then instead of clearly describing the specific subject-matter of a patent right, it described a broader objective of industrial property,[112] as "inter alia to ensure to the holder, so as to recompense the creative effort of the inventor, the exclusive right to utilise an invention with a view to manufacture and first putting into circulation of industrial products, either directly or by the grant of licences to third parties, as well as the right to oppose any infringement".[113]

(3) "Independent" rights   8–054

Deutsche Grammophon[114] involved the exercise of an intellectual property right in order to block the intra-Community cross border circulation of a product put on the Community market with the consent of the holder of the right.

The Court was more perceptive and permissive in cases where conflicting rights in two Member States arose independently from each other.

---

[109] *Centrafarm BV v Sterling Drug Inc* (15/74) [1974] E.C.R. 1147.
[110] *Centrafarm BV v Sterling Drug Inc* (15/74) [1974] E.C.R. 1147, para.7.
[111] *Centrafarm BV v Sterling Drug Inc* (15/74) [1974] E.C.R. 1147, para.8.
[112] Note the distinction between industrial and intellectual property. In its earlier case law the Court discriminated between rights according to their perceived importance. In *Sirena SRL v Eda SRL* (40/70) [1971] E.C.R. 69, a competition case, it appeared to place trade mark rights at the bottom of the hierarchy.
[113] *Centrafarm BV v Sterling Drug Inc* (15/74) [1974] E.C.R. 1147, para.9.
[114] *Deutsche Grammophon* (78/80) [1971] E.C.R. 487.

In *Terrapin*[115] the Court considered the exercise of trade mark rights. Terranova, a German company, was the holder of a number of "Terra" marks registered in Germany for building materials. Terrapin, an English company, that manufactured and marketed "Terrapin" prefabricated houses, had failed to overcome Terranova's opposition and obtain a registration in Germany. Following prolonged litigation between the parties the question referred to the Court of Justice sought to clarify whether the rights of a company in one Member State can be used to stop the marketing of products from another Member State that bear lawfully a distinguishing name which may be confused with the commercial name and trade mark that are protected in the first Member State, when there is no link between the two entities and their national trade mark rights arose "autonomously" and "independently" of one another.[116]

8–055   Advocate General Henri Mayras followed a cautious integrationist approach; in the absence of positive integration the crux of the case was identifying the forum and criteria for determining trade mark protection.[117] Following an analysis of the prevailing trade mark theories in Europe he conceded that it was for the Member States to delineate the scope of protection and for national courts to apply it, but the national discretion should still be within the limits imposed by the Treaty: the right could be enforced unless enforcement constituted arbitrary discrimination or a disguised restriction on trade between Member States. His reasoning was analogous to that regarding public policy expressed in *Van Duyn*.[118]

The Court concurred with the Advocate General but failed to discuss in any detail the specific subject-matter of trade mark rights. It repeated that the Treaty does not affect the existence of rights arising from national industrial and commercial property legislation but may restrict their exercise, inasmuch as "it provides an exception to one of the fundamental principles of the Common Market, Article [30] in fact admits exceptions to the free movement of goods only to the extent to which such exceptions are justified for the purpose of safeguarding rights which constitute the specific subject-matter of that property".[119]

According to the then current state of Community law "an industrial or commercial property right legally acquired in a member-State may legally

---

[115] *Terrapin (Overseas) Ltd* (119/75) [1976] E.C.R. 1039; [1967] 2 C.M.L.R. 482.
[116] The timeline of the dispute is indicative of the determination of the parties. Terrapin applied in 1961; litigation regarding the registration went on until 1967 when the Federal Patent Court prohibited registration. In 1968 Terranova brought infringement actions and Terrapin brought an action asking the court to order Terranova to stop objecting to the use of its trade name and trade marks. Appeals and cross appeals culminated in the reference to the Court of Justice dated October 31, 1975. Note that the two companies coexisted in other Member States.
[117] [1976] 2 C.M.L.R. 482 at 495.
[118] *Van Duyn v Home Office* (41/74) [1974] E.C.R. 1337.
[119] *Terrapin (Overseas) Ltd* (119/75) [1976] E.C.R. 103, para.5.

be used to prevent under the first sentence of Article [30] of the Treaty the import of products marketed under a name giving rise to confusion where the rights in question have been acquired by different and independent proprietors under different national laws".[120]

4. FREE MOVEMENT OF GOODS AND TRADE MARK LAW

(1) The early days—the essential function and the specific subject-matter of trade marks

8–056

The Court described the essential function of a trade mark and the specific subject-matter of a trade mark right in *Centrafarm v Winthrop*.[121] The essential function is to guarantee the identity of the origin of the marked product and the specific subject-matter of the right is that the owner of a trade mark has the exclusive right to use it when putting the marked product for the first time into circulation. Essentially, protection is against competitors selling products illegally bearing the mark.

Sterling Drug held registrations for Negram in the United Kingdom and The Netherlands; the Dutch registration was in the name of one of its subsidiaries, Winthrop. In both jurisdictions the drug was put on the market by subsidiaries of Sterling Drug. Centrafarm, once again, imported Negram to The Netherlands from the United Kingdom. Could Sterling Drug employ the Dutch registration and block the imports?

The Court referred to the general principle constructed in *Centrafarm v Sterling Drug*[122] and went on to adapt it to fit trade mark law:

"As regards trade marks, the specific object of commercial property is inter alia to ensure to the holder the exclusive right to utilise the mark for the first putting into circulation of a product, and to protect him thus against competitors who would take advantage of the position and reputation of the mark by selling goods improperly bearing the mark."[123]

It then acknowledged that the "existence" of national provisions "that the right of the trade mark holder is not exhausted by the marketing in another Member State of the product protected by the mark ... may constitute an obstacle to the free movement of goods"[124] and held that this would not be justified "when the product has been lawfully put, by the holder himself or with his consent, on the market of the Member State from which it is

8–057

---

[120] *Terrapin (Overseas) Ltd* (119/75) [1976] E.C.R. 103, para.7.
[121] *Centrafarm BV v Winthrop BV* (156/74) [1974] E.C.R. 1183.
[122] *Sterling Drug Inc* (15/74) [1974] E.C.R. 1147.
[123] *Winthrop BV* (16/74) [1974] E.C.R. 1183, para.8.
[124] *Winthrop BV* (16/74) [1974] E.C.R. 1183, para.9.

imported in such a way that there can be no question of abuse or infringement of the mark".[125] Because otherwise, the holder would be "enabled to partition the national markets and thus to maintain a restriction on the trade between the Member States without such a restriction being necessary for him to enjoy the substance of the exclusive right deriving from the mark".[126]

Consent had become the key word.

8–058 **(2) Developing the concept of consent**

The two *Hag* cases illustrate two developing trends in the trade mark jurisprudence of the Court of Justice.

First, they evidence the growing appreciation of what a trade mark does in the marketplace and the willingness of the Court to adapt protection accordingly and link consent much more accurately with the subject-matter and justification of the right. Secondly, they depict the continuum applied by the Court in its everlasting balancing between free movement of goods and the establishment of a single market on one side and trade mark rights on the other. These two trends persuaded the Court to take a sharp turning and depart from its previous rulings, a bold example of admitting rather than disguising change.

8–059 **(3) Hag I—a restrictive approach**

In *Hag I*[127] registrations of the trade mark "Hag" for decaffeinated coffee in Belgium, Germany, and Luxembourg were originally held by a German company, Hag AG. In 1927 the rights for Belgium and Luxembourg were transferred to a Belgian subsidiary. German property in Belgium was sequestered following the end of the Second World War, and the subsidiary, according to the Court's terminology, became independent as a result of an act by a public authority. Control passed to Belgian hands and the company was later sold to Van Zuyelen Frères who objected to the marketing of Hag coffee originating from the German Hag company on the basis of their trade mark rights.

The Court accepted that the competition provisions did not apply because there was no legal, financial, technical, or economic link. It turned to free movement of goods rules and considered the specific subject-matter of trade mark rights from a negative perspective, first, by noting that trade mark laws protect against "infringement on the part of persons who lack any legal title"[128] and, secondly, by highlighting that the exercise of trade mark rights contributes to the partitioning of markets given, in particular, that they are not subjected to time limitations.

---

[125] *Winthrop BV* (16/74) [1974] E.C.R. 1183, para.10.
[126] *Winthrop BV* (16/74) [1974] E.C.R. 1183, para.11.
[127] *Van Zuylen Frères v Hag AG* (192/73) [1974] E.C.R. 731.
[128] *Van Zuylen Frères* (192/73) [1974] E.C.R. 731, para.11.

4. FREE MOVEMENT OF GOODS AND TRADE MARK LAW

In two short paragraphs the Court managed to misleadingly limit the scope of the right and accentuate its territorial effect and life-cycle. The Court overlooked the fact that a legal title can be used to defend against infringement proceedings but does not always trump a trade mark right. And trade mark rights are not unlimited in terms of time; registration can be renewed perpetually but for specified periods of time and non-use renders a registration liable to cancellation proceedings.

Following its analysis the Court stressed that "one cannot allow the holder of a trade mark to rely upon the exclusiveness of a trade mark right—which may be the consequence of the territorial limitation of national legislations—with a view to prohibiting the marketing in a Member State of goods legally produced in another Member State under an identical trade mark having the same origin".[129]

8–060

It observed that both products were lawfully marketed and although "the indication of origin of a product covered by a trade mark is useful, information to consumers on this point may be ensured by means other than such as would affect the free movement of goods".[130]

It held that "to prohibit the marketing in a Member State of a product legally bearing a trade mark in another Member State, for the sole reason that an identical trade mark having the same origin exists in the first state, is incompatible with the provisions providing for free movement of goods within the common market."[131] The Court also held that if the holder of a trade mark in one Member State could market the marked product in another Member State the same applied to any third party who had duly acquired the product in the first Member State.

(4) Terrapin—consent and independent rights

8–061

As we have seen above in *Terrapin*[132] the Court reconsidered its approach without altering the principles because the "independence" of the trade marks allowed a more logical outcome.

In that case the Court restated that the:

"proprietor of an industrial or commercial property right protected by the law of a member-State cannot rely on that law to prevent the importation of a product which has lawfully been marketed in another member-State by the proprietor himself or with his consent. It is the same when the right relied on is the result of the subdivision, either by voluntary act or as a result of public constraint, of a trade mark right which originally belonged to one and the same proprietor. In these cases the basic

---

[129] *Van Zuylen Frères* (192/73) [1974] E.C.R. 731, para.12.
[130] *Van Zuylen Frères* (192/73) [1974] E.C.R. 731, para.14.
[131] *Van Zuylen Frères* (192/73) [1974] E.C.R. 731, para.15.
[132] *Terrapin (Overseas) Ltd* (119/75) [1976] E.C.R. 103.

function of the trade mark to guarantee to consumers that the product has the same origin is already undermined by the subdivision of the original right."[133]

Common origin appeared to prevail again over consent. Still, the Court was given the opportunity to reconsider its position on consent in two patent cases.

8–062 **(5) Merck v Stephar—lack of protection**

In *Merck v Stephar*[134] the pharmaceutical product in question was protected by a patent in Holland held by Merck. The same company marketed the product in Italy where at the time there was no patent protection available for pharmaceutical products. Stephar bought the product in Italy and imported it to Holland. Merck argued that there was a crucial difference from *Centrafarm*.[135] In Italy it did not have the opportunity to enjoy the benefits of exclusivity deriving from patent protection. This in turn meant that its patent rights in Holland had not been exhausted by the circulation of the product in Italy. The Court rejected this line of argument. Consent prevailed over the absence of protection:

> "It is for the proprietor of the patent to decide, in the light of all the circumstances, under what conditions he will market his product, including the possibility of marketing it in a Member State where the law does not provide patent protection for the product in question. If he decides to do so he must accept the consequences of his choice as regards the free movement of the product within the Common Market, which is a fundamental principle forming part of the legal and economic circumstances which must be taken into account by the proprietor of the patent in determining the manner in which his exclusive right will be exercised".[136]

8–063 **(6) Pharmon v Hoechst—compulsory licence**

Pharmon v Hoechst[137] provided a more elaborate factual scenario. Hoechst owned patents for a pharmaceutical product in Holland and the United Kingdom. In the United Kingdom another company, DDSA, obtained a compulsory licence to manufacture and market the product according to

---

[133] *Terrapin (Overseas) Ltd* (119/75) [1976] E.C.R. 103, para.6.
[134] *Merck v Stephar* (187/80) [1981] E.C.R. 2063; reconfirmed in *Merck & Co Ltd v Primecrown Ltd* (C-267/95 & C-268/95) [1996] E.C.R. I-6285.
[135] *Winthrop BV* (15/74) [1974] E.C.R. 1183.
[136] *Merck* (187/80) [1981] E.C.R. 2063, para.11.
[137] *Pharmon BV v Hoechst AG* (19/84) [1985] E.C.R. 2281.

4. FREE MOVEMENT OF GOODS AND TRADE MARK LAW

the law in the United Kingdom that also provided that the licence was non-assignable and that goods under the licence were not to be exported. DDSA breached the second condition and sold the pharmaceutical product to Pharmon, a Dutch company.

Surely, Hoechst argued, there was no consent in this case and its rights in Holland had not been exhausted.

Pharmon, on the other hand, supported that there was no difference between a compulsory and a voluntary licence; in both cases the licensor received remuneration.

The Court this time agreed with the patent holder: 8–064

> "It is necessary to point out that where . . . the competent authorities of a Member State grant a third party a compulsory licence which allows him to carry out manufacturing and marketing operations which the patentee would normally have the right to prevent, the patentee cannot be deemed to have consented to the operation of that third party."[138]

It went on to describe the core of the right:

> ". . . the substance of a patent lies essentially in according the inventor an exclusive right of first placing the product on the market so as to allow him to obtain the reward for his creative efforts. It is therefore necessary to allow the patent proprietor to prevent the importation and marketing of products manufactured under a compulsory licence in order to protect the substance of his exclusive rights under his patent."[139]

(7) Centrafarm v American Home Products—changing direction 8–065

In *Centrafarm v American Home Products Corp*[140] the Court again favoured the holder of the right. American Home Products was the holder of a number of national trade mark registrations for the same pharmaceutical product. Centrafarm imported the product to Holland under the mark Serenid, removed the trade mark affixed to the product and replaced it with the mark Seresta that Centrafarm had registered and been using in Holland.

The Court repeated that in "relation to trade-marks, the specific subject-matter is in particular the guarantee to the proprietor of the trade-mark that he has the exclusive right to use that trade-mark for the purpose of putting a product into circulation for the first time and therefore his protection against competitors wishing to take advantage of the status and reputation of the mark by selling products illegally bearing that trade-mark"[141] and

---

[138] *Pharmon BV v Hoechst AG* (19/84) [1985] E.C.R. 2281, para.25.
[139] *Pharmon BV* (19/84) [1985] E.C.R. 2281, para.26.
[140] *Centrafarm BV v American Home Products Corp* (3/78) [1978] E.C.R. 1823.
[141] *Centrafarm BV* (3/78) [1978] E.C.R. 1823, para.11.

that the essential function of a trade mark is "to guarantee the identity of the origin of the trade-marked product to the consumer or ultimate user".[142]

The Court then linked the essential function of a trade mark with the exclusivity of a trade mark right, finding that only the "proprietor may confer an identity upon the product by affixing the mark",[143] and the scope of the right, stating that the guarantee of origin would be jeopardised if it were "permissible for a third party to affix the mark to the product, even to an original product".[144]

8–066　　Accordingly, national laws could prevent third parties from "usurping the right"[145] to affix the trade mark or change the affixed trade mark irrespective of whether "the different parts of the production, bearing different marks, come from two different Member States"[146] and this would fall within the specific subject-matter of the trade mark.

The Court noted that choosing different marks for the same product in different Member States was lawful unless it constituted an attempt to partition national markets artificially. It would then be considered a disguised restriction on intra-Community trade.

8–067　**(8)　HAG II—the concept of consent, the role and function of trade marks**

This gradual change of approach culminated to an unequivocal u-turn by the Court that revisited the facts of *HAG I*[147]—this time Belgian coffee found its way into Germany—in HAG II.[148]

8–068　*(a)　The Opinion of the Advocate General*

Advocate General Jacobs considered the position adopted in *Terrapin*.[149] He accepted the logic behind the four principles developed by the Court: the existence/exercise dichotomy, the concept of the specific subject-matter, the principle of exhaustion, and the parallel application of competition rules. But he questioned the reasoning and justification behind the judicial structure of common origin raised by the Court in *HAG I*,[150] identifying four major flaws. First, the reliance on the second sentence of art.30 that was not relevant in the case; secondly, the failure to delineate the specific subject-matter of the right; thirdly, the unwarranted discrimination between trade marks and other intellectual property rights; and fourthly, the weakness of

---

[142] *Centrafarm BV v American Home Products Corp* (3/78) [1978] E.C.R. 1823, para.12.
[143] *American Home Products Corp* (3/78) [1978] E.C.R. 1823, para.13.
[144] *American Home Products Corp* (3/78) [1978] E.C.R. 1823, para.14.
[145] *American Home Products Corp* (3/78) [1978] E.C.R. 1823, para.15.
[146] *American Home Products Corp* (3/78) [1978] E.C.R. 1823, para.16.
[147] *Van Zuylen Frères v Hag AG* (192/73) [1974] E.C.R. 731.
[148] *SA CNL-SUCAL NV v Hag GF AG* (C-10/89) [1990] E.C.R. I-3711.
[149] *Terrapin (Overseas) Ltd* (119/75) [1976] E.C.R. 103.
[150] *Van Zuylen Frères* (192/73) [1974] E.C.R. 731, paras 6–15.

4. FREE MOVEMENT OF GOODS AND TRADE MARK LAW

the link between reasoning and conclusion, that the Court tried to hide behind the invention of common origin.

Terrapin[151] was:

"a valiant attempt to legitimise the doctrine of common origin, but the logic on which it is based is ... fallacious. It is true that the essential function of a trade mark is 'to guarantee to consumers that the product has the same origin'. But the word 'origin' in this context does not refer to the historical origin of the trade mark; it refers to the commercial origin of the goods. The consumer is not ... interested in the genealogy of trade marks; he is interested in knowing who made the goods that he purchases. The function of a trade mark is to signify to the consumer that all goods sold under that mark have been produced by, or under the control of, the same person and will, in all probability, be of uniform quality. That basic function of the 'HAG' mark has never been undermined in Germany, where it has, since its inception, been in the hands of one company. Nor had it been undermined in Belgium and Luxembourg until the Court's judgment in Hag I ... throughout its history (until 1974, that is) the mark had, in each territory, been in the exclusive ownership of a single person who had the power either to build up the goodwill associated with it by maintaining the quality of the product or to destroy that goodwill by allowing the quality to deteriorate. Once the owner of the mark is deprived of his exclusive right to its use, he loses the power to influence the goodwill associated with it and he loses the incentive to produce high-quality goods. Looking at matters from the consumer's point of view, the result of all this is thoroughly unsatisfactory because the trade mark no longer acts as a guarantee of origin. At best he is confused; at worst he is misled. In the circumstances, it is difficult not to conclude that the essential function of the mark is compromised, its specific subject-matter is affected and—most seriously of all—its very existence is jeopardised. But none of those consequences ensued from the fragmentation of the 'HAG' trade mark in 1944; they ensued from the Court's judgment in Hag I".[152]

Given the almost unprecedented call for a change in direction, A.G. Jacobs attempted to make it more palatable and justify the position of the Court in *HAG I* based on the lack of cases that would allow the Court to build fully worked out principle. Since that judgment however, the Court had developed both the concept of "specific subject matter"[153] and the principle of exhaustion.[154]

---

[151] *Terrapin (Overseas) Ltd* (119/75) [1976] E.C.R. 103.
[152] *SA CNL-SUCAL NV v Hag GF AG* (C-10/89) [1990] E.C.R. I-3711, point 24.
[153] See para.8–053, above.
[154] *Merck v Stephar* (187/80) [1981] E.C.R. 2063.

Note too that at the time of *HAG II* the Advocate General could also refer to positive integration in the form of a legislative text regulating trade marks. Article 5(1) of the Trade Mark Directive conferred on the proprietor the exclusive right to prevent use of a sign that is confusingly similar with the protected sign without its consent. The European legislator had accepted the principle that trade mark rights can block cross-border trade opting for a broad test involving confusion rather than total identity. How could this be reconciled with the outcome of *HAG I*? His analysis, however, accepted that the Directive did not have direct effect and was inconclusive regarding exhaustion of rights. The Court would have to reconsider its own jurisprudence rather than hide behind the intent of the legislator.

8–069   He went on to undermine the, summarily accepted by the Court in *HAG I*, claim that two signs could co-exist and be distinguished from each other on the same market aided by additional markings.

First, he highlighted the historical and doctrinal limitations of the common law doctrine of honest concurrent use that was developed by the courts in a bygone era of localised trade.

And secondly, he discussed in greater detail the actual difficulties of applying additional distinguishing matter. According to the Advocate General "everything must of course depend on the facts".[155] In practice, it would be more difficult to distinguish between identical marks. And the nature and style of additional matter should also be taken into account; a sticker placed next to the trade mark disclaiming any connection with another trader's products could be tolerated, a sticker obliterating and replacing the trade mark would create a negative impression for the product.[156]

8–070   *(b)   The judgment of the Court*

The Court responded to the plea of the Advocate General. It considered the essential function of a trade mark and the specific subject-matter of the right[157] and, linking the factual scenario with its judicial doctrine, noted that a situation such as that described by the national court, "the decisive fact is the absence of any element of consent, on the part of the owner of the trade mark right protected by national legislation, to the marketing in another member-State, under a mark which is identical or may cause confusion, of a similar product manufactured and marketed by an enterprise which has no tie of legal or economic dependence with that owner".[158]

The owner of the right should be allowed to exercise the "option under national law to prevent the importation of the similar product under a name

---

[155] Point 43 of the Opinion of A.G. Jacobs.
[156] See *Frits Loendersloot* (C-349/95) [1997] E.C.R. I-6227, see paras 8–170 and following, below.
[157] See paras 8–056 and following, above.
[158] *Hag II*, para.15.

4. FREE MOVEMENT OF GOODS AND TRADE MARK LAW

likely to be confused with his own mark"[159] irrespective of whether the offending mark originally belonged to the same owner but changed hands as a result of expropriation. The Court admitted that from the date of expropriation the two marks functioned independently from each other as guarantees of distinct sources in spite of their common origin.

(9) Ideal Standard—voluntary assignment 8–071

The Court went further and considered the result of a voluntary assignment in *Ideal Standard*.[160] In this case a parent company held, through its subsidiaries, registrations of Ideal Standard covering sanitary fittings and heating equipment in France and Germany. In the process of insolvency proceedings the French subsidiary sold the heating equipment part of the business together with the trade mark registration for heating equipment to another French company. The German subsidiary brought infringement proceedings against the new proprietor for marketing in Germany Ideal Standard products relying on its registration for sanitary fittings.

The Court repeated its finding in *Deutsche Renault*[161] that application of national law, in that case the provision for establishing confusion, remained in the jurisdiction of the national court. It had added however that the assessment of similarity should not lead to arbitrary discriminations or disguised restrictions.

Regarding the territorial split of the rights it accepted the submission that trade mark rights are not only territorial but also independent of each other,[162] and that the French registration could be assigned on its own, without the related business or goodwill, as provided by French law but also without the parallel German registration.[163]

As a result the Court looked at the effect of the transfer of the trade mark. 8–072

If, despite the transfer, control remains in the hands of a single body—the group of companies in the case of products put into circulation by a subsidiary, the manufacturer in the case of products marketed by the distributor, or the licensor in the case of products marketed by a licensee—the origin of the product is the same and the exercise of national trade mark rights would be against the free movement provisions of the Treaty.

---

[159] *Hag II*, para.16.
[160] *IHT Internationale Heiztechnik GmbH and Uwe Danzinger v Ideal-Standard GmbH and Wabco Standard GmbH* (C-9/93) [1994] E.C.R. I-2789.
[161] *Deutsche Renault AG v AUDI AG* (C-317/91) [1993] E.C.R. I-6227.
[162] It referred to art.6(3) of the Paris Convention providing that: "A mark duly registered in a country of the Union shall be regarded as independent of marks registered in other countries of the Union".
[163] To back up its position the Court referred to art.6quater of the Paris Convention, providing that when according to national law assignment of the relevant goodwill or business is required whenever a trade mark is assigned it suffices to assign the national portion of such business or goodwill, and to art.9ter of the Madrid Agreement providing that partial, in terms of jurisdictional coverage, assignment of an international registration is possible.

8–073 The Court added that the possibility of control by a single body would suffice; for example, a national law allowing the licensor to oppose the importation of products marketed by the licensee on the basis of their quality would be considered contrary to arts 28 and 30; "if the licensor tolerates the manufacture of poor quality products, despite having contractual means of preventing it, he must bear the responsibility".[164]

Unitary control was contrasted with the effect of a transfer to an undertaking which has no economic link with the original holder of the right; "a contract of assignment by itself, that is in the absence of any economic link, does not give the assignor any means of controlling the quality of products which are marketed by the assignee and to which the latter has affixed the trade mark".[165]

In this case the Court felt that the assignor could exercise its national rights in order to stop the importation of products marketed by the assignee.

It rejected the submission, by the Commission, that the assignment implied consent by the assignor and juxtaposed between consent that is implicit in an assignment and consent that leads to the exhaustion of a right. The latter went together with the ability to determine the products to which the trade mark may be affixed in the exporting State and to control their quality.

8–074 The Court followed the logic of *Hag II*[166] and reiterated that trade mark rights are territorial and accordingly the function of a trade mark has to be assessed by reference to the respective territory, and decided that the outcome should be the same irrespective of whether the split in ownership was the result of a voluntary or a mandatory transfer. The Court took into account the development of the Community Trade Mark regime highlighting the statement in the fifth recital in the preamble to the Community Trade Mark Regulation that the "the Community law relating to trade marks ... does not replace the laws of the Member States on trade marks".[167]

Further, art.8 empowered the proprietor of an earlier national right with the right to oppose subsequent conflicting Community Trade Mark applications. This combination meant that the Regulation did not render void assignments of national trade mark rights.

The Court stressed that such a measure could only be introduced by the legislature through the adoption of a Directive, not through case law. It "would have the effect of imposing on the States a positive obligation, namely to embody in their laws a rule rendering void assignments of national trade marks made for part only of the Community".[168]

---

[164] *Ideal Standard*, para.38.
[165] *Ideal Standard*, para.41.
[166] *SA CNL-SUCAL NV v Hag GF AG* (C-10/89) [1990] E.C.R. I-3711.
[167] Note that the Court chose to describe the relationship as one where the "Community trade mark is merely superimposed on the national rights", para.56, rather than one where they exist in parallel.
[168] *Ideal Standard*, para.57.

4. FREE MOVEMENT OF GOODS AND TRADE MARK LAW

It also underlined that competition law could have a role to play in the case of assignments intending to enable a market sharing agreement. However, art.81 EC should not be applied mechanically to every assignment. "Before a trade-mark assignment can be treated as giving effect to an agreement prohibited under art.[81], it is necessary to analyse the context, the commitments underlying the assignment, the intention of the parties and the consideration for the assignment."[169]

(10) Repackaging and parallel imports—Hoffmann-La Roche— setting the principles 8–075

In *Hoffmann-La Roche*[170] the Court set the foundations of its repackaging case law.

The German subsidiary of Hoffmann-La Roche had been marketing Valium Roche (the brand name for Diazepam, a psychopharmacological drug) in Germany in small packets of 20 or 50 tablets; for hospital use five small packets were combined in new packaging containing 100 or 250 tablets. The trade mark Valium was registered in the name of another Hoffmann-La Roche company and its use licensed to the German subsidiary. In the United Kingdom the local subsidiary marketed Valium in packages of 100 or 500 tablets, at a lower price than in Germany.

The German subsidiary of Centrafarm bought Valium Roche tablets from its Dutch parent company, which, in turn, had purchased them in the United Kingdom and repackaged them in The Netherlands in batches of 1,000 tablets, and started marketing them in Germany. On the new packaging appeared the Valium and Roche signs, in a slightly different format from that used in the United Kingdom and Germany, the registration number of the entry on the German register for pharmaceutical products, the name Centrafarm, and the words "Marketed by Centrafarm GmbH, 4444 Bentheim-1, Telephone: 05922–2525". In each packet there was an information leaflet in German, signed Hoffmann-La Roche, that repeated the notice that the medicinal preparation was marketed by Centrafarm. Centrafarm also intended to repackage the tablets in smaller packets for sale to individuals.

Note that Centrafarm was also manufacturing its own Diazepam 8–076 preparation.

Hoffmann-La Roche considered this to constitute trade mark infringement. It obtained an interim injunction and the case reached the Landgericht (District Court) Freiburg that referred the following questions to the Court of Justice:

"1. Is the person entitled to a trade mark right protected for his benefit both in member-State A and in member-State B empowered under Article [30]

---

[169] *Ideal Standard*, para.59.
[170] *Hoffmann-La Roche & Co AG and Hoffmann-La Roche AG* (102/77) [1978] E.C.R. 1139.

of the EEC Treaty, in reliance on this right, to prevent a parallel importer from buying from the proprietor of the mark or with his consent in member-State A of the Community medicinal preparations which have been put on the market with his trade mark lawfully affixed thereto and packaged under this trade mark, from providing them with new packaging, affixing to such packaging the proprietor's trade mark and importing the preparations distinguished in this manner into member-State B?"[171]

"2. Is the proprietor of the trade mark entitled to do this or does he thereby infringe provisions of the EEC Treaty—in particular those contained in Article [81] thereof—even if he acquires a dominant position within the market in member-State B with regard to the medicinal preparation in question, when prohibition on imports of a repacked product to which the proprietor's trade mark has been affixed has in actual fact a restrictive effect on the market, because different sizes of packages are used in countries A and B and because the importation of the product in another manner has not yet in fact made any appreciable progress on the market, and when the actual effect of the prohibition is that between the member-States there is maintained a substantial—in certain circumstances disproportionate—price differential, without its being possible to prove that the owner of the mark is using the prohibition solely or mainly to maintain this price differential?"[172]

8-077   (a)   *The Opinion of the Advocate General*

Advocate General Capotorti acknowledged that the balance attempted by art.30 was a delicate and difficult exercise and that the Court had been trying to contribute to the gradual definition of the limits to the protection of individual claims based on trade mark rights; limits that reflected the constraints imposed by Community law on national systems of protection that had been developed independently and preceded the Community legal order.

He digested the existing case law of the Court of Justice[173] by describing the basic concept, the Treaty did not prejudice the existence of the rights conferred, but free movement of goods rules impinged on their exercise. The derogation of art.30 applied only when it was essential to the safeguarding of rights which constituted the specific subject-matter of the mark that was in turn linked with its essential function to guarantee to consumers the identity of the origin of the product.

The peculiarity of this case, however, was the repackaging of the product. Hoffmann-La Roche would not object to the importation of Valium from the

---

[171] *Hoffmann-La Roche*, para.5.
[172] *Hoffmann-La Roche*, para.15.
[173] Citing *Deutsche Grammophon v Metro* (78/70) [1971] E.C.R. 487; *Van Zuylen Frères AG* (192/73) [1974] E.C.R. 731; *Sterling Drug* (15/74) [1974] E.C.R. 1147; *Centrafarm BV v Winthrop BV* (16/74) [1974] E.C.R. 1183; and *Terrapin (Overseas) Ltd* (119/75) [1976] E.C.R. 1039.

4. FREE MOVEMENT OF GOODS AND TRADE MARK LAW

United Kingdom in their original packaging. So according to the principles already developed by the Court what needed to be established in this case was whether there was a necessary connection between the essential function of the mark and the right that German law appeared to grant to Hoffmann-La Roche in Germany to prevent the marketing of the imported tablets on the ground that the importer had, without authorisation, altered their packaging and reapplied the trade mark.

He found that the injunction sought by the trade mark proprietor would restrict the free movement of the tablets within the Community. Before considering whether the barrier could be justified he rejected two preliminary arguments raised by Hoffmann-La Roche, both linked with consumer protection and perception.

(i) Public health and the guarantee of quality function. First, he rejected the argument that the barrier could be justified on the basis of consumer and public health protection. These aims should be obtained in their own proper field, according to the relevant legislation, not by the means of trade mark rights.[174]

8–078

The second had to do with consumer expectations regarding specific and constant product quality consumer expectations based on trade marks. Seeking support in the views of two prominent academics in this field, Beier and Vanzetti, he concluded that trade mark law protected only the guarantee of origin function, indeed this principle constituted the common element of all the Member States' national systems of protection.[175] Consumer expectations were to be protected under unfair competition and criminal laws.

And in any case, the ancillary functions would face the same limitations with those imposed in relation to the primary function.

(ii) The position in the Member States. Turning to how Member States would have dealt with unauthorised alterations in the packaging of a product he found that in most cases the trade mark proprietor would be entitled to object; however this did not appear to be unconditional but based on confusion as to origin. He remarked that in the United Kingdom, Ireland, and Denmark chemists could take the product out of its packaging and supply it to the consumer in their own packets. In the Benelux there was case law that a finding of "passing off" would require the alteration of the product itself rather than its packaging. And the actual position in German law had been disputed by the Commission and Hoffmann-La Roche.

8–079

(iii) The scope of article 30. But what should be truly decisive was the scope of art.30 that was linked with the essential function of a trade mark.

8–080

---

[174] *Winthrop BV* (16/74) [1974] E.C.R. 1183.
[175] Beier, "La Territorialité du Droit des Marques et des Echanges Internationaux" [1971] Journal du Droit International 19; and Vanzetti, "La Funzione E la Natura Giuridica del Marchio" [1961] I Rivista del Diritto Commerciale 16.

In general the substitution of packaging could affect the identification of origin, even when the trade mark had been re-affixed. The circumstances of each case did matter, for example affixing the trade mark on the inner packaging or the product itself would reduce the risk of confusion. However, in order to eliminate all such risks it would be necessary to eliminate any interference with the packaging.

This, he found:

> "would entail sanctioning restrictions on the movement of goods which seem incommensurate with the objective pursued by Article [30] of the Treaty, that is to protect the essential function of the trade mark. Since, however, the restrictions on the free movement of goods permitted under that provision, which is a derogatory and exceptional provision, must be contained within the limits strictly necessary for that objective, I consider that it is incompatible with Community law to concede a general power to the proprietor of the mark to prohibit the repackaging of the product even where the attainment of the essential objective of the mark is not in fact jeopardised."[176]

The only concession he was willing to make was in respect of cases that "having regard to the type of product, any change in the container thereof entails an actual risk of a modification of the essential characteristics of the product itself such as to affect its identity".[177]

The market conditions, for example price discrepancies between Member States and methods of sale, should also be taken into account as counterbalancing factors to a general risk of confusion.

8–081 **(iv) Product quality and liability considerations.** Another point raised by Hoffmann-La Roche had to do with the responsibility of the trade mark proprietor for the quality of the product; it should be able to check both the manufacture and packaging of the product. More importantly, once the product was repackaged it should not be answerable for the quality of the product.

The Advocate General noted that the party altering the quality of the product should carry the liability burden. He recognised, however, that this was a legitimate concern and suggested that an obligation should be imposed on the importer to indicate on the new packaging that the repackaging was carried out by the importer.

8–082 **(v) Dominance, trade mark rights and competition.** Advocate General Capotorti underlined that following his submissions in respect of the first question would render the issues raised in the second question superfluous. Still, he proposed some guidelines.

---

[176] Point 8 of the Opinion of A.G. Capotorti.
[177] Point 8 of the Opinion of A.G. Capotorti.

4. FREE MOVEMENT OF GOODS AND TRADE MARK LAW

First, he suggested that the exercise of trade mark rights should not in itself constitute an abuse under art.82 EC. "The exercise of a trade mark within the limits which are necessary to protect its essential function, as has been set out above, cannot be precluded for a given undertaking merely because it occupies a dominant position."[178]

However, should the exercise of the rights exceed the limits set by art.30 then art.82 might also be infringed:

"an endeavour to rely on the trade mark right, with regard to a product of the kind in question in the present proceedings, in order to achieve a general and complete prohibition on imports solely on the basis of an alteration in the packaging is not justified under Aricle [30]. Such unjustified exercise of a trade mark right by an undertaking occupying a dominant position may accordingly, together with other factors, constitute an infringement of Article [82] of the Treaty if it is instrumental in allowing that undertaking to exploit the market in which it operates".[179]

He believed that the situation described in the second question referred to the Court would probably fall under art.82, since the abuse should not consist merely in restraining competition by the prevention of parallel imports on the basis of trade mark rights. It should be seen in the context of a more complex pattern of behaviour, with the price discrepancy being a decisive factor.

(b) The judgment of the Court

8–083

(i) The first question—repackaging and free movement. The Court repeated that the Treaty did not affect the existence of the rights, but the exercise of those rights might be restricted by the prohibitions contained in the Treaty, and that the exceptions to the fundamental principles should be tolerated only to the extent they were justified for the purpose of safeguarding the rights which constituted the specific subject-matter of that property:

"In relation to trade marks, the specific subject-matter is in particular to guarantee to the proprietor of the trade mark that he has the exclusive right to use that trade mark for the purpose of putting a product into circulation for the first time and therefore to protect him against competitors wishing to take advantage of the status and reputation of the trade mark by selling products illegally bearing that trade mark."[180]

The question had to be answered keeping in mind the "essential function of the trade mark, which is to guarantee the identity of the origin of the

---

[178] Point 11 of the Opinion of A.G. Capotorti.
[179] Point 11 of the Opinion of A.G. Capotorti.
[180] *Hoffmann-La Roche*, para.7.

trade-marked product to the consumer or ultimate user, by enabling him without any possibility of confusion to distinguish that product from products which have another origin".[181]

8–084 **(ii) Repackaging and the guarantee of origin.** The Court appeared at this stage to take a stance favouring trade mark owners by acknowledging that the guarantee of origin meant that the consumer or ultimate user could be certain that the trade marked product had not been subject to unauthorised interference by a third party at a previous stage of marketing. Preventing this should form part of the specific subject-matter of the right. But, the balance shifted once again through the notion of a "disguised restriction on trade" between Member States.

Putting a product on the European market in various packages and employing trade mark rights to prevent repackaging even if it were done in a way that would not affect the identification of origin and the original condition of the product would be such a restriction.

8–085 **(iii) Affecting the original condition of the product.** So the critical question for the Court was whether the repackaging was capable of affecting the original condition of the product.

This would depend on the circumstances of the case. The Court underlined that the nature of the product and the method of repackaging should be the two decisive factors.

There could be cases where the original condition of the product would not be affected. For instance where the manufacturer marketed the product in double packaging and the repackaging affected only the external packaging, leaving the internal packaging intact.

8–086 **(iv) The general rule—the first repackaging condition.**

"Where the essential function of the trade mark to guarantee the origin of the product is thus protected, the exercise of his rights by the proprietor of the trade mark in order to fetter the free movement of goods between member-States may constitute a disguised restriction within the meaning of the second sentence of Article [30] of the Treaty if it is established that the use of the trade mark right by the proprietor, having regard to the marketing system which he has adopted, will contribute to the artificial partitioning of the markets between member-States."[182]

8–087 **(v) The limitations to the general rule—three additional conditions.** The Court accepted that the above finding amounted to giving to the importer a certain licence that in normal circumstances would be reserved for the proprietor.

---

[181] *Hoffmann-La Roche*, para.7.
[182] *Hoffmann-La Roche*, para.10.

5. FREE MOVEMENT OF GOODS AND THE NEW TRADE MARK REGIME

Accordingly it should be, first, shown by the importer that the repackaging could not adversely affect the original condition of the product.

Secondly, the importer should give prior notice to the trade mark proprietor. Note that this was viewed as a measure protecting consumers for being misled, although the Court also stated that this would be in the proprietor's interest.[183]

Thirdly, the importer should indicate on the new packaging that the product had been repackaged by the importer.

(vi) The second question—article 30 and competition. The Court dealt with the second question in a summary way, by observing that to the extent to which the exercise of a trade mark right was lawful in accordance with art.30, the exercise of trade mark rights would not be contrary to art.82 on the sole ground that it was the act of an undertaking occupying a dominant position on the market if the trade mark right had not been used as an instrument for the abuse of such a position.

8–088

5. FREE MOVEMENT OF GOODS AND THE NEW TRADE MARK REGIME

(1) Bristol Myers Squibb and the related cases—article 7 of the Directive and the free movement of goods rules—the fifth repackaging condition

8–089

In *Bristol Myers Squibb*[184] the Court looked at repackaging, for the first time after the introduction of the Directive. Advocate General Jacobs delivered a joint Opinion covering a number of cases referred to the Court from Danish and German courts. The Court joined the cases in two judgments.

(a) The Danish cases

8–090

There were three references from Denmark; the first two[185] were references from the So-og Handelsret (Commercial Court), Copenhagen, the third[186] was a reference from the Hojesteret (Supreme Court).

In the first case[187] Paranova, an importer and distributor of pharmaceutical products, imported a number of Bristol Myers Squibb products that it

---

[183] Compare with the Opinion of A.G. Jacobs in *Frits Loendersloot v George Ballantine & Son* (C-349/95) [1997] E.C.R. I-6227, see paras 8–170 and following, below.
[184] *Bristol Myers Squibb v Paranova A/S* (C-427/93) and *CH Boehringer Sohn, Boehringer Ingelheim KG and Boehringer Ingelheim A/S v Paranova A/S* (C-429/93) and *Bayer Aktiengesellschaft and Bayer Danmark A/S v Paranova A/S* (C-436/93) [1996] E.C.R. I-3457.
[185] C-427/93 and C-429/93.
[186] C-436/93.
[187] C-427/93.

had purchased in Member States other than Denmark, repackaged them, and marketed them in Denmark. The repackaging involved the following: repackaging of blisters in new external packaging, bearing the "Bristol Myers Squibb" yellow and green colours, application of the names under which the product were sold in Denmark but without the ® symbol, and a statement indicating that the goods were manufactured by Bristol Myers Squibb but imported and repackaged by Paranova; removal of phials from their original padding, application of a label bearing the name of the product without the ® symbol and a similar statement, the phials were then put back into their padding and packed in new external packaging bearing the Bristol Myers Squibb colours and trade marks and the same importation information, the original instructions leaflet was removed and a Danish version with the Bristol Myers Squibb trade marks inserted; removal of flasks from their outer packaging, placement of a similar label as above, repackaging in new external packaging as above but this time together with a spray not manufactured by Bristol Myers Squibb.

Bristol Myers Squibb brought trade mark infringement proceedings and the So-og Handelsret referred the following questions to the Court:

"1. Is Article 7(1) of Council Directive 89/104 to approximate the laws of the Member States relating to trade marks to be interpreted as meaning that unless Article 7(2) applies the proprietor of a trade mark who has put goods into circulation in a Member State under a trade mark cannot prevent a third party from importing the goods into another Member State in order to market the goods there under the same trade mark even if that third party has attached to the inner packaging of the goods labels on which the trade mark is affixed and substituted for the original outer packaging a new packaging on which the trade mark is affixed?

It is stressed that the question does not seek a ruling on cases in which the second sentence of Article [30] of the Treaty might justify repackaging and reaffixing a mark in accordance with the principles set out in Case 102/77 but only on whether Article 7(1) is to be construed as meaning that apart from laying down the general principle of the exhaustion of trade mark rights within the European Community it also entails a general limitation on the rights otherwise conferred on trade mark proprietors regarding use of the trade mark for which the trade mark proprietor has not given his consent.

2. If the answer to Question 1 is affirmative, does Article 7(2) of Directive 89/104, after implementation, entail that the case law of the Court of Justice as set out in Case 102/77 and developed subsequently comes to be of subsidiary importance since the right to repackage will primarily fall to be determined in application of national provisions corresponding to Article 7(2) of the said Directive?

3. On the premise that Article 7(1) of the said Directive is intended to permit parallel importers to reaffix trade marks, must the fact that goods

5. FREE MOVEMENT OF GOODS AND THE NEW TRADE MARK REGIME

are repackaged be regarded as 'legitimate reasons' for the purposes of Article 7(2)?

In particular, does it make any difference that it is only the outer packaging that has been repackaged and remarked but not the inner packaging?

4. With regard to the derogating provision in the second sentence of Article 36 of the Treaty and in the light of the judgment of the Court of Justice in Case 102/77, what may be described as a partitioning of the market for a specific product and, in particular, what distinguishing factors are to be taken into account in assessing whether an artificial partitioning of markets between the Member States can be said to exist for a specific product in connection with the sales system applied by the trade mark proprietor?"[188]

8–091 In the second case[189] Paranova bought products produced by Boehringer in a Member State other than Denmark, imported, repackaged, and marketed them in Denmark. On the new packaging Boehringer was indicated as the producer and included an informational leaflet in Danish. Note that in this case Paranova had registered the pharmaceutical products with the relevant authorisation authorities using the Boehringer names.

The So-og Handelsret referred to the Court two questions with the same wording as the first two questions indicated above.[190]

The third case[191] involved Bayer products; Paranova followed similar repackaging procedures. One additional complication was that, according to Bayer, a warning to keep the product away from the light was added, following the manufacturer's notification to Paranova. Paranova disputed whether the original packaging bore a warning to that effect.

8–092 The case reached the Hojesteret, that referred the following questions to the Court:

"1. Must the possibility for a trade mark proprietor to oppose a parallel importer's action in replacing wholly or in part the original packaging of his goods by new packaging on which the parallel importer reaffixes the trade mark be determined under national trade mark law only in conjunction with Article 7(1) and (2) of the First Council Directive (89/104) to approximate the laws of the Member States relating to trade marks or also in conjunction with the first and second sentences of Article [30] E.C.?

2. In assessing the legal steps that may be taken by the trade mark proprietor, is it significant whether there may be said to exist an 'artificial

---

[188] Reproduced in Point 15.
[189] C-429/93.
[190] See fn.188 above and accompanying text.
[191] C-436/93.

partitioning of the markets for trade in the goods in question? If so, the Court is asked to specify what is the significance as regards such steps.

3. If Question 2 is answered in the affirmative, is it significant for the rights of the trade mark proprietor whether he had the intention to create or exploit such an artificial partitioning of the markets? If so, the Court is asked to specify what is the significance as regards those rights.

4. In connection with Question 3, must the parallel importer show or else establish a probability that there was intent or must the trade mark proprietor show or establish a probability that there was no intent?

5. Is the reaffixing of the trade mark, as described in Question 1, in itself sufficient 'legitimate reason' within the meaning of Article 7 of the Directive or must the trade mark proprietor in addition show further circumstances, for example that the condition of the goods is changed or impaired when they are put on the market by the parallel importer?"[192]

8–093 *(b) The German cases*

In the first of three cases joined by the Court[193] Beiersdorf manufactured a pharmaceutical product under a licence granted by a French company that was the proprietor of the trade mark in Germany. In France the product was marketed in packages containing two blister strips with 14 pills each, in order to comply with national legislation. At the back of the blister appeared the days of the week in French, one for each pill. In Germany the standard sizes were packets of 50 or 100 pills. Eurim-Pharm, the parallel importer bought the product in France, cut some strips in order to achieve the number 50 or 100 (inevitably interrupting the series of week days that appeared at the back), and repackaged them in a new box, some strips still in their own original box and others outside their original box. The new packaging had a small hole from which the original trade mark was visible as it appeared on one of the original packets. On the outer new packaging there was information about the active ingredients and a statement that the goods have been imported, packed and distributed by Eurim-Pharm.

Beiersdorf, authorised by the French company, started infringement proceedings. The case reached the Bundesgerichstshof that referred the following questions to the Court:

"1. Is the proprietor of an internationally registered trade mark (I R mark) having effect in Member State A entitled under Article [30] E.C., in reliance upon the trade mark, to prevent an importer from buying medicinal products which have been marketed under the trade mark in Member State B by the proprietor of the trade mark and which require a

---

[192] Reproduced in Point 21.
[193] *Eurim-Pharm Arzneimittel GmbH v Beiersdorf AG* (C-71/94), *Boehringer Ingelheim KG* (C-72/94) and *Farmitalia Carlo Erba GmbH* (C-73/94) [1996] E.C.R. I-3603.

5. FREE MOVEMENT OF GOODS AND THE NEW TRADE MARK REGIME

prescription in Member State A, from repackaging them in conformity with the prescribing practices of medical practitioners in Member State A, which are based on a recommendation by prominent organisations (including those representing the pharmaceutical industry) on therapeutically desirable sizes and which differ from the packaging sizes prescribed by statute in Member State B, and from marketing them in Member State A in external packaging styled by the importer, if such packaging contains an original packet with original blister strips from Member State B and a number of additional blister strips which have been cut up and the new packaging has a window through which the I R mark on the original packaging is visible and displays a reference to the packaging and marketing by the importer but no reference to the manufacturer? Is it of relevance for the purposes of the answer to the question that information printed on the back of the original blister strip refers (in, for Member State A, a foreign language) to the days of the week for a 14-day period, which when the blister is cut becomes incomplete?

2. Is it sufficient, for the purpose of establishing a disguised restriction on trade between Member States within the meaning of Article [30] E.C., that the use of the national trade mark in conjunction with the marketing system adopted by the proprietor of the I R mark objectively leads to a partitioning of the markets between Member States, or is it necessary for that purpose to show that the proprietor of the I R mark exercises his trade-mark right in conjunction with the marketing system which he employs with the object of bringing about an artificial partitioning of the markets?"[194]

The second case[195] involved Boehringer products marketed in Germany in boxes of 20, 50, or 100 capsules, in blister strips of 10, and in France in boxes of 30 capsules, each containing three blister strips of 10. Eurim-Pharm placed in new outer packaging original French boxes—adding stickers with information about the active ingredients and the importer details—and made the numbers up to 50 or 100 by adding blister strips that were taken out from their original French packaging. It also included a leaflet with information in German. The packaging had a hole revealing the trade mark that was originally applied on one of the French packets.

The Bundesgerichtshof referred two questions to the Court:

"1. Is the proprietor of an internationally registered trade mark (I R mark) having effect in Member State A entitled under Article [30] E.C., in reliance upon the trade mark, to prevent an importer from buying medicinal products which have been marketed under the trade mark in

---

[194] Reproduced in Point 25 of the opinion of A.G.
[195] Case C-72/94.

Member State B by the proprietor of the trade mark and which require a prescription in Member State A, from repackaging them in conformity with the prescribing practices of medical practitioners in Member State A, which are based on a recommendation by prominent organisations (including those representing the pharmaceutical industry) and which differ from the packaging sizes prescribed by statute in Member State B, and from marketing them in Member State A in external packaging styled by the importer, if such packaging contains an original packet with original blister strips from Member State B and a number of additional blister strips which have been cut up and if the new packaging has a window through which the I R mark on the original packaging is visible and displays a reference to the packaging and marketing by the importer but no reference to the manufacturer?"[196]

8–094 The second question was identical to the second question of the first reference reproduced above.[197]

In the third case[198] Eurim-Pharm imported Farmitalia products from Portugal and marketed them repackaging them in packets of 50 or 100 capsules. Similarly with above the new packets contained some original packets and loose strips to make up the numbers. The difference was that at the back of each strip it added a sticker with the word "forte" so that the name would correspond with that used in Germany, "Sermion forte". The word "forte" was printed underneath the hole from which one could see the trade mark as it appeared on the original packet. In the case of imports from Spain, where the product was marketed in packets of 45 capsules, Eurim-Pharm added to the packet a cut strip and placed on the packet a sticker with information about the product and the details of the importer.

The Bundesgereichtshof referred two questions to the Court, the second being identical with the second question reproduced above[199]:

"1. Is the proprietor of an internationally registered trade mark (I R mark) having effect in Member State A entitled under Article [30] E.C., in reliance upon the trade mark, to prevent an importer from buying medicinal products which have been marketed under the trade mark in Member State B by an undertaking belonging to the same group as the proprietor of the trade mark and which require a prescription in Member State A, from repackaging them in conformity with the prescribing practices of medicinal practitioners prevailing in Member State A, which are based on a recommendation by prominent organisations (including those representing the pharmaceutical industry) on therapeutically

---

[196] Reproduced in point 28. The A.G. noted that the reference to severed strips was probably a clerical error.
[197] See para.18–093.
[198] Case C-73/94.
[199] See para.8–093, fn.194, above and accompanying text.

5. FREE MOVEMENT OF GOODS AND THE NEW TRADE MARK REGIME

desirable sizes and which differ from the standard sizes in Member State B and:

(a) from marketing them in Member State A in external packaging styled by the importer, if such packaging contains an original packet with original blister strips from Member State B and a number of additional original blister strips and the new packaging has a window through which the trade mark on the original packet is visible and displays a reference to the repackaging and marketing by the importer but no reference to the manufacturer, or

(b) from marketing them in Member State A in the original trade-marked packaging from Member State B if it is supplemented by the importer with stickers showing his firm's name and further particulars (batch number, use-by date, registration number, etc.) and with a strip containing five capsules cut from an original blister strip?"[200]

The third German case[201] involved the importation of Rhône-Poulenc products to Germany by MPA. The blister strips were removed from their original packaging and put into new packaging. On the sides of the new packet there was information about the manufacturer, the importer, and the product whereas in the packet itself it introduced a leaflet with information in German.

8–095

The Oberlandesgericht Köln referred two questions to the Court, the first being identical with the second question reproduced above[202]:

"2. Is there a presumption of a 'disguised restriction on trade between Member States' within the meaning of the second sentence of Article [30] E.C. where the proprietor of a trade mark protected in Member States A and B relies on its national trade mark in order to prevent an importer from buying medicinal products which have been marketed under the trade mark in Member State B by an undertaking belonging to the same group as the proprietor of the trade mark and which are available only on prescription in Member State A, from repackaging them and marketing them in Member State A in external packaging which the importer designs and to which he affixes the trade mark without the consent of the proprietor of the mark, if the exercise of the trade mark right results in a partitioning of the markets between the Member States, if it is demonstrated that the repackaging cannot impair the original condition of the product and the proprietor of the trade mark was informed in advance of the offering of the repackaged product for sale, and also if not only the

---

[200] Reproduced in point 33.
[201] *MPA Pharma GmbH v Rhône-Poulenc Pharma GmbH* (C-232/84) [1996] E.C.R. I-3671.
[202] Case C-71/94, para.8–093; the only difference being that it referred to a national rather than an international registration.

manufacturer and importer are indicated on the new packaging, but also the person responsible for the repackaging, even though:

(a) the information as to who repackaged the product is not set out on the external packaging with sufficient clarity, with the result that it may be overlooked by user groups; and/or

(b) neither the information concerning the repackaging itself nor the layout of the external packaging in general indicates that the repackaging was carried out by the importer without the consent of the proprietor of the trade mark or its associated undertaking?"[203]

8-096 *(c) The Opinion of the Advocate General*

Advocate General Jacobs started his analysis by comparing the position under art.28 EC and art.30 EC and that under art.7 of the Directive.[204]

8-097 **(i) Free movement of goods and repackaging—the basic principles.** He started by the principle of exhaustion of rights, referring to *Deutsche Grammophon v Metro*[205] and *Ideal Standard*[206]; a trade mark right could not be invoked in order to prevent the importation and sale of goods which had been placed on the market with the consent of its owner in another Member State.

Hoffmann-La Roche[207] set out the principles and conditions for repackaging and he cited all the relevant extracts from the judgment regarding the four conditions.

---

[203] Reproduced in point 36.
[204] Regarding the effect of the Directive at that time he noted that, although directives did not have direct effect, courts were under a duty to interpret national legislation in the light of a directive so as to ensure, wherever possible, that the result prescribed by the directive was attained, citing amongst others *Marshall v Southampton and South West Hampshire Area Health Authority* (152/84) [1986] E.C.R. 723; and *Von Colson and Kamann v Land Nordrhein-Westfalen* (14/83) [1984] E.C.R. 1891. That applied to other provisions of national law, including those adopted before the Directive. Regarding its temporal application it was directly relevant in Denmark that had adopted the relevant implementing legislation. In the case of Germany, where it had still not been implemented he noted that the marketing and the acts of importation occurred before December 31, 1992, the effective date of the Directive, and found that this would be relevant only for any decision regarding damages. However, "[a]ny injunction granted by the national courts after a preliminary ruling is delivered in the present cases will necessarily relate to the period subsequent to December 31, 1992. After that date the national courts' duty to interpret domestic law in the light of the Directive applies not just to specific implementing legislation but to all provisions of domestic law. Thus, in deciding whether to grant the injunctions sought by the trade mark owners, the German courts should seek to interpret the relevant provisions of German law in such a way as to ensure that the result prescribed by the Directive is attained" (para.58).
[205] *Deutsche Grammophon v Metro* (78/70) [1971] E.C.R. 487.
[206] *IHT Internationale Heiztechnik GmbH and Uwe Danzinger v Ideal-Standard GmbH and Wabco Standard GmbH* (9/93) [1994] E.C.R. I-2789.
[207] *Hoffmann-La Roche & Co AG and Hoffmann-La Roche AG* (102/77) [1978] E.C.R. 1139.

5. FREE MOVEMENT OF GOODS AND THE NEW TRADE MARK REGIME

He also referred to *Pfizer v Eurim-Pharm*[208] where the Court reconfirmed the *Hoffmann-La Roche* conditions. He identified two particular points made by the Court in that judgment:

> "No use of the trade mark in a manner liable to impair the guarantee of origin takes place in a case such as the one in point where, according to the findings of the national court and the terms of the question submitted by it, a parallel importer had repackaged a pharmaceutical product merely by replacing the outer wrapping without touching the internal packaging and by making the trade mark affixed by the manufacturer on the internal packaging visible through the new external wrapping."[209]

The Court noted that in such circumstances the original condition of the product would not be affected.

8–098

The second point was the finding that inserting in the external packaging a leaflet containing information relating to the medicinal product would not affect the above condition.

The third case he found relevant was *Centrafarm v American Home Products*.[210] A trade mark proprietor was entitled to prevent the marketing of a product by a third party in a Member State even if that product had been lawfully marketed in another Member State under another mark by the same proprietor. The Court accepted that it might be lawful to use different trade marks for the same product in different Member States; but it also stressed that if that choice formed part of a system of marketing intended to partition the markets artificially it would constitute a disguised restriction on intra-Community trade.

Finally, A.G. Jacobs referred to *HAG II*,[211] the case that had opened a new direction for the trade mark jurisprudence of the Court since it accepted that trade marks were an essential element in the system of undistorted competition envisaged by the Treaty:

> "Under such a system, an undertaking must be in a position to keep its customers by virtue of the quality of its products and services, something which is possible only if there are distinctive marks which enable customers to identify those products and services. For the trade mark to be able to fulfil this role, it must offer a guarantee that all goods bearing it have been produced under the control of a single undertaking which is accountable for their quality."[212]

---

[208] *Pfizer Inc v Eurim-Pharm GmbH* (1/81) [1981] E.C.R. 2913.
[209] *Pfizer v Eurim-Pharm*, para.10.
[210] *Centrafarm BV v American Home Products* (3/78) [1978] E.C.R. 1823.
[211] *SA CNL-SUCAL NV v Hag GF AG* (C-10/89) [1990] E.C.R. I-3711.
[212] *Hag II*, para.13.

8-099　**(ii) Article 7—exhaustion of rights and the Directive.** The Advocate General noted that the epithet "first" in the title of the Directive as well as the Third Recital of the Preamble showed that the approximation envisaged therein was not complete. But, once the Community legislature had adopted specific provisions dealing with exhaustion then the issue should be considered in the terms of the relevant legislation:

> "That does not however mean that Articles [28] and [30] of the Treaty may be disregarded entirely. On the contrary, the Directive must be interpreted in the light of the Treaty provisions. If there were any conflict between them and the Directive, the conflict would have to be resolved by giving precedence to the Treaty provisions, which are a primary source of law. Clearly a directive adopted under Article 95 of the Treaty for the purpose of approximating the laws of the Member States could not derogate from the fundamental rules of the Treaty on the free movement of goods."[213]

However, as his Opinion would show, there was no such conflict between the free movement of goods rules and the provisions of the Directive.

8-100　**(iii) Exhaustion of rights and repackaged goods—a detailed analysis.** Under the free movement of goods rules the Treaty applied a Community wide doctrine of exhaustion: any sale within the territory of the Community, made with the consent of the owner of an intellectual property right, exhausted the right:

> "The justification for that approach is that if the proprietor of the right could preclude the importation and sale of products marketed in another Member State by him or with his consent, he would be able to partition the national markets and thus restrict trade between Member States, even though such a restriction is not necessary to protect the substance of the right... What matters for the application of the exhaustion principle, according to the case law of the Court, is not whether the owner of the right obtains a fair reward from the sale, but whether he consents to it."[214]

In all the cases before the Court the trade mark proprietors were part of the same group of companies, accordingly they were deemed to have consented.

He identified two types of repackaging. In situation A the internal packaging was not altered and the products were placed in a new external packaging on which the importer affixed the trade mark. In situation B the

---

[213] Point 54 of the Opinion of A.G. Jacobs.
[214] Point 61, citing *Merck v Stephar and Exler* (187/80) [1981] E.C.R. 2063; *Pharmon v Hoechst* (19/84) [1985] E.C.R. 2281; and *Sterling Drug* (15/74) [1974] E.C.R. 1147.

5. FREE MOVEMENT OF GOODS AND THE NEW TRADE MARK REGIME

new packaging was designed in such a way that the original trade mark applied on the internal packaging remained visible. The second scenario was examined in *Pfizer v Eurim-Pharm*[215] and found not to impair the trade mark's function as a guarantee of origin; according to his reading of the case the Court did not even have to consider the application of the second sentence of art.30

He believed that the same reasoning should be applied for situation A because the crucial factor was not whether the parallel importer affixed the trade mark to the goods or merely allowed the original mark to remain visible, but whether it interfered with the goods in such a way that it is was no longer possible to be certain that their original condition had not been affected. And *Hoffmann-La Roche*[216] appeared to confirm that interpretation.

8–101

From those two cases he deduced that "the trade mark cannot be used to prevent the sale of repackaged goods where the use of different packages in different Member States has led to a partitioning of the market and where it is established that the repackaging cannot affect the original condition of the goods".[217]

(iv) The scope of article 30—the fundamental interests protected by trade mark rights. In order to identify the scope of art.30 in a positive way he turned to the justification of trade mark protection. The scope of trade mark systems was twofold, to enable traders to protect the reputation of their goods and prevent the theft of their goodwill by unscrupulous competitors and enable consumers to make informed purchasing choices on the basis of the assumption that goods sold under the same name emanated from the same source and would, in normal circumstances, be of uniform quality:

8–102

> "Thus trade mark law seeks to protect the interests, not only of the trade mark proprietor, but also of the consumer. In so far as the trade mark protects the interests of its proprietor by enabling him to prevent competitors from taking unfair advantage of his commercial reputation, the exclusive rights conferred on the proprietor are said, in the language of the Court's case law, to constitute the specific subject-matter of the trade mark. In so far as the trade mark protects the interests of consumers by acting as a guarantee that all goods bearing the mark are of the same commercial origin, that is known, in the Court's terminology, as the essential function of the trade mark. Those two aspects of trade mark protection are of course two sides of the same coin."[218]

---

[215] *Pfizer Inc* (1/81) [1981] E.C.R. 2913.
[216] *Hoffmann-La Roche & Co AG and Hoffmann-La Roche AG* (102/77) [1978] E.C.R. 1139.
[217] Point 70 of the Opinion of A.G. Jacobs.
[218] Point 72 of the Opinion of A.G. Jacobs.

Compartmentalising the Common Market, on the other hand, was not the purpose of trade mark law. He accepted that trade mark proprietors would feel aggrieved when price differentials were caused by direct or indirect price controls that were outside their control. However, according to the case law of the Court, price controls would not justify the exercise of trade mark rights in order to block parallel imports.[219] For trade marks in particular, where the reward issue did not underlie the right in the way it did patents, "none of the interests protected by a trade mark ... is affected by rules which restrict the trade mark owner's freedom to fix his own selling prices. The trade mark's ability to function as a guarantee of origin is not impaired simply because the exhaustion principle is applied to goods which have been placed on the market at a regulated price".[220]

Article 30, being a derogation from art.28, had to be construed narrowly and, in order to determine what the provision allowed, courts would have to balance between the fundamental principle of free movement of goods and the fundamental interests behind trade mark rights.

8–103 **(v) The main criteria for the application of article 30.** Accordingly he suggested that the following criteria would be relevant for assessing whether art.30 should be applied.

First, had the condition of the goods been so modified that they could no longer truthfully be described as the goods of the trade mark owner, with the result that the parallel importer would unfairly be taking advantage of the reputation of the trade mark?

Secondly, had the condition of the goods been modified in such a way that their further marketing under the trade mark might unfairly damage the reputation of the trade mark?

8–104 Thirdly, would consumers be misled, in the sense that they would assume that the goods had been produced under the control of the trade mark owner and so possess the quality normally associated with the trade mark when in fact, as a result of the repackaging, the goods have been interfered with in such a way that their original quality may have been impaired?

The answers to the above questions would at the end provide the answer to the ultimate question: had the trade mark's function as a guarantee of origin been compromised? He suggested that an affirmative answer to any of the three questions would justify the exercise of trade mark rights against parallel imports.

8–105 **(vi) Partitioning the market.** Responding to the argument raised by trade mark proprietors that the starting point should be whether they

---

[219] Citing *Winthrop BV* (16/74) [1974] E.C.R. 1183 for trade marks; and *Sterling Drug Inc* (15/74) [1974] E.C.R. 1147 for patents.
[220] Point 76 of the Opinion of A.G. Jacobs.

5. FREE MOVEMENT OF GOODS AND THE NEW TRADE MARK REGIME

had deliberately chosen different packaging in order to partition the market artificially, A.G. Jacobs appeared to support that this was a secondary issue:

> "If the repackaging is done in such a way that it does not compromise the trade mark's function as a guarantee of origin and does not impair the reputation of the trade mark, there seems no valid reason for saying that the parallel importer should only be allowed to sell the repackaged goods if he can show that the trade mark owner has deliberately used different packaging with a view to artificially partitioning the market."[221]

It was a mistake to construe the second sentence as an exception to a general rule laid down in the first sentence. A better interpretation would be to read the two sentences of art.30 jointly, as a whole:

> "Either a measure is justified on one of the grounds listed in Article [30] or it is not justified. One of the factors to be taken into account in assessing justification is whether the measure leads to a disguised restriction, in other words whether the measure, though ostensibly intended to safeguard industrial property, is really designed to achieve some other purpose unconnected with trade mark protection. If a trade mark owner uses the trade mark in order to exclude parallel imports of his own goods when the sale of those goods does not threaten the interests protected by the specific subject-matter of the trade mark and does not compromise the essential function of the trade mark by preventing it from acting as a guarantee of origin, then the presumption inevitably arises that the trade mark is being used for some other purpose..."[222]

Accordingly, the fact that the partitioning of the markets occurred because of national rules governing size was irrelevant.[223]

(vii) Prior notice and indication of repackaging—the additional criteria. Finally the Advocate General considered the scope of the last two conditions imposed by Hoffmann-La Roche.

8–106

Here there were two particular issues he had to examine. Should the repackaged product indicate that the repackaging had taken place without the consent of the proprietor?[224] And should failure to mention the name of

---

[221] Point 81 of the Opinion of A.G. Jacobs.
[222] Point 82 of the Opinion of A.G. Jacobs.
[223] He accepted that para.10 of *Hoffmann-La Roche* [1978] E.C.R. 1139 was ambiguous on this issue; however he saw it as implying an essentially objective test. And in any case the Court had appeared to move more clearly towards that direction in *Centrafarm v American Home Products Corp* [1978] E.C.R. 1823.
[224] As mentioned in *MPA Pharma GmbH v Rhône-Poulenc Pharma GmbH* (C-232/94) [1996] E.C.R. I-3671.

the manufacturer on the new packaging justify the exercise of trade mark rights?[225]

The Advocate General noted that there might be cases where the prior notice requirement might be superfluous. However, it did appear to be a reasonable requirement, in particular in relation to pharmaceuticals, making it easier for the trade mark proprietor to fight counterfeiters.

8–107   He suggested that in addition to the notification the parallel importer should also provide the trade mark proprietor with a sample of the new packaging, in order to point out any deficiencies and demand them to be corrected. Otherwise it should be allowed to object to the marketing of the repackaged product.[226]

The requirement that the entity responsible for the repackaging should be indicated on the packaging was also justified. Otherwise, consumers would have the impression that the trade mark proprietor was responsible for the repackaging, including defects.

But he did not deem it necessary to indicate that the product had been repackaged without the authorisation of the trade mark proprietor. This would taint the product as not entirely legitimate.

Similarly, he suggested that indicating the manufacturer on the product should not be essential, at least where the manufacturer was identified on the original internal packaging.

8–108   **(viii) The position under the directive—exhaustion of the rights conferred by a trade mark.** The position would not differ at all under the directive. Article 7 was modelled according to the Advocate General on the free movement of goods rules. Its heading and language confirmed this.

Article 7(1) provided the general principle and art.7(2) recognised that the principle would not apply where there existed "legitimate reasons . . . especially where the condition of the goods is changed or impaired after they have been put on the market". It reflected *Hoffmann-La Roche*[227] and *Pfizer v Eurim-Pharm*.[228]

In addition the vagueness of art.7(2) required it to be interpreted following the jurisprudence of the Court in this area.

8–109   He also suggested that the brevity of the provision was evidence that its purpose was not to codify the existing case law. The Advocate General doubted whether the Council had the authority to "codify" in the first place; he believed that the Council wanted to let the case law evolve in this area. The word "especially" strengthened this argument showing the non exhaustive nature of the provision.

---

[225] As suggested in Joint Cases C-71/94 to C-73/94.
[226] He noted that some information should, in any case, be provided on the packaging according to Council Directive 92/97 on the labelling of medicinal products for human use and on package leaflets [1992] OJ L113/8.
[227] *Hoffmann-La Roche & Co AG and Hoffmann-La Roche AG* (102/77) [1978] E.C.R. 1139.
[228] *Pfizer Inc* (1/81) [1981] E.C.R. 2913.

5. FREE MOVEMENT OF GOODS AND THE NEW TRADE MARK REGIME

In common with the Treaty the Directive sought to strike a balance between the free movement of goods and the protection of trade mark rights. In essence the Directive would remove any conflict between national law and the Treaty that might had existed in the past in the field of trade mark law.

He rejected the argument that the Directive had tilted the balance towards trade mark proprietors in that exhaustion covered only goods marketed in their original state. This, he found, would make it difficult to reconcile art.7(1) with art.7(2)—in particular following his analysis on situations where there would be no legitimate reason for blocking parallel imports—and would disregard the fact that art.7 had been modelled on the free movement of goods jurisprudence of the Court; finally it would go against the aim of the Directive and raise rather than remove trade barriers.[229]

(ix) The burden of proof. Balancing the impact of his Opinion he rejected the submission of the UK Government that had intervened in the proceedings claiming that art.7 had reversed the burden of proof: the onus should now be on the trade mark proprietor to demonstrate the existence of legitimate reasons for opposing further marketing of the repackaged goods.

8–110

He found both the provision and the free movement of goods case law to be silent on this issue. *Hoffmann-La Roche* appeared to suggest that in principle the trade mark owner had the right to object and would only lose the right in exceptional circumstances.

However, he viewed this as an interference with a procedural matter that should remain under the remit of national autonomy, according to the principle of procedural autonomy. In the absence of any specific rules of Community law it was for the domestic legal system of each Member State to determine the conditions governing the implementation of directly effective Community law, provided that the procedural rules applicable to claims founded on Community law were not less favourable than those governing similar actions of a domestic nature and would not render the exercise of rights arising from Community law practically impossible or excessively difficult.[230]

Considering whether in the cases before the Court the application of rules as to the burden of proof might have the effect of making virtually impossible or excessively difficult the exercise of the right of the trade mark proprietor to prevent unjustified use of its trade mark by a third party, compared with the right of the parallel importer to market trade marked goods, provided that no harm was done to the legitimate interests of the trade mark owners he noted that none of the parties should be subject to

8–111

---

[229] Submitted in relation to the German cases.
[230] Citing *Deutsche Milchkontor v Germany* (205/82 to 215/82) [1983] E.C.R. 2633, for an extensive discussion of this issue see A.G. Sharpston's Opinion in paras 8–255 and following, below.

a probatio diabolica: be compelled to prove something which could not be proved or could only be proved with the utmost difficulty. This could be the case for a parallel importer that would have to prove that the repackaging could not affect the original condition of the goods, because proving a negative would be extremely difficult.

It would not, however, be unreasonable to be required to show that it had taken adequate safeguards when repackaging goods.

On the other hand a trade mark proprietor of an intellectual property right should do more than make a general reference to the industrial property exception. "A coherent argument is required, showing precisely how the interest in question will be impaired. I do not think that the Court means to lay down technical rules about the incidence of the burden of proof or about the standard of proof."[231]

8–112   **(x) Identifying the issues.** Having established the basic principles he identified the relevant issues in each particular case.

In Case C-427/93[232] Paranova's repackaging affected only the outer packaging of the products; in the two most intrusive instances a label was placed on the inner packaging and a spray manufactured by Paranova was included together with the original product in the new outer packaging.

The Advocate General suggested that replacing the outer packaging and placing the trade mark on the new packaging did not appear to affect the interests protected by trade mark rights:

> "No theft of Bristol-Myers Squibb's goodwill takes place. Arguably, if the external packaging were shoddy or defective, it might damage the reputation of the trade mark, but that does not seem to be contended by Bristol-Myers Squibb."[233]

8–113   Further, the repackaging did not appear to affect the original condition of the products. The only reservations he had concerned the insertion of a product emanating from a different source; the national court would have to determine, first, whether the statement appearing on the packaging of the product was sufficiently clear to disperse the impression that the products emanated from the same source and, secondly, responsibility for the additional product might still be attributed to the trade mark owner irrespective of the statement.

In respect of Case C-429/93[234] the Advocate General suggested that the repackaging of the inhalers appeared to be unproblematic. He identified

---

[231] Point 105, citing, *Sandoz* (174/82) [1983] E.C.R. 2445, a case concerning the marketing authorisation of food products enriched with vitamins in The Netherlands, as an example of the balanced approach sought by the Court regarding the application of art.30.
[232] The first of the Danish cases.
[233] Point 109 of the Opinion of A.G. Jacobs.
[234] The second of the Danish cases.

5. FREE MOVEMENT OF GOODS AND THE NEW TRADE MARK REGIME

three possible problems that the national court had to consider as questions of fact: the chance of misprinting the use-by date on the new label; the possibility of mistakes in the translation of the instructions; and the risk of contamination of the inhalers during their repackaging.

Regarding Case C-436/93 the national court would have to consider the relevance of the non-inclusion of the photo-sensitivity warning, taking into account whether the information appeared on the original packaging.

In Case C-71/94 the national court would have to focus on three issues. **8–114**

First, the effect that the severed blister packs and the window on the packaging would have on the image of the mark rather than the condition of the product. He accepted that "part of the function of the trade mark is to enable its proprietor to protect his commercial reputation"[235] and accordingly there could be cases where trade could be relied upon against the marketing of shoddily repackaged products. The type of the product could influence the decision on the presentation of the product. For the Advocate General it might be more important for luxury than for functional— including pharmaceutical—goods. Another relevant factor would be the way the product reached the consumer; appearance could be less important for a pharmacist dispensing the product than a consumer reaching for the product on a shelf.

Secondly, whether the severing of the blister packs involved a risk of contamination, noting that according to the evidence it appeared that in some cases the severing of the pack occurred too close to the pills themselves.

Thirdly, whether the interruption of the series of days of the week at the **8–115** back of the pack and the repetition of particular days could adversely affect the way the pills were consumed resulting to overdoses.

The only objectionable issue in Case C-72/94 would be the effect of the window on the image of the trade mark.

In Case C-73/94, the first issue related to the effect the severing of the packs would have both on the image of the trade mark and the actual condition of the product.

The second concerned the addition of the word "forte" as an indication **8–116** that the imported products corresponded to the stronger version of the locally marketed version. The Advocate General distinguished this case from *American Home Products v Centrafarm*[236] because here the starting point was the use of a common trade mark.[237]

So if in principle the parallel imported product could be resold in Germany then it would indeed be necessary to add the word "forte" in order to alleviate any possibility of consumer confusion regarding the strength of the product.

---

[235] Point 115 of the Opinion of A.G. Jacobs.
[236] The third of the Danish cases.
[237] An issue that has been revisited by A.G. Jacobs from a different perspective: see paras 5–139 and following, above.

Finally, in Case C-232/94 the Advocate General focused on the information regarding repackaging that appeared on the package. Ultimately the adequacy or not of the content and the presentation of the information was for the national court to decide. Still, he believed that the actual content was sufficient; as to presentation he remarked that if "the information is written in such a way that a consumer with normal eyesight, exercising a normal degree of attentiveness, would be able to understand who is responsible for the repackaging, that is sufficient".[238]

8–117 **(xi) Applying the principles.** Advocate General Jacobs chose to respond to the questions submitted to the Court by providing first a set of general propositions, a framework that national courts could apply and only then by suggesting a number of specific rulings. He noted that both were applicable in interpreting both art.7 of the Directive and the free movement of goods provisions of the Treaty.

8–118 *Joined Cases C-427/93, C-429/93 & C-436/93*

(a) The general propositions The trade mark proprietor should not invoke its rights in order to block the marketing of parallel imported goods placed in new external packaging unless the repackaging was capable of affecting the original condition of the goods or otherwise impairing the reputation of the trade mark.

In the case of pharmaceuticals the party carrying out the repackaging of the goods should in principle inform the trade mark proprietor and provide a specimen of the repackaged product.

It should also indicate on the repackaged product that it is responsible for the repackaging but did not have to mention the manufacturer of the goods or state that the proprietor of the trade mark has not authorised the repackaging

Whether repackaging was capable of affecting the original condition of the goods or otherwise impairing the reputation of the trade mark was a question of fact to be determined by the national court in accordance with its own domestic rules regarding procedural matters, including the burden and the standard of proof and the admissibility of evidence. Those rules should not treat claims founded on Community law less favourably than claims founded on national law or make the enforcement of rights arising from Community law unduly difficult.

8–119 *(b) The specific rulings* In the case of pharmaceuticals originally packaged in blister packs, phials, flasks or aerosol containers and where the person responsible for the repackaging simply removed the packs, etc. from their original external packaging and placed them in new external packaging

[238] Point 128 of the Opinion of A.G. Jacobs.

5. FREE MOVEMENT OF GOODS AND THE NEW TRADE MARK REGIME

without cutting or opening them, in suitable premises, with competent staff, and taking all reasonable safeguards, there was not in principle any ground for finding that the original condition of the goods might be affected, and the national court was precluded from making such a finding in the absence of specific evidence.

The fact that the party responsible for the repackaging used the same colour scheme for the repackaged product as the owner of the trade mark was irrelevant.

Where the party responsible for the repackaging inserted in the new packaging additional goods the trade mark proprietor might in principle object to the further marketing of the repackaged goods under the trade mark, unless the origin of the additional material was indicated in such a way as to dispel any impression that the trade mark proprietor was responsible for it.

Joined Cases C-71/94 & C-73/94   8–120

(a) The general propositions The Advocate General covered with the same general principles the case where the goods were repackaged in such a way that the trade mark affixed to the internal packaging remained visible.

(b) The specific rulings He repeated the first ruling mentioned above, but   8–121
added that if the blister packs were severed, the trade mark proprietor was entitled to object to the further marketing of the goods if the national court considered that practice was capable of affecting the original condition of the goods.

The trade mark proprietor was entitled to object to the further marketing of repackaged goods not only where the repackaging affected the technical quality of the goods but also where it gave them a shoddy appearance capable of damaging the reputation of the trade mark.

The same would apply where the severing of the blister packs affected information printed on their backs allocating the pills to specific days of the week for a certain period of time, if the national court considered that the interruption of the series of days caused unacceptable confusion for the consumer or endangered his health or was detrimental to the reputation of the trade mark.

A trade mark owner that sold two versions of a product in Member State A under the names "Sermion" and "Sermion forte" and sold in Member State B under the name "Sermion" a product which corresponded to "Sermion forte" in Member State A, could not invoke its trade mark rights in order to prevent the resale in Member State A of goods which it had placed on the market in Member State B, even though the reseller described them as "Sermion forte".

Case C-232/94 The Advocate General added to the general propositions   8–122
mentioned above that the indication as to who was responsible for the

repackaging should be written in such a way that a person with normal eyesight, exercising a normal degree of attentiveness, would be able to understand it.

8–123   *(d)   The Judgment of the Court in Joined Cases C-427, 429 & 436/93*[239]

The Court constructed its judgment starting from the basic principles—the relationship between art.7 and the free movement of goods rules and its interpretation—and then moving to the factual scenarios of the joined cases. Accordingly, it dealt with the questions in a logical rather than formalistic sequence.

8–124   **(i) Article 7 of the Directive and article 30 EC.** The Court started its analysis by looking at the first question in Case C-436/93[240] in order to untangle the relationship between art.7 of the Directive and the free movement of goods rules of the Treaty.

It restated that where Community directives provided for the harmonisation of measures ensuring the protection of the interests covered by art.30, "any national measure relating thereto must be assessed in relation to the provisions of that directive and not Articles [28] to [30] of the Treaty".[241]

Article 7 clearly constituted such a provision–it was worded in general terms and regulated comprehensively the exhaustion of trade mark rights for products traded in the Community[242]—and national exhaustion rules had to be assessed accordingly.

8–125   Albeit, art.7 itself had to be interpreted in the light of art.30, since it constituted part of secondary legislation.[243]

Accordingly the answer to that question should be that the reliance on trade mark rights in order to prevent intra-Community parallel imports where the importer had repackaged the product and reaffixed the trade mark without the owner's authorisation should be assessed on the basis of the combined provisions of national trade mark law and art.7 of the Directive, interpreted in the light of art.30.

---

[239] *Bristol Myers Squibb v Paranova A/S* (C-427/93), *CH Boehringer Sohn, Boehringer Ingelheim KG and Boehringer Ingelheim A/S v Paranova A/S* (C-429/93); and *Bayer Aktiengesellschaft and Bayer Danmark A/S v Paranova A/S* (C-436/93) [1996] E.C.R. I-3457.
[240] See paras 8–091–8–092 and accompanying text.
[241] *Bristol Myers Squibb*, para.25, citing *Tedeschi v Denkavit* (5–77) [1977] E.C.R. 1555; *Van Bennekom* (227/82) [1983] E.C.R. 3883; *Vanacker and Lesage* (C-37/92) [1993] E.C.R. I-4947; and *Centre d' Insémination de la Crespelle v Coopérative de la Mayenne* (C-323/93) [1994] E.C.R. I-5077.
[242] Note that the Court avoided stating that art.7 regulated exhaustion of trade mark rights in general. At this stage it appeared to limit its scope to intra-Community exhaustion.
[243] Citing *Delhaize v Promalvin* (C-47/90) [1992] E.C.R. I-3669; and *Verband Sozialer Wettbewerb v Clinique Laboratoires and Estée Lauder* (C-315/92) [1994] E.C.R. I-317.

5. FREE MOVEMENT OF GOODS AND THE NEW TRADE MARK REGIME

(ii) The interpretation of article 7(1). The Court then moved to the interpretation of art.7 through its answer to the first question in Cases C-427/93 and 429/93.[244]

8–126

Article 7(1) provided the general rule and it was framed in analogy with art.28 and art.30 of the Treaty and the case law of the Court that the owner of a trade mark protected by the legislation of a Member State could not rely on that legislation to prevent the importation or marketing of a product which was put on the market in another Member State by the proprietor or with its consent.[245]

The Court rejected the argument favouring trade mark proprietors that the provision conferred on the parallel importer only the right to resell the products in the form in which the trade mark owner had put them on the market in another Member State and that the proprietor's exclusive right to affix the trade mark was not exhausted.

Subjugating the provision to the power of its case law, the Court stressed that the exclusive right to affix a trade mark to a product should in certain circumstances be regarded as exhausted in order to allow parallel imports.[246] To accept the contrary argument would imply a major alteration to the Treaty's free movement of goods rules:

8–127

"There is nothing to suggest that art.7 of the Directive is intended to restrict the scope of that case law. Nor would such an effect be permissible, since a directive cannot justify obstacles in intra-Community trade save within the bounds set by the Treaty rules. The Court's case law shows that the prohibition on quantitative restrictions and measures having equivalent effect applies not only to national measures but also to those emanating from Community institutions."[247]

Accordingly the answer to that question should be that, with the exception of the circumstances defined in art.7(2), art.7(1) precluded the owner of a trade mark from relying on its rights to prevent an importer from marketing a product which had been put on the market in another Member State by the owner or with its consent, even if that importer had repackaged the product and reaffixed the trade mark to it without the owner's authorisation.

---

[244] See paras 8–091–8–092 above and accompanying text.
[245] *Centrafarm BV v Winthrop BV* (16/74) [1974] E.C.R. 1183; *SA CNL-SUCAL NV v Hag GF AG* (C-10/89) [1990] E.C.R. I-3711; and *IHT Internationale Heiztechnik GmbH and Uwe Danzinger v Ideal-Standard GmbH and Wabco Standard GmbH* (9/93) [1994] E.C.R. I-2789.
[246] *Hoffmann-La Roche & Co AG and Hoffmann-La Roche AG v Centrafarm Vertriebsgesellschaft Pharmazeutischer Erzeugnisse mbH* (102/77) [1978] E.C.R. 1139; *Centrafarm v American Home Products Corp* (3/78) [1978] E.C.R. 1823; and the judgments delivered by the Court on the same day with the current judgment in *Eurim-Pharm Arzneimittel GmbH v Beiersdorf AG* (C-71/94), *Boehringer Ingelheim KG* (C-72/94) and *Farmitalia Carlo Erba GmbH* (C-73/94) [1996] E.C.R. I-3603; and in *MPA Pharma GmbH v Rhône-Poulenc Pharma GmbH* (C-232/94) [1996] E.C.R. I-671.
[247] *Bristol Myers Squibb*, para.36, citing *Meyhui v Schott Zwiesel Glaswerke* (C-51/93) [1994] E.C.R. I-3879.

8–128   (iii) **The interpretation of article 7(2).** The Court brought together the remaining questions in order to define the art.7(2) circumstances it had mentioned above. It considered jointly the second question in Cases C-427/93 and C-429/93, the third and fourth questions in Case C-427/93 and the second, third, fourth and fifth questions in Case C-436/93.

It identified three particular issues that troubled the national courts. First, whether the art.30 case law of the Court remained relevant; secondly, the significance of the concept of artificial partitioning of the markets; and, thirdly the significance and interpretation of the concept of the adverse effect on the original condition of the product. And it added a fourth part where it discussed the remaining conditions that had to be fulfilled.

In terms of language analysis the Court highlighted the use of the word "especially". This indicated that the situation described in the provision was only an example.

8–129   It then positioned art.7 in its wider context, in order to delineate properly the role of art.7(2). Article 7 pursued the same aim with art.30 EC; it intended to reconcile the fundamental interest in protecting trade mark rights with the fundamental interest in the free movement of goods.

As a result the two provisions should be interpreted in the same way and the art.30 case law of the Court should be the basis for determining the scope of art.7(2).

8–130   *Article 7(2) and the case law of the court* According to that case law, derogations from the free movement of goods principle were allowed only to the extent they were justified in order to safeguard the rights that constitute the specific subject-matter of the industrial and commercial property in question. For trade marks the Court repeated its findings on their essential function and specific subject-matter it had established in cases like *HAG II*,[248] *Ideal Standard*,[249] *Winthrop*,[250] and *Hoffmann-La Roche*.[251]

The effect of this definition of the specific subject-matter was that the owner of a national trade mark right could not rely on the relevant national legislation in order to oppose the importation or marketing of a product which had been put on the market in another Member State by the owner or with its consent. Trade mark rights, the Court stressed, were not intended "to allow their owners to partition national markets and thus promote the retention of price differences".[252] It recognised the peculiarities

---

[248] *SA CNL-SUCAL NV v Hag GF AG* (C-10/89) [1990] E.C.R. I-3711.
[249] *IHT Internationale Heiztechnik GmbH and Uwe Danzinger v Ideal-Standard GmbH and Wabco Standard GmbH* (9/93) [1994] E.C.R. I-2789.
[250] *Centrafarm BV v Winthrop BV* (16/74) [1974] E.C.R. 1183.
[251] *Hoffmann-La Roche & Co AG and Hoffmann-La Roche AG v Centrafarm Vertriebsgesellschaft Pharmazeutischer Erzeugnisse GmbH* (102/77) [1978] E.C.R 1139.
[252] *Bristol Myers Squibb*, para.46.

5. FREE MOVEMENT OF GOODS AND THE NEW TRADE MARK REGIME

of the market for pharmaceuticals where price differences might be the result of other factors, but repeated that "distortions... must be remedied by measures of the Community authorities and not by another Member State introducing measures which are incompatible with the rules on the free movement of goods".[253]

Turning to the guarantee of origin function the Court re-stated its findings in *Hoffmann-La Roche*[254] and the conditions it had established therein regarding the exercise of trade mark and supplemented in the other two simultaneous parallel import cases.[255]

Artificial partitioning of the markets between Member States The Court's starting point was that blocking the marketing of repackaged products would contribute to the partitioning of markets between Member States in particular where the owner had placed the same product on the market in several Member States in various forms of packaging, and the product might be imported from one Member State and put on the market in another by a parallel importer. 8–131

Accordingly, the trade mark proprietor could not oppose repackaging in new external packaging or the modification of the contents of an original external packet when the size of the packaging in the exporting Member State could not be marketed in the importing Member State:

> "by reason, in particular, of a rule authorising packaging only of a certain size or a national practice to the same effect, sickness insurance rules making the reimbursement of medical expenses depend on the size of the packaging, or well-established medical prescription practices based, inter alia, on standard sizes recommended by professional groups and sickness insurance institutions".[256]

The Court went further holding that the same principle should apply even if the trade mark owner used in the importing Member State a number of sizes of packaging and one of those sizes was also used in the exporting Member State. "Partitioning of the markets would exist if the importer were able to sell the product in only part of his market."[257]

Balancing between the rights of trade mark proprietors and the interests of parallel importers the court clarified that repackaging would not gain automatic clearance. 8–132

---

[253] *Bristol Myers Squibb*, para.46 citing *Winthrop BV* (16/74) [1974] E.C.R. 1183.
[254] *Hoffmann-La Roche & Co AG and Hoffmann-La Roche AG* (102/77) [1978] E.C.R. 1139.
[255] *Eurim-Pharm Arzneimittel GmbH v Beiersdorf AG* (C-71/94), *Boehringer Ingelheim KG* (C-72/94) and *Farmitalia Carlo Erba GmbH* (C-73/94) [1996] E.C.R. I-3603; and *MPA Pharma GmbH v Rhône-Poulenc Pharma GmbH* (C-232/94) [1996] E.C.R. I-3671.
[256] *Bristol Myers Squibb*, para.53.
[257] *Bristol Myers Squibb*, para.54.

The owner could oppose it when the importer could achieve the packaging that might be marketed in the importing Member State by less intrusive means. For example by affixing to the original external or inner packaging new labels in the language of the importing Member State, by adding new user instructions or information in that language, or by replacing an additional article not capable of gaining approval in the importing Member State with a similar approved article:

> "The power of the owner of trade mark rights protected in a Member State to oppose the marketing of repackaged products under the trade mark should be limited only in so far as the repackaging undertaken by the importer is necessary in order to market the product in the Member State of importation."[258]

Taking a step back, the Court added that "artificial partitioning" did not require the importer to prove that the trade mark proprietor had deliberately sought to partition the markets by using different forms of packaging. Employing once again the essential function of a trade mark, this time as a tool for limiting protection, the Court added that it had been using the concept with the intention to stress that the owner of a trade mark might always rely on its rights to oppose the marketing of repackaged products when such action was justified by the need to safeguard the essential function of the trade mark. In this case the partitioning would not be artificial.

8–133 *Adverse effect on the original condition of the product* The Court, first, noted that the concept referred to the condition of the product inside the packaging. It reminded us that in *Hoffmann-La Roche*[259] it had held that in order to determine whether there was a risk of the product being exposed to tampering or to influences affecting its original condition account should be taken of the nature of the product and the method of repackaging.

Following the principles developed in the same case in respect of pharmaceutical products the Court ruled that "the mere removal of blister packs, flasks, phials, ampoules or inhalers from their original external packaging and their replacement in new external packaging cannot affect the original condition of the product inside the packaging".[260]

It rejected the specific claims of the trade mark owners—for example the risk of combining blister packs with different use-by dates in the same outer packaging—outright. "It is not possible for each hypothetical risk of isolated error to suffice to confer on the trade mark owner the right to oppose any repackaging of pharmaceutical products in new external packaging."[261]

---

[258] *Bristol Myers Squibb*, para.56.
[259] *Hoffmann-La Roche & Co AG and Hoffmann-La Roche AG* (102/77) [1978] E.C.R. 1139.
[260] *Bristol Myers Squibb*, para.61.
[261] *Bristol Myers Squibb*, para.63.

5. FREE MOVEMENT OF GOODS AND THE NEW TRADE MARK REGIME

The same applied to the remaining contested operations: the fixing of self-stick labels to flasks, phials, ampoules or inhalers, the addition to the packaging of new user instructions or information in the language of the Member State of importation, or the insertion of an extra article from a source other than the trade mark owner. It found that they would not affect the original condition of the product inside the packaging. **8–134**

Giving some recognition to the arguments of trade mark owners it accepted that:

> "the original condition of the product inside the packaging might be indirectly affected where, for example: the external or inner packaging of the repackaged product, or a new set of user instructions or information, omits certain important information or gives inaccurate information concerning the nature, composition, effect, use or storage of the product, or an extra article inserted into the packaging by the importer and designed for the ingestion and dosage of the product does not comply with the method of use and the doses envisaged by the manufacturer".[262]

Ultimately this was a question that the national court had to consider. However, the Court indicated that such problems could be resolved by the parallel importer providing additional information.

(iv) The remaining requirements. The Court acknowledged that the above conclusion conferred "on the importer certain rights which, in normal circumstances, are reserved for the trade mark owner himself".[263] **8–135**

To safeguard the interests of trade mark proprietors against any misuse of those rights the Court reiterated the requirements it had established in *Hoffmann-La Roche*.[264]

Indication of repackaging It started with the requirement of including an indication on the outer packaging of who was responsible for the repackaging of the product. It agreed with the Advocate General that the national court had to assess whether the indication was printed in such a way as to be understood by a person with normal eyesight, exercising a normal degree of attentiveness. **8–136**

It did not, though, consider the content that would satisfy the requirement in a positive way. It simply held that it was not necessary to make a further express statement that the repackaging occurred without the

---

[262] *Bristol Myers Squibb*, para.65.
[263] *Bristol Myers Squibb*, para.68; note the language used by the Court. The parallel importer appears to obtain a right rather than a licence to perform some actions that would otherwise constitute an infringement.
[264] *Hoffmann-La Roche & Co AG and Hoffmann-La Roche AG* (102/77) [1978] E.C.R. 1139.

authorisation of the trade mark owner. Such a statement would imply that the repackaged product was not entirely legitimate.

And when an extra article from a source other than the trade mark owner had been added into the packaging then the parallel importer should ensure that its origin was clearly indicated, dispelling any impression that the trade mark proprietor was responsible for it.

8–137 *Indication of manufacturer* Citing *Pfizer*[265] it added that it might also be required to incorporate on the external packaging a clear indication as to who manufactured the product. Apart from its informational value this would also serve the interests of the trade mark proprietor ensuring that the consumer of the product would not be led to believe that the importer was the owner of the trade mark or that the product was manufactured under its supervision.

8–138 *The fifth condition—inappropriate presentation and reputation* The Court gave some ground to trade mark proprietors by recognising that the reputation of a trade mark might suffer from an inappropriate presentation of the repackaged product:

> "In such a case, the trade mark owner has a legitimate interest, related to the specific subject-matter of the trade mark right, in being able to oppose the marketing of the product. In assessing whether the presentation of the repackaged product is liable to damage the reputation of the trade mark, account must be taken of the nature of the product and the market for which it is intended."[266]

For pharmaceuticals in particular the presentation of a product might be capable of inspiring public confidence; "defective, poor quality or untidy packaging could damage the trade mark's reputation".[267]

Taking another step back, this time towards the position of parallel importers, the Court indicated that the channels of trade for the particular product should also be taken into account. For products sold to hospitals presentation would be of little importance. For those reaching the consumers through pharmacies presentation would be more significant, even if the product had been prescribed by a doctor.

8–139 *Advance notice* The final requirement was that the parallel importer should give advance notice to the trade mark proprietor. The proprietor might also require to be given a specimen of the repackaged product in order to ensure that the repackaging would not directly or indirectly affect the original

---

[265] *Pfizer Inc* (1/81) [1981] E.C.R. 2913.
[266] *Bristol Myers Squibb*, para.75.
[267] *Bristol Myers Squibb*, para.76.

5. FREE MOVEMENT OF GOODS AND THE NEW TRADE MARK REGIME

condition of the product and that the presentation would not be likely to damage the reputation of the trade mark.

(e)   The judgment of the Court in joined cases C-71/94 to C-73/94[268]   **8–140**

This time the Court focused on the questions from the perspective of the free movement of goods rules rather than the Directive. In essence, however, the viewpoint remained the same. The national court had not mentioned the Directive in the questions it referred to the Court; still it reminded us that although a directive would not of itself impose obligations on an individual[269] when applying national law, whether adopted before or after the Directive, the national court that had to interpret that law should do so, as far as possible, in the light of the wording and the purpose of the directive. And in any case the Court had just decided in *Bristol Myers Squibb*[270] that art.7 of the Directive and art.30 of the Treaty shared a common purpose but also the same interpretive principles.

Indeed the Court repeated the analysis it had followed in *Bristol Myers Squibb* almost verbatim; the distinguishing feature in this case was the way the original trade mark became visible to the public, and the Court found that this did not really make a difference:

> "With regard to the arguments raised in these cases, there is no reason in principle to distinguish between the situation where a third party reaffixes the trade mark after repackaging the product, and the situation where, after the product has been repackaged, he uses the trade mark affixed to the original packaging by the manufacturer by leaving it visible through new external packaging or by retaining the original external packaging itself."[271]

In all these cases the critical question remained the same: whether, having regard to the essential function of a trade mark, the power of the owner to oppose the use of the trade mark by a third party after the product had been repackaged fell within the specific subject-matter of the trade mark right.

The additional point made by the Court in this case was that it was for the national court to ascertain whether the insertion into single external packaging of both original external packaging and loose blister packs

---

[268] *Eurim-Pharm Arzneimittel GmbH v Beiersdorf AG* (C-71/94); *Boehringer Ingelheim KG* (C-72/94) and *Farmitalia Carlo Erba GmbH* (C-73/94) [1996] E.C.R. I-3603.

[269] *Marshall v Southampton and South-West Hampshire Area Health Authority* (152/84) [1986] E.C.R. 723; *Marleasing v La Comercial Internacional de Alimentacion* (C-106/89) [1990] E.C.R. I-4135; and *Faccini Dori v Recreb Srl* (C-91/92) [1994] E.C.R. I-3325.

[270] *Bristol Myers Squibb v Paranova A/S* (C-427/93), *CH Boehringer Sohn, Boehringer Ingelheim KG and Boehringer Ingelheim A/S v Paranova A/S* (C-429/93) and *Bayer Aktiengesellschaft and Bayer Danmark A/S v Paranova A/S* (C-436/93) [1996] E.C.R. I-3457.

[271] C-71/94 to C-73/94, para.38.

constituted an untidy form of packaging liable to damage the reputation of the trade mark. The same applied to the severing of the blister packs.

8–141 *(f) The judgment of the Court in Case C-232/94*[272]

Here the Court simply restated the five principles having stressed that the trade mark could not oppose repackaging in new external packaging when the packet size used by the owner in the Member State where the importer purchased the product could not be marketed as a result of a national rule, national practice, sickness insurance rules, or well-established medical prescription practices.

6. PHARMACIA & UPJOHN—REPLACING THE TRADE MARK—THE REQUIREMENT OF NECESSITY

8–142 The links between free movement of goods and the replacing of a trade mark were re-examined by the Court in *Pharmacia & Upjohn SA v Paranova A/S*,[273] a reference from the Danish Maritime and Commercial Court.

The Upjohn Group marketed in the Community the antibiotic clindamycin in a variety of forms using the trade marks "Dalacin" in Denmark, Germany, and Spain, "Dalacine" in France, and "Dalacin C" in the remaining Member States. The variations were due to an agreement concluded in 1968 between the Upjohn Group and American Home Products Corp, another pharmaceutical company. Paranova purchased "Dalacine" capsules in packets of 100 in France in order to market them in smaller batches in Denmark as "Dalacin". Further, it imported "Dalacin C" injection phials from Greece and marketed them as "Dalacin" in Denmark.

When the Upjohn Group initiated trade mark infringement proceedings Paranova argued that the different trade marks used in Denmark, France, and Greece were in essence the same trade mark; this meant that the Upjohn Group's rights had been exhausted. And as a second defence it supported that a marketing system built on variants of the same mark amounted to artificial partitioning of the markets.

8–143 The Danish court referred the following questions to the Court.

"1. Do Article 7 of Council Directive 89/104/EEC of 21 December 1988 to approximate the laws of the Member States relating to trade marks and/or Articles [28] and [30] of the EC Treaty preclude the proprietor of a trade mark from relying on its right under national trade-mark law as the basis for opposing a third party's purchasing a pharmaceutical

---

[272] *MPA Pharma GmbH v Rhône-Poulenc Pharma GmbH* (C-232/94) [1996] E.C.R. I-3671.
[273] *Pharmacia & Upjohn v Paranova A/S* (C-337/95) [1997] E.C.R. I-6013.

product in a Member State, repackaging it in that third party's own packaging, to which it affixes trade mark X belonging to the trade-mark proprietor, and marketing the product in another Member State, in the case where the pharmaceutical product in question is marketed by the trade-mark proprietor or with its consent in the Member State of purchase under trade mark Y and an identical pharmaceutical product is marketed by the trade-mark proprietor or with its consent in the abovementioned second Member State under trade mark X?

2. Does it have any bearing on the reply to Question 1 whether the trade-mark proprietor's use of different trade marks in the country in which the importer purchases the product and in that in which the importer sells the product is attributable to subjective circumstances particular to the trade-mark proprietor? If the answer is yes, is the importer required to adduce evidence that the use of different trade marks is or was intended artificially to partition the markets (reference is made in this connection to the Court's judgment of 10 October 1978 in Case 3/78 Centrafarm v American Home Products Corporation)?

3. Does it have any bearing on the reply to Question 1 whether the trade-mark proprietor's use of different trade marks in the country in which the importer purchases the product and in that in which the importer sells the product is attributable to objective circumstances outside the control of the trade-mark proprietor, including, in particular, requirements of national health authorities or the trade-mark rights of third parties?"[274]

(a) The Opinion of the Advocate General

8–144

Advocate General Jacobs noted that the main reason behind the reference was the uncertainty of the national court regarding the intent of the trade mark proprietor to partition the market, following *Bristol Myers Squibb*.[275]

(i) Rejecting the requirement of intention. Reviewing the case law of the Court he explained that possible inconsistencies between the position in *American Home Products*,[276] where according to one view the Court required some sort of intention to partition the market, and *Hoffmann-La Roche*[277] where it leaned towards a more objective test, had been resolved by *Bristol Myers Squibb*:

8–145

---

[274] Reproduced in para.11.
[275] *Bristol Myers Squibb v Paranova A/S* (C-427/93), *CH Boehringer Sohn, Boehringer Ingelheim KG and Boehringer Ingelheim A/S v Paranova A/S* (C-429/93) and *Bayer Aktiengesellschaft and Bayer Danmark A/S v Paranova A/S* (C-436/93) [1996] E.C.R. I-3457.
[276] The A.G. considered that in *Centrafarm v American Home Products Corp* (3/78) [1978] E.C.R. 1823 the difference in the formulation was deliberate. The aim was to deal with specific arguments developed by the parties regarding intent.
[277] *Hoffmann-La Roche & Co AG and Hoffmann-La Roche AG v Centrafarm Vertriebsgesellschaft Pharmazeutischer Erzeugnisse GmbH* (102/77) [1978] E.C.R. 1139.

"The scope of a parallel importer's right to repackage where the trade-mark owner markets goods in different forms of packaging in different Member States is, since Bristol-Myers Squibb, now governed by a body of coherent and clearly articulated principles hinging on objective factors. In my view, it would be anomalous and illogical for the scope of the importer's right to affix a different trade mark where the trade-mark owner markets goods under different marks in different Member States to continue to be governed by a separate set of principles dependent upon the subjective element of intention . . . the new criteria laid down by the Court in Bristol-Myers Squibb for repackaging by the parallel importer should be applied equally to such cases."[278]

For the Advocate General the prevalence of the essential function of the trade mark and the specific subject-matter of the right, compared with the subjective concept of intention, underpinned further the position adopted by the Court.

Similarly, the factors that led the trade mark proprietor to adopt different marks in different Member States should be irrelevant when considering whether the importer might affix a different trade mark. He repeated what he had supported in *Bristol Myers Squibb*, that it would be illogical to link the legality of the parallel importer's conduct with the subjective behaviour of the trade mark proprietor.

Intention on the other hand should be relevant where it could be shown that the trade mark proprietor's practice was indeed intended to partition markets, "that will in itself be sufficient to preclude reliance by him on his trade-mark rights to oppose affixing of a different mark by the importer".[279] This was after all what the Court said, or at least meant to say, in *American Home Products*.[280]

8–146   **(ii) The requirement of necessity.** The Advocate General observed on the other hand that the Court had indicated in *Bristol Myers Squibb*[281] and Ballantine[282] that the requirement of necessity should act as a balancing factor between the rights of the trade mark proprietor and those of the parallel importer.

---

[278] Point 35 of the Opinion of A.G. Jacobs.
[279] Point 42 of the Opinion of A.G. Jacobs.
[280] According to the A.G. para.28 of the judgment in *Frits Loendersloot v George Ballantine & Son* (C-349/95) [1997] E.C.R. I-6227, confirmed this: "Article [30] does not permit the owner of the trade mark to oppose the reaffixing of the mark where such use of his trade-mark rights contributes to the artificial partitioning of the markets between Member States and where the reaffixing takes place in such a way that the legitimate interests of the trade-mark owner are observed".
[281] *Bristol Myers Squibb v Paranova A/S* (C-427/93), *CH Boehringer Sohn, Boehringer Ingelheim KG and Boehringer Ingelheim A/S v Paranova A/S* (C-429/93) and *Bayer Aktiengesellschaft and Bayer Danmark A/S v Paranova A/S* (C-436/93) [1996] E.C.R. I-3457.
[282] *Frits Loendersloot v George Ballantine & Son* (C-349/95) [1997] E.C.R. I-6227.

6. PHARMACIA & UPJOHN—REPLACING THE TRADE MARK

He suggested that the principle should be applied to re-branding.

For repackaging the Court had already referred to rules or national practices, sickness insurance rules governing the reimbursement of medical expenses, and well-established medical prescription practices as reasons justifying repackaging.

Necessity and re-branding The same reasoning should apply to re-branding; he suggested however that there might be circumstances where repackaging would not be justified, but re-branding could be; "rebranding will more often be needed in order to avoid confusion in the importing State where ex hypothesi an identical product has previously been sold under a different mark".[283]   8–147

At the same time there might be circumstances where re-branding would be likely to cause rather than alleviate confusion, for example if the inner and the outer packaging bore different marks.

He was against rigid categorisations of factors that should be seen as necessary commercial risks rather than reasons necessitating re-branding. Ultimately, the decisive test was "whether in a given case prohibiting the importer from rebranding would constitute an obstacle to effective access by him to the markets of the importing State".[284] It was for the national court to assess where each specific factor should be located.

He indicated that in general where the importer used the trade mark applied by the proprietor in the importing Member State for identical products the criterion should be satisfied, because re-branding would ensure that there would be no confusion.

The time for assessing necessity He suggested that whether re-branding was necessary should be assessed at the time of the re-branding. He noted that the mere act of registration of a trade mark would not in itself constitute an impediment to importation; it was the exercise of the rights to oppose re-branding by the importer that should count.   8–148

(iii) Further conditions for re-branding. The Advocate General doubted whether the same conditions that applied to repackaging should also apply to re-branding.   8–149

Intrusive re-branding—for example sticking labels with the new trade mark on the inner packaging—that could affect the condition of the product would constitute repackaging rather than re-branding.

He also rejected the argument that there should be an indication on the outer packaging regarding the identity of the party responsible for the re-branding; such an indication would contribute to customer confusion.

---

[283] Point 50 of the Opinion of A.G. Jacobs.
[284] Point 54 of the Opinion of A.G. Jacobs.

8–150   He accepted, though, that re-branding should be done in a way that it would not be liable to damage the reputation of the trade mark.

Similarly, the importer should give notice to the trade mark proprietor and provide a specimen if required.

8–151   **(iv) The burden of proof.** Here, he referred to his views expressed in *Bristol Myers Squibb*.[285] This was a procedural matter that should be governed by national law provided that the procedural rules applicable to claims founded on Community law were not less favourable than those governing similar actions of a domestic nature and were not such as to render the exercise of rights flowing from Community law practically impossible or excessively difficult.

(b)   The judgment of the Court

8–152   **(i) The case law of the Court.** The Court referred first to its "consistent"[286] case law; following a thorough review of its case law on trade mark exhaustion it cited in relation to the concept of artificial partitioning of the markets its judgment in *Bristol Myers Squibb*: there was no requirement to show that the trade mark proprietor had deliberately sought to partition the markets between Member States.

And it repeated that reliance on trade mark rights to oppose marketing under the relevant trade mark of products repackaged by a third party would contribute to the partitioning of markets between Member States, in particular where the proprietor had placed an identical pharmaceutical product on the market in several Member States in various forms of packaging and the product might not, in the condition it had been marketed in one Member State, be imported and placed on the market in another Member State by a parallel importer. The power of the trade mark proprietor should be limited only in so far as the repackaging undertaken by the importer was necessary in order to market the product in the importing Member State.

It then looked at the *American Home Products*[287] judgment on re-branding. It accepted that it had held that the essential function of the trade mark would be jeopardised if it were permissible for a third party to affix the mark even to the original product and that the right to prohibit any unauthorised affixing of the trade mark fell within the specific subject-matter of the trade mark. It stressed though that it had also held that such a prohibition would constitute a disguised restriction on trade if it were established that using different trade marks for the same product in different Member States was for the purpose of artificially partitioning the markets.

---

[285] *Bristol Myers Squibb* (C-427/93), *CH Boehringer Sohn, Boehringer Ingelheim KG and Boehringer Ingelheim A/S* (C-429/93) and *Bayer Aktiengesellschaft and Bayer Danmark A/S* (C-436/93) [1996] E.C.R. I-3457.
[286] *Pharmacia & Upjohn*, para.13.
[287] *American Home Products Corp* (3/78) [1978] E.C.R. 1823.

(ii) Re-branding and repackaging. For deciding whether the principles that applied to repackaging covered re-branding the Court had to examine whether re-branding was different from repackaging. It found that there was no objective difference between reaffixing a trade mark after repackaging and replacing the original trade mark by another that was capable of justifying the condition of artificial partitioning being applied differently. 8–153

Both practices led to the partitioning of the market on the one hand and unauthorised use of a trade mark by a third party on the other.

Accordingly, the condition of artificial partitioning applied to both concepts in the same way. This, the Court found, also meant that there was no requirement to assess the intention of the trade mark proprietor.

On the other hand, the replacement of the trade mark had to be objectively necessary. The assessment of this requirement remained in the jurisdiction of the national courts. The Court elaborated a bit more on what the national court would have to establish in order to assess the condition of the necessity. 8–154

From a positive perspective it held that it would be:

"satisfied if, in a specific case, the prohibition imposed on the importer against replacing the trade mark hinders effective access to the markets of the importing Member State. That would be the case if the rules or practices in the importing Member State prevent the product in question from being marketed in that State under its trade mark in the exporting Member State. This is so where a rule for the protection of consumers prohibits the use, in the importing Member State, of the trade mark used in the exporting Member State on the ground that it is liable to mislead consumers".[288]

It would not be satisfied though if the replacement was "explicable solely by the parallel importer's attempt to secure a commercial advantage".[289]

7. BOEHRINGER—REVISITING REPACKAGING

The same motif characterised *Boehringer Ingelheim Pharma KG v Swingward Ltd*[290] and *Merck, Sharp and Dohme GmbH v Paranova Pharmazeutica Handels GmbH*.[291] 8–155

In the first case capsules and inhalers were repackaged by parallel importers in the United Kingdom that employed a diverse number of tactics,

---

[288] *Pharmacia & Upjohn*, para.43.
[289] *Pharmacia* para.44.
[290] *Boehringer Ingelheim Pharma KG v Swingward Ltd* (C-143/00) [2002] E.C.R. I-3759.
[291] *Merck, Sharp and Dohme GmbH v Paranova Pharmazeutica Handels GmbH* (C-443/99) [2002] E.C.R. I-3703.

like the application of stickers that did not obscure the trade mark but contained relevant to the product information, marketing in new boxes with a reproduction of the original trade mark, or marketing in new boxes with the generic name but not the original trade mark—parallel importers had not tampered with the original trade mark on the capsules, but had covered the trade mark on the inhaler with a sticker bearing a generic name.

The High Court referred the following questions to the Court:

"1. Can a proprietor of a trade mark use his trade mark rights to stop or hinder the import of his own goods from one Member State into another or to hinder their subsequent marketing or promotion when the importation, marketing or promotion causes no, or no substantial, harm to the specific subject-matter of his rights?

2. Is the answer to the previous question different if the ground relied on by the proprietor is that the importer or subsequent dealer is using his mark in a way which, although not prejudicial to its specific subject-matter, is not necessary?

3. If an importer of the proprietor's goods or a dealer in such imported goods needs to show that his use of the proprietor's mark is necessary, is that requirement met if it is shown that the use of the mark is reasonably required to enable him to access (a) part only of the market in the goods, or (b) the whole of the market in the goods; or does it require that the use of the mark was essential to enabling the goods to be placed on the market and if none of these, what does necessary mean?

4. If the proprietor of a mark is, prima facie, entitled to enforce his national trade mark rights against any use of his mark on or in relation to goods which is not necessary, is it abusive conduct and a disguised restriction on trade in accordance with the second sentence of Article 30, to use that entitlement in order to hinder or exclude parallel imports of his own goods which do not threaten the specific subject-matter or essential function of the trade mark?

5. Where an importer or someone dealing in imported goods intends to use the proprietor's trade mark on or in relation to those goods and such use does and will not prejudice the specific subject matter of the mark, must he nevertheless give the proprietor advance notice of his intended use of the mark?

6. If the answer to the previous question is in the affirmative, does that mean that failure of the importer or dealer to give such notice has the effect of entitling the proprietor to restrain or hinder the importation or further commercialisation of those goods even though such importation or further commercialisation will not prejudice the specific subject-matter of the mark?

7. If an importer or someone dealing in imported goods must give prior notice to the proprietor in respect of uses of the trade mark which do not prejudice the specific subject-matter of the mark, (a) does that

requirement apply to all such uses of the trade mark, including in advertising, re-labelling and repackaging or, if only some uses, which? (b) must the importer or dealer give notice to the proprietor or is it sufficient that the proprietor receives such notice? (c) how much notice must be given?

8. Is a national court of a Member State entitled, at the suit of the proprietor of trade mark rights, to order injunctions, damages, delivery up and other relief in respect of imported goods or the packaging or advertisements therefor where the making of such an order (a) stops or impedes the free movement of goods placed upon the market within the EC by the proprietor or with his consent but (b) is not for the purpose of preventing harm to the specific subject-matter of the rights and does not help to prevent such harm?"[292]

The second case concerned tablets imported into Austria. The blister packs were being repackaged in new outer boxes on which the original trade mark was reaffixed; the boxes also contained leaflets with information on use and other necessary details for the marketing of the product in Austria.

The Oberlandesgericht Wien (Higher Regional Court, Vienna) referred the following question to the Court:

8–156

"Must Article 7(2) of the First Council Directive of 21 December 1988 to approximate the laws of the Member States relating to trade marks (89/104/EEC) be interpreted as meaning that a trade mark owner may oppose the marketing of a pharmaceutical product put on the market under his trade mark where the importer has repackaged it and reaffixed the trade mark and has complied with the other requirements set forth in the Court of Justice judgment in Joined Cases C-427/93, C-429/93 and C-436/93 (the product inside the packaging must not be affected, the manufacturer and origin must be clearly indicated, the reputation of the trade mark or its owner must not be damaged as a consequence of poor packaging, and the trade mark owner must be given notice before the repackaged pharmaceutical product is put on sale), but the marketability of the product would be jeopardised without such repackaging solely because a significant proportion of the consumers of pharmaceutical products in the State of importation is suspicious of pharmaceutical products which have clearly been produced for the market of another State (in which a different language is spoken) and are inside packagings which have been adapted merely by means of self-stick labels to the domestic provisions governing the sale of pharmaceutical products?"[293]

---

[292] Reproduced in Point 58.
[293] Reproduced in Point 61.

8-157   (a)   *The Opinion of the Advocate General*

Advocate General Jacobs rejected the insinuation that the repackaging requirements set by the Court were inconsistent or incoherent; perhaps such an impression was due to the fact that those requirements were relevant at different stages in the analysis of the question whether a trade mark owner might rely on its trade mark rights to prevent a parallel importer from repackaging trade marked goods.

8-158   **(i) Framing the position of the Court.** Following a review of the case law of the Court he described its position in the following terms.

The trade mark owner was prima facie justified in preventing an importer from affixing the trade mark on the new packaging. However, in certain circumstances the exercise of that right might be unlawful because it would constitute a disguised restriction. For instance, adopting different packaging in different Member States and then using trade mark rights to stop repackaging that would not affect the identification of origin of the product, the original condition of the product, and the reputation of the trade mark and of its proprietor, should be considered an attempt to partition national markets artificially. In such cases repackaging would in principle be allowed.

He observed though that the Court had held that it was essential to consider whether the repackaging was objectively necessary in order to market the product in the importing Member State. This requirement would be clearly satisfied in cases of specific rules or national practices, sickness insurance rules on reimbursement of medical expenses, and medical prescription practices.

8-159   This was in contrast with cases where repackaging aimed to achieve a commercial advantage for the parallel importer.

Albeit, in less clear and less extreme cases, the existence and extent of necessity remained an uncharted territory.

8-160   **(ii) The uncertainties of the necessity requirement.** The Advocate General accepted that the necessity requirement meant that trade mark proprietors might in principle assert their trade mark rights even in the absence of actual harm or risk of harm; hence, he described the balancing between the interests of trade mark proprietors and parallel importers the Court aimed to achieve:

> "[I]t is clear from the terms of the relevant provisions of the Treaty as interpreted by the Court that interference by a third party, such as a parallel importer, with intellectual property rights, such as the rights of a trade mark owner, will be capable of justification by virtue of Community law only where the unfettered exercise of those rights would have an adverse effect on the free movement of goods. By importing the criterion

of necessity, and hence justifying all such interference which is necessary for effective access to the market in the importing State, the Court has developed a formula which precisely reflects that balance".[294]

He underlined that repackaging in principle constituted a particularly intrusive form of trade mark infringement. And that in most cases it concerned pharmaceuticals, a type of product that portrayed special features regarding quality and consumer expectations.

He also stressed that if it was shown that the trade mark owner's practice of using different marks in different Member States was intended to partition markets, that would in itself be sufficient to preclude the exercise of trade mark rights to oppose affixing of a different mark by the importer.

Attempting to accommodate these factors within the general principles developed by the Court he added:

8–161

"... repackaging may correctly be regarded as objectively necessary in other less black and white situations. If the national court finds as fact ... that there is widespread and substantial resistance to over-stickered boxes by the relevant consumers, and if the effect of such resistance is that the parallel importer would be effectively excluded from the market unless permitted to repackage, repackaging would to my mind certainly be regarded as objectively necessary for effective market access in the sense that is reasonably required for such access."[295]

Repackaging on the other hand should not be considered necessary if another, less intrusive, method could be found to give effective market access. The Court should also take account of the peculiarities of each product market; for example, in the case of pharmaceuticals, factors like price controls and public health considerations.

To illustrate the above guidelines he referred to the factual scenario of the Austrian case. If there was no doubt that some pharmacists would not purchase over-stickered products because some of their customers would not accept them he would accept that repackaging was necessary because otherwise the product would be excluded from the national market.

(iii) The advanced notice requirement. On the requirement of advanced notice the Advocate General suggested that it should be given by the parallel importer in all cases, even where the importation was licensed by the appropriate national authorities dealing with pharmaceutical products.

8–162

It should not be dependent on whether there was actual prejudice to the specific subject-matter of the mark. Failure to give notice should automatically

---

[294] Point 97 of the Opinion of A.G. Jacobs.
[295] Point 110 of the Opinion of A.G. Jacobs.

render the repackaging an infringement. Regarding what would constitute adequate notice he suggested that a three- to four-week period should be reasonable.

8–163   *(b) The judgment of the Court in Boehringer*

8–164   **(i) The specific subject-matter and the necessity requirement.** The Court joined the first, second, fourth and eighth questions of the English case as essentially seeking clarifications of the concept of the specific subject-matter of the trade mark.

It repeated its case law on what constitutes the specific subject and citing *Bristol Myers Squibb*[296] it found that "it is clear from settled case law that the change brought about by any repackaging of a trade-marked pharmaceutical product—creating by its very nature the risk of interference with the original condition of the product—may be prohibited by the trade mark proprietor unless the repackaging is necessary in order to enable the marketing of the products imported in parallel and the legitimate interests of the proprietor are also safeguarded".[297]

The third question focused on the circumstances that could render repackaging necessary. First it clarified that it was necessary to take account of the circumstances prevailing at the time of marketing in the importing Member State which made repackaging objectively necessary for the product to be placed on that State's market.[298] "The trade mark proprietor's opposition to the repackaging is not justified if it hinders effective access of the imported product to the market of that State."[299]

8–165   It then referred to its findings in *Bristol Myers Squibb*.[300] Such circumstances could be the result of national rules or practices relating to packaging, or where sickness insurance rules made reimbursement of medical expenses dependent on a certain packaging or where well-established medical prescription practices were based, inter alia, on standard sizes recommended by professional groups and sickness insurance institutions. But not when the repackaging was based solely on the parallel importer's attempt to secure a commercial advantage.

In the same case it had held that the trade mark proprietor might oppose replacement packaging where the parallel importer could reuse the original packaging by affixing an additional label to it.

---

[296] *Bristol Myers Squibb* (C-427/93), *CH Boehringer Sohn, Boehringer Ingelheim KG and Boehringer Ingelheim A/S* (C-429/93) and *Bayer Aktiengesellschaft and Bayer Danmark A/S* (C-436/93) [1996] E.C.R. I-3457.
[297] *Boehringer*, para.34.
[298] *Pharmacia & Upjohn S* (C-337/95) [1997] E.C.R. I-6013.
[299] *Boehringer*, para.46.
[300] *Bristol Myers Squibb*(C-427/93), *CH Boehringer Sohn, Boehringer Ingelheim KG and Boehringer Ingelheim A/S* (C-429/93) and *Bayer Aktiengesellschaft and Bayer Danmark A/S* (C-436/93) [1996] E.C.R. I-3457.

7. BOEHRINGER—REVISITING REPACKAGING

(ii) Effective market access. Here though the Court appeared to adopt a more conservative stance. The case law of the Court required the relabelled pharmaceutical product being able to have effective access to the relevant market.

8–166

Applying the familiar technique of one step backwards and then another forwards the Court first remarked that "[r]esistance to relabelled pharmaceutical products does not always constitute an impediment to effective market access such as to make replacement packaging necessary".[301]

Then again there may exist on a market, or on a substantial part of it, such strong resistance from a significant proportion of consumers to relabelled pharmaceutical products that there must be held to be a hindrance to effective market access. In those circumstances, repackaging of the pharmaceutical products would not be explicable solely by the attempt to secure a commercial advantage. The purpose would be to achieve effective market access.

National courts would have to determine the applicability of the concept of effective access that was linked with the necessity requirement either as a new requirement or, at least, as determining factor.

(iii) Advance notice. The response to the fifth, sixth, and seventh question was that the purpose of advance notice and furnishing a sample on request was to safeguard the legitimate interests of trade mark proprietors. Fulfilling it should not pose any real practical problems for parallel importers provided that the proprietors reacted within a reasonable time to the notice.

8–167

If the parallel importer failed to satisfy that requirement, the trade mark proprietor might oppose the marketing of the repackaged pharmaceutical product.

As to the method of giving notice the Court required the parallel importer itself to give notice to the trade mark proprietor of the intended repackaging; notification from another source would not suffice.

Finally, regarding the timing of the notice the Court held that it was appropriate to allow a reasonable time for the trade mark proprietor to react to the intended repackaging; on the other hand the parallel importer's interest in actually marketing the pharmaceutical product as soon as possible after obtaining the necessary licence from the competent authority should also be taken into account.

8–168

The balancing between the two interests was for the national court to achieve, however the Court—referring to the facts of the case—considered that a period of 15 working days seemed reasonable where the parallel importer had given notice to the trade mark proprietor and supplied simultaneously a sample of the repackaged pharmaceutical product.

---

[301] *Boehringer*, para.51.

8-169   (c)   *The judgment of the Court in Merck*[302]

The Court took a parallel path with that followed in *Boehringer I*.[303]

In this case the problem identified by the Austrian court was that Austrian consumers were not accustomed to pharmaceutical products that had been put on the market in another Member State with a different language. The Court repeated the above analysis and held that it was for the national court to decide whether this resistance made repackaging necessary in order to obtain effective access in the Austrian market.

8. BALLANTINE—TRADE MARK INFRINGEMENT AND POLICING CHANNELS OF TRADE

8-170   In *Frits Loendersloot v George Ballantine & Son Ltd*[304] the Court considered a challenge of the whisky producers' practice of affixing identification numbers on the labels, bottles, and packaging of their products. In a way it opened the line of free movement of goods cases under the new European trade mark regime.[305] The judgment is fundamental as it re-considers the rapport between trade mark rights and free movement of goods on a background newly dominated by positive integration.

Whisky producers started trade mark infringement proceedings in The Netherlands against Loendersloot, a transport and warehousing firm active in parallel imports. Loendersloot was removing the labels and, according to the destination market, re-affixing them or replacing them with copies having removed the identification numbers, the word "pure", and the name of the authorised importer, occasionally substituting it with the name of another importer. The products where then shipped to France, Spain, the United States of America and Japan.

8-171   Loendersloot's defence was two-pronged.

First, it argued that preventing a third party from removing or reapplying a trade mark was not part of the specific subject-matter of a trade mark right.

Secondly, it placed trade mark law within the context of free movement of goods rules and claimed that the whisky producers exercised their rights in order to eliminate parallel imports.

8-172   On this second point the whisky producers counter argued that the application of identification numbers intended to enable the identification of

---

[302] *Merck, Sharp and Dohme GmbH* (C-443/99) [2002] E.C.R. I-3703.
[303] *Boehringer Ingelheim Pharma KG v Swingward Ltd* (C-143/00) [2002] E.C.R. I-3759.
[304] *Frits Loendersloot* (C-349/95) [1997] E.C.R. I-6227.
[305] It can be taken as a starting point because any injunction granted by the national court would have taken effect after the effective date of the Directive. See the Opinion of the A.G. at para.8-177, below.

defective and counterfeit products; and that, in any case, it did not raise a barrier in intra-Community trade since the products could circulate within the Community in their original condition.

The Hoge Raad found that Loendersloot's interference with the labels constituted trade mark infringement according to Benelux trade mark law. Still, it stayed proceeding and made a reference to the Court of Justice on the application of art.30.

"1. Is the specific subject-matter of the rights attaching to a trade mark to be regarded as including the possibility afforded to the proprietor of a trade mark under national law to oppose, with regard to alcoholic drinks manufactured by him, the removal by a third party of labels affixed by the proprietor on bottles and on the packaging containing them, and bearing his mark, after the drinks have been placed by him on the Community market in that packaging, and the subsequent reapplication of those labels by that third party or their replacement by similar labels, without thereby in any way damaging the original condition of the product?

2. In so far as the labels are replaced by other similar labels, is the position different where the third party omits the indication 'pure' appearing on the original labels and/or, as the case may be, replaces the importer's name with another name?

3. If Question 1 falls to be answered in the affirmative, but the proprietor of the trade mark avails himself of the possibility referred to in that question in order to prevent the third party from removing the identification marks which the trade mark proprietor has affixed on or underneath the labels in order to enable the trade mark proprietor to detect shortfalls within his sales organisation and thus to combat, parallel trade in his products, must such an exercise of the trade mark right be regarded as a 'disguised restriction on trade between Member States' aimed at achieving an artificial compartmentalisation of the markets?

4. To what extent is the answer to Question 3 affected where the trade mark proprietor has affixed those identification marks either pursuant to a legal obligation or voluntarily, but in any event with a view to making a 'product recall' possible and/or in order to limit his product liability and/or to combat counterfeiting, or, as the case may be, solely in order to combat parallel trade?"[306]

(a) The Opinion of the Advocate General

Advocate General Jacobs viewed this case as a variation on the theme of repackaging, this time covering alcoholic beverages rather than pharmaceutical products.

---

[306] Reproduced in para.13.

He started by reviewing the principles developed by the Court. It is worth referring to this review in detail as a concise reminder of the case law of the Court until *Ballantine*.

8–174 **(i) The general principles.** The exercise of trade mark rights amounted to a measure having equivalent effect to a quantitative restriction on imports or exports.

Article 30 however provided for an exception to the rule of art.28 only to the extent to which the exceptions were necessary for the purpose of safeguarding rights that constituted the specific subject-matter of the relevant industrial or commercial property. For trade marks the specific subject-matter included the guarantee to the owner of the trade mark that it had the right to use that trade mark for the purpose of putting a product into circulation for the first time and therefore to protect it against competitors wishing to take advantage of the status and reputation of the trade mark by selling products illegally bearing that mark.

Once the product had been lawfully put on the market by the owner or with its consent the exclusive right to use the mark would be exhausted, otherwise the owner of trade mark rights would be able to partition off national markets.[307]

8–175 However, there were circumstances where a trade mark owner could prevent further marketing. This was linked with the essential function of a trade mark, namely to guarantee the identity of origin of the marked product to the consumer or ultimate user by enabling him without any possibility of confusion to distinguish that product from products which have another origin.[308]

Trade marks, he added allowed their owners to attract and retain customers by the quality of their products and services; trade marks made that possible by allowing them to be identified[309]:

> "It follows that, notwithstanding the fact that a product bearing a mark has been lawfully marketed by the owner or with his consent, the owner of a trade mark may oppose any use of the mark which is liable to impair the guarantee of origin so understood."[310]

---

[307] *Deutsche Grammophon v Metro* (78/70) [1971] E.C.R. 487; *Centrafarm BV v Winthrop BV* (16/74) [1974] E.C.R. 1183; *Pharmon v Hoechst* (19/84) [1985] E.C.R. 2281; and *SA CNL-SUCAL NV v Hag GF AG* (C-10/89) [1990] E.C.R. I-3711.

[308] *Hoffmann-La Roche & Co AG and Hoffmann-La Roche AG* (102/77) [1978] E.C.R. 1139; *American Home Products Corp* (3/78) [1978] E.C.R. 1823; [1979] 1 C.M.L.R. 326; and *SA CNL-SUCAL NV v Hag GF AG* (C-10/89) [1990] E.C.R. I-3711.

[309] *Bristol Myers Squibb v Paranova* (C-427/93); *CH Boehringer Sohn, Boehringer Ingelheim, Boehringer Ingelheim* (C-429/93) *Bayer Aktiengesellschaft, Bayer Danmark v Paranova* (C-436/94) [1996] E.C.R. I-3457; [1997] 1 C.M.L.R. 1151; *Eurim-Pharm Arzneimittel v Beiersdorf, Boehringer Ingelheim and Farmitalia Carlo Erba* (C-71/94 to C-73/94) [1996] E.C.R. I-3603; [1997] 1 C.M.L.R. 1222, and *MPA Pharma GmbH v Rhône-Poulenc Pharma GmbH* (C-232/94) [1996] E.C.R. I-3671.

[310] Point 17 of the Opinion of A.G. Jacobs.

(ii) The application of the general principles on repackaging. In *Hoffmann-La Roche*[311] the Court applied the above principles to the repackaging of pharmaceutical products. 8–176

The starting point in that case was that a trade mark owner could rely on its rights in one Member State to prevent an importer from marketing a product put on the market in another Member State by the owner or with its consent, where that importer had repackaged the product in new packaging to which the trade mark had been reaffixed.

There was one exception to that principle. The trade mark owner would not be able to rely on his rights, where:

(i) it was established that the use of the trade mark right by the owner, having regard to the marketing system which it had adopted, would contribute to the artificial partitioning of the markets between Member States;

(ii) it was shown that the repackaging could not adversely affect the original condition of the product;

(iii) the owner of the mark had received prior notice before the repackaged product was put on sale; and

(iv) it was stated on the new packaging by whom the product had been repackaged.[312]

(v) A fifth requirement had been added by the Court in *Bristol Myers Squibb*: the presentation of the repackaged product, in particular defective, poor quality or untidy packaging, should not damage the reputation of the trade mark.[313]

Note that the parallel importer does not appear to enjoy an automatic entitlement to repackage. The trigger is the behavior of the trade mark proprietor.[314]

(iii) The legislative context of the Directive. Advocate General Jacobs noted that the questions referred to the Court focused exclusively on the interpretation of art.30. 8–177

He suggested that from a procedural perspective the Directive was relevant because any injunction granted by the national court would relate to a post-Directive period.

---

[311] *Hoffmann-La Roche & Co AG and Hoffmann-La Roche AG* (102/77) [1978] E.C.R. 1139.
[312] Hoffmann-La Roche, para.14.
[313] *Bristol Myers Squibb v Paranova A/S* (C-427/93), *CH Boehringer Sohn, Boehringer Ingelheim KG and Boehringer Ingelheim A/S* (C-429/93) and *Bayer Aktiengesellschaft and Bayer Danmark A/S* (C-436/93) [1996] E.C.R. I-3457, para.75.
[314] Note that the same point is reiterated by A.G. Jacobs from the negative starting point of the trade mark proprietor who cannot rely on its rights; see para.8–179, below.

From a substantive perspective, he remarked that the Court had indicated in *Bristol Myers Squibb*[315] that art.7(2) of the Directive was to be given the same interpretation as that given to art.28 and art.30 of the Treaty.

8-178 **(iv) The applicability of article 28.** One of the main arguments introduced by *Ballantine* was to refute from the outset the applicability of art.28, partly because there was no obstacle to exporting to third countries or circulate within the European Union whisky bottles that had not been relabelled and partly because art.28 should not be an issue in the case of exports of relabelled bottles to third countries.

The Advocate General rejected that argument; under art.234 EC the Court was bound to answer the questions referred to it unless they were manifestly irrelevant to the dispute before the referring national court. Here the Hoge Raad had, at least, assumed that the injunctions would restrict the free movement of goods and would need to be justified under art.30. There was no reason to challenge the stance of the national court.

As to whether relabelling was necessary or not, this was a question that the national court had to consider. At this stage "the Hoge Raad's questions have to be considered on the hypothesis that parallel trade in the products concerned would not be possible unless they were relabelled. If that hypothesis is correct (which is a matter for the national courts to establish), then reliance by Ballantine and others on their trade mark rights in order to prevent relabelling clearly operates as a barrier to trade which must be justified under Article [30] of the Treaty".[316]

8-179 **(v) The essential principle of the Court's jurisprudence.** In order to respond to the questions the Advocate General delineated the core, the essential principle, of *Hoffmann-La Roche*[317] and *Bristol Myers Squibb*[318]:

"a trade mark owner cannot rely on his trade mark rights to prevent a parallel importer from repackaging goods bearing the trade mark and from re-applying the trade mark to the repackaged goods where it is established that the use of the trade mark right by the owner will contribute to the artificial partitioning of the markets between Member States; provided that in the course of such repackaging: (i) the guarantee of origin is not impaired; (ii) the original condition of the product is not adversely affected; and (iii) the reputation of the trade mark is not damaged".[319]

---

[315] *Bristol Myers Squibb* (C-427/93), *CH Boehringer Sohn, Boehringer Ingelheim KG and Boehringer Ingelheim A/S* (C-429/93) and *Bayer Aktiengesellschaft and Bayer Danmark A/S* (C-436/93) [1996] E.C.R. I-3457, para.50.
[316] *Ballantine*, para.26.
[317] *Hoffmann-La Roche & Co AG and Hoffmann-La Roche AG* (102/77) [1978] E.C.R. 1139.
[318] *Bristol Myers Squibb v Paranova A/S* (C-427/93), *CH Boehringer Sohn, Boehringer Ingelheim KG and Boehringer Ingelheim A/S* (C-429/93) and *Bayer Aktiengesellschaft and Bayer Danmark A/S* (C-436/93) [1996] E.C.R. I-3457.
[319] Point 28 of the Opinion of A.G. Jacobs.

He noted that the third point was also linked with the origin function because consumers confronted with inappropriate packaging might be confused regarding the origin of the product.

The remaining two conditions—notice and labelling information—were more specific and more detailed compliance provisions, in particular in relation to pharmaceuticals.[320]

(vi) Pharmaceuticals and whisky. The principles of the Court had, until then, been developed in cases involving pharmaceuticals. But there was no reason to make any distinction according to product category in respect of the essential principle. The underlying rationale remained the same. 8–180

However, the nature of the product would characterise the circumstances of the case. And in some cases particular considerations would be more poignant than in others, for example labelling information could be more critical for pharmaceuticals than alcoholic drinks:

> "In any event, this Court would ... be going beyond its functions under Article 234 of the Treaty if it were to rule on all aspects of repackaging and relabelling which might be undertaken by parallel importers in relation to different types of product. Once the Court has spelt out the essential principle or principles, it must be left to the national courts to apply those principles in the cases before them."[321]

(vii) Reputation considerations. He accepted that for a product like whisky any form of shoddy repackaging or relabelling would damage the reputation of the trade mark. 8–181

On the other hand he noted that relabelling would be permissible only to the extent necessary to facilitate parallel imports.

In this case it appeared to involve less interference than in *Bristol Myers Squibb*.[322] The national court would have to be that "there was a significant impairment of the presentation of the product which could affect the reputation of the trade mark".[323]

(viii) Partitioning of the markets. The three specific questions raised by the national court—the omission of the word "pure" from the relabelled products, the replacement of the importer's name with another name, and the removal of identification marks—were linked with the starting point of 8–182

---

[320] Contrast with the Opinion of A.G. Sharpston in para.8–259, below.
[321] Point 33. A point that has been made in other cases as well, see for example, para.8–256, below.
[322] *Bristol Myers Squibb* (C-427/93), *CH Boehringer Sohn, Boehringer Ingelheim KG and Boehringer Ingelheim A/S* (C-429/93) and *Bayer Aktiengesellschaft and Bayer Danmark A/S* (C-436/93) [1996] E.C.R. I-3457.
[323] Point 35 of the Opinion of A.G. Jacobs.

parallel import cases: artificial partitioning of the markets between Member States.

8–183 *Removal of "pure"* Loendersloot had argued that the word "pure" had to be removed from the label for the product to be allowed to circulate in some Member States.

The Advocate General referred to *Bristol Myers Squibb* in some detail.[324]

One of the instances where the exercise of trade mark rights could contribute to partitioning was where the owner had placed an identical pharmaceutical product on the market in several Member States in various forms of packaging, and the product could not, in the condition that it had been marketed by the trade mark owner in one Member State, be imported and put on the market in another Member State by a parallel importer.

8–184 The Court had contrasted between two cases. Where repackaging was necessary because the product was marketed in one size in one Member State but could not be marketed in the same size at another Member State the owner would be unable to rely on its rights.

8–185 To the contrary, the owner should be able to oppose repackaging in cases where the importer would be able to satisfy the marketing conditions by affixing new labels or adding information in the language of the Member State of importation.

The principle was that the "power of the owner of trade mark rights protected in a Member State to oppose the marketing of repackaged products under the trade mark should be limited only in so far as the repackaging undertaken by the importer is necessary in order to market the product in the Member State of importation".[325]

National courts would have to apply the above principle and determine whether the removal of the word "pure" was indeed necessary.

8–186 *Replacement of the importer's name—removal of identification numbers* Here the Advocate General believed that the Court would have to provide further clarifications to respond to Loendersloot's argument that these details had to be removed in order to prevent whisky producers from suffocating parallel trade.

Ballantine counter-argued that the details served legitimate purposes, for example they could facilitate product recalls.

The Advocate General supported the argument of the parallel importers. According to the basic principle described above:

---

[324] In particular paras 52–56 of *Bristol Myers Squibb* (C-427/93), *CH Boehringer Sohn, Boehringer Ingelheim KG and Boehringer Ingelheim A/S* (C-429/93) and *Bayer Aktiengesellschaft and Bayer Danmark A/S* (C-436/93) [1996] E.C.R. I-3457.
[325] *Bristol Myers Squibb*, para.56.

"it is clear that, subject to compliance with the conditions designed to safeguard the origin, quality and reputation of the product, an importer must be able to relabel products where that is necessary in order to effect parallel trade; otherwise the owner of a trade mark would be able, by relying on his trade mark right, artificially to partition the markets of the Member States. It is for the national courts to determine whether that requirement is met in the present case".[326]

He sought support for his statement from the Court's account of "artificial partitioning of the markets" in *Bristol Meyers Squibb*.[327] The Court did not require a deliberate endeavour to partition the markets between Member States. Rather, its intention was to stress that the owner of a trade mark might always rely on its rights when its opposition to parallel imports would be justified by the need to safeguard the essential function of the trade mark, in which case the resultant partitioning could not be regarded as artificial.

"Marking" obligations Responding to the final question he accepted that at least numbers identifying the lot to which a product belonged might serve legitimate public interests, in particular that of consumer protection. Community law had explicitly recognised that for specific product markets[328]: 8–187

"However, the extent to which a parallel importer may lawfully remove an identification number, applied either voluntarily or by virtue of a Community or national rule, on the ground that it is used for the purpose of tracking parallel imports is a separate issue going beyond the scope of the Hoge Raad's questions, which are concerned solely with the exercise of trade mark rights. It is clear that the removal of such identification numbers cannot be resisted by virtue of trade mark rights taken alone."[329]

Concluding he suggested that a trade mark proprietor could not exercise its rights in all the instances cases described by the Hoge Raad where it was established that the use of the trade mark right by the proprietor would contribute to the artificial partitioning of the market between Member States.

He required that the relabelling should not impair the guarantee of origin, not affect adversely the original condition of the product, and not damage the reputation of the trade mark.

---

[326] Point 41 of the Opinion of A.G. Jacobs.
[327] *Bristol Myers Squibb* (C-427/93), *CH Boehringer Sohn, Boehringer Ingelheim KG and Boehringer Ingelheim A/S* (C-429/93) and *Bayer Aktiengesellschaft and Bayer Danmark A/S* (C-436/93) [1996] E.C.R. I-3457, para.57; Point 42.
[328] For example Council Dir.89/396 on indications or marks identifying the lot to which a foodstuff belongs: [1989] OJ L186/21.
[329] Point 43 of the Opinion of A.G. Jacobs.

8–188   *(b)   The judgment of the Court*

The four questions were reformulated by the Court as essentially asking "whether Article [30] of the Treaty is to be interpreted as meaning that the owner of trade mark rights may, even if that constitutes a barrier to intra-Community trade, rely on those rights to prevent a third party from removing and then reaffixing or replacing the mark which the owner has himself affixed to products he has put on the Community market, where the original condition of the products is not affected".[330]

The Court acknowledged that according to the evidence and the position adopted by the Dutch courts Loendersloot's actions constituted infringement under the Benelux law, adopted according to the Directive. However, it held that the case should be resolved according to the Directive. The exhaustion provisions of the Directive had the same primary scope with art.30, to reconcile trade mark protection with free movement of goods; they were destined to produce analogous results.

It accepted that in principle an injunction would raise a trade barrier. The Court noted that art.30 allows derogations from the fundamental principle expressed in art.28 to the extent that they safeguard the specific subject-matter of the relevant right, which for trade marks was, "in particular to guarantee to the owner that he has the exclusive right to use that mark for the purpose of putting a product on the market for the first time and thus to protect him against competitors wishing to take unfair advantage of the status and reputation of the trade mark by selling products illegally bearing it".[331]

8–189   This led to the restatement that the holder of a trade mark right in one Member State could not exercise the right to block the importation or marketing of a product that had been put on the market in another Member State by itself or with its consent.

Here, the Court relied on its case law on repackaging, adding one additional caveat. The party relabelling the product must also ensure that the reputation of the trade mark was not harmed by "inappropriate presentation".[332] The national court should take into account "in particular the interest of Ballantine in protecting the luxury image of their products and the considerable reputation they enjoy".[333] This would be in addition to the requirements the Court had set in its earlier jurisprudence.[334]

---

[330] *Ballantine*, para.19.
[331] *Ballantine*, para.22, referring in particular to *Hoffmann-La Roche & Co AG and Hoffmann-La Roche AG* (102/77) [1978] E.C.R. 1139.
[332] *Ballantine*, para.33.
[333] *Bristol Myers Squibb* (C-427/93), *CH Boehringer Sohn, Boehringer Ingelheim KG and Boehringer Ingelheim A/S* (C-429/93) and *Bayer Aktiengesellschaft and Bayer Danmark A/S* (C-436/93) [1996] E.C.R. I-3457.
[334] The trade mark owner must be notified; a specimen must be made available on demand; and the particulars of the person responsible for the relabelling must appear on the product.

9. DIOR—BEYOND THE ORIGIN FUNCTION

The Court also accepted the finding of the Dutch court that removal of the identification numbers was not necessary for the cross-border trading and marketing of whisky. Where it is established that they impede parallel imports then the parallel trader must turn to the competition provisions of the EC Treaty.

Finally, regarding the removal of the word "pure" and the importer's name from the labels the Court decided that such acts should be tolerated only if it could be proved that they constituted requirements for the lawful marketing of whisky in a national market, since at this stage the European Union had not reached full harmonisation on labelling issues.[335] In such case, relabelling should cause the minimum possible prejudice to the specific subject-matter of the right.

9. DIOR—BEYOND THE ORIGIN FUNCTION

8–190 The Court reinforced the new approach in *Parfums Christian Dior SA and Parfums Christian Dior v Evora*,[336] another reference from Dutch courts. The Dior companies held a number of Benelux trade mark registrations for the containers and packaging of cosmetic products and were seeking to enforce their rights against Evora, a company operating a chain of chemists' shops that was not part of Dior's distribution network. Evora's promotional campaign incorporated in advertising leaflets pictures of containers and packaging that related clearly and directly to Dior products offered for sale. This manner of advertising was common amongst similar retailers.

Dior complained that the advertising campaign was not in accordance with the luxurious and prestigious image of Dior's brands. It argued that the expression "condition of the goods" articulated in art.7(2) of the Directive covered the physical as well as the "mental condition" of the goods, referring to the "allure, prestigious image and aura of luxury surrounding the goods, resulting from the manner in which the trade mark owner has chosen to present and advertise the goods using his trade mark rights".[337]

Evora argued, first, that advertising in a manner that was customary to retailers in the relevant sector would not infringe the Dior's rights and, secondly, that the provisions of the Directive and the free movement of goods provisions of the Treaty should preclude Dior from relying on its rights in order to stop its advertising campaign.

8–191 The Hoge Raad referred a number of questions to the Court of Justice, despite the fact that at the time of the reference the Directive had not yet been implemented into Benelux law. The implementation deadline had

---

[335] Council Directive 79/112/EEC, [1979] OJ L33/1.
[336] *Parfums Christian Dior SA* (C-337/95) [1997] E.C.R. I-6013; see also *Bayerische Motorwerke AG and BMW Nederland BV* (C-63/97) [1999] E.C.R. I-905, paras 6–094 and following.
[337] Point 12 of the Opinion of A.G. Jacobs.

passed and it considered that the interpretation of the provisions of the Directive would be of utmost urgency and relevance.

"(a) Where, in proceedings relating to trade marks in one of the Benelux countries in connection with the interpretation of the Uniform Benelux Act on Trade Marks, a question relating to the interpretation of the First Council Directive 89/104 to approximate the laws of the Member States relating to trade marks arises, is the highest national court or the Benelux Court to be regarded as the court or tribunal of the Member State against whose decisions there is no remedy under national law and which is therefore obliged under the third paragraph of Article 234 EC to make a reference to the Court of Justice?

(b) Is it in keeping with the system of the aforementioned Directive, in particular Articles 5, 6 and 7 thereof, to assume that, where it is a question of the resale of goods which have been put on the market in the Community under a trade mark by the trade mark proprietor or with his consent, the reseller is also free to use that trade mark for the purposes of bringing such further commercialisation to the attention of the public?

(c) In the event that question (b) is answered in the affirmative, do exceptions exist to that rule?

(d) In the event that question (c) is answered in the affirmative, is there room for an exception where the advertising function of the trade mark is endangered by the fact that, as a result of the manner in which the reseller uses the trade mark in order to attract public attention in that way, he damages the luxurious and prestigious image of the trade mark?

(e) Can there be said to be 'legitimate reasons' within the meaning of Article 7(2) of the directive where, as a result of the way in which the reseller advertises the goods, the 'mental condition' of the goods—that is to say, their allure, prestigious image and aura of luxury resulting from the manner in which the trade mark proprietor has chosen to present and advertise the goods using his trade mark rights—is altered or detracted from?

(f) Do the provisions of Articles [28] and [30] E.C. preclude the proprietor of a (picture) trade mark or a holder of copyright relating to the bottles and packaging used for his goods from making it impossible, by invoking the trade mark right or copyright, for a reseller who is free further to commercialise those goods to advertise the goods in a manner customary to retail traders in the relevant sector? Is this the case also where the reseller, as a result of the manner in which he uses the trade mark in his advertising material, damages the luxurious and prestigious image of the trade mark or the publication or reproduction takes place in circumstances such that damage may be done to the person entitled to the copyright?"[338]

---

[338] Reproduced in para.14.

9. DIOR—BEYOND THE ORIGIN FUNCTION

(a) The Opinion of the Advocate General   8–192

Advocate General Jacobs described the essential question of the case as whether a trade mark proprietor could prevent the advertising of goods placed on the market by itself or with its consent, "in circumstances in which such advertising damages the luxurious and prestigious image of his mark. In particular, is the prevention of such advertising possible if the reseller is merely advertising in a manner customary to his trade"?[339]

This time the Directive was discussed in greater detail. The Advocate General started by referring to the relevant provisions of the Directive and then turned to the questions referred by the Hoge Raad.

The relevant provisions were art.5(3)(d) including the right to prevent all third parties not having the proprietor's consent from using the mark in advertising to the rights of the trade mark proprietor; art.6 providing the limitations to the exercise of trade mark rights; and art.7 on the exhaustion of rights.

(i) Question 1—a procedural peculiarity. He found the question to be   8–193
admissible, at least as a tool for resolving future cases. The peculiarity was the existence of the Benelux Court that functioned similarly to the Court of Justice way in relation to the Uniform Benelux Act on Trade Marks. The issue was whether Hoge Raad, the Dutch court, was bound to refer the questions to the Benelux Court or the Court of Justice.

The Advocate General favoured the second option. It would suffice for the purposes of art.234 EC that the national court would adopt a final decision at the national level. It would also be in the interests of procedural economy for the Court to be given the opportunity to rule in advance of the proceedings before the Benelux Court.

(ii) Question 2—exhaustion and advertising. Article 7 incorporated   8–194
into the Directive principles that had already been developed by the Court.[340]

Here, A.G. Jacobs looked at the language of art.7(1). The provision precluded a trade mark owner from prohibiting "use" of a trade mark in relation to goods which have been put on the market in the Community under that trade mark by the proprietor or with his consent.

He suggested that if "a reseller is free to sell products placed on the market by the trade mark owner or with his consent, it must follow that he is free, in principle, to advertise the goods also".[341] Otherwise the reseller's would be rendered virtually meaningless. Even more so if we included to advertising point of sale material and displays of the product.

---

[339] Point 1 of the Opinion of A.G. Jacobs.
[340] Citing as an example *Bristol Myers Squibb* (C-427/93), *CH Boehringer Sohn, Boehringer Ingelheim KG and Boehringer Ingelheim A/S* (C-429/93) and *Bayer Aktiengesellschaft and Bayer Danmark A/S* (C-436/93) [1996] E.C.R. I-3457.
[341] Point 31 of the Opinion of A.G. Jacobs.

8-195   The wording of art.5(3)(d) supported his interpretation. It referred to "using the sign on business papers and in advertising". It would be logical to assume that the concept of "use" in art.7(1) covered advertising as well.

Concluding, he suggested that the answer to the first question should be that a reseller should be free, as a matter of general principle, not only to resell those goods but also to use that trade mark for the purposes of bringing such sale to the attention of the public.

8-196   **(iii) Questions 3, 4, and 5—the exceptions to the general principle.** The Advocate General found the *Bristol Myers Squibb* judgment[342] to be a useful precedent. There the Court found that damage to a trade mark owner's reputation could be a "legitimate reason" within the meaning of art.7(2):

> "If a trade mark owner is entitled to oppose shoddy repackaging which damages his reputation, I do not see why he should not be entitled in certain circumstances to oppose shoddy advertising which damages his reputation."[343]

Still, he drew some distinctions between the two situations. Repackaging constituted a more direct interference with the rights of the trade mark owner. However, it would only affect the perception of those viewing the repackaged products. Advertising by a reseller could reach a wider audience and have a greater effect on the reputation of the brand.

He then found that the word "commercialization" in art.7(2) should be seen either as having the same meaning with "use" in art.7(1), in the sense that it referred to further marketing of the goods, or as clearly incorporating advertising into its meaning. Accordingly he rejected one of Evora's main arguments.

At the same time he disagreed with the argument suggested by Dior that the reference to the "condition of the goods" in art.7(2) extended to the "mental condition" of the goods. The Court in *Bristol Myers Squibb*[344] had indicated that it covered the actual condition of the goods in their packaging.

8-197   **(iv) Reputation and the functions of a trade mark.** Advocate General Jacobs conceived the protection of reputation as a free standing concern.

---

[342] *Bristol Myers Squibb* (C-427/93), *CH Boehringer Sohn, Boehringer Ingelheim KG and Boehringer Ingelheim A/S* (C-429/93) and *Bayer Aktiengesellschaft and Bayer Danmark A/S* (C-436/93) [1996] E.C.R. I-3457.

[343] Point 36 of the Opinion of A.G. Jacobs.

[344] *Bristol Myers Squibb* (C-427/93), *CH Boehringer Sohn, Boehringer Ingelheim KG and Boehringer Ingelheim A/S* (C-429/93) and *Bayer Aktiengesellschaft and Bayer Danmark A/S* (C-436/93) [1996] E.C.R. I-3457.

9. DIOR—BEYOND THE ORIGIN FUNCTION

He agreed with the emphasis the Court placed on the function of a trade mark as an indicator of origin. However, he suggested broadening the framework of protection that was characterised by the function of a trade mark.

According to his reading of *Bristol Myers Squibb*[345] the Court had indicated that it would not have necessarily required that consumers believed that the trade mark owner was in any way responsible for or connected with the undertaking which carried out the shoddy repackaging. "It therefore seems reasonable to conclude that, in circumstances such as those of the present case, the trade mark owner need only show risk of significant damage to his reputation, and need not show that the public believe the retailer to be connected to or authorised by him."[346]

8–198

He cautiously remarked however that his discussion of origin in likelihood of confusion cases remained valid.[347] Choosing the middle ground, he noted that "the origin theory, understood more broadly, recognises that marks deserve protection because they symbolise qualities associated by consumers with certain goods or services and guarantee that the goods or services measure up to expectations. It is in that broader sense that the origin function has been understood by the Court . . . in HAG II".[348]

All the other functions, be it communication, investment, or advertising, were derivatives of the origin function. "Accordingly, it follows that the circumstances in which a trade mark owner can invoke his trade mark rights in order to protect his reputation should not be construed too widely."[349]

In order to accommodate this middle ground approach the Advocate General mediated his willingness to protect the reputation of a trade mark by adding the requirement that there should be a risk of significant damage to it.

Concentrating on the market for luxury perfumes he cited a statement of the Commission in a decision exempting a selective distribution network: "the distribution system notified allows the exclusive character of the contract products to be safeguarded, such exclusive character being the main reason why consumers choose them. The consumer is thus assured that the luxury product will not become an everyday product as a result of the downgrading of its image and a decrease in the level of creation".[350]

8–199

---

[345] Referring for example to para.47 of that judgment.
[346] Point 49 of the Opinion of A.G. Jacobs.
[347] Citing his Opinion in *SABEL BV v Puma AG* (C-251/95) [1997] E.C.R. I-6191.
[348] Point 41, citing *SA CNL-SUCAL NV v Hag GF AG* (C-10/89) [1990] E.C.R. I-3711.
[349] Point 42 of the Opinion of A.G. Jacobs.
[350] Commission Decision 92/428 of July 24, 1992 relating to a proceeding under art.85 EEC Case No.IV/33.542—*Parfums Givenchy System of Selective Distribution* [1992] OJ L236/11, at p.20 para.IIB(3); Commission Decision 92/33/EEC of December 16, 1991 relating to a proceeding under art.85 EEC IV/33.242—*Yves Saint Laurent Parfums* [1992] OJ L12/24, at pp.32–33 para.IIB(3). The position had been upheld by the Court of First Instance in *Groupement D'Achat Edouard Leclerc v EC Commission* (T-19 & 88/92) [1996] E.C.R. II-185.

Distinguishing this case from selective distribution agreement cases he noted that here the products had been put on the market by the trade mark owner. As a result, "trade mark rights may be invoked to object to advertising by parallel traders only if there is a risk of significant damage to the trade mark and that risk is properly substantiated".[351]

8–200 *Factors for Assessing the Risk of Significant Damage* Advocate General Jacobs suggested that the assessment of the risk would be a question of fact for the national court. To assist he suggested a number of factors that courts could take into account.

First, whether the authorised distributors had advertised in similar ways without a complaint from the trade mark proprietor.

Secondly, evidence that the selective distribution system set up by the trade mark owner would be objectionable under the competition provisions of the Treaty, because it would not be necessary for the relevant type of product in question.

8–201 Thirdly, the fact that the trade mark proprietor had not attempted to set up a watertight distribution system.

Qualifying further the damage to reputation risk, he noted that trade mark owners "should not, as a general rule, be entitled to object to respectable advertising by respectable traders, even if it can be shown that there is some damage to the product's luxurious image by virtue of the fact that such advertising is inferior to that of selected distributors".[352]

Towards the other extreme he accepted that the advertising of sale of luxury perfumes at cut prices joined with rolls of toilet paper and toothbrushes would be objectionable. In some cases, for example a "novelty" shop in a seedy area, some establishments should not be able to market luxury products.

Concluding, he submitted that the owner of the trade mark might oppose use of its trade mark by a reseller in advertising that would be liable to damage significantly the reputation of the trade mark and of its owner. In the case of luxury goods such as perfumes, the damage might consist in damage to the luxurious image of the goods. In any case the risk of significant damage to the reputation of the trade mark should be properly substantiated.

8–202 **(v) Question 6—the application of article 28 and article 30—copyright considerations.** The Advocate General reminded that copyright would fall within the scope of art.30, in particular when exploited commercially.[353]

---

[351] Point 46 of the Opinion of A.G. Jacobs.
[352] Point 51 of the Opinion of A.G. Jacobs.
[353] *Musik-Vertrieb Membran v GEMA* (55 & 57/80) [1981] E.C.R. 147.

9. DIOR—BEYOND THE ORIGIN FUNCTION

Following the above analysis the Advocate General supported that both trade mark rights and copyrights should be taken into account in order to prevent advertising liable to damage significantly the reputation of the relevant product. The risk of significant damage to the reputation of the trade mark should be properly substantiated.

(b) *The judgment of the Court*

(i) Question 1—the admissibility issue. Following an analysis of the respective roles of the Benelux Court and the Hoge Raad the Court of Justice held that when a question relating to the interpretation of the Directive was raised in proceedings in one of the Benelux Member States concerning the interpretation of the Uniform Benelux Act on Trade Marks, a court against whose decisions there was no remedy under national law— this covered both the Benelux Court and the Hoge Raad—had to make a reference to the Court of Justice under art.234. However, that obligation would lose its purpose when the question raised was substantially the same as a question which had already been the subject of a preliminary ruling in the same national proceedings.

8–203

(ii) Question 2—exhaustion and advertising. For the Court, the second question focused on the link between the resale of parallel imported products and advertising. It asked whether resellers, who are otherwise free to resell them, are also free to use the products' respective trade marks in order to communicate to consumers this further commercialisation.

The Court of Justice turned to arts 5 and 7 of the Directive for an answer. It stated unequivocally that the right to prohibit use of a trade mark was exhausted once the marked product has been put on the market by the proprietor or with its consent and that the same should apply to the right to use the trade mark for letting consumers know that the marked product was being resold.

Whether the right had been exhausted would be decided according to the Directive; however, art.7 should be interpreted in the light of the free movement of goods principle. Otherwise, the exhaustion principle set in art.7 would be undermined. "When trade-marked goods have been put on the Community market by the proprietor of the trade mark or with his consent, a reseller, besides being free to resell those goods, is also free to make use of the trade mark in order to bring to the public's attention the further commercialisation of those goods".[354]

8–204

(iii) Questions 3, 4, and 5—the exceptions to the general principle. The Court then considered the possible exceptions to this rule.

8–205

---

[354] *Dior*, para.38.

According to its interpretation the Hoge Raad wanted to learn whether any exceptions were allowed, in particular:

> "where the advertising function of the trade mark is endangered by the fact that the reseller damages the luxurious and prestigious image of the trade mark, as a result of the manner in which he uses the trade mark in order to attract public attention, and where the 'mental' condition of the goods, that is to say the allure, prestigious image and aura of luxury which they have as a result of the manner in which the trade mark owner has chosen to present and advertise the goods using his trade mark rights, is changed or impaired, as a result of the way in which the reseller advertises the goods".[355]

Note that the reference to the advertising function of a trade mark appeared in the elucidation by the Court of the questions referred by the Hoge Raad rather than in its own interpretation of art.7(2).

Still, the response of the Court to this question appears to broaden the scope of trade mark protection, whilst using a neutral and restrained language. According to art.7(2) the exhaustion of rights rule of art.7(1) did not apply where there were legitimate reasons for the proprietor to oppose further commercialisation of trade marked goods, altering or impairing the original condition of the goods would constitute one, but the legitimate reasons were not depleted there. The use of the word "especially" in art.7(2) combined with the jurisprudence of the Court suggested that alteration or impairment was given only as an example.

8–206 According to the Court, the purpose of art.7(2) was to reconcile two, now equal, interests; the "fundamental interest in the protection of trade mark rights with the fundamental interest in the free movement of goods within the common market".[356]

This case involved prestigious, luxury goods and the reseller should "not act unfairly in relation to the legitimate interests of the trade mark owner".[357] Expressed positively, this meant that the re-seller must endeavour to prevent the relevant advertising from affecting the value of the trade mark "by detracting from the allure and prestigious image of the goods in question and from their aura of luxury".[358]

But the Court then went on to limit the scope of the obligation by adding that a reseller who habitually marketed articles of the same kind—rather than of the same quality or prestige—could use methods of advertising that are customary in the relevant trade sector, even if these methods are not the same with those of the trade mark owner. The final proviso added by the

---

[355] *Dior*, para.39.
[356] *Dior*, para.42.
[357] *Dior*, para.45.
[358] *Dior*, para.45.

10. SILHOUETTE—THE TERRITORIAL SCOPE OF EXHAUSTION

Court expanded again the scope of protection available to the trade mark owner: such advertising would not, in any case, seriously damage the reputation of the trade mark.[359]

(iv) The sixth question—the application of article 28 and article 30—copyright considerations. The essence of the question according to the Court was whether a prohibition such as that sought in the main proceedings might be allowed under art.30. 8–207

Following its analysis above and the ruling in *Bristol Myers Squibb*[360] that art.7 and the free movement of goods rules should be interpreted in the same way the Court found that the proprietor of a trade mark might not oppose the use of the trade mark, by a reseller who habitually marketed articles of the same kind, but not necessarily of the same quality, as the trademarked goods, in ways customary in the reseller's sector of trade, for the purpose of bringing the further commercialisation of those goods to the public's attention, unless it was established that, given the specific circumstances of the case, the use of the trade mark for this purpose seriously damages the reputation of the trade mark.

Regarding copyright it underlined that art.30 did cover copyright under industrial and commercial property and that commercial exploitation of copyright raised the same issues as that of any other industrial or commercial property.[361]

Accordingly it held that the protection conferred by copyright as regards the reproduction of protected works in a reseller's advertisement should not, in any event, be broader than that conferred on a trade mark owner in the same circumstances and repeated its holding regarding trade marks this time covering copyright. 8–208

10. SILHOUETTE—THE TERRITORIAL SCOPE OF EXHAUSTION

Silhouette,[362] a reference from the Austrian Oberster Gerichtshof, presented to the Court the scenario of territorial versus international exhaustion. Silhouette, a producer of designer spectacles and spectacle frames exercised its national trade mark rights, arising from registration of "Silhouette", 8–209

---

[359] Note that according to the judgment the exercise of copyright covering an imported product would raise similar concerns; accordingly, the exclusive right of exploitation conferred by copyright should not prevent or restrict, for example, the importation of sound recordings of protected works that have been lawfully marketed in another Member State by the owner of the right or with its consent.

[360] *Bristol Myers Squibb* (C-427/93), *CH Boehringer Sohn, Boehringer Ingelheim KG and Boehringer Ingelheim A/S* (C-429/93) and *Bayer Aktiengesellschaft and Bayer Danmark A/S* (C-436/93) [1996] E.C.R. I-3457.

[361] *Musik-Vertrieb Membran v GEMA* (55 & 57/80) [1981] E.C.R. 147; and *Warner Brothers Inc and Metronome Video ApS v Erik Viuff Christiansen* (158/86) [1988] E.C.R. 2605.

[362] *Silhouette International Schmied GmbH & Co KG v Hartlauer Handelsgesellschaft mbH* (C-355/96) [1998] E.C.R. I-4799.

against Hartlauer, a retailer known for its low prices. Hartlauer had obtained genuine "Silhouette" frames from a Bulgarian company to which Silhouette had sold part of its out-of-fashion stock. Silhouette had instructed its representative to agree with the purchasers of this stock that it would be made available only in Bulgaria and states of the former Union of Soviet Socialist Republics and not exported to other countries.[363]

Silhouette claimed that the frames had not been put on the market of the European Economic Area by itself or with its consent. Hartlauer responded that Silhouette had not sold the frames subject to any prohibition of re-importation.

The Oberster Gerichtshof posed two questions. First, whether the true meaning of art.7(1) of the Directive is "that the trade mark entitles its proprietor to prohibit a third party from using the mark for goods which have been put on the market under that mark in a State which is not a Contracting State",[364] and, secondly, whether a trade mark proprietor may "seek an order that the third party cease using the trade mark for goods which have been put on the market under that mark in a State which is not a Contracting State"[365] based exclusively on art.7(1).

8–210 *(a) The Opinion of the Advocate General*

Advocate General Jacobs described first the framework for exhaustion set by the Directive and the provisions of the Treaty as interpreted by the Court. He then looked at the concepts of territorial and international exhaustion before considering the position adopted by the Directive. The starting point was the principle of Community wide exhaustion established by the Court for intellectual property rights and trade marks in particular.[366] This was reflected in art.7(1).

8–211 **(i) Article 7(1)—territorial scope.** The Advocate General demarcated the scope of the first question by assuming that Silhouette had not consented to its products being resold within the EEA; in addition the referring court had not suggested that there were any legitimate reasons for Silhouette to oppose the resale of its spectacles in Austria under art.7(2).

The Court had to decide whether the Directive precluded Member States from adopting the principle of international exhaustion.

---

[363] The factual scenario of the case raised a number of uncertainties; first, Austrian courts were unable to establish whether the representative had acted according to its instructions; and, second, the itinerary of the frames from a warehouse in the United Kingdom to Sofia combined with a cloud over where the sale had been concluded meant that the case could be viewed as a case of re-importation of products into the EEA.
[364] Reproduced in para.14.
[365] Reproduced in para.14.
[366] *Winthrop BV* (16/74) [1974] E.C.R. 1183, extended to the EEA following the Agreement on the EEA.

10. SILHOUETTE—THE TERRITORIAL SCOPE OF EXHAUSTION

The wording and legislative history of article 7(1) He remarked that according to its wording art.7(1) provided only for Community wide, not for international, exhaustion. It did not require Member States to provide for international exhaustion; the ambiguity in its interpretation was whether it allowed Member States to adopt international exhaustion.

8–212

Turning to the history of the provision he noted that the original proposal provided for international exhaustion; subsequently the Commission changed its stance and limited the scope of the provision to goods that had been put on the market in the Community.

And the language of the provision indicated that the Directive precluded international exhaustion:

"Article 7(1) spells out the circumstances in which the trade-mark rights are exhausted: it is naturally read as doing so exhaustively. In providing that the rights are exhausted when the goods are marketed in the Community, Article 7(1) is naturally understood as meaning that the rights are not exhausted when the goods are marketed in a third country. It is true that the Directive does not specifically preclude international exhaustion, but that effect can reasonably be inferred from the language. I accept that there are arguments which go the other way, but those arguments derive little support from the language of the Directive."[367]

Still, only by delineating the scope of art.7(1) it would become clear what principle the Directive went for. "Since the terms of the Directive are not conclusive, the aims and scope of the Directive are of crucial significance in interpreting its provisions."[368]

The scope of article 7(1)—derogating from article 5(1) Interestingly, he viewed art.7(1) as a derogation from the rights conferred by art.5(1). And derogations should not be construed broadly; accepting that art.7(1) allowed international exhaustion would introduce another, implied, derogation.[369]

8–213

He admitted that the Recitals appeared contradictory; on the one hand the Directive did not aim to undertake full-scale approximation but rather to approximate the national provisions that most directly affected the functioning of the Common Market.[370] On the other, it intended to provide for trade marks the same protection under the legal systems of all the Member States.[371] Proponents of international exhaustion stressed the first element, opponents the second.

---

[367] Point 33 of the Opinion of A.G. Jacobs.
[368] Point 35 of the Opinion of A.G. Jacobs.
[369] Regarding the starting point in this debate see also para.8–257, below.
[370] Point 4 of the Opinion of A.G. Jacobs.
[371] Citing the Third Recital to the Preamble.

The Advocate General viewed art.7 as having a broader role rather than that of a simple codification tool of the case law of the Court, which appeared to leave free Member States to choose a principle of exhaustion provided that they respected Community wide exhaustion:

> "If the Directive is seen as establishing the essential terms and effects of trade-mark protection, it is difficult to argue that it leaves Member States free to opt for international exhaustion. The scope of the exhaustion principle is after all central to the content of trade-mark rights."[372]

8–214 He reached the same conclusion from the perspective of the functioning of the internal market. If some Member States adopted international exhaustion and others did not there would be barriers to trade within the internal market, whereas the aim of the Directive was to remove such barriers.

He accepted the argument that if Member States were free to adopt international exhaustion then the same products could be the subject of parallel imports into one Member State but not into another, a result incompatible with the internal market. Accepting that once goods were imported into an international exhaustion Member State should be allowed to circulate freely throughout the Community, would indirectly impose international exhaustion on all Member States.[373]

8–215 **(ii) The "competence" of the Directive.** He also rejected the submission of the Swedish Government that the choice of an exhaustion principle remained outside the scope of a Directive based on art.95[374] because it concerned the relations between the Member States and third countries.

The Advocate General looked at the Directive from a narrower perspective. Its aim was not to regulate relations between Member States and third states but only to lay down the rights of trade mark proprietors in the Community; precluding international exhaustion would have an effect on external trade but it would not actually regulate it. It was inevitable that internal market measures would affect imports from third countries.

The Swedish argument was supplemented by the claim that the external competence in matters of intellectual property was not exclusive to the Community.[375] Here the Advocate General noted that the issue would arise

---

[372] Point 40 of the Opinion of A.G. Jacobs.
[373] Contrast with the approach of the EFTA Court that opted for international exhaustion in Case *Mag Instrument Inc v California Trading Co Norway, Ulsteen* (E-2/97) [1998] 1 C.M.L.R. 331 EFTA.
[374] Now art.95.
[375] Opinion 1/94 on the WTO Agreement [1994] E.C.R. I-5267. The A.G. observed that some Member States and some third countries had not opted for international exhaustion and that had not been held to be contrary to the General Agreement on Tariffs and Trade. Indeed, the World Trade Organisation Agreement left, in art.6 of the Agreement on Trade-related aspects of Intellectual Property Rights (TRIPs), the exhaustion issue an open question. On how TRIPs affects provisional measures, see *HERMÈS International v FHT Marketing Choice BV* (C-53/96) [1998] E.C.R. I-3603.

10. SILHOUETTE—THE TERRITORIAL SCOPE OF EXHAUSTION

only if negotiations were to be undertaken with third countries to deal with international exhaustion. Indeed, commercial policy and reciprocity considerations were among the reasons why the original provision for international exhaustion had been amended. These considerations however did not limit the material scope of a measure based on art.95.

(iii) Commercial policy considerations. The final Swedish argument for international exhaustion was based on the case law of the Court on the function of a trade mark as an indicator of origin. Trade mark rights, it argued, should not become tools for dividing and compartmentalising the global market. International exhaustion would break down the barriers and promote price competition. 8–216

He accepted that these arguments were attractive, albeit not persuasive. First, the case law of the Court had been developed in the context of the Community and the development of a common market rather than the global market.[376]

In a way, the Advocate General admitted that trade mark rights had been limited through the origin function because they impeded the establishment of a common market; the wider role of trade marks had not really influenced the case law of the Court. International exhaustion, as he had argued above, would erect rather than bring down intra Community barriers and distort price competition within the internal market because only consumers in the international exhaustion Member States would benefit.

He accepted that there was a powerful argument for international exhaustion based on the concern for free trade; however this was a commercial policy consideration that remained outside the function of the Court.

(iv) Exhaustion and competition policy. Finally he reminded the Court that whatever they decided on exhaustion it would not affect the application of the competition provisions of the Treaty. He highlighted the outcome of cases like *EMI v CBS*[377] and *Javico International*.[378] 8–217

(v) Exhaustion and the Community Trade Mark Regulation. Since the Community Trade Mark Regulation formed part of the Community Trade Mark regime A.G. Jacobs noted that art.13, the exhaustion provision of the Regulation, was worded in identical terms with art.7 of the Directive. Again, the original proposal provided for international exhaustion but it was then amended to cover only goods that had been put on the market in the Community. Given the nature of the Regulation it was clear that it did not 8–218

---

[376] *EMI Records v CBS United Kingdom* (51/75) [1976] E.C.R. 811 where the Court had held that its free movement of goods rules case law could not be transposed to imports from third countries.
[377] *EMI Records* (51/75) [1976] E.C.R. 811.
[378] Citing the Opinion of A.G. Tesauro in *Javico International and Javico AG v Yves Saint Laurent Parfums SA* (C-306/96) [1998] E.C.R. I-1983.

leave the adoption of an exhaustion principle in relation to the Community Trade Mark to the discretion of the Member States.

Could the two provisions be interpreted differently?[379] The answer was negative since the Directive and the Regulation shared the same context: the Community's internal market.

Even if one were to accept that their respective objectives were distinct there was clear support for the view that the Directive precludes international exhaustion.

Accordingly, he concluded that art.7(1) "is to be interpreted as meaning that the proprietor of a trade mark is entitled to prevent a third party from using the mark for goods which have been put on the market under that mark outside the territory of the EEA. Member States are accordingly precluded from adopting the principle of international exhaustion".[380]

8–219 **(vi) The effect of the Directive in the national legal order.** The second question queried whether an injunction could be granted solely on the basis of art.7(1) of the Directive.

At the time there was no right to a prohibitory injunction in respect of trade mark infringement under Austrian trade mark law. An injunction could only be granted on the basis of the Austrian law on unfair competition. The referring court had noted that art.7 had been copied verbatim into Austrian law; however art.5(1)(a) had yet not been implemented.

The Advocate General identified the principles established by the Court:

"whether or not the specific provisions of a directive has been implemented in national law, and independently of the possible direct effect of those provisions—which, if not implemented, can be invoked only against the State or a public body—the national courts are under a duty to take account of all provisions of national law so as to ensure, wherever possible, that the result prescribed by the directive is attained. That duty applies as regards not only national legislation specifically introduced in order to implement a directive but also other provisions of national law, including those adopted before the directive."[381]

8–220 In *MPA Pharma*[382] the Court had already stated in relation to art.7(1) that when applying national law, whether adopted before or after the Directive, the national court had to interpret it, as far as possible, in the light of the wording and the purpose of the directive so as to achieve its results and comply with the third paragraph of art.189 EC.

---

[379] He cited *Polydor Ltd v Harlequin Record Shops Ltd* (270/80) [1982] E.C.R. 329, as an example of identical provisions being construed differently according to their respective context, the EC Treaty on the one hand and the EFTA agreement on the other.
[380] Point 63 of the Opinion of A.G. Jacobs.
[381] Point 68, citing *Marleasing v La Comercial Internacional de Alimentación* (C-106/89) [1990] E.C.R. I-4135.
[382] *MPA Pharma GmbH v Rhône-Poulenc Pharma GmbH* (C-232/94) [1996] E.C.R. I-3671.

10. SILHOUETTE—THE TERRITORIAL SCOPE OF EXHAUSTION

From the above it was clear that the national legislation had to be interpreted consistently with the Directive. "Provided that the legislation is capable of being interpreted in that way, the national courts are under a duty to give trade marks the same protection as if each of the provisions of the Directive had been specifically and explicitly transposed into national law."[383]

Austrian courts had to interpret the Austrian legislation in the light of art.5(1)(a) that indicated that the trade mark proprietor should be entitled to a court order. If such an order were available under national law, even under unfair competition rather than trade mark law, it should also be made available for cases falling under art.5(1)(a).

The Advocate General went further and reminded that the Court had also held that interim relief should also be provided for the protection of Community rights even where they would be unable to do so under national law.[384] The same should apply to a final injunction, a measure that would be equally necessary to ensure the effective protection of Community rights.

(b) The judgment of the Court   8–221

(i) The territorial scope of article 7(1). Presenting the context for its answer to the first question the Court noted that exhaustion of the exclusive rights conferred by registration was subject to two conditions: first, that the goods had been put on the market by the proprietor or with its consent; secondly, that the relevant market was that of the EEA.

The second point had been contested by Hartlauer and the Swedish Government that maintained that art.7 had not resolved comprehensively the issue of exhaustion failing to delineate between EEA and international exhaustion. According to their interpretation EEA exhaustion should be seen as the minimum required by the Directive, abolishing national exhaustion principles. International exhaustion provided a broader context incorporating the EEA.

The Court though sided with the position of the Commission, supported by Austria, France, Germany, Italy, and the United Kingdom. The Directive, according to its Preamble, demanded harmonisation in relation to substantive rules of central importance in the sphere of trade mark law. Accordingly, art.5, art.6 and art.7 should be construed as embodying the principle of complete harmonisation and interpreted strictly. Article 7 did not leave Member States free to adopt wider than EEA exhaustion. This interpretation, the Court noted, would also be consistent with the establishment of an internal market.

The second argument submitted by the Swedish Government that the Directive, adopted according to art.95 of the EC Treaty, could not interfere with relations between Member States and non-member countries was also

---
[383] Point 69 of the Opinion of A.G. Jacobs.
[384] *R. v Secretary of State for Transport Ex p. Factortame* (C-231/89) [1990] E.C.R. I-2433.

rejected by the Court. It remarked that art.7 simply delineated the rights of trade mark proprietors in the Community. Community authorities could in the future conclude international agreements adopting international exhaustion.

8–222   **(ii) The effect of the Directive in the national legal order.** On the second question, regarding the direct applicability of art.7(1), the Court stated that Directives did not in themselves impose obligations on individuals and, as a result, they should not be relied upon in actions against individuals. National courts, though, applying national law should interpret national law, as far as possible, in the light of the wording and the purpose of the Directive.[385]

11. SEBAGO—"SPECIFIC" CONSENT

8–223   The qualitative assessment of consent started with *Sebago Inc and Ancienne Maison Dubois et Fils SA v GB-Unic SA*,[386] a reference from the Brussels Court of Appeal. Sebago, the registered proprietor of "Sebago" and "Docksides" for shoes in the Benelux, started trade mark infringement proceedings against GB-Unic which marketed and advertised the sale of Sebago and Docksides shoes in its hypermarkets. The shoes were genuine, manufactured in El Salvador and supplied to GB-Unic by a parallel trader.

Sebago claimed that the unauthorised importation of goods from outside the EEA constituted infringement. GB-Unic supported that once goods that are similar to those imported have been marketed in the EEA by the proprietor or with its consent then its rights have been exhausted in relation to all goods of that brand. Sebago responded that consent must relate to each individual consignment imported at a particular time by a particular importer.

GB-Unic's second line of defence was that Sebago had not prohibited the licensee in El Salvador from exporting its products to the Community and that this accounted to implied consent to the marketing of the shoes in the Community.[387]

8–224   The Cour d' Appel (Court of Appeal), Brussels, referred the following questions to the Court:

"Is Article 7(1) ... to be interpreted as meaning that the right conferred by the trade mark entitles its proprietor to oppose the use of his trade

---

[385] *Marleasing v LA Comercial Internacional de Alimentnación* (C-106/89) [1990] E.C.R. I-4135; and *Faccini Dori v Recreb Srl* (C-91/92) [1994] E.C.R. I-3325.
[386] *Sebago Inc and Ancienne Maison Dubois & Fils SA v G-B Unic SA* (C-173/98) [1999] E.C.R. I-4103.
[387] Interestingly the existence and scope of the licence has not been established before the Belgian courts.

mark in relation to genuine goods which have not been put on the market in the European Economic Community (extended to ... the European Economic Area) by the proprietor or with his consent, where:

> the goods bearing the trade mark come directly from a country outside the European Community or the European Economic Area,
>
> the goods bearing the trade mark come from a Member State of the European Community or the European Economic Area in which they are in transit without the consent of the proprietor of the trade mark or his representative,
>
> if the goods were acquired in a Member State of the European Community or of the European Economic Area in which they were put on sale for the first time without the consent of the proprietor of the trade mark or his representative,
>
> either where goods bearing the trade mark—which are identical to the genuine goods bearing the same trade mark but imported in parallel either directly or indirectly from countries outside the European Community or the European Economic Area—are, or have already been, marketed within the Community or the European Economic Area by the proprietor of the trade mark or with his consent,
>
> or where goods bearing the trade mark—which are similar to the genuine goods bearing the same trade mark but imported in parallel either directly or indirectly from countries outside the European Community or the European Economic Area—are, or have already been, marketed within the Community or the European Economic Area by the proprietor of the trade mark or with his consent."[388]

(a) The Opinion of the Advocate General 8–225

Advocate General Jacobs identified two main issues. The first, the territorial scope of exhaustion, had been settled in *Silhouette*. Here the Court would have to resolve the second issue, whether consent in relation to the marketing of one batch of goods meant that the trade mark proprietor had exhausted its rights in relation to other batches of identical or similar goods bearing the same trade mark.

In order to set the background for answering the question, the Advocate General referred to the relevant exhaustion principle the Court had been applying in an intra-Community context. "If a trade-mark proprietor places on the market one particular batch of goods it is only that batch of goods which he puts into circulation: obviously he does not thereby put into circulation all other batches of identical (or similar) goods remaining in his warehouse, and so he retains, in respect of those remaining batches, all such rights as he may enjoy to impose conditions of retail sale."[389]

---

[388] Reproduced in Point 10.
[389] Point 21 of the Opinion of A.G. Jacobs.

He then turned to the contested provision. Reading together art.7(1) with art.7(2) he supported that the loose wording of the first provision should be linked with the reference to "further commercialization" in the second. The French wording "commercialisation ulterieure" made it even clearer that it referred to "subsequent dealings with individual products following first sale".[390] The Court too had referred to the exhaustion of the "right of resale" in *Dior*[391] and "la commercialisation ulterieure" in *BMW*.[392]

8–226   He noted that holding that the trade mark proprietor did not have the right to prevent the importation of a particular batch of goods that had been marketed, by him or with his consent, outside the EEA would stand legislation on its head. If the approach of the Directive was mistaken then it should be amended or the scope of exhaustion should be extended on the basis of international agreements.

Article 7(1) however should be interpreted as meaning that where goods "have been marketed by the trade-mark owner or with his consent within the EEA, he is not thereby precluded from exercising his trade-mark rights to oppose the importation into the EEA of other identical or similar goods bearing his mark".[393]

8–227   *(b)   The judgment of the Court*

The Court of Justice restated that trade mark rights were exhausted only in respect of the individual items that had been put on the market in the EEA with the consent of the trade mark proprietor who might prohibit the use of the trade mark with regard to other individual items of the same product put on the market in the same territory without its consent.

This conclusion according to the Court was justified by the language of art.7(2) of the Directive referring to the "further commercialization". The relevant goods were not the product as an abstract concept but specific individualised goods that had been put on the market with the consent of the trade mark proprietor. The principle of EEA exhaustion would become devoid of substance if the rights were exhausted by the marketing of identical or similar products.

12.   DAVIDOFF—"CLEAR" CONSENT

8–228   What constitutes consent had been discussed further in Joined Cases *Zino Davidoff SA v A&G Imports Ltd and Levi Strauss & Co v Tesco Stores and Costco Wholesale UK Ltd*.[394]

---

[390] Point 22 of the Opinion of A.G. Jacobs.
[391] *Parfums Christian Dior SA* (C-337/95) [1997] E.C.R. I-6013.
[392] *Bayerische Motorenwerke AG and BMW Nederland BV* (C-63/97) [1999] E.C.R. I-905.
[393] Point 31 of the Opinion of A.G. Jacobs.
[394] *Levi Strauss & Co and Levi Strauss (UK) Ltd* (C-414/99), *Costco Wholesale UK Ltd* (C-415/99) and *Zino Davidoff SA* (C-416/99) [2001] E.C.R. I-8691.

12. DAVIDOFF—"CLEAR" CONSENT

Davidoff and Levi Strauss had brought separately trade mark infringement proceedings in the United Kingdom in order to prevent the sale of products that parallel importers had obtained from distributors outside the EEA. The parallel importers supported that since the two trade mark owners had not specifically restricted their distributors they had implicitly consented to the importation of their products.

In *Davidoff*,[395] the function of batch code numbers that the importer had removed was also contested. The trade mark owner claimed that this altered the characteristics of the product whereas the importer viewed them as tools for policing trade channels.

The High Court referred the following questions to the Court of Justice: 8–229

"(A) Insofar as the Directive refers to goods being put on the market in the Community with the consent of the proprietor of a mark, is it to be interpreted as including consent given expressly or implicitly and directly or indirectly?

(B) Where:

(i) a proprietor has consented to or allowed goods to be placed in the hands of a third party in circumstances where the latter's rights to further market the goods are determined by the law of the contract of purchase under which that party acquired the goods, and

(ii) the said law allows the vendor to impose restrictions on the further marketing or use of the goods by the purchaser but also provides that, absent the imposition by or on behalf of the proprietor of effective restrictions on the purchaser's right to further market the goods, the third party acquires a right to market the goods in any country, including the Community,

then, if restrictions effective according to that law to limit the third party's rights to market the goods have not been imposed, is the Directive to be interpreted so as to treat the proprietor as having consented to the right of the third party acquired thereby to market the goods in the Community?

(C) If the answer to Question (B) is in the affirmative, is it for the national courts to determine whether, in all the circumstances, effective restrictions were imposed on the third party?

(D) Is Article 7(2) of the Directive to be interpreted in such a way that legitimate reasons for the proprietor to oppose further commercialisation of his goods include any actions by a third party which affect to a substantial extent the value, allure or image of the trade mark or the goods to which it is applied?

---

[395] See *Zino Davidoff SA (No.1)* [1999] 2 C.M.L.R. 1056; and *Zino Davidoff SA (No.2)* [2000] 2 C.M.L.R. 750.

(E) Is Article 7(2) of the Directive to be interpreted in such a way that legitimate reasons for the proprietor to oppose further commercialisation of his goods include the removal or obliteration by third parties (in whole or in part) of any markings on the goods where such removal or obliteration is not likely to cause any serious or substantial damage to the reputation of the trade mark or the goods bearing the mark?

(F) Is Article 7(2) of the Directive to be interpreted in such a way that legitimate reasons for the proprietor to oppose further commercialisation of his goods include the removal or obliteration by third parties (in whole or in part) of batch code numbers on the goods where such removal or obliteration results in the goods in question

- (i) offending against any part of the criminal code of a Member State (other than a part concerned with trade marks) or
- (ii) offending against the provisions of Directive 76/768/EEC?"[396]

In Levi Strauss it added the following:

"(1) Where goods bearing a registered trade mark have been placed on the market in a non-EEA country by the trade mark proprietor or with his consent and those goods have been imported into or sold in the EEA by a third party, is the effect of Directive 89/104/EEC (the Directive) that the trade mark proprietor is entitled to prohibit such importation or sale unless he has expressly and explicitly consented to it, or may such consent be implied?

(2) If the answer to Question 1 is that consent may be implied, is consent to be implied from the fact that the goods have been sold by the proprietor or on his behalf without contractual restrictions prohibiting resale within the EEA binding the first and all subsequent purchasers?

(3) Where goods bearing a registered trade mark have been placed on the market in a non-EEA country by the trade mark proprietor:

- [A] to what extent is it relevant to or determinative of the issue whether or not there was consent by the proprietor to the placing of those goods on the market within the EEA, within the meaning of the Directive, that:

    - (a) the person placing the goods on the market (not being an authorised retailer) does so with the knowledge that he is the lawful owner of the goods and the goods bear no indication that they may not be placed on the market in the EEA; and/or
    - (b) the person placing the goods on the market (not being an authorised retailer) does so with knowledge that the trade

---

[396] Reproduced in Point 14.

mark proprietor objects to those goods being placed on the market within the EEA; and/or
(c) the person placing the goods on the market (not being an authorised retailer) does so with the knowledge that the trade mark proprietor objects to them being placed on the market by anyone otherwise than an authorised retailer; and/or
(d) the goods have been purchased from authorised retailers in a non-EEA country who have been informed by the proprietor that the proprietor objects to the sale of the goods by them for the purposes of resale, but who have not imposed upon purchasers from them any contractual restrictions on the manner in which the goods may be disposed of; and/or
(e) the goods have been purchased from authorised wholesalers in a non-EEA country who have been informed by the proprietor that the goods were to be sold to retailers in that non-EEA country and were not to be sold for export, but who have not imposed upon purchasers from them any contractual restrictions on the manner in which the goods may be disposed of; and/or
(f) there has or has not been communication by the proprietor to all subsequent purchasers of its goods (i.e. those between the first purchaser from the proprietor and the person placing the goods on the market in the EEA) of its objection to the sale of the goods for the purposes of resale; and/or
(g) a contractual restriction has or has not been imposed by the proprietor and made legally binding upon the first purchaser prohibiting sale for the purposes of resale to anyone other than the ultimate consumer?

[B] Does the issue of whether or not there was consent by the proprietor to the placing of those goods on the market within the EEA, within the meaning of the Directive, depend on some further or other factor or factors and, if so, which?"[397]

In essence, there were two issues the Court had to decide. First, whether the proprietor's consent to import or sell the product had to be expressed or it sufficed to show implied consent. Secondly, if implied consent was considered sufficient, what factors could be used to imply consent, in particular whether consent could be implied from indications on the goods, contractual restrictions prohibiting re-sale binding the first and subsequent purchasers, or knowledge on behalf of the importer or re-seller of the position of the trade mark proprietor.

---

[397] Reproduced in Point 24.

8–230 *(a) The Opinion of the Advocate General*

(i) **The existing background.** Advocate General Stix-Hackl referred both to *Silhouette*[398] and *Sebago*[399] in order to settle parts of the questions that the Court had covered in those cases but also in order to provide the necessary background. The Directive according to that case law intended to enable trade mark proprietors within the EEA to oppose the importation of goods bearing their trade marks which were first placed on the market outside the EEA; and art.5, art.6 and art.7 provided for complete harmonisation.

In this case the first contested issue was whether the existence of consent should be determined by reference to national law or Community law. Subsequently, the Court would have to elaborate on the type and characteristics of consent that would contribute in exhausting the rights of a trade mark owner.

8–231 (ii) **Consent—a Community concept.** The Advocate General noted that in the *Davidoff*[400] case the national court had assumed that consent had to be defined according to the law that was applicable to the first contract.

But this approach would go against the harmonisation aim of the Directive and, given the number of transactions along the distribution chain, could reintroduce international exhaustion through a presumption of consent.

Moving towards a definition of consent by elimination, she suggested that exhaustion had to be determined independently of the question of the national law governing the contract.[401]

8–232 She then rejected the line of parallel importers' arguments based on property and the legitimate expectations following a change of ownership. "That trader does not receive the trade mark right in se; the sole question is whether he can exploit the products bearing that mark. It is only within that context that the question of protection of legitimate expectations can arise."[402]

Further, even the right to property could be restricted in its exercise provided that the restrictions corresponded to Community objectives of general interest and did not constitute a disproportionate and intolerable interference in relation to the aim pursued impairing the very substance of the rights.[403]

---

[398] *Silhouette International Schmied GmbH & Co KG v Hartlauer Handelsgesellschaft mbH* (C-355/96) [1998] E.C.R. I-4799.

[399] *Sebago Inc and Ancienne Maison Dubois & Fils SA v G-B Unic SA* (C-173/98) [1999] E.C.R. I-4103.

[400] *Zino Davidoff SA (No.1)* [1999] 2 C.M.L.R. 1056.

[401] Following a line of argument the Court had developed in a case regarding the harmonisation of national laws relating to self-employed commercial agents; *Ingmar Gb Ltd v Eaton Leonard Technologies Inc* (C-381/98) [2000] E.C.R. I-9305.

[402] Point 62 of the Opinion of A.G. Stix-Hackl.

[403] Case C-200/96 *Metronome Musik GmbH* [1998] E.C.R. I-1953.

As a result she proposed that only an interpretation that focused on the meaning and purpose of art.7(1) would make it possible to provide an answer that took proper account of the content and function of the concept of consent.

Consent had to be examined from the perspective of Community law.

(iii) Delineating consent. Examining first the wording of the provision she eliminated its narrow definition as an expression of intent made for the purposes of concluding a contract; "such a construction would fail to take sufficient account of the distinction in Article 7(1) ... between the marketing of goods by the trade mark proprietor and the marketing of such goods with his consent".[404]

8–233

Examining the development of the concept in the case law of the Court she identified two main characteristics.

The first had to do with the territorial extent of consent. The Court's case law "extended the barrier of exhaustion in the sense that consent to the placing of goods on the market could no longer relate solely to the territory of one Member State but to the entire territory of the Community".[405]

The second, with the qualities of consent: "consent within the framework of the Court's exhaustion theory does not relate to an expression of intent by the trade mark proprietor concerning transfer but rather to the question of accountability for the sale—or marketing—of the trade-marked products".[406]

8–234

What needed to be ascertained in each case was whether the placing of the goods on the EEA market could be attributed to the proprietor. "The Community interpretation of the concept of consent must accordingly have as its object the search for criteria of attribution."[407]

Another essential prerequisite for consent was that the proprietor had, or could have availed of, the opportunity to exercise its rights within the EEA. On the other hand there was no need to actually exercise the right one way or the other, the mere possibility that it might have been exercised would suffice.

The Advocate General then distinguished between goods marketed inside and outside the EEA, from a teleological perspective:

8–235

"Indiscriminate application of Article 7(1) ... to trade within the Community, on the one hand, and to trade from non-member countries,

---

[404] Point 67 of the Opinion of A.G. Stix-Hackl.
[405] Point 70, citing cases like *Winthrop BV* (16/74) [1974] E.C.R.1183.
[406] Point 73, citing *Keurkoop BV v Nancy Kean Gifts BV* (144/81) [1982] E.C.R. 2853; and *IHT Internationale Heiztechnik GmbH and Uwe Darzinger v Ideal-Standard GmbH and Wabco Standard GmbH* (C-9/93) [1994] E.C.R. I-2789.
[407] Point 73. On the other hand she also noted that consent could be equally linked with entitlement, citing the Opinion of A.G. Roemer in *Deutsche Grammophon Gesellschaft mbH v Metro-SB-Grossmarkte GmbH & Co KG* (78/80) [1971] E.C.R. 487. It appears that this alternative approach strengthened her view that at the end all the circumstances of each individual case had to be taken into account.

on the other, would fail to take account of the differences in the respective initial positions: in the case of parallel imports within the Community, transfer of the power of disposal over the trade-marked goods coincides with the placing of those goods on the market within the EEA, whereas these do not coincide in the case of parallel imports into the Community from non-member countries. This necessarily gives rise to different possibilities in regard to control over distribution, of which appropriate account must be taken when balancing the requirements of trade mark protection against the interests of free-flowing trade."[408]

Accordingly, the trade mark proprietor's rights would be exhausted in the case of parallel imports from non-member countries if it was able, or could have been able, to control the distribution of the marked goods within the EEA.

Having explored two possible links that could lead to a presumption of consent—economic linkage and control—she found that ultimately they related to a single criterion: control over the initial distribution within the EEA. She reminded that it was not the actual exercise of the right that was determinative, but the mere possibility that it might have been exercised.[409]

She suggested that if the first instance in which the products bearing the trade mark were placed on the market on the one hand and their initial distribution within the EEA on the other did not coincide, the trade mark proprietor might, when those products were first placed on the market, control their initial distribution within the EEA by waiving its exclusive right to control distribution.

8–236   **(iv) Assessing consent.** Trade mark proprietors had an exclusive right to control the distribution of their goods first marketed outside the EEA unless their conduct at the time of marketing would lead subsequent purchasers justifiably to believe that they had waived their rights. Consent could be implied rather than explicit and its assessment by national courts should be based on Community law and a consideration of all the circumstances of each individual case. She also remarked that the Court in its case law had constantly been trying to balance between the interests underlying free movement of goods on the one hand,[410] and the rights of trade mark proprietors on the other.

She cautioned, though, national courts to apply reasonable standards and resist making "presumptions of consent"; it should not become practically

---

[408] Point 84 of the Opinion of A.G. Stix-Hackl.
[409] Citing *Merck & Co Inc, Merck Sharp & Dohme Ltd and Merck Sharp & Dohme International Services BV v Primecrown Ltd and Beecham Group Plc v Europharm of Worthing Ltd* (C-267/95 & C-268/95) [1996] E.C.R. I-6285.
[410] Note that the A.G. avoided referring to the "rights" of parallel importers.

impossible for the trade mark owner to rely on its exclusive right. Article 7(1), in principle, precluded the application of a national rule which constituted a general presumption of waiver.

(v) Damage to reputation—the removal of batch codes. She went on to suggest that where there was a risk of serious damage to the reputation, image, or allure of a trade mark this could be the basis for opposing further commercialisation of the marked products under art.7(2).[411]

8–237

Finally, in relation to the *Davidoff* code numbers and the argument that their removal could damage its reputation she stated:

> "[The] trade mark proprietor has a legitimate interest in being able to remove such products from circulation. Consequently, it would also be necessary in the national proceedings to examine whether the damage to the reputation of the trade mark is rendered sufficiently serious by the removal or obliteration of the prescribed batch code numbers. An infringement of the cosmetics directive would be relevant in the context of trade mark rights only under this aspect."[412]

Ultimately, the legitimate reasons which might justify a trade mark proprietor in opposing further commercialisation of products bearing the trade mark did not include the actions of third parties or circumstances that did not affect the rights constituting the specific subject-matter and essential function of the rights conferred by the trade mark.

(b)   The judgment of the Court

8–238

The Court focused on the questions relating to art.7(1). Its answers meant that the questions relating to art.7(2) did not have to be answered, at least at this stage.

(i) The article 7(1) questions—interpreting the concept of consent. Having repeated the main points it had resolved in *Silhouette*[413] and *Sebago*[414] the Court focused on the requirements for establishing consent.

8–239

Before considering whether consent might be implied the Court dealt with the fundamental issue of whether the concept had to be interpreted uniformly throughout the community legal order. Being a major component of art.7, consent constituted the decisive factor in the extinction of the rights arising from art.5(1):

---

[411] Citing *Parfums Christian Dior SA* (C-337/95) [1997] E.C.R. I-16013.
[412] Point 121 of the Opinion of A.G. Stix-Hackl.
[413] *Silhouette International Schmied GmbH & Co KG* (C-355/96) [1998] E.C.R. I-4799.
[414] *Sebago Inc and Ancienne Maison Dubois & Fils SA* (C-173/98) [1999] E.C.R. I-4103.

> "If the concept of consent were a matter for the national laws of the Member States, the consequence for trade mark proprietors could be that protection would vary according to the legal system concerned. The objective of the same protection under the legal systems of all the Member States set out in the ninth recital ... would not be attained."[415]

It was clear that consent had to be interpreted uniformly.

8–240　**(ii) The requirements for consent.** The first requirement—and in essence the answer to the first question of the *Levi* cases—was that because of its effect consent "must be so expressed that an intention to renounce those rights is unequivocally demonstrated".[416] An express statement of consent would normally satisfy this requirement. However in some cases consent might be inferred from facts and circumstances prior to, simultaneous with, or subsequent to the placing of the goods on the market outside the EEA which, in the view of the national court, "unequivocally demonstrate that the proprietor has renounced his rights".[417]

The second requirement, that also constituted the answer to the second question in both the *Levi* and the *Davidoff* references, was that consent had to be expressed positively; this led to five more specific requirements ensuring that courts would not find deemed consent to be sufficient.

For implied consent this meant that the factors taken into consideration should unequivocally demonstrate that the trade mark proprietor had renounced any intention to enforce his exclusive rights.

8–241　For the burden of proof, it meant that it was for the trader alleging consent to prove it and not for the trade mark proprietor to demonstrate its absence.

Thirdly, it led to the finding that implied consent could not be inferred from the mere silence of the trade mark proprietor.

Fourthly, implied consent could not be inferred from the fact that a trade mark proprietor had not communicated its opposition to marketing within the EEA or from the fact that the goods did not carry a warning that it was prohibited to place them on the market within the EEA.

8–242　And finally, consent could not be inferred from the fact that the trade mark proprietor transferred ownership of the goods bearing the mark without imposing contractual reservations or from the fact that, according to the law governing the contract, the property right transferred included, in the absence of such reservations, an unlimited right of resale or a right to market the goods subsequently within the EEA.

The next condition had to do with the consequences of the importer's ignorance of the trade mark proprietor's expressed opposition to the

---

[415] *Sebago*, para.42.
[416] *Sebago*, para.45.
[417] *Sebago*, para.46.

13. PEAK HOLDING—THE CONCEPT OF "PUTTING GOODS ON THE MARKET"

imports, a response to question 3(a)(ii)–(v) of the *Levi* reference. The Court found that since consent could not be inferred from silence, the exclusive rights of the trade mark proprietor should not depend on an express prohibition of marketing in the EEA or the repetition of such a prohibition in the product's distribution chain. The fact that the importer was unaware of the proprietor's objections should not be relevant in the assessment of consent:

> "The national rules on the enforceability of sales restrictions against third parties are not, therefore, relevant to the resolution of a dispute between the proprietor of a trade mark and a subsequent trader in the distribution chain concerning the preservation or extinction of the rights conferred by the trade mark."[418]

13. PEAK HOLDING—THE CONCEPT OF "PUTTING GOODS ON THE MARKET"

Peak Holding AB v Axolin-Elinor AB[419] looks at the concept of putting goods on the market for the purposes of art.7(1) of the Directive following an often intricate itinerary.

8–243

Factory Outlet, a Swedish company controlled by Axolin-Elinor, marketed in Sweden genuine "Peak Performance", a trade mark held by Peak Holding, garments; the garments belonged to earlier collections and were sold at half price. Peak Holding brought trade mark infringement proceedings targeting the marketing conditions of the sale. The case focused on a particular consignment of garments, that according to Peak Holding, consisted of garments that had been originally offered for sale by Peak Holding in Denmark; the garments that were not sold were returned to the warehouse and subsequently sold to COPAD, a French company, under restrictions regarding resale; mainly that the goods were not to be resold in European countries, except Russia and Slovenia, with the further exception of 5 per cent that could be resold in France. Factory Outlet on the other hand supported that it had acquired the consignment from a Swedish company and was not aware of any restrictions regarding resale. According to the evidence of the case the consignment never left the territory of the EEA during the contested period of time.

The Swedish referring court posed the following questions. First, whether goods are considered to have been put on the market when the trade mark proprietor has imported them into the common market with the intention of selling them but the sale has not materialised. Secondly, if the answer to the first question is in the affirmative, whether exhaustion

---

[418] *Sebago*, para.65.
[419] *Peak Holding AB v Axolin-Elinor AB* (C-16/03) [2004] E.C.R. I-11313.

can be interrupted by returning the goods to a warehouse. Thirdly, whether goods that have been sold to another company in the common market with a resale restriction are considered to have been put on the common market. And, fourthly, whether the contractual exception to the resale restrictions should affect the answer to the third question.

In respect of the first question Peak Holding, supported by the Commission in this, submitted that rights are exhausted by actual sales rather than hypotheses. Axolin-Elinor focused on customs' procedures supporting that rights are exhausted by importation, customs clearance and warehousing of the goods in the EEA with a view to sale; in any case offering, even without success, for sale should suffice.

8–244 *(a) The Opinion of the Advocate General*

The Advocate General examined art.7(1) first from a literal perspective concluding that internal transactions, for example the transfer of goods bearing the mark to a retail subsidiary, or preparatory acts, like the importation by the proprietor of goods from non-member countries which have been manufactured there on its behalf, did not put the goods on the market. For goods manufactured outside the EEA she added that the trade mark proprietor might have not yet decided upon importation whether the goods were to be sold for the first time in the EEA; so offering the goods in the EEA should not necessarily mean putting the goods on the market.

To resolve this she turned to systematic interpretation of the provision linking it with art.5(3) that inter alia prohibited "offering the goods, or putting them on the market or stocking them for these purposes under that sign . . .". Whether the meaning was the same in both provisions remained unanswered and as a last resort she employed a teleological interpretation; in essence a balancing exercise. From an economic point of view the critical point was the disposal of the goods bearing the mark.

It should be pointed out that a change of ownership also leaves open the question whether the trade mark proprietor can obtain an economic benefit from the mark. In other words, the change of ownership of the marked goods must be irrelevant if the necessary economic approach is to be followed. From a legal perspective the critical point was the transfer of the right of disposal rather than a change in legal ownership.

Regarding the third and the fourth question the Advocate General suggested that once the goods bearing the mark are put on the market in the EEA by the trade mark proprietor itself exhaustion of rights arose by operation of law, irrespective of the contract between the proprietor and the purchaser. Breach of territorial restrictions on sale which the proprietor might have imposed on purchasers might only give rise to claims under the contract of sale but would be irrelevant under trade mark law.

14. CLASS INTERNATIONAL—GOODS IN TRANSIT

(b) The judgment of the Court   8–245

The Court started its analysis by noting the complete harmonisation effect of arts 5–7 of the Directive; whether goods were "put on the market" was decisive in the application of these provisions and should be interpreted in a uniform manner. And since the wording of the term did not in itself solve the interpretive dilemma the Court had to turn to the scheme and objectives of the Directive. Article 5 provides the general rule, that trade mark rights are exclusive rights that include the prevention of imports; art.7 is the exception to the general rule providing for exhaustion. The Community legislature allowed the trade mark proprietor to control the initial marketing of the marked goods in the EEA but not their further marketing.

The mechanism of exhaustion would be triggered by a "sale which allows the proprietor to realise the economic value of his trade mark".[420] Importing the goods with a view to selling them or offering them for sale in the EEA would not be enough:

"Such acts do not transfer to third parties the right to dispose of the goods bearing the trade mark. They do not allow the proprietor to realise the economic value of the trade mark. Even after such acts, the proprietor retains his interest in maintaining complete control over the goods bearing his trade mark, in order in particular to ensure their quality".[421]

Offering a product for sale without actually selling it did not satisfy the exhaustion requirements.

Regarding the third question the arguments put before the Court   8–246
contested whether the contractual imposition of a resale prohibition is equivalent to retaining trade mark rights or whether exhaustion takes place by operation by law and breaching the prohibition should be considered simple breach of contract.

The Court observed that art.7(1) of the Directive does not refer to an additional requirement of consent regarding further marketing. "Exhaustion occurs solely by virtue of the putting on the market in the EEA by the proprietor".[422] Contractual stipulations do not preclude exhaustion.

14. CLASS INTERNATIONAL—GOODS IN TRANSIT

Class International[423] looked at the notions of exhaustion and consent   8–247
regarding original Unilever goods located in the Community in "transit

---

[420] *Peak Holding*, para.40.
[421] *Peak Holding*, para.42. The Court also referred to the wording of art.5(3)(b) and (c) distinguishing between offering the goods, putting them on the market, stocking them for those purposes, and importing them.
[422] *Peak Holding*, para.53.
[423] *Class International BV v Colgate-Palmolive Co, Unilever NV, SmithKline Beecham Plc and Beecham Group Plc* (C-405/03) [2005] E.C.R. I-8735.

procedure" or "customs warehousing" by Class International. The case is important not only because it reconsiders parallel trade and exhaustion concepts but also because its factual scenario positions the Community in a global trading context where its territory functions as a transit location.

The referring court, the Gerechtshof te's-Gravenhage, held that the interpretation of arts 5(1) and (3)(b) and (c) of the Directive and arts 9(1) and (2)(b) and (c) of the Regulation was necessary to decide the case, and sought a preliminary ruling for the following. First, whether the proprietor of a trade mark can oppose the introduction of goods from third countries into the territory of a Member State in the context of transit trade. Secondly, whether "using a sign in the course of trade" covers the storing, in a customs office or warehouse within the territory of a Member State, of original branded goods which have the customs status of non-Community goods. Thirdly, whether knowledge, or its absence, of the final destination of those goods carries any significance regarding the first two questions. Fourthly, whether there are any other additional circumstances that the Court may consider relevant. The fifth question was linked with the first and inquired whether the term "offering" in the relevant provisions of the Directive and the Regulation covers the offering for sale of original branded goods which are stored in a customs office or warehouse within the territory of a Member State. The final, sixth, question focused on whether the trade mark proprietor or the importer carried the burden of proof.

Apart from trade mark law, the relevant legislation in this area is Regulation 2913/92.[424] Article 91(1) provides that the external transit procedure "shall allow the movement from one point to another within the customs territory of the Community of ... non-Community goods, without such goods being subject to import duties and other charges or to commercial policy measures". Article 92 provides that the external transit procedure is to end "when the goods and the corresponding documents are produced at the customs office of destination in accordance with the provisions of the procedure in question".

(a) The Opinion of the Advocate General

8–248 According to A.G. Jacobs goods in transit procedure are considered not to have entered the Community. And the essential purpose of customs warehouses is to provide for the storage of goods and not to permit the goods to pass from one stage of marketing to another. On the other hand, the exercise of trade mark rights must be reserved to cases in which a third party's use can affect the functions of the trade mark, in particular its essential function of guaranteeing to consumers the origin of the goods.

---

[424] [1992] OJ 302/1. Note that the Customs Code has no effect in the EFTA countries that are part of the EEA. The Court also observed that the Directive—though not the Regulation—is referred to in Annex XVII to the EEA Agreement under the common rules applicable therein.

14. CLASS INTERNATIONAL—GOODS IN TRANSIT

Goods in the transit procedure are not in free circulation within the Community and thus are not liable to affect the functions of the trade mark; "... trade mark proprietor may not oppose the entry into the customs territory of the Community without his consent of non-Community goods bearing his trade mark and subject to the Community external transit procedure on the basis that such entry alone constitutes 'using [the mark] in the course of trade' within the meaning of Article 5(1) of the First Council Directive".[425]

Finally, his conclusion on who carries the burden of proof in infringement cases appears to narrow the scope of *Zino Davidoff*[426] creating a, narrower than many would have thought, factual and jurisprudential context for the case. In the current state of Community law, where a trade mark proprietor brings infringement proceedings national procedural rules determine which party bears the burden of proof "... except with regard to the question whether the goods were put on the market in the European Economic Area under that trade mark with the proprietor's consent. The exception is the result of Zino Davidoff where the Court ruled that it was for the trader alleging consent to prove it and not for the trade mark proprietor to demonstrate its absence."[427] Still, *Zino Davidoff* must be seen as a specific exception to the rule due to "cogent reasons". The Court had stated that consent must be expressed in such a way that an intention to renounce the exclusive trade mark rights is unequivocally demonstrated because of consent's serious effect in extinguishing trade mark rights. Thus it was necessary to provide a uniform interpretation. In the current case, however, there were no cogent reasons for a uniform interpretation and national rules on the burden of proof should apply.

(b) The judgment of the Court 8–249

The Court deliberated sitting as a Grand Chamber. It examined the questions in two stages. Its reasoning followed the pattern of delineating the positions of parallel traders and trade mark proprietors in broad terms—here favouring parallel traders—whilst providing for a special case favouring trade mark proprietors. The final balancing detail would be the rule on the burden of proof.

---

[425] Point 37. Note that in *Administration des Douanes et Droits Indirects v Rioglass SA* (C-115/02) [2006] 1 C.M.L.R. 12, the Court had already decided that art.28 EC precluded the implementation, pursuant to a legislative measure of a Member State concerning intellectual property, of procedures for detention by the customs authorities of goods lawfully manufactured in another Member State and intended, following their transit through the territory of the first Member State, to be placed on the market in a non-member country.

[426] *Levi Strauss & Co and Levi Strauss (UK) Ltd* (C-414/99), *Costco Wholesale UK Ltd* (C-415/99) and *Zino Davidoff SA* (C-416/99) [2001] E.C.R. I-8691.

[427] Point 79 of the Opinion of A.G. Jacobs.

8–250　　**(i) The concept of "importing".** First it looked at the scope of the term "importing" in the context of art.5(3)(c) of the Directive and art.9(2)(c) of the Regulation. It started by linking it with the, codetermining the rights of the proprietor, requirement that it must entail "using [the mark] in the course of trade" within the meaning of art.5(1) of the Directive and art.9(1) of the Regulation. So "importing" requires introduction of the goods into the Community for the purposes of putting them on the market therein.

For goods coming from non-EEA countries this would in turn require their release for free circulation according to art.24 EC. The Court made a distinction between goods in customs procedures such as external transit, waiting to be transferred to a non-EEA destination, or customs warehousing, stored while awaiting a final destination, on the one hand, and goods in customs procedures leading to their release for free circulation and the conferment of Community goods customs status according to art.79 of the Customs Code. However, at any stage a trader could switch from one procedure to another under art.58(1) of the Customs Code:

> "As long as that option is not chosen and the requirements of the customs-approved treatment or use, other than release for free circulation, under which the goods have been placed are satisfied, the mere physical introduction of those goods into the territory of the Community is not 'importing' ... and does not entail 'using [the mark] in the course of trade' ..."[428] and the trade mark proprietor cannot "oppose that introduction ... or make it conditional on the existence of a final destination already specified in a third country, possibly pursuant to a sale agreement".[429]

As to the scope of art.58(2) of the Customs Code, providing that the choice of customs treatment does not preclude prohibitions or restrictions justified on grounds of industrial and commercial property, the Court viewed the provision under a restrictive light as covering:

> "only ... cases in which the customs-approved treatment or use would adversely affect industrial and commercial property rights. Placing non-Community goods under a suspensive customs procedure does not make it possible for them to be put on the market in the Community in the absence of release for free circulation. In the field of trade marks, such placing of original goods bearing a mark is not therefore, per se, interference with the right of its proprietor to control the initial marketing in the Community".[430]

---

[428] *Class International*, para.44.
[429] *Class International*, para.45. The very nature of this process rejected the argument that there was a risk that goods in external transit or customs warehousing would be released for free circulation since this was one of the options available to traders.
[430] *Class International*, para.47.

14. CLASS INTERNATIONAL—GOODS IN TRANSIT

(ii) The concepts of offering and putting on the market. The Court 8–251
then moved to the second stage of its analysis, examining whether
"offering" and "putting on the market" the goods under art.5(3)(b) of the
Directive and art.9(2)(b) of the Regulation covers, "respectively, offering
and selling original goods bearing a trade mark and having the customs
status of non-Community goods, when the offering is made and/or the sale
is effected while the goods are placed under the external transit procedure
or the customs warehousing procedure".[431]

Here the Court was more lenient towards trade mark proprietors making
what appears to be a practical distinction. The sale to a party in a third
country of goods that were in external transit or warehousing did not affect
adversely the "trade mark proprietor's right to control the initial marketing
in the Community".[432] This was not the case when the sale "necessarily
entails putting goods bearing the mark on the market in the Community"[433];
this would be considered "using [the mark] in the course of trade" within
the meaning of art.5(1) of the Directive and art.9(1) of the Regulation and
could be opposed by the trade mark proprietor. But trade mark rights
should be asserted on the basis of cogent evidence rather than assumptions
based on the involvement of the trader in parallel trade. A trade mark proprietor could not "rely on his right against a trader who offers or sells those
goods to another trader on the sole ground that that trader is likely then to
put them on the market in the Community".[434]

(iii) The burden of proof. Finally the Court considered the question of 8–252
which party carries the burden of proof. Note that the Commission had
submitted that it was up to the Member States to establish the applicable
rules of procedure, adding though that setting too strict requirements would
render the right to use the Community as a territory of transit illusory.

The Court started by the general position that as long as the conditions
of the customs suspensive procedures were complied with, the situation of
the trader concerned is, in principle, lawful. It then moved to the stage of
"pleading interference"[435] with the exclusive trade mark rights. It noted that
according to its findings in *Zino Davidoff*[436] divergent procedural rules
could lead to divergent levels of protection in an area of law that has been
described as fundamental. Accordingly, following the principles of *Zino
Davidoff*, "the onus of proving interference must lie with the trade mark
proprietor who alleges it. If that is proven, it is then for the trader sued to

---

[431] *Class International*, para.51.
[432] *Class International*, para.57.
[433] *Class International*, para.58.
[434] *Class International*, para.60.
[435] *Class International*, para.70.
[436] *Levi Strauss & Co and Levi Strauss (UK) Ltd* (C-414/99), *Costco Wholesale UK Ltd* (C-415/99) and *Zino Davidoff SA* (C-416/99) [2001] E.C.R. I-8691.

prove the existence of the consent of the proprietor to the marketing of the goods in the Community".[437]

15. BOEHRINGER II—REVISITING REPACKAGING, OVERSTICKERING AND REBOXING

8-253 The judgment of the Court in *Boehringer I*[438] was not the end of the story. The Court of Appeal came back seeking further clarifications.[439]

The High Court, perhaps provocatively, interpreted *Boehringer I* as laying down two propositions:

> "first, that damage to the specific subject-matter ... must be assumed to result from repackaging, even where there was in fact no damage either to the quality of the goods or to the mark's function as an indication of origin; and second, that the necessity test applied ... also ... to determine the type of repackaging which was permissible, so that the only permissible repackaging was that which from a trade mark point of view was as unobtrusive as possible. The High Court accordingly concluded that both debranding and cobranding infringed the claimants' trade marks."[440]

The Court of Appeal felt that a number of points regarding the meaning of "necessary", the burden of proof, and the consequences of failure to give notice, required further clarifications and referred a number of detailed questions to the Court of Justice.

8-254 "1. Where a parallel importer markets in one Member State a pharmaceutical product imported from another Member State in its original internal packaging but with a new exterior carton printed in the language of the Member State of importation (a 'reboxed' product): (a) does the importer bear the burden of proving that the new packaging complies with each of the conditions set out in [*Bristol Myers Squibb*] or does the trade mark proprietor bear the burden of proving that those conditions have not been complied with or does the burden of proof vary from condition to condition, and if so how? (b) does the first condition set out in [*Bristol Myers Squibb*] as interpreted in [*Pharmacia & Upjohn*] and [*Boehringer I*], namely that it must be shown that it is necessary to repackage the product in order that effective market access is not hindered, apply merely to the fact of reboxing (as held by the EFTA Court in Case E-3/02 *Paranova v Merck*) or does it also apply to the precise manner and style

---

[437] *Class International*, para.74.
[438] *Boehringer Ingelheim Pharma KG v Swingward Ltd* (C-143/00) [2002] E.C.R. I-3759.
[439] [2004] EWCA Civ 757, CA.
[440] Point 26; [2003] EWHC 110 (Ch).

of the reboxing carried out by the parallel importer, and if so how? (c) is the fourth condition set out in [*Bristol Myers Squibb*], namely that the presentation of the repackaged product is not such as to be liable to damage the reputation of the trade mark or its owner, only infringed if the packaging is defective, of poor quality or untidy or does it extend to anything which damages the reputation of the trade mark? (d) if the answer to question 1(c) is that the fourth condition is infringed by anything which damages the reputation of the trade mark and if either (i) the trade mark is not affixed to the new exterior carton ('debranding') or (ii) the parallel importer applies either his own logo or a house-style or get-up or a get-up used for a number of different products to the new exterior carton ('co-branding') must such forms of box design be regarded as damaging to the reputation of the trade mark or is that a question of fact for the national court? (e) If the answer to question 1(d) is that it is a question of fact, on whom does the burden of proof lie?

2. Where a parallel importer markets in one Member State a pharmaceutical product imported from another Member State in its original internal and external packaging to which the parallel importer has applied an additional external label printed in the language of the Member State of importation (an 'overstickered' product): (a) do the five conditions set out in [*Bristol Myers Squibb*] apply at all? (b) if the answer is question 2(a) is yes, does the importer bear the burden of proving that the overstickered packaging complies with each of the conditions set out in [*Bristol Myers Squibb*] or does the trade mark proprietor bear the burden of proving that those conditions have not been complied with or does the burden of proof vary from condition to condition? (c) if the answer to question 2(a) is yes, does the first condition set out in [*Bristol Myers Squibb*] as interpreted in [*Pharmacia & Upjohn*] and [*Boehringer I*], namely that it must be shown that it is necessary to repackage the product in order that effective market access is not hindered, apply merely to the fact of overstickering or does it also apply to the precise manner and style of overstickering adopted by the parallel importer? (d) if the answer to question 2(a) is yes, is the fourth condition set out in [*Bristol Myers Squibb*], namely that the presentation of the repackaged product is not such as to be liable to damage the reputation of the trade mark or its owner, only infringed if the packaging is defective, of poor quality or untidy or does it extend to anything which damages the reputation of the trade mark? (e) if the answer to question 2(a) is yes and the answer to question 2(d) is that the fourth condition is infringed by anything which damages the reputation of the trade mark, is it damaging to the reputation of a trade mark for this purpose if either (i) the additional label is positioned so as wholly or partially to obscure one of the proprietor's trade marks or (ii) the additional label fails to state that the trade mark in question is a trade mark owned by the proprietor or (iii) the name of the parallel importer is printed in capital letters?

3. Where a parallel importer has failed to give notice in respect of a repackaged product as required by the fifth condition of [*Bristol Myers Squibb*], and accordingly has infringed the proprietor's trade mark(s) for that reason only: (a) Is every subsequent act of importation of that product an infringement or does the importer only infringe until such time as the proprietor has become aware of the product and the applicable notice period has expired? (b) Is the proprietor entitled to claim financial remedies (i.e. damages for infringement or the handing over of all profits made by infringement) by reason of the importer's acts of infringement on the same basis as if the goods had been spurious? (c) Is the granting of financial remedies to the proprietor in respect of such acts of infringement by the importer subject to the principle of proportionality? (d) If not, upon what basis should such compensation be assessed given that the products in question were placed on the market within the EEA by the proprietor or with his consent?"[441]

8-255   (a)   *The Opinion of the Advocate General*

The reference gave the opportunity to A.G. Sharpston to sum up the current position regarding repackaging and overstickering.[442]

8-256   **(i) The purpose of the Court of Justice.** However, her starting robust remark was about the purpose and function of the Court of Justice. Once the principles were established, national courts should "play their part robustly in applying the principles to the facts before them without further requests to fine-tune the principles. Every judge knows that ingenious lawyers can always find a reason why a given proposition does or does not apply to their client's situation. It should not however in my view be for the Court of Justice to adjudicate on such detail for evermore."[443]

8-257   **(ii) The Legal Context.** The Advocate General first constructed the legal framework. Regarding the specific subject-matter of a trade mark she noted that the jurisprudence of the Court had developed two components: "First, there is the right to use the mark for the purpose of putting products

---

[441] Reproduced in point 27.
[442] *Boehringer Ingelheim KG Boehringer Ingelheim Pharma GmbH & Co KG, Glaxo Group Ltd v Swingward Ltd and Boehringer Ingelheim KG, Boehringer Ingelheim Pharma GmbH & Co KG, Glaxo Group Ltd, Smithkline Beecham Plc, Beecham Group Plc Smithkline and French Laboratories Ltd, Eli Lilly and Co, The Wellcome Foundation Ltd v Dowelhurst Ltd* (C-348/04) [2007] E.C.R. I-3391.
[443] Point 3, noting that a similar point had been made by A.G. Jacobs in *Frits Loendersloot v George Ballantine & Son* (C-349/95) [1997] E.C.R. I-6227. Advocate General Sharpston accepted however that the principles were not entirely clear; referring to overstickering for example she found that there were conflicting indications in the more recent case law, illustrated by the fact that both the claimants and the defendants relied on *Frits Loendersloot v George Ballantine & Son* (C-349/95) [1997] E.C.R. I-6227 and *Boehringer Ingelheim Pharma KG v Swingward Ltd* (C-143/00) [2002] E.C.R. I-3759, so it was worth re-establishing them.

protected by it into circulation for the first time in the EC, after which that right is exhausted. Second, there is the right to oppose any use of the trade mark which is liable to impair the guarantee of origin, which comprises both a guarantee of identity of origin and a guarantee of integrity of the trademarked product."[444] These two components were also reflected in the Trade Marks Directive, with art.7(1) qualifying the application of art.5(1). She viewed them as counterbalancing provisions rather than an exception to a general rule. Article 7(2) on the other hand should be seen as an exception to the art.7(1) and, being an exception, should "not be generously construed"[445]; as a result "legitimate reasons" and the notion of the "condition" of the goods being "changed or impaired" should be interpreted narrowly.

She suggested that the jurisprudence of the Court on art.5, art.6, and art.7 had settled the following principles: (i) they effected a complete harmonisation; (ii) art.30 should be the basis for the application of art.7(2) in respect of repackaged products to which the original trade mark had been reaffixed; (iii) the same "canons of interpretation must apply to other variants of repackaging"[446]; and (iv) the Directive should be construed in accordance with the Treaty framework and the core rights developed by the Court.

She also appeared to suggest however, that since the interpretive principles were settled it was time to move on and look at the Directive rather than art.30.

(iii) Reformulating the Bristol Myers Squibb propositions. To achieve this she started by reformulating the propositions of *Bristol Myers Squibb*[447] within the language and structure of the Directive, stressing that, in a post-*Silhouette*[448] reading, art.7(2) did not create an independent right of action but was linked with the exercise of art.5:

8–258

> "To summarise the BMS conditions in a way that fits clearly within the structure and language of the Directive, repackaging—or at least certain types of repackaging—will constitute a 'legitimate reason' within the meaning of Article 7(2) unless (i) the repackaging is necessary for market access; (ii) the repackaging cannot affect the original condition of the product; (iii) the new packaging shows the name of the importer and the manufacturer; (iv) the presentation is not such as to be liable to

---

[444] Point 9 of the Opinion of A.G. Sharpston.
[445] Point 13 of the Opinion of A.G. Sharpston.
[446] Point 14 of the Opinion of A.G. Sharpston.
[447] *Bristol Myers Squibb* (C-427/93), *CH Boehringer Sohn, Boehringer Ingelheim KG and Boehringer Ingelheim A/S* (C-429/93) and *Bayer Aktiengesellschaft and Bayer Danmark A/S* (C-436/93) [1996] E.C.R. I-3457.
[448] *Silhouette International Schmied GmbH & Co KG* (C-355/96) [1998] E.C.R. I-4799.

damage the reputation of the mark and its owner; and (v) the importer gives notice to the owner."[449]

8–259   **(iv) The six essential questions.** The next step was to suggest how these principles should be applied in relation to the questions referred to the Court. She divided her Opinion by providing the answers to six questions that reflected the essence of the reference.

8–260   *The conditions of Bristol Myers Squibb and overstickered products* (1) Do the five conditions set out in *Bristol Myers Squibb apply* to overstickered products?

The answer according to the Advocate General should be no. Both in *Bristol Myers Squibb* and *Loendersloot*[450] the Court had hinted that overstickering should be tolerated; this in turn implied that overstickering did not amount to repackaging. Still, *Phytheron*[451] appeared to indicate that some conditions also apply to overstickering, in particular the second and fourth conditions of *Bristol Myers Squibb*. However, in *Bristol Myers Squibb* itself the Court had accepted that the second condition was not breached by overstickering the inner packaging; so it could be validly argued that overstickering the outer packaging should also not be considered a breach; even more so since *Phytheron* was not a pharmaceuticals case.

In order to resolve the interpretive contradictions she turned to basic principles. *Hoffmann-La Roche*[452] linked the proprietor's right with impairment of the trade mark as a guarantee of origin. Looking at the facts of the case—perhaps surprisingly given her views on detailed adjudication by the Court of Justice—she stated:

> "Whatever the Court's historical approach to the risks attached to replacing external packaging, the overstickering at issue in the present case does not appear to me to constitute such use of the trade mark. The mark is being affixed to genuine goods with no risk of affecting the original condition of the product itself... In my view, where there is no risk that the guarantee of origin is impaired, as in the case of applying an additional external label to the original external packaging while retaining the original internal packaging, the BMS conditions do not apply."[453]

---

[449] Point 20 of the Opinion of A.G. Sharpston.
[450] *Frits Loendersloot v George Ballantine & Son* (C-349/95) [1997] E.C.R. I-6227.
[451] *Phytheron International SA v Jean Bardon SA* (C-352/95) [1997] E.C.R. I-1729 37; the Court had ruled that the addition on the label of a product of information that is necessary "the mere addition on the label of a number of statements designed to comply with the laws of the Member State where the product is imported would not constitute a legitimate reason within the meaning of art.7(2) of the Trade Marks Directive, unless the "the label so altered does not omit important information or give inaccurate information and its presentation is not liable to damage the reputation of the trade mark and that of its owner" (para.23). Indeed *Bristol Myers Squibb* had been cited in *Phytheron*.
[452] *Hoffmann-La Roche & Co AG and Hoffmann-La Roche AG v Centrafarm Vertriebsgesellschaft Pharmazeutischer Erzeugnisse mbH* (102/77) [1978] E.C.R. 1139.
[453] Point 40 of the Opinion of A.G. Sharpston.

15. BOEHRINGER II—REVISITING REPACKAGING, OVERSTICKERING

Attempting to narrow down the scope of the five provisions she added: 8–261

> "That approach to my mind best reflects the appropriate balance between the primary Treaty principle of free movement of goods and the rights of trade mark owners in relation to parallel imports. Where there is no risk to the guarantee of origin as defined by the Court, free movement of goods must prevail. Where on the facts a trade mark owner can demonstrate that overstickering risks impairing the guarantee of origin as so understood, then by way of derogation from the free movement of goods, the trade mark owner's rights may exceptionally prevail. That follows from the Court's definitions of the core rights and specific subject-matter of a trade mark."[454]

Note that Advocate General based her negative answer primarily on the facts of the case:

> "I accordingly conclude on question 2(a) that the BMS conditions do not apply where a parallel importer markets in one Member State a pharmaceutical product imported from another Member State in its original internal and external packaging to which the parallel importer has applied an additional external label printed in the language of the Member State of importation."[455]

The necessity requirement and the style of reboxing (2) Does the requirement 8–262
that repackaging be necessary apply merely to the fact of reboxing or to the precise manner and style of the reboxing and if so, how?

The contrast between the positive position of the High Court and the claimants on the one hand and the negative position of the Court of Appeals, the defendants, and the Commission on the other, all based on *Boehringer I*[456] and *Loendersloot*[457] evidenced the ambiguity—real or apparent—of the jurisprudence of the Court on these issues.

Here the Advocate General chose to be more provocative. She supported that the necessity requirements applied to reboxing itself rather than its precise manner and style; the Court's statement in *Boehringer I* that "it is the repackaging of the trade-marked pharmaceutical products in itself which is prejudicial to the specific subject-matter of the mark, and it is not necessary in that context to assess the actual effects of the repackaging by the parallel importer"[458] had misread *Hoffmann-La Roche*.

According to the Advocate General the guarantee of origin was narrowly 8–263
construed by the Court in *Hoffmann-La Roche*: the trade mark should

---

[454] Point 41 of the Opinion of A.G. Sharpston.
[455] Point 42 of the Opinion of A.G. Sharpston.
[456] *Boehringer Ingelheim Pharma KG* (C-143/00) [2002] E.C.R. I-3759.
[457] *Frits Loendersloot* (C-349/95) [1997] E.C.R. I-6227.
[458] *Boehringer I*, para.30.

enable the consumer to be certain that the marked product had not been subject to unauthorised interference by a third party "such as to affect [its] original condition".[459] "That suggests that the precise manner and style of reboxing which affects only the outer packaging would not impair the guarantee of origin."[460] This stance was closer to her initial position regarding the scope of the exceptions in art.7(2).

From an interpretive perspective she sought support in the travaux préparatoires for the Directive[461]: "... the Commission originally intended the necessity requirement to apply to the fact of repackaging; and envisaged that the parallel importer should enjoy a degree of freedom as to how precisely he repackaged, provided that he met the requirements laid down in Hoffmann-La Roche. There is nothing to suggest that that intention did not survive the legislative process".[462]

The treatment of *Paranova v Merck*,[463] a relevant decision of the EFTA court, was also relevant in terms of substance but also as an example of the weight EFTA court decisions can carry. Distilling the principles of the Court of Justice the EFTA court decided that once the right to repackage is established and the parallel importer has achieved effective access to the market the necessity requirement should not be decisive for interpreting "legitimate reasons", "[I]mposing the necessity requirement on the market conduct of the parallel importer after having gained market access, in particular on its strategy of product presentation, such as advertising or packaging design, would constitute a disproportionate restriction on the free movement of goods".[464] The Advocate General accepted the logic of the proportionality argument and suggested that the Court itself had hinted something similar in *Pharmacia & Upjohn*.[465]

8-264   Finally the Advocate General stressed the burden a stricter interpretation would impose on national courts that would have "to take numerous decisions on trivial details of pattern and colour which are not obviously within their judicial remit".[466]

8-265   *What causes damage to reputation* (3) Is the fourth *Bristol Myers Squibb* condition infringed only if the packaging is defective, of poor quality or untidy or does it extend to anything which damages the reputation of the trade mark?

---

[459] *Hoffmann-La Roche*, para.7.
[460] Point 46 of the Opinion of A.G. Sharpston.
[461] Explanatory Memorandum to the Proposal for a first Council Directive to approximate the laws of the Member States relating to trade marks (COM(80) 635 final, November 19, 1980), commentary on art.6.
[462] Point 49 of the Opinion of A.G. Sharpston.
[463] *Paranova AS v Merck & Co Inc* (E-3/02) [2003] 3 C.M.L.R. 7, EFTA.
[464] *Paranova* para.45.
[465] *Pharmacia & Upjohn S v Paranova A/S* (C-337/95) [1997] E.C.R. I-6013.
[466] Point 54 of the Opinion of A.G. Sharpston.

15. BOEHRINGER II—REVISITING REPACKAGING, OVERSTICKERING

Here the Advocate General gave some comfort to the pharmaceutical companies. There was no reason to limit the fourth condition; it was clear that the Court in *Bristol Myers Squibb* referred to defective, poor quality or untidy packaging as examples of "inappropriate presentation". Other cases—like *Dior*[467] and *BMW*[468]—went even further and considered inappropriate use and damage to the reputation in advertising.

Damage to reputation—a question of fact (4) Are certain (specified) methods of repackaging necessarily damaging to the reputation of a trade mark or is damage to reputation a question of fact?   8–266

The methods specified by the Court of Appeals were "debranding", not applying the trade mark to the new packaging, and "cobranding", adding the parallel importer's to the packaging.

Advocate General Sharpston agreed with the position of the Commission that national courts had to carry out a detailed factual appraisal in order to determine whether the repackaging damaged the reputation of the trade mark owner; in principle both debranding—leading to inappropriate presentation of the mark—and cobranding—incorrectly suggesting a commercial link with the trade mark owner could be damaging. In *Dior*[469] the Court held that only serious damage to reputation would amount to a legitimate reason under art.7(2) and in *BMW*[470] that determining whether there is a link between the advertisement and the impression of a commercial connection between the parties was a question of fact.

These two rulings should create general principles. "Whether a given circumstance (e.g. damage to reputation) may in principle constitute a 'legitimate reason' is a question of law, but whether in a given case that circumstance obtains is a question of fact".[471]

The effect of giving notice (5) What is the effect of failing to give notice as required by the fifth *Bristol Myers Squibb* condition?   8–267

Advocate General Sharpston distinguished between the first four conditions that were substantive and based on the Treaty and the fifth condition that was of procedural nature and introduced by the Court.

Initially, the rationale behind it, as developed in *Hoffmann-La Roche*,[472] was to reduce the risk of consumers being misled. But, as is almost always the case in the development of trade mark and unfair competition law, the

---

[467] *Parfums Christian Dior SA* (C-337/95) [1997] E.C.R. I-6013, one of the few instances that *Dior* had been cited by the Court.
[468] *Bayerische Motorenwerke AG and BMW Nederland BV* (C-63/97) [1999] E.C.R. I-905.
[469] *Parfums Christian Dior SA* (C-337/95) [1997] E.C.R. I-6013.
[470] *Bayerische Motorenwerke AG and BMW Nederland BV* (C-63/97) [1999] E.C.R. I-905.
[471] Point 65 of the Opinion of A.G. Sharpston.
[472] *Hoffmann-La Roche & Co AG and Hoffmann-La Roche AG* (102/77) [1978] E.C.R. 1139.

Court introduced in *Bristol Myers Squibb*[473] the interests of the proprietor; the notice enabled the proprietor to ensure that the repackaging did not affect the original condition and presentation of the product. And *Boehringer I*[474] stressed that it strengthened anti-counterfeiting protection.

8–268　　Accordingly, she supported, "breach of the notice requirement attracts a sanction distinct from the sanctions applicable if the other, substantive, BMS conditions are breached".[475]

She then distinguished between two scenarios: no or inadequate notice without breach of the other conditions and no or inadequate notice with breach of one or more of the other conditions. Breaching the notice requirement should be sanctioned in both cases in an effective and dissuasive way, because the breach would, almost always, be deliberate disregard of a straightforward condition. However, it would be disproportionate to apply the same sanction under both scenarios.

Finally she suggested a number of balancing parameters national courts would have to explore before determining the appropriate sanction. Where delay in commencing proceedings might be deliberate in order to increase financial awards for infringement, the sanction should not make it practically impossible for the parallel importer to exercise what in essence was a Community right. Deliberate breach of the condition would be an aggravating factor, if it allowed the parallel importer to access the market before the trade mark owner was given a chance to enforce its rights.

8–269　　*The burden of proof* (6) Who bears the burden of proof?

The Advocate General acknowledged that the Court's ruling in *Boehringer I*,[476] that the burden of proof was a procedural matter, that remained in the jurisdiction of national court provided that its exercise is non-discriminatory, was insufficiently precise.

She suggested a more intricate distinction. The Court should indicate who carried the burden of proof in respect of each of the five conditions. National procedural and evidential rules would then determine how this burden would be discharged.

She deemed it essential to differentiate between each condition for conceptual and practical reasons. Requiring the parallel importer to discharge all five conditions would tilt the balance from the principle of free movement of goods to its exception, the recognition of intellectual property rights. On the other hand, requiring the same from the trade mark owner would lumber the exercise of rights under art.7(2). Further, because the conditions differed in terms of complexity and individual requirements it

---

[473] *Bristol Myers Squibb* (C-427/93), *CH Boehringer Sohn, Boehringer Ingelheim KG and Boehringer Ingelheim A/S* (C-429/93) and *Bayer Aktiengesellschaft and Bayer Danmark A/S* (C-436/93) [1996] E.C.R. I-3457.
[474] *Boehringer Ingelheim Pharma KG* (C-143/00) [2002] E.C.R. I-3759.
[475] Point 72 of the Opinion of A.G. Sharpston.
[476] *Boehringer Ingelheim Pharma KG* (C-143/00) [2002] E.C.R. I-3759.

15. BOEHRINGER II—REVISITING REPACKAGING, OVERSTICKERING

was worth exploring for which of the two parties would be more practicable to gather the necessary evidence.

(i) Necessity It was implicit in the logic of the requirement that the parallel importer had to demonstrate necessity. The parallel importer would also be familiar with the market conditions and regulatory requirements and had the commercial incentive to research consumer perceptions regarding overstickering and reboxing. 8–270

(ii) No adverse effect on condition of product The parallel importer again would have to prove this, because it determined and controlled the repackaging process. This would not be a disproportionate burden because the parallel importer would also have to satisfy national regulatory authorities that repackaging would not affect the condition of the original product. 8–271

(iii) Clear identification of importer and manufacturer Again, the parallel importer determined and controlled the repackaging process and should carry the burden of showing that both the trade mark owner and the parallel importer were clearly identified on the repackaged product. 8–272

(iv) Presentation not damaging to reputation presentation The trade mark owner was in the best position to assess whether there was such a risk, to consider whether it was serious, and present the relevant evidence. 8–273

(v) Notice The parallel importer controlled whether, when and how the trade mark owner had been informed and would have to carry the burden of proof. 8–274

(b) The judgment of the Court 8–275

In its preliminary observations the Court reviewed its discussion in *Boehringer I*.[477]

(i) The concept of repackaging. It started its specific analysis by examining question 2(a) and the concept of "repackaging". Looking again at *Boehringer I*[478] it found that the concept of repackaging included relabelling and that relabelling, just like reboxing, was prejudicial to the specific subject-matter of the mark. Accordingly it was not necessary to assess the actual effects of the activity performed by the parallel importer: 8–276

> "The change brought about by any new carton or relabelling of a trade-marked medicinal product creates by its very nature real risks for the

---
[477] *Boehringer Ingelheim Pharma KG* (C-143/00) [2002] E.C.R. I-3759.
[478] *Boehringer Ingelheim Pharma KG* (C-143/00) [2002] E.C.R. I-3759.

guarantee of origin which the mark seeks to protect. Such a change may thus be prohibited by the trade mark proprietor unless the new carton or relabelling is necessary in order to enable the marketing of the products imported in parallel and the legitimate interests of the proprietor are also safeguarded."[479]

It followed according to the Court that the five requirements set out in *Bristol Myers Squibb*[480] should be applied and, if met, prevent the proprietor from opposing further commercialisation of a pharmaceutical product.

Accordingly, the answer to question 2(a) should be:

"that Article 7(2) of Directive 89/104 must be construed as meaning that the proprietor may legitimately oppose further commercialisation of a pharmaceutical product imported from another Member State in its original internal and external packaging with an additional external label applied by the importer, unless

— it is established that reliance on trade mark rights by the proprietor in order to oppose the marketing of the overstickered product under that trade mark would contribute to the artificial partitioning of the markets between Member States;

— it is shown that the new label cannot affect the original condition of the product inside the packaging;

— the packaging clearly states who overstickered the product and the name of the manufacturer;

— the presentation of the overstickered product is not such as to be liable to damage the reputation of the trade mark and of its proprietor; thus, the label must not be defective, of poor quality, or untidy; and

— the importer gives notice to the trade mark proprietor before the overstickered product is put on sale, and, on demand, supplies him with a specimen of that product."[481]

8-277   **(ii) The manner and style of repackaging—the necessity requirement.** The Court then considered questions 1(b) and 2(c): the application, as regards the manner and style of repackaging, and the condition that there must be a need to repackage the product.

The Court offered two views:

"That condition that repackaging be necessary is fulfilled if the rules or practices in the importing Member State prevent the product in question

---

[479] *Boehringer I*, para.30.
[480] *Bristol Myers Squibb* (C-427/93), *CH Boehringer Sohn, Boehringer Ingelheim KG and Boehringer Ingelheim A/S* (C-429/93) and *Bayer Aktiengesellschaft and Bayer Danmark A/S* (C-436/93) [1996] E.C.R. I-3457.
[481] *Boehringer II*, para.32.

from being marketed in that State in the same packaging as that in which those products are marketed in the exporting Member State. Conversely, the condition that it be necessary is not fulfilled if repackaging of the product is explicable solely by the parallel importer's attempt to secure a commercial advantage."[482]

The condition was directed only at the fact of repackaging the product, and the choice between a new carton and oversticking, for the purposes of allowing that product to be marketed in the importing State and not at the manner or style in which it had been repackaged.[483]

Accordingly the answer to questions 1(b) and 2(c) should be that the condition that the repackaging of the pharmaceutical product, either by reboxing the product and re-applying the trade mark or by applying a label to the packaging containing the product, be necessary for its further commercialisation in the importing Member State, as one of the conditions which, if fulfilled, prevent the proprietor under art.7(2) of Directive 89/104 from opposing such commercialisation, is directed solely at the fact of repackaging and not at the manner and style of the repackaging.

(iii) Damaging the reputation—turning back to Dior. Moving to questions 1(c) and 2(d) the Court found, following the application of the five conditions, that the carton or the label should not be defective, of poor quality, or untidy. However, this referred only to certain cases in which inappropriate presentation of the repackaged product was liable to damage the reputation of the trade mark and of its proprietor.

8–278

The Court held that "a repackaged pharmaceutical product could be presented inappropriately and, therefore, damage the trade mark's reputation in particular where the carton or label, while not being defective, of poor quality or untidy, are such as to affect the trade mark's value by detracting from the image of reliability and quality attaching to such a product and the confidence it is capable of inspiring in the public concerned".[484]

The answer to questions 1(c) and 2(d) was that the condition that the presentation of the pharmaceutical product should not be such as to be liable to damage the reputation of the trade mark and of its proprietor from legitimately opposing further commercialisation of a pharmaceutical product, where the parallel importer had either reboxed the product and re-applied the trade mark or applied a label to the packaging containing the product—is not limited only to cases where the repackaging is defective, of poor quality, or untidy.

---

[482] *Boehringer II*, paras 36–37, citing *Upjohn* (C-379/97) [1999] E.C.R. I-6927.
[483] Citing the EFTA Case *Paranova v Merck* (E-3/02) [2003] EFTA Court Report 2004, p.1.
[484] *Boehringer II*, para.43, citing *Bristol Myers Squibb* and *Parfums Christian Dior* (C-337/95) [1997] E.C.R. I-6013.

It went on to examine question 1(d) and question 2(e) on the circumstances likely to damage the trade mark's reputation. The Court here decided that the effect of the specific acts mentioned in the questions was for the national court to determine:

> "... precisely as with the question whether advertising is liable to create the impression that there is a commercial connection between the reseller and the trade mark proprietor and, therefore, constitute a legitimate reason within the meaning of Article 7(2) of Directive 89/104 ... the question whether the circumstances referred to in the previous paragraph of the present judgment are liable to damage the trade mark's reputation is a question of fact for the national court to decide in the light of the circumstances of each case."[485]

8-279 **(iv) The burden of proof.** On the burden of proof, covered in questions 1(a) and (e) and 2(b), the Court stated that where it was established that the parallel imported medicinal products had been repackaged, it was for the parallel importers to prove the existence of the conditions that would prevent the proprietors from lawfully opposing their further commercialisation.

As to whether the repackaging affected the original condition of the product inside the packaging, it should be sufficient that the parallel importer furnishes evidence that leads to the reasonable presumption that that condition has been fulfilled:

> "This applies a fortiori also to the condition that the presentation of the repackaged product must not be such as to be liable to damage the reputation of the trade mark and of its proprietor. Where the importer furnishes such initial evidence that the latter condition has been fulfilled it will then be for the proprietor of the trade mark, who is best placed to assess whether the repackaging is liable to damage his reputation and that of the trade mark, to prove that they have been damaged."[486]

8-280 **(v) Prior notice—the requirements.** In its analysis of the third question the Court held that prior notice was a requirement that the parallel imported had to fulfil. It was not sufficient that the proprietor be notified by other sources.

If a parallel importer had failed to give prior notice to the trade mark proprietor concerning a repackaged pharmaceutical product, he would infringe the right of that proprietor on the occasion of any subsequent importation of that product, so long as he had not given the proprietor such notice.

---

[485] *Boehringer II*, para.46, citing *BMW* (C-63/97) [1999] E.C.R. I-905.
[486] *Boehringer II*, para.53.

(vi) The absence of prior notice—the consequences. On the **8–281**
consequences of failure to give prior notice the Court held that where
Community law did not lay down specific sanctions it was incumbent on the
national authorities to adopt appropriate measures to deal with such a
situation. Those measures had to be proportionate, but also sufficiently
effective and a sufficient deterrent to ensure that Directive 89/104 was fully
effective.[487]

Accordingly, a national measure under which the trade mark proprietor
was entitled to claim financial remedies on the same basis as if the goods
had been spurious, would not in itself be contrary to the principle of proportionality. It was for the national court, however, to determine the amount of
the financial remedies according to the circumstances of each case, in the
light in particular of the extent of damage to the trade mark proprietor
caused by the parallel importer's infringement and in accordance with the
principle of proportionality.

16. WELLCOME V PARANOVA—IS THERE A REQUIREMENT OF MINIMUM INTERVENTION?—THE EXTENT OF DISCLOSURE

Two of the *Boehringer* issues were revisited in *The Wellcome Foundation Ltd* **8–282**
v Paranova Pharmazeutika Handels GmbH.[488] This time the reference came
from the Austrian Oberster Gerichtshof.

Wellcome, the proprietor of the trade mark ZOVIRAX, registered in
Austria for pharmaceutical products, started proceedings against Paranova,
who had imported ZOVIRAX products from Greece. The product had to be
sold in Austria in packs of 60 tablets whereas in Greece it was sold in packs
of 70. Paranova repackaged the product in packs of 60. On the new packaging the statement "Repackaged and imported by Paranova" appeared on
the front, in bold type and block capitals. Wellcome was mentioned on the
sides and the back in normal type. And a blue strip, commonly used by
Paranova, appeared at the edges. Paranova did inform Wellcome regarding
the importation of the product in Austria. Wellcome required additional
information regarding the State of export and a requested a sample, rather
than prints, of the packaging.

The case came before the Oberster Gerichtshof, which referred two
questions, to an extent overlapping with *Boehringer II*, to the Court. The
case was suspended and following the judgment in *Boehringer II* the
national court maintained two sub-questions, that had not been answered in
that case, concerning the presentation of repackaging and the importer's
obligation to notify the trade mark owner of its intention to repackage.

---

[487] *Adeneler* (C-212/04) [2006] E.C.R. I-6057.
[488] *The Wellcome Foundation Ltd v Paranova Pharmazeutika Handels GmbH* (C-276/05) [2009] E.T.M.R. 20.

8-283 *(a) The Opinion of the Advocate General*

Advocate General Sharpston limited her initial citations of earlier case law to the five conditions established in *Bristol Myers Squibb*,[489] the concept of necessity developed in *Boehringer I*,[490] and the burden of proof and the consequence of failure to give notice discussed in *Boehringer II*.[491]

8-284 **(i) Minimum intervention v damage to reputation.** Relying on *Loendersloot*[492] the national court queried first whether the presentation of the new packaging had to be considered against the legal background of minimum intervention or that of damage to reputation. It understood minimum intervention to mean that relabelling and/or repackaging should be done in a way causing as little prejudice as possible to the specific subject-matter of the trade mark right.

The Advocate General started her analysis by highlighting the differences between *Loendersloot* and *Boehringer II*, for example that the second concerned a pharmaceutical product a point specifically recognised in *Loendersloot*.

She reminded the point she had made in *Boehringer II* that the specific subject-matter of a trade mark had two components: the right to use the mark for the purpose of putting products protected by it into circulation for the first time in the EEA, after which that right is exhausted, and the right to oppose any use of the trade mark which is liable to impair the guarantee of origin, which comprised both a guarantee of identity of origin and a guarantee of integrity of the trade-marked product.

8-285 In the current case the first right had been exhausted. Regarding the second, she noted, that the Court had dealt with the guarantee of identity of origin in the context of co-branding as an aspect of reputation. "If the principle of minimum intervention had applied, there would have been no need for such an approach. It would have sufficed to state that co-branding was unlawful per se."[493]

Looking at the jurisprudence of the EFTA Court,[494] *Boehringer II*, and *Merck, Sharpe & Dohme*[495] she argued that repackaging that went beyond minimum intervention should not be automatically unlawful.

She rejected Wellcome's argument that without the principle of minimum intervention the parallel importer would be able to repackage for the sole purpose of obtaining a commercial advantage. Albeit, obtaining such an

---

[489] *Bristol Myers Squibb* (C-427/93) and *CH Boehringer Sohn, Boehringer Ingelheim KG and Boehringer Ingelheim A/S* (C-429/93) and *Bayer Aktiengesellschaft and Bayer Danmark A/S* (C-436/93) [1996] E.C.R. I-3457.
[490] *Boehringer Ingelheim Pharma KG* (C-143/00) [2002] E.C.R. I-3759.
[491] *Boehringer Ingelheim Pharma KG* (C-143/00) [2002] E.C.R. I-3759.
[492] *Frits Loendersloot* (C-349/95) [1997] E.C.R. I-6227.
[493] Point 32 of the Opinion of A.G. Sharpston.
[494] Case *Paranova v Merck* (E-3/02) [2003] EFTA Court Report 2004 1.
[495] *Merck v Paranova* (C-443/99) [2002] E.C.R. I-3703.

advantage would not be enough as the Court had already held in *Boehringer II*: "repackaging solely for a commercial advantage will be neither more nor less permissible depending on whether the principle of minimum intervention is or is not the relevant criterion for determining whether specific repackaging is permissible. Such repackaging is in any event impermissible."[496]

(ii) The duty of notification. The Austrian court had also questioned whether the duty of notification required the identification of the State of export and a statement of the precise reasons for the repackaging. 8–286

She suggested that identifying the State of export was not necessary. The parallel importer had to prove the existence of the five *Bristol Myers Squibb* conditions. *Boehringer II* set that the necessity condition was directed at the fact of repackaging and not at the manner and style of the repackaging. The parallel importer had to give the trade mark proprietor information that objectively demonstrated that the repackaging was necessary. Such information might have to cover the State of export but this was not a requirement as such.

(b) The Judgment of the Court 8–287

The Court too started its analysis by referring to *Bristol Myers Squibb*.[497] It viewed the notification requirement as a condition that enables the proprietor, first, to check that the repackaging does not directly or indirectly affect the original condition of the product and, secondly, that it is not likely to damage the reputation of the trade mark.

(i) The necessity condition—repackaging and presentation. It added that in *Boehringer II* it had held that the necessity requirement was directed only at the fact of repackaging the product, and not at the manner or style in which it had been repackaged. "Thus, the condition of necessity is directed only at the fact of repackaging the product, inter alia by reboxing it, and not at the presentation of that new packaging."[498] The Court also held that since the presentation of the new packaging of the product should not be assessed against the condition of necessity for the further marketing of the product, it should also not be assessed against the criterion that the adverse affect on the trade mark rights should be the minimum possible. The trade mark proprietor would be adequately protected by the requirement that the presentation of the repackaged product must not be such as to be liable to damage the trade marks or its proprietor reputation. Accordingly art.7(2) of the Directive should be interpreted "as meaning 8–288

---

[496] Point 40 of the Opinion of A.G. Sharpston.
[497] *Bristol Myers Squibb* (C-427/93) and *CH Boehringer Sohn, Boehringer Ingelheim KG and Boehringer Ingelheim A/S* (C-429/93) and *Bayer Aktiengesellschaft and Bayer Danmark A/S* (C-436/93) [1996] E.C.R. I-3457.
[498] *Wellcome v Paranova* (C-276/05), para.26.

that, where it is established that repackaging of the pharmaceutical product is necessary for further marketing in the Member State of importation, the presentation of the packaging should be assessed only against the condition that it should not be such as to be liable to damage the reputation of the trade mark or that of its proprietor".[499]

8–289   **(ii) Prior notice—the extent of disclosure.** Here the Court added that following *Boehringer I*[500] and in order to ensure the adequate functioning of the notice system presupposed that the interested parties would make sincere efforts to respect each other's legitimate interests. Accordingly it held, "it is for the parallel importer to furnish the proprietor of the trade mark with the information which is necessary and sufficient to enable the latter to determine whether the repackaging of the product under that trade mark is necessary in order to market it in the Member State of importation".[501]

The kind of information required would depend on the factual context of each case and, in exceptional cases, could involve disclosing the Member State of export, where the absence of that information would prevent the proprietor of the trade mark from evaluating the need to repackage.

To balance this the Court added that competition provisions of the EC Treaty could cover cases where the details provided by the importer were used by the proprietor to enable him to police his distribution and sale networks and combat parallel trade.[502]

17. CONCLUSION

8–290   This chapter looked at the interaction between free movement of goods rules and the exercise of trade mark rights. This has been an area where the Court has willingly undertaken a policy role. At the early stages the balance tilted heavily towards the free movement principle; but as the common market grew in strength the Court started acknowledging the beneficial effects of trade mark rights.

The free movement principle remains the starting point throughout the jurisprudence of the Court in free movement and exhaustion cases, it is the rule to which the property right over a trade mark is an exception that must be interpreted narrowly, even in the most recent cases involving repackaging and rebranding. At the same time, though, the Court has recognised that both trade mark rights and the free movement of goods rules are there to protect fundamental interests. And, gradually it has started accommodating

---

[499] *Wellcome*, para.30.
[500] *Boehringer Ingelheim Pharma KG* (C-143/00) [2002] E.C.R. I-3759.
[501] *Wellcome*, para.34.
[502] Citing *Frits Loendersloot* (C-349/95) [1997] E.C.R. I-6227.

17. CONCLUSION

the idea of trade marks deserving to be protected not only as indications of origins but also as indicators of reputation and prestige. Note that in *Boehringer II*[503] the Court chose to refer to *Dior*[504] in order to describe the reputation interests of the proprietor.

Looking at the exhaustion provisions of the Directive and the Regulation the Court followed the rationale it had developed in its free movement of goods case law. It opted for a territoriality principle: the general rule is that the right is exhausted once the marked product is put on the market within the EEA. At the same it developed a set of conditions for establishing whether and delineating the extent that trade mark rights can still be used in order to stop intra-Community trade.

---

[503] *Boehringer Ingelheim Pharma KG* (C-143/00) [2002] E.C.R. I-3759.
[504] *Parfums Christian Dior SA* (C-337/95) [1997] E.C.R. I-6013; see also *Bayerische Motorwerke AG and BMW Nederland BV* (C-63/97) [1999] E.C.R. I-905.

CHAPTER 9

COMPETITION AND TRADE MARKS

1.	Introduction	9–001
2.	Competition Rules	9–004
3.	The Scope of the Competition Provisions	9–005
	(1) The multiple tasks of European competition law	9–005
	(2) Direct applicability	9–008
4.	The Application of Article 81	9–014
	(1) The concept of undertakings	9–014
	(2) The scope and the form of an agreement	9–016
	(3) Concerted practices	9–022
	(4) Hugin—the boundaries between Community and national competition law	9–023
	(5) Consten and Grundig—the interaction with trade mark law—the starting point	9–024
	(6) Société Technique Minière—a rule of reason analysis?	9–035
	(7) Volk v Vervaecke—significant effect	9–036
	(8) Beguelin—the relevance of context	9–037
	(9) Delimitis—a web of agreements—closer to a rule of reason analysis	9–038
	(10) EMI and Nungesser—existence and the way the right is exercised	9–052
	(11) Pronuptia de Paris—the benefits of franchising agreements	9–057
	(12) BAT—competition and trade mark law—delimitation agreements	9–062
	(13) The position of the Commission on delimitation agreements	9–064
	(14) The Commission on repackaging bans	9–066
	(15) Campari—an example of the application of article 81(3) by the Commission	9–067
	(16) Javico—the Contrast with Silhouette	9–072
5.	The Application of Article 82	9–079
	(1) Dominance	9–079
	(2) Dominance and intellectual property	9–088
	(3) Der Grüne Punkt—dominance and trade marks—the function of the sign	9–121
6.	Conclusion	9–134

1. INTRODUCTION

9–001 In this chapter we will examine briefly the formal interaction between trade marks and competition law. We have seen that competition questions were raised in the previous chapter in respect of the potential function of trade mark rights as tools for compartmentalising the common European market into national markets. More importantly for the development of trade mark law we have also highlighted the competition arguments and rationale considered by the Court first in determining what constitutes a protectable trade mark and second in delineating the scope of protection.[1]

Here the focus shifts on how trade marks rights and agreements involving trade marks are weighed up by competition law. The two primary competition rules, that are described below, deal with anticompetitive collusion (art.81) and abuse of market dominance (art.82).

For the purposes of competition law, and art.81 in particular, there is another legal tool that we must also take into account, that of block exemptions; a mechanism that European law has employed often, in order to ease the tension between the exclusive nature of intellectual property rights and competition principles. Historically, the exemptions covered specific rights or types of agreement. For example, Regulation 2349/84[2] covered patent licences whereas Regulation 556/89[3] followed the same route for know-how licences. Gradually the scope of the exemptions broadened, in parallel with the growing completion of the common market project and responding to changes in economic thinking. Regulation 240/96[4] amalgamated the two exemptions mentioned above and became known as the Technology Transfer Regulation for patent, know-how, and mixed patent and know-how licences.

9–002 The Commission, feeling that its approach has become too formalistic, expanded further the ambit of the exemptions by adopting Regulation 2790/99,[5] the vertical agreements block exemption, and Regulation 772/2004,[6] the new technology transfer block exemption.

Intellectual property transactions might also fall under the umbrella of other block exemptions relating to types of agreements, like the Research

---

[1] Indeed, Ghidini notes that the main competition related trade mark issue is the transformation of their basis for protection from distinguishing symbols issue to assets in themselves and the power of advertising: see Ghidini, *Intellectual Property and Competition Law: the Innovation Nexus* (E. Elgar, 2006); see for example the opinion of the A.G. in *Dyson Ltd* (C-321/03), discussed in Ch.4.
[2] Reg.2389/84 [1984] OJ L 219/15.
[3] Reg.556/89 [1989] OJ L 61/1.
[4] Reg.240/96 [1996] OJ L 31/2.
[5] Commission Reg.2790/99 on the application of art.81(3) of the Treaty to categories of vertical agreements and concerted practices [1999] OJ L 336. For an overview see Korah and O'Sullivan, *Distribution Agreements under the EC Competition Rules* (Hart, 2002).
[6] Commission Reg.772/2004 on the application of art.81(3) of the Treaty to categories of technology agreements [2004] OJ L123/11. For an overview see Fine, *The EC Competition Law on Technology Licensing* (Sweet and Maxwell, 2005); and for a comparative perspective Byrne and McBratney, *Licensing Technology* (Jordans, 2005).

1. INTRODUCTION

and Development Regulation,[7] the Specialisation Regulation,[8] or even specific product markets like car trade.[9] Note that only one block exemption may apply to any agreement.

Transactions involving trade marks will have to satisfy the requirements of the relevant block exemption in order to benefit from its application. For example, according to the Guidelines issued by the Commission, trade mark licensing is not covered by Regulation 772/2004, unless and to the extent that the trade marks are directly related to the exploitation of the licensed technology and do not constitute the primary objective of the agreement. Still, signs that constitute trade marks but also enjoy design protection can be covered directly by the Regulation. The same applies to Regulation 2790/99; according to the guidelines the intellectual property clauses of the agreement must be part of the vertical agreement rather than constitute its primary object.

The general principle is the same for all the block exemptions: agreements that satisfy the conditions of the relevant regulation are automatically exempted under art.81(3). To avoid abuse of the system there are market thresholds above which the exemptions do not apply and lists of clauses that would not be exempted in any case. For example, under the Vertical Agreements Block Exemption, setting maximum or recommended prices would be allowed, however fixing or setting minimum prices would not be tolerated.

9–003

The way the competition rules are applied has been transformed following the introduction of Regulation 1/2003,[10] the aim of which is to obtain the direct, decentralised, and uniform application of European competition law by national courts and competition authorities with the Commission retaining its primacy in respect of decision making powers through a right of intervention.[11] This new path of enforcement also means that national authorities should take into account the Guidelines and other Notices issued by the Commission in a more direct way. In many ways the Regulation attempts to formalise the informal system of co-operation between the Commission, on the one hand, and the national courts and competition authorities, on the other, established by the Court in cases like *Delimitis*[12] and *HB Ice Cream*.[13]

---

[7] Commission Reg.2659/2000 on the application of art.81(3) of the Treaty to categories of research and development agreements [2000] OJ L304/7.
[8] Commission Reg.2658/2000 on the application of art.81(3) of the Treaty to categories of specialisation agreements [2000] OJ L304/3.
[9] Commission Reg.1400/2002 on the application of art.81(3) of the Treaty to categories of vertical agreements and concerted practices in the motor vehicle sector [2002] OJ L203/30.
[10] Council Reg.1/2003 on the implementation of the rules on competition laid down in arts 81 and 82 of the Treaty, [2003] OJ L 1/1.
[11] See Roitman, "Legal Uncertainty for Vertical Distribution Agreements: the Block Exemption Reg.2790/1999 and Related Aspects of the New Reg.1/2003" [2006] E.C.L.R. 261.
[12] *Stergios Delimitis v Henninger Bräu AG* (C-234/89) [1991] E.C.R. I-935.
[13] *HB Ice Cream Ltd v Masterfoods* (C-344/98) [2000] E.C.R. I-11369.

Finally, a cautionary note. The cases discussed below aim to give the reader a flavour of the interface between trade marks, or by way of example other intellectual property rights, and competition from a European competition law angle; the perspective however remains that of a trade mark lawyer. They do not purport to be an authoritative, or even comprehensive, picture of European competition law.

2. COMPETITION RULES

9–004 Article 3(g) of the EC Treaty states that one of the deeds of the Community is the establishment of a system ensuring that competition in the internal market is not distorted. The primary tools for achieving this are provided by the joint application of art.81 and art.82.

Article 81 EC is the provision that aims to stop anti-competitive collusion between market players:

"1. The following shall be prohibited as incompatible with the common market; all agreements between undertakings, decisions by associations of undertakings and concerted practices which may affect trade between Member States and which have as their object or effect the prevention, restriction or distortion of competition within the common market, and in particular those which:

(a) directly or indirectly fix purchase or selling prices or any other trading conditions;
(b) limit or control production markets, technical development, or investment;
(c) share markets or sources of supply;
(d) apply dissimilar conditions to equivalent transactions with other trading parties, thereby placing them at a competitive disadvantage; and
(e) make the conclusion of contracts subject to acceptance by the other parties of supplementary obligations which, by their nature or according to commercial usage, have no connection with the subject of such contracts.

2. Any agreements or decisions prohibited pursuant to this Article shall be automatically void.

3. The provisions of para.1 may, however, be declared inapplicable in the case of:

— any agreement or category of agreements between undertakings;
— any decision or category of decisions by associations of undertakings; and
— any concerted practice or category of concerted practices;

which contributes to improving the production or distribution of goods or to promoting technical or economic progress, while allowing consumers a fair share of the resulting benefit, and which does not:

(a) impose on the undertakings concerned restrictions which are not indispensable to the attainment of these objectives; and
(b) afford such undertakings the possibility of eliminating competition in respect of a substantial part of the products in question."

Article 82 targets the concentration of economic power when combined with abusive behaviour:

"Any abuse by one or more undertakings of a dominant position within the common market or in a substantial part of it shall be prohibited as incompatible with the common market in so far as it may affect trade between Member States. Such abuse may, in particular, consist in:

(a) directly or indirectly imposing unfair purchase or selling prices or unfair trading conditions;
(b) limiting production, markets or technical development to the prejudice of consumers;
(c) applying dissimilar conditions to equivalent transactions with other trading parties, thereby placing them at a competitive disadvantage; and
(d) making the conclusion of contract subject to acceptance by the other parties of supplementary obligations which, by their nature or according to commercial usage, have no connection with the subject of such contracts."

3. THE SCOPE OF THE COMPETITION PROVISIONS

(1) The multiple tasks of European competition law

The Court of Justice has described the negative effect of monopolies, in *United Brands*,[14] as:

9–005

"... a position of economic strength enjoyed by an undertaking which enables it to prevent effective competition being maintained on the relevant market by giving it the power to behave to an appreciable extent independently of its competitors, customers and ultimately of its consumers".[15]

---

[14] *United Brands Co and United Brands Continental BV v Commission* (27/76) [1978] E.C.R. 207.
[15] *United Brands*, para.2.

Competition law in a "national market" environment aims to inject to trade, the fuel of the market engine, an efficiency additive that benefits both consumers and marketers. Resources are allocated productively and efficiently, consumer welfare is enhanced, and the dynamism of smaller players is protected from the abuse of stronger opponents.

In Europe competition law has undertaken an additional role, to facilitate the creation of a single market.

9–006 From a historical perspective the application of the competition provisions of the Treaty can be divided into three stages that broadly correspond with the establishment, development, and strengthening of the common market.[16]

Wesseling convincingly argues that at the first stage the framers of the Treaty wanted to preclude private undertakings from replacing the prohibited public obstacles to inter state trade. At the second stage competition law became a tool serving the establishment of a broader Community industrial policy granting preferential treatment to forms of trans-national co-operation that promoted integration or other policy aims. At the third stage the focus turned to the control of corporate mergers and the liberalisation of State-dominated sectors. The system adapted, accepting the broad policy trends but without conforming to a strict hierarchy of objectives. Accordingly, each case has to be viewed in its own economic and historical context.

The current theme is uniform, but less formalistic, decentralised application of competition rules. The breadth of competition policy objectives is exemplified by the Commission's Competition Report back in 1972. It had declared that its competition policy:

"... endeavours to cut monopoly profits, to ensure that the economy remains adaptable to circumstances and to stimulate innovation",[17] and "to maintain or create effective conditions of competition by means of rules applying to enterprises ... Such a policy encourages the best possible use of productive resources for the greatest possible benefit of the economy as a whole and for the benefit, in particular, of the consumer".[18]

9–007 Integration was another objective:

"... restrictions on competition and practices which jeopardise the unity of the Common Market are proceeded against with special vigour".[19]

---

[16] See Wesseling, *The Modernisation of EC Antitrust Law* (Hart, Oxford, 2000); and, for intellectual property rights in particular, Greaves, "Herschel Smith Lecture 1998: Article 86 [82] of the EC Treaty and Intellectual Property Rights" [1998] E.I.P.R. 379; and Maher, "Competition Law and Intellectual Property Rights: Evolving Formalism" in Craig and De Burca (eds), *The Evolution of EU Law* (Oxford: Oxford University Press, 1999).
[17] European Commission, Second Report on Competition 1972, p.9.
[18] European Commission, Second Report on Competition 1972, p.12.
[19] European Commission, Second Report on Competition 1972, p.15.

3. THE SCOPE OF THE COMPETITION PROVISIONS

But, competition law was also perceived as a regulatory tool:

> "Even though the operation of market forces is an irreplaceable factor for progress and the most appropriate means of ensuring the best possible distribution of production factors, situations can nevertheless arise when this in itself is not enough to obtain the required results without too much delay and intolerable social tension. When the decisions of the enterprises themselves do not make it possible for the necessary changes to be made at an acceptable cost in social terms, then recourse to relatively short-term and limited intervention is necessary in order to direct such decisions towards an optimal economic and social result".[20]

Competition law in Europe is not only about corporate efficiency; it affects trade integration, the approximation of the economies of the Member States, the development of targeted sectors of the European economy and specific geographical regions, and, ultimately, the creation and support of an integrated European economy.

(2) Direct applicability

Articles 81 and 82 are directly applicable. In *BRT*[21] the Court ruled that they had direct effect in the national legal orders, they "apply to relationships between individuals and create rights directly in respect of the individuals concerned which national courts must safeguard. Articles [81] (1) and [82] are therefore part of the national legal order and can be pleaded before a national court either as a case of action and/or as a defence".[22]

9–008

"To deny ... the national courts' jurisdiction to afford this safeguard, would mean depriving individuals of rights which they hold under the Treaty itself."[23]

However, the direct applicability of the two provisions created competence conflicts.

(i) HB Ice Cream v Masterfood—the dominant role of the Commission. The Court described the traditional roles of the Community actors in *HB Ice Cream*.[24] The case concerned agreements entered into by HB, the larger manufacturer and distributor of ice cream in Ireland cornering 70 per cent of the market, in connection with the distribution of "impulse" ice cream in Ireland and the provision of freezer cabinets to retailers. The agreements incorporated an exclusivity clause providing that the freezers would be used exclusively for its own products.

9–009

---

[20] European Commission, Second Report on Competition 1972, p.17.
[21] *Belgische Radio en Televisie v SV SABAM and NV Fonior* (127/73) [1974] E.C.R. 51, para.16.
[22] Greaves (1998), p.380.
[23] *Belgische Radio en Televisie* (127/73) [1974] E.C.R. 51, para.17.
[24] *HB Ice Cream Ltd* (C-344/98) [2000] E.C.R. I-11369.

Masterfoods challenged, unsuccessfully, the clause before the Irish courts when HB warned retailers stocking Masterfood's Mars ice cream bars in the freezers supplied by HB that they would have to comply with the clause. The High Court granted an injunction restraining Masterfoods from inducing retailers to store its products in freezers supplied by HB.

In parallel Masterfoods lodged a complaint with the Commission, which accepted the complaint and issued a statement of objections. As a result HB proposed some changes into its system of distribution; the Commission at the end found that the changes were not enough and that the exclusivity clause constituted an infringement of art.81(1).[25] HB challenged the Decision before the Court of First Instance.

9-010   The case in Ireland reached the Irish Supreme Court that had to deal with a conflict between the decision of the national court and a decision of the Commission that in turn had been challenged before the Court of First Instance. It chose to stay proceedings and refer to the Court a number of questions: first it enquired what a national court should do under the circumstances and secondly, depending on the answer to the first question, whether HB's practices infringed the competition provisions of the Treaty.

The Court of First Instance suspended the operation of the Commission's decision until the Court of Justice issued its judgment.[26]

9-011   *Delineating the division of powers* The Court started by delineating the—pre-Regulation 1/2003—division of powers between the Commission and the national courts.

The Commission carried the task of ensuring the application of the art.81 and art.82 principles and the responsibility for defining and implementing the orientation of the competition policy. "It is for the Commission to adopt, subject to review by the Court of First Instance and the Court of Justice, individual decisions in accordance with the procedural rules in force and to adopt exemption regulations. In order effectively to perform that task, which necessarily entails complex economic assessments, it is entitled to give differing degrees of priority to the complaints brought before it."[27]

It had exclusive competence to adopt decisions implementing art.81(3) and shared competence to apply art.81(1) and art.82 with the national courts.[28]

---

[25] Commission Decision 98/531 (*Van den Bergh Foods Limited*) [1998] OJ L246/1; [1998] 5 C.M.L.R. 530. Note that the Commission had initially indicated that the amended agreements deserved exemption under art.81(3), however it changed its stance following a re-examination of the market.
[26] The Court of first Instance reached a decision (*Van den Bergh Foods Ltd v Commission* (T-65/98R) [2003] E.C.R. II-4653) following the judgment of the Court, against which Unilever, the parent of HB, appealed before the Court of Justice, *Unilever v Commission* (C-552/03P) [2004] OJ C59/13.
[27] *HB Ice Cream*, para.46, citing *Stergios Delimitis v Henninger Bräu AG* (C-234/89) [1991] E.C.R. I-935; and *Ufex v EC Commission* (C-119/97 P) [1999] E.C.R. I-1341.
[28] Citing *Delimitis v Henninger Braü AG* (C-234/89) [1991] E.C.R. I-935.

3. THE SCOPE OF THE COMPETITION PROVISIONS

Article 81 and art.82 produced direct effects in relations between individuals and created direct rights that national courts had to safeguard. Accordingly national courts continued to have jurisdiction to apply the provisions even after the Commission had initiated a procedure under Regulation 17.[29]

The role of the Commission—the principle of sincere co-operation. However the Court gave ultimate precedence to the decisions of the Commission: 9–012

> "Despite that division of powers, and in order to fulfil the role assigned to it by the Treaty, the Commission cannot be bound by a decision given by a national court in application of Articles [81](1) and [82] of the Treaty. The Commission is therefore entitled to adopt at any time individual decisions under Articles [81] and [82] of the Treaty, even where an agreement or practice has already been the subject of a decision by a national court and the decision contemplated by the Commission conflicts with that national court's decision."[30]

On the other hand Member States carried the duty under art.10 EC to take all appropriate measures to ensure fulfilment of the obligations arising from Community law and to abstain from any measure which could jeopardise the attainment of the objectives of the Treaty. This was binding on all the authorities of Member States including courts.[31]

Having set the competence boundaries the Court turned into resolving the instances of contradiction.

Under art.249 EC the decisions of the Commission implementing the competition provisions were binding in their entirety upon those to whom they were addressed. Accordingly, national courts should avoid giving decisions which would conflict with a decision of the Commission[32]: 9–013

> "It is even more important that when national courts rule on agreements or practices which are already the subject of a Commission decision they cannot take decisions running counter to that of the Commission, even if the latter's decision conflicts with a decision given by a national court of first instance."[33]

The Court added that acts of the Community institutions were in principle presumed lawful until annulled or withdrawn; and a decision to suspend

---

[29] Citing *Belgische Radio en Televisie* (127/73) [1974] E.C.R. 51.
[30] *HB Ice Cream*, para.48.
[31] Citing *Societa Italiana Petroli SpA v Borsana* (2/97) [1998] E.C.R. I-8597.
[32] Citing *Stergios Delimitis v Henninger Bräu AG* (C-234/89) [1991] E.C.R. I-935.
[33] *HB Ice Cream*, para.52.

proceedings had purely provisional effect; it did not neutralise the subsequent decision in the main action.[34]

Finally, according to the principle of sincere co-operation when the outcome of the dispute before the national court depended on the validity of the Commission decision, the national court should stay its proceedings pending final judgment in the action for annulment by the Community Courts, unless it considered that it had to make a reference to the Court of Justice. Taking the first option the national court would have to examine whether it was necessary to order interim measures in order to safeguard the interests of the parties pending final judgment.

In this case it was clear that the maintenance of the injunction of the High Court depended on the validity of the Decision of the Commission. The Supreme Court would have to follow one of the above two options.

4. THE APPLICATION OF ARTICLE 81

(1) The concept of undertakings

9–014 In *Hoefner*[35] the Court held that the term undertaking covers any entity engaged in an economic activity:

> "... in the context of competition law, ... the concept of an undertaking encompasses every entity engaged in an economic activity, regardless of the legal status of the entity and the way in which it is financed".[36]

Distinct entities may be treated as one when there is a strong link between them. For example a parent company may be considered as one economic unit with its subsidiary.

In *Béguelin*,[37] for example, the Court held that in such cases the contested agreement could fall outside the scope of art.81:

> "Article [81] (1) prohibits agreements which have as their object or effect an impediment to competition."[38]
>
> "This is not the position in the case of an exclusive sales agreement when in fact the concession granted under that agreement is in part transferred from the parent company to a subsidiary which, although having separate legal personality, enjoys no economic independence."[39]

---

[34] Citing Case *Commission v BASF* (C-137/92 P) [1994] E.C.R. I-2555; and *Commission v Atlantic Container Line* (C-149/95 P (R)) [1995] E.C.R. I-2165.
[35] *Hoefner and Elser v Macrotron GmbH* (C-42/90) [1991] E.C.R. I-1979.
[36] *Hoefner*, para.21.
[37] *Béguelin Import v GL Import-Export* (22/71) [1971] E.C.R. 949.
[38] *Béguelin*, para.7.
[39] *Béguelin*, para.8.

4. THE APPLICATION OF ARTICLE 81

"Accordingly the relationship between the companies cannot be taken into account in determining the validity of an exclusive dealing agreement entered into between the subsidiary and a third party."[40]

The Court, however, will not hesitate to lift the corporate veil and decide the opposite if it finds that the subsidiary enjoys a sufficient degree of autonomy from its parent.[41]

9–015

The same applied to other forms of collaboration. In *Volkswagen*[42] the Court rejected the argument that because dealers acted as intermediaries they formed one integrated economic unit with their provider:

"... Representatives can lose their character as independent traders only if they do not bear any of the risks resulting from the contracts negotiated on behalf of the principal and they operate as auxiliary organs forming an integral part of the principal's undertaking[43] ... However, the German VAG dealers assume, at least in part, the financial risks linked to the transactions concluded on behalf of VAG Leasing, in so far as they repurchase the vehicles from it upon the expiry of the leasing contracts. Furthermore, their principal business of sales and after-sales services is carried on, largely independently, in their own name and for their own account."[44]

(2) The scope and the form of an agreement

(a) The Quinine Cartel—gentlemen's agreements

The *Quinine Cartel*[45] case shows the willingness of the Court to consider the scope rather than the form of the agreement as the decisive criterion.

9–016

The entities involved concluded an agreement setting prices in, and dividing markets of, non-Member States (the export agreement). Sales within the common market were covered by an informal gentlemen's agreement. They argued that this did not constitute an agreement within the meaning of art.81(1), that in any event it had ceased to exist for a long time, and that there was no indication that they continued the restrictions on competition originally envisaged in the gentlemen's agreement.

---

[40] *Béguelin*, para.9.
[41] See for example *Stora Kopparbergs Bergslags AB v Commission* (C-286/98 P) [2000] E.C.R. I-9925.
[42] *Bundeskartellamt v Volkswagen AG and VAG Leasing GmbH* (C-266/93) [1995] E.C.R. I-3477.
[43] The Court referred to *Cooperative Vereniging "Suiker Unie" UA v Commission* (40/73 to 48/73, 50/73, 54 to 56/73, 111/73, 113/73 and 114/73) [1975] E.C.R. 1663.
[44] *Volkswagen*, para.19.
[45] *ACF Chemiefarma NV v Commission* (41/69) [1970] E.C.R. 661; *Buchler & Co v Commission* (44/69) [1970] E.C.R. 733; and *Boehringer Mannheim GmbH v Commission* (45/69) [1970] E.C.R. 769.

The Court was not convinced. Having noted that the parties to the export agreement had conceded that they declared themselves willing to abide by the gentlemen's agreement until the end of October 1962 it found that this document "amounted to the faithful expression of the joint intention of the parties to the agreement with regard to their conduct in the Common Market".[46] Equally damning was the provision in the gentlemen's agreement that its infringement would ipso facto constitute an infringement of the export agreement.

9–017 The Court went on to evaluate the evidence regarding the post-1962 effect of the agreement holding that the parties continued to abide by the gentlemen's agreement. Their behaviour could not be justified on the basis of independent economic reasoning. Incidentally, one of the suggested, but not accepted by the Court, explanations for the low volume of trade in quinine products was the divergence between national legislations "governing pharmaceutical products under trade-mark".[47]

The informal agreement had a parasitic, but effective, existence that the Court recognised without any difficulty.

(b) Bayer (Adalat)—tacit agreement and unilateral conduct

9–018 *Bayer*[48] is a recent judgment on competition in the market of pharmaceuticals. It considered in particular the distinction between tacit agreements and unilateral conduct.

Bayer marketed throughout the European Union a drug treating cardiovascular disease under the trade name Adalat or Adalate. Price differences—the prices in most Member States were fixed by national health authorities—led to parallel importation that hurt Bayer considerably. Bayer then stopped supplying some wholesalers in Spain and France, two of the cheaper jurisdictions; in turn the affected wholesalers complained to the Commission that decided that Bayer, in essence, imposed an export ban to wholesalers, infringing art.81(1). It supplied only those wholesalers that had practically, through their conduct, agreed not to export from their own jurisdiction. Bayer supplied only those wholesalers that had been ordering at a level that corresponded—or in some cases calculated to appear to correspond—with the needs of their traditional market according to Bayer's calculations. It refused to supply those that placed excessive orders.

Bayer appealed to the Court of First Instance that annulled the decision holding that the Commission had incorrectly assessed the facts as to whether there had been an agreement—"a meeting of minds"—between

---

[46] *Quinine Cartel*, para.112.
[47] *Quinine Cartel*, para.121.
[48] *Bundesverband der Arzneimittel-Importeure eV and Commission of the European Communities v Bayer AG* (C-2/01 P and C-3/01 P) [2004] E.C.R. I-23. The cases were appeals against a judgment of the Court of First Instance in *Bayer AG v Commission* (T-41/96) [2000] E.C.R. II-3383 annulling Commission Decision 96/478/EC (ADALAT), [1996] OJ L 201/1.

4. THE APPLICATION OF ARTICLE 81

Bayer and the wholesalers it continued to supply. Bayer's behaviour constituted unilateral conduct rather than a tacit agreement between a supplier and acquiescing wholesalers.

(c) The burden of proof

The Court reconfirmed that "it is for the Commission to prove the infringement which it has found and to adduce evidence capable of demonstrating to the requisite legal standard the existence of circumstances constituting an infringement".[49] The documents submitted by the Commission did not establish that "the wholesalers had wished to give Bayer the impression that, in compliance with its declared intention, they were willing to reduce their orders to a given level".[50]

9–019

(d) The factors establishing the existence of an agreement

The Court held that the finding of the Court of First Instance regarding the lack of a system of monitoring and penalties on behalf of Bayer was simply a position on the facts of the case rather than an imposition of a new precondition for establishing that an agreement consisted an export ban:

9–020

> "the Court of First Instance did not in any event consider that the absence of a system of subsequent monitoring and penalties in itself implied the absence of an agreement prohibited by Article [81](1) of the Treaty. On the other hand, such an absence was regarded as one of the relevant factors in the analysis concerning Bayer's alleged intention to impose an export ban and, therefore, the existence of an agreement in this case. In that regard, although the existence of an agreement does not necessarily follow from the fact that there is a system of subsequent monitoring and penalties, the establishment of such a system may nevertheless constitute an indicator of the existence of an agreement".[51]

The Court went further to hold that the "mere fact that the unilateral policy of quotas implemented by Bayer, combined with the national requirements on the wholesalers to offer a full product range, produces the same effect as an export ban does not mean either that the manufacturer imposed such a ban or that there was an agreement prohibited by Article [81](1) of the Treaty".[52]

Also, the judgment of the Court of First Instance, according to the Court of Justice, did not impose a requirement that in order to fall under art.81(1) an agreement must demand a particular line of conduct rather than identify

---

[49] *Bayer*, para.62.
[50] *Bayer*, para.54.
[51] *Bayer*, para.83.
[52] *Bayer*, para.88.

a concurrence of wills between at least two parties. The Court of First Instance did not require proof of an express ban.

9–021 The Court accepted that the existence of an agreement can be deducted from conduct of the parties but distinguished this from a unilateral expression of a wish:

> "For an agreement within the meaning of Article 81(1) of the Treaty to be capable of being regarded as having been concluded by tacit acceptance, it is necessary that the manifestation of the wish of one of the contracting parties to achieve an anti-competitive goal constitute an invitation to the other party, whether express or implied, to fulfil that goal jointly, and that applies all the more where, as in this case, such an agreement is not at first sight in the interests of the other party, namely the wholesalers".[53]

Commenting on the facts of the case the Court noted that the wholesalers' strategy to make Bayer believe that the needs of the national markets had grown went against establishing a meeting of minds.

Finally, on the relevance of the wholesalers' acquiescence the Court held that the mere co-existence of an agreement which is in itself neutral, with a unilaterally imposed measure restricting competition does not amount to an agreement prohibited by that provision; "the mere fact that a measure adopted by a manufacturer, which has the object or effect of restricting competition, falls within the context of continuous business relations between the manufacturer and its wholesalers is not sufficient for a finding that such an agreement exists".[54]

(3) Concerted practices

9–022 In *ANIC*[55] the Court accepted that describing the borders between an agreement and a concerted practice is not an exact science. It turned to the scope of art.81(1) stating that both are intended to catch forms of collusion that had the same nature and differed only in respect of intensity and the forms they manifest themselves:

> "It follows that, whilst the concepts of an agreement and of a concerted practice have partially different elements, they are not mutually incompatible. Contrary to Anic's allegations, the Court of First Instance did not therefore have to require the Commission to categorise either as an agreement or as a concerted practice each form of conduct found but was right to hold that the Commission had been entitled to characterise some of those forms of conduct as principally 'agreements' and others as 'concerted practices'."[56]

[53] *Bayer*, para.102.
[54] *Bayer*, para.141.
[55] *Commission v ANIC Partecipazioni SpA* (C-49/92 P) [1999] E.C.R. I-4125.
[56] *ANIC*, para.132.

4. THE APPLICATION OF ARTICLE 81

In *ICI*,[57] a case questioning the pricing practices of the dyestuffs industry, the Court defined what constituted a concerted practice by juxtaposing it with contract on the one hand and independent parallel behaviour on the other.

> "By its very nature ... a concerted practice does not have all the elements of a contract but may inter alia arise out of coordination which becomes apparent from the behaviour of the participants."[58]

The Court conceded that parallel behaviour and concerted practice did not necessarily coincide. It is the effect of parallel behaviour that counts: "it may ... amount to strong evidence of such practice if it leads to conditions of competition which do not correspond to the normal conditions of the market, having regard to the nature of the products, the size and number of the undertakings and the volume of the said market".[59]

This would be especially the case if the "parallel conduct is such as to enable those concerned to attempt to stabilize prices at a level different from that to which competition would have led, and to consolidate established positions to the detriment of effective freedom of movement of the products in the Common Market and of the freedom of consumers to choose their suppliers."[60]

> "Therefore the question whether there was concerted action in this case can only be correctly determined if the evidence upon which the contested decision is based is considered, not in isolation, but as a whole, account being taken of the specific features of the market in the products in question."[61]

(4) Hugin—the boundaries between Community and national competition law

The Court set the boundaries between Community and national competition law in *Hugin*.[62] The criterion was the effect on interstate trade:

9–023

> "the interpretation and application of the condition relating to effects on trade between Member States contained in Articles [81] and [82] of the Treaty must be based on the purpose of that condition which is to define, in the context of the law governing competition, the boundary between

---

[57] *Imperial Chemical Industries v Commission* (48/69) [1972] E.C.R. 619.
[58] *ICI*, para.65.
[59] *ICI*, para.66.
[60] *ICI*, para.67.
[61] *ICI*, para.68.
[62] *Hugin Kassaregister AB and Hugin Cash Registers Ltd v Commission* (22/78) [1979] E.C.R. 1869.

the areas respectively covered by Community law and the law of the Member States. Thus Community law covers any agreement or any practice which is capable of constituting a threat to freedom of trade between Member States in a manner which might harm the attainment of the objectives of a single market between the Member States, in particular by partitioning the national markets or by affecting the structure of competition within the common market. On the other hand conduct the effects of which are confined to the territory of a single Member State is governed by the national legal order."[63]

Greaves notes, however, that as far as the actual outcome of the application of the *Hugin* criteria is concerned *Hugin* is the exception rather than the rule. For art.82 in particular, it would be extremely rare for the Court to decide to dismiss a case because the abusive behaviour did not affect trade between Member States.

This is particularly relevant for intellectual property rights. "In view of the territorial nature of intellectual property rights, it is extremely unlikely that a situation could be envisaged often where an argument could be sustained that the behaviour of the owner of the right did not affect trade between Member States."[64]

(5) Consten and Grundig—the interaction with trade mark law—the starting point

9–024   *Consten and Grundig*[65] is the starting point in the interaction between competition and trade mark law in Europe. It was also the first time that a decision of the Commission regarding the application of art.81(1) and art.81(3) on an individual case was challenged before the Court.

Consten was the sole distributor of Grundig products in France and had undertaken not to stock competing products. It provided an after-sales service and was responsible for the national marketing campaigns in France. In order to protect the territorial integrity of the licence Consten had also undertaken not to sell Grundig products outside the territory covered by the licence.

9–025   Grundig, the German manufacturer of electronic products, had similar arrangements with other "national" distributors in Europe. To enable the enforcement of these agreements Grundig had assigned to Consten the registration of the trade mark GINT in France. UNEF, a parallel importer, who bought Grundig products in Germany and imported them to France,

---

[63] *Hugin*, para.17.
[64] Greaves (1998), p.381. Note that in *EMI Records v CBS United Kingdom* (51/75) [1976] E.C.R. 811, the Court held that a restrictive agreement between traders within the common market and competitors in third countries could isolate the common market as a whole and affect adversely the conditions of competition.
[65] *Etablissements Consten SARL and Grundig-Verkaufs-GmbH v Commission* (56 and 58/64) [1966] E.C.R. 299.

4. THE APPLICATION OF ARTICLE 81

responded to Grundig's trade mark infringement action by claiming that the agreement between Grundig and Consten violated art.81 and complained to the Commission.

Grundig too notified to the Commission the sole agency agreements. The Commission found that the contract concluded between Grundig and Consten constituted an infringement of art.81 and refused to grant an exemption under art.81(3).[66]

The Decision was challenged before the Court of Justice.

(a) The interpretation of article 81 and article 82—vertical agreements

9–026

The Court started its consideration by noting that arts 81 and 82 did not have distinct areas of application. Article 81 could be applied to an agreement between competitors as well as to an agreement between non-competing entities operating at different levels of the supply chain, even if the latter did not constitute an abuse of a dominant position. Competition might be distorted by agreements limiting competition that might take place between one of the parties to the agreement and third parties.

It held that sole distribution agreements should be examined under the light of art.81(1), excluding, in principle, only cases where a sole undertaking integrated its own distribution network into its business organisation.

Revealing the Court's priorities it added that:

> "an agreement between producer and distributor which might tend to restore the national divisions in trade between Member States might be such as to frustrate the most fundamental objections of the Community. The Treaty, whose preamble and content aim at abolishing the barriers between states, and which in several provisions gives evidence of a stern attitude with regard to their reappearance, could not allow undertakings to reconstruct such barriers. Article [81](1) is designed to pursue this aim, even in the case of agreements between undertakings placed at different levels in the economic process."[67]

(b) Capable of constituting a threat

9–027

As to whether an agreement affects trade between Member States, the factor triggering the application of Community rather than national law, the Court identified as particularly important "whether the agreement is capable of constituting a threat, either direct or indirect, actual or potential, to freedom of trade between Member States in a manner which might harm the attainment of the objectives of a single market between states".[68]

---

[66] Commission Decision 64/566 (Grundig) [1964] C.M.L.R. 489; [1964] OJ 2545.
[67] *Consten and Grundig*, p.340. The reader should note that the Court viewed art.81 as a tool for breaking down barriers between States.
[68] *Consten and Grundig*, p.341.

It followed that an agreement preventing, first, other, than the sole distributor, undertakings from importing Grundig products into France and then the sole distributor from re-exporting Grundig products from France to other Member States fell within the scope of art.81.

The Court however equated to such an agreement the limitations that "might ensue for third parties from the registration in France by Consten of the GINT trade mark".[69]

(c) The relevant product market

9–028 The Court then considered the relevant product market. Grundig and the German Government supported that the Commission had failed to follow a "rule of reason" analysis by looking only at the market for Grundig products rather than the market of similar products of different makes. Vertical sole distributorship agreements would increase rather than harm competition between different brands.

The Court disagreed. "The principle of freedom of competition concerns the various stages and manifestations of competition. Although competition between producers is generally more noticeable than that between distributors of products of the same make, it does not thereby follow that an agreement tending to restrict the latter kind of competition should escape the prohibition of Article [81](1) merely because it might increase the former."[70]

(d) Object and effect

9–029 And, against a "rule of reason" analysis, the Court added that for an agreement that had as its object the prevention, restriction or distortion of competition there was no need to take account of its concrete effects.

Still, it considered the agreement within its economic and legal context, concluding that it aimed to isolate the French market for Grundig products and maintain artificially separate national markets within the Community.

The Court stressed that this would be in relation to products of a very well-known brand. It rejected the relevance of economic data, including price differences between France and Germany, the character of the considered products, and the level of Consten's overheads, in potentially justifying the agreement from a commercial perspective as well as the possibility of other beneficial effects.

It also decided that although it was desirable for the Commission to take into account the views of other parties affected by its Decision, for example other Grundig licensees, this did not mean they had a right to be part to the Consten and Grundig proceedings.

---

[69] *Consten and Grundig*, p.341.
[70] *Consten and Grundig*, p.342.

4. THE APPLICATION OF ARTICLE 81

(e) The validity of the agreement 9–030

The only concession the Court made was deciding that only the parts of the agreement that were against art.81(1) should be considered automatically void, unless these parts were not severable from the overall agreement in which case it should be considered void in its totality. Thus, the Commission had to justify its decision specifically in respect of each one of the clauses of the agreement.

(f) The effect of the trade mark registration 9–031

Part of the argument against the Decision of the Commission was based on the role of the trade mark registration. The argument was that the effect on competition was the result of the trade mark registration; the contested Decision would take away from Consten the power to assert its trade mark rights.

The Court however took a step back noting that the French registration was the result of the agreement between Grundig and Consten that should be prohibited according to art.81(1). Allowing Consten to use the trade mark registration assigned to it by Grundig to achieve the objective of the agreement would render the prohibition ineffective.

(g) Property, article 30 and the competition provisions 9–032

The Court then considered the Treaty provisions relied upon by Consten and Grundig. Article 30 was linked with the liberalisation of trade rather than competition, and could not limit the application of art.81. Further, there was no conflict with art.295 providing that the Treaty shall not prejudice the rules in Member States governing the system of property ownership, because the Decision did not interfere with the grant of property rights but only limited "their exercise to the extent necessary to give effect to the prohibition under art.[81](1). The power of the Commission to issue such an injunction . . . was in harmony with the nature of the Community rules on competition which have immediate effect and are directly binding on individuals".[71] It concluded that such "a body of rules, by reason of its nature described above and its function, does not allow the improper use of rights under any national trade-mark law in order to frustrate the Community's law on cartels".[72]

(h) The exemption requirements 9–033

The Court then looked at the grounds for applying art.81(3). The Court recognised that, as a matter of good administration, the Commission had to contribute to the process for determining whether an exemption is justified

[71] *Consten and Grundig*, p.345.
[72] *Consten and Grundig*, p.346.

rather than expect from the parties to prove that the art.81(3) requirements were fulfilled.

The ultimate decision on this involved complex economic evaluations and the Court in its judicial review should confine itself to an examination of the relevance of the facts on which the evaluations are based and of the legal consequences which the Commission deduces from those facts.

The Court—looking once again at the wider picture—decided that the existence of a compensating improvement in the production or distribution of the relevant goods could only be decided in the spirit of art.81; the advantages had to be generally indisputable, render the agreement indispensable in all respects, and be appreciable and objective.

9-034 *(i) The quality function*

One specific argument linked with the quality function of a trade mark was that the Commission did not examine whether it would be possible to provide guarantee and after-sales services without absolute territorial protection, taking into account Grundig's reputation in respect of these services.

Allowing parallel imports could compel Consten to refuse them in respect of parallel imported products whereas those provided by parallel importers could be unsatisfactory.

Here the Court took another step back and looked at the actual market place, finding that UNEF's services were comparable to Consten's. Their services did not seem to have harmed Grundig's reputation. It added that Consten could inform potential consumers about the advantages of dealing with the official distribution network.

As to the need to compensate Consten through exclusivity for taking the risk for launching the products into the French market the Court found that this was linked with its decision to accept the agreement but not with the improvement in distribution mentioned in art.81(3). Similarly the Court rejected the argument that Consten deserved exclusivity because some of the products were specially adapted for the French market; indeed the Court considered this to be an advantage for a sole distributor.

9-035 **(6) Société Technique Minière—a rule of reason analysis?**

Société Technique Minière[73] offers a contemporaneous comparative context for comprehending the effect and limitations of *Grundig*.

Again, the contested contract covered an "exclusive right of sale" agreement. Société Technique Minière was the exclusive distributor in France of grading equipment produced by Maschinenbau Ulm. Typically, the validity of the contract according to art.81 became an issue when a dispute arose between the parties.

---

[73] *Société Technique Minière v Maschinenbau Ulm GmbH* (56/65) [1965] E.C.R. 235.

4. THE APPLICATION OF ARTICLE 81

The crucial difference with *Grundig* was that the French market had not been compartmentalised: Société Technique Minière could export to other Member States, parallel imports could reach the French market, and intellectual property rights were not raised as cross-border barriers.

Accordingly the Court felt comfortable enough to consider the benefits of such an agreement. It noted that according to art.81 "object" and "effect" are alternative rather than cumulative conditions and described a two-step analysis.

First, the precise purpose of the agreement had to be sought within its economic context. "Where, however, an analysis of the said clauses does not reveal the effect on competition to be sufficiently deleterious, the consequences of the agreement should then be considered and for it to be caught by the prohibition it is then necessary to find that those factors are present which show that competition has in fact been prevented or restricted or distorted to appreciable extent."[74]

This examination followed the principles of a "rule of reason" analysis:

"The competition in question must be understood within the actual context in which it would occur in the absence of the agreement in dispute. In particular it may be doubted whether there is an interference with competition if the said agreement seems really necessary for the penetration of a new area by an undertaking. Therefore, in order to decide whether an agreement containing a clause 'granting an exclusive right of sale' is to be considered as prohibited by reason of its object or of its effect, it is appropriate to take into account in particular the nature and quantity, limited or otherwise, of the products covered by the agreement, the position and importance of the grantor and the concessionnaire on the market for the products concerned, the isolated nature of the disputed agreement or, alternatively, its position in a series of agreements, the severity of the clauses intended to protect the exclusive dealership or, alternatively, the opportunities allowed for other commercial competitors in the same products by way of parallel re-exportation and importation."[75]

The context of subsequent cases allowed the Court to adopt subtly more nuanced positions.

(7) Volk v Vervaecke—significant effect   9–036

In *Volk v Vervaecke*[76] the Court considered an exclusive distribution agreement for washing machines covering the territories of Belgium and Luxembourg. The agreement provided that only if the distributor would fail

---

[74] *Société Technique Minière*, p.249.
[75] *Société Technique Minière*, p.250.
[76] *Volk v Etablissements J Vervaecke SPRL* (5/69) [1969] E.C.R. 295.

to sell the agreed number of products would the manufacturer supply other traders in the same territory.

The validity of the agreement was challenged before the Oberlandesgericht, Munich, that sought from the Court to clarify whether in order to assess the application of art.81(1) the part of the market which the plaintiff in fact held or had sought to win in the relevant Member States, the ceded territory, should be taken into account.

The Court held that to be capable of affecting trade between Member States:

> "the agreement must, on the basis of a collection of objective legal or factual factors, permit a reasonably probable expectation that it could exercise an influence, direct or indirect, actual or potential, on the trade trends between member-States in a direction which would harm the attainment of the objectives of a single market between States. Furthermore, the prohibition in Article [81] (1) may apply only on condition that the agreement in question also has the object or effect of preventing, restricting or distorting competition in the Common Market. These conditions should be understood by reference to the actual context in which the agreement exists".[77]

From the opposite perspective, an agreement would escape art.81(1) if it only affected the market insignificantly, taking into account the weak position of the parties in the relevant product market. It found that it was possible that "an exclusive concession agreement, even with absolute territorial protection, may in view of the weak position of the parties on the market in the products in question in the territory which is the subject of the absolute protection escape the prohibition".[78]

9-037 **(8) Beguelin—the relevance of context**

In *Beguelin*,[79] the Court again considered the overall context of the agreement rather than the agreement in isolation. On the one hand it required from the national courts to examine not only the rights and obligations derived from the clauses of the agreement but also its economic and legal context, and particularly the possible existence of similar agreements concluded by the same producer with concessionnaires established in other Member States:

> "More particularly, an exclusive agency agreement is capable of affecting trade between member-States and may have the effect of hindering

---

[77] *Volk v Vervaecke*, para.3.
[78] *Volk v Vervaecke*, para.3.
[79] *Beguelin Import Co v GL Import Export SA* (22/71) [1971] E.C.R. 949.

4. THE APPLICATION OF ARTICLE 81

competition where the concessionnaire can prevent parallel imports from other member-States into the conceded territory by means of a combination of the agreement with the effects of national law on unfair competition."[80]

However, for art.81 to apply "the agreement must affect noticeably the trade between member-States and competition."[81] Courts should consider the relevant factors "in the real context in which they would be in the absence of the agreement in the case".[82]

The Court added that in assessing whether the agreement could escape the application of art.81(1) courts should look:

"at the nature and limited or unlimited quantity of the products covered by the agreement, the position and importance of the grantor, the position and importance of the concessionnaire on the market in the products in question, the isolated nature of the agreement in question or its place among a network of agreements, the severity of the clauses intended to protect the exclusive right or the possibilities left open to other commercial dealings in the same products through re-export or parallel imports."[83]

(9) Delimitis—a web of agreements—closer to a rule of reason analysis

9–038

Delimitis[84] offered the Court the opportunity to deal with the effect of restrictive practices adopted by a network of similar beer supply agreements. The case is also relevant from the aspect of market definition, contrasting between beer supplied through retail channels and beer supplied through public houses and restaurants.

Note that at the time the Commission had adopted Regulation 1984/83[85] on the application of art.81(3) to certain categories of exclusive purchasing agreements, including long-term exclusive purchasing agreements for the resale of beer in premises used for sale and consumption of drinks. Article 6 of the Regulation defined the agreements eligible for block exemption as agreements between only two undertakings (a supplier and a reseller), whereby the reseller agreed with the supplier to purchase only from the supplier certain beers, or certain beers and certain other drinks specified in the agreement, for resale in designated premises in consideration for according special commercial or financial advantages. According to a Notice

---

[80] *Beguelin*, para.14.
[81] *Beguelin*, para.16.
[82] *Beguelin*, para.17.
[83] *Beguelin*, para.18.
[84] *Stergios Delimitis v Henninger Bräu AG* (C-234/89) [1991] E.C.R. I-935.
[85] [1983] OJ L173/5.

issued by the Commission the drinks covered in such agreements should be specified by brand or denomination.

The contested agreement was between Henninger, the supplier, and Delimitis, the reseller. The supplier let a café to Delimitis who undertook to obtain, exclusively, draught, bottled, and canned beer from Henninger and soft drinks from its subsidiaries.

9–039   The purchase of beers and soft drinks from other undertakings established in the Federal Republic of Germany or from undertakings established in non-Member States was prohibited. However, the agreement allowed the tenant to purchase beer and soft drinks from undertakings in other Member States.

Once again, the validity of the agreement was challenged upon termination. Henninger deducted from the initial deposit an amount that it considered it was owed by Delimitis. Delimitis disagreed and contended that the contract was contrary to art.81(1) and was not covered by the block exemption. The case reached the Oberlandesgericht (Higher Regional Court), Frankfurt am Main that referred a number of questions to the Court on the interpretation of art.81(1) and the Block Exemption Regulation.

9–040   **(i) Object and effect.** The Court repeated that even if the agreements did not have the object of restricting competition within the meaning of art.81(1), it remained necessary to ascertain whether they had the effect of preventing, restricting or distorting competition. Citing *Brasserie de Haecht*,[86] it noted that they had to be assessed in the context in which they occurred; this included the issue whether they might combine with others to have a cumulative effect on competition.

In order to ascertain the effects of beer supply agreements the Court first defined the relevant market and then looked at the function and effect of the supply agreements.

9–041   **(ii) The definition of the relevant market.** The starting point was identifying the nature of the economic activity in question, in this case the sale of beer.

The second step was to identify the channels of trade: retail channels and premises for the sale and consumption of drinks, in particular public houses and restaurants. The second method of sale was distinguished from the first on the basis of price elasticity; consumption was not necessarily dependent on price because the sale of beer was linked with the provision of services. "The specific nature of the public house trade is borne out by the fact that the breweries organise specific distribution systems for this sector which require special installations, and that the prices charged in that sector are generally higher than retail prices."[87]

It accepted that there was some overlap between the two channels, in particular that retail sales allowed new players to get into the wider market

---

[86] *Brasserie de Haecht v Wilkin* (23/67) [1967] E.C.R. 407.
[87] *Delimitis*, para.16.

4. THE APPLICATION OF ARTICLE 81

for beer, make their brands known, and then use their reputation to gain access into the second market, but found that it had to define the relevant market narrowly as the market for beer distribution in premises for the sale and consumption of drinks.

The third step was to identify the geographical limits of the relevant market. Since most beer supply agreements covered the national level, it concluded that account is to be taken of the national market for beer distribution in premises for the sale and consumption of drinks.

(iii) The object and effect of the agreements. The fourth step was to examine the nature and extent of the beer supply agreements in their totality, comprising all similar contracts tying a large number of points of sale to several national producers[88]:

9–042

"The effect of those networks of contracts on access to the market depends specifically on the number of outlets thus tied to national producers in relation to the number of public houses which are not so tied, the duration of the commitments entered into, the quantities of beer to which those commitments relate, and on the proportion between those quantities and the quantities sold by free distributors."[89]

(iv) A multi-factor article 81(1) test. However, the existence of a bundle of agreements would not in itself be enough for a finding that the relevant market was inaccessible. The Court saw the bundle as one amongst a number of factors that had to be considered in the examination of "whether there are real concrete possibilities for a new competitor to penetrate the bundle of contracts by acquiring a brewery already established on the market together with its network of sales outlets, or to circumvent the bundle of contracts by opening new public houses".[90]

9–043

The factors included the legal rules and agreements on the acquisition of companies and the establishment of outlets, the minimum number of outlets necessary for the economic operation of a distribution system, and the presence of beer wholesalers not tied to producers.

The fifth step, in essence a parallel enquiry, should consider the actual conditions under which competitive forces operated on the relevant market. This covered the number and the size of producers present on the market, the degree of market saturation, brand loyalty, and the trend in beer sales in the retail trade.

If the above examination revealed that it was difficult to gain access to the relevant market then—and this would be the sixth step—"it is necessary to assess the extent to which the agreements entered into by the brewery in

9–044

---

[88] Citing *Bilger v Jehle* (43/69) [1970] E.C.R. 127.
[89] *Delimitis*, para.19.
[90] *Delimitis*, para.21.

question contribute to the cumulative effect produced in that respect by the totality of the similar contracts found on that market".[91]

According to the competition rules of the Community the responsibility for closing off the market would fall on the breweries which made an appreciable contribution thereto. Agreements by breweries with an insignificant contribution to the cumulative effect would remain outside the scope of art.81(1).

The critical question for this assessment would be the market position of the contracting parties, determined by the market share held by the brewery and any group to which it might belong and the number of tied outlets in relation to the total number of premises for the sale and consumption of drinks in the relevant market.

However, courts would also have to consider the contribution of the individual contracts. Here, their duration would be the most important issue. If it were manifestly excessive in relation to the average duration of such agreements generally in the relevant market, the individual contract would fall under the prohibition of art.81(1):

> "A brewery with a relatively small market share which ties its sales outlets for many years may make as significant a contribution to a sealing-off of the market as a brewery in a relatively strong market position which regularly releases sales outlets at shorter intervals."[92]

9–045 **(v) The relevance of the access clause.** The Court then looked at the relevance of the access clause authorising the reseller to obtain supplies from other Member States. It accepted that it mitigated the scope of the prohibition in favour of beers from other Member States. However, the scope of the clause should be assessed in the light of its wording and its economic and legal context.

It noted that the wording of the actual clause appeared limited, allowing the reseller to purchase competing beers in other Member States but not to sell beers imported from other Member States by other undertakings.

The economic and legal context encompassed questions about the minimum quantity of beer the reseller was obliged to obtain from the supplier and the overall sales it could achieve. This would reveal whether the access clause had any practical meaning, in particular where failure to reach the target also meant payment of financial penalties.

If the effect of the clause was non-existent or insignificant the agreement would be treated in the same way as a classic supply agreement without an access clause for the purposes of art.81(1). If, on the other hand, the clause could give a national or foreign supplier of beers from other Member States a real possibility of supplying the relevant outlet, then the agreement would fall outside the scope of art.81(1).

---

[91] *Delimitis*, para.24.
[92] Point 26.

4. THE APPLICATION OF ARTICLE 81

(vi) Block exemptions—exemptions to the rule. The Court found   9–046
that an agreement could not benefit from Regulation 1984/83 if it failed to
identify specifically the beers and drinks it related to. An agreement that
referred to a list of products which might be unilaterally altered by the
supplier would fail to satisfy the above requirement.

(vii) The validity of the agreement. Citing *Société Technique Minière*[93]   9–047
the Court reminded us that in principle only those aspects of the agreement
that were prohibited by art.81(1) would be void. The agreement as a whole
would be void only if those parts were not severable from the agreement
itself.

It added that according to the Community legal order an agreement that
did not enjoy the protection of a block exemption regulation could always be
exempted individually.

(viii) The role of the national Court. The national court had also   9–048
sought guidance in relation to the division of competences. What should a
national court do in regard to an agreement that did not satisfy the
conditions for the application of Regulation 1984/83, since the Commission
was responsible for the implementation of competition policy?

The Court held that it was for the Commission to adopt, subject to review
by the Court of First Instance and the Court of Justice, individual decisions;
this entailed complex economic assessments, in particular in order to
assess whether an agreement fell under art.81(3).

At the same time the Commission shared with national courts the competence to apply art.81(1) and art.82.[94] "Articles [81](1) and [82] produce
direct effect in relation between individuals and create rights directly in
respect of the individuals concerned which the national courts must safeguard."[95]

The same principle applied to Block Exemption Regulations; however, in   9–049
the case of such Regulations courts could not extend their application to
agreements not covered by them because any extension "whatever its
scope, would affect the manner in which the Commission exercises its
legislative competence".[96]

The problem as identified by the Court has a wider, than competition law,
significance:

> "It now falls to examine the consequences of that division of competence
> as regards the specific application of the Community competition rules
> by national courts. Account should here be taken of the risk of national
> courts taking decisions which conflict with those taken or envisaged

---

[93] *Société Technique Minière v Maschinenbau Ulm GmbH* (56/65) [1965] E.C.R. 235.
[94] Citing *Belgische Radio en Televisie v SV SABAM and NV Fonior* (127/73) [1974] E.C.R. 51.
[95] *Delimitis*, para.45.
[96] *Delimitis*, para.46.

by the Commission in the implementation of Articles [81](1) and [82], and also of Article [81](3). Such conflicting decisions would be contrary to the general principle of legal certainty and must, therefore, be avoided when national courts give decisions on agreements or practices which may subsequently be the subject of a decision by the Commission."[97]

The agreement was clearly outside the scope of Regulation 1762[98] to enjoy provisional validity. Still the Court held that in order to avoid conflicting decisions the national court should consider a number of alternatives whilst applying art.81.

9–050 First, if the conditions for the application of art.81(1) were clearly not satisfied and there was not a genuine risk of the Commission taking a different decision, the national court might continue the proceedings and rule on the agreement in issue.

The same principle should apply where the agreement was clearly against art.81(1) and according to the exemption regulations and the decision practices of the Commission the agreement, "may on no account be the subject of an exemption decision under Article [81](3)".[99]

The second option would cover agreements that satisfied the formal requirements and that the court considered, again according to the rules and practices of the Commission, that they could be the subject of an exemption decision. The court might then decide to stay proceedings or adopt interim measures.

9–051 The court should follow the same route when it envisaged a risk of conflicting decisions in the context of the application of arts 81(1) and 82.

A parallel option would be to contact the Commission regarding the state of any proceedings undertaken by it or in order to obtain the necessary economic and legal information. The Commission would be bound to assist the national court according to the duty of sincere cooperation.[100]

The final option available to the national court would be to stay proceedings and make a reference to the Court for a preliminary ruling.

9–052 **(10) EMI and Nungesser—existence and the way the right is exercised**

In *Nungesser*[101] the Court considered the exercise of plant breeders' rights. The French Institut National de la Recherche Agronomique (INRA) had given Eisele exclusive propagating and selling rights over certain varieties of

---

[97] *Delimitis*, para.47.
[98] Reg. 17/62 [1962] OJ L13/204, covering agreements that were in existence prior to March 13, 1962 and notified to the Commission.
[99] Point 50.
[100] According to art.10 EC; *Zwartveld* (C-2/88R) [1990] I-E.C.R. 3365.
[101] *LC Nungesser KG and Kurt Eisele v Commission* (258/78) [1985] E.C.R. 2015.

4. THE APPLICATION OF ARTICLE 81

hybrid maize seeds it had developed in respect of Germany. Eisele, and through him Nungesser, enjoyed absolute territorial protection in Germany: INRA had undertaken not to sell the seed to other undertakings in Germany and through its agreements with other, similar to Eisele, national distributors would ensure that they too would not export the seed to Germany. Eisele could enforce the restriction outside the contractual agreement, through the exercise of German plant breeders' rights assigned to him by INRA. In return Eisele had undertaken not to sell the seed outside Germany. The Commission found that the agreement infringed art.81(1).[102]

Note that under the relevant German legislation an owner of breeders' rights established outside Germany would be unable to enjoy them in Germany. Thus the assignment of the rights to a German entity appeared to be objectively necessary outside the context of the licensing agreement.

The Court considered that all the agreements between INRA and Eisele should be considered as part of an indivisible whole. In economic terms, Eisele was INRA's exclusive licensee in Germany.

Challenging the Commission's Decision before the Court, Eisele and INRA argued that the exclusive licence was commercially essential to allow INRA to enter a new national market and compete with products that were not identical but comparable. INRA would be unable to find a licensee without guaranteeing protection from competition from itself, as licensor, and other licensees. A further argument raised by the applicants was that the exclusive licence constituted the most appropriate means of attaining the objectives of the Common Agricultural Policy, leveraging one fundamental European policy with another.

(a) Rights and contract—existence and exercise 9–053

The Court repeated its two familiar distinctions: first, between the contractual agreement and plant breeders' rights, and, secondly, between the existence and the exercise of the rights developed in cases like *EMI*.[103] There the Court had found that cross licensing of trade marks between competitors leading to market sharing should be prohibited. A trade mark right as such did not possess the necessary elements of contract or concerted practice. Still, the exercise of that right might fall within the ambit of the competition prohibitions "if it were to manifest itself as the subject, the means, or the consequence of a restrictive practice."[104]

Back in *Nungesser* the Court confirmed that an "industrial or commercial property right, as a legal entity, does not possess those elements of contract or concerted practice referred to in Article [81] (1) of the Treaty, but the exercise of that right might fall within the ambit of the prohibitions

---

[102] Commission Decision 78/823 (breeders' maize seed) [1978] OJ L286/23; [1978] 3 C.M.L.R. 434.
[103] *EMI Records v CBS United Kingdom* (51/75) [1976] E.C.R. 811.
[104] *EMI*, para.27.

contained in the Treaty if it were to manifest itself as the subject, the means or the consequence of an agreement".[105]

In particular "where an agreement granting exclusive rights to utilize an industrial or commercial property right in a certain territory, in conjunction with an agreement appointing the licensee sole distributor for that territory, has the effect of ensuring absolute territorial protection for the licensee by preventing parallel imports."[106]

9–054 Turning to the nature and economic characteristics of the product the Court acknowledged that the development of new seeds involved considerable financial risks; however it limited their relevance by finding that they were encountered at the time of production of the basic seeds.

Once the new variety had reached the stage that the seeds were capable of being officially certified and marketed, trade rules, including competition provisions, should in principle be applied. According to the Court, the technical complications were not dissimilar to those encountered in the field of food or pharmaceutical products, possibly protected by patent or trade mark rights, and were not sufficient to justify a special system for breeders' rights in relation to other industrial or commercial property rights.

(b) Open exclusive and exclusive licences

9–055 The Court then looked at the nature of the agreement. It distinguished between an open exclusive licence, the case where the licensor undertakes not to compete with the licensee in a defined territory directly or indirectly by granting licences to others, and an exclusive licence with absolute territorial protection, providing the means for eliminating all competition by third parties.

So, it was necessary to examine the situation between licensor and licensees asking whether "the exclusive nature of the licence, in so far as it is an open licence, has the effect of preventing or distorting competition within the meaning of Article [81] (1) of the Treaty".[107]

At this more specific stage the Court appeared willing to look at the substantive arguments it has rejected as grounds for treating plant breeders' rights separately from other commercial and industrial property rights.

9–056 The product took years of research and experimentation and it was unknown to German farmers before INRA and Eisele started cooperating. "For that reason the concern... as regards the protection of new technology is justified."[108] It accepted that assurances regarding competition might be necessary for the licensee to take the risk of cultivating and marketing that product; not granting licences "would be damaging to the

---

[105] *Nungesser*, para.28.
[106] *Nungesser*, para.29, citing *TEPEA BV v Commission* (28/77) [1978] E.C.R. 139.
[107] *Nungesser*, para.54.
[108] *Nungesser*, para.56.

4. THE APPLICATION OF ARTICLE 81

dissemination of a new technology and would prejudice competition in the Community between the new product and similar existing products".[109]

It concluded that having "regard to the specific nature of the products in question, ... in a case such as the present, the grant of an open exclusive licence, that is to say a licence which does not affect the position of third parties such as parallel importers and licensees for other territories, is not in itself incompatible with Article [81] (1) of the Treaty".[110]

However the position of the Court shifted when it introduced into the picture the position of third parties not bound by the contractual agreement, in particular parallel importers. It repeated its findings in *Grundig*[111] that "absolute territorial protection granted to a licensee in order to enable parallel imports to be controlled and prevented results in the artificial maintenance of separate national markets, contrary to the Treaty".[112] For example, the clauses of the agreement seeking to prevent third parties buying seeds in France from exporting them to Germany were found to be against art.81(1).

The Court then considered what was required in order to grant an exemption under art.81(3). This time the importance of the product was used by the Court as an argument against the grant of an exemption. The seeds would be used by a large number of farmers for the production of maize, an important foodstuff. Accordingly "absolute territorial protection manifestly goes beyond what is indispensable for the improvement of production or distribution or the promotion of technical progress".[113]

(11) Pronuptia de Paris—the benefits of franchising agreements 9–057

In *Pronuptia de Paris*[114] the Court looked at a franchising agreement for wedding dresses and accessories within the context of competition rules. It was the nature of the agreement that the Court considered of particular importance.

(a) Franchising agreements 9–058

According to the agreement the franchisor undertook: to grant the franchisee the exclusive right to use the Pronuptia de Paris trade mark for a specified area for marketing the relevant products; not to open any other Pronuptia shops or to provide goods or services to third parties in that area; to assist the franchisee in successfully setting up and operating the franchise

---

[109] *Nungesser*, para.57.
[110] *Nungesser*, para.58.
[111] *Etablissements Consten SARL and Grundig-Verkaufs-GmbH v Commission* (56 & 58/64) [1966] E.C.R. 299.
[112] *Grundig*, para.61.
[113] *Nungesser*, para.77.
[114] *Pronuptia de Paris GmbH v Pronuptia de Paris Irmgard Schillgallis* (161/84) [1986] E.C.R. 353.

and with the commercial aspects of the business, advertising, staff training, fashion and products, purchasing and marketing, and other aspects of the business.

The franchisee remained the owner of its business but undertook: to sell the relevant products using the Pronuptia de Paris trade mark, only in the shop specified in the contract, and maintain the shop according to the franchisor's instructions; to purchase from the franchisor 80 per cent of wedding dresses and accessories; to pay the franchisor a royalty on sales; to regard the prices suggested by the franchisor as recommended retail prices, but retaining its freedom to fix its own prices; to advertise in the contract territory only with the franchisor's agreement; to apply the business methods imparted by the franchisor; and, to refrain from competing in any way with other Pronuptia shops. Following a dispute between the parties, the franchisee challenged the validity of the agreement on the back of the competition provisions.

The Court highlighted the variety of franchising agreements and distinguished in particular between service franchises, where the franchisee offers a service under the business name or trade mark and in accordance with the instructions of the franchisor, production franchises, where the franchisee manufactures products according to the instructions of the franchisor and sells them under the franchisor's trade mark, and distribution franchises, where the franchisee sells products in a shop with the franchisor' business name or symbol.

9–059 *(b) The relevance of the specific agreement*

The contested agreement fell under the third category, however the Court stressed that its compatibility with art.81 should be determined on the basis of its specific provisions rather than its categorisation.

It recognised the benefits of this type of agreement that was something more than a simple method of distribution. From the franchisor's perspective it was a way for an undertaking to derive financial benefit from its expertise without investing its own capital. For the franchisee, it gave a trader without the necessary experience the opportunity to exploit the franchisor's proven business methods and the reputation:

> "Franchise agreements for the distribution of goods differ in that regard from dealerships or contracts which incorporate approved retailers into a selective distribution system, which do not involve the use of a single business name, the application of uniform business methods or the payment of royalties in return for the benefits granted. Such a system, which allows the franchisor to profit from his success, does not in itself interfere with competition".[115]

[115] *Pronuptia de Paris*, para.15.

4. THE APPLICATION OF ARTICLE 81

The Court then found that there were two conditions that had to be met for a franchise agreement to work and accordingly would not violate art.81.

(c) The essential clauses   9–060

First, the franchisor should be able to support the franchisee without the risk that its know-how might benefit competitors, directly or indirectly. This would cover clauses that were essential to avoid that risk, including clauses that: prohibit the franchisee during the term of the agreement and for a reasonable period after its termination from opening a similar shop in an area covered by a member of the franchise; prohibit the franchisee to transfer its shop without the approval of the franchisor.

Secondly, the franchisor must be able to maintain the identity and reputation of the network bearing its business name or symbol. This would cover: provisions which establish the means of control necessary for that purpose, including clauses that require the franchisee to: apply the franchisor's business methods and know-how; follow the franchisor's specifications regarding the location and appearance of its shop and seek approval for all advertising; seek authorisation regarding assignment of the franchise; sell only products supplied by the franchisor or by selected suppliers, but without preventing the franchisee from obtaining those products from other franchisees, in order to enable the public to find at the franchises products of the same quality and the franchisor to protect the reputation of the network.

Note the open-ended language of the Court; it simply described some types of clauses that appeared to be essential linking them with the purpose they ought to fulfil without providing a closed list.

(d) The anti-competitive clauses   9–061

The Court then went on to consider provisions that restrict competition between the members of the network without being necessary for satisfying the two conditions mentioned above in particular those that share markets between the franchisor and the franchisees or between franchisees or prevent price competition between franchisees.

By way of example, the Court considered the effect of the clause prohibiting a franchisee from opening a second shop combined with the franchisor's obligation to ensure that the franchisee has the exclusive use of the indicia identifying the network—i.e. business names, symbols, and trade marks—within the context of the web of agreements of the franchising network. They could result to the sharing of markets and the restriction of competition within the network. Following *Grundig*[116] "a restriction of that kind constitutes a limitation of competition for the purposes of Article [81] (1) if it concerns a business name or symbol which is already

---

[116] *Etablissements Consten SARL and Grundig-Verkaufs-GmbH* (56 & 58/64) [1966] E.C.R. 299.

well-known".[117] It added that even if such agreements covered the territory of a single Member State they were liable to affect trade between Member States if they prevent franchisees to establish themselves in other Member States. Extrapolating on the viability of the franchise network without such provisions became for the Court an issue for the national courts to determine from the perspective of art.81(3).

Similarly price guidelines should not become a concerted network practice to set prices.

Finally, the Court decided that franchising agreements did not fall within the scope of Regulation 67/67[118] by underlining four characteristics of the block exemption established in the Regulation. First, it covered contracts defined by reference to obligations of supply and purchase, which might or might not be reciprocal, and not by reference to the franchising factors analysed by the Court. Secondly, the wording of art.2 covered expressly only exclusive dealing agreements. Thirdly, art.2 listed the restrictions and obligations of the exclusive distributor rather than those that were imposed on franchisors. Fourthly, art.2 did not include the obligation to pay royalties or other obligations pertaining in franchising.

9–062 **(12) BAT—competition and trade mark law—delimitation agreements**

In *BAT*[119] the Court of Justice held that trade mark law should not be used improperly, to undermine European competition law.

BAT, the proprietor of the trade mark "Dorcet" that had been registered in Germany but not used commercially, opposed the registration of "Toltecs" by Segers. Segers entered into negotiations and signed an agreement with BAT regarding the specification of his application without challenging BAT's registration on the basis of non-use.

At a later stage BAT and Segers disagreed regarding the definition of the products covered by the agreement. Segers did not apply to German courts to rectify the ambiguity, because according to the Commission he was not in a position to risk costly litigation with BAT. Because of the ongoing difficulties with BAT Segers stopped using the trade mark in Germany and applied to the Commission claiming that BAT had infringed arts 81 and 82. The Commission issued a Decision against BAT,[120] which in turn challenged it before the Court of Justice.

According to the Court the scope of the agreement was objectively ambiguous as a result of the wording suggested by Segers himself. BAT

---

[117] *Pronuptia de Paris*, para.24.
[118] Reg. 67/67 [1967] OJ L57/849.
[119] *BAT Cigaretten-Fabriken GmbH v Commission of the European Communities* (35/83) [1985] E.C.R. 363.
[120] Commission Decision 82/897 (TOLTECS/DORCET) [1982] OJ L379/19; [1983] 1 C.M.L.R. 412.

4. THE APPLICATION OF ARTICLE 81

took advantage of this ambiguity in order to block Segers from marketing in Germany the only kind of tobacco he produced. According to BAT the agreement constituted a "delimitation" agreement that contained a no-challenge clause "intended to consolidate the position of the Dorcet mark even after it had ceased to be legally protected"[121]: its validity should be judged according to German law.

(a) Risk of confusion and competition 9–063

The Commission had found that there was no "serious" risk of confusion between the two marks and accordingly no basis for the agreement whereas BAT argued that according to the principles of German law there was a real risk of confusion. The German government supported BAT's general argument; in relation to confusion it claimed that there was a real risk because of the phonetic similarity between the signs.

The Court accepted that delimitation agreements are "lawful and useful if they serve to delimit, in the mutual interest of the parties, the spheres within which their respective trade marks may be used, and are intended to avoid confusion or conflict between them. That is not to say, however, that such agreements are excluded from the application of Article [81] of the Treaty if they also have the aim of dividing up the market or restricting competition in other ways".[122] However, the relevant agreement imposed obligations on Segers in return of an obligation on behalf of BAT that proved to be fictitious. Without even considering the confusion criteria the Court noted that "on the one hand, Segers is the proprietor of a trade mark legally acquired and used in a Member State and BAT, on the other, is the proprietor of an unused, dormant, trade mark which is liable to be removed from the register upon application by any interested party, BAT's opposition, as part of its efforts to control the distribution of Segers's products, constitutes an abuse of the rights conferred upon it by its trade mark ownership".[123] BAT's overall aggressiveness confirmed that it aimed to prevent Segers from entering the German market rather than protect its dormant trade mark.

(13) The position of the Commission on delimitation agreements 9–064

Note that the position of the Commission on delimitation agreements varied according to the effect of the agreement. In *Sirdar*[124] an agreement between a French and an English undertaking not to use their trade marks on each other's respective territory was found to infringe art.85(1). The French trade mark was LE PHIL D'ART (and its phonetic equivalent PHILDAR)

---

[121] *BAT*, para.26.
[122] *BAT*, para.33.
[123] *BAT*, para.35.
[124] Commission Decision 75/297 (*Re the Agreement of Sirdar Ltd*) [1975] OJ L125/27; [1975] 1 C.M.L.R. D93; [1975] F.S.R. 492.

whereas the UK registration was for SIRDAR; the agreement covered PHILDAR and SIRDAR for knitting yarns and its validity was challenged by the French firm following the accession of the United Kingdom to the EEC. The Commission noted that the two signs coexisted in all the other Member States and found that the object of the agreement was to restrict competition in the common market, rejecting the argument that the French company could import its products into the UK market under a different trade mark. Use of another trade mark would deprive the French company of the impact of its advertising campaign and would be financially impossible for other prospective importers to undertake since the yarn was sold in 50 gramme packs contained in larger packages. The Commission stressed that even likelihood of confusion between the two signs would not justify market sharing between the two companies. It rejected the claim that the agreement deserved to be exempted holding that in fact it hindered distribution of the relevant products by obstructing cross border trade and harmed consumers by denying them choice between competing products.

In *Persil*[125] however, where ownership of the same trade mark throughout Europe has been split between two undertakings, an agreement to allow each other's products to circulate freely subject to distinctive colouring was found not to infringe art.81. The agreement covered only the appearance of the two trade marks and aimed to ensure that there can be no confusion about the difference between the relevant products, this, according to the Commission, allowed the products to circulate freely within Europe without either party having to give up a well-established trade mark.

In *EEC v Syntex*[126] the Commission reconfirmed that it remained in the jurisdiction of Member States to decide whether there was a risk of confusion between different trade marks.

However, art.81(1) would still be applicable to trade mark delimitation agreements where it was evident that the holder of an earlier trade mark could have recourse to national law to prevent the holder of the later mark from using it in one or more Member States, and in particular where the result was to divide the territory of the Union into various territories.[127]

Similarly, an agreement that provided for field of use restrictions could also fall under art.81(1). In *Bayonox*[128] a German chemical producer distributed additives for animal feedstuffs direct to the feed manufacturers through local subsidiaries or licensees.

---

[125] *Re the Persil Trade Mark* [1978] 1 C.M.L.R. 395; [1978] F.S.R. 348.
[126] *EEC v Syntex Corp* [1990] 4 C.M.L.R. 343; [1990] F.S.R. 529.
[127] In the particular case the Commission considered that the risk of confusion between the trade marks of two pharmaceutical companies did not justify a delimitation agreement that covered the United Kingdom and other non-member countries and that it should be caught by art.81(1). It closed its investigation once the companies agreed to amend the agreement, allowing their trade marks to co-exist in all Member States.
[128] *EEC v Bayer AG (Bayo-N-ox)* [1990] 4 C.M.L.R. 930; [1991] F.S.R. 168; the Decision of the Commission was challenged, without success, before the Court of Justice in *Bayer AG v Commission* (C-195/91 P) [1994] E.C.R. I-5619.

4. THE APPLICATION OF ARTICLE 81

The Commission held that an agreement with its German customers that they would use supplies of a particular additive exclusively for their own feedstuff production in return for reduced prices was against art.81(1). The selective distribution network would not be objectionable only if there was freedom to trade within the network.

(14) The Commission on repackaging bans 9–066

In *Bayer Dental*[129] the Commission found excessive repackaging bans to be against art.81(1); even if notified they would not be exempted under art.81(3). Dental, a division of Bayer AG, was the distributor of Bayer's dental products in a number of Member States either directly, in Germany and to an extent in Denmark, or through wholly owned subsidiaries, in other Member States.

In its wholesale price lists in Germany it incorporated the following objectionable clauses: (1) original packages of the seller bearing a registered trade mark could be supplied to a third party only in unopened form; (2) the preparations were intended for distribution solely in the Federal Republic of Germany. Their resale abroad might constitute an infringement of industrial property rights.

The Commission found Bayer Dental's subsequent amendments acceptable; however it issued a decision in order to indicate that irrespective of the intention of the parties a provision would still infringe art.81(1) if its effect, objectively considered, would be to restrict exports of the products concerned.

(15) Campari—an example of the application of article 81(3) by the Commission 9–067

Campari[130] is another decision of the Commission. Campari-Milano was the holder of the international trade marks, Bitter Campari and Cordial Campari for aperitifs that were manufactured using special mixtures of crushed herbs. To promote its aperitifs Campari set up a network of exclusive product and trade mark licenses that proved to be quite successful.

Bitter Campari was the only product manufactured both by the licensor and its licensees at that stage. The alcoholic strength and analogies of ingredients varied from country to country. The bottles used for the product followed the same design but varied in terms of size.

The agreements were notified to the Commission that went on to examine them according to art.81.

---

[129] Commission Decision 90/645 (*Re Bayer Dental*) [1990] OJ L351/46.
[130] Commission Decision 78/253 (*Re the Agreements of Davide Campari-Milano SpA*) [1978] OJ L70/69; [1978] 2 C.M.L.R. 397; [1978] F.S.R. 528. See also Commission Decision 90/186 (*Moosehead and Whitbread's Agreement*) [1990] OJ L100/32, where a restriction imposed on the licensee not to produce or promote any other beer identified as a Canadian beer (when the licensed Moosehead beer was a Canadian beer) was exempted by the Commission. The same applied to a no challenge clause regarding the validity of a trade mark.

Its views on trade mark licensing appeared restrictive:

"The proprietor of a trade mark has the exclusive right to use the distinctive mark on first sale and to protect the product against infringement of the mark. The proprietor of the trade mark may by licence authorise the use of the protected mark by third parties.

However, if he undertakes only to allow one single undertaking to use his trade mark in a particular territory and to refrain himself from manufacturing products bearing his trade mark there, he loses his freedom to respond to other requests for licences and the competitive advantage to be gained from manufacture by himself in this territory.

In the case in point, the exclusive nature of the licence entails a restriction upon Campari-Milano's freedom to use its marks as well as preventing third parties, particularly manufacturers of alcoholic beverages, from using them as licensees, however much they may find it in their interests to do so."[131]

9-068 Accordingly, the Commission found that the obligation on licensees not to handle competing products for the duration of the licensing agreement restricted competition under art.81(1).

The same applied to a ban on the licensor and the licensees engaging in active sales outside their territories, although passive sales were permitted, and the obligation on the licensees to supply the grantor's Campari product rather than their own Campari to diplomatic customers, ships' provision suppliers, and other organisations with duty-free facilities:

"The ban on engaging in an active sales policy outside their respective territories prevents Campari-Milano and its licensees from freely disposing throughout the Common Market of the Bitter they have manufactured, restricting them to their exclusive territories, and thus affects international trade in the product. The obligation to supply certain consumers with the original Italian product rather than that which they themselves manufacture means that the licensees have to obtain supplies of Bitter Campari from Italy and thus affects international trade in the product."[132]

It found though that a prohibition on licensees exporting that product to countries outside the European Union would not affect competition under art.81(1) where re-importation was unlikely because of economic factors. A similar approach was taken in relation to export prohibitions to EFTA States. The Commission deemed re-importation unlikely because potential buyers could obtain the product within the borders of the Union directly from the licensor or its licensees. In addition economic factors such as the accumulation of trade margins and the combination of excise duties and taxes on

---

[131] *Campari*, paras 51–52.
[132] *Campari*, para.56.

4. THE APPLICATION OF ARTICLE 81

alcohol levied by importing countries with the duties charged on crossing the borders of the Union made re-importation financially unattractive.

9–069 Restriction of a manufacturing licence to plants that were capable of guaranteeing the quality of the product were not covered by art.81 (1) provided that they did not go beyond a legitimate concern for quality control; indeed the licensor could object only on the basis of product quality criteria.

The Commission appeared to be influenced by the link between quality control with the licensed trade marks. This contributed to making the obligation on licensees to follow the licensor's instructions regarding the manufacture of the product and the quality of the ingredients and to buy certain secret raw materials from the licensor compatible with art.81(1). Note that the agreements covered only the ingredients that were essential for the qualities of the product. The Commission accepted that the qualities of the licensed product had to be controlled by the licensor who had been marketing the original product in the first place. Further, the licensor should not be required to reveal its trade secrets to its licensees.

9–070 Similarly an obligation on licensees not to divulge the licensed manufacturing process to third parties was compatible with art.81(1).

The obligation on licensees to maintain continuous contact with customers and to spend a standard minimum sum on advertising also passed the hurdle of art.81(1).

The same applied to the prohibition of license assignments. The licensor was simply safeguarding its freedom to select its licensees.

The Commission found that the exclusivity granted by Campari-Milano benefited the production and distribution of Campari Bitter and could be exempted under art.81(3). The Commission was influenced by the evidence showing that the web of licensing agreements had been successful in practice in creating a decentralised and rational system of production within the Union.

9–071 Note that even the obligation to supply certain customers with Campari-Milano's product was accepted by the Commission. The Commission accepted that there might be taste variations between the products; the purpose of the clause was to ensure product consistency for the customers that had to move frequently from one country to another. In essence it multiplied rather than restricted choice:

> "By restricting licensees' freedom to supply the products they manufacture themselves it makes sure that particular categories of consumers, who are deemed to be outside the licensee's territory and are usually required to move frequently from one territory to another, can always purchase the same original product with all its traditional features as regards both composition and outward appearance. Even though quality standards are observed, it is impossible in particular to avoid differences in taste between the products of the various manufacturers. This obligation is thus designed to prevent these consumers from turning

to other competing products and to ensure that they continue to buy Bitter Campari, with the facility of being able to obtain stocks from their local dealer. Further, such consumers are not prevented from freely obtaining the licensees' own products even though any such purchase would be on the normal trading conditions applicable to non-duty-free purchasers."[133]

Finally, in respect of arbitration clauses and awards the Commission in granting an exemption under art.81(3) required to be informed of any relevant arbitral awards. It was concerned that the agreements might be interpreted without regard for the Commission's Decision and that the Commission might have to amend it:

"There is a greater risk at arbitration than in the ordinary courts that interpretation of the agreement may go beyond the limits imposed by the exemption, particularly where the arbitrators, whose function, as in this case, is to produce an amicable settlement, are not bound by the substantive law. Furthermore, review of arbitral awards for their compatibility with Articles [81] and [82], inasmuch as these fail to be regarded as part of EEC public policy, is not necessarily available in non-member-States."[134]

9–072 **(16) Javico—the contrast with Silhouette**

Javico[135] is evidence of how much the legislative context of a case can influence its outcome. Despite the apparent analogies with *Silhouette*[136] the competition context led to a different conclusion.

The case came before the Court as a reference from the Cour d' Appel, Versailles. Yves Saint Laurent Parfums (YSL) had set up a selective distribution network for its products in the European Union that was granted an exemption under art.81(3).[137] For Eastern European markets YSL had concluded with Javico, a company that was not part of YSL's selective distribution network, two distribution contracts one for Russia and Ukraine and the other for Slovenia that was not then a member of the Union.

The Russia and Ukraine agreement included a number of detailed provisions aiming to ensure that the YSL products covered therein were destined solely for those markets. The Slovenia agreement included a more general

---

[133] *Campari*, para.74.
[134] *Campari*, para.87.
[135] *Javico International and Javico AG v Yves Saint Laurent Parfums SA* (C-306/96) [1998] E.C.R. I-1983.
[136] *Silhouette International Schmied GmbH & Co KG v Hartlauer Handelsgesellschaft mbH* (C-355/96) [1998] E.C.R. I-4799.
[137] Commission Decision 92/33 (*Yves Saint Laurent Parfums*) [1992] OJ L12/24. Part of the decision was declared void by the Court of First Instance, *Leclerc v EC Commission* (T-19/92) [1996] E.C.R. II-1851; [1997] 4 C.M.L.R. 995; this related to an unrelated to the current case provision, the remaining parts of the Decision were upheld by the Court of First Instance.

4. THE APPLICATION OF ARTICLE 81

clause to that effect. Both were not notified to the Commission for the purposes of art.81(3).

Once YSL had spotted in the EU market products originally sold to Javico it terminated the contracts and sought compensation before the French courts. The case reached the Cour d' Appel where Javico argued that the relevant clauses infringed art.81(1) and that the exemption granted by the Commission was irrelevant. The French court stayed proceedings and referred the following questions to the Court.

"(1) Where an undertaking (the supplier) situated in a Member State of the European Union by contract entrusts another undertaking (the distributor) situated in another Member State with the distribution of its products in a territory outside the Union, must Article [81](1) of the Treaty establishing the European Community be interpreted as prohibiting provisions in that contract which preclude the distributor from effecting any sales in a territory other than the contractual territory, and hence any sale in the Union, either by direct marketing or by re-exportation from the contractual territory?

(2) In the event that the said Article [81](1) prohibits such contractual provisions, must it be interpreted as not being applicable where the supplier otherwise distributes his products on the territory of the Union by means of a selective distribution network which has been the subject of an exemption decision under Article [81](3)?"[138]

(a) The Opinion of the Advocate General

(i) The interpretation of article 81(1). Advocate General Tesauro identified two distinct obligations imposed on Javico through the contested clauses. The first was to export the products to the specified countries; the second was a prohibition of marketing outside the contractual territories.

9–073

He found that the Block Exemption Regulation 1983/83[139] was irrelevant, since art.1 clearly provided that it only covered agreements relating to the whole or parts of the European Union; this was viewed by the Court as an essential condition.[140]

Accordingly the object and effect of the clauses had to be examined under the light of art.81(1).[141] The intention of the parties was clearly to prevent the distribution in the Common Market of the products sold to Javico. "That allows YSL to oppose parallel imports into the Common Market, where it

---

[138] Reproduced in para.9.
[139] [1983] OJ L 173/1.
[140] Citing *Hydrotherm Geratebau GmbH v Compact del Dott. Ing. Mario Andreoli & C. Sas.* (170/83) [1984] E.C.R. 2999.
[141] He cited *Goettrup-Klim Grovvareforeninger v Dansk Landbrugs Grovvareselskab AmbA (DLG)* (C-250/92) [1994] I-5641; and *Stergios Delimitis v Henninger Bräu AG* (C-234/89) [1991] E.C.R. I-935. The object and effect were considered as alternatives not cumulatively according to *Ferriere Nord SpA v Commission* (C-219/95 P) [1997] E.C.R. I-4411.

operates through a selective distribution network whose efficacy might be undermined by the presence on the market of products distributed by resellers not belonging to the network."[142]

9-074   The Advocate General found that the clauses pursued an essentially anti-competitive aim and in order to gauge their necessity he looked at the two agreements rather than YSL's selective distribution network: "those clauses are not in fact necessary to ensure that the distribution contract fulfils the economic function assigned to it: that of facilitating penetration of [YSL] products into the East European market. The export clauses must therefore in principle be regarded as prohibited as far as their purpose is concerned".[143]

The next step was to consider whether the agreements had an appreciable effect on competition in the Common Market.[144] In order to discern the factors the national court had to take into account A.G. Tesauro looked at the decisions of the Commission regarding destination clauses: the impact of the customs duties which must be paid on the product upon reimportation into the European Union; the existence of a difference between the prices charged within the Union and in non-Member countries large enough to cover the greater costs of transport and the profit margins of those involved in re-importation and distribution within the Union; and the level of inter-brand competition in the Community.[145] The additional requirement for the application of art.81(1) was the finding of an adverse impact on trade between Member States.[146]

The applicability or not of art.81(1) remained in the jurisdiction of the national court, however the Advocate General appeared to believe that the lack of parallel imports from outside the Community was anti-competitive, "in this case, the possibility and economic advantage of reimporting the contractual products is not in doubt, if only because reimportation has in fact occurred. It is undisputed that large volumes of the contractual products are present on the market in the United Kingdom, Belgium and the Netherlands, and are being distributed at significantly lower prices by resellers outside the [YSL] distribution system, a fact which clearly indicates the advantageousness, and therefore the possibility, of parallel imports".[147]

---

[142] Point 10 of the Opinion of A.G. Tesauro.
[143] Point 10, citing the analogies in *Compagnie Royale Asturienne des Mines SA and Rheinzink GmbHC and Rheinzink v EC Commission* (29 & 30/83) [1984] E.C.R. 1679; Commission Decision 82/866 (*Rolled Zinc Products and Zinc Alloys*) [1982] OJ L362/40; [1983] 2 C.M.L.R. 285; and Commission Decision 68/376 (*Rieckermann/AEG*) [1968] OJ L276/25.
[144] *Société Technique Minière v Maschinenbau Ulm* (56/65) [1966] E.C.R. 235; *Brasserie de Haecht v Wilkin* (23/67) [1967] E.C.R. 407; *Stergios Delimitis v Henninger Bräu AG* (C-234/89) [1991] E.C.R. I-935; and *Völk v Ets Vervaecke SPRL* (5/69) [1969] ECR 295.
[145] He referred to a number of decisions including Commission Decision 78/253 (*Re the Agreements of Davide Campari-Milano SpA*) [1978] OJ L70/69; [1978] 2 C.M.L.R. 397; [1978] F.S.R. 528 and the Commission Notice under art.19(3) of Reg. 17 in *Chanel* [1994] OJ C334/11.
[146] Citing *Etablissements Consten SARL and Grundig-Verkaufs-GmbH* (56 & 58/64) [1966] E.C.R. 299.
[147] Point 14 of the Opinion of A.G. Tesauro.

4. THE APPLICATION OF ARTICLE 81

(ii) The interpretation of article 81(3). Advocate General Tesauro stressed that the exemption of the selective distribution network under art.81(3) did not require or mean that it should remain immune to competition and parallel imports.[148] To the contrary, he viewed parallel imports as a way "for tempering excess rigidity of the system, particularly as regards prices".[149]

9–075

Indeed, the Advocate General was a strong supporter of parallel trade: "... parallel trade—far from being the result of a sort of perverse economic opportunism, still less unlawful opportunism, as many tend maliciously to depict it—is a guarantee of the overall vitality of the distribution system which, alongside selective networks, ultimately is beneficial to the final consumer, whose interests are in any event (at least) one of the objectives of Article [81](1) and (3)".[150]

Apart from that general stance the Advocate General added a more concrete argument. The exemption decision could not cover distribution agreements that had not been themselves examined by the Commission; it was a derogation from the fundamental rule of art.81(1) and should be construed restrictively.[151] That approach would also ensure that the Commission would be able to fulfil its role as competition enforcer,[152] a competence that belonged to the Commission rather than the national court.

(b) The judgment of the Court

(i) The interpretation of article 81(1). The Court repeated that art.81(1) covered agreements between economic operators at different levels of the economic process.[153]

9–076

The Court had already decided that agreements that were destined to apply within the Community and deprived a reseller of its commercial freedom were against art.81(1).[154] The same applied to agreements with the aim of exclusion of parallel imports within the Community and consequently of restriction of competition in the common market.[155] Accordingly "[s]uch provisions, in contracts for the distribution of products within the Community, therefore constitute by their very nature a restriction of competition".[156] For art.81(1) to apply, these agreements should also be capable of affecting

---

[148] Citing *Metro SB-Großmärkte GmbH v Cartier SA* (C-376/92) [1994] E.C.R. I-15.
[149] Point 18 of the Opinion of A.G. Tesauro.
[150] Point 18 of the Opinion of A.G. Tesauro.
[151] Citing *Bundeskartellamt v Volkswagen AG and VAG Leasing GmbH* (C-266/93) [1995] E.C.R. I-3477.
[152] Citing *Stergios Delimitis v Henninger Bräu AG* (C-234/89) [1991] E.C.R. I-935.
[153] Citing *Société Technique Minière* (56/65) [1966] E.C.R. 235; and *Etablissements Consten SARL and Grundig-Verkaufs-GmbH v Commission* (56/64 & 58/64) [1966] E.C.R. 299.
[154] Citing *Hasselblad (GB) Ltd v Commission* (86/82) [1984] E.C.R. I-883; and *Bayerische Motorenwerke AG v ALD Auto-Leasing D GmbH* (C-70/93) [1995] E.C.R. I-3439.
[155] Citing *Tipp-Ex GmbH & Co KG v Commission* (C-279/87) [1990] E.C.R. I-261.
[156] *Javico*, para.14, citing *Miller International Schallplatten GmbH v Commission* (19/77) [1978] E.C.R. 131.

trade between Member States in a significant way.[157] The position and importance of the parties in the relevant market were significant factors in that assessment.[158]

Here, the Court had to determine whether similar considerations applied to agreements covering a territory outside the Community. The starting point was different. The Court, too, considered the purpose of such agreements but reached a different conclusion from the Advocate General:

> "[i]n the case of agreements of this kind, stipulations of the type mentioned in the question must be construed not as being intended to exclude parallel imports and marketing of the contractual product within the Community but as being designed to enable the producer to penetrate a market outside the Community by supplying a sufficient quantity of contractual products to that market. That interpretation is supported by the fact that, in the agreements at issue, the prohibition of selling outside the contractual territory also covers all other non-member countries".[159]

9–077 Accordingly, an undertaking to sell the contractual products on a market outside the Community should not be regarded as having the object of appreciably restricting competition within the common market or as being capable of affecting, as such, trade between Member States. "Similarly, the provisions of the agreements in question, in that they prohibit direct sales within the Community and re-exports of the contractual product to the Community, cannot be contrary, by their very nature, to art.[81](1) of the Treaty."[160]

Article 81(1) would still be applied if, according to the national court, the agreements had the effect of preventing, restricting, or distorting competition within the common market irrespective of their object. This was an assessment for the national court taking account of their economic and legal context.[161]

The Court underlined the following issues that should be seen as part of that context. First, whether the relevant market was an oligopoly; secondly, whether there was an appreciable difference between the Community and the non-Community prices of the contractual products; thirdly, if there was an effect it had to be an appreciable effect on the pattern of trade between the Member States such as to undermine attainment of the objectives of the common market:

> "In that regard, intra-Community trade cannot be appreciably affected if the products intended for markets outside the Community account for

---

[157] *Völk v Ets Vervaecke SPRL* (5–69) [1969] E.C.R. 295.
[158] *Lancôme and Cosparfrance Nederland BV v Etos BV* (99/79) [1980] E.C.R. I-2511; and *Musique Diffusion Française v Commission* (100/80 to 103/80) [1983] E.C.R. 1825.
[159] *Javico*, para.19.
[160] *Javico*, para.21.
[161] Citing *Gemeente Almelo v NV Energiebedrijf Ijsselmij* (C-393/92) [1994] E.C.R. I-1477.

only a very small percentage of the total market for those products in the territory of the common market."¹⁶²

(ii) The interpretation of article 81(3). The Court underlined that the individual exemption decision related only to standard YSL selective distribution contracts for the retail sale of its products in the Community; it could not affect agreements concerning their distribution outside the Community. Indeed art.1 of Regulation 1983/83 made it clear that the block exemption could not even apply to such agreements.

9–078

As to whether the contested provisions could escape art.81(1) because their aim was to protect an exempted selective distribution network the response of the Court was categorically negative. The decision provided for an exemption to the fundamental rule and should be interpreted restrictively so as to ensure that its effects would not be extended to situations that it was not intended to cover.¹⁶³

5. THE APPLICATION OF ARTICLE 82

(1) Dominance

The Court of Justice described dominance as:

9–079

"a position of economic strength enjoyed by an undertaking which enables it to prevent effective competition being maintained on the relevant market by affording it the power to behave to an appreciable extent independently of its competitors, customers and ultimately of its consumers".¹⁶⁴

(a) Identifying the relevant product market

9–080

From a trade mark perspective identifying dominance is a particularly topical issue because the primary issue is identifying the relevant product market.

(i) Continental Can—the interchangeability criterion. In *Continental Can*¹⁶⁵ the Court indicated that interchangeability of products was the decisive criterion:

9–081

---

¹⁶² *Javico*, para.26.
¹⁶³ Citing *Bayerische Motorenwerke AG v ALD Auto-Leasing D GmbH* (C-70/93) [1995] E.C.R. I-3439.
¹⁶⁴ *United Brands Co and United Brands Continental BV v Commission* (27/76) [1978] E.C.R. 207, paras 65 and 66.
¹⁶⁵ *Europemballage Corp and Continental Can Co Inc v Commission* [1973] E.C.R. 215.

"... the possibilities of competition can only be judged in relation to those characteristics of the products in question by virtue of which those products are particularly apt to satisfy an inelastic need and are only to a limited extent interchangeable with other products".[166]

The Commission had failed to show why and how three markets for food containers—"light containers for canned meat products", "light containers for canned seafood", and "metal closures for the food packing industry"—differed from each other in the first place and, secondly, from the general market for "light metal containers, namely the market for metal containers for fruit and vegetables, condensed milk, olive oil, fruit juices and chemico-technical products".

The Court added that in order:

"to be regarded as constituting a distinct market, the products in question must be individualized, not only by the mere fact that they are used for packing certain products, but by particular characteristics of production which make them specifically suitable for this purpose. Consequently, a dominant position on the market for light metal containers for meat and fish cannot be decisive, as long as it has not been proved that competitors from other sectors of the market for light metal containers are not in a position to enter this market, by a simple adaptation, with sufficient strength to create a serious counterweight".[167]

9–082   Further, the Court took into account the argument that competition from containers made of other material was possible, opening up the concept of the relevant product market. It also looked at potential competition in a geographical context. Parts of the case focused on the German market and the Court rejected the Commission's argument that plants in neighbouring countries should not be considered as competitive because they were located too far away from most German consumers as unsubstantiated. And, finally, it considered the potentiality of competition from large consumers of containers, food producers who were manufacturing their own containers.

Once the market is identified, the most common criteria for establishing dominance are market share, whether market power constitutes a sufficient barrier to entry, and the conduct of the undertaking.

The Court accepted that superior technology, access to financial resources, and intellectual property rights can function as barriers to entry.

---

[166] *Continental Can,* para.32. Greaves (1998), p.380: "Interchangeability is established by looking primarily at the demand side substitutability (e.g. physical characteristics; price; intended use) but the supply substitutability should also be considered".
[167] *Continental Can,* para.33.

5. THE APPLICATION OF ARTICLE 82

(b) United Brands—the market for bananas   9–083

United Brands[168] considered whether bananas were part of a larger market for fresh fruit or constituted a market of their own. United Brands argued that cross elasticity in demand between bananas and other fresh fruit was high, the Commission argued that it was low.

The Court started its analysis by noting that establishing whether there was a distinct market for bananas rested on whether it was possible for the banana "to be singled out by such special features distinguishing it from other fruits that it is only to a limited extent interchangeable with them and is only exposed to their competition in a way that is hardly perceptible".[169]

One of its characteristics was that ripening took place the whole year round so it was always available in sufficient quantities. So the Court had to examine whether it could be replaced by other fruits throughout the year.

The Court looked at the market for seasonal fruits and found that limited substitutability existed between bananas on the one hand and peaches and table grapes on the other in only one Member State; this meant that there was some—but minimal—price interaction. It then considered oranges and apples that were also available throughout the year finding that there was no link with oranges and only a limited one with apples. After the analysis of the market conditions it attempted to identify the reasons behind them, focusing on the product's special characteristics. "The banana has certain characteristics, appearance, taste, softness, seedlessness, easy handling, a constant level of production which enable it to satisfy the constant needs of an important section of the population consisting of the very young, the old and the sick."[170] It concluded that the banana market is a market which is sufficiently distinct from the market for other fresh fruits.

(c) Hugin—the market for spare parts   9–084

The delineation of the relevant product market in *Hugin*[171] is particularly topical from a trade mark law perspective.[172]

According to the Commission Hugin, a manufacturer of cash registers, was in breach of art.82 because it refused to supply spare parts to Liptons, a company that competed with Hugin in the market for servicing Hugin registers. The Commission had defined the relevant market as the market for spare parts for Hugin cash registers required by independent repairers, where Hugin was by definition the dominant player. Hugin supported that

---

[168] *United Brands Co and United Brands Continentaal BV v Commission* (27/76) [1978] E.C.R. 207.
[169] *United Brands*, para.22.
[170] *United Brands*, para.31.
[171] *Hugin Kassaregister AB and Hugin Cash Registers Ltd v Commission* (22/78) [1979] E.C.R. 1869.
[172] See paras 7–007 and following, above.

the product market should be the wider market for cash registers, a much more open and competitive market, and argued that charging anti-competitive price for its spare parts would influence negatively its position as a manufacturer of cash registers.

The Court agreed with the Commission.

It started its analysis by the finding of fact that the servicing of Hugin registers was a specialist's job:

> "there exists a separate market for Hugin spare parts at another level, namely that of independent undertakings which specialize in the maintenance and repair of cash registers, in the reconditioning of used machines and in the sale of used machines and the renting out of machines. The role of those undertakings on the market is that of businesses which require spare parts for their various activities. They need such parts in order to provide services for cash register users in the form of maintenance and repairs and for the reconditioning of used machines and for re-sale and renting out. Finally, they require spare parts for the maintenance and repair of new or used machines belonging to them which are rented out to their clients. It is, moreover, established that there is a specific demand for Hugin spare parts, since those parts are not interchangeable with spare parts for cash registers of other makes".[173]

Hugin admitted that in this narrow market it had a monopoly in new spare parts, but supported nevertheless that the purchase and dismantling of used machines disputed an alternative source of supply. The Court held that this was not a sufficient alternative.

9-085   (d) *Crossing market boundaries*

In *L'Oreal*[174] the Court described the definition of the market as an issue of fundamental significance. "Indeed, the possibilities of competition must be judged in the context of the market comprising the totality of the products which, with respect to their characteristics, are particularly suitable for satisfying constant needs and are only to a limited extent interchangeable with other products."[175]

In *AKZO*[176] the Court applied this test in a case where the Commission had found AKZO dominant in a particular market, the organic peroxides market (including the benzoyl peroxide used in the plastics industry) because that was the market from which AKZO sought to exclude in the long run one of its competitors, supporting that, alternatively, abuse also

---

[173] *Hugin*, para.7.
[174] *NV L'Oreal and SA L'Oreal v PVBA De Nieuwe AMCK* (31/80) [1980] E.C.R. 3775.
[175] *L'Oreal*, para.25.
[176] *AKZO Chemie BV v Commission* (C-62/86) [1991] E.C.R. I-3359.

5. THE APPLICATION OF ARTICLE 82

occurred in the flour additives market (including the benzoyl peroxide used in the milling sector) in the United Kingdom and Ireland.

The Court concurred with the Commission primarily because the same organic peroxide was used in both markets. In addition AKZO's competitor historically had been more active in the flour additives sector which was of limited importance to AKZO that was able to subsidise its losses in that market with its profits from the plastics sector.

9–086

According to the evidence AKZO's intention was to preserve its position in the plastics sector by preventing its competitor entering this market. "The Commission was in those circumstances justified in regarding the organic peroxides market as the relevant market, even though the abusive behaviour alleged was intended to damage ECS's main business activity in a different market."[177]

The Court also rejected the argument that the definition of the market was not precise enough because the category of organic peroxides contained more than one product:

> "organic peroxides may, indeed, be individualized with regard to their formula, their concentration or their presentation in order to meet the particular requirements of customers. Nevertheless, 90% of their use is in various operations in the plastics industry and they are therefore suitable for satisfying constant needs ... Moreover, they are not exposed to competition from other products, such as sulphur-based compounds used in the limited field of vulcanization of synthetic rubber, since the latter products cannot replace them completely as they do not have all the technical properties required".[178]

(e) Derivative markets

9–087

Note that the Court had already considered the effect of dominance in one market in other derivative markets in *Commercial Solvents*.[179] There the Court found that abuse of a dominant position in a market of raw materials—aminobutanol—could have anti-competitive effects in the market on which derivatives are sold—ethambutol, an anti-tuberculosis drug—that should be taken into account regarding the applicability of art.82. Commercial Solvents had also argued that ethambutol was only one amongst a number of anti-tuberculosis drugs but the Court held that its holding covered even the case of a second market that did not constitute a self-contained market.

The particular facts of the case were relevant to the outcome because Commercial Solvents was active only in the market for raw materials before

---

[177] *AKZO*, para.45.
[178] *AKZO*, para.52.
[179] *Instituto Chemioterapico Italiano SpA and Commercial Solvents Corp v Commission* (6/73 & 7/73) [1974] E.C.R. 223.

deciding to start manufacturing the derivative pharmaceutical product and thus compete with its former customers: "an undertaking which has a dominant position in the market in raw materials and which, with the object of reserving such raw material for manufacturing its own derivatives, refuses to supply a customer, which is itself a manufacturer of these derivatives, and therefore risks eliminating all competition on the part of this customer, is abusing its dominant position within the meaning of Article [82]".[180]

9-088 **(2) Dominance and intellectual property**

(a) Exclusivity and dominance

Because of their exclusive nature, intellectual property rights can lead to dominance. However, exclusivity should not lead to automatic conclusions.

In *Parke, Davis v Probel*[181] the Court considered whether in itself the existence of an intellectual property right constituted a problem for competition. The referring Dutch court had noted that the owner of a patent could block all commercial dealings in a Member State in the product covered by the patent coming from another Member State that did not grant an exclusive right to manufacture and sell that product and that the price of the patented product was higher than that of a similar, but not covered by a patent, product. The judgment was partly based on the fact that at that stage there was no harmonisation of the national rules relating to industrial property and drew from analogies with free movement of goods cases; for "similar reasons, the exercise of the rights arising under a patent granted in accordance with the legislation of a Member State does not, of itself, constitute an infringement of the rules on competition laid down by the Treaty".[182]

In respect of art.81(1), in particular, a patent taken by itself and independently of any agreement of which it may be the subject "... is the expression of a legal status granted by a state to products meeting certain criteria, and thus exhibits none of the elements of contract or concerted practice required by Article [81](1). Nevertheless it is possible that the provisions of this Article may apply if the use of one or more patents, in concert between undertakings, should lead to the creation of a situation which may come within the concepts of agreements... within the meaning of Article [81](1)".[183]

9-089 And regarding art.82 it added that although a "patent confers on its holder a special protection at national level, it does not follow that the exercise of the rights thus conferred implies the presence together of all the three [dominance, abuse, and effect on trade between Member States]

---

[180] *AKZO*, para.25.
[181] *Parke, Davis and Co v Probel, Reese, Beintema-Interpharm and Centrafarm* (24/67) [1968] E.C.R. 55.
[182] *Parke, Davis v Probel*, p.71.
[183] *Parke, Davis v Probel*, p.71.

5. THE APPLICATION OF ARTICLE 82

elements in question. It could only do so if the use of the patent were to degenerate into an abuse of the abovementioned protection".[184] Price differences between patented and unpatented products did not necessarily constitute an abuse.

In *EMI* the Court adopted the same principle in respect of trade marks:

"Although the trade-mark right confers upon its proprietor a special position within the protected territory this, however, does not imply the existence of a dominant position within the meaning of the abovementioned Article, in particular where, as in the present case, several undertakings whose economic strength is comparable to that of the proprietor of the mark operate in the market for the products in question and are in a position to compete with the said proprietor".[185]

(b)   Volvo v Veng—spare parts and intellectual property   9–090

Volvo v Veng[186] reconsiders the markets for spare parts, only this time an intellectual property right is involved. Volvo, the car manufacturer, employed its UK registered design right for body panels against Veng, an importer of infringing panels. The Patents Court referred three questions to the Court of Justice: did a car manufacturer in Volvo's position hold a dominant position in the relevant market for spare parts; would refusal to license third parties to supply spare parts in return for a reasonable royalty constitute prima facie an abuse of a dominant position; would this be considered to affect trade between Member States where the parts derived from another Member State.

Advocate General Mischo, without mentioning *Hugin*,[187] suggested that Volvo indeed held a dominant position. A Volvo owner simply had to buy a body panel identical to the original Volvo panel and any substitutable product would infringe Volvo's design right. The combination of these two facts meant that potential competitors faced a barrier that was impossible to mount. In essence Volvo enjoyed a double monopoly, one over the car as a whole and another over the parts of the car as spare parts.

(i) Reversing the order. The Court however chose a surprisingly   9–091 different route. Instead of considering first the issue of dominance and then the question of abuse—as a proper economic analysis would require—it started and finished its analysis by focusing on the second question of the Patent Court. It highlighted the absence of harmonisation of national laws

---

[184] *Parke, Davis v Probel*, p.72.
[185] *EMI Records* (51/75) [1976] E.C.R. 811.
[186] *AB Volvo v Eric Veng (UK) Ltd* (238/87) [1988] E.C.R. 6211.
[187] *Hugin Kassaregister AB and Hugin Cash Registers Ltd v Commission* (22/78) [1979] E.C.R. 1869.

in this particular field repeated its earlier holding that in such cases national laws determine the subject-matter and scope of protection.[188] So, given the scope of the national right, "an obligation imposed upon the proprietor of a protected design to grant to third parties, even in return for a reasonable royalty, a licence for the supply of products incorporating the design would lead to the proprietor thereof being deprived of the substance of his exclusive right, and that a refusal to grant such a licence cannot in itself constitute an abuse of a dominant position".[189]

The Court then went further and identified hypothetical types of conduct by the proprietor of an industrial design that would still constitute an abuse, to the extent that they affected trade between Member States: the arbitrary refusal to supply spare parts to independent repairers; the fixing of prices for spare parts at an unfair level; a decision to stop the production of spare parts for car models still in circulation in substantial numbers.

Irrespective of the actual outcome of the case the anomaly in the judicial reasoning is obvious. It appears that, uncharacteristically, the Court felt uneasy with the antagonistic relationship between national intellectual property rights and European competition law and chose to hide behind the lack of harmonisation. But then immediately rediscovered its interventionist appetite and identified hypothetical anti-competitive situations. Keeling expresses his disbelief in the following words:

> "The Court's performance in Volvo v Veng was extraordinary. The question whether a dominant position exists is surely preliminary to the question whether a dominant position is abused. Presumably the Court thought that the question whether ownership of an intellectual property right could by itself give rise to a dominant position was so horrendously controversial and difficult that it was preferable to say that, even if a dominant position existed, it was not abused simply because the owner of an exclusive right exercised it. If anything though, the latter question was surely the more controversial of the two. Moreover, if the Court was anxious to avoid making unnecessary pronouncements in this field, why did it choose to identify certain forms of conduct not mentioned by the national court and condemn them as abusive of a (purely hypothetical) dominant position?"[190]

It is suggested that the Court, facing a difficult judicial and political dilemma, attempted another balancing exercise choosing to ignore the route that a court facing a competition question would normally take, like it itself did in *Hugin*.[191] It is worth repeating that even in the more orthodox

---

[188] Referring to *Keurkoop v Nancy Kean Gifts* (144/81) [1982] E.C.R. 2853.
[189] *Volvo v Veng*, para.8.
[190] DT Keeling, *Intellectual Property Rights in EU Law—Volume I* (Oxford: Oxford University Press, 2003), p.373.
[191] *Hugin Kassaregister AB and Hugin Cash Registers Ltd* (22/78) [1979] E.C.R. 1869.

5. THE APPLICATION OF ARTICLE 82

approach of the Advocate General there was no reference to *Hugin*. *Volvo v Veng* is perhaps the most telling example of the difference an intellectual property right can make but also of the willingness, and perhaps of the need, of the Court to take into account the ever changing nature of the European project in its judicial reasoning.

(c) Renault—a lenient approach

9–092

Renault[192] reconfirmed that, per se, the sale of components protected by an industrial property right at a higher price than that charged for the same components by independent manufacturers is not deemed to be an abuse. The Italian referring court had underlined that a return for the proprietor of the rights was already guaranteed by the exclusive rights covering the bodywork as a whole and suggested that protection of the components of the bodywork was unjustified.

The Court of Justice held that a higher price for the protected component than its unprotected equivalent "does not necessarily constitute an abuse, since the proprietor of protective rights in respect of an ornamental design may lawfully call for a return on the amounts which he has invested in order to perfect the protected design".[193]

(d) Hilti—anti-competitive exploitation of a patent

9–093

In *Hilti*[194] the Court confirmed on appeal the decision of the Court of First Instance[195] identifying one instance of abuse: Hilti held a patent and protracted the process for granting to a competitor a license of right, available according to UK law, by making excessive royalty demands:

"As far as [Hilti's] policy on the grant of licences of right is concerned ... it is clear ... that ... Hilti was not prepared to grant licences on a voluntary basis and that during the proceedings for the grant of licences of right it demanded a fee approximately six times higher than the figure ultimately appointed by the Comptroller of Patents. A reasonable trader, as Hilti claims to have been, should at least have realized that by demanding such a large fee it was needlessly protracting the proceedings for the grant of licences of right, and such behaviour undeniably constitutes an abuse."[196]

---

[192] *Consorzio Italiano della Componentistica di Ricambio per Autoveicoli and Maxicar v Regio Nationale des Usines Renault* (53/87) [1988] E.C.R. 6039.
[193] *Volvo v Veng*, para.17.
[194] *Hilti AG v Commission* (C-53/92) [1994] E.C.R. I-667.
[195] *Hilti AG* (T-30/89) [1991] E.C.R. II-1439.
[196] *Hilti AG* (T-30/89) [1991] E.C.R. 11-1439, para.99.

It also agreed with the Court of First Instance that the relevant market was consumables, nails and cartridge strips, for Hilti nail guns rather than the wider market of nail guns as supported by Hilti.

9-094 *(e) Magill—copyright, exclusivity, and dominance*

In *Magill*[197] the Court revisited the issue whether the exercise of an intellectual property right can constitute an abuse of a dominant position.

Magill published a weekly television guide listing the programmes of British and Irish broadcasters without seeking their authorisation. The latter claimed copyright in the listings of their programmes and refused to license Magill to publish them. Note that they too were publishing separate weekly television guides. The gap in the market was obvious: broadcasters had become publishers of guides that did not compete with each other since each guide was based on the content of its own broadcaster/publisher. They only allowed daily newspapers to publish daily guides, or information for 48 hours when the next day was a public holiday, and weekly highlights. Magill introduced a new product combining the listings of all broadcasters and competing with all the existing guides. Magill's complaint that the broadcasters' refusal constituted an abuse of a dominant position was upheld by the Commission, that considered the market for advance weekly listings as the relevant market, in which the broadcasters/publishers enjoyed a dominant position that they abused by refusing to license Magill to publish the listings.[198]

The broadcasters/publishers challenged the Commission's decision before the Court of First Instance. They supported that the relevant market was the market for all advance programme information, both weekly and daily, and there was a high degree of substitutability between the various information platforms. Indeed the majority of viewers relied on daily newspapers rather than weekly listings.

9-095 The Court of First Instance concurred with the Commission.[199] It characterised the markets for weekly and daily listings as sub-markets of a wider market for television programme information and found that there was a specific demand for information on a weekly basis.

The Court of First Instance clearly acknowledged that copyright in their listings transformed the broadcasters/publishers to dominant players: the applicant:

"enjoyed, as a consequence of its copyright in its programme listings, the exclusive right to reproduce and market those listings. It was thus able, at the material time to secure a monopoly over the publication of its

---

[197] *Radio Telefis Eireann (RTE) and Independent Television Publications Ltd (ITP) v Commission* (C-241/91 P & C-242/91 P) [1995] E.C.R. I-808.
[198] Commission Decision 89/205 *Magill* [1989] OJ L78/43.
[199] *Radio Telefis Eireann (RTE) v Commission* (T-69/89) [1991] E.C.R. II-485.

weekly listings in ... [its own] magazine specializing in its own programmes. Consequently, the applicant clearly held at that time a dominant position both on the market represented by its listings and on the market for the magazines in which they were published ...".[200]

RTE and ITP appealed further to the Court of Justice.

(i) De facto monopoly. The Court recognised the competition issues but, in order to avoid considering the potential conflict between national copyright law and European competition law, it chose to take a step back and stated that the dominance of the broadcasters/publishers was due to their "de facto monopoly over the information used to compile listings for the television programmes".[201] 9–096

It repeated that mere ownership of an intellectual property cannot confer a position of dominance.

Greaves notes that the Court "did its utmost to distance itself from the controversial issue of reconciling national copyright law with the Community's competition rules ... The fact that [basic information] was not available from another source, mainly because of the copyright, was conveniently ignored".[202]

(ii) Factors establishing abusive conduct. However, the Court added that the exercise of an intellectual property right could still be reviewed under the light of art.82. Turning to the facts of the case it agreed with the Court of First Instance that the following constituted abusive conduct: 9–097

(i) there was no actual or potential substitute for a weekly television guide offering information on the programmes for the week ahead whilst "there was a specific, constant and regular potential demand on the part of consumers"[203];

(ii) the broadcasters/publishers, "who were, by force of circumstance, the only sources of the basic information on programme scheduling ... gave viewers wishing to obtain information on the choice of programmes for the week ahead no choice but to buy the weekly guides for each station, and draw from each of them the information they needed to make comparisons"[204];

(iii) the broadcasters/publishers' refusal "to provide basic information by relying on national copyright provisions ... prevented the appearance

---

[200] *Magill*, para.63.
[201] *Radio Telefis Eireann (RTE) and Independent Television Publications Ltd (ITP) v Commission* (C-241/91 P & C-242/91 P) [1995] E.C.R. I-808, para.47.
[202] Greaves (1998), p.381.
[203] *Magill*, para.52.
[204] *Magill*, para.53.

of a new product... which the appellants did not offer and for which there was a potential consumer demand"[205];

(iv) "there was no justification for such refusal either in the activity of television broadcasting or in that of publishing television magazines"[206]; and

(v) the broadcasters/publishers "by their conduct, reserved to themselves the secondary market of weekly television guides by excluding all competition on that market... since they denied access to the basic information which is the raw material indispensable for the compilation of such a guide".[207]

The Court also rejected the plea that the Commission's decision would violate the obligations of the Member States under the Berne Convention[208] based on its jurisprudence regarding the effect of international agreements, without having to examine the substance of the argument. The Community was not a member of the Berne Convention and the provisions of an agreement concluded prior to entry into force of the Treaty or prior to a Member State's accession cannot be relied on in intra-Community relations if the rights of non-Member countries are not involved.[209]

9-098   (f)   *Bronner—exporting the principles of Magill*

Bronner[210] is not an intellectual property and competition law case but it relied on *Magill*[211] and provided a new perspective that the Court used in subsequent judgments involving intellectual property rights.

The reference was from an Austrian court, the Oberlandesgericht Wien, and involved the refusal by the publisher of the biggest national newspapers, that also operated the only home delivery scheme in Austria, to allow access to the scheme to Bronner, a smaller rival competitor.

The Court accepted that this could be seen as a national rather than Community competition law case but this would not preclude it from considering the reference; it was also possible for the same situation to fall under both national and Community law. The circumstances concerning the

---

[205] *Magill*, para.54.
[206] *Magill*, para.55.
[207] *Magill*, para.56.
[208] In particular art.9(1) conferring an exclusive right of reproduction and art.9(2) allowing a signatory State to permit reproduction only in certain special cases, provided that such reproduction did not conflict with normal exploitation of the work and did not unreasonably prejudice the legitimate interests of the copyright owner.
[209] Referring to *Ministere Public v Deserbais* (286/86) [1988] E.C.R. 4907.
[210] *Oscar Bronner GmbH & Co KG v Mediaprint Zeitungs-und Zeitschriftenverlag GmbH & Co KG, Mediaprint Zeitungsvertriebsgesellschaft mbH & Co KG and Mediaprint Anzeigengesellschaft mbH & Co KG* (C-7/97) [1998] E.C.R. I-7791.
[211] *Radio Telefis Eireann (RTE) and Independent Television Publications Ltd (ITP) v Commission* (C-241/91P and C-242/91P) [1995] E.C.R. I-808.

5. THE APPLICATION OF ARTICLE 82

applicability of art.82 to the factual situation of the main proceedings fell within the scope of the assessment by the national court; they were irrelevant for determining admissibility.

Bronner argued that postal delivery did not constitute an alternative to Mediaprint's home delivery scheme because it took place later and that it would be entirely unprofitable to set up a competing delivery service, on its own or in collaboration with other publishers, because of its small number of subscribers. Bronner sought access to Mediaprint's service, characterised as an "essential facility", for a reasonable fee. Mediaprint argued that irrespective of its dominant position in principle it was entitled to decide freely to whom it wished to allow access to its facilities and that there were no exceptional circumstances leading to the application of art.82. In any case its refusal was justified because opening the scheme to its rivals would be a challenge for its capacity.

9–099

The Court started its analysis by defining the relevant market. In principle it comprises all the products or services which are particularly suited to satisfy constant needs and are only to a limited extent interchangeable with other products or services, but it remained for the national court to decide whether home delivery schemes constituted a separate market from other methods for selling newspapers. The next step would be to establish whether Mediaprint's refusal deprived its competitor "of a means of distribution judged essential for the sale of its newspaper".[212]

Revisiting *Magill*[213] it read it as an intellectual property case and held that:

> "even if that case-law on the exercise of an intellectual property right were applicable to the exercise of any property right whatever, it would still be necessary ... not only that the refusal of the service comprised in home delivery be likely to eliminate all competition in the daily newspaper market on the part of the person requesting the service and that such refusal be incapable of being objectively justified, but also that the service in itself be indispensable to carrying on that person's business, inasmuch as there is no actual or potential substitute in existence for that home-delivery scheme."[214]

Turning to the facts of *Bronner* the Court found that other methods of distribution did exist. Perhaps they were less advantageous but this would not be enough. Further, there were no technical, legal, or economic obstacles capable of making it impossible or unreasonably difficult, for any other publisher to establish, alone or in co-operation with others publishers, its own nationwide home delivery scheme. The argument that such a scheme

---

[212] *Bronner*, para.37.
[213] *Radio Telefis Eireann (RTE) and Independent Television Publications Ltd (ITP)* (C-241/91P and C-242/91P) [1995] E.C.R. I-808.
[214] *Bronner*, para.41.

would not be economically viable because of the small circulation of the newspapers to be distributed was not enough for the Court. It accepted the view of A.G. Jacobs that in order to regard access to the scheme as indispensable "it would be necessary at the very least to establish ... that it is not economically viable to create a second home-delivery scheme for the distribution of daily newspapers with a circulation comparable to that of the daily newspapers distributed by the existing scheme".[215]

9-100   (g)   *IMS Health*—*importing the principles of Bronner*

Following *Bronner*,[216] the attitude of the Court of Justice towards the balance between intellectual property rights and competition is reflected in the *IMS* case[217] a reference from the Landgericht Frankfurt am Main.

IMS provided information on sales of pharmaceutical products in Germany using a brick structure. Each brick corresponded to a geographic area and its boundaries were set according to a variety of criteria relevant to the market for pharmaceuticals, e.g. postcodes, distribution of pharmacies, and distribution of doctors' surgeries. There were two brick formats, the basic consisting of 1,860 bricks and a secondary consisting of 2,847 bricks. At an early stage IMS and other users of the formats had collaborated in developing the formats. IMS marketed the two formats to its clients but also distributed them free of charge to pharmacies and surgeries to the extent that they have become the industry standard to which its clients adapted their information and distribution systems.

A former employee of IMS set up a company, marketing similar information. He used a format consisting of 2,201 bricks. Potential clients however had become accustomed to the IMS model and he switched to two formats of 1,860 and 3,000 bricks similar to the IMS ones. His company was acquired by NDC. German courts described the formats as databases protectable under copyright law and granted an order prohibiting NDC from using formats deriving from the basic 1,860 brick format. The referring court however held that IMS should not be allowed to exercise its right if it acted in an abusive manner, according to art.82, by refusing to grant a licence to NDC. So, in essence, it sought from the Court of Justice to indicate whether IMS's behaviour fell within the scope of art.82.

9-101   Referring to *Bronner*[218] the Court noted that in order to establish that a product is indispensable for enabling an undertaking to operate in a

---

[215] *Bronner*, para.46.
[216] *Oscar Bronner GmbH & Co KG v Mediaprint Zeitungs- und Zeitschriftenverlag GmbH & Co KG, Mediaprint Zeitungsvertriebsgesellschaft mbH & Co KG and Mediaprint Anzeigengesellschaft mbH & Co KG* (C-7/97) [1998] E.C.R. I-7791.
[217] *IMS Health GmbH & Co OHG v NDC Health GmbH & Co KG* (C-418/01) [2004] E.C.R. I-5039.
[218] *Oscar Bronner GmbH & Co KG v Mediaprint Zeitungs- und Zeitschriftenverlag GmbH & Co KG, Mediaprint Zeitungsvertriebsgesellschaft mbH & Co KG and Mediaprint Anzeigengesellschaft mbH & Co KG* (C-7/97) [1998] E.C.R. I-7791.

5. THE APPLICATION OF ARTICLE 82

particular market it must be determined whether there are products that offer alternative, even less advantageous, solutions and whether there are technical, legal, or economic obstacles capable of making it impossible or at least unreasonably difficult to create these alternatives, possibly in co-operation with others. This remained in the jurisdiction of the national court; in this case the court should take into account the fact that pharmaceutical laboratories have contributed substantially to the improvement of the basic brick format. This has created a dependency that could render competition, through use of an alternative format, unviable.

As to whether refusal to grant a licence in such circumstances constituted an abuse the Court referred to *Volvo*[219] and *Magill*[220] setting that the exclusive right of reproduction, being part of an intellectual property right, meant that in itself refusal did not constitute an abuse. Additional circumstances however could reverse this finding: "it is sufficient that three cumulative conditions be satisfied, namely, that that refusal is preventing the emergence of a new product for which there is a potential consumer demand, that it is unjustified and such as to exclude any competition on a secondary market".[221]

The Court looked at the third condition first. Deciphering *Bronner*[222] the Court noted that in order to assess indispensability it is relevant to distinguish between an upstream market, constituted by the product or service in question and a secondary, downstream, market "on which the product or service in question is used for the production of another product or the supply of another service".[223] It is sufficient that a potential or even hypothetical market can be identified, but it is "determinative that two different stages of production may be identified and that they are interconnected, inasmuch as the upstream product is indispensable for the supply of the downstream product".[224]

In, admittedly, one of its most impenetrable holdings, the Court concluded that transposed "to the facts of the case in the main proceedings, that approach prompts consideration as to whether the 1,860 brick structure constitutes, upstream, an indispensable factor in the downstream supply of German regional sales data for pharmaceutical products"[225] and left it to the national court to decide whether IMS's refusal constituted an abuse.

---

[219] *AB Volvo v Eric Veng (UK) Ltd* (238/87) [1988] E.C.R. 6211.
[220] *Radio Telefis Eireann (RTE) and Independent Television Publications Ltd (ITP)* (C-241/91P & C-242/91P) [1995] E.C.R. I-808.
[221] *IMS Health*, para.38.
[222] *Oscar Bronner GmbH & Co KG v Mediaprint Zeitungs- und Zeitschriftenverlag GmbH & Co KG, Mediaprint Zeitungsvertriebsgesellschaft mbH & Co KG and Mediaprint Anzeigengesellschaft mbH & Co KG* (C-7/97) [1998] E.C.R. I-7791.
[223] *IMS Health*, para.42.
[224] *IMS Health*, para.45.
[225] *IMS Health*, para.46.

9–102   **(i) Intellectual property and competition—tilting the balance.** As to the first condition, relating to the emergence of a new product, the Court held that the balance will tilt from intellectual property towards competition when refusal to grant a licence prevents the development of the secondary market to the detriment of consumers: the undertaking which requested the licence must intend to offer, "on the market for the supply of the data in question, new products or services not offered by the owner of the intellectual property right and for which there is a potential consumer demand".[226] So, according to the Court, intellectual property prevails when the potential competitor intends to duplicate what the owner of the intellectual property right is already offering. The statement is significant because the Court appears to accept as uncontroversial the exclusivity that lies in the heart of the intellectual property right.

In respect of the second condition, the Court stated only that it is for the national court to examine whether the refusal of the request for a licence is justified by objective considerations.

9–103   *(h)   Microsoft—interoperability, bundling and intellectual property*

The CFI considered the concept of interoperability and revisited the friction between intellectual property rights and art.82 in *Microsoft*.[227]

The case goes back to the end of 1998 when the Commission started investigating Microsoft following a complaint by Sun Microsystems (Sun), and found it had abused its market dominance in the client PC operating systems market and in the work group server operating systems market by (i) restricting interoperability between Windows and non-Microsoft work group servers; and (ii) tying its own media player with its personal computer operating system. The Commission imposed a record fine, an obligation to bring an end to infringement, a requirement to divulge all necessary interface information, and a requirement to update the disclosed information in parallel with the circulation of new versions of its relevant products. From an intellectual property perspective information protected by copyright would be given to competitors under a compulsory licence, with reasonable remuneration calculated on non-discriminatory terms. In 2006 the Commission imposed a further fine for non-compliance.

The CFI stated from the outset it would focus on the decision from the perspective of checking the accuracy of the facts, the completeness of the evidence, and whether the evidence supported the conclusions; however

---

[226] *IMS Health*, para.52.
[227] *Microsoft Corp v Commission of the European Communities* (T-201/04) [2007] 5 C.M.L.R. 11. This was an application for annulment of Commission Decision 2007/53/EC of 24 March 2004 relating to a proceeding pursuant to art.82 EC and art.54 of the EEA Agreement against Microsoft Corp. (Case COMP/C-3/37.792—*Microsoft* [2007] OJ L32/23).

5. THE APPLICATION OF ARTICLE 82

insofar as the Commission's decision was the result of complex technical appraisals, Community Courts should not substitute their own assessment of matters of fact for the Commission's.

(i) The indispensability requirement. The first part of the judgment focused on the indispensability of the interface protocols. Following an essential facilities reasoning, the CFI concurred with the Commission that Microsoft's operating system has become the de facto standard and access to it was necessary for the operators in the market for work servers.

9–104

Consequently the Court accepted that there was a risk of eliminating competition in the market for work servers.

(ii) The applicable standard. Here Microsoft had argued that in cases involving intellectual property rights a stricter test had to be applied requiring a "high probability" to eliminate competition. The court rejected the argument:

9–105

> "Microsoft's complaint is purely one of terminology and is wholly irrelevant. The expressions 'risk of elimination of competition' and 'likely to eliminate competition' are used without distinction by the Community judicature to reflect the same idea, namely that Article 82 EC does not apply only from the time when there is no more, or practically no more, competition on the market. If the Commission were required to wait until competitors were eliminated from the market, or until their elimination was sufficiently imminent, before being able to take action under Article 82 EC, that would clearly run counter to the objective of that provision, which is to maintain undistorted competition in the common market and, in particular, to safeguard the competition that still exists on the relevant market."[228]

The CFI added that because the market was characterised by significant network effects and the elimination of competition would be difficult to reverse.

Further what had to be established was the likelihood of eliminating all effective competition on the market; "a marginal presence in certain niches on the market cannot suffice to substantiate the existence of such competition".[229]

(iii) Refusal to licence an intellectual property right. Revisiting the *Volvo v Veng*[230] and *IMS*[231] discussion the CFI accepted that:

9–106

---

[228] *Microsoft*, para.561.
[229] *Microsoft*, para.563.
[230] *AB Volvo* (238/87) [1988] E.C.R. 6211.
[231] *IMS Health GmbH & Co OHG v NDC Health GmbH & Co KG* (C-418/01) [2004] E.C.R. I-5039.

> "the fact that the holder of an intellectual property right can exploit that right solely for his own benefit constitutes the very substance of his exclusive right. Accordingly, a simple refusal, even on the part of an undertaking in a dominant position, to grant a licence to a third party cannot in itself constitute an abuse of a dominant position within the meaning of Article 82 EC. It is only when it is accompanied by exceptional circumstances such as those hitherto envisaged in the case-law that such a refusal can be characterised as abusive and that, accordingly, it is permissible, in the public interest in maintaining effective competition on the market, to encroach upon the exclusive right of the holder of the intellectual property right by requiring him to grant licences to third parties seeking to enter or remain on that market. It must be borne in mind that it has been established above that such exceptional circumstances were present in this case."[232]

The CFI also rejected an argument based on the secrecy of the relevant technology. It accepted the finding of the Commission that it was normal practice for operators in the industry to disclose to third parties the information which would facilitate interoperability with their products and Microsoft itself had followed that practice until it was sufficiently established on the work group server operating systems market.

Note, too, the broad approach followed by the CFI as in relation to the new product argument:

> "The circumstance relating to the appearance of a new product, as envisaged in Magill and IMS Health, paragraph 107 above, cannot be the only parameter which determines whether a refusal to license an intellectual property right is capable of causing prejudice to consumers within the meaning of Article 82(b) EC. As that provision states, such prejudice may arise where there is a limitation not only of production or markets, but also of technical development."[233]

9–107   In any case the CFI had also stressed that the existence of potential consumer demand could satisfy the new product condition.

It found that Microsoft had not demonstrated the existence of any objective justification for its refusal to disclose the interoperability at issue and that the exceptional circumstances identified by the Court of Justice in *Magill*[234] and *IMS Health* were also present in this case.

9–108   **(iv) The media player bundling.** The CFI accepted the Commission's finding that software developers who wrote applications that relied on a media player had incentives to write foremost to Windows Media Player. The

---

[232] *Microsoft*, para.691.
[233] *Microsoft*, para.647.
[234] *Radio Telefís Eireann (RTE) and Independent Television Publications Ltd (ITP)* (C-241/91 P & C-242/91 P) [1995] E.C.R. I-808

5. THE APPLICATION OF ARTICLE 82

ubiquity of the Windows Media Player, by virtue of the bundling, also had effects on adjacent markets, such as media players on wireless information devices, set-top boxes, DRM solutions and online music delivery.

The CFI also paid attention to the considerable rise of the market share of the media player that had contributed to the bundling.

In short it accepted that Windows was used as a distribution channel to ensure a significant competitive advantage on the media players market; because of the bundling Microsoft's competitors were a priori at a disadvantage even if their products were inherently better than Windows Media Player; Microsoft interfered with the normal competitive process which would benefit users by ensuring quicker cycles of innovation as a consequence of unfettered competition on the merits; bundling increased the content and applications barriers to entry, which protected Windows, and facilitated the erection of such barriers for Windows Media Player; Microsoft shielded itself from effective competition from vendors of potentially more efficient media players who could challenge its position, and thus reduced the talent and capital invested in innovation of media players; through bundling, Microsoft could expand its position in adjacent media-related software markets and weaken effective competition, to the detriment of consumers; and, through bundling, Microsoft sent signals which deterred innovation in any technologies in which it might conceivably take an interest and which it might tie with Windows in the future.

Following a similar analysis to the one regarding interoperability the Court rejected Microsoft's argument that its behaviour could be objectively justified.

(i) Syfait—refusal to supply 9–109

As we have already seen in the chapter on parallel imports[235] the market for pharmaceutical products continues to challenge the efficacy of the common market and test both the functions and the limitations of intellectual property rights in Europe. There are still wide price variations between Member States. This has meant increased activity from parallel importers and a significant body of European jurisprudence in this area. The same applies to the Court's jurisprudence on competition.

In *Syfait v GlaxoSmithKline*[236] the Court considered the applicability of art.82 on GlaxoSmithKline's refusal to supply wholesalers in Greece with its products branded under Imigran, Lamictal, and Serevent. Because the prices in Greece were significantly lower these wholesalers were parallel exporting

---

[235] See for example the Opinion of A.G. Sharpston in *Boehringer Ingelheim KG, Boehringer Ingelheim Pharma GmbH & Co KG, Glaxo Group Ltd v Swingward Ltd and Boehringer Ingelheim KG, Boehringer Ingelheim Pharma GmbH & Co KG, Glaxo Group Ltd, Smithkline Beecham Plc, Beecham Group plc, Smithkline and French Laboratories Ltd, Eli Lilly and Co, The Wellcome Foundation Ltd v Dowelhurst Ltd* (C-348/04), discussed in Ch.8.
[236] *Synetairismos Farmakopoion Aitolias & Akarnanias (Syfait) v GlaxoSmithKline Plc* (C-53/03) [2005] E.C.R. I-4609.

805

the products to other Member States. The wholesalers complained to the national Greek Competition Commission which referred two questions to the Court of Justice.

The first question asked whether a dominant player's refusal to supply constitutes an abuse of its dominant position in all cases even where the relevant national market is distorted by State intervention. If this was not an abuse in all cases, the second question sought to clarify the criteria for establishing whether it constituted an abuse in specific cases, referring, for example, to the percentage of exported products relative to national demand, the loss of the manufacturer relative to its turnover, the benefit to the patient, or the interest of national insurance bodies.

9–110 Advocate General Jacobs started by admitting that whether the Greek Competition Commission constituted a "court or tribunal" entitled to make a reference under art.234 was a difficult, he accepted however that its decision would be of a judicial nature and turned to the substance of the case.

Following *IMS*[237] he found that refusal to supply, even where the intention behind it is to limit parallel trade, does not necessarily constitute an abuse of a dominant position. The ultimate question should be whether "such a refusal is in all circumstances justified".[238]

Turning to the second question he identified three relevant factors: regulation of price and distribution, impact on manufacturers, and impact on purchasers and patients.

9–111 Regarding regulation of price and distribution he noted that Member States influence the price of pharmaceutical products leading to price differences between Member States. At the same time there are obligations imposed on manufacturers and wholesalers under national and Community[239] laws to guarantee the availability of pharmaceutical products. These obligations influence both the manufacturers' ability to refuse to supply a market and the wholesalers' ability to parallel export.

The Advocate General then conducted a thorough economic analysis of the market for pharmaceuticals in order to delineate the second factor. The price of pharmaceuticals reflects the relatively low marginal cost of production but also the high fixed costs of research and development, including risk. It can be uniform or it can vary between markets:

"It is therefore rational for an undertaking to supply its products on any market where the price is fixed above variable cost. The mere fact that a product is marketed on a given market at a given price does not mean that a pharmaceuticals undertaking could recoup its total costs if that price were generalised across the whole of the Community."[240]

---

[237] *IMS Health GmbH & Co OHG v NDC Health GmbH & Co KG* (C-418/01) [2004] E.C.R. I-5039.
[238] Point 71 of the Opinion of A.G. Jacobs.
[239] Directive 2001/83 [2001] OJ L311/67 as amended by Directive 2004/27 [2004] OJ L136/34.
[240] Point 89 of the Opinion of A.G. Jacobs.

5. THE APPLICATION OF ARTICLE 82

Manufacturers may accept a lower price in certain markets, but will not do so if the products are then exported to a higher price market, because parallel exports would undermine recoupment of the fixed costs by higher priced sales. He recognised that forcing manufacturers to supply wholesalers in lower price markets would lead to higher prices, withdrawal of products, or delays in product launches in these markets. Consumer welfare would suffer in these cases.

9–112 The finding on consumer welfare led to the Advocate General's finding in respect of the third factor, the impact on purchasers and patients. He noted that distributors benefit more than consumers or purchasers from parallel trade. Purchasers are often public bodies that can set prices and parallel trade may undermine the agreed prices. The consumers are patients that often and to varying degrees do not pay for pharmaceutical products directly; for them the impact from parallel trade is limited.

Advocate General Jacobs concluded that "a restriction of supply by a dominant pharmaceutical undertaking in order to limit parallel trade is capable of justification as a reasonable and proportionate measure in defence of that undertaking's commercial interests".[241] He stressed though that this conclusion was "highly specific to the pharmaceutical industry in its current condition and to the particular type of conduct at issue in the present proceedings".[242] In particular it was highly unlikely that restrictions of supply could be justified in other sectors, even in the pharmaceutical sector conduct "which more clearly and directly partitioned the common market would not be open to a similar line of defence".[243]

Unfortunately, the Court chose not to look at the substance of the questions. The case fell in the first obstacle, as the Court did not follow the finding of the Advocate General that the Greek Competition Commission constituted a court or a tribunal under art.234. The Commission was not wholly independent of the Greek Government and its proceedings would not lead to a decision of a judicial nature.

(j) Lelos—revisiting Syfait

9–113

The issue of refusing to supply wholesalers engaged in parallel imports resurfaced in *Lelos v GlaxoSmithKline*.[244]

---

[241] Point 100 of the Opinion of A.G. Jacobs.
[242] Point 101 of the Opinion of A.G. Jacobs.
[243] Point 103 of the Opinion of A.G. Jacobs.
[244] *Sot Lelos & Sia EE* (C-468/06), *Farmakemporiki AE* (C-469/06), *Konstantinos Xidias & Sia OE* (C-470/06), *Farmakemporiki AE* (C-471/06), *Ionas Stroumsas EPE* (C-472/06), *Ionas Stroumsas EPE* (C-473/06), *Farmakapothiki Farma-Group Messinias AE* (C-474/06), *KP Marinopoulos AE* (C-475/06), *KP Marinopoulos AE* (C-476/06), *Kokkoris D Tsanas K EPE* (C-477/06), *Kokkoris D Tsanas K EPE* (C-478/06) *v GlaxoSmithKline AEVE*, formerly Glaxowellcome AEVE.

As described above in *Syfait*,[245] GSK, the Greek subsidiary of GlaxoSmithKline, the holder of marketing authorisations in Greece for a number of pharmaceutical products, including Imigran, Lamictal, and Serevent, available in Greece on prescription only. Lelos and the other appellants were buying the GSK products for distribution in Greece and other Member States. GSK at some point stopped supplying the appellants—claiming there were shortages for which it was not responsible—and started supplying itself the Greek market. At a later stage GSK started supplying again the appellants but with limited quantities. GSK had applied to the Competition Commission for a negative clearance according to Greek law whereas the appellants had also applied for a declaration that GSK's policy constituted an abuse of a dominant position.

Following court proceedings and the intervention of the National Organisation for Medicines a case came before Efetio Athinon (Court of Appeal, Athens). In the meantime the Competition Commission had referred the Syfait[246] questions that the Court had declined to answer. The Court of Appeal however decided to stay proceeding and refer the following questions:

"1. Where the refusal of an undertaking holding a dominant position to meet fully the orders sent to it by pharmaceuticals wholesalers is due to its intention to limit their export activity and, thereby, the harm caused to it by parallel trade, does the refusal constitute per se an abuse within the meaning of Article 82 EC? Is the answer to that question affected by the fact that the parallel trade is particularly profitable for the wholesalers because of the different prices, resulting from State intervention, in the Member States of the European Union, that is to say by the fact that pure conditions of competition do not prevail in the pharmaceuticals market, but a regime which is governed to a large extent by State intervention? Is it ultimately the duty of a national competition authority to apply Community competition rules in the same way to markets which function competitively and those in which competition is distorted by State intervention?

2. If the Court holds that limitation of parallel trade, for the reasons set out above, does not constitute an abusive practice in every case where it is engaged in by an undertaking holding a dominant position, how is possible abuse to be assessed?
In particular:

(a) Do the percentage by which normal domestic consumption is exceeded and/or the loss suffered by an undertaking holding a

---

[245] *Synetairismos Farmakopoion Aitolias & Akarnanias (Syfait) v GlaxoSmithKline Plc* (C-53/03) [2005] E.C.R. I-4609.
[246] *Synetairismos Farmakopoion Aitolias & Akarnanias (Syfait)* (C-53/03) [2005] E.C.R. I-4609.

5. THE APPLICATION OF ARTICLE 82

dominant position compared with its total turnover and total profits constitute appropriate criteria? If so, how are the level of that percentage and the level of that loss determined (the latter as a percentage of turnover and total profits), above which the conduct in question may be abusive?

(b) Is an approach entailing the balancing of interests appropriate, and, if so, what are the interests to be compared?
In particular:

   (i) is the answer affected by the fact that the ultimate consumer/patient derives limited financial advantage from the parallel trade and

   (ii) is account to be taken, and to what extent, of the interests of social insurance bodies in cheaper medicinal products?

(c) What other criteria and approaches are considered appropriate in the present case?"[247]

(a) The Opinion of the Advocate General 9–114

Advocate General Ruiz-Jarabo Colomer characterised the case as a boomerang that came back to the Court and expressed his trepidation about having to write a second Opinion that appeared to be "the second part of somebody else's novel".[248]

The Advocate General started by expressing some criticism regarding the formulation of the questions. First, there was an issue as to whether GSK indeed held a dominant position in relation to some of the products concerned according to the view of the Competition commission. He stressed that if that was the case then the Court should have narrowed the scope of the questions. "As investigating the position of an undertaking in a particular market and defining the relevant market entail an examination of the facts, it must be left to the referring court and there can be no question of the Court of Justice giving its view on the matter."[249] Secondly, the expression "to meet fully the orders" did not describe accurately the factual context of the case. He believed that the questions should move back from a broader theoretical context to that characterised by the circumstances that gave rise to the legal questions.

Accordingly he attempted a practical reformulation of the questions by introducing headings and providing a broader legal contextual analysis.

He started by considering the relevant Community case law, highlighting 9–115 the parallels between the current case and *Commercial Solvents* on the one

---

[247] Lelos, para.23.
[248] Point 3 of the Opinion of A.G. Ruiz-Jarabo Colomer.
[249] Point 28 of the Opinion of A.G. Ruiz-Jarabo Colomer.

hand[250] and *United Brands* on the other.[251] The case law showed that a dominant undertaking which avoided supplying goods, particularly when there are no substitutes, and reserved to itself the parallel export market, is committing an abuse under art.82 EC.

To determine whether this constituted an abuse per se he considered a number of factors.

He accepted that abuse was an objectively assessed concept according to the case of the Court. Still, subjective elements could indicate that an anti-competitive outcome is being sought and, also, in order to demonstrate that a breach of art.82 EC has taken place it was sufficient to prove that the abusive conduct of the dominant undertaking tended to restrict competition or, in other words, was capable of having such an effect.[252] "Therefore, the closer the undertaking in a dominant position is to hindering competition in the market, the stronger the presumption of abuse."[253]

9–116 Despite the strong inference of infringement he went on to identify a methodology for recognising abuse.

There were three types of behaviour that the Court had considered in its jurisprudence to be anti-competitive: imposing exclusive supply obligations on purchasers by a dominant company; loyalty rebates; and, predatory pricing. The Court had always been prepared to listen to arguments defending the above.[254] "However, apart from specific statements focusing on the circumstances of each individual case, the Court has not given any general rules indicating that abuses per se do not fall within the article of the Treaty dealing with abuse of a dominant position."[255] He then went on to try and identify and delineate some relevant rules.[256]

Following this analysis he suggested that the answer to the first question should be that "abusive conduct per se does not sit well with Article 82 EC, and consequently the first question put by the Efetio Athinon should not be answered in the affirmative".[257]

9–117 In order to respond to the second question, A.G. Ruiz-Jarabo Colomer suggested three routes that had to be explored: grounds relating to the market in which they are operating; the legitimate protection of their business interests; and proof of net positive economic effect.

Accordingly the answer to that question should be that:

"when an undertaking in a dominant position reduces the number of wholesalers' orders which it processes to the levels necessary to meet demand in

---

[250] *Instituto Chemioterapico Italiano SpA and Commercial Solvents Corp v Commission* (6/73 & 7/73) [1974] E.C.R. 223.
[251] *United Brands Co and United Brands Continental BV v Commission* (27/76) [1978] E.C.R. 207
[252] Citing *British Airways v Commission* (C-95/04 P) [2007] E.C.R. I-2331.
[253] Point 51 of the Opinion of A.G. Ruiz-Jarabo Colomer.
[254] Citing for example *DLG* (C-250/92) [1994] E.C.R. I-5641.
[255] Point 61 of the Opinion of A.G. Ruiz-Jarabo Colomer.
[256] See Point 65 of the Opinion of A.G. Ruiz-Jarabo Colomer.
[257] Point 76 of the Opinion of A.G. Ruiz-Jarabo Colomer.

5. THE APPLICATION OF ARTICLE 82

a domestic market, with the intention of preventing parallel imports to other Member States by such wholesalers, this in principle constitutes an abuse of a dominant position within the meaning of Article 82 EC. However, the potentially abusive undertaking can point to any matters it considers relevant in order to justify its behaviour objectively ..."[258]

(b) The judgment of the Court   9–118

The Court, sitting in Grand Chamber, accepted that the refusal by an undertaking occupying a dominant position on the market of a given product to meet the orders of an existing customer constituted abuse of that dominant position "where, without any objective justification, that conduct is liable to eliminate a trading party as a competitor".[259] This would also cover cases involving exports to other Member States and the Court underlined the pro-parallel import stance it had often adopted. Parallel imports enjoy a certain amount of protection in Community law because they encourage trade and help reinforce competition.

It was willing however to consider the peculiarities of the market for pharmaceutical products.

It turned first to the consequences of parallel trade for the ultimate consumers of medicinal products and accepted that:

"even in the Member States where the prices of medicines are subject to State regulation, parallel trade is liable to exert pressure on prices and, consequently, to create financial benefits not only for the social health insurance funds, but equally for the patients concerned, for whom the proportion of the price of medicines for which they are responsible will be lower. At the same time, as the Commission notes, parallel trade in medicines from one Member State to another is likely to increase the choice available to entities in the latter Member State which obtain supplies of medicines by means of a public procurement procedure, in which the parallel importers can offer medicines at lower prices".[260]

It then considered the other side of the coin, the impact of State price and   9–119
supply regulation in the pharmaceuticals sector. It highlighted that this remained a non-harmonised area but also acknowledged that the control exercised by Member States over the selling prices or the reimbursement of medicinal products did not entirely remove the prices of those products from the law of supply and demand. It also reminded that market integration was amongst the objectives of the Treaty.

---

[258] Points 121–122 of the Opinion of A.G. Ruiz-Jarabo Colomer.
[259] *Lelos*, para.34, citing *Istituto Chemioterapico Italiano, Commercial Solvents v Commission* (6/73 & 7/73) [1974] E.C.R. 223; and *United Brands and United Brands Continentaal v Commission* (26/76) [1978] E.C.R. 207.
[260] *Lelos*, para.56.

So, "there can be no escape from the prohibition laid down in Article 82 EC for the practices of an undertaking in a dominant position which are aimed at avoiding all parallel exports from a Member State to other Member States, practices which, by partitioning the national markets, neutralise the benefits of effective competition in terms of the supply and the prices that those exports would obtain for final consumers in the other Member States."[261]

Balancing its approach it added that the application of competition rules could not be precluded, nevertheless State intervention was one of the factors triggering parallel trade.

9–120 It concluded that: "even if the degree of regulation regarding the price of medicines cannot prevent any refusal by a pharmaceuticals company in a dominant position to meet orders sent to it by wholesalers involved in parallel exports from constituting an abuse, such a company must nevertheless be in a position to take steps that are reasonable and in proportion to the need to protect its own commercial interests."[262]

For the appraisal of whether the refusal by a pharmaceuticals company to supply wholesalers involved in parallel exports constituted a reasonable and proportionate measure in relation to the threat that those exports represent to its legitimate commercial interests, it had to be ascertained whether the orders of the wholesalers were out of the ordinary.[263]

Within the context of the pharmaceutical industry the Court held that:

"although a pharmaceuticals company in a dominant position, in a Member State where prices are relatively low, cannot be allowed to cease to honour the ordinary orders of an existing customer for the sole reason that that customer, in addition to supplying the market in that Member State, exports part of the quantities ordered to other Member States with higher prices, it is none the less permissible for that company to counter in a reasonable and proportionate way the threat to its own commercial interests potentially posed by the activities of an undertaking which wishes to be supplied in the first Member State with significant quantities of products that are essentially destined for parallel export."[264]

The answer to the questions:

"as a whole should be that Article 82 EC must be interpreted as meaning that an undertaking occupying a dominant position on the relevant market for medicinal products which, in order to put a stop to parallel exports carried out by certain wholesalers from one Member State to

---
[261] *Lelos*, para.66.
[262] *Lelos*, para.69.
[263] See, to that effect, *United Brands and United Brands Continentaal v Commission*.
[264] *Lelos*, para.71.

5. THE APPLICATION OF ARTICLE 82

other Member States, refuses to meet ordinary orders from those wholesalers is abusing its dominant position. It is for the national court to ascertain whether the orders are ordinary in the light of both the size of those orders in relation to the requirements of the market in the first Member State and the previous business relations between that undertaking and the wholesalers concerned."[265]

(3) Der Grüne Punkt—dominance and trade marks—the function of the sign

9–121

A case involving a logo, *Der Grüne Punkt—Duales System Deutschland GmbH v Commission of the European Communities*[266]—is one of the most recent cases in which the Court dealt with the abuse of a dominant position. The case came before the Court as an appeal against a judgment of the Court of First Instance.[267]

Under German law manufacturers and distributors of packaging were required to take back the packaging they had placed on the German market. Duales System Deutschland (DSD) provided such a service and allowed them to benefit from an "exemption system" rather than "self manage" packaging as provided in the relevant Ordinance. The "exemption system" had to be approved by the relevant state authority. To benefit from the exemption system they had to place the Der Grüne Punkt logo (DGP)—a registered trade mark—on their packaging and pay DSD a fee. DSD's exemption system covered the entire territory of Germany through a number of subcontractors; it employed a standard trade mark agreement covering use of the logo and payment of the corresponding fee that was calculated on the basis of the weight and volume of the packaging and the type of material used. The fee aimed to cover collection, sorting, recovery, and administrative costs.

Following proceedings before the Commission DSD had committed to measures assuring that users of alternative exemption systems or those who self managed their packaging would not have to pay the fee; however it required evidence in cases of part recovery of packaging. According to the Commission the fact that the fee charged by DSD was not determined according to actual use of its system but calculated on the basis of the number of packages bearing the DGP trade mark constituted an abuse of a dominant position, since in a number of possible scenarios involving both DSD and another exemption or self-management system, manufacturers and distributors would have to place the logo on all the packaging and pay

---

[265] *Lelos*, para.77.
[266] Case C-385/07 P
[267] *Duales System Deutschland v Commission* (T-151/01) [2007] E.C.R. II-1607 that concerned a challenge of a decision of the Commission Decision on an art. 82 proceeding, Case COMP D3/34493—*DSD* ([2001] OJ L166/1).

9–122 the fee for the whole packaging although DSD would only recover part of it or provide for separate production lines and distribution channels.

Accordingly, the principal measure imposed on DSD was the requirement not to charge any licence fee for quantities of packaging put into circulation in Germany carrying the DGP logo for which the exemption service was not used and for which the obligations imposed by Packaging Ordinance had demonstrably been fulfilled in another way.

DSD challenged the decision before the Court of First Instance without success and appealed further to the Court of Justice. The Court had to consider a number of issues focusing from a substantive perspective on whether DSD could rely on the logo to justify the fee and from a procedural perspective on whether the CFI had failed to decide the case within a reasonable time since the proceedings covered a period of five years and nine months.

9–123 *(a) The Opinion of the Advocate General*

Following a thorough review of the factual context and the judgment of the CFI, A.G. Bot looked at the abuse of the dominant position issue.

Reviewing the judgment of the CFI he agreed that the DGP logo had an economic value and that merely placing that logo on packaging was likely to have a price however a distinction had to be made between a fee that covered only the costs associated with the actual use of the system and a fee for merely using the DGP logo, "which, being different in nature, is merely a possibility for negotiation in a completely different sphere and extraneous to the matter before the Court of First Instance".[268]

9–124 **(i) The trade mark agreement.** Specifically on the trade mark agreement he adopted the CFI's position that it was the fee that was considered to be abusive not the requirement that the manufacturer or distributor wishing to use the DSD system had to affix the DGP logo to each piece of notified packaging; in particular the imbalance between the fee and the service actually provided, since DSD charged a fee even where certain packaging was taken back by a competitor system. According to the system the fee should cover the costs of collecting, sorting and recovering the packaging, and administrative costs.

The CFI, according to the Advocate General, had not interpreted the Trade Mark Agreement as having the effect of granting a licence to use the DGP logo to the participating undertakings for the packaging not taken back or recovered by the DSD system. Indeed, the logo had no relationship with the Trade Mark Agreement, it played an identifying role and informed the consumer as to what he had to do with the packaging.

---

[268] Point 97 of the Opinion of A.G. Bot.

5. THE APPLICATION OF ARTICLE 82

The peculiar function of the logo meant that it could co-exist with other logos, allowing manufacturers or distributors to participate in other exemption or self management programmes, meaning that the decision of the Commission did not constitute "a disproportionate impairment of the trade mark right or, in any event, an impairment which is not justified by the need to prevent an abuse of a dominant position within the meaning of Article 82 EC".[269]

9–125 DSD had argued against coexistence and in favour of exclusivity claiming that consumers would be deceived as a result of contradictory information appearing on the packaging. However, the Trade Mark Agreement concerned manufacturers and distributors of packaging rather than consumers.

DSD further argued that if packaging not disposed of by its own system was allowed to carry the DGP logo there was a risk that the logo would lose its distinctiveness. Advocate General Bot agreed with the CFI regarding the function of the logo. The possibility of cumulative marking simply meant that DSD and another system could be applied for the same piece of packaging.

9–126 **(ii) The effect of trade mark law—the function of the logo.** Turning his attention more closely to the effect of trade mark law the Advocate General said that the specific object of trade mark law was, in particular, to guarantee to the owner that he had the exclusive right to use that mark for the purpose of putting a product on the market for the first time and thus to protect him against competitors wishing to take unfair advantage of the status and reputation of the trade mark by selling products illegally bearing it. This was linked with the exclusive rights of the trade mark proprietor entitling to stop third parties from using identical or similar signs.

However, in this case the undertakings participating in the DSD system for only part of their packaging or for packaging placed on the market of another Member State could not be regarded as competitors of DSD or as third parties improperly selling goods covered by the DGP logo. In the first two cases the manufacturers and distributors had entered into an agreement with DSD; in the third case they were holders on the territory of another Member State of a licence to use the logo. This was the essence of the system as devised by DSD.

In practice, here, the essential function of the logo was to ensure that the packaging could be taken back by the DSD system. The logo did not fit into the classic scheme of trade mark law that allowed consumers to choose between products. He accepted that it could be closer to the scheme if it indicated a characteristic of the product, for example that it was recyclable.

9–127 **(iii) The competition issues.** The Advocate General highlighted that, according to the CFI, the abuse consisted in requiring payment of a fee for

---
[269] Point 131 of the Opinion of A.G. Bot.

the total quantity of packaging carrying the DGP logo and put into circulation in Germany. Accordingly the obligations imposed by the Commission did not amount to an obligation to grant a licence to use the mark "but merely to require it not to charge a fee on the total amount of packaging bearing [that] logo where it is shown that all or only some of that packaging has been taken back or recovered through another system".[270] He also agreed with the CFI that there was no need to insert an explanatory text on the packaging according to the principle of proportionality. The function of the sign combined with the unpredictability characterising consumer behaviour would render it irrelevant.

9–128 **(iv) The "reasonable time" claim.** The Advocate General accepted that where "where the stakes are high in financial terms, the case must ... be dealt with rapidly".[271] In this case however DSD had not been fined by the Commission and the decision had not affected its activities:

> "The importance of the case is therefore, in my view, real for DSD, as it necessarily has an impact on that undertaking, but it is not fundamental, as it does not threaten the economic survival of its activity."[272]

On the other hand the complexity of the case did not justify the length of the proceedings. And the behaviour of DSD had contributed, albeit not drastically, to the delay. Overall, the period of the delay should be considered unreasonable.

Failure to observe the reasonable time requirement could only give rise to a claim for compensation for the harm caused. Here though there was no economic harm. The only satisfaction DSD could enjoy was the recognition of breach of a Community principle. DSD, he accepted, could still bring an action for compensation before the CFI.

9–129 *(b) The judgment of the Court*

The Court delivered its judgment sitting in a Grand Chamber and considering systematically all the grounds of appeal.

First, it rejected the claim that there were contradictions in the judgment of the CFI considering the fee charged by DSD. It found that the fee that DSD might charge for use of the logo on its own was a separate issue from the fee it charged in respect of the packaging that was actually taken back and recovered by DSD under the Trade Mark Agreement.

It also accepted the CFI's reading of the Trade Mark Agreement and the fact that its provisions concerning the fee were regarded to be abusive.

---

[270] Point 224 of the Opinion of A.G. Bot.
[271] Point 273 of the Opinion of A.G. Bot.
[272] Point 279 of the Opinion of A.G. Bot.

5. THE APPLICATION OF ARTICLE 82

The decision of the Commission had not criticised the requirement that manufacturers or distributors wishing to use the DSD system had to affix the logo to each piece of notified packaging intended for domestic consumption.

Thirdly, it agreed with the CFI that the question whether an item of packaging did, or did not, bear the DGP logo was not determinative, the only point at issue was whether the quantities of material for recovery put into circulation by the manufacturer or distributor were actually taken back and recovered. It also found that DSD had not established that the affixing of the DGP logo to packaging processed under a different system ran counter to that objective of transparency. "The affixing of that logo to packaging notified to DSD indicates clearly to consumers and to the relevant authorities, irrespective of the question whether that packaging will actually be processed under that system or under another system, that the packaging in question is no longer covered by the obligation that it be taken back at points of sale or in the immediate vicinity of them but has been notified to DSD."[273] In essence this was the function of the logo.

(i) The exclusive trade mark use argument. The fourth plea concerned the challenges based on Community Trade Mark law. Here the Court elaborated further on use and distinguished between the use of the DGP logo by DSD's contractual partners and its possible use by other third parties.

9–130

In relation to the first type of use the Court noted that art.5 of Directive 89/104 did not cover circumstances in which a third party uses a trade mark with the consent of its proprietor. Clearly, DSD could not rely on that provision. The Court noted that according to art.8(2) of Directive 89/104 a trade mark proprietor might invoke its rights against a licensee contravening the terms of the licensing agreement. However, in this case DSD itself had set up the system serviced by the Trade Mark Agreement.

Further it rejected the claim that the measures imposed by the Commission allowed partial free use of the logo. The decision had targeted solely the fee charged for services not provided by DSD. And, at the end, if there was a price for the application of the logo on its own this could be negotiated between the parties.

Finally, the court noted, use of the DGP logo by third parties was not covered in the Commission's decision and the judgment of the CFI.

(ii) The competition argument. The fifth ground of appeal was based on art.82 EC. The Court reminded that setting a disproportionate value of the services provided fee was an abuse of dominance.[274] Charging a fee for a service that was not provided should be seen under the same light.

9–131

---

[273] *Der Grüne Punkt*, para.118.
[274] Citing *British Leyland v Commission* (226/84) [1986] E.C.R. 3263 as an example.

And obliging DSD not to charge any licence fee for partial quantities of sales packaging bearing the DGP logo and put into circulation in Germany, but for which (i) the exemption service was not used and (ii) the obligations imposed by the German authorities had demonstrably been fulfilled in another way, was the consequence of the finding of an abuse of a dominant position and of the exercise of the Commission's power to put an end to the infringement. This did not constitute a compulsory licence since it did not affect DSD's freedom to choose the parties with which it entered into a Trade Mark Agreement.

9–132   (iii) **The principle of proportionality.** The Court repeated that there was no obligation imposed on DSD to grant the licence to use the DGP logo. It also agreed with the CFI that it was impossible to make the a priori distinction DSD wanted to make between packaging bearing the logo that would be processed by the DSD system on the one hand and mixed or self-managed systems on the other. It was impossible to determine in advance the route that an item of packaging would follow.

9–133   (iv) **Procedural irregularities—reasonable time.** The Court rejected the seventh plea focusing on CFI's request for additional evidence. The Court held that this fell well within the jurisdiction of the CFI.

On the final point regarding the right to have the case dealt with within a reasonable time the Court noted that it was entrusted with the jurisdiction to verify whether a breach of procedure adversely affecting the appellant's interests was committed by the CFI and that the general principles of Community law have been complied with.[275] The right to a fair and public hearing within a reasonable time by an independent and impartial tribunal established by law was covered in art.6(1) of the European Convention on the Protection of Human Rights and Fundamental Freedoms, recognised in art.47 of the Charter of Fundamental Rights of the European Union, and acknowledged by the jurisprudence of the Court.[276]

The reasonableness of the period for delivering judgment had to be appraised in the light of the circumstances specific to each case. The relevant criteria included the complexity of the case and the conduct of the parties but the list was not exhaustive and the assessment of reasonableness did not require a systematic examination of all of them where the duration of the proceedings appeared justified in the light of one of them.[277]

Here, the length of the proceedings, five years and approximately 10 months, were not justified and there was a failure in the proceedings

---

[275] Citing *Baustahlgewebe v Commission*; and *TEAM v Commission* (C-13/99 P) [2000] E.C.R. I-4671.
[276] Citing *Chronopost and La Poste v UFEX* (C-341/06 P & C-342/06 P) [2008] E.C.R. I-0000.
[277] Citing, amongst others, *Efkon v Parliament and Council* (C-146/08 P); and *Limburgse Vinyl Maatschappij v Commission* (C-238/99 P, C-244/99 P, C-245/99 P, C-247/99 P, C-250/99 P to C-252/99 P & C-254/99 P) [2002] E.C.R. I-8375.

6. CONCLUSION

before the CFI. However, and following a purposive application of art.61 of the Statute of the Court of Justice that dealt with the effect of procedural irregularities, the Court held that in "so far as there is nothing to suggest that the failure to adjudicate within a reasonable time may have had an effect on the outcome of the dispute, the setting aside of the judgment under appeal would not remedy the infringement of the principle of effective legal protection committed by the Court of First Instance".[278]

In addition the Court could not allow an appellant to reopen the question of the existence of an infringement, on the sole ground that there was a failure to adjudicate within a reasonable time, where all the other pleas were unfounded.

The only potential remedy for DSD was to raise a claim for damages brought against the Community under arts 235 and 288 EC.

6. CONCLUSION

There are three particular points that need to be highlighted. **9–134**

First, that the starting point in the antagonistic relationship between trade mark law on the one hand and free movement of goods and competition rules on the other was competition. The fact that the majority of subsequent cases have been decided under the free movement rules does not mean that competition has become redundant. Following the case law of the Court the existence of intellectual property rights, including trade marks, is not in itself anti-competitive. The Court also appears to increasingly accept that there are benefits that the owner of an intellectual property enjoys, for example the opportunity to charge a higher price, that in themselves are not anti-competitive. What counts is whether the way these rights are exercised falls under what the Court will consider to be infringing the rules on competition.

Secondly, that a particular factual scenario could be decided one way under trade mark rules but another under competition rules.

Thirdly, that a number of competition considerations have been internalised into trade mark law. For example, as we have seen in Ch.4, whether a functional product feature or a geographical name can be protected as trade marks are, ultimately, competition questions the answer for which can be found in trade mark law.

---

[278] *Der Grüne Punkt*, para.193.

CHAPTER 10

THE SPILLOVER EFFECT

1.	Introduction	10–001
2.	Comparative Advertising	10–002
	(1) Toshiba—the interplay between trade marks and comparative advertising	10–005
	(2) Pippig—the contradictions of article 7(2) of Directive 84/450	10–025
	(3) Siemens—reconfirming the Court's permissive approach	10–040
	(4) DeLandtsheer Emmanuel—designations of origin—the competitive relationship	10–049
	(5) O2—use of a similar sign—the indispensability challenge	10–059
	(6) L'Oréal v Bellure—taking a step back?	10–065
3.	Geographical Indications	10–072
	(1) Feta—consumer confusion and a misappropriation rationale	10–072
	(2) Bavaria—the coexistence between trade mark and geographical indication protection	10–091
	(3) Grana Padano—trade marks v geographical indication—the concept of genericity	10–103
4.	The Budweiser Tetralogy	10–106
	(1) Geographical indications, bilateral agreements, and free movement of goods	10–107
	(2) Bud II—replaying Bud I	10–119
	(3) European trade mark law and the TRIPs Agreement—protecting trade names	10–133
	(4) The European Court of Human Rights—geographical indications, trade marks and property rights	10–155
5.	Conclusion	10–166

1. INTRODUCTION

Competition law and the free movement of goods principles have characte‑ **10–001**
rised the development of trade mark law in Europe. The aim of this chapter
is to provide examples of other interrelationships.

The first part considers the use of trade marks in comparative advertise‑
ments. We have seen in Ch.6 how comparative advertising rules have
affected the drawing of the limits of trade mark law. Here the other side of
the relationship is examined.

Chapter 4 considered whether a geographical name can function and be
protected as a trade mark and the limits of such protection. The second part

of this chapter gives a flavour of the system of protecting product designations as geographical indications of origin.

The third part is a good example of how one dispute between distinguishing signs can become the common theme of distinct and varied plots replayed before different European legal audiences and against revolving legal backgrounds.

2. COMPARATIVE ADVERTISING

10–002 Comparative advertising can be indirectly comparative, when an advertisement refers directly only to one brand but there is also indirect reference to competing products without mentioning specific brands, or directly comparative, when the comparison is between specific brands. In the latter case the advertisement may contain explicit references to a competing product or simply enable the viewer to recognise it without specifically mentioning it. Non-competing "referential" advertising refers to more than one brand but the products are not competing directly with each other; often the aim is to benefit from the "aura" of the better-known product.

Member States viewed comparative advertising from divergent perspectives with Germany, the most restrictive, and the United Kingdom, the most liberal, occupying the antithetical corners.

Finally, in 1997 the Misleading Advertising Directive (84/450) was amended by the Comparative Advertising Directive (97/55) in order to allow and regulate comparative advertising.[1] Being the result of a compromise the amendments could be read either way.

10–003 Article 2 defines advertising as "the making of a representation in any form in connection with a trade, business, craft or profession in order to promote the supply of goods or services, including immovable property, rights and obligations".

Article 2a defines comparative advertising as "any advertising which explicitly or by implication identifies a competitor or goods or services offered by a competitor".

According to art.2(2) misleading advertising is "any advertising which in any way, including its presentation, deceives or is likely to deceive the persons to whom it is addressed or whom it reaches and which, by reason of its deceptive nature, is likely to affect their economic behaviour or which, for those reasons, injures or is likely to injure a competitor".

10–004 Article 3 includes a list of factors that should, in particular, be considered for determining whether the advertisement is misleading; the list covers information regarding:

---

[1] Council Directive 84/450/EEC relating to the approximation of the laws, regulations and administrative provisions of the Member States concerning misleading advertising [1984] OJ L250/17 as amended by Directive 97/55/EC amending Directive 84/450/EEC concerning misleading advertising so as to include comparative advertising [1997] OJ L290/18.

2. COMPARATIVE ADVERTISING

"(a) the characteristics of goods or services, such as their availability, nature, execution, composition, method and date of manufacture or provision, fitness for purpose, uses, quantity, specification, geographical or commercial origin or the results to be expected from their use, or the results and material features of tests or checks carried out on the goods or services; (b) the price or the manner in which the price is calculated, and the conditions on which the goods are supplied or the services provided; (c) the nature, attributes and rights of the advertiser, such as his identity and assets, his qualifications and ownership of industrial, commercial or intellectual property rights or his awards and distinctions."

Article 3(a)(1) provides that comparative advertising shall "as far as the comparison is concerned, be permitted when the following conditions are met:

(a) it is not misleading according to Articles 2(2), 3 and 7(1);

(b) it compares goods or services meeting the same needs or intended for the same purpose;

(c) it objectively compares one or more material, relevant, verifiable and representative features of those goods and services, which may include price;

(d) it does not create confusion in the market place between the advertiser and a competitor or between the advertiser's trade marks, trade names, other distinguishing marks, goods or services and those of a competitor;

(e) it does not discredit or denigrate the trade marks, trade names, other distinguishing marks, goods, services, activities, or circumstances of a competitor;

(f) for products with designation of origin, it relates in each case to products with the same designation;

(g) it does not take unfair advantage of the reputation of a trade mark, trade name or other distinguishing marks of a competitor or of the designation of origin of competing products;

(h) it does not present goods or services as imitations or replicas of goods or services bearing a protected trade mark or trade name."

Note too that art.7 leaves some freedom to Member States:

"1. This Directive shall not preclude Member States from retaining or adopting provisions with a view to ensuring more extensive protection, with regard to misleading advertising, for consumers, persons carrying on a trade, business, craft or profession, and the general public.

2. Paragraph 1 shall not apply to comparative advertising as far as the comparison is concerned.

3. The provisions of this Directive shall apply without prejudice to Community provisions on advertising for specific products and/or services or to restrictions or prohibitions on advertising in particular media.

4. The provisions of this Directive concerning comparative advertising shall not oblige Member States which, in compliance with the provisions of the Treaty, maintain or introduce advertising bans regarding certain goods or services, whether imposed directly or by a body or organization responsible, under the law of the Member States, for regulating the exercise of a commercial, industrial, craft or professional activity, to permit comparative advertising regarding those goods or services. Where these bans are limited to particular media, the Directive shall apply to the media not covered by these bans.

5. Nothing in this Directive shall prevent Member States from, in compliance with the provisions of the Treaty, maintaining or introducing bans or limitations on the use of comparisons in the advertising of professional services, whether imposed directly or by a body or organization responsible, under the law of the Member States, for regulating the exercise of a professional activity."

10–005 **(1) Toshiba—the interplay between trade marks and comparative advertising**

Toshiba[2] was the first comparative advertising case brought before the Court following the adoption of Directive 97/55. It came as a reference from the Landgericht Düsseldorf (Regional Court, Düsseldorf).

Toshiba manufactured and marketed spare parts and consumables for its photocopiers. Katun used Toshiba's product numbers for its own, equivalent to Toshiba's, products that could be used for Toshiba photocopiers. In its catalogues it listed next to Toshiba's order numbers (displayed in a column under the heading "OEM Product Number" with OEM being used as an acronym for "Original Equipment Manufacturer") its own order numbers (under the column "Katun Product Number"); the third column listed the description of each product, and the fourth referred to the photocopier models for which the product was intended. For some products the catalogues included advertising statements regarding price and performance like "you can reduce your costs without loss of quality or performance".

Toshiba relied on German jurisprudence and claimed before the German courts that the listing of its own product numbers next to Katun's product

---

[2] *Toshiba Europe GmbH v Katun Germany GmbH* (C-112/99) [2001] E.C.R. I-7945.

numbers was not indispensable; it would suffice to refer to the models of the Toshiba photocopiers. Also, it was not essential in order to compare its own prices with Toshiba's prices. Katun referred to the numbers of the original products in order to boost its own products. It added that Katun could use detailed diagrams to identify the products. Lastly, the use of Toshiba product numbers is not necessary in order to compare the prices of the products. For these reasons Katun's actions constituted acts of unfair competition.

Katun challenged the compatibility of this view with Directive 97/55. Responding to Toshiba's specific arguments it added that its catalogues targeted a specialised audience aware that its products were not Toshiba products, that the reference to the number of each Toshiba product was objectively necessary because for each photocopier model there was a large number of corresponding spare parts and consumables, that and it would also facilitate customers to compare prices.

10–006

The German court stayed proceedings and referred the following questions to the Court:

"1. Is advertising by a supplier of spare parts and consumable items for an equipment manufacturer's product to be regarded as comparative advertising within the meaning of Article 2(2a) of the Directive if the advertising indicates the manufacturer's product numbers (OEM numbers) for the relevant original spare parts and consumable items for reference purposes in order to identify the supplier's products?

2. If Question 1 is to be answered in the affirmative:

(a) Does the display of the equipment manufacturer's product numbers (OEM numbers) alongside the supplier's own order numbers constitute a comparison of goods permissible under Article 3a(1)(c) of the Directive, in particular a comparison of the prices?

(b) Are the product numbers (OEM numbers) distinguishing marks of a competitor within the meaning of Article 3a(1)(g)?

3. If Question 2 is to be answered in the affirmative:

(a) What are the criteria to be used when assessing whether an advertisement within the meaning of Article 2(2a) takes unfair advantage of the reputation of a distinguishing mark of a competitor within the meaning of Article 3a(1)(g)?

(b) Is the fact that the equipment manufacturer's product numbers (OEM numbers) appear alongside the supplier's own order numbers sufficient to justify an allegation that unfair advantage is being taken of the reputation of the distinguishing mark of a competitor within the meaning of Article 3a(1)(g), if the third party competitor could instead indicate in each case the product for which the consumable item or spare part is suitable?

(c) When assessing unfairness, does it matter whether a reference (solely) to the product for which the consumable item or spare part is suitable, rather than to the product number (OEM number), is likely to make sale of the supplier's products difficult, particularly because customers generally go by the equipment manufacturer's product numbers (OEM numbers)?"

(a) The Opinion of the Advocate General

Advocate General Léger started with an analysis of the concept of comparative advertising. He accepted that it could be justified by functional considerations but chose to highlight its potentially negative points. This is perhaps evidence of the more restrained continental approach towards this type of advertising. Marketers might be tempted to denigrate or derive unfair advantage from the comparisons with their competitors' products and it might expose commercial relationships to the constant threat of unfair practices. He then moved to the definition of comparative advertising according to Directive 97/55.

10-007   **(i) "Defining" comparative advertising.** Without attempting to define the concept of advertising he found that the catalogues were created with a view to the promotion and sale of Katun's products, by providing consumers—the term included both end consumers and trade customers—with information on replacement parts and consumable items required to operate Toshiba photocopiers.

He then opted for a broad interpretation of the concept of comparative based on the wording and the purpose of the Directive. Article 2(2a) referred to any advertising which explicitly or by implication identified a competitor or goods or services offered by a competitor. There was no reference to a requirement of an express comparison. "It may be concluded that a comparison, in the broadest sense, begins where two competing economic operators are associated in an advertisement, even in a non-descriptive way."[3] And, further, there was no requirement that the competitor be expressly identified. This conclusion was also supported by the Sixth Recital stating that "it is desirable to provide a broad concept of comparative advertising to cover all modes of comparative advertising".

It remained in the jurisdiction of the national court to determine whether the advertising complained of constituted comparative advertising, however the Advocate General suggested that there was an, at least, implicit identification of a competitor in the eyes of an ordinary well-informed person to identify Toshiba's products.

He then looked at what an objective comparison would entail, in order to answer the first part of the second question.

---

[3] Point 30 of the Opinion of A.G. Léger.

2. COMPARATIVE ADVERTISING

(ii) Objective comparisons. According to the Eleventh Recital the conditions of art.3a(1) were cumulative and should be respected in their entirety. Advocate General Léger divided the provisions into positive and negative, with the requirement of making an objective comparison belonging to the first category.

10–008

What he found problematic was that Katun had not included any comparative description of the relevant products. Still, he accepted that in Katun's advertising "one sees the double justification for comparative advertising—improving the information available to consumers and stimulating competition".[4] The combined display indicated that the products were technically identical. He found that the implicit comparison satisfied the comparative requirement but he added that the comparison should also be verifiable according to art.3a(1)(c).

The comparison was objective in relation to the purpose or use of the products. He also found the price comparisons—that the provision specifically mentioned by way of example—to be objective. The catalogues contained a suggestion that Katun's prices were lower but no direct price comparisons. It was the absence of any indication that the suggestion was not objective that counted:

"A competitor who has been harmed can show perfectly well that the prices actually charged rebut the statements in the advertisement. Consumers can also verify the truth of this information by recourse to other sources, such as price lists issued by the two competing suppliers."[5]

What was missing was a wider comparison of the characteristics of the products:

10–009

"If the implicit nature of the comparison is not in itself enough to render the advertising unfair, the same is not so of its general character. The passive juxtaposition of the products is an invitation to treat as equivalent characteristics which are not all capable of being identified. If one ignores the price or the purpose of the supplies in question, the advertising appears to convey a desire by the advertiser to confer on his product all the virtues of the competing product, including those which belong to the competitor's trade mark itself."[6]

The advertisement suggested that the quality of the competing products was identical; however it lacked the necessary information to back up the suggestion.

Having identified one of the problem areas, he noted:

---

[4] Point 45 of the Opinion of A.G. Léger.
[5] Point 53 of the Opinion of A.G. Léger.
[6] Point 56 of the Opinion of A.G. Léger.

"The objectivity of the information is masked by the impossibility of listing the features on which the comparison is based, and consequently of verifying the merits claimed for them. Seen from this perspective and having regard to the documents before the Court, advertising of this kind does not appear ... to comply with the requirement for an objective presentation of the goods."[7]

10-010 He required the advertisement to provide "a precise and concrete description of the merits or deficiencies of the advertised products, such as their durability, reliability or ease of use".[8]

He added that claiming that the products were of the same quality without indicating the verifiable features supporting that claim would render an advertisement even less objective.

10-011 **(iii) The misuse of reputation.** The remaining questions introduced trade mark law considerations. The Advocate General noted that by its nature comparative advertising involved use of a competitor's trade marks that could in turn lead to an unfair advantage.

Article 3a(1)(g) of Directive 97/55 aimed to eliminate this risk. To interpret the provision the Advocate General looked first at the concept of "distinguishing marks".

10-012 *The concept of distinguishing marks* Here the Advocate General referred first to the Trade Marks Directive. Citing the Twelfth and the Thirteenth Recitals he noted that the approach of the Community legislature was to favour objective comparisons between goods or services while at the same time maintaining trade mark rights. For comparative advertising on the other hand reference to a competitor's trade mark or trade name appeared indispensable.

In order to avoid "parasitic business conduct"[9] he suggested that the concept of "distinguishing marks" should be interpreted very broadly. Accepting the opposite view could strip of legal protection identifying signs that competitors might use for their comparisons without directly referring to a trade mark. Indeed the provision referred to a trade mark, trade name or other distinguishing marks.

So the national court would have to establish whether the order numbers allowed the identification of Toshiba; if they did they should be considered to be distinguishing marks.

10-013 *Unfair advantage of the reputation* Advocate General Léger accepted that comparative advertising included the risk of the advertiser taking a share of its competitor's reputation. Accordingly, the provision prohibited only the unfair taking of reputation.

---

[7] Point 59 of the Opinion of A.G. Léger.
[8] Point 60 of the Opinion of A.G. Léger.
[9] Point 68 of the Opinion of A.G. Léger.

2. COMPARATIVE ADVERTISING

He indicated that if the only aim of the advertiser would be to take advantage of the reputation of its competitor the advertising should be considered unfair. But there would not be an unfair advantage where the content of the advertisement could be justified by reference to certain conditions.

From his perspective the right to use a competitor's distinguishing marks was an exception that should be interpreted narrowly; "derogations from the protected rights of proprietors should only be allowed within limits which are strictly necessary to achieve the object of the Directive, which is to make possible a comparison of the objective characteristics of the products".[10]

10–014 The lawfulness of the use should be determined according to a test of necessity: when the reference itself to the competitor or the manner in which it is done is not necessary in order to inform customers of the respective qualities of the goods compared the advertisement would be unlawful; if the comparison could not be made without making reference to the competitor it would be lawful.

Turning to the facts of the case he characterised the indication of order numbers alongside one another as an ambiguous method of advertising. On the one hand it indicated the purpose of the products, on the other hand it might also be perceived as suggesting that the products were in fact interchangeable, but without indicating in what respect this is so.

The Advocate General disapproved the aggressiveness of such advertising. "Seen from this perspective, it is more evidently competitive, particularly when, in addition to the parallel references, it mentions a more favourable selling price for Katun's products of the same quality. As regards this last point, there is a risk of presenting the products as being equal which is not permissible if not justified by the informative purpose of the advertising."[11]

He supported that the indication of compatibility with the Toshiba photocopiers did not necessitate a comparative advertisement; it could be achieved in other descriptive ways that would fall under the permitted uses of art.6(1)(c) of Directive 89/104. Note that the Advocate General used that provision in order to limit the scope of allowable comparative advertising.

10–015 *The necessity factors* The Advocate General referred to the following factors that should be examined as part of the assessment of the necessity test.

The first one was the purpose of the products where he balanced between effective communication of information on the one hand and limited use of the competitor's reputation on the other. He concluded that "account may be taken of the consequences of not being able to refer to the product number of the competing product only if no other solution is available whereby the advertiser may use comparative advertising".[12]

---

[10] Point 84 of the Opinion of A.G. Léger.
[11] Point 89 of the Opinion of A.G. Léger.
[12] Point 106 of the Opinion of A.G. Léger.

The second was price. Here he required the advertisement to specify the relative prices explicitly, "comparative advertising whose aim is price comparison may not use the distinguishing mark of a competitor without explicitly mentioning the prices of each of the products compared".[13]

10-016 *(b) The judgment of the Court*

The Court too made the link between trade mark law and comparative advertising; however this led to diametrically opposing conclusions from those of the Advocate General.

10-017 **(i) Defining comparative advertising.** The Court noted that according to art.2(1) of Directive 84/450 as amended, "advertising" meant "the making of a representation in any form in connection with a trade, business, craft or profession in order to promote the supply of goods or services, including immovable property, rights and obligations".

This broad definition meant that advertising, including comparative advertising, could take different forms.

The comparative element of the concept was described in equally broad terms by reference to art.2(2a) and the Sixth Recital of the preamble to Directive 97/55, which stated that the intention was to introduce a broad concept of comparative advertising that would cover all its forms; "it is therefore sufficient for a representation to be made in any form which refers, even by implication, to a competitor or to the goods or services which he offers. It does not matter that there is a comparison between the goods and services offered by the advertiser and those of a competitor."[14]

10-018 **(ii) The conditions for comparative advertising.** The conditions according to which comparative advertising would be lawful were indicated in art.3a of Directive 84/450 as amended.

Here the Court moved away from a literal interpretation and looked at the provisions from a teleological perspective, showing how practical it could become in interpreting the law:

"It follows from a comparison of Article 2(2a) of Directive 84/450 as amended, on the one hand, and Article 3a of that Directive, on the other, that, on a literal interpretation, they would render unlawful any reference enabling a competitor, or the goods or services which he offers, to be identified in a representation which did not contain a comparison within the meaning of Article 3a. That would have to be the case where there were mere mention of the trade mark of the manufacturer of the original

---

[13] Point 116 of the Opinion of A.G. Léger.
[14] *Toshiba*, para.31.

2. COMPARATIVE ADVERTISING

models or of the reference numbers of models for which the spare parts and consumable items are manufactured."[15]

Article 6(1)(c) of the Trade Marks Directive became the interpretive catalyst; the relevant case law of the Court clearly provided that use of another party's trade mark might be legitimate where it was necessary to inform the public of the nature of the products or the intended purpose of the services offered.[16]

10–019

Because a literal interpretation of Directive 84/450 would result in a contradiction with Directive 89/104 that the Community legal order would not tolerate the Court held that it was necessary to take account of the objectives of Directive 84/450 as amended. Those were indicated in the Second Recital of the Preamble to Directive 97/55 stating that comparative advertising would help demonstrate objectively the merits of the various comparable products and thus stimulate competition between suppliers of goods and services to the consumer's advantage:

"For those reasons, the conditions required of comparative advertising must be interpreted in the sense most favourable to it."[17]

Following this analysis the Court concluded that displaying the product numbers of the equipment manufacturer alongside a competing supplier's product numbers enabled the public to match precisely the corresponding products:

"Such an indication does, however, constitute a positive statement that the two products have equivalent technical features, that is to say, a comparison of material, relevant, verifiable and representative features of the products within the meaning of Article 3a(1)(c) of Directive 84/450 as amended."[18]

(iii) The answer to question 1 and question 2(a). Note that the actual answer of the Court was very heavily based, in term of wording, on the facts of the case:

10–020

"The answer to Question 1 and Question 2(a) must therefore be that, on a proper construction of Articles 2(2a) and 3a(1)(c) of Directive 84/450 as amended, the indication, in the catalogue of a supplier of spare parts and consumable items suitable for the products of an equipment manufacturer, of product numbers (OEM numbers) by which the equipment manufacturer designates the spare parts and consumable items which he himself sells may constitute comparative advertising which objectively

---

[15] *Toshiba*, para.33.
[16] *Bayerische Motorenwerke AG and BMW Nederland BV* (C-63/97) [1999] E.C.R. I-905.
[17] *Toshiba*, para.37.
[18] *Toshiba*, para.40.

compares one or more material, relevant, verifiable and representative features of goods." (para.40)

10-021 **(iv) The concept of distinguishing marks.** The Court referred to its case law on trade mark distinctiveness[19] in order to support its holding that a sign used by an undertaking may be a "distinguishing mark" "if the public identifies it as coming from a particular undertaking".[20]

It expressed doubts as to whether the alphanumeric combinations in question would be seen as distinguishing signs without the OEM reference at the top of the column.

Still this was for the national court to decide, once it had considered perception of an average individual, reasonably well informed and reasonably observant and circumspect. It added that the average individual should reflect the persons targeted by the advertisement, in this case specialist traders who would be much less likely to associate the reputation of the equipment manufacturer's products with those of the competing supplier.

10-022 **(v) Unfair advantage.** In the case that the national court would find the codes to be distinguishing marks it would also have to have regard to the Fifteenth Recital of the Preamble to Directive 97/55, stating that use of a trade mark or distinguishing mark did not breach the right to the mark where it complied with the conditions of Directive 84/450 as amended, "the aim being solely to distinguish between the products and services of the advertiser and those of his competitor and thus to highlight differences objectively".[21]

From that the Court concluded that an advertiser should not be considered as taking unfair advantage of the reputation of his competitor's distinguishing marks if effective competition on the relevant market was conditional upon a reference to them. And the Court reminded us that it had already held that one of the ways that a third party's use of a mark might take unfair advantage of the distinctive character or the reputation of the mark or be detrimental to them could be by giving the public a false impression of the relationship between the advertiser and the trade mark owner.[22]

It repeated that the way the codes were displayed could be seen as a positive statement that the technical features of the two products were equivalent, however the national court would also have to determine whether the public would associate the equipment manufacturer with the competing suppliers, in that the public might associate the reputation of that manufacturer's products with the products of the competing supplier.

10-023 The Court held that the overall presentation of the advertising at issue should be considered. For example the manufacturer's product number might be one of several combined indications relating to that manufacturer

---

[19] Citing *Lloyd Schuhfabrik Meyer & Co GmbH* (C-342/97) [1999] E.C.R. I-3819.
[20] *Toshiba*, para.49.
[21] *Toshiba*, para.53.
[22] Citing *Bayerische Motorenwerke AG and BMW Nederland BV* (C-63/97) [1999] E.C.R. I-905.

2. COMPARATIVE ADVERTISING

and his products or the trade mark of the competing supplier might be highlighted "in such a way that no confusion or association is possible between the manufacturer and the competing supplier or between their respective products".[23]

In this case it appeared, first, that Katun would have difficulty in comparing its products with Toshiba's without referring to the order numbers and, secondly, that a "clear distinction is made between Katun and Toshiba Europe, so that they do not appear to give a false impression concerning the origin of Katun's products".[24]

(vi) The answer to question 2(b) and question 3. Again it is worth reproducing here the actual answer of the Court, as its wording was influenced by the facts of the case: 10–024

"In the light of those considerations, the answer to be given to Question 2(b) and Question 3 is that, on a proper construction of Article 3a(1)(g) of Directive 84/450 as amended, where product numbers (OEM numbers) of an equipment manufacturer are, as such, distinguishing marks within the meaning of that provision, their use in the catalogues of a competing supplier enables him to take unfair advantage of the reputation attached to those marks only if the effect of the reference to them is to create, in the mind of the persons at whom the advertising is directed, an association between the manufacturer whose products are identified and the competing supplier, in that those persons associate the reputation of the manufacturer's products with the products of the competing supplier. In order to determine whether that condition is satisfied, account should be taken of the overall presentation of the advertising at issue and the type of persons for whom the advertising is intended."[25]

(2) Pippig—the contradictions of article 7(2) of Directive 84/450
10–025

The Court reconsidered the basic principles of comparative advertising in *Pippig*[26] where it reconfirmed its pro-comparative advertising stance; the case was a reference from the Oberster Gerichtshof (Supreme Court) of Austria.

Pippig Augenoptik (Pippig) was a specialist optician firm running three shops in Linz. Hartlauer was a retailer that sold spectacles—usually obtained through parallel trade—at low prices and followed a two-fold advertising campaign. First it used in a marketing campaign a leaflet highlighting the price differences between its own prices and those charged by specialist

---

[23] *Toshiba*, para.58; note the reference to "confusion or association".
[24] *Toshiba*, para.59; note here the insistence to "impression concerning the origin".
[25] *Toshiba*, para.60.
[26] *Pippig Augenoptik GmbH & Co KG v Hartlauer Handelsgesellschaft mbH* (C-44/01) [2003] E.C.R. I-3095.

opticians like Pippig; the general claim was supported by the more specific claim that for a clear Zeiss lens, opticians made a profit of 717 per cent. The advertising leaflet also contained a direct comparison between Pippig's prices for a particular frame fitted with Zeiss lenses and the price charged by Hartlauer for the same model, albeit with lenses of another brand; the comparison was based on a test purchase. Secondly, the latter price comparison was also used in television and radio advertisements. The television advertisements showed one of Pippig's shop fronts.

Pippig claimed before the Austrian Courts that Hartlauer's advertising was misleading and discrediting; it argued that the price difference between the identical models was largely due to the price of the Zeiss lenses for that particular model and that the same model was made available at Hartlauer's at a later date and only in a limited number of colours. The case reached the Oberster Gerichtshof that stayed proceedings and referred the following questions to the Court.

"(1) Is Article 7(2) of Directive 97/55 of the European Parliament and of the Council of October 6, 1997 amending Directive 84/450 concerning misleading advertising so as to include comparative advertising (the directive) to be interpreted to the effect that comparative advertising, as far as the comparison is concerned means the statements regarding the product offered by the advertiser himself, the statements regarding the product offered by the competitor and the statements regarding the relationship between the two products (the result of the comparison)? Or is there a comparison within the meaning of Article 7(2) of the directive only in so far as the statements are made regarding the result of the comparison, with the consequence that misconceptions regarding other features of the compared goods/services may be assessed on the basis of a national standard governing misleading statements which is possibly more strict? Is the reference in Article 3a(1)(a) of the directive to Art.7(1) of the directive a lex specialis in relation to Article 7(2) of the directive, with the result that a national standard governing misleading statements which is possibly more strict may be applied to all elements of the comparison? Is Article 3a(1)(a) of the directive to be interpreted as meaning that the comparison of the price of a brand-name product with the price of a no-name product of equivalent quality is not permitted where the name of the manufacturer is not indicated, or do Article 3a(1)(c) and Article 3a(1)(g) of the directive preclude indication of the manufacturer? Is the image of a (brand-name) product a feature of the product/service within the meaning of Article 3a(c) of the directive? Does it follow from a (possible) negative answer to this question that any (price) comparison of a brand-name product with a no-name product of equivalent quality is not permitted?

(2) Is Article 7(2) of the directive to be interpreted as meaning that differences in the procurement of the product/service whose features are

2. COMPARATIVE ADVERTISING

compared with features of the advertiser's product/service must also be assessed solely on the basis of Article 3a of the directive? If this question is answered in the affirmative: Is Article 3a of the directive to be interpreted as meaning that a (price) comparison is permitted only if the compared goods are procured through the same distribution channels and are thus offered by the advertiser and his competitor(s) in a comparable selection?

(3) Is comparison within the meaning of Article 7(2) of the directive to be construed as including the creation of the bases for comparison through a test purchase? If this question is answered in the affirmative: Is Article 3a of the directive to be interpreted as meaning that the deliberate initiation of a (price) comparison which is favourable to the advertiser through a test purchase which is made before the beginning of the advertiser's own offer and is arranged accordingly makes the comparison unlawful?

(4) Is a comparison discrediting within the meaning of Art.3a(1)(e) of the directive if the advertiser selects the goods purchased from the competitor in such a way that a price difference is obtained which is greater than the average price difference and/or if such price comparisons are repeatedly made with the result that the impression is created that the prices of the competitor(s) are generally excessive? Is Art.3a(1)(e) of the directive to be interpreted as meaning that the information on the identification of the competitor must be restricted to the extent absolutely necessary and it is therefore not permitted if, in addition to the competitor's name, its company logo (if it exists) and its shop are shown?"[27]

(a) The Opinion of the Advocate General
10–026

Advocate General Tizzano considered each one of the issues raised by the Austrian Court.

(i) Indicating the names of manufacturers. The Advocate General concurred with the argument maintained by Pippig and the Commission and supported by the Austrian Government that the brand of the lenses was one of the factors influencing consumers; accordingly comparing prices without indicating the brand names of the respective lenses appeared to be misleading. He noted that according to art.2(2) a likelihood of deceiving consumers would suffice to render the advertisement unlawful.

10–027

Turning to the facts of the case he found it obvious that comparing the retail price whilst stating that the frames were the same and that the lenses had the same features, but not indicating that the lenses had different brand names—one more known to the public than the other—would be misleading. On the basis of the particular facts he rejected Hartlauer's

[27] Reproduced in para.21.

argument that such a finding would require for example indicating the manufacturers of all the parts and accessories of two cars when comparing their prices and would make it very difficult to use comparative advertising. This would not be the case here.

He sought further support for his argumentation from the underlying principle that competitors were allowed to use the brand names of their competitors. Note that he referred to the findings of the Court in *BMW*[28] and *Toshiba*[29] as supporting his restrictive view of comparative advertising, stressing that both art.3a(1)(c) and art.3a(1)(g) did not preclude use of a brand name in comparative advertising. He believed that the absence of the reference to the brand name was critical.

10–028 **(ii) Stricter national standards.** Advocate General Tizzano noted that the wording of this part of the first question was so imprecise that it could be rejected as hypothetical and inadmissible; the referring court was uncertain as to whether the Austrian standards were indeed stricter than those imposed by the Directive. In addition, if the Court were to adopt his stance regarding the indication of the manufacturers' names there would be no conflict between the two systems.

Still, in the spirit of co-operation between the Court and national courts, he gave his views on this issue. He acknowledged that there appeared to be a contradiction between art.3a(1)(a) of the Directive, which referred to art.7(1) in defining the conditions permitting comparative advertising, and art.7(2), which precluded the application of art.7(1) "to comparative advertising as far as the comparison is concerned".

His starting point was that the primary purpose of Directive 84/450 was to protect consumers and traders against misleading advertising. For that reason art.7(1) did not preclude more extensive protection. Article 3a(1)(a) provided that comparative advertising should not be misleading according to the relevant provisions of the Directive or to any stricter national provisions adopted according to art.7(1).

10–029 At the same time the amendments introduced by Directive 97/55 and Directive 84/450 itself aimed to lift the national barriers to trade that could be raised as a result of comparative advertising's regulatory differences. This is why art.3a was added to Directive 84/450, providing that comparative advertising was, "as far as the comparison is concerned", to be permitted in all the Member States according to the conditions specified in that article. This was also reflected by art.7(2).

Now, his interpretation of art.7(2) could restrict the scope of allowing comparative advertising; art.7(2) did not preclude the application to comparative advertising of a national standard that would be stricter than the Community rules in respect of the definition of comparative advertising,

---

[28] *Bayerische Motorenwerke AG and BMW Nederland BV* (C-63/97) [1999] E.C.R. I-905.
[29] *Toshiba Europe GmbH v Katun Germany GmbH* (C-112/99) [2001] E.C.R. I-7945.

2. COMPARATIVE ADVERTISING

"the sole purpose of that article is to prevent the permissibility of comparative advertising 'as far as the comparison is concerned' from being subject to conditions over and above those laid down in Article 3a. In other words, what it means is that the conditions under which comparative advertising is permitted are exhaustive, precisely because the purpose of the directive is to ensure that, under the conditions specified, such comparisons may be made and released in all the Member States".[30] But, the conditions of art.3a(1) precluded misleading advertising and the concept of "misleading" could vary according to stricter national standards.

He supported that his suggested solution would resolve the contradiction and reconcile the purposes of the Directive, rejecting the opposite view expressed by Hartlauer and the Commission as assuming without "any objective justification that consumers, traders and the general public are being afforded different and less extensive protection against the danger of anything misleading in advertising material only in cases where the material makes a comparison between competing products or services".[31]

(iii) The relevance of channels of trade—a challenge to parallel imports. The Advocate General noted that there was no provision in art.3a setting that that price comparisons should cover only goods following the same trade channels, it seemed obvious that "Member States cannot indiscriminately prohibit any advertising that compares the price charged for certain products by competing traders who obtain their supplies through different distribution channels".[32]

10–030

He admitted though that in some cases such a comparison could be misleading under art.3a(1)(a). He gave three examples: first, when spare parts or aftersales service were important for the consumer, in which case a more direct relationship between the trader and the manufacturer of the product might be relevant; secondly, when the advertisement falsely suggested that the advertiser offered a similar selection of products; and thirdly, when the product was offered by the advertiser on an occasional basis in which case art.3a(2) could be applied.

He stressed however, that in all three cases it would be the misleading nature of the information rather than the channels of trade that would make the advertisement unlawful.

(iv) The context of the test purchase—acceptability of additional conditions. Advocate General Tizzano repeated that art.7(2) provided that Member States could not subject the permissibility of comparative advertising to conditions over and above those of art.3a. So, providing that comparative advertising would not be permitted in the case of test

10–031

---

[30] Point 44 of the Opinion of A.G. Tizzano.
[31] Point 46 of the Opinion of A.G. Tizzano.
[32] Point 50 of the Opinion of A.G. Tizzano.

purchases as described in the third question was not an option for the national authorities.

The comparison could not be regarded misleading merely because it was based on a test purchase, made before the products concerned were offered for sale by the advertiser, or because the products selected were being sold at different prices by competitors.

However, he considered that the advertisement would be misleading under art.3a(1)(a) were the advertisement to be released before the products were offered at the price quoted or where the comparison was presented in such a way as to suggest falsely that the price difference also applied to other products.

10–032 **(v) The context of price comparisons.** In relation to the third question the Advocate General repeated that comparison between the prices charged for certain products by two or more competing traders might be misleading under art.3a1(a) if it gave the false impression that the price difference indicated also applied to other products. "Comparing products sold by different traders at very different prices is in itself likely to create the impression that the same difference applies to other products."[33] The frequency of the advertisement would not in itself be likely to create that impression.

Finally, he suggested that the content and presentation of the advertisement would determine whether it was discrediting or not. But, identifying a competitor by pictures of a shop or a company logo should not as such be considered discrediting under art.3a(1)(e).

10–033 *(b) The judgment of the Court*

Once again the Court appeared to be more supportive of comparative advertising.

10–034 **(i) The interpretation of article 7(2).** The Court stressed that in *Toshiba*[34] it had already held that art.2(2)(a) provided a broad definition of comparative advertising; a statement referring even by implication to a competitor or to the goods or services offered by a competitor would suffice. Its approach was pragmatic:

> "All comparative advertising is designed to highlight the advantages of the goods or services offered by the advertiser in comparison with those of a competitor. In order to achieve that, the message must necessarily underline the differences between the goods or services compared by describing their main characteristics. The comparison made by the advertiser will necessarily flow from such a description."[35]

[33] Point 66 of the Opinion of A.G. Tizzano.
[34] *Toshiba Europe GmbH* (C-112/99) [2001] E.C.R. I-7945.
[35] *Pippig*, para.36.

2. COMPARATIVE ADVERTISING

Accordingly it was not necessary "to establish distinctions in the legislation between the various elements of comparison, that is to say the statements concerning the advertiser's offer, the statements concerning the competitor's offer, and the relationship between those two offers."[36]

As to the scope of the Comparative Advertising Directive the starting point for the Court was different from that of the Advocate General. In relation to comparative advertising its objective was the establishment of conditions in which comparative advertising should be regarded as lawful in the context of the internal market.

Article 3(a) included amongst the conditions to be satisfied that the comparative advertisement should not be misleading according to art.2(2), art.3 and art.7(1). It conceded that art.7(1) allowed Member States to apply stricter national standards since the harmonisation undertaken by the Directive was minimal. However, it observed, art.7(2) expressly provided that art.7(1) did not apply to comparative advertising in respect of the comparison. It acknowledged the "apparent textual contradiction"[37] and in order to resolve it, it held that the provisions had to be interpreted in such a way as to take account of the objectives of Directive 84/450 and in the light of *Toshiba*,[38] where the Court had held the conditions required of comparative advertising should be interpreted in the sense most favourable to it.

10–035

The Preamble to Directive 97/55 underlined that differences in the recognition or not of comparative advertising at the national level could raise obstacles to free movement of goods and distort competition. The Eighteenth Recital excluded stricter national provisions on misleading advertising:

"It follows that Directive 84/450 carried out an exhaustive harmonisation of the conditions under which comparative advertising in Member States might be lawful. Such a harmonisation implies by its nature that the lawfulness of comparative advertising throughout the Community is to be assessed solely in the light of the criteria laid down by the Community legislature. Therefore, stricter national provisions on protection against misleading advertising cannot be applied to comparative advertising as regards the form and content of the comparison."[39]

(ii) Indicating the names of manufacturers. The Court underlined that Directive 84/450 allowed an advertiser to state in comparative advertising the brand of a competitor's product. This was made clear in the Preamble to Directive 97/55 and through the application of art.3a(1)(d), (e) and (g) of Directive 84/450, "where the comparison does not have the

10–036

---

[36] *Pippig*, para.37.
[37] *Pippig*, para.42.
[38] *Toshiba Europe GmbH* (C-112/99) [2001] E.C.R. I-7945.
[39] *Pippig*, para.44.

intention or effect of giving rise to such situations of unfair competition, the use of a competitor's brand name is permitted by Community law".[40] The Court had also accepted this in *Toshiba*.[41]

Now, the omission of such a statement might also be capable of misleading:

> "In cases where the brand name of the products may significantly affect the buyer's choice and the comparison concerns rival products whose respective brand names differ considerably in the extent to which they are known, omission of the better-known brand name goes against Article 3a(1)(a) of Directive 84/450, which lays down one of the conditions for comparative advertising to be lawful."[42]

This was for the national court to decide taking into account the presumed expectations of an average consumer who is reasonably well informed and reasonably observant and circumspect.[43]

10–037 **(iii) The relevance of the channels of trade.** Given that the Court had already decided that the harmonisation was exhaustive it notes that the conditions comparative advertising had to satisfy were set out in art.3a(1). The requirement that the products had to be obtained through the same distribution channels was not amongst them; in addition such a requirement would be against the objectives of the internal market and of Directive 84/450. Parallel imports prevented the compartmentalisation of national markets and comparative advertising empowered consumers to exploit the opportunities offered by the internal market.

10–038 **(iv) Test purchases.** Again, since a test purchase by the advertiser before putting on the market its own competing product was not in itself prohibited, the advertisement would be unlawful only if it failed to comply with one of the art.3a(1) conditions.

10–039 **(v) The context of price comparisons.** The Court started by accepting that price comparison was at the core of comparative advertising. Accordingly, in itself it did not constitute discrediting or denigration of a competitor within the meaning of art.3a(1)(e).

Restricting price comparisons to the average prices of the products offered by the advertiser and those of its competitor would, according to the Court, be contrary to the objectives of the Community legislature.

---

[40] *Pippig*, para.49.
[41] *Toshiba Europe GmbH* (C-112/99) [2001] E.C.R. I-7945.
[42] *Pippig*, para.53.
[43] Citing *Esteé Lauder GmbH & Co OHG v Lancaster Group GmbH* (C-220/98) [2000] E.C.R. I-117.

2. COMPARATIVE ADVERTISING

And based on objectivity, a requirement for comparative advertising identified in the Second Recital in the Preamble to Directive 97/55, the Court concluded that the audience of the advertisement should be capable of knowing the actual price differences between the compared products rather than merely the average differences.

Finally, regarding the use of the picture of the competitor's shop front and logo the Court noted that according to the Fifteenth Recital in the Preamble to Directive 97/55, use of another's trade mark, trade name, or other distinguishing marks would not breach the respective exclusive right where it complied with the conditions laid down by the Directive.

(3) Siemens—reconfirming the Court's permissive approach   10–040

Siemens[44] is another recent decision of the Court on comparative advertising. Siemens manufactured and marketed programmable controllers under the name "Simatic" using a system of alphanumeric combinations as order codes for the controllers and their add-on components. VIPA manufactured and marketed components that were compatible with "Simatic" controllers; the codes were identical with those used by Siemens, with the only difference being that VIPA used its own acronym in the first part of the codes. For example whereas a Siemens product carried the code 6ES5 928-3UB21 the VIPA equivalent displayed VIPA 928-3UB21.

The codes were also used in VIPA's trade catalogue. In the catalogue VIPA linked the codes with the Siemens products. It stated: "Please check the order number of the memory modules you require in the handbook for your module or call us. The order numbers correspond to those of Siemens programme modules".[45]

Siemens claimed before the German courts that VIPA took unfair advantage of the reputation of its products. The case reached the German Bundesgerichtshof (Federal Court of Justice) that stayed proceedings and referred to the Court the following questions in relation to the interpretation of Directive 84/450.

> "(1) Is the reputation of an 'other distinguishing mark' within the meaning of Article 3a(1)(g) of Directive 84/450/EEC taken advantage of unfairly where an advertiser adopts in identical form the core elements of a distinguishing mark of a competitor (in this case, a system of order numbers) which is known in trade circles, and refers to those identical elements in advertising?
>
> (2) In determining whether unfair advantage is taken of a reputation for the purposes of Article 3a(1)(g) of Directive 84/450/EEC, is the benefit

---

[44] *Siemens AG v VIPA Gesellschaft Für Visualisierung und Prozeßautomatisierung mbH* (C-59/05) [2006] E.C.R. I-2147.
[45] Reproduced in para.9.

to the advertiser and the consumer procured by the adoption of the identical system a relevant factor?"[46]

10–041 *(a) The judgment of the Court*

The Court decided to proceed without considering an Opinion and looked at the two questions jointly.

The link between comparative advertising and trade mark law was considered by the Court as settled case law:

> "It is settled case law that it is necessary, when assessing whether the condition laid down in art.3a(1)(g) of Directive 84/450 has been observed, to have regard to recital 15 in the preamble to Directive 97/55, which states that the use of a trade mark or distinguishing mark does not breach the right to the mark where it complies with the conditions laid down by Directive 84/450, the aim being solely to distinguish between the products and services of the advertiser and those of his competitor and thus to highlight differences objectively."[47]

For the Court it was clear that a manufacturer would not take unfair advantage of the reputation of its competitor's marks by referring to them if that was a condition for effective competition. From the opposite perspective there would be an unfair advantage if the reference gave to the public a false impression about the relationship between the two entities.

In this case it was apparent that VIPA was using the codes for informing the public that the products had equivalent technical features. The Court viewed this as a comparison within the meaning of art.3a(1)(c) of Directive 84/450. Still, it went on to consider whether the adoption of the code would associate VIPA and its products with the reputation of Siemens products. There were three reasons for giving a negative answer.

10–042 *The importance of the relevant public* Following *Toshiba*[48] it found that given that the products were intended for a specialist public it would be much less likely for that public, than final consumers to associate the reputation of Siemens products with VIPA's products.

10–043 *Use of VIPA's acronym* The use of its own acronym combined with the statement in the catalogue would ensure further that there would be no false impression either as to the origin of VIPA products or of an association between those two companies.

---

[46] Reproduced in para.11.
[47] *Siemens*, para.14, citing *Toshiba Europe GmbH* (C-112/99) [2001] E.C.R. I-7945.
[48] *Toshiba Europe GmbH* (C-112/99) [2001] E.C.R. I-7945

2. COMPARATIVE ADVERTISING

The relevance of the technical function Finally, the technical nature of the codes weakened further the argument of Siemens. The codes had to be programmed into the assembly system in order to operate the controller. **10–044**

(i) The significance of the benefits of comparative advertising. The reference to the benefits to the advertiser and the consumer allowed the Court to elaborate further on the policies underlying comparative advertising. **10–045**

The benefits to the consumer The Court reminded us that in *Pippig*[49] it had held that comparative advertising was designed to enable consumers to make the best possible use of the internal market and that the Second Recital to the Preamble of the Directive 97/55[50] indicated that amongst the aims of comparative advertising was to stimulate competition between suppliers of goods and services to the consumer's advantage: **10–046**

> "It follows that the benefit of comparative advertising to consumers must necessarily be taken into account in determining whether an advertiser is taking unfair advantage of the reputation of a trade mark, trade name or other distinguishing marks of a competitor."[51]

The benefits to the advertiser The benefits to the advertiser however, although self-evident, "cannot alone be determinative of whether the conduct of such an advertiser is lawful".[52] **10–047**

(ii) The importance of the circumstances of the case. *Siemens* was another case that the Court was unable to untangle its response from the factual scenario of the case. It found that if a different code was used by VIPA the users of the components would have to refer to comparative listings. That would be disadvantageous, both to consumers and to VIPA. From that it deduced that the possibility that there would be restrictive effects on competition in the market for add-on components to the controllers manufactured by Siemens could not be excluded. **10–048**

---

[49] *Pippig Augenoptik GmbH & Co KG v Hartlauer Handelsgesellschaft mbH* (C-44/01) [2003] E.C.R. I-3095.
[50] "Whereas the completion of the internal market will mean an ever wider range of choice; whereas, given that consumers can and must make the best possible use of the internal market, and that advertising is a very important means of creating genuine outlets for all goods and services throughout the Community, the basic provisions governing the form and content of comparative advertising should be uniform and the conditions of the use of comparative advertising in the Member States should be harmonized; whereas if these conditions are met, this will help demonstrate objectively the merits of the various comparable products; whereas comparative advertising can also stimulate competition between suppliers of goods and services to the consumer's advantage".
[51] *Siemens*, para.24.
[52] *Siemens*, para.25.

The Court concluded that "art.3a(1)(g) of Directive 84/450 must be interpreted as meaning that, in circumstances such as those in the main proceedings, by using in its catalogues the core element of a manufacturer's distinguishing mark which is known in specialist circles, a competing supplier does not take unfair advantage of the reputation of that distinguishing mark".[53]

10–049 **(4) DeLandtsheer Emmanuel—designations of origin—the competitive relationship**

DeLandtsheer Emmanuel SA[54] reached the Court as a reference from the Cour d'Appel de Bruxelles (Brussels Court of Appeal). De Landtsheer had been marketing beer varieties in Belgium under the trade mark "MALHEUR". One of its beers, "Malheur Brut Réserve" was brewed according to a method for producing sparkling wine. On the label and the packaging of the product a number of statements highlighted this particular characteristic: "The First BRUT Beer in the World", "Light Beer Produced according to the Traditional Method, Reims-France", and a reference to the wine-growers of Reims and Epernay. Whilst presenting the beer the company often used the term "Champagnebier", a reference to the champagne method used for the production of the beer. The company also referred to the qualities of the beer in the media using champagne comparisons or contrasts. The Comité Interprofessionnel du Vin de Champagne (CIVP) and Veuve Clicquot brought an action based on the Belgian law concerning misleading and comparative advertising. They got a partial injunction, covering references to "Reims-France" and the "Traditional Method" and any other reference to Champagne producers and product characteristics.

De Landtsheer appealed and the Brussels Court of Appeal referred the following questions to the Court:

"1. Does the definition of comparative advertising cover advertisements in which the advertiser refers only to a type of product, so that in those circumstances such advertisements must be regarded as referring to all undertakings which offer that type of product, and each of them can claim to have been identified?

2. With a view to determining whether there is a competitive relationship between the advertiser and the undertaking to which reference is made within the meaning of Article 2(2a) of Directive 84/450:

(a) On the basis in particular of a comparison of Article [2(2a)] with Article [3a(1)(b)], should any undertaking which can be identified in the advertising be regarded as a competitor within the meaning of Article 2(2a), whatever the goods or services it offers?

---

[53] *Siemens*, para.27.
[54] *De Landtsheer Emmanuel SA v Comité Interprofessionnel du Vin de Champagne and Veuve Clicquot Ponsardin SA* (C-381/05) [2007] E.T.M.R. 69.

2. COMPARATIVE ADVERTISING

(b) In the event of a negative response to that question and if other conditions are required in order for a competitive relationship to be established, is it necessary to consider the current state of the market and drinking habits in the Community or is it necessary also to consider how those habits might evolve?

(c) Must any investigation be confined to that part of the Community territory in which the advertising is disseminated?

(d) Is it necessary to consider the competitive relationship in relation to the types of products being compared and the way in which those types of products are generally perceived, or is it necessary, in order to assess the degree of substitution possible, to take into account also the particular characteristics of the product which the advertiser intends to promote in the advertising concerned and of the image he intends to give it?

(e) Are the criteria by which a competitive relationship within the meaning of Article 2(2a) can be established identical to the criteria for verifying whether the comparison satisfies the condition referred to in Article [3a(1)(b)]?

3. Does a comparison of Article 2(2a) of Directive 84/450 with Article 3a of that directive mean that

(a) either any comparative advertising is unlawful which enables a type of product to be identified where a competitor or the goods offered by him cannot be identified from the wording?

(b) or the lawfulness of the comparison must be considered in the light only of national legislation other than that by which the provisions of the directive on comparative advertising are transposed, which could lead to reduced protection for consumers or undertakings offering the type of product being compared with the product offered by the advertiser?

4. If it should be concluded that there has been comparative advertising within the meaning of Article 2(2a), must it be inferred from Article 3a(1)(f) of the Directive that any comparison is unlawful which, in respect of products without designation of origin, relates to products with designation of origin?"

The length and detailed nature of the questions referred to the Court is evidence of the uncertainty characterising the national court's approach.

(a) The Opinion of the Advocate General   10–050

Before dealing with individual questions A.G. Mengozzi made a general point noting that the Court was not in fact required to give a ruling on whether the advertising messages constituted comparative advertising or were indeed lawful, but simply to assist the national court in interpreting the provisions of Directive 84/450.

10-051 **(i) The first question—reference to a type of product.** The Advocate General supported that the broad nature of the definition of comparative advertising should not of itself be conclusive for answering the question. He turned instead to the recitals to the Directive and the judgment of the Court in *Toshiba*:[55] comparative advertising should identify, explicitly or by implication, a competitor or goods or services offered by a competitor. He acknowledged that whether the Directive covered types of as well as specific products was not clear. A literal reading would probably not agree with a teleological approach. A compromise would be to decide that "the test for comparative advertising must be that the message refers, albeit only by implication, to one or more specific competitors or the corresponding goods or services".[56] An oligopolistic market might facilitate such a finding but at the end it was for the national court to decide whether the contested signs functioned in that way.

10-052 **(ii) The second question—the competitive relationship.** Here the Advocate General supported that the language of the provision was clear: "in order for comparative advertising to exist, the advertising must make it possible to identify a competitor undertaking (or the related goods or services) and not just any undertaking (or its related goods or services)".[57] The products of the two parties had to be identified and taken into account.

He added that there was no need for competition between the products. "What matters is that the advertising make it possible to identify that there is competition between the advertiser and the other undertaking (or its product) in relation to any part of the range of goods or services they each offer."[58] He argued against taking a narrow approach focusing on defining product markets according to competition law principles; instead the Court should embrace a broader interpretation taking into account a contemporary view of advertising and its functions. Actual or potential competition in relation to segments of the relevant markets or even a degree of demand substitutability could suffice.

10-053 **(iii) The third question—the scope of the Directive.** The Advocate General strongly supported that advertising which did not meet the requirements to be classified as comparative advertising should not be considered automatically illegal pursuant to the provisions of Directive 84/450; it would simply fall outside its scope.

---

[55] *Toshiba Europe GmbH* (C-112/99) [2001] E.C.R. I-7945.
[56] Point 46 of the Opinion of A.G. Mengozzi.
[57] Point 61 of the Opinion of A.G. Mengozzi.
[58] Point 63 of the Opinion of A.G. Mengozzi.

2. COMPARATIVE ADVERTISING

(iv) The fourth question—article 3(a)1(f). Here the Advocate General referred to the Twelfth Recital in the Preamble to Directive 97/55 stating that the conditions for comparative advertising "should include, in particular, consideration of the provisions resulting from Council Regulation (EEC) No 2081/92 of 14 July 1992 on the protection of geographical indications and designations of origin for agricultural products and foodstuffs, and in particular Article 13 thereof, and of the other Community provisions adopted in the agricultural sphere". Accordingly, art.3a(1)(f) should "be interpreted as meaning that comparative advertising which relates to a product with designation of origin is lawful only if the comparison refers to another product with the same designation of origin".[59]

10–054

(b) The judgment of the Court

(i) The first question—reference to a type of product. The Court repeated that a statement relating even by implication to a competitor or to the goods or services which it offered could suffice to render the advertisement comparative. "The mere fact that an undertaking solely refers in its advertisement to a type of product does not mean that the advertisement in principle falls outside the scope of the directive."[60] It went on to hold that it should be irrelevant that the reference to a type of product might, given the circumstances of the case and, in particular, the structure of the market in question, enable a number of competitors, or the goods or services that they offer, to be identified.

10–055

(ii) The second question—the competitive relationship. To answer the first part of the question the Court noted that identification of a "competitor" of the advertiser or of the goods and services which it offered was the key element of comparative advertising. The competitive relationship depended on the substitutable nature of the goods or services that they offered on the market.

10–056

The specific assessment of the degree of substitution depended on a number of factors and fell within the jurisdiction of national courts. The Court held here that it was necessary to consider not only the present state of the market but also the possibilities for development within the context of free movement of goods at the Community level and the further potential for the substitution of products for one another which could be revealed by intensification of trade.

In short the following should be considered:

"—the current state of the market and consumer habits and how they might evolve;

---

[59] Point 125 of the Opinion of A.G. Mengozzi.
[60] *DeLandtsheer Emmanuel*, para.18.

- the part of the Community territory in which the advertising is disseminated, without, however, excluding, where appropriate, the effects which the evolution of consumer habits seen in other Member States may have on the national market at issue, and

- the particular characteristics of the product which the advertiser seeks to promote and the image which it wishes to impart to it."[61]

Regarding the third part of the question the Court accepted that arts 2(2a) and 3a(1)(b) served different purposes. The first delimited the scope of the Directive, the second provided one of the conditions that had to be satisfied. Accordingly the criteria for their application should be distinct.

10–057   (iii) **The third question—the scope of the Directive.** The Court held that the conditions set out in Article 3a(1) were applicable only to advertisements which are comparative in character. The question of the permissibility of an advertisement which referred to a type of product without, however, identifying a competitor or the goods offered by that competitor did not fall within the scope of comparative advertising. National law and Community law on misleading advertising should then be taken into account.

10–058   (iv) **The fourth question—article 3a(1)(f).** The Court held that for products without a designation of origin, any comparison which related to products with a designation of origin should not be permitted:

"Comparative advertising helps to demonstrate objectively the merits of the various comparable products and to stimulate competition between suppliers of goods and of services to the consumer's advantage. In the wording of recital 5 in the preamble to Directive 97/55, comparative advertising, when it compares material, relevant, verifiable and representative features and is not misleading, may be a legitimate means of informing consumers of their advantage".[62]

The Court added that art.3a(1)(f) had to be read in conjunction with art.3a(1)(g).

10–059   (5)   **O2—use of a similar sign—the indispensability challenge**

In *O2*[63] the Court considered the conditions for comparative advertising focusing on whether a sign similar to a competitor's trade mark can be used

---

[61] *DeLandtsheer Emmanuel*, para.42.
[62] *DeLandtsheer Emmanuel*, para.62.
[63] *O2 Holdings Ltd, O2 (UK) Ltd v Hutchison 3G UK Ltd* (C-533/06) [2008] E.C.R. I4231.

2. COMPARATIVE ADVERTISING

in a comparative advertisement. O2, a mobile telephone services provider, had been using bubble images in their advertising and had registered two pictures of bubbles for telecommunication services and apparatus. They brought a trade mark infringement action against Hutchison 3G (H3G) targeting a television advertisement with price comparisons. The advertisement began by using the name "O2" and moving black-and-white bubble imagery, followed by "Threepay" and "3" imagery (H3G's trade marks), together with a message on price differences. O2 accepted that the comparisons were true and the advertisement was not misleading. However, they maintained that use of the bubble imagery was unnecessary. The action was dismissed, O2 filed an appeal, and the English Court of Appeal referred three questions to the Court of Appeal.

The first question regarded the concept of use in the context of art.5(1) of the Trade Mark Directive. The second and the third questions queried whether there was an indispensability requirement.

"1. Where a trader, in an advertisement for his own goods or services, uses a registered trade mark owned by a competitor for the purpose of comparing the characteristics (and in particular the price) of goods or services marketed by him with the characteristics (and in particular the price) of the goods or services marketed by the competitor under that mark in such a way that it does not cause confusion or otherwise jeopardise the essential function of the trade mark as an indication of origin, does his use fall within either (a) or (b) of Article 5[(1)] of Directive 89/104?

2. Where a trader uses, in a comparative advertisement, the registered trade mark of a competitor, in order to comply with Article 3a[(1)] of Directive 84/450 . . . must that use be 'indispensable' and if so what are the criteria by which indispensability is to be judged?

3. In particular, if there is a requirement of indispensability, does the requirement preclude any use of a sign which is not identical to the registered trade mark but is closely similar to it?"[64]

(a) The Opinion of the Advocate General 10–060

Advocate General Mengozzi conceded that there had been, at least at first sight, inconsistencies in the case law of the Court on the interpretation of art.5(1)(a) and (b) of the Directive. As an example he contrasted the approach taken in *BMW*[65] with that followed in *Hölterhoff*[66] and *Adam Opel*[67]:

---

[64] Reproduced in para.28.
[65] *Bayerische Motorenwerke AG and BMW Nederland BV* (C-63/97) [1999] E.C.R. I-905
[66] *Hölterhoff v Freiesleben* (C-2/00) [2002] E.C.R. I-4187.
[67] *Adam Opel AG v Autec AG* (C-48/05) [2007] E.C.R. I-1017.

"the use of another's trade mark by a third party to distinguish the goods or services supplied by the proprietor of the trade mark, which does not cause confusion regarding the origin of those goods or services and the third party's goods or services, may apparently fall within the ambit of Article 5(1) of Directive 89/104 on the basis of BMW, and may escape it on the basis of Hölterhoff and Adam Opel, while . . . in order to determine whether or not the said use is caught by that provision, it must be ascertained whether it is liable to affect a function of the trade mark other than the essential function of providing a guarantee of origin".[68]

Instead, the Advocate General chose to focus on the regulation of comparative advertising and the exhaustive harmonisation introduced by Directive 84/450.[69] He supported that the use of a competitor's trade mark in a comparative advertisement was specifically and exhaustively covered by art.3a of Directive 84/450. "It is prohibited only if does not comply with the conditions laid down in that article. In that case, it is prohibited under that article and not under Article 5(1)(a) or (b) of Directive 89/104. Conversely, if it complies with those conditions, it cannot be held to be prohibited under the provisions contained in Article 5(1)(a) or (b) of Directive 89/104."[70]

Since the use complained of fell clearly within the scope of Directive 84/450 and Directive 97/55 there was little point in wondering whether that conclusion would also have been reached in the absence of Directive 97/55, because that use did not in any case fall within the scope of art.(1) of Directive 89/104.

10-061
(i) **The indispensability requirement.** Advocate General Mengozzi supported that there was no indispensability requirement. He reminded that in *Pippig*[71] the Court had concluded that art.3a(1)(e) of Directive 84/450 did not prevent the competitor's logo and a picture of its shop front if the advertising complied with the conditions laid down by Community law. He added that art.3a, which provided an exhaustive harmonisation of the conditions for comparative advertising, did not refer to indispensability.

Article 3a(1)(g) prohibited only taking unfair advantage of the reputation of a trade mark or other distinguishing marks of a competitor or of the designation of origin of competing products. In *Toshiba*[72] Advocate General Léger had discussed a condition of necessity, however the Court appeared to disregard this approach and take a narrower approach as to when there is an unfair advantage covering only cases where the effect of the reference

---

[68] Point 26 of the Opinion of A.G. Mengozzi.
[69] Citing *Pippig Augenoptik GmbH & Co KG* (C-44/01) [2003] E.C.R. I-3095.
[70] Point 34 of the Opinion of A.G. Mengozzi.
[71] [2003] E.C.R. I-3095.
[72] Case C-59/05 [2006] ECR I-2147.

is to create in the mind of the targeted audience an association between the manufacturer whose products were identified and the competing supplier, in that they associated the reputation of the manufacturer's products with the products of the competing supplier.

The same considerations should also apply to use of a sign which is not identical but similar to a competitor's trade mark. Turning to the factual context of this case he added: "if a link with the competitor is already established by means of the reference to O2's trade mark, without any objection on the subject from O2, I do not see what unfair advantage H3G could gain from the additional use in the advertisement at issue of signs similar to the bubbles trade marks likewise owned by O2".[73]

And the fact that the H3G bubbles were a distorted version of the O2 bubbles was irrelevant unless it did not comply with the art.3a conditions. He noted that art.3(a) did cover discrediting or denigration and the taking unfair advantage of the reputation of a trade mark. If the distortion were presenting the O2 trade marks or O2's image in a negative light, O2 could complain. He stressed though that art.3a did not cover the protection of the distinctive character of the trade mark and contrasted this with the approach taken by Directive 89/104 and Regulation 40/94. "This must represent a deliberate choice by the Community legislature, which clearly considered that it had a duty to prefer the interest in effective comparative advertising which acts as an instrument to inform consumers and a stimulus to competition between suppliers of goods and services... to the interest of protecting the distinctive character of trade marks".[74]

(b) The judgment of the Court

(i) The relationship between Directives 89/104 and 84/450. The Court started its analysis by clarifying the relationship between the two Directives. Article 5(1) and (2) of Directive 89/104 provide for the exclusive rights of the trade mark proprietor. Article 5(3)(d) states that the proprietor may prevent all third parties from using such a sign in advertising. So, use in a comparative advertisement, of a sign identical with, or similar to, a competitor's mark may constitute use within the meaning of art.5(1) and (2).

10–062

The aim of Directive 97/55, on the other hand, is to promote comparative advertising and this meant that trade mark rights had to be limited to a certain extent. "Such a limitation of the effects of the mark for the purposes of promoting comparative advertising appears necessary not only in the case of use, by the advertiser, of a competitor's actual mark, but also in the case of use of a sign similar to that mark."[75]

---

[73] Point 61 of the Opinion of A.G. Mengozzi.
[74] Point 65 of the Opinion of A.G. Mengozzi.
[75] *O2*, para.40.

The Court added that the broad definition of comparative advertising in art.2(2a) of Directive 84/450 covered cases where a reference to a competitor or its products was made even by implication.[76] "Comparative advertising" means any advertising which explicitly or by implication identifies a competitor or goods or services offered by a competitor. This would also cover use of a sign similar to the mark of a competitor of the advertiser perceived by the average consumer as a reference to that competitor or its goods and services:

> "Consequently, in order to reconcile the protection of registered marks and the use of comparative advertising, Article 5(1) and (2) of Directive 89/104 and Article 3a(1) of Directive 84/450 must be interpreted to the effect that the proprietor of a registered trade mark is not entitled to prevent the use, by a third party, of a sign identical with, or similar to, his mark, in a comparative advertisement which satisfies all the conditions, laid down in Article 3a(1) of Directive 84/450, under which comparative advertising is permitted."[77]

10-063   The Court then made the link between art.5(1)(b) of Directive 89/104 and art.3a(1)(d) of Directive 84/450 both covering cases where there is a likelihood of confusion.

So, art.5(1) and (2) of Directive 89/104/EEC and art.3a(1) of Directive 84/450 had to "be interpreted as meaning that the proprietor of a registered trade mark is not entitled to prevent the use by a third party of a sign identical with, or similar to, his mark, in a comparative advertisement which satisfies all the conditions, laid down in Article 3a(1) of Directive 84/450, under which comparative advertising is permitted."[78] But, where the conditions required in art.5(1)(b) of Directive 89/104 were met then the condition of art.3a(1)(d) of Directive 84/450 would not be met.

10-064   **(ii) Use of a sign similar to a trade mark.** The Court noted that the factual context of the case meant that only art.5(1)(b) of Directive 89/104 had to be interpreted.

However, some concepts had to be clarified in a uniform way for the purpose of art.5(1). "Use" was one of them and reviewing its case law the Court identified four conditions:

— that use must be in the course of trade;

— it must be without the consent of the proprietor of the mark;

---

[76] *O2*, para.42, citing *Pippig Augenoptik* (C-44/01) [2003] E.C.R. I-3095; and *De Landtsheer Emmanuel* (C-381/05) [2007] E.C.R. I-3115.
[77] *O2*, para.45.
[78] *O2*, para.51.

— it must be in respect of goods or services which are identical with, or similar to, those for which the mark is registered; and

— it must affect or be liable to affect the essential function of the trade mark, which is to guarantee to consumers the origin of the goods or services, by reason of a likelihood of confusion on the part of the public.[79]

Turning to the facts of the case the Court made the following remarks: H3G's use was use in the course of trade, without the consent of O2, for services identical with those for which those marks were registered, but did not give rise to a likelihood of confusion.

Accordingly, the answer to the first question should be that:

"Article 5(1)(b) of Directive 89/104 is to be interpreted as meaning that the proprietor of a registered trade mark is not entitled to prevent the use, by a third party, in a comparative advertisement, of a sign similar to that mark in relation to goods or services identical with, or similar to, those for which that mark is registered where such use does not give rise to a likelihood of confusion on the part of the public, and that is so irrespective of whether or not the comparative advertisement satisfies all the conditions laid down in Article 3a of Directive 84/450 under which comparative advertising is permitted."[80]

The Court held that it did not have to consider the other two questions since it had not answered the first question in the affirmative.

(6) L'Oréal v Bellure—taking a step back?

(a) The factual context 10–065

The Court appears to be taking a step back in the discourse on comparative advertising with its judgment in *L'Oréal v Bellure*.[81]

Bellure and the other respondents referred to the trade marks of the appellants in comparative lists in which they paired, according to similarity of smell, their own much cheaper products with the established luxury perfumes; the lists had been circulated to retailers. Some of the smell-alike products were also sold in packaging similar in terms of appearance to the packaging of their luxury paired perfumes, although it had been accepted that it was unlikely that either retailers or consumers would be misled as to origin.

---

[79] *O2*, para.57, citing *Arsenal Football Club; Anheuser-Busch* (C-245/02) [2004] E.C.R. I-10989; Medion; Adam Opel; and Céline.
[80] *O2*, para.69.
[81] *L'Oréal SA, Lancôme Parfums et Beauté & Cie, Laboratoire Garnier & Cie v Bellure NV, Malaika Investments Ltd, Starion International Ltd* (C-487/07).

The case reached the English Court of Appeal that referred five questions to the Court. In the first four questions the balancing between the interests of trade mark proprietors and the use of trade marks in comparative advertising was an issue. Questions one and two covered primarily aspects of art.5(1) of Directive 89/104; question five considered art.5(2) and it has been covered earlier in this book.[82]

The remaining two focused more, either directly or indirectly, on Directive 84/450:

> "(3) In the context of Article 3a[1](g) of Directive [84/450], what is the meaning of 'take unfair advantage of' and in particular, where a trader in a comparison list compares his product with a product under a well-known trade mark, does he thereby take unfair advantage of the reputation of the well-known mark?
>
> (4) In the context of Article 3a[1](h) of the said directive, what is the meaning of 'present[ing] goods or services as imitations or replicas' and in particular does this expression cover the case where, without in any way causing confusion or deception, a party merely truthfully says that his product has a major characteristic (smell) like that of a well-known product which is protected by a trade mark?"[83]

10–066 *(b) The Opinion of the Advocate General*

Advocate General Mengozzi expressed some reservations in respect of the findings of the Court of Appeal, for example he doubted whether the parties were real competitors in the market place for perfumes but accepted that following *De Landtsheer Emmanuel*, where he too delivered the Opinion,[84] the acts of the respondents could still constitute comparative advertising since potential competition and how markets and consumers might evolve should also be taken into account. He conceded though that in the absence of clear evidence to the contrary it was necessary to accept the premise adopted by the Court of Appeal that the lists constituted comparative advertising within the meaning of art.2(2a) of Directive 84/450.

10–067 **(i) The first two questions.** He then proceeded in reminding the Court that they had held in *O2*[85] that use of a third party's trade mark in comparative advertisements could be regarded as use for the advertiser's own goods and services for the purposes of art.5(1) and (2) of Directive 89/104, however the trade mark proprietor was not entitled to prevent such use provided it satisfied art.3a(1) of Directive 84/450.

---

[82] See paras 5–230 and following and para.6–056.
[83] Reproduced in Point 15.
[84] *De Landtsheer Emmanuel* (C-381/05) [2007] E.C.R. I-3115.
[85] *O2 Holdings Ltd, O2 (UK) Ltd v Hutchison 3G UK Ltd* (C-533/06) [2008] E.C.R. I4231

2. COMPARATIVE ADVERTISING

According to the Advocate General "[C]ompliance with the conditions under which comparative advertising is permitted under Article 3a(1) of Directive 84/450 constitutes, in my view, an independent ground of defence, in addition to those in Articles 6 and 7(1) of Directive 89/104, which is capable of defeating an action brought against a comparative advertisement based on national provisions implementing Article 5(1) or (2) of Directive 89/104".[86]

Focusing on the first two questions the Advocate General noted that elements, and at least the first question, had been answered in terms of principles by *O2* but still felt he had to consider in the light of the factual context.

Following an analysis of the jurisprudence of the Court in respect of the essential function of a trade mark A.G. Mengozzi suggested that the answer to first two questions should be that art.5(1)(a) of Directive 89/104 should be interpreted as meaning "that the proprietor of a trade mark is not entitled to prohibit use by a third party in comparative advertising of a sign that is identical with that mark for goods or services which are identical with those for which the mark is registered where such use does not affect or is not liable to affect the mark's essential function of providing a guarantee of origin or any of the mark's other functions and that is the case even if such use plays a significant role in the promotion of the advertiser's goods and, in particular, permits that advertiser to take unfair advantage of the mark's reputation".[87]

10–068

However, the stated use could still be prohibited under art.5(2) of Directive 8/104 or art.3a(1) of Directive 84/450.

He then went on to discuss questions three and four.

(ii) The comparative advertising questions. Starting his question 3 analysis A.G. Mengozzi suggested that the legislature used the word "unfair" in art.3a(1)(g) "because it considered that the fact that there may be an advantage for the advertiser deriving from the reputation of the competitor's distinctive signs is not sufficient in itself to justify prohibiting comparative advertising ... In order for it to be prohibited, it is necessary for that advantage to be classified as 'unfair' ".[88] Accordingly, the second part of the question should be answered in then found to be negative.

10–069

Attempting to identify the criteria according to which a comparative advertisement could be classified as unfair he supported that "it will be necessary first of all to ascertain whether such advertising may cause the public at whom it is directed to make an association with the reputation of the competitor's mark by way of extension";[89] the overall presentation of the

---

[86] Point 25 of the Opinion of A.G. Mengozzi.
[87] Point 61 of the Opinion of A.G. Mengozzi.
[88] Point 66 of the Opinion of A.G. Mengozzi.
[89] Point 74 of the Opinion of A.G. Mengozzi.

advertising and the type of audience targeted by the advertisement would be factors that should be taken into account. The second step would be to determine whether the advantage was unfair, for this reference to the individual circumstances of each case had to be made. Even an advertisement with genuine informative content could be found to confer an unfair advantage "where, when an association with the reputation of another person's mark is made by way of extension, that content is, viewed objectively, of limited value, the competitor's mark enjoys a high degree of brand recognition and the funds invested for the purpose of promoting the advertiser's product are fully utilised in advertising which makes a comparison with the product identified by that mark".[90] The assessment was of a factual nature, a matter for the national court to determine.

Turning to the fourth question, on art.3a(1)(g) of Directive 84/450, he suggested that the provision:

> "does not even appear to be intended to prohibit a positive statement that the advertiser's product or one of its characteristics and the product protected by another person's mark or one of its characteristics are equivalent. Accordingly, where the advertiser simply states that his product is equivalent (or has an equivalent characteristic) to the product protected by another person's mark (or to one of that product's characteristics), without, however, alluding to the fact that that equivalence is the result of copying the latter mark (or one of its characteristics), it does not seem to me that one product is being presented as an imitation or replica of another".[91]

Choosing a strict interpretation he added that the provision covered only "a statement of the fact that the advertised product has been manufactured in a process involving the making of an imitation or replica of the model for the product bearing the protected trade mark".[92]

(c) The judgment of the Court

10–070 **(i) The first two questions.** The Court concurred with the Advocate General that the broad definitions of advertising and comparative advertising in art.2(1) of Directive 84/450 could cover varied advertising patterns and made the same points regarding its findings in O2.[93]

Following a review of its case law on the functions of a trade mark the Court concluded that:

---

[90] Point 77 of the Opinion of A.G. Mengozzi.
[91] Point 84 of the Opinion of A.G. Mengozzi.
[92] Point 88 of the Opinion of A.G. Mengozzi.
[93] *O2 Holdings Ltd, O2 (UK) Ltd* (C-533/06) [2008] E.C.R. I4231

2. COMPARATIVE ADVERTISING

"Art. 5(1)(a) of Directive 89/104 must be interpreted as meaning that the proprietor of a registered trade mark is entitled to prevent the use by a third party, in a comparative advertisement which does not satisfy all the conditions, laid down in Article 3a(1) of Directive 84/450, under which comparative advertising is permitted, of a sign identical with that mark in relation to goods or services which are identical with those for which that mark was registered, even where such use is not capable of jeopardising the essential function of the mark, which is to indicate the origin of the goods or services, provided that such use affects or is liable to affect one of the other functions of the mark".[94]

(ii) The comparative advertising questions. The Court examined questions three and four together. 10–071

It held that the art.3a(1)(a) to (h) list of factors had to be applied cumulatively and that they should be interpreted in the sense most favourable to permitting advertisements which objectively compare product characteristics.[95] It followed, "that the use of a competitor's trade mark in comparative advertising is permitted by Community law where the comparison objectively highlights differences and the object or effect of such highlighting is not to give rise to situations of unfair competition, such as those described inter alia in Article 3a(1)(d), (e), (g) and (h) of Directive 84/450".[96]

Turning to art.3a(1)(h) the Court found that "it is not only advertisements which explicitly evoke the idea of imitation or reproduction which are prohibited, but also those which, having regard to their overall presentation and economic context, are capable of implicitly communicating such an idea to the public at whom they are directed".[97] The Court then considered art.3a(1)(g) taking into account the factual context and its own approach towards art.3a(1)(h). Accordingly, it held that:

"the answer to the third and fourth questions is that Article 3a(1) of Directive 84/450 must be interpreted as meaning that an advertiser who states explicitly or implicitly in comparative advertising that the product marketed by him is an imitation of a product bearing a well-known trade mark presents 'goods or services as imitations or replicas' within the meaning of Article 3a(1)(h). The advantage gained by the advertiser as a result of such unlawful comparative advertising must be considered to be an advantage taken unfairly of the reputation of that mark within the meaning of Article 3a(1)(g)".[98]

---

[94] *L'Oreal v Bellure*, para.65.
[95] *De Landtsheer Emmanuel* (C-381/05) [2007] E.C.R. I-3115.
[96] *L'Oreal v Bellure*, para.72.
[97] *L'Oreal v Bellure*, para.75.
[98] *L'Oreal v Bellure*, para.80.

3. GEOGRAPHICAL INDICATIONS

10-072 (1) Feta—consumer confusion and a misappropriation rationale

The judgment of the court in *Feta*[99] represented another challenge to the European regime for the protection of geographical indications and designations of origin. The issue was whether the term "feta" constituted a generic description of a type of cheese or a designation of origin.

For our purposes the judgment of the Court reveals the wider applicability of consumer confusion and misappropriation rationales. It also provides the opportunity to compare the Community Trade Mark system with another Community-wide system of protection of distinguishing signs that has to deal with analogous problems, in this case what constitutes a generic description.

10-073 *(a) The framework of protection*

The framework of protection based on registration is provided by Council Regulation (EEC) 2081/1992.[100]

Article 2(2)(a) defines a designation of origin as "the name of a region, a specific place or, in exceptional cases, a country, used to describe an agricultural product or a foodstuff:—originating in that region, specific place or country, and—the quality or characteristics of which are essentially or exclusively due to a particular geographical environment with its inherent natural and human factors, and the production, processing and preparation of which take place in the defined geographical area".

Article 2(3) equates to designations of origin certain traditional geographical or non-geographical names designating an agricultural product or a foodstuff originating in a region or a specific place, which fulfils the same conditions.

10-074 According to art.3(1) generic names should not be registered. A name that relates to the place or the region where this product or foodstuff has been originally produced or marketed but has become the common name of an agricultural product or a foodstuff is considered to have become generic.

To determine whether a name has become generic all relevant factors are taken into account, and in particular the existing situation in the Member State in which the name originates, in areas of consumption, and in other Member States, as well as the relevant national or Community laws. A "Register of Protected Designations of Origin and Protected Geographical

---

[99] *Federal Republic of Germany and Kingdom of Denmark v Commission* (C-465/02 & C-466/02) [2005] E.C.R. I-9115.
[100] Council Reg.(EEC) 2081/92 on the Protection of Geographical Indications and Designations of Origin for Agricultural Products and Foodstuffs, [1992] O.J. L 208/1.

3. GEOGRAPHICAL INDICATIONS

Indications" is maintained by the Commission. The process has been subsequently repealed by Council Regulation (EC) No.692/2003.[101]

A committee of representatives from Member States assists the Commission in respect of measures to be taken according to the Regulation. Disagreement between the Commission and the committee triggers a process that involves the Council. The Commission has also set up a scientific committee to examine technical problems relating to the application of the Regulation.

(b) The history of Feta's protection 10–075

"Feta" had been registered as a designation of origin in 1996 according to earlier Regulations,[102] albeit the Court annulled the registration in 1999[103] on the ground that the Commission had not taken into account all the factors it had to consider, in particular the situation in other Member States.

Subsequently the Commission conducted a survey on the manufacture, consumption, and reputation of "feta" in each of the Member States on the basis of which the scientific committee concluded that "feta" was not generic.

As a result the Commission reintroduced "feta" into the list of protected designations of origin through the adoption of the contested Regulation 1829/2002 (the Regulation)[104] that, to an extent, followed a "misappropriation" rationale.

The finding on consumer confusion was influenced by the evidence of free riding. According to the Twentieth Recital, most "feta" cheeses made explicit or implicit reference to Greek territory, culture or tradition, irrespective of their actual origin, by adding text or drawings with a Greek connotation. The link was considered to be "deliberately suggested and sought as part of a sales strategy that capitalises on the reputation of the original product, and this creates a real risk of consumer confusion".[105] 10–076

In addition the Regulation incorporated a broad range of criteria; legal, historical, cultural, political, social, economic, scientific, and technical information contributed to its justificatory basis.

The geographical area covered by the Regulation was broadly delineated: the relevant natural and human factors applied throughout the mainland and the island of Lesvos.

---

[101] Council Reg.(EC) 692/2003 Amending Regulation (EEC) 2081/92 on the Protection of Geographical Indications and Designations of Origin for Agricultural Products and Foodstuffs, [2003] OJ L 99/1.
[102] Commission Reg.(EC) 1107/96 on the Registration of Geographical Indications and Designations of Origin under the Procedure laid down in art.17 of Reg.2081/92, [1996] OJ L148/1.
[103] *Kingdom of Denmark* (289/96), *Federal Republic of Germany* (293/96) and *French Republic* (299/96) *v Commission* [1999] E.C.R. I-1541.
[104] Commission Regulation (EC) 1829/2002 amending the Annex to Regulation (EC) 1107/96 with regard to the name "Feta" [2002] OJ L277/10.
[105] *Feta*, para.21.

10-077   However, the revised product specification submitted by the Greek authorities included a balancing limitation: milk used to produce "feta" must come from ewes and goats of local breeds reared traditionally and whose feed is based on the flora present in the pastures of eligible regions.

This, coupled with the traditional method of production, in particular the straining without pressure process, gave to the end product its specific aroma and flavour and as a result its international reputation.

10-078   *(c)   The Opinion of the Advocate General*

There were main points in the substantive analysis of A.G. Ruiz-Jarabo Colomer.[106]

First, he described the reasoning behind the protection of geographical names as the reward for the efforts of those manufacturing a product in a particular way that bestows the product a reputation deserving to be protected through an industrial property right. The aim is to prevent financial injury but also the unjust enrichment of third parties. Citing his Opinion in *Canadane* he reminded the Court that "geographical names are legally protected by national laws on industrial and commercial property. The legal protection of a geographical name confers a collective monopoly over its commercial use upon a particular group of producers by reference to their geographical location–in contrast, a trade mark can only be used by the owner".[107]

Reviewing the jurisprudence of the Court in this area he concluded:

> "All those judgments reflect the tendency of European legislation to put the emphasis on the quality of the products, within the framework of the common agricultural policy, in order to improve their reputation . . . they attribute a dual purpose to appellations of origin: to guarantee the origin of the particular product and act as a barrier against the deceptive use of the appellation and in parallel to protect the industrial and commercial property which has become increasingly more in relation to the principle of free movement of goods."[108]

10-079   Secondly, he repeated his conclusion in *Canadane* regarding the principle of protecting the designation "feta":

> "(1) Legislation of a Member State which prevents the marketing, under the sales description 'feta', of a cheese lawfully produced and marketed under that name in another Member State is a measure having equivalent

---

[106] The Opinion was available to the author in French and Greek.
[107] Point 36 of *Canadane Cheese Trading AMBA and Adelfi G Kouri Anonymos Emoriki Kai Viomichaniki Etaireia v Hellenic Republic* (C-317/95) [1997] E.C.R. I-4681.
[108] Point 82 of the Opinion of A.G. Ruiz-Jarabo Colomer.

3. GEOGRAPHICAL INDICATIONS

effect to a quantitative restriction, contrary to Article [28] of the EC Treaty.

(2) Legislation of a Member State which restricts to national products the use of the name 'feta' is not justified on the grounds of consumer protection or fair trading.

(3) Legislation of a Member State intended to protect the rights which are the specific subject-matter of a geographical name, such as the name 'feta', is justified on the ground of protection of industrial and commercial property referred to in Article [30] of the EC Treaty."[109]

Thirdly, he suggested that in ascertaining consumer perception the view of Greek consumers should be taken into account since there was partial overlap between the place of origin and the place of consumption. Greek consumers perceived "feta" as a domestic product that enjoyed a high degree of reputation. And a large part of consumers in other Member States associated "feta" with Greece to the extent that the overwhelming majority of labelling of "feta" included references to the Greek cultural identity.

Fourthly, he suggested that the views of consumers in Germany, Denmark, and France on "feta"—countries that produced "feta"-like cheeses using cows' milk—should be taken into account but not dominate the overall assessment that should consider the position throughout the Union and take account of all relevant factors. The situation in other countries, outside the Union, constituted another factor to be taken into account; he suggested though that it should be accorded less relevance in the absence of a specific international agreement. He noted that the use of cows' milk rather than goats' or sheeps' milk, as a result of chemical and organoleptic differences, meant that the cheese produced in those countries differed in terms of appearance, taste, and aroma. Feta made from sheeps' milk is pure white, whereas that from cows' milk is a yellowish white, which can be made pure white only by the addition of chemical substances. Cows' milk feta has fewer holes than that made from sheeps' milk because the effect of the brine is different. The original feta has an oily, salty, slightly acidic taste and a strong aroma, whereas cows' milk feta is sweeter in taste and less aromatic.

10–080

Fifthly, he underlined the intertemporal context of use; going back to Homer's Odyssey and the account of the cheese produced by the cyclop Polyphemus.[110] There was a historical link with Greece that should not be overlooked. Looking at the link from another angle he posed the rhetorical question: "Why do the manufacturers of white cheese made from cows' milk in brine choose to call it 'feta'? Without a doubt, in order to use a

10–081

---

[109] Point 79 of *Canadane Cheese Trading AMBA and Adelfi G Kouri Anonymos Emoriki Kai Viomichaniki Etaireia v Hellenic Republic* (C-317/95) [1997] E.C.R. I-4681.
[110] See the historical analysis in *Canadane*.

designation that means something to consumers ... they sought the name that would allow them to maximize sales."[111]

Following the consideration of all relevant factors under the light of the five points described above he proposed that the challenge to the Regulation should be rejected.

10-082 *(d) The Judgment of the Court*

(i) The procedural point. The first issue raised by Germany was on a point of procedure. The documents to be discussed by the regulatory committee at one of its meetings were, first, not notified to the German authorities within a 14-day period prior to the discussion and, secondly, not notified in German. The Court rejected the claim given that Germany had in any case managed to raise an objection to the adoption Regulation at the particular meeting. "A procedural irregularity of this nature could entail annulment of the act ultimately adopted only if, were it not for that irregularity, the procedure could have led to a different result."[112]

10-083 **(ii) The attack against Feta—etymology and geographical coverage.** The second German claim was based on the Italian etymological origin of the word "feta"; it meant "slice" and was used in Balkan and Middle East countries in relation to a cheese in brine. Accordingly, the Commission should have taken a further step back and examined whether the word had acquired a geographic meaning in the first place.

In addition, the breadth of the geographical area—one particular point made was that almost the entire country was covered—appeared, according to Germany, to be arbitrarily set and not linked with the quality and characteristics of "feta".

The Danish attack too focused on the geographical area covered by the Regulation supporting on the one hand that the required link with "feta" did not exist because "feta" was used throughout the Balkans and on the other that morphological and climatological differences within the designated area resulted to variations of "Greek fetas", as the Danes put it. The product's international reputation, they claimed, was partly due to the production and exports of other Member States.

10-084 *Geographical coverage* The Court started by noting that art.2(3) of the basic application referred to art.2(2)(a); their joint application meant that "the designated area must therefore, present homogenous natural factors which distinguish it from the areas adjoining it".[113]

---

[111] Point 176 of the Opinion of A.G. Ruiz-Jarabo Colomer.
[112] *Feta*, para.37; referring inter alia to *Belgium v Commission* (C-142/87) [1990] E.C.R. I-959.
[113] *Feta*, para.50; the Court cited *Commission v Germany* (12/74) [1975] E.C.R. 181.

3. GEOGRAPHICAL INDICATIONS

According to the Court the relevant Greek legislation identified the geographical area that satisfied the criteria of art.2(3) and excluded a significant part of the territory of Greece, namely all the islands except Lesvos. It did not cover the entirety of Greece. Accordingly, the Court had only to consider whether the designated area was determined in an artificial manner.

10–085

The Greek legislation provided that: "the milk used for the manufacture of feta must come from breeds of ewes and goats raised using traditional methods and adapted to the region of manufacture of the feta and the flora of that region must be the basis of their feed".[114]

According to the specifications submitted in 1994 the demarcation of the geographical area was based on its homogeneous geomorphology, climate, and botanical characteristics. The excluded territories did not display the same features.

There was evidence that "feta" was also produced in some of the smaller Aegean islands, however this was not found to constitute a problem since, according to the Commission, those islands were part of the department of Lesvos.

On the basis of the above the Court rejected the claim that the geographical area was not defined according to art.6(2) of the Regulation.

Geography and product characteristics Another claim targeting the geographical coverage of the Regulation was that feta's quality and characteristics were not essentially or exclusively due to a particular geographical environment, as required by art.2(2)(a) of the basic regulation.

10–086

The Court rejected this claim since the Preamble to the Regulation referred to a list of factors supporting that the characteristics of feta were essentially or exclusively due to a particular geographical environment. The specifications submitted by the Greek Government focusing, amongst others, on the amount of sunshine, temperature changes, the practice of transhumance, extensive grazing, and vegetation reinforced the statement in the Preamble.

(iii) The generic nature of feta. The Court also rejected the plea that the Regulation infringed art.3(1) of the basic regulation because "Feta" was a generic name within the meaning of art.3(1).

10–087

One of the specific arguments under this plea was that the likelihood of consumer confusion referred to in the Twentieth Recital in the Preamble had no bearing on the issue of whether a name was generic. Another had to do with identifying the party that carried the burden of proof.

The Court noted that although white cheeses soaked in brine had been produced for a long time in other countries they were known in those countries under other names than "feta".

---

[114] Article 2(1)(e) of Ministerial Order No.313025, cited in para.56.

10–088 In Greece itself, until 1987, cheese produced from cows' milk and according to non-traditional methods was produced under the name "feta" and, until 1988, imported under the same name from other countries. If this were to continue inevitably the name would have become generic, however through a number of measures these practices were discontinued.

The Court accepted that the fact that a product that had been lawfully marketed under a name in some Member States might constitute a factor in the assessment of whether that name had become generic. However, it noted, although the production in the other countries had been relatively large and of substantial duration, the production of "feta" had remained concentrated in Greece. Lawful production in other countries was only one of the factors that had to be taken into account.

Consumption on the other hand occurred predominantly in Greece. 85 per cent of Community consumption of "feta" was concentrated in Greece, where the majority of consumers considered the name to carry a geographical rather than a generic connotation. In Denmark, the opposite outcome was reached.

10–089 What weakened the evidence regarding the allegedly generic use of "feta" in Member States other than Greece was that it was commonly marketed with labels referring to Greek cultural traditions and civilisation. It was legitimate to infer that consumers perceived "feta" as a cheese associated with Greece irrespective of its place of production.

All the above suggested that "feta" was not generic and that it was not incorrect to state that the link between the name "feta" and Greece was deliberately suggested; accordingly the German Government contention was unfounded.

Even the national legislation in Denmark, the Court remarked, referred to "Danish feta" rather than "feta", a fact that suggested that even in Denmark the name had a Greek connotation.

Note that the Court did not consider the burden of proof argument, once it found that the statement was correct.

10–090 **(iv) The sufficiency of the statement of reasons.** Finally the Court found that the Commission's analysis, as reflected in the Preamble, was adequately detailed and substantiated.[115] The Commission was free to refer any relevant questions to the committee and then to decide to what extent it would follow the opinion provided by the committee. In this case, it chose to follow the advice of the committee.

---

[115] Citing *Weber v Freistaat Bayern* (C-328/00) [2002] E.C.R. I-1461; and *Commission v Chambre Syndicale Nationale des Entreprises de Transport de Fonds et Valeurs (Sytraval) and Brink's France SARL* (C-367/95 P) [1998] E.C.R. I-1719.

3. GEOGRAPHICAL INDICATIONS

(2) Bavaria—the coexistence between trade mark and geographical indication protection

In Case C-343/07, *Bavaria NV, Bavaria Italia Srl v Bayerischer Brauerbund eV*[116] the Court considered the coexistence between trade mark and protected geographical indication protection.

10-091

The case came before the Court as a reference from the Italian Corte d'Appello di Torino (Turin Court of Appeal). The questions posed by the Italian court focused on whether the name "Bayerisches Bier" constituted a valid protected geographical indication (PGI), registered by a German association, and whether such protection would affect the validity and use of existing trade marks for beer incorporating the name "Bavaria" registered in Italy by a Dutch controlled group of companies.[117]

(a) The Opinion of the Advocate General

In his opinion Advocate General Mazák[118] looked first at whether the Dutch group was entitled to challenge the validity of Regulation No 1347/2001[119] having missed the chance to challenge it before the ECJ within the period set by art.230 EC. According to the ECJ's case law "a person is prevented from pleading the illegality of a Community act before the national court and from challenging its validity indirectly under Article 234 EC only if his entitlement to seek the annulment of that act under Article 230 EC was both plain and beyond doubt".[120] Here, however, everything depended on the scope of protection of the PGI that was neither plain nor beyond doubt.

10-092

(i) The validity of the PGI registration. Turning to the substantive arguments of the parties he accepted that beer could be considered a "foodstuff", defined in art.2 of Regulation No 178/2002[121] as "any substance or product, whether processed, partially processed or unprocessed, intended to be, or reasonably expected to be ingested by humans". And having rejected all the challenges based on procedural aspects he moved to the crux of the dispute: whether the term was generic, and as such should

10-093

---

[116] *Bavaria NV, Bavaria Italia Srl v Bayerischer Brauerbund eV* (C-343/07) [2009] E.T.M.R. 61.
[117] Proceedings in *Bavaria v Council* (T-178/06) and *Bayerischer Brauerbund* (C-120/08) pending before the CFI and the ECJ respectively have been stayed until delivery of the judgment in the present case.
[118] Opinion of A.G. Makák [2009] E.T.M.R. 61.
[119] Council Regulation (EC) No 1347/2001 of 28 June 2001 supplementing the Annex to Commission Regulation (EC) No 1107/96 on the registration of geographical indications and designations of origin under the procedure laid down in Article 17 of Council Regulation (EEC) No 2081/92 ([2001] OJ L182/3) and of Council Regulation (EEC) No 2081/92 of 14 July 1992 on the protection of geographical indications and designations of origin for agricultural products and foodstuffs ([1992] O.J. L208/1). Note the narrow scope of the Regulation.
[120] Para 36, citing *TWD Textilwerke Deggendorf* (C-188/92) [1994] E.C.R. I-833.
[121] Regulation 178/2002 laying down the general principles and requirements of food law, establishing the European Food Safety Authority and laying down procedures in matters of food safety [2002] OJ L31/1.

be precluded from registration.[122] The Dutch group supported that the term referred to a widespread method of production rather the origin of the product, highlighting that "Bavaria" was a common element of company names trade marks in a number of countries, including Germany, and a synonym for beer in Denmark, Sweden, and Finland.

However, he accepted that the term has been accepted for registration because of the particular reputation of beer produced in Bavaria, the result of tradition and legal measures that went back to 1516. "What is decisive, for the purposes of registering a PGI, is not whether the quality, reputation or other characteristic of a specific type or brand of beer is attributable to its geographical origin, but whether such a link can be established between the beverage 'beer' and the geographical origin concerned. Similarly, PGIs are not designed to distinguish a specific product or producer but can be used by all producers and with regard to all products, in this case by all types of beer, which emanate from the geographical area concerned and which satisfy the relevant product specifications."[123] And as we have seen above,[124] in order to assess the generic character of a name, it is necessary to take into account the position both inside and outside the Member State which obtained the registration of the contested name. He also stressed that even if the term had become generic at some point it could regain its indication of origin significance; in this case there was evidence "Bayerisches Bier" functioned as such an indicator after 1940.

The other critical, for our purposes, validity point had to do with whether use of the term has become misleading in the light of the reputation of the registered trade marks.[125] According to the Advocate General the purpose of art.14(3) was to "prevent a product bearing a PGI from being confused by the consumer with a given trade mark product".[126] However this had already been considered at the time the PGI was registered and there was no evidence that the finding of the Commission was incorrect. Note the point made by the Advocate General that "the higher the reputation or renown of a mark, and thus the stronger its distinctiveness, the lower will be the likelihood that consumers may be misled to the extent of ascribing a product with a given PGI to that trade mark".[127]

10–094 **(ii) The effect of the PGI registration on pre-existing trade marks—another aspect of coexistence.** To answer that question the Advocate General focused on the actual relevant provision of the Regulation

---

[122] According to arts 2(2)(b), 3(1) and 17(2) of Regulation No 2081/92 and citing *Warsteiner* (C-312/98) [2000] E.C.R. I-9187.
[123] *Bavaria*, para.112.
[124] *Bavaria*, para.00000, citing *Germany and Denmark v Commission* (C-465/02 & C-466/02) [2005] E.C.R. I-9115; and *Commission v Germany* (C-132/05) [2008] E.C.R. I-957.
[125] According to art.14(3) of Regulation No 2081/92.
[126] *Bavaria*, para.128.
[127] *Bavaria*, para.133.

3. GEOGRAPHICAL INDICATIONS

No 1347/2001, art.14, rather than the Recitals in its Preamble.[128] Article 14(3): "offers... protection to pre-existing trade marks in so far as it prevents the registration of an indication or designation, the use of which would result in a likelihood of confusion with an earlier trade mark".[129] It was a barrier to registration and did not cover "all the situations in which, according to the scope of protection afforded under Article 13 of the regulation, trade marks may encroach on names registered under that regulation".[130]

Coexistence in this case meant that a trade mark which conflicts with a protected geographical indication or designation of origin for the purposes of art.13 of Regulation No 2081/92 could be continued to be used "only on condition that, first, that trade mark was registered in good faith before the date on which the application for registration of a designation of origin or a geographical indication was lodged and, secondly, provided that there are no grounds for the invalidity or revocation of the trade mark as laid down under Article 3(1)(c) and (g) and Article 12(2)(b) of the Trade Marks Directive".[131] Whether the facts of the case fell under the provision was for the national court to determine.[132]

(b) The judgment of the Court

10–095

The Court[133] to a large extent followed the Opinion of Advocate General Mazák.

It accepted that it cannot be claimed that Bavaria and Bavaria Italia are undoubtedly directly affected by Regulation No 1347/2001 and accordingly did not undoubtedly have standing to bring an action for annulment. It could accordingly challenge the Regulation at a later stage.

Given that Regulation No 2081/92 does not provide a definition of the term "foodstuff" the Court found no reason why beer should be excluded. From a positive perspective the Court added that in other Community legislation beer is covered by the definition of "foodstuff"[134] and the Court had already decided that arts 33 and 37 EC also apply to products that are not covered in Annex I to the Treaty.[135] Note that the Court also paid attention

---

[128] See in particular the Third and the Fourth Recitals, referring to the trade marks in question.
[129] *Bavaria*, para.151.
[130] *Bavaria*, para.153.
[131] *Bavaria*, para.156.
[132] Citing *Consorzio per la tutela del formaggio Gorgonzola v Kaserei Champignon Hofmeister and Eduard Bracharz* (C-87/97) [1999] E.C.R. I-1301.
[133] [2009] E.T.M.R. 61. See also *Commission v Germany* (C-132/05) [2008] E.C.R. I-957 on the conflict between Parmiggino Reggiano and Parmesan.
[134] Citing art.2 of Regulation (EC) No 178/2002 of the European Parliament and of the Council of 28 January 2002 laying down the general principles and requirements of food law, establishing the European Food Safety Authority and laying down procedures in matters of food safety ([2002] OJ L31/1).
[135] Citing *Commission v Council* (C-11/88), para.15; and *United Kingdom v Commission* (C-180/96) [1998] E.C.R. I-2265.

to the argument that although beer is not expressly mentioned in the annex, most of its ingredients are.

10–096 **(i) Subsidiarity and the social aspects of agriculture.** Turning to the procedures established by Regulation No 2081/92 the Court, probably following the principle of subsidiarity, accepted the division of powers between Member States and the Commission "the decision to register a designation as a PDO or as a PGI may only be taken by the Commission if the Member State concerned has submitted to it an application for that purpose and that such an application may only be made if the Member State has checked that it is justified".[136] And regarding its own jurisdiction it added that "while the Court has jurisdiction to analyse whether a name registered under Regulation No 2081/92 complies with the conditions set out in that regulation, it is for the national courts alone to review the verification of that compliance initiated by the competent national authorities".[137]

In this case the evidence established that the PGI was registered after extensive assessment regarding its compliance indication with the conditions in Regulation No 2081/92.

The Court added that arts 34 and 37 EC bestowed the Community a broad discretion in matters of agricultural policy; accordingly, "the lawfulness of a measure adopted in that sphere can be affected only if the measure is manifestly inappropriate, having regard to the objective which the competent institution is seeking to pursue".[138]

10–097 And looking at the issue from a social perspective it added that:

"[w]hen implementation by the Council or the Commission of the Community's agricultural policy necessitates the evaluation of a complex economic or social situation, their discretion is not limited solely to the nature and scope of the measures to be taken but also, to some extent, to the finding of basic facts. In that context, it is open to the Council or the Commission to rely if necessary on general findings".[139]

Accordingly, and given that the assessment made by the German authorities did not appear to be vitiated by manifest error, the Council or the Commission could rightly assume that the PGI in question satisfied the conditions set out in art.17(1) of Regulation 2081/92 for registration under the simplified procedure.

---

[136] *Bavaria*, para.66.
[137] *Bavaria*, para.70.
[138] *Bavaria*, para.81, citing *Germany v Council* (C-280/93) [1994] E.C.R. I-4973; and *SMW Winzersekt* (C-306/93) [1994] E.C.R. I-5555.
[139] *Bavaria*, para.84, citing *Commission v Council* (C-122/94) [1996] E.C.R. I-881; *NIFPO and Northern Ireland Fishermen's Federation* (C-4/96) [1998] E.C.R. I-681; *Spain v Council* (C-179/95) [1999] E.C.R. I-6475; and *Italy v Council* (C-120/99) [2001] E.C.R. I-7997.

3. GEOGRAPHICAL INDICATIONS

(ii) The generic nature of the term. As to the generic or not nature of the term the Court accepted that the German authorities were best placed to make the complex and detailed assessment that had not been challenged before a national court.

It also rejected the argument that Bavaria was the name of a state and hence exceptional conditions had to be established in order to be protected as a PGI finding that it did not constitute the name of a "country", as indicated in the Regulation, but an infra-State body.

Looking at the reasons for granting PGI protection the Court found that neither purity nor the traditional brewing method were in themselves the bases for the registration of the term, "it was rather the reputation of beer originating in Bavaria that was determinative".[140] Admittedly, the above qualities that now have become widespread have contributed in building up the reputation, but it was also the reputation of Bavarian beer that contributed to the worldwide acceptance of those qualities.

10–098

The Court found those arguments to be more relevant for the claims regarding the generic nature of the term. It repeated that:

10–099

> "when assessing the generic character of a name, it is necessary, under Article 3(1) of Regulation No 2081/92, to take into account the places of production of the product concerned both inside and outside the Member State which obtained the registration of the name at issue, the consumption of that product and how it is perceived by consumers inside and outside that Member State, the existence of national legislation specifically relating to that product, and the way in which the name has been used in Community law".[141]

Following this it rejected all the specific contentions regarding genericity.

The analysis of the Court on the purpose of the PGI registration system to prevent a term becoming generic may, by analogy, be also relevant in trade mark cases. The system is "designed ... to prevent the improper use of a name by third parties seeking to profit from the reputation which it has acquired and, moreover, to prevent the disappearance of that reputation as a result of popularisation through general use outside its geographical origin or detached from a specific quality, reputation or other characteristic which is attributable to that origin and justifies registration".[142]

> "Therefore, as regards a PGI, a name becomes generic only if the direct link between, on the one hand, the geographical origin of the product and, on the other hand, a specific quality of that product, its reputation or

---

[140] *Bavaria*, para.97.
[141] *Bavaria*, para.101, citing *Commission v Germany* (C-132/05) [2008] E.C.R. I-957.
[142] *Bavaria*, para.106.

another characteristic of the product, attributable to that origin, has disappeared, and that the name does no more than describe a style or type of product."[143]

Looking at the facts of the case the Court found that the name has not become generic. Note that it considered the existence between 1960 and 1970 of the collective marks Bayrisch Bier and Bayrisches Bier as evidence supporting its findings.

10–100 **(iii) Reputation, trade marks, and PGIs.** The Court stated that according to the 3rd Recital the Council had found that registration of the name "Bayerisches Bier" was not liable to mislead the consumer as to the true identity of the product and that, consequently, the geographical indication "Bayerisches Bier" and the trade mark "Bavaria" were not in the situation referred to in art.14(3) of Regulation No 2081/92.

It noted that the finding did not appear to be manifestly inappropriate and there was no argument against it.

Regarding the effect of the registration of the PGI on the Bavaria trade marks the Court noted that art.14 of Regulation No 2081/92 specifically governs that relationship.

10–101 Article 14(3) covers:

"the conflict between a PDO or a PGI and a pre-existing trade mark where registration of the name at issue would, in the light of the trade mark's reputation, renown and the length of time for which it has been used, be liable to mislead the consumer as to the true identity of the product. The consequence provided for in the event of such a conflict is that registration of the name must be refused. This is therefore a rule which implies that there must be an analysis, intended inter alia for the Community institutions, prior to registration of the PDO or PGI."[144]

Its aim is to prevent the possibility of a mistake on the part of the consumer. On the other hand:

"... Article 14(2) of Regulation No 2081/92 refers to a situation of conflict between a registered PDO or a PGI and a pre-existing trade mark where the use of that trade mark corresponds to one of the situations referred to in Article 13 of Regulation No 2081/92 and the trade mark was registered in good faith before the date on which the application for registration of the PDO or PGI was lodged. The consequence provided for in that situation is that use may continue notwithstanding the registration of

---

[143] *Bavaria*, para.107.
[144] *Bavaria*, para.118.

3. GEOGRAPHICAL INDICATIONS

the name, where there are no grounds for invalidity or revocation of the trade mark as provided respectively by Article 3(1)(c) and (g) and Article 12(2)(b) of First Directive 89/104. This is therefore a rule which implies that there must be an analysis, intended inter alia for the authorities and courts called upon to apply the provisions in question, after registration."[145]

Here, the "analysis ... involves ascertaining whether the use of the trade mark corresponds to one of the situations referred to in Article 13 of Regulation No 2081/92; whether the trade mark was registered in good faith before the date on which the application for registration of the name was lodged; and, if appropriate, whether there are grounds for invalidity or revocation of the trade mark as provided respectively by Article 3(1)(c) and (g) and Article 12(2)(b) of First Directive 89/104."[146] This requires an examination of facts that the national court must undertake.

10–102

According to the Court the two provisions have separate objectives and functions and are subject to different conditions. The fact that the marks according to the 3rd Recital do not fall under art.14(3) does not affect the examination of the conditions which make it possible for the mark and the PGI to co-exist as set out in art.14(2).

In particular, the fact that "there is no likelihood of confusion does not mean that it is not necessary to ascertain that the trade mark in question was registered in good faith before the date on which the application for registration of the PDO or PGI was lodged".[147]

(3) Grana Padano—trade marks v geographical indication—the concept of genericity

10–103

It is also worth referring to a CFI case[148] that looks at the concept of genericity from the geographical indication perspective.

The case involved an application by the Consorzio per la tutela del formaggio Grana Padano (the Consorzio) for the invalidation of the Community Trade Mark "Grana Biraghi" registered for cheese on the basis of the registration of the words "grana padano" as a protected denomination of origin. The Cancellation Division accepted that the trade mark registration was invalid, Biraghi, the trade mark proprietor, successfully appealed against OHIM's decision before the Board of Appeal.[149] The Board based primarily on Italian dictionaries and internet searches found, in turn, that

---

[145] *Bavaria*, para.119.
[146] *Bavaria*, para.121.
[147] *Bavaria*, para.125.
[148] *Consorzio per la tutela del formaggio Grana Padano v Office for Harmonisation in the Internal Market (Trade Marks and Designs) (OHIM)* (T-291/03) [2007] E.C.R. II-3081.
[149] Case R 153/2002-1.

the term "grana" was generic from a PDO perspective and, as such, did not preclude the registration of the trade mark.

Before the CFI the Consorzio argued that "grana" was not a generic name, since the PDO "grana padano" was protected under Italian law and at Community level under Regulation No 1107/96[150] and Regulation No 2081/92. Originally, it supported, the term functioned as geographical designation for a small stream in Valle Grana and has now become part of the designation "grana padano". Further, the Court had already ruled against the argument that mere parts of complex names of origin are generic in nature.[151] OHIM observed that the Board of Appeal did not appear to have consulted the competent Italian or Community authorities or to have carried out an in-depth examination of the Italian market and the markets of other Member States. From a "jurisdictional" perspective it noted that once a PDO is registered serves it may not be considered generic, unless the Commission or the competent Community or national judicial authorities decided that it has become generic.

10–104 The core of Biraghi's contention was that the term "grana" was generic, literally describing the granular structure of a type of cheese rather than its geographical origin.

The CFI started by art.142 of Regulation No 40/94 providing that the CTM Regulation does not affect the provisions of Regulation No 2081/92. Accordingly, OHIM was bound to apply the CTM Regulation "in such a way as not to affect the protection granted to PDOs by Regulation No 2081/92".[152] So, a CTM registration of a mark covered by art.13 of Regulation No 2081/92 had to be declared invalid.

However, according to art.13(1) of Regulation No 2081/92, "where a registered name contains within it the name of an agricultural product or foodstuff which is considered generic, the use of that generic name on the appropriate agricultural product or foodstuff shall not be considered to be contrary to (a) or (b) in the first subparagraph".

10–105 The CFI accepted that the Board of Appeal was competent to determine whether part of the PDO was generic and refuse to grant protection to that part. "Since this is not a question of declaring a PDO to be invalid in itself, the fact that the second subparagraph of Article 13(1) of Regulation No 2081/92 precludes the protection of generic names in a PDO authorises the Board of Appeal to ascertain whether the term in question actually constitutes the generic name of an agricultural product or foodstuff."[153] However, the analysis had to verify that a certain number of

---

[150] Commission Regulation (EC) No 1107/96 of 12 June 1996 on the registration of geographical indications and designations of origin under the procedure laid down in Article 17 of Regulation No 2081/92, [1996] OJ L148/1.
[151] *Bigi* (C-66/00) [2002] E.C.R. I-5917.
[152] *Grana Padano*, para.55.
[153] *Grana Padano*, para.60.

conditions have been met; this required, to a great extent, detailed knowledge both of matters particular to the relevant Member State but also other Member States; in short the Board of Appeal was required to carry out a detailed analysis of all the factors which could establish that generic character, including legal, economic, technical, historical, cultural and social evidence, consumer surveys, and any other relevant factor including the definition of the name as generic in the Codex alimentarius.[154]

Here the CFI found, the Board had overlooked the criteria identified by Community case law and covered in art.3 of Regulation No 2081/92.

The CFI then considered in detail the relevant Italian legislation against its historical context; originally it referred to different granas (parmigiano-reggiano, lodigiano, emiliano, lombardo and veneto), all produced in the area of the plain of the Po. Subsequent legislation introduced the name "grana padano" and abandoned the earlier names; this indicated that "grana is a cheese traditionally produced in numerous areas of the plain of the Po, which the Italian legislature therefore, at a certain point in time, identified by the term 'padano' so as to simplify the framework of rules and to include in one single name the various previous names, all originating in the Padanian Valley".[155]

Note too the point made by CFI regarding the use of "grana" on other cheese intended for export to countries where the name "grana" was not protected: "that argument is irrelevant, in accordance with the principle of territoriality recognised by the Court in the area of intellectual property rights".[156]

The CFI annulled the decision of the Board of Appeal.

4. THE BUDWEISER TETRALOGY

The four cases covered here deal with aspects of the same dispute played before different European fora. The *Budweiser* cases are perhaps the best example of the interplay between trade mark and other laws at the Community level. The effect of a bilateral agreement on the free movement of goods, the relationship between European trade mark law and the TRIPs Agreement, and the limitations on the right of property from a human rights perspective have all become factors in a dispute involving distinguishing signs.

10–106

---

[154] Citing amongst others *Carl Kühne* (C-269/99) [2001] E.C.R. I-9517; *Denmark v Commission* (C-289/96, C-293/96 & C-299/96) [1999] E.C.R. I-1541; and *Guimont* (C-448/98) [2000] E.C.R. I-10663.
[155] *Grana Padano*, para.77.
[156] *Grana Padano*, para.80, citing *Exportur*.

(1) Geographical indications, bilateral agreements, and free movement of goods

10–107 The first *Budweiser* case[157] came before the Court as a reference from the Handelsgericht Wien (Commercial Court, Vienna).

The case is important not only because it assisted in setting the context regarding the protection of geographical indications but also because the approach of the Court highlighted the critical difference between the system for protecting geographical indications and that for protecting trade marks.

Both are centralised systems based on registration and providing uniform protection throughout the Union. Both co-exist with national systems of protection. However, the development of trade mark law is also influenced by the Harmonisation Directive that brought closer national systems of protection.

Budvar, the Czech brewer using the names Budějovický Budvar and Budweiser Budvar, started proceedings in Austria against Ammersin that marketed in Austria a beer called American Bud, produced by the US brewer Anheuser-Busch.

It claimed, first, that the Austrian trade mark American Bud should be annulled on the basis of its own earlier registrations in Austria of Budweiser, Budweiser Budvar and Bud.

And, secondly, that use of the designation American Bud for a beer from a state other than the Czech Republic was contrary to the provisions of a bilateral convention between Austria and Czechoslovakia.[158]

The Austrian Court noted that there had been parallel proceedings in Austria against the importer of the American Bud that highlighted the uncertainties surrounding aspects of the case—in particular whether simple indications of geographical source should be considered to fall under the scope of art.30 in the absence of consumer confusion–and referred to the Court the following questions.

"(1) Is the application of a provision of a bilateral agreement concluded between a Member State and a non-member country, under which a simple/indirect geographical indication which in the country of origin is the name neither of a region nor a place nor a country is accorded the absolute protection, regardless of any misleading, of a qualified geographical indication within the meaning of Regulation No 2081/92 compatible with Article 28 EC and/or Regulation No 2081/92, if on application of that

---

[157] *Budějovický Budvar v Rudolf Ammersin GmbH* (C-216/01) [2003] E.C.R. I-13617.
[158] Agreement on the protection of indications of source, designations of origin and other designations referring to the source of agricultural and industrial products, Vienna, June 11, 1976; annexed protocol, Vienna, November 30, 1977; BGBl. 1981, 75. The Agreement between Austria and Czechoslovakia provided amongst others that the parties would protect a number of designations, including Bud, Budjovicke pivo, Budvicke pivo, Budvar, and Budjovický Budvar, for beer.

provision the import of a product which is lawfully put on the market in another Member State may be prevented?

(2) Does this apply also where the geographical indication which in the country of origin is the name neither of a region nor a place nor a country is not understood in the country of origin as a geographical designation for a specific product, and also not as a simple or indirect geographical indication?

(3) Do the answers to Questions 1 and 2 apply also where the bilateral agreement is an agreement which the Member State concluded before its accession to the European Union and continued after its accession to the European Union with a successor State to the original other State party to the agreement by means of a declaration of the Federal Government?

(4) Does the second paragraph of Article 307 EC oblige the Member State to interpret such a bilateral agreement, concluded between that Member State and a non-member country before the Member State's accession to the EU, in conformity with Community law as stated in Article 28 EC and/or Regulation No 2081/92, so that the protection laid down therein for a simple/indirect geographical indication which in the country of origin is the name neither of a region nor a place nor a country comprises merely protection against misleading and not the absolute protection of a qualified geographical indication within the meaning of Regulation No 2081/92?".[159]

The two first questions are particularly relevant for the purposes of this book.

(a) The Opinion of the Advocate General 10–108

Advocate General Tizzano started by casting away any doubt as to admissibility. The Court was asked to interpret art.28 and art.30, rather than the provisions of the bilateral agreement, between a Member State, Austria, and a non-Member State (the Czech Republic joined the Union on May 1, 2004). He also rejected the submission of the Commission that the reference concerned a hypothetical situation. It was for the national court to determine the need for a preliminary ruling and the relevance of the questions to its case; the Court should consider the reference, unless it was obvious that the interpretation of Community law had no relation to the actual nature of the case or the subject-matter of the main action.[160]

(i) The first question. The Advocate General started by considering whether Regulation No.2081/92[161] precluded the application of the 10–109

---

[159] Reproduced in para.43.
[160] Citing *Guimont* (C-448/98) [2000] E.C.R. I-10663; and *Bigi* (C-66/00) [2002] E.C.R. I-5917.
[161] Council Regulation (EEC) 2081/92 on the Protection of Geographical Indications and Designations of Origin for Agricultural Products and Foodstuffs, [1992] OJ L 208/1.

provisions of the bilateral agreement. He conceded that the classification of the designation required the interpretation of the rule that implemented the relevant provision of the agreement into Austrian law. The interpretation of national rules remained a matter for the national courts.[162] However, he expressed his support for the view that the agreement provided for absolute protection of a simple geographical indication. This remained outside the scope of Regulation No. 2081/92.[163]

The second point concerned the applicability of the free movement of goods rules. All parties accepted that the application of the agreement had the potential to hinder the intra-Community circulation of products that have been placed on the market lawfully in other Member States by precluding their importation into Austria. The challenge lay in the applicability of art.30.

He reminded the Court that in *Exportur*[164] the Court had accepted that art.30 covered in principle the protection of simple geographical designations provided for in a bilateral international agreement. There it had observed primarily that the aim of such protection was to prevent taking advantage of the reputation attaching to the products of the undertakings in the protected designations even though no particular or distinctive quality was necessarily linked to the origin of the product. Article 30 should not be applied though when the designations had become, either at the time of the entry into force of the agreement or subsequently, generic in the country of origin.

The Austro-Czechoslovak agreement pursued the same objective, "it aims to prevent persons not established in the Czech Republic from using for the marketing of beer a Czech geographical designation, and more precisely an indication which refers to the Bohemian city of Budweis, thus taking advantage of the reputation attaching to the beer produced in that place",[165] and its compatibility with art.30 should be judged following the above stated principles.

10–110   **(ii) The second question.** All the parties concurred that if there was no link between the designation and the product then its protection would constitute a quantitative restriction without benefiting from the exemption of art.30 EC.

Citing again *Exportur*[166] and using the language of Regulation No. 2081/92 he asserted that the protection of generic designations could not be

---

[162] Citing *Vanacker* (C-37/92) [1993] E.C.R. I-4947.
[163] Citing *Schutzverband gegen Unwesen In der Wirtschaft eV v Warsteiner Brauerei Haus Cramer GmbH & Co KG* (C-312/98) [2000] E.C.R. I-9187.
[164] *Exportur v LOR and Confiserie du Tech* (C-3/91) [1992] E.C.R. I-5529; also followed in *Consorzio per la tutela del formaggio Gorgonzola v Kdserei Champignon Hofmeister and Eduard Bracharz* (C-87/97) [1999] E.C.R. I-1301.
[165] Point 83 of the Opinion of A.G. Tizzano.
[166] *Exportur v LOR and Confiserie du Tech* (C-3/91) [1992] E.C.R. I-5529.

justified under art.30 EC; he defined generic designations by referring to art.3 of the Regulation, as an indication which "although it relates to the place or the region where this product or foodstuff was originally produced or marketed, has become the common name of an agricultural product or a foodstuff".[167]

Expanding on this theme he stated that it covered designations that had either become generic or never been capable of establishing a link between a product and its geographical origin.

There would be no public interest in protecting such a designation. "It is quite clear that, if any possibility of consumers being misled as to the origin of the product can be ruled out, as on the assumption put forward by the national court, the designation in question would not be able to result in, even potentially, either a luring away of customers or wrongful exploitation of a reputation which, by definition, does not exist."[168]

10–111

He doubted though whether Bud was such a designation. Being an abbreviation of the name of the city of Budweis it was capable of evoking the Bohemian origin of the product by associating it with that city. Albeit, this was for the national court to explore.

(iii) The remaining two questions. From a broader interpretive perspective A.G. Tizzano's discussion of the applicability of art.307 EC[169] reveals the range of sources the Court can employ in order to delineate general principles.

10–112

The agreement was signed in 1977; on January 1, 1993, Czechoslovakia was split into the Czech and Slovak Republics; Austria became a member of the Community on January 1, 1995; and on July 31, 1997 the Federal Chancellor of Austria (Bundeskanzler) officially declared the agreement in force between Austria and the Czech Republic. The Advocate General considered a variety of sources before coming to a conclusion regarding the effect of the agreement. He considered the 1978 Vienna Convention on Succession of States in respect of Treaties, despite the fact that neither Austria nor any other Member State had at the time become members of that convention, viewing as a codification of general, and potentially binding, international law; looking not only at its text but also at the travaux preparatoires drawn by the International Law Commission. A principle of conti-

---

[167] Point 90 of the Opinion of A.G. Tizzano.
[168] Point 93 of the Opinion of A.G. Tizzano.
[169] Article 307 EC provides: 1. The rights and obligations arising from agreements concluded before January 1, 1958 or, for acceding States, before the date of their accession, between one or more Member States on the one hand, and one or more third countries on the other, shall not be affected by the provisions of this Treaty. 2. To the extent that such agreements are not compatible with this Treaty, the Member State or States concerned shall take all appropriate steps to eliminate the incompatibilities established. Member States shall, where necessary, assist each other to this end and shall, where appropriate, adopt a common attitude.

nuity[170] began to emerge that he then tested against the practice of international relations from all available perspectives: the Czech and Slovak Republics; the states that emerged from the dissolution of the Union of Soviet Socialist Republics and Yugoslavia; contracting third States; Community institutions; and academic opinion.

It appeared that Austria had moved away from the more traditional tabula rasa principle to a nuanced principle of continuity. Following the split up of Czechoslovakia it chose to denounce the future effect of specific agreements and remain silent about others until it declared at a later stage their continuous effect.

10–113   He concluded that the fact that Austria had not explicitly confirmed that the agreement remained in force until after Austria's entry into the Community did not affect the application of art.307 EC and that it prevailed over any provisions to the contrary of Community law.

Note that Austria and all the Member States that intervened in the proceedings went for such an interpretation of art.307 EC that would strengthen their own position rather than that of the Union.

The fourth question concerned the application of the balancing exercise between the first and the second paragraph of art.307 EC that recognised the supremacy of the international obligations arising from agreements concluded by a Member State before its accession to the Community; at the same time it urged an interpretation of the provisions in conformity with substantive Community law, following the principle of loyal co-operation. The Advocate General added that this should not go against the limits set by general international law on the interpretation of treaties according to the principles of good faith and in accordance with the ordinary meaning to be given to the terms of the treaty in their context and in the light of its object and purpose, following art.31 of the Vienna Convention on the Law of Treaties.

The national court had to apply those principles, but their actual application involved the interpretation of the national law that implemented into Austrian law the obligations arising from the agreement. This remained within the jurisdiction of the national court.

(b)   The judgment of the Court

10–114   The Court rejected in an outright way the inadmissibility arguments. Where the questions submitted by a national court concerned the interpretation of

---

[170] Article 34(1) of the Vienna Convention provides: When a part or parts of the territory of a State separate to form one or more States, whether or not the predecessor State continues to exist: (a) any treaty in force at the date of the succession of States in respect of the entire territory of the predecessor State continues in force in respect of each successor State so formed; (b) any treaty in force at the date of the succession of States in respect only of that part of the territory of the predecessor State which has become a successor State continues in force in respect of that successor State alone.

4. THE BUDWEISER TETRALOGY

Community law, the Court of Justice was, in principle, bound to give a ruling. It could only refuse where it was quite obvious that the interpretation sought had no relation to the actual facts of the main action or its purpose, where the problem was hypothetical, or where the Court did not have before it the factual or legal material necessary to give a useful answer.[171]

The questions here concerned the correct interpretation of art.28 EC, art.30 EC, art.307 EC and Regulation No. 2081/92, in order to enable the national court to determine the compatibility of the national rules at issue with Community law.

(i) The first question. The Court started by describing the two hypotheses implied by the wording of the first question. First, that the name Bud constituted a simple and indirect indication of geographical source; a name in respect of which there was no direct link between a specific quality, reputation or other characteristic of the product and its specific geographical origin.[172] And, secondly, that it was not in itself a geographical name but was at least capable of informing the consumer that the product bearing that indication came from a particular place, region or country.[173] 10–115

The function of the name was considered relevant for deciding whether Regulation 2081/92 precluded or not protection of a name that fell outside its net. Budvar argued that the distinction was irrelevant because the Regulation itself was irrelevant when considering purely national protection accorded by a bilateral convention. Anmersin on the other hand argued that the Regulation precluded protection at the national level of names that failed to meet its strict requirements.

The Court restated its analysis of the scope of the Regulation, originally made in *Warsteiner*.[174] It provided a uniform Community wide system of protection based on registration. But it co-existed with, rather than replaced, national systems of protection. The absolute nature of the Austrian system that provided protection without requiring evidence of confusion did not affect that interpretation.

Accordingly the Regulation did not preclude the application of a provision of a bilateral agreement between a Member State and a non-member country under which a simple and indirect indication of geographical origin from that non-member country was accorded protection in the importing Member State, whether or not there was any risk of consumers being 10–116

---

[171] Citing *PreussenElektra AG v Schleswag AG* (C-379/98) [2001] E.C.R. I-2099.
[172] Outside the scope of art.2(2)(b) of Reg.No.2081/92 according to *Schutzverband gegen Unwesen In der Wirtschaft eV v Warsteiner Brauerei Haus Cramer GmbH & Co KG* (C-312/98) [2000] E.C.R. I-9187.
[173] Citing *Exportur v LOR and Confiserie du Tech* (C-3/91) [1992] E.C.R. I-5529.
[174] *Schutzverband gegen Unwesen In der Wirtschaft eV v Warsteiner Brauerei Haus Cramer GmbH & Co KG* (C-312/98) [2000] E.C.R. I-9187.

misled, and the import of a product lawfully marketed in another Member State might be prevented.

However, the outcome could be different form the perspective of art.28 EC.

Given the US origin of the American Bud the Court clarified that art.28 EC and art.30 EC applied without distinction to products originating in the Community and to those admitted into free circulation in any of the Member States irrespective of the real origin of the latter category[175] and found the prohibition on marketing beer from countries other than the Czech Republic under the name of Bud in Austria capable of becoming an intra-Community barrier to trade. Such rules, without always precluding in an absolute manner the importation of the "protected" products into the Member State concerned made their marketing more difficult, impeding trade between Member States.[176]

The Court then followed A.G. Tizzano's proposition. It concluded that art.30 EC covered the application of the provisions of the bilateral agreement, unless the name was generic at the date of the entry into force of the agreement or had subsequently become generic in the state of origin.

10–117 **(ii) The second question.** The answer to the second question followed the same logic. If the national court found that according to the perception prevailing in the Czech Republic the name Bud did not directly or indirectly identify any region or place in the territory of that State it would come outside the scope of art.30 EC, at least under the industrial or commercial property exemption.[177] Note that here the Court appeared to refer to the status of the name in abstract, as a geographical indication as such, rather than as an indication of source for a specific product.

The Court would then have to examine whether the barrier could be justified by an imperative requirement in the general interest such as fairness in commercial transactions or consumer protection. Taking a more neutral stance than the Advocate General the Court responded using itself a hypothetical scenario:

> "If it were established that the name Bud does not contain any reference to the geographical source of the products that it designates, the Court would have to hold that none of the information supplied to it by the national court shows that protection of that name is susceptible of preventing economic operators from obtaining an unfair advantage or consumers from being misled as to any of the characteristics of those products."[178]

---

[175] Citing *Nijman* (125/88) [1989] E.C.R. 3533.
[176] Citing *Guimont* (C-448/98) [2000] E.C.R. I-10663.
[177] Citing *Exportur v LOR and Confiserie du Tech* (C-3/91) [1992] E.C.R. I-5529; and *Pistre v France* (C-321/94 & C-324/94) [1997] E.C.R. I-2343.
[178] *Bud I*, para.110.

4. THE BUDWEISER TETRALOGY

Recovering the function of the name as a link between the product and its origin it concluded that art.28 EC precluded the application of a provision of a bilateral agreement between a Member State and a non-Member country under which a name which in that country did not directly or indirectly refer to the geographical source of the product that it designated was accorded protection in the importing Member State, whether or not there was any risk of consumers being misled, and the import of a product lawfully marketed in another Member State might be prevented.

(iii) The remaining questions. The Court started by describing the aim of art.307 EC. "The purpose of that provision is to make clear, in accordance with the principles of international law, that application of the EC Treaty does not affect the duty of the Member State concerned to respect the rights of non-member countries under an earlier agreement and to perform its obligations thereunder."[179] What had to be established was whether that agreement imposed on Austria obligations whose performance might still be required by the Czech Republic. 10–118

The Court referred to the analysis of the Advocate General and stated that the national court would have to ascertain whether the two parties actually intended to apply the principle of the continuity of treaties to that particular agreement and whether there was any relevant evidence during the period between the date of the break-up and that of the Republic of Austria's accession to the European Union.

The national court also had to ascertain whether a possible incompatibility between the Treaty and the agreement could be avoided by interpreting the agreement, to the extent possible and in compliance with international law, in such a way that it is consistent with Community law. If that was not possible then Austria had to apply the agreement but remained obliged to eliminate the incompatibilities. The Court noted that an obligation to denounce an agreement that could not be reconciled with Community law could not be excluded.

(2) Bud II—replaying Bud I

The same Budweiser saga was behind the most recent judgment of the Court on geographical indications.[180] The Handelsgericht Wien (Commercial Court, Vienna), referred more questions to the Court following its judgment in the original *Bud I* reference.[181] The Opinion of A.G. Ruiz-Jarabo Colomer provides a comprehensive summary of the history and the disputes between the US and Czech breweries. 10–119

Following *Bud I* the Austrian court had found that the Czech public did not associate the name "Bud" with a specific geographical location and that, as a

---

[179] *Bud I*, para.145, citing *Commission v Portugal* (C-84/98) [2000] E.C.R. I-5215.
[180] *Budějovický Budvar National Corp v Rudolf Ammersin GmbH* (C-478/07).
[181] *Budějovický Budvar* (C-216/01) [2003] E.C.R. I-13617.

result, it should not be protected as a geographical indication following art.28 EC. The Oberster Gerichtshof, the Austrian Supreme Court, however annulled that judgment and found that the term was at least capable of conveying a message regarding geographical origin and that the Commercial Court had to determine whether "Bud" functioned as a simple and indirect geographical indication. The Commercial Court found that it did not function in that way following a consumer survey.

There was then a further appeal to the Oberlandesgericht Wien (Higher Regional Court, Vienna), which sent the case back to the Commercial Court suggesting a more focused survey targeting Czech consumers. This triggered the Commercial Court's current round of questions, in particular following the Czech Republic's new membership of the European Union.

10-120 *(a) The Opinion of the Advocate General*

The Advocate General started his analysis by commenting on the judicial politics of the reference, suggesting that the Commercial Court had hoped that its own position would be endorsed by the Court. "However, the Court of Justice should not take up the challenge. In Bud I it expressly made the evaluation in question the responsibility of the national court and there is no reason for it now to change its mind or to bring into play different criteria or clarifications additional to those it made in the past."[182]

Advocate General Ruiz-Jarabo Colomer also distinguished between "simple and indirect", on the one hand, and "qualified", on the other, geographical indications:

"Simple geographical indications do not require products to have any special characteristics or element of renown deriving from the place from which they come, but they must be capable of identifying that place. In contrast, geographical indications which designate a product having a quality, reputation or other characteristic related to its origin are qualified geographical indications. As well as the geographical link, they have another, qualitative, link, less strong than that of designations of origin, which are reserved to products whose particular characteristics are due to natural or human factors relating to their place of origin. Community law protects only designations of origin and qualified geographical indications."[183]

He noted that whereas in *Bud I* the Court had found "Bud" to constitute a simple geographical indication the Austrian court employed both concepts in its questions. The Advocate General queried whether the Court should decline responding to what can be seen as hypothetical questions but given

---

[182] Point 54. A poignant indirect response to those critics who target the Court's judicial processes and delays but tend to overlook the games played by advocates and national courts.
[183] Point 57 of the Opinion of A.G. Ruiz-Jarabo Colomer.

4. THE BUDWEISER TETRALOGY

the genuine uncertainty regarding the meaning of "Bud" in the Czech Republic decided to deal with their substance.

(i) The first question: establishing the association. The first question focused on paras 101–107 of *Bud I*. The Advocate General noted that there may be "indirect" geographical indications, not comprising actual geographical names, that can still indicate to consumers a link between the product and a geographical location. This should suffice; in "the situation under analysis, it must be ascertained whether 'Bud' makes it clear to Czech citizens that beer with that name comes from the town of České Budějovice, which does not mean that the name performs that role of geographical indication when it is mentioned together with the product in question, and only then".[184]

10–121

As to whether the three requirements mentioned in *Bud I*[185] must be assessed cumulatively or independently from each other A.G. Ruiz-Jarabo Colomer prefers the first interpretation. Paragraph 101 meant that Czech consumers had to associate "Bud" with a particular place or region, as stated above, "without particular 'circumstances' having to be present".[186]

On the value of consumer surveys he observed that the Court had accepted such surveys.[187] At the end it was for the national court to determine the evidentiary tools it required.

The national court had also enquired whether the geographical indication had to indicate a number of undertakings or a single undertaking. The Advocate General made a distinction between trade marks and geographical indications. Both protected commercial reputation "against potential unlawful usurpation by third parties, focussing on its geographical or its business origin respectively. They differ in that a trade mark safeguards a private interest, that of its holder, whereas a geographical indication protects the interests of all producers established in the relevant area".[188] However this did not mean it had to be used in parallel by several undertakings. He accepted though that in the Community system there was "a certain underlying preference for the former, perhaps because they protect the public interest in consumers knowing the provenance and characteristics of goods".[189] Regulation No 510/2006[190] provided that the application for

10–122

---

[184] Point 69 of the Opinion of A.G. Ruiz-Jarabo Colomer.
[185] See paras 10–116—10–117 above.
[186] Point 75 of the Opinion of A.G. Ruiz-Jarabo Colomer.
[187] Citing *Gut Springenheide and Tusky* (C-210/96) [1998] E.C.R. I-4657; *Estée Lauder Cosmetics* (C-220/98) [2000] E.C.R. I-117; and *Windsurfing Chiemsee* (C-108/97 & C-109/97) [1999] E.C.R. I-2779.
[188] Point 82 of the Opinion of A.G. Ruiz-Jarabo Colomer.
[189] Citing amongst others N Resinek, "Geographical indications and trade marks: Coexistence or 'first in time, first in right' principle?" [2007] E.I.P.R. 446; and A von Mühlendhal, "Geographical indications and trade marks in the European Union: conflict or coexistence", Festskrift till Marianne Levin, 2008, p.401.
[190] [2006] OJ L93/12.

registration of trade marks will be refused if they correspond to protected designations of origin or geographical indications, whilst trade marks registered earlier or acquired by established use in good faith will coexist with indications subsequently registered in accordance with European law. And the Harmonisation Directive and the CTM Regulation prohibit the use of signs which may mislead as to the geographical origin of the product.

Again, the conflict had to be resolved by the national court, in accordance with the bilateral agreement.

10–123　**(ii) The exclusivity of the Community system.** The second question, as to whether national protection for an indication that has not been notified to the Commission becomes void when it is found to be a qualified geographical indication, focused, according to A.G. Ruiz-Jarabo Colomer, on whether the Community system is exclusive or not.

Bud I and *Warsteiner*[191] had settled that simple geographical indications were considered to be part of "industrial property" regimes, exempted according to art.30 EC, without being covered by the Community system:

> "There remain designations of origin and qualified geographical indications, which do satisfy the requirements of the European legislation and may, therefore, be registered and enjoy protection under Regulation No 510/2006. However, unless they are registered at Community level, it is uncertain that Member States can protect them with their own arrangements or that that regulation is exclusive and precludes any intervention at State level within the formal and material scope of its application."[192]

In other words does the Community system pre-empt national measures?

According to the Advocate General an exclusive Community system is more coherent with the wording of the Community provisions, with their purpose, and with the case law of the Court of Justice in contrast with the trade mark regime where there is a Community and national systems of protection. Taking into account the history and objectives of the 1992 and the 2006 Regulations and the transitional nature of the Community legislation referring to national measures he supported that they can be achieved only with a single European instrument. Whilst he accepted that the case law of the Court had not fully determined the issue he observed that "Gorgonzola,[193] Chiciak,[194] and Fol[195] highlight the limitations to which

---

[191] *Schutzverband gegen Unwesen In der Wirtschaft eV v Warsteiner Brauerei Haus Cramer GmbH & Co KG* (C-312/98) [2000] E.C.R. I-9187.
[192] Point 92 of the Opinion of A.G. Ruiz-Jarabo Colomer.
[193] *Consorzio per la tutela del formaggio Gorgonzola v Kdserei Champignon Hofmeister and Eduard Bracharz* (C-87/97) [1999] E.C.R. I-1301.
[194] *Chiciak and Fol* (C-129/97 & 130/97) [1998] E.C.R. I-3315.
[195] *Chiciak and Fol.*

Member States are subject from the moment they apply to the Commission to register a name".[196] And according to *Warsteiner*[197] the purpose of Regulation No 2081/92 could not be undermined by the parallel application of national rules falling outside its scope. "On an a contrario interpretation, that assertion means that a national system governing qualified geographical indications, which are covered by the Community regulation, could indeed jeopardise attainment of the purpose of the European provision."[198] The same principle should cover, and even more so, systems of protection extended bilaterally to another Member State.

"Accordingly, a name which is within that scope and which has not been notified to the Commission cannot obtain protection from one or more Member States independently, and is unprotected. However, that circumstance does not derive solely, as the wording of the question referred for a preliminary ruling would seem to suggest, from non-registration of the indication, but from the fact that the Community system is exclusive."[199]

Considering the last question posed by the Commercial Court he supported that "the fact that a name, unlike other names for the same foodstuff with the same provenance, is not on the list in the Accession Treaty so as to have protection at Community level, is not, in theory, an obstacle to its national or bilateral protection, unless it is a shortened version or a part of any of the notified geographical indications. That assertion has no practical consequences, however, given the exclusive nature of Regulation No 510/2006."[200]

(b) The judgment of the Court   10–124

The Court delivered its judgment on September 8, 2009.[201]

(i) Judicial co-operation. Starting from a judicial co-operation perspective the Court described in detail first the ambiguities of its first judgment and secondly the changes in circumstances that made the Commercial Court refer the case back to the Court of Justice.   10–125

It approached under a similar light the admissibility argument as to whether the reference was a based on a hypothetical scenario. The Court stressed:

---

[196] Point 116 of the Opinion of A.G. Ruiz-Jarabo Colomer.
[197] *Schutzverband gegen Unwesen In der Wirtschaft eV v Warsteiner Brauerei Haus Cramer GmbH & Co KG* (C-312/98) [2000] E.C.R. I-9187.
[198] Point 119 of the Opinion of A.G. Ruiz-Jarabo Colomer.
[199] Point 129 of the Opinion of A.G. Ruiz-Jarabo Colomer.
[200] Point 138 of the Opinion of A.G. Ruiz-Jarabo Colomer.
[201] Available following the links at *http://curia.europa.eu* [Accessed November 3, 2009].

"it should... be borne in mind that, according to settled case-law, questions on the interpretation of Community law referred by a national court in the factual and legislative context which that court is responsible for defining, and the accuracy of which is not a matter for the Court to determine, enjoy a presumption of relevance. The Court may refuse to rule on a question referred by a national court only where it is quite obvious that the interpretation of Community law that is sought bears no relation to the actual facts of the main action or its purpose, where the problem is hypothetical, or where the Court does not have before it the factual or legal material necessary to give a useful answer to the questions submitted to it".[202]

It accepted that the approach taken by the national court on whether "Bud" must be classified as a designation of origin differed from the approach that led to the first reference but also diverged within the current reference between the first question on the one hand and the second and third on the other. However, it rejected the claim that the first question concerned a hypothetical situation; "..., the possibility cannot be ruled out that, in reality, those are two distinct and, a priori, possible theories and that, at this stage, the national court does not wish definitively to discard that of a simple and indirect indication of geographical provenance, with the result that it referred the first question in order to allow for the possibility that it might, none the less, accept that theory".[203]

10-126 (ii) **Clarifying Bud I.** In order to clarify *Bud I* the Court adopted a contextual type of analysis. It had considered "Bud" to be a simple and indirect geographical designation. "Simple" meant a name in respect of which there was no direct link between a specific characteristic of the product and its specific geographical origin. "Indirect" meant a designation not in itself a geographical name but at least capable of informing the consumer that the product comes from a particular place, region or country. A simple and indirect designation fell outside the scope of art.2(2)(b) of Regulation 2081/92. It had then viewed the bilateral agreement as aiming to ensure fair competition and within the sphere of industrial and commercial property under art.30 EC, provided that the names covered in the agreement had not, at the time of the entry into force of that agreement or subsequently, become generic in the country of origin.

Against that background the Court reviewed the contestable elements of para.101 in *Bud I*.

First, the reference to factual circumstances and perceptions prevailing in the Czech Republic, had to be understood "in the particular context of the

---

[202] *Bud II*, para.63, citing *Régie Networks* (C-333/07) [2008] E.C.R. I-0000.
[203] *Bud II*, para.66.

mechanism for protection of the designation 'Bud' under the bilateral instruments at issue, which rests in the fact that that mechanism ... is based on an extension of the protection provided in the Member State of origin, in the present case the Czech Republic, to the importing Member State, here the Republic of Austria".[204] Accordingly, the national court had to examine the circumstances and perceptions prevailing in the Czech Republic; if the designation was not at least capable of evoking the geographical provenance of the product then its protection could not be justified.

Secondly, the reference to the art.30 EC criteria meant that the national court had also to ascertain whether the designation had, at the time of the entry into force of the bilateral instruments or subsequently, become generic the Czech Republic.

Thirdly, for a simple and indirect geographical designation that has not become generic arts 28 and 30 EC "do not preclude national protection ... nor, moreover, the extension of that protection by way of a bilateral agreement to the territory of another Member State".[205]

(iii) Consumer surveys—the principles of equivalence and effectiveness. The Court repeated that Community law does not provide for procedural rules in this matter:

10-127

10-128

"it is for the domestic legal system of each Member State to designate the courts and tribunals having jurisdiction and to lay down the detailed procedural rules governing actions for safeguarding rights which individuals derive from the direct effects of Community law, provided that such rules are not less favourable than those governing similar domestic actions (the principle of equivalence) and that they do not render practically impossible or excessively difficult the exercise of rights conferred by Community law (the principle of effectiveness)".[206]

Accordingly it was for the national court to decide whether a consumer survey should be commissioned and set the parameters for what would be sufficiently significant when assessing its results.[207]

(iv) Use as a designation v use as a trade mark. As to whether the evidence had to show use as a geographical indication by a number of undertakings and not use solely as a trade mark by a single undertaking the Court responded that art.30 EC did not contain "specific requirements as to both the quality and the duration of the use made of a designation".[208]

10-129

---

[204] *Bud II*, para.78.
[205] *Bud II*, para.85.
[206] *Bud II*, para.88, citing *Kempter* (C-2/06) [2008] E.C.R. I-411.
[207] Citing *GutSpringenheide and Tusky* (C-210/96) [1998] E.C.R. I-4657.
[208] *Bud II*, para.91.

Once the art.30 EC requirements were satisfied, the provision did not preclude the extension, according to the bilateral agreement, of the specific protection for "Bud" to the territory of another Member State provided art.30 did not lay down specific requirements as to the quality and the duration of the use of the designation. National law and the bilateral agreements would determine whether any such requirements had to be applied in the context of the specific dispute.

10-130 **(v) The nature of the Regulation 510/2006 system.** The Court first noted that the accession of the Czech Republic meant that bilateral agreements including provisions contrary to the rules of the Treaty could not be applied.[209] From an international perspective it added that the case concerned a designation that was protected as an appellation of origin under the Lisbon Agreement in the Czech Republic. Both the Regulation and the Lisbon Agreement had adopted essentially the same definition for designation of origin—under the Regulation—and an appellation of origin—under the Lisbon Agreement; however whether the fact that Regulation No. 510/2006 was exhaustive in nature precluded protection under the Lisbon Agreement did not arise in this case since Austria was not a member of Lisbon.

In the absence of an application for registration of the designation under the Regulation the Court noted that what the national court was seeking to ascertain was whether the exhaustive nature of Regulation No. 510/2006 precluded national protection and extension of that protection to the territory of another Member State.

The Court set the protection of geographical designations within the broader context of protection of industrial and commercial property rights. The aim was to protect against improper use by third parties seeking to profit from their reputation and guarantee that the product bearing them comes from a specified geographical area and displays particular characteristics. The Court made a causative link between the two; the characteristics were the reason for gaining reputation.

10-131 According to the Court:

"Regulation No 510/2006, adopted on the basis of Article 37 EC, constitutes an instrument of the common agricultural policy essentially intended to assure consumers that agricultural products bearing a geographical indication registered under that regulation have, because of their provenance from a particular geographical area, certain specific characteristics and, accordingly, offer a guarantee of quality due to their geographical provenance, with the aim of enabling agricultural operators to secure higher incomes in return for a genuine effort to improve quality and of preventing improper use of those designations by third parties

[209] Citing *Ravil* (C-469/00) [2003] E.C.R. I-5053.

seeking to profit from the reputation which those products have acquired by their quality".[210]

But if Member States allowed the use of indications:

"which are reserved, under Article 8 of Regulation No 510/2006, for designations registered under that regulation, on the basis of a national right which could meet less strict requirements than those laid down in that regulation for the products in question, the risk is that that assurance of quality, which constitutes the essential function of rights conferred pursuant to Regulation No 510/2006, could not be guaranteed. That also carries the risk, in the internal market, of jeopardising the aim of fair competition between producers of products bearing those indications or symbols and, in particular, would be liable to harm rights which ought to be reserved for producers who have made a genuine effort to improve quality in order to be able to use a geographical indication registered under that regulation."[211]

The Court also highlighted the difference between the geographical designation and trade mark regimes in that the first had not adopted the principle of harmonising national systems in parallel with the creation of a Community system.

Following the two fundamental reasons favouring the exhaustive nature of the Community system the Court considered a number of additional grounds.

10–132

First, the registration procedure was based on powers shared between the Member State concerned and the Commission. "The national registration procedures are therefore incorporated in the Community decision-making procedure and constitute an essential part thereof. They cannot exist outside the Community system of protection."[212]

Secondly, the Community system provided for transitional arrangements for existing national designations or in Member States where there was no system of protection. In this case Regulation 918/2004[213] was specifically relevant. National protection of existing qualified geographical indications would be permitted subject to conditions, including the condition to submit an application for registration within six months. The Czech authorities had failed to do so.

Turning back to the broader principle the Court repeated that the Community system of protection was exhaustive in nature and decided that

---

[210] *Bud II*, para.111.
[211] *Bud II*, para.112.
[212] *Bud II*, para.117.
[213] Commission Regulation of April 29, 2004 introducing transitional arrangements for the protection of geographical indications and designations of origin for agricultural products and foodstuffs in connection with the accession of the Czech Republic, Estonia, Cyprus, Latvia, Lithuania, Hungary, Malta, Poland, Slovenia and Slovakia ([2004] OJ L163/88).

this precluded the application of a system of protection laid down by agreements between two Member States conferring protection on a designation, recognised under the law of a Member State as constituting a designation of origin, in another Member State despite the fact that an application for registration of that designation had not been made.

10–133 **(3) European trade mark law and the TRIPs Agreement— protecting trade names**

The third *Budweiser* case[214] concerned the interpretation of art.2(1),[215] art.16(1),[216] and art.70[217] of the Agreement on Trade-Related Aspects of Intellectual Property Rights (TRIPs).

Anheuser-Busch was the proprietor in Finland of the trade marks Budweiser, Bud, Bud Light and Budweiser King of Beers, for beer. The application filing date for Budweiser, the earlier of the marks, was October 24, 1980. Budvar had two registrations for the trade marks Budvar and Budweiser Budvar for beer since May 21, 1962 and November 13, 1972 respectively that had been cancelled for non-use. Budvar had also registered the following trade names in the Czechoslovakian commercial register since 1967: "Budějovický Budvar, národní podnik", "Budweiser Budvar, National Corporation", and French "Budweiser Budvar, Entreprise nationale".

---

[214] *Anheuser-Busch v Budejovický Budvar, narodni podnik* (C-245/02) [2004] E.C.R. I-10989.
[215] Article 2 of TRIPs provides: "1. In respect of Parts II, III and IV of this agreement, Members shall comply with Articles 1 through 12, and Article 19, of the Paris Convention (1967). 2. Nothing in Parts I to IV of this agreement shall derogate from existing obligations that Members may have to each other under the Paris Convention, the Berne Convention, the Rome Convention and the Treaty on Intellectual Property in Respect of Integrated Circuits."
[216] Article 16(1) of TRIPs provides: "The owner of a registered trade mark shall have the exclusive right to prevent all third parties not having the owner's consent from using in the course of trade identical or similar signs for goods or services which are identical or similar to those in respect of which the trade mark is registered where such use would result in a likelihood of confusion. In case of the use of an identical sign for identical goods or services, a likelihood of confusion shall be presumed. The rights described above shall not prejudice any existing prior rights, nor shall they affect the possibility of Members making rights available on the basis of use."
[217] Article 70 of TRIPs provides: "1. This agreement does not give rise to obligations in respect of acts which occurred before the date of application of the Agreement for the Member in question. 2. Except as otherwise provided for in this agreement, this agreement gives rise to obligations in respect of all subject-matter existing at the date of application of this agreement for the Member in question, and which is protected in that Member on the said date, or which meets or comes subsequently to meet the criteria for protection under the terms of this agreement.... 4. In respect of any acts in respect of specific objects embodying protected subject-matter which become infringing under the terms of legislation in conformity with this agreement, and which were commenced, or in respect of which a significant investment was made, before the date of acceptance of the WTO Agreement by that Member, any Member may provide for a limitation of the remedies available to the rightholder as to the continued performance of such acts after the date of application of this agreement for that Member. In such cases the Member shall, however, at least provide for the payment of equitable remuneration...."

4. THE BUDWEISER TETRALOGY

Anheuser-Busch started infringement proceedings before the Helsingin käräjäoikeus (Helsinki District Court) in order to stop use of the marks Budějovický Budvar, Budweiser Budvar, Budweiser, Budweis, Budvar, Bud and Budweiser Budbraü for beer. It also sought to stop use of the trade names that Budvar had been using. Budvar counter-argued that there was no confusion and, further, that the registration of its trade names constituted an earlier right according to art.8 of the Paris Convention.[218]

10–134 The Helsinki District Court found that there was no trade mark infringement and that Budvar was entitled to use its trade names in the way it did—BREWED AND BOTTLED BY THE BREWERY BUDWEISER BUDVAR national enterprise as the trade name of the brewery rather than in a trade mark sense, because there was evidence that they were well known in the relevant trade circles at the time Anheuser-Busch's marks were registered in Finland.

The Helsingin hovioikeus (Helsinki Court of Appeal) set aside only the second part of the judgment of the Helsinki District Court regarding the well-known status of Budvar's trade name. Both parties appealed to the Korkein oikeus (Supreme Court).

The Supreme Court observed that the Court of Justice had pointed out in *Dior*[219] that it had jurisdiction to interpret a provision of the TRIPs Agreement in cases where the Community had already adopted legislation in the relevant field.

10–135 Accordingly it referred the following, rather detailed, questions to the Court of Justice:

"1. If the conflict between a trade mark and a sign alleged to infringe it is situated at a point in time before the entry into force of the TRIPs Agreement, do the provisions of the TRIPs Agreement apply to the question of which right has the earlier legal basis, when the alleged infringement of the trade mark is said to continue after the date on which the TRIPs Agreement became applicable in the Community and the Member States?

2. If the answer to Question 1 is affirmative:

(a) Can the trade name of an undertaking also act as a sign for goods or services within the meaning of the first sentence of Article 16(1) of the TRIPs Agreement?

---

[218] Article 8 of the Paris Convention provides: "A trade name shall be protected in all the countries of the Union without the obligation of filing or registration, whether or not it forms part of a trade mark."

[219] *Parfums Christian Dior SA v Tuk Consultancy BV* (C-300/98) and *Assco Geruste GmbH and Rob van Dijk v Wilhelm Layher GmbH & Co KG and Layher BV* (C-392/98) [2000] E.C.R. I-11307. It added that in *Schieving-Nijstad VF v Groenveld* (C-89/99) [2001] E.C.R. I-5851 the Court had ruled that the TRIPs Agreement was applicable in so far as the infringement of intellectual property rights continued beyond the date on which TRIPs became applicable with regard to the Community and the Member States.

(b) If the answer to Question 2(a) is affirmative, on what conditions may a trade name be regarded as a sign for goods or services within the meaning of the first sentence of Article 16(1) of the TRIPs Agreement?

3. If the answer to Question 2(a) is affirmative:

(a) How is the reference in the third sentence of Article 16(1) of the TRIPs Agreement to existing prior rights to be interpreted? May the right to a trade name also be regarded as an existing prior right within the meaning of the third sentence of Article 16(1) of the TRIPs Agreement?

(b) If the answer to Question 3(a) is affirmative, how is the said reference in the third sentence of Article 16(1) of the TRIPs Agreement to existing prior rights to be interpreted in the case of a trade name which is not registered or established by use in the State in which the trade mark is registered and in which protection is sought for the trade mark against the trade name in question, having regard to the obligation under Article 8 of the Paris Convention to afford protection to a trade name regardless of whether it is registered and to the fact that the Permanent Appellate Body of the WTO has regarded the reference in Article 2(1) of the TRIPs Agreement to Article 8 of the Paris Convention as meaning that WTO members are obliged under the TRIPs Agreement to protect trade names in accordance with the latter article? When assessing, in such a case, whether a trade name has a legal basis prior to a trade mark for the purposes of the third sentence of Article 16(1) of the TRIPs Agreement, may it thus be considered as decisive:

(i) whether the trade name was well known at least to some extent among the relevant trade circles in the State in which the trade mark is registered and in which protection is sought for it, before the point in time at which registration of the trade mark was applied for in the State in question; or

(ii) whether the trade name was used in commerce directed to the State in which the trade mark is registered and in which protection is sought for it, before the point in time at which registration of the trade mark was applied for in the State in question; or

(iii) what other factor may decide whether the trade name is to be regarded as an existing prior right within the meaning of the third sentence of Article 16(1) of the TRIPs Agreement?"[220]

---

[220] Reproduced in para.39.

4. THE BUDWEISER TETRALOGY

(a) The Opinion of the Advocate General   10–136

Advocate General Tizzano noted that the case raised a number of admissibility issues together with the substantive interpretive questions. The two, however, where interwoven in such a way that could only be answered together.

(i) The first question. Regarding the first question the Advocate   10–137
General supported that the effect of the TRIPs agreement was ratione temporis, covering infringing acts that had started before the agreement but continued after its effective date.[221]

(ii) The second question. In his analysis of the second question he had   10–138
no doubt that a trade name could constitute a sign for the purposes of art.16(1) of TRIPs; the requirements for the application of that provision however were less straightforward.

The use as a trade mark requirement He suggested that the function of a   10–139
trade name was to identify an undertaking whereas the function of a trade mark was to distinguish the products of one undertaking from those of other undertakings. In principle, there should be no risk of confusion between a sign used as a trade name and another used as a trade mark.

However, a trade name could also fulfil the essential function of a trade mark, to create a link between the product and the undertaking responsible for its manufacture or distribution; in that case there could be a likelihood of confusion.

For the Advocate General, according to art.16(1) of TRIPs, use of a sign as trade mark constituted one of the essential requirements for the exercise of the exclusive rights arising from registration. When the trade mark and the sign were not identical the next requirement that had to be satisfied was the establishment of a risk of confusion between the sign and the trade mark.

Compatibility with Community law The next consideration was the   10–140
compatibility between art.16 of TRIPs and Community law, since national laws had to conform to TRIPs, but even more so to Community legislation. The Court had ruled in *Dior*[222] that although TRIPs provisions do not have a direct effect on the Community legal order national courts would have to act, to the extent that is possible, according to the letter and the scope of the relevant TRIPs provisions.

---

[221] Citing *Schieving-Nijstad VoF v Groeneveld* (C-89/99) [2001] E.C.R. I-5851.
[222] *Parfums Christian Dior SA v Tuk Consultancy BV* (C-300/98) and *Assco Geruste GmbH and Rob van Dijk v Wilhelm Layher GmbH & Co KG and Layher BV* (C-392/98) [2000] E.C.R. I-11307.

Article 16 provided the minimum standard of protection that had to be guaranteed by the national laws of the Member States of the World Trade Organisation.[223] Since he had found that use of the sign as a trade mark constituted the essential requirement for its application he went on to consider the position of the Court on the function of a trade mark as a guarantee of origin.[224] The national court would have to examine accordingly the nature of the function of the trade name Budvar. If it functioned in that way then the court would have to consider the likelihood of confusion according to its national law following the criteria set by art.5 of the Trade Marks Directive and the relevant jurisprudence of the Court of Justice.

The Advocate General expressed his certainty that the Community regime was fully compatible with the minimum standard of protection envisaged by TRIPs.

Comparing the respective TRIPs and Trade Mark Directive provisions he noted that even the wording was similar.

(iii) The third question

10-141 *The status of trade names* The first point raised in the third question was whether trade names constituted existing prior rights. Budvar, the Finnish Government, and the Commission argued that they did. The Advocate General was closer to the negative stance of Anheuser-Busch. He believed that earlier rights could be established only in relation to signs that functioned as trade marks; he accepted though that those signs could also function in other ways, for example as trade names. He stressed that there should be an analogy between the scope of protection, discussed above, and the obstacles to gaining that protection.

Narrowing further the scope of the limitation he suggested that in order to satisfy the "existing prior" condition only prior rights based on uninterrupted trade mark registrations should be taken into account. Any other interpretation, he added, would go against the scope of TRIPs, the elimination of trade barriers raised by the differences between national industrial property regimes.

10-142 **(iv) The third question—requirements for protecting a trade name.** The second point of the third question concerned the availability and the requirements of protection for a trade name that had not been registered or established through use in a Member State of the World Trade Organisation, taking into account art.2 of TRIPs and art.8 of the Paris Convention that provides for the obligation of Member States to protect foreign trade names irrespective of registration.

---

[223] Citing WT/DS176/AB/R, http://www.wto.org, point 186, as supporting his interpretation from the World Trade Organisation's perspective.
[224] Citing *Arsenal Football* (C-206/01) [2002] E.C.R. I-10273 as a recent restatement on that.

4. THE BUDWEISER TETRALOGY

Advocate General Tizzano found that the art.2 of TRIPs reference to the Paris Convention meant that the issue of trade name protection fell within the scope of TRIPs and thus the question was admissible in terms of subject-matter.[225]

Regarding the jurisdiction of the Court he noted that although in principle it would appear that it did not cover TRIPs provisions on trade names because the Community had not legislated in that area it might still be argued that the extension of protection to the holder of a trade name could indirectly affect the protection granted to a trade mark proprietor, an area that had been regulated by Community law.

As the facts of the case showed such a conflict was possible when a trade name functioned in a trade mark way; accordingly, the jurisdiction of the Court, at least in the context of that conflict, should not be precluded and the scope of the question of the referring court be limited accordingly.

10–143

He explored the criterion for determining the stronger right according to art.16 of TRIPs and art.4 of the Directive. The priority between the two rights should be established according to the date the trade name, that functioned as a trade mark, became well known in the Member State where protection was sought, based on art.4(2)(d) of the Directive, or the date that because of its use it gave rise to a right under art.4(4)(b) of the Directive and according to the relevant legislation of the Member State where protection was sought. This interpretation would also be in accordance with the fundamental principle that priority could only exist between the same types of right.

The application of the above rule to the facts of the case remained in the jurisdiction of the national court; however he doubted whether the trade name of Budvar had become well known in Finland according to the evidence of the case.

(b) The judgment of the Court

(i) The admissibility issues. Citing *Dior*,[226] the Court reaffirmed that it had assumed jurisdiction to interpret a provision of the TRIPs Agreement when national courts had to apply their national rules "with a view to ordering measures for the protection of rights created by Community legislation which fall within the scope of that agreement"[227] and that the Community was under an obligation to interpret its trade mark legislation, as far as possible, in the light of the wording and purpose of TRIPs.[228]

10–144

---

[225] Citing the Omnibus Appropriations Act 1998 case, WT/DS176/AB/R, available at http://www.wto.org from the World Trade Organisation's perspective.
[226] *Parfums Christian Dior SA* (C-300/98) and *Assco Geruste GmbH and Rob van Dijk v Wilhelm Layher GmbH & Co KG and Layher BV* (C-392/98) [2000] E.C.R. I-11307.
[227] *Budweiser*, para.41.
[228] Citing *Heidelberger Bauchemie GmbH* (C-49/02) [2004] E.C.R. I-6129.

Accordingly the interpretation of art.16(1) fell within the jurisdiction of the Court.

It viewed the first question as a further admissibility issue, linked with the temporal applicability of the TRIPs provision. Applying the rule adopted in *Schieving-Nijstad*,[229] it found that the provision was applicable because Budvar's acts commenced in Finland before the date the TRIPs Agreement gained effect but they continued thereafter. Article 70(1) of TRIPs excluded the imposition of obligations in respect of "acts which occurred" before the Agreement's date of application but it did not exclude such obligations in respect of situations that continued beyond that date. Whereas "subject-matter" that existed at the time TRIPs became effective was specifically covered according to art.70(2).[230]

10–145 **(ii) The effect of TRIPs—a balancing exercise.** On the one hand, the Court repeated that although the TRIPs Agreement did not have direct effect national courts were required in areas where the Community had already legislated to take them into account and any relevant measures should be taken, as far as possible, in the light of the wording and purpose of the relevant provisions.[231]

On the other, it stressed that the competent authorities had to apply and interpret the relevant national law, as far as possible, in the light of the wording and the purpose of the Harmonisation Directive.[232]

Accordingly, the relevant national provisions had to be applied and interpreted, as far as possible, in the light of the wording and purpose of both the TRIPs Agreement and the Directive.

10–146 **(iii) Trade marks and trade names.** The answers to the remaining two questions can be divided into three parts: first, it considered whether a trade name could infringe a trade mark right under art.16(1) of TRIPs; secondly, it looked at the limitations of trade mark protection that could be relevant in that case; thirdly, it considered whether a trade name might constitute an earlier right.

10–147 *Trade names as "signs"* The question whether a trade mark might constitute a sign for the purposes of art.16(1) of TRIPs was answered by the Court by reference to its judgment in *Arsenal*,[233] departing from the Opinion of the

---

[229] Citing *Schieving-Nijstad VoF v Groeneveld* (C-89/99) [2001] E.C.R. I-5851.
[230] Citing, from the World Trade Organisation's perspective, the Report of the WTO Appellate Body, Canada—Term of Patent Protection (AB-2000-7), WT/DS170/AB/R, available following the links at http://www.wto.org, paras 69, 70 and 71.
[231] Citing *Parfums Christian Dior SA* (C-300/98) and *Assco Geruste GmbH and Rob van Dijk v Wilhelm Layher GmbH & Co KG and Layher BV* (C-392/98) [2000] E.C.R. I-11307.
[232] Citing *Henkel KGaA* (C-218/01) [2004] E.C.R. I-1725.
[233] *Arsenal Football Club Plc* (C-206/01) [2002] E.C.R. I-10273.

4. THE BUDWEISER TETRALOGY

Advocate General that viewed use of the sign in a trade mark sense as an essential condition.

Repetition made the tautology of *Arsenal* even more obvious: "the exclusive right conferred by a trade mark was intended to enable the trade mark proprietor to protect his specific interests as proprietor, that is, to ensure that the trade mark can fulfil its functions and that, therefore, the exercise of that right must be reserved to cases in which a third party's use of the sign affects or is liable to affect the functions of the trade mark, in particular its essential function of guaranteeing to consumers the origin of the goods".[234]

Using the sign in such a way as to create the impression of a material link in trade between the third party's goods and the undertaking from which the original goods originated.

The ambiguities of *Arsenal* became even more apparent by the following statement of the Court. "It must be established whether the consumers targeted, including those who are confronted with the goods after they have left the third party's point of sale, are likely to interpret the sign, as it is used by the third party, as designating or tending to designate the undertaking from which the third party's goods originate".[235] The Court here appeared to include post-sale confusion to the gamut of actionable behaviour; a position from which it pulled back later in *Picasso*.[236] 10–148

At any rate this is what the national court had to establish, in relation to the labelling used by Budvar in Finland. The Court seemed to take for granted that Budvar's use was "use in the course of trade" and "in relation to goods", noting that the national court ultimately needed to confirm these two points.

The next step would be to determine whether the signs and the goods were identical in which case protection was absolute or similar and there was the additional requirement to prove confusion.[237]

The Court highlighted that if use of the sign was other than for the purposes of distinguishing goods or services further protection might be available under Finnish law. Article 5(5) of the Directive left to the Member States to decide the availability, extent, and nature of trade mark protection in that case. Note that it failed to mention that art.5(5) required use to without due cause take unfair advantage of, or be detrimental to, the distinctive character or the repute of the trade mark.[238] 10–149

---

[234] *Budweiser*, para.59, citing paras 51 and 54 of *Arsenal Football Club Plc v Matthew Reed* (C-206/01) [2002] E.C.R. I-10273.
[235] *Budweiser*, para.60, citing paras 56 and 57 of *Arsenal*.
[236] *Claude Ruiz-Picasso* (C-361/04 P) [2006] E.C.R. I-643.
[237] Citing *Davidoff & Cie SA and Zino Davidoff SA* (C-292/00) [2003] E.C.R. I-389; and *LTJ Diffusion SA v Sadas Vertbaudet SA* (C-291/00) [2003] E.C.R. I-2799.
[238] Citing *Robelco* (C-23/01) [2002] E.C.R. I-10913.

The next step for the Court was to consider the compatibility of the approach suggested above with the minimum standards of protection set by TRIPs.

It approached this from a teleological perspective: the primary objective of TRIPs was to strengthen and harmonise the protection of intellectual property on a worldwide scale and at the same time reduce distortions and impediments to international trade.[239]

It found that there was a close link between TRIPs and the Directive. A combined reading of art.16 and art.15 of TRIPs led to the conclusion that TRIPs, like art.2 and art.5 of the Directive, laid down a guarantee of origin as the essential function of a trade mark. So, the "interpretation of the relevant provisions of the national trade-mark law so far as possible in the light of the wording and purpose of the relevant provisions of Community law . . . is not prejudiced by an interpretation in keeping with the wording and purpose of the relevant provisions of the TRIPs Agreement".[240]

10-150 *The limitations to trade mark protection* The Court felt that in this case it had to broaden the remit of the question originally set by the national court; assessing its authority it reminded that "it is for the Court to provide the national court with all the elements of interpretation of Community law which may be of assistance in adjudicating on the case pending before it, whether or not that court specifically refers to them in its questions".[241]

It went on to consider art.17 of TRIPs and the limitations to trade mark protection. Use of a sign in good faith by a third party, in particular where the sign was part of that party's name or address could be fair use of a descriptive term, outside the scope of trade mark protection. A similar provision, art.6(1)(a) was included in the Directive.

The Council of the European Union and the Commission had indicated in a joint declaration that the provision covered only natural persons' names; however, as the declaration itself acknowledged, it had no legal significance since it was not mentioned in the wording of the provision.[242]

10-151 According to the Court the application of art.6(1)(a) provided to a third party an entitlement to use a sign for the purpose of indicating its trade name, even if that use would constitute an infringement of a registered trade mark; the only assessment criterion was that such use should be made in accordance with honest practices in industrial or commercial matters.[243]

The Court appeared to accept that Budvar in principle was entitled to use its trade name and that the burden of proof was carried by Anheuser-Busch

---

[239] See also *Schieving-Nijstad VoF v Groeneveld* (C-89/99) [2001] E.C.R. I-5851.
[240] *Budweiser*, para.70.
[241] *Budweiser*, para.75, citing *Trojani v Centre Public d'Aide Sociale de Bruxelles* (C-465/02) [2004] E.C.R. I-7573.
[242] Citing *Heidelberger Bauchemie GmbH* (C-49/02) [2004] E.C.R. I-6129 on the non-effect of the declaration.
[243] Citing *Gerolsteiner Brunnen GmbH & Co v Putsch GmbH* (C-100/01) [2004] E.C.R. I-691.

by noting that it was for the national court to determine, following an overall assessment of all the relevant circumstances, whether Budvar competed unfairly with Anheuser-Busch.

It offered three factors that should be examined together with all the other circumstances.

First, the extent to which the use of the third party's trade name was understood by the relevant public, or at least a significant section of that public, as indicating a link between the third party's goods and the trade mark proprietor.

10–152

Secondly, the extent to which the third party ought to have been aware of that.

Thirdly, whether the trade mark enjoyed a reputation in the relevant Member State from which the third party might profit in selling its own products.

Trade names as prior rights The third sentence of art.16(1) meant that "where the proprietor of a trade name has a right falling within the scope of the TRIPs Agreement which arose prior to that conferred by the trade mark with which it is alleged to conflict and which entitles him to use a sign identical or similar to that trade mark, such use cannot be prohibited by virtue of the exclusive right conferred by the trade mark on its proprietor under the first sentence of Article 16(1) of the TRIPs Agreement".[244]

10–153

Exploring the applicability of the provision the Court suggested five steps that a national court had to take.

First, decide whether the right to a trade name fell within the substantive scope of TRIPs. A joint reading of art.2(1) of TRIPs with art.8 of the Paris Convention led to the clear conclusion that members of the World Trade Organisation were under an obligation to protect trade names.[245]

The second and the third step dealt with time. It would be for the national court to determine whether the right fell within the temporal scope of the TRIPs Agreement and then whether it was still protected at the time it was relied on by its proprietor.

10–154

This led to the fourth step: determining whether the right was an "existing" right. According to art.8 of the Paris Convention protection of a trade name should be guaranteed without any registration requirement. However, art.16(1) did not preclude Finnish law to impose conditions relating to minimum use or minimum awareness of the trade name.

The fifth step would be to determine priority. This meant that "the basis for the right concerned must have arisen at a time prior to the grant of the trade mark with which it is alleged to conflict".[246]

---

[244] *Budweiser*, para.89.
[245] Citing again the Report of the WTO Appellate Body, United States—Section 211 of the Omnibus Appropriations Act, for a similar conclusion from the perspective of the World Trade Organisation.
[246] *Budweiser*, para.98.

The approach of the Court diverged from that of the Advocate General. It did not require the trade name to be used in a trade mark way, nor it did it impose the requirement of being well known in the jurisdiction where protection for the competing trade mark was being sought.

(4) The European Court of Human Rights—geographical indications, trade marks and property rights

10–155 The fourth case considered the interrelationship between geographical indications and trade mark rights on the one side and the concept of property on the other. This time the game was played in Portugal, the challenge was based on the rules of the Convention for the Protection of Human Rights and Fundamental Freedoms, and the adjudicator was the European Court of Human Rights.

The Convention for the Protection of Human Rights and Fundamental Freedoms became effective in 1953, drafted by the Council of Europe following the principles set by the 1948 Universal Declaration of Human Rights. The Convention listed a number of civil and political rights and freedoms and provided for a mechanism of collective enforcement that was assigned by the Contracting States to the European Commission of Human Rights, the European Court of Human Rights, and the Committee of Ministers of the Council of Europe (composed of the Ministers of Foreign Affairs of the Contracting States). The European Court of Human Rights (the Court, in this chapter) was established in 1959.[247]

The scope of the Convention and the jurisdiction of the Court expanded through the adoption of a number of Protocols. Recognition of the right of individual application that was originally optional became compulsory according to Protocol 11 and Protocol 2 empowered the Court to give advisory opinion.

10–156 In *Anheuser-Busch Inc v Portugal*,[248] Anheuser-Busch applied for the registration of the trade mark BUDWEISER for beer back in 1981. The application was opposed by Budějovický Budvar on the basis of its registration of "Budweiser Bier" as an appellation of origin in Portugal. The parties failed to reach an agreement and the applicant started cancellation proceedings regarding the registration of the appellation of origin in 1989. The Lisbon Court of First Instance cancelled the registration on March 8, 1995 and subsequently the Portuguese Intellectual Property Office granted the trade mark registration on June 20, 1995. Budějovický Budvar counter-attacked on the basis of a bilateral agreement concluded in 1986 between Czechoslovakia and Portugal protecting a number of appellations of origin.

---

[247] For an overview of proceedings in the ECtHR see Ovey and White, Jacobs and White, *The European Convention of Human Rights* (OUP, 2006), Ch.24.
[248] *Anheuser-Busch Inc v Portugal* [2006] E.T.M.R. 43, 2005 WL 3935702 ECtHR.

4. THE BUDWEISER TETRALOGY

The Court of First Instance rejected the claim but the judgment was reversed by the Lisbon Court of Appeal.

The case reached the Portuguese Supreme Court where Anheuser-Busch argued that the decision went against art.2 and art.24(5) of TRIPs.[249] The Supreme Court rejected the claim on two grounds. First, it found that the applicant had failed to discharge the burden of proving it had acted in good faith, as required by art.24(5). Secondly, it ruled that TRIPs, effective since January 1, 1996 in Portugal, did not cover in terms of time the 1986 bilateral agreement.

Anheuser-Busch also claimed that the bilateral agreement covered the term "Ceskebudejovicky Budvar" and its translation into Portuguese rather than the German expression "Budweiser". The Supreme Court took the intention of the two contracting parties as its starting point. They wanted to protect their respective national products, including cases where a translation of the protected names was used. The appellation of origin "Ceskebudejovicky Budvar" and its translations in German that indicated a beer coming from that region should be protected.

Finally, the Supreme Court rejected a third ground of appeal regarding the constitutionality of the agreement.

(a)   The arguments of the parties   **10–157**

Before the Court Anheuser-Busch supported that the judgment of the Supreme Court contravened art.1 of Protocol 1 to the Convention providing that:

> "Every natural or legal person is entitled to the peaceful enjoyment of his possessions. No one shall be deprived of his possessions except in the public interest and subject to the conditions provided for by law and by the general principles of international law. The preceding provisions shall not, however, in any way impair the right of a State to enforce such laws as it deems necessary to control the use of property in accordance with the general interest or to secure the payment of taxes or other contributions or penalties."

It sought from the Court to set aside the judgment of the Supreme Court. It claimed that the right to use a trade mark fell within the scope of indisputably constituted "possessions" and should be protected from the date the application for registration was filed, back in 1981. It was dispossessed by a

---

[249] Article 24(5) provides: Where a trademark has been applied for or registered in good faith, or where rights to a trademark have been acquired through use in good faith either: (a) before the date of application of these provisions in that Member as defined in Part VI; or (b) before the geographical indication is protected in its country of origin; measures adopted to implement this Section shall not prejudice eligibility for or the validity of the registration of a trademark . . . on the basis that such a trademark is identical with, or similar to, a geographical indication.

subsequent third party right produced by the 1986 bilateral agreement. It noted that the judgment of the Supreme Court had relied exclusively on the provision of New Code on Industrial Property that precluded registration when the sign was in conflict with another rule of law but had failed to refer to the Code's provision on confusion.

In effect, it argued, its mark had been expropriated without any compensation and this interference with its right of property was against the general principles of international law and based on a wrong interpretation of the 1986 agreement, targeting the Supreme Court's willingness to protect against use of a translation of the term in a language other than Portuguese. In any case the interference did not pursue a legitimate aim, in the apparent absence of a risk of confusion, and was disproportionate failing to strike a fair balance between the general interest and the right of individuals.

10-158   Finally, it submitted that insisting on the application of the 1986 agreement the Supreme Court had overlooked TRIPs and the Community legal order that could provide the tools for resolving a conflict between a trade mark and an indication of source.

The Portuguese Government challenged the assertion that the application for registration constituted a "possession" in the first place prior to registration. In any case, it added, it certainly did not constitute an "existing" possession that could be protected by the European Court of Human Rights.

10-159   But, even supposing that there had been an interference with the right of property, such interference amounted to control of the use of property rather than deprivation of possessions and was based on an agreement that had become part of the Portuguese legal order.

Regarding the risk of confusion argument it supported that the judgment had taken into account in its reasoning the risk of confusion but conceded that it had not relied on the relevant provision of the Code. Even if there was any interference it was entirely proportionate given that states enjoyed a wide margin of appreciation states when determining the public interest.

The final point made by the Portuguese Government had to do with the function of the European Court of Human Rights. It argued that by granting the remedy sought the Court would transform itself into a court of fourth instance, contrary to the aim and spirit of the Convention.

10-160   (b)   *The analysis of the Court*

The Court started its analysis with a comparative review of the national laws of the Member States of the Council of Europe regarding the rights linked with an application for a trade mark registration. Then the Court presented the arguments of the parties and moved into its own assessment of the case, answering first whether the applications constituted possessions and then assessing the interference.

4. THE BUDWEISER TETRALOGY

(i) The rights arising from an application for trade mark registration. The general principle was that trade mark rights were conferred by registration. However an application for registration also conferred a number of rights: in most cases registration conferred retrospective protection going back to the filing date of the application; in some cases the application itself functioned as a provisional registration; international priority was determined according to the application filing date; and, in some jurisdictions the mark applied for might be assigned, licensed, or used as security.

10-161

In terms of procedural steps the Court noted that in most countries a notice of the application was published triggering an opposition period, although in some jurisdictions registration followed immediately the examination of the application as to formalities and substantive requirements.

In its consideration of Portuguese law there were three points worth highlighting: the application for registration could be the subject of an assignment, with or without consideration, or a licence; there was a process for third parties adversely affected by the registration to appeal against the decision of the national Office; and, that according to earlier Portuguese jurisprudence the application conferred on the applicant a protectable "legal expectation".[250] This last principle had been adopted by art.5 of the New Code on Industrial Property that afforded provisional protection to an applicant through an action in damages.

(ii) Trade mark applications and the concept of "possessions". The Court reminded us that according to its case law the concept of "possessions" had an autonomous meaning, not limited to ownership of physical goods and independent from the formal classification in domestic law. "The issue that needs to be examined in each case is whether the circumstances of the case, considered as a whole, conferred on the applicant title to a substantive interest protected by Article 1 of Protocol 1."[251]

10-162

Intellectual property had the status of possessions and enjoyed the protection of art.1[252]; the status of an application however was more uncertain. The Commission had found that an unsuccessful patent application meant that the applicant had been denied a protected intellectual property right but not deprived of its existing property; the case went to the Court that had not examined and ruled on that particular issue.[253]

---

[250] In para.31 the Court noted that in a judgment of May 10, 2001 (Colectanea de Jurisprudencia, 2001, Vol.III, p.85), the Lisbon Court of Appeal held that the mere filing of an application for registration conferred on the applicant a "legal expectation" that warranted the protection of the law.

[251] *Anheuser-Busch Inc v Portugal*, para.42, citing as examples *Beyeler v Italy* [GC], no.33202/96, E.C.H.R. 2000–1; and *Broniowski v Poland* [GC], no.31443/96, at E.C.H.R. 2004–v.

[252] *Smith Kline and French Laboratories Ltd v The Netherlands* (12633/87), October 4, 1990, Decisions and Reports (DR) 66.

[253] *British-American Tobacco Co Ltd v The Netherlands* (A/331-A) [1996] 21 E.H.R.R. 409.

The Court appeared to be influenced by the financial repercussions of the legal position of an applicant for the registration of a trade mark. The particular sign enjoyed an international reputation; the application could be assigned or licensed; Portuguese law, according to case law prior to 1993 and expressly with the New Code on Industrial Property thereafter provided that unlawful or fraudulent use by a third party of a mark applied for registration entitled the applicant to compensation in certain circumstances; and, filing the application conferred a priority right.

10–163   All the above created a pecuniary interest, albeit "the company's position in law was not sufficiently strong to amount to a 'legitimate expectation' attracting the protection of Article 1 of Protocol 1".[254] That provision applied only to existing possessions and according to the Court's case law future income could not be considered "possessions" unless it had already been earned or was definitely payable. In order to dissolve any doubt that could be raised by the complicated history of the application the Court added that the hope that a long-extinguished property right might be revived could not be regarded as a "possession"; the same applied to a lapsed conditional claim.[255]

In this case the applicant "had a conditional right, which was extinguished retrospectively for failure to satisfy the condition, namely that it did not infringe third-party rights".[256] Budějovický Budvar had contested the application from the beginning and Anheuser-Busch had entered into negotiations before challenging the registration of the geographical origin. The Court noted that commercial enterprises always carried an element of risk and Anheuser-Busch was or should have been aware that there was a possibility that its application would be rejected.

The Court concluded that a trade mark constituted a "possession" only after its final registration.

10–164   **(iii) The dissenting opinions.** Contrary to the practice of the European Court of Justice, the dissenting members of the European Court of Human Rights can publicise their opinions. Based on the right of priority the dissenting members in this case supported that the applicant company was entitled to expect that its application would be examined in accordance with the priority rule and the other rules governing intellectual property in force at the time of the original application for registration. They viewed the provision of the New Code of Industrial Property regarding the entitlement of an applicant for registration to seek compensation in some cases as strengthening their argument.

They believed that Anheuser-Busch had a legitimate expectation that was sufficiently strong to attract the protection of art.1 of Protocol 1 and that the refusal to register the mark amounted to interference its right of property.

---

[254] *Anheuser-Busch Inc v Portugal*, para.48.
[255] *Gratzinger and Gratzingerova v The Czech Republic* [GC], no.39794/98, E.C.H.R. 2002-VII.
[256] *Anheuser-Busch Inc*, para.50.

5. CONCLUSION

This was not a case of deprivation of ownership but still the effect of the denial to register the mark was to prevent the applicant from using the mark.

In order to be acceptable the interference had to satisfy three requirements: comply with the rule of law, pursue a legitimate aim, and strike a "fair balance" between the demands of the general interest of the community and the requirements of the protection of the individual's fundamental rights.[257]

Here it was the "fair balance" requirement that appeared problematic. Its assessment required an overall examination of the interests of all the actors involved. The state had an undisputed right to enter into such international agreements but it also had to take into account the rights of private parties, especially if they are non-nationals because "there may well be legitimate reason for requiring nationals to bear a greater burden in the public interest than non-nationals".[258]

10–165

By essentially making registration impossible the Portuguese authorities had passed to Anheuser-Busch an individual and excessive burden that upset the "fair balance" between the general interest and the protection of the right to the peaceful enjoyment of the individual's possessions.

5. CONCLUSION

This chapter has followed the same theme as Chs 8 and 9, looking at the interaction between trade mark law and other areas of law.

10–166

The comparative advertising cases have shown how the Court used advertising rules to define the scope of trade mark rights on the one hand and trade mark provisions to establish what should be allowed under comparative advertising on the other. They have also shown that according to the context of the case signs other than trade marks could also function as distinguishing indicia.

The geographical indication cases have shown how the regulation of another type of distinguishing signs deals with descriptiveness and genericity issues. They have also indicated that messages about the geographical origin of a product can be conveyed by distinguishing signs that do not as such possess a geographical meaning.

Following the same line we have seen a geographical name having the potential to function and be protected as a geographical indication, a trade name, and a trade mark. Note that conflicts between trade marks and trade names or geographical indications have also been considered in Ch.5. Finally, the property element of trade marks highlighted that there is yet another angle under which a trade mark dispute can be perceived.

---

[257] *Iatridis v Greece* [GC], no.31107/96, E.C.H.R. 1999–11.
[258] Opinion referring to *Lithgow v UK* (1986) 8 E.H.R.R. 329, para.17.

CHAPTER 11

THE CONTEMPORARY JURISPRUDENCE OF THE US SUPREME COURT

1. Introduction — 11–001
   (1) Unfair competition foundations — 11–001
   (2) The distinction between registered trade mark infringement and unfair competition — 11–002
   (3) Introduction to unfair competition — 11–003
   (4) Registered trade marks — 11–006
   (5) The jurisprudence of the Supreme Court — 11–015
2. The Trade Dress Cases — 11–016
   (1) Two Pesos—a permissive approach — 11–016
   (2) Qualitex—a state of ambivalence — 11–026
   (3) Wal Mart—taking a step back — 11–032
3. Traffix—Functionality — 11–037
   (1) Functionality as a public policy — 11–037
   (2) The judgment in Traffix — 11–041
4. Other Limitations to Trade Mark Protection — 11–047
   (1) Dastar—the scope of section 43(a) and copyright — 11–047
   (2) KP Permanent—a balancing exercise — 11–053
5. Victoria's Secret—The Uncertainties of Dilution — 11–058
   (1) The basics of dilution — 11–058
   (2) The Gay Olympic Games—protecting the Olympic symbols — 11–060
   (3) The 1995 Act—section 43(c) — 11–068
   (4) Establishing dilution — 11–070
   (5) Victoria's Secret—the sceptic's stance — 11–071
6. Parallel Imports — 11–077
   (1) The exhaustion principle—universality v territoriality — 11–077
   (2) Legislative context — 11–081
   (3) The competition question — 11–082
   (4) Material differences — 11–083
   (5) K MART—parallel imports — 11–084
7. Conclusion — 11–101

1. INTRODUCTION

(1) Unfair competition foundations

11–001 In the United States, trade mark law is viewed as one aspect of unfair competition law. Passing off, or palming off as it is otherwise known, is also considered to be the foundation of the modern law of registered trade mark infringement. Individual States have their own unfair competition laws, however for products in inter-State commerce (i.e. goods or services travelling from one State to another) and products imported into the US protection arises under legislation at the Federal level according to the United States Constitution that places the "regulation of foreign and interstate commerce"[1] within the jurisdiction of the Federal government.

Authoritative information regarding the level and methods of protection against unfair competition is provided by the Restatement of Unfair Competition, a review and analysis of the current state of the law that is periodically undertaken by lawyers, judges, and academics. Its position is persuasive but not binding.

(2) The distinction between registered trade mark infringement and unfair competition

11–002 Section 16 of the Restatement (Third) of Unfair Competition (1995), states that there:

> "is, however a fundamental distinction to be drawn between trademark infringement and unfair competition. Trade mark infringement rests on a relatively narrow principle compared to unfair competition. The essential element of a trademark is the exclusive right of its owner to use a word or device to distinguish his product. On the other hand, a claim of unfair competition considers the total physical image given by the product and its name together. Thus, unfair competition exists if the total impression of the package, size, shape, color, design and name upon the consumer will lead him to confuse the origin of the product."[2]

In this chapter references to cases are only indicative of the views of US courts.

(3) Introduction to unfair competition

11–003 Unfair competition is a common law tort that has been partially developed by State courts, partially codified by State statute, and partially codified by Federal statute.[3]

---

[1] See para.11–006.
[2] Restatement of the Law Third, Unfair Competition (ALI, 1995).
[3] *Fashion Two Twenty Inc v Steinberg*, 339 F. Supp. 836, 172 USPQ 102 (E.D.N.Y. 1971).

1. INTRODUCTION

Unfair competition is intertwined with competition; the latter is considered to be the rule and the former its exception. From the large number of cases repeating this proposition McCarthy refers to *Eastern Wine Corp*[4] for the assertion that there is a basic public policy, deep rooted in the US economy and respected by the courts, resting on the assumption that social welfare is best advanced by free competition.

As a result there is no general rule against copying. To the contrary the general principle is that there is a freedom to copy and compete, unless what is copied is protected by a specific right—copyright or trade mark and patent rights for example—or the specific act of copying constitutes an act of unfair competition.

(a) Unfair competition—particular types of behaviour

Unfair competition targets particular types of behaviour. "Liability is imposed under this Section, and under this Restatement generally, only in connection with harm resulting from particular methods of competition determined to be unfair".[5]

11-004

McCarthy, taking into account state case law, has devised the following chart of acts that could constitute unfair competition[6]: infringement of trade and service marks; trade mark dilution; use of confusingly similar corporate, business and professional names; use of confusingly similar titles of literary works on other literary property, and on commercial goods; the appropriation of distinctive literary and entertainer characterisations; simulation of a container or product configuration and of trade dress and packaging; infringement of the right of publicity; misappropriation of valuable business values; "bait and switch" selling tactics; false representations and false advertising; "palming off" goods by unauthorised substitution of one brand for the brand ordered; theft of trade secrets; filing a groundless lawsuit or administrative challenge as an aggressive competitive weapon; sending cease and desist letters charging patent infringement before a patent has been granted; sending cease and desist letters to customers of a competitor charging patent infringement without having a reasonable basis for a belief that there was infringement; an unreasonable rejection of goods shipped under contract; and physically obstructing entrance to a competitor's place of business and harassing its customers.

The list is indicative; new causes of action may be created in the future.[7] At the same time the historical development of case law under some of the types of behaviour listed above is rather limited.

---

[4] *Eastern Wine Corp v Winslow Warren Ltd*, 137 F.2d 955, 57 USPQ 565 (2nd Cir. 1943).
[5] Restatement (Third) of Unfair Competition, s.1, comment a (1995).
[6] McCarthy, *McCarthy on Trademarks and Unfair Competition* (Looseleaf, Thomson), ch.25.
[7] "When a scheme is evolved which on its face violates the fundamental rules of honesty and fair dealing, a court of equity is not impotent to frustrate its consummation because the scheme is an original one. There is a maxim as old as law that there can be no right without

In the field of trade marks s.43 of the Lanham Act reflects the current position on unfair competition. The provision covers registered and unregistered trade marks alike. Section 43(a) provides the classic confusion and deception scenarios.[8] Section 43(b) covers the importation of infringing goods.[9] Section 43(c) covers the expansion of the scope of protection to cover dilution.[10] And s.43(d) introduces protection against cyber-piracy.[11]

11–005 In 1974 Gilson had described the Lanham Act as "a broad, flexible instrument of federal trademark policy. In many ways it is like a constitution, and the courts are being increasingly innovative as they apply it to new fact situations."[12]

Indeed, the interpretation, application and expansion of the Lanham Act is evidence of the development of trade mark law from its early days, where protection was limited against use of similar marks on similar products when there was confusion as to source, to a law that recognises the value of trade marks on their own and protects them against dilution, has expanded the scope of confusion to cover more than the traditional origin link, and covers new arenas of infringement like the world wide web.

---

a remedy, and in searching for a precise precedent, an equity court must not lose sight, not only of its power, but of its duty to arrive at a just solution of the problem" (*American Philatelic Soc v Claibourne*, 3 Cal. 2d 689, 46 P.2d 135 (1935)): McCarthy 1:12.

[8] The Lanham Act is found in Title 15 of the US Code. In this chapter references to Sections of the Lanham Act will follow the numbering of the Act rather than that of the US Code. Section 43 false designations of origin and false descriptions forbidden:

(a) Civil action.
  (1) Any person who, on or in connection with any goods or services, or any container for goods, uses in commerce any word, term, name, symbol, or device, or any combination thereof, or any false designation of origin, false or misleading description of fact, or false or misleading representation of fact, which—
    (A) is likely to cause confusion, or to cause mistake, or to deceive as to the affiliation, connection, or association of such person with another person, or as to the origin, sponsorship, or approval of his or her goods, services, or commercial activities by another person, or
    (B) in commercial advertising or promotion, misrepresents the nature, characteristics, qualities, or geographic origin of his or her or another person's goods, services, or commercial activities, shall be liable in a civil action by any person who believes that he or she is or is likely to be damaged by such act.
  (3) In a civil action for trade dress infringement under this Act for trade dress not registered on the principal register, the person who asserts trade dress protection has the burden of proving that the matter sought to be protected is not functional.

[9] Section 43 (b) Importation. Any goods marked or labeled in contravention of the provisions of this section shall not be imported into the US or admitted to entry at any customhouse of the US. The owner, importer, or consignee of goods refused entry at any customhouse under this section may have any recourse by protest or appeal that is given under the customs revenue laws or may have the remedy given by this Act in cases involving goods refused entry or seized.

[10] On which see paras 11–058 and following, below.

[11] For an overview see Maniatis, "Trade Mark Use on the Internet", Philips and Simon (eds), *Trade Mark Use* (Oxford University Press, 2005).

[12] In the introduction of Gilson, *Trademark Protection and Practice* (Looseleaf, Matthew Bender).

1. INTRODUCTION

(4) Registered trade marks

As mentioned above all signs functioning as trade marks enjoy the broad protection of s.43 of the Lanham Act. The establishment of ownership in trade marks requires either registration or actual use of the mark in commerce. The benefits of registration include: prima facie evidence of exclusive right to use; incontestability; constructive notice of rights and constructive use at the Federal level; remedies against the importation of infringing goods. Section 32 provides for infringement and remedies; there are direct analogies with s.43.

11–006

The first Federal Act providing for trade mark registration irrespective of use was adopted in 1870; however in 1879 the Supreme Court[13] decided that there was no constitutional basis for the 1870 Act. For patents and copyright art.1 para.8 cl.8 of the US Constitution gave Congress the power to "promote the progress of science and the useful arts, by securing for limited times to authors and inventors the exclusive right to their respective writings and discoveries". Trade marks, however, were simply founded on priority of appropriation. In order to overcome the constitutionality problem Congress turned to art.1 para.8 cl.3 of the Constitution. Under its Commerce Power it could "regulate commerce with foreign nations, and among the several states, and with the Indian Tribes". This led in 1881 to the adoption of a statute providing for registration of trade marks used in commerce with foreign nations and the Indian tribes; there was no registration requirement for trade marks used in interstate commerce. The 1905 Act introduced a system of registration covering also trade marks used in interstate commerce but only when they were "technical common law trademarks"; this meant that descriptive trade marks, geographical names, personal names, names of firms, and names of corporations were excluded from protection, unless they had been in actual and exclusive use for at least a 11-year period prior to the adoption of the 1905 Act. In 1920 registration of non-technical trade marks became available.

A draft modernising Bill, the Vestal Bill, was introduced in 1921. Following a long period of discussions and amendments a new version of the Vestal Bill, the Lanham Bill, was introduced by congressman Fritz Garland Lanham as a draft before the Congress. The Lanham Act was adopted in 1946 and became effective on July 5, 1947.

Subsequently, it had been amended a number of times, including the following. In 1962, in order to expand the scope of confusion. In 1984, to provide (i) for ex parte seizure orders and mandatory monetary remedies in counterfeiting cases; and (ii) that trade marks may be considered to distinguish a product even where its source is unknown by name to customers. In 1988, by introducing (i) a bona fide "intent to use" basis for applications; (ii) reducing the registration period from 20 to 10 years; and (iii) adding trade libel and product disparagement to s.43(a). In 1989 by providing that a

---

[13] *Trade Mark Cases*, 100 U.S. 82, 25 L. Ed. 550 (1879).

trade mark is infringed by use of another sign that "is likely to cause confusion, or to cause mistake, or to deceive as to the affiliation, connection, or association" of the later user with the earlier user. In 1993, to provide that geographically misdescriptive trade marks will not be registered even where they have acquired secondary meaning, in order to comply with the North American Free Trade Agreement. In 1994, to provide (i) that geographical indications for wine or liquor will not be registered if they identify a place other than the product's place of origin; and (ii) extend the period of non-use that is considered to be a presumption of abandonment from two to three years. In 1995, introducing s.43(c). In 1996, in order to strengthen the anti-counterfeiting provisions. In 1999, to introduce into the text of the Act the concept of "functionality", a public policy doctrine that had been applied extensively by the courts; and in 2000, introducing s.43(d). Most recently, in October 2006, the provision on dilution, s.43(c), has been amended as a consequence of the jurisprudence of the Supreme Court.

11–007 The Federal Registration system comprises two Registers: the Principal Register and the Supplemental Register.

Registration on the Principal Register provides protection at the Federal level. Examination is for formalities, absolute grounds, and conflict with prior applications and registrations. Section 13 provides that any party who believes that it would be damaged can oppose an application for registration. Oppositions must be filed within 30 days following the publication of the application.

The Supplemental Register allows US trade mark owners to obtain a registration they can use as a "basis" home registration enabling them then to register the same marks abroad in countries where home registration is required. The only requirement is that the mark is capable of distinguishing; there is no provision for publication of an application or for opposition proceedings. The trade mark is published upon registration and any person who believes that it will be damaged by the registration may at any time institute cancellation proceedings.

(a) Use in commerce—the basic requirement

11–008 According to s.1 the basic requirement for registration on the Principal Register is use in commerce, actual or intended. There are three ways to satisfy this requirement. First, actual use in commerce that must be indicated and evidenced on the application form. Secondly, bona fide intention to use in commerce; once the trade mark application is accepted the applicant must, within a six-month period (extendable), file a statement and evidence of the mark as used in commerce. If the statement of use is accepted then the mark is registered with the original filing date. Thirdly, the applicant may claim the benefit of a foreign registration (or an application for registration) in its country of origin, on the basis of international conventions to which the United States is a party or reciprocity. In this case

1. INTRODUCTION

the application must state the applicant's bona fide intention to use the mark in commerce, but use in commerce is not required prior to registration.

In any case the registered proprietor must file an affidavit and evidence of use within the one-year preceding the expiration of the sixth year of registration or show that non-use was due to special circumstances and not its intention to abandon the mark. The mark as used may not present a different commercial impression from the mark as registered, which would constitute an impermissible "material alteration" in the mark. Alterations are material if the change would require republication in order to present the mark fairly for purposes of opposition.

(b) *Additional registrability requirements*

According to s.2 the following are excluded from registration: immoral, scandalous, and disparaging signs; coats of arms; names of living individuals, unless there is written consent (with a special provision for US Presidents); marks confusingly or deceptively similar to marks already on the Register; descriptive or deceptively misdescriptive marks; geographically descriptive or deceptively misdescriptive names; and marks that are primarily surnames.

11–009

Descriptive terms can be registered once they have acquired secondary meaning.

The fundamental positive requirement is that the trade mark must be one "by which the goods of the applicant may be distinguished from the goods of others".[14]

A mark is considered distinctive if it is (i) inherently distinctive; or (ii) has acquired distinctiveness through secondary meaning. According to case law and practice signs can be generic, descriptive, suggestive, and arbitrary or fanciful. Suggestive, arbitrary and fanciful signs are prima facie registrable (inherently distinctive). Generic terms can not be protected as trade marks. Protectability of descriptive terms relies on secondary meaning.

The difficulty lies in separating borderline suggestive from descriptive signs. According to the Supreme Court, distinctiveness is always a question of fact.[15] In order to draw the line courts have been applying three tests, considering each time: the degree of imagination; competitors' need to use the sign; competitors' actual use of the sign.

11–010

According to McCarthy[16] there are six questions that courts must consider in a combined and comprehensive approach. First, how much imagination is required on behalf of the consumer in order to get a direct message from the mark about the quality, ingredients, or characteristics of the relevant product, keeping in mind that the attention of consumers will vary according to the product. Secondly, whether the mark directly conveys a real and unequivocal idea of some characteristic, function, quality or ingredient

---

[14] Lanham Act s.2.
[15] See para.11–016.
[16] See Ch.11 of McCarthy.

of the product or service to a reasonably informed potential buyer. Thirdly, whether the mark is closely linked with the product that other marketers would be likely to use the mark. Fourthly, whether the mark is used by other traders. Fifthly, whether the mark also brings to mind an arbitrary connotation despite its descriptive meaning. Finally, whether consumers perceive the sign as an indication of source or as an advertising message.

(c) Conflicts between marks

11-011   In order to resolve traditional conflicts between trade marks "likelihood of confusion" is the touchstone.

According to an early judgment of the Supreme Court likelihood of confusion means probable confusion. "Under the facts, we are of opinion that it does not appear that the use of the word as a trade-mark upon the goods of the plaintiff will probably confuse or deceive the public, to the injury of the defendant or of any other corporation."[17] Lower courts had held that if one mark simply calls to mind another mark this would not be enough to establish likelihood of confusion.[18]

However, the concept of confusion has been broadened considerably throughout the years.

11-012   In terms of the text of the law, in 1962 by taking out of s.43 the sentence "of purchasers as to the source of origin of such goods or services" and in 1989 by providing that use which "is likely to cause confusion, or to cause mistake, or to deceive as to the affiliation, connection, or association" of the later user with the earlier user would constitute an infringement.

In terms of application of the law by the courts a number of "types" of confusion had been held actionable. The traditional forms of confusion include "forward confusion" when customers perceive the later user's goods as goods of the earlier user and "reverse confusion" when customers perceive the earlier user's goods as goods of the later user.

But confusion of end users,[19] pre-sale confusion,[20] initial interest confusion,[21] and post-sale confusion[22] had been recognised by the courts.

---

[17] *American Steel Foundries v Robertson*, 269 U.S. 372 (1926), at 384.
[18] Although call to mind surveys could be used as supporting evidence. In *Re Ferrero*, 178 U.S.P.Q. 167 (C.C.P.A. 1973) the court employed the traffic light example, according to their sequence one colour in traffic lights will call to mind the next one. This does not mean that there is any confusion between the colours.
[19] For example, *In re Artic Electronics Co*, 220 U.S.P.Q. 836 (T.T.A.B. 1983).
[20] For example, *McNeil—PPC v Guardian Drug Co*, 45 U.S.P.Q.2d 1437 (E.D. Mich. 1997).
[21] For example, *Mobil Oil Corp v Pegasus Petroleum Corp*, 2 U.S.P.Q.2d 1677 (2nd Cir. 1987).
[22] For example in *Mastercrafters Clock & Radio Co v Vacheron & Constantin—Le Coultre Watches*, 105 U.S.P.Q. 160 (2nd Cir. 1955) the Court of Appeals held that some customers would buy the later user's cheaper clock for acquiring the prestige gained by displaying a prestigious article. In essence it was the confusion of third parties visiting the homes of the buyers that rendered the conduct of the copyist actionable. Similarly with the viewing public's confusion in *Hermes Intern v Lederer de Paris Fifth Ave Inc*, 55 U.S.P.Q.2d 1360 (2nd Cir. 2000) where the seller of copies informed the buyers that the products were copies. If

1. INTRODUCTION

(d) The test for establishing confusion

Courts have been using two multi factor tests for establishing the likelihood of confusion. **11–013**

The first deals with competing products[23]; it covers the following factors:

1. the similarity or dissimilarity of the marks in their entireties as to appearance, sound, connotation and commercial impression;
2. the similarity or dissimilarity and nature of the goods or services as described in an application or registration in connection with which a prior mark is in use;
3. the similarity or dissimilarity of established, likely-to-continue trade channels;
4. the conditions under which and buyers to whom sales are made;
5. the fame of the prior mark (sales, advertising, length of use);
6. the number and nature of similar marks in use on similar goods;
7. the nature and extent of any actual confusion;
8. the variety of goods on which a mark is or is not used;
9. the length of time during and conditions under which there has been concurrent use without evidence of actual confusion;
10. ,the market interface between the applicant and the owner of the mark (consents; agreements aiming to limit confusion; assignments; goodwill; estoppels);
11. the extent to which the applicant has a right to exclude others from use of its marks on its goods;
12. the extent of potential confusion (de minimis or substantial); and
13. any other established fact probative of the effect of use.

The second covers products that are not competing with each other,[24] although it is also used in cases of competing products. The following factors have to be considered:

1. the strength of the mark;
2. the degree of similarity of the marks;

---

there are too many "knockoffs" in the market, sales of the originals might suffer because the public would have doubts as to whether what they are purchasing is an original and because the scarcity value the product has for the purchaser of an original would diminish.

[23] *In re El Du Pont de Nemours & Co*, 476 F.2d 1357, 177 U.S.P.Q. 563 (C.C.P.A. 1973).
[24] *Polaroid Corp v Polarad Electronics Corp*, 287 F.2d 492, 128 U.S.P.Q. 411 (2dn Cir. 1961).

3. the degree of closeness of the products;
4. the likelihood that the senior user would expand;
5. actual confusion;
6. the defendant's motive and good faith;
7. the quality of defendant's product; and
8. the sophistication of the buyer class.

McCarthy notes that the ultimate question in the case of use on non-competing goods or services, must be "Is the reasonably prudent purchaser likely to be confused not only as to source, but also as to sponsorship, affiliation or connection?"[25]

11-014 He summarises the factors that we have to look at, according to the Restatement (Third) of Unfair Competition, as follows:

1. the degree of resemblance between the conflicting designations;
2. the similarity of the marketing methods and channels of distribution;
3. the characteristics of the prospective purchasers and the degree of care they exercise;
4. the degree of distinctiveness of the senior user's mark;
5. where the goods or services are not competitive, the likelihood that prospective buyers would expect the senior user to expand into the field of the junior user;
6. where the goods or services are sold in different territories, the extent to which the senior user's designation is known in the junior user's territory; and
7. the intent of the junior user; and
8. evidence of actual confusion.

However, according to the Restatement no "mechanistic formula or list can set forth in advance the variety of elements that comprise the market context from which likelihood of confusion must be determined."

(5) The jurisprudence of the Supreme Court

11-015 Following this very brief introduction this chapter will look at the relatively recent decisions of the Supreme Court in the field of trade marks. They covered five particular areas: the protection of trade dress, functionality, other limitations to trade mark protection, dilution, and parallel imports.

---

[25] McCarthy, 24:1.

2. THE TRADE DRESS CASES

(1) Two Pesos—a permissive approach

In *Two Pesos*[26] the Supreme Court looked at the issue of distinctiveness of trade dress. The Court considered the case, an appeal from the Fifth Circuit,[27] in order to resolve a conflict between the Circuits as to whether trade dress could be inherently distinctive or in order to be protected it required evidence that it has acquired a new secondary meaning.[28]

11–016

Taco Cabana, a chain of Mexican fast-food restaurants, argued that the trade dress of its restaurants should be protected against simulation by Two Pesos under s.43(a) of the Lanham Act.[29] It described its—unregistered—trade dress as:

"a festive eating atmosphere having interior dining and patio areas decorated with artifacts, bright colors, paintings and murals. The patio includes interior and exterior areas with the interior patio capable of being sealed off from the outside patio by overhead garage doors. The stepped exterior of the building is a festive and vivid color scheme using top border paint and neon stripes. Bright awnings and umbrellas continue the theme."[30]

The Court of Appeals had followed its own line of precedent setting that proof of secondary meaning was required only for trade marks that were not sufficiently inherently distinctive and that the same principle should also be applied to trade dress. It noted however that its position disagreed with that adopted by other Courts of Appeals that insisted on secondary meaning for unregistered trade marks and trade dresses.[31]

The Supreme Court granted certiorari and endorsed the approach of the Fifth Circuit. Note however that it considered exclusively the question of

---

[26] *Two Pesos, Inc v Taco Cabana, Inc*, 505 U.S. 763, 23 U.S.P.Q.2d 1081 (1992).
[27] *Two Pesos Inc v Taco Cabana, Inc*, 932 F.2d 113 (5th Cir. 1991).
[28] According to s.13 of the Restatement (Third) of Unfair Competition a term has acquire secondary meaning when it "has come through use to be uniquely associated with a specific source". According to the Supreme Court, to "establish secondary meaning, a manufacturer must show that, in the minds of the public, the primary significance of a product feature or term is to identify the source of the product rather than the product itself", *Inwood Laboratories, Inc v Ives Laboratories, Inc*, 456 U.S. 844 (1982), at 851.
[29] Lanham Act s.43(a) (it has since been amended) provided: "Any person who shall affix, apply, or annex, or use in connection with any goods or services, or any container or containers for goods, a false designation of origin, or any false description or representation, including words or other symbols tending falsely to describe or represent the same, and shall cause such goods or services to enter into commerce, and any person who shall with knowledge of the falsity of such designation of origin or description or representation cause or procure the same to be transported or used in commerce or deliver the same to any carrier to be transported or used, shall be liable to a civil action by any person doing business in the locality falsely indicated as that of origin or in the region in which said locality is situated, or by any person who believes that he is or is likely to be damaged by the use of any such false description or representation".
[30] 932 F.2d 1113 (5th Cir. 1991), at 1117.
[31] In particular the Second Circuit, for example in *Vibrant Sales, Inc v New Body Boutique Inc* 652 F.2d 299 (2nd Cir. 1981).

distinctiveness, it did not examine whether Taco Cabana's trade dress was functional.

The way the Supreme Court built its judgment is revealing in terms of interpretive techniques and substantive trade mark law; it is worth examining it in detail for its substance but also in order to give an example of the mechanics and style of the Supreme Court.

(a) The main issue

11–017 Justice White delivered the opinion of the Court and started by describing the issue and the background of the case: "The issue in this case is whether the trade dress of a restaurant may be protected under §43(a) of the Trademark Act of 1946 (Lanham Act) ... based on a finding of inherent distinctiveness, without proof that the trade dress has secondary meaning".[32]

To delineate the concept of trade dress he referred to the judgments of the District Court and the Court of Appeals under appeal, other judgments, and the Restatement of Unfair Competition. He employed a number of definitions; the first one was linked with the facts of the case whereas the other two were more abstract:

(i) According to the District Court: " '[T]rade dress' is the total image of the business. Taco Cabana's trade dress may include the shape and general appearance of the exterior of the restaurant, the identifying sign, the interior kitchen floor plan, the decor, the menu, the equipment used to serve food, the servers' uniforms and other features reflecting on the total image of the restaurant".[33]

(ii) The Court of Appeals accepted this definition and also quoted from another case: "The 'trade dress' of a product is essentially its total image and overall appearance".[34]

(iii) Justice White also cited the definition employed by another Circuit and the Restatement (Third) of Unfair Competition. Trade dress "involves the total image of a product and may include features such as size, shape, color or color combinations, texture, graphics, or even particular sales techniques".[35]

---

[32] 505 U.S. 763, at 764–765.
[33] 505 U.S. 763, fn.1.
[34] 505 U.S. 763, citing *Blue Bell Bio-Medical v Cin-Bad, Inc*, 864 F.2d 1253 (5th Cir. 1989), at 1256.
[35] 505 U.S. 763, citing *John H Harland Co v Clarke Checks, Inc*, 711 F.2d 966 (11th Cir. 1983), at 980 and s.16 of the Restatement (Third) of Unfair Competition.

2. THE TRADE DRESS CASES

(b) The legislative context

He then considered the purpose of the Act and the relevant provision within the Act.

11–018

The Lanham Act, according to s.45, was intended to make "actionable the deceptive and misleading use of marks" and "to protect persons engaged in ... commerce against unfair competition". Following the Supreme Court's jurisprudence s.43(a), a wider unfair competition provision, prohibited a broader range of practices than s.32 that covered exclusively registered trade marks.[36] However, according to Justice White, it was common ground that the s.2 registrability conditions were also "for the most part" applicable in determining whether an unregistered mark was entitled to protection under s.43(a).[37] The basic registration requirement a trade mark had to satisfy was to be capable of distinguishing the applicant's goods from those of others.

Justice White then referred to a widely accepted classification of trade marks according to distinctiveness, noting that it had also been followed by the Court of Appeals and accepted by the petitioner. Trade marks might be: (1) generic; (2) descriptive; (3) suggestive; (4) arbitrary; or (5) fanciful.[38] He dealt first with what appeared to be less controversial. Suggestive, arbitrary, and fanciful marks, because of their intrinsic nature, identified the source of a product, were deemed inherently distinctive, and were entitled to protection. At the other end generic marks, "refe[r] to the genus of which the particular product is a species"[39] and were not entitled to protection.[40]

Descriptive marks lay in the middle; because they were descriptive of a product they did not inherently identify a particular source and they could not be protected. Section 2 though opened the possibility of protection if the descriptive mark "has become distinctive of the applicant's goods in commerce", or, as the courts put it, had acquired a secondary meaning.[41]

The secondary meaning requirement for descriptive marks had consistently been applied to s.43(a) cases.[42] To complete the picture he added that

---

[36] Citing again *Inwood Laboratories, Inc v Ives Laboratories, Inc*, 456 U.S. 844 (1982), at 858.
[37] 505 U.S. 763, at 768, citing two judgments from two Circuits: *AJ Canfield Co v Honickman*, 808 F.2d 291 (3rd Cir. 1986) and *Thompson Medical Co v Pfizer Inc*, 753 F.2d 208 (2nd Cir. 1985).
[38] Citing *Abercrombie & Fitch Co v Hunting World, Inc*, 537 F.2d 4 (2nd Cir. 1976).
[39] 505 U.S. 763, at 9.
[40] He actually refers to registration rather than entitlement to protection citing the Supreme Court's own judgment in *Park 'N Fly, Inc v Dollar Park and Fly, Inc*, 469 U.S. 189, 224 U.S.P.Q.2d 327 (1985).
[41] Citing *Inwood Laboratories, Inc v Ives Laboratories, Inc*, 456 U.S. 844 (1982) and a much earlier Supreme Court judgment on trade dress, *Kellogg Co v National Biscuit Co*, 305 U.S. 111 (1938). He also referred to s.13 of the Restatement (Third) of Unfair Competition and *Park 'N Fly* at 194.
[42] By way of example Justice White cited two Court of Appeals decisions from different Circuits, *University of Georgia Athletic Assn v Laite*, 756 F.2d 1535 (11th Cir. 1985) and (a second time) *Thompson Medical Co v Pfizer Inc*, 753 F.2d 208 (2nd Cir. 1985).

non-functionality[43] and likelihood of confusion[44] were the additional requirements under s.43(a).

(c) The context of the case

11-019   Justice White then turned to the case before the Supreme Court separating the issues according to what the Court would and would not consider, starting from the latter.

The District Court and the Court of Appeals had ruled that the jury that had decided that Taco Cabana's trade dress was, first, inherently distinctive and, secondly, non-functional had been properly instructed according to the principles that Justice White had identified and that the evidence supported its verdict. These rulings remained outside the scope of the current judgment: "None of these rulings is before us in this case, and for present purposes we assume, without deciding, that each of them is correct".[45]

What the Supreme Court would do is affirm that the position of the Court of Appeals that inherently distinctive trade dress was entitled to protection despite the lack of proof of secondary meaning was correct. Justice White noted that this position had been adopted by the Court of Appeals in an earlier case[46] that the Supreme Court had at the time refused to consider.

There was one contradictory complication in the findings of the jury however: it had found that the trade dress had not acquired a secondary meaning but, nevertheless, was still inherently distinctive.

(d) The reasoning of the Court

11-020   According to Justice White setting a general requirement of secondary meaning for trade dress would be at odds with the principles generally applicable to infringement actions under s.43(a); so, there ought to be a persuasive argument for this derogation.

The first argument was based on the apparently inconsistent findings of the jury on distinctiveness. Justice White rejected it accepting the Court of Appeals' view on this issue:

"While the necessarily imperfect (and often prohibitively difficult) methods for assessing secondary meaning address the empirical

---

[43] Citing, by way of example, *Inwood Laboratories, Inc v Ives Laboratories, Inc*, 456 U.S. 844 (1982), and a number of cases from the Circuits: *Brunswick Corp v Spirit Reel Co*, 832 F.2d 513 (10th Cir. 1987); *First Brands Corp v Fred Meyers, Inc*, 809 F.2d 1378 (9th Cir. 1987); *Stormy Clime Ltd v ProGroup, Inc*, 809 F.2d 971 (2nd Cir. 1987); *AmBrit, Inc v Kraft, Inc*, 812 F.2d 1531; *American Greetings Corp v Dan-Dee Imports, Inc*, 807 F.2d 1136 (3rd Cir. 1986).
[44] Citing *Brunswick Corp, v Spirit Reel Co*, 832 F.2d 513 (CAIO (10th Cir. 1987) 1987); *AmBrit*, ibid; *First Brands, Corp v Fred Meyers, Inc*, F.2d 1378 (9th Cir. 1987); *Stormy Clime, Ltd v ProGroup, Inc*, 809 F.2d 971 (2nd Cir. 1987); and, *American Greetings, Corp v Dan-Dee Imports, Inc*, 807 F.2d 1136 (3rd Cir. 1986).
[45] 505 U.S. 763, at 770.
[46] *Chevron Chemical Co v Voluntary Purchasing Groups, Inc*, 659 F.2d 695 (5th Cir. 1981).

2. THE TRADE DRESS CASES

question of current consumer association, the legal recognition of an inherently distinctive trademark or trade dress acknowledges the owner's legitimate proprietary interest in its unique and valuable informational device, regardless of whether substantial consumer association yet bestows the additional empirical protection of secondary meaning."[47]

There are two points to underline here. First, the recognition that assessing secondary meaning is a very difficult exercise because the court has to identify consumer perceptions in the market place at a given point of time. Secondly, the acceptance that the starting point when we are dealing with something inherently distinctive is the proprietary interest of its owner rather than consumer perception.[48]

The way the petitioner had supported the argument weakened it further; having accepted that trade dress can be inherently distinctive it claimed that protection should be limited until it acquired secondary meaning. However, Justice White agreed with the Court of Appeals that the termination of protection of trade dress that was neither functional nor descriptive for failure to gain secondary meaning would not be based on the failure of the dress to retain its fanciful, arbitrary, or suggestive nature, but on the commercial failure of its user in the marketplace whereas the "user of such a trade dress should be able to maintain what competitive position it has and continue to seek wider identification among potential customers".[49]

The judge then turned to the argumentation developed by the Second Circuit. He rejected outright the holding that unregistered trade marks required secondary meaning to qualify for protection because they lacked the presumptive source association that registered trade marks had[50]; "there are plainly marks that are registrable without showing secondary meaning. These same marks, even if not registered, remain inherently capable of distinguishing the goods of the users of these marks".[51] This sweeping view of unregistered trade marks had been reversed by the Second Circuit itself[52]; it continued however to refuse inherent distinctiveness in respect of trade dress.[53]

11–021

Justice White though could not see the reason for and the purpose of the distinction. If trade dress was capable of identifying the source of a product, secondary meaning should not be required. This was the line followed by the Fifth Circuit but also accepted by the Eleventh and the Ninth Circuits.

Turning to the language of s.43(a) he supported that it, too, provided no justification for such a distinction between trade dress and other signs

---

[47] 932 F.2d 1113, at 1120.
[48] Compare with the approach adopted by the Court of Justice on this issue in *Arsenal Football Club Plc* (C-206/01) [2002] E.C.R. I-10273.
[49] 505 U.S. 763, at 771.
[50] *Vibrant Sales, Inc v New Body Boutique, Inc*, 652 F.2d 299 (2nd Cir. 1981).
[51] 505 U.S. 763, at 772.
[52] *Thompson Medical Co v Pfizer Inc*, F.2d 208 (2nd Cir. 1985).
[53] See for example *LeSportsac, Inc v K Mart Corp*, 754 F.2d 71 (2nd Cir. 1985).

because the provision did not even mention trade marks or trade dress on the one hand and secondary meaning on the other. Secondary meaning was a s.2 requirement for descriptive marks.

From a purposive angle he observed that adding a superfluous requirement to s.43(a) would undermine the Lanham Act. He cited *Park 'N Fly*[54] on the desirability of trade mark protection and broadened the scope of the ruling to cover trade dress as well as ordinary trade marks. "By making more difficult the identification of a producer with its product, a secondary meaning requirement for a nondescriptive trade dress would hinder improving or maintaining the producer's competitive position".[55]

11–022   Competition implications, he repeated, would be covered by the doctrine of functionality, so the claim that the first user of any shape or trade dress would eliminate competition remained unpersuasive. To the contrary, a secondary meaning requirement could prove anticompetitive, first by adding to start-up costs.

Justice White introduced another consideration at this stage:

"It would present special difficulties for a business, such as respondent, that seeks to start a new product in a limited area and then expand into new markets. Denying protection for inherently distinctive nonfunctional trade dress until after secondary meaning has been established would allow a competitor, which has not adopted a distinctive trade dress of its own, to appropriate the originator's dress in other markets and to deter the originator from expanding into and competing in these areas".[56]

Accordingly, the Court affirmed the decision of the Court of Appeals.

(e)   Concurring Opinions

11–023   The opinion of the Court was expressed by Justice White; two justices concurred in the judgment following a different route.

Justice Stevens believed that the textual analysis of s.43(a) did not support the conclusion of the Court. However, Federal courts have transformed the provision. This was in accordance with the purpose of the Act and the legislative intent of Congress.

Reviewing the jurisprudence of the Court on s.43(a)[57] he noted that the provision protected against using either a "false designation of origin" or a "false description or representation" in connection with any goods or services; the term "origin" referred to the geographical origin of the goods.

---

[54] *Park 'N Fly, Inc v Dollar Park and Fly, Inc*, 469 U.S. 189, 224 U.S.P.Q.2d 327 (1985).
[55] 505 U.S. 763, at 774.
[56] 505 U.S. 763, at 775.
[57] Citing by way of example *Moskal v United States*, 498 U.S. 103, 111 S.Ct. 461 (1990), *K Mart Corp v Cartier Inc, et al. 47th Street Photo Inc*, 486 U.S. 281, 108 S.Ct. 1811 (1988); and *United States v Turkette*, 452 U.S. 576, 101 S.Ct. 2524.

2. THE TRADE DRESS CASES

Historically, both harmful acts were construed narrowly covering false advertising and passing off. Secondary meaning was relevant only to passing off actions. Gradually the federal courts expanded the scope of the provision.[58] Likelihood of confusion became the test for liability, common for both wrongs. He cited a case from the Ninth Circuit that typified the new approach: "[U]nder the Lanham Act [§43(a)], the ultimate test is whether the public is likely to be deceived or confused by the similarity of the marks ... Whether we call the violation infringement, unfair competition or false designation of origin, the test is identical—is there a 'likelihood of confusion?' ".[59] And the Circuits, with the exception of the Second Circuit, also agreed that inherently distinctive trade dress could be protected under s.43(a) without evidence of secondary meaning.[60]

He found, however, that the transformation of s.43(a) was consistent with the general purposes of the Lanham Act. Referring to Congressman Lanham, who sponsored the bill, he mentioned the interests of businesspeople and consumers and highlighted the federal nature of the Act. Federal courts applied and interpreted the law and Congress had followed the direction drawn by them,[61] without introducing a secondary meaning requirement to s.43(a).[62] Congress "explicitly extended to any violation of §43(a) the basic Lanham Act remedial provisions whose text previously covered only registered trademarks".[63] He concurred in the judgment but not in the Opinion of the Court.

Justice Thomas relied on a language analysis of s.43(a) in order to concur in the judgment of the Court. He agreed that the provision codified common law torts of technical trade mark infringement and passing off that were both linked with misrepresentations regarding a product's source of production.[64]

11–024

---

[58] Citing two farsighted cases: *L'Aiglon Apparel, Inc v Lana Lobell Inc*, 214 F.2d 649 (3rd Cir. 1954); and *Maternally Yours, Inc v Your Maternity Shop, Inc*, 234 F.2d 538 (2nd Cir. 1956).
[59] *New West Corp v NYM Co of California, Inc*, 595 F.2d 1194 (9th Cir. 1979), at 1201.
[60] Citing, amongst other examples of the common approach, two cases that certiorari had been denied by the Supreme Court, *AmBrit, Inc v Kraft, Inc*, 805 F.2d 974 (11th Cir. 1986), cert. denied, 481 U.S. 1041, 107 S.Ct. 1983 (1987); and *Chevron Chemical Co v Voluntary Purchasing Groups, Inc*, 659 F.2d 695 (5th Cir. 1981), cert denied, 457 U.S. 1126, 102 S.Ct. 2947. And as an example of the Second Circuit's early approach, influenced by common law, he cited *Crescent Tool Co v Kilborn and Bishop Co*, 247 F. 299 (1917); the Second Circuit continued to demand evidence of secondary meaning, however he remarked, most of the cases where the Second Circuit had pronounced this requirement were not inherent distinctiveness cases. Some involved products that where both functional and non distinctive—a velcro belt in *Vibrant Sales, Inc v New Body Boutique, Inc*, 652 F.2d 299 (2nd Cir. 1981), cert. denied, 455 U.S. 909, 102 S.Ct. 1257. Others linked functionality with distinctiveness—a rainjacket was found to be closer to the functionality rather than the distinctiveness end in *Stormy Clime Ltd v ProGroup, Inc*, 809 F.2d 971 (2nd Cir. 1987). Others were functionality cases were distinctiveness should be irrelevant—*LeSportsac, Inc v K Mart Corp*, 754 F.2d 71 (2nd Cir. 1985).
[61] The Trademark Law Revision Act of 1988, 102 Stat. 3935, provided a good example.
[62] He cited *Tiger v Western Investment Co*, 221 U.S. 286, 31 S.Ct. 578, where the Court ruled that subsequent legislation may assist in the interpretation of prior legislation on the same subject.
[63] 505 U.S. 763, at 784.
[64] Citing *Inwood Laboratories, Inc v Ives Laboratories, Inc*, 456 U.S. 844, (1982); *Chevron Chemical Co v Voluntary Purchasing Groups, Inc*, 659 F.2d 695 (5th Cir. 1981), cert. denied, 457 U.S. 1126, 102 S.Ct. 2947; *Yale Electric Corp v Robertson*, 26 F.2d 972 (2nd Cir. 1928); *American Washboard Co v Saginaw Mfg Co*, 103 F.281 (6th Cir. 1900).

Originally common law was more restrictive in respect of trade dress:

"Trade dress, which consists not of words or symbols, but of a product's packaging (or 'image', more broadly), seems at common law to have been thought incapable ever of being inherently distinctive, perhaps on the theory that the number of ways to package a product is finite. Thus, a user of trade dress would always have had to show secondary meaning in order to obtain protection".[65]

11-025 However, gradually, courts started accepting that trade dress could follow the same distinctiveness classification with words or symbols.[66] So, according to Justice Thomas, from the language of s.43(a) and without having to take registrability provisions into account it was apparent that a particular trade dress could serve as a representation or designation of source and the first user of an arbitrary package should be entitled to the "presumption that his package represents him".[67]

Finally, Justice Scalia concurred with Justice Thomas on the language of s.43(a) under the light of its common law derivation but found it complementary, to rather than inconsistent with, the Opinion of the Court as expressed by Justice White.

There were two weaknesses in the *Two Pesos* decision.[68] First, the scope of the decision regarding the subject matter of protection was uncertain. Justice White, describing the main issue of the case had referred specifically to the trade dress of a restaurant. Secondly, the Supreme Court failed to provide a test for determining trade dress distinctiveness.

(2) Qualitex—a state of ambivalence

11-026 *Qualitex*[69] offered to the Court the opportunity to resolve these problems.

Qualitex had been manufacturing, for nearly 50 years, dry cleaning press pads in a particular shade of green-gold. Jacobson started using a similar colour on its own pads. Qualitex claimed that this constituted unfair competition; in order to strengthen its position it successfully registered the green-gold colour as a trade mark and added trade mark infringement as a further count. The District Court accepted Qualitex's claims; however on appeal the Ninth Circuit decided that under the Lanham Act it is not possible to register a colour as such as a trade mark.[70]

---

[65] 505 U.S. 763, at 786 citing, as examples, *Crescent Tool Co v Kilborn & Bishop Co*, 247 F. 299 (2nd Cir. 1917); *Flagg Mfg Co v Holway*, 178 Mass. 83 (1901); *Philadelphia Novelty Mfg Co v Rouss*, 40 F. 585 (CC SDNY 1889). He also referred to early authoritative commentators on trade mark law and the Third Restatement.

[66] Citing, by way of example, *AbBrit, Inc v Kraft, Inc*, 812 F.2d 1531 (11th Cir. 1986), cert. denied, 481 U.S. 1041, 107 S.Ct. 1983, 95 L.Ed.2d 822 (1987).

[67] 505 U.S. 763, at 787.

[68] See Dinwoodie, "The Trademark Jurisprudence of the Rehnquist Court", 8 Marquette Intellectual Property Law Review 187 (2004).

[69] *Qualitex Co v Jacobson Products Co*, 514 U.S. 159, 34 U.S.P.Q.2d 1161 (1995).

[70] 13 F.3d 1297 (9th Cir. 1994).

2. THE TRADE DRESS CASES

This time the Court reached a unanimous, albeit vacillating, decision. Justice Breyer delivered the Opinion of the Court on whether the Lanham Act permits "registration of a trademark that consists, purely and simply, of a color".[71]

(a) The legislative context

Justice Breyer explained that the Court took the case because the Circuits had not been following a cohesive approach.[72]

11–027

His analysis of the Lanham Act started by the exclusive right of the owner of a trade mark to register it and prevent its competitors from using it. Turning to what can constitute a trade mark he noted that the language of the Lanham Act and the underlying principles of trade mark law did not preclude the protection of colours as trade marks.

From a textual perspective the Lanham Act was permissive, including symbols and devices next to words and names the traditional types of signs.[73] "Since human beings might use as a 'symbol' or 'device' almost anything at all that is capable of carrying meaning, this language, read literally, is not restrictive". Colours should be in the same league with three dimensional shapes, sounds, and scents.[74]

Combining his textual analysis with basic principles he found that colours satisfied the statutory requirement that a trade mark must be used in order to identify and distinguish the products of its proprietor. He accepted however that in practice there were differences between types of signs. "True, a product's color is unlike 'fanciful', 'arbitrary', or 'suggestive' words or designs, which almost automatically tell a customer that they refer to a brand ... But, over time, customers may come to treat a particular color on a product or its packaging ... as signifying a brand. And, if so, that color would have come to identify and distinguish the goods—i.e. 'to indicate' their 'source'—much in the way that descriptive words on a product."[75] So,

---

[71] 514 U.S. 159, at 160–161.
[72] *In re Owens-Corning Fiberglas Corp*, 774 F.2d 1116 (CA Fed. 1985) the colour pink has been accepted as a trade mark for insulation material (fibreglass); however, the Seventh Circuit held that there was an absolute prohibition against registration of a colour on its own in *NutraSweet Co v Stadt Corp*, 917 F.2d 1024 (7th Cir. 1990); and then came the Eighth Circuit refuting that there was a per se prohibition against generating trade mark protection to a colour on its own in *Master Distributors, Inc v Pako Corp*, 986 F.2d 219 (8th Cir. 1993).
[73] Lanham Act s.45.
[74] 514 U.S. 159, at 162. He added that the US Patent and Trademark Office had already accepted registrations of shapes, sounds, and scents referring as examples to the Coca-Cola bottle, the NBC's three chimes, and Celia Clarke's plumeria blossom trade mark for knitting yarn and sewing thread (*In re Clarke*, 17 U.S.P.Q.2d 1238 (TTAB 1990).
[75] 514 U.S. 159, at 162–163, citing *Abercrombie & Fitch Co v Hunting World, Inc*, 537 F.2d 4 (2nd Cir. 1976) and *Two Pesos, Inc v Taco Cabana, Inc*, 505 U.S. 763, 112 S.Ct. 2753 as examples of word and design trade marks; *J Wiss & Sons Co v WE Bassett Co*, 59 C.C.P.A. 1269 (Pat.), 462 F.2d 569 (1972) and *Car-Freshner Corp v Turtle Wax, Inc*, 268 F.Supp 162 (SDNY 1967) were examples of signs that acquired distinctiveness. Finally *Inwood Laboratories, Inc v Ives Labooratories, Inc*, 456 U.S. 844, 102 S.Ct. 2182 was cited in order to introduce the concept of secondary meaning.

if trade mark law permitted a descriptive word with secondary meaning to function and be protected as a trade mark it should also permit a color, under similar circumstances, to do the same. So, unequivocally, it should be possible to protect colours under trade mark law. However, Justice Breyer appeared less certain and clear as to whether colours deserved trade mark protection automatically, without evidence of secondary meaning.

11-028   He then considered the basic objectives of trademark law in relation to colours that have attained secondary meaning, rather than distinctive colours. Referring to the two most established trade mark works in the United States and the classic article on the economics of trade marks[76] he concluded that it "is the source-distinguishing ability of a mark—not its ontological status as color, shape, fragrance, word, or sign—that permits it to serve these basic purposes".[77] But again the language of the Opinion was much less than not unequivocal: "it is difficult to find, in basic trademark objectives, a reason to disqualify absolutely the use of a color as a mark".[78]

On functionality[79] Justice Breyer remarked that in some—but not all—instances colour might be functional. Where a colour was not essential to a product's use or purpose and did not affect its cost or quality there would be no reason to apply the doctrine.

Summing up, he stated that, at least sometimes, colour alone can act as a symbol that distinguished a firm's products and identified their source, without serving any other significant function.[80]

(b)   The context of the case

11-029   Having described the legislative context and applied it on colours in abstract terms Justice Breyer turned to the actual case before the Court. According to the findings of the District Court the green-gold colour had acquired a secondary meaning and was not functional. So, following a similar judicial path with that taken in *Two Pesos*[81] he noted that, in the absence of a compelling reason to the contrary, Qualitex's colour should be protected as a trade mark.

---

[76] McCarthy, *McCarthy on Trademarks and Unfair Competition* (3rd edn. Thomson West, 1994); Altrman, *Callmann on Unfair Competition, Trademarks and Monopolies* (4th edn. St. Paul Minnestoa 1983); and Landes and Posner, "The Economics of Trademark Law", 78 T.M. Rep. 267 (1988) esp. at 290.
[77] 514 U.S. 159, at 164.
[78] 514 U.S. 159, at 164.
[79] In his analysis of the doctrine he cited *Kellog Co v National Biscuit Co*, 305 U.S. 111, 59 S.Ct. 109 (1938); and *Inwood Laboratories, Inc v Ives Laboratories, Inc*, 456 U.S. 844, (1982) on the tension between the objectives of trade mark law and those of patent law and the basic principles of the doctrine.
[80] Referring with approval to the position adopted by the US Patent and Trademark Office expressed in the US Dept. of Commerce, Patent and Trademark Office, Trademark Manual of Examining Procedure § 1202.04(e), p.1202–13 (2d edn. May, 1993).
[81] See *Two Pesos, Inc v Taco Cabana, Inc*, 505 U.S. 763, 23 U.S.P.Q.2d 1081 (1992).

2. THE TRADE DRESS CASES

(c)   The reasoning of the Court

In order to determine whether there was such a compelling objection Justice Breyer examined the reasons suggested by Jacobson.   **11–030**

The first was based on a practical issue that could have repercussions on the scope of protection. Shades of colours changed according to lighting conditions; accordingly, determining similarity between colours would be a more difficult—but also different—exercise from the case of more traditional signs.

Justice Breyer remarked that courts had been deciding difficult similarity questions in respect of all types of signs, so this was not a special colour problem[82]; in cases where colour constituted an element of a composite mark courts had already conducted colour comparisons.[83] He also cited McCarthy who, reviewing the case law on confusion, had observed that strong marks with greater secondary meaning enjoyed broader protection than weak marks.

The second reason suggested by Jacobson was based on the colour depletion theory. Colours were in limited supply and if traders were allowed to appropriate particular colours then the available palette of colours would be depleted.[84] This would be exacerbated first by the fact that the number of appealing or suitable colours for a particular product could be limited and second because of the cautiousness that competitors would have to exercise in order to avoid infringing registered colours. At the end some competitors would be put at a comparative disadvantage.

Justice Breyer found the argument unpersuasive for two reasons. First, it   **11–031**
relied on an occasional problem to justify a blanket prohibition.[85] And secondly, the application of the functionality doctrine would resolve the problem anyway. The Court had already stated, for example, that competitors might be free to copy the colour of a pill where the colour was a functional indicator of the kind of medication the pill was about.[86] And, lower

---

[82] Citing amongst others *Dial-A-Matress Franchise Corp v Page*, 880 F.2d 675 (2nd Cir. 1989) where the Court of Appeals compared two alpha-numeric telephone numbers: "Mattres" and "1-800-Mattres".

[83] For example, in *Youngstown Sheet & Tube Co v Tallman Conduit Co*, 149 U.S.P.Q. 656 (TTAB 1966) a gold stripe on a sewer pipe; in *Amsted Industries, Inc v West Coast Wire Rope & Rigging Inc*, 2 U.S.P.Q.2d 1755 (TTAB 1987) a yellow strand of wire rope; and, *In re Hodes-Lange Corp*, 167 U.S.P.Q. 256 (TTAB 1970), a brilliant yellow band on ampoules.

[84] In *Campbell Soup Co v Armour & Co*, 175 F.2d 795 (3rd Cir. 1949) for example a combination of white with red had been denied protection on the basis of this theory.

[85] And the evidence according to existing precedents was that in practice there were alternative colours to be used as trade marks by competitors, *In re Owens-Corning Fiberglas Corp*, 774 F.2d 1116 (CA Fed. 1985).

[86] *Inwood Laboratories, Inc v Ives Laboratories, Inc*, 456 U.S. 844, at 850, fn.10. An interesting related remark was a reference to commentators supporting that drug colour cases had to do more with public health policy rather than trade mark law (Ginsburg, Goldberg, and Greenbaum, *Trademark and Unfair Competition Law Lexis*, 1991, at 194–195).

courts were used dealing with functional colours.[87] Where colours had a function other than that of a trade mark[88] courts should "examine whether its use as a mark would permit one competitor (or a group) to interfere with legitimate (non trademark-related) competition through actual or potential exclusive use of an important product ingredient".[89]

The third line of argument was particularly challenging from an interpretive perspective as it exploited the earlier jurisprudence of the Supreme Court. Historically the Court started from a permissive position; the common law definition of a trade mark included names, symbols, letters, figures, forms, or devices.[90] Gradually however the Court became more restrictive. In dicta, it had questioned whether colours on their own could be valid trade marks and had suggested that a product, including its colour, should be free for other competitors to make.[91]

The Court distinguished these earlier cases from its current position on the basis of the Lanham Act, adopted in 1946, that opened up trade mark protection to descriptive words that had acquired secondary meaning and endorsed the position of the Federal Circuit that the jurisprudence developed under the Lanham Act—if a mark was capable of being or becoming distinctive of the applicant's goods in commerce then it was also capable of serving as a trade mark—permitted the protection of a colour as a trade mark.[92] Note that at this point Justice Breyer appeared to cover both instances of distinctiveness, inherent and acquired through secondary

---

[87] For example black had been rejected as a trade mark for outboard boat motors because black makes large objects appear smaller and is compatible with other colours, *Brunswick Corp v British Seagull Ltd*, 35 F.3d 1527 (CA Fed. 1994); blue had been rejected as a trade mark for fertilizer because blue indicates the presence of nitrogen, *Nor-Am Chemical v O.M. Scott & Sons Co*, 4 U.S.P.Q.2d 1316 (ED Pa. 1987). Perhaps more controversially, the Eighth Circuit had allowed competitors to copy the green colour applied on farm machinery because consumers would prefer their farm equipment to match, *Deere & Co v Farmland, Inc*, 560 F. Supp. 85 (721 F.2d 253 (8th Cir. 1983). Justice Breyer also referred to the doctrine of aesthetic functionality: a particular design (and presumably colour) is functional if it confers a significant benefit that cannot duplicated by alternative designs. According to the Restatement the "ultimate test of aesthetic functionality is whether the recognition of trademark rights would significantly hinder competition", Restatement (Third) of Unfair Competition § 17, Comment c, at 176. Justice Breyer noted that the examination of whether a design (or colour) is functional should not discourage firms from creating esthetically pleasing mark designs (or colours); it remains open to their competitors to do the same, citing by way of example *WT Rogers Co v Keene*, 778 F.2d 334 (7th Cir. 1985).

[88] Functional, for example distinguishing a type of medicine from another, or aesthetic, for example satisfying the "noble instinct for giving the right touch of beauty to common and necessary things", an unusual non-legal reference to Chesterton, *Simplicity and Tolstoy* (1912), at p.61.

[89] 514 U.S. 159, at 170.

[90] *McLean v Fleming*, 96 U.S. 245 (1878).

[91] Citing respectively *A Leschen & Sons Rope Co v Broderick & Bascom Rope Co*, 201 U.S. 166, 26 S.Ct. 425 (1906); and *Coca-Cola Co v Koke Co of America*, 254 U.S. 143, 41 S.Ct.113 (1920). Lower Courts took theses cases as precluding protection of a colour as a trade mark; he referred to *Life Savers Corp v Curtiss Candy Co*, 182 F.2d 4 (7th Cir. 1950) as such an example.

[92] *In re Owens-Corning Fiberglas Corp*, 774 F.2d 1116 (CA Fed. 1985), at 1120.

2. THE TRADE DRESS CASES

meaning. He added that in the 1988 amendment of the Act, subsequent to Owens-Corning and the adoption of a policy by the Patent and Trademark Office to accept registrations of colours, Congress did not change the relevant language—"any word, name, symbol, or device"—suggesting that there was no reason to exclude colours from registrability.

The final argument submitted by Jacobson relied on the existence of trade dress protection under s.43(a) that could cover colour as an element of a trade mark questioning whether there is a need to provide further protection of a colour as such as a trade mark. Justice Breyer remarked that there might be cases where it is more practical to use a colour on its own as a trade mark. And in terms of scope, trade mark registration and protection covered areas that trade dress protection based on confusion did not. For, example it constituted prima facie evidence of validity and ownership.

Consequently, the judgment of the Ninth Circuit was reversed.

(3) Wal-Mart—taking a step back

In *Wal-Mart*[93] the Court took another, this time more restrictive, turn distinguishing between product design and product packaging.   11–032

Samara Brothers were designers and manufacturers of children's clothing. They started proceedings under s.43(a) against Wal-Mart, who were selling copies of their clothes; the particular product was a line of spring/summer one-piece seersucker outfits decorated with appliqué of hearts, flowers, and fruits. The copies were manufactured by Wal-Mart's suppliers on the basis of photographs of Samara clothes. The supplier and other retailers selling similar copies settled with Samara Brothers out of court. The District Court found for Samara and the Second Circuit confirmed that clothing designs could be protected as distinctive trade dress under s.43(a).[94]

The case reached the Supreme Court and Justice Scalia delivered the Opinion for a unanimous Court.

(a) *The main issue*

Justice Scalia described what the case was all about as "under what circumstances a product's design is distinctive, and therefore protectible, in an action for infringement of unregistered trade dress under § 43(a) of the Trademark Act of 1946 (Lanham Act)".[95]   11–033

---

[93] *Wal-Mart Stores, Inc v Samara Bros, Inc*, 529 U.S. 205, 54 U.S.P.Q.2d 1065 (2000).
[94] 969 F.Supp. 895 (S.D.N.Y. 1997) and 165 F.3d 120 (2nd Cir. 1998), respectively, certiorari 528 U.S. 808, 120 S.Ct. 308 (1999).
[95] 529 U.S. 205, at 207.

(b) The legislative context

11–034 Justice Scalia in his analysis of the legislative context of the case referred to a number of cases that had expanded the subject matter of protection. Trade dress originally covered the packaging or "dressing" of the product but courts had expanded the concept to cover product design.[96] He accepted that the legislative development of the provision by the addition of s.43(a)(3) referring to "civil action[s] for trade dress infringement under this chapter for trade dress not registered on the principal register" reinforced this expansion. He added, citing *Two Pesos*,[97] that distinctiveness was the primary condition for protection and that the general registrability requirements under s.2 should also be applied under s.43(a), and reminded the grades of inherent distinctiveness[98] that warranted automatic protection but also the possibility of protection following the establishment of secondary meaning.[99]

The Lanham Act also distinguished between inherently distinctive marks; s.2 referred to marks "by which the goods of the applicant may be distinguished from the goods of others" whereas s.2(f) provided that "nothing in this chapter shall prevent the registration of a mark used by the applicant which has become distinctive of the applicant's goods in commerce".

However he noted, s.2 did not demand "the conclusion that every category of mark necessarily includes some marks 'by which the goods of the applicant may be distinguished from the goods of others' without secondary meaning—that in every category some marks are inherently distinctive".[100] And according to his reading of *Qualitex*[101] the Supreme Court had already decided that at least for one category of marks secondary meaning should always be required.

Justice Scalia then stated that design, like colour, was not inherently distinctive and contrasted design with packaging, which, like words, could be inherently distinctive. In most cases "the very purpose of attaching a particular word to a product, or encasing it in a distinctive packaging, is most often to identify the source of the product".[102]

---

[96] For example bedroom furniture, *Ashley Furniture Industries, Inc v Sangiacomo N.A., Ltd*, 187 F.3d 363 (4th Cir. 1999); sweaters, *Knitwaves, Inc v Lollytogs, Ltd*, 71 F.3d 996 (2nd Cir. 1995); and notebooks, *Stuart Hall Co, Inc v Ampad Corp*, 51 F.3d 780 (8th Cir. 1995). He noted that the Supreme Court, too, had noted that the language of the provision was not restrictive; see *Qualitex Co v Jacobson Products Co*, 514 U.S. 159, 34 U.S.P.Q.2d 1161 (1995).
[97] *Two Pesos, Inc v Taco Cabana, Inc*, 505 U.S. 763, 112 S.Ct. 2753.
[98] *Abercrombie & Fitch Co v Hunting World, Inc*, 537 F.2d 4 (2nd Cir. 1976).
[99] He felt however that, at least for reasons of clarity, a distinction had to be made between word marks and other types of signs. Words possess a primary meaning so the term "secondary meaning" aptly described their new trade mark significance. For other signs, that lack such a meaning, "acquired meaning" would probably be a better term.
[100] 529 U.S. 205, at 211.
[101] *Qualitex Co v Jacobson Products Co*, 514 U.S. 159, 34 U.S.P.Q.2d 1161 (1995).
[102] 529 U.S. 205, at 212.

2. THE TRADE DRESS CASES

Even where word marks were suggestive or packaging designed to attract the attention of the consumer, source identification remained their predominant function. Re-using the terminology that the Court had expressed in *Qualitex*[103] he suggested that consumers are predisposed to regard words and packaging as indication of the producer, they "almost automatically tell a customer that they refer to a brand", and "immediately ... signal a brand or a product 'source' ".[104]

11–035

For product design however, "as in the case of color, we think consumer predisposition to equate the feature with the source does not exist. Consumers are aware of the reality that, almost invariably, even the most unusual of product designs—such as a cocktail shaker shaped like a penguin—is intended not to identify the source, but to render the product itself more useful or more appealing".[105]

This time the principles behind the functionality doctrine reinforced the exclusion:

> "Consumers should not be deprived of the benefits of competition with regard to the utilitarian and esthetic purposes that product design ordinarily serves by a rule of law that facilitates plausible threats of suit against new entrants based upon alleged inherent distinctiveness. How easy it is to mount a plausible suit depends, of course, upon the clarity of the test for inherent distinctiveness, and where product design is concerned we have little confidence that a reasonably clear test can be devised."[106]

Justice Scalia rejected the suggestion that elements of a distinctiveness test for packaging[107] might be used for determining the inherent distinctiveness of product design because "such a test would rarely provide the basis for summary disposition of an anticompetitive strike suit".[108]

He accepted that applying the doctrine of functionality should resolve some competition questions. Albeit, "[C]ompetition is deterred ... not merely by successful suit but by the plausible threat of successful suit, and given the unlikelihood of inherently source-identifying design, the game of allowing suit based upon alleged inherent distinctiveness seems to us not worth the candle."[109] After all, he suggested, there were alternative ways for

---

[103] *Qualitex Co*, 514 U.S. 159, 34 U.S.P.Q.2d 1161 (1995).
[104] 529 U.S. 205, at 212–213.
[105] 529 U.S. 205, at 213.
[106] 529 U.S. 205, at 213.
[107] *Seabrook Foods, Inc v Bar-Well Foods, Ltd*, 568 F.2d 1342 (1977), "whether it was a 'common' basic shape or design, whether it was unique or unusual in a particular field, [and] whether it was a mere refinement of a commonly-adopted and well-known form of ornamentation for a particular class of goods viewed by the public as a dress or ornamentation for the goods", at 1344.
[108] 529 U.S. 205, at 214.
[109] 529 U.S. 205, at 214.

11-036 protecting an "inherently source identifying (if any such exists)"[110] under patent, design, and copyright laws.

Finally, he had to deal with the *Two Pesos*[111] precedent, the scope of which proved to be limited. Two Pesos established that trade dress in general—rather than product-design trade dress—can be inherently distinctive. And the décor of a restaurant did not constitute product design; it was either product packaging or else "some tertium quid that is akin to product packaging and has no bearing on the present case".[112]

He accepted that making the distinction between product packaging and product design could be a difficult exercise and urged courts to err on the side of caution when they are uncertain about the type of trade dress in front of them and require evidence of secondary meaning. He concluded with a sweeping comment: "The very closeness will suggest the existence of relatively small utility in adopting an inherent-distinctiveness principle, and relatively great consumer benefit in requiring a demonstration of secondary meaning".[113]

The judgment of the Second Circuit was reversed.

3. TRAFFIX—FUNCTIONALITY

(1) Functionality as a public policy

11-037 The Restatement (Third) of the Law of Unfair Competition provides that:

"The exclusion of functional designs from the subject matter of trade mark law is intended to insure effective competition, not just by the defendant, but also by other existing and potential competitors."[114]

Functionality had relatively recently become a statutory ground for refusal under s.2(e)(5)[115]; nevertheless, it had historically been vigorously applied by the courts as a public policy doctrine limiting the scope of trade mark rights.

According to McCarthy functionality "is a potent public policy, for it trumps all evidence of actual consumer identification of source and all evidence of actual consumer confusion caused by an imitator".[116]

---

[110] 529 U.S. 205, at 214.
[111] *Two Pesos, Inc*, 505 U.S. 763, 23 U.S.P.Q.2d 1081 (1992).
[112] 529 U.S. 205, at 215.
[113] 529 U.S. 205, at 215.
[114] Restatement (Third) of the Law of Unfair Competition para.17.
[115] Amendment introduced in 1998.
[116] McCarthy, 7:63.

3. TRAFFIX—FUNCTIONALITY

According to s.33(b)(8) of the Lanham Act functionality is a defence to the charge of infringement of, even, an incontestable trade mark.

The essence of functionality was described in *Inwood Laboratories*.[117] A product feature was functional if it was essential to the use or purpose of the article or if it affected the cost or quality of the article.

(a) De jure functionality

11–038 The courts often refer to "de jure functionality". The term covers what the courts consider to be functional and fall outside the scope of trade mark law. De jure functionality may be either utilitarian, considering the utility of the design, or aesthetic, considering the aesthetic appeal of the design.

A commonly used "functionality" test was established in *Morton Norwich*.[118] First, it settled that functionality and distinctiveness were two distinct issues. Secondly, it identified four factors that courts should examine: the existence of a utility patent which disclosed the utilitarian advantage of the design; whether the originator of the design promoted the utilitarian advantages of the product through advertising; whether there were alternative designs available; and whether the design was more economical than an alternative design.

The third factor proved to be the most controversial and equally resilient, despite the disapproval of the Supreme Court in *TrafFix*.[119]

(b) Utilitarian functionality

11–039 *Kellogg*[120] provided an early example of utilitarian functionality. A shredded wheat biscuit shape, the "pillow shape", was functional according to Justice Brandeis because the cost of the biscuit would be increased and its high quality lessened if some other form were substituted for the "pillow shape".

In *Morton-Norwich*[121] a Court of Appeals noted that the availability of equally satisfactory alternatives for a particular feature, and not its inherent usefulness, was often the pivotal question. The court having defined "utilitarian" as superior in function (de facto) or economy or manufacture, added that superiority was analogous to the competitive necessity to copy.

(c) Aesthetic functionality

11–040 Aesthetic functionality was described in the 1938 Restatement of Torts:

---

[117] *Inwood Laboratories Inc v Ives Laboratories*, 436 U.S. 844, 214 USPQ 1 (1982).
[118] *Re Morton Norwich Products Inc*, 671 F2d 1332, 213 U.S.P.Q. 9 (C.C.P.A. 1982).
[119] See for example *Valu Enginnering, Inc v Rexnord Corp*, 278 F.3d 1268, 61 U.S.P.Q.2d 1422 (Fed. Cir. 2002).
[120] *Kellogg Co v National Biscuit Co*, 305 U.S. 111, 83 L. Ed. 73, 59 S. Ct. 109 (1938).
[121] *Re Morton Norwich Products Inc*, 671 F2d 1332, 213 U.S.P.A. 9 (C.C.P.A. 1982).

"When goods are bought largely for their aesthetic value, their features may be functional because they definitely contribute to that value and thus aid the performance of an object for which the goods are intended. The determination of whether or not such features are functional depends upon the question of fact whether the prohibition of imitation by others will deprive the others of something which will substantially hinder them in competition. So for example a candy or a chocolate box in the shape of a heart could be functional in an aesthetic sense."[122]

The Restatement (Third) of Unfair Competition (1995) s.17, comment (c) avoided to reject the doctrine of aesthetic functionality as such but narrowed down its scope by redefining it:

"A design is functional because of its aesthetic value only if it confers a significant benefit that cannot practically be duplicated by the use of alternative designs."[123]

The distinction between two very similar cases with seemingly opposing outcomes exemplifies the above statement. In *Pagliero*,[124] Wallace China could not prevent Pagliero from copying floral designs on plates and selling the plates as replacements for broken dishes to restaurants and hotels. The designs were functional because "functional" might be said to connote a purpose other than a trade mark purpose. If the particular feature was an important ingredient in the commercial success of the product, the interest in free competition permitted its imitation in the absence of copyright or a patent right. In *Villeroy & Boch*[125] "the basket design" that a hotel had adopted for its chinaware was not found to be functional. The key fact was that the defendant had not showed that it was at a competitive disadvantage in making the initial sale without the "basket design".

(2) The judgment in TrafFix

11–041   *TrafFix*[126] gave the Supreme Court the opportunity to look again at trade dress and the uneasy relationship between patent and trade mark law from a functionality perspective.

Marketing Displays, the manufacturer of WindMaster outdoor sign stands brought a trade mark and trade dress infringement action against TrafFix Devices, a competitor manufacturing similar WindBuster stands.

---

[122] Restatement of Torts (1938).
[123] The narrowing of the scope of aesthetic functionality was the result of a line of cases, like *Qualitex Co*, 514 U.S. 159, 34 U.S.P.Q.2d 1161 (1995), accepting that marketers should not be discouraged from creating aesthetically pleasing trade mark designs.
[124] *Pagliero v Wallace China Co*, 198 F.2d 339, 95 U.S.P.Q. 45 (9th Cir. 1952).
[125] *Villeroy & Boch Keramiche Werke KG v THC Sys, Inc*, 999 F.2d 619, 27 U.S.P.Q.2d 1866 (2nd Cir. 1993).
[126] *TrafFix Devices, Inc v Marketing Displays, Inc*, 532 U.S. 23, 58 U.S.P.Q.2d 1001 (2001).

3. TRAFFIX—FUNCTIONALITY

Marketing Displays held an expired utility patent for the mechanism—a dual-spring design—that kept the sign upright in adverse wind conditions. It claimed that the same mechanism constituted protectable trade dress. TrafFix had copied the mechanism following the expiration of the utility patent.

The District Court found that there was trade mark but not trade dress infringement because the mechanism had not acquired secondary meaning and, in any case, was functional; Marketing Displays had not proven that the design of the mechanism was not functional.[127] The Court of Appeals affirmed in part and reversed in part, considering that the expired utility patent was not determinative; finding a way round the design would not be that difficult and accordingly granting trade dress protection would not put TrafFix at a significant disadvantage.[128]

Justice Kennedy delivered the Opinion for a unanimous Court.

(a) The main issue

The Supreme Court granted certiorari, because of the disagreement on functionality between the Circuits highlighted by the Court of Appeals.[129] **11–042**

The part of the case that the Court would consider was the trade dress question, and in particular the functionality issue. Whether the mechanism did or did not possess secondary meaning would be irrelevant if it were functional. "The principal question in this case is the effect of an expired patent on a claim of trade dress infringement."[130]

(b) The legislative context

Justice Kennedy acknowledged that trade dress was protectable under Federal law. This time however the Court appeared to be even more cautious: "The design or packaging of a product may acquire a distinctiveness which serves to identify the product with its manufacturer or source; and a design or package which acquires this secondary meaning, assuming other requisites are met, is a trade dress which may not be used in a manner likely to cause confusion as to the origin, sponsorship, or approval of the goods".[131] **11–043**

One of the requisites developed by the courts, recognised by the Supreme Court in all its most recent jurisprudence on trade dress, and

---

[127] 967 F.Supp. 953 and 971 F.Supp. 262 (E.D.Mich. 1997) respectively.
[128] 200 F.3d 929 (6th Cir. 1999).
[129] Cases like *Sunbeam Products, Inc v West Bend Co*, F.3d 246 (5th Cir. 1997) looked for a significant non reputation-related comparative disadvantage; whilst cases like *Vornado Air Circulation Systems, Inc, v Duracraft Corp*, 58 F.3d 1498 (10th Cir. 1995) found the existence of a utility patent determinative in preventing trade dress protection for the same design.
[130] 532 U.S. 23, at 29.
[131] 532 U.S. 23, at 28.

explicitly stated in the Lanham Act was that "[I]n a civil action for trade dress infringement under this chapter for trade dress not registered on the principal register, the person who asserts trade dress protection has the burden of proving that the matter sought to be protected is not functional".[132]

The starting point is that there is no prohibition against copying of products unless there is an intellectual property right[133] or the product deserves trade dress protection.[134]

Regarding the effect of an expired patent the Court ruled that it should have "vital significance in resolving the trade dress claim",[135] as strong evidence that the features claimed in the patent are functional.

"If trade dress protection is sought for those features the strong evidence of functionality based on the previous patent adds great weight to the statutory presumption that features are deemed functional until proved otherwise by the party seeking trade dress protection. Where the expired patent claimed the features in question, one who seeks to establish trade dress protection must carry the heavy burden of showing that the feature is not functional, for instance by showing that it is merely an ornamental, incidental, or arbitrary aspect of the device."[136]

Note however, that the Court declined to decide whether the Patent Clause of the Constitution[137] precludes the holder of an expired utility patent from claiming trade dress protection. "We need not resolve this question. If, despite the rule that functional features may not be the subject of trade dress protection, a case arises in which trade dress becomes the practical equivalent of an expired utility patent, that will be time enough to consider the matter."[138]

(c) The context of the case

11–044 In this case the dual spring design, the essential element of the trade dress, was also at the heart of the expired utility patent. The dual function negated any possibility of protection: "The rule we have explained bars the trade

---

[132] Lanham Act s.43(a) (3).
[133] *Bonito Boats, Inc v Thunder Craft Boats, Inc*, 489 U.S. 141, 109 S.Ct. 971 (1989), at 160: "Reverse engineering of chemical and mechanical articles in the public domain often leads to significant advances in technology".
[134] Reminding us that in *Wal-Mart Stores, Inc v Samara Bros, Inc*, 529 U.S. 205, 54 U.S.P.Q.2d 1065 (2000) the Court cautioned against the misuse or overextension of trade dress, referring to the finding of the Count that product design almost invariably serves purposes other than source identification.
[135] 532 U.S. 23, at 29.
[136] 532 U.S. 23, at 29–30.
[137] Constitution Art.I §8 cl.8.
[138] 532 U.S. 23, at 35.

dress claim, for MDI did not, and cannot, carry the burden of overcoming the strong evidentiary inference of functionality based on the disclosure of the dual-spring design in the claims of the expired patents."[139]

Justice Kennedy accepted that there were visual differences between the design of the trade dress and the design of the patent—the springs were closer in the trade dress than in the patent—however this was not considered legally significant; the critical element was the existence of the two springs and under the doctrine of equivalents applicable in the United States both designs would have been covered by the claims of the patent.[140]

(d) The reasoning of the Court

11–045
The Court found the case to be a good example of why disclosing the advantages of a feature in the patent constituted strong evidence of functionality. According to the specifications of the relevant patents the combination of the two springs was a central issue for the functioning of the stand; it also affected the cost of the product because it was acknowledged that the stand could use three springs, but this would raise the cost of the product unnecessarily.

The error of the Court of Appeals according to Justice Kennedy was that it failed to give sufficient recognition to the importance of the expired utility patent. Claiming that this was the result of a wider misinterpretation of trade dress principles he took the opportunity to restate these principles.

First, irrespective of whether there a previous patent or not, in the case of unregistered trade dress the party seeking protection has to establish that it is not functional.

11–046
Secondly, the reference in *Qualitex*[141] to a significant "non-reputation disadvantage" was linked with aesthetic functionality. It did not mean that the relevant product configuration had to be a competitive necessity, as interpreted by the Court of Appeals.[142] Re-contextualising *Qualitex* according to its facts Justice Kennedy remarked that it did not aim to change the traditional rule that a feature is also functional when it is essential to the use or purpose of the device or when it affects the cost or quality of the device. The "significant non-reputation-related disadvantage" was appropriate for determining aesthetic functionality, that was the central question in *Qualitex*. "Where the design is functional under the Inwood

---

[139] 532 U.S. 23, at 30.
[140] Indeed in previous litigation a design that looked like the current version of the trade dress was found to infringe the patent under the doctrine of equivalents, *Sarkisian v Winn-Proof Corp*, 697 F.2d 1313 (9th Cir. 1983).
[141] *Qualitex Co*, 514 us 159, 34 U.S.P.Q. 2d (1995).
[142] See also *Vornado Air Circulation Systems, Inc, v Duracraft Corp*, 58 F.3d 1498 (10th Cir. 1995), at 1507: "Functionality, by contrast, has been defined both by our circuit, and more recently by the Supreme Court, in terms of competitive need".

formulation there is no need to proceed further to consider if there is a competitive necessity for the feature."[143]

Thirdly, there is no need to consider secondary meaning once functionality is established. In *Two Pesos*[144] where the Court granted protection to inherently distinctive trade dress the Court had acted on the assumption that the protectable trade dress was not functional.

Fourthly, there is no need for the courts to enquire about other design possibilities, for example in this case whether three or more springs might serve the same function and be adequately dissimilar from the original design. If the design is functional competitors do not have to explore other configurations.

Fifthly, for functional designs there is no need for competitors to explore ways for concealing the configuration. It would be a paradox to require concealing a design that informs consumers about the function of the product.

Sixthly, it could be possible to protect as trade dress "arbitrary, incidental, or ornamental aspects of features of a product found in the patent claims, such as arbitrary curves in the legs or an ornamental pattern painted on the springs ... There the manufacturer could perhaps prove that those aspects do not serve a purpose within the terms of the utility patent".[145] This was not the case here.

The judgment of the sixth Circuit was reversed.

4. OTHER LIMITATIONS TO TRADE MARK PROTECTION

(1) Dastar—the scope of section 43(a) and copyright

11-047 The relationship between copyright and trade mark protection was considered by the Court in *Dastar*.[146]

Twentieth Century Fox (Fox) claimed that the unaccredited copying of a television series constituted copyright and trade mark infringement. The inspiration behind Fox's original television series was a work by General Eisenhower, Crusade in Europe, published by Doubleday that granted exclusive television rights to Fox. The series in respect of which Fox owned the copyright was broadcasted in 1949. Doubleday renewed copyright in respect of the book in 1975. However, Fox failed to renew copyright in respect of the television series[147]; copyright protection expired in 1977 and the television series came into the public domain. In 1988 Fox acquired

---

[143] 532 U.S. 23, at 33.
[144] *Two Pesos, Inc v Taco Cabana, Inc* 505 U.S. 763, 23 U.S.P.Q. 2d 1081.
[145] 532 U.S. 23, at 34.
[146] *Dastar Corp v Twentieth Century Fox Film Corp*, 539 U.S. 23, 123 S.Ct. 2041 (2003).
[147] In his closing remarks Justice Scalia noticed Fox's failure to renew.

once again the television rights in the book, including the right to distribute the television series on video that it then granted to two other companies that restored the negatives of the television series and remarketed the series on videotapes.

Dastar took tapes of the original version of the television series, copied and edited them, and produced a video set, World War II Campaigns in Europe, marketed at a considerably lower price than the Fox video set. Dastar's set had no reference to the original television series and no attribution to Fox.

The District Court gave summary judgment for Fox, accepting that Dastar's set infringed Doubleday's copyright in the book, Fox's exclusive television rights, and also constituted "reverse passing off", meaning that someone else's product is passed off as the infringer's. The Court of Appeals reversed in respect of copyright but affirmed in respect of the Lanham Act claim, based on the notion of "bodily appropriation".[148]

The Supreme Court granted certiorari[149] and Justice Scalia delivered the Opinion of the Court.

(a) The main issue

The Court considered whether s.43(a) of the Lanham Act prevented the unaccredited copying of a work; it did not look at the copyright claims of the case.

11–048

(b) The legislative context

This time s.43(a) would be construed more cautiously and closer to its text. The Lanham Act was intended to protect against unfair competition and s.43(a) did go beyond trade mark protection. Still, it did not have "boundless application as a remedy for unfair trade practices".[150] Because of its wording it applied only to certain unfair trade practices indicated in the provision. This case fell under the "origin of goods" part of the provision.

11–049

Justice Scalia accepted that the concept of origin went further than the geographical origin of a product, covering also the "origin of source or

---

[148] "Dastar copied substantially the entire Crusade in Europe series created by Twentieth Century Fox, labeled the resulting product with a different name and marketed it without attribution to Fox, therefore committed a 'bodily appropriation' of Fox's series", 34 Fed. Appx 312 (9th Cir. 2002), at 314.
[149] 537 U.S. 1099, 123 S.Ct. 816 (2003).
[150] Citing *Alfred Dunhill, Ltd v Interstate Cigar Co*, 499 F.2d 232 (2nd Cir. 1974), at 237; and referring to McCarthy stating that s.43(a) can never be a federal codification of the overall law of unfair competition, McCarthy, *Trademarks and Unfair Competition* (4th edn, 2002), at 27-14. In his closing remarks Justice Scalia reminded the Court that if the producer of a video that substantially copied the Crusade series gave consumers the impression that the video was quite different from that series, then there might be a cause of action for misrepresentation under the "misrepresents the nature, characteristics [or] qualities" provision of s.43(a)(1)(B).

manufacture"[151] as well as "reverse passing off".[152] This was acknowledged by the courts but also evidenced by the legislative amendments of the provision always broadening its scope. Here, however the origin related question was how far back in the life of the product the Court had to go in order to establish its origin for the purposes of s.43(a). Did origin refer to the manufacturer or producer of the videotapes, the actual physical product, or did it go further back to the creator of the underlying work?

From a linguistic perspective "origin of goods" meant "source of wares"; in more concrete terms the producer of the "tangible product sold in the marketplace, in this case the physical Campaigns videotape sold by Dastar",[153] or even the trade mark owner who commissioned or assumed responsibility for the videotapes.[154] But it did not go further back to whoever originated the ideas or communications contained in the products. This according to Justice Scalia would be against a linguistic analysis of the provision, outside the history and scope of the Act, and inconsistent with precedent.

(c) The reasoning of the Court

11–050 **(i) Consumer psychology.** Now, before turning to the analysis of the scope of the Act and the precedents that were raised as obstacles to this expansive interpretation of s.43(a), Justice Scalia chose a hypothetical example employing the most iconic of products in the United States—cola—in order to demonstrate what s.43(a) is all about.

Section 43(a) would stop Coca-Cola passing off its cola as Pepsi-Cola or reverse passing off Pepsi-Cola as its own cola. However, according to Justice Scalia, the brand-loyal consumer chooses one cola over the other:

> "while he believes that that company produced (or at least stands behind the production of) that product, surely does not necessarily believe that that company was the 'origin' of the drink in the sense that it was the very first to devise the formula. The consumer who buys a branded product does not automatically assume that the brand-name company is the same entity that came up with the idea for the product, or designed the product—and typically does not care whether it is. The words of the

---

[151] Citing *Federal-Mogul-Bower Bearings, Inc v Azzof*, 313 F.2d 405 (6th Cir. 1963), at 408.
[152] Referring amongst others to *Bangor Punta Operations, Inc v Universal Marine Co*, 543 F.2d 1107 (5th Cir. 1976); *Smith v Montoro*, 648 F.2d 602 (9th Cir. 1981), and *ALPO Petfoods, Inc v Ralston Purina Co*, 913 F.2d 958 (C.A.D.C. 1990).
[153] 539 U.S. 23, at 3.
[154] The legislator had followed the jurisprudence of the courts and the post-1988 s.43(a) provided protection against the use of any "word, term, name, symbol, or device", or "false or misleading description of fact" that is likely to cause confusion as to "affiliation, connection, or association ... with another person", or as to "sponsorship, or approval" of goods.

4. OTHER LIMITATIONS TO TRADE MARK PROTECTION

Lanham Act should not be stretched to cover matters that are typically of no consequence to purchasers".[155]

This journey into the realm of consumer psychology also encompassed the distinction between ordinary—valued for their physical qualities—and communicative—valued for their intellectual content—products. Should "origin of goods" cover not only the producer of the physical product abut also the creator of the content conveyed by the physical product? After consumers would care more about the author rather than the publisher of a work. Without answering the question from the Lanham Act perspective, Justice Scalia identified as a barrier the conflict that an affirmative answer would cause between the Lanham Act and copyright law.

(ii) The scope of the Lanham Act. The Supreme Court had already decided that the right to copy, even without attribution, passes to the public once copyright has expired.[156] And more recently it reiterated that an item that is not covered by an intellectual property right is subject to copying.[157] He reminded the "carefully crafted bargain"[158] that ensured that inventions and works protected by copyright following the expiration of the set period of protection were free for all to copy. The purpose of the Lanham Act on the other hand was to protect "source-identifying marks"[159] rather than reward innovation.[160] Expanding its scope to cover the source of the creative work conveyed by the videos "would create a species of mutant copyright law",[161] whereas the original copyright law was limited and focused in describing the subject matter and scope of protection. The express right of attribution, for example, was developed with much more specificity than the concept of origin; it "attaches only to specified 'work[s] of visual art', ... is personal to the artist, ..., and endures only for 'the life of the author', ... Recognizing in 43(a) a cause of action for misrepresentation of authorship of noncopyrighted works (visual or otherwise) would render these limitations superfluous".[162] From an interpretive perspective rendering another statute superfluous should be avoided.[163]

11–051

Turning to a more practical problem he queried where should courts stop in their origin identifying quest: those that created the original war footage?

---

[155] 539 U.S. 23, at 32–33.
[156] *Sear, Roebuck & Co v Stiffel Co*, 376 U.S. 225, 84 S.Ct. 784 (1964).
[157] *TrafFix Devices, Inc v Marketing Displays, Inc*, 532 U.S. 23, 121 S.Ct. 1255 (2001).
[158] The public enjoyed a federal right to copy and use the invention or copyright work, *Bonito Boats, Inc v Thunder Craft Boats, Inc*, 489 U.S. 141, 109 S.Ct. 971 (1989), at 165.
[159] *Qualitex Co v Jacobson Products Co*, 514 U.S. 159, 34 U.S.P.Q.2d 1161 (1995), at 163.
[160] *TrafFix Devices, Inc v Marketing Displays, Inc*, 532 U.S. 23, 121 S.Ct. 1255 (2001).
[161] 539 U.S. 23, at 34.
[162] 539 U.S. 23, at 34–35.
[163] Citing *Mackey v Lanier Collection Agency & Service, Inc*, 486 U.S. 825, 108 S.Ct. 2182 (1988).

From the manufacturer's perspective he identified another potential dilemma that would become inherent in the Lanham Act following an expansive interpretation of origin: "[O]n the one hand, they would face Lanham Act liability for failing to credit the creator of a work on which their lawful copies are based; and on the other hand they could face Lanham Act liability for crediting the creator if that should be regarded as implying the creator's 'sponsorship or approval' of the copy".[164]

11-052 (iii) **The conflict with precedents.** Citing *Wal Mart*[165] and *Inwood Laboaratories*[166] Justice Scalia noted that the Supreme Court required secondary meaning in order to protect the design of a product in order to ensure that the design identified the source of the product rather than the product itself. This limitation would become pointless if the original producer of the design would be able to use s.43(a) for a reverse passing off action in order to protect the origin of the design rather than the origin of the product. Similar concerns would be raised in respect of the unpatented boat hulls designs in *Bonito Boats*[167] and the expired patents in *TrafFix*.[168]

He concluded that "origin of goods" in accordance with the Lanham Act's common-law foundations that were not linked with creativity and innovation and in light of copyright and patent laws referred to the producer of the tangible goods that are offered for sale, and not to the author of any idea, concept, or communication embodied in those goods. An expansive interpretation would be "akin to finding that §43(a) created a species of perpetual patent and copyright, which Congress may not do".[169]

(2) KP Permanent—a balancing exercise

11-053 *KP Permanent Make-Up, INC, v Lasting Impression I, Inc, et al*[170] is the most recent judgment of the Supreme Court in the field of trade marks. The Court again appeared cautious and restrictive in respect of the scope of protection a trade mark can afford.

Both parties had been using versions of the term "micro color" for permanent cosmetic makeup. KP Permanent's use of "microcolor" started in 1990 but Lasting registered the words "Micro Colors" as part of a composite trade mark in 1992. The registration became incontestable in 1999. The case came before the Supreme Court as an appeal from the Ninth Circuit. The Court of Appeals[171] had reversed the decision of the District Court that

---

[164] 539 U.S. 23, at 36.
[165] *Wal-Mart Stores, Inc v Samara Bros, Inc*, 529 U.S. 205, 54 U.S.P.Q.2d 1065 (2000).
[166] *Inwood Laboratories Inc*, 436 U.S. 844, 214 USPQ 1 (1982).
[167] *Bonito Boats, Inc v Thunder Craft Boats, Inc*, 489 U.S. 141, 109 S.Ct. 971 (1989), at 160.
[168] *TrafFix Devices, Inc v Marketing Displays, Inc*, 532 U.S. 23, 121 S.Ct. 1255 (2001).
[169] 539 U.S. 23, at 37, citing *Eldred v Ashcroft*, 537 U.S. 186, 123 S.Ct. 769.
[170] 543 U.S. 111, 125 S.Ct. 542.
[171] 328 F.3d 1061 (9th Cir. 2003).

found KP Permanent's continuous use of "microcolor" since 1990—before the trade mark registration—fair and in good faith use in a descriptive sense rather than use as a trade mark because the District Court had failed to consider whether it caused confusion in the marketplace. The Court of Appeals appeared to require from the party claiming a fair use defense to prove that there is no likelihood of confusion.

Justice Souter delivered the Opinion of an almost unanimous Court. Justice Scalia joined as to all with the exception of fnn.4 and 5 and Justice Breyer joined as to all but fn.6; they both supported the textual and jurisprudential analysis of the Court.

(a) The main issue

Justice Souter described the main issue as to "whether a party raising the statutory affirmative defense of fair use to a claim of trademark infringement ... has a burden to negate any likelihood that the practice complained of will confuse consumers about the origin of the goods or services affected".[172] The Court did not consider whether the sign was generic or whether it was descriptive but had acquired secondary meaning; the same applied to the Court of Appeals's discussion of the concept of "nominative fair use".[173]

11–054

The Court granted certiorari[174] in order to resolve the disagreement between the Circuits on the significance of confusion for fair use.[175]

(b) The legislative context

Justice Souter started by reviewing the rights of the trade mark proprietor. Registration was an option open to the user of a trade mark. Once it materialises, and provided it satisfies certain conditions including use for a five year period, registration becomes incontestable.[176] Registration conferred an exclusive right to use the sign and a civil action against use that is likely to cause confusion, mistake or deception with the plaintiff bearing the burden of proof.[177] Incontestability was considered conclusive evidence of the registrant's right to use the mark but the registrant still had to establish

11–055

---

[172] 543 U.S. 111, at 114–115.
[173] 328 F.3d 1061, at 1071–1072.
[174] 540 U.S. 1099, 124 S.Ct. 981 (2004).
[175] Citing as examples *PACCAR Inc v Telescan Technologies, LLC*, 319 F.3d 243 (6th Cir. 2003); and *Zatarains, Inc v Oak Grove Smokehouse*, 698 F.2d 786 (5th Cir. 1983) making confusion an obstacle to a finding of fair use on the one hand; and *Cosmetically Sealed Industries, Inc v Chesebrough-Pond's USA Co*, 125 F.3d 28 (2nd Cir. 1997); *Shakespeare Co v Silstar Corp of Am*, 110 F.3d 234 (4th Cir. 1997); and *Sunmark, Inc v Ocean Spray Cranberries, Inc*, 64 F.3d 1055 (7th Cir. 1995) ruling that confusion does not preclude a fair use defence.
[176] Lanham Act s.15.
[177] Lanham Act s.32.

confusion about the origin of the relevant products in order to succeed in the civil action. Confusion remained the touchstone for infringement.[178]

From the alleged infringer's perspective "fair use" was one amongst a number of defenses available against an infringement action. Section 1115(b)(4) (s.33(b)(4) of the Lanham Act) provided that "use of the name, term, or device charged to be an infringement is a use, otherwise than as a mark, . . . of a term or device which is descriptive of and used fairly and in good faith only to describe the goods or services of such party, or their geographic origin . . .".

Starting his analysis from a textual perspective Justice Souter noted that whilst proving likelihood of confusion was essential for establishing infringement the legislator did not include it in the provision regarding fair use. So applying the interpretive principle that " '[W]here Congress includes particular language in one section of a statute but omits it in another section of the same Act, it is generally presumed that Congress acts intentionally and purposely in the disparate inclusion or exclusion",[179] he found it improbable that a fair use defense entailed a burden to negate confusion.

He also rejected the claim that the term "used fairly" was an "oblique incorporation of a likelihood-of-confusion test developed in the common law of unfair competition".[180] The reading of the relevant cases by the Court was more nuanced; they were linked with degrees of confusion and competing audacity rather than the existence of confusion as such.[181]

11-056   It became clear that the Court preferred approaching each case on its merits rather than creating sweeping interpretive rules. "While these cases are consistent with taking account of the likelihood of consumer confusion as one consideration in deciding whether a use is fair . . . they do not stand for the proposition that an assessment of confusion alone may be dispositive. Certainly one cannot get out of them any defense burden to negate it entirely".[182]

The way a trade mark infringement action is usually argued supported the logic of the Court's analysis. The plaintiff makes a prima facie case; the

---

[178] Citing *Two Pesos, Inc*, 505 U.S. 763, 23 U.S.P.Q. 2d 1081 (1992). Section 21 Comment a of the Restatement (Third) of Unfair Competition (1995); and *Lone Star Steakhouse and Saloon, Inc v Alpha of Virginia, Inc*, 43 F.3d 922 (4th Cir. 1995).

[179] Citing *Russello v United States*, 464 U.S. 16, 104 S.Ct. 296, quoting, at 23, *United States v Wong Kim Bo*, 472 F.2d 720 (5th Cir. 1972) at 722. In fn.4. Justice Souter added that the legislative history of the provision reinforced his position, because a proposal to limit the scope of the defense to uses that are unlikely to deceive the public was rejected during the legislative process.

[180] 543 U.S. 111, at 119.

[181] He cited *Baglin v Cusenier Co*, 221 U.S. 580, 31 S.Ct. 669 (1911); and *Herring-Hall-Marvin Safe Co v Hall's Safe Co*, 208 U.S. 554, 28 S.Ct. 350 (1908) as examples of a fair use defense that failed; and *William R Warner & Co v Elli Lilly & Co*, 265 U.S. 526, 44 S.Ct. 615 (1924); and *Canal Co v Clark*, 13 Wall. 311, 20 L.Ed. 581 (1872) as examples of tolerating some confusion when a deceptive intent is lacking.

[182] 543 U.S. 111, at 119–120.

defendant offers rebutting evidence—for example that there is no likelihood of confusion—and raises available affirmative defenses if the plaintiff's prima facie case is sound. "But it would make no sense to give the defendant a defense of showing affirmatively that the plaintiff cannot succeed in proving some element (like confusion); all the defendant needs to do is to leave the factfinder unpersuaded that the plaintiff has carried its own burden on that point".[183] Clearly if the defendant manages to undermine the effectiveness of the plaintiff's evidence on confusion there will be, in most cases, no need to employ an affirmative defense. If to the contrary litigation reaches the stage where an affirmative defense is required it would be irrational to require from the defendant to prove something—no likelihood of confusion—that, if proven, would have made the claim of the plaintiff redundant in the first place, irrespective of whether there is good faith or not. "A defendant has no need of a court's true belief when agnosticism will do."[184]

Lasting attempted to support its claim through a legalistic route. The requirement for proprietors of incontestable trade marks to prove infringement was introduced into the Lanham Act in 1988.[185] Before 1988 it argued, there was no need to prove likelihood of confusion, this is why the case law required defendants to prove its absence when they made use of a fair use defense. The revision however failed to relieve the defendant from that burden. The Court rejected the argument both as an interpretive technique but also in its substance. First, "it would be highly suspect in leaving the claimed element of Section 1115(b)(4)[186] redundant and pointless, because the Court had adopted a "rule against superfluities".[187] Secondly, the majority courts did require, even before 1988, the proprietors of incontestable trade marks to prove infringement.[188]

Having established that defendant had no "free-standing need to show confusion unlikely" it followed for the Court "that some possibility of consumer confusion must be compatible with fair use, and so it is".[189] The next step for Justice Souter was to legitimise this conclusion from a first principles perspective. The common law's tolerance of confusion was the

---

[183] 543 U.S. 111, at 120.
[184] 543 U.S. 111 at 120, citing *Shakespeare Co v Silstar Corp*, 110 F.3d 234, at 243 (4th Cir. 1993), "[I]t defies logic to argue that a defense may not be asserted in the only situation where it ever becomes relevant".
[185] Trademark Law Revision Act of 1988 s.128(b)(1), 102 Stat. 3944.
[186] Providing that "the use of the name, term, or device charged to be an infringement is a use, otherwise than as a mark, of the party's individual name in his own business, or of the individual name of anyone in privity with such party, or of a term or device which is descriptive of and used fairly and in good faith only to describe the goods or services of such party, or their geographic origin".
[187] Citing *Hibbs v Winn*, 542 U.S. 88, 124 S.Ct 2276 (2004).
[188] Referring to McCarthy, *Trademarks and Unfair Competition*, 32:154 (4th edn, 2004); and by way of example to *Beer Nuts Inc v Clover Club Foods Co*, 805 F.2dn 920 (10th Cir. 1986); and *United States Jaycees v Philadelphia Jaycees*, 639 F.2d 134 (3rd Cir. 1981).
[189] 543 U.S. 111, at 121–122.

11-057 result of the originally descriptive nature of the sign—implicitly a weak trade mark—and the "undesirability of allowing anyone to obtain a complete monopoly on use of a descriptive term simply by grabbing it first".[190]

The Lanham Act too had adopted safeguards to prevent commercial monopolisation of language.[191] First, registration comes only if the term has acquired a secondary meaning; and secondly, it is the secondary rather than the descriptive meaning that is protected. Or, in the words of McCarthy, "[T]he only aspect of the mark which is given legal protection is that penumbra or fringe of secondary meaning which surrounds the old descriptive word".[192] So in some cases, "[I]f any confusion results, that is a risk the plaintiff accepted when it decided to identify its product with a mark that uses a well known descriptive phrase".[193]

Finally, Justice Souter described the limits of the Court's ruling that mere risk of confusion should not rule out fair use. Resisting the advice of commentators and amici the Court did not rule on "the relevance of the extent of any likely consumer confusion in assessing whether a defendant's use is objectively fair"[194] as well as the relevance of the extent of acquired distinctiveness in determining whether the defendant's use had indeed been descriptive.[195] The Court also did not rule on whether the "used fairly" requirement required only that the descriptive term described the goods accurately.[196] Referring to s.28 of the Restatement and the factors stated therein—accuracy, commercial justification, and the strength of the plaintiff's mark—Justice Souter appeared to indicate, by stating that door is not closed to them, that the requirement was an intricate one that required multiple considerations. "In sum, a plaintiff claiming infringement of an incontestable mark must show likelihood of consumer confusion as part of the prima facie case . . . while the defendant has no independent burden to negate the likelihood of any confusion in raising the affirmative defense that a term is used descriptively, not as a mark, fairly, and in good faith."[197]

---

[190] Citing *Canal Co v Clark*, 80 U.S. 311 (1872).
[191] *Park'N Fly, Inc v Dollar Park and Fly, Inc*, 469 U.S. 189, 105 S.Ct. 658 (1985).
[192] McCarthy, s.11:45
[193] *Cosmetically Sealed Industries, Inc v Chesebrough-Pond's USA Co*, 125 F.3d, at 30; he also cited *Car-Freshner Corp v SC Johnson & Son*, Inc, 70 F.3d 267 (2nd Cir. 1995), at 269, stressing the need to "protect the right of society at large to use words or images in their primary descriptive test". In fn.5 Justice Souter referred to the testimony of Wallace Martin, Chairman, American Bar Association Committee on Trade-Mark Legislation: "Everybody has got a right to the use of the English language and has got a right to assume that nobody is going to take that English language away from him".
[194] 543 U.S. 111, at 123.
[195] For example *Shakespeare Co v Silstar Corp*, 110 F.3d 234 (4th Cir. 1997); and *Sunmark, Inc v Ocean Spray Cranberries, Inc*, 64 F.3d 1055 (7th Cir. 1995) appeared to link the extent of confusion with the finding on fairness. Indeed in fn.6 the Court hinted that whether use of the contested sign in this case had been descriptive or not in all instances was a contested issue.
[196] Referring to s.28 of the Restatement (Third) of Unfair Competition (1995)).
[197] 543 U.S. 111, at 124.

5. VICTORIA'S SECRET—THE UNCERTAINTIES OF DILUTION

(1) The basics of dilution

11–058
Schechter introduced a "qualitative" shift in the basis of trade mark protection. Trade mark laws should aim to protect the mark as such. The harm they should be targeting was dilution, the "gradual whittling away" or "dispersion of the identity" and "hold upon the public mind" of the mark by its use on non competing goods.[198] However, not all trade marks deserved this expanded form of protection against dilution; to qualify trade marks should be famous, well-known, or reputable.

In 1947 Bay State Massachussetts adopted the first anti-dilution statute and 24 States followed until 1996 whereas three States recognised dilution as part of their common law developed by courts.

Trade mark proprietors and practitioners promoted extensively the United States Trade Mark Association (now International Trade Mark Association—INTA) Model State Trade Mark Bill that provided:

> "Likelihood of injury to business reputation or of dilution of the distinctive quality of a mark registered under this Act, or a mark valid under common law, or a trade name valid at common law, shall be a ground for injunctive relief, notwithstanding the absence of confusion as to source of goods or services."

Most of the State statutes followed the Model Bill and provided for protection against injury to business reputation, dilution by tarnishment, and dilution of the distinctive quality of the trade mark, dilution by blurring.

Courts were uncertain about how confusion fitted in this new scheme. Although there was no requirement to prove confusion, a number of courts would still require some evidence on confusion whereas others would not use dilution when there was evidence of confusion.[199]

11–059
The position on dilution was crystallised in the Restatement (Third) of Unfair Competition that provided:

---

[198] FI Schechter, "The Rational Basis of Trademark Protection", 40 Harvard L. R. 813 (1927).
[199] See for example *Nikon, Inc v Ikon Corp*, 987 F. 2d 91, 25 U.S.P.Q. 2d 2021 (2d Cir. 1993); and *AHP Subsidiary Holding Co v Stuart Hale Co*, 1 F. 3d 611, 27 U.S.P.Q. 2d 1758 (7th Cir. 1993). *Mead Data Central Inc v Toyota*, 875 F.2d 1026, 10 U.S.P.Q.2d 1961 (2nd Cir.) considered the conflict between Lexus, for luxury cars, and Lexis, for the provision of information services. The court found that a mental association had to be made in the mind of the reasonable buyer between the two parties and the mark. Back then, Lexis was not distinctive enough to be diluted by Lexus used on Toyota cars. The case also exemplifies that it might be difficult to establish dilution in the absence of tarnishment. In its assessment the court employed a number of factors, including some that pointed towards the existence of confusion rather than dilution: similarity of the products; similarity of the marks; consumer sophistication; predatory intent; renown of the senior mark; renown of the junior mark.

"For dilution to occur, purchasers or prospective customers must make a mental connection between the plaintiff's mark and the mark as used by the defendant.

The connection, however, is not that which serves as the basis of trade mark infringement—the mistaken belief that the plaintiff is in some way associated with defendant's goods—but rather is the accurate recognition that a mark once associated exclusively with the plaintiff is now also in use as an identifying symbol by others".[200]

Some consumer might be confused as to the existence of some sort of link between the entities behind the two trade marks; others might see the association but not be confused. The same person would not be confused and not confused at the same time; confusion and dilution could co-exist, but not in the mind of the same person at the same time.[201]

Before the introduction of dilution in the Lanham Act the Court considered the concept in the Gay Olympics case.

(2) The Gay Olympic Games—protecting the Olympic symbols

11–060   *San Francisco Arts & Athletics, Inc v United States Olympic Committee*[202] provided early evidence that dilution would be a complex and controversial issue. The case also dealt with two other challenging questions, first the status of the world "Olympic" and the limits of trade mark law in its uneasy relationship with freedom of speech.

The United States Olympic Committee (USOC) and the International Olympic Committee (IOC) were awarded a permanent injunction by the District Court restraining use of the term "Olympics" by a non-profit corporation, the San Francisco Arts & Athletics, Inc (SFAA), under the Amateur Sports Act of 1978.[203] SFAA used the term "Gay Olympic Games" to describe a sports competition and on promotional merchandising products. The competition would be an international event that employed parallels with the Olympic Games; for example, the organisers planned a "Gay Olympics Torch" relay to light the "Gay Olympic Flame". Successful "Gay Games I" and "Gay Games II" had already been held in 1982 and 1986 respectively.

The Court of Appeals affirmed the injunction.[204]

---

[200] Restatement (Third) of Unfair Competition para.25.
[201] *Coca Cola v Gemini Rising*, 346 F. Supp. 1183, 175 U.S.P.Q. 56 (E.D.N.Y. 1972), the "Enjoy cocaine" in a Coca-Cola script exemplifies that confusion and dilution can coexist in the market place. There was some evidence of confusion in the market place but the court also found that the association between the plaintiff and an illegal drug would be particularly injurious.
[202] 483 U.S. 522, 3 U.S.P.Q.2d 1145 (1987).
[203] 36 U.S.C. §§ 371–396.
[204] 781 F.2d 733 (9th Cir. 1986). The Supreme Court granted certiorari 479 U.S. 913, 107 S.Ct. 312 (1986).

5. VICTORIA'S SECRET—THE UNCERTAINTIES OF DILUTION

Justice Powell gave the Opinion of the Court, joined by Chief Justice Rehnquist, and Justice White, Justice Stevens, and Justice Scalia. Justice O'Connor filed an Opinion concurring in part and dissenting in part in which Justice Blackmun joined, whereas Justice Brennan filed a dissenting Opinion joined by Justice Marshall.

(a) The main issue

The Court granted certiorari to review statutory and constitutional interpretation issues decided by the Court of Appeals.   11–061

(b) The legislative context

Section 110 of the Amateur Sports Act (Act) granted USOC an exclusionary right: 11–062

> "Without the consent of the [USOC], any person who uses for the purpose of trade, to induce the sale of any goods or services, or to promote any theatrical exhibition, athletic performance, or competition—
>
> (1) the symbol of the International Olympic Committee ...;
> (2) the emblem of the [USOC] ...;
> (3) any trademark, trade name, sign, symbol, or insignia falsely representing association with, or authorization by, the International Olympic Committee or the [USOC]; or
> (4) the words 'Olympic', 'Olympiad', 'Citius Altius Fortius', or any combination or simulation thereof tending to cause confusion, to cause mistake, to deceive, or to falsely suggest a connection with the [USOC] or any Olympic activity;
>
> shall be subject to suit in a civil action by the [USOC] for the remedies provided in the ... Lanham Act ...".
>
> (b) The [USOC] may authorize contributors and suppliers of goods or services to use the trade name of the [USOC] as well as any trademark, symbol, insignia, or emblem of the International Olympic Committee or of the [USOC] in advertising that the contributions, goods, or services were donated, supplied, or furnished to or for the use of, approved, selected, or used by the [USOC] or United States Olympic or Pan-American team or team members.
> (c) The [USOC] shall have exclusive right to use the name 'United States Olympic Committee'; the symbol described in subsection (a)(1) of this section; the emblem described in subsection (a)(2) of this section; and the words 'Olympic', 'Olympiad', 'Citius Altius Fortius' or any combination thereof subject to the preexisting rights described in subsection (a) of this section."

(c) The reasoning of the Court

11–063 Given the ambiguity of subs.4 above[205] Justice Powell started his analysis by setting the provision in its historical context rather than resorting to a textual analysis. Before the adoption of s.110 unauthorised use was punishable by criminal sanctions; there was a criminal intent requirement—that made the application of the provision more difficult—but no need to establish confusion. He switched however immediately to a textual analysis as the main reason for rejecting the argument that the reference to Lanham Act remedies also covered the defenses included therein. So, protection of the Olympic words and symbols differed from traditional trade mark protection in that, first, it did not require proving likelihood of confusion two respects and, secondly, the normal statutory defenses were not available.

The SFAA argued that this two pronged divergence was unconstitutional under the First Amendment[206]; first because the word "Olympic" had become generic and second because unauthorised use was not likely to cause confusion.

The Court had already acknowledged the tension in its jurisprudence by referring to a "substantial risk of suppressing ideas" when words were protected.[207] However, Justice Powell counterbalanced this statement with the principle that a limited property right in a word may be obtained when a word acquires value as "the result of organization and the expenditure of labor, skill, and money".[208] He also noted that this type of protection had also been made available for other distinctive words or symbols, for example the American National Red Cross, Boy and Girl Scouts, and veterans' organisations.

A short overview of the history of the modern Olympic Games led to the conclusion that the commercial and promotional value of the word "Olympic" was the result of the USOC's and the IOC's efforts. Accordingly, there was no need to decide whether Congress could grant a private entity an exclusive right over a generic word because Congress could reasonably find that the word since 1896 had acquired a secondary meaning; a limited property right fell "within the scope of trademark law protections, and thus certainly within constitutional bounds".[209]

The absence of a confusion requirement was also considered to be justified.

---

[205] Does "tending to cause confusion" apply to the word "Olympic" alone (as suggested by the SFAA) or to "any combination or simulation thereof". Despite having earlier ruled that "[T]he starting point in every case involving construction of a statute is the language itself", *Blue Chip Stamps v Manor Drug Stores*, 421 U.S. 723, 95.S.Ct. 1917 (1975), at 756.

[206] "Congress shall make no law respecting an establishment of religion, or prohibiting the free exercise thereof; or abridging the freedom of speech, or of the press; or the right of the people peaceably to assemble, and to petition the government for a redress of grievances."

[207] *Cohen v California*, 403 U.S. 15, 91 S.Ct. 1780 (1971), at 26.

[208] *International News Service v Associated Press*, 248 U.S. 215, 39 S.Ct. 68 (1918), at 239.

[209] 483 U.S. 522, at 535.

5. VICTORIA'S SECRET—THE UNCERTAINTIES OF DILUTION

First, the Government was entitled to regulate deceptive or misleading commercial speech.[210]

11–064

And, secondly, to the extent that s.110 applied only to trade uses, its application was to commercial speech that received limited protection under the First Amendment.[211] However, the section also covered the promotion of theatrical and athletic events, potentially bringing its scope outside the "strictly business" context.[212] And the scope of the "Gay Olympics" was, according to its organisers, to make a political statement about the status of homosexuals.

Justice Powell, however, noted that s.110 simply restricted the manner in which the SFAA could communicate its message rather than the communication as such of its message.[213]

"The restrictions on expressive speech properly are characterized as incidental to the primary congressional purpose of encouraging and rewarding the USOC's activities... The appropriate inquiry is thus whether the incidental restrictions on First Amendment freedoms are greater than necessary to further a substantial governmental interest."[214]

He suggested that the public interest behind the protection of the Olympic signs was broader than the production of quality products that underpins trade mark protection: participation in the Olympic Games and all the goals, interests, and activities that coalesce and culminate towards participation.

11–065

And the restrictions of s.110 were not broader than necessary. Although the Lanham Act was, then, focusing on confusion, that was not a requirement under s.110 because "Congress reasonably could conclude that most commercial uses of the Olympic words and symbols are likely to be confusing. It also could determine that unauthorized uses, even if not confusing, nevertheless may harm the USOC by lessening the distinctiveness and thus the commercial value of the marks".[215] The dilution rationale behind the provision is obvious.

---

[210] *Virginia Pharmacy Bd v Virginia Citizens Consumer Council, Inc*, 425 U.S. 748, 96 S.Ct. 1817 (1976).
[211] Citing *Posadas de Puerto Rico Assoc v Tourism Company of Puerto Rico*, 478 U.S. 328, 106 S.Ct. 2968 (1986), at 340.
[212] *Friedman v Rogers*, 440 U.S. 1, 99. S.Ct. 887 (1979), at 11.
[213] Adding that purely expressive uses of the word "Olympic" could be outside the scope of the provision, referring, by way of example, to *Stop the Olympic Prison v United States Olympic Committee*, 489 F.Supp. 1112 (S.D.N.Y. 1980).
[214] *United States v O'Brien*, 391 U.S. 367, 88 S.Ct. 1673 (1968); and *Central Hudson Gas & Electric Corp v Public Service Comm'n of New York*, 447 U.S. 557, 100 S.Ct. 2343 (1980). Responding to Justice Brennan's position that the Act was unconstitutionally overbroad he supported that there was no basis in the record to believe that the Act would be applied against non commercial speech rights, there was no realistic danger that the statute would affect First Amendment rights of other parties that were not before the Court, citing *City Council of Los Angeles v Taxpayers for Vincent*, 466 U.S. 789, 104 S.Ct. 2118 (1984).
[215] 483 U.S. 522, at 539, referring to Schechter, "The Rational Basis of Trademark Protection" 40 Harv.L.Rev. 813 (1927).

SFAA's activities would harm USOC in a variety of ways. First there was the possibility of confusion as to sponsorship. Secondly, looking at SFAA's motives, it was suggested that it intended to exploit the "commercial magnetism" of the symbols[216]; this would affect USOC's commercial strategy "since much of the word's value comes from its limited use. Such an adverse effect on the USOC's activities is directly contrary to Congress' interest. Even though this protection may exceed the traditional rights of a trademark owner in certain circumstances, the application of the Act to this commercial speech is not broader than necessary to protect the legitimate congressional interest and therefore does not violate the First Amendment".[217]

Equally justified was the treatment of promotional uses of "Olympic" in relation to athletic or theatrical events:

> "The image the SFAA sought to invoke was exactly the image carefully cultivated by the USOC. The SFAA's expressive use of the word cannot be divorced from the value the USOC's efforts have given to it. The mere fact that the SFAA claims an expressive, as opposed to a purely commercial, purpose does not give it a First Amendment right to appropriat[e] to itself the harvest of those who have sown. The USOC's right to prohibit use of the word 'Olympic' in the promotion of athletic events is at the core of its legitimate property right."[218]

11–066 We will not deal in detail here with the claim put forward by SFAA based on the nature of the USOC, since it is outside the scope of this book.

Briefly, it supported that the USOC was a governmental actor and that its enforcement policy was discriminatory, targeting particular groups, in violation of the Fifth Amendment. It suffices to say that the Court found it to be a private actor. One issue that is related to trade mark law is the relevance of the grant by Congress of the exclusive right to use the word "Olympic".

The Court noted: "All enforceable rights in trademarks are created by some governmental act, usually pursuant to a statute or the common law. The actions of the trademark owners nevertheless remain private. Moreover, the intent on the part of Congress to help the USOC obtain funding does not change the analysis. The Government may subsidize

---

[216] *Mishawaka Rubber & Woolen Mfg Co v SS Kresge Co*, 316 U.S. 203, 62 S.Ct. 1022 (1942).
[217] 483 U.S. 522, at 539–540.
[218] 483 U.S. 522, at 540–541, citing *International News Service v Associated Press*, 248 U.S. 215, at 239–240. He also rejected SFAA's claim that as a non-profit corporation it should enjoy a superior right. Citing a case on copyright fair use he repeated in fn.19: "The crux of the profit/non-profit distinction is not whether the sole motive of the use is monetary gain but whether the user stands to profit from exploitation of the [protected] material without paying the customary price", *Harper & Row Publishers, Inc v Nation Enterprises*, 471 U.S. 539, 105 S.Ct. 2218 (1985), at 562.

5. VICTORIA'S SECRET—THE UNCERTAINTIES OF DILUTION

private entities without assuming constitutional responsibility for their actions."[219]

Note however that the dissenting Opinion of Justice Brennan carried considerable support in relation to the nature of the USOC and the character of its actions. He claimed that the USOC "performs a distinctive, traditional governmental function: it represents this Nation to the world community".[220] So, the USOC should be seen as either a pure Government actor or at least a private actor acting together—in a symbiotic relationship—with the Government; Congress had granted, through s.110, an unprecedented right in order to enhance USOC's fundraising ability. Whether the USOC acted discriminatory deserved further investigation; the judgment of the Court of Appeals should have been reversed and the case remanded to the District Court to decide on this issue.

He also disagreed with the findings of the majority regarding the balancing between the right and the First Amendment. The statute was overbroad first, because it provided the remedies of the Lanham Act without its defenses and, secondly, because it extended to non commercial or expressive activities.

Further he noted that "[C]haritable solicitation and political advocacy by organizations such as SFAA may in part consist of commercial speech regulated by trademark law, but the expressive element of such speech has been sheltered from unconstitutional harm by Lanham Act defenses. Without them, the Amateur Sports Act prohibits a substantial amount of noncommercial speech".[221] The limitations and defenses of the Lanham Act delimited the scope of trade mark rights; without them there was a risk that non commercial speech would be affected. Even dilution he noted, available then only at the State level, had limitations that were not imposed by s.110.[222]

He concluded that:

"[L]anguage, even in a commercial context, properly belongs to the public, unless the Government's asserted interest is substantial, and unless the limitation imposed is no more extensive than necessary to serve that interest... The Lanham Act is carefully crafted to prevent commercial monopolization of language that otherwise belongs in the public domain... the SFAA therefore is entitled to use the word

---

[219] Citing *Blum v Yaretsky*, 457 U.S. 991, 102 S.Ct. 2777 (1982); and *Rendell-Baker v Kohn*, 457 U.S. 830, 102 S.Ct. 2764 (1982).
[220] 483 U.S. 522, at 550; the decision of the US to boycott the 1980 Moscow Olympic Games exemplified the political, to an extent, nature of the Games.
[221] 483 U.S. 522, at 563–564.
[222] Note that his discussion of dilution in fn.25 reveals his concerns regarding the expansion of trade mark protection; at some point he appears to favour a requirement of likelihood of confusion even in the case of dilution.

'Olympic' in a nonconfusing and nonmisleading manner in the noncommercial promotion of a theatrical or athletic event, absent proof of resultant harm to the USOC".[223]

(3) The 1995 Act—section 43(c)

11–068 The 1989 revision of the Lanham Act failed to introduce Federal protection against dilution because there was strong opposition based on the vagueness of the concept, its potentially anti-competitive aspects and freedom of speech consideration.

In 1995 however the defences against dilution had been defused and the anti-dilution Act sailed swiftly through the US legislative process.

Dilution was defined as the lessening of the capacity of a famous mark to identify and distinguish goods or services, regardless of the presence or absence of competition between the owner of the famous mark and any likelihood of confusion, mistake or deception. Note that there was no direct reference to dilution by tarnishment.

The Act provided no guidance on how similar the marks should be for leaning towards a finding of dilution. A Court of Appeals had suggested in *Nabisco*[224] that the marks should be of sufficient similarity so that, in the mind of the consumer, the junior mark would conjure an association with the senior.

11–069 The starting point for obtaining protection was establishing that a mark was "distinctive and famous". The Act introduced eight factors:

1. the degree of inherent or acquired distinctiveness of the mark;

2. the duration and extent of use of the mark in connection with the goods or services with which the mark is used;

3. the duration and extent of advertising and publicity;

4. the geographical extent of the trading area in which the mark is used (the Act does not require use by the plaintiff in interstate commerce);

5. the channels of trade for the goods or services with which the mark is used;

6. the degree of recognition of the mark in the trading areas and channels of trade used by the mark's owner and the person against whom the injunction is sought;

7. the nature and extent of use of the same or similar marks by third parties; and

8. and, whether the mark is the subject of a Federal Registration.

---

[223] 483 U.S. 522, at 573.
[224] *Nabisco, Inc v PF Brands, Inc*, 51 U.S.P.Q.2d 1882 (2nd Cir. 1999).

5. VICTORIA'S SECRET—THE UNCERTAINTIES OF DILUTION

Note that Federal Registration is not a requirement.

(4) Establishing dilution

The *Nabisco* decision[225] advocated a cautious approach towards finding dilution by blurring and suggested a 10 point test. The test had been criticised for introducing unnecessary confusion questions into the assessment of dilution. The court identified the following factors:

11–070

1. The degree of distinctiveness.
2. The similarity of the marks.
3. The proximity of the products and likelihood of bridging the gap.
4. Balancing the above factors.
5. Overlap between consumers in terms of product market and geographic location.
6. Sophistication of consumers.
7. Actual confusion.
8. Adjectival or referential quality of the junior use.
9. Harm to the junior user and delay by the senior user.
10. Senior user's failure to protect the mark. It also suggested that the predatory intent of the junior user must be taken into account.

(5) Victoria's Secret—the sceptic's stance

The question of what is required in order to establish dilution reached the Court in *Moseley v V Secret Catalogue*.[226]

11–071

The owners of Victoria's Secret trade mark for lingerie started trade mark infringement proceedings, claiming traditional trade mark infringement and dilution, against Victor Moseley who run a shop under the name "Victor's Little Secret" selling adult videos, novelty products, and lingerie; the original name of the shop, "Victor's Secret", was changed following a letter from the lawyers of V. Secret Catalogue. Victoria's Secret was an established brand with outlets throughout the United States and a very popular mail order business.

Note that part of the evidence, and what triggered the case, was a letter from a retired army colonel that exemplified dilution: he saw an advertisement for "Victor's Secret" and although he realised that there is no

---

[225] *Nabisco, Inc* 51 U.S.P.Q.2d 1882 (2nd Cir. 1999).
[226] 537 U.S. 418, 123 S.Ct. 1115.

connection between the two entities sent the advertisement to the owners of Victoria's Secret to warn them that their trade mark was used to sell questionable merchandise.

In the absence of evidence of actual confusion the District Court found that there was no likelihood of confusion. It found, however, that "Victor's Little Secret" would tarnish the Victoria's Secret trade mark. The Court of Appeals affirmed finding the case a classic example of dilution:

> "While no consumer is likely to go to the Moseleys' store expecting to find Victoria's Secret's famed Miracle Bra, consumers who hear the name 'Victor's Little Secret' are likely automatically to think of the more famous store and link it to the Moseleys' adult-toy, gag gift, and lingerie shop. This, then, is a classic instance of dilution by tarnishing (associating the Victoria's Secret name with sex toys and lewd coffee mugs) and by blurring (linking the chain with a single, unauthorized establishment)."[227]

The Supreme Court granted certiorari[228] and Justice Stevens delivered the Opinion for the Court. The Court was unanimous for the majority of the Opinion. Justice Kennedy filed a concurring Opinion for one part and Justice Scalia did not join the majority for the same part.

(a) The main issue

11–072   The Court granted certiorari because the Circuits had been expressing differing views on whether actual harm to the mark must be shown in order to obtain protection against dilution.

(b) The context of the case

11–073   Justice Stevens noted that the Court of Appeals had applied the test for determining dilution devised by the Second Circuit[229] and considered two particular aspects of the case. There was no controversy regarding the finding that Victoria's Secret was both famous and distinctive. The second issue however was more controversial. The Court of Appeals did not follow

---

[227] 259 F.3d 464 (6th Cir. 2001), at 477.
[228] 535 U.S. 985, 122 S.Ct. 1536 (2002).
[229] *Nabisco, Inc* 191 F.3d 208 (2nd Cir. 1999); adopted by the Sixth Circuit in *Kellogg Co v Exxon Corp*, 209 F.3d 562 (6th Cir. 2000). The test comprised ten non exclusive factors: distinctiveness; similarity of marks; proximity of the products and the likelihood of bridging the gap; interrelationship among the distinctiveness of the senior mark, the similarity of the junior mark, and the proximity of the products; shared consumers and geographic limitations; sophistication of consumers; actual confusion; adjectival or referential quality of the junior use; harm to the junior user and delay by the senior user; and the effect of the senior's prior laxity in protecting the mark. The reference to confusion is of course puzzling and points to the conceptual difficulties courts have with dilution; if there is confusion then this is a case of traditional trade mark infringement.

5. VICTORIA'S SECRET—THE UNCERTAINTIES OF DILUTION

the Sixth and the Fourth Circuits that required evidence of actual dilution[230]; it characterised the requirement of actual loss of revenues or consumer surveys as evidence of actual dilution as an arbitrary and unwarranted limitation of the methods of proof.

(c) *The reasoning of the Court*

Justice Stevens viewed traditional trade mark infringement law as part of the law of unfair competition with a dual purpose, to protect consumers from being misled as a result of confusion but also to protect from the unfair practices of imitating competitors.[231] Dilution on the other hand required neither consumer confusion nor a competitive relationship between the parties. Protection against dilution was not motivated by "an interest in protecting consumers".[232] He then juxtaposed Schechter's concept of dilution, the preservation of the uniqueness of a famous trade mark,[233] with the legislative developments at the state level where dilution covered both tarnishment and blurring. Note that Justice Stephens conducted an indirect—through Schechter's work—but detailed analysis of the German *Odol* case.

Turning to the 1995 Act he noted the provisions that aimed to placate the opposition against dilution that had succeeded back in 1988. In order to overcome concerns based on the First Amendment s.43(c)(4) incorporated two exceptions, one allowing fair use of a trade mark in comparative advertising and the second excluding non commercial uses of a trade mark from the scope of anti-dilution protection.

He also highlighted the contrast between state laws and the Lanham Act regarding the nature of the injury and the scope of the provision. State statutes referred to both "injury to business reputation" (tarnishment) and "dilution of the distinctive quality of a trade name or trademark" (blurring). The Lanham Act referred only to the latter. This could mean that the scope of protection at the Federal level was narrower.

Another critical difference was that state statutes referred to a likelihood of dilution whereas s.43(c)(1) provided protection against commercial use of a trade mark that "causes dilution of the distinctive quality" of the famous mark. This time the Court favored a textual analysis: "This text unambiguously requires a showing of actual dilution, rather than a likelihood of dilution."[234]

11-074

---

[230] *Ringling Bros–Barnum & Bailey Combined Shows, Inc v Utah Division of Travel Dev*, 170 F.3d 449 (4th Cir. 1999); and *Nabisco, Inc* 191 F.3d 208 (2nd Cir. 1999).
[231] Citing *Qualitex Co*, 514 U.S. 159, 34 U.S.P.Q.2d 1161 (1995) at 163–164.
[232] 123 S.Ct. 1115, at 1122.
[233] Schechter, (1927).
[234] 123 S.Ct. 1115, at 1124. The contrast in s.45 between "the lessening of the capacity" and the "likelihood of confusion" strengthened this analysis. "The term 'dilution' means the lessening of the capacity of a famous mark to identify and distinguish goods or services, regardless of the presence or absence of—(1) competition between the owner of the famous mark and other parties, or (2) likelihood of confusion, mistake, or deception."

11–075 This did not mean that the consequences of dilution, for example loss of sales, had also to be proven. However:

> "at least where the marks at issue are not identical, the mere fact that consumers mentally associate the junior user's mark with a famous mark is not sufficient to establish actionable dilution. As the facts of [Ringling Bros] that case demonstrate, such mental association will not necessarily reduce the capacity of the famous mark to identify the goods of its owner, the statutory requirement for dilution under the FTDA... 'Blurring' is not a necessary consequence of mental association. (Nor, for that matter, is 'tarnishing.')"[235]

Justice Stephens interpreted the factual context of Victoria's Secret in the same way. The army officer on whose evidence the case was built was offended by the advertisement but this did not change his perception of Victoria's Secret.

He accepted that obtaining evidence of actual dilution could be a difficult and expensive exercise. "It may well be, however, that direct evidence of dilution such as consumer surveys will not be necessary if actual dilution can reliably be proved through circumstantial evidence—the obvious case is one where the junior and senior marks are identical. Whatever difficulties of proof may be entailed, they are not an acceptable reason for dispensing with proof of an essential element of a statutory violation."[236]

The judgment was reversed and the case remanded.

(d) A concurring opinion

11–076 Justice Kennedy concurred, but wished to comment further on the term "capacity", incorporated in the definition of dilution as "the lessening of the capacity of a famous mark to identify and distinguish goods or services". He felt that the term introduced into the provision the potential power of the famous mark to identify and distinguish goods. Accordingly "[D]iminishment of the famous mark's capacity can be shown by the probable consequences flowing from use or adoption of the competing mark... A holder of a famous mark threatened with diminishment of the mark's capacity to serve its purpose should not be forced to wait until the damage is done and the distinctiveness of the mark has been eroded".[237]

---

[235] 123 S.Ct. 1115, at 1124–1125.
[236] 123 S.Ct. 1115, at 1125.
[237] 123 S.Ct. 1115, at 1126; and according to the Supreme Court injunctive relief aimed to "prevent future wrong, although no right has yet been violated", *Swift & Co v United States*, 276 U.S. 311, 48 S.Ct. 311, at 326.

6. PARALLEL IMPORTS

(1) The exhaustion principle—universality v territoriality

In the United States the general rule is that trade mark rights are exhausted following the first sale of the marked. Given that the same trade mark can be owned by the same entity or connected entities in different jurisdictions the first sale doctrine was affected by the application of two divergent doctrines dealing with parallel imports.

According to the territoriality doctrine a trade mark has a separate existence in each jurisdiction in which it is registered or legally recognised as a mark. According to the universality doctrine a trade mark signifies the same source, the manufacturer of the product, wherever the mark is used in the world.

11–077

(a) A shift towards territoriality

The initial approach favoured the universality doctrine. However in 1923 a judgment of the Supreme Court marked a shift towards the territoriality doctrine based on how the trade mark functioned in the United States. In *A Bourjois & Co v Katzel*[238] it held that for American consumers the trade mark signified that the relevant cosmetic products came from the plaintiff as distributor. The importation and sale of even genuine goods by anyone else would be likely to cause confusion as to source. The mark indicated in law that the goods came from the plaintiff although not made by it. It staked the reputation of the plaintiff upon the character of the goods.

11–078

An extract from a case from a lower court evidences the shift towards the territoriality doctrine.

The focus is on the party who owns the goodwill in the United States rather than the actual, in terms of manufacture, source of the product:

"The universality principle has faded and has been generally supplanted by the principle of 'territoriality,' upon which the [earlier] rulings were based. This principle recognizes that a trademark has a separate legal existence under each country's laws, and that its proper lawful function is not necessarily to specify the origin or manufacture of a good (although it may incidentally do that), but rather to symbolize the domestic goodwill of the domestic mark-holder so that the consuming public may rely with an expectation of consistency on the domestic reputation earned for the mark by its owner, and the owner of the mark may be confident that his goodwill and reputation (the value of the mark) will not be injured through use of the mark by others in domestic commerce."[239]

---

[238] 260 U.S. 689, 43 S. Ct. 244 (1923).
[239] *Osawa & Co v B & H Photo*, 589 F. Supp. 1163, 223 U.S.P.Q. 124 (S.D.N.Y. 1984) at 1171.

This was considered to be in accordance with art.6(3) of the Paris Convention providing that "a mark duly registered in a country of the Union shall be regarded as independent of marks registered in other countries of the Union, including the country of origin".

11–079 According to s.29 of the Restatement (Third) of Unfair Competition (1995) the source indicated by a trademark may be the firm perceived by consumers as assuring the consistent quality of the goods.

The factual question was existed as to whether the trade mark identifies the domestic trade mark owner or the foreign manufacturer.

If the trade mark identified the domestic owner, rather than the foreign manufacturer, then the source of the imported "gray market" product was not accurately identified by the trade mark. Their sale would constitute an infringement.

(b) "Gray market" goods

11–080 "Gray market" or "gray" goods have become the most common terms for describing parallel imported products in the United States. The term can misleadingly imply that the imported products are somewhere between genuine and counterfeit products.

In reality these goods are legally purchased abroad and imported into the United States without the consent of the US trade mark holder.

An extract from a lower court discusses the psychological effect of the term.

> "[Defendants] in the present case note that the term 'gray-market' unfairly implies a nefarious undertaking by the importer, and that the more accurate term for the goods at issue is 'parallel import.' We agree that the term parallel import accurately describes the goods and is, perhaps, a better term because it is devoid of prejudicial suggestion. For that reason, we use that term in this discussion. However, we also employ the term 'gray-market' goods because, for better or worse, it has become the commonly accepted and employed reference to the goods at issue."[240]

(2) Legislative context

11–081 There are two legislative backgrounds dealing with parallel imports.

Section 42 of the Lanham Act provides that:

> "no article of imported merchandise shall be admitted to entry at any customhouse of the US if:

---

[240] *Weil Ceramics & Glass, Inc v Dash*, 878 F.2d 659, 11 USPQ2d 1001 (3d Cir. 1989).

6. PARALLEL IMPORTS

(1) it bears a trademark which shall copy or simulate a trademark registered on the Principal Register of the federal Lanham Act;
(2) it bears a name which shall copy or simulate the name of any domestic manufacturer or trader, or of any manufacturer or trader located in any foreign country which, by treaty, convention or law affords similar privileges to citizens of the United States; and
(3) it bears a name or mark calculated to induce the public to believe that the article is manufactured in the United States or that it is manufactured in any foreign country or locality other than the country or locality in which it is in fact manufactured."

Protection is also available under the Tariff Act that regulates Customs authorities. Trade marks may be recorded with Customs. An imported mark which is likely to be associated with a mark registered under the Lanham Act is deemed to "copy or simulate" the registered mark.

Customs may act ex parte. Unrecorded trade marks may be seized if importation constitutes the crime of "trade mark counterfeiting". Goods bearing a counterfeit mark ("a spurious mark which is identical with, or substantially indistinguishable from, a registered mark") are automatically seized and forfeited.

In order to focus their efforts on the importation of counterfeit goods Customs started imposing the "common control" and "authorisation" exceptions. *K-Mart*[241] was the response of the Supreme Court to these exceptions.

(3) The competition question

The anti-competitive effect of the compartmentalisation of the global market on the basis of trade mark rights came close to being considered by the Supreme Court in *United States v Guerlain, Inc.*[242]   11–082

The Department of Justice convinced a district court that the US part of a single international company should not be allowed to invoke customs' seizure provisions against parallel imports. This would be against the Sherman Act (competition legislation).

The case was discontinued by the government while on appeal to the Supreme Court. Subsequently, a bill aiming to limit the Tariff Act and the Lanham Act failed.

(4) Material differences

Goods made by an affiliate of the US trade mark owner can also be blocked from being marketed in the jurisdiction because of material differences between the imported goods and the goods made for circulation in the United States.   11–083

---

[241] *K MART Corp v Cartier Inc, et al. 47th Street Photo Inc*, 486 U.S. 281, 108 S.Ct. 1811 (1988).
[242] 78 S. Ct. 285, 19 USPQ 501 (1958).

For example in *Lever Bros Co v United States*[243] it was argued without success that the importation of goods made by an affiliate of a US trade mark owner cannot "copy or simulate" a US registered trade mark because the goods are by definition genuine. This was rejected.

The foreign trade mark was applied to physically different goods. It was not a genuine trade mark from the perspective of an American consumer.

Affiliation between the producers did not reduce likelihood of confusion. In this case Lever US and Lever UK manufactured SHIELD brand soap. The US SHIELD soap produced more foam, had an antibacterial agent, and had a different scent from the UK SHIELD soap. The products were not of the same quality.

It is against this background that K MART must be read.

(5)   K MART—parallel imports

11-084   *K MART*[244] is the most recent judgment of the Supreme Court that considers the issue of parallel imports. It is a good review of the changes in the position of the Supreme Court regarding exhaustion; it is also a good example of the interpretive tools the Supreme Court uses in order to position a specific provision within a wider framework of rules.

Finally, the way it was constructed is evidence of the striking differences in style between the judgments of the Supreme Court on the one hand and the Court of Justice on the other. The differences between individual personalities are made public in the case of the Supreme Court; the cross responses in the Opinions are closer to full fronted attacks rather than veiled criticisms. The collective nature of the judgments of the Court of Justice hides these differences behind a common language; textual nuances accommodate diverging opinions in a way that is probably meaningful only to the judges that participated in the judgment.

The case started with an action brought by the Coalition to Preserve the Integrity of American Trademarks (COPIAT, an association of trade mark holders) seeking a declaration that s.133.21(c)(1)–(3) (1987) of the Customs Service Regulations was invalid and an injunction against its enforcement. K MART and 47th Street Photo intervened as defendants. The District Court upheld the Customs Service Regulations, the Court of Appeals reversed.[245] The Supreme Court granted certiorari[246] to resolve a conflict between the Courts of Appeals.

11-085   Justice Kennedy announced the judgment of the Court and delivered an opinion, with the other members joining parts of the opinion, issuing concurring in part or dissenting in part opinions, or joining the opinions of the other two members.

---

[243] 981 F.2d 1330, 25 USPQ2d 1579 (D.C. Cir. 1993).
[244] *K MART Corp v Cartier, Inc, et al. 47th Street Photo, Inc*, 486 U.S. 281, 108 S.Ct. 1811 (1988).
[245] *COPIAT v United States*, 252 U.S.App.D.C. 342, 790 F.2d 903 (1986).
[246] 479 U.S. 1005, 107 S.Ct. 642, (1986).

6. PARALLEL IMPORTS

In Pts I and II-A, Chief Justice Rehnquist, and Justice White, Justice Blackmun, Justice O'Connor, and Justice Scalia, joined Justice Kennedy in the opinion of the Court. In respect of Pt II-B, only Justice White joined. In respect of Pt II-C, Chief Justice Rehnquist and Justice Blackmun, Justice O'Connor, and Justice Scalia, joined Justice Kennedy in the Opinion of the Court.

Justice Brennan filed an opinion concurring in part and dissenting in part, in which Justice Marshall and Justice Stevens, joined, and Justice White joined in part; Justice Scalia filed an opinion concurring in part and dissenting in part, in which Chief Justice Rehnquist and Justice Blackmun and Justice O'Connor, joined.

(a) The Opinion of Justice Kennedy

(i) Part I. Part I of the Opinion of Justice Kennedy dealt with the general framework regarding "gray market" goods. Justice Kennedy described three gray market scenarios.

11–086

The "prototypical" scenario (case 1) would involve a US firm purchasing from an independent foreign firm the rights to register and use the latter's trade mark as a US trade mark. Allowing the foreign manufacturer, or a third party that had obtained the trade marked products from the foreign manufacturer outside the US, to import the trade marked products in the United States would create strong intra-brand competition; "a gray market that could jeopardize the trademark holder's investment".[247]

The second scenario focused on a US firm registering the US trade mark for products that were manufactured abroad by an affiliate. There were three variations on the same theme here. First (case 2a), where a foreign entity incorporates a subsidiary in the United States that in turn registers the trade mark in its own name and a third party or the affiliate imports trade marked products in the United States. Secondly (case 2b), where a US-based entity establishes abroad a manufacturing subsidiary corporation or, the third variation (case 2c), its own unincorporated manufacturing division to produce products bearing the US trade mark that it then imports into the United States for domestic distribution; gray market goods would compete with those marketed by the holder of the trade mark.

The third scenario (case 3) would involve an agreement with a third party outside the United States. The domestic holder authorises an independent manufacturer to use the trade mark, usually in relation to a specific geographical area and with the condition that the products will not be imported in the United States. If these products found their way into the American market they would compete with the holder's products intended for the same market.

---

[247] 486 U.S. 281 at 286.

11-087   The regulation of parallel imports was triggered by the Court of Appeals decision in *Bourjois & Co v Katzel*.[248] Congress adopted s.526 of the Tariff Act of 1922, that subsequently became s.526 of the 1930 Tariff Act, 19 U.S.C.§1526.[249]

The Customs' Regulations implementing s.526 however provided for an exception to the broad rule introduced by that provision. Section 133.21(c) of the Regulations provided that the restrictions described in the Regulations would not apply when:

> "(1) Both the foreign and the U.S. trademark or trade name are owned by the same person or business entity;
>
> (2) The foreign and domestic trademark or trade name owners are parent and subsidiary companies or are otherwise subject to common ownership or control. . . .
>
> (3) The articles of foreign manufacture bear a recorded trademark or trade name applied under authorization of the U.S. owner . . .".

A majority of the Court held that s.133.21(c)(1)–(2) (1987) was consistent with s.526 whereas a different majority held that s.133.21(c)(3) (1987), was inconsistent with s.526.

11-088   **(ii) Part II—A.** Justice Kennedy started the review of the implementing regulations by setting the interpretive framework of the review.

If the statute was clear and unambiguous it should be given precedence in a case of conflict with an agency regulation because the statute reflected the intent of the legislator. The plain meaning of the statute should be ascertained by looking at the wording of the particular provision but also at the language and design of the statute as a whole.

If the statute was silent or ambiguous then "the question becomes whether the agency regulation is a permissible construction of the statute".[250]

11-089   **(iii) Part II—B.** Justice Kennedy found s.133.21(c)(1) and s.133.21(c)(2) (1987) to be permissible constructions designed to resolve statutory ambiguities.

---

[248] 275 F. 539 (2nd Cir. 1921), rev'd, 260 U.S. 689, 43 S.Ct. 244 (1923).

[249] Tariff Act of 1922 s.526(a) provided: "Except as provided in subsection (d) of this section [personal use exception], it shall be unlawful to import into the United States any merchandise of foreign manufacture if such merchandise, or the label, sign, print, package, wrapper, or receptacle, bears a trademark owned by a citizen of, or by a corporation or association created or organized within, the United States, and registered in the Patent and Trademark Office by a person domiciled in the United States, under the provisions of sections 81 to 109 of title 15, and if a copy of the certificate of registration of such trademark is filed with the Secretary of the Treasury, in the manner provided in section 106 of said title 15, unless written consent of the owner of such trademark is produced at the time of making entry".

[250] 486 U.S. 261 at 292.

He noted that there was no disagreement between the members of the Court regarding case 1 and case 2a. Customs could interpret the statute as barring importation of gray-market goods in case 1 and permitting importation in case 2a because of the indeterminacy of the entity the words "owned by" referred to, because in some cases the domestic could be wholly owned by its foreign parent.

Justice Kennedy found that equally ambiguous was the reference to "merchandise of foreign manufacture"; it could cover goods manufactured in a foreign country, goods manufactured by a foreign company, or goods manufactured in a foreign country by a foreign company. This meant that the regulations could be sustained to the extent that they applied to case 2b and case 2c. Customs should be entitled to interpret the provision as stating that goods manufactured by a foreign subsidiary or division of a domestic company were not covered by the concept of "merchandise of foreign manufacture".

(iv) **Part II—C.** Kennedy J. however held that s.133.21(c)(3) of the Regulations should not be upheld. The ambiguous statutory references cited above were irrelevant to the prohibition contained in subs.(3). "Under no reasonable construction of the statutory language can goods made in a foreign country by an independent foreign manufacturer be removed from the purview of the statute."[251]

11–090

The subsection could be severed from the Regulations, leaving the remaining parts unaffected.

(v) **Part III.** Part III was the operative part of the judgment.

The Court held that the Customs Service Regulation was consistent with s.526 to the extent that it exempted from the importation ban goods that were manufactured abroad by the "same person" that held the US trade mark or by a person who was "subject to common ... control" with the US trade mark holder.

11–091

The authorised-use exception under s.133.21(c)(3) was in conflict with the plain language of the statute and could not stand.

(b) The Opinion of Justice Brennan

The Opinion of Justice Brennan followed a more sceptical route, viewing s.526 as providing extraordinary protection to trade mark proprietors. "A United States trademark holder covered by Section 526 can prohibit or condition all importation of merchandise bearing its trademark, thereby gaining a virtual monopoly, free from intrabrand competition, on domestic distribution of any merchandise bearing the trademark."[252]

11–092

---

[251] 486 U.S. 2b 294.
[252] 486 U.S. 281 at 295.

As a result of the long standing policy of the Treasury, expressed with the Regulations, a multi-billion parallel importation industry had emerged. It was against that industry that COPIAT "most of whom are United States trademark holders or affiliates of United States trademark holders that compete against the gray market"[253] have waged a full-scale battle at all the available fora, legislative, executive, and administrative.

Underlining that COPIAT had been unsuccessful in the political branches, Justice Brennan viewed this litigation as an aspect of the battle fought before the courts.[254]

He agreed that case 1 was undisputed.

He also concurred with the stance of the Court regarding the common-control exception but followed a different reasoning from Justice Kennedy However, he disagreed with and dissented from the judgment regarding the authorised-use exception.[255]

11-093 (i) **Part I.** Looking at the language of the provision Justice Brennan noted that the tone of the provision hinted that Congress had not intended to extend s.526 protection to affiliates of foreign manufacturers, in essence the scenarios covered under case 2. He found the flavour of the provision to be protectionist, even jingoist.

A foreign manufacturer would fail because the trade mark would not be "registered in the Patent and Trademark Office"; registration would be unobtainable because it would not be "a person domiciled in the United States"; even if it hired a domiciliary to obtain registration it would not be "organized within... the United States"; even a subsidiary would not provide a solution if the foreign parent remained the owner of the trade mark.

The barriers appeared high, but would be fragile if it were possible to overcome them through a transfer of the trade mark to a local "shell" subsidiary.

This is why it made sense that the Customs Service had exploited the ambiguities of the provision and interpreted it the way it did through the regulations. In all the scenarios under case 2 "it cannot be confidently discerned either which entity owns the trademark or whether the goods in question are 'of foreign manufacture' ".[256]

11-094 In case 2a the ambiguity was the result of the parent and subsidiary relationship, its extent as agreed between the two parties but also its legal recognition and treatment.

---

[253] 486 U.S. 281 at 295; the language is telling. It is COPIAT that competes with the gray market, not the other way round.
[254] Citing as examples *Olympus Corp v United States*, 792 F.2d 315 (2nd Cir. 1986), aff'g 627 F.Supp. 911 (EDNY 1985); *Vivitar-Corp v United States*, 761 F.2d 1552 (CA Fed. 1985), aff'g 593 F.Supp. 420 (Ct.Int'l Trade 1984); and *Lever Brothers Co v United States*, 652 F.Supp. 403 (DC 1987) that had not yet reached the Court of Appeal.
[255] Justice White did not join the dissenting part of the Opinion.
[256] 486 U.S. 281 at 298.

6. PARALLEL IMPORTS

In cases 2b and 2c there was no ambiguity regarding this relationship because the domestic parent would own the trade mark registered in its own name; however, it was unclear whether products manufactured abroad constituted "merchandise of foreign manufacture".

Accordingly, he had to move from the language analysis to the purpose and legislative history of the provision in order to interpret the provision, finding that Congress had intended not to provide s.526 protection to foreign manufacturers.

The main support and context for his finding came from the "the controversial judicial opinion that spawned"[257] s.526: *A Bourjois & Co v Katzel*.[258]

The provision was the hasty Congressional reaction to a judgment of the Court of Appeal; Congress reacted without even waiting for the Supreme Court to consider the case, and eventually reversed the Court of Appeal, because US trade mark holders, many of which had purchased foreign trade marks from unrelated foreign corporations, demanded a legislative response to *Bourjois v Katzel*.

The considerations in *Bourjois v Katzel*, however, were different from those underlying the current case.

Bourjois had purchased the US trade mark rights at arm's length from an independent manufacturer and the importation of genuine Katzel products by third parties undermined the anticipated benefits of the transaction:

"In contrast, a United States trademark holder that acquires identical rights from an affiliate (case 2a) or creates identical rights itself and permits them to be used abroad by an affiliate (cases 2b and 2c) does not have the same sort of investment at stake."[259]

Bourjois had no direct control over the importation of Katzel competing goods or over Katzel's sales to third parties abroad:

"In contrast, if the gray market harms a United States trademark holder in case 2a, 2b, or 2c, that firm and its foreign affiliate (whether a parent, subsidiary, or division) can respond with a panoply of options that are unavailable to the independent purchaser of a foreign trademark. They could, for example, jointly decide in their mutual best interests that the manufacturer (1) should not import directly to any domestic purchaser other than its affiliate; (2) should, if legal, impose a restriction against resale (or against resale in the United States) as a condition on its sales abroad to potential parallel importers; or (3) should curtail sales abroad entirely."[260]

11–095

---

[257] 486 U.S. 281 at 300.
[258] 275 F. 539 (2nd Cir. 1921), rev'd, 260 U.S. 689, 43 S.Ct. 244 (1923).
[259] 486 U.S. 281 at 302.
[260] 486 U.S. 281 at 302.

11–096 Following an exhaustive analysis of the, short, legislative history of the provision he supported that the provision was intended to respond to a very specific situation and should be read in that context. It did not have the sweeping effect supported by COPIAT:

> "In sum, the legislative history and purpose of Section 526 confirm ... that if Congress had any particular intent with respect to the application of Section 526 to trademark owners affiliated with foreign manufacturers, it was to exclude them from its shield. At the very least, that interpretation— which forms the basis of the Customs Service regulation—is reasonable."[261]

The longevity of the substance of what was covered in the regulations was another factor he took into account, finding that for a 50-year period Treasure had been applying the common control exception despite the changes in the form and language of the regulations.

For these reasons he supported that s.133.21(c)(3) (1987) was not inconsistent with the plain language of s.526. The supposition that the domestic firm in a case 3 scenario still "own[s]" its trade mark "bespeaks stolid anachronism not solid analysis. It follows only from an understanding of trademark law that established itself long after the 1922 enactment and 1930 reenactment of Section 526".[262]

Then the law considered a trade mark to function as an indication of the product's physical source or origin.[263] A trade mark was linked with the source of the product in the physical sense. Authorising a third party to use the trade mark could result in a relinquishment of ownership.[264] Similarly, there was very limited evidence that the principle that a trade mark could be assigned for one geographical area but retained for another was recognised.[265]

11–097 The law had been gradually changing until it recognised with the 1946 Lanham Act that a trade mark functioned in different ways, for example as an indicator of product quality, and the exploitation regime had become more permissive.

So, the term "owned by", he suggested had a different meaning for the legislators that adopted s.526. "At the very least, it seems ... plain that Congress did not address case 3 any more clearly than it addressed case 2a, 2b, or 2c."[266]

---

[261] 486 U.S. 281 at 309, citing *INS Cardoza-Fonseca*, 480 U.S. 421 (1987), at 445–449.
[262] 486 U.S. 281 at 312.
[263] Citing as an example *Macmahan Pharmacal Co v Denver Chemical Mfg Co*, 113 F. 468, 475 (8th Cir. 1901).
[264] For example *Everett O Fisk & Co v Fisk Teachers' Agency, Inc*, 3 F.2d 7, (8th Cir. 1924).
[265] For example *Independent Baking Powder Co v Boorman*, 175 F. 448, (CC NJ 1910); and cf. *Scandinavia Belting Co v Asbestos & Rubber Works of America, Inc*, 257 F. 937, (2nd Cir. 1919).
[266] 486 U.S. 281 at 315.

Once the ambiguity had been established, the analysis he employed for the case 2 scenarios led Justice Brennan to conclude that the authorised-use exception should also be upheld as reasonable.

(c) The Opinion of Justice Scalia

11–098 Justice Scalia argued that not only subs.(c)(3) but subs.(c)(1) and (c)(2) of the Regulation were also in conflict with the clear language of s.526.

He accepted that the phrase "owned by" could be ambiguous when applied to domestic subsidiaries of foreign corporations (case 2a). However, he noted this had been irrelevant in the application of the regulation. "In fact ... that has never been asserted to be the theory of the regulation, and is assuredly not its only, or even its principal, effect."[267]

For Justice Scalia in case 2b and case 2c it would be impossible not to conclude that a trademark owned by a US corporation and applied abroad either by the corporation or its foreign subsidiary was "owned by" anyone other than a US corporation.

It was even more difficult for him to understand how the majority of the Court found the concept of merchandise "of foreign manufacture" to be ambiguous. "Foreign" had a number of meanings but in the particular context the phrase "of foreign manufacture" was in common usage and well understood to mean "manufactured abroad". The regulations simply distinguished between goods "of foreign or domestic manufacture".

11–099 He suggested that the application of the regulations with the majority's interpretation could also produce results that would go against s.526(a) in case 1 scenarios:

> "Not uncommonly a foreign trademark owner licenses an American firm to use its trademark in the United States and also licenses one or more other American firms to use the trademark in other countries. In this situation, the firm with the United States license could not keep out gray-market imports manufactured abroad by the other American firms, since, under the majority's interpretation, the goods would not be 'of foreign manufacture'."[268]

The interpretation of the majority, intended to save the regulation, would undermine even the core of the statute.

He then submitted that the majority's "queer"[269] reading was based on the supposed construction adopted by the Customs Service. However, the

---

[267] 486 U.S. 281 at 318.
[268] 486 U.S. 281 at 320. Justice Kennedy had responded to this argument by supporting that the regulation resolved this hypothetical by allowing a company justifiably invoking the protection of the statute to bar the importation of goods of foreign or domestic manufacture. Justice Scalia however could not see how the regulation could bar something that the statute would not.
[269] 486 U.S. 281 at 320.

Government's petition for writ of certiorari had clearly stated that s.526(a) did not deal with goods manufactured by foreigners, but rather with "goods manufactured abroad", "genuine foreign-made goods", "genuine goods manufactured abroad", and "goods produced abroad". "It is a strange sort of deference to agency interpretation which adopts a view of the statute that the agency clearly rejects."[270]

A further problem he identified was that the majority's interpretation could cause problems with the interpretation of commercial treaties. "I doubt, in any case, that our trade partners will look favorably upon a regulation which, as now interpreted, treats goods manufactured by American companies on their soil more favorably than goods manufactured there by their own nationals."[271]

Justice Scalia then attacked the approach of Justice Brennan regarding the case 3 scenarios, in particular his purposive interpretive principle. Courts, according to Justice Scalia should not ignore the statutory language attempting to perpetuate the purpose of the statute. This would go against the democratic principles requiring from legislators to adapt the laws to changing circumstances when they consider it appropriate.

11–100   And his own view of the historical context of development of trade mark law at the time s.526 was adopted differed from the assessment of Justice Brennan Circumstances had not changed in a way that could justify the re-interpretation of s.526. He doubted, for example, whether trade marks could still be assigned apart from their associated goodwill on the one hand, and whether trade mark law did not recognise that unrelated businesses could own and use an identical trade mark in different and distinct regions back then.[272] A trade mark holder doing business in two distinct territories, he asserted was free to assign the business, goodwill, and rights to the trade mark in one of the regions.[273]

He finally scorned the distinctions drawn by Justice Brennan on the basis of the interests that were supposed to be protected in cases like *Bourjois v Katzel*.[274] The US assignee's innocent vulnerability to gray market imports was analogous to that of the US trade mark proprietor who assigned the right to use its trade mark right abroad:

"In sum, while congressional attention to the problem addressed by Section 526(a) may have been prompted by the gray-marketeering represented by A. Bourjois & Co. v. Katzel . . . the language of the statute goes

---

[270] 486 U.S. 281 at 322.
[271] 486 U.S. 281 at 322.
[272] Citing for example *Hanover Star Milling Co v Metcalf*, 240 U.S. 403, 415, 36 S.Ct. 357, 361 (1916).
[273] Citing for example *Scandinavia Belting Co v Asbestos & Rubber Works of America, Inc*, 257 F. 937, 953–956 (2nd Cir. 1919).
[274] *A Bourjois & Co v Katzel*, 260 U.S. 689, 43 S. Ct. 244 (1923).

well beyond that narrow case to cover the same inequity in other contexts. Even if Congress could not have envisioned those other contexts I would find no reasonable basis to disregard what the statute plainly says; but to make the case complete, it surely must have envisioned them."[275]

7. CONCLUSION

This chapter attempted to draw a picture of the most recent case law of the US Supreme Court[276]; the aim is to provide a comparative background for the case law of the Court of Justice.

The Supreme Court faced the same dilemmas with the Court of Justice. Turnarounds regarding the subject matter and scope of protection, balancing exercises between competing interest, considerations about the interface of trade marks with other intellectual property rights on the one hand and competition law on the other, the positioning of a national—but federal—regime within a global market, and the interaction with other areas of law (in the case of Olympic symbols for example) have been troubling the Supreme Court for decades.

Its current stance appears to be sceptical towards the overexpansion of rights. Still, trade mark law is currently at a crossroad. The result of the Supreme Court's jurisprudence on dilution has been the expression of uncertainty from lower courts[277] and a new law amending s.43(c).[278]

The new law attempts to resolve the "likelihood of dilution" problem by providing protection through the new s.43(c)(1) against "use of a mark or trade name in commerce that is likely to cause dilution by blurring or dilution by tarnishment of the famous mark, regardless of the presence or absence of actual or likely confusion, of competition, or of actual economic injury". Note here that the Act provides for a "likelihood of dilution" standard but counterbalances this with the requirement that the diluting use must be use "in commerce".

The starting point is that the mark for which protection is sought must be famous; this appears to require wide recognition: a mark "is famous if it is widely recognized by the general consuming public of the United States as a designation of source of the goods or services of the mark's owner".

11-101

11-102

---

[275] 486 U.S. 281 at 328.
[276] Dinwoodie, "The Trademark Jurisprudence of the Rehnquist Court", 8 Marquette Intellectual Property Law Review 187 (2004), provides an excellent similar analysis.
[277] See for example *Autozone, Inc, et al v Tandy Corp*, 71 U.S.P.Q.2d 1385 (6th Cir. 2004).
[278] The Trade Mark Dilution Revision Act of 2005, in 2006. The text of the Act can be found following a search at *http://firstgovsearch.gov*. It is worth considering three cases that have been brought under the new Act: (i) *Starburcks Corp v Wolfe's Borough Coffee Inc* 477 F.3d 765 (2nd cir. 2007); (ii) *Louis Vuitton v Harte Diggity Dog* 507 F.3d 252 (4th cir. 2007); (iii) *Nike v Nikepal* 2007 WL 2782030 (E.D. Cal. 2007).

On the other hand it narrows down the types of actionable dilution to dilution by blurring, defined as the "association arising from the similarity between a mark or trade name and a famous mark that impairs the distinctiveness of the famous mark" and dilution by tarnishment, defined as the "association arising from the similarity between a mark or trade name and a famous mark that harms the reputation of the famous mark".

The Act takes up one of the tools commonly employed by the Supreme Court and provides multifactor tests for determining fame, blurring, and tarnishment.

In terms of limitations the Act provides that when "trade dress" dilution is claimed for unregistered trade marks the claimant will carry the burden of proving that the trade dress, taken as a whole, is not functional and is famous and if the claimed trade dress includes any mark or marks registered on the principal register, that the unregistered matter, taken as a whole, is famous separate and apart from any fame of such registered marks.

11–103 From the perspective of defenses, and in addition to the "use in commerce" requirement, there is provision for fair use defenses, including use in comparative advertising, parody, criticisms and comments.

Will this satisfy the Supreme Court? We will have to wait for at least a couple of years for an answer. The Supreme Court has the advantage of being able to pick its cases, unlikely the Court of Justice. Right now it appears that it wishes to take a step back.[279]

---

[279] In *Gibson Guitar Corp v Paul Reed Smith Guitars, LP*, 126 S.Ct. 2355 (2006) it refused to consider an appeal against a decision of the 6th Circuit; *Gibson Guitar Corp v Paul Reed Smith Guitars, LP*, 423 F.3d 539 (6th Cir. 2005) involving the trade dress of a guitar and initial interest and post-sale confusion.

Chapter 12

CONCLUSION

The Court of Justice has considered within a relatively short period of time a large number of trade mark cases from two perspectives: as an interpretive court for the purposes of the Directive and a supreme court of appeal under the Regulation. In both contexts it interpreted and applied provisions that were essentially identical. However, under the Regulation the Court also had to be supportive of the new Community Trade Mark right and the institutions administering it. For example, by strengthening the role of the Boards of Appeal[1] the Court could achieve a number of things: make the registration process more efficient, raise the level of dependency on the institutions of OHIM, make the appeal route more difficult, and lessen the burden imposed on the Court of First Instance and the Court of Justice.

12–001

At the same time the Community Trade Mark has been a success. Its "peculiarities" that have been described in Ch.2—the architecture of co-existence, conversion, and seniority—combined with competitive pricing and membership of the Madrid Protocol have made it a very attractive right. The story appears even more successful if one considers the long history of its inception and, as we have seen in Chs 4, 5, and 6 the delicate balancing exercises that aimed at reconciling fundamentally different systems of protection and at satisfying a variety of stakeholders, including existing trade mark owners, new applicants (European and foreign large corporations but also small enterprises), and trade mark lawyers, bureaucracies, and courts with heightened national sensitivities. It should also be reminded that the Community Trade Mark is in essence a federal right in a European Union that shies away from being perceived to be a federation. In many ways it is the closest we can get to a European "national" right, applied by national courts that play the role of Community courts.[2]

Throughout this analysis of the trade mark jurisprudence of the Court of Justice it has become apparent that it, too, has been attempting to perform two balancing exercises: first, between the rights of trade mark proprietors and the interests of competitors and consumers; secondly, between the subject-matter and the extent of protection.

In terms of registrability there is a body of case law that appears to embrace a broader concept of functionality, similar to that applied by the US

---

[1] See for example, *Sergio Rossi SpA v Office for Harmonisation in the Internal Market (Trade Marks and Designs)* [2006] E.C.R. 000, paras 5–106 and following.
[2] See paras 6–141 and following.

CONCLUSION

Supreme Court,[3] in order to accommodate the interests of competitors. Having initially rejected the applicability of general public policy doctrines[4] the Court started looking for the public interest or policy behind each specific provision,[5] sometimes introducing arguments very heavily influenced by the public policy doctrine it had rejected in the first place. Conceptually, there is no inconsistency in that tactic since the Court made it clear that the specific grounds in the registrability provisions had been adopted in response to the same questions that were previously covered by general doctrines; however, the adoption of overbroad policy considerations dilutes the character of each specific provision. For, example the Court had shown that it takes seriously the provisions on three-dimensional signs[6] but lacking the tools to expand their rationale to cover signs that are not three-dimensional it relied on the fundamental question of what constitutes a sign and the distinctiveness and graphical representation requirements.[7] It also had to make assumptions regarding the function of particular types of signs in the marketplace.[8]

In the same area of trade mark law the Court has assimilated the appearance of a product with the appearance of its packaging,[9] following an initially more nuanced distinction based on whether the product had an innate shape or not.[10] This is perhaps a rushed conclusion that could make the registration of packaging more difficult without any obvious justification. Again, a clearer position on functionality would make these issues easier to resolve.

Functionality questions illustrate another issue that will keep on coming before the Court. Chapters 8 and 9 have shown that trade mark law has to some extent internalised competition and free movement of goods questions. In addition there is considerable case law in this field re-establishing the free movement of goods principle and the related case law of the Court as the starting point for the exhaustion cases. From a competition perspective though what will keep on coming back before the Court is the relationship between trade mark and other intellectual property rights and the effect of simultaneous protection; a policy issue that will be difficult for the Court to resolve.[11]

Turning to relative grounds and the scope of protection the Court has consistently required evidence of likelihood of confusion. And the hurdle is high: likelihood of confusion must be genuine and substantiated. It has drawn the essential tests for assessing sign and product similarity and views

---

[3] See paras 11–037 and following.
[4] See paras 4–336 and following.
[5] See for example paras 4–350 and 4–511.
[6] See paras 4–503 and following.
[7] See para.4–013 and following.
[8] See para.4–210; the Supreme Court has made similar assumptions, paras 11–032 and following.
[9] See para.4–311 and following and contrast with paras 11–032 and following.
[10] See para.4–228 and following.
[11] See para 4–506.

CONCLUSION

the two similarity conditions as cumulative. In any case it is clear that there must be some evidence of similarity between the products and between the signs in order to make the overall assessment of confusion.[12]

Where the Court faces some difficulty is dealing with distinct variations of confusion. In *Arsenal*[13] it appeared to include post sale confusion in what it found to be actionable. But then in subsequent case law it chose to review the *Arsenal* judgment and take a step back.[14] The Court's pragmatic approach in delineating the scope of protection taking into account the specific factual context of each case and its wish to counterbalance the expansion of exclusionary rights with the need to keep markets open and competitive are factors that explain its reluctance to embrace doctrinally solid but rigid solutions. Instead the Court so far has opted for a more flexible—but narrower in terms of scope—approach. Its judgments are often embedded against a context that is characterised by the relevant product market, the facts of the case, parallel developments in other areas of law, and the setting of the trade mark within a broader and hierarchical system of rules.

In the future the Court will also have to refine further the types of use that remain outside the scope of protection. The concept of use has served in Ch.4 as a factor that is determinative of trade mark protection: the way a sign is used will dictate the possibility and scope of protection. In Chs 5 and 6 the nature of use by the alleged infringer has determined whether there is a question of infringement in the first place and then, even if the conditions of infringement are satisfied, whether there is a defence that can be raised. So far, the Court has been consistent in requiring use in trade and interpreting the defences from a permissive angle.[15] This will probably be challenged further in relation to the extended protection enjoyed by marks with a reputation with freedom of commercial and political speech arguments being introduced into the debate. Again, the indications from the Court's case law on comparative advertising are that it would be unwilling to expand the scope of trade mark protection. *L'Oreal*[16] appeared to be a signpost indicating a change of direction; still the Opinion of A.G. Maduro in *Google*[17] shows that the discourse has not yet been settled.

A parameter of the above is use of trade marks on the internet. This is another area of law that the Court will have to explore further, taking into account the jurisdictional problems raised by such use.

In terms of style the Court appears to favour multi factor tests. However, these tests are sometimes lost in the narrative of the judgment. This is

---

[12] See paras 5–038 and following.
[13] See para 10–134 and following.
[14] See para 5–094 and following.
[15] See for example chaps 8, 9 and 10.
[16] see 6–056 *L'Oreal* (C-487/07) E.C.R. [2009] 00.
[17] See 6–066 *Google* (C-237/08 and C-238/08) [2009] E.C.R. 0.

indicative of a more intricate problem. The Court has proven to be quite pragmatic and practical in its approach. But the difficulty it faces is that it only views snippets, often distorted, of the cases before the referring courts. And it has a limited jurisdiction over appeals against the judgments of the Court of First Instance. So, often it deals only with an aspect of the case that is sometimes characterised by very particular and specific facts. The wider significance of the judgment of the Court can be lost because the audience focuses on the answer to the specific question or issue under appeal. A solution, proposed to and followed by the Court in a number of cases,[18] is to take a step back, detach itself from the facts of the case, and attempt giving an answer from basic principles. On the other hand, as shown in Ch.6, context is everything in the interpretation and application of trade mark law. Accepting this more explicitly could allow the Court to reconcile what appear to be inconsistencies in its trade mark jurisprudence and give back to national court the jurisdiction to decide how its jurisprudence affects the application of the basic principles established by the Court.

The Court of Justice does not have the luxury of choosing its cases. Re-establishing, restating, and insisting on the basic principles could relieve the burden carried by the Court and contribute to the development of a European trade mark law.

---

[18] See paras X–XXX and following.

INDEX

Absolute grounds for protection
competition issues, 4-643
overview
  devoid of distinctive character, 4-001, 4-005
  distinctiveness, 4-001, 4-005
  registration, 4-002
ECJ jurisprudence, 4-002, 4-643, 4-644
public policy, 4-643
shapes, 4-001
see also **Shapes**
signs, 4-001
see also **Signs**

Abuse of market dominance
abuse of dominant position, 9-004
direct applicability, 9-008
dissimilar conditions, 9-004
dominance (generally)
  abuse of dominant position, 9-094, 9-114, 9-115, 9-121
  crossing market boundaries, 9-085, 9-086
  definition, 9-079
  derivative markets, 9-087
  distinct market, 9-081, 9-083
  intellectual property, 9-088, 9-089
  interchangeable products, 9-081
  market share, 9-082
  relevant product market, 9-080, 9-082, 9-084
dominance (intellectual property)
  abuse of dominant position, 9-094, 9-114, 9-115, 9-121
  abusive conduct, 9-097
  anti-competitive exploitation, 9-093, 9-116
  bundling, 9-103, 9-108
  business interests, 9-117
  consumer welfare, 9-112
  control of distribution, 9-111
  copyright, 9-094, 9-095, 9-103
  customer demand, 9-107
  de facto monopoly, 9-096
  essential facility, 9-099
  exclusivity, 9-088, 9-089
  exercise of rights, 9-094, 9-100
  indispensable product, 9-101, 9-104
  interoperability, 9-103
  positive economic effect, 9-117
  price regulation, 9-111
  refusal of access, 9-098
  refusal to licence, 9-098, 9-100–9-102, 9-106
  refusal to supply, 9-109–9-120
  relevant market, 9-094, 9-099
  separate market, 9-099
  supply of spare parts, 9-090–9-092
economic power, 9-004
limiting production, 9-004
supplementing obligations, 9-004
trade mark law
  effects, 9-126
  function of sign, 9-121–9-124
  trade mark agreements, 9-124, 9-125
unfair trading conditions, 9-004

Acquisition through use
consumer perception, 4-608
date of application/registration, 4-636
distinctive character, 4-587, 4-591, 4-596, 4-597–4-600, 4-606, 4-610, 4-618, 4-625
see also **Distinctive character**
evidence of use, 4-619, 4-620
geographical designation, 4-587, 4-592
geographical extent, 4-622, 4-624
market share, 4-622, 4-623
national trade marks, 4-632–4-634
promotion investment, 4-622
public perception, 4-622
slogans, 4-596, 4-600
three dimensional signs, 4-610, 4-613–4-615
time for acquisition, 4-636

977

INDEX

Adam Opel
Advocate General's Opinion
availability of descriptive signs, 6-139
balance of interests, 6-139
basis, 6-025
distinct product market, 6-139
honest commercial practices, 6-140
indication of type/quality, 6-139
legal context, 6-029–6-032
limitations (trade mark rights), 6-139, 6-140
product market, 6-029, 6-030
uses of sign, 6-026–6-028
background, 6-024
ECJ decision
description by reference to other product, 6-037–6-039
likelihood of confusion, 6-039
prohibited use, 6-034
public perception, 6-034, 6-035
threat to other functions, 6-036
uses of sign, 6-033
identical signs/goods or services
limits of protection, 6-024
scope of protection, 6-024
preliminary ruling, 6-024

Adidas v Fitnessworld
Advocate General's Opinion, 5-202, 5-205
ECJ decision, 5-203, 5-206
reputed marks
similarity between marks, 5-201
use as trade mark, 5-204

Administrative examination system
Boards of Appeal (OHIM), 3-053–3-056, 3-058, 12-001
Community judicature, 3-053
scope of proceedings, 3-058, 3-059

Alcan
acronyms, 4-482
Court of First Instance, 4-483–4-485
customary signs/indications, 4-482
ECJ decision
determining invalidity, 4-489
evidence, 4-488
findings of fact, 4-488
interpretation, 4-486, 4-487
Order of the Court, 4-485

Anheuser-Busch v Budejovický
Advocate General's Opinion
Community law compatibility, 10-140
protection of trade names, 10-142, 10-143
status of trade names, 10-141
trade names as sign, 10-138
TRIPS Agreement, 10-137, 10-138, 10-140, 10-142, 10-143
use as trade mark, 10-139, 10-140
ECJ decision
admissibility, 10-144
trade mark protection, 10-150–10-152
trade marks, 10-146–10-154
trade names as prior rights, 10-153, 10-154
trade names as signs, 10-147–10-149
TRIPS Agreement, 10-144, 10-145
geographical indications
trade mark registration, 10-133
TRIPS Agreement, 10-133
preliminary ruling, 10-135
use of trade names, 10-133, 10-134

Anheuser-Busch v Portugal
cancellation proceedings, 10-156
ECJ decision
balance of interest, 10-164, 10-165
concept of possessions, 10-160, 10-162, 10-163
dissenting opinions, 10-164
legitimate aim, 10-164
legitimate expectation, 10-164
national laws, 10-160
pecuniary interests, 10-163
property right, 10-164
trade mark registration, 10-160, 10-161
European Convention on Human Rights, 10-157
geographical indications
appellations of origin, 10-156
arguments, 10-157–10-159
bilateral agreements, 10-156
registration, 10-156
risk of confusion, 10-157, 10-159
TRIPS Agreement, 10-158
property right, 10-157

Ansul
Advocate General's Opinion
genuine use, 7-013–7-016
interpreting use, 7-010–7-016
legislative framework, 7-009
background, 7-007, 7-008
challenging and maintaining registration

composite marks, 7-007
concept of use, 7-007
ECJ decision
  basis, 7-017
  competence of national court, 7-024
  concept of use, 7-019
  uniform interpretation, 7-018, 7-019
  use of directly related goods/ services, 7-023
  use of integral parts, 7-022
  preliminary ruling, 7-008

Anti-competitive collusion
agreements
  access clauses, 9-045
  agreements between undertakings, 9-004
  anti-competitive agreements, 9-074
  exclusive dealing agreements, 9-014
  exclusive right of sale, 9-035
  existence of agreement, 9-020, 9-021
  gentleman's agreements, 9-016, 9-017
  informal agreements, 9-017
  limiting/controlling production, 9-004
  market sharing, 9-004
  price fixing, 9-004
  prohibited agreements, 9-004, 9-014
  scope/form of agreement, 9-016, 9-017
  sole agency agreements, 9-024–9-026
  tacit agreements, 9-018
  tying agreements, 9-038–9-040, 9-044
  validity, 9-030, 9-047
  vertical agreements, 9-026
  void agreements, 9-004
  web of agreements, 9-038–9-043
assignment of rights, 9-052, 9-053
block exemptions, 9-046, 9-049
  see also **Block exemptions**
boundaries of law, 9-023
burden of proof, 9-019
competing/non-competing entities, 9-026
competitive disadvantage, 9-004
concerted practices, 9-004, 9-022
contextual relevance, 9-037
corporate veil, 9-015

delimitation agreements
  ambiguity, 9-062
  Commission position, 9-064, 9-065
  risk of confusion, 9-063
direct applicability, 9-008
dissimilar conditions, 9-004
distortion of competition, 9-004, 9-029, 9-040
distribution networks, 9-072, 9-075
economic characteristics, 9-054
economic dimension, 9-029
exclusive licence, 9-052, 9-055, 9-056, 9-067–9-071
exemptions
  consumer benefit, 9-004
  economic/technical progress, 9-004
  requirements, 9-033
exercise of rights, 9-052, 9-053
existence of rights, 9-052
franchising agreements
  anti-competitive clauses, 9-061
  benefits, 9-057, 9-058
  essential clauses, 9-060
  specific agreement, 9-059
marketing prohibitions, 9-073
national courts, 9-048–9-051
quality function, 9-034
relevant product market, 9-028, 9-041, 9-043, 9-044
repackaging bans, 9-066
rule of reason analysis, 9-035, 9-038
significant effect, 9-036
supplementing obligations, 9-004
threat to trade, 9-027
trade liberalisation, 9-032
trade mark law, 9-024, 9-025
trade mark registration, 9-031
undertakings, 9-014, 9-015
unilateral conduct, 9-018

Architecture of coexistence
national trade mark rights, 2-010
national trade mark systems, 2-010

Armafoam
Court of First Instance, 5-164
similarity/confusion
  impact on conversion, 5-167, 5-168
  linguistic considerations, 5-164
unitary character of Community trade marks, 5-165, 5-166

Arsenal
Advocate General's Opinion
  concept of use, 6-016, 6-017
  legal context, 6-015

INDEX

trade mark proprietor's interest,
  6-018
ECJ decision
  consumer protection, 6-021
  guarantee of origin, 6-019
  trade mark proprietor's interest,
    6-020
  unauthorised use, 6-019
  use in course of trade, 6-019
identical signs/goods or services
  evidence of confusion, 6-014
  indication of origin, 6-014
  passing off, 6-014
  trade mark infringement, 6-014
  unauthorised products, 6-014
referral back to national court, 6-022,
  6-023
Baby-Dry
Advocate General's Opinion
  ellipsis, 4-366
  grammatical structure, 4-366
  incompleteness, 4-366
  inventiveness, 4-366
  legal context, 4-360–4-362
  procedural aspects, 4-358
  public interest, 4-363
  registration, 4-364, 4-365
  scope of appeal, 4-359
  suggested approach, 4-367
Court of First Instance, 4-356
descriptive signs or indications
  composite words, 4-355
  distinctiveness, 4-355
  linguistic differences, 4-355
  registration process, 4-357
ECJ decision
  admissibility, 4-368
  composite marks, 4-371
  descriptiveness, 4-369, 4-370, 4-372
  lexical inventions, 4-373
  registration, 4-373
  suggested approach, 4-374
  unusual juxtaposition, 4-373
Bad faith
effects, 4-576–4-586
Bainbridge
challenging and maintaining
    registration
  defensive registrations, 7-066, 7-069
  earlier marks, 7-066, 7-067
  'family' of marks, 7-066
ECJ decision
  continuous use, 7-070
  defensive registrations, 7-069

distinctiveness, 7-072, 7-073
'family' of marks, 7-068
simultaneous use/similar marks,
  7-070–7-073
Ballantine
Advocate General's Opinion
  exports to third countries, 8-177
  identification marks, 8-181, 8-185
  identity of origin, 8-174
  legal principles, 8-173, 8-175
  legislative context, 8-176
  market partitioning, 8-181–8-184
  marking obligations, 8-186
  measures having equivalent effect,
    8-173
  product categories, 8-179
  repackaging, 8-172, 8-175, 8-178,
    8-179, 8-183
background, 8-169
ECJ decision, 8-187, 8-188
free movement of goods, 8-169
parallel imports
  defective/counterfeit goods,
    8-171
  identification numbers, 8-169,
    8-171
  intra-Community trade, 8-171
  positive integration, 8-169
  removal/reapplication of trade
    mark, 8-170
  specific subject matter, 8-170
preliminary ruling, 8-171
BAT
anti-competitive collusion, 9-062
delimitation agreements
  ambiguity, 9-062
  risk of confusion, 9-063
Bavaria
Advocate General's Opinion
  legal challenge, 10-092
  protected geographical indication,
    10-093, 10-094
ECJ decision
  agricultural policy, 10-096, 10-097
  basis, 10-095
  generic nature of term, 10-098,
    10-099
  protected geographical indication,
    10-100–10-102
  reputation, 10-100–10-012
  subsidiarity, 10-096
geographical indications, 10-091
protected geographical indication,
  10-091

980

INDEX

Bellure
　Advocate General's Opinion,
　　5-223–5-235, 6-057–6-061
　ECJ decision, 5-236–5-238, 6-062–6-065
　facts in main proceedings, 5-231,
　　5-232
　identical signs/goods or services
　　prohibited use, 6-056
　　scope of protection, 6-056
　　use of signs, 6-056
　reputed marks
　　get-up imitation, 5-239
　　unfair advantage, 5-230, 5-232,
　　　5-239

Benetton
　ECJ decision, 4-516–4-518
　facts of main proceedings,
　　4-513–4-515
　functional shapes
　　aesthetic functionality, 4-512
　　distinctive design, 4-512
　　product shape, 4-512

BioID
　Advocate General's Opinion
　　assessment of sign, 4-138
　　burden of proof, 4-141
　　case law interpretation, 4-135, 4-136
　　consumer perception, 4-136
　　distinctive character, 4-135, 4-136,
　　　4-139
　　overall impression, 4-137, 4-138
　　registrability, 4-143
　　registration of comparable marks,
　　　4-142
　　relevant public, 4-137
　　scope of appeal, 4-134
　　words/figurative elements, 4-140
　background, 4-132
　biometrical identification, 4-132, 4-133
　computer-aided identification, 4-132
　Court of First Instance, 4-133
　distinctive character, 4-132
　ECJ decision
　　burden of proof, 4-146
　　common usage, 4-148
　　distinctive character, 4-149, 4-150
　　overall impression, 4-145, 4-150
　　registrability, 4-149
　　registration of comparable marks,
　　　4-147
　　separate claims, 4-144

Block exemptions
　automatic exemption, 9-003
　generally, 9-001
　market thresholds, 9-003
　research and development, 9-002
　specific products, 9-002
　technology transfer, 9-002
　trade marks, 9-002
　vertical agreements, 9-002

BMW
　Advocate General's Opinion
　　aura of quality, 6-100
　　exhaustion of rights, 6-099
　　legal context, 6-096
　　role of Court, 6-097
　　use in relation to goods,
　　　6-098–6-100
　　use in relation to services,
　　　6-101–6-105
　background, 6-094
　ECJ decision
　　basis, 6-106
　　distinguishing goods/services,
　　　6-109
　　exercise of rights, 6-111–6-115
　　informing the public, 6-109
　　legal effect, 6-107
　　legislative framework, 6-108
　　sale of goods, 6-110
　limitations (trade mark rights), 6-094
　preliminary ruling, 6-095

Boehringer
　Advocate General's Opinion
　　advance notice requirement, 8-161
　　necessity requirement, 8-159, 8-160
　　position of the Court, 8-157
　　repackaging, 8-157, 8-158, 8-160
　ECJ decision
　　advance notice requirement, 8-166,
　　　8-167
　　market access, 8-165
　　necessity requirement, 8-163, 8-164
　　specific subject matter, 8-163
　parallel imports, 8-154
　preliminary ruling, 8-154
　repackaging, 8-154

Boehringer II
　Advocate General's Opinion
　　basis, 8-252
　　burden of proof, 8-265
　　clear identification, 8-268
　　condition of product, 8-267
　　function of the Court, 8-253
　　legal context, 8-254
　　legal principles, 8-256–8-270
　　necessity requirement, 8-259,
　　　8-266

INDEX

notice requirement, 8-263, 8-264, 8-70
overstickering, 8-257, 8-258
previous case law, 8-255
re-boxing, 8-259, 8-260
repackaging, 8-260
reputation, 8-261, 8-262, 8-269
ECJ decision
  burden of proof, 8-25
  necessity requirement, 8-273
  prior notice, 8-276, 8-277
  repackaging, 8-272, 8-273
  reputation, 8-274
parallel imports
  burden of proof, 8-250, 8-251
  necessity requirement, 8-250
  overstickering, 8-251
  re-boxing, 8-251
  repackaging, 8-250
  reputation, 8-251
  specific subject matter, 8-250
preliminary ruling, 8-251

Bravo
Advocate General's Opinion
  distinctive character, 4-475, 4-476
  interpretation, 4-473
  legislative framework, 4-472
  link between sign/goods or services, 4-474–4-477
  registration, 4-478
  strength of association, 4-477
background, 4-471
customary signs/indications
  link with specification, 4-471
  registration, 4-471
ECJ decision
  excluded signs, 4-481
  legislative framework, 4-479
  link with specification, 4-480
preliminary ruling, 4-471

Bristol Myers Squibb
Advocate General's Opinion
  applying the principles, 8-116–8-121
  burden of proof, 8-109, 8-110
  exhaustion of rights, 8-096, 8-098–8-100, 8-107
  free movement rules, 8-096
  original condition of product, 8-097
  relevant issues, 8-111–8-115
  repackaging, 8-096, 8-105, 8-106
  scope of protection, 8-101–8-103
ECJ decision
  advance notice, 8-138
  basis, 8-122

free movement rules, 8-139
importer's rights, 8-134
inappropriate presentation/reputation, 8-137
indication of manufacturer, 8-136
indication of repackaging, 8-135
legal context, 8-123, 8-124
legal interpretation, 8-125–8-130
market partitioning, 8-130, 8-131
original condition of product, 8-132
repackaging, 8-131–8-133, 8-139, 8-140
specific subject matter, 8-139
joined cases
  Danish case referrals, 8-089–8-091
  German case referrals, 8-092–8-094
parallel imports
  repackaging, 8-058, 8-059
  trade mark infringement, 8-089
preliminary ruling, 8-089–8-094

Bronner
abuse of market dominance
  essential facility, 9-099
  refusal of access, 9-098
  refusal to licence, 9-098
relevant market, 9-099
separate market, 9-099

BUD I
Advocate General's Opinion 10-108–10-113
geographical indications
  bilateral agreements, 10-106, 10-107, 10-109, 10-112, 10-113
  earlier registrations, 10-107
  free movement of goods, 10-106
  rights of property, 10-106
  TRIPS Agreement, 10-106
ECJ decision
  admissibility, 10-114
  bilateral agreements, 10-116, 10-117
  consumer protection, 10-117
  direct/indirect identification, 10-11
  geographical indication, 10-115
  geographical names, 10-115
  geographical origin, 10-115
  international agreements, 10-118
  international law, 10-118
human rights concerns, 10-106
national systems of protection, 10-106
preliminary ruling, 10-107
public interest, 10-111
quantitative restriction, 10-110

INDEX

BUD II
  Advocate General's Opinion
    establishing the association, 10-121, 10-122
    exclusivity of Community system, 10-123
    geographical indications, 10-120, 10-122
    judicial politics, 10-120
  ECJ decision
    bilateral agreements, 10-126, 10-127, 10-130
    consumer surveys, 10-128
    effectiveness principle, 10-128
    equivalence principle, 10-128
    geographical designations, 10-130, 10-131
    geographical indications, 10-132
    geographical names, 10-126
    indirect geographical indication, 10-126
    judicial cooperation, 10-125
    national registration procedures, 10-132
    simple/indirect designation, 10-126
    use as designation/trade mark, 10-129
  geographical indications, 10-119
  geographical origin, 10-119
BVBA
  Advocate General's Opinion
    national authorities, 4-442
    product by product approach, 4-443, 4-444
    registration, 4-442
    specification, 4-447–4-449
    time limits, 4-442, 4-445, 4-446
  descriptive signs or indications
    distinctive character, 4-439, 4-440
    inconsistent jurisprudence, 4-440
    specification, 4-439
  ECJ decision
    basis, 4-453
    Community Trade Mark, 4-457, 4-458
    national rules, 4-455
    specific reasoning, 4-454
    time considerations, 4-456
  preliminary ruling, 4-441
Canon
  Advocate General's Opinion, 5-018, 5-035, 5-074–5-076
  background, 5-017

  comparing goods/services, 5-074–5-077
  earlier rights
    association, 5-017
    confusion, 5-017, 5-035
    distinctiveness, 5-017
    global appreciation test, 5-035, 5-036, 5-073, 5-077
    likelihood of confusion, 5-077
    product similarity, 5-017, 5-035
  ECJ decision, 5-019, 5-036, 5-077
Céline
  Advocate General's Opinion, 6-086–6-089
  background, 6-084, 6-085
  ECJ decision
    basis, 6-090
    company names, 6-091, 6-092
    honest practice exception, 6-093
  preliminary ruling, 6-085
  trade names/trade marks
    distinguishing function, 6-084
    signs as trade marks, 6-084
Celtech
  Court of First Instance, 4-465
  descriptive signs or indications
    burden of proof, 4-464
    descriptiveness, 4-464
    distinctiveness, 4-464
    technical/scientific terms, 4-464
  ECJ decision, 4-466–4-467
Centrafarm v American Home Products
  national laws, 8-065
  origin
    guarantee of origin, 8-065
    identity of origin, 8-065
  parallel imports
    exclusive right, 8-065
    specific subject matter, 8-065
Challenging and maintaining registration
  see also **Registration**
  challenges, 7-001
  commercial failure, 7-025
  composite marks, 7-007
  defensive registrations, 7-066, 7-069
  earlier marks, 7-001, 7-051, 7-066, 7-067, 7-075
  ECJ jurisprudence, 7-089
  maintaining registration, 7-001, 7-025
  non-profit making services, 7-052
  product comparison, 7-088
  'proper reasons' defence, 7-062–7-065

relevant market, 7-028
Trade Marks Directive
  grounds for
    invalidity/refusal/revocation,
    7-004, 7-005
  posteriori invalidity, 7-006
  sanctions for non-use, 7-003
  use of trade marks, 7-002
unfair advantage, 7-050
use
  absence of proof, 7-074
  actual use, 7-027
  advertising use, 7-046
  application for revocation, 7-030
  burden of proof, 7-074, 7-082, 7-083,
    7-084
  concept, 7-001, 7-007, 7-019
  continuous use, 7-070
  directly related goods/services,
    7-023
  evidence of use, 7-074, 7-075
  genuine use, 7-013–7-016, 7-020,
    7-021, 7-027–7-029, 7-049–7-052,
    7-054, 7-074, 7-082, 7-083,
    7-086, 7-087
  guarantee of origin, 7-044
  non-profitable activities, 7-031
  non-use, 7-003, 7-025, 7-054
  proof of use, 7-052
  reference market, 7-045
  simultaneous marks/similar use,
    7-070–7-073
  start of use requirement, 7-054
  types of use, 7-027–7-029
  without payment, 7-038
Class International
  Advocate General's Opinion, 8-245
  ECJ decision
    basis, 8-246
    burden of proof, 8-249
    concept of importing, 8-247
    concept of offering, 8-248
    putting goods on the market, 8-248
  parallel imports
    consent, 8-244
    exhaustion of rights, 8-244
    goods in transit, 8-244, 8-245
  preliminary ruling, 8-244
Clinique
  background, 4-543
  deceptive trade marks
    cosmetic products, 4-546, 4-548,
      5-549
    misleading character, 4-543

ECJ decision
  consumer protection, 4-547
  legal context, 4-544, 4-545
  public interest, 4-546
  scope of prohibition, 4-547, 4-548
  unfair competition, 4-547
free movement of goods, 4-543, 4-547
preliminary ruling, 4-543
Codacons
  ECJ decision
    basis, 8-041
    free movement rationale, 8-044
    interrelation of Community
      measures, 8-043
    vertical application, 8-042
  free movement of goods, 8-040
  genetically modified organisms, 8-040
  labelling requirements, 8-040
Colour(s)
  abstract combinations, 4-079, 4-080,
    4-081, 4-083
  clarity/precision, 4-073
  colour combinations, 4-082, 4-189,
    4-190, 4-191
  concept, 4-175
  devoid of distinctive character,
    4-069
  distinctiveness, 4-069, 4-076, 4-080,
    4-174, 4-176, 4-178, 4-181, 4-186,
    4-188, 4-192, 4-197
  external appearance, 4-196, 4-198
  graphical representation, 4-069–4-072,
    4-074–4-078, 4-080
  perception, 4-175, 4-187, 4-198
  registration, 4-008, 4-069, 4-177, 4-182,
    4-184, 4-192, 4-196
  sensation, 4-175
  signs, 4-008
  systematic arrangement, 4-085
  trade marks, 4-070, 4-075, 4-076,
    4-078, 4-180, 4-190
Commission v Ireland
  ECJ decision, 8-046
  free movement of goods, 8-045
  precious metals/hallmarking,
    8-045
Community law
  indirect effect, 3-046
  judicial interpretation, 3-069, 3-070
  judicial protection
    equivalence, 3-027
    formalisation, 3-027
    fundamental rights, 3-052
    selective deference, 3-027

principles
  case law, 3-026
  direct effect, 3-026, 3-028–3-040
  fundamental rights, 3-026
  proportionality, 3-027
  subsidiarity, 3-027
  supremacy doctrine, 3-026, 3-041–3-045

Community Trade Mark
acquisition through use, 2-013
see also **Acquisition through use**
coexistence principle, 2-027, 2-025, 12-001
consumer choice, 2-002
conversion, 2-023, 12-001
definition, 2-011
development
  federal path, 2-001
  harmonisation, 2-001, 2-003
  historical perspective, 2-002, 2-003
  intention, 2-004
  international dimension, 2-003
earlier rights
see also **Earlier rights**
  earlier registration, 2-013
  grounds for refusal/invalidity, 5-002
  identical marks, 5-002
  similar marks, 5-002
enforcement, 6-151
see also **Enforcement**
equal effect, 2-011
free movement of goods, 2-014
see also **Free movement of goods**
generally, 1-001
genuine use, 2-014
indivisible entity, 2-011
invalidation proceedings, 2-014, 7-074
judicial review
see **Judicial review**
legislative framework, 2-027
licensing, 2-011
opposition proceedings, 2-013
procedural matters
  applications for registration, 2-015
  court proceedings, 2-020
  enforcement, 2-020
  EU enlargement, 2-021, 2-022
  examination procedure, 2-018, 2-019, 2-020
  expansion, 2-021, 2-022
  jurisdiction, 2-020
  language rules, 2-015, 2-016, 2-017
refusal of registration, 2-012

registration, 2-011, 2-012
see also **Challenging and maintaining registration; Registration**
revocation, 2-011, 7-074
seniority, 2-024
success, 12-001
sufficient use, 2-014
surrender, 2-011
third party use, 2-014
transfer, 2-011
unitary right, 2-011
working language, 2-003

Community Trade Mark Regulation
architecture of coexistence
  national trade mark rights, 2-010
  national trade mark systems, 2-010
earlier rights
  identical marks, 5-003
  relative grounds of refusal, 5-003
  similar marks, 5-003
scope of protection, 2-009
  exclusive rights, 6-004
  generally, 2-009
  limitations, 6-007
  prohibited use, 6-004–6-006
  reproduction in dictionaries, 6-005
  rights conferred, 6-004
  use in course of trade, 6-007
unitary right, 2-009

Companyline
Advocate General's Opinion
  descriptiveness, 4-111
  distinctive character, 4-108
  grounds of appeal, 4-112
  judicial function, 4-107
  OHIM practice, 4-113
  perceptible differences, 4-108
  public interest considerations, 4-105
  registrability, 4-109, 4-110
  structure of signs, 4-105
composite marks, 4-103, 4-105, 4-106
Court of First Instance, 4-104
descriptiveness, 4-103, 4-111
distinctive character, 4-103
ECJ decision
  appraisal of facts, 4-114
  distinctiveness, 4-115, 4-116
  inadmissibility, 4-114
  new pleas, 4-114

Comparative advertisements
acronyms, 10-043
advertising statements, 10-005, 10-006

benefits, 10-045–10-047
channels of trade, 10-030, 10-037
comparative advertising rules,
　10-001, 10-007, 10-017–10-020,
　10-025, 10-040, 10-054, 10-053,
　10-059, 10-065–10-071
competitive relationship, 10-052,
　10-056
concept of use, 10-059
consumer benefit, 10-046
designations of origin, 10-054, 10-058
distinguishing marks, 10-012, 10-021,
　10-024
ECJ jurisprudence, 10-166, 12-003
equivalent technical features, 10-041
geographical indications, 10-054
imitations/replicas, 10-065
indicating names of manufacturers,
　10-027, 10-036
indirectly comparative, 10-002
indispensability requirement, 10-059,
　10-061
interplay with trade marks, 10-005
legislative provisions, 10-002–10-004
Member States' position, 10-002
misleading advertising, 10-025,
　10-049, 10-059
misuse of reputation, 10-011–10-015
national standards, 10-028, 10-029
necessity factors, 10-015
non-competing referential
　advertising, 10-002
objective comparisons, 10-008, 10-009
price differentials, 10-025, 10-032,
　10-039
reference to type of product, 10-051,
　10-055
relevant public, 10-042
similar packaging, 10-065
test purchases, 10-031, 10-038
unfair advantage, 10-013, 10-040,
　10-041, 10-065
unfair competition, 10-005
use of similar sign, 10-059, 10-064
use of trade mark, 10-065, 10-067
Comparing goods/services
　see also **Confusion; Earlier rights**
　consumer perception, 5-081, 5-083
　distinctive character, 5-079, 5-085,
　　5-086
　economic significance, 5-081
　generally, 5-074–5-077
　global assessment, 5-077
　likelihood of confusion, 5-077, 5-078

timing of assessment, 5-078, 5-088,
　5-089
Competition law
　abuse of market dominance, 9-001
　see also **Abuse of market
　　dominance**
　anti-competitive collusion, 9-001,
　　9-134
　see also **Anti-competitive
　　collusion**
　block exemptions, 9-001
　see also **Block exemptions**
　competition rules
　　cooperation, 9-003
　　implementation, 9-003
　ECJ jurisprudence, 9-134
　generally, 9-001
　know-how, 9-001
　patents, 9-001
　scope of provisions
　　Commission's role, 9-009–9-013
　　competition policy, 9-006
　　conflicting competences. 9-008
　　consumer benefit, 9-005
　　corporate efficiency, 9-007
　　direct applicability, 9-008
　　division of powers, 9-011
　　integration, 9-007
　　inter-State trade, 9-006
　　monopoly control, 9-005
　　sincere cooperation principle,
　　　9-012, 9-103
　　Single Market objective, 9-005,
　　　9-006
　Technology Transfer Regulation,
　　9-001
Composite marks
　descriptiveness, 4-103, 4-111
　devoid of distinctive character, 4-103,
　　4-105, 4-106
　distinctiveness, 4-115, 4-116
Conflict
　see **Trade names/trade marks
　　(conflict)**
Confusion
　see also **Comparing
　　goods/services; Earlier
　　rights; Similarity/confusion**
　abstract figures, 5-011
　alternative concepts, 5-011
　average consumer, 5-030, 5-249
　composite trade mark, 5-011
　concept, 5-017, 5-020, 5-023, 5-248
　distinctiveness, 5-248

ECJ jurisprudence, 12-003
factual context, 12-003
geographical names, 4-337
global assessment test, 5-007, 5-009,
    5-032, 5-034, 5-035, 5-036, 5-073,
    5-046, 5-047
likelihood of confusion, 4-337, 5-001,
    5-009, 5-010, 5-011, 5-013, 5-020,
    5-030, 5-032, 5-035, 5-039, 5-041,
    5-042, 5-052, 5-066, 5-248, 12-003
pictorial trade mark, 5-011
post sale confusion, 5-094, 5-101,
    5-104, 5-105, 12-003
presumption of confusion, 5-247
reputation, 5-248
reputed marks, 5-249
    see also **Reputed marks**
risk of confusion, 5-013, 5-033, 5-071
substantive/genuine confusion,
    5-020, 5-247
surnames, 5-106
tests for confusion, 5-031–5-033,
    5-248
timing of assessment, 5-078
total identity, 5-247

Consent
concept, 8-058
consent/independent rights, 8-061
consent/subject matter link, 8-058,
    8-067
restrictive approach, 8-059

Consten v Grundig
anti-competitive collusion
    exemption requirements, 9-033
    relevant product market, 9-028
    sole agency agreements, 9-024,
        9-025
    threat to trade, 9-027
    validity of agreement, 9-030
    vertical agreements, 9-026
background, 9-024
distortion of competition, 9-029
quality function, 9-034
trade liberalisation, 9-032
trade mark registration, 9-031

Continental Can
abuse of market dominance, 9-081
distinct market, 9-081
interchangeable products, 9-081
market share, 9-082
relevant market, 9-082

Cotonelle
background, 4-554
deceptive trade marks

deceptive use, 4-554
unfair competition, 4-554
ECJ decision
    quantitative restriction, 4-556
    scope of provision, 4-556, 4-557
    unfair competition, 4-556, 4-558
free movement of goods, 4-554
preliminary ruling, 4-555
territorial nature of trade marks,
    4-555

Court of First Instance
appeals, 3-022
composition, 3-024
creation, 3-022
direct actions, 3-022
jurisdiction, 3-022
jurisprudence, 1-001
procedural rules, 3-025
role, 3-022
status, 3-022

Customary signs and indications
acronyms, 4-482
consumer perception, 4-490
distinctive character, 4-497, 4-498
distinctiveness, 4-490, 4-494–4-497
excluded signs, 4-481
'in the trade' concept, 4-493, 4-497
indication of origin, 4-494
language considerations, 4-495
link(s)
    sign/goods or services, 4-474–4-477
    specification, 4-471, 4-480
registration, 4-471

Dastar
copyright protection, 11-053, 11-054
reverse passing off, 11-054
Supreme Court decision
    conflict with previous cases,
        11-059
    consumer psychology, 11-057
    judicial reasoning, 11-057–11-059
    legislative context, 11-056
    legislative scope, 11-058
    main issue, 11-055
trade mark protection, 11-053

Davidoff III
Advocate General's Opinion
    consent issues, 8-228–8-233
    damage to reputation, 8-234
    legal context, 8-227
    removal of batch codes, 8-225
enforcement
    Community Trade Mark, 6-151
    seizure of goods, 6-151

ECJ decision,
  basis, 6-153, 6-154, 8-235
  burden of proof, 8-238
  concept of consent, 8-236
  implied consent, 8-238
  requirement for consent, 8-237–8-239
facts of main proceedings, 6-152
parallel imports
  clear consent, 8-225
  implicit consent, 8-225
  policing trade channels, 8-225
  removal of batch codes, 8-225
preliminary ruling, 6-152, 8-226

Davidoff v Gofkid
Advocate General's Opinion
  contradictory meaning, 5-193
  literal interpretation, 5-194
  protection gap, 5-194
  reputed marks, 5-192, 5-193
ECJ decision, 5-196
reputed marks
  identical/similar goods or services, 5-191
  likelihood of confusion, 5-191
  well-known marks, 5-191

Deceptive trade marks
advertising messages, 4-550
assignment of trade mark, 4-519, 4-520
consumer protection, 4-533, 4-547
cosmetic products, 4-546, 4-548, 4-549
deception
  deceptive effect, 4-520
  deceptive use, 4-523, 4-524, -528, 4-529, 4-554
  determining deception, 4-525
  effect on trade, 4-539
  product presentation, 4-550, 4-551
  free movement of goods, 4-536, 4-541, 4-542, 4-453, 4-551, 4-554
misleading character, 4-543
personal names, 4-529
proportionality, 4-540
public interest, 4-533, 4-546
public perception, 4-520, 4-534, 4-535
purchasing behaviour, 4-520
quantitative restriction, 4-537
unfair competition, 4-519, 4-541, 4-547, 4-550, 4-554, 4-556, 4-558
use of symbol, 4-537, 4-540

DeLandtsheer Emmanuel
Advocate General's Opinion
  comparative advertising, 10-053, 10-054

competitive relationship, 10-052
designation of origin, 10-054
geographical indications, 10-054
interpretative issue, 10-050
reference to product type, 10-051
scope of legislation, 10-053
comparative advertising
  misleading advertising, 10-049
  production method, 10-049
ECJ decision
  competitive relationship, 10-056
  designation of origin, 10-058
  reference to product type, 10-055
  scope of legislation, 10-057
preliminary ruling, 10-049

Delimitis
anti-competitive collusion
  access clauses, 9-045
  distortion of competition, 9-040
  relevant market, 9-041, 9-043, 9-044
  tying agreements, 9-038–9-040, 9-042
  validity of agreement, 9-047
  web of agreements, 9-038–9-043
block exemptions, 9-046, 9-049
national courts, 9-048–9-051

Der Grűne Punkt
abuse of market dominance
  abuse of dominant position, 9-121
  function of sign, 9-121
  packaging/exemption system, 9-121, 9-122
Advocate General's Opinion
  basis, 9-123
  competition issues, 9-127
  legal effect, 9-126
  reasonable time, 9-128
  trade mark agreements, 9-124
ECJ decision
  basis, 9-129
  exclusive use, 9-130
  competition issues, 9-131
  procedural irregularities, 9-132
  proportionality, 9-132
  reasonable time, 9-132, 9-133

Descriptive signs or indications
burden of proof, 4-464, 4-468
composite marks, 4-355, 4-371, 4-375, 4-419, 4-420, 4-421, 4-432
consumer goods, 4-468
descriptiveness, 4-336, 4-369, 4-370, 4-372, 4-377, 4-380–4-387, 4-394, 4-400–4-403, 4-421, 4-432, 4-464, 4-468

devoid of distinctive character, 4-429, 4-468
distinctive character, 4-336, 4-355, 4-394, 4-421, 4-439, 4-440, 4-464, 4-470
  free movement issues, 4-459
  geographical indication, 4-339, 4-354
  geographical names, 4-336
  geographical origin, 4-353, 4-351
  grammatical structure, 4-366
  incompleteness, 4-366
  inventiveness, 4-366, 4-429
  likelihood of confusion, 4-337
  linguistic differences, 4-355
  marketing practices, 4-470
  multi-factor test, 4-380–4-387, 4-390
  national rules, 4-455
  need to leave free, 4-337, 4-338, 4-345, 4-423
  public interest, 4-350–4-352, 4-363, 4-414
  registration, 4-364, 4-365, 4-373, 4-389, 4-393, 4-397–4-399, 4-008–4-411, 4-414, 4-442, 4-450 – 4-452
  relevant public, 4-424
  specification, 4-425–4-427, 4-439, 4-447–4-449
  technical/scientific terms, 4-464
  three dimensional signs, 4-468
  time limits, 4-442, 4-445, 4-446, 4-456
  unusual juxtaposition, 4-373

Designs
  abstract designs, 4-241
  distinctive character, 4-241

Develey
  Court of First Instance, 4-469
  descriptive signs or indications
    burden of proof, 4-468
    consumer goods, 4-468
    descriptiveness, 4-468
    devoid of distinctive character, 4-468
    distinctive character, 4-470
    marketing practices, 4-470
    three dimensional signs, 4-468
  ECJ decision, 4-469

Devoid of distinctive character
  abstract designs, 4-241
  aesthetic functionality, 4-241, 4-242
  burden of proof, 4-141, 4-146
  colours, 4-068, 4-174
  common usage, 4-148
  composite marks, 4-103, 4-105, 4-106

computer-aided identification, 4-132, 4-133
consumer perception, 4-136
descriptive signs or indications, 4-429, 4-468
  see also **Descriptive signs or indications**
descriptiveness, 4-103, 4-111
distinctive character
  abstract designs, 4-241
  biometrical identification, 4-132, 4-135, 4-136, 4-139, 4-149, 4-150
  composite marks, 4-103, 4-108, 4-115, 4-116
  products of different origins, 4-118, 4-119, 4-122, 4-123, 4-127–4-129
  slogans, 4-164, 4-172
  surnames, 4-154, 4-155, 4-156
overall impression, 4-137, 4-138, 4-145, 4-150
packaging of goods, 4-228
permissive perspective, 4-120, 4-121
products of different origins, 4-119
public interest, 4-105, 4-129
registration, 4-109, 4-110, 4-124, 4-130, 4-131, 4-148, 4-149
registration of comparable marks, 4-147
relevant public, 4-1264-137
shapes, 4-199, 4-215, 4-228
signs, 4-003, 4-007, 4-014, 4-014
slogans, 4-160, 4-164, 4-172
surnames, 4-151, 4-154, 4-155, 4-156

Dior
  Advocate General's Opinion
    admissibility, 8-192
    advertising, 8-193–8-195
    condition of goods, 8-195
    copyright considerations, 8-201
    exceptions to general principles, 8-195
    exhaustion of rights, 8-193
    function of trade mark, 8-196, 8-197
    legal context, 8-191
    procedural issues, 8-192
    repackaging, 8-195
    reputation, 8-196–8-200
    reselling, 8-194
    risk of significant damage, 8-198–8-200
  ECJ decision
    admissibility, 8-202
    advertising, 8-203
    copyright considerations, 8-205

exceptions to general rule, 8-204
exhaustion of rights, 8-203
parallel imports
  advertising materials, 8-189
  condition of goods, 8-189
  free movement provisions, 8-189
  packaging, 8-189
  preliminary ruling, 8-190
Direct effect
Decisions, 3-040
Directives, 3-033–3-039
discretionary restrictions, 3-034, 3-035
estoppel, 3-035
generally, 3-028
horizontal direct effect, 3-037, 3-038
incidental horizontal effect, 3-039
public policy considerations, 3-034
Regulations, 3-032
treaties, 3-029–3-031
vertical effect, 3-034, 3-037
Directives
direct effect, 3-033–3-039
horizontal direct effect, 3-037, 3-038
incidental horizontal effect, 3-039
vertical direct effect, 3-034, 3-037
Distinctive character
see also **Devoid of distinctive character**
absolute grounds for protection, 4-001
abstract designs, 4-241
acquired by use, 4-587, 4-591, 4-596, 4-597–4-600, 4-606, 4-610, 4-618, 4-625
biometrical identification, 4-132, 4-135, 4-136, 4-139, 4-149, 4-150
composite marks, 4-103, 4-108, 4-115, 4-116
customary signs/indications, 4-497, 4-498
functional shapes, 4-508, 4-512
products of different origins, 4-118, 4-119, 4-122, 4-123, 4-127–4-129
slogans, 4-164, 4-172
surnames, 4-154, 4-155, 4-156
Distinctiveness
see also **Devoid of distinctive character**
absolute grounds for protection, 4-001, 4-005
capability of distinguishing
  arbitrary/capricious additions, 4-089, 4-094

continuum of distinctiveness, 4-093, 4-099
devoid of distinctive character, 4-086, 4-099
functionality, 4-086, 4-087, 4-089
three dimensional signs, 4-086, 4-094
requirement, 4-086–4-089, 4-095, 4-096
colour, 4-069, 4-076, 4-080, 4-096
customary signs/indications, 4-490, 4-496
descriptive signs or indications, 4-355
functional shapes, 4-501, 4-512
public interest considerations, 4-097
signs, 4-013, 4-017, 4-028, 12-002
Dominance
see **Abuse of market dominance**
Doublemint
Advocate General's Opinion
  descriptiveness, 4-377, 4-380–4-387
  keeping free for others to use, 4-388
  meaning of exclusivity, 4-378
  multiplicity of meanings, 4-379
  multi-factor test, 4-380–4-387
  registration (other jurisdictions), 4-389
Court of First Instance, 4-376
descriptive signs or indications
  composite words, 4-375
  descriptiveness, 4-377, 4-380–4-387
  exclusivity, 4-378
ECJ decision
  future/potential use, 4-392
  multi-factor test, 4-390
  registration, 4-393
  restatement of principles, 4-391
Duties and taxes
see also **Free movement of goods**
charges having equivalent effect, 8-003, 8-006
comparisons
  beer/wine, 8-009
  types of fruit, 8-010
  whisky/liqueurs, 8-010
competition/substitution, 8-008, 8-009
ECJ jurisprudence, 8-006
product similarity, 8-007–8-009
prohibition of new duties/charges, 8-006
Dyson
Advocate General's Opinion
  competition issues, 4-026

INDEX

distinctive character, 4-017, 4-020–4-022
distinguishing function (signs), 4-017
functionality, 4-019, 4-021–4-024, 4-027
fundamental requirements (signs), 4-016
graphical representation, 4-018
intellectual property rights, 4-025, 4-026
registration, 4-025
technical innovation, 4-024, 4-026
transfer of technology, 4-024
unfair advantage, 4-016
ECJ decision
definition of trade mark, 4-028
distinctiveness, 4-028
non-specific subject matter, 4-029
requirement for signs, 4-029, 4-030
unfair advantage, 4-029
legal background, 4-013
signs
colour, 4-008
context, 4-008, 4-009
devoid of distinctive character, 4-003, 4-007, 4-014
distinctiveness, 4-013, 4-017
functionality, 4-013
fundamental requirement, 4-006, 4-007, 4-013
graphical representation, 4-003, 4-006, 4-008, 4-010, 4-013
mere concept, 4-006
non-visual signs, 4-012
registration, 4-014
signs in the abstract, 4-009
undistinguishable, 4-007, 4-008, 4-010

Earlier rights
association
concept, 5-013, 5-017
likelihood of association, 5-001, 5-012, 5-014, 5-015
non-origin association, 5-013, 5-014
Community Trade Mark Regulation
identical marks, 5-003
relative grounds of refusal, 5-003
similar marks, 5-003
comparing goods/services
see **Comparing goods/services**
comparing the marks, 5-042, 5-043
composite marks, 5-008
conflict resolution, 5-001
confusion
see **Confusion**
global assessment test, 5-007, 5-009, 5-032, 5-034, 5-035, 5-036, 5-073, 5-046, 5-047
identical marks, 5-001, 5-004, 5-005
identity between marks, 5-001, 5-004
identity of origin, 5-009
national rights, 5-001
participation rules, 5-001
reputation, 5-001
similar marks, 5-001
similarity
aural similarity, 5-045
cumulative similarity, 5-038, 12-003
goods/services, 5-010
phonetic similarity, 5-039, 5-069
signs, 5-010
Trade Marks Directive
grounds for refusal/invalidity, 5-002
identical marks, 5-002
similar marks, 5-002
unfair advantage, 5-001

Elizabeth Emanuel
Advocate General's Opinion
admissibility, 4-521
commercialisation of trade names, 4-522
deceptive use, 4-523, 4-524, -528, 4-529
determining deception, 4-525
interpretation, 4-526, 4-527, 4-530
personal names, 4-529
Appointed Person, 4-520
assignment of trade mark, 4-519, 4-520
background, 4-519
deceptive trade marks
deceptive effect, 4-520
public perception, 4-520
purchasing behaviour, 4-520
unfair competition, 4-519
ECJ decision
consumer perception, 4-534, 4-535
consumer protection, 4-533
interpretation, 4-532
procedural issues, 4-531
public interest, 4-533

Enforcement
adequate enforcement, 6-141
Community Trade Mark, 6-151
continuing infringement, 6-141, 6-142

national laws, 6-147–6-150
procedural issues, 2-020
seizure of goods, 6-151
'special reasons' condition, 6-144–6-147
Erpo
  Advocate General's Opinion
    burden of proof, 4-167
    distinctive character, 4-164, 4-166
    distinctiveness, 4-164
    interpretative criteria, 4-163
    legal context, 4-163
    registration of slogans, 4-165–4-168
  Court of First Instance, 4-161
  ECJ decision
    distinctiveness, 4-172
    error of law, 4-173
    function of slogans, 4-170, 4-171
    registration of slogans, 4-169, 4-171
  slogans
    distinctive character, 4-164, 4-166
    function, 4-170, 4-171
    registration, 4-160, 4-165–4-169, 4-171
Eurocermex
  background, 4-301, 4-302
  Court of First Instance, 4-303–4-305
  ECJ decision
    overall impression, 4-307, 4-308
    parameters for appeal, 4-309, 4-310
  product concept, 4-301
  three dimensional shapes, 4-301
European Convention on Human Rights
  civil/political rights, 10-155
  collective enforcement, 10-155
  legitimate aim, 10-164
  legitimate expectation, 10-164
  right of property, 10-157, 10-158, 10-164
  scope of protection, 10-155
European Court of Human Rights
  balance of interests, 10-164, 10-165
  establishment, 10-155
  opinions, 10-164
European Court of Justice
  see also **Forms of action**
  acte claire doctrine, 3-047
  Advocate Generals' Opinions, 3-015
  appeals, 1-001, 3-008, 3-062, 3-063, 12-001
  Community law principles
    case law, 3-026
    direct effect, 3-026, 3-028–3-040
    fundamental rights, 3-026, 3-050–3-052
    indirect effect, 3-046
    interpretation, 3-069, 3-070
    proportionality, 3-027
    subsidiarity, 3-027
    supremacy principle, 3-026, 3-041–3-045
    validity of Community acts, 3-048
  competence, 3-026, 3-047, 3-048
  composition, 3-013
  constitutionalisation process, 3-026
  costs, 3-017
  direct actions, 3-014–3-017
  expedited procedure, 3-021
  interlocutory proceedings, 3-020
  interpretative function, 12-001
  judicial activism, 3-003
  judicial process, 3-014–3-017
  judicial protection
    equivalence, 3-027
    formalisation, 3-027
    fundamental rights, 3-052
    selective deference, 3-027
  judicial review, 3-055–3-058, 3-062–3-063
  jurisdiction, 3-003, 3-048
  jurisprudence
    anti-competitive measures, 2-001
    comparative advertisements, 12-003
    confusion, 12-003
    functionality, 12-002
    generally, 1-001, 3-012, 3-026, 3-069, 12-001, 12-002
    scope of protection, 12-003
  majority decisions, 3-017
  multi-factor tests, 4-380–4-387, 4-594, 4-595, 12-004
  referrals
    essence of legal questions, 3-049
    increase, 1-001
    interpretation, 1-001
    notice of action, 3-014
    preliminary rulings, 3-003, 3-009–3-012, 3-018, 3-019, 3-048
    unwieldy questions, 3-049
  reports, 3-014
  role, 3-001, 3-002, 12-001
  substantive rulings, 3-017
European institutions
  Council, 3-001
  Court of Auditors, 3-001
  European Commission, 3-001

European Court of Justice, 3-001
European Parliament, 3-001
failure to act, 3-005
Europolis
  acquisition through use, 4-625
  Advocate General's Opinion
    legal context, 4-627–4-630
    national trade marks, 4-632–4-634
    territorial scope of assessment, 4-631
  ECJ decision, 4-635
  preliminary ruling, 4-626
Exhaustion of rights
  competition policy, 8-214
  domestic, 8-049
  intellectual property rights, 8-067
  international, 8-049, 8-206–8-212, 8-218
  national legal order, 8-216, 8-217, 8-219
  parallel imports, 8-096, 8-098–8-100, 8-107, 8-193, 8-203, 8-240, 8-242, 8-244, 8-280, 8-281, 8-286
  see also **Parallel imports**
  territorial exhaustion, 8-206–8-212, 8-222–8-224
Exhaustion of rights (USA)
  general rule, 11-089, 11-098
  Paris Convention, 11-091
  territoriality doctrine, 11-089, 11-090
  universality doctrine, 11-089, 11-090
Feta
  Advocate General's Opinion
    consumer perception, 10-079
    context of use, 10-080
    etymology, 10-083
    geographical coverage, 10-083–10-085
    geographical names, 10-078
    protecting the designation, 10-079
  ECJ decision
    generic nature, 10-087–10-089
    procedural issues, 10-082
    product characteristics, 10-086
    statement of reasons, 10-090
  geographical indications
    consumer confusion, 10-072, 10-076
    designations of origin, 10-072
    misappropriation, 10-072
    protection, 10-073–10-077
Fincas Tarragona
  Advocate General's Opinion, 5-177
  ECJ decision, 5-178, 5-179
  facts in main proceedings, 5-175, 5-176
  reputed marks, 5-173, 5-174

Fitnessworld
  Advocate General's Opinion, 5-198, 5-199
  ECJ decision, 5-200
  reputed marks
    identical /similar goods or services, 5-197
    likelihood of confusion, 5-197
    similarity between marks, 5-197, 5-201
    usage as embellishment, 5-197
Flexi Air
  background, 5-066
  Court of First Instance, 5-067–5-069
  earlier rights
    likelihood of confusion, 5-066
    multifactor assessment, 5-066
  ECJ decision
    degree of distinctiveness, 5-071
    distinctive character, 5-071
    inadmissibility, 5-073
    likelihood of confusion, 5-072
    reasoned order, 5-070–5-072
    risk of confusion, 5-071
Forms of action
  actions against Community institutions, 3-005
  actions against Member States, 3-004
  annulment actions, 3-006, 3-007
  appeals, 3-008
  preliminary rulings, 3-009–3-012, 3.018, 3-048
Franchising agreements
  anti-competitive clauses, 9-061
  benefits, 9-057, 9-058
  essential clauses, 9-060
  specific agreement, 9-059
Free movement of goods
  consent concept, 8-058, 8-059, 8-061, 8-067
  distortion of competition, 8-001
  duties and taxes
  see **Duties and taxes**
  ECJ jurisprudence, 8-286
  economic purpose, 8-001
  equality proviso, 8-028, 8-029
  exclusive right, 8-060, 8-065
  fundamental principle, 8-01, 8-006
  genetically modified organisms, 8-040
  import restrictions, 8-001
  intellectual property rights
  see **Intellectual property rights**
  labelling requirements, 8-040
  legislative framework

charge having equivalent effect, 8-003
customs duties, 8-003
duties and charges, 8-002, 8-003
exemptions, 8-005
quantitative import/export restrictions, 8-002, 8-004
national laws, 8-057, 8-065
necessity requirement, 8-145
origin
  common origin, 8-060, 8-067
  concept, 8-018–8-021
  discrimination based on origin, 8-016, 8-017
  guarantee, 8-065
  indication of origin, 8-018, 8-056, 8-060, 8-065
policy issues, 8-286
public policy considerations
  derogations, 8-030
  domestic product market, 8-032
  protection of health/human life, 8-036–8-039
  public morality, 8-031
  public policy, 8-033, 8-034
  public security, 8-035
quantitative restrictions
  see **Quantitative restrictions**
replacing trade marks, 8-144, 8-145, 8-153
Single Market objectives, 8-001
socio-political purpose, 8-001
specific subject matter, 8-059, 8-065, 8-067
trade mark law
  compulsory licences, 8-063, 8-064
  essential function, 8-056
  exclusive right, 8-056
  identity of origin, 8-056
  lack of protection, 8-062
  national provisions, 8-057
  subject matter/trade marks, 8-056

Functional shapes
alternatives, 4-504–4-506, 4-511
distinctive character, 4-508
distinctiveness, 4-501, 4-512
functionality, 4-501, 4-505, 4-507, 4-512
product shape, 4-512
public interest, 4-509
technical features, 4-502
technical result, 4-501

Functionality
acquisition through use, 4-086, 4-088, 4-505, 4-507
distinctive character, 4-019, 4-021–4-024, 4-027
distinctiveness, 4-086, 4-087, 4-089
registration, 12-002
shapes, 4-501, 4-505, 4-507, 4-512
  see also **Functional shapes**
signs, 4-013, 4-019, 4-021–4-024, 4-027, 4-086

Functionality (USA)
aesthetic functionality, 11-044
de jure functionality, 11-042
defence, 11-041
ground for refusal, 11-040
legislation, 11-040
public policy, 11-040
utilitarian functionality, 11-043

Fundamental rights
Community measures, 3-051, 3-052
ECJ jurisprudence, 3-050–3-052
equal treatment, 3-052, 3-056, 3-066
human rights protection, 3-051
international treaties, 3-052
judicial deference, 3-050
judicial protection, 3-052
legal certainty, 3-052
legitimate expectations, 3-052, 3-065
proportionality, 3-052, 3-069
rights of defence, 3-052
Treaty of the European Union, 3-050

General Motors
Advocate General's Opinion, 5-170
assessing reputation, 5-1269
ECJ decision, 5-171, 5-172
reputed marks, 5-169

Geographical indications
see also **Geographical names**
bilateral agreements, 10-106, 10-107, 10-109, 10-112, 10-113, 10-116, 10-117, 10-126, 10-127, 10-130, 10-156
consumers
  confusion, 10-072, 10-076
  perception, 10-079
  protection, 10-117
  surveys, 10-128
denomination of origin, 10-103
designations of origin, 10-054, 10-058, 10-072, 10-130, 10-131
direct/indirect identification, 10-117, 10-126
earlier registrations, 10-107
ECJ jurisprudence, 10-166
effectiveness principle, 10-128
equivalence principle, 10-128

free movement of goods, 10-106
generic names, 10-103–10-105
genericity concept, 10-103
geographical coverage, 10-083–10-085
geographical names, 4-339, 4-354
geographical origin, 4-351, 4-353, 10-115, 10-119
historical context, 10-105
human rights concerns, 10-106, 10-155, 10-157, 10-164, 10-165
indications of origin, 4-279, 10-001, 10-078
international agreements, 10-118
international law, 10-118
misappropriation, 10-072
national systems, 10-106, 10-132, 10-160
property rights, 10-106, 10-157, 10-164
protection (generally), 10-073–10-077, 10-079
public interest, 10-111
quantitative restriction, 10-110
trade mark protection
  balance of interests, 10-164, 10-165
  cancellation proceedings, 10-156
  designation as trade mark, 10-129
  generic nature of term, 10-098, 10-099
  limitation, 10-150–10-152
  protected geographical indication, 10-091, 10-100–10-102
  registration, 10-133, 10-156, 10-160, 10-161
  reputation, 10-100–10-102
  subsidiarity principle, 10-096
  TRIPS Agreement, 10-106, 10-137, 10-138, 10-140, 10-142, 10-143
trade names
  prior rights, 10-153, 10-154
  protection, 10-142, 10-143
  signs, as, 10-138, 10-147–10-149
  status, 10-142
  use, of, 10-133, 10-134, 10-138–10-140

Geographical names
descriptive signs or indications, 4-336
distinctive character, 4-336
geographical origin, 4-351, 4-353, 10-115
indications of origin, 4-279, 10-001, 10-078
likelihood of confusion, 4-337

Gerolsteiner Brunnen
Advocate General's Opinion
  honest commercial practices, 6-122
  legal context, 6-117, 6-118, 6-121
  schematic classification, 6-119, 6-120
  teleological analysis, 6-121
background, 6-116
ECJ decision, 6-123, 6-124
limitations (trade mark rights), 6-116
preliminary ruling, 6-116

Gillette
Advocate General's Opinion
  advertisers, 6-133
  function of trade mark, 6-127
  honest commercial practices, 6-131, 6-132
  legal context, 6-126
  necessary use, 6-129–6-131
  proprietors/consumers' interests, 6-130
background, 6-125
ECJ decision
  honest commercial practices, 6-137, 6-138
  necessary use, 6-134–6-136
limitations (trade mark rights)
  impression of authorisation, 6-125
  indicating compatibility, 6-125
  link between products, 6-125
  misleading impression, 6-125
  necessary use, 6-125

Glaverbel
abstract designs
  aesthetic functionality, 4-241, 4-242
  distinctive character, 4-241
Court of First Instance, 4-242
ECJ decision, 4-241

Google
Advocate General's Opinion
  basis, 6-068
  contributory infringement / liability, 6-069
  display use, 6-071–6-073
  infringing use, 6-070
  liability exemption for hosting, 6-077
  prohibited use, 6-079
  relevance to reputation, 6-074, 6-075
  'selection' use, 6-070
  third party use, 6-076
  use by advertisers, 6-078
  use of keywords, 6-079
identical signs/goods or services
  advertisements by competitors, 6-067

factual context, 6-067
third party advertisements, 6-066, 6-067
use of keywords, 6-066, 6-067
Grana Padano
Court of First Instance, 10-015
geographical indications
denomination of origin, 10-103
generic names, 10-103–10-105
historical context, 10-105
Graphical representation
accessible, 4-047
clarity/precision, 4-046, 4-073
colours, 4-069–4-072, 4-074–4-078, 4-080
durable, 4-048
general conditions, 4-032
intelligible, 4-047
non-visual signs, 4-032
objective, 4-049
purpose, 4-032
requirement, 4-031
scents, 4-032
self-contained, 4-047
signs, 4-003, 4-006, 4-008, 4-010, 4-013, 4-018, 4-029, 4-268, 12-002
see also **Signs**
sounds, 4-052, 4-049
unequivocal, 4-049
Hag I
common origin, 8-060
consent concept, 8-059
exclusive right, 8-060
free movement rules, 8-059, 8-060
indication of origin, 8-060
specific subject matter, 8-059
Hag II
additional markings, 8-068
Advocate General's Opinion, 8-067
common origin, 8-067
consent concept, 8-067
ECJ decision, 8-069
honest concurrent use, 8-068
specific subject matter, 8-067
Harmonisation
development, 2-001, 2-003
Harmonisation Directive
grounds for refusal
identical marks/identical goods, 2-006
similar marks/similar goods, 2-006
subsequent similar marks, 2-006
indication of origin, 2-005
internal market considerations, 2-005

Member States
court procedures, 2-008
discretion, 2-008
ownership provisions, 2-008
registration systems, 2-008
regulation of rights, 2-008
national laws
equal protection, 2-005
mandatory implementation, 2-005, 2-006
purpose, 2-005
scope, 2-007
trade mark protection, 2-005, 2-006
Heidelberger Bauchemie
Advocate General's Opinion
colour combinations, 4-082, 4-083
colours in abstract, 4-081
ECJ decision, 4-084, 4-085, 4-191
colours
abstract combinations, 4-079, 4-080
combinations, 4-189, 4-190, 4-191
distinctiveness, 4-080
graphical representation, 4-080
Henkel
Advocate General's Opinion
availability of signs, 4-264, 4-265
consumer attention/perception, 4-260, 4-261
distinctive character, 4-233, 4-234, 4-254–4-256, 4-262, 4-263
legal context, 4-230, 4-253
legal interpretation, 4-257, 4-258
packaging and content, 4-231, 4-232
registration, 4-235
similar products, 4-258, 4-259
territoriality, 4-234
ECJ decision
availability of signs, 4-266, 4-270–4-273
consumer attention/perception, 4-266, 4-269, 4-274
distinctive character, 4-239, 4-266–4-269, 4-275
graphical representation, 4-268
packaging/content, 4-236–4-238
public interest, 4-238
registration, 4-240
packaging of goods, 4-228
preliminary ruling, 4-229
product shapes, 4-228
public interest, 4-228
three dimensional marks, 4-228

INDEX

Hoffmann-La Roche Case
  Advocate General's Opinion
    basis, 8-076
    dominant position, 8-081
    free movement rules, 8-079
    guarantee of quality, 8-077
    liability, 8-080
    Member States' position, 8-078
    product quality, 8–080
    public health considerations, 8-077
  background, 8-074, 8-075
  ECJ decision
    additional conditions, 8-086
    dominant position, 8-097
    free movement rules, 8-082
    guarantee of origin, 8-083
    original condition of product, 8-084
    repackaging, 8-082, 8-083, 8-085
  parallel imports
    repackaging, 8-074
    trade mark infringement, 8-075
  preliminary ruling, 8-075
Hölterhoff
  Advocate General's Opinion
    Comparative Advertising Directive, 6-012
    legal context, 6-011
    negative exclusionary rights, 6-011
    positive ownership rights, 6-011
  background, 6-009
  ECJ decision, 6-013
  identical signs/goods or services, 6-009
  limits on protection, 6-009
  preliminary ruling, 6-009, 6-010
Human rights
  see also **European Convention on Human Rights; Fundamental rights**
  legitimate expectations, 3-052, 3-065
  judicial protection, 3-051
Identical signs/goods or services
  advertisements by competitors, 6-067
  availability requirement, 6-040, 6-046–6-048, 6-050
  concept of use, 6-016, 6-017
  consumer protection, 6-021
  contributory infringement/liability, 6-069
  evidence of confusion, 6-014
  exclusionary rights, 6-011
  generally, 6-008
  guarantee of origin, 6-019
  likelihood of confusion, 6-039
  limits of protection, 6-009, 6-024
  passing off, 6-014
  positive ownership rights, 6-011
  product market, 6-029, 6-030
  public perception, 6-034, 6-035
  third party advertisements, 6-066, 6-067
  third party use, 6-076
  trade mark proprietor's interest, 6-018, 6-020
  use
    advertisers, 6-078
    course of trade, 6-019
    display use, 6-071–6-073
    intermediaries, 6-051
    keywords, 6-066, 6-067, 6-079
    prohibited use, 6-034, 6-056
    signs, 6-056
    unauthorised use, 6-019
IMS
  abuse of market dominance
    exercise of rights, 9-100
    indispensable product, 9-101
    refusal to licence, 9-100–9-102
  database formats, 9-100
Indirect effect
  development, 3-046
  European Court of Justice, 3-046
Intel
  Advocate General's Opinion
    blurring, 5-215, 5-16
    consumer's economic behaviour, 5-216
    dilution doctrine, 5-210
    free riding, 5-214
    link/infringement relationship, 5-211–5-213
    tarnishment, 5-217
  ECJ decision
    assessment of detriment, 5-224, 5-225
    dilution by blurring, 5-218
    existence of link, 5-221–5-223
    relevant public, 5-219
    standard/burden of proof, 5-220
  facts in main proceedings, 5-208, 5-209
  repercussions, 5-226–5-229
  reputed marks
    detriment to distinctiveness, 5-207
    proof of dilution, 5-207
Intellectual property rights
  derogations, 8-050, 8-052
  dominance (anti-competitive behaviour)

abuse of dominant position, 9-094, 9-114, 9-115, 9-121
abusive conduct, 9-097
anti-competitive exploitation, 9-093, 9-116
bundling, 9-103, 9-108
business interests, 9-117
consumer welfare, 9-112
control of distribution, 9-111
copyright, 9-094, 9-095, 9-103
customer demand, 9-107
de facto monopoly, 9-096
essential facility, 9-099
exclusivity, 9-088, 9-089
exercise of rights, 9-094, 9-100
indispensable product, 9-101, 9-104
interoperability, 9-103
positive economic effect, 9-117
price regulation, 9-111
refusal of access, 9-098
refusal to licence, 9-098, 9-100–9-102, 9-106
refusal to supply, 9-109–9-120
relevant market, 9-094, 9-099
separate market, 9-099
supply of spare parts, 9-090–9-092
exclusionary nature, 8-047, 8-049
exhaustion of rights, 8-067, 8-049
see also **Exhaustion of rights**
existence/exercise dichotomy, 8-051–8-053, 8-067
free movement rules, 8-050, 8-067
see also **Free movement of goods**
importation of products, 8-049
independence, 8-048, 8-054, 8-055
infringement of rights, 8-049
national markets, 8-049
proprietary nature, 8-048
specific subject matter, 8-053, 8-067
territorial existence, 8-047, 8-073

Javico
anti-competitive agreements, 9-074
anti-competitive collusion
consumer interests, 9-075
distribution networks, 9-072, 9-075
marketing prohibitions, 9-073
block exemptions, 9-073
ECJ decision
block exemptions, 9-078
commercial freedom, 9-076
distorting competition, 9-077
relevant market, 9-077
restriction of competition, 9-076, 9-077

selective distribution network, 9-078
legislative context, 9-072
Judicial review
Boards of Appeal (OHIM), 3-053–3-058, 12-001
case precedents, 3-064–3-068
court proceedings, 3-057, 3-058, 3-060, 3-061
European Court of Justice, 3-055–3-058, 3-062–3-063
K Mart
background, 11-098, 11-099
judicial differences, 11-099–11-115
legislative interpretation, 11-102–11-106, 11-108, 11-110
parallel imports
customs regulations, 11-101
exhaustion of rights, 11-098
foreign manufacture, 11-109, 11-110, 11-115, 11-116
'gray' goods, 11-100, 11-103, 11-106
indication of origin, 11-113
KP Permanent Make-Up
Supreme Court decision
legislative context, 11-062–11-064
main issue, 11-061
trade mark protection, 11-060
Kit-Kat
acquisition through use
distinctive character, 4-600
slogans, 4-600
Advocate General's Opinion, 4-061–4-604
ECJ decision, 4-605
KWS
Advocate General's Opinion
external appearance, 4-196
public perception, 4-196
registrability, 4-196
colours
distinctive character, 4-192
registration, 4-192
Court of First Instance, 4-193–4-195
ECJ decision
distinctive character, 4-197
external appearance, 4-198
inadmissibility, 4-197
public perception, 4-198
statement of reasons, 4-197
L'Oréal v Bellure
Advocate General's Opinion
comparative advertising, 10-066–10-069

INDEX

legal interpretation, 10-068
use of trade marks, 10-067
comparative advertising
  imitations/replicas, 10-065
  similar packaging, 10-065
  unfair advantage, 10-065
  use of trade marks, 10-065
ECJ decision
  comparative advertising, 10-070, 10-071
  legal interpretation, 10-070

La Española
Court of First Instance, 5-160, 5-161
ECJ decision, 5-162, 5-163
similarity/confusion
  composite marks, 5-159
  figurative elements, 5-159
  get-up imitation, 5-159

Laboratoire de la Mer
background, 7-025
challenging and maintaining registration
  commercial failure, 7-025
  maintaining registration, 7-025
  revocation for non-use, 7-025
ECJ (reasoned order)
  actual use, 7-027
  applications for revocation, 7-030
  basis, 7-026
  genuine use, 7-027–7-029
  relevant market, 7-028
  types of use, 7-027–7-029
preliminary ruling, 7-025

Language rules
procedure, 2-015, 2-016, 2-107

Legal certainty
fundamental rights, 3-052
importance, 3-069

Lelos
abuse of market dominance
  marketing authorisations, 9-113
  refusal to supply, 9-113
Advocate General's Opinion
  abuse of dominant position, 9-114, 9-115
  anti-competitive behaviour, 9-116
  business interests, 9-117
  positive economic effect, 9-117
ECJ decision, 9-118–9-120

Levi Strauss
Advocate General's Opinion
  consumer perception, 5-081, 5-083
  economic significance, 5-081
  loss of distinctive character, 5-085, 5-086
  scope of protection, 5-084, 5-085
  timing of assessment, 5-082, 5-083
  trade mark protection, 5-081
background, 5-078, 5-079
comparing goods/services
  distinctive character, 5-079
  likelihood of confusion, 5-078
  timing of assessment, 5-078
ECJ decision
  scope of protection, 5-090–5-093
  style of judgment, 5-087
  timing of assessment, 5-088, 5-089
  vigilant conduct, 5-091, 5-092
preliminary ruling, 5-080

Libertel
Advocate General's Opinion
  colours as trade marks, 4-070, 4-073, 4-075
  competition considerations, 4-179
  distinctiveness, 4-176, 4-177
  graphical representation, 4-070–4-072, 4-074, 4-075
  legal certainty, 4-075
  legal context, 4-070, 4-072
  registration, 4-177
  relevant law, 4-070
background, 4-069
colours
  clarity/precision, 4-073
  concept, 4-175
  devoid of distinctive character, 4-069, 4-174
  distinctiveness, 4-069, 4-174, 4-176, 4-178
  graphical representation, 4-069
  perception, 4-175
  registration, 4-177
  sensation, 4-175
  trade marks, 4-070, 4-073, 4-075, 4-174, 4-180
ECJ decision
  colours as trade marks, 4-076, 4-078, 4-180
  competition considerations, 4-183
  distinctiveness, 4-076, 4-181, 4-186, 4-188
  graphical representation, 4-076–4-078
  legal context, 4-076
  public interest, 4-183–4-185
  public perception, 4-187
  registration, 4-182, 4-184

preliminary ruling, 4-069
public policy considerations, 4-069
Lidl
  Advocate General's Opinion, 7-057–7-059
  challenging and maintaining registration
    genuine use, 7-054
    non-use, 7-054
    start of use requirement, 7-054
  ECJ decision
    basis, 7-060
    proper reasons defence, 7-062–7-065
    start of five year period, 7-061
  facts of main proceedings, 7-055, 7-051
  preliminary ruling, 7-056
Limitations (trade mark rights)
  advertisers, 6-133
  availability of descriptive signs, 6-139
  balance of interests, 6-139
  distinct product market, 6-139
  distinguishing goods/services, 6-109
  exercise of rights, 6-111–6-116, 6-139
  exhaustion of rights, 6-099
  function of trade mark, 6-127
  general principles, 6-094
  indication of type/quality, 6-139
  link between products, 6-125
  misleading impressions, 6-125
  sale of goods, 6-110
  use of mark
    honest commercial practices, 6-122, 6-125, 6-131, 6-132, 6-137, 6-138, 6-140
    necessary use, 6-125, 6-129–6-131, 6-134–6-136
    relation to goods, 6-098–6-100
    relation to services, 6-101–6-105
Limoncello
  Court of First Instance, 5-153, 5-154
  similarity/confusion, 5-153
Linde, Winward and Rado Cases
  Advocate General's Opinion
    availability of sign, 4-220, 4-221
    distinctiveness, 4-217–4-219
    exclusive rights, 4-223
    product shapes, 4-222
    public interest, 4-219, 4-223
    substantial value, 4-223, 4-224
    technical result, 4-223
  ECJ decision
    distinctiveness, 4-225
    public interest, 4-226, 4-227
    three dimensional shapes, 4-225, 4-226
  preliminary ruling, 4-216
  shapes
    distinctiveness, 4-215, 4-216
    product shapes, 4-215
    three dimensional marks, 4-215, 4-216
Lindt & Sprüngli
  Advocate General's Opinion, 4-580–4-582
  bad faith, 4-576
  ECJ decision, 4-583–4-586
  facts of main proceedings, 4-577–4-579
  preliminary ruling, 4-579
Lloyd Schuhfabrik
  Advocate General's Opinion, 5-021, 5-028, 5-046
  earlier rights
    aural similarity, 5-045
    concept of confusion, 5-020
    consumer perception, 5-047
    distinctiveness factors, 5-028
    global assessment test, 5-047
    likelihood of confusion, 5-020, 5-030
    substantive/genuine confusion, 5-020
  ECJ decision, 5-022, 5-029, 5-047
LTJ Diffusion
  Advocate General's Opinion
    composite marks, 5-008
    freedom of trade, 5-005
    global assessment test, 5-007
    identity/similarity, 5-006, 5-008
    legal context, 5-008
    meaning of identical, 5-005
  background, 5-004
  earlier rights
    identical marks, 5-004
    identity between marks, 5-004
  ECJ decision
    global assessment test, 5-009
    identity of origin, 5-009
    likelihood of confusion, 5-009
Mag
  Advocate General's Opinion
    distinctiveness, 4-202–4-205
    legal context, 4-201
    right to hearing, 4-206
  Court of First Instance, 4-200
  ECJ decision
    appraisal of facts, 4-210
    distinctive character, 4-209, 4-211

INDEX

evidence, 4-211, 4-212
general propositions, 4-214
grounds of appeal, 4-207–4-214
overall impression, 4-208
product shape marks, 4-209
right to hearing, 4-213
shapes
distinctiveness, 4-199
registration, 4-199
Magill
abuse of market dominance
abuse of dominant position, 9-094
abusive conduct, 9-097
de facto monopoly, 9-096
exercise of right, 9-094
copyright issues, 9-094
Court of First Instance, 9-095
relevant market, 9-094
Maple Leaf
Advocate General's Opinion
confusion as to endorsement, 4-568
functions of emblems, 4-565, 4-566
heraldic/geometric description, 4-567
heraldic imitation, 4-571–4-573
Paris Convention, 4-569, 4-570
background, 4-561
Court of First Instance, 4-562, 4-563
ECJ decision
heraldic imitation, 4-571–4-573
service marks, 4-574, 4-575
state emblems
legislative framework, 4-560
Paris Convention, 4-559, 4-560
scope of protection, 4-559
Marca II
Advocate General's Opinion, 6-043–6-045
availability requirement, 6-040
ECJ decision
availability requirement, 6-046–6-048, 6-050
scope of protection, 6-046–6-049
facts in main proceedings, 6-041, 6-042
identical signs/goods or services, 6-040
order for reference, 6-041, 6-042
preliminary ruling, 6-042
Marca Mode
Advocate General's Opinion, 5-024, 5-025
background, 5-023
confusion, 5-023

earlier rights, 5-023
ECJ decision, 5-026, 5-027
Marks with a reputation
see **Reputed marks**
Mars
background, 4-550
deceptive trade marks
advertising messages, 4-550
deceptiveness, 4-550
product presentation, 4-550, 4-551
unfair competition, 4-550
ECJ decision
consumer protection, 4-552, 4-553
scope of prohibition, 4-552, 4-553
free movement of goods, 4-551
Matratzen
Advocate General's Opinion, 4-460
Court of First Instance, 5-057–5-059
descriptive signs or indications
anti-competitive effects, 4-459
free movement issues, 4-459
earlier rights
figurative/word marks, 5-056
global assessment test, 5-061–5-063
similarity of marks, 5-056
ECJ decision, 4-461–4-463, 5-060–5-065
free movement of goods, 5-065
Medion
Advocate General's Opinion, 5-139
confusion/similarity
global appreciation test, 5-137
importance of dominant elements, 5-137, 5-138
likelihood of confusion, 5-137, 5-138
overall impression, 5-137
product markets, 5-138
ECJ decision, 5-140
Merck, Sharp and Dohme v Paranova
ECJ decision, 8-168
parallel imports, 8-155
preliminary ruling, 8-155
repackaging, 8-155
Microsoft
abuse of market dominance
bundling, 9-103, 9-108
indispensability, 9-104
interoperability, 9-103
market dominance, 9-103
refusal to licence, 9-106
copyright issues, 9-103
customer demand, 9-107
elimination of competition, 9-105

1001

Mühlens
Advocate General's Opinion
  balancing the factors, 5-050, 5-051
  likelihood of confusion, 5-052
  national laws, 5-052, 5-053
background, 5-048
Court of First Instance, 5-049
ECJ decision, 5-054, 5-055
similarity of marks, 5-048

Nasdaq
challenging and maintaining registration
  complementary services, 7-049, 7-052, 7-053
  earlier marks, 7-051
  genuine use, 7-049–7-052
  non-profit making services, 7-052
  proof of use, 7-052
  unfair advantage, 7-050
Court of First Instance, 5-242, 5-243
ECJ decision, 5-244, 5-246, 7-053
reputed marks
  detrimental link, 5-245
  figurative signs, 5-240
  reputation of earlier mark, 5-240, 5-246
  unfair advantage, 5-240, 5-245

National laws
development, 2-003

Nichols
Advocate General's Opinion
  distinctive character, 4-154, 4-155
  distinctiveness, 4-152
  registration of surnames, 4-153
ECJ decision
  competition considerations, 4-159
  consumer perception, 4-158
  distinctive character, 4-156
  distinctiveness, 4-156
  uniform criteria, 4-157
preliminary reference, 4-151
surnames, 4-151, 4-153

Nokia
Advocate General's Opinion
  basis, 6-143
  national laws/measures, 6-147–6-150
  'special reasons' condition, 6-144–6-147
background, 6-141, 6-142
enforcement
  adequate enforcement, 6-141
  continuing infringement, 6-141, 6-142
preliminary ruling, 6-142

Nungesser
anti-competitive collusion
  assignment of rights, 9-052, 9-053
  economic characteristics, 9-054
  exclusive licence, 9-052, 9-055, 9-056
  exercise of rights, 9-052, 9-053
  existence of right, 9-052
background, 9-052

O2
Advocate General's Opinion
  inconsistent case law, 10-060
  indispensability requirement, 10-061
  legal context, 10-060
  unfair advantage, 10-061
comparative advertising
  concept of use, 10-059
  indispensability requirement, 10-059
  misleading advertising, 10-059
ECJ decision
  legal context, 10-062, 10-063
  use of similar sign, 10-064

Office for Harmonisation in the Internal Market
administrative examination system, 3-053, 3-055
Boards of Appeal, 3-053–3-058, 12-001
dependency, on, 12-001
location, 2-003, 2-011

Packaging
comparative advertising, 10-065
packaging/exemption scheme, 9-121, 9-122
parallel imports, 8-169, 8-171, 8-189
registration, 12-002
shapes, 4-228, 4-279, 4-320
similar packaging, 10-065

Pago
Advocate General's Opinion
  local reputation, 5-187, 5-188
  reputation in the Community, 5-183–5-186
reputed marks, 5-180, 5-189, 5-190

Pall
background, 4-537
deceptive trade marks
  effect on trade, 4-539
  proportionality, 4-450
  quantitative restriction, 4-537
  unfair competition, 4-541
  use of symbol, 4-537, 4-540
free movement of goods, 4-541, 4-542

legislative context, 4-538
scope of prohibition, 4-539
Parallel imports
see also **Free movement of goods**
advance notice requirement, 8-138, 8-161, 8-166, 8-167, 8-276, 8-277, 8-285
advertising materials, 8-189, 8-192, 8-203
burden of proof, 8-109, 8-110, 8-150, 8-249, 8-250, 8-251, 8-265, 8-275, 8-279
clear identification, 8-268
condition of goods, 8-189, 8-195, 8-267
consent
   assessment of consent, 8-220
   clear consent, 8-225
   concept, 8-236
   effect, 8-228–8-233
   implicit consent, 8-225, 8-238
   individual consignments, 8-220
   requirements, 8-237–8-239
copyright considerations, 8-201, 8-205
defective/counterfeit products, 8-171
dominant position, 8-081, 8-087
exhaustion of rights, 8-096, 8-098–8-100, 8-107, 8-193, 8-203, 8-240, 8-242, 8-244, 8-280, 8-281, 8-286
   see also **Exhaustion of rights**
exports to third countries, 8-177
extent of disclosure, 8-278, 8-285
goods in transit, 8-244, 8-245
guarantee of origin, 8-083, 8-280
identification marks/numbers, 8-169, 8-171, 8-181, 8-185
identity of origin, 8-174, 8-280
importer's rights, 8-134
inappropriate presentation/reputation, 8-137
indication of manufacturer, 8-136
intra-Community trade, 8-171
liability, 8-080
market access, 8-165
market partitioning, 8-130, 8-131, 8-144, 8-151, 8-181–8-184
measures having equivalent effect, 8-173
minimum intervention, 8-278, 8-280, 8-281
necessity requirement, 8-145–8-147, 8-159, 8-160, 8-163, 8-164, 8-250, 8-259, 8-266, 8-273, 8-279, 8-284
original condition of product, 8-084, 8-097, 8-132
overstickering, 8-251, 8-257, 8-258
packaging, 8-169, 8-171, 8-189
policing channels of trade, 8-169, 8-225
product quality, 8-077, 8-080
public health issues, 8-077
putting goods on the market, 8-240, 8-242, 8-248
re-boxing, 8-251, 8-259, 8-260
re-branding, 8-146, 8-148, 8-149, 8-151, 8-152
re-labelling, 8-280
removal/reapplication of trade mark, 8-170
repackaging, 8-074, 8-082, 8-083, 8-085, 8-088, 8-089, 8-096, 8-105, 8-106, 8-131–8-133, 8-135, 8-139, 8-140, 8-152, 8-154, 8-155, 8-157, 8-158, 8-160, 8-172, 8-175, 8-178, 8-179, 8-183, 8-195, 8-250, 8-260, 8-272, 8-273, 8-278, 8-280, 8-284
replacing trade marks, 8-141, 8-144, 8-153
reputation, 8-196–8-200, 8-251, 8-261, 8-262, 8-269, 8-274, 8-280
reselling, 8-194, 8-240, 8-243
risk of damage, 8-198–8-200
scope of protection, 8-101–8-103
specific subject matter, 8-139, 8-144, 8-163, 8-170, 8-280
trade mark infringement, 8-075, 8-089, 8-141
Parallel imports (USA)
competition issues, 11-095
customs regulations, 11-101
exhaustion of rights, 11-089, 11-090
foreign manufacture, 11-109, 11-110, 11-115, 11-116
'gray' goods, 11-092, 11-100, 11-103, 11-106
indication of origin, 11-113
legislative context, 11-093, 11-094
material differences, 11-096, 11-097
seizure of goods, 11-094
Parfums Christian Dior
see **Dior**
Peak Holding
   Advocate General's Opinion, 8-241
   ECJ decision, 8-242, 8-243
   parallel imports
      exhaustion of rights, 8-240, 8-242

putting goods on the market, 8-240, 8-242
resale restrictions, 8-240, 8-243
preliminary ruling, 8-240
Pharmacia v Upjohn
Advocate General's Opinion
basis, 8-143
burden of proof, 8-150
market partitioning, 8-144
necessity requirement, 8-145–8-147
re-branding, 8-146, 8-148, 8-149
replacing trade marks, 8-144
requirement of intention, 8-144
specific subject matter, 8-144
ECJ decision
market partitioning, 8-151
previous case decisions, 8-151
re-branding, 8-152
replacing trade marks, 8-153
parallel imports
replacing trade marks, 8-141
trade mark infringement, 8-141
preliminary ruling, 8-142
Philips
Advocate General's Opinion
arbitrary additions, 4-089
distinctiveness, 4-087–4-089
functionality, 4-088, 4-505
legal context, 4-087, 4-503
relevance of alternatives, 4-504–4-506
technical features, 4-502
technical result, 4-089
acquisition through use, 4-596
ECJ decision
acquisition through use, 4-597–5-599
capricious additions, 4-094
categories of trade mark, 4-092
consumer perspective, 4-102
continuum of distinctiveness, 4-093, 4-099
devoid of distinctive character, 4-099
distinctive character, 4-508
distinctiveness, 4-095–4-097
function of trade mark, 4-091
functionality, 4-507
independent grounds, 4-098
indication of origin, 4-597, 4-598
legal framework, 4-508, 4-510
link with specification, 4-100
procedural issue, 4-090
public interest, 4-097, 4-509
public perspective, 4-101

public recognition, 4-597, 4-598
relevance of alternatives, 4-511
three dimensional signs, 4-094
timing, 4-102
functionality, 4-501
three dimensional signs
devoid of distinctive character, 4-086
distinctiveness, 4-086, 4-501, 4-596–4-599
functionality, 4-086
technical result, 4-501
Picasso/Picaro
Advocate General's Opinion
conceptual similarity, 5-098
concluding remarks, 5-102
distinctiveness, 5-099
post sale confusion, 5-101
post sale effect, 5-100
subject matter of case, 5-097
background, 5-095
Court of First Instance, 5-096
ECJ decision
distinctiveness, 5-103
phonetically similar marks, 5-103
post sale effect, 5-104, 5-105
public attention, 5-104
phonetically similar marks, 5-095, 5-096
Pippig
Advocate General's Opinion
channels of trade, 10-030
indicating names of manufacturers, 10-027
national standards, 10-028, 10-029
price comparisons, 10-032
test purchases, 10-031
comparative advertising
misleading advertising, 10-025
price differentials, 10-025
ECJ decision
channels of trade, 10-037
indicating names of manufacturers, 10-036
legal interpretation, 10-034, 10-035
price comparisons, 10-039
test purchases, 10-038
preliminary ruling, 10-025
Postkantoor
Advocate General's Opinion
descriptiveness, 4-400–4-403
form/meaning, 4-405, 4-406
language considerations, 4-404
neologism, 4-405, 4-406
registration, 4-397–4-399

scope of protection, 4-396
scope of reference, 4-395
background, 4-394
descriptive signs or indications
  descriptiveness, 4-394
  distinctive character, 4-394
ECJ decision
  composite marks, 4-419, 4-420
  examination procedures, 4-413
  interpretation, 4-414–4-417
  overlapping provisions, 4-418
  public interest, 4-414
  registration, 4-408–4-411, 4-414
  specification/disclaimers, 4-412
  structure of judgment, 4-407

Praktiker
Advocate General's Opinion, 5-142–5-144
ECJ decision, 5-145
similarity/confusion
  registration of services, 5-141
  retail services, 5-141

Procordia
Advocate General's Opinion
  distinctiveness, 4-494, 4-495, 4-497, 4-498
  'in the trade' concept, 4-493, 4-497
  indication of origin, 4-494
  language considerations, 4-495
  legal context, 4-491, 4-492, 4-494, 4-495
background, 4-490
customary signs/indications
  consumer perception, 4-490
  distinctiveness, 4-490
ECJ decision, 4-499, 4-4500

Proctor & Gamble
ECJ decision
  consideration of trade mark as a whole, 4-276, 4-277
  consumer attention, 4-276
  criterion for use, 4-276, 4-277
  distinctive character, 4-276
  inlaid washing tablets, 4-251, 4-252, 4-278

Pronuptia de Paris
anti-competitive agreements, 9-061
franchising agreements
  benefits, 9-057, 9-058
  essential clauses, 9-060

Pure Digital
acquisition through use
  date of application/registration, 4-636

distinctive character, 4-636
relevant time, 4-636
background, 4-637
Court of First Instance, 4-638
ECJ decision, 4-639–4-632

Qualitex
background, 11-028
Supreme Court decision
  general context, 11-031
  judicial reasoning, 11-032, 11-033
  legislative context, 11-029, 11-030
  trade mark registration, 11-028
trade dress, 11-028
trade mark registration, 11-028
unfair competition, 11-028

Quantitative restrictions
see also **Free movement of goods**
consumer protection, 8-023, 8-025
derogation, 8-019
equivalent measures, 8-019
exceptions, 8-013
import/export restrictions, 8-001
interpretation of provisions, 8-015
intra-Community trade, 8-014
intra-State trade, 8-014
measures having equivalent effect, 8-011
origin
  concept, 8-018–8-021
  discrimination based on origin, 8-016, 8-017
  indication of origin, 8-018
price controls, 8-025, 8-026
principle, 8-012
product characteristics, 8-022, 8-023
product market, 8-020
public health considerations, 8-023
selling arrangements, 8-024–8-026
unfair competition provision, 8-021

Quicky
Court of First Instance, 5-155
ECJ decision, 5-156, 5-157
similarity/confusion
  likelihood of confusion, 5-158
  unclear dominance, 5-155, 5-156

Radetsky
Advocate General's Opinion, 7-034
challenging and maintaining registration, 7-031
ECJ decision, 7-035–7-037
facts in main proceedings, 7-031, 7-032
non-profitable activities, 7-031
respective arguments, 7-033

INDEX

Registration
see also **Challenging and maintaining registration**
absolute grounds for protection, 4-002
application procedure, 2-015
colour, 4-008, 4-069, 4-177, 4-182, 4-184, 4-192, 4-196
Community Trade Mark, 2-011, 2-012
consumer perspective, 4-102
customary signs/indications, 4-471, 4-478
descriptive signs/indications, 4-364, 4-365, 4-373, 4-389, 4-393, 4-397–4-399, 4-008, 4-411, 4-414, 4-442, 4-450 – 4-452
devoid of distinctive character, 4-109, 4-110, 4-124, 4-130, 4-131, 4-148, 4-149
functionality, 12-002
grounds for refusal, 4-004, 4-005
link with specification, 4-100, 4-471
non-registrability, 4-005
packaging, 12-002
public interest, 12-002
public perspective, 4-101
public policy, 12-002
shapes, 4-199
signs, 4-003
slogans, 4-160
surnames, 4-151
three dimensional signs, 12-002

Reputation
see **Reputed marks**

Reputed marks
assessing reputation, 5-169
blurring, 5-215, 5-216, 5-218
burden of proof, 5-220
consumer behaviour, 5-216
detriment to distinctiveness, 5-207, 5-224, 5-225
dilution doctrine, 5-201
free riding, 5-214
identical/similar goods or services, 5-191, 5-197
likelihood of confusion, 5-191, 5-197
local reputation, 5-187, 5-188
proof of dilution, 5-207
reputation in the Community, 5-180
reputed marks, 5-173, 5-174, 5-191, 5-207
similarity between marks, 5-197, 5-201
unfair advantage, 5-230, 5-232, 5-239, 5-240, 5-245

usage as embellishment, 5-197
well-known marks, 5-173, 5-174, 5-191

Robelco
Advocate General's Opinion, 6-081, 6-082
background, 6-080
ECJ decision, 6-083
trade names/trade marks
conflict with earlier marks, 6-080
identical/similar signs, 6-080
likelihood of association, 6-080
likelihood of confusion, 6-080

Rossi
Advocate General's Opinion
appreciation of facts, 5-130
assessment of facts, 5-130
new evidence, 5-128, 5-129
procedural points, 5-125
scope of appeal, 5-126, 5-127
background, 5-106
confusion/similarity
global assessment test, 5-106
likelihood of confusion, 5-107, 5-108
registration process, 5-106, 5-107
surnames, 5-106
Court of First Instance
global assessment test, 5-117
likelihood of association, 5-122
likelihood of confusion, 5-108, 5-117, 5-121, 5-123
product similarity, 5-109–5-111, 5-113–5-117
similarity between marks, 5-118–5-120
targeted public, 5-112
ECJ decision
evidential matters, 5-131, 5-136
inadmissibility, 5-131
likelihood of confusion, 5-132
procedural challenge, 5-124
procedural infringements, 5-134–5-136
registration process, 5-136
scope of appeal, 5-133

Sabel
Advocate General's Opinion
comparing the marks, 5-043
concept of association, 5-013
guarantee of origin, 5-012
identity of origin, 5-033
likelihood of association, 5-012, 5-014, 5-015
likelihood of confusion, 5-013

non-origin association, 5-013, 5-014
risk of confusion, 5-013, 5-033
similarity of marks, 5-033
test for confusion, 5-033
background, 5-011
earlier rights
  abstract figures, 5-011
  alternative concepts, 5-011
  comparing the marks, 5-043
  composite marks, 5-011
  conceptual similarity, 5-044
  confusion, 5-011, 5-032
  consumer perception, 5-044
  global appreciation test, 5-032, 5-034, 5-044
  likelihood of confusion, 5-013, 5-044
  pictorial marks, 5-011
ECJ decision, 5-016, 5-034, 5-044

San Francisco Arts & Athletics Inc v United States Olympic Committee
Supreme Court decision
  constitutional considerations, 11-071, 11-072, 11-076
  enforcement policy, 11-075
  judicial reasoning, 11-071–11-077
  legislative context, 11-070
  main issue, 11-069
trade mark protection
  commercial speech, 11-073, 11-077
  confusion, 11-071, 11-074
  distinctive words/symbols, 11-071, 11-074
  Olympic symbols, 11-068, 11-071
  public interest, 11-073

SAT.2
Advocate General's Opinion
  distinctive character, 4-122, 4-123
  distinctiveness, 4-118, 4-119, 4-122, 4-123
  legal context, 4-118, 4-119
  non-discrimination principle, 4-125
  permissive perspective, 4-120, 4-121
  products of different origins, 4-119
  registrability, 4-124
Court of First Instance, 4-117
devoid of distinctive character, 4-116
distinctiveness, 4-116
ECJ decision
  distinctive character, 4-127–4-129
  distinctiveness, 4-127
  essential function/trade marks, 4-126

public interest, 4-129
registrability, 4-130, 4-131
relevant public, 4-126

Scents
consumer perspective, 4-035
graphical representation, 4-032, 4-041, 4-042, 4-047, 4-048
indication of origin, 4-043
message capable of perception, 4-037
olfactory signs, 4-038, 4-050, 4-051

Scope of protection
concept of use, 12-003
ECJ jurisprudence, 6-155, 12-003
enforcement
  see **Enforcement**
generally, 6-001
identical signs/goods or services
  see **Identical signs/goods or services**
infringement/enforcement, 6-001
Community Trade Mark Regulation
  exclusive rights, 6-004
  limitations, 6-007
  prohibited use, 6-004–6-006
  reproduction in dictionaries, 6-005
  rights conferred, 6-004
  use in course of trade, 6-007
market context, 6-155
Trade Marks Directive
  exclusive rights, 6-002
  limitations, 6-003
  prohibited use, 6-002
  rights conferred, 6-002
  use in course of trade, 6-002

Sebago
Advocate General's Opinion
  basis, 8-222
  exhaustion of rights, 8-222, 8-223
ECJ decision, 8-224
parallel imports
  advertising, 8-220
  assessment of consent, 8-220
  consent/individual consignments, 8-220
  exhaustion of rights, 8-222–8-224
  preliminary ruling, 8-221

Shapes
see also **Functional shapes**
absolute grounds for protection, 4-001
availability, 4-220, 4-221
basic geometric shapes, 4-285
consumer attention/perception, 4-260, 4-261, 4-276, 4-316

distinctiveness, 4-199, 4-202–4-204,
    4-209, 4-211, 4-215–4-219, 4-225
indications of origin, 4-279
innate shapes, 12-002
packaging, 4-228, 4-279, 4-320
product shapes, 4-215, 4-222, 4-228,
    4-311, 4-330, 4-512, 4-607
public interest, 4-219, 4-223, 4-226,
    4-227, 4-228
registration, 4-199
three dimensional shapes, 4-215,
    4-216, 4-225, 4-226, 4-228, 4-279,
    4-286, 4-287, 4-301, 4-311, 4-319
substantial value, 4-223, 4-224

Shield Mark
Advocate General's Opinion
    copyright, 4-063
    descriptions of sounds, 4-061
    graphical representation,
        4-058–4-060
    musical notation, 4-060
    need for precision, 4-058
    policy considerations, 4-062
    scope of reference, 4-056
    sounds as trade marks, 4-055, 4-057
    trade mark rights, 4-063
ECJ decision
    graphical representation, 4-067,
        4-068
    representation of sounds, 4-067,
        4-068
    scope of reference, 4-064
    sounds as trade marks, 4-065
    visual perception, 4-066
background, 4-052, 4-053
preliminary ruling, 4-054
sounds
    graphical representation, 4-052,
        4-054
    registration, 4-052, 4-053
unfair competition, 4-054

Sieckmann
Advocate General's Opinion
    consumer perspective, 4-035
    graphical representation, 4-038
    messages capable of perception,
        4-037
    visual/olfactory signs, 4-038
background, 4-032, 4-033
ECJ decision
    function of trade mark, 4-043
    graphical representation,
        4-045–4-048
    indication of origin, 4-043
    legal context, 4-043
    non-visual signs, 4-044
    olfactory scents, 4-050, 4-051
    registration, 4-043
scents
    graphical representation, 4-032,
        4-034
    wording of signs, 4-032

Siemans
comparative advertising, 10-040
ECJ decision
    acronyms, 10-043
    benefits of comparative
        advertising. 10-045–10-047
    circumstances of the case, 10-048
    equivalent technical features,
        10-041
    previous case law, 10-041
    relevant public, 10-042
    technical function, 10-044
    unfair advantage, 10-041
preliminary ruling, 10-040
unfair advantage, 10-040

Signs
see also **Customary**
    signs/indications; Descriptive
    signs or indications
absolute grounds for protection,
    4-001
colour, 4-008
concept, 4-001
confusion, 5-010
devoid of distinctive character, 4-003,
    4-007, 4-014
distinctiveness, 4-013, 4-017, 4-028,
    12-002
function, 9-121–9-124
functionality, 4-013, 4-019, 4-021–4-024,
    4-027
fundamental requirement, 4-006,
    4-007, 4-013, 4-017, 4-029, 4-030
graphical representation, 4-003, 4-006,
    4-008, 4-010, 4-013, 4-018, 4-029,
    4-268, 12-002
    see also **Graphical representation**
identical signs/goods or services
    see **Identical signs/goods or**
        services
mere concept, 4-006
non-visual signs, 4-012, 4-032, 4-044
olfactory signs, 4-038
registration, 4-003, 4-008, 4-014
signs in the abstract, 4-009
similarity, 5-010

structure of signs, 4-105
technical innovation, 4-024, 4-026
three dimensional signs, 4-086, 4-094,
    4-468, 4-610, 4-613–4-615, 12-002
undistinguishable, 4-007, 4-008, 4-010
unfair competitive advantage, 4-016,
    4-029
use of similar signs, 10-059, 10-064
visual perception, 4-066
wording, 4-032

Silberquelle
Advocate General's Opinion
    basis, 7-043
    use as guarantee of origin, 7-044
    use in advertising, 7-046
    use in reference market, 7-045
challenging and maintaining
    registration
    use of promotional items, 7-038
    use without payment, 7-038
ECJ decision, 7-047, 7-048
facts in main proceedings, 7-039,
    7-040
order for reference, 7-039
principal arguments, 7-041, 7-042

Silhouette
Advocate General's Opinion
    commercial policy considerations,
        8-213
    Community Trade Mark
        Regulation, 8-215
    competition policy, 8-214
    legal context, 8-207
    international/territorial
        exhaustion, 8-207–8-212
    national legal order, 8-216, 8-217
background, 8-206
ECJ decision
    international/territorial
        exhaustion, 8-218
    national legal order, 8-219
exhaustion of rights
    international exhaustion, 8-206
    territorial exhaustion, 8-206
preliminary ruling, 8-206

Similarity/confusion
see also **Confusion**
composite marks, 5-152, 5-159
conceptual similarity, 5-098
consumer attention, 5-146
figurative elements, 5-152, 5-159
get-up imitation, 5-159
global assessment test, 5-106, 5-117,
    5-137

likelihood of confusion, 5-072, 5-078,
    5-108, 5-117, 5-121, 5-123, 5-132,
    5-137, 5-138, 5-146, 5-152, 5-158
linguistic considerations, 5-164
marks with reputation
    see **Reputed marks**
mediation, 5-148
non-negligible word elements, 5-153
overall impression, 5-137
phonetically similar marks, 5-095,
    5-096, 5-103
post sale confusion, 5-094, 5-101,
    5-104, 5-105
product markets, 5-138
product similarity, 5-249
public attention, 5-104
registration of services, 5-141
retail services, 5-094, 5-141
similarity
    aural similarity, 5-045
    cumulative similarity, 5-038, 12-003
    goods/services, 5-010
    phonetic similarity, 5-039, 5-069
    signs, 5-010
threshold of confusion, 5-146
unclear dominance, 5-155, 5-156
verbal elements, 5-152

SiSi-Werke
Advocate General's Opinion
    absence of justification, 4-288,
        4-289
    basic geometric shapes, 4-285
    distinctive character, 4-282–4-284
    interests of competitors, 4-290
    legal context, 4-281
    three dimensional marks, 4-286,
        4-287
Court of First Instance, 4-280
ECJ decision
    context of assessment,
        4-291–4-295
    distinctive character, 4-291, 4-296
    monopolisation, 4-297–4-300
    third party interests, 4-291,
        4-297–4-300
indications of origin, 4-279
packaging, 4-279
three dimensional marks, 4-279

Slogans
acquisition through use, 4-600
devoid of distinctive character, 4-160
distinctive character, 4-164, 4-166,
    4-172
registration, 4-165–4-169, 4-171

Smirnoff
ECJ (reasoned order), 6-054, 6-055
facts of main proceedings, 6-052, 6-053
identical signs/goods or services, 6-051
preliminary ruling, 6-053
use by intermediaries, 6-051
Sounds
descriptions, 4-061
graphical representation, 4-052, 4-054, 4-058–4-060, 4-067, 4-068
musical notation, 4-060
registration, 4-052, 4-053
representation, 4-068, 4-069
trade marks, 4-053, 4-055, 4-057, 4-065
unfair competition, 4-054
Specialist tribunals
European Civil Service Tribunal, 3-023
Patent Tribunals, 3-023
State emblems
endorsement, 4-568
functions, 4-565
heraldic/geometric description, 4-567
heraldic imitation, 4-571–4-573
Paris Convention, 4-559, 4-560, 4-569, 4-570
service marks, 4-574, 4-575
Stork I
acquisition through use
  consumer perception, 4-608
  distinctive character, 4-606
  product shape, 4-607
Advocate General's Opinion
  acquisition through use, 4-610
  admissibility considerations, 4-315
  consumer perception, 4-316
  distinctive character, 4-316, 4-317
  three dimensional signs, 4-610
  time for determining distinctiveness, 4-612, 4-612
Court of First Instance, 4-312–4-314, 4-607–4-609
ECJ decision
  admissibility considerations, 4-318
  three dimensional shapes, 4-319, 4-613–4-615
  time for determining distinctiveness, 4-616, 4-617
product shape, 4-311, 4-607
three dimensional shapes, 4-311
Stork II
acquisition through use, 4-618

Advocate General's Opinion
  distinctive character, 4-25–4-329
  evidence of use, 4-619, 4-620
  geographical extent, 4-619, 4-621
  product shape, 4-325
  re-assessment of facts, 4-324
ECJ decision
  admissibility considerations, 4-334, 4-335
  general interest, 4-331
  geographical extent, 4-622, 4-624
  market share, 4-622, 4-623
  product shape, 4-330
  promotion investment, 4-622
  public perception, 4-622
  re-assessment of facts, 4-332, 4-333
Court of First Instance, 4-321, 4-322
packaging, 4-320
product shapes, 4-320
sales figures in abstract, 4-618
Streamserve
background, 4-421
Community Trade Mark, 4-428
Court of First Instance, 4-422
descriptive signs or indications
  composite marks, 4-421
  descriptiveness, 4-421
  devoid of distinctive character, 4-429
  distinctiveness, 4-421
  inventiveness, 4-429
  need to leave sign free, 4-423
  relevant public, 4-424
  specification, 4-425–4-427
division of powers, 4-422
ECJ Order, 4-430, 4-431
Sunrider
background, 7-075
challenging and maintaining registration
  absence of proof, 7-074
  burden of proof, 7-074
  earlier marks, 7-075
  evidence of use, 7-074, 7-075
  genuine use, 7-074
Court of First Instance, 7-076, 7-077
ECJ decision
  admissibility of OHIM response, 7-079
  basis, 7-078
  burden of proof, 7-082–7-084
  dealing with new grounds, 7-080, 7-081

genuine use, 7-082, 7-083, 7-085–7-087
product comparison, 7-088
Supremacy doctrine
application, 3-041
development, 3-041–3-045
EC Treaty, 3-041
European Court of Justice, 3-041–3-045
Surnames
devoid of distinctive character, 4-151
distinctive character, 4-154, 4-155, 4-156
registration, 4-151
Syfait
abuse of market dominance
control of distribution, 9-111
price regulation, 9-111
refusal to supply, 9-109
consumer welfare, 9-112
jurisdiction, 9-110
Telefon & Buch
Court of First Instance, 4-433, 4-434
descriptive signs or indications
composite marks, 4-432
descriptiveness, 4-432
ECJ Order, 4-435–4-438
Toshiba
Advocate General's Opinion
comparative advertising, 10-007
distinguishing marks, 10-012
misuse of reputation, 10-011–10-015
necessity factor, 10-015
objective comparisons, 10-008, 10-009
unfair advantage, 10-013
background, 10-005
comparative advertising
advertising statements, 10-005, 10-006
unfair competition, 10-005
ECJ decision
basis, 10-016
comparative advertising, 10-017–10-020
distinguishing marks, 10-021, 10-024
pro-comparative position, 10-025
unfair advantage, 10-022, 10-023
preliminary ruling, 10-006
Trade dress (USA)
design/product packaging, 11-034
distinctiveness, 11-016, 11-017
protection, 11-016, 11-028, 11-045

registration, 11-028
unregistered, 11-016
Trade Mark law
abuse of market dominance
effects, 9-126
function of sign, 9-121–9-124
trade mark agreements, 9-124, 9-125
consent concept, 8-058, 8-059, 8-061, 8-067
consumer protection, 1-001
development, 1-001, 1-003
disparate systems, 1-001
enforcement
see **Enforcement**
exclusive right, 8-056, 8-060, 8-065
free movement provisions
compulsory licences, 8-063, 8-064
essential function, 8-056
exclusive right, 8-056
identity of origin, 8-056
lack of protection, 8-062
national provisions, 8-057
subject matter/trade marks, 8-056
harmonisation, 1-001
interaction, 1-003
national courts, 1-001
national laws, 1-001, 8-065
origin
common origin, 8-060, 8-067
guarantee of origin, 8-065
indication of origin, 8-060, 8-065
scope of protection
see **Absolute grounds of protection; Scope of protection**
subject matter, 8-056, 8-058. 8-059, 8-065, 8-067
territorial aspects, 8-073
unitary control, 8-072
voluntary assignment, 8-070–8-073
Trade Mark law (USA)
Federal protection, 11-001
passing off (palming off), 11-001
Restatement of Unfair Competition, 11-001, 11-002
State laws, 11-001
trade mark infringement, 11-001
unfair competition law, 11-001
Trade mark protection
see **Enforcement; Registration; Scope of protection**
Trade mark protection (USA)
business reputation, 11-065, 11-066

commercial speech, 11-073, 11-077
confusion, 11-071, 11-074, 11-082
copyright protection, relationship
    with, 11-053, 11-054
dilution
    actual dilution, 11-084
    basics, 11-065–11-067
    establishing, 11-080, 11-081,
        11-085–11-087
    likelihood of dilution, 11-118
dispersion of identity, 11-065
distinctive words/symbols, 11-071,
    11-074
extent, 11-068–11-077, 11-118,
    11-119
legislative protection, 11-078, 11-079
limitations, 11-053
reverse passing off, 11-054
scope of protection, 11-060, 11-117
tarnishment, 11-082
trade mark infringement, 11-081,
    11-085
Trade Marks Directive
challenging and maintaining
    registration
    grounds for
        invalidity/refusal/revocation,
        7-004, 7-005
    posteriori invalidity, 7-006
    sanctions for non-use, 7-003
    use of trade marks, 7-002
earlier marks
    grounds for refusal/invalidity,
        5-002
    identical marks, 5-002
    similar marks, 5-002
scope of protection
    exclusive rights, 6-002
    limitations, 6-003
    prohibited use, 6-002
    rights conferred, 6-002
    use in course of trade, 6-002
Trade Marks (USA)
additional registrability
    requirements, 11-009
commercial use, 11-008
conflicts between marks, 11-011,
    11-012
confusion
    concept, 11-011, 11-012
    test for confusion, 11-103, 11-014
descriptive signs, 11-010
distinctive marks, 11-010
geographical indications, 11-007

legislation, 11-006, 11-007
oppositions, 11-007
ownership, 11-006
period on non-use, 11-007
protection, 11-006, 11-007
registration system, 11-006
Supreme Court jurisprudence,
    11-015, 11-117, 11-119
Trade names/trade mark (conflict)
company names, 6-091, 6-092
conflict with earlier marks, 6-080
distinguishing function, 6-084
honest practice exception, 6-093
likelihood of association, 6-080
likelihood of confusion, 6-080
signs
    identical/similar signs, 6-080
    performing as trade marks, 6-084
TrafFix
functionality, 11-045
Supreme Court decision
    context of case, 11-049
    judicial reasoning, 11-050–11-052
    legislative context, 11-047, 11-048
    main issue, 11-046
trade dress, 11-045
Travatan
Advocate General's Opinion, 5-149
ECJ decision, 5-150, 5-151
similarity/confusion
    consumer attention, 5-146
    likelihood of confusion, 5-146
    mediation, 5-148
    threshold of confusion, 5-146
Two Pesos
Supreme Court decision
    basis, 11-017, 11-018
    concurring opinions, 11-024–11-027
    general context, 11-020
    judicial reasoning, 11-021–11-024
    legislative context, 11-019
trade dress
    distinctiveness, 11-016, 11-017
    protection, 11-016
Unfair competition (USA)
common law tort, 11-003
copying, 11-003
generally, 11-003
trade mark infringement,
    distinguished, 11-002
types of behaviour, 11-00, 11-005
United Brands
abuse of market dominance, 9-083
distinct market, 9-083

INDEX

United States Supreme Court
jurisprudence, 11-015, 11-117, 11-119
Vedial
Advocate General's Opinion
delimiting the dispute, 5-040
likelihood of confusion, 5-041
earlier rights
cumulative similarity, 5-038
likelihood of confusion, 5-039
phonetic similarity, 5-039
ECJ decision
comparing the marks, 5-042
delimiting the dispute, 5-042
likelihood of confusion, 5-042
Victoria's Secret
Supreme Court decision
concurring opinion, 11-088
judicial reasoning, 11-085–11-087
legal context, 11-084
main issue, 11-083
trade mark protection
actual confusion, 11-082
actual dilution, 11-084
establishing dilution, 11-081, 11-085–11-087
likelihood of confusion, 11-082
tarnishment, 11-082
trade mark infringement, 11-081, 11-085
Wal-Mart
background, 11-034
design/product packaging, 11-034
Supreme Court decision
legislative context, 11-036–11-039
main issue, 11-035
trade dress, 11-034
Washing tablet cases
see also **Henkel; Proctor & Gamble**
graphical representation, 4-268
inlaid tablets, 4-251, 4-252
speckled tablets, 4-248–4-250
two-layered tablets, 4-244–4-247
Wellcome v Paranova
Advocate General's Opinion
basis, 8-279
burden of proof, 8-279

exhaustion of rights, 8-280, 8-281
guarantee of origin, 8-280
identity of origin, 8-280
minimum intervention, 8-280, 8-281
necessity requirement, 8-279
notice requirement, 8-279, 8-282
re-labelling, 8-280
repackaging, 8-280
reputation, 8-280
specific subject matter, 8-280
ECJ decision
basis, 8-283
extent of disclosure, 8-285
necessity condition, 8-284
prior notice, 8-285
repackaging, 8-284
parallel imports, 8-278
preliminary ruling, 8-278
repackaging, 8-278
Windsurfing Chiemsee
Advocate General's Opinion
acquisition by use, 5-588–4-590
conditions for application, 4-342–4-347
geographical indication, 4-339
German doctrine, 4-345
legal context, 4-340
background, 4-336, 4-337
ECJ decision
acquisition by use, 4-591
distinctive character, 4-593–4-595
geographical indication, 4-354, 4-592
geographical origin, 4-351, 4-353
German doctrine, 4-349
multi-factor test, 4-594, 4-595
need to leave free, 4-348, 4-349, 4-591
public interest, 4-350–4-352
geographical names
acquisition by use, 4-587
descriptiveness, 4-336
distinctive character, 4-336, 4-587
need to leave free, 4-337, 4-338, 4-345
preliminary ruling, 4-338, 4-587